THE PAPERS OF
James Madison

Heitman, *Historical Register.*   Francis B. Heitman, *Historical Register and Dictionary of the United States Army, from Its Organization, September 29, 1789, to March 2, 1903* (2 vols.; Washington, 1903).

Kline, *Papers of Burr.*   Mary-Jo Kline, ed., *Political Correspondence and Public Papers of Aaron Burr* (2 vols.; Princeton, 1983).

Lipscomb and Bergh, *Writings of Jefferson.*   Andrew A. Lipscomb and Albert Ellery Bergh, eds., *The Writings of Thomas Jefferson* (20 vols.; Washington, 1903–4).

Madison, *Writings* (Hunt ed.).   Gaillard Hunt, ed., *The Writings of James Madison* (9 vols.; New York, 1900–1910).

Mayo, *Instructions to British Ministers.*   Bernard Mayo, ed., *Instructions to British Ministers to the United States, 1791–1812,* Annual Report of the American Historical Association of the Year 1936, vol. 3 (Washington, 1941).

OED.   *Oxford English Dictionary.*

Parliamentary Debates.   *Hansard Parliamentary Debates,* 1st ser. (41 vols.; London, 1804–20).

PJM.   William T. Hutchinson et al., eds., *The Papers of James Madison* (1st ser., vols. 1–10, Chicago, 1962–77, vols. 11–17, Charlottesville, Va., 1977–91).

PJM-PS.   Robert A. Rutland et al., eds., *The Papers of James Madison: Presidential Series* (5 vols. to date; Charlottesville, Va., 1984–).

PJM-SS.   Robert J. Brugger et al., eds., *The Papers of James Madison: Secretary of State Series* (6 vols. to date; Charlottesville, Va., 1986–).

PMHB.   *Pennsylvania Magazine of History and Biography.*

Riverside.   G. Blakemore Evans, ed., *The Riverside Shakespeare* (Boston, 1974).

Robinson, *Admiralty Reports.*   Christopher Robinson, *Reports of Cases Argued and Determined in the High Court of Admiralty (Great Britain)* (6 vols.; Philadelphia, 1801–10).

Rowland, *Claiborne Letter Books.*   Dunbar Rowland, ed., *Official Letter Books of W. C. C. Claiborne, 1801–1816* (6 vols.; Jackson, Miss., 1917).

Senate Exec. Proceedings.   *Journal of the Executive Proceedings of the Senate of the United States of America* (3 vols.; Washington, 1828).

Shaw and Shoemaker.   R. R. Shaw and R. H. Shoemaker, comps., *American Bibliography: A Preliminary Checklist for 1801–1819* (22 vols.; New York, 1958–66).

U.S. Statutes at Large.   *The Public Statutes at Large of the United States of America . . .* (17 vols.; Boston, 1848–73).

VMHB.   *Virginia Magazine of History and Biography.*

WMQ.   *William and Mary Quarterly.*

Madison Chronology

1812

27 August	JM leaves Washington for Montpelier.
29 August	JM returns to Washington after receiving news of Hull's surrender at Detroit.
2 September	JM leaves Washington for Montpelier.
12 September	JM leaves Montpelier for Washington.
14 September	JM arrives in Washington.
2 November	Second session of Twelfth Congress begins.
4 November	JM delivers annual message to Congress.
3 December	William Eustis resigns as secretary of war.
30 December	Paul Hamilton resigns as secretary of the navy.

1813

8 January	JM nominates John Armstrong as secretary of war and William Jones as secretary of the navy.

Significant Federal Officers

1812–February 1813

President Madison's Cabinet

Secretary of State	James Monroe
Secretary of War	William Eustis / James Monroe (acting) / John Armstrong
Secretary of the Treasury	Albert Gallatin
Secretary of the Navy	Paul Hamilton / Charles Goldsborough (acting) / William Jones
Attorney General	William Pinkney

Supreme Court

Chief Justice	John Marshall
Associate Justices	Gabriel Duvall
	William Johnson
	Henry Brockholst Livingston
	Joseph Story
	Thomas Todd
	Bushrod Washington

Other Ranking Positions

Speaker of the House of Representatives	Henry Clay
U.S. Minister to France	Joel Barlow
Postmaster General	Gideon Granger
Chief Clerk, State Department	John Graham

From Jeremiah Anderson

May it please your Excellency   Baltimore July 10th. 1812

Since my last address[1] I have been induced to make an observation to your Excellency that an most rigid precaution is necessary to be taken with the Blacks amongst us I beg you will recollect they have an Emperor amongst them—this I pray your Excellency will particularly notice.

A further explanation I can give if necessary.

I beg your Excellency will recollect that I look up to you as a father and the representative of his children. As such, I presume to call myself Your Excellencys very humble Servant.

Jeremiah Anderson

RC (DNA: RG 45, Misc. Letters Received).

1. See Anderson to JM, 9 July 1812, *PJM-PS*, 4:582.

From Jeremiah Anderson

May it please your Excellency   Baltimore July 10. 1812

Since I had the pleasure of addressing you this Morning—I have had a conversation with Sergeant Forrest of the Marine Corps and I pray your Excellency will allow me to observe that it is not his friendly disposition which makes him hold his present Situation.

I pray you will excuse this but as I look up to you as a father—I consider I have a right to make an observation in where my Countrys interest is in view. Your Excellencys &a.

Jeremiah Anderson

RC (DNA: RG 45, Misc. Letters Received).

From John Murray Forbes

Agency of the U. S. of America

Sir,   Copenhagen 10th July 1812.

Fully aware of your unceasing and important occupations and duly Sensible how presumptuous it is in me to obtrude my personal interests on those moments which are wholly devoted to my Country, I look only for indulgence to your benignity of Character and hope that the great and pressing importance (even to the continuance of my life) of the Subject of the present will ensure me your forgiveness. I have taken the liberty to represent to Mr. Monroe, to whom I have long had the honor to be known, that my health is So compleatly destroyed by ten years residence in the unfriendly climate of Hamburgh, joined to a vast deal of vexation brought on me by the Strict and Conscientious discharge of my public duty, that I have but a Short and very wretched existence to expect in remaining here.[1] Mr. Erving our late Special Minister here also witnessed and even reported my Sufferings to the Secretary of State[2] and when he proposed to me to undertake this Agency I consented to do it only during the summer in which Season I had a right to expect Something like a return of my health; in this hope I have, however, been disappointed. I have frequently and pressingly Solicited an appointment in a Southern and milder Climate and have taken the liberty to name Several Situations which were desireable.

I have just learned that the Situation which I Should prefer to every other is now vacated, I mean the *Consulate* of *Lisbon*, which I am assured Mr. Jefferson has determined to relinquish. If, Sir, you would have the goodness to Confer this appointment on me, you would recall me from death unto life and would Sweeten and Solace the remainder of my days. I would take the liberty to observe that it is only on account of Climate that Lisbon is to be preferred to Hamburgh and the latter Consulate would amply indemnify any one on whom you might be disposed to Confer the other; thus, Sir, without injury to any one it depends on you to make me happy beyond expression. I have the honor to be, with the greatest respect, Your Obedient Servant

J: M: Forbes

RC (DNA: RG 59, LAR, 1809–17, filed under "Forbes"); RC (DNA: RG 59, CD, Copenhagen, vol. 2). Second RC marked duplicate.

1. Forbes had complained of his health to Monroe on a number of occasions, requesting that he be reassigned to a warmer climate (Forbes to Monroe, 24 Feb., 6 Apr., 31 May, 6 June, and 8 July 1812 [ibid.]). Monroe later forwarded to JM two further letters he had received advancing Forbes's candidacy for the Lisbon consulate (Forbes to Monroe, 20 Aug. 1812, and James Lloyd to Monroe, 26 Nov. 1812 [DNA: RG 59, LAR, 1809–17, filed under "Forbes"; both docketed by Monroe "For the President"]).

2. U.S. special minister to Denmark George W. Erving had explained to Monroe in a 10 Nov. 1811 dispatch that he "had invited Mr. Forbes from Hamburg with a view to place him on my departure from hence in communication with this government as '*agent*,' that he might be thus enabled more effectually to assist the captains of whatever vessels may be captured hereafter," noting that Forbes "was detained by ill health and did not arrive 'till the 5th. of September" (DNA: RG 59, DD, Denmark, vol. 1A). Though Erving acknowledged in his 17 Apr. 1812 dispatch to Monroe that "Mr Forbes's health will not admit of his passing another winter here," he continued to press for Forbes's appointment as agent in his 14 May dispatch (ibid.).

From Zebulon Montgomery Pike

S<small>IR</small>,   W<small>ASHINGTON</small> C<small>ITY</small> 10th July 1812.

I presume that I shall be pardoned in addressing to you this letter, when it is understood that motives of respect for an aged Father and veteran officer are the causes which induced me to intrude on you. Major Zebulon Pike of the [. . .] ⟨In⟩fantry, enter⟨ed⟩ th⟨e⟩ military service of our country in 1775 and served to the peace of 1783, when he held the rank of Captain of Dragoons for five years; He again entered the army in 1791 and was in the action with the savages under Genl. St. Clair. He continued in actual service untill 1806 or 7 when his infirmities arising from the ardent pursuit of the profession of Arms for twenty three years rendering him unable to perform the duties of his station, he received an unlimited furlough. In consequence of his infirmity it was thought proper to promote Major Richard Sparks over his head, to the rank of Lieut: Colonel, who will now succeed to the command of the 2nd. Regt. of Infantry vice Col: Cushing promoted: I have therefore been emboldened to request from the generosity of the President; that the twenty nine years services (& I may with pride say honorable ones) may be rewarded by a Brevet commission; as He never can take the field, this will only serve to shew him he is held in consideration by the Chief Magistrate of his country and will gratify the Pride of an old soldier.[1] Suffer me on my part to assure you sir of my profound respect & sincere veneration,

Z. M. P<small>IKE</small>[2]

Col. 15 Iny

RC (DNA: RG 107, LRRS, P-173:6). In a clerk's hand, signed by Pike; docketed as received in the War Department on 15 July 1812. A note at the foot in Pike's hand reads: "NB. Majr. Pike was promoted to that rank 21 March 1800." Torn.

1. Zebulon Pike Sr. (d. 1834) was promoted to the rank of brevet lieutenant colonel on 10 July 1812 (Heitman, *Historical Register*, 1:792).

2. Zebulon Montgomery Pike (1779–1813) of Lamberton, New Jersey, was both an explorer and a soldier. As a lieutenant under Brig. Gen. James Wilkinson, Pike led a mission in 1805 to explore portions of the Louisiana Purchase in a fruitless attempt to locate the source of the Mississippi River. He was then assigned to search for the headwaters of the Red and Arkansas Rivers in 1806, when he found occasion to attempt the peak outside of Pueblo, Colorado, that would eventually be named for him. Suspicious of his intentions, the Spanish authorities terminated Pike's explorations and forced him to return to the U.S. After 1807 Pike continued to serve on the southwestern frontier, from which post Orleans territorial governor William C. C. Claiborne in March 1812 enthusiastically recommended him to the *"further patronage"* of JM as "a faithful soldier, & an excellent Citizen." While it is uncertain whether the president ever received that recommendation, Pike's subsequent advance was rapid. He served as deputy quartermaster general in the spring of 1812 before being promoted to colonel and stationed on the northern frontier. After another promotion, to brigadier general in March 1813, he led the successful attack on York, Upper Canada, on 27 Apr., where he was killed by the explosion of a British magazine (*Niles' Weekly Register* 7 [1814–15],

supplement, 1–8; Claiborne to JM, 1 Mar. 1812, in Rowland, *Claiborne Letter Books*, 6:65; Heitman, *Historical Register*, 1:792).

From William Pope

DEAR SIR,   VIRGINIA July 10th. 1812

I have taken the liberty to write to you Occasionally on the subject of our public concerns, for all which you will please to forgive me, their would never have been any necissity of writing a line or saying a word, if all matters, and things, had been exlusively under your controle—however "alls well that ends well." Congress have done their duty at last and will become as famous as the congress of 1776, but a great many of your countrymen give all the credit to you, they say (and I believe with truth,) that if it had not been for your instrumentality nothing decisive would have been done at last; you have politically regenerated the nation, and washed out the stain in their national charactor, inflicted on it by England; Since the declaration of war, their appears to be an entirely different aspect presented by the people of this country ever since the 18th of June makeing an allowance for the arrival of the news, all has been life, and vivacity in Virginia; the federalists appear to be uniting fast with the republicans, and if the war is carried on with life, and spirit all parties will be united except the Randolphits. In the County of powhatan their is only one tory, and he is a scotchman, and three Randolphits, but they will soon be obliged to give up their leader as he appears to be proscribed, and execrated by his countrymen universally; John Randolph has certainly done more injury to our country than all the tories, and discontented persons beside. I concienciously beleive that he has contributed greatly to forward on the war, and if the vengence of heaven does not fall on him, the hand of his country will at last overtake him; Your communication to congress on the first of June[1] is more read, and admired than any state paper I ever knew, it is more highly prized than the valledictory address of Washington or the enorgural Speech of Jefferson. I was in the City of Richmond when the declaration of War arrived, I never saw more joy, and exultation among the republicans and friends of their Country, and never more disconsolation, and consternation among the Tories &c &c. Their was a full band of music through the City of Richmond, they saluted the governor, they then agreed with one consent, that they would salute Mr W Wirt[2] as he had always been the best of friends to the admin[i]stration, and country; I believe that Mr Wirt is the most popular man in Virginia, and any appointment that he could meet with in the Army would be highly pleasing to the people of Virginia independant of which, he would make a most excellent officer. I heard Mr Jefferson say about 3 or 4 years ago, that he thought Mr Wirt one of the best Orators in

America and that he did not doubt, but that Mr Wirt possessed high military talents, what lead to the conversation was, that Mr. Wirt had lately before that been appointed a Collonel by the Executive of Virginia, Mr Wirt is not inferior to any man in Ameri[c]a in speaking and writing, a political peice of his, called one of the people in answer to the protest of the minority was one of the most unanswerable argument in favor of the administration; and called down on him all the resentment, and vengence of the minority. I beleive he would cheerfully go into service if called on by his country. If any of the E, S, should give back, or give themselves any airs the government has only to call down on them the southern, Western and middle states, and they will be as easily quelled as the wisky insurgents. If the Government attemps to parry, and temporise with them, the Union is gone for ever, the repeal of the first embargo was the most unfortunate step that was ever taken in America, by Congress, nothing like Energy in Washington, and Madison, If during the recess of Congress the president of the U, S, would visit the Eastern states on the sea board, and view their fortifications it would have the hapiest Effect, in consiliating the affections of the Eastern people, independant of all which, it would be an agreeable relax[a]tion from the fatigues of the Cabinet which you have unceasingly sustained for nearly 7 months. I am yr Excellency's most Obedient humble Servant.

WILLIAM POPE

RC (DLC). Docketed by JM.

1. JM to Congress, 1 June 1812, *PJM-PS*, 4:432–38.
2. William Wirt (1772–1834) served for three sessions as clerk in the Virginia House of Delegates and in the spring of 1800, along with George Hay and Philip Norborne Nicholas, served as counsel for James Thomson Callender in his trial before Justice Samuel Chase under the Sedition Act. In 1803 Wirt published the first of "The Letters of the British Spy" in the Richmond *Argus*. While living in Richmond in 1807, he assisted in the prosecution of Aaron Burr. The following year he was elected to the House of Delegates, but he retired after serving only one term, preferring the literary life to politics. In 1810 Wirt started publication of another series of essays entitled "The Old Bachelor." In 1816 he argued his first case before the U.S. Supreme Court and shortly thereafter was appointed by JM as U.S. attorney for the District of Richmond. Named attorney general of the U.S. by James Monroe in 1817, he served in that position for twelve years (Kennedy, *Memoirs of the Life of William Wirt* [1850 ed.], 1:13, 16, 79–80, 105, 149, 152, 226, 235, 263, 353–54, 2:29).

From the Republican Delegates of New Jersey

SIR,   TRENTON (N J.) July 10th 1812

Believing it would be pleasing to you, at this crisis, to be acquainted with the sentiments and views of your constituents in every part of the Union;

the Convention of Republican delegates, from the several Counties of the State of New Jersey, take the liberty of addressing you, on behalf of their constituents and themselves. They have seen with approbation, the long continued, and often repeated efforts of the Government of the United States, to preserve to the Country, the blessings of peace, and, at the same time, to maintain the honor and Independence of the nation. Negociation has at length been abandoned, as hopeless; Resistence has been commenced, as the last resort. To retreat now from the contest, would indeed, justly subject our Government to the stigma of pusillanimity, and our People, to the charge, of a want of patriotism.

On behalf of the Republican citizens of this State, and of ourselves, we, therefore Sir, assure you, that we are now, as much in favour of a vigorous prosecution of the war, untill our wrongs are redressed, and our rights respected; as we have heretofore been of the preservation of peace, while it could be maintained without a sacrafice of our rights and interests: and we are fully of opinion, that the confidence of the friends of Government, in New-Jersey, will be encreased, rather than diminished, by the measures adopted by the General Government, for the support of our unquestionable and unalienable rights. Permit us Sir, to add, that your conduct, as well in your endeavours to preserve peace, as in your final recommendation of a resort to arms, meets with our most decided approbation. By order of the Convention.

BENJ'N. LUDLOW President
GEO: CASSEDY. Secretary.

RC (DLC). Docketed by JM. Printed in the *National Intelligencer*, 4 Aug. 1812.

From Jonathan Williams

SIR   NEW YORK July 10 1812

Since my Letter to you of the 21 June,[1] Brigre General Bloomfield communicated to me an order from the Secretary of War, which in substance agreed with the request, I had the honour to make to you, and of which you have a Copy inclosed.[2] After compleating some official duties at Philadelphia I returned to New-York and reported myself ready to take such command as might "comport with my rank."

General Bloomfield was about to issue the requisite order when he received a communication, of which I also enclose a Copy, being a remonstrance against the measure signed by eighteen company officers.[3]

Far be it from me, Sir, to create any division among men whose profession of all others should form a well connected & affectionate Brother-hood; but I must be permitted to judge for myself in what relates to me personally, therefore it only remains to do the last, and only, act that can be done consistently with my honour, and a desire to preserve harmony among the officers of the Army, and I hereby resign my Commission.

The Case is too imperious to need much argument; but it may not be improper to observe that after having resigned on a former occasion, I was called again into Service upon an express stipulation which was afterwards made Law by the 63d Article of the Rules & Regulations for the Government of the Army.[4] This being the condition, *upon which alone* I accepted my Commission, I hold myself absolved from all obligation the moment it ceases to operate. The loss of an Officer in his sixty third year may not be considered of great importance when compared with that of eighteen Officers in the vigour of youth, for by the tone of the remonstrance it is to be presumed that this consequence would follow if the order were to be enforced. I have the honour to be with the highest deference & respect Sir Your obedient Servant[5]

JONA WILLIAMS

RC and enclosures (DNA: RG 107, LRRS, W-196:6); draft (InU: Jonathan Williams Papers). RC docketed as received in the War Department on 15 July 1812. For enclosures, see nn. 2 and 3.

1. *PJM-PS*, 4:495.

2. The enclosure is a copy of William Eustis to Joseph Bloomfield, 23 June 1812 (1 p.) (see ibid., 4:495 n. 3).

3. The enclosure is a copy of a remonstrance of eighteen officers to Col. Henry Burbeck, 8 July 1812 (3 pp.) (see ibid., 4:495 n. 3).

4. In the draft statement concerning his resignation (see n. 5, below), Williams claimed to have turned in his lieutenant colonel's commission when the secretary of war ruled on 20 June 1803 that engineers were "not entitled to any command of ports." Williams returned to service on 19 Apr. 1805, after a general order restored command privileges to him. The order was codified the following year in Article 63 of "An Act for Establishing Rules & Articles for the Government of the Armies of the United States," which reads: "The functions of the engineers being generally confined to the most elevated branch of military science, they are not to assume, nor are they subject to be ordered on any duty beyond the line of their immediate profession, except by the special order of the President of the United States, but they are to receive every mark of respect, to which their rank in the army may entitle them respectively, and are liable to be transferred at the discretion of the President, from one corps to another, regard being paid to rank" (*U.S. Statutes at Large*, 2:367). Williams's statement detailed recent events that had led him to believe that this article was no longer in effect.

5. Filed with the draft is a copy of Williams to Eustis, 10 July 1812 (1 p.), in which Williams resigned his commission, and a draft statement (3 pp.) of Williams's reasons for resigning (see n. 4, above).

§ From the Inhabitants of Charlemont, Massachusetts. *10 July 1812*. "The memorial & remonstrance of the Inhabitants of the Town of Charlemont in the County of Franklin & Commonwealth of Massachusetts humbly sheweth; that they hold in the highest estimation the right Solomnly guarranteed to them as free Citizens of a great Republic by the Constitution of their Country; of peaceably assembling together & of expressing their Opinion, of the measures adopted by their public agents, tho we have not the advantage of viewing the whole ground of our relations & connections with foreign Nations and may therefore have formed mistaken apprehensions of the conduct of our Rulers, & may have been led to believe it erronious when in fact it is correct, yet having read and considered with great attention, such documents & correspondence as the Government have been pleased to make public and from them formed our deliberate & settled opinions we deem it not only our right, but in the present important calamitous & distressing crisis of our national affairs, we feel it a Solemn duty that we owe to our Country, our selves, & to those to whom we wish to transmit unimpaired the rights & priviledges of freemen, to let our sentiments be known to our Rulers, that they be not decieved by calculating on the volentary & hearty coopperation of the citizens in the cause in which they are engaged, when their hearts are far from it; the serv[i]ce of the Citizens when forced or grudgingly bestowed; cannot be productive of those efficient & ben[e]ficial effects as when they are volentary and flow from a hearty conviction of the rectitude of the cause in which they are ingaged. It would afford us much satisfaction in a crisis like the present, to have it in our power to express to our Rulers, our approbation of their conduct; our concurrence in the measures they have adopted; and to tender to them, what little property we possess, together with our personal services to assist them in the conflict they are about to engage in; but our candor, our sincerity, and our sense of duty to ourselves & our Country compel us to declare that all the information our Rulers have seen fit to communicate to the Public has not enabled us to perceive in their conduct, that wisdom, that firmness, that impartiality, and that high sense of national honor which ought to Characterize a free, Independant & neutral State; for we perceive that in their correspondence with the french Government, they have suffered themselves & through themselves the People of the United States to be branded & disgraced as a mean, degenerate & dastardly People; a nation without energy, without spirit, & without Just political views, who would not fight for their honor tho they might be compeled to for their Interest. We would also remark it as a singular fact, & one which deserves particular attention that in all communications of the french Government with that of the United States we have been permitted to see only extracts, not a single letter have we seen entire; enough however has been published to satisfy us that if the United States are to war with any nation, it becomes us first to redeem our National honor from the deep disgrace heeped on her by french insolence, first to wipe of[f] the stigma of penury & cowa[r]dice with which we have been branded, then may we have confidence to contend for our Interest.

"In examining the alledged grounds of the war lately declared against Great Britain we have been led to the following r[e]marks, with respect to their instigating the Indians to commit hostilities on our frontiers; it is acknowledged by the committee of foreign r[e]lations who bring forward the charge that they have no evidence to support it,[1] while by the British Government it is expressly denied; and we think those hostilities may in a great measure be accounted for, by the want of punctuality on the part of the United States in performing the stipulations of their treaties.

"The blockading Order of may eighteen hundred & six we believe has not til lately been considered by our Government as a cause of complaint much less as a cause of war.[2] With regard to the secret mission of John Henry we have not been furnished with evidence to shew that the British Government had any agency in the enterprize of Henry; or efforded him any encouragement or assistance in it,[3] but so contrary is the fact that he has been obliged to look to our own Government for the reward of his iniquity, to that Government which he says he was employed to undermine & to destroy! With respect to the impressment of our Seamen it is an injury not to be put up with by a nation jealous of its honor and unless abandoned or equitably aranged by treaty to the satisfact[i]on of the United States ought to be retaliated by all the energies of the nation; we cannot however but remark that the British Government, have repeatedly expressed a willingness to settle that subject by treaty so as to remove all grounds for complaint & do expressly disclaim all pretence of a right thus to exercise power contrary to right.

"The Orders in Council so much complained of & so injurious to our trade unless repealed might under some circumstances justify a war to obtain their repeal; but besides having a just cause of war, we ought to be satisfied that the object to be obtained will more than compensate for sacrafices to be made in the attempt, and that we have a reasonable prospect of obtaining that object, that our means are adequate to the end & that victory should we obtain it would not involv[e] us with our enemy in one common ruin. War is an evil greatly to be deprecated, we sincerely lement that it has been proclaimed, & we earnestly entreat that it may be speedily brought to a close, that peace may again return to our borders, to brighten our prospects & to chase away the gloom that now surrounds us. We cannot but view with painful apprehension the collecting & stationing bodies of regular troops in the interior parst [sic] of our Country while the Militia at the time are called to do duty at places distant from their homes.

"Among the evils with which we view ou[. . .] threatened & exposed; none strikes us with more dismay than the prospect of a more intimate connextion & alliance with the cruel despot who holds beneath his Iron sway the distressed nations of continental Europe.

"War, & pestilence, & famine & sword, would be hailed as the sure mercies of Heaven when compaired to such an alliance, and we humbly pray almighty God that he would so far turn the hearts of our Rulers to himself as that they may be induced to avoid such a connextion."

"Voted by the Inhabitants" of Charlemont "that the foregoing Memorial be . . . forwarde⟨d⟩ to the President of the United States."

RC (DNA: RG 59, ML). 3 pp.; signed by Abel Wilder, moderator, and Andrew Rudd, town clerk; postmarked Northampton, 16 July. Damaged by removal of seal.

1. The 3 June 1812 report of the House committee on foreign relations declared that its members had not been "disposed to occupy much time" in investigating "Whether the British Government has contributed by active measures to excite against us the hostility of the savage tribes on our frontiers," adding that "Certain indications of general notoriety may supply the place of authentic documents, though these have not been wanting to establish the fact in some instances" (*ASP, Foreign Relations*, 3:569).

2. For Fox's blockade, see *PJM-PS*, 2:108 n. 4.

3. For the mission of John Henry, see ibid., 4:117 n. 2.

From William Tatham

Sir,   Mr. O'Neals, Washington, 11th. July 1812.

I have come up from Norfolk prepared to offer proofs to government of that unabating zeal for the public safety & prosperity which your late proclamation recommends; and to demonstrate to Administration that I am in a condition to be useful at the present crisis in many particulars resulting from singular pursuits, exclusive knowledge of our military & maritime topography, and many years personal & zealous investigation.

The services most immediately applicable, and over which I feel a power, seem to me to be the following:

1. To furnish the War office with the original British plans sections elevations &c of the several Barracks, store-houses &c, formerly built at Albany in the wars against the French & Indians which were closed by the Treaty of 1763: These, with some of their Estimates, are at least elucidatory & exemplary documents, if they do not prove so applicable to the national change of circumstances as to expedite the Military works which, I have understood, are contemplated there.

2. To furnish the chief part, or all of, the topographical surveys; military plans, fortifications, operations, charts drawings &c, whi⟨ch⟩ were done by the British Engineers under General Wolfe, Amherst, Monkton, &c; and which apply to illustrate the whole of Knox's Journal,[1] Rogers Journal,[2] and those five years Campaigns preceeding the treaty of 1763, &c.

3. To furnish similar documents of the British operations & works in Florida; with Surveys of the Environs of Mobile, Pensacola, St. Augustine, the Plan of Fort St. Marks &c, &c, including originals; & admiralty copies of valuable unpublished Charts of Spiritu Santo Bay, & other Bays Bars & Harbours along the Coast of Florida, taken by G. Gauld & other Maritime Engineers in the British Admiralty service.[3]

4. To demonstrate, from my own, and collected, manuscript surveys, how far we are deficient in a knowledge of the Maritime frontiers of N. Carolina Virginia & Maryland; The powers & influence of these coasts in a general defence of the U. States against Maritime invasion; and certain measures which occur to me as essential towards attaining better information, & greater security.

5. To prepare, from my own Surveys & personal recollection of the posts of Norfolk, Kempsville, & Lynnhaven, a more complete topographical Map of those countries than any existing: th⟨is?⟩ to answer, as a temporary information, till the whole is rendered more perfect by completing my Surveys.

6. To furnish such Ichnographic, or touri⟨ng⟩ plans as the Navy or War departments may desire to possess from my collection.

7. To complete, as far as practicable, several Canadian Surveys yet unfinished, and ⟨s⟩ome of them still in pencil.[4]

8. To complete the equipment and modification of a Boat of peculier construction which I came here in alone, and in which I have singly navigated the Maritime waters of Virginia and Carolina for about two years past; so as to render her the model of a new & powerful military system whereby the whole expense of the war will be economized: particularly in dispensing with the wear & tear of baggage waggons, packhorses, marching and countermarching of troops &c. I propose (as heretofore communicated) that each Boat shall carry sixteen men, with their officers & baggage; that they shall pass out to sea, over the Sea banks, up Creeks or small rivers, cross the Chesapeake in any weather which other vessels can do, run into shallow water, pass (by land) along any road where a common waggon can go, without a necessity for using quadrupeds to convey them, perform Evolutions on the water as if on land; and, ultimately, hang upon a Maritime Enemy (as a Hornets nest) from their Entering our Capes through the whole of their depradations. I estimate that such boats, sails & equipments complete, can be built for three hundred dollars each; and carefully managed, under officers bred & experienced in their Management, they may be preserved for Thirty Years.

My Boat is 24 ft. 8 in. long, 5 ft. 5 in. Wide, and two men have carried her.

Thus, an Army would require a smaller number of men to defend a penninsulated country; because, when a vehicle of conveyance is rendered capable of passing one & the same army over land or water (indifferently) in the nearest line of direction, it will neither be necessary to march round by distan⟨t?⟩ [*illegible*], or to employ a seperate army on each seperate penninsula, as in former wars.

9. To demonstrate (by models) a new, and impregnable system of fortification; whereby power, & situation, will be commanded, and expenditure economised.

If, Sir, any advantage can be derived from my personal communications of what may concern the defenceless situation of Norfolk & adjacent parts, or if my impressions of the state of popular opinion at the present juncture may be deemed useful, I am ready to enter on any specific explanations which the respective departments may require of me. I have the honor to be, Sir, Your obt H Servt.

WM TATHAM

RC (DNA: RG 107, LRRS, T-121:6). Docketed as received in the War Department on 18 July 1812; torn.

1. John Knox, *An Historical Journal of the Campaigns in North-America, for the Years 1757, 1758, 1759, and 1760: Containing the Most Remarkable Occurrences of That Period; Particularly the Two Sieges of Quebec* (2 vols.; London, 1769).

2. Robert Rogers, *Journals of Major Robert Rogers: Containing an Account of the Several Ex-*

cursions He Made under the Generals Who Commanded upon the Continent of North America, during the Late War (London, 1765).

3. Tatham could have been in possession of any number of published and unpublished surveys by British cartographer George Gauld. For a checklist of Gauld's surviving work, including a copy of a survey of Pensacola and its environs, the original of which was in Tatham's possession in 1813, see John D. Ware and Robert R. Rea, *George Gauld: Surveyor and Cartographer of the Gulf Coast* (Gainesville, Fla., 1982), 235–41.

4. This was not the first time Tatham had offered JM materials on West Florida, Norfolk, and Canada. See Tatham to JM, 18 Aug. 1809, in McPherson, "Letters of William Tatham," *WMQ*, 2d ser., 16 (1936): 383–87 (calendared in *PJM-PS*, 1:332), and Tatham to JM, 1 Jan. 1811 and 26 June 1812, *PJM-PS*, 3:89–90, 4:513.

§ From Daniel D. Tompkins. *11 July 1812, Albany*. Bears "unqualified testimony" in favor of Samuel Russell[1] of New York, who will be recommended to the president for the office of deputy commissary general.

Printed copy (Hugh Hastings, ed., *Public Papers of Daniel D. Tompkins, Governor of New York, 1807–1817: Military* [3 vols.; New York and Albany, 1898–1902], 3:25–26).

1. On 9 Nov. 1812 JM nominated Samuel Russell to be deputy commissary of purchases; the Senate confirmed the appointment on 10 Nov. 1812 (*Senate Exec. Proceedings*, 2:299, 302; Heitman, *Historical Register*, 1:853).

From Albert Gallatin

[ca. 12 July 1812]

Agenda

1. Organise regularly the encampment at Albany by marching there all the recruits, those intended for Niagara excepted[1]
2. Invite offers of volunteers every where, but not giving orders to march (those intended for Niagara excepted) until the number in most places be ascertained, and it be known whether the changes in England will produce immediate peace[2]

    The inviting offers as aforesaid through letters to Gen. Dearborn & Pinkney and to several Governors.[3]

    Preparatory steps to be taken for the march & supplies of volunteers, so that any part wanted may be ready within one month after issuing the orders to march.
3. Direct immediately a force to Niagara to take the British fort there & co-operate with Gen. Hull. That force to consist of recruits & volunteers from Kentucky, West Pennsylva. & West New York & to amount to 3000 men.[4]

The object of these measures is 1. to take without any delay possession of Canada from Niagara upwards. 2. to prepare for attacking Montreal late in fall or early in winter with the force consisting of all the regulars who can be collected, of the troops which shall have reduced Niagara, and of number of volunteers who, according to the amount of opposing force, may be wanted. 3. to delay immediate attack on Montreal until trial has been made of possibility of immediate peace

4. On return of our frigates, keep them on our coast, which will but protect our commerce and prevent any but properly defensive engagements with enemy.

5. Communicate immediately to British ministry our disposition for peace[5] on following basis. 1. mutual restoration of territory occupied & public vessels taken. 2. repeal of orders of council & definition of blockade as agreed heretofore by them. 3. Restoration of seamen on both sides & abolition of impressments, on condition of restoration of deserters and non-employment of subjects of other nation as heretofore agreed proposed. 4 Mutual promise not to occupy Florida east of Perdido, it being understood that America may acquire it by convention

Armistice as heretofore mentioned

6. Immediate evacuation of E. Florida occupancy being now altogether illegal & calculated as cause or pretence for preventing peace (Holland to Joy)[6]

7. Checking un-necessary expence. This can be done only by Sec. of War & Navy. It appears for that purpose absolutely necessary that they should suspend or discontinue whatever is not actually necessary at this time—regulate *themselves* the amount & nature of each expence, leaving no general discretion to Generals, Quarter Masters, Commissarys, Agents, &c. to call militia, purchase, or build without *special* authority for each such act from Department—make no advances beyond what is strictly necessary nor unless accounts of former ones are rendered—limit most strictly the authority to draw on them—systematize as soon as possible every branch of expenditure where it is not yet done—submit to the President all measures of general nature requiring considerable expence.

Queries. 1. Effect of revocation of orders in Council on non-importation.
2. Addit. appn. defence of maritime frontier—also clause intended to forbid transfers.

RC (DLC: Rives Collection, Madison Papers). Undated; date assigned here on the basis of evidence presented in nn. 1–4 and Gallatin's departure from Washington on 14 July 1812 (*National Intelligencer*, 16 July 1812). Addressee not indicated.

1. On 26 June 1812 Eustis had informed Dearborn in Boston of JM's wish that he relocate to Albany to "prepare the force to be collected at that place for actual Service." On 15 July, Eustis repeated the request (DNA: RG 107, LSMA).

2. An announcement of a new British cabinet may have been the "changes in England" to

which Gallatin referred (*National Intelligencer*, 11 July 1812). A note in the left margin in Gallatin's hand reads: "Acknowledge offers."

3. On 15 July 1812 Eustis informed Dearborn that in addition to giving him "the authority to require of the Governors detachments of the militia for defence, and with a view to offensive operations," JM had authorized him "to accept Volunteers from New England, New York, & Pensylvania." Eustis enclosed copies of the 6 Feb. and 6 July 1812 Volunteer Acts, and Dearborn was instructed to give the state governors "such notice, or invitation" as he might "deem expedient" (DNA: RG 107, LSMA).

4. The forces preparing to invade the Niagara peninsula were so slow to organize that they were unable to divert the British from Detroit and in fact did not launch a full-scale attack in 1812. On 15 July, Eustis requested that upon arriving in Albany, Dearborn should direct his attention "to the Security of the Northern frontier by the Lakes," but Dearborn did little to organize a Niagara campaign and all but refused to consider the Niagara force as under his command (ibid.). New York militia and volunteers gathered for service under Stephen Van Rensselaer throughout the summer, but local political conflicts made it difficult for him to take the field. For his part, Eustis did not request Pennsylvania volunteers from Governor Snyder until 13 Aug. (ibid.). By that time, Kentucky forces were under orders to march directly to Detroit to aid Hull (Eustis to the Governor of Kentucky, 26 July 1812 [ibid.]).

5. Monroe's instructions to Jonathan Russell of 26 June 1812 had outlined terms upon which the U.S. would agree to an armistice. Russell was advised that "If the orders in council are repealed, and no illegal blockades are substituted for them, and orders are given to discontinue the impressment of seamen from our vessels, and to restore those already impressed, there is no reason why hostilities should not immediately cease." Monroe continued: "As an inducement to the British Government to discontinue the practice of impressments from our vessels, you may give assurance that a law will be passed (to be reciprocal) to prohibit the employment of British seamen in the public or commercial service of the United States" (extract printed in *ASP, Foreign Relations*, 3:585–86). On 27 July, Monroe repeated the terms of his previous letter, explaining that by authorizing Russell "to secure these objects" he had not intended to restrict Russell "to any precise form in which it should be done." Monroe emphasized the desirability of achieving an armistice even if only an informal agreement could be reached (printed ibid., 3:586).

6. For Lord Holland's 14 May 1812 letter to George Joy, enclosed in Joy to JM, 16 May 1812, see *PJM-PS*, 4:390 n. 5.

§ From the Merchants of New York. *12 July 1812*. "Understanding that the office of Consul General of Portugal will become vacant in consequence of the return of George Jefferson Esquire to America, and that an application is about to be made for the appointment, in behalf of Richard M Lawrence Esquire a Native Citizen of the State of New York now and for two years past a resident in Lisbon:[1] The Subscribers from a knowlege of Mr. Lawrence's talents integrity and mercantile information, and of the unblemished character he has always sustained, recommend him to the President of the United States as a proper person to fill the aforesaid office."

RC (DNA: RG 59, LAR, 1809–17, filed under "Lawrence"). 2 pp.; signed by John Hone and thirty others.

1. Lawrence was the subject of an extensive letter-writing campaign. Monroe received letters on his behalf from New York senator John Smith and New York representative Samuel Latham Mitchill, both dated 14 July 1812, and from New York representative William Paulding, dated 15 July. New Jersey representative Lewis Condit wrote to Monroe in support of

Lawrence on 31 July, as did New Jersey senator John Condit on 29 July, enclosing a supporting letter from Asa Hillyer, dated 28 July (ibid.).

§ From Constant Taber and Asher Robbins. *12 July 1812, Newport.* Recommend that Capt. David Bartlett be awarded the rank of first captain for Rhode Island and state that Bartlett believes he is entitled to that rank because he has held a commission as a field officer, which the other captain from the state has not. Inform JM that Bartlett has forwarded or will forward evidence of his commission to the president.[1]

RC (DNA: RG 94, Letters Received, filed under "Bartlett"). 1 p.

1. On 6 July 1812 Bartlett sent Alexander Macomb, the acting adjutant general, notification of his rank and service (ibid.). Bartlett's bid to be listed first of the Rhode Island captains in the Twenty-fifth Infantry Regiment failed. William Battey, the only other Rhode Islander, preceded Bartlett in that regiment's list (Thomas H. S. Hamersly, ed., *Complete Regular Army Register of the United States for One Hundred Years [1779 to 1879]* . . . [Washington, 1880], 80). Eustis also received letters on Bartlett's behalf from Charles Collins and James De Wolf, dated 15 July 1812, and from Jeremiah B. Howell and James Kennin, dated 16 July 1812 (DNA: RG 94, Letters Received, filed under "Bartlett").

From Albert Gallatin

[ca. 13 July 1812]

The monies approprd. by 1st. Sect. of Act herein mentioned, not being stated to be for the use of the navy cannot by the Secy. of the Treasury be ordered for that purpose.[1]

It must on the contrary be observed that the words used are the same wh. have in former laws been exclusively applied to fortifications & been accordingly placed under the controul of the Secy. of War.

A. G.

RC (DLC). Docketed by JM: "July: 1812." Undated; date assigned by the editors on the basis of evidence presented in n. 1.

1. Gallatin wrote this note on the verso of a letter from Navy Secretary Paul Hamilton to Gallatin, dated 13 July 1812, which requested that Gallatin issue $50,000 to the "Treasurer of the navy," Thomas Tucker, under the terms of a 5 July 1812 act "for the purposes of fortifying & defending the ports, harbours, & maritime frontier of the United States." The first section of that act appropriated $500,000 for naval fortification and defense but did not stipulate that the money was to be channeled directly to the Navy Department (*U.S. Statutes at Large*, 2:776–77).

From Elbridge Gerry

private[1]

My dear Sir,   Cambridge 13th July 1812

    I addressed a line to you on the 5th,[2] & am happy to learn that Colo Porter has the command of Fort Independence; that he has upwards of three hundred men; & that he is daily receiving reinforcements. Sure I am, that nothing will be wanting on the part of the Republicans in this State, to aid General Dearborn, & to promote the veiws & orders of the national Government.

    It is impossible to say, what are the objects of Governor Strong, in regard to the line of conduct he is pursuing. But this is so extraordinary, & wears such an aspect, as to leave no doubt in my mind, of the expediency & policy, on the part of the friends of Government to provide for the worst. I have therefore urged the Republicans, in their private capacitees to such measures as shall be warrantable, for ascertaining with precision, every man in the State, who will enroll himself, for supporting at all hazards the national Gove[r]nment, in conducting the war, & also every *recusant;* for having the former armed & equipped, to repair with proper officers at a moments warning to the respective places of Rendezvous; for having regular returns thereof; & for having the men so enrolled, officered & equipped, at the command, when requisite, of an officer who may be entrusted for defence. The conduct of Governor Strong, under a pretext, in changing two of the Major Generals who were Republicans (& appointed for commanding two of the divisions of the detachments, by the former Executive) for two high federal Major Generals;[3] in reserving to himself, the command of the whole militia of the State, including the detachments;[4] & in manifesting an intention of placing it, in case of an invasion, under the command of a veteran federal Major General; in forming with Governor Griswold, who has departed from his declared intentions, respecting the detachments of that State, a coalition for opposing the national administration;[5] & in its using such an extraordinary proclamation for a fast,[6] justifies apprehensions of the most inimical nature, in case of an attack by the british, & authorizes measures for guarding against every possible hostile event. It appears to me, that it would be an unpardonable neglect, for the republicans in this State, with folded arms, to leave it in the power of such a disaffected Executive, to deliver up our fortresses to the Enemy; to enable those, who may be disposed to rebel, to unite with our foes; to aid them, in making a diversion, of our western army & to subject the State to be overawed by a few traitors; for I verily beleive, that the friends of the national Government in Massachusetts, are sufficiently powerful, to drive every malecontent out of the State; & before the trial is made, I think the republicans would be very unwilling to call on any of our Sister States for aid. Notwithstanding this, it may be well to have in them a commanding force, & to let this be known, in order to keep in check the tories & tory federalists on this Quarter. I beleive their number to be very small, when compared with the whole number of federalists.

Of the final result of these measures, I cannot judge at present; but the republicans of Boston & the Vicinity, who are to meet this evening, will probably come to some decision.[7] I pray your Excellency to be assured of my highest esteem & respect, & that I have the honor to remain, Dear Sir, yours very sincerely

E. GERRY

RC (DLC); FC (MHi: Elbridge Gerry Papers). RC docketed by JM.

1. JM added "& important" here.

2. *PJM-PS*, 4:560.

3. Strong appointed Ebenezer Malton and Henry Sewall (Strong to Dearborn, 3 July 1812, enclosed in Dearborn to Eustis, 5 July 1812 [DNA: RG 107, LRRS, D-105:6]). For the major generals originally appointed by Gerry, see Gerry to JM, 25 Apr. 1812, *PJM-PS*, 4:349–50.

4. For Strong's refusal to detach the militia, see Memorandum from an Unidentified Correspondent, post 1 July 1812, and Dearborn to JM, 3 July 1812, ibid., 4:538, 541 n. 1, 543, 544 n. 1.

5. Connecticut governor Roger Griswold had written to Eustis on 17 June promising to comply with presidential requests made through Dearborn to supply detached militia. He then convened a special meeting of the governor's council on 29 June in Hartford to receive advice. Lt. Gov. John Cotton Smith informed Eustis on 2 July that Griswold had decided not to supply the militia. Griswold argued that the promise of compliance was made on the assumption that it would not violate the U.S. Constitution (*ASP, Military Affairs*, 1:325–26).

6. On 26 June 1812 Governor Strong issued a proclamation calling for a day of public fasting, humiliation, and prayer in Massachusetts. The proclamation treated the declaration of war as divine punishment and called upon the citizens to seek forgiveness and pray for peace (Boston *Columbian Centinel*, 27 June 1812).

7. The Republican meeting scheduled for 13 July was held at the Exchange Coffee House, but so many Federalists turned out that the room was too small to contain the crowd. The meeting adjourned and reconvened on 15 July, when Federalists took it over and passed a series of antiwar resolutions (ibid., 15 and 18 July 1812).

From the Inhabitants of Lyman, District of Maine

LYMAN July the 13th 1812

At a legal Town meeting of the Inhabitance of the Town of Lyman in the county of york for the Purpose of Expressing our minds on the Desstressing situation of our Publick affairs in regard to the Declaration of war with great Britain and the great Provibilaty of our alliance with france at a very full meeting, the question was then taken to know who was for Peace and who was for war, a motion was then made to Pole the house and Every one Present voted there Disapprobation of the Present war, and wished for a speedy Restoration of Peace and then chose a committee to Draw up a memorial to send and lay before the President of the United States, Expressing our sintiments in regard to the Present war, we would therefore respectfully represent, that a war with great Britain in our Canded opinion, is a measure Destructive and ruinous, of our Independence, and of our futer Prosspect of rank and Destintion as a Nation, we therefor⟨e⟩ most harttily say, that we Disaprove of the Present war, with that Power, a Power solely Possesing the means to annoy and Injuer us, Congress must have mistaken the sentiments and feelings of the grate body of the yeomanry of this Country, for in our opinion we are unprepeared, for a contest, the End of which is beyond the reach of mortal Eye; we would not wish to be understood to mean that great Britain has not injuered us, but we Do say that there has bin times in which all the Disputes between us and that Nation might have bin settled on honourable terms, and we Do say and belive that france has Insulted us much more and we view war a serious calamity and we have Ever considered the Present war as no ordinery Event and anliance with france is the natural result of it, from which Evil may the good Lord Diliver us for we should Prefer the lot of the three hebrews in the fire furnice or the lot of Daniel in the lions Den, reather than fall a sacrifice to that Despot but relieing on your candor and Infermation we subscribe our selves obedient subjects to Peace and good order hopeing that you will Immediately order a sisation of all hostillities and we as in Duty bound shall Ever Pray.

JOHN LOW
ISACHAR DAM } A committee
JACOB WATERHOUSE
JEREMIAH ROBERTS
NATHAN SMITH

RC (DNA: RG 59, ML).

From Elisha Tyson

RESPECTED FRIEND   BALTO 7 mo 13 1812

It is only under the apprehension of its being my duty, that I am induced to address a letter to thee upon the present occasion.

The Spanish Privateer schooner Genl. Morla, with 32 affrican negroes on board, having put into this Port, under the pretext of being in distress, was libeled for a breach of the laws of the U. S. In a conversation which I have just had with the collector of this District on the subject, he has informed me, that representations had, or would be made, to the Government for the release of the Vessel & People on board,[1] and not doubting but that every artifice and misrepresentation will be resorted to by those interested in geting her off, in order to mislead and deceive; I have believed it right to communicate to thee, the information which has reached me, from a credible person who was on board of the Vessel, and had some conversation with one of the crew. He states, that he learned that this Privateer had been a considerable time out, from a piratical cruise, during which time she commited numerous depredations, and amongst others, plundered these negro⟨es⟩ and about 220 others from a Guineaman on the Coast of Cuba, and that they had succeeded in landing and selling about 200 along the shores of South Carolina & Georgia: This fact if established would I presume independent of all other considerations, preclude any claim upon the Government.

I forbear to annimadvert at the present time on the barbarous & inhuman practices inseperable from this trade, it is sufficient that the laws of our Country forbid it, and altho the exercise of the Clemency of Government is right when employed for the relief of suffering innocence, it surely never could have been intended to be applied in a case similar to the present, but even should it be deemed proper to remit the forfeiture of the Vessel, and penalties on the Master, does not a just and humane policy forbid that the suffering victims on board should be deliverd up to the captors. They can have right of property in them by the laws of nature, and the municipal laws of our Country deny them any. Without attempting any further appology for this letter I am respectfully Thy real friend

ELISHA TYSON[2]

RC (DNA: RG 59, ML).

1. The collector of the port of Baltimore, James H. McCulloch, had evidently told Tyson that the captain of the *General Morla*, P. Brugman, had petitioned JM (not found) for the release of the vessel. Monroe wrote to McCulloch on 17 July 1812 acknowledging receipt of Brugman's petition, which claimed that the *General Morla* had been "forced from her destination and brought into the Port of Baltimore by unavoidable circumstances," where she was seized because of the Africans on board. Monroe informed McCulloch that it was JM's "intention to cause the Vessel to be released, provided such a disposition is made of the Africans in question as may be conformable with the laws of the State of Maryland." He explained that JM had made it clear, however, that the Africans should not "be exported in the same Vessel" (DNA: RG 59, DL, vol. 16).

2. Elisha Tyson (1749–1824) was a Maryland Quaker who was actively involved in curtailing slave trading ([John S. Tyson], *Life of Elisha Tyson, the Philanthropist* [Baltimore, 1825], 3, 7–8, 14–15, 37, 121).

§ From the Inhabitants of Riverhead, New York. *13 July 1812*. "Whereas it highly concerns the Citizens of this Town, in union with the whole family of the United States at large; to take into serious and deliberate consideration our present situation relative to the high & aggravated injustice which this nation hath repeatedly experienced from the British Government; and for which purpose this meeting is now convened. Therefore, Resolved, that we most cordially approve of the measure, which the constituted Authorities of these United States have adopted, relative thereunto.

"Resolved, that we hold it as our indispensible, religious, and bounden duty; to rally around the Standard of our common country, with a firm & determined resolution, to the last cent of our treasure, & the last drop of our blood and upon our sacred honor to defend her as far as in us lies.

"Resolved, that in our opinion all party distinctions and animosities ought at this critical juncture to be laid aside; and every real American and friend to the palladium of our Liberty, use his utmost endeavors and exertions to promote union and concord, throughout the great American Family.

"Resolved, that we will use every legal effort to detect, and hold up to Public contempt, and bring to due punishment, every act of internal enemies, (if such there should be, which God forbid) again[s]t the Just Cause in which we are engaged.

"Resolved, that we hold in the highest estimation, the Candidates recommended by the members of Congress, at Washington for President and Vice President.[1]

"Resolved, that the proceedings of this meeting be . . . transmitted to the President of the United States, and through him to Congress."

RC (DNA: RG 59, ML). 2 pp.; signed by Josiah Reeve as chairman and John Wells as secretary of the meeting.

    1. For the proceedings of the congressional caucus, see *PJM-PS*, 4:398 n. 1.

§ From the Residents of Buckland, Massachusetts. *13 July 1812.* "Resolved, that we view with sorrow, a departure from our neutral, or Washingtonian principles. 1st. Because it is destructive to our interests and the peace and happiness of the community. 2d. Because it has a direct tendency to enslave those Nations who are struggling for their liberty on the Continent of Europe.

"Resolved, that we do not so much dread a war with Great-Britain, as we do too near an approach to that Vortex which has carried down every Political Institution that has come within its power.

"Resolved, That we shall ever be ready to take up arms against any Nation that may invade us; and we also feel disposed to use all lawful endeavours to place in office, Men, who will regard the interests of our County [*sic*] and restore us to the prosperous Situation in which we were left at the close of the Washingtonian administration.

"Done in Legal Town Meeting. . . . And voted almost Unanimously."

RC (DNA: RG 59, ML). 2 pp.; signed by Gardner Wilder and Joseph Griswold, selectmen, and Samuel Taylor, clerk.

From Joel Barlow

Sir   Paris 14 July 1812

Sir   Paris 14 July 1812

The Bearer of this Mr. Nancrede[1] a naturalized citizen of the U. S. will be passing thro Washington on his way to the western country. I have desired him to solicit the honor of an interview with you to impart what he knows of the conduct of Aaron Burr while in this place.[2] Mr. Nancrede had occasion to see him much & perhaps became as well acquainted with his projects as any individual, without however any disposition, as I presume, to afford them any aid. He is a man of fair character & good connections, & as such I beg leave to commend him to the favor of your protection & kindness. I have the honor to be Sir with great respect yr. obt. St.

                                       J. Barlow

RC (DLC).

1. Paul Joseph Guérard de Nancrède (ca. 1760–1841) served in the French army at Yorktown before taking a position as a French instructor at Harvard College. He opened a printing shop in Boston in the 1790s, later moving it to Philadelphia (Fernand Baldensperger, "Le Premier 'instructeur' de français à Harvard College: Joseph Nancrède," *Harvard Advocate*, 5 Dec. 1913, 76–79).

2. For a discussion of Burr's visit to Paris in March 1810, see "Aaron Burr and Napoleon's Court," in Kline, *Papers of Burr*, 2:1099–1102.

From Matthew Livingston Davis

Private.

Sir   New York July 14 1812

I inclose you a letter recd. two days since from Mr. Nathl. W. Strong.[1] You will perceive, Sir, that it is a private letter, and not intended for the inspection of any person but myself. I have, however, deemed it the most correct and honorable mode, to let you understand explicitly and frankly, how far I am interested in the appointment of Mr Strong.

Should our affairs be settled with Great Britain (which I fear will not be the case) the commercial advantages and facilities which Mr Strongs residence in Lisbon, would afford the house of Strong & Davis, are very great.

Should the war continue, and the trade to that country be permitted under Spanish & Portuguese flags, we should also derive an advantage from his situation, by his having an opportunity to procure consignments to me. Thus far my *interest* is concerned. My feelings are also deeply engaged in the prosperity and success of my friend.

I pray, however, to be understood, that it is not my wish, nor the wish of Mr Strong, to supplant Mr. Jefferson. The present application is predicated upon a firm conviction that Mr. J. does not intend to return to Lisbon; and this information I derive from what I consider a highly respectable and authentic source in this City, well acquainted with the feelings and views of Mr. J.

I have been nearly nine years the copartner of Mr. Strong—consequently, know him well.

He is a native of Orange County, in the State of New York. The son of Capt. Strong, of our revolutionary army. He is, and has ever been, a decided republican, of irreproachable character. He is an intelligent, discriminating merchant: Not ignorant of our foreign relations. He has travelled much. Has resided nearly two years in the French West India Islands; Three years in London, and has been in Portugal and Sweeden. He possesses a degree of energy and promptness, which, in my opinion, at this crisis, adds to his other qualifications for the situation to which he wishes to be appointed. On the whole, I think he would make a good public officer, and most sincerely hope he may receive your approbation. With sentiments of respect & Esteem Your friend

MAT. L. DAVIS

P. S. Nothing new, except what is to be found in the Eastern papers.

RC and enclosure (DLC). Docketed by JM. For enclosure, see n. 1.

1. Davis enclosed a four-page letter from Lisbon, dated 3 June 1812, in which Strong reported a shortage of bread and high wheat prices in the city, which he supposed had been caused by the American embargo. He noted that he would "not be surprised if the people here, in case bread gets much higher, . . . should turn against the English and force them to leave the Country," an event that he believed would lead to a "speedy redress for all our complaints against England." In response to the departure of the U.S. consul, Strong requested that Davis solicit the position for him. JM received a further letter on Strong's behalf from Isaac Clason, dated 30 Oct. 1812 (DNA: RG 59, LAR, 1809–17, filed under "Strong"), and on 31 May 1813 nominated him to be consul at Saint-Barthélemy (*Senate Exec. Proceedings*, 2:347).

From the Inhabitants of Holden, Massachusetts

July 14. 1812

The memorial of the inhabitants of the Town of Holden in the State of Massachusetts—

Humbly shews That your petitioners would have found a very particular pleasure in perceiving the measures adopted by the general government of the United States, such as they could cordially approve, & trust that none would be more ready than they to cooperate in carrying such measures into effect. Nothing can be farther from thier wish than to impede the wheels of government, were they bearing on the nation at large to honor, peace, & happiness. They desire to think & speak well of the powers that be in the land so far as truth & reason demand. But the right of private judgment they hold too dear to be sacrific'd to any consideration whatever, & they regard it, as the right & duty of the freemen of America, with a manly & decent freedom to express their disapprobation of measures which they soberly, & solemnly believe are fraught with evil, & may be followed by consequences, shocking to their feelings, subversive of their prosperity, & productive of general misery. & they do now explicitly declare their disapprobation of a war at this time with Great-Britain. They will now submit to the candor of those whom they address the reasons of this declaration. War is confessedly a very great calamity, & the charge of cruelty, & the unrighteous shedding of human blood must rest somewhere in case of war, & this is a very heavy charge. We apprehend that those who declare war against any nation ought to be able, in sincerity, to appeal to the Great Arbiter of nations & searcher of human hearts that in such a declaration they have not been governed by motives of avarice, & ambition—that they have no desire to aggrandise themselves by unrighteous depredations of the property of others—that they have felt, & exhibited a pacific disposition, & spared no reasonable exertion for an honorable compromise of existing disputes & that they sincerely deprecate any war but that of self defence.

That the present war was unavoidable except by the sacrifice of our honor, & interest as a nation we find no reason to believe. Let the disposition of the people of Great-Britain be what it may. They have a mighty host of enemies to combat & to struggle against all the artifice, & power of a most formidable, & inveterate foe. They know that 'tis for their interest as a nation to be at peace with America, & can have no wish to add to the mighty pressure of present burdens. Every motive urges them against a state of hostility with the United States of America. & they have come forward with the olive branch to meet us—have made reparation for the injury done to the Chesapeak—have declar'd their readiness to give up every american Seaman that may have been press'd aboard their vessels of war, & explicitly declare the repeal of their obnoxious orders of Council, when it shall be made to appear that the no less obnoxious decrees of France are actually, & in fact removed.

The british Goverment have also declar'd, in official communications, that to constitute a blockade, particular ports must be actually invested, & previous warning given to vessels bound to them, not to enter, & have not british ships of war in many cases prov'd an asylum to our merchant vessels from french rapacity? Taking those & other things that might be mention'd into consideration we cannot say that we believe a war with Great Britain is wise, & righteous or necessary to secure our honor as an independent nation. We wish we could say that there is apparent in the mea-

23

sures & movements of our general Government a noble, & magnanimous impartiality respecting the belligerent nations of Europe, but we dare not, till further evidence of it shall appear. Among the evils we dread as a consequent of the present war is an alliance offensive & defensive with France. We say not that this is contemplated by any: But one evil often produces another still more fatal. & was such an alliance to take place, we should consider it as a mortal stab to our liberties as a people. For what stress can we lay on those that have paid so little regard to a solemn treaty already in existence. To hope for protection, & stable friendship from one that has committed the most flagrant outrage on every principle of equity, & devour'd, like the grave, the freedom of millions would be as absurd as to expect that fire had lost its power to burn & that we might safely venture without any call, into a flaming furnace. We feel a willingness to venture life & property to ward off the attacks of any invading foe, that shall threaten to desolate our country & wrest from us our rights as freemen, but wish not to plunge the sword into the breasts of those that covet to be at peace with us, tho' they may have fail'd of giving all the demonstration of it which they might, or ought. We have no desire to exculpate any thing that is wrong in the British Government but cannot say that they are obstinately bent to resist all overtures for a state of honorable peace.

Whenever we enter the lists with an enemy our request is to have the Lord of armies on our side—approving the motives by which we are govern'd: for we are aware that the race is not always to the swift, nor the battle to the strong, that safety is of the Lord. & we cannot promise ourselves the aid of an omnipotent arm when engag'd in a war that we are not satisfied is wise, & righteous, & necessary to secure our existence, & prosperity as a people. We do therefore express our deep, & ardent solicitude that nothing, within the bounds of propriety, may be left unattempted for the restoration of peace, & preventing an increase of publick & individual distress. We believe that many to whom we apply ourselves at this time coincide with us in the sentiments we have express'd. & 'tis our most fervent desire that the period may soon arrive when some happy expedient may be discover'd that shall arrest the fatal progress of war—sweep away the multiplied embarrasments that rest on our Country & commerce—prevent a dreadful load of taxes & brighten the countenance of every citizen with Joy. & should this event take place, may those who shall be active instruments of producing it, have their reward not only in the approbation of their own consciences, & the applause of grateful millions, but in that blessed state where the guilt, & miseries of war are not known, & true peace reigns forever triumphant. & your petitioners as in duty bound shall ever pray In the name & behalf of the Town

ETHAN DAVIS Moderator
LEMUEL DAVIS Clerk. P. T

N. B. The vote of the Town in favor of the above Memorial was unanimous—one dissentient excepted.

RC (DNA: RG 59, ML). Addressed "To The president, Senate & House of Representatives."

From Lemuel Taylor

SIR   BALTIMORE July 15th. 1812.

On the 29th. of May I had the honor of inclosing a letter from Mr. Wilmer, Supercargo of the Ploughboy.[1] My fears then expressed that no revision of the sentence would take place, have been realized by his arrival.

It is already known to you that Mr. Barlow, impressed with the justice of the case, had warmly espoused my cause in remonstrating against the injustice of the decision, & claiming a revision of the same.[2] It is also known by the Public prints, that reiterated assurances had been received that his request should be complied with.[3] The enclosed letter & notification of sale will however prove the melancholy truth, that *verbal* assurances are not always sacred.[4] Mr. Barlow's interference is the best proof that no existing decree has been violated & renders it unnecessary to comment on the absurdity of the sentence.

Allow me also to observe that at the departure of Mr. Wilmer from France (the 3d. of June)[5] no reply had been received by Mr. Barlow to a renewed claim of the Ship *Two Friends & Cargo.* This case has been represented to H. E. James Monroe under date 22d. November 1811 and of which the enclosed outlines will prove that I am truly the victim of injustice.[6] I also adjoin a copy of the 10th. clause of the treaty between France & Holland which renders the former government responsible for such vessels as were ceded in virtue thereof.[7]

After most respectfully begging your attention to the documents herewith, it remains for me to say, that as I have at all times conformed to the laws of my country, my government will not allow such unprecedented injustice to sink in oblivion.

My great plea is—"an American citizen stripped of the fruit of many years toil & anxiety by his good faith in the law of nations, & whose only hope & resource (under existing circumstances) is protection from his government.["]

As to the means of redress, it would be presumption in me to dictate. Whatever steps may be deemed necessary to obtain the desired end, will call forth the most grateful sentiments of Your unfortunate & most Obt. Servt.

LEMUEL TAYLOR

RC and enclosures (DNA: RG 76, Preliminary Inventory 177, entry 143, France, State Department Records Relating to the Adjudication of Unsettled Spoliation Claims, Unbound Records, no. 431). For enclosures, see nn. 4, 6, and 7.

    1. See Lemuel Taylor to JM, 29 May 1812, *PJM-PS*, 4:424 and n. 2.

    2. Though Barlow did not address Taylor's case specifically, his correspondence with Monroe between 29 Sept. 1811 and 22 Apr. 1812, which was printed in the *National Intelligencer* on 28 May 1812, outlined his efforts to obtain redress for captured vessels.

    3. Taylor was probably referring to Barlow's 22 Apr. 1812 letter to Monroe, which noted that urging France to acknowledge U.S. claims of indemnity was "dull work, hard to begin and difficult to pursue," but that French officials had "consented to give it a discussion" and the minister had assured Barlow "that something shall be done to silence the complaints" (printed ibid.).

    4. Taylor enclosed a 16 Apr. 1812 letter (1 p.) to John R. Wilmer from Parish and Company of Hamburg, which contained a newspaper clipping (in French) announcing the sale of the cargo of the *Ploughboy*.

    5. "In the Whosp" is interlined here in an unidentified hand.

    6. Taylor enclosed copies of Wilmer to Barlow, 12 Oct. 1811 (2 pp.) and 13 Apr. 1812 (1 p.), chronicling Wilmer's efforts to gain restoration or compensation from the French government for the cargo of Taylor's brig *Two Friends*. Wilmer hoped that Barlow would justly represent his claims. The latter letter was submitted to substantiate Taylor's case that the ship *Two Friends* had been ceded to the French government. In 1827 Taylor's representatives were still seeking redress for the January 1810 capture of his brig at Amsterdam, "in conformity to the treaty signed between France and Holland, at Paris, 16th March, 1810" (*ASP, Foreign Relations*, 6:449).

    7. Taylor enclosed a copy (1 p.) of a clause (in French) from Article 10 of the 16 Mar. 1810 treaty between France and the Netherlands stipulating that all merchandise entering the ports of the Netherlands in American vessels would be sequestered and handed over to France to be disposed of according to current circumstances and the state of political relations with the U.S. (de Clercq, *Recueil des traités de la France*, 2:330).

§ From the Delegates from Towns in Franklin, Hampshire, and Hampden Counties, Massachusetts. *15 July 1812*. "In the exercise of the inestimable privilege of peaceably assembling and petitioning government for a redress of grievances, your memorialists, delegates from towns in the Counties of Franklin, Hampshire and Hampden, within the Commonwealth of Massachusetts, legally appointed in regular town meetings, warned for that purpose, except in the four instances of West-Springfield, Leverett, Bernardston & Northfield, (said Counties comprising a population of about Eighty thousand souls) take the liberty of addressing the chief Magistrate of the Union upon subjects of vital importance to the public interest; and penetrated, as well with a conviction, that the people are the source of power, as with a sense of the veneration due to the several branches of their government, they would approach your Excellency with the freedom of independent citizens and at the same time with respect.

"From the nature of our government it is obviously requisite to its just administration, that it should be much guided and governed in its operations by public opinion; not that the wild caprice or impassioned and hasty sentiments of the people should impel their rulers into systems of policy morally wrong, or divert them from a course of measures wisely calculated to advance the public happiness; but that the deliberate voice of the people, in relation to subjects, of which they have the means of judging correctly, and in which they are immediately interested, should be listened to, with the most careful attention, by their 'substitutes and agents' in public office.

"Thus in the language of the Constitution of this Commonwealth, 'the end of the institution, maintenance, and administration of government is to secure the existence of the body politic; to protect it; and to furnish the individuals, who compose it, with the power of enjoying, in safety and tranquility, their natural rights and the blessings of life; and whenever these great objects are not obtained, the people have a right to alter the government, and to take measures necessary for their safety, prosperity and happiness.'[1] But the shades of injustice, of which Rulers may be guilty, are at once so various and so indefinitely blended, extending from mere omissions of duty to a continued course of 'injuries and usurpations' that it becomes of the utmost importance to a government, conceding and founded upon these great first principles and 'self evident truths,' that its measures should correspond, as far as may be, with the wishes and enlightened judgment of the people.

"A supposed common interest is, in the apprehension of your Memorialists, the basis of the Federal Union; and if in consequence of the proceedings of the government, any particular section of our country should be induced to consider its own interests, as sacrificed to aid the ambition or appease the jealousy of other sections, it cannot, and it ought not to be concealed, that by the habitual indulgence of such feelings, which measures partial in their effects cannot fail to produce, the Union itself would eventually be endangered. Your Memorialists, therefore, ardently attached from principle, as well as habit, to their present form of government, and sincerely desirous of transmitting it unimpaired to posterity, as under God the choicest of all temporal blessings, cannot forbear to express to your Excellency the sentiments of many thousands of their friends and fellow citizens on the subject of the restrictive measures of Congress and the existing War with Great Britain.

"For many years after the establishment of the present government, the prosperity and happiness of the people of the United States were great beyond example. But since the attempts on the part of the government in 1807 to protect commerce by withdrawing it from the ocean, enterprise has lost its activity and industry its hope of reward. Jealousies have been excited by repeated measures of Congress, tending to the depression and extinction of our commercial rights; and the people of New England, in consequence of the severe pressure of commercial restrictions, have almost seemed to view those, who should be to them 'nursing fathers,' as enemies and not friends. But notwithstanding the long series of evils, which have been experienced of late years, in a peculiar degree, by the Northern and Commercial States, your Memorialists feel themselves still bound to believe that the government will not persist in a course of measures, hitherto inefficient either in redressing the wrongs committed against the United States or in protecting any part of the property of her citizens, when experimentally convinced of its disastrous influence upon the rights and interests of a large portion of the people.

"After the able and satisfactory examination of the alledged causes of War against Great Britain, contained in an 'Address of Members of the House of Representatives of the Congress of the United States to their Constituents,'[2] it can hardly be expected that your Memorialists should detail to your Excellency the particular grounds of their belief that the war is neither just, necessary, nor expedient. While they would not therefore attempt a discussion of the alledged grounds of hostilities, they would congratulate your Excellency and the friends of peace throughout the Union upon the recent appearance of a Decree of the government of France, repealing her Decrees of Berlin and Milan, and the probable consequent removal of the principal alledged cause of War, the British orders in Council. At the same time your Memorialists cannot repress their indignant emotions, while contemplating the manifest attempt on the part of France to deceive the American people to their ruin.

"The Berlin and Milan decrees were alledged to have been repealed in November 1810; but Great Britain, in justification of her refusal to withdraw her Orders in Council, has invariably considered the promise of repeal, made in the month of August preceding, as dependent on our determination to *cause our rights to be respected by the commencement of hostilities against the English*. In vain, for more than eighteen Months, did the citizens of the United States wait the ordinary and proper evidence of that repeal—the repealing Decree; in vain did Great Britain promise a repeal of her orders, whenever that evidence should be furnished; the condition of the promise of repeal had not then been performed, *the United States being at peace with Great Britain*. But in the judgment of your Memorialists, it is a singular and alarming fact, *that within thirty days after the declaration of War against Great Britain, a Decree of repeal, bearing date April 1811. (more than a year previous to its formal promulgation) was received in the United States!*[3] It is singular, because it displays a boldness of deception, hitherto unparallelled in the intercourse of independent States; and it is alarming, inasmuch as 'he that runs may read,'[4] that Bonaparte, from the imposition of the first Embargo down to the declaration of War against Great Britain, has anticipated with more exactness the proceedings of our public Councils, than Americans themselves. But could the Emperor of France have believed, that the government of the United States was about to be entangled in his toils and irresistibly drawn into the Continental system and the Embraces of an Alliance? Is it possible he should have imagined, that a War, commenced against Great Britain on the ground of her obnoxious orders in Council, would be persisted in when those orders were removed by the removal of his decrees, upon which they were founded? Is it conceivable that he has issued this decree, affixing to it a false date, in order to deceive the American people as to the time of the repeal itself?

"Why the repeated declaration, since the month of November 1810, that the Berlin and Milan decrees were fundamental Laws of the French Empire, confirmed, as it has been, by an indiscriminate capture of American property and the total ignorance of the judicial & ministerial officers of the French government as to the fact of any revocation; and now for the first time the promulgation of a decree, whereby the Emperor would seem to have expressed his gracious pleasure, in April 1811, that those decrees should be repealed? Why is a Decree of repeal, purporting on the face of it, to have been adopted in consequence of a Law of Congress of March 1811, now published to the world, as conclusive evidence of the existence of that repeal in the month of November 1810. Why, your Memorialists respectfully ask, why this dark & mysterious conduct on the part of France? Why this mixture of falsehood & hypocrisy? Why her alternate caresses and indignities? Why are we at one time told, that 'his Majesty loves the Americans,' and that 'their prosperity & commerce are within the scope of his policy';[5] and at another, that they are 'men without just political views, without honor, and without energy'?[6] Why, we ask, but that France would hurry *us* into the same snares, into which the governments of the Continent have already fallen, by the united agency of flattery, fraud & menace?

"Impressed, therefore, with the importance of the crisis, as it respects the justice, impartiality, and honor of the National government, about to be evidenced, by the course of its measures, in the new relation, supposed to be now subsisting between the belligerents of Europe and the United States, your memorialists do not hesitate to express their conviction, that measures should be immediately taken, in the event of the repeal of the British orders in Council, to bring the War, in its infancy, to an honorable termination; and that a persistence in hostilities, after the removal of this, the leading & only recent ground of War against Great Britain, would be viewed of necessity, by all classes of the people, as deeply alarming to the liberties and independence of the United States.

"But whatever may be the course of Great Britain, in consequence of this fraudulent attempt on the part of France to bind us indissolubly to her Empire, your Memorialists cannot consider the War, in which we are engaged, as required by the interest, security or honor of the American people. If prosecuted for the protection of commerce, the friends of commerce have invariably deprecated restrictions & War as indescribable evils, and would gladly exchange them, upon any terms, for free trade & honorable peace. If War has been declared to cleanse the honor of the government, should not that power have been selected as our enemy, which imprinted the stain? Which, while it has declared the Americans to be 'more dependent than Jamaica, which at least has its Assembly of Representatives & its privileges,'[7] has practically expressed her contempt of our government & her disregard of national Law, by seizing, scuttling, & burning our Merchant Vessels, without even the forms of regular adjudication?[8] Admitting, however, our honor to have been tarnished by Great Britain, our rights to have been withholden, and the personal liberty of our citizens to have been infringed; how, your memorialists respectfully inquire, are our seamen to be protected by exposing them to capture as prisoners of War? How are our injuries to be redressed by throwing our wealth within the grasp of Great Britain, and authorising depredations on the part of her subjects? Or how is our honor to be brightened by a War, which must terminate, if persisted in, either in ruin or disgrace.

"Under these circumstances your Memorialists earnestly pray your Excellency, that Commissioners may be forthwith appointed, on the part of the United States, to negociate and conclude a Treaty of Peace with Great Britain upon just, safe, and honorable terms."

RC (DNA: RG 59, ML). 11 pp.; signed by eighty-six representatives from fifty-six towns.

1. The delegates quoted the opening paragraph of the preamble to the 1780 Massachusetts Constitution.
2. For this address, see *PJM-PS*, 4:496 n. 2.

3. For the Decree of St. Cloud, see Joel Barlow to JM, 12 May 1812, ibid., 4:379 and n. 2.

4. In the Old Testament the prophet Habakkuk is instructed, while waiting for an answer to his prayers concerning iniquity in the world, to write the answer he receives plainly on tablets "that he may run that readeth it" (Hab. 2:2).

5. The memorialists quoted from a 5 Aug. 1810 letter from the duc de Cadore to John Armstrong (*ASP, Foreign Relations*, 3:386–87).

6. The memorialists quoted from a 14 Feb. 1810 letter from the duc de Cadore to Armstrong (ibid., 3:380–81).

7. Ibid., 3:381.

8. On 20 June 1812 the Boston *Columbian Centinel* reported that Capt. James T. S. Mather had been captured by a French squadron on a return cruise from Lisbon. Mather was released and required to take on board seventeen captured seamen from five American vessels the French squadron had "*captured*, sunk, or BURNT": the *Mercury*, the *Pizarro*, the *Happy-Couple*, the *Sally*, and the *Iris*. The *National Intelligencer* of 27 June 1812 printed a report Mather had received from the commander of the French squadron listing the "English and Americans" they had captured and were returning on Mather's ship. Mather reported that twenty-seven American vessels had been "taken, burnt or sunk" during the squadron's cruise and that French officers had orders "to burn and destroy all American vessels going to or coming from an enemy's port."

From the Inhabitants of New Braintree, Massachusetts

MAY IT PLEASE YOUR EXCELLENCY,   July 16th. 1812.

We your memorialists, beg leave to improve a constitutional privilege, in expressing our views and feelings, with respect to the late *Declaration* of *War*, by our government, against Great-Britain. While we would treat the opinion and measures of our Rulers with deference, we feel it to be a right and a duty which we owe to ourselves and to our Country, to express our sentiments at this time with freedom. We shall not undertake to state *all* the objections we have to this War. They are such, however, as have come before your Excellency from other quarters. The usual calamities of War are so dreadful, that they ought always to be avoided, if possible. But we should not shrink from these calamities, did we feel ourselves impelled to them, by duty and necessity. But after having carefully attended to the public documents, relating to the existing difficuilties [*sic*] between the government and the Belligerent Powers, we can see no sufficient reasons, for this Nation to plunge itself into that vortex, which has destroyed most of the civilized nations of the world. Nor can we confidently appeal to *Him* for aid, in this war, who has respect to justice and righteousness, while we are avenging ourselves of *one nation*, for injuries and wrongs, which have principally been occasioned by *another*. And that virtua⟨l⟩ coalescence with France, in spreading misery and wretchedness among the human race, which is *more* than *implied*, in a war with Great Britain at the present time, is most abhorrent to our feelings, and can never be cordially complied with.

Add to all other circumstances, the want of unanimity, both among the Councils and the people of this nation, in the prosecution of this war, and we are constrained to view it as most impolitick, even if it were just. When we consider that *that* part of the Union whence the resources in war must chiefly come, and which must be viewed as the *nerves* and *sinews* of the nation, is strongly disinclined to the present war, we tremble for the fate of the Nation. We are ready to believe that Government have mistaken the feelings of the efficient part of the community, with respect to war.

Wherefore, your petitioners pray your Excellency to take into serious consideration, the present dangers and calamities of the country, arising from the late declaration of War, against Great-Britain, and to adopt speedy measures for the restoration of peace. And as in duty bound, your memorialists will ever pray.

JAMES WOODS Moderator of sd. Meeting
Attest. PHILIP DELANO Town Clerk

RC (DNA: RG 59, ML).

From George S. Kavenagh

TERITORY OF ORLEANS

HONOURED SIR   BAYOU SARAH July 16th 1812.

The High Station you fill in the Hearts of your Counterymen Has Induced Me to adress My self to you in Preference to Making Interest through others and as My Statement is Certain Facts I Expect that Justice which Has Ever Marked with Honour your Precedency will be Extended in My Present application.

Your Excellency may well Recollect the Decided Step Taken by you to Save from Ruin West Florida which from Necessity Renounced its Alegeance to Spain; and onely looked for Succour from the United States;[1] when Endeavouring to Place ourselves in the best Posible Sittuation of Defence after the Taking of Batton Rouge and fitting out an Expedition against Pensacola I was Directed By the Convention to Have a Number of Cannon mounted at as Early a Period as Posible there being no funds to advance, I undertook to Perform for our Common Welfare and in Hopes our Troubles would be Crowned with Liberty which from your Guardianship we were not disappointed in. Some of the Cannon were mounted and Delivered up in Batton Rouge to Governor Claiborne and some are yet in My Custody Amongst which are one of A Very Supperior Quality, it being A Brass Six-Pounder Neatly finished and Counter Bored and thought by Judges to be of the best Kind.

War Having been declared from the best Information Here I Have thought it Proper to Acquaint your Excellency Hoping that the Cannon May be Serviceable on the Present Occasion.

My Reason for Not Having Delivered the Cannon at the Time Posession was Taken Here by your Excellencies forces, was that as I Had Never Received any Compensation for the work that I Had furnished which was Taken by the United States Troops in the fort and as all the work by Me furnished was Ultimately for the benefit and Interest of the United States that when these Pieces of Cannon now in My Hands would be delivered that the United States would Sanction the Payment of a debt wherein they were onely Interested in its benefits and as they Alone Have Received all the benefits Ariseing from My Having Mounted said Cannon and Cariages Limbers &c that at the delivery of the Cannon Now in My Hand that I May be Indemnified for Said Services So Rendered the United States.

Under our Convention there was a Millitary Agent appointed[2] and Having Examined My bill of Services Has Accepted it for upwards of Seventeen Hundred Dollars which work was on the Most Reasonable Terms our Eoconomy Could Sudgest yet after the Manner & form of those of the United States I Hope your Excellency will Excuse My want of Judgement Should this application be Improperly Made as Perhaps it ought to Have been directed to the Secretary of War yet as the Cannon might be usefull to My Cuntery; and Confiding in your Excellencies Goodness I Trust Such Etiquett will not Injure the Good Intentions your (Execllency) [sic].

I Need Not Make a Plea of My Necessity, by being Deprived of the Money Expended by Me to aid at that Critical Moment our little Country but Had it Not been for the Timely Asistance of Governor Claiborne in conferring on Me an office of Small Profit I must Certainly Have been Reduced to the Last Extremity as I Had Extended My Credit for Many Materials furnished.

I Have the Honour Still to be a [. . .] of the Felecianna Troop of Horse who Made the Decent uppon Batton Rouge and am joined by My brave Comrades in offering our Services in all Times of Exegencies to Support the Honor and Interest of our Cuntery. I Have the Honor to be your Excellencies Most Devoted Humble Servt.

GEORGE. S. KAVENAGH[3]

RC (DNA: RG 107, LRRS, K-37:6). Docketed as received in the War Department on 15 Aug. 1812. Damaged by removal of seal.

1. Kavenagh referred to JM's annexation of West Florida on 27 Oct. 1810 (Presidental Proclamation, 27 Oct. 1810, PJM-PS, 2:595–96).

2. Kavenagh referred to James Neilson (ibid., 3:102 n. 2).

3. George Kavenagh was the sheriff of Feliciana Parish, his term commencing on 19 Jan. 1811 (Carter, Territorial Papers, Orleans, 9:986).

From Jeremiah Anderson

MAY IT PLEASE YOUR EXCELLENCY   BALTIMORE July. 17th. 1812

I am the unhappy young man to say again that I have not received an answer yet to my last dates[1]—which grieves, me to the quick by Keeping me in suspence. I pray your Excellency will be so good to Send me my documents by return of Post together with an answer or without an answer—as may please your Excellency best.

'Ere' I close I beg to impress on your mind the observation which I have already made with respect to the Blacks—as I am in the habit of mixing with all classes—merely for information—I have an opportunity of making observations & remarks & this I remark—in my different excursions in and about Baltimore—that there is an old woman roving about the town, whom the people call insane in consequence of her carrying always in her hands a Bible & in her pockets Books for children, but believe me there is no more insanity in that old womans head than there is in your Excellencys. I have seen her in all parts of the town & Suburbs—not only the bible but sometimes a "hoe" in her hand and seemingly very busy—and believe me it is my opinion that there are some whites who call themselves Christia⟨ns⟩ in this, or what your excellency may please to call it. I pray your excellency will please to notice these as merely observations.

I consider my case hard, (not only myself but others, men of talents, who have perused the case, private as well as public).

And I wish it relived by—Your Excellency's very humble Servant.

JEREMIAH ANDERSON

RC (DNA: RG 45, Misc. Letters Received).

1. See Anderson to JM, 10 July 1812 (two letters). Anderson also wrote on 15 July: "My anxiety remains yet unbelieved [*sic*], by answer from my last dates, respecting my fate. I consider my case hard, and I pray to be relieved by an answer from or by your direction at an early hour. The sentiment of my whole heart is before your Excellency" (ibid.; 1 p.).

From Paul Carrington Jr.

SIR   CHARLOTTE July. th[e] 17th. 181⟨2⟩

Conformably to an order of a general meeting of the people of Charlotte at their Court-house I transmit to you a Copy of their Proceedings. The Coincidence of your order, and the people's sentiments, is satisfactory evidence of their truth, and justice; and I am the more gratifyed, as I am forceably reminded of our early acquaintance in 1786, and 1787, when we generally concurred in important measures of State policy.[1]

Being forced into the n[e]cessary resistance of the war waged against us by Great Brittain, the freedom of the St Lawrance may be gained with little loss of blood, or treasure, and all the confines of the territories of the United States will be marked by natural and secure boundaries. It gives me pleasure to state ⟨tha⟩t my Eldest son, and three nephews, the sons of my Brother the late Genl Carrington are equipped in volunteer Companies, and are ready to march for any part of the Continent at a moments warning. Permit me to sollicit your acceptance of my esteem, and profound respect.

PAUL CARRINGTON JR.[2]

P. S. Will you be so indulgent as to excuse a father for speaking of his son, or for requesting you, if your time will permit to Peruse Edward Carrington's speech delivered to the people of Halifax the 4th of July.[3]

PCJR.

[Enclosure]

§ From the Citizens of Charlotte County, Virginia. *15 July 1812.* "In all free governments it is the privilege & duty of the people to assemble & express freely their sentiments on great & important subjects. To resist by remonstratrance [*sic*] encroachments on their liberties, and by a proper expression of Confidence, to Strengthen & Support the government in trying & difficult emergences. A more interesting period has not been Witnessed since the formation of the government, and a more Suitable occasion for an expression of the public Opinion, has not presented itself. Our Country after a series of years of peace, quietness, & prosperity, is compelled to relinquish these blessings, and encounter the evils & Calamities of War.

"We had Cherished a love of peace & had Cultivated a friendship for all Nations. In return we had a right to expect from them a regard and respect for our rights as a Nation, and a Strict observance of the laws of Nations towards Neutrals. Our expectations have been disappointed; & in return, we have met with insults, & injuries, too enormous to be borne by a Nation, jealous of it's character, proud of it's independance, & boasting of it's liberties. To submit, would be a loss of National Character, a surrender of National independance, and would produce a state of self degradation, in which we should value neither our personal, nor National liberties. A state imediately preparitory, to Slavery, & despotism, not to be endured by free Men.

"To prevent an appeal to Arms, our government has resorted to all those measures, which it believed would sensibly affect the belligerants, & produce a respect for our rights. With France it has been encouraged to continue Negotiation, now rendered almost hopeless by the late dispatches of our envoy, and by the repeated Accounts of the burnings, & distruction of our Vessels at Sea. With England, every expedient has failed. Negotiation with her, has only served to unfold her vast & encreasing pretentions. It would be now useless to enumerate the various provocations & injuries received from her. They have been borne with a patience, to be Accounted for only, by our love of peace, & the dread of the Calamities of War. They have encreased with our anxiety for peace, and were we now, to yield, She would but advance in her demands. No other Nation would have so long borne such provocations, such wrongs, such aggressions on it's rights. But there is a point of endurance beyond which it would be dangerous, we cannot go.

"Resolved therefore, that we the Citizens of Charlotte will unite in the support of the government in carrying on the war declared against Great Britain, beleiving that the Causes are just, & trusting that a good & righteous providence will protect us in it & crown our Arms with success.

"Resolved that bare submission to the laws is but a duty, a Virtue of the Negat[i]ve kind. That in a contest with a foreign Nation, great & powerful as our enemy, we will not only obey the requisitions of the law, but Cordially support the government by giving it every aid in our power. That we will forget all party distinctions, and unite heart & hand against the Common foe. That we will endeavour to promote harmony & concord, among our fellow Citizens, and Shew to our enemy, that she will not have to fight a part, but the whole of the nation.

"Resolved, that it is the opinion of this meeting, that to ensure a speedy, just, & honourable, peace, the War should be prosecuted with the utmost vigour, both by Sea & Land. For this purpose, we trust that all the energies of the government will be exercised, & all the means of annoying our enemy be used. That the Nation ought to know it's strength, and it's enemies be made to feel it.

"Resolved, that as in peace we have felt & experienced the happy effects of our government, in the security of our rights & best interests, in the maintenance of order, in the encouragement of Moral & Virtuous principles, & in the unexampled promotion of our prosperity: so in war, we will endeavour to shew it's efficacy, & convince the world that a free government, to which the people are attached is not only calculated for a State of peace, but Sufficient to afford defence & protection to its citizens & to carry them safely through the storms & difficulties of a war, with one of the most powerful Nations On earth—and that thus our love & attachment to it's principles may be encreased, & our Confidence in it's institutions Confirmed.

"Resolved, that whatever may be the result of our present Negotiation with France, we ought to fear & avoid an Alliance with her—that close Alliances with foreign Nations are at all times dangerous, but more especially in this unexampled state of the world, and with a despot, who has envariably made his Allies, his subjects, & Slaves; that should the Negotiation fail in producing a just redress of our grievances, we are equally ready to support the government in any measures of defence & coertion, which in its wisdom it may adopt towards that Nation."

RC (DLC); enclosure (DNA: RG 59, ML). RC docketed by JM; torn. Enclosure 4 pp.; signed by Paul Carrington Jr., chairman, and Thomas Read Jr., secretary. A shorter letter of 17 July from Carrington, possibly to JM, also mentions enclosing the resolutions of the citizens of Charlotte County (ibid.; 1 p.).

1. Carrington and JM crossed paths on at least two occasions during the 1780s. In 1786 JM introduced a bill in the Virginia General Assembly that supported Carrington's petition to allow the executors of the will of Joseph Mayo to free Mayo's 176 slaves (The General As-

sembly Session of October 1786, *PJM*, 9:147–51). As a member of Virginia's ratifying convention in 1788, Carrington was among those JM counted on to vote in favor of ratification (see Archibald Stuart to JM, 21 Oct. 1787, and JM to Jefferson, 24 Oct. 1787, *PJM*, 10:202, 206–19).

2. Paul Carrington (1733–1818) was one of the first judges to be appointed in 1779 to the Virginia Supreme Court of Appeals, on which he served until his retirement in 1807. Carrington was a member of the House of Burgesses from 1765 to 1775 and represented Charlotte County on several committees of safety and in state conventions between 1775 and 1788 (Alexander Brown, *The Cabells and Their Kin: A Memorial Volume of History, Biography, and Genealogy* [Boston, 1895], 204–7).

3. In the right margin of the postscript Carrington added: "at the request of the people directed to be published in the 'Enquirer' at Richmond." The Richmond *Enquirer* reported on Edward Carrington's speech on 24 July 1812 but did not print it.

From George Joy

DEAR SIR,   LONDON July 17th. 1812.

Leaving Town for a few days I sent to Lord Sidmouth the letter of which I take the liberty to enclose copy herein.[1] I returned on the 11th. Instant & found a card of Mr Russell subjoining a request in pencil that I would call on him on my return.

My letters have been regularly sent me; but of this card I knew nothing though it had lain a week at my lodgings and on calling I found he had left town the day before for a fortnight. I have written him to Cheltenham; but find by Mr Beasley that he was absent on the arrival of my letter and as the bag by which I send this Via Norfolk will close before I can hear from him I am left to conjecture his special object. The most probable that presents itself is some consequence of my reference of Lord Sidmouth to him in my letter of the 22nd. of June 1812[2] as he could have received no letters from you for me from the time of my departure 'till the day he left his card.

Mr R. & myself have frequently missed each other of late owing chiefly to his occasional absence from town. I have not seen him once since the revocation of the Orders in Council.

A remark of the Lord Chancellor in the House of Lords on (I think) monday last[3] relating to the extent of his duties and among others, that of examining the cases of criminals that may be proper subjects of mercy has reminded me of a subject, which, as exhibiting something of the character of Sir Wm. Scott is not altogether uninteresting in the perspective of the agency of reclamation the uncertain emoluments of which I hope to have attached to the barren product of the Consulship & agency for seamen, if that place should be alotted for me.

A man by the name of Jemott had been condemned at the Admiralty sessions under circumstances which made it the duty of the Judge in passing sentence to leave him without hopes of mercy. My nephew (a student at Lincolns Inn) hearing accidentally of the peculiar domestic misery involved in the case, and of certain circumstances which struck him as unknown or misconceived at the trial, made an effort to save the man's neck, and obtained an appointment with the Judge who spent with him more than two hours, went over all his notes on the trial, and informed him that the case had already gone thro' the usual process of reconsideration before the Chancellor and others of the Council, who had reported for the execution clearly & unanimously. He had therefore a difficulty as to the means of interference, thought himself altogether the wrong person to be even consulted, but with an evident uneasiness and desire to have the pardon accomplished he added if it were possible in any way it could only be by the intervention of the parties aggrieved by the robbery. Much interest and exertion were made in which several persons humanely lent a hand, much difficulty was encountered but finally the underwriters and all the jurors having been prevailed on to join in the petition the pardon was obtained; being a singular, and as some say an unique, instance of acquittal, at such a period, on the merits of the Case.

Besides the personal intercourse there was some correspondence between my nephew & Sir William who went to Bath in the time, a part of which, (a letter from Sir William,) I subjoin chiefly to show that if he can be petulant and peevish, as sometimes occurs, his temper knows how to taper off and yield to the control of better dispositions.

Copy

"Sir,

You must give me leave to say that this is putting me into an unfair situation. I have done the whole of my duty in this matter; and shall as I have already informed you take no further part. If the matter stated by the committee (and of the grounds of which I am wholly ignorant) shall appear to the Council of sufficient weight in itself, and sufficiently supported by evidence, the unfortunate person will have such benefit from it as the Council may think due. But it never can justify my interposition that one body of men have come to conclusions, upon evidence of which I am totally unacquainted, and that another body of men (the Jury) may *possibly* adopt those conclusions. And I cannot help thinking that, under such circumstances, a very undue advantage is attempted to be taken of my private feelings. I am Sir, Your Obdt. St.

W: SCOTT.

The utmost that I can do (and I do it without any alteration of my opinion that the application made to me is by no means a justifiable one to be made to a person who has any responsibility for the administration of public justice) is to send your letter to my brother telling him that I am totally ignorant of the facts stated in this letter; (which comes from a respectable person;) that it will be for the Regent's council to decide (if such petitions are presented) how far it may be proper to extend mercy to the unfortunate person, upon any disclosed change of circumstances from those that appeared in the original evidence. From mere motives of humanity I shall not regret if their decision should take that course, certainly otherwise, as far as such motives can operate; but no efforts of mine can go farther.

Henry, H: Joy Esqre.

  Lincolns Inn."

I take no notice of the analogy, (in respect to the "change of circumstances from those that appeared in the original evidence") between this case and that of the Fox & others because, to be honest, there is none.[4] I have been informed that it was in contemplation to date the decree of April 1811[5] in November at Paris. Nor do I contemplate any great advantage from fixing it between the 2nd. of March & the 30th. of May, as I wrote you before;[6] but I believe that property, and a great deal more, ought to be restored; and that at least may be with management; nor should I utterly dispair, but for the inefficiency of the strong efforts of Mr Monroe & Mr Pinkney, of some compensation being obtained in those cases of condemnation which followed the Polly-Laskey[7] without previous warning. But I repeat that I should prefer the attempt in the lifetime of Sir Wm. Scott. I am alway's very respectfully, your friend & Servant.

G. Joy.

RC and enclosure (DLC: Rives Collection, Madison Papers). RC in a clerk's hand, signed by Joy; postmarked Boston, 2 Sept.; docketed by JM. For enclosure, see n. 1.

  1. Joy's three-page letter to Sidmouth, dated 30 June 1812, expressed his concern over "the mischief that may ensue if the valuable cargoes now preparing should be suffered to proceed to the U. S." Joy cited U.S. terms for revocation of trade restrictions as evidence that the repeal of the orders in council would prove ineffective in restoring Anglo-American trade so long as Fox's blockade of May 1806 remained in force.
  2. In Joy's 23 June letter to Sidmouth, which he enclosed in a 23 June letter to JM, Joy suggested that Russell "would corroborate" his belief that the blockade of May 1806 should be revoked (DLC: Rives Collection, Madison Papers; *PJM-PS*, 4:499–500 and n. 1).
  3. Joy was probably referring to a speech given by Lord Chancellor John Scott on 13 July 1812 concerning an appellant jurisdiction and court of chancery bill (*Parliamentary Debates*, 1st ser., 23:997).
  4. The *Fox* was an American merchantman captured under the orders in council on 15 Nov. 1810 (*PJM-PS*, 3:412 n. 3).
  5. Joy referred to the Decree of St. Cloud of 28 Apr. 1811.
  6. Joy believed that dating the supposed French repeal between the passage of the Nonintercourse Act of 2 Mar. 1811 and Wellesley's 30 May 1811 decision that court proceedings would be carried out against the *Fox* would "operate in some degree inversely to what a genuine document of that date would effect" (Joy to JM, 25 May 1812, ibid., 4:418–21).
  7. The *Polly*, under the command of Captain Laskey, had been captured by the British on 16 Oct. 1799 while carrying a cargo of Cuban sugar to Spain from Marblehead, Massachusetts. The case revised Sir William Scott's strict interpretation of the notion of "continuous

voyage" by allowing the vessel's brief stop in Massachusetts to qualify as a bona fide break in its voyage between Cuba and Spain (Robinson, *Admiralty Reports* [Shaw and Shoemaker 584], 2:295–304; Bradford Perkins, "Sir William Scott and the *Essex*," *WMQ*, 3d ser., 13 [1956]: 171–73).

From Robert Martin

DEAR SIR   CASWELL COTY No. CAROLINA 17th. July 1812
In your fathers liftime Capt. Scott—your father and one or two Others, agreed to let my Grandfather Ro. Martin have a Certain quantity of land, adjoining Capt. Scott & others; which was in his possession a Considerable time; he lived & died upon it—but your father for some Cause detaind the land [(]the part he was to give) & profered to give to the representatives of Robert Martin so much money: say 60 or 70. dollars; and detain the right of the land. He stated that he woud pay it over to any of the Legatees who was properly authorised under law to receive it. Being so far; & no one of them wer[e] willing to undertake the Journey, & expences that might accru[e] it hath remain unsettled. I understand you are Executor of you[r] fathers will. If you recoll[e]ct any thing relative to this afair, & you Consider there is any thing due us, from your father, or his estates; you will Confer a particular favour to inform us to what amot. if any thing—how and where we are to apply for it.[1] I shoud not Call on you at this late period for information Concern[i]ng it—but if any thing is due; it will be of Considerable service to me at present, having procured a relinqu[i]shmnt of the Int. of all the legatees—to the same, which I will produce properly Certified in any manner requ[i]red. If you Consider nothing is due us from your father nothing more will be named Concerning it—it remains with yourself—please inform me accordingly. Respectfully yr. Obt Srvt
ROBERT MARTIN

The particular information Concer[n]ing this business is received by a Mr. French who Conversed with your father on this subject. Perhaps it may be Known to you.

RC (DLC). Docketed by JM.

1. The will of James Madison Sr. makes no mention of Martin's claims (DLC).

From Caleb Nichols

[ca. 17 July 1812]

The earnest Petition of Caleb Nichols of Plattsburgh in the State of N. Y. humbly Showeth, that Whereas the U. S. have Declared war against G. B. And Whereas Canada and Novascotia, Nay Hallifax alone, are worth continuing the war for. And Whereas it is reported, which report your Petitioner believes to be true, that the British orders in Council have been recinded.[1] And Whereas the British Ministry will expect that the U. S. will make peace merely because G. B. has recinded her orders. And Whereas the U. S. ought by all means to possess themselves of those Promises before they permit G. B. to make any overtures for Peace. And Whereas it is of infinite importance to the Commerce of the U. S. that G. B. Should not, but that the U. S. Should possess Hallifax. And Whereas G. B. is unable to remunerate the U. S⟨.⟩ in Cash for her Spoliations on that Commerce. And Whereas peace ought not to be made with G. B. without payment, in Some way, for all the damages Sustained by them on the ocean. And Whereas after the Conquest of those Provinces and their erection into a State or States of the U. S. it will not be Necessary to keep on foot a Standing army. And Whereas while G. B. is in possession of those Provinces and whenever the U. S. have any difference with her it will always be necessary to keep a Standing army, which may aid Some a[m]bitious popular individual to divide the Northern from the Southern States and to usurp the Government of the former. And Whereas after the Conquest of Canada the Indians will be absolutely dependant on the U. S. Therefore your Petitioner humbly prays that the War may be Continued until C. and N. are Conquered and that at the Conclusion of a Peace they may continue in the possession of the U. S. as part of the indemnity for Spoliations and to deprive the British Navy of Timber and an Assylum in North America. And Whereas it is important that the best plan for the Conquest of Canada Should be Addopted. And Whereas your Petitioner from a long residence on the frontiers has become acquainted with the Strength oppinions and feelings of the Inhabitants of Upper and lower Canada and therefore ought to be a better Judge of the Point and Manner of Attack than those Who have not a particular knowledge of those circumstances. And Whereas it is your Petitioners decided oppinion that it will be more difficult to conquer the Upper than the lower, except Quebect, Province, because the Subjects of the former are infinitely More loyal than those of the latter, unless by the conquest of Montreal, by which to cut off the Communication between the upper and lower Province, when the former would fall of Course without Sending a Single Soldier into it. Your Petitioner ther⟨e⟩for reiterates his humble Prayer that the troops and Melitia of the U. S. May be, especially the old Regiments, immediately except enough of the Melitia to guard our frontiers on upper Canada from depredations, collected at Plattsburg⟨h⟩ and from thence Marched directly to the River S't Lawrence in the Neigh-bourhood of Montreal or dow[n] Lake Champlain to S't Johns in the Boats which are now building and then cross by Land to the River S't L. and Carry the Boats to the latter River to Carry the Troops over to Montreal. Twelve Thousand Regulars with as Many Melitia would be able to take Montreal in a week or a fortnight from the time they Started from Platts-burgh. The Regulars could winter in Montreal in the British Barracks &c and keep the upper Province in Check and their places being Supplied by Melitia, March in the Spring to the Siege of Quebect.

CALEB NICHOLS[2]

RC (DNA: RG 107, LRRS, N-42:6). Undated; date assigned here on the assumption that the letter was mailed in Plattsburgh, New York, approximately ten days before being docketed as received in the War Department on 27 July 1812.

1. For the terms of the 23 June 1812 repeal of the orders in council, see *PJM-PS*, 4:488–89 n. 2. Unofficial news of the repeal, with some variation from the actual order, arrived in Washington on 8 Aug. (see JM to Gallatin, 8 Aug. 1812).

2. Caleb Nichols was a Plattsburgh lawyer and occasional informant for the War Depart-ment (Allan S. Everest, *The War of 1812 in the Champlain Valley* [Syracuse, N.Y., 1981], 52).

From William Pinkney

MY DEAR SIR.   BALTIMORE. 17h. July 1812.

From the enclosed Extract from the "American" it would seem that our Consul at Lisbon has retired from his Station;[1] and it is possible that he may not wish to return to it. If that should be so, will you permit me to mention my eldest Son (William) for your Consideration as his Successor in Case one shd. be appointed. He can have the best Recommendation from Merchants and others of all parties. He has been twice at Lisbon, and is there at this Moment.

I take the Liberty to name him to you rather by his own Desire than mine—and I beg to be understood as not intending in any Degree to press his Interests upon you. On the contrary it is my unfeigned wish that he may not even be thought of, if any Reason whatever exists against it. I have the Honour to be with true Respect & Attachment Dear Sir, Your faithful & Ob Servant

WM PINKNEY

RC (DLC). Docketed by JM.

1. Enclosure not found, but on 17 July 1812 the Baltimore *American and Commercial Daily Advertiser* reported that the American consul at Lisbon had taken passage aboard a ship for Baltimore in anticipation of the declaration of war.

From William Wirt

Dear Sir.   Richmond. July 17. 1812.

On passing through the county of Powhatan two days ago, I had the mortification to learn from a friend of mine that he had, with a kind yet ill-judged officiousness, written to you in my behalf, recommending me for a military appointment.[1] I was aware that you had lately received a similar intimation, through Mr. Brent, from another quarter; and 'though I had explained, immediately, to Mr. Brent how the thought came into circulation, yet I am fearful that congress had risen & that he had left the city, before he received my letter and had an opportunity of correcting his first statement to you. If this should have been the case, the mistaking kindness of my friends, will have left me presented before you as a candidate for a military commission: You will excuse me, therefore, I hope for stating that however strong my desire to enter the service of my country, actively, the situation of my private affairs will not permit it: circumstanced as I am, such a step would be a sacrafice not called for by the posture of the country and therefore wholly incompatible with my duties both as a husband and a father. I beg you to accept the assurance of my respect & devotion.

WM. WIRT

RC (DLC). Docketed by JM.

1. See William Pope to JM, 10 July 1812, and n. 2.

§ From William Farquhar.[1] *17 July 1812, Natchez*. Asks that JM permit him "to remain peacably untill He can dispose of his property lawfully aquired here; Pay his debts which are but few; and retire, to oppose in another land Napoleon the Tyrant the plague of Europe."[2]

RC (DNA: RG 59, War of 1812 Papers, Letters Received regarding Enemy Aliens). 1 p.; docketed by JM.

1. William Farquhar of Natchez was described on the State Department alien enemies list compiled between 25 Aug. and 1 Sept. 1812 as a forty-two-year-old shopkeeper with no family who had submitted no application for naturalization (Carter, *Territorial Papers, Mississippi*, 6:309).
2. In July 1812 several American newspapers reprinted the "Act respecting Alien Enemies" of 6 July 1798, which stated that "all natives, citizens, denizens, or subjects" of nations with which the U.S. was at war "shall be liable to be apprehended, restrained, secured and removed, as alien enemies," at the discretion of the president (*U.S. Statutes at Large*, 1:577). Farquhar may have believed that this act was still in force, but it had in fact expired in 1801. In 1812 enemy aliens were required to comply with a 7 July 1812 directive from the State Department requesting that British subjects in the U.S. report to U.S. marshals their names, ages, places and duration of residence, occupations, names of family members, and whether they had applied for naturalization (*National Intelligencer*, 8 July 1812).

§ From Richard Rush. *17 July 1812*. Requests that JM "accept a copy of the discourse the delivery of which, on the 4th of July, he was so obliging as to witness."[1]

RC (PHi). 1 p. Enclosure not found, but see n. 1.

1. On 8 July 1812 the *National Intelligencer* reported that JM, along with his family and the
heads of departments, had been escorted to the Capitol on 4 July to hear Rush's address. Afterward, JM's party returned to the president's house, "where an unusually numerous assemblage of ladies and gentlemen, including a large portion of the members of Congress, soon
collected to offer and to interchange their personal respects," while militia performed ma-
neuvers and a marching salute in front of the house. The newspaper published Rush's address
on 28 July, and it was also printed in pamphlet form (*An Oration, Delivered in the Hall of the
House of Representatives . . . Washington, July 4, 1812* [Washington, 1812; Shaw and Shoemaker
26671]).

From James Barbour

SIR,   RICHMOND, July 18th 1812.

I have just learned through Colo. Coles that he has received Orders to
cause the recruits of the regular Army in this State, as well those now in the
Forts of Norfolk, as those hereafter to be enlisted, to repair forthwith, to
Carlisle, as a place of general rendezvous.[1] This arrangement I presume has
been made after due deliberation and the wisdom thereof, it does not become me to question. The effect of the measure as immediately connected
with the defence of this State I am however at liberty to regret. As I had
heretofore received assurances from the Secretary of War that this portion
of the regular force should remain in this State and that in addition thereto
a portion of the Militia in requisition should be called into actual service if
necessary it was to me a subject equally of regret and Surprize that a
Change of System, so radically affecting the Security of Virginia, should
not have been Communicated to this Department and that it should have
reached me through a Channel so informal.

Presuming however that the Course which has been adopted in relation
to the regulars is irrevocable the unpleasant task devolves upon me to invite your attention to the exposed situation of our Maratime Frontier. I
have heretofore addressed to the Secretary of War several letters exhibiting in detail our Condition, so defenceless that its very weakness, invites
aggression.[2] I solicited of him a view of the plan adopted by the General
Government for our defence and also asked what were its expectations as
to the exertions we were to make. I took the liberty also to point out Certain measures calculated to facilitate our defensive operations. I wrote also
to the Secretary of State and requested of you, through him, for a discretionary power to be lodged in this Department, to call forth such portions
of the Militia as the exigency of our affairs might make necessary.[3] To these

letters and representations (I would fain beleive from higher Claims to the attention of these Gentlemen) I have received no Satisfactory answer. In the mean time I have daily to listen to the lamentations of the People flying from the maritime Frontier, abandoning their homes and their property and who Clamorously call for protection. To shield myself from their upbraidness I am Constrained to expose the entire inadequacy of this Department to extend to them relief without the sanction of the General Government.

Thus Circumstanced and deeply impressed with their hardships and the Justice of their Claims I am Compelled (tho' reluctantly) to address myself directly to you. Hoping that you will discover in the embarrassment of my situation a sufficient apology for the trespass I Commit upon your time and attention.

For the purpose however of presenting to you a more Comprehensive view of our wants and expectations than the limits of a letter would admit I have requested the Hon: Chas. K Mallory[4] a member of the Council of State to wait on you in person who will give you such information as may be wanting relatively to the best means of defence and who will report with fidelity to us such Communications as you may think advisable to impart.

I beg leave to recommend this Gentleman to your polite attention. I am very respectfully your Fellow Citizen

Js: BARBOUR

RC (DLC); letterbook copy (Vi: Executive Letterbook). RC in a clerk's hand, except for Barbour's complimentary close and signature; docketed by JM.

1. On 9 July 1812 acting adjutant general Alexander Smyth gave orders to this effect to Isaac A. Coles of the Twentieth Infantry Regiment. However, Coles was prevented from immediately carrying out these orders by confusion over precisely which troops came under his command (Smyth to Coles, 9 July 1812 [DNA: RG 94, Letters Sent]; Coles to Smyth, 19 July 1812, and Coles to Thomas Cushing, 31 July and 7, 15, and 24 Aug. 1812 [DNA: RG 94, Letters Received, filed under "Coles"]).

2. On 17 Apr. and 19 May 1812 Barbour had written to Eustis to draw attention to the need to provide defense on the Virginia coast (DNA: RG 107, LRRS, B-217:6, B-251:6).

3. Barbour's 23 June 1812 letter to Monroe requested authority to call out the militia. Barbour also sought sanction for an act of the Virginia legislature related to the defense of the coast that was soon to be submitted to Congress for approval, a copy of which he enclosed (NN: Monroe Papers).

4. Charles K. Mallory (1781–1820), a former member of the Virginia General Assembly, was elected to the Virginia Executive Council in 1808. He served as lieutenant governor of Virginia during the War of 1812 and upon leaving that office became the customs collector for Norfolk and Portsmouth (*Richmond Compiler*, 22 Apr. 1820; *CVSP*, 10:190, 192).

From Thomas Claxton

Honored Sir   Washington July 18, 1812

At the South End of the South Wing of the Capitol there is a gang way or platform which serves for the entrance of the Galleries of the Ho of Reps—this passage, Sir was at first built of perishable Materials and is now almost impassable and in times of a Crowd, very dangerous, its elevation being about twelve feet from the ground. Having learnt that you are about to cause the expenditure of some money on the building this Summer, I have conceived it my duty to give you this information. The Speaker also deemed it proper for me to communicate the circumstance to you. Without this way, Sir, the entry of the Galleries is impracticable, and unless rebuilt this Summer, that will be the situation of things here next winter. If a permanent platform should be deemed most expedient, I think there will be plenty of money left after it is erected to finish the Caps. of the Column[s], for which four thousand dollars were appropriated. A Long passage between the two wings wants strong Shoaring to secure it in times of Storms. Some other external repairs are wanting, altho' of less moment, absolutely necessary. I flatter myself Sir that you will pardon the liberty I have taken. Long experience has taught me that it is necessary for one perfectly acquainted with the wants about the House, to point them out in order that things may be comfortable and convenient. I have the honor to be Sir Your Humble Servant

Thos. Claxton.[1]

RC (DNA: RG 42, Records of the District of Columbia Commissioners, Letters Received and Drafts of Letters Sent by the Superintendent of the City of Washington, vol. 21).

1. Thomas Claxton was doorkeeper of the House of Representatives from 1795 to 1821 (*Records of the Columbia Historical Society . . . 1969–1970* [1971], 192).

From Ebenezer Sage

Sr.   Sag harbor. L Island July 18th. 1812

On my return to this place I found that the Citizens had assembled in a number of places, and appointed Committees to devise the most effectual means of defence, in the event of an attack from the enemy. This port lies near Gardiners Bay: the best harbor for a fleet in the United States and where the british usually wintered their fleets in the time of the revolution. On Application, some years since, the G[o]vernment built us a Magazine & Arsenal, and furnished with four heavy cannon, and promised that if war should take place we should be provided with three or four Gunboats, for

45

the defence of the harbor, for which kind of defence it is extremely well calculated, admitting vessels no larger than two or three hundred tons, and through a long narrow & crooked channel. The Secretary of the Navy assured me before I left Washington, that he would order on three Gun boats. In this little system of defence one very essential thing is still wanting, Men. Four companies have been detached from Gen. Rose's brigade[1] in this vicinity, and the people here have instructed their Committee to pray you through the Secretary of War, that those four companies may be stationed for the defence of this coast, one company at this port, and the others in such places as shall be deemed best.[2] We have also in this place a small company of Artillery, half of which have lately been drafted and ordered to New York; this appears to the people improper, as our shores are more exposed & have less means of defence than any portion of the Sea Board of the State. The people here almost unanimously approve and will support the measures of the Government, they are organizing and arming themselves, from the veterans of 60, to the youth of 16. All they ask, is that the draft from the Militia, more immediately designed for defence may be stationed near their own homes, and in this they think they are justified, by the exposed situation of this part of the country. With the highest respect I am Sir your most Obt Servt

E SAGE

RC (DNA: RG 94, Letters Received, filed under "Dering"). Docketed as received in the War Department on 25 July.

1. Brig. Gen. Abraham Rose of Suffolk County, New York, was in command of the Thirty-third Brigade of infantry militia (Hastings, *Military Minutes of the N.Y. Council of Appointment*, 2:1401).

2. Filed with this letter is a one-page memorial dated 18 July from a committee of the inhabitants of Sag Harbor addressed to Secretary of War William Eustis, which complained of the exposed situation of the town and requested that defensive measures be taken that included stationing men in Sag Harbor from Rose's brigade. Eustis acknowledged receipt of the memorial on 28 July and informed the committee that it had been transmitted to the commanding general in New York, Joseph Bloomfield, for consideration (DNA: RG 94, Letters Received, filed under "Dering").

From Hugh White

ALBEMARLE CHARLOTTESVILLE July 18th *1812*

It is hoped that your Excellency will not be offended with the freedom taken by a citizen in sending you a few of his meditations & mental discussions on subjects which in a greater or less extent have occupied the rational faculties of the human race since the origin of the world.[1]

Relaxations, intermissions and unbending of the human mind from intenseness of study may be profitable both to the internal & external man.

N B The writer of the pamphlet in the year 75 was a Tutor of your brother General William. With due respect yours &c

HUGH WHITE[2]

RC (DLC). Docketed by JM.

1. Enclosure not found.

2. Hugh White (d. 1827) was a Baptist minister and landholder in Charlottesville and Milton (Woods, *Albemarle County in Virginia*, 178, 401).

§ From the Citizens of Darlington District, South Carolina. *18 July 1812*. Approve the declaration of war against Great Britain and report the following resolutions, "which were unanimously adopted." "To avenge insult, and repel injury, is characteristic of a great and magnanimous people: To Suffer them with impunity, bespeaks pusillanimity, and invites to repetition. Great Britain compelled to acknowledge us independent, has always manifested towards us, a Spirit of hostility. No sooner than she had signed the treaty of Eighty three, than she determined to evade it; she retained the Post on the Lakes contrary to the express stipulations thereof, in order to let loose the Savage hordes upon us—repress the extension of our frontier Settlements, and if occasion presented, to be in a situation to make an easy descent upon these States. The carrying trade which promised much gain, we were forbid to enjoy in it's full extent, whilst she traded direct from the West India Islands to the Continent of Europe, & her own dominions, we were obliged after purchasing in those Islands, to sail from thence to the United States—pay a specified duty—reship the commodity, before we could carry it to Europe; by means of which restriction, she expected that her merchants would have been enabled, to undersell us in the European market: Notwithstanding these difficulties the activity and enterprise of our merchants, soon surmounted all obstacles, and wealth in a few years afterwards was pouring her abundance into our land. Great Britain under the influence of a selfish policy, grew alarmed at our growing prosperity, and determined it's distruction. The opinions of Sheffield and Stevens,[1] are reduced to practice, and rigidly enforced. The doctrines of her navigation laws, merely municipial regulations, are enlarged, and an effort is made, to abrogate the laws of Nations, and to make them a Substitute. She styles herself the mistress of the Ocean, & arrogantly assumes to herself the supremacy thereof. By her Orders in Council, [the] whole coast of a continent is blockaded, without the semblance of a force to effect it, and our commerce is forbid to approach it. The next year we are insultingly told, that we will be permitted to trade to places interdicted by her Orders, but we must under penalty of Condemnation, touch at her ports—pay the charges thereof, and purchase at immense cost a license from her to do so: Her rapacity not yet satisfied, the license is now withheld and condemnation awaits every American Sail that Whitens the Ocean. Our Vessels are now taken—carried into her ports and condemned, and with the same papers, or some that are forged, ordered to their places of Origina⟨l⟩ destination. Not content with making spoliations upon our Commerce, our personal rights are infringed—Our Seamen torn from the service of their employers—forced on board British Ships of War, and obliged to fight against their Country. Almost every wind that blows, wafts from Seas far & near, the complaints of our Countrymen thus cruelly enslaved. Frequently our Government have interfered to effect their liberation, but in Vain; few or none have ever been released: And unhappy men, if ever they dare to appeal to British Justice to regain their liberty, their Complaints are answered, not by consolation, but with Stripes and with insults. They not only injure us abroad, but approach our own coast—come within our own waters, and regardless of the laws either of nations or hospitality, harass our coasting trade—stop our Vessels—send some to Halifax for adjudication—fire upon others, and murder our Cit[i]zens. The murder of Pierce[2] lies unatoned and unrevenged: A mere mockery of trial was had upon Whitby the perpetrator of the deed, in which Justice was insulted, the Just expectation of our Government disappointed, & Whitby so far from receiveing a punishment adequate to so flagrant an outrage, was acquited, honored & advanced. In time of peace national armed Vessels are regarded as part of terra firma, and as such held inviolable: notwithstanding this received & established opinion, in profound peace, and in the midst of professions of friendship, the Chesapeake a national armed Vessel, was attacked by a British armed vessel of superior force—Our Citizens were murdered, and O! degrading Spectacle, our seamen serving on board said Vessel, was upon beat of drum, and by order of a British Officer, paraded on board of our own Vessel, and Several of them were forcibly taken from our service. Had Great Britain paid a Just regard to her own character, and had promptly not only disavowed authorising the deed, but had tendered to this Government, a compensation & apology in some measure commensurate with the insult and injury, the transaction might have been regarded as the unauthorised act of an individual; but the want of a manifestation of such conduct on her part, induces a presumption, that Humphries[3] acted on that occasion by her Orders. To this black catalogue of insults and injuries, our Government has manifested a moderation, unparalleled in the History of nations: Sensible that a State of neutrality, was most compatible with the happiness and prosperity of these States, it has uniformly, and impartially practized it; And under the influence of an ardent desire for the maintainance of peace, have made frequent advances to the British Government for the continuance of so desirable an object—presented to her attention the extent of our rights, and have remonstrated for years, though in vain, against their frequent infraction. To such representations, she has at some times insidiously opened the door of negotiation, (as in the Case of Erskines Arrangement) until she had obtain'd her wishes, then would disavow the deed—triumph in her degradation, and smile at our credulity in her plighted faith. At other times she would treat such advances & representations, with marked indifference, & insulting silence: And it is now in proof, that amidst all these professions of friendship, & regard for our national welfare, she was perfidiously plotting our destruction in the very bosom of our Country: Her secret agent Henry endeavoured to effect resistance to the laws of the land—set father against son, son against father, and stir up among us, that worst of all national evils, Civil War; in which nothing but faction, outrage & discord, would reign triumphant; And in which some aspiring chief might take advantage of the times—triump over the liberties of the people, & ascend to empire. The Yell of the Savage, mingled with the sighs of widows & orphans, is heard from beyond the mountains: Tis' Britains deed; more cruel than the Savage foe, she excites them to murder our defenceless women & children: And finally we are told that unless we compel France, not only to rescind her decrees as they affect our commerce, but as they relate to other neutral States, so as to afford her an opportunity to send her manufactures to the French empire, we must not expect a repeal of her Orders in Council. At conduct so fraught with insult & injury, we can forbear no longer. Our patience is exhausted, & we are forced to resistance. Our honor and interest demands War, and our constituted authorities have decreed it against Great Britain & her dependencies.

"1st. Therefore Resolved, That honorable War, is preferable to the dishonorable and ruinous peace which we have suffered, & although we much deprecate the evils, which will necessarily result from war, we highly approbate the conduct of the General Government in having declared it.

"2d. Resolved, That in our opinion, the attack upon the Frigate Chesapeake was Just cause of War; it was War on the part of Great Britain; for we Know of no name but that of War, with which to characterize the conduct of a nation, that will attempt by force of Arms, to obtain from another a real or imaginary right.

"3d. Resolved, That the plea of Justification by Great Britain, of her Orders in Council, that she was obliged to injure us, an innocent & unoffending neutral, for the purpose of affecting her enemy, was as insulting to our understanding, as injurious to our interest.

"4th. Resolved, That unless France does us the Justice which we have a right to expect; we hope that our Government will assume as firm a stand against her, as against Great Britain; For the purpose of obtaining a redress of the grievancies which we have received from her, and that the Voice of prejudice and Calumny, may no longer dare to impeach the purity, & impartiality of our Councils.

"5th. Resolved, That we are determined to support our Government in its prosecution of the War against Great Britain, & if required against France."

Conclude with three resolutions that praise JM for manifesting "a firmness and integrity of character, worthy the chief magistrate of a great people"; approve of the "firm & patriotic conduct" of their congressional representative, David R. Williams; and determine that the resolutions should be printed in the *Carolina Gazette* and copies sent to JM and their congressional delegate.

RC (DNA: RG 59, ML). 5 pp.; signed by Samuel Benton, chairman, and William Zimmerman, secretary. Enclosed in Samuel Benton to JM, 27 Aug. 1812 (ibid.; 1 p.), in which Benton explained that he was proud to concur with his "Old Revolutionary friends," who ordered him as their elected chairman "to transmit the Inclosed resolutions as a faint testimony of the high sense of approbation they entertain of the measures persued by the Executive ⟨of⟩ Our choice—the majority of both H⟨o⟩uses of Congress, and our immediate Representation from South Carolina."

1. John Baker Holroyd, first earl of Sheffield, was the author of *Observations on the Commerce of the American States* (Philadelphia, 1783; Evans 17976), a pamphlet which argued that the newly independent U.S. should be treated as a foreign nation, subject to all British commercial restrictions, particularly with regard to the West Indies trade. He claimed that Canada and other colonies of the British empire could provide the goods that had traditionally come from the U.S., while American dependence upon Great Britain for finished products

would make it impossible for the U.S. to break off commercial relations. James Stephen was the author of *War in Disguise; or, The Frauds of the Neutral Flags* (London, 1805). For this pamphlet, see *PJM-PS*, 1:129 n. 1.

2. In April 1806 the British vessel *Leander* fired a warning shot at an American vessel off New York, inadvertently killing crewman John Pierce. The incident sparked protest in New York and resulted in the recall of the captain of the *Leander*, Henry Whitby. Whitby was acquitted of wrongdoing at his court-martial hearing the following April (*New-York Evening Post*, 26 Apr. 1806; Perkins, *Prologue to War*, 107–8 and n. 11).

3. Salusbury P. Humphreys was the captain of the British vessel *Leopard*. He gave orders to fire upon the U.S. vessel *Chesapeake* on 22 June 1807 in an effort to retrieve British seamen (ibid., 141).

§ From the Citizens of Greenville District, South Carolina. *19 July 1812*. Submit "the following address and Resolutions," which were drafted by a committee of thirteen and "Unanimously adopted." "Secluded as our happy Country has been from the horrors and privations of War, Indicative of that firm & Decorous Stand, as a nuteral [*sic*] which she long since adopted, as the best policy for a Republic to persue, under which policy, the American States from a few Feeble depressed colonys, have arisen to be the praise and envious Emulation of the whole earth. Is it not fresh in the Recollection of our Venerable Revolutioners? And our Young-Men breathing the same air, have caught the same Spirit, that G. Britain has long envied our rising prosperity, and have never fail'd by every means in her Power, (no odds how unjustly) to retard & blast that growth, and notwithstanding all her Bosted Prowess, and superior Maratime preponderence, she was forced to recognise our Independence, altho' with a Sullen and sower Heart. And the same evil Spirit that Dictated and influenced the Council of Lord North, hath more or less pervaded the Cabinet ever since, Bursting out sometimes in One shape and then another, by impresment of our seamen to fight in their bloody Wars, in support of a Tottering Despot. By their Vexatious orders in council, By searching our Free ships, which shou'd make free goods. By false Editors Slumping and publishing the most preposterous absurdities—thereby ingendering Strife, Contention and disunion amongst our Citizens. By their emmissarys, engaged in treasonable plots, By their murdering our Citizens, in our own Waters, and Finally by Instigating the yelling and heideous Savages, to murder and Massacree our unoffending Inhabitants, on our Defenceless frontiers. Against all of which our Pacific Government have borne and borne, & Continued to Bare, have try'd every effort, have offer'd negociation by different Extraordinary Envoys, have opened it on every apparent, Vulnarable Point, all have proved ineffectual. The Cup of Conciliation being at length drean'd Dregs and all. The Man of the People, has at length arizen like a Lyon from the swellings of Jordon, and Communicated in thundering accents, to the Congress, that America aught to be Free. The Representatives of the only Free people now under the Canopy of heaven, hath Joined with the Illustrious Madison and declared, that, under the auspices of a ruling providence, she *shall* be free. Fond of peace but bold and Magnanimus in War, hath at length resorted to the last alternative, to Retrieve our Injured charactor; and Redress the Ten thousand rongs heaped upon us by our Inveterate Enamy G. Britain. Therefore Resolved—1st That James Madison President of the United States has our most unbounded Confidence, and that the Message bareing date the 1st. of June,[1] shou'd be engraven in pillars of Adamant, as it conveys in Minature, the complicated outrages Committed, on our Flag, and otherwise, and Demands Redress, which will Certainly be the Cap Stone of his Administration.

"2nd. Resolved, That the Republican Members in the Congress, are and aught to be Respected, by every true American, and that we hereby pledge our lives and Fortuns, in the most Sacred and Inviolate manner, to support the Measures they have adopted, Which Measures will shortly cause the British Lyon, to Gnaw and Bite his galling bonds, and like a surly Mastiff, Bark at the Moon, whose rising he cannot prevent.

"3rd. Resolved, That we cherish, and Foster, by all the Means in our Power, the Union of the States, wishing to go into the contest against Our Ennamy, as a Band of Brothers, having the same Interests, views, aims, and Ends, and Finally may we be United like David and Jonothon in a Reciprocal Covenant, That will never be Broken nor forgotton.

"4th. Resolved, That a Copy of these proceedings be transmitted, to the Executive of the United States, and his Excellency of this State, and that they be Published in the State & South Carolina Gazetts.

"5. Resolved, That the thanks of this meeting be given to the Chairman and Secretary, for their Vigorous Exertions in Carrying Our wishes into Execution."

RC (DNA: RG 59, ML). 3 pp.; signed by John Alexander, chairman, and Joel E. Grace, secretary. Undated; cover addressed from "Fork Shoal July the 19."

1. *PJM-PS*, 4:432–38.

§ From Frederick Stump. *19 July 1812, Davidson County, Tennessee.* "I tender you by the unanimous voice of the Company of Cavalry sixty four in Number our Services to be included in the fifty Thousand Volunteers or at your Exlency will and disposial." Was appointed a cavalry captain by Tennessee governor John Sevier in 1808. Informs JM that his company is "in good order and well Equiped." Adds in a postscript that he encloses a list of the names of the men under his command.

RC and enclosure (DNA: RG 107, LRRS, S-315:6). RC 2 pp.; docketed as received in the War Department on 12 Aug. 1812. The enclosure is a one-page list of sixty-three volunteers.

From Anthony Morris

Dear Sir   Philada July 20th. 1812.

Among the numerous applications which you must receive for various appointments none perhaps have caus'd more difficulty on your part to decide upon, than I have found on mine to add to the number or weight of your perplexities on this Subject by mentioning my wishes for an appointment to some southern port of Europe, or South America, in which commercial advantages might be probably connected with change of Climate and Scene, which I have some years past been advis'd to try the efficacy of;[1] the reported vacancy of the Lisbon Consulate has lately reviv'd this Subject in my wishes, and induc'd me to overcome the reluctance which many circumstances have heretofore prevented my mentioning directly to yourself; in now taking this liberty, Sir, be assur'd that no personal considerations could induce me to wish for any deviation from the various motives which on your part must be so imposing in making every choice; with wishes the most sincere & fervent for your health and happiness I am truly, and most respectfully, yr much obligd & obt. Servt.

ANTHONY MORRIS[2]

RC (DLC). Docketed by JM.

1. Morris also wrote to his longtime friend Dolley Payne Madison on 20 July, describing a desire for "a total change of Scene, to my health, my feelings, and my Interests." He mentioned his request for an appointment, claiming that should he be refused he would reconcile himself "to a disappointment which will come with healing on its Wings" (DLC: Dolley Madison Papers). In a 29 July letter to Morris's daughter Phoebe, Dolley Madison explained that "Mr. M is anxious to employ your Papa in some good place, entirely within his own gift, when we should not be subject to the political or personal objections of a capricious Senate (allmost treason my dear) but it is really true that M has but a small voice, at present, in appointments that go into the House" (owned by Dumbarton House, Washington, D.C., 1995).

2. Anthony Morris (1766–1860), a Philadelphia lawyer and merchant, had been the Speaker of the Pennsylvania Senate in 1793–94 and director of the Bank of North America from 1800 to 1806. On 5 May 1813 JM offered Morris a position as confidential agent at Cádiz, which Morris filled until George W. Erving was appointed minister to Spain in 1814 (Robert C. Moon, *The Morris Family of Philadelphia: Descendants of Anthony Morris, Born 1654–1721 Died* [5 vols.; Philadelphia, 1898–1909], 2:528–35; JM to Morris, 5 May 1813 [ViFreJM]).

§ From the Inhabitants of Brewster, Massachusetts. *20 July 1812.* "The Inhabitants of the town of Brewster, in the County of Barnstable & Commonwealth of Massachusetts in legal town meeting assembled, respectfully represent, that when our most valuable earthly interests are at stake we trust that it will not be considered as an act of rebellion to exercise the privilege granted to us by the Constitution of this Commonwealth, which asserts that the people have a right in an orderly & peaceable manner to assemble to consult upon the common good.

"As the more immediate representatives of the people are not now in session we feel impell'd by the present exigency of the times to address ourselves, during the recess of both houses in Congress, to the supreme Executive of the Union whose duty it is to look with an impartial eye upon every section of the United States, and whose inclination, we hope, will lead him to listen to the petitions of each portion of the Citizens who peaceably demean themselves since if any member suffer every member must more or less suffer with it.

"Although we constitute but a small and inconsiderable portion of the community, yet bearing in mind that as mighty rivers are composed of smaller tributary streams so the voice of numerous small societies contribute to an expression of the public sentiment, we are encouraged to address the Chief Magistrate from an idea that he wou'd acertain the public opinion.

"We presume not to be versed in the more intricate and ardious duties of legislation, but upon subjects which come home familiarly to every man's bosom and vitally affect our essential interests we trust we shall be excused if we deem it the privilege and duty of free Citizens to enquire and judge of public proceedings: and we indulge a hope that no suspicion of treason will be attached to us if we frankly express our disapprobation of measures which our public Agents may think proper to adopt when those measures are of such a ruinous nature as we cannot in conscience approve.

"We deeply regret that the proceedings of our rulers shou'd, at any time, be such as to render it difficult to reconcile our honest views and feelings with the confidence which we wish to repose in the constituted authorities.

"Of this complexion it appears to us are some of the recent proceedings of our national legislators. Under this painful conviction we beg leave respectfully to state that feeling in common with our fellow citizens in other parts of the Union a deep interest in whatever may affect the prosperity and happiness of our Country, We cannot view with unconcern the awful crisis that has befallen our beloved country by a declaration of War with Great Britian [*sic*]—a crisis for which we appear to be so greately unprepar'd. Convinced that War at any time and under any circumstances is an evil which cannot fail seriously to affect a nation, we had flattered ourselves that our rulers wou'd not have resorted to so destructive a measure at this time and with that power which, in all probability, can do us the most essential injury.

"Consternation and astonishment accompanied the tidings of this declaration of war! We look around and ask for the reasons which have hurried us into this disastrous expedient at a moment so unexpected and under circumstances peculiarly unfavourable. Called to encounter a naval power which possesses in a great degree the command of the Ocean, we look around with anxiety for the means of defence. We have embraced the opinion and hope it will not be judged indecorous or criminal to express it, that the duties of rulers and the ruled are reciprocal—that if the former may exact respect & obedience to the constituted authorities the latter have an equal right to claim protection and defence from their rulers. Pardon us, Sir, if we are strengthened in this opinion by the preamble of the Constitution of the United States which explicitly declares that among other purposes for which Government is instituted it is expressly one, 'to provide for the common defence'—are we inexcusable then in expecting ample provisions for the defence of our lives and property before we are plunged into a ruinous war? We know not how to restrain the expression of our Opinion respecting the impolicy of permitting our commerce to remain so long in a defenceless state amid the long continued aspect of the dangers to which it has been exposed. Neither can we conceal our surprise that the very portion of the community which is the least concerned in commercial pursuits shou'd appear unusually zealous for the preservation of Commerce by the very means, which commercial men are well satisfied, tend to its destruction. We had once anticipated the pleasing idea that our little Navy wou'd have been nourished and fostered and permitted to grow with our national growth, that increasing years might have witnessed its increasing glory and ability to protect our maritime rights; and we must deplore the refusal to grant appropriations for this purpose in the full season of our prosperity as eminently at variance with sound policy and unfriendly in its Operation to our maritime pursuits.

"In attending to the reasons for the present state of Warfare as exhibited to our view by public[1] we lament that they do not furnish to our minds satisfactory evidence of its propriety. We feel no disposition to indulge antipathy or prejudiceis in regard to foreign nations if on one hand we are driven to the detainments & Captures occasioned by the British Orders in Council, we are not more inclined on the other hand to suffer the Captivity of our friends and the destruction of our property by a nation professedly in amity with us, who in the face of solemn and[2] treaties and even since the public declaration of the revocation of the Berlin & Milan decrees, does not hesitate to *sink, burn* and *destroy* the *vessels* of our Citizens.[3] We are constrain'd to ask ourselves from a power that will freely violate its former treaties what security have we for good faith in the observence of new ones.

"An alliance with such a power we greatly fear will be one of the fatal consequences of the present war. We feel ourselves solemnly admonish'd by facts allready recorded in the pages of modern history to deprecate as one of the most serious evils which can befall our beloved Country, an alliance with a foreign power whose malignant influence has been destructive to the prosperity of all who have submitted to its protection.

"We ask leave in conclusion to state that about three fourths of our townsmen depend on the sea for the means of subsistence for themselves & families. By the present declaration of war more than that proportion is liable to fall into the hands of the enemy with a large proportion of their property and many of their wives and Children may thereby be reduced to extreme poverty. We wou'd be permitted further to remark that out of this large proportion of Seamen belonging to this town, We have but *four* detained by foreign nations, viz. two impress'd by the English with out *protections* and two detain'd as prisoners in France.[4] Judging from this circumstance & from our own personal observations in other cases, we cannot believe it necessary to enter into war for the protection of Seamen at this time, more especially when we consider that a much greater number thereby must be enevitably exposed to captivity without previous warning: nor can we believe it necessary or expedient to engage in war for Commercial interests while our merchants have property to so large amount afload [*sic*] and in foreign countries.

"We feel it, therefore, most strongly incumbent upon us by all lawful and constitutional methods to seek for a speedy termination of the present war, by the restoration of a safe & honourable peace. And as in duty bound shall ever pray.

"The foregoing memorial was accepted unanimously by the town & it was voted that the Selectmen sign the same for and in behalf of the town and the town Clerk to Attest the same."

RC (DNA: RG 59, ML). 7 pp.; signed by Isaac Clark and Thomas Seabury, selectmen, and attested by Joseph Smith, town clerk.

1. The authors may have omitted a word here.
2. The authors may have omitted a word here.
3. See Delegates from Towns in Franklin, Hampshire, and Hampden Counties, Massachusetts, to JM, 15 July 1812, and n. 8.
4. One of the signatories of this document, Isaac Clark, was involved in the Massachusetts

General Court's investigation of impressment. The resulting report, based on evidence sub-mitted by Clark and leaders of other towns, estimated that only 35 seamen had been impressed from American vessels by the British in the years preceding the declaration of war, rather than 6,057, as JM's administration claimed (Massachusetts General Court, *Impressed Seamen* [Boston, 1812; Shaw and Shoemaker 25995]).

§ From the Inhabitants of Plymouth, Massachusetts. *20 July 1812*. Submit "the fol-lowing memorial," which "was unanimously adopted and voted to be . . . forwarded to the president of the United States."

"The inhabitants of the town of Plymouth in the Commonwealth of Massachu-setts, in legal town meeting assembled, respectfully shew.

"That having recently united with their fellow-citizens in the vicinity, in memo-rializing congress,[1] upon the menacing aspect of their public relations, solicitously tho' ineffectually supplicating the national legislature, to remove the impolitic re-strictions, that had almost annihilated a once lucrative commerce, and especially to avert the host of calamities that in rapid succession will follow a war with Great Britain, they now address you, Sir to interpose your presidential powers and influence, that in a great measure controul the destinies of the nation, to rescue them from scenes of horror, from the mere prospect of which, hope the solace of the wretched flies away, and which in their serious apprehensions, will endanger the existence of the social compact.

"When the rulers of a people, deliberately and obstinately persevere in a system of measures dire[c]tly tending (if not intentionally devised) to depress a large and respectable section of the country, to gratify the unfounded jealousies, and restless envious passions of another, and the irritation produced by the operation of such partial system, begins to discover its natural effects, it is unquestionably the part of wisdom, seasonably to contemplate the possible consequences.

"What must be the extent and degree of suffering, before avowed resistance to the constituted authorities, becomes a duty, cannot be accurately defined, but the awful, though sometimes necessary decision, must be submitted to the judgement and feelings of the sufferers themselves.

"They have the authority of Mr. Madison, that even the unpopularity of a war-rantable measure of the federal government, in particular states, will justify a refusal of concurrence.[2] What then, they would enquire, is the justifiable mode of opposi-tion, to an unwarrantable measure of that government, not only unpopular, but fraught with degradation and ruin? Surely, in the opinion of Mr. Madison such an efficient counteraction by regular and constitutional means, as will ensure redress.

"The enumeration of wrongs, inflicted by Great Britain on the United States, ex-hibited by the committee of foreign relations, recapitulated in the manifesto, and assigned as the causes of war, by their vivid colouring, and sublimated extravagance, evidently betrays the vagaries of an overheated imagination. Allusions are made to injuries, that have been honourably adjusted, & to swell the catalogue of wrongs, the stale vulgar story of Indian hostilities, stimulated by British agents, and the mis-erable tale of John Henry, are introduced, which affect your memorialists in the same ludicrous manner, as the declaration of war against Great Britain by a former king of Spain, where he estimated the injuries he had received, at the precise num-ber of *one hundred*.

"Divest these pretended causes of war of all specious & artificial representation, consult the history of all the wars among commercial belligerents, for the last two centuries, contrast the injuries heaped upon neutrals, in these wars with those sustained by the United States from Great Britain, take into the account, the peculiar ferocious character of the war that raged in Europe almost without interuption, for more than twenty years, the notorious partialities shewn to France, during the administration of your immediate predecessor, and your memorialists pronounce with much confidence, that no legitimate causes of war exist against Great Britain. In the convulsed unnatural state of society, consequent on war, from the principles of policy assumed by belligerents, arising from their varying relative situations, evils and embarrassments, always have been & always will be incident to Neutrals, unwilling to encounter any impediments in their pursuit if [*sic*] wealth, which if considered as just causes of war, the inevitable result will be, that a long continued conflict between two great maritime powers, will embroil the whole commercial world.

"Conceiving this to be a correct view of the subject, it would be easy to multiply observations upon the manifest impolicy and injustice of war with Great Britain, commenced at a period and under auspices the most unfavourable to the eastern States, exposing them to immense losses, and accumulated distresses; but they will not trespass on your time as these losses and distresses, have been depicted in numerous addresses, with a force of reasoning & splendor of eloquence, that have seldom been equalled.

"From the circumstances and manner, in which the revocation of the Berlin and Milan decrees, was lately made known, they have the most mortifying suspicion, that a war with Great Britain, was the express condition of their revocation, nor can they suppress their indignation, at the imposition attempted to be practiced on the credulity of their government, by the disgusting pretext, that these obnoxious decrees were revoked in April 1811, and had a retrospect to the November before, in direct contradiction of every act, public and private of the court of St. Cloud—a legerdemain worthy indeed of that *prostituted court*, where the basest perfidy is openly rewarded and a man of integrity an[d] honour finds no ticket of admission.

"Among the innumerable train of evils, that a war with Great Britain will produce, the one conspicuous above all others, as pregnant with universal, political, and moral ruin, and which cannot be too often repeated and deprecated, is an alliance with the French empire—at the head of which, is placed a desperate adventurer, who to accomplish his infernal purposes of avarice and ambition, would waste countless millions of money, and destroy whole generations of men. They sicken at the thought of their fellow-citizens being amalgamated with the slaves of this monster, and of cooperating with them, in sweeping from the globe the residue of virtuous freedom that yet remains. They invoke the genius of their fathers to save them from this base and contaminating confederacy, and if they are destined to be wretched, that their wretchedness may not be embittered, by a servile connection with profligate and infidel France.

"Thus, Sir, with much brevity, but with a frankness that the magnitude of the occasion demanded, they have expressed their honest sentiments, upon the existing offensive war with Great Britain, a war, by which their dearest interests as men and christians, are deeply effected, and in which they deliberately declare, as they cannot *conscientiously*, so they *will not* have any *voluntary* participation. They make this declaration with that paramount regard to their civil and religious obligations which become the deciples of the prince of peace, whose kingdom is not of this world, and before whose impartial tribunal, Presidents and Kings will be upon a level, with the meanest of their fellow-men and will be responsible for all the blood they shed in wanton and unnecessary wars.

"Impressed with these solemn considerations, with an ardent love of country, and high respect for the union of the states, your memorialists entreat the President immediately to begin the work of peace, with that unaffected dignity, and undisguised sincerity, which distinguished one of your illustrious predecessors, and they have the most satisfactory conviction, that upright and sincere efforts will be crowned with success, while the land is undefiled with the blood of its citizens, & before the demon of slaughter, thirsting for human victims, 'cries havock and lets slip the dogs of War.'"[3]

RC (DNA: RG 59, ML). 4 pp.; signed by William Jackson, moderator, and Ephraim Spooner, town clerk.

1. On 14 May 1812 Representative Charles Turner of Massachusetts presented a petition of the inhabitants of the county of Plymouth requesting the repeal of the embargo against Great Britain (*Annals of Congress*, 12th Cong., 1st sess., 1427).

2. The memorialists were probably referring to JM's 1798 Virginia Resolutions (see Virginia Resolutions, 21 Dec. 1798, and Editorial Note, *PJM*, 17:185–90).

3. Shakespeare, *Julius Caesar*, 3.1.273 (*Riverside*).

§ Executive Pardon. *20 July 1812*. "Whereas it has been made to appear to me that a certain D. McKenny, a private in the Marine Corps of the United States, has been sentenced, by a Court Martial to suffer death—Now be it known, That I James Madison, President of the UStates, for divers good causes and considerations, do by these presents pardon and remit the sentence aforesaid; requiring all persons whom it may concern to Govern themselves accordingly."[1]

Letterbook copy (DNA: RG 59, PPR). 1 p.

1. JM also remitted the death penalty for several other offenders in the early months of the war: Privates Daniel, Leonard, Conroy, McDonald, Jones, Green, and Howard, 22 July 1812; James Grant and Martin Johnson, 6 Aug. 1812; James Barrett, 6 Aug. 1812; John Miller, Robert Bennet, Theodorus Vanilestine, and Rowland Jeffery, 21 Aug. 1812; John McCormick, 26 Oct. 1812; John Ryan, 14 Nov. 1812; and James Whitehurst, 1 Dec. 1812 (ibid.). In addition, JM remitted lesser penalties and discharged prosecutions in the cases of several others: Francis Breuel, 15 Aug. 1812; Amasa Kingsborough, 18 Aug. 1812; and Josiah Rogers, 8 Oct. 1812 (ibid.). The procedure for handling pardons changed, however, with a 5 Sept. 1812 general order that stipulated: "The proceedings of General Courts Martial, which in time of peace are to be submitted to the President of the U. States, before the same can be carried into execution, will, during the continuance of the war, be laid before the general officer having the command of the Department, within which such general courts martial may be held, for his confirmation or disapproval and orders in the case; agreeably to the provisions of the 65th article of the act entitled 'An Act for establishing Rules and Articles for the government of the Armies of the United States'" (*National Intelligencer*, 8 Sept. 1812). That article required that "no sentence of a general court martial, in time of peace, extending to the loss of life, or the

dismission of a commissioned officer, or which shall, either in time of peace or war, respect a general officer, be carried into execution, until after the whole proceedings shall have been transmitted to the Secretary of War, to be laid before the President of the United States, for his confirmation or disapproval, and orders, in the case" (*U.S. Statutes at Large*, 2:367). The order of 5 Sept. 1812 notwithstanding, death penalty cases continued to come to JM's attention throughout the War of 1812.

¶ From Anthony Morris. Letter not found. *20 July 1812*. Mentioned in Morris to Dolley Payne Madison, 20 July 1812 (DLC: Dolley Madison Papers). Introduces Samuel Mifflin to JM and enumerates his "recommendations."

To St. George Tucker

DR. SIR   WASHINGTON July 21. 1812

 I was duly favored with yours of the 8th. on the subject of the B. officer arrested near Norfolk.[1] The circumstances which attracted your notice very justly exposed him to suspicion; and it is more than possible that he had the views tho' not the full character of a Spy. It was thought best however to commence the war with an example of liberality, and he was permitted as a mere alien Enemy to depart for his own Country.

 The papers inclosed contain specimens of the political Spirit which reigns at Boston; and of the manner in which a British Cabinet is made up.[2] Accept assurances of my great esteem and friendly respects

             JAMES MADISON

RC (DLC). Docketed "ansd. 27th."

 1. *PJM-PS*, 4:576–77.

 2. JM may have enclosed the 11 and 14 July 1812 issues of the *National Intelligencer*. In the "Address of the Senate, to the People of the Commonwealth of Massachusetts," reprinted there on 11 July 1812, the senators decried war in principle but said they understood its necessity in light of the seemingly unprovoked attacks by the British. They requested that all citizens of the state support the war. The newspaper also reported on that day that the British ministry had resigned and on 14 July speculated that it might be reconstituted under Lord Wellesley and George Canning.

From Albert Gallatin

DEAR SIR   PHILADA. 21 July 1812

 It is said that the Consulship of Lisbon is vacant. If so, permit me to recommend with more than common earnestness Pemberton Hutchinson the son of my former friend Doctr. Hutchinson.[1] The name is dear to every republican in this State both in city & country. And I am assured that the son by his talents & standing deserves the appointment. In one respect he has an advantage, that of being already on the spot, connected with one of the most respectable houses in this city. I had not intended to write until I could give you some account of my success; but understanding that one of the Mifflins goes by to day's stage to Washington to solicit the office,[2] would not let the mail go without writing in favour of Hutchinson for whose appointment I feel truly anxious.

We have arrived here safe & intend to proceed to New York as soon as I have done what can be effected here with respect to money.[3]

Mrs. G. presents her best respects to Mrs. Madison.

Do you still want volunteers? I could easily have set the thing going here. Respectfully Your obedt. Servt.

ALBERT GALLATIN

RC (DLC). Docketed by JM.

1. Gallatin referred to Israel Pemberton Hutchinson, who received the consulship in Lisbon on 15 Jan. 1813 (*Senate Exec. Proceedings*, 2:313, 316). He was the son of Dr. James Hutchinson, who died in the Philadelphia yellow fever epidemic of 1793, leaving Gallatin to raise funds to support his widow and children (Harry Marlin Tinkcom, *The Republicans and Federalists in Pennsylvania, 1790–1901* [Harrisburg, 1950], 53–54).

2. Gallatin probably referred to Samuel Mifflin of Philadelphia, who had sought appointment to the consulate in Malta on 5 May 1811 and had recently been introduced to JM by Anthony Morris (DNA: RG 59, LAR, 1809–17, filed under "Mifflin"; Morris to JM, 20 July 1812 [second letter]).

3. Gallatin had embarked upon a trip to Baltimore, Philadelphia, and New York to meet with businessmen and bankers to raise war loans (Raymond Walters Jr., *Albert Gallatin: Jeffersonian Financier and Diplomat* [New York, 1957], 254–55).

From David Bailie Warden

SIR,   PARIS, 21 July, 1812

I have the honor to send you a *Brochure* "on the principles, and laws of armed neutrality,"[1] of which the contents, from particular circumstances, are highly interesting to the United States.

The Head quarters of the Emperor of France are already Twenty leagues beyond Wilnaw.[2] It is generally believed, that Russia will make but a feeble resistance against his immense army, supported by Austria, Poland, Prussia, Turkey, and the Confederation of the Rhine.

May I take the liberty, Sir, of requesting you to present my respects to Mrs. Madison, and Mr Coles, your Secretary. I am, Sir, with profound respect your most obedt and very humble Servant

DAVID BAILIE WARDEN

59

RC (DLC); letterbook copy (MdHi: Warden Papers).

1. Enclosure not identified.
2. Napoleon's army entered Vilna, in Russia, at the end of June 1812 (Tulard, *Dictionnaire Napoléon*, 1728).

From Joel Barlow

DEAR SIR   PARIS 22 July 1812

The copy of the encyclopedie in the president's library goes no farther than the 56th. livraison inclusive. I take the liberty to enclose herewith a moniteur which will give you the present state of that work & the promise of its continuance & completion.[1] There is no doubt but it will be when done a most complete & useful set of Dictionaries, on all the sciences.

If you will please to let me know whether you wish to have me procure & send the 21 livraisons wanting in your set to bring it up to the 77 already out, & to continue to receive the future ones, I will carefully follow your orders. I have the honor to be Dr. Sir your faithful servt.

J. BARLOW

RC (DLC). Docketed by JM.

1. Barlow probably enclosed the 22 July 1812 edition of the Paris *Moniteur universel*, which ran an advertisement for the seventy-seventh volume of the *Encyclopédie méthodique*.

From Elbridge Gerry

secret
MY DEAR SIR   CAMBRIDGE 22d. July 1812

Since my recovery from indisposition, I have had an interview with General Dearborn, who informed me that he was soon to depart from Boston; & being informed by him of the state of our Castle, I enquired what was to prevent the Enemy, if apprized of our defenceless situation, from embarking all its regular troops at Nova Scotia, in transports trusting its defence for a short period to their militia & with a ship or two [of] the line & such other naval force as they could command, from attacking our Castle & carrying it by a Coup de main, & from sacking afterwards the town of Boston? His answer was, *nothing*. He expressed great uneasiness on the subject & said he would write to You immediately on the Subject. If General Varnum could be put into the command, it appeared to be General Dearborn's opinion, as well as my own, that he would secure the Castle, by his division & artillery companies in particular, on whom he could rely.[1]

William Little Esq of Boston, a very excellent Character, I find is considered by the Republicans, as a proper candidate for the office of Commissary of prisoners. If no one has the preferrence for any particular reasons, I am sure he would give general Satisfaction.[2] I am with the highest
esteem & respect dear Sir, your unfeigned friend & obedt Sevt

E GERRY

RC (DLC). Docketed by JM.

1. The editors have been unable to locate any correspondence between Dearborn and JM
matching this description. However, Dearborn wrote to Eustis on 17 July 1812 to discuss the
preparations for his departure from Boston and his concern that the seacoast remained unde-
fended. He explained that he continued to request militia detachments from New England
governors but had also begun to look to volunteer troops to defend the seacoast. He expressed
his opinion that Senator Joseph B. Varnum of Massachusetts was the best choice to gather a
division of volunteers for that purpose (DNA: RG 107, LRRS, D-114:6). Dearborn wrote to
Eustis again on 22 Aug. to discuss his plans for an invasion of Canada and to suggest that Varnum be ordered "to march with a Sufficient number of his Divisions, to occupy the works in
Boston Harbour, Salem, Marblehead, & Cape Ann" (NHi: Dearborn Letterbooks).
2. William Little was also recommended by Dearborn to Eustis as an appropriate candidate for the position in a 21 July letter, but the post was filled by John Mason (DNA: RG 107,
LRRS, D-115:6; *ASP, Miscellaneous*, 2:337).

From William Jones

PROVIDENCE July 22d 1812

SIR

I have the honor to enclose to your Excellency a Resolution of the General Assembly of this State pass'd on the 8th Inst[1] and in conformity there-
with permit me to request your Excellency to give orders to the proper
officer to furnish me with two thousand stand of arms & six pair of Field
peices vizt two pair of six pounders & four pair of four pounders with such
quantities of ammunition &c for the use of this State as your Excellency
shall deem proper.

I now beg leave to observe to your Excellency that there is no State in
the Union in proportion to its limits more (if as much) exposed to a foreign
Enemy as Rhode Island, that our Militia are but in part Armed, that the
small arms they have are indifferent in quality & of various sizes which may
answer for parade but cannot be relied on in action & that as our Shores
are extensive & much exposed an additional number of Field peices are
highly necessary—fully relying on your Excellencys readiness to afford the
aid & protection our exposed situation requires I have the honor to be respectfully Your Excellencys Obedient servant

WM. JONES

RC and enclosure (DNA: RG 107, LRRS, J-212:6); RC (ibid., J-240:6); RC and enclosure (ibid., J-306:6). First RC docketed as received in the War Department on 28 July 1812. Second RC written on the verso of Jones to JM, 22 Aug. 1812. For enclosure, see n. 1.

1. The enclosure is a copy (1 p.) of an 8 July 1812 resolution of the Rhode Island General Assembly requiring the governor to request that JM furnish him with "arms, ammunition and ordnance for the use of the militia of this State."

§ From the Inhabitants of Barre, Massachusetts. *23 July 1812.* "The Inhabitants of the Town of Barre in the County of Worcester & State of Massachusetts, beg leave to represent.

"That in a government like ours, which is instituted, & established, for the protection, safety, prosperity & happiness of the People, they have a Right at all times to assemble in a peacable Maner, to consult upon the Common good, & to express their Sentiments & Opinions respecting the proceedings & acts, of the Constituted Authorities.

"And when Measures are adopted & pursued, which in their opinions have a direct tendency to destroy the peace, & harmony of Society, sap the foundation of our free government, and eradicate every vestage of Liberty; and to introduce poverty & distress, anarchy and tyrany: duty to themselves, to their Families, to their Country & their God, imperiously demands, that they Should, by the exercise of all Constitutional Means, endeavor to avert the Evils which hover over their heads, and rescue their devoted Country from inevitable Ruin.

"As we have not been indifferent Spectators of the Scenes that have been passing before us for a succession of years, we believe the present portentous Crisis of our public affairs, demands, that we Should, without fear, express *our* opinions of the Measures which have been pursued by the general Government.

"And it is with Sentiments & feelings prompted by a love of Country, and of national Liberty, and with due deferen[c]e to the authority of the general Government with deep Regret we have noticed, that the late negociations entered into by the government of the United States, with an *avowed* intention on their part, to effect a settlement of the existing differences with the Beligerent Nations, & to obtain a due respect for our Neutral Rights, and a Repeal of their pernicious Edicts, have entirely failed of Success, and we are now pr[e]cipitately plunged into a war with Great Brittian; an event awful & unexpected, which is menacing to our Liberties, hostile to our Interest & revolting to our feelings. The Clangor of Arms is now heard in our streets, & our Brothers & our Sons are now Summoned to the field. And to what extent the Cries & tears of Widows & Orphans, Parents & Brothers, will be carried God only knows.

"In a struggle for Conquest on the one hand, & for existance on the other, it was not to be expected that America would be entirely exempt from encroachments on her Neutral Rights, by the Contending Powers, and it is too true that by endeavouring to annoy each other, they have greatly effected the Interest of the United States; the one in the exercise of a Right which She Claims of taking her seamen and by her Orders in Couscil [*sic*], the other by her pernicious Decrees, notwithstanding their pretended repeal.

"We will not undertake to determine, by what Motives a Small Majority of Congress were actuated in voting for a Declaration of War, and the President in recommending and Sanctioning Such a Measure—Nor will we deny that if it were expedient for the United States to go to war for honor, they have ample Causes against both the beligerents, and that those causes have long existed, yet we believe, that at this important Crisis, when the whole World Seems to be in Confusion, that a war with either of the Beligerents, is unwise & impolitic, and more especially a War with Great Brittian; as it will eventually annihilate the little Remainder of our Commerce which has escaped the pernicious & palsying effects of our own restrictive System; by a wide and wasteful Sweep of all our floating property; but what we have most reason to fear, is, that it will inevitably lead to an alliance with the Tyrant of Europe, who, under the pretence of giving liberty to the Republics of the old world, has wrested, from them every Vestage of freedom and annexed them to the great nation & their Names are blotted out from among the Nations of the Earth. Happy indeed will it be for America if she take warning, and escape the deathly grasp of his iron hand.

"And to us it is matter of surprise, that our government should, at this time, Select England as the only object of our resentment, when, it is acertained by 'proof as Strong as holy writ,'[1] that the United States, have greater Cause of War against France, than against her—and this Surprise is increased when we consider that the Brittish government, has repeatedly declared that; whenever the French De[c]rees shall be repealed by any authentic document duely promulgated, their orders in Council would be revoked (which orders are considered as a principal Cause of war). Yet no such document, it is presumed ever existed, as had that been the Case it would have been Communicated. Besides it is proved, not only by the Capture & Condemnation of our Vessels & Cargoes; but by the repeated declarations of the French Government, & even so late as the tenth of March last,[2] that those decrees are considered to be in force, & the *Supreme law of the Land.*

"Further, as to our impressed seamen, the British Government, through their Minister Mr Foster, has lately disclaimed all Right to take native Americans, and offered to deliver up every Individual in the Brittish service, upon proof that they were such.[3] Indeed Brittan never has Claimed a Right to take native Americans.

"Without being more particular, we are constrained to believe, that, in order to obtain a repeal of the French Decrees, altho. prior in date & more pernicious in their Consequences, than the Brittish orders; We must, not only relinquish all trade with Great Brittian & her dependencies, but we must resist with force & arms the Right of Search and even a vissit from a Brittish Vessel. To have enjoyed the Boon & secure the love & Friendship of the great & good Napoleon we must resort to open Hostilities.

"We believe that it is for the Interest of the United States, to Cultivate peace with all Nations, & avoid entangling alliances with any; and that if our government had relinquished, or rather never introduced, their restrictive System, authorised our Merchants to arm for defence, fostered and increased our Navy, husbanded our resourses, and entered into the Negociations, with a Spirit & disposition for accomodation our differences with Great Brittian would long since have been amicably adjusted, and our Citizens would now enjoy peace in their Borders & prosperity in their Habitations.

"We therefore request you to endeavour by all fair & honorable means, to bring the present War to a Speedy & honorable termination.

"At a Legal Meeting of Said Inhabitants holden on thursday July 23, 1812. Voted by a large Majority that the foregoing address be signed by the Moderator and Town Clerk and Communicated to the President of the United States."

RC (DNA: RG 59, ML). 4 pp.; signed by Samuel Lee Jr., moderator, and Ephraim Russell, town clerk.

 1. "Trifles light as air / Are to the jealous [*sic*] confirmations strong / As proofs of holy writ" (Shakespeare, *Othello*, 3.3.322–24 [*Riverside*]).
 2. For this report, see *PJM-PS*, 4:361 n. 2.
 3. For Foster's statements concerning impressment, see ibid., 4:438 n. 1 and 462 n. 1.

§ From the Republican Citizens of Plymouth, Massachusetts. *23 July 1812*. Submit the following address, which was "unanimously adopted."

"It is with the most painful emotions on the present occasion, that we feel it our duty to address the President of the United States. We should not interrupt his uniform, firm procedure in establishing & securing the rights of his Country; but we are constrained to this measure to evince to him, to the administration generally, & to the legislative body, our contempt, indignation, & abhorrence at the modes of conduct exhibited by the majority of this town, who have undertaken to give an expression of the sentiments of its inhabitants:[1] & *that* in a tone & language as if we were all ripe for rebellion against the constituted authorities: as if we were ready to succumb to the infamous claims of the most insolent nation on earth; & to return to that barbarous state of colonization from which we were so lately emancipated by the fortitude, the swords & the blood of our Ancestors.

"Be assured, Sir, that in our opinion, those resolutions, & the memorial accompanying them, emanated from a virulent principle of faction & toryism that has attached to the rulers of this town from the end of the Revolution to this moment. That some of those leaders have been uniform Tories, born & nurtured in the principles; & others, professing patriotism, but who are apostates of the bitterest cast.

"We are in a minority at the *Hustings*, & our opposers shew votes procured by means we should blush to adopt; yet the *Federal* Administration may rest satisfied that the inhabitants of the ancient town of Plymouth, the moment they see the views & designs of the federal faction will abandon them. And even at this moment, while we are surrounded with threats, menaces & abuse we have sufficient moral sentiment, civil & municipal feelings, & physical strength to evince to these people that the virulence of their British principles must evaporate & expire on their paper resolutions.

"Be assured, Sir, that there are sixty thousand free born citizen soldiers of Massachusetts who are convinced that we have drank the British cup of humiliation to its last dregs: & that we are ready to show that nation, & the rebellious incendiaries of our own Country, that having once had fortitude sufficient to procure our emancipation, we have firmness enough to maintain our Independence.

"We embrace the opportunity forced on us by the oppositionists to Government to express our deep regret that such causes should propel us to address you: But the deepest conviction of the duty we owe ourselves—our families—our Country—& our God makes it irresistible. And while we deplore the infatuated counsels of men who seem to merge all pride of character, all dignity of human nature, all moral sentiment, & all religious principle, either in mercantile cupidity, or an *avarice of Am-*

bition, still more detestable, we pledge ourselves that we will support the constituted authorities; the individuals who compose them; & *above all*, the precious instrument under which they act, that Constitution sanctioned & signed by a Washington—a Franklin—& other departed worthies, whose indignant shades frown with a severity, that interrupts their heavenly enjoyments, upon a set of men—factionists—terrorists & *almost* rebels, who in language, in action, expression & sentiment totally depart from the legacy of the *Father of his Country*, whose name they daily blaspheme by professing to be his disciples. Were they such, would they violate his last expressions of Union?[2] Would they attempt, contrary to his injunctions, to sever the union of these States? Would they contemplate a *New England monarchy*? Would they mark the Hudson as the boundary of the *Northern Confederacy*? Would they distinguish the Alleghany mountains as a line drawn by Providence beyond which the power even of the benevolence of Deity should not extend the freedom & happiness of man; & that the citizens who have peopled that wilderness, & made it to blossom as the rose, should be considered as the outcasts of society? No, Sir! we cherish them as brethren, we revere them as Patriots, & respect them for their manly exhibit of freedom of sentiment, & of action.

"Nor will be [*sic*] forbear to utter our sentiments of horror on, not only the impolicy, but the wickedness discoverable in the malignant observations in conversation & in the public gazettes, on our Sister States, south of the Delaware;[3] & the virulent effusions of wrath against their distinguished & enlightened inhabitants: a separation from whom, either by territorial limits, or the broader expansion of fraternal affection—we should deplore as the greatest of all calamities.

"We further embrace this moment to express our utmost detestation of an avowed necessity & determination to divide these States, as announced without disguise in the shameless papers of Boston.[4] Nor can we avoid to revolt at the idea of Governor Strong's expression in his proclamation for a fast in this Commonwealth that Great Britain has 'for generations been the bulwark of the religion we profess.'[5] We feel this to be a deep & insidious reflection on the character of our Ancestors, whose memories we revere: who landed on this desolate spot, in a dreary season, fleeing from the persecutions of *British hierarchical* tyranny; & no sooner having escaped *that*, were pursued with all the civil abuse, rigor & oppression that a powerful nation could pour on a young weak & powerless people. But while yet young, so dreadful was this oppression, that we rose, like Hercules from his cradle and strangled the snake. And though like the Hydra it renews itself, yet *again*, like Hercules we will assist you to destroy the monster, & to *cleanse the Augean stable:* and if they reduce us to the deplorable necessity we will lift the Club, which if we *must do*, shall be wielded with effect that will be *truly* Herculean.

"The suggestions in the Plymouth memorial & resolutions, relative to French connection, we conceive only introduced to excite popular feeling. We are conscious that it is not only your policy, but the genius & feeling of the American people, in the language of the immortal Jefferson, to have 'Peace with all nations, entangling alliances with none.'[6] Happily our distance, separated by an immense ocean, frees us from the necessity of any alliance with European nations but on principles of commercial reciprocity. And we equally detest the abuses on our Commerce from one belligerent as from another. But still we consider there are gradations of political feeling, of national sentiment—& of general violation, that create a marked & distinguished exhibition of national character. And while France has been making daily inroads on our commerce, which touches the sensibilities of the nation in a keen point; yet the similar violence of Great-Britain as to property, & the thousand-fold horror of their impressment of our seamen seem to sink the commercial aggressions of the former power comparatively to nothing. Sir, we consider property as a bauble to freedom, we consider the inestimable privilege of one citizen to his inheritance 'to roam the world at large,' as paramount to uncounted wealth.

"Sir, take with you, if you please, with this address the assurances of our personal respect for your character—for the bland manners that surround you in private life—for the mild, yet dignified sentiments of your political conduct, while *yet* in deliberative assemblies—& for the cool fortitude which exhibits you to the admiration of the world in your present situation of first magistrate of the Independent States of America."

RC (DNA: RG 59, ML). 7 pp. Enclosed in Henry Warren and others to JM, 25 July 1812 (ibid.; 1 p.; signed by Henry Warren, William Sturtevant, Benjamin Warren, Salisbury Jackson, and Zabdiel Sampson as a "Committee of the Republican citizens of the town of Plymouth").

1. See Inhabitants of Plymouth, Massachusetts, to JM, 20 July 1812.

2. The memorialists referred to Washington's 19 Sept. 1796 farewell address (Fitzpatrick, *Writings of George Washington*, 35:214–38).

3. The memorialists may have referred to the report of a 2 July town meeting in Hampshire County, Massachusetts, printed in the Boston *Columbian Centinel* on 15 July 1812. The notice observed that "if a spirit pervades the country similar to that which animates the county of *Hampshire*, the Administration will find *'that the people will not go to war,'* at the *dictum* of Southern slave holders, nor of Lawyers—who never saw the ocean but on a map, nor a ship but such as have been rotting in JEFFERSON's dry dock in *Washington*."

4. The memorialists probably referred to an 18 July 1812 article in the Boston *Columbian Centinel* entitled "The Duty of the Northern States." It argued that the country had become too large to have its divergent interests represented by a single government and that commercial and noncommercial states could never "be satisfied with the same laws." The article also hinted that western states were best not governed by Atlantic states, pointing out that "the Mountains form a natural line of division—and moral and commercial habits would unite the western people," while "the moral and commercial habits of the Northern and Middle States would naturally link them together; as would the like habits of the Slaveholding States."

5. The memorialists quoted from Strong's 26 June 1812 proclamation of a day of public fasting, humiliation, and prayer (see Gerry to JM, 13 July 1812, n. 6).

6. In his first inaugural address, Jefferson called for "peace, commerce, & honest friendship with all nations, entangling alliances with none" (Ford, *Writings of Jefferson*, 8:4).

From John G. Jackson

DEAR SIR   CLARKSBURG July 24th 1812

I received by the last Mail a commission from the Executive of Virginia appointing me in conjunction with Genls. Porterfield[1] & Trigg[2] Commissioners on the part of the State of Virginia to superintend &c the line between the Virginia Military reservation, & the lands ceded to the U States by the State of Virginia.[3] Altho' I feel anxious to undertake the duty of that office, so important to a meritorious class of our Citizens, yet unless the time of the meeting of the Commissioners is delayed for three weeks after the 5th. October it will be impossible for me to do so, without the neglect of very important business in our Courts confided to me solely; which no *civil* employment would justify me in failing to attend to. As I perceive the act of Congress authorises you to postpone the commencement of surveying the line, & no public disadvantage can result from three weeks delay, I am induced to solicit that accommodation, preparatory to my acceptance of the appointment: And will esteem it a favor to receive an early answer. Your Mo Obt

J G JACKSON

RC (DLC). Docketed by JM.

1. Robert Porterfield (1752–1843), a militia general in the War of 1812, was a Revolutionary War veteran and an active political leader in Augusta County, Virginia (Stuart Lee Butler, *A Guide to Virginia Militia Units in the War of 1812* [Athens, Ga., 1988], 307).

2. Abram Trigg (b. 1750) had served in the Revolutionary War and was a delegate to the Virginia constitutional ratifying convention in 1788. He was a member of the Fifth through Tenth Congresses (*PJM*, 15:125 n. 2).

3. Virginia governor James Barbour had requested that Jackson serve on a commission to survey the northwestern boundary between the Virginia Military District and Ohio, which had been in dispute at least since 1802, when Gallatin had first urged Congress to conduct a survey. Jackson's request for a postponement was granted, but he nevertheless turned down the commission (William Thomas Hutchinson, *The Bounty Lands of the American Revolution in Ohio* [New York, 1979], 211–12; Jackson to JM, 21 Oct. 1812).

From Richard M. Johnson

BLUE SPRING. SCOTT COUNTY. KENTUCKY.

SIR,   July 24th. 1812

From the communications received from & the personal application made by the officers of the detachment of militia in this state I am induced to suggest the propriety of calling into actual service at least a portion of our quota composed altogether of volunteers & men who would do honor to any cause worthy to be defended by fre[e]men. The measures of the Government have been supported with a zeal, to which we have been strangers even in the western states which should be fostered by giving action to the military ardour manifested among us. The administration has never recd. such universal applause—we are a united people in our confidence in the executive, with a very few exceptions; and the inquiry is made among all classes, "when will our President permit our volunteers to serve in the glorious cause of their Country." "Is it possible that we will not be permitted to share the glory, the toil & the danger." The people of this state are accustomed to prompt & active measures; they are a spirited people and nothing can satisfy them but some military enterprise to engage at least a part of our men. If they should be disappointed in these expectations I am sure great injury will be done to that noble & patriotic ardour which has prompted our people to volunteer, whatever may be the reasons to prevent the use of six months men so far from the scene of action. But all the objections considered I do not hesitate to advise an immediate call for a part; one Redgiment if no more. In thirty days we could be at detroit. The Governor has just informed me that the next mail will carry a return of a well organized force of near 6,000. They will go South, west or North on account of health they prefer west or North. The people here are anxious to take Malden this year. It forms the point of rendevous for indians to get supplies of arms &c. and the hot bed of encitement to murder our families. The hearts of our troops are fired upon such an enterprize & the officers stand pledged that no scruples will be made on account of boundary. The Rifle Redgiment for instance under the command of Col. John Allen,[1] the first man in the state for learning talents &c. are composed of officers & men who would not be inferior to any body of men in talents, learning respectabil[it]y & firmness. Col. Allen informs me that his Redgiment have not expended less than ten thousand dollars in preparation besides the purchase of guns—& besides the time & expences of musters & encampments for 3 or 4 days successivly to be better acquainted with actual service. The other volunteers are equaly meritorious. In fact the officers & men expected, to be called into the field; & have therefore thrown themselves out of business—and if none of them should be employed at this time, the whispers of our enemies here that government did not intend to employ them after all their sacrifices will be verified. The officers have in several instances given their men assurances that a portion of our forces would be called upon by the first of Sept. I have written thus freely that you may have the views of the people here—by which you will be enabled to act as you may deem most consistent with the public good, which has so long formed the polar Star of your political life. In haste—accept assurances of My sincere friendship.

RH: M. JOHNSON

RC (DLC).

1. John Allen (1771–1813) was born in Rockbridge County, Virginia, and moved to Kentucky with his family sometime before 1780. After studying law with Archibald Stuart in Virginia, he returned to Kentucky, where he practiced law and served in the state legislature. He was killed at the Battle of the River Raisin in January 1813 (G. Glenn Clift, *Remember the Raisin! Kentucky and Kentuckians in the Battles and Massacre at Frenchtown, Michigan Territory,*

in the War of 1812 [1961; reprint, with *Notes on Kentucky Veterans of the War of 1812*, Frankfort, Ky., 1995], 113–14).

From the Officers of the Sixth Regiment of South Carolina Cavalry

CAMDEN So. Ca. July 24. 1812.

The officers of the 6th. regiment of South Carolina cavalry, had not intended to offer to the government our sentiments on the present situation of our country, believing that no assurance would be necessary, but that it would be taken for granted, that in a war into which we have been reluctantly forced by the injustice of our enemy, every part of the military were ready to discharge their duty. We have however been induced to address you, in consequence of perceiving that there exists in some parts of the union a disposition, if not to oppose, at least to withhold from the government all voluntary aid in support of the measures which the present crisis demands. An expression of our sentiments we conceive has thus become a duty. We are aware that on the measures of administration in a free government, the opinions of all cannot coincide, but while all cannot unite in approving every measure which the constituted authorities may adopt, yet on the great subject of national defence, there ought not to exist and with us there does not exist any division. We all unite in sentiments of inviolable attachment to the union, and a determination to support by every exertion in our power, such measures as are deemed necessary for a vigorous prosecution and speedy termination of the war.

We are compelled to consider the present as a war which could not be avoided but by a surrender of our honor and our independence, and therefore both just and necessary. And when we take a review of the measures of aggression and insult towards us, which Great Brittain has invariably pursued, and which has been encreased only by a disposition on our part to retain the relations of friendship, we can discover no course by which to avoid national degradation and a sacrafice of our best interests, but the one which our government has adopted. We are, always disposed to regard war as an evil, but on the present occasion we are compelled to consider it as an evil infinitely less than the one intended to be prevented by it.

Animated by sentiments exclusively American, we hesitate not to express our conviction, that in selecting an enemy, government has alone had regard to the certainty that all hopes of an honorable peace with Great Brittain were past and that when the same certainty shall exist as it respects France, the same measure will be persued in relation to that power. We are equally convinced, that with her no accommodation will be made, while the immense capital of our merchants, which with lawless violence she has plundered, remains unrestored. When we consider the state of the old world, engaged in a war, which to human view presents no prospect of an end but in the distruction of one of the great contending parties, and the inordinate ambition of the sovereign who rules the distinies of the land, under whose pretended friendship, the independence of every power, within the reach of his influence or of his arms, has been distroyed, We are convinced that our government will not connect itself with France by an alliance which shall preclude a termination of the present war, whenever we may have an oppertunity of ending it with advantage and honor to ourselves.

Signed by the unanimous order of the officers of the regiment

THOS. HUTCHINSON
Lieut Col.

RC (DNA: RG 59, ML). Enclosed in Thomas Hutchinson to JM, 24 July 1812 (ibid.; 1 p.).

From Thomas Shepherd

SIR   No. HAMPTON, MASSTS. 24th July 1812

In obedience to the vote of a convention composed of Republican Delegates convened at No. Hampton on the 20th. Instant from fifty one Towns in the Counties of Hampshire Franklin & Hampden (late Hampshire County), I herewith transmit you the report and resolutions adopted by that convention on the subject of the present war with Great Brittain.

It is with pleasure that I do this, as this convention is a true organ not only of their own sentiments but also of the sentiments of more than four thousand six hundred republican citizens of these Counties.

Accept Sir, my most ardent wishes for your health and happiness. I am respectfully your most obedient & hble servant

THOMAS SHEPHERD

[Enclosure]

§ From the Republican Delegates from Towns in Hampshire, Franklin, and Hampden Counties, Massachusetts. *24 July 1812.* "At a convention of republican delegates, consisting of one hundred and forty two members, from fifty one towns, in the late County of Hampshire comprising the counties of Hampshire, Franklin, and Hampden, convened at the Court-House in Northampton on the twentieth day of July inst. at eleven o'clock A.M. to counteract the effects of a convention holden at the same place on the 14th. inst.[1] Samuel Buffington Esquire was unanimously chosen Moderator, and Thomas Shepherd, Secretary of the Convention. The following report and resolutions were unanimously adopted.

"The Committee appointed by a delegation of republican citizens assembled at West Springfield on the 13 inst. to take into consideration the causes of the present war with Great-Britain and the combinations which are believed to exist to dissolve the present happy Union of the States, and to present the result of their deliberation to a republican convention to be held at Northampton on the 20th. inst. from all the towns in the former county of Hampshire, have attended that service and beg leave to submit the following report and resolutions: After an attentive perusal of the documents submited to Congress by the president of the United States, it most clearly appears, that both England and France have, for several years, violated the neutral rights, insulted the flag, and depredated upon the lawful commerce of the United States on the high seas. That Great Britain in addition to the outrages done on the ocean, has committed the most atrocious violences within our own waters, impressed our seamen and excited the savages to an indiscriminate massacre of the inhabitants of our frontiers.

"The goverment of the United States actuated by a sincere disposition to remain at peace with all the world, have attempted by negociation commenced and prosecuted in a spirit of amity and impartiality, to settle all our differences with both the belligerents. Those powers, blind to their true policy, and regardless of justice, have refused to comply with our reasonable terms of accommodation. France, inflamed by a blind rage against England, is resolved to destroy British commerce, and England, governed not only by a mortal hatred against France, but jealous of the prosperity of the American republic, is determined to establish for herself a monopoly of commerce and the dominion of the seas. That this view of the designs of Great Britain is correct, we need only advert to the notorious fact, that while she has been cutting up American commerce by the roots, while she has been depriving us of an adequate market for the great staples of our country, while she has seized our merchantmen and condemned our property in her prize Courts, under the pretext of retaliating, on her enemy, she has herself carried on an extensive trade with that enemy under licences and forged papers. In many instances the very cargoes of American property, owned and freighted by American citizens, after being condemned in England under the Orders in Council, has been shipped to the contine[n]t of Europe and sold for the benefit of the captors.

"In this way does England retaliate on her enemy by seeking every corrupt opportunity of trading with her in the merchandize plundered from the citizens of the United States. To submit to such injustice while we have the power to resist would be to surrender our independence without a struggle. A degree of degradation to which the United States ar[e] not reduced, and by the permission of the Almighty we trust they never will be. When by the valor of the American people crowned by the blessing of God, the United States were severed from the British yoke; they acquired all the rights and privileges of an independant nation. After the expulsion of the British from our shores, those rights and privileges were acknowledged to belong to our republic by the powers of the world, not excepting Great Britain herself.

"Among those rights thus guaranteed, those of navigating the ocean under the known laws of nations, and of protecting the lives, liberty and property of our citizens in the persuit of a lawful commerce, were always deemed most sacred.

"To violate these by any nation is an act of war, and to refuse to make reparation for the wrong by the offending party is a just and righteous cause for war on the part of the injured. There is no doubt then, that the United States have just cause of war against England and France; but sound policy required that we should not be burthened by a war with two powerful nations at once, Congress therefore wisely selected England as our enemy, she being the first and the greatest aggressor. England by her orders in council has given a fatal stab to the freedom of commerce, has violated the laws of nations and under pretexts the most futile has exercised the rights of sovereignty over us. In the impressment of seamen sailing under the protection of the American flag she has trampled upon the personal liberty of the citizen and entered with ruthless violence the sanctuary of our independence, dragging her victims to slavery and to death. In employing the savages to murder our people, a fact which is confirmed by the testimony of Governor Harrison, and which no one can doubt who knows the influence the British have over the Indian tribes, she has shewn that she disregards those maxims which ought to govern civilized nations. In sending a secret agent among us to plot with the disaffected a dismemberment of the Union; she has convinced the world that she makes use of means to accomplish her nefarious purposes, at once the most atrocious and the most despicable. With these just grounds for war, with such powerful inducements to rally round the ark of our independence and defend it; it is a matter of astonishment to us that any men that claim to be Americans should be so entangled in the Coils of party, so lost to themselves, so dead to the injuries inflicted upon their country as to deny the justice of this war altogether. Your committee are fully convinced that the present war is not only just but necessary and unavoidable. Even however did they doubt of the necessity or policy of the war they should hold it to be their duty, now that war has been resorted to, to support the government in it, in order that our rulers might have a fair chance to obtain an acknowledgement of our rights. Every other expedient has been tried in vain to bring belligerents to a sense of justice, and nothing remained to choose but war or unconditional and base submission.

"If the war of the revolution was just, this war is not less so. That was a war against arbitrary taxation of the British Parliament. It was a war for Independence. It was a war for liberty and equal rights. It was begun in honor and ended in glory. At the commencement of it, clouds and darkness hung over the country, our internal enemies, those ill omened birds of night were continually croaking around; ruin, devastation and death were the burthen of their song; but genius of America triumphed and left her sons, a rich inheritance, cemented by the blood of her heroes. Let no one say that this prize was not worth contending for. We have reason to thank God that the noble virtues and exemplary courage of the revolutionary worthies del[i]vered us from British bondage, and rescued this nation from the thraldom of a corrupt hierarchy, from the tyranny of a mad King and of a proff[l]igate Prince.

"The present war is a contest undertaken in defence of rights not less essential and for privileges not less dear.

"It is commenced under circumstances by far more auspicious and promising a happy issue. With perseverance union and courage on the part of our citizens, the result we may venture to predict will be equally glorious.

"Under these circumstances is it not absurd to withhold our support to government because another power besides England has injured us? Do the decrees of France afford a justification of the orders in Council? By this mode of reasoning the United States are made the football of the belligerents. On this subject the ground taken by the Congress of the United States is the true American ground, and the only one which a nation that respects itself should take. In the language of Congress we repeat 'that the United States must act as an independant nation and assert their rights, and avenge their wrongs according to their own estimation of them, with the party who commits them, holding it responsible for its own misdeeds, unmitigated by those of another.'[2]

"Your Committee are not insensible to the calamities of war, neither are they dead to the rights and independance of their Country. They view war as an evil, but as an evil infinitely less then [sic] the surrender of our rights, or a quiet submission to the violation of them. For thirty years the United States have enjoyed peace; so long have they enjoyed it and so patient have they been in the endurance of wrongs that the belligerents have believed that the love of peace and the desire of gain were paramount to every other consideration with the American people. The British Government has believed that the people of the United States were so dependent upon British commerce, so wedded to foreign luxuries and so base in principle that to use a vulgar expression of an ignoble mind 'they could not be kicked into a war.'[3]

"Have we not reason to believe the disavowal of Erskine's agreement by the British government[4] was mad[e] in consequence of the opposition made to the Embargo, and in consequence of the belief that the United States would not go to war? Indeed, we should be warranted in declaring, that all the embarrassments this country now suffers, and the necessity of the present war, has been produced by the unreasonable opposition to the measures of our own government. This consideration alone is sufficient to induce a more general support of it. Opposition at this time should be discountenanced as productive only of national calamnity. Let it be remembered that the restless men who now exclaim against the goverment, have been as hostile to every measure it has adopted as they now are to the war. They opposed the Embargo before it could have an effect, they have opposed the war before it could be known in Europe. Their only desire seems to be [to] aggrandize themselves on the ruins of the Union, and their only fear that the British goverment would be compelled to do us justice. They know that their existence as a party depends upon British aggression.

"Your committee have no doubt that there is a settled determination on the part of certain leading and influential federal men in New England to dissolve the union of the States. It is a cause of pain and regret to us that any men in our country have so contemptible an opinion of the United States and such a blind attachment to Britain as to harbour so nefarious a design. But the proofs of this conspiracy are so clear that its existance cannot now be denied. It has been long matured and the faction concerned in it, have only waited for a period of national calamity to carry their des[i]gns into execution. With this view they have attempted to make the national government odious, to represent that the eastern states are oppressed and to hold up the government of Britain, our ancient oppressor, as the champion not only of liberty but of religion. In confirmation of our statement we need only refer to the proceedings of the legislature of this Commonwealth in 1809, and to the resolvs of

various towns during that year, recommending a resistance to the laws and a seperation of the States.[5] The transactions of the leaders of the opposition, since the declaration of war, prove that this plan of division has not been abandoned. A convention has been held by the federal party in this county, professedly to oppose the
war[6] but in the opinion of your committee it was set on foot to prepare the minds
of the people for the sad catastrophe of a dissolution of the Union. A state convention has been proposed by that body, and this too in a Commonwealth where the
choice of officers is annual, and immediately subsequent to an election.

"A convention unknown to the Constitution, and without an object as your committee conceive, unless it be to concert means to resist the government and prostrate the Union. Your Committee have no fears of the result—the struggle for the
Union may be an arduous one, but the fabric of Washington is not to be overturned
by desperate party men.

"Without making proffessions of patriotism which they do not feel, without
claiming any higher respect for the honor and independence of the Country than
should belong to every citizen of the republic; your Committee recommend an
united an ardent support of the national goverment, as they conceive that not only
patriotism, but duty and personal security require it.

"Considering that one of those occurrences, pointed out by the great father of
his country, in his parting address, may produce commotions we cannot forbear to
recommend to all classes of people, of whatever political party, a frequent recurrence and a filial reverence of his advice. And to pause, and ponder upon that part
wherein he says, that 'In contemplating the causes which may disturb our union, it
occurs as matter of serious concern, that any ground should have been furnished for
charactizing parties by geographical discriminations. Northern and Southern Atlantic and Western: whence designing men may endeavour to excite a belief that
there is a real difference of local interests and views—one of these expedients of
party to acquire influence within particular districts, is to misrepresent the opinions
and aims of other districts. You cannot shield yourselves to[o] much against the jealousies and heart burnings which spring from those misrepresentations; they tend
to render alien to each other those who ought to be bound together by fraternal
affection.

"'All obstructions to the execution of the laws, all combinations and associations,
under whatever plausible character, with the real design to direct controul, counteract, or awe the regular deliberation and action of the constituted authorities are
destructive of this fundamental principle and of fatal tendency. They serve to organize faction; to give it an artificial force; to put in the place of the delegated will
of the nation the will of a party often a small but artful and enterprising minority
of the community; and according to the alternate triumphs of different parties, to
make the public administration the mirror of the ill-concerted and incongruous
projects of faction rather than the organ of consistent and w[h]olesome plans, digested by common council, and modified by mutual interests.'[7]

"If justice should mark the footsteps of the new ministry of England we shall hail
the day as a jubilee when we can with honor renew the ties of friendley intercourse
with England. But a change of ministry in England, heretofore has produced very
little alteration in her commercial and mar[i]time systems. It is a fair conclusion
that the orders in council against which America has uniformly complained have

become so odious and destructive to England as well as America as to have been the great cause of the change of Ministry. Still this system may not be abandoned, and our joy at the removal of the most corrupt ministry that ever disgraced a nation, may be without much foundation and a ministry may be formed that will adopt measures towards us which will call for the opposing energies of the people of United America.

"The public mind ought to be directed at this time, to the correspondence between the Secretary of State Mr. Munroe, and the British Minister Mr. Foster immediately preceding the declaration of War—and which may be considered as the pivot upon which that important question turned. The President haveing been satisfied that the Milan and Berlin Decrees were revoked, or modified so as not to effect America the American Government in that event required of the British Government a repeal of the orders in Council; to which this unequivocal answer was given by Mr. Foster; 'America as the case now stands has not a pretence for claiming from Great-Britain, a repeal of her orders in council. She must recollect that the British Government never for a moment countenanced the idea that the repeal of these, could depend upon any partial or conditional repeal of the decrees of France. What she always avowed was her readiness to recind her orders in council as soon as France rescinded absolutely and unconditionally her decrees'[8]—Thereby involving America in the European conflict from which, France has been willing and has proved by the most solem avowal, that she is ready to consider America as an exception.

"A revocation therefore of the French decrees, as it respects America, will not be followed by a repeal of the orders in council, unless the new ministry should listen to the voice of justice, and of the English nation, and abandon the old wicked system. A tame and quiet submission to these orders of the British Cabinet, would be a satire upon the principles of the revolution, and would start from their peaceful abodes, the shades of Washington, and the heroes of the revolution.

"These orders of the British cabinet have been condemned by a formidable part of the people of England, and are, it is presumed, at this time, without advocates on the other side of the atlantic. But in the County of Hampshire, a section of the country, least affected by commercial restrictions, the orders in council still find warm and able advocates, and the old ministry are not yet g[i]ven up.

"Upon this view of the domestic situation of the United States, and of our relations with foreign powers, your committee reccommend to this convention the adoption of the following resolutions.

"Resolved, That the veneration and gratitude of the whole American nation, are justly due to the present administration of the general government for their 'ceaseless and solicitous exertions for the welfare of our common country'; that we have never felt at any former period, a more cordial zeal in seconding their measures; that we hasten to declare to this administration, our unqualified approbation of this just and necessary war; that we give them our hands and hearts at such an eventful crisis, pledging ourselves in behalf of every democratic citizens in the counties we represent, that they will support a government so dear to them, in resisting foreign aggression, or in crushing domestic treason.

"Resolved, That whereas the government of Great Britain commenced a war against the United States in the year 1806, and have continued it to this time, although they have withheld the declaration thereof, we cannot view without indignation the base assertion that 'the government of the United States have plunged our country into an offensive war,' which is daily reiterated in the British prints in the United States, and by their influential patrons in public and private life; solemnly denouncing the same as a treacherous and malignant falshood.

"Resolved, That the opposition to the existing measures of the national government in these counties has in its extent been grossly misrepresented, that it is in a great measure factitious, far exceeding in its clamorous and blustering tone and manner, any thing of the kind ever before exhibited by that faction; that we can assure the government and our fellow citizens at large, that this opposition is not so very formidable and alarming, even in this La Vendée of the American union, and the declaration so often repeated by Tories, that any of the 'former friends' of the general administration here are abandoning them, at this important crisis, is another disgraceful falshood.

"Resolved, That the charge that the American government have in any public measure, been under the dominion of a partiality to France, is founded in the suspicion only of their enemies, the partizans of Britain and contradicted by positive evidence contained in the public documents, and that we do not entertain the least doubt, that our government is determined to avenge the wrongs inflicted upon our country by France, unless the negociations now pending should speedily eventuate in an honorable adjustment of her unjustifiable aggressions upon our commerce.

"Resolved, That we cannot conscientiously approve of the proceedings of the majority of the house of representatives in this Commonwealth at the late session,[9] relative to our national affairs, considering them neither wise nor patriotic, as they have a tendency to disunite the people, to counteract the supreme law of the land, to encourage our foreign enemy and to prolong the calamities of war.

"Resolved, That the recent address of the Senate of Massachusetts to their constituents, comprizes the principles which ought to animate every state government and every citizen of the union, and that it deserves our warmest applause.[10]

"Resolved, That in the present state of our country, threatened by foreign and domestic enemies, we deem it highly expedient as well as our imperious duty, to appoint committees of safety and correspondence in every town in these counties and to raise a fund to defray the unavoidable expences connected with a measure of this nature.

"Resolved, That we consider all meetings and conventions for the purpose of opposing the general government and the laws of the union, as dangerous during the existence of the present war and highly criminal, and that in case the leaders of the federal party should call a state or New-England convention according to their contemplated plan, we solemnly declare that we shall regard such an act as a preparatory step on the part of our domestic enemies to organize a force for the destruction of every thing dear to us and that we shall take such decisive measures as so alarming a crisis will imperiously demand.

"Resolved, That we view with inexpressible abhorrence, the recent attempts made in this section of the union to oppose the constituted authorities of the nation, in pursuance of the orders of a few restless and unprincipled individuals in the town of Boston, being the same factious citizens who in April 1811 declared that a law of the United States must and would be resisted, and that the tories of the last war, are now foremost in aiding those disorganizers in the circles in which we have had an opportunity of witnessing the proceedings of their coadjutors and slaves.[11]

"Resolved, That we deem it too late as well as wholly irrelavant to be told at this unexampled crisis by the miserable apologists for the wrongs inflicted upon our beloved country, by the corrupt government of Great Britain, (wrongs which cry even to Heaven for vengeance) 'that we are the descendants of the British nation—and that she is the bulwark of the religion we profess,'[12] a nation that has for ages sustained the character of lawless conquerors and pirates; which whenever her power would admit, has carried the terror of her arms to every land and sea; which, in a barbarous seven years war in conjunction with her natural alies the American Indians burnt our cities and towns, slaughtered our armies, butchered and scalped our defenceless men, women and children; which has annihilated the independence of the brave and generous people of Ireland, and doomed her worthiest citizens to the scaffold; which, has laid waste the fairest provinces of India, and murdered millions of her inoffensive inhabitants; which has in latter times without any pretext but that of tyrannical violence, impressed thousands of our seamen, and consigned them to the most ignominious servitude on board her floating castles of cruelty; which has swept American commerce from the ocean, has attempted to rally the traitors of our Country under the banner of John Henry, to dismember the union, and thereby to produce a civil war and a re-colinization of the New England states, and has again let slip the dogs of savage war, to spread dessolation and havoc among the citizens of our frontiers, and under whose fatal alliances the continent of Europe is now bleeding to death—with a government already exhibiting a decaying mass of corruption, which will probably soon become food for worms, and be consigned to the same just grave that has swallowed up other despotisms.

"Resolved, That this report and resolutions be signed by the Moderator and Secretary of this convention—and that the Secretary be directed to forward a copy thereof to the President of the United States, and to cause the same to be published in the Democrat printed in Northampton."

RC and enclosure (DNA: RG 59, ML). Enclosure 17 pp.; signed by Samuel Buffington, moderator, and Thomas Shepherd, secretary.

1. See Delegates from Towns in Franklin, Hampshire, and Hampden Counties, Massachusetts, to JM, 15 July 1812.

2. The delegates quoted from the 3 June 1812 report of the House committee on foreign relations (*ASP, Foreign Relations*, 3:570).

3. The delegates quoted loosely from Josiah Quincy's 19 Jan. 1809 speech in the House of Representatives, in which he expressed his opinion that "no insult, however gross, offered to us by either France or Great Britain," could force the House to declare war. In his view the majority "could not be kicked into such a declaration by either nation" (*Annals of Congress*, 10th Cong., 2d sess., 1112).

4. For the British disavowal of Erskine's agreement, see Presidential Proclamation Restoring Commerce with Great Britain, 15–19 Apr. 1809, John Armstrong to JM, 6 June 1809, and JM to Jefferson, 12 June 1809, *PJM-PS*, 1:117–18, 228–31, 239–40 and n. 1.

5. In January 1809 the Massachusetts legislature received a number of petitions requesting that action be taken to nullify the effects of the Embargo and Enforcement Acts. The Massachusetts legislature subsequently wrote a memorial to Congress protesting the embargo

and threatening noncompliance (see *The Patriotick Proceedings of the Legislature of Massachusetts* ... [Boston, 1809; Shaw and Shoemaker 18040]).

6. See Delegates from Towns in Franklin, Hampshire, and Hampden Counties, Massachusetts, to JM, 15 July 1812.

7. See Washington's farewell address (Fitzpatrick, *Writings of Washington*, 35:223, 224–25).

8. Foster to Monroe, 30 May 1812, *ASP, Foreign Relations*, 3:454–57.

9. See *Address of the House of Representatives to the People of Massachusetts* (Boston, 1812; Shaw and Shoemaker 25978).

10. The Massachusetts Senate remained under Republican control after the April 1812 elections. The delegates referred to a senate address in favor of the declaration of war (see *Report of the Committee of the Senate of Massachusetts; Comprising the President's Message of the 1st of June; the Report of the Committee of Foreign Relations; the Act Declaring War; . . . and the Address of the Senate to the People of This Commonwealth* [Boston, 1812; Shaw and Shoemaker 26011]).

11. The memorialists most likely referred to widely distributed resolutions passed at a meeting of the citizens of Boston on 31 Mar. 1811. The meeting declared that the imposition of nonintercourse against Great Britain on 2 Mar. 1811 was a "tyrannical act . . . and that the only means short of an appeal to force to prevent such a calamity . . . is the election of such men to the various offices in the State government, as will oppose by peaceable, but firm measures, the execution of Laws, which if persisted in, must and will be resisted" (Boston *Columbian Centinel*, 27 Apr. 1811).

12. The delegates quoted from Caleb Strong's proclamation for a day of fasting, humiliation, and prayer (see Gerry to JM, 13 July 1812, n. 6).

Statement of Appropriations
for the Navy and Marine Corps

	Balances in the hands of the Secy of Treasury	Balances in the hands of Treasurer	Over
	July 24th 1812		
Pay &c of Officers & Seamen [1]	780 119 95	25.810 65	
Provisions [2]	289.757	6 822 52½	
Medicines &c	19.000	446 37	
Repairs of Vessels		2.329 24	
Contingent &c	11.000		1.222 79½
Navy yards	28.000	230 68	
Ordnance [3]	293.000	7.689 74	
Sulpher & Salt petre	180.000	9.072 11	
Repairs of Constellation &c	55.000		3.356 81
Purchase of timber &c	200 000		388 53
Torpedo Experiment	2.500		
Putting & keeping in Service the Constellation &c	71.250		

Repairs of vessels damaged in action	400 000		
Equipping &c captured vessels	428.750		
Marine corps—			
Pay &c of M. corps	95.725 10	1.909 61	
Clothing M Corps	32.577 20	3.300 17	
Military Stores "	2.572 50	105 93	
Medicines &c — "	5.500	2 16 60	
Qr Masters Dept	7.000		1.885. 4
	2.901.751 75	57.933 62½	6 853 17½
			57.933.62½
			6 853.17½
Balance, in the hands of the Treasurer			51.080.45
Balance in the hands of the Secretary of Treasury			2.901.751.75
			2.952.832.20

Ms (DLC). In a clerk's hand; docketed by JM.

1. After this item is written in pencil "200,000."
2. After this item is written in pencil "100,000."
3. After this item is written in pencil "150,000."

§ From the Inhabitants of Gerry, Massachusetts. *24 July 1812.* "The Inhabitants of the Town of Gerry, in the County of Worcester, and Commonwealth of Massachusetts, in legal Town-meeting assembled, beg leave respectfully to present the following . . . *Memorial.*

"We have viewed, with anxious eye, the proceedings of our National Council, since the days of the retirement of our beloved and illustrious *Washington.*

"We have endeavored to examine, with that patriotic jealousy, to which the love of our Country prompted, all the acts of Administration, which have come to our knowledge. As far as they respected the great political relations of our nation, we have tried by the standard of our national Saviour, in his '*farewel*' advice to his fellow-citizens.

"Whenever we have discovered what we considered a deviation from the principles of that excellent manuel—principles on which, we deem, our political redemption and salvation rest—we have been distressed for our people, & the cities of our GOD! With all the deference to the wisdom of the Chief Magistrate of this great nation, which his character and station demand, we have been obliged to differ in opinion from your Excellency, especially in the *momentous* Manifesto, presented to Congress, the first of June last,[1] and which was the precursor of that declaration, that has involved us in a war with the only nation under Heaven, capable of doing us any great and essential injury!

"Had your Excellency's Manifesto included the wrongs done us by France, the knowledge of which, by *official* documents, has been pouring in upon the nation for a series of years; and had it been productive of a declaration of War against *both* the Great Belligerents of the East, we cannot but believe it would have met the approbation of far greater numbers of your fellow-citizens; for the evidence from documents, now in the Secretary's Office, is too glaring to remain unnoticed, that our causes for war on the part of France are far more aggravating than those on the part of Great-Britain.

"We cannot disguise our fears that the present policy of Administration is tending directly to an alliance with France, which we consider one of the greatest calamities that can befall our Country: for we have seen that the friendship of the Emperor to other nations has been their ruin: and can expect nothing better for our own.

"In the Northern section of the Union, we feel more sensibly the weight of those calamities, which are always attendant on war, than it is possible our Southern Brethren should feel: In the vicinity of a great province of the *declared* enemy; with hundreds of miles of unprotected sea-coast, on which stand many of our wealthiest and most populous Towns; in a state of almost entire want of preparation for War, both by sea & land, with millions of our property afloat, and thousands of our fellow-citizens exposed to capture, imprisonment, and death! we tremble for the event!!!

"We apply to your Excellency, as the Great source, under GOD, of our relief from anxiety, & the burden of our fears! We pray your Excellency to consider the distressed situation of these Northern States; the hopeless event of a long struggle against Great-Britain; the happy consequences of a speedy return of peace; and to use all those energies, and that influence, with which your Excellency is possessed, and for the exercise of which your Country loudly calls, to bring to a termination the present unhappy contest, before our Citizens are reduced to a condition in which peace would scarcely be a blessing!!!

"Done at Gerry this 24th. of July 1812, in very full meeting of the Inhabitants. *Nemine contradicente!*" [2]

RC (DNA: RG 59, ML). 3 pp.; signed by Elijah Gould, moderator, and Nahum Ward, town clerk.

1. *PJM-PS*, 4:432–38.
2. *Nemine contradicente:* no one contradicting.

§ From James Jefferis. *Ca. 24 July 1812.* Claims that in 1809 he and John Dauphin, both of the District of Delaware, put up security for James Brobson to serve as marshal.[1] Explains that at that time there was little business for the marshal to perform, that they believed Brobson was solvent and of good character, and that Jefferis and Dauphin were both men of considerable means. "Your Memorialist however respectfully represents, that . . . things have undergone an entire change, and the confidence of the Parties as well as the security of the United States completely vanished. The buisness [*sic*], from a state in which a few suits only annually marked the records of the Courts, has augmented in a degree almost unparalleled, and the responsibility of the officer has itself grown to treble the amount of the security required at the time of his appointm[e]nt. From a condition of solvency, the Marshall too has become notoriously indigent, and . . . it is also his fate to have parted with the confidence which he once possessed." Notes that Dauphin suffered financial ruin and died, leaving his family without support. "And your Memorialist . . . has also had his share of ill fortune," which has diminished his means. Under these circumstances, has repeatedly applied to the marshal to be released from his obligation but has been refused. Has been "instructed by the advise of Counsel that there exists no remedy so likely to be effectual & easy, and at the same time so regardfull of the feelings of the individual concerned, as by a representation of the facts of the case to his Excellency the President of the United States on the grounds of which he presumes to ask that his Excellency would be pleased to release him from his future liability as the security aforesaid, either by removing the said officer under the permission to receive the office a second time upon his giving New and Substantial securities, or in any other manner most agreeable to the President." Gives JM "due notice of the condition of an officer in whom neither his securities or the United States are safe." Will avail himself of "all the benifit of such notice" should any attempt be made to make him liable for the marshal's "losses or Misconduct."[2]

RC (DNA: RG 59, ML). 4 pp. Enclosed in Richard Rush to Monroe, 28 July 1812 (ibid.). Undated; date assigned here on the assumption that Rush forwarded the letter shortly after receiving it in the comptroller's office in Washington. Rush pointed out that "no order can be taken upon [the memorial] at this department" and requested that it be laid before JM at Monroe's discretion. Rush added that "complaints of a similar nature have heretofore reached this office from the same quarter."

1. JM nominated Brobson to be marshal of the Delaware district on 25 May 1809. He nominated him for another four-year term on 29 May 1813 (*Senate Exec. Proceedings*, 2:122, 347).

2. Brobson wrote to Monroe on 12 Aug. 1812 to give "a statement of facts, for the information of the President, as an explanation of the charges" against him (DLC; docketed by Monroe: "For the President / answer & vindication of the Marshall of Delawre."; docketed by JM).

To Benjamin Ludlow

SIR   WASHINGTON July 25. 1812

I have recd. the address from "The Convention of Republican Delegates from the several counties of the State of New Jersey,"[1] explaining the sentiments entertained at this crisis, by that portion of my Constituents. The sentiments are worthy the character of Citizens, who know the value of the national rights at stake in the present contest; and who are willing to do justice to the sincere & persevering efforts which have been employed to obtain respect to them, without a resort to arms.

The conduct of the nation agst. whom this resort has been proclaimed, left no choice but between that & the greater evil of a surrender of our Sovereignty on the Element, on which all nations have equal rights, and in the free use of which, the U. S. as a nation whose agriculture & commerce are so closely allied, have an essential interest.

The appeal to force, in opposition to the force so long continued against us, had become the more urgent, as every endeavor short of it, had not only been fruitless; but had been followed by fresh usurpations & oppressions.

The intolerable outrages committed agst. the crews of our vessels which at one time were the result of alledged searches for deserters from British Ships of War, had grown into a like pretension, first as to all British Seamen, and next as to all British subjects; with the invariable practice of seizing on all neutral seamen of every nation; and on all such of our own seamen, as British officers interested in the abuse, might please to demand.

The blockading orders in Council, commencing on the plea of retaliating injurys, indirectly done to G. Britain, through the direct operation of French Decrees, agst. the trade of the U. S. with her; and on a professed disposition to proceed step by step with France in revoking them, have been since bottomed on pretensions more & more extended and arbitrary; till at length it is openly avowed, as indispensible to a repeal of the orders as they affect the U. States, that the French Decrees, be repealed as they affect G. Britain directly, and all other neutrals, as well as, the U. States. To this extraordinary avowal is superadded abundant evidence, that the real object of the orders is not to restore freedom to the American Commerce with G. B. which could indeed be little interrupted by the decrees of France, but to destroy our lawful commerce, as interfering with her own unlawful commerce with her enemies. The only foundation of this attempt to banish the American flag from the high way of nations, or to render it wholly subservient to the commercial views of the B. Govt. is the absurd & exploded doctrine, that the Ocean not less than the land, is susceptible of occupancy & dominion: that this dominion is in the hands of G. Britain; and that her laws, not the law of nations, which is ours as well as hers, are to regulate our maritime intercourse with the rest of the world.

When the U. S. assumed & established their rank among the nations of the Earth, they assumed & established a common Sovereignty on the high seas, as well as an exclusive sovereignty within their territorial limits. The one is as essential as the other, to their Character as an Independent nation. However conceding they may have been on controvertible points, or forbearing under casual and limited injuries, they can never submit to wrongs irreparable in their kind, enormous in their amount, and indefinite in their duration; and which are avowed and justified on principles degrading the U: States from the rank of a sovereign & independent Power. In attaining this high rank, and the inestimable blessings attached to it, no part of the American people, had a more meritorious share, than the people of N. Jersey. From none therefore may more reasonably be expected a patriotic zeal in maintaing by the sword the unquestionable & unalienable rights, acquired by it; and which it is found, can no otherwise be maintained.

Draft (DLC, filed at 25 June 1812). Written on the cover of a 15 July 1812 letter to JM addressed from "Orange C. h Va." Addressed to "Ludlow. B. (Chairman[)]." A note in the margin in JM's hand reads: "answer to Address / Convention of Republican delegates N. Jersey / July 25. 1812." Printed in the *National Intelligencer*, 18 Aug. 1812.

1. See Republican Delegates of New Jersey to JM, 10 July 1812.

From John Allen

I am unknown to you and therefore this address may seem improper. My apology is that several years ago I was among those who forwarded Resolutions pledging ourselves &c to Endeavor to support all lawful measures taken by Govrment to vindicate our rights.[1] I considered it a Solemn promise which aught to be performed But besides that obligation I heartily approve of the measure taken. I only regret that it was not sooner & that It had not extended to France Also. My best feelings Are alive for my Countrys Cause And deeming a communication necessary from what you will herein after discover I have thought it no time to indulge qualms about form or Ceremony. Should there be Any thing improper I hope it will be pardoned for the intention's sake.

In the war office you have my name as the Comdt. of the rifle regiment raised in this State as part of the detachment of the militia of 100,000 under the Act of Congress of the 10th. of April 1812. That regiment is altogeth[e]r Volunteer they have been raised on fair and open terms for marching into Canada if required. They are men who will not hesitate on passing the boundary line if required leaving it to others if they please to discuss the right of the president to call militia beyond the United States.

But a Considerable point is this, there are persons who Endeavour to discourage the service first by dissuading men from Volunteering by a variety of Arguments—And now by—endeavouring to impress the belief that they will not be called for that their parade will only tend to Expose them As the dupes of an inefficient administration &c. &c. The Credit of the officers &c. have yet been proof agt. these attemps—but should the Volunters be passed unnoticed it will materially injur the Countrys Cause And add Strength to the opposition. The extent of its effects I am unable to point out—but this far at least might be expect that it would be in vain attempt to get Volunteers (and by the by 1 Volunteer is as good as 4 or 5 ordinary drafts).

I would not be understood as representing the dispositions of the reg[i]ments Generally—as to passing the boundary line. I do not Know them particulary and therefore cannot make a representation but presume from the General disposition here that all would serve in Canada, with alacrity. My Own Regiment I Know & pledge them as willing. They were raised in the Spring and are only provided with Summer Cloathing—they would want some provision for winter Cloathing if called into Canada for a cold Season. My regiment is pretty well armed—but some of the rifles are rather too Small in the bore, could we be aided a litt[l]e in that way it would be An advantage—but if not convenient we can do with what we have.

Notwithstanding the attemps agt. Gov. Harrison[2] he stands well with the offic[e]rs in this state. I do not Know one who would be dissatisfied with serving under him but believe all would be pleased with it And a large proportion highly Gratified—in case the Govermental Arrangements placed them under him.

Should not the Service this year requ[i]re the whole detachment on Any enterprize of Great importance would it not bee for the Genl. Good to employ a part in some minor way to secure that degree of confidence which is necessary in times like the present.[3] I mix here with the officers & Soldiers & think I perceive their feelings. With High respect yr. Hbl. Svt.

JOHN ALLEN

This I mark as conf[i]dential, not as containing any Secret—but that it may meet the prst. own eye before that of Any of his clerks—& then to be disposed of at [*sic*] he shall think right.

JA.

RC (DNA: RG 107, LRRS, A-139:6). Cover marked *"(confidential)."* Docketed as received in the War Department on 4 Aug. 1812.

1. The editors have been unable to identify these resolutions.

2. The conduct of William Henry Harrison during the Battle of Tippecanoe on 7 Nov. 1811 had been the subject of criticism in frontier areas, particularly by friends and associates of Joseph H. Daviess of Kentucky, who had been killed in the action (see Harrison to Charles Scott, 13 Dec. 1811, and Harrison to Eustis, 28 Dec. 1811, in Esarey, *Messages and Letters of William Henry Harrison*, Indiana Historical Collections, 1:666–72, 686–88).

3. On 5 Aug. 1812 Eustis responded to this letter, informing Allen that Brig. Gen. James Winchester had been authorized to reinforce Hull in Upper Canada with such volunteers as the governor of Kentucky might approve. Eustis recommended that Allen redirect his request to the governor (DNA: RG 107, LSMA).

From George Joy

DEAR SIR,   LONDON 25th. July 1812.

Mr. Russell being still absent; and having, in addition to the anxiety expressed in my last, a desire to know the operation of the late news from America on this Government, I obtained on Thursday an appointment to meet Lord Sidmouth yesterday morning, when I spent about an hour with him.

In conformity with the mode, which I took the liberty to suggest to you some years ago, & which I have not unfrequently practised since, I had left to the correspondence to which I had previously referred his Lordship to demonstrate *more palpably* than I had asserted the necessity for adopting the measure I was urging on this occasion: however I took with me the extracts, of which I cover copy, underlined in the same manner,[1] and called his particular attention to that of Mr. Foster to Mr. Monroe of the 26th. of July,[2] which I treated as a pledge of the Government in the Secretaryship of Marquis Wellesley which the Prince would most assuredly redeem, when fairly before him if not already done.

He told me he thought the conversation we had formerly had together was not quite right although he declared most solemnly that he had not the least doubt that he could fully confide in me. He said I must know that these subjects were best discussed in the department to which they belonged. He had thought it his duty to hand what I had written him to Lord Castlereigh and he presumed, that the call of Mr. Russell (which I had mentioned to him, as well as his absence) resulted from that communication.

What further passed on this subject, though certainly nothing like a state secret, was not to be repeated neither would it be any information to you when this shall reach you.

With respect to the other object of my visit he expressed a decided opinion that the American Government had been too precipitate in voting for War when they knew it had been agreed to refer the petitions on the Orders in Council to a committee, and that there was an accession of members to the Government favorably disposed to the United States. At this time, too, when France was on the eve of a War with Russia, he could not but think that the President had precipitated the measure; lest the news he might expect should make it out of his power to obtain the consent of the legislature. To the charge of precipitancy I opposed the length of time the subject was debating in Congress. I found that the approval by the President had not yet reached this Country.

I observed to him that every thing before the Govert. of the U. S. at the time indicated a determination here to persist in the hostile measure of the Orders in Council; that it was not even certain that the reference of the subject to a committee was known at Washington and if it were it must be accompanied with the confidence of Ministers in the result of the enquiry being favorable to their views, and the reflections arising out of the consequences of the former investigation. That the speech of Mr Perceval in reply to Mr. Canning[3] which was before the Government was any thing but favorable to the hopes of accomodation and if he would look to appearances as between Russia and France at the time, to say nothing of the difficulties that Mr. Barlow had encountered in his efforts to obtain redress for the later enormities of France,[4] he would see no reason for the surmise of any connivance between the French Government & that of the United States.

That moreover there was all the evidence that could be reasonably de-

sired of the most friendly dispositions between Russia & the U. S. To seize
on news-paper reports, he observed, (referring to the speech of Perceval)
was not the best indication of a pacific disposition. I told him it was not a
news-paper report, but the report of Mr Russell who was himself in the
house & heared it;[5] and though I did not perceive any material difference
between this & the news-paper reports; Mr. R. had assigned the deficiency
of these last as a reason for sending the M. S.

A comparison of dates, for want of which, owing to the distance of the
U. S, many ideas are confounded, seem'd to obviate his notions of hostility
and he evidently considered the speech of Mr. Perceval in the official form
of a letter from Mr. Russell as a more proper subject for the consideration
of congress than a news-paper report. He wondered that the newspapers
here did not copy more from those of America (in one of which I had told
him I had read this communication).

He had seen some excellent speeches of the members of our legislature,
recited with considerable emphasis a part of one of Mr Giles[6] in which he
stated that this Govt: knew very little of human nature, if they expected to
soothe the feelings of the Americans by insulting their understanding,
which he charactarized as very eloquent & most just. Finally, he hoped we
should have to shake hands on a friendly adjustment of all the matters in
difference between the two countries to which he trusted I was sensible
from the past that no reasonable efforts on his part would be wanting.

I have a more extensive stenographic minute of this conversation, but
will here only add that if there are members of the administration that
nothing will shake from the unwarrantable identification of French &
American Politics, I cannot consider Lord Sidmouth as one of them. In
speaking of blockade, he admitted the necessity of a *stationary* force anticipating the word, or emphasising it in reference to the quotation in my letter of 24th. of April;[7] but in respect to French pretensions he quoted an expression of Lord Nelson. "If we lay a straw there & the French tell us to
pick it up, we must for that reason let it lie." I rest, always very faithfully,
dear sir, Your Friend & Servant

GEO: JOY.

RC (DLC: Rives Collection, Madison Papers). In a clerk's hand, signed by Joy; postmarked
Boston, 22 Oct.

1. Enclosure not found.

2. In this 1811 letter Foster explained that the blockade of May 1806 would not be auto-
matically rescinded should the orders in council be repealed. The British minister stated that
the blockade "will not continue after the repeal of the orders in council, unless His Majesty's
Government shall think fit to sustain it by the special application of a sufficient naval force;
and the fact of its being so continued or not will be notified at the time." In the interim he
asked that all further reference to the blockade be suspended, as it was not germane to a discussion of the orders in council (*ASP, Foreign Relations*, 3:443–45).

3. On 3 Mar. 1812 Henry Brougham, a longtime parliamentary opponent of the orders in council, had raised the question of their repeal in the House of Commons, generating a lengthy debate. George Canning claimed that the orders were retaliatory only and amounted to an actual blockade, which was undermined by Great Britain's attempts to trade with its enemy. Perceval responded that the orders in council were indeed retaliatory and that Great Britain was within its rights to respond to France's aggression. In his opinion the orders in council could continue so long as the Berlin and Milan Decrees remained in force against Great Britain, regardless of their application against the U.S. Late that evening the House of Commons voted 216 to 144 to continue the orders (*Parliamentary Debates*, 21:1092–1164).

4. Barlow had engaged in a protracted struggle with French officials for the release of vessels captured after the alleged repeal of the Berlin and Milan Decrees and to negotiate a commercial treaty (see Barlow to JM, 1 Jan. 1812, JM to Barlow, 24 Feb. 1812, Barlow to JM, 3 Mar., 22 Apr., and 2 May 1812, *PJM-PS*, 4:110 and nn., 199–202, 222–23 and n. 1, 337–38 and n. 1, 359–60 and nn.).

5. For Jonathan Russell's report on Perceval's speech, see Russell to Monroe, 4 Mar. 1812, *ASP, Foreign Relations*, 3:426–27.

6. This was probably William Branch Giles's speech in the Senate on 8 Dec. 1809 in support of resolutions condemning Francis James Jackson (*Annals of Congress*, 11th Cong., 2d sess., 484–509).

7. Joy's 24 Apr. 1812 letter to Lord Sidmouth was published as *A Letter, from a Calm Observer, to a Noble Lord* (see *PJM-PS*, 4:389 n. 1). In that letter Joy quoted from JM's 27 Oct. 1803 letter to Edward Thornton (*PJM-SS*, 5:580–82), in which JM had argued that the law of nations was clear on the subject of paper blockades. Here JM quoted from the fourth part of Article 3 of the June 1801 convention between Great Britain and Russia: "in order to determine what characterizes a blockaded port, that denomination is given only to a port where there is, by the dispositions of the power which attacks it with Ships stationary or sufficiently near, an evident danger in entering."

From John Coape Sherbrooke

SIR,   GOVERMENT HOUSE HALIFAX 25th. July 1812
    There being at present no public functionary of the British Goverment, within the United States, to whom I could address myself in a case of humanity, of high interest to both Countries, I take the freedom, however irregular or informal it may be, of Submitting to your Excellency's consideration the subject of the inclosed Affidavit.[1] It respects the Capture of a British Vessel, taken by an American Privateer, while in the Act of transporting Provisions for the support of the Establishment on the Isle of Sable, in the maintenance of which all nations and individuals that can feel for the miseries of Shipwreck must be particularly interested. I am convinced that Your Excellency will cheerfully adopt any measure that can prevent the recurrence of captures so inconsistent with the common principles of humanity, and it is under this impression that I leave the consideration of the greivance as well as the discussion of the remedy to the wisdom and

benevolence of Your Goverment. I have the Honor to be Your Excellencys most Obedient and Humble Servant.

J. C. SHERBROOKE[2]
Lt. Govr. of Nova Scotia

RC (DNA: RG 59, ML).

1. Enclosure not found.
2. Sir John Coape Sherbrooke (1764–1830) served as lieutenant governor of Nova Scotia from July 1811 to April 1816. While building up his colony's defenses and supporting an extensive privateering campaign, Sherbrooke remained on friendly terms with the New England states, continuing trade under a licensing system throughout the War of 1812. He also led a campaign that resulted in the occupation of parts of the District of Maine for eight months in 1814 (Halpenny, *Dictionary of Canadian Biography*, 6:712–16).

§ From Frederick Freeman. *25 July 1812, Milledgeville, Baldwin County, Georgia.* Informs JM that the "Baldwin Troop of Light Dragoons 5th. Squadron, 3d. Regiment of Georgia Cavalry" have observed the "belligerent outrages" that have interrupted "equitable commerce" between the U.S. and Europe for "the last three years." Convinced that the claims of the U.S. government were just, "the members of the troop entertained a fond hope that the violated rights of their Country would have been immediately restored on terms acceptable to freemen and to patriots." While they "deplore the consequences of disappointment, in expectations so reasonable, and so interesting to the peaceful enjoyments of civil life, the Officers and privates of the troop are prompt in declaring their determination to meet, with alacrity and firmness, every privation and danger which a successful vindication and support of the late highly approved measures of their government may require." "The Adjutant General, in making a detail of this States quota of the 100,000 militia, to be raised in conformity with the act of Congress for that purpose,[1] has required no part of the Cavalry from the Regiment to which they are attached." "They, therefore, disdaining the inglorious safety of domestic retirement whilst others are fighting the battles of their Country," tender their services to JM, according to the 5 Feb. 1812 Volunteer Act.[2]

RC and enclosure (DNA: RG 107, LRRS, F-94:6). RC 3 pp.; signed by Capt. Frederick Freeman "for himself, the Subaltern Officers and the privates of the before described troop"; docketed as received in the War Department on 8 Aug. 1812. The enclosure (2 pp.) is a list of the forty members of the Baldwin Volunteer Troop, with an appended note by Freeman stating that several applicants waiting to join would soon "be equipped ready for the service, so that the Captain entertains no doubt but that, by the time they can be called upon, he will have a full company."

1. See *U.S. Statutes at Large*, 2:705–7.
2. The statute was dated 6 Feb. 1812. See ibid., 2:676–77.

§ From John Morris. *25 July 1812, Erie.* "Some time this Spring, myself & Company under my Command, tendered our Services, to you, through Mr Lacock, [(]under the Law Feb. 6, 1812) upon Certain conditions viz, mer[e]ly for the Protection of this frontier of Pena,[1] Should the terms upon Which we offerd, not be acceptable, I would beg Leave to with Draw the papers."

RC (DNA: RG 107, LRRS, M-343:6). 1 p.; docketed as received in the War Department on 4 Aug. 1812. A note on the cover in Eustis's hand reads: "the President is not authorised by Law to accept Volunteers on the condition proposed."

    1. Letter not found, but it is listed in the Registers of Letters Received by the Secretary of War (DNA: RG 107) as a letter from Abner Lacock to Eustis dated 26 June 1812 and received 29 June. Eustis responded to Morris's letter on 4 Aug. 1812, explaining that the provisions for accepting volunteers had been delineated in federal acts and that as his offer of service specified "other Conditions, the Original is returned" as requested (DNA: RG 107, LSMA).

From William Tatham

SIR,   July 26th. 1812.

    I have had repeated conferences with the honl. the Secretaries, heads of departments aiding the Executive of the United States, on the subjects communicated in my letter to you dated the 11th. instant; and find, in reference to my propositions No. 1. 2. & 3. exclusive of any other subject matter claim or proposal, that we have the same view of the great importance of the British and other original manuscripts aplicable to Canada, to Nova Scotia, to Florida, and other Countries with which we are, or are likely to be, at war, and which are only to be found in my collection.

    The honl. the Secretary at war (most particularly) is impressed with the great advantage of deriving speedy aid from various inestimable military originals in my posession, and seems to accord with me in opinion of the utility of all which may apply in his Department, either as matter of superior military information or as examples for the instruction of our rising Army; and this idea is expressly approved by the Resolution of the Committee of the House of Representitives on this subject, reported in April 1806,[1] as well as stimulated by your late proclamation.[2]

    The difficulty which impedes the public accommodation, in this particular, is that, the late legislature, having no foreknowledge that so great an acquisition would be so timeously offered to the executive assistance as one which immediately tends to ⟨e⟩lucidate the measures directed against Canada, have neither provided a specific or contingent fund for the occasion; yet anxious to contribute all, on my part, which prudence and a just regard for those who have claims on me by nature or equity will allow, I am willing to meet the magnanimity of the nation on terms of liberality. Hence, as there remains no doubt that the whole accumulation is a matter of great public acquisition, I propose,

    1. That the sum of ____[3] dollars be advanced me on account; being an

amount necessary to my present occasions, and to carry on the work till the legislature shall have convened, and acted on the premises.

2dly. I will immediately fix an office for the purpose of completing such copies of original surveys, plans, maps, charts, or drawings, as the respective appartments may desire for their particular occasions: each of which Copies shall be specially charged on account, according to its nature and description, and delivered on the receipt of the particular Department.

3dly. The heads of Departments, respectively, will adjust with me the rule for a reasonable discrimination of such works as entitle me to recieve, on an equitable rate, the value of originals, the value of Copies, or the value of works published & in print, each under their peculier circumstances; and such fair statements of existing facts, so certified, shall be deemed competent vouchers for the performance of a service whereon I trustfully confide in the wisdom and justice of Congress for a comensurate compensation.

Under such mutual liberality in the case which now occurs, I have no doubt, Sir, the affairs of the United States will become more prosperous; and that their Armies will be placed in a condition to face their enemies with superior knowledge of their Country, & well digested plans for our military operations. I have the honor to be, Sir, Your hble. Servt.

WM TATHAM

RC (DNA: RG 107, LRRS, T-130:6). Docketed as received in the War Department on 28 July 1812; torn.

1. On 1 Apr. 1806 the House of Representatives received a report dealing with the books, papers, and models in the possession of William Tatham, accompanied by a resolution that "in addition to the appropriation made by law, a sum not exceeding —— dollars be appropriated as a part of the fund for the purchase of books, maps, and charts, for the Department of War, to enable the Secretary of War to purchase from William Tatham such parts of his collection as may be . . . of public use, to be paid out of any money in the treasury not otherwise appropriated" (*ASP, Miscellaneous*, 1:456–57).

2. Presidential Proclamation, 19 June 1812, *PJM-PS*, 4:489–90.

3. Blank left in RC.

From William Ray

ELIZABETHTOWN, ESSEX COUNTY, N. Y. July 27, 1812

Permit me, Sir, without unnecessary apologies, to tender my services to the United States, in any station that may make provision for myself and a small family.

I must confess that my patriotism is not unmixed with selfish views—my circumstances are indigent, and amidst these barren mountains, I find it difficult to subsist, with the strictest industry and frugality. I have suffered every thing but death itself in the service of my country, and am willing to expose myself again, rather than remain in my present state of want. I hold no office, at present, but that of county magistrate, and have no employment but that of an Editor to a newspaper,[1] devoted, Sir, to your interest; the profits of which scarcely affoard me decent support. If there is any office or employment at your disposal, I most humbly solicit your assistance. If not, a small *pecuniary* donation would not be rejected. As I am unable to labor, this might aid me in my present business, and perhaps not injure the cause I have espoused. I should, however, prefer some appointment, like that of paymaster or quartermaster. You doubtless remember the Book I sent you.[2]

Judge Pond, our representative to congress, will, probably, write to you on my account. My last request is, Sir, that I may not linger in suspense for an answer. I am, Sir, with due Consideration & Respect, Your most obedient humble Servant,

WILLIAM RAY.

RC (DLC). Docketed by JM.

1. Ray was the editor of the Elizabethtown *Reveille* (Brigham, *History of American Newspapers*, 1:570).

2. Ray placed an asterisk here and wrote at the bottom of the page, "Horrors of Slavery." On 22 Mar. 1809 Ray had sent JM a copy of his *Horrors of Slavery; or, The American Tars in Tripoli* (*PJM-PS*, 2:2–3 and n. 1).

From Samuel Thurber

HOND. SIR,   PROVIDENCE R I 27th. July 1812.

Feeling zealous to support the Constitution of our Country, and being ready with Three Sons, who I have instructed to be always ready to do evry thing in their power agreable to Law in defence of it, as are a few, say from 80 to 100 others in this town, A part of whom have undertaken to build one Vessel, and to repair an other for the purpose of Privateers. We are threatned with distruction if we persew it. As the threats did not deter, they began to execute. On Monday night last week, the smallest of the two, the one repairing, being calculated for onley twenty men with Swivels &c was taken away, scutled and sunk. She however is up again, and under a guard repaired and sent down the river last eavening. The circumstance I think was a fortunate one, as it will lead us to guard the other which is of much greater magnitude. The same Villens who sunk, or encouraged the sinking the one, would Burn, Sink or destroy the other and the Constitution of the United States with it if they could.

As such conduct seems to meet with encouragement, commotions are great and the opposition to government such, that I very much apprehend, the fitting our privateers will be the cause of very serious troubles with some. If the day of vengence must come, let it come in my day, if it is to fall on me, let it fall while in the defence of my Country, in order that you may have a further and a more full idea of the subject I refer you to the enclosed Gazette,[1] particularly to Osgoods remonstrance, Which for the want of health (as is said) in Wm. Edds, one of the popular preachers in this town, or the want of ingenuity to form something worse, he red in his Pulpit on Thursday last a day appointed by our State as a day of Fasting &c. I am told that an other popurlar preacher in this town, a Paddey by the name of Wilson gave a treat to a large audeance, it was pleasant food to most of them, it being (if possible) more rebellious and much more sevear then the other.

If Sir, our Government hath not energy enough to check such Hellish Monsters, the credulas people of New England, will from an idea of gitting to HEAVEN through their means, go on as directed to oppose Government in evry shape and in evry thing. I Sir, Wish you to think of those things, then apply such remedy as in your Wisdom is concluded to be most consistant with the general good. With Evry Sentement of Respect. Sir. your Very Humbe. Sarvt.

SAML. THURBER

NB. It is from an idea of duty that I am under to my Government that I make this communication.

S T.

RC and enclosure (DNA: RG 59, ML). For enclosure, see n. 1.

1. Thurber enclosed the 25 July issue of the *Providence Gazette*, which printed "a solemn protest" against the war by David Osgood, minister of the Medford, Massachusetts, Congregational Church.

From St. George Tucker

DEAR SIR,   WILLIAMSBURG July 27th. 1812.

Be pleased to accept my acknowledgements for your favor of the 21st. in answer to my former Letter. I sincerely wish that the example of Liberality which has been set by our Government may be followed by our Enemies. It is more than I expect.

I am mortified to observe, from the papers you did me the favor to enclose, the probable predominance of a faction in Boston, whose designs have long been suspected by me; and whose present determination seems to be, either to rule, or to dissolve, the Union. Whether there is virtue enough in the State at large to resist their Machinations, or not, is what I possess too little knowledge of the actual state of political opinion in that quarter of the Union to conjecture: but without the spirit of prophecy, I may venture to say, that the ambition of certain characters in the eastern states seems at present to threaten the Union. May their pernicious designs be percieved by their Country time enough to defeat their success! Accept the most sincere assurances of my respectful Esteem, & good wishes.

ST: G: TUCKER

RC (DLC). Docketed by JM.

§ From the Inhabitants of Biddeford, District of Maine. 27 *July 1812*. "The Freeholders & other Inhabitants of the Town of Biddeford, in the District of Maine, in legal Town Meeting assembled, having seen your Manifesto, the Act of Congress declaring War against the United Kingdom of Great Britain & Ireland, and your Proclamation of the same, feel in Duty bound respectfully to state some of our Ideas respecting this subject; Some of us bore a heavy burthen in the Revolution, which acheived our Independence; but our heads are now hoary & our limbs enervated by time; our young Men have heard what their Fathers have told them concerning these days of Old, these former years of Visitation; the most of us look back with Pleasure on the prosperous years that succeeded the adoption of our Federal Constitution and ask, why has our Gold become dim? Why are those happy, thrice happy times changed? We see no sufficient Reason for it; the great belligerents of Europe ever cordially hated each other, their trade & their Delight is in War, and when they get engaged therein the smaller States & Kingdoms are obliged to give way in smaller Matters; the Emperor of France is at this time making monstrous Strides over the Continent of Europe; we view with horror & regret the fate of Holland reduced to a Province of France as well as the other republics on the continent of Europe; nay several of the Kingdoms of Europe are obliged to bow to this Mighty Emperor. We see him sheding the blood of millions to gain Supremacy over Spain and Portugal; we view Great Britain as fighting at this time for her very existance; if this mighty Emperor subjugates Europe, we shudder, we tremble at the thought, when will his pride be satiated? Will he be satisfied with Europe? Will he not spread his Conquests round the Atlantic? We tremble when we contemplate on these things; we abhor an Alliance with a Nation whose ambition knows no bounds, we remember what our Father Washington said 'why, by interweaving our Destiny with that of any part of Europe, entangle our Peace & Prosperity in the Toils of European Ambition'[1] we frequently hear how this Monarch daily treats us, by burning, sinking & destroying our Commerce on the Ocean; without any legal Process, but by the Caprice of an individual Master of an Armed Vessel belonging to this aspiring Usurper for universal Dominion; we also see many things arbitrary in the conduct of the Government of Great Britain; we see the commanders of the British armed Vessels donineering [*sic*] over our unarmed Merchantmen, pressing & forcibly carrying away our seamen, their Government (as we understand) never justified such conduct, but always restored the men as soon as it was ascertained that they were Americans, and we are taught to believe, that they ever have been ready, willing & forward to make such arangements with our Government as to prevent abuses on this Subject: we know that a number of our sea-faring brethren in this port have been pressed & restored as above stated; another great Grieveance is stated to be the British Orders in Council, we find upon examination that the French decrees of Berlin & Milan were anterior to these orders in Council, and that they were to be recinded in their very nature, whenever these decrees should be revoked, being only retaliatory; As to their stiring up the Savages against us we see no proof; The United States being then in treaty with all those tribes & under Obligations to supply them with all the necessaries of Life. As to the Henry Plot we see no evidence of his, with any person or persons, affecting a seperation of our happy Union, this would strike us with Horror & Detestation. In viewing the whole Ground we see no sufficient reason to justify this Declaration of War; we are rather led to believe the President has been misinformed by artfull designing men, who surround his person; we therefore, knowing that it is his province to send Ambasidors to make peace earnestly supplicate him to take constitutional measures to bring about this most desirable Object, and restore the United States to peace if it can be done on honerable terms; & then break the fetters on Commerce, which will restore our Revenue to its wonted Channel, and again fill our exhausted Treasury; then set up a strict impartiality with all Nations; and we confidently hope & trust under Divine Providence, we shall again set, as in the days of Washington, under our own Vines & our own Figtrees & have none to make us afraid, and the Inhibants [*sic*] of the Town of Biddeford will ever pray."

RC (DNA: RG 59, ML). 3 pp.; signed by Israel Lassell, moderator, Jeremiah Hill, selectman, and Edmund Coffin, town clerk.

1. The memorialists quoted from Washington's farewell address (Fitzpatrick, *Writings of Washington*, 35:234).

§ From the Inhabitants of Wells, Massachusetts. *27 July 1812*. "The disign of our National Government being 'to form a more perfect union, establish justice, ensure domistic tranquility, provide for the common defence, promote the general welfare & secure the blessings of peace to ourselves and our posterity[']—The Inhabitants of the Town of Wells, in the County of York & Common-wealth of Massachusetts in legal Town-Meeting assembled . . .

"*Respectfully represent*, that while we revere the union of the States as the rock of our Political safety—while we respect its laws a[s] legitimate commands & admire its institutions as proud Monuments of rational liberty, we do not forget that it is '*the right of the People peacibly* to *assemble* & *petition* the Government for redress of grievances'—A right secured by the articles amendatiory to the Constitution of the United States & that not to exercise it, when laws are made or measures adopted, which bear the stamp of being unequal, unnecessary, ruinous and oppressive, would be a base diraliction of duty, injustice to our-selves & trechery to posterity.

94

"In reviewing the foreign relations of our Country, with the two great Beligerents, *Your memorialists* can not but be mortified at the contrast which it exhibits. Under the two first administrations altho' wrongs & injuries were received, altho' our Maratime rights were invaded & war threatened, yet the Nation assumed a bold & commanding Attitude, its Government met the crisis with firmness & decission & the cloud was dissipated. To the two succeeding administrators it has been reserved under similar circumstances to recede from danger to shrink at insult—to manacle our own Citizens, to practice visionary & imbesile experiments at the expence of our-selves & after having impoverished & half ruin'd the nation to plunge it into an offensive war. To us the acts which have marked the course of the present & next preceeding administration, having the character of novelty & being the reverse of those practiced in the days of Washington & Adams, have been wrap'd in mistery. That our Rulers have been ploting our ruin by disign, that they were plunging the Nation into an Abyss of misery, from ignorance & incapacity to govern, or that they were lending their aid to a foreign despot to subjugate the world & assisting to rivet his chains on their fellow-citizens, we have been and still are unwilling to believe.

"In vindication of our Maratime & Commercial rights, as we have been told, we have had Embargoes with paucity in their train, we have witnessed Bankruptcies in company with nonimportations & nonintercourse, & we now behold war with its numerous calamities treading close on their heels. Without entering into a detail of the grounds assigned for waging hostilities against Great Britain, without travailing thro' the long catalogue of causes contained in the war Manifesto, we regret to say, that it is our belief, that the aggressions complained of, have been magnified so that acts considered ⟨friendly?⟩ at the time of their Adoption are no⟨w⟩ [. . .] being big with hostility & an abridgment of neutral rights.

"That a spirit of honest accomodation upon principles of reciprocity—that an ardent & sincere wish of adjustment which would have been honourable to our selves has not been pursued by our own government.

"Your Memorialists must be permited to enquire that if the government had resolved that a crisis has arrived when an appeal to the last resort of Nations was indispensable, whethe[r] the many outrages on our rights, whether the burnings, sinkings, sequestrations & imprisonments, whether the duplicity & trechery & the vandal warfare on civil cociety [*sic*] by the tirant of Europe were all forgotten & if not what motive led to a selection of great Britain as the soul Object of American vengeance. To draw us into the vortex of European Politics & make us a party in the war—to induce the United States to aid him in enforcing his continental sistem has undoubtedly been the object of Napoleon & his purpose we fear is too far accomplished. But any alliance in defence of maritime or of territorial rights with this scourge of the human race & also to the inexpediency & folly of the present War we enter our most solemn Protest—to assign any reasons for the former would be an insult to the whole American People, To the latter we give the following.

"1st. Want of unanimity in the national councils & the aversion of the people to war.

"2d. The almost total deficiency in land & Naval preparations.

"3d. The impoverished State of the Treasury & the enormous public burdens which must follow.

"4th The imense amount of american property afloat & in foreign Countries & which is put in jeopardy.

"5th. The ruin of thousands of our Citizens & the general distress & poverty which must follow a protra[c]ted war.

"6th. The almost certain failure of obtaining the Objects for which the Government have avow[ed] they have drawn the sword.

"Deeply impressed with these considerations & already feeling many of the inconveniencies & in some measure inticipating the distresses which a war of any considerable duration must bring upon us & believing as we do that Great Britain has neither inclination nor interest to be at war with us—Your Memorialists therefore recommend and earnestly pray that on the formation of a new Ministry in England should the Orders in Council as modified in 1809 be revoked or be so modified anew as not to embarrass our commerce a negociation on our part may be immediately set on foot to restore to our common Country the blessings of peace & to our suffering fellow Citizens their former prosperity & happiness."

RC (DNA: RG 59, ML). 4 pp.; signed by John Storer, moderator, and Nathaniel Wells, town clerk; torn.

From James Maury

Dr Sir,   Liverpool 29th July 1812

The free shipping of Goods to the United States subsequent to the revocation of the orders in council suggested to me that some chease might not be unacceptable & I have, *without order*, sent you two by the Argo for Alexandria, which I hope you will recieve in good condition: to insure which they are in Lead as before. I inclose the bill of parcels.[1]

All your Tobaccoe ℔ Adeline is on hand. I wait for the chance of a more favorable opportunity of selling than has yet presented. With great respect & esteem I have the honor to be your obliged friend & Servant

JAMES MAURY

RC and enclosure (DLC). RC docketed by JM. For enclosure, see n. 1.

1. The enclosure (1 p.) is a bill dated 28 July 1812 for one "Fine Dolphin [Dauphin] Cheese" and one Cheshire cheese purchased from "Metcalfe & Parker, Cheese-Factors," of Liverpool.

§ To Albert Gallatin. *29 July 1812*. In accordance with the 3 Mar. 1809 "act further to amend the several acts for the establishment & regulation of the Treasury, War & Navy Departments,"[1] directs that $450,000 "be applied out of the following appropriations Viz Pay & subsistence of the Navy two hundred thousand dollars, Provisions one hundred thousand dollars, ordnance one hundred & fifty thousand dollars, to Repairs of Vessels."

Letterbook copy (DNA: RG 45, entry 4, Letters to Secretary of Treasury). 1 p.

1. *U.S. Statutes at Large*, 2:535–37.

§ From the Citizens of Natchez, Mississippi Territory. *29 July 1812*. Present the resolutions adopted at a meeting in Washington, Mississippi Territory, of which Beverly R. Grayson was appointed chairman and Capt. Hunter Holmes was appointed secretary.

"Whereas it is the opinion of this meeting that our Government, after having exhausted the peaceful course of dignified remonstrance, and having done all that justice could require or wisdom dictate, to maintain the peace of the nation, has been ultimately compelled to vindicate the rights essential to the sovereignty and independance of our country against the unjust pretensions and aggressions of the British Government by an appeal to the last resort of injured nations, and it becomes the people of the United States to meet the solemnity of the crisis with the most patriotic intrepidity, and to manifest their vigilance and zeal in the discharge of all those duties incident to the occasion; as also to prepare to endure the deepest sacrifices, and efficiently to unfold those energies which have been perhaps from a native love of peace too long quiescent—Therefore,

"*Resolved*, That as a constituent part of those people, we hold it an inviolable duty to proclaim to our fellow citizens, and to the world, our sincere approbation of the conduct of the government; and that in life, we will not be classed with those who may ingloriously shrink from the contest before us—a contest forced upon us by the boundless arrogance of an insulting foe, & marked in the strongest hostility to our personal safety and neutral rights.

"*Resolved*, That whatever course 'the rights, the interest and the honor of our country' may require of Congress towards the government of France, we will in the plenitude of American feelings and pride, support with a promptitude and energy co-extensive with our lives, our fortunes and our dearest reputations.

"*Resolved*, That the present moment is propitious for an ample developement and systematic display of the internal resources of our country; and that in our growing manufactories and internal improvements we recognize the best succedaneum for the temporary sufferings of our commerce, which we will encourage by discarding from our use every possible article of British production.

"*Resolved*, That as this southern section of our union is considered most susceptible of hostile intrusion, and doubtless from its fertility of soil, and other local advantages is a strong temptation to European ambition and cupidity, we acknowledge the wisdom and policy of our government for extending to our benefit the talents, experience and approved patriotism of General *James Wilkinson* who is destined by the order of our parent government to act in unison with our worthy and sensible Executive, Governor Holmes, in whom we confidently rely, and will cheerfully obey; believing that in the concurrence of such virtues and principles we distinctly see the presages of safety and of victory.

"*Resolved*, That although we have no distinct participation in the election of a President of the United States, yet we acknowlege an enlivened interest in so important an event; and confiding as we do most cordially in the abilities, firmness and virtues of James Madison, we approbate the prudential recommendation, made by gentlemen of Congress in their individual capacities, of his re-election as Chief Magistrate of the Union, more especially at such an eventful period of national trial, when experience in the great national administration ought to prevail over the hazards incident to a change of men, and innovation of system.

"*Resolved,* That although the tenor of our principles and the habits of our lives are opposed to violations of regular order, yet the opposite characteristics of peace and war, marking widely the range of propriety in speech and action, we hold it not only an absolute duty, but it shall be our pride to resist and hush to silence in time of war, ther [*sic*] utterance of sentiments and doctrines tending to sow the seed of discontent & sedition among our citizens, or the encouragement of our enemies by persons who live in the bosom of our land, fatten upon the blessings of our government, soil and clime; and, that in the '*Whiggery*' and examples of our forefathers, as well as in the manly check of recent treason, we observe precedents of laconic energy, which we may find expedient to emulate if the intrusions of '*Toryism*' should be pressed upon us.

"*Resolved,* That the preceding resolutions be published in the Chronicle, Mississippi Republican and National Intelligencer, and that a copy thereof be sent to the President of the U. States, and to the Executive of this Territory, subscribed by the names of the chairman and secretary."

Printed copy (*National Intelligencer,* 1 Sept. 1812).

§ From William Gamble. *29 July 1812, Capitol Hill.* Refers to a conversation with JM regarding a letter of recommendation written on Gamble's behalf by Richard M. Johnson on 19 May.[1] Hoped his application "would not be unattended to"; points out that "nothing but the most urgent want, could induce me to make such application." Admits that his "little resources are entirely exausted." Reflects upon "the Government I helped to raise by the exertions of my early life . . . and the sacrafices of a handsome Patrimonial Estate"; mentions the current military service of his sons, four of them under Commodore Rodgers. Asks to be placed "in any situation in which I might render service to my Country (for which I may be found competent,) which may put me beyond the reach of want."

RC (DNA: RG 107, LRRS, G-124:6). 2 pp.; docketed as received in the War Department on 30 July 1812.

1. *PJM-PS,* 4:402.

§ From James Simrall.[1] *29 July 1812, Shelbyville, Kentucky.* Is authorized by the Kentucky volunteer cavalry regiment to offer their services to march as soon as possible "to Canada or any other point where our Services may be wanting." This regiment "is upwards of 400 strong they are well acquipt in everry thing but arms." Has been informed by Col. John Allen that his regiment was named in Allen's letter to JM.[2] He and Allen have communicated with JM "in consiquen[ce] of letters being recev'd by his Excellen[c]y Govr. Scott from the War department, to furnish aid to the Governors of the Territoreys with Men . . . Which from t[he] present Situation of the Indians their is but little probability of being calld for on that service."[3] Will call upon Governor Scott to request that he provide JM with information concerning the cavalry.

RC (DNA: RG 107, LRRS, S-309:6). 2 pp.; docketed as received in the War Department on 18 Aug. 1812.

1. James Simrall (1781–1823) of Pennsylvania relocated to Virginia and then to Kentucky in 1792. Simrall's Kentucky volunteers participated in the Mississinewa expedition of December 1812 before the regiment was disbanded. Simrall formed another regiment in 1813 and participated in the Battle of the Thames, where it fell to him to supervise British prisoners (Esarey, *Messages and Letters of William Henry Harrison*, Indiana Historical Collections, 2:145 n. 3, 253–62).

2. John Allen to JM, 25 July 1812.

3. On 9 July 1812 William Eustis informed Scott that if an emergency arose "requiring an additional Military force on the frontiers of the Indiana & Illinois Territories," Eustis was authorized by the president to request detachments of Kentucky militia (DNA: RG 107, LSMA).

From William Pope

Dear Sir   Virginia July 30th. 1812

I wrote to you some time ago, and also to the secretary at War,[1] on the great inactivity their was in this part of Virginia in the recruiting of men; I can assure you, that I have never seen a fife or Drum, in the county of Goochland, or Powhatan beating up for recruits. I consienciously beleive that 25000 men might have been raised 2 months a go in Virginia alone if the officers had gone from county court, to county court, their was the greatest oppertunity last spring afforded the officers they could have wished, all the regiments in Virginia were drawn out to see whether they would Volunteer or submit to a draft; I never saw a band of music or even a fife or drum on those Occasions; what a golden opportunity was afforded ⟨for⟩ the inlistment of men the secretary at war was apprised of this, but no exertions made to inlist; if the people would go to Manchester, Lynchburgh Winchester, and one or two other places they might have gone into the service; but it was the business of the recruiting officers to come among the people from county to county; I wrote, and spoke to a great many officers to adopt that plan, but they observed they had no music, and were obliged to stay at their different placces of rendesvous for the purpose of receiving communications from the Secretary at war, the best patriots in this country lament, the great inactivity observed in the inlistment of men, in Virginia and if the same plans have been persued all Over the united states it has been misarably conducted indeed, we know the arduous duties of your Office Sir and know that they have never been so well ⟨atten⟩ded to since the formation of the Government you are vigilent, and indefatigable to all the duties of your office; I heard a member of congress say that you had not, been off the presidential square intil the 4th. of last July (when you went to the Capitol to hear the oration) for 8 or 9 months back, I would to god that the other departments of Government in all its ramifications would act, thus; I trust, and hope, that their will be more activity in the feild now the armies of the U States are in motion every thing depends now on decisive measures and that orders will be given to attack in the enemy instantly in all his ⟨vinsiable?⟩ points, as soon as one battle is faught the federal band will be as light as possible, an Idea seems to have gone forth that movements are slow in the war department, this opinion ought to be instantly removed. If Genl Hull would fight only one battle you would hear no more discontent to the North. Their is great expectation formed in favour of the Energy of our naval department, but one battle fought on the continent would make the people of the U States almost rise en mass and all opposition then would immediately subside. I am your excellencies most Obed Hun Sert

WILLIAM POPE

RC (DLC). Postmarked 5 Aug.; docketed by JM; damaged by removal of seal.

1. See Pope to JM, 10 July 1812. The editors have been unable to locate Pope's letter to Eustis.

From Charles Scott

SIR,   FRANKFORT (KY) July 30th. 1812

In a time like the present it is hoped no apology will be necessary for laying before you my Ideas of what may Contribute in any wise to the Success of the Contest in which we are engaged, and which may be truly regarded as our Second Struggle for independence. And before I proceed further permit me to bring the name of Govr. William H. Harrison to your notice. I know of no man at this time among us who Surpasses him in Military merit. But what is more, even than this, he has the confidence and attachment, as a Commander, of the great Body of the Western People. The people of this State in particular would sooner serve under him than any man in the Union. And I have reason to believe the same of Ohio; of his own, and the Illinois Territories. His fame has justly risen above the Calumny of his enemies.

I am well convinced if Volunteers are employed, his name alone in this quarter of the Union will raise more men than their expectation of Compensation. And it would give me the highest pleasure to see a man promoted to an efficient Command, who promises to be one of the greatest Military men of the time—and whose Zeal in the service of his Country is equal to his talents.

With this man's merits, I presume however, you are well acquainted, perhaps not so well with his popularity. The information I wish to give you, ought probably to have been sooner made known to you; that is, that as to the Militia of this State there need exist no difficulty in marching them beyond the limits of the U. S. for there will be as many Volunteers as the Government will have occasion for, from it. And their impatience to be employed in immediate Service is extreme.

Many have uniformed and equipped themselves at Considerable expence—and have waited in momentary expectation of orders for about two or three months past. Their patience seems almost exhausted and their ardor I fear, unless they have something to do, will finally grow Cool. The inconvenience of young men mechanics and others without fortune, remaining idle and disengaged, to be ready to march whenever Called on, is very great.

Indeed the situation of a great number of them will render it almost impossible they should continue long in such a state of preparation. Their eyes are hourly turned toward an Indian or Canadian Campaign as may be required. If you will pardon the presumption of an old man just retiring from office and who will likely not again trouble you, I would suggest it as my opinion, that a strong Campaign against the North Western Indians, while Genl. Hull was operating against Upper Canada, would have brought them to our feet—with more certainty of their permanent Neutrality, than any treaty which can now be held with them. The acquaintance I have had with the character of that people, and my opportunity of knowing it, has not been inconsiderable, has impressed me with the belief, that their faith is no farther to be depended upon, than their interest, which must be composed in a great degree of fear, is concerned. And their uniform practice is to treat, while they secure the means of striking with effect, the meditated blow. A small reverse in our success, unless they have been severely scourged out of their hostile attitude and intentions, will, I very much fear, bring them thick upon us.

Since writing the above, I have received a letter from Govr. Edwards, of the 21st. Inst. stating, that he has procured an authentic and detailed account of a most formidable combination of the Indians; and their meditated system of attacking and destroying the Territories in that quarter; excited by the British, and waiting merely for instructions from their agents, to be executed.

This seems to add strength to my Conjecture above. I suppose he had not then received information that he is authorized to require Troops from this State. They may give us some trouble, but must ultimately feel the overwhelming weight of our Arms, and their own blindness and folly by the destruction of their towns and people.

I shall upon the earliest information afford the necessary supply of Troops, agreeably to your order, through the Secretary of War. With my best wishes for your health, I have the honor to be with high respect Yr. Excellency's Obt. servt.

CHS. SCOTT

RC (DLC). Docketed by JM.

§ From Matthew Magee and Others. *30 July 1812, Pittsburgh.* "At a meeting of the Pittsburgh Blues held in the absence of Captain Butler on the 27th of July Inst. after taking into consideration the situation of the Company as it respected its relations with the general government under the Act of Congress of February 6th. 1812 and its Supplement of July 2nd. 1812,[1] it was unanimously resolved that a Committee be appointed to remonstrate against the provisions of that supplement being a flagrant violation of those rights the Company enjoyed under the Act of the 6th. and entirely derogatory to the principles under which the Company tendered their Services. Sir, the Company's Committee regret the necessity of an address. They regret that any circumstances should arise to require any communication from the Company, but a declaration of their prompt obedience to the wishes and orders of the constituded authorities.

"But Sir, it is a right, nay it is the duty of the citizen even if not immediately interested to enquire into the expediency of the measures of our Government and see that they do not overleap the bounds of the Constitution or wantonly infringe the rights and preveleges of the Citizen. Then we may ask if it is the right—if it is the duty of the individual not immediately interested to enquire into and remonstrate against such measures of the government as are improper—impolitic and unconstitutional—is it not more particularly the rights—is it not more particularly a duty of the citizen whose rights and preveleges are immediately affected by acts of the Government, a duty which he owes himself as well as posterity, spiritedly to remonstrate and lay his grievances before those who have the means of redressing them.

"Sir, Impressed with the idea of the correctness of the premises permit us to lay before your excellency in the most decent and respectful terms the grievances of the Company. The 1st Section of the Act of the 6th of February, or as it is generally called the Original Act, gives to Volunteers the right of choosing their own officers, and of supplying any vacancies that may hereafter take place by election. This was, and is considerd by the Company the dearest prevelege the citizen soldier could enjoy, to be commanded by men in whom they knew they might place confidence, and in whose hands they could repose their personal safety and liberty without a dread of being decieved. This prevelege being granted to them was a sufficient, and indeed the principle inducement to their Volunteering. But unfortunately for us, and unfortunately for the interest and service of our Country, your Excellency with the National Congress have though[t] proper by a supplementary Act to deprive the volunteers of this highly prized prevelege. We say unfortunately for us, as it has placed the Company in the unbecoming attitude of opposition to the orders of Government when those orders are founded on the provisions of this supplement. We say unfortunately for the interest and service of our Country, as it is the prevailing opinion that if the Volunteers generally have a proper notion of what is their rights, they will not submit themselves to the provision of this abhored supplement. The Company say the supplement is an ex post facto law as it respects their tender—they never volunteered under it, and do not consider themselves bound by it.

"The Company declare their willingness to march under the act of the 6th. of February 1812, but absolutely refuse to move should the provision of the Supplement be contemplated to be exercised upon them.

"We have at length accomplished the disagreeable task of complaint set us by the Company; We proceed to the more pleasing duty of enquiry, the result of which may heal the wounds inflicted on the minds of the members. The Company instruct the Committee to enquire of your Excellency whether the intention of the supplement is merely to *commission* officers only, and not appoint them as is the opinion of some. And to ascertain should the supplement vest in your Excellency the right of appointment as well as commissioning, whether the provisions of the supplement will be strictly exercised against the Volunteers."

RC (DNA: RG 107, LRRS, M-361:6). 4 pp.; signed by Magee and four others; docketed as received in the War Department on 13 Aug. 1812.

1. Magee referred to the Volunteer Act of 6 July 1812 (see *PJM-PS*, 4:522 n. 2).

From Edward E. Davis

RESPECTED SIR   NEW YORK July 31st. 1812.

I now beg leave to address you again with boldness, for the Love I have for my Country & my fellow Soldiers & Sailors that stands in defence of the Same. The many disease's thats common to the Army & Navy is undertaken to be cure'd by Physicians under the Pay of Government is only sporting with the life's of this Class of Citizens which are so much wanted for the good of the Country, the expence of Hospitals in Navy & Army is great to the United State's & her Citizens are Kept lingering by improper practice, in this time of War & the Doctors in Navy & Army who practice study not the Climate with the complaint & therefore Keep diseases reigning these who practice are not content with the pay of Government but have a Charge, when they report them of $5. which was never known in any nation & discourage's our Men, & makes them discontented & turn against the Country, by such extortion & makes them unquiet because they are imposed upon & rob's the funds of the United States. I conceive some body acquainted with the Business, ought to be appointed for Mens lifes are not to be triffled, with at any time & particularly at this period for a Soldiers or Sailors life is as good as an Officers if he is virtuous to his Country. This I dont send to the Honorable first Magistrate of my Country, of the imposition. But because I am requested by the individuals in Uniform of Army & Navy under the difficultys, come to my Shop from them, to be cured.

I herewith enclose another Handbill[1] at the same time remarking I am near the Navy yard & Garrison's & ready for my Country, and wish you would give a hint to both Secretary of Army & Navy, while I subscribe your Respected & obedt Humble Servant

EDWD. E. DAVIS
Indian Physicians

NB I dont do this because of want of employ because I have enough but for the good of my Country I was wounded in have constant call of many different complaints of Medical in Society, but I mention it because I think it a Duty due my Country & the Saviour & Father of the same believe me sentimentaly

EDWD. E DAVIS Indian Physician

As to Surgery, I am call'd far and near & turn my back to not any Man my Charecter is well Known throughout the United States. I am sorry to see our Country making Speculations of this filling their Pockets & not having the Country or its Citizens at Heart. This is the fifth letter I have wrote.[2] If the President wishes to see me inform me & I[']ll come to Washington immediately on receipt of the Letter with one Leg.

RC (DLC). In the hand of Rosewell Saltonstall.

1. Enclosure not found.
2. The editors have located only one other letter to JM from Davis, dated 4 Jan. 1812 (*PJM-PS*, 4:119).

From Rosewell Saltonstall

WORTHY FRIEND & AMERICAN   NEW YORK July 31st. 1812

In America the Land of my nativity which ought to be grateful to every being who drew his first breaths, in it. Permit me to address you again[1] & to observe, the Dignitys of & in my Country causes me bitter pangs to hear the acramonious in foul printers presses throughout our Union, stabbing its Rulers. The Charecter of Presidents Govenors General's Naval Commanders. Not any power can escape the censorious *Types*, while every true Born American feels circulating in his blood affection for his Government who can suppress *Mobs in City's* or give obedience to judicial Power, therein that hears these Sedisious expressions untill the ax is laid to the tree where evil arises, nothing can abate this solid inward affection of Republicans. Heaven grant The President & Executive may issue mandate's of Emancipation, on our English Printers, while the Sun shine's in the firmament, may heaven endow me to rule the Pen with shafts of Satirical to lash with tongues, those that insult the Authoritys of my native Country. Inclose'd accept of my Productions as a Specimen of my reverence. I loudly solicit the first Magistrate of America to let them, be put into the National Intelligencer,[2] and trust that the other Productions of mine, will by the respected Genl Bloomfield, meet the President, truly do I hope every Gardian eye in Americans brain's will use fedility to our present cause and spread the wings of Union, over our fertile Land with blessings on The President & his Lady. I have the honor to be with due respect Your Very obedient Humble St.

ROSEWELL SALTONSTALL[3]

NB Its devoutly to be wishd the President will remember the ingenuity & Medical Knowledge & good Sence of the Indian Physician he has Knowledge & Patriotizm[4]

RC and enclosures (DLC). RC postmarked New York, 9 Aug.; docketed by JM. For enclosures, see n. 2.

1. The editors have been unable to locate another letter to JM from Saltonstall subsequent to one of 20 Dec. 1808 (DNA: RG 59, ML). Saltonstall may have referred to the letter in his hand of this date under the name of Edward E. Davis.

2. Saltonstall enclosed two letters in his hand; they were not published in the *National Intelligencer*. One, dated 31 July and titled "Dog in the manger," is a two-page letter, signed "An American of 1776," criticizing New Englanders for opposing the war. The other, an undated three-page letter with the same signature, is a response "To the Author of the piece in the New york Even'g Post of Wednesday July 22nd. 1812." The letter accused that author of "treasonable expressions of & against The Honble Js. Madison," including his comment that those who "defend Madisons encroachments on the constitution" are "base & stupid." Saltonstall reproached the publisher of the *Post* for bowing to "Federal & quaker Faction" by printing anti-Madisonian sentiments. That issue of the *Post*, however, contained no articles matching this description.

3. Rosewell Saltonstall (d. 1840?) was a sailor from New London, Connecticut, who settled in New York and dabbled at being an amateur inventor (Rosewell Saltonstall, *Concise History and Biography of Sir Richard Saltonstall* . . . [New York, 1812; Shaw and Shoemaker 26688], 4, 5–6, 7; Peterson, *Minutes of the Common Council of the City of New York*, 12:710, 13:290, 348–49, 361, 723, 15:19, 131).

4. Saltonstall referred to Edward E. Davis.

§ From the Citizens of Pittsylvania County, Virginia. *31 July 1812.* "At this important juncture when the nation is called upon to vindicate its injured rights by war, and a difference of opinion is believed to exist among the people on the policy of the measure, a portion of the citizens of Pittsylvania, voluntarily assembled, conceive that they discharge a duty as well as exercise a right in making this public expression of their sentiments.

"In common with the rest of our fellow citizens, we awaited with the most anxious interest the decision of our representatives on the question of Peace or War. With them too we considered the situation of the Country as highly dangerous and alarming. But our *chief* fear was, that the guardians of our rights, mistaking the clamour of a party for the voice of the people, might surrender the honour of the nation: and we considered that the worst danger was over, when Congress had finally determined on an appeal to arms.

"We had indeed long since abandoned the dream of obtaining a willing reparation from the government of Great Britain. If her recent conduct to other nations; if our own former experience had warranted the expectation, the history of her present controver[s]y with the United States would have forbidden it. We find her gradually advancing in her claims under the successive pretexts of temporary usage; of doubtful principles of national law; and of forced applications of these principles. Then laying aside the law of nations as affording no further colour to her usurpations, she claims the sanction of her enemy's example for the right of injuring us, and finding us still patient, she bold[l]y advances pretensions which would cancel the whole code of neutral rights; would annihilate the commerce of these States, and finally render their dear bought sovereignty but a shadow and a name.

"We here take occasion to observe with the frankness of men who feel their own honour involved in the conduct of their Government, that some of the claims advanced by Great Britain are such as ought to preclude discussion. Too palpably absurd to require formal refutation, and too insolent to deserve it, they should always be rejected with prompt disdain. To treat them in a different way is derogatory to the dignity of the nation. Nor is this all. By deigning to enter into a discussion of their merits, we embolden the British Nation to advance in its arrogant pretensions, and familiarize ourselves to the debasing sentiments of inferiority and submission.

"Considering War to have been long ago imperiously dictated by the conduct of Great Britain, we should be disposed to censure the representatives of the nation for their too patient forbearance, if we were not aware that they could not have counted upon the undivided support of the community.

"In this country where the road to public favour is the road to honour, and that road is open to all, the Government will probably always meet with considerable opposition in every important measure. But in none is it likely to be so strong as in a controversy with Great Britain. From the sameness of language, of manners and laws, and still more from an extensive commercial intercourse great numbers of her subjects are always resident among us, and possess a degree of influence unknown to foreigners in any other country, and to any other foreigners in this. As may be expected these generally side with their native country in all disputes with this Government; aid and encourage the party in opposition; and often, by means of the press, dictate its course.

"The effects of this unpropitious union of parties have been but too successful in dividing our citizens, by making plausible appeals to their avarice, their fears, and their well known attachment to peace.

"Far be it from us to undervalue the benefits of peace. Good in itself, it is particularly recommended to us by the genius of our laws—the situation of our country—the habits and inclinations of our citizens. But it unfortunately does not depend solely upon ourselves to preserve it. The British Government has long since made war upon our commerce, and the persons of our countrymen, and the only question with us was whether we should return the blow. To have doubted about the answer to this question, nay to have longer hesitated, would have made us contemptible in the eyes of others, base and perfidious in our own. If the path we have chosen leads to danger, it also leads to glory. If it risques disappointment, it does not incur disgrace.

"Having thus unsheathed the sword, we trust that the same manly virtues which carried these States successfully through their struggle for independence, will attend them in the present contest, and finally conduct them to victory. With three times the population, with ten times the resources, and the means of commanding them that we then possessed, we feel confident of our superiority on this continent: Nor is the period very distant when we shall humble Great Britain on that element where she now boasts her power and glories in its abuse. In less than the ordinary term of human life, fifty millions of freeborn Americans, will, without an effort, wrest the sceptre of the ocean from its present usurpers, and after taking ample retribution for their country's wrongs, establish on the seas the same freedom, which under the smiles of approving Heaven, is fast overspreading the whole Western Hemisphere.

"Whilst we make active resistance to the more aggravated injuries of Great Britain, we are not unmindful of the hostile conduct of France. Her aggressions have been in many instances such as to justify retaliation by war, and it is due to ourselves to demand of her ample reparation, and if it be refused or delayed, to shew her and the world that we know no difference between nations except as they differ in their treatment of us.

"In the present contest we are prepared to expect some inconvenience—some privation—some loss. To these we submit with cheerfulness, because we know that they are our rights which are to be defended—our wrongs which are to be avenged. Our honor which has been preserved. And it is not to be forgotten that our losses will probably not exceed those our commerce has long since sustained from British freebooters, and that our internal manufactures will receive an encouragement in War which will soon make them adequate to our more important demands.

"We hope that however some of our citizens may have doubted about the policy of the War, they will join with us in manly efforts to bring it to a speedy and honorable termination. We are now embarked in a common cause, and must all gain or lose alike. Let then the jar of civil strife cease for a time, whilst in one firm and compact phalanx we meet our haughty foe. Let us cordially unite in aiding and encouraging our gallant defenders by sea and land. If our hopes do not deceive us they are about to add new trophies to their country's fame. They know that the eyes of a grateful nation are upon them, and they will not act unworthy the spirit of their ancestors; the noble liberty their country now enjoys; and the high destinies which await it.

"Such being the views and sentiments of this meeting it is by them therefore Resolved, That the Congress of the United States in preferring War to an unprofitable, a precarious and ignominious peace, have consulted the interest as well as the honour of the nation, and are entitled to the thanks of their countrymen.

"Resolved, That the President of the United States deserves the continuance of our confidence and support: and that in his zealous and indefatigable maintenance of our national rights; his scrupulous impartiality to all foreign nations; and his readiness to risque the favor of his countrymen on the chances of war, We behold the same disinterested patriotism which elevated him to the highest of all honors, that of being the chief of a free people.

"Resolved, That as we consider the present War to have been dictated by a becoming respect for ourselves, and a just consideration of our interests, we hope that the nation will not lay down its arms, until Great Britain shall solemnly recognize our rights as declared by the law of nations, and more especially the entire immunity of our citizens when under the protection of the national flag.

"Resolved. That it is equally due to our justice, our consistency, and our honor to insist upon immediate reparation for the injuries we have sustained from France.

"Resolved. That we will cheerfully submit to the additional claims on our purses and our services which the occasion demands; that we will aid and assist, to the best of our ability, the operations of the Government, and that we will practise and encourage individual industry and frugality as the best means of encreasing the national resources and strength."

RC (DNA: RG 59, ML). 4 pp.; signed by Daniel Coleman, chairman, and William Tunstall, secretary. Enclosed in Tunstall to JM, 1 Aug. 1812 (ibid.; 1 p.). Printed in the *National Intelligencer*, 15 Aug. 1812.

§ From James Russel. *31 July 1812, Washington, North Carolina.* Had arranged for the arrival of his family from Great Britain in November; however, "by the circumstances attending on a state of war between these countries, this cannot take place." Has "determined to return to them by the first suitable opportunity." Requests JM's "permission, and the protection of the United States to cover a small vessel belonging to this port to be cleared out from hence to Bermuda, New Providence, or Jamaica; or to a british port on this continent."

RC (DNA: RG 59, War of 1812 Papers, Requests for Permission to Sail from the U.S.). 1 p. Enclosed in Russel to Monroe, 31 July 1812 (ibid.).

§ From Daniel Tuttle and Others. *31 July 1812, Boston.* Represent that they are the owners of the *Mechanic*, a vessel equipped for regular passage between Boston and Liverpool. Are informed that "a number of English prisoners of war, now in the town of Boston and its vicinity are desirous of being exchanged according to the usages of Nations at War, and that the Government of the United States are probably desirous to effect such exchange; And . . . that several American citizens inhabitants of the said town of Boston & its vicinity are extremely solicitous to embark for different ports in Great Britain for the purpose of bringing to an adjustment, large and important concerns of a commercial nature." Request that the *Mechanic* "may be permitted by the Government of the United States to proceed from the port of Boston to any port in Great Britain in the character of a Cartel and with the privileges and immunities properly appurtaining to Vessels in that employment; On such terms and conditions as to your Excellency may seem expedient."

RC (DNA: RG 59, ML). 1 p.; signed by Daniel Tuttle, William F. Salter, and Joseph M. Salter. On the verso is a 1 Aug. statement by George Blake, U.S. attorney for the Massachusetts district, certifying that Tuttle and the Salters were respectable merchants "deserving of faith and credit."

From Mathew Carey

Sir,   Philadelphia, August 1. 1812

I have had considerable hesitation about a second trespass upon your time & attention.[1] And nothing but the extreme delicacy & difficulty of the existing state of affairs wd. have induced me.

The press, one of the greatest blessings of mankind, when properly conducted, has for four or five years been the greatest curse & scourge of this Country, particularly of the New England section of it. The American press is incomparably more profligate & abandoned than that of England. Many of Our printers have abandoned all sense of honour, shame, or decency. There is no falsehood too base for them to assert—& such is the awful delusion of the public mind, that the detection of twenty gross & abominable lies, does not prevent credulity from opening wide her ears, for the twenty first.

It is easy to point out an evil—&, in many cases, not very difficult to point out remedies. But it is very frequently extremely difficult to apply those remedies. And I must confess that the present case is to my mind nearly a hopeless one.

The mass of the federalists are as good citizens as ever existed. They are however made tools of by men who have the very worst views. They have been led on step by step, through fraud and misrepresentation, till they have arrived at the verge of civil war, the most horrible of all calamities that ever scourged the human race.

A man of powerful talents, ardent zeal, & pure patriotism, might prevent the catastrophe that now threatens us. A luminous detail of the views & conduct of the leaders of the federal party, from their application to congress respecting the British restrictions on the Colonial Trade, till the present time, could not fail to convert many of the honest men of the one party, & to confirm the wavering of the other—that is, provided it could be forced into circulation.[2] So far as respects the latter object, there wd. be no difficulty. But in the prostrate situation of the press, there wd. be difficulty to procure access to the other side.

In the Weekly Register of last Saturday (25th. July), there is an admirable essay on this subject—but it is too concise.[3] I send by this day's mail, a pamphlet, of which I cannot say "materiam superabat opus";[4] for the materials are excellent—but the execution very clumsy. In the hands of a man of talents, this wd. be of infinite service. With respect & esteem, Your obt. hble servt

MATHEW CAREY[5]

P S. I wish this, like my former letter, destroyed.

RC (DLC). Docketed by JM.

    1. The editors have been unable to locate any letters from Carey to JM for several years preceding the date of this one.

    2. Carey himself undertook this task in 1814, publishing his widely read work *The Olive Branch; or, Faults on Both Sides, Federal and Democratic: A Serious Appeal on the Necessity of Mutual Forgiveness and Harmony, to Save Our Common Country from Ruin* (Philadelphia, 1814; Shaw and Shoemaker 31090).

    3. Carey probably referred to an article entitled "Original Principles," published on 25 July 1812 (*Niles' Weekly Register* 2 [1812]: 346–48). The article faulted the Federalists for claiming that the war was offensive rather than defensive in nature. The author quoted from Federalist petitions against Fox's blockade of 1806 proclaiming British trade restrictions to be unjust and questioning how "those who felt so much zeal to *defend* the right of the United States to the *carrying trade*, affect to believe that we are now engaged in an OFFENSIVE war, seeing the same nation has assumed to itself, (and actually exercised) the right to regulate the whole foreign commerce of the U. States, by a mere *order in council?*"

    4. "The workmanship was more beautiful than the material" (Ovid, *Metamorphoses*, trans. Frank Justus Miller, Loeb Classical Library [2 vols.; London, 1916], 1:61).

    5. Mathew Carey (1760–1839), Philadelphia writer and publisher, immigrated to the U.S. from Ireland in 1784. In 1802 he accepted a post as director of the Bank of Pennsylvania and, always reluctant to submit to party doctrine, came under fire from his fellow Republicans for defending the First Bank of the United States during the recharter debate of 1810–11. Throughout the War of 1812 he corresponded with JM, urging measures to combat disunionist activity in New England. In defense of his nonpartisan principles and Unionist ideals, in 1814 he wrote and published *The Olive Branch*, the work for which he is best known. He retired as the country's foremost publisher in 1822 (Edward C. Carter II, "Mathew Carey and 'The Olive Branch,' 1814–1818," *PMHB* 89 [1965]: 399, 400, 401–2, 405, 414).

From William Eustis

[ca. 1 August 1812]

    John Wait (with his son) a gloomy federalist from Boston a plain man travelling thro' the city in a single horse waggon is very desirous to see the President—and will call on the Secy War at 12 Oclock for that purpose.

    "Then Mr Wait they will seperate from the Union" "O no Sir they cling to the Union"—"but they have said it and will do it"—"No. unless they see commerce entirely destroyed & themselves ruined"—"unless the Laws are unconstitutional"—"and they, the minority are to be the judges"—inter-rupted—perhaps he is the most perfect representative, as far as his charac-ter extends of the Mass: feds that ever came to this place.

RC (DLC). Unsigned; undated; dated 1812 in the *Index to the James Madison Papers;* con-jectural date assigned here on the assumption that the conversation described by Eustis may have taken place after news had broken of a 14 and 15 July meeting of delegates from Hamp-shire, Franklin, and Hampden Counties, Massachusetts, which began a movement to select delegates to a state convention in protest of the war and possibly to consider secession (see Banner, *To the Hartford Convention,* 308–10; Samuel Eliot Morison, *The Life and Letters of Harrison Gray Otis, Federalist, 1765–1848* [2 vols.; Boston, 1913], 2:60–61).

§ From the Inhabitants of Attakapas, Louisiana. *1 August 1812.* "Since our excellent Government has no other foundation than the interests and affections of the people, since without the sanction of their will every measure must be feeble & inefficacious, since the destinies of this nation are now risen to a Crisis which re-quires the support of every voice & the strength of every arm, we therefore the in-habitants of Attacapas, think it our duty to express our sense of the justice of the war to which the nation is driven & our determination to support the government in every measure for the effectual prosecution thereof.

"England, with whom we have to contend, is not only the enemy of this nation, but of the liberties & comm[e]rce of every other nation on the globe. Possessing the means of annoyance at a distance, there is no where a port accessible to attack, that has not felt the power of her navy. She has hunted down the last remnant of com-merce from the five seaes of the earth and now roams their naked surface as the Arab his sandy desert, in pursuit of his prey. With her, the laws of nations are a nulity: she has blotted out from their sacred pages, the well Known rules of warfare, & the rights of neutrals, & levelled to the dust that system, the proudest monument of the wisdom & justice of man. She has particularly aim'd at this nation every wrong in her power to inflict. Even before a declaration of war had issued, or a hos-tile blow been struck, her emissaries had penetrated into the councils of every tribe of Indians on our frontiers, & renew'd the horrors of the scalping Knife & tomma-hawk from Pensicola to the lake of the woods. It has been with the deepest appro-hension we have seen the American people submit to so long a course of injury that submission had almost become habitual. They have endured without redress, their property to be tax'd & plunder'd on the high seas; the jurisdiction of their Terri-tory to be violated with every species of abomination; their chara[c]ter insulted, their ships seiz'd, & their countrymen murder'd within their own waters; & above all more than 7000 American Citizens impress'd by the enemy to fight their battles or perish in the pestilential vapours of the East or West Indies; or if they survive, it is only to deplore the loss of an ungreatful Country that has hitherto refused to pro-tect them. And though we view war as the chief of human calamities, and though we believe that no part of the whole line of American coast is more expos'd than our own, yet it [is] with pleasure we see the Spirit of '76 awakned anew, & that thirty years of commercial prosperity has not yet extinguish'd that sacred love of country, which onc⟨e⟩ placed the American name in the foremost files of a courageous people. Therefore we resolve

"1. That to have longer delay'd a war with Gr. Britain, would have been to endanger the liberties of this nation a reproach upon the American name.

"2. That we have entire confidence in [the] wisdom & patriotism of the general government, & are prepared at all sacrafices to support every measure for the effectual prosecution of the war.

"3. That all those who oppose the declaration of war, & are not ready at all times to aid the government in the maintenance of its rights, ought to be held under suspicion & view'd as enemies to their country."

RC (DNA: RG 59, ML). 4 pp.; signed by Peter Regnier, chairman, and John Wilkinson, secretary. Enclosed in Nathan Kemper and others to JM, 1 Aug. 1812 (ibid.; 1 p.).

From William C. C. Claiborne

DEAR SIR,   NEW-ORLEANS August 2nd, 1812

I have the honor to inform you, that on the 30h Ultimo, I entered upon the duties of the office of Governor of Louisiana, to which I have been called by a Vote of the people of the State and of the General Assembly.

Yielding to the feelings of a Grateful Heart, I eagerly seize this occasion to return you my sincere thanks for the high confidence you were pleased to repose in me, during the late Territorial Government, and to assure you, that in the course of my Services as Governor of Louisiana, there is nothing I more desire, than to promote the views of your wise & Virtuous Administration, and to give you individually, proofs of my most faithful and respectful Attachment.

WILLIAM C. C. CLAIBORNE

RC (DLC). Docketed by JM.

From John Armstrong

Private.

DEAR SIR,   NEW YORK Augt. 3d. 1812.

I arrived here on friday last and have this day taken the command.[1] Gen. Bloomfield left us this morning.[2] He has been both frank and friendly & I should do wrong were I not to make this acknowlegment, as well to you as to him. Before we parted, he wished me to suggest, that he thought it adviseable under all circumstances, that he should be left in New Jersey untill the 25th. of September next. All the measures of state policy, with which he has connexion, & in the management of which his presence may be useful, will then have been taken. Having occasion to see Mr. Gallatin, this circumstance became a subject of conversation between us, and we supposed, that it would be well to reinstate the General in the direction of the recruiting service within the States of Jersey & Pennsylvania & order Col. Izzard to his place. I have one motive the more for presenting this subject thus early to your own consideration, as I understand from Gen. Bloomfield, that Gen. Dearborn has intimated to him in a letter of the 31st. Ult. a wish, that he would repair to Albany as early as his convenience would allow. I shall employ the first days of this week in examining the different posts & their respective garrisons, when I shall have the honor of addressing an official letter to the Secretary of the War Department in relation to them. I am with the greatest respect & esteem, Your faithful & obedient servant

J ARMSTRONG.

RC (DLC). Docketed by JM.

1. On 20 July 1812 Eustis ordered Armstrong to take command of the city and port of New York (DNA: RG 107, LSMA).

2. Joseph Bloomfield (1753–1823), who had served as a major in the Revolutionary War, renounced his Federalist leanings in 1800 and was subsequently elected Republican governor of New Jersey. Bloomfield resigned this post after receiving a brigadier general's commission in March 1812. Initially assigned to the command of the city and port of New York, Bloomfield requested a leave of absence to meet with the New Jersey legislature in August. After discharging this duty, he reported to Dearborn in Albany. He was then assigned the command of troops in Plattsburgh, New York (Sobel and Raimo, *Biographical Directory of the Governors*, 3:1010; Eustis to Bloomfield, 18 July and 4 Aug. 1812 [DNA: RG 107, LSMA]; Dearborn to Eustis, 24 Nov. 1812 [DNA: RG 107, LRRS, D-254:6]).

From James Fenner

Sir   Providence August 3rd. 1812

I am informed that Judge Barnes of this District, in consequence of a severe malady under which he is now suffering without hope of recovery, has sent forward his resignation as District Judge.

Presuming the report to be true, I take the liberty of nominating the Hon David Howell, at present our District Attorney, as the Successor of Judge Barnes.[1] Your knowledge of Mr Howell renders it unnecessary for me to mention the several honorable appointments which he has held from both the National and State Governments. He was one of the Commissioners appointed by President Washington for ascertaining the St. Croix boundary; and is now a Commissioner under Massachusetts for settling the conflicting land titles in the Province of Maine. As a literary Gentleman and a Lawyer he is without a rival in this State; I think, therefore, that his appointment would give general satisfaction. With highest respect and Esteem, Your Obt Servt.

J FENNER

RC (DNA: RG 59, LAR, 1809–17, filed under "Howell, David").

1. Fenner had already recommended Howell for the office of judge of the district court of Rhode Island in 1810, when he hoped that David Leonard Barnes would vacate the office by replacing William Cushing on the Supreme Court. JM received letters from the following on Howell's behalf: Benjamin Howland, 8 Aug. 1812, Isaac Wilbour, 8 Aug. 1812, Elisha Mathewson, 12 Aug. 1812, Elbridge Gerry, 12 Oct. 1812, Asa Messer, 3 Nov. 1812, John Pitman, 5 Nov. 1812, and Jeremiah B. Howell, 9 Nov. 1812, enclosing Stephen Gano to Howell, 4 Nov. 1812 (ibid.). JM nominated Howell for the position on 12 Nov., and the Senate approved him on 16 Nov. 1812 (Fenner to JM, 3 Dec. 1810, *PJM-PS*, 3:44–45; *Senate Exec. Proceedings*, 2:303, 304).

From James Monroe

DEAR SIR   ALBEMARLE Augt. 4. 1812

We arrived here on sunday last, & had the good fortune to meet Mr Hay[1] & our daughter on their way to the springs. Mrs. Monroe had intended to accompany them there, but will remain here, with the younger part, being not far from indisposition, & too much fatigued to pursue the journey. We took the Dumfries route, & breakfastd at Lansdowne's, the worst house we ever saw. The upper route by Fauquier cthouse is far preferable to this. I intend to set out back, the beginning of the ensuing week.

We hear nothing certain of Com: Rogers,[2] & the accounts of the affair at Baltimore[3] still leave it in much obscurity. However much to be regretted & censur'd popular movments of this kind always are, nothing can be said in favor of a party organised for the purpose of its combating the mob, unknown to the law, equally in defiance of it, and which could not fail, by the excitment it was sure to produce, to bring on the contest. Mobs however must be prevented, & the punishment even of such men as the Editors of that paper must be inflicted by law, not mob movments. It would do credit to the Executi⟨ve⟩ of Maryland to reestablish that paper, and the credit wod. be in proportion to its past & future excesses. I fear that if some distinguished effort is not made, in favor of the authority of the law, there is danger of a civil war, which may undermine our free system of govt. I am dear Sir very sincerely & respectfully your friend.

JAS MONROE

RC (DLC: Rives Collection, Madison Papers).

1. George Hay (1765–1830), Monroe's son-in-law, was appointed U.S. attorney for the district of Virginia in 1803 and was the prosecutor in the treason trial of Aaron Burr. He

served in the Virginia House of Delegates from 1816 to 1817 and spent four years in the state senate before receiving an appointment in 1825 to the U.S. District Court of Eastern Virginia (*PJM*, 7:75 n. 12).

2. For Rodgers's pursuit of the British fleet, see *PJM-PS*, 4:503 n. 2.

3. Monroe referred to the Baltimore Riots. On 22 June 1812 Republicans destroyed the Gay Street office of the Baltimore *Federal Republican and Commercial Gazette*, a Federalist newspaper that had published editorials in opposition to the war. On 27 July the editor of the *Federal Republican*, Alexander Hanson, put out an edition featuring a scathing critique of the hostile climate in the city, under a masthead with a new address at 45 Charles Street. A crowd soon gathered in front of the paper's new offices, threatening to charge the building. Hanson and his supporters, anticipating trouble, had gathered inside and armed themselves. A militia company barely kept peace through the night. Finally, Baltimore's mayor, Edward Johnson, negotiated a compromise whereby the Federalists were escorted from the building and held in protective custody in jail on the promise of causing no further trouble. However, the crowd destroyed the house and gathered at the jail. By the evening of 28 July, the crowd took on the character of a lynch mob. Calling for blood, they pulled Federalists from the jail and beat them severely, killing Gen. James M. Lingan and wounding at least nine others, among them Light-Horse Harry Lee. In the weeks that followed, Federalists demanded government protection while Republicans persisted in their quest to rid the city of "tories." Hanson published another edition of the paper on 3 Aug., which he intended to distribute by mail. A crowd gathered at the post office to prevent the paper from being delivered. This time, however, the city's officials acted swiftly to prevent further violence, calling out the militia and conducting a cavalry charge to disperse the crowd. Increased patrolling then brought a tentative peace (*Report of the Committee of Grievances and Courts of Justice of the House of Delegates of Maryland, on the Subject of the Recent Mobs and Riots in the City of Baltimore, Together with the Depositions Taken before the Committee* [Annapolis, 1813; Shaw and Shoemaker 29064]; *Interesting Papers relative to the Recent Riots at Baltimore* [Philadelphia, 1812; Shaw and Shoemaker 25720]). See also Frank A. Cassell, "The Great Baltimore Riot of 1812," *Maryland Historical Magazine* 70 (1975): 241–59; Donald R. Hickey, "The Darker Side of Democracy: The Baltimore Riots of 1812," *Maryland Historian* 7 (1976): 1–19; and Paul A. Gilje, "The Baltimore Riots of 1812 and the Breakdown of the Anglo-American Mob Tradition," *Journal of Social History* 13 (1979): 547–64.

From Thomas Jefferson

DEAR SIR   MONTICELLO Aug. 5. 12.

In a letter of May 6. from Foronda is this passage. 'No remito a Vm exemplares de mis papelitos para el ilustrado y sabio Madison, aunque le tributo todos mis respetos: pero es Presidente, y las vilas almas, lexos de conocer que esto seria un acto de Cortesania que no tiene relacion con la presidencià, me tacharian tal vez de poco afecto à la patria, alegando que tenià consideraciones con quien nos ha tomado à Baton rouge.'[1] You will draw the inferences both personal & public from this paragraph which it authorises. He nevertheless sent me duplicates of his publications, and I have no doubt I fulfill his wish in sending you one of them.

The inclosed letter to Kosciusko[2] is important to him as covering a bill of exchange, the proceeds of his funds here. A safe conveyance is more important than a speedy one. If you can have it so disposed of in the office of state as to give it the protection of Barlow's cover, it will serve one of our most genuine foreign friends.

I am glad of the reestablishment of a Percival ministry. The opposition would have recruited our Minority by half way offers. With Canada in hand we can go to treaty with an offset for spoliations before the war. Our farmers are chearful in the expectation of a good price for wheat in autumn. Their pulse will be regulated by this, and not by the successes or disasters of the war. To keep open sufficient markets is the very first object towards maintaining the popularity of the war which is as great at present as could be desired. We have just had a fine rain of $1\frac{1}{4}$ I. in the most critical time for our corn. The weather during harvest was as advantageous as could be. I am sorry to find you remaining so long at Washington. The effect on your health may lose us a great deal of your time: a couple of months at Montpelier at this season need not lose us an hour. Affectionate salutations to mrs Madison and yourself.

Th: Jefferson

RC (DLC: Rives Collection, Madison Papers); FC (DLC: Jefferson Papers).

1. "I do not send you examples of my little papers for the enlightened and wise Madison, although I offer him all my respects: but he is President, and mean spirits, far from recognizing that this would be an act of courtesy that has no relation to the presidency, would perhaps accuse me of little affection for my native country, alleging that I had consideration for him who has robbed us at Baton Rouge" (editors' translation).

2. Jefferson enclosed his 5 Aug. 1812 letter to Kościuszko (DLC: Jefferson Papers).

From John Morris

Sir,   Erie Penna. Augt. 5th. 1812

The tender of voluntary service which I had the honour to offer on behalf of the officers and privates of my company[1] having been invited as well by previous assurances and recommendations communicated by Mr Lacock and others, as by special and peculiar circumstances which recommended that course for the most prompt and efficacious mean of defending their own frontier, those assurances have been implicitly relied upon: But from the terms of a letter to me from the Brigadier & Inspector general of the 14 July last, directing me to organize my company, *Arm* and equip and expect orders to march, and containing no indication that he was apprised of any special assurance having been given; Some doubts have arisen whether in the immensity of your official avocations it has been adverted to or the Inspector General made aware of it. I am therefore called upon as well by the express desire of the company as by a sense of their situation and of the considerations which have influenced them; to make a direct communication to you recapitulating the circumstances conditions and assurances which induced and enabled them to unite in this tender of their services for a special purpose.

An opinion had long prevailed here that in the event of a war with Great Britain, the frontier of Pennsylvania on Lake Erie unless in a State of preparation for defence would be exposed to various danger so long as the former commanded exclusively the Navigation of all the lakes upon which are a very considerable number of Armed and unarmed Vessels, possessing also an extensive influence over numerous tribes of Indians, and Strong Military posts at each of the Streights: During the late session of congress the probability of such a war was sufficiently strong to awaken the inhabitants of this frontier to a sense of danger and of their unprepared condition; but the danger was not deemed to be clearly of that description which would Authorize the State government to embody an armed force inasmuch as there was no actual invasion apprehended except upon the contingency of war being declared by the General Government: In this view of the Subject an application to the President of the United States in the first instance was considered best suited to the case, and was accordingly made through Mr Lacock in March last.[2] The President declined to interfere for reasons which he assigned, refering to the State government; upon which Mr Lacock wrote to the Governor of Pennsylvania on the Subject generally of defending this frontier and particularly on that of issuing the arms of the state to the militia of its vicinity. The State legislature had adjourned and the governor in answer informed Mr Lacock that he was not authorised by law to make any distribution of the State Arms other than to Arm such companies as had or might tender voluntary service to the President under some of the acts of congress. Mr. Lacock and others then wrote to Sundry Persons here recommending an early and general tender of services by the Militia of this quarter as the best or only means of obtaining Arms for their own defence, adding that Mr Lacock was further Authorised (by the President as was clearly understood) positively to assure any companies of this part of Pennsylvania so volunteering that they would not be called upon duty elswhere but be left to defend their homes. In the mean time a number of persons to the number of eighty or ninety men of the immediate vicinity had united in a memorial to the President, and a communication to the Governor which being prepared were forwarded on the same day the foregoing advices from Mr. Lacock were received; upon the receipt of them it was concluded that the objects of the Memorial were anticipated, which subsequently proved to be the case, and without entirtaining any further expectations from that, Consultations were immediately gone into on the subject of voluntary Service agreeably to the recommendation of Mr Lacock, with a view to the object exclusively contemplated by his letter and all the previous Correspondence and with full reliance upon the assurance above mentioned communicated by him from the President. It was found that no tender of service through the governor of Pennsylvania could be made by any company without a degree of preparation required by the State laws that would occasion great delay at least, and more probably amount to an insuperable difficulty: this course therefore was declined as impracticable or at best unsuitable to the present occasion; and the only altarnatives were to abandon the hope [of] adopting any efficient plan, or to make the tenders of Service directly to the president under the act of Congress Authorising the President to accept and organize certain Volunteer Military Corps; but as Some uncertainty was Suggested whether the President would accept the services of any companies offering as apart of these Corps and at the same time relying upon the assurances given them previously of being employed in the defence of the frontier of their own State exclusively; it was therefore not deemed advisable to form many Companies of this description until it could be ascertained whether any distinction was intended by the president between this and other corps proposed by him to be so exclusively employed. And that no misunderstanding should possibly take place the only tender so made at this place (that by my company) was accompanied with two or three other communications to Mr. Lacock Explicitly recognizing the assurances relied upon; stating expressly that without the fullest reliance on that assurance they would not have been enabled, how ever will [sic] disposed, to Serve their country, as Volunteers; and requiring definitely that the president in case he should find or apprehend any difficulty in a compliance with the conditions proposed would in that case not accept, but return their communication. In due time advice was received from Mr Lacock that the president in answer to the proposition had deliberately and explicitly complied with the wishes of the company—and had no hesitation in assuring them that if called into actual Servic[e] it would be on their own frontier and not elswhere. Thus having accompanied their tender of service with merely a condition which for special reasons had been offered to them by the President, and not by themselves originated; having in express terms left it to the more deliberate choice of the President, to confirm that condition or decline the acceptance of their Services, and having received through their Representative the Presidents deliberate Answer, explicitly saying that although not strictly conformable to the express provisions of the law nor the arrangements of the war department yet in the exercise of his discretion as commander in chief he would in the present instance comply with their wishes; The officers and privates of this company cannot therefore entertain a reasonable doubt of the Presidents intention to realize fully his promise: Their only apprehension is that it might not be adverted to in the general arrangement and distribution of the Army.

Should you deem it proper Sir to enable me directly to reassure my company that they are not to be marched away from their own frontier, it will contribute much to the tranquility of their families; to the relief of Sundry individuals who with myself are pledged for the faithful observance of the assurances heretofore relied on; and so far as this company forms a part of the Strength of the frontier will contribute also to that object.

The Supplement of the act of Congress of February last Said to have passed is not yet published here nor its terms known to us of course we are guided solely by the law as it originally stood. It would have been desirable to have received from the Brigadier & Inspector Genl. some further detail explanatory of our duty under that part of his order requiring us to "Arm."

I will barely add that a quantity of arms for this frontier are ordered by the Governor of Pennsylvania and now on the road, and I have no reason to doubt will afford a Supply to my Company if wanted notwithstand[ing] the provision of the act of Congress. I have the Honour to be Sir—Your Obt Huml Servt.

JOHN MORRIS

RC (DNA: RG 107, LRRS, M-375:6).

1. See Morris to JM, 25 July 1812, and n. 1.
2. Lacock first alerted Eustis to the concerns of inhabitants of the Pennsylvania frontier on 7 Apr., but when he received no response from the War Department, he sought JM's aid (Lacock to JM, 11 Apr. and 18 May 1812, *PJM-PS*, 4:311–12 and n. 1, 395 and n. 1).

§ From the Inhabitants of Rockingham County, New Hampshire. *5 August 1812.* Represent over 1,500 inhabitants who assembled at Brentwood to express their opinion on the present state of national affairs. Observe with regret that the "system of policy pursued by the General Government, from the Embargo of 1807 to the present time," has encouraged "the destruction of the *Commerce* of these States." "We have not been indifferent spectators," as commerce is "a leading pursuit . . . intimately blended with all our other interests and occupations." Believe that the U.S. Constitution was intended to protect the interests of each section of the nation. Have therefore perceived with "alarm and apprehension" the government's "disposition to embarrass and enthral *Commerce*, by repeated Restrictions, . . . to *make War*, by shutting up *our own ports*," and to admonish citizens *"finally to retire from the seas."* Believe that the declaration of war against Great Britain "will be productive of evils of incalculable magnitude." Are not reluctant to endure the privations and dangers of war, as long as the war is just, unavoidable, and expedient. Argue that the present war will not "bear the test of these principles."

Believe that the impressment of American seamen has been "the subject of great misrepresentation." Are convinced that "the number of these cases has been *ex-*

travagantly exaggerated." Explain that if impressment were widespread, it would most affect the citizens of coastal states, yet those states have been unable "to discover instances of impressment, in any degree equal to the alledged numbers." Note that the strongest feelings on impressment and war "are entertained by the Representatives of those States which *have no Seamen at all of their own;* while those sections of the Community, in which *more than three fourths* of the mariners of the United States have their homes, are, by great majorities, *against* that War." Argue that Great Britain claims no right to impress American seamen but only "a right to the service of *her own subjects,* in time of war." Ask whether the U.S. would "plunge into a ruinous War, in order to settle a question of relative right between the Government of a foreign Nation and the subjects of that Government." Believe it would be fatal to the "interests of the Navigating States, if the consequence of this War should be, that the American Flag shall give the American character to all who sail under it, and thus invite thousands of *foreign* seamen to enter into our service, and thrust aside our own native Citizens!" Point out that Great Britain has been willing to make adjustments on this subject if the U.S. would prohibit its officers from granting protections to British subjects. Ask why, after so many years, impressment has become an issue of "sudden and unusual importance."

Argue that "The Blockade, and Orders in Council, the other causes of War, bear no better examination than the subject of Impressment." Ask by what train of reasoning the blockade, which was regarded initially "as a measure *favorable* to our interests . . . is now turned into an *injury* . . . of such magnitude as to justify *War.*" Are "unsatisfied with the arguments used to prove that the Decrees of France were *repealed* in November 1810—and that therefore, without departing from *impartial* policy, we are justified in undertaking to compel Great Britain, by War, to abandon her Orders in Council." Argue that the recent transmission of the French decree of 28 Apr. 1811, which declared that the Berlin and Milan Decrees were repealed "*in consequence* of measures adopted by our Government against Great Britain, *in March 1811,* . . . proves beyond contradiction, that those Decrees *were not* repealed at the time when our Government adopted measures against Great Britain, *founded on their supposed repeal.*" "We cannot but lament, that the Declaration of War was *forced* and *hurried,* as if to put us *beyond the benefit of favorable events.*"

"As none of the complaints against Great Britain are of *recent* origin . . . it was reasonably expected, that if Government intended *War,* it would have made adequate provision and preparation for that event. In this expectation we have been *disappointed.* The Nation is totally unprepared for War: we say *totally* unprepared, because the degree of preparation bears no definable relation to the magnitude of the occasion, or the greatness of the interests which are at stake."

Emphasize "the exposed state of our *Sea Coast,* and our *Commerce.*" "It is unheard of, and beyond imagination strange, in our opinion, that such great and important interests as *the Navigation and Commerce of a whole Country* should be put to hazard—nay, to certain loss—for want of that protection which it was in the power, and which we presume to say it was the *duty,* of Government to have afforded.

"On the subject of *Naval Defence,* we . . . hold it to be our *Right,* to *demand,* at the hand of the General Government, adequate protection to our lawful *Commerce.* When the Constitution empowered the Government to *build and maintain a Navy,* . . . it was confidently expected, that that power would be exercised as cheerfully as the power to levy and collect taxes. We consider protection on the *Sea* to be as solemnly guaranteed to us by the Constitution, as protection on the *Land*. . . .

"When the Commercial and Navigating States surrendered to the General Government the riches of their Custom-Houses, and thereby parted with the fairest portion of their revenue, leaving to themselves nothing to defray the expenses of their own establishments, but an unpleasant resort to Direct Taxation, they had a *right* to expect, and they *did* expect, from the Wisdom and Justice of that Government, adequate and ample means of Protection and Defence." Observe that "a *distinguished Advocate*[1] for the *Union* of these States urged the adoption of the Federal Constitution upon the inhabitants of the Atlantic Frontier, in the following manner."

"'The palpable necessity of the power to *provide and maintain a Navy*, has protected that part of the Constitution against a spirit of censure which has spared few other parts. It must be numbered among the greatest blessings of America, that as her *Union* will be the only source of her *Maritime Strength*, so this will be the principal source of her security against danger from abroad.'"[2]

"The same *distinguished Gentleman*, at a later period, gave . . . a solemn and official *Pledge* of his sentiments on this important subject . . . in the following emphatic manner:

"'I consider an *Acquisition of Maritime Strength essential* to this Country; should we ever be so unfortunate as to be engaged in *War*, what but *this* can defend our towns and cities upon the *Sea Coast?* Or what but this can enable us to repel an *invading enemy?*'"[3]

Observe that in spite of these promises, "It is notorious that we have *not* this Navy; we are *not* protected; we *cannot* be quiet, or secure; our Maritime Towns are *not* safe against invasion and burning; our best interests are at the mercy of our enemies, and we can *do nothing* but sit still and see the fruits of thirty years of laborious industry swept away with the besom of destruction!"

Claim to be attached "to the *substance*, and not to the *form*" of the union. "If the time should ever arrive, when this Union shall be holden together by nothing but the authority of Law; when . . . we shall be *one*, not in interest and mutual regard, but in *name* and *form* only; we, Sir, shall look on *that hour* as the closing scene of our Country's prosperity!" "We shrink from the separation of the States," but if such a separation "*should* take place, it will be on some occasion when one portion of the Country undertakes to control, to regulate, and to *sacrifice*, the interests of another."

Lament the war most of all as "the harbinger of *French Alliance!*" Will not "assist in uniting the Republics of America with the Military Despotism of France." "It only remains for us . . . to supplicate the Government to adopt such a system as shall restore to us the blessings of *Peace* and of *Commerce*."

RC (DNA: RG 59, ML). 17 pp.; signed by Samuel Tenney, chairman, and William Austin Kent, secretary. Enclosed in Tenney to JM, 17 Aug. 1812 (ibid.; 1 p.), which notes that the memorial was composed at a meeting of the "Friends of Peace," that it was approved "with one dissenting voice," and that the mailing of the memorial was delayed by the necessity of copying it and obtaining the signature of the secretary in a remote part of the state. Printed in Charles M. Wiltse, ed., *The Papers of Daniel Webster*, ser. 4, *Speeches and Formal Writings* (2 vols.; Hanover, N.H., 1986) 1:6–17.

1. The memorialists placed an asterisk here and noted at the bottom of the page, "Mr. Madison himself."

2. The memorialists here quoted from *The Federalist* No. 41 (*PJM*, 10:395).

3. The memorialists placed an asterisk here and noted at the bottom of the page, "Mr. Madison's speech in Congress—1789." The authors quoted from a 21 Apr. 1789 speech (*PJM*, 12:101–2).

From William Duane

SIR   PHILA. Aug. 6. 1812

I have been just informed by Mr Carswell that he means to signify by the morning's Mail, that he cannot accept the office of Commissary General.[1] There is no man more honest than Mr Carswell, and it is the sense which he entertains of the importance of the station which induces him to decline its acceptance. The same idea of its importance induces me to take the liberty of addressing you.

A little attention to the duties which must devolve on the Commissary general during a war will shew that it requires something more than a mere accountant or merchant; during a peace any office may be filled by common qualifications without danger, but it is otherwise in such a crisis as the present—and the more necessary it is to carry on the war with vigor in order to make it short and decisive, so much more indispensible will it be to have men in such stations as can give vigor to the public arm. A Commissary General should have a knowlege of Military affairs—he should know their habits—their wants and their privations in camp and quarters—the esprit de Corps or that sympathy which arises out of association—a knowlege of the country not merely on the map, but of its roads and means of communication its people and peculiar products and resources—a knowlege of arms and equipments of every kind, he should know at sight what is fit, what not; he should know the quality and quantity of ammunition and stores—and his zeal should be always guarded so as to avert the consequences of those momentary disasters from which no war can be exempted—he should be as a second soul to the war department, and serve as a kind of instinct to that department and the army: a very honest man might fill the office, and with only an innocent incapacity, debilitate the army endanger the public force and ruin himself.

In thus sketching the qualifications of a fit man permit me to suggest, with the most respectful deference, the name of a gentleman who unites with all the qualifications I have described the stern integrity of a private and public character, such a man as the public voice would applaud, the army confide in, and such as would render credit to yourself. I mean the present Superintendant of Military stores, Mr C. Irvine,[2] son of the late General Wm. Irvine. He has served in the army is known and esteemed in private and public. His zeal for the public service is every where known, and his probity would be a guarantee to the public and to you, such as is not always to be found in candidates for public office; and I am told that at this moment there is a stir making to press upon you a person of the name of Duncan,[3] a broker of this city, a man whose profession as an agent of Usury, is not exactly that which is best adapted for a great trust in critical times.

I shall only add that I have neither seen nor conversed with Mr Irvine on this subject—I consider myself as performing an act of duty to the public, and should I be so fortunate as to have brought into your view the man qualified & he shall be appointed, I shall feel great pride and pleasure in the consciousness that I shall have rendered a public service to the country, to the army, and to the government of my country.

As this note is intruded on you without the knowlege of a second person—I beg leave to say, that whatever may be its fate—it shall remain known only to myself and I keep no copy. I am Sir Your very obed Sert

WM DUANE

RC (DLC). Docketed by JM.

1. For the circumstances of Carswell's nomination and refusal, see JM to Gallatin, 28 June 1812, *PJM-PS*, 4:517–18 and n. 1.

2. Callender Irvine (1775–1841) of Pennsylvania was appointed superintendent of military stores on 24 Oct. 1804 and held that post until his promotion to the commissary general's office, where he served for the remainder of his life (Risch, *Quartermaster Support*, 125).

3. Duane probably referred to William Duncan (1772–1864), a Philadelphia merchant who was appointed superintendent of military stores in the place of Callender Irvine on 26 Aug. 1812. As part of an effort to streamline the War Department, this office was abolished in early 1813, and Duncan applied for the newly created office of superintendent general of military supplies, for which Richard Cutts was confirmed on 3 June 1813. Duncan was also a brigadier general and adjutant general in the Pennsylvania militia during the War of 1812. JM appointed him collector of direct taxes in Philadelphia on 21 Jan. 1814 (ibid., 140–41, 151; *Senate Exec. Proceedings*, 2:349, 455–56, 460).

From Benjamin Henry Latrobe

SIR,   WASHINGTON Augt. 6t. 1812

I beg leave to submit to you, & to solicit your approbation of these accounts,[1] the only ones relating to the public buildings on which I have occasion to give you any trouble, because unless allowed by you they cannot pass the treasury, and must stand as a charge against me personally.

1. Of the first, the enclosed affidavit[2] explains the nature perfectly, and I will only add that altho' the custom of all public buildings obliged me on extraordinary occasions to treat the workmen it is the only treat which I have charged the public with in the S. Wing of the Capitol. Mr Stelle[3] has received of the Superintendent 100$ on acct.

2. The second is also for a treat on compleating the Vaults of the North wing. I promised it to the Workmen during your absence in July 1809 to induce them to strike the centers of the great arch, to do which they were afraid, the first arch having fallen down. To avoid dispute I contracted for 50$ for a supper for about 80 Men, including Liquors. I have paid the amount.

3. The third item is for the Assistance necessarily required for the Estimates called for by the House of Representatives in Jany. 1809, on which occasion I explained its necessity in a letter to You,[4] and also had a verbal conversation on the subject.

Mr Hadfield[5] has received 150$ of Mr. Munroe & 150 from me as he could not wait for the appropriation. Altho' the Estimate of the timber part was not laid before Congress, it was made in great detail & required much labor.

I beg leave to refer to the Superintendent of the city for further information & am with high respect Yrs.

B HENRY LATROBE

FC and FC of enclosure (MdHi: Latrobe Letterbooks). For surviving enclosure, see n. 2.

1. Enclosure not found.

2. In his 6 Aug. 1812 affidavit, Latrobe described his request that the workmen be treated to a dinner on 17 Oct. 1807, after the completion of the south wing of the Capitol. He claimed that Jefferson initially agreed to the request and that Pontius D. Stelle was contracted to purchase and prepare the food and drink for the event. However, a disagreement over the price of the dinner led Jefferson to refuse payment to Stelle. The superintendent of the city, Thomas Munroe, paid Stelle $100, and the Commercial Company of Washington eventually verified the rest of the charges. At that point Jefferson claimed a lapse of memory about the entire event and declined again to sanction the account.

3. Pontius D. Stelle (1763–1826) was a Washington innkeeper with an establishment near the Capitol. From 1812 to 1818 he served as secretary to the Common Council of Washington (Van Horne, *Papers of Benjamin Henry Latrobe*, 2:97 n. 1).

4. Letter not found.

5. George Hadfield (1763–1826), an architect trained at the Royal Academy in England, was the brother of Jefferson's friend Maria Cosway. He was appointed superintendent of the U.S. Capitol in 1795, where he served for three years before being dismissed (ibid., 1:50 n. 1).

From Andrew Hull Jr.

Sir   Cheshire August 7th. 1812

At this interesting crisis of our beloved country I take the liberty, to address a few lines to the perusal of your Exelency as it hath ben reported by those who are unfriendly to the measures adopted by the goverment that the War is unpopalar even among the republicans in the New-england States, having Traveled lately in the States of Massechusets New Hamshire and Vermont, am confident of its not being the fact, and I am certain that the republicans of Connecticut are alive to their duty and that they will at the hazard of their lives and all that is dear to them on the earth support the constituted Athorities of our common country and defend its rights Against external and internal enemies there is in this state a sufficient number that will readily voluntere to meet any force that could be raised to oppose the general goverment, but in case of such an event it would be important that arms and amunition should be kept in reserve in this part of the United States to furnish those that Are destitute, as the State Legislator while Threatning to disregard if not to oppose the laws of the Union have ben procuring a supplussage of Arms and placing them under the care of the Governor—being a member of our Legislator at the time the Resolve passd to procure Arms, I well recollect the hints given by Federal members what Use they might be wanted for—our Governor And Council are now in Session at Hartford As it is Said to decide whether the quota of Militia shall be called out.[1] David Dagget[2] of New-Haven one of the Governor council expres.d himself at the Post Office before he went to Hartford with a degree of warmth that he would oppose their being called out and said many hard things of the President of the United States for making three wars. (Viz) against Spain—the Indians and England and Baltimore Mob, but his violent invectives will do no harm as it respects the government. I do not apprehend the least danger of any serious opposition from the federal party—their Main object is to gain the Assendency in the Government of the United States, or sever the Union. I was at Washington three years ago last January and in conversation with your Exellency observd that the opposition in the N. England States to the then embargo laws was in my opinion to Frighten the government from the stand they had taken and to make them Unpopalar. Th[e]y now begin to Shrink from their violent opposition after seing the determined Stand the Republi[c]ans are about to take as they are organ[i]zing themselves and will be prepared to meet them in case of any opposition that might be made in case the Rebublicans [sic] can have Arms from the United States. I have commanded A brigade of Militia in this State for several Years which office I resighned about Six years ago, but am ready to step forth as a Private if nessesary.[3] I

am with sentiments of the highest Esteem and Respect Your Exellencies
Obt. Servt

ANDREW HULL JUNR.

RC (DLC). Enclosed in Hull to JM, 7 Aug. 1812 (second letter).

1. Eustis and Dearborn, on 14 and 17 July, respectively, had renewed their requests for detached militia from Connecticut. The governor responded by convening his council on 4 Aug.
to consider the propriety of complying (*ASP, Military Affairs*, 1:325–26; Hartford *Connecticut
Mirror*, 10 Aug. 1812).

2. David Daggett (1764–1851) was a Federalist member of the Connecticut governor's
council from 1797 to 1804 and again from 1809 to 1813. He was elected to the U.S. Senate
in 1813 to serve the remainder of Chauncey Goodrich's term. Upon leaving the Senate in
1819, Daggett returned to Connecticut, where he variously pursued a private law practice,
taught law at Yale, served as New Haven's mayor, and held the position of state supreme court
judge (Dexter, *Biographical Sketches of the Graduates of Yale College*, 4:260–61).

3. Andrew Hull Jr. served in the Connecticut state legislature in the late 1790s, distinguishing himself as one of two members willing to endorse the Kentucky Resolutions. JM
nominated Hull as collector for the Third Connecticut District on 13 Dec. 1813 (Harold J.
Bingham, *History of Connecticut* [4 vols.; New York, 1962], 1:398–400; *Senate Exec. Proceedings*, 2:438, 439).

From Andrew Hull Jr.

SIR   NEW HAVEN Augt. 7th. 1812

Since writing the Inclosed[1] I here learn that the governor and council
have refused to comply with the Requisition of the Secretary at war in calling out the drafted Militia and to summon the Members of the house of
Representetives to mete at this place two weeks from next Tuesday.[2] With
sentiments of high consid[e]ration Your Obt Servt

ANDW. HULL JUNR.

RC (DLC).

1. Hull to JM, 7 Aug. 1812 (first letter).
2. On 10 Aug. the Hartford *Connecticut Mirror* printed a report of the 4 Aug. meeting of
the governor and council. The report expressed the council's support for Governor Griswold's view that Dearborn's request for militia violated the 10 Apr. 1812 law stipulating that
militia could be called into national service only to enforce the laws of the nation, to suppress
insurrection, or to repel invasion. The council claimed to be willing to comply with requests
consistent with the Constitution but insisted that since no evidence of invasion existed, calling out the militia would be a violation of its terms. The newspaper also reported that Griswold had summoned the Connecticut General Assembly to meet on 25 Aug. 1812.

From William Pinkney

Dear Sir. Baltimore August 7. 1812

I do not perceive that the General Government could well interfere upon the subject of the Letter, which you did me the Honour to enclose to me[1] even if it were desirable that it should; but I am quite sure that it will be wholly unnecessary. There is no Disposition to Riot here except with a mere Handful of low people, who can and will be restrained by the Authority of the Majistracy of the Place aided by a proper Show of Force on the part of the Militia.

I hope to be able to pay my respects to you in person in the Course of the next Week. A Prize-Cause detains me in Baltimore at present. I have the Honour to be with sincere Respect and Attachment—Dear Sir Your faithful & Obt Servant

Wm Pinkney

RC (DLC). Docketed by JM.

1. Letter not found.

To Richard Cutts

Dear Sir Washington Aug. 8. 1812

I have had the pleasure of receiving yours of the 25th. Ult:[1] The rancorous opposition in some of the E. States to the war, is peculiarly unfortunate, as it has the double effect of crippling its operations, and encouraging the Enemy to withold any pacific advances otherwise likely to be made. It appears that the B. Cabinet has been forced into a reconsideration of their refusal to repeal the Orders;[2] but whether they will adopt such a repeal as will be an effective step towards adjustment; or whether they will repeal at all after a knowledge of the war, and above all, of the factious proceedings agst. it remains to be seen. Their delay in removing the Orders out of the way, may have the advantage of letting our vessels in England hear of the war before they avail themselves of the removal and anticipated repeal of the Non: Imp: act. In that case, they will surely be prudent eno' not to encounter the risks without passports that will make them perfectly safe. Hull has raised the standard with some eclât on the Canada shore. He was preparing cannon & Mortars for the Attack on Malden. The Indians seem to be pretty generally in that quarter withdrawing from their allies.[3] At Niagara there is or will be a force which I hope will effectually co-operate with Hull. But what are we to do as to the main expedition towards Montreal, under the manoeuvering counteractions of Strong & Griswold, and the general chill diffused by federalism throughout the region from which the requisite force was to be drawn? I wish the zeal of the S. & W. could be imparted to that region. It overflows so much in Kent:y: & Tenns. &c. that if disaffection takes place, it will be from disgust & disappt. at not being called into active service. We all join in Affece. remembrance to Mrs. C & the little family. Yrs. sincerely

J. MADISON

RC (MHi); Tr (NjP: Crane Collection). RC docketed by Cutts.

1. Letter not found.

2. JM had been discussing with the British chargé d'affaires, Anthony St. John Baker, Foster's recently received instructions from Lord Castlereagh, dated 17 June 1812, announcing that the orders in council would be repealed as of 1 Aug. 1812 (see JM to Gallatin, 8 Aug. 1812). Castlereagh explained that the orders would resume on 1 May 1813 if the French government failed to modify its conduct and also that they would be restored two weeks after formal notification if the U.S. continued to exclude British ships of war from American ports and persisted in restricting British trade. The instructions specified that a formal notification of this policy would follow in a matter of days (Mayo, *Instructions to British Ministers*, 381–83).

3. After Hull's entry into Upper Canada, James Taylor wrote to Eustis from Sandwich on 14 July, informing him that "the american Eagle was hoisted on the bank of this province amid the acclimations [*sic*] of our Patriotic little army and the shouts of the Inhabitants of Detroit." Hull subsequently reported on 14 and 19 July that he was fortifying his position, obtaining control of the rivers, and preparing for an attack on Fort Malden. The Indians, he declared, had reacted to the invasion of Canada by returning to their villages, and a meeting with several nations in Brownstown would result in their neutrality. The Canadians, he continued, were receptive to his 13 July proclamation, which promised them protection and invited their help against the British. He concluded that disaffection at Fort Malden was so pronounced that "in a day or two, I expect the whole will desert" (*Michigan Historical Collections* 40 [1929]: 409–11, 412–15, 418–19).

To Albert Gallatin

DEAR SIR   WASHINGTON Aug. 8. 1812

The communications from the B. Govt. lately recd. thro' Baker are of a curious character. They promise that the O. in C. would cease on the 1st. Aug: with a right reserved to renew them in May next, in case the conduct of France and of the U. S. should require it; and particularly in case the Non-Imp: Act should not be repealed within 14 days after a notification of the actual repeal should be made to this Govt: The communication was so informal, that it was not only not in writing, but not permitted by Baker to be taken down in his presence by Mr. Graham. It is not improbable that the vessel was despatched, in consequence of the notice, from Foster by the May Packet[1] (referred to in his despaches lately found on board the Tulip)[2] that war would be declared, and in the hope that the expectation of a repeal of the orders thus authorized, would arrest the declaration. In the mean time they would have an oppy. of learning the issue in Congs. and might govern themselves by it. Baker professes however to expect another arrival immediately making a further & more particular communication on the subject, and that it will contain the act of repeal. He states also that the B. Authorities at Halifax with the sanction of Foster, are willing to fix a day in concert with this Govt. after which all captures at sea, are to be hung up in the Courts for the final decision of the two Govts: this arrangement to be accompanied by a suspension of military operations in Canada, which Foster has advised the Govr. there to propose to the adverse Commander. It may be inferred from the whole, that the British Cabinet is in some agitation, and that it is believed at Halifax that the road to peace cannot be made too short; whilst they are careful, to effect it by a bargain as safe & advantageous as possible. Perhaps it may be a ruse only to exhibit that side as anxious to stop hostilities, and throw on ours the foreseen rejection of the proposal.

The latest information from Hull is in the last Nat: Intellgr. He finds it necessary to prepare heavy cannon (24s.) and mortars in order to take Malden without a bloody storm. He allowed himself two weeks to make the preparation.[3] A re-inforcement is ordered to him from the Ohio.[4] He seems to have severed the Indians from their Allies, for the present. But without a conspicuous success in his Military progress, there is reason to apprehend an extensive combination agst the Frontiers of Ohio and all the neighboring Territories. Should he be able to descend upon Niagara, and an adequate co-operation be there afforded, our prospect as to upper Canada may be good eno'. But what is to be done with respect to the expedition agst. Montreal? The enlistments for the regular army fall short of the most moderate calculation. The volunteer act is extremely unproductive. And even the Militia detachments are either obstructed by the disaffected Governors, or chilled by the federal spirit diffused throughout the region most convenient to the Theatre. I see nothing better however than to draw on this resource as far as the detachments consist of volunteers who it may be presumed will cross the line without raising constitutional or legal questions. An experiment must if possible, be made for cutting off all British communications with the Indians. If this cannot be done by occupying Montreal, is it impossible to do it, by some other operation that will put the communication thro' the Utiwas under our controul? The Secy. of State is on a visit to his Farm. He will be back in the course of this week; when, ⟨I find?⟩, I must follow his example.[5] I am much worne down, and feel the approach of my bilious visitor on tide water. I have also some very pressing calls for my presence on my farm. Accept my affece. respects

JAMES MADISON

It is the wish of Baker that his communications may be regarded as confidential, till more definite and formal ones shall arrive.

If you have an oppy. obtain from J. Lewis[6] information leading to a use of the ports of Hayiti for our cruisers. Perhaps he wd. be a good missionary for that purpose.

RC (NHi: Gallatin Papers). Docketed by Gallatin.

1. Foster had warned in his 3 and 5 May 1812 letters to Castlereagh that a declaration of war was imminent (PRO: Foreign Office, ser. 5, 85:273–78, 296–99).

2. The British brig *Tulip* was captured while carrying one of Foster's messengers bearing dispatches to England. The vessel was ruled a lawful prize by the District Court of Pennsylvania on 11 Sept. 1812 (*Niles' Weekly Register* 3 [1812–13]: 60).

3. The 8 Aug. 1812 edition of the *National Intelligencer* reported that letters from Hull dated 21 and 22 July had been received. The first letter explained that a vote for neutrality concluded the Brownstown Indian council and that Col. Duncan McArthur had successfully repelled an attack by British and Indian forces. Hull's 22 July letter to Eustis, not summarized in the newspaper, mentioned a two-week delay in the attack on Fort Malden to allow for the building of wagons for large cannon (DNA: RG 107, LRRS, H-332:6).

4. On 22 June, James Winchester had been ordered to lead Ohio and Kentucky volunteers to reinforce Hull, but his troops did not depart until 20 Aug. (Adjutant General [Thomas Cushing] to Winchester, 26 July 1812 [DNA: RG 94, Letters Sent]; Winchester to Eustis, 19 Aug. 1812 [DNA: RG 107, LRRS, W-274:6]; Eustis to Return Jonathan Meigs, 26 July 1812 [DNA: RG 107, LSMA]).

5. JM did not begin his annual trip to Montpelier until 27 Aug. (Richard Rush to Charles Jared Ingersoll, 28 Aug. 1812, *The Letters and Papers of Richard Rush*, ed. Anthony M. Brescia [microfilm ed.; 29 reels; Wilmington, Del., 1980], reel 1). Dolley Madison noted that she and her husband had traveled as far as Dumfries, Virginia, before news of Hull's surrender reached them on the evening of 28 Aug., forcing a brief return to Washington (Dolley Madison to Edward Coles, 31 Aug. 1812 [owned by Charles E. Feinberg, Detroit, Mich., 1961]). JM set out for Montpelier a second time on 1 Sept. 1812, but he remained there for little more than a week before returning to Washington again on 14 Sept. (Brant, *Madison*, 6:73–74, 75, 85).

6. Jacob Lewis (1764–1824) was a Massachusetts-born merchant who had been engaged in trade with French colonies in the Caribbean and the Indian Ocean. In 1797 and 1802 he received consular appointments at Île de France and Calcutta, respectively, but never actually held either position. Thereafter he moved to New York, where he engaged in trade with Haiti as well as participating in the schemes of Samuel Ogden and Francisco de Miranda against Venezuela in 1806 (Kline, *Papers of Burr*, 2:810; *PJM-SS*, 2:40 n. 5; Rayford W. Logan, *The Diplomatic Relations of the United States with Haiti, 1776–1891* [Chapel Hill, N.C., 1941], 173, 180, 215 n.).

From Charles Hall

SIR   NEW YORK, August 8th: 1812

I have conversed with several passengers who arrived here last week in the Ship William direct from London, and who are not employed by the

English Government, consequently do not endeavour to make their miserable condition appear to be desirable.

These passengers represent the disaffection of the Natives of England to their Government as extreme, and the wretchedness and misery of the great body of the People as to surpass description. Percival's death seems to have been the signal for the People to express their sentiments, and among many reproaches to their Government they state the Orders of Council relative to America as one of the causes (and the principal one) of their wretchedness.

Under these circumstances Sir, I am not in the least surprised at their sending instructions to their Minister to *patch-up* an accommodation with the United States.[1] I would call your attention to the speeches in Parliament on occasion of an address being moved to the Regent relative to the Orders in Council. In the House of Com. Mr. Brougham's and Mr. Whitbread's speeches, and in short all the speeches on that occasion are worth attention. They state that, 'forbearing to exercise their right (as they term it) to capture Neutral Vessels does not give up the right, and that they can resort to it at any future period.'[2] These sentiments are expressed by men who are generally considered as friendly to America, and show the caution that ought to [be] taken in wording any arrangement with the English, so that they may not resort to their pretended rights *when their necessities are less urgent* than they are at present.

With respect to the Orders in Council of the English, one Nation cannot be bound by the Laws of another Nation unless the Government of that Nation agrees to it by Treaty. This Government has not agreed by Treaty to allow the English to capture American Vessels, consequently the English have no such right. The English Council *derives its authority from the English Parliament*, the English Parliament has no authority *but of a Municipal nature*, consequently cannot impart to another Body, authority which it does not itself possess.

It therefore clearly appears that the authority by which the English Privy Council take upon themselves to issue Edicts to affect the Persons and Property of American Citizens, is a self-created authority, not founded on right nor Justice.

I have given in, on Oath, my intention to become an American Citizen as soon as the Laws will allow it, and will be glad to be employed in the mean time in any way that I can be of service to the Government. I would be glad to write in one of the news Papers in this or any other City, in support of your Administration; they are in general very badly Edited. I wrote to Mr. Jefferson from Philadelphia but do not know if he recd. my letter.[3] This Sir, is a private letter to you, if you can get me employed I will thank you; please to let me know by your private Secretary and I will return him his letter. Please to direct under cover to Messrs. Kelso & Crump No. 55 South Street N. York. I have the Honour to be, Sir, Your very obedt. ser.

CHARLES HALL

RC (NN). Docketed by JM.

1. For Foster's instructions, see JM to Richard Cutts, 8 Aug. 1812, n. 2.
2. Henry Brougham used words to this effect in a 16 June 1812 speech calling for repeal of the orders in council (*Parliamentary Debates*, 23:511–13). Accounts of Brougham's motion for repeal and responding speeches, including Samuel Whitbread's, were printed in the *National Intelligencer* on 4 Aug. 1812. For more on Brougham's motion, see George Joy to JM, 19 June 1812, *PJM-PS*, 4:488 and n. 2.
3. Jefferson noted the 1 July receipt of a 25 June 1812 letter from Hall, which he marked as "enclosd to Pr. US." (Jefferson's Epistolary Record [DLC: Jefferson Papers]). The editors have been unable to locate the letter.

§ From the Chester Republican Cavalry. *8 August 1812, "Chester Ct. House, So Ca."* Have observed that the supplement to the Volunteer Act empowers the president to appoint and commission officers in the volunteer corps, "apparently contravening a certain clause of the first Act," which allowed militia companies already organized to retain their commanding officers in the volunteer service. "We were and still hold ourselves ready & willing to march at a moments warning, but if our officers are removed and succeeded by others whose confidence & disposition we Know little or Nothing of we can not nor do not Consider ourselves as volunteers without further arrangements respecting the service." Transmit the names of the forty-seven enrolled members of the corps of cavalry.

RC (DNA: RG 107, LRRS, M-380:6). 3 pp.; docketed as received in the War Department on 24 Aug. 1812.

§ From John Morris. *8 August 1812, Erie, Pennsylvania.* His volunteer company having been ordered by the governor into service in defense of the frontier bordering on Lake Erie, as was their sole object when they tendered their service to the president, "this company now consider the motive of the President as well as their own at an end in the accomplishment of its object; and through me beg leave to signify their wish to be discharged from their engagement to the President." Adds that the act supplementary to the Volunteer Act "Seems to present an additional consideration in favour of this application, from the probability that the Volunteers who have or may originate or renew their tender of Service So as to come under the provisions of this, will be preferred."

RC (DNA: RG 107, LRRS, M-375:6). 1 p.; docketed as received in the War Department on 21 Aug. 1812. A note on the cover in Eustis's hand reads: "The company may remain at Erie as originally proposed."

To Henry Dearborn

No. 60.

DEAR SIR   WASHINGTON Augst. 9. 1812

The last of your favors which I have to acknowlege is that of the 3d. Ult: from Boston.[1] I am glad to see that you are again at Albany; where your presence will aid much in doing all that can be done for the reputation of the campaign. The lapse of time & the unproductiveness of the laws, contemplating a regular force, and volunteers for an entire year, under federal commissions, compel us to moderate some of our expectations. It was much to have been desired that simultaneous invasions of Canada at several points, particularly in relation to Malden, and Montreal, might have secured the great object of bringing all Upper Canada, & the channels communicating with the Indians, under our Command; with ulterior prospects towards Quebec flattering to our arms. This systematic operation having been frustrated, it only remains to pursue the course that will diminish the disappt. as much as possible. Genl. Hull, as you will have learnt, is preparing a force for the attack of Malden: And that he may descend towards Niagara with greater effect, and be the more secure agst. Indian dangers, a reinforcement of 1500 men, is ordered; which will be promply [*sic*] supplied by the overflowing zeal of the detached Militia of Ohio & Kentucky. We hope that your arrangements with Govr. Tomkins[2] will have provided an effective cooperation for subduing the hostile force opposite ours at Niagara, and preparing the way for taking possession of the Country at the other extremity of L. Ontario.[3] In these events, we shall have in our hands, not only all the most valuable parts of the Upper Province: but the important command of the Lakes. It appears that Genl. Hull was making an effort to overpower the B. force on Lake Erie; his success in which will be critically useful in several respects.

In addition to these measures, it is essential, notwithstanding the advance of the Season, and the difficulties thrown in the way, that the expedition agst. Montreal should be forwarded by all the means in our power. The number of regulars that can be procured for it, cannot even yet be ascertained; but it is sufficiently ascertained that an extensive auxiliary force will be wanted; and it is nearly as certain that this will not be furnished by the volunteer Act of Feby. unless a sudden ardor overcoming the objections to it, should be inspired by the vicinity of the object, & the previous conquests. The last resource therefore on which we are to depend, is that portion of the detached & other Militia which may be within reach, will comply with the call; and voluntarily unite with their officers, in rejecting geographical limits to their patriotism. To this resource I hope you will turn your full attention, with a view to the immediate steps proper to be taken for making it supply the deficit of regulars & volunteers; with respect to the latter of which, as far as they are within a practicable distance, the number known here to be in readiness is very inconsiderable. From the Vermont & N. Hampshire Militia, favorable expectations are indulged, the State Authorities being well disposed to promote the service. As to Massachts. & Connecticut even, notwithstanding the obstructions created by the Govrs. it is not yet decided that the spirit of some of the detached or other Corps, may not give effect to your requisitions. Should an adequate force be attainable from the whole or part of the sources referred to, you will be the best judge how far a demonstration towards Quebec may be proper in aid of the measures agst. Montreal; which if we can take by means of any sort, we shall find the means of holding. Should it be found impracticable to take it, this campaign; will it be possible to occupy any other spot that will cutt off the intercourse with the Indians through the Utiwas river?

You will have noticed the arrival of a dispach vessel from the B. Govt. Nothing is disclosed from that quarter that ought in the slightest degree, to slacken our military exertions.

The Secy. of State is on a visit to his Farm where he will leave his family. On his return, which will take place in a few days, I propose a like respite. I find myself much worne down, and in need of an antidote to the accumulating bile of which I am sensible, & which I have never escaped in Augst. on tide water. Accept Dr Sir my respects & best regards

JAMES MADISON

We are aware of the scantiness with which you can be supplied with Genl. Officers, as well as of the disadvantages produced by the tardiness of Congs. in providing for the Staff establishments. The evil has been increased by the successive refusals of those appointed to the Commissareate. Carswell, last appointed Commissary Genl. has followed the example, or rather has resigned on acct. of ill-health, after being prevailed on to accept. The office has just been offered to Callender Irvine, whose determination is not yet known. Those are difficulties in which we all sympathize with you; and which we must all cooperate in overcoming.

RC (MeHi); draft (DLC); Tr (MeHi). RC docketed as received 15 Aug. 1812.

1. *PJM-PS*, 4:543–44.

2. Daniel D. Tompkins (1774–1825) had been a New York state representative from 1803 to 1804 and a state supreme court justice from 1805 to 1807. He resigned from the court when he was elected governor of New York, an office he filled as an ally of the Madison administration until 1817. He served as James Monroe's vice president from 1817 to 1825 (Sobel and Raimo, *Biographical Directory of the Governors*, 3:1072).

3. After his arrival in Albany at the end of July, Dearborn wrote to Eustis on 7 Aug. 1812 that he had been "making Arrangements with Governor Tompkins for having Reinforcements Sent to Niagara Ogdensburg & Plattsburg." He mentioned that Tompkins readily complied with his requests for militia and had reassured him that the militia would "cheerfully Consent to cross the Boundary" into Canada (NHi: Dearborn Letterbooks).

From John Montgomery

SIR   BALTIMORE 9th August 1812.

I presume you have seen the Statement with the Documents subjoined, Made under a resolve of the City Council of Baltimore, published in the American of yesterday,[1] this gives the origin progress & extent of the late disturbances in this Place.

With regard to the Alarm for the safety of the Post Office here, the Very general Military Assemblage of all ranks for its protection, & the general sentiment expressed that it should not be Violated Affords evidence either that there was not any Very strong grounds for the Alarm, or if Any Attack was ever Meditated, it Must have been confined to a Very few. Should however any Violence be offered to this establishment, I am satisfied, it would be instantly put down by a Very large proportion of the people of Baltimore, who speak in terms of the greatest indignation against such an Outrage, perhaps an attempt, even the slightest, would be gratifying, to a certain political description of Men, as promoting, in their View, particular Objects to them desireable, but I decidedly think & trust, they will be disapointed.

Having information that a correspondence from this place is kept up with Washington between characters, who May Misrepresent, exaggerate, & Mislead, I have thought proper to communicate the above, that if Apprehensions Are entertained for the safety of the Post office, they May in some degree be Allayed. With the highest consideration your obt. Servt.

J MONTGOMERY.[2]

RC (DLC). Docketed by JM.

1. Montgomery referred to a committee report submitted to the city council on 6 Aug. 1812 and reprinted in the Baltimore *American and Commercial Daily Advertiser* on 8 Aug. that described the recent Baltimore riots.

2. John Montgomery (1764–1828) was elected as a Republican to the Tenth, Eleventh, and Twelfth Congresses but resigned his seat on 29 Apr. 1811. He served as attorney general of Maryland from 1811 to 1818 and participated in the Battle of North Point in 1814 as the captain of an artillery company. He was mayor of Baltimore from 1820 to 1822 and from 1824 to 1826 (Melvin G. Holli and Peter d'A. Jones, eds., *Biographical Dictionary of American Mayors, 1820–1980: Big City Mayors* [Westport, Conn., 1981], 258–59).

§ From Matthew Walton. *9 August 1812, Prince Edward.* "Some time ago a Vacancy was occationed in upper Louis[i]ana by the Death of Judge Shraider, Shortly after Several Recommendations was sent on Recommending Mr. Richard Cocke of Washington County Kentucky,[1] & as yet have Received no answer." Supposes that the appointment has been overlooked in "the great press of war Business." Assures JM that Cocke's appointment would "do honour to the Goverment." "This man has practised law in Virginia Some years with Honour & Success he is a firm & bold Republican."

RC (DNA: RG 59, LAR, 1809–17, filed under "Cocke"). 2 pp.

1. See Cocke to JM, 19 Dec. 1811, *PJM-PS*, 4:78 and n. 2.

From Thomas Jefferson

Dear Sir   Monticello Aug. 10. 12.

The death of my much valued friend & relation George Jefferson will doubtless produce many competitors for the office of Consul at Lisbon. Among these a neighbor of mine, mr David Higginbotham[1] wishes to be considered. He is a merchant of Milton, of very fair character, steady application to business, sound in his circumstances, and perfectly correct in all his conduct. He is a native of this part of the country, brought up to mercantile business, of a temper and manners entirely conciliatory and obliging, and would, I am persuaded execute the duties of the office with all the diligence and zeal in his power. Should no person of better qualifications be proposed his appointment would gratify his many friends here as well as, Dear Sir Your affectionate friend & servt.

Th: Jefferson

[Enclosure]

Dear Sir   Monticello Aug. 10. 12.

The letter within which this is inclosed contains the truth: there is not a word in it that is not so, but while the sollicitations of a friend have obliged me to present his case, duty to yourself & the public oblige me to say it does not contain the whole truth. One single circumstance is to be added. This candidate for the office of Consul at Lisbon, who often has to transact diplomatic business with that government, as we have no minister there, is not qualified by education or understanding for the duties of the office. He is uninformed & unlettered, & so much so as to be entirely insensible of it himself. His understanding is equal to the business he is in, but not to that which would be incumbent on him at that post. His letter now inclosed[2] is a specimen by which you can judge, which after perusal be so good as to return under cover to me, without taking the trouble of saying a word on the subject. My outer letter will probably go on your files; I have written this separately that it may not do so, but remain among your private papers, unwilling to make a public record of it in the case of so good a man.

Constant rains are detracting from the produce of our harvest, by rendering it impossible to thresh, and in the mean time injuring the grain in the stacks. Ever affectionately yours

Th: Jefferson

RC (DNA: RG 59, LAR, 1809–17, filed under "Higginbotham"); enclosure (DLC); FC and FC of enclosure (DLC: Jefferson Papers).

1. David Higginbotham (1775–1853) was a merchant in Charlottesville and Milton. Beginning in 1798, Jefferson traded with and borrowed money from Higginbotham extensively (William Montgomery Sweeny, "Higginbotham Family of Virginia," *WMQ*, 1st ser., 27 [1918–19]: 124).

2. Enclosure not found, but it was probably one of two letters Jefferson had received from Higginbotham, dated 26 and 27 June 1812 (Jefferson's Epistolary Record [DLC: Jefferson Papers]). JM returned the enclosure in his 17 Aug. letter to Jefferson. JM also received a letter from Higginbotham, dated 12 Aug. 1812, offering his services in the Lisbon consulate (DNA: RG 59, LAR, 1809–17, filed under "Higginbotham").

From William Woods

STATE OF TENNESSEE GILES COUNTY

[ca. 10 August 1812]

DEAR SIR

Since the commencement of the last Session of Congress I have with unremitted attention noticed the procedings of the same so fare as in my power lay, and it has been with pleasure I have markd there procedings from step to step, I do confess that it is my opinion that the members of Congress have felt the weight of there high responcibility while Transacting buisness for the Goverment which has been of so much inportance Laterly, and I do think the it dose become every individual whose interest is at stake and that have any desire to secure peace and happyness to the goverment and preserve the life or lives of those that are nere and dear to them to make use of all the means put in there power to obtain the same, and for my part I do not see any surer way to do this than ⟨t⟩o cause a proper unison to take place with the different ⟨m⟩embers constituting a govrment and as there is no other medium through which we can have a union of communication than this I do humbly Conceive it my duty as one who is dependant on the goverment to use my best endevours to promote the intrest of the same and I would wish to do that which would bee advantegious to my fellow citizans at all times but more espacially when Extream circumstances and kneacessity Calls for it and yet have it not in my power under the impression that it is better perhaps to sustain considerable loss than to Violate the ruls of Goverment when I do conceive them to be so holy and pure, yet I see that there is a number of that body which is set a part to dictatee for the people at largee is not Void of thee same feelings of my self I discover that there is considerable complaint with them respecting the impressment of our see men which I must acknowledg is perfectly right and in addition to this there is great burdens to be born from Robery on the high seas that path which the god of nature in my opinion have garrented to all Nations Equally alike and this is a burden to intolarable to be born, but sir we who are planted at so remote a Distance from those procedings cannot nor do not feel the weight of them like those who are more immedately under there influence, But be asured of this truth we have more grevious burdens to be borne than this when we could extricate ourselves from them just at a nod or wink from the govrment, which do cause great complaint in all those back cuntries if we may call them so to think of mem [*sic*] being taken and put a bord of a Vessel and there compeld to fight a gainst there cuntrymen contrary to there will I must [*sic*] is Enough to rouse to action the powers that can prevent it if any there bee yet I do confess that my fealings could sleep under those circumstances with more propriety than not to ⟨bee?⟩ [*illegible*] with all the powers of action under circumstances that do occur with us and that frequently when we see the Indians come in to our houses there to tomhack our wives and Children Stab and Scelp the same because we ar absent on some buisness or other a few hours, some they will bear a way with them and you cannot be ignorant how they are treated by those Savage hell howns and yet they will keep suing for peace and promise to punish the offenders, why sir it is Enough to Chill the blod of any man to have a relation of a Circumstance that took place a mong us not long since by some of the Creeks and yet they are neglected as agressors, and I am sure if anything in this wourld would prejudice me a gainst goverment it would be n[e]glecting to punish those who dare to act in this maner and all those concernd, for not less than Eleven of those savages by force went in to a house where two weaman and some children was one who had a few day previous to that past through the pangs of labour and yet in bead with the babe of innocence in her arms and in this situation was mad the first object of there Victom then the rest of the children, and if inocence that have never been Capable of evil must be treated thus God forbid the progress of the Embrio in the Womb whilst the mother must View her ofspring with agony treated thus, and then bee compeld to trace the steps of a heathen in flight through a rough rockey mountaineous wilderness to the native cuntry of those that have her in possession there to bear the treatment that would cause the tear to flow to here a relation of thee same which has been the case with us lately, and sir I would ask you if this had taken place with those who you are most closely connected with if you suppose that we could have heard the screams of the weoman and Children from the City of Washington to Giles no we could not but I will Venture to say if setch should occur with you that your Vengance against the perpetrators and there adherants while one of them was in existance was not the life of Belingham as dear to him as that of Percival Was to him the answer is obvious to every man who knows a wagon from a Cart yes sir and when the arms of a Tender wife pillows the head of faithfull husband when she wipes from his brow the duw of Desolveing nature I wonder if it would not almost cause infinite Venganc to k⟨ind⟩le against those that dare to harme Sir a proof of this is To me is [. . .]t when goverment calls on men from this section of the cuntry the [. . .] that we cannot nor we will not goo from home till setch times as our wives and Children is mad safe from the hands of those our enemies the Creek indians if the[y] do not as a nation come against us we do know that as parties the[y] steal and murder and make prisoners and then the people say the next news is a lenthy whurang we have in the news papers a bout setch amicable ajustments as has taken place betwen the war department and the agent of that nation which they are tired of and have been long since and in fact we do sufer to much from this way of doing buisness and I do beleve that the peoples minds are more dissatisfyed with goverment in this way than any other and the reason is because the[y] realy do feel the dyer affects of it with centiments of a steem I would subscribe my self your loyal subject & &c &c

WILLIAM WOODS 2nd Majr. of
the 37 Regement of this State

P.S Sir I would humbly thank you for your centiments on this subject by a letter and will feel my self undr obligations

WMWOODS

RC (DNA: RG 107, LRRS, W-277:6). Undated; date assigned here on the basis of the cover, which is addressed from "Polaski T / 10 Augt." Docketed as received in the War Department on 1 Sept. 1812; damaged by removal of seal. A note on the cover in a clerk's hand reads: "appears much enraged that an attack has not been made on the Creek nation."

§ From the Inhabitants of Templeton, Massachusetts. *10 August 1812.* "The Memorial and Remonstrance of the Town of Templeton in the County of Worcester and Commonwealth of Massachusetts . . . Humbly shews—

"That we have seen, with the most painful anxiety and regret, the Declaration of War by Congress against Great Britain. We profess the most firm and unshaken attachment to our Common Country, and to that Constitution and Republican form of Government, under which, if duly and impartially administer'd, we might enjoy all the blessings of rational Liberty—and we are ready at all times to defend the same, against every hostile attempt of Foreign or Domestic Foes, at the expence of our lives, our fortunes, and every thing we hold dear. But, Sir, in the present awful and alarming state of our Country, we hold it to be no less our Constitutional right, than our sacred duty to ourselves and posterity, to enquire into the causes of a Declaration, which threatens to bring innumerable evils and calamities upon every class of our Citizens; and involve us all in a contest, the issue of which no human foresight can divine, or power controul—but which, we seriously fear, may endanger, if not destroy, that invaluable inheritance, which descended to us from our Fathers, and which they purchased for us at the expence of so much blood and treasure. We consider in a Republican Government as ours *now* is, that those who administer it, are servants of the People, from whom all their authority is derived, for whose use it was entrusted to them, and to whom they are at all times accountable, for the use or abuse of that trust—and the only way to prevent such a Government, in process of time, from becoming a Despotism, is to encourage the diffusion of knowledge among the people, a watchful jealousy of their Rulers, and a free, candid and impartial examination of all their official conduct—and this is the more especially necessary in times like these, when such Rulers have seen fit to veil so much of their doings in secret and nocturnal Sessions. And it is the inalienable right of every Citizen, and more especially of Towns and Cities in their corporate capacity (notwithstanding the opinions of unprincipled Demagogues to the contrary) freely to express or publish their sentiments, and proper and respectful languague, of the wisdom or folly of the measures of Government—to the end that the people may be inform'd of their danger before it is too late, and thereby be enabled, in the exercise of their Constitutional franchise, to rescue their endanger'd Government from the hands of a set of men who have abused their ill-plac'd confidence, and intrust it with those, who both understand and respect their rights. War is an evil of such fearful magnitude, that no Nation having a due regard to the Laws of God or happiness of Men, will ever resort to it, but in the last extremity. Offensive war we hold to be unjust in every case. And no wise Nation will ever appeal to arms, even in self defence, whilst there remains any probability of obtaining redress for the wrongs they suffer, by impartial and honest negotiation. In examining the causes of war against Great Britain, as submitted to the world in a late Manifesto by the Executive of the United States,[1] we are unable to discover anything, upon which we believe the Administration themselves lay any serious stress, except the Blockade of May 16th. 1806—the Orders in Council, and the Impressment of American Seamen—as to the Agency of John Henry in an attempt to effect a disunion of the States, and the instigation of our Savage neighbours to commence hostilities upon our Western frontier, we are unable to perceive the slightest evidence that either of them are justly chargeable upon the British Government—and the very mention of them in so formal a manner by the Executive is proof to us of the want of more serious causes of complaint. And moreover as both have been formally disavow'd by Mr. Foster, the late British Minister, we think that the common courtecy, which one civilised Nation owes to another, and without which it is impossible to preserve a friendly intercourse, demands that we give credit to his assurance made in behalf of his Government. As to the Blockade of May 1806, we confess our astonishment, at this late day, to find it *conjurd* up into a cause of war—for nothing can be more clear than the fact, that our Government view'd it in a very different light, at the time of its promulgation, as fully and undeniably appears from the correspondence between the two Governments at the time, and betwixt our Minister, then in London, and our own Goverment. Mr. Munroe, our Minister, then at the British Court, in a letter address'd to Mr. Madison, then Secretary of State, dated May 19. 1806, observes, speaking of this Blockade, that it 'must be view'd in a favourable light'[2]—and again in another letter, written soon afterwards, he says, 'he was strengthen'd in the opinion, that the order of the 16th. was drawn with a view to the question of our trade with Enemies colonies, and that it promises to be highly satisfactory to our commercial interest.'[3] How comes it to pass then, permit us to ask, that this Blockade should be considerd in so favourable a point of view at this *early* period; and moreover so *late* as the time of the arrangement with Mr. Erskine

was not even consider'd a cause of complaint, when now, six years after its first existence, it should all at once become a cause of war? There is no dispute at all betwixt this Country and England as to the true and lawful principles of Blockade—
both admit the necessity of the special application of a competent naval force—or
at least they have both agreed in this so far as their opinions have come to our
knowledge—and we believe it to have become, by general consent, the Law of Nations. We know very well, that the doctrine, which the Emperor of France has endeavour'd to impose upon the world, (on account of his own weakness and imbecility at sea) is very different—and we lament to find such a cordial disposition in
the Government of our own Country, to co-operate with him in his ambitious and
Tyranical views. He would fain conquer all the naval forces of Europe by paper
Blockades and empty threats—thereby vainly hoping to impose upon the world by
the terror of his name the principles, which, he says, have become the Law of Nations by being found in the Treaty of Utrecht—a part of which is that no Blockade
is justifiable, unless the place be invested by Land as well as Sea nor even then, unless the place, so blockaded, be a fortified City. But it is perfectly evident to every
unprejudiced mind, that these principles are no less absurd than new—for the
practice of all civilised Nations, when at war, has been different for Centuries. And
shall we endanger our very existence as a Nation in order to assist France in the establishment of her novel and extravagant doctrines, which she never would have
thought of but for his mortal enmity to that country, which alone stands betwixt her
and Universal Dominion? Must the United States be driven into a war contrary to
the wishes and interest of a vast majority of the Inhabitants—wherein defeat is
more than probable, and nothing to be expected from success but the probable loss
of their liberties, and the priviledge of being added to the number of the slaves and
vassals of the Tyrant of France? What secret charm has French friendship and alliance, that so infatuates our Councils, and seems to lead us with irresistable force
to unite our destinies with those of France? Are the manners and Customs of
Frenchmen, their Religion, Laws, and form of Government so congenial with our
own, that we should wish to throw our weight into the scale with her in an attempt
to overthrow the power of that Country which gave birth to our Forefathers, and
where they inhaled with their breath those principles of Freedom and abhorence of
Tyranny, which, being transmitted to their children, at length gave Independence
to this, their now flourishing and happy Country?

"With regard to the Orders in Council, we feel no disposition to justify them
upon the principles of retaliation, assumed by the British Government—still we
are of opinion, that no principle of sound policy in the present state of the world,
and more particularly of our own Country, would warrant or justify a resort to war
nor are we at all convinced, that every reasonable concession on the part of great
Britain could not be obtained by fair and impartial negotiation—for surely that
Country is not in a situation to multiply her Enemies unnecessarily. At war already
with most of Europe, and contending for her own existence, and as we humbly conceive, for the rights of mankind, against the most powerful Despot, that ever dis-
grac'd a Throne, it is our most serious and solemn conviction, that it is her sincere
desire, to conciliate America by every reasonable concession, consistent with her
own salvation as a Nation; and that it is her most ardent wish, as it is manifestly for
her interest, to seale with us a permanent and durable peace—provided she could

be met by us 'in the spirit of peace.' Had the United States, agreeably to the Neutral character, which she had assumed, and let it be added, agreeable to justice and that respect, which she ow'd to herself, resisted, in a determin'd manner, the scandalous and outrageous principle contained in the Berlin Decree, we might, from that period until now have enjoy'd an uninterupted peace with England. This Decree, as is apparent to us, was the first trespass upon our Neutral rights—and directly too, in violation of a solemn Treaty, then in force betwixt this Country and France. And altho', perhaps, it may be said, that the injuries and insults, offer'd us by France, are no justification for those of England, yet it ill-becomes us, (all the while pretending to be Neutral) after having submitted to every dishonour from the 'Great Emperor' without resistence, or even the language of complaint, now to be so 'tenderly alive' to the wrongs of another power, when they are not only far more recent in point of time, but bare no more proportion in amount to the indignities, heaped upon us by France, than a mole-hill to a mountain. Why is it, we would ask that for years past, the American people have been permitted to know so little, *officially*, of our diplomatic intercourse with France while that with England has been publish'd at large? Why has every insult and abuse, which we have received so bountifully from our 'Loving Emperor,' been polluted or conceal'd, whilst the invasions of our rights by the British have been agravated and blazon'd from pole to pole? If it were necessary for us to resort to war to wipe off the stain from our injur'd honour, why not select that Enemy, who has done most to tarnish it? If a war were call'd for to protect Commerce, why select that power for an enemy, who alone could destroy the little remnant that remain'd to us? Who has forgot that this same Emperor, 'who loves the Americans,'[4] has undertaken to declare war for us—that he has declar'd us 'men without just political views, without honour and without energy'?[5] Who is ignorant of his baseness and hypocricy in pretending to revoke his Decrees, when his whole object was to deceive us by a *sham* revocation, in order to draw us into a war with England—well-knowing, had they been *in fact* revoked, that the British Orders in Council would have been at an end also, and thereby the principle cause of war with that power remov'd. Who is ignorant, that our vessels without number have been burnt on the Ocean, our Citizens robb'd and taken captive, and their property, to an immense amount, been condemn'd by virtue of these very Decrees ever since their pretended repeal? And who, even now, can doubt, that their revocation at last, is purchased at no less a price than a Declaration of war by us against Great Britain?

"The remaining cause of war to be consider'd, is the Impressment of American Seamen. This is a subject, which has fill'd the Newspapers for a long time, and has been agravated and misrepresented with all the bitterness and violence of which party spirit is capable—were it indeed true, to the extent, that some have pretended, it would be a sufficient cause of war—and would, as it ought to, rouse the whole continent to arms. But this is not the case. It is perfectly well known to every man who has given the subject the least attention, that Great Britain makes no pretention to the right of search, except in Merchant vessels, and then only to find her own deserters. And what Nation is there that does not claim the same right? Whilst Great Britain claims it herself, she is willing to allow us the same priviledge. There is no difficulty attending the subject, other than what has existed for many years—the same complaint, which is now made under the administration of Mr. Madison, was made by all his Predecessors—yet none of them thought it a case to be remedied by war. We know, and have no hesitation in admitting, that in the exercise of this right, claim'd by the British, many and flagrant abuses are practised by some of her petty officers in the Navy—but we know also, that the evil is much less than has been represented—and that from the circumstance of the same language being common to both, some injuries may have been sustain'd, when none were intended. Add to this the great number of American Seamen who have voluntarily enlisted aboard the British Navy, *for want of employment at home,* and the frauds and deceptions, attempted to be practised, and too often with success, by British Runaways, who have afterwards procured false protections, and the subject of Impressment will be strip'd of many of the seeming evils, which party spirit has endeavour'd to attach to it. And moreover the British Government have ever profess'd a readiness to unite with us in concerting the best possible system of measures of which the subject is capable, to remove the evils attending it. And we have the strongest assurance, that no instance can be adduced of an American Seaman's being detain'd by the British, when after proper application, it has been prov'd he was an American. England has made repeated proposals to America on this subject—and such as we believe it would have been for the interest of America to have accepted—for Mr. Munroe, in a letter to Mr. Madison dated Feby. 28. 1808[6] expressly says, speaking of these offers, that 'they were both honourable and advantageous to the United States.' As for the *French* doctrine, that the flag covers and protects every thing sailing under it, we believe the contrary is admitted by every Nation in Europe, France excepted—and her *practise* is as oposite as her professions and practises usually are. But it is unnecessary to multiply words upon this, or either of the foregoing subjects, after the able and lucid exposition of them, lately exhibited to the world by a Minority in Congress, and address'd to the people of the United States.[7] And we are happy in this opportunity of expressing our most cordial approbation of this & their other exertions to rescue their Country from the horrors of an impending war. From the best and most impartial view of the whole subject, we have been able to take, we have no hesitation in declaring it as our solemn conviction that the war, recently declared by Congress against Great Britain, is *unnecessary* and *impolitic,* if not unjust—unnecessary, because we believe our rights can be more permanently and effectually secured by negotiation than war—Impolitic, because the finances of the Country are in no situation to support it—and more especially, because it will have a direct tendency to produce (if it has not already) an alliance with France—for as much as we deprecate a war with England, we seriously consider it, with all its calamities, as a mercy from heaven, compar'd with such an alliance—for what Country in Europe, having allied herself to that, has not been despoil'd of her Independence, and her surviving Inhabitants become slaves to their Conquerer? Their names alone remain to shew they were once Independent States. Wherefore we humbly pray, and would fain indulge the hope, that immediate measures may be taken to restore to our distracted Country its former peace, prosperity & happiness.

"At a Legal meeting of the Male Inhabitants of the Town of Templeton legally convened in Town Meeting on Monday the tenth day August 1812 upon a motion to accept the within Memorial & Remonstrance, and forward the same to the

President of the United States—eighty six in the affirmative & twenty two in the negative."

RC (DNA: RG 59, ML). 12 pp.; signed by Adam Jones, moderator, and Moses Wright, town clerk.

1. The memorialists referred to JM's 1 June 1812 message to Congress (*PJM-PS*, 4:432–38).
2. Monroe to JM, 17 May 1806, *ASP, Foreign Relations*, 3:124–25.
3. Monroe to JM, 20 May 1806, ibid., 3:125–26.
4. Duc de Cadore to Armstrong, 5 Aug. 1810, ibid., 3:386–87.
5. Duc de Cadore to Armstrong, 14 Feb. 1810, ibid., 3:380–81.
6. Ibid., 3:173–83.
7. For the address of the Federalists in Congress, see *PJM-PS*, 4:496 n. 2.

§ From John Mason. *10 August 1812, Indian Office.* Recommends assistant agent Robert P. Bayly[1] for the office of Indian agent at the trading house on Chickasaw Bluffs, left vacant by the death of John B. Treat. Recommends William M. Stewart[2] as assistant agent at Fort Madison, to fill the vacancy left by the resignation of Asa Payne.

RC (DLC); letterbook copy (DNA: RG 75, Letters Sent by the Superintendent of Indian Trade). RC 2 pp.; in a clerk's hand, signed by Mason; docketed by JM.

1. Bayly was appointed the same day (Mason to Bayly, 10 Aug. 1812 [ibid.]).
2. Stewart was appointed the same day but declined the position (see Mason to JM, 27 Aug. 1812).

To Joel Barlow

Dear Sir   Washington Aug. 11. 1812

As I write on short notice and in cypher, I must be very brief.

The conduct of the F. Govt. explained in yours of May. 12.[1] on the subject of the *decre⟨e⟩ of April ⟨18⟩11 will be an everlasting reproach to it.* It is the *more shameful* as, *departing from* the *declar⟨a⟩tion to general armstrong*[2] of which the *enforcement of the non importation was the effect* the *revoking decre⟨e⟩ assumes* this as the *cause and itself as the effect* and thus *transfersa* [sic] *to this government the inconsistency of its author.*[3]

The *decre⟨e⟩ of April* may nevertheless be *used by Great Britain as A pretexte for revoking* ⟨her⟩ *orders;* not *withstanding the* contrary *language of castelreagh in parlement.*[4] An *authentic tho informal communication* has *just arrived in a dispatch ship from England importing* that the *orders* were to be *revoked on the first of August;* subject to *renewal if* required *by the conduct of France and the U. States;* particularly if the *non importation should not be forthwith re-⟨s⟩cinded* on *the arrival of the act of revocation.* As this *pledge* was given before the *declaration of war was known* it may *not be adher⟨e⟩d to.* It is not *improba-*

ble however that it was hurried off as a *chance for* preventing an *apprehended war;* and that the same *dislike to the war* may possibly produce *advances for terminating it which if the terms be admissable will be immediately*[5] embraced.

In the event of a *pacification with G. B. the full tide of indignation* with which the public *mind here is boiling will* be *directed against France* if not *obviated by a due* ⟨reparation of⟩[6] *her wrongs. War will be* called for by the *nation* almost *una voce.* Even without a *peace with England* the further *refusal* and[7] *prevarications of France* on the subject of *red⟨ress⟩*[8] *may be* expected to *produce measures* of *hostility* at the *ensuing session of ⟨Congs.⟩*[9] This result is the more probable as the general *exasperation will* coincide with the *calculation of not a few* that a *double war is the shortest road to peace.*[10]

I have been the more disposed to furnish you with these *prospects* that you may *turn them to account if possible* in *your discussions with the French government* and be not *unprepared to retire* from *them altogether on a sudden notice so to do.* Your *return home* ⟨may⟩ possibly be *directed even before the meeting of Congress if the intermediate* information should *Continue to present the French conduct* in the *provoking light* in which it *has hitherto appeared.*

The Secretary of State is absent; but you will receive from Mr. Graham the usual supply of current intelligence, to which I refer you. I have not time to write to Genl. F.[11] With my best regards to him, tell ⟨him that⟩ Congs. rose without deciding as to the validity of the remaining locations near Pointe Coupee. Affecte respects

JAMES MADISON

RC (DLC); draft (DLC). Italicized words are those encoded by JM and decoded interlinearly by a clerk; key not found. Missing words and letters are supplied within angle brackets from the draft.

1. *PJM-PS,* 4:379.
2. For the letter from the duc de Cadore about the revocation of the Berlin and Milan Decrees, see Armstrong to JM, 5 Aug. 1810, ibid., 2:460–62, 463 n. 1.
3. For the spurious Decree of St. Cloud on 28 Apr. 1811 repealing the Berlin and Milan Decrees, see Barlow to JM, 12 May 1812, ibid., 4:379 and nn. 2 and 3.
4. On 22 May 1812 Lord Castlereagh gave a speech declaring the 28 Apr. 1811 decree "disgraceful to the government of any civilized nation." He pointed out that the decree did not meet the terms of the prince regent's order in council of 21 Apr. 1812 because it repealed the Berlin and Milan Decrees only with regard to the U.S. while leaving them in force against other nations, thereby making "no manner of alteration in the question of the Orders in Council" (*Parliamentary Debates,* 23:287–88).
5. Draft has "readily."
6. Interlinear decoding has "dru."
7. Draft has "or."
8. Interlinear decoding has "red exams."
9. Interlinear decoding has "em."
10. These sentiments about the possibility of war with France, along with a discussion of the peace terms required from Great Britain, appeared in a 4 Aug. 1812 *National Intelligencer* editorial that Irving Brant has attributed to JM (see Brant, *Madison,* 6:59–61, and Brant, "Joel

Barlow, Madison's Stubborn Minister," *WMQ*, 3d ser., 15 [1958]: 445–46). The basis for this claim was Jean-Baptiste Petry's remark to the duc de Bassano on 26 Aug. 1812 that the editorial had been written "by Mr. Madison himself" and that "He has avowed it in a private letter which he wrote to Mr. Barlow on August 11." While there is little reason to doubt that the 4 Aug. editorial reflected the president's thinking, and while it is by no means impossible that he had a hand in its publication, the contents of JM's 11 Aug. letter to Barlow are hardly sufficient to support Brant's contention. Brant assumed that JM was the author of the editorial because the secretary of state was absent from Washington at the time of its appearance, but there are other candidates for its authorship, including Richard Rush, the clerks in the State Department, and Joseph Gales and William Seaton of the *National Intelligencer* itself. Any one of these could have written the editorial, possibly after a conversation with JM to the effect that the appearance of such views would suit the purposes of the administration.

    11. Draft has "Fayette" (Lafayette).

From Orchard Cook

MAY IT PLEASE YOUR EXCELLY.   WISCASSET August 11th. 1812

    The Merchants of this Place—who were Republicans lately forwarded to your Excely an address—requesting a cessation of Arms &c.[1] This was done in haste, immediately on the reception, at this Port, of the revocation of the Orders in Council. I wish to assure Your Excellency, that it would be the last of our Wishes that any of the Rights or Honour of the U. S should be sacrificed to G. B. for the sake of a premature Peace. Had Congress seen fit to have increased the Navy to a respectable State, The Adminisn. would be more popular here than ever. A respectable Navy would be the great Peace Maker between the S. & W States & the N & Eastern States. I hope & I trust that this Peace offering will be withheld no longer than the next Session of Congress. With profound respect I am your ever devoted & hum. Servt.

                                        ORCHARD COOK

RC (DLC).

    1. Letter not found.

From William Willis

RESPECTED SIR   WESTMINSTER VERMONT August 11th 1812

    I have had considerable oppertunities since the declaration of the present war, of finding the sentiments of the people respecting that measure; both on the Atlantic, and in the interior. And if some fortunate event dous [*sic*] not present itself soon to reconcile the Citizens of these States to the war, the ensuing elections will be much affected, And I fear that if many disastrous circumstances occur, that the Minds of the people will too generally not only become exasperated against the advisers of the resort to war, but become disaffected to the Union, which must be one of the most alarming circumstances, that can present itself to those, who have looked on the Union as the rock of our safety.

You perhaps Sir know enough of the formation of my mind, to know, that I have never been so much an Idolater of any of our administrations, as not to think I saw errors in them. Even in that of Washington I saw somthing that I could not approve of and in all I have seen somthing to approve. I am not one of those who see in every error a corruption of the heart. Surrounded as you Sir, and all our Presidents have been, by men, some of whom no doubt have been influenced by private & personal interests, or influenced themselves by others who had private or personal interests to promote. Placed in this situation it would require supernatural powers and faculties to avoid error in all transactions.

I have been a particular observer of events since my arrival from Europe, and with regret I must say that there has at all times been but little of that Patriotism realizd which has been promisd. This state appear'd to wish for war more than either of the other no[r]thern states. It appear'd by some public resolutions that the inhabitants only wished for an oppertunity to invade Canady, that permission was all they wanted. But now permiss[i]on is given them I do not suppose that two thousand in the whole state and perhaps not one thousand can be found ready to realize the encour[a]gement they had given. How can the expected result of a measure be realizd when those who call the loudest for it thus deceive their administrators of Government? They and not the administration are responsible for the disasters, should any serious ones attend the War.

The change of political sentiment has been more conspicuous on the atlantic than in the interior, which will continue to be the case untill the tax bills are presented to the people of the interior. There seems to have been but little change yet in the Local situation where I now am. But I am inform'd that there is more in the west part of the state. The friends of the present Administration in this quarter are however very Sanguine that they shall succeed in the choice of their Candidate for the Federal Legislature. And it is my opinion also that they will succeed especially if nothing disastrous should occur to change the political Sentiment. They have I believe fix'd upon Wm R Bradley Esqr.[1] who is a very popular man with the Democratic party.

Altho party feelings run high in this quarter, and warm express⟨ions⟩ appear in News papers Yet their does not appear to be any danger that the public peace will be invaded. And if An invasion by the Enemy should take place party distinctions would be forgotten, and all would unite to repel it. Altho there is such a reluctance discovered to turn out to invade Canady.

I shall leave this place in a few days for New Hampshire & Boston and shall as a friend of my Country use all my inf[l]uence to discourage any disaffection to the Union, and safety, of the United States whether I approve or disapprove of the acts of Administration. And whether those acts have a temporary effect to check the activity and prosperity of myself & fellow Citizens or not; I shall not be dispos'd to accuse the Authors, of being actuated by improper motives. I am Sir very Respectfully Your Hble Servt

WILLM WILLIS

RC (DLC). Docketed by JM.

1. Willis probably referred to William Czar Bradley (1782–1867), son of the U.S. senator from Vermont, Stephen Row Bradley. The younger Bradley was elected as a Republican to the Thirteenth Congress.

From Mathew Carey

SIR,   PHILADA. August 12. 1812

I take up my pen once more, for probably the last time, on the subject of the present crisis.

Many persons suppose that the determination to dissolve the Union, which has been formed by the leaders of the federal party in New England, has arisen from the measures of the last and present administration. It is an utter error, & a belief in it has a tendency to lead to ruinous results. To apply remedies to disorders, moral or physical, their sources must be traced.

Men who on small stages act the part of Richards, Othellos, Romeos & Coriolanii, on large ones sink down to those of servants, or battleaxe men, or perhaps Candle snuffers. And many, who, if the Union were dissolved, & three or four distinct confederacies formed, wd. be presidents, or vice presidents, or secretaries, cannot in the existing order of things emerge beyond state senators or members of assembly. To such men a separation is "a consummation devoutly to be wished."[1]

As early as 1793, the necessity of a separation was advocated by an assemblage of the highest talents & greatest influence Connecticut could produce. The essays were signed "Pelham." S. H. Smith, who republished them, can give you an account of the project they disclosed.[2]

To this project every thing has been rendered subservient. It is impossible to devise any system of policy, that wd. silence or satisfy the leaders of the party. But a complete exposure of their conduct & views wd detach from them many of those by whose countenance & support alone they are formidable.

There are two modes, & two only, by which the impending calamity may be prevented—one, such a complete exposure of the party as I referred to in my last—& this exposure universally circulated—the other a complete counter current throughout the state of Ms patronized & encouraged, & impelled forward by every means at the command of the government. This is the sovereign remedy. And thanks to heaven, I see by this morning's paper, that it has been begun in the County of Middlesex.[3] It now behoves (pardon my freedom) the administrators of the affairs of eight millions of men, to use all their energies; &, in as excellent cause as ever excited the ardour of mankind, use a portion of the industry & activity displayed by those who are engaged in one of the worst. I cannot help thinking, that three fourths of our danger has arisen from the pernicious the fatal idea, that the good Sense of mankind is a fair match for the Machinations of the wicked. Every page of history proves the destructive fallacy of this opinion. A corrupt or wicked press, (I mean the press at large) wd. write down a government of angels & archangels, that did not use the proper means to defend itself. Had Mr. Jefferson been a Nero, & you a Caligula, you could not be more completely abhorred & detested than you are in such parts of New England as are under the influence of the Boston Gazette & the Repertory.

A law of ten lines, making any attempt to dissolve the union, a high crime & misdemeanor, subject to a severe penalty, wd. have probably arrested the evil in an early stage. Better late than never. Such a law ought to be one of the first enacted at next session.

I enclose a few extracts from papers published at the commencement of the first embargo.[4] These fully develope the nefarious views of the leaders of the party. I remain, with due respect, Your obt. hble servt

MATHEW CAREY

RC and enclosure (DLC). RC docketed by JM. For enclosure, see n. 4.

1. Shakespeare, *Hamlet*, 3.1.62–63 (*Riverside*).

2. The first of the "Pelham" essays, appearing in the Hartford *Connecticut Courant* on 21 Nov. 1796 and reprinted in the Philadelphia *Aurora General Advertiser* the following month, expressed antislavery and antisouthern sentiments and argued that New England could survive as a republic separated from the South (see Joseph Jones to JM, 8 Jan. 1797, *PJM*, 16:448–49 and n. 3). At that time Samuel Harrison Smith was the printer of the Philadelphia *New World*, which may have reprinted the "Pelham" essays as well (Brigham, *History of American Newspapers*, 2:1484).

3. On 12 Aug. 1812 the Philadelphia *Aurora General Advertiser* reprinted from the *Boston Patriot* a 5 Aug. notice from the Republicans of Middlesex County, Massachusetts, which expressed their support of the war, observed the rising tide of antiwar and secessionist sentiment, and called for a 10 Aug. meeting to determine a course of action.

4. Carey enclosed a newspaper clipping entitled "Bold Language." The clipping included extracts from three Federalist newspapers, headed by a statement that the reader might "judge

whether *open rebellion*, *British alliance*, and a *separation of the States*" were clearly recommended therein.

To John Montgomery

DEAR SIR   August. 13. 1812

I have recd. and thank you for your favor of the 9th. I never considered an assault by the mob on the post office as probable, nor allowed myself to doubt that, if made, the local authority was both able and willing to crush it. The case was brought to my attention, as was natural eno'; the post office being under the sanction of the U. S., but I was not aware, that any defensive measures, were within the Executive sphere; if less confidence had been felt in the means & the disposition to employ them, on the spot. The report of the Come. of investigation is a seasonable antidote to the misrepresentations propagated by those, who knowing the pestilent tendencys of all mobs, seek the double purpose of casting the reproach of them on the friends of true liberty, and using them as instruments of factious ambition. Accept my friendly respects

JAMES MADISON

RC (MdBJ-G).

From Tench Coxe

SIR ————————————————— PHILADELPHIA Augt. 13. 1812

It is with sincere reluctance, that I trouble you upon the subject of a vacancy which I am told has been created, this day. It is understood that Capt. C. Irvine has been appointed Commissary Genl.

I submit myself to your consideration for the office of Supt of military stores, of the duties of which I have had many occasions to think and much opportunity to acquire information.

Tho it is not connected with the consideration of the Senate, yet I beg leave to assure you that Mr. Gilman of that body made me a visit of his own motion on his ride from Washington to New Hampshire, and in the course of a voluntary conversation on his part he took occasion to declare to me that the Senate would have approved my appointment as deputy Commy if I had been nominated again after Capt. Jones had declined the office of Commissary General.[1] He thought the government ought to have nominated me again, but I told him it was impossible for the government to know that disposition in the Senate. He said it was false that there had been

150

an unanimous rejection by the Senate, as had been published, that no objection had been mentioned to my conduct, but that after Mr. Jones had been nominated & approved as Commissary Genl. my nomination was expressly objected to because two officers were not wanted in Philadelphia. He added expectations that I would receive attention at the next Session, and expressed opinions decidedly favorable to the issue.

I am sensible, Sir, of very considerable delicacy in addressing you in this manner, but conscious that I have destroyed the interests of my family but [sic] a laborious course of public exertions, I am obliged to submit to you exact views of things according to my best Judgment, that my situation may receive such consideration as the public interests may be found to admit. I have the honor to be, with unaltered attachment and respect, Sir your most obedient & most humble Servt.

                                                          TENCH COXE

RC (DLC). Docketed by JM.

1. Coxe's term as purveyor of public supplies had ended on 1 June 1812, following the elimination of the office by the creation of the new position of commissary general of purchases, which had been offered to William Jones on 3 Apr. 1812. On 1 Apr. 1812 JM had nominated Coxe as a deputy commissary, but he was not appointed to that or any other post in military supply (Risch, *Quartermaster Support*, 139, 145; *Senate Exec. Proceedings*, 2:242, 243).

From Albert Gallatin

DEAR SIR   NEW YORK 13th Augt. 1812

I received yours, of 7th[1] only by yesterday's mail. What I can do at this time here with respect to money is nearly completed. But I had intended before my return to Washington, to go to Albany in order to see Gen. Dearborn & Govr. Tompkins together and to be able to give you a better account of the situation & prospect of our affairs there. It is also necessary that I should spend one week longer in Philada. in fiscal arrangemts.

The tenor of your letter, your intended departure, the magnitude of the questions to be immediately decided at Washington & the account of the capture of Michillimakinac[2] have however induced me to alter my plan. Being indisposed and obliged to take medicine, I cannot with all possible diligence reach Washington before Thursday 20th inst., as I must necessarily spend Monday in Philada. I presume that the actual revocation of the orders in Council, and the necessity of deciding on the important questions connected with that act, will as well as the critical situation of Gen. Hull keep you in the city till my arrival.

I will only state with respect to the first subject, that independent of the answer to Gr. Britain & of the measures proper to be adopted with that country, eight or ten millions of Dollars worth of British merchandize may be shortly expected, & that some general rule must be pursued towards that unexpected mass of goods.[3]

As to Gen. Hull, hemmed as he is, behind by the Indian & Canadian force (in the employment of the ⟨fur?⟩ companies) which has taken Michillimakinac, and in front by the mixed force at Malden which may in a few days be strengthened by that near Niagara; it appears to me that, unless he shall have taken Malden before he is attacked by the Indians & succours from Niagara, the utmost he can do is to keep on the defensive; and that he can only be extricated by an immediate concentration of all our disposible troops & militia at Niagara, and by the capture of the British fort & settlements there. An attack upon Montreal must probably be delayed. It is true that the communication from that quarter with the Indians cannot be completely cut off without taking Montreal itself. But once complete masters of Niagara & of the settlements along Lake Erie to Malden, a corps may be marched to the Ottowa river from Niagara & obstruct if not interrupt altogether that communication.

From Queenstown opposite to Niagara, the distance to York near the western extremity of Lake Ontario is about 35 miles; & thence northwardly there is an indian road to the Ottowa river distant about 70 miles. By that road, expresses go from York to Fort St Joseph on Lake Huron in four or five days. With sincere respect & attachment Your obedt. Servt.

ALBERT GALLATIN

RC (DLC: Rives Collection, Madison Papers). Docketed by JM.

    1. Gallatin probably referred to JM's letter of 8 Aug.

    2. On 29 July 1812 Hull informed Eustis that he had received a report from two Chippewa that a British force supported by nearly a thousand Indian troops had taken the American post at Michilimackinac (or Mackinac). Hull expressed his belief that as a result of the fall of the post, "a large body of hostile Indians may soon be expected here from the north." On 4 Aug., after receiving confirmation that the fort had surrendered on 17 July, Hull wrote again to emphasize that his situation at Detroit had become perilous (DNA: RG 107, LRRS, H-331:6, H-336:6).

    3. On 26 Aug. 1812 Gallatin attempted to resolve this issue by releasing a circular concerning the status of ships and cargoes that had left Great Britain on the assumption that the repeal of the orders in council would lead to the termination of nonimportation. Gallatin stated, "The Non-importation Act being still in force, must, in every respect, be carried into effect." He directed customs collectors "to seize and libel British merchandize in whatever manner and by whomsoever it may be brought or sent into the United States, with the exception only of property captured from the enemy; the importation of which is permitted by the fourteenth section of the act concerning letters of marque, prizes and prize goods." Relief, he noted, could be obtained only by a special act of Congress or by "application for a remission of the forfeiture in the manner prescribed by law" (*National Intelligencer*, 8 Sept. 1812).

    This proved to be only a temporary solution. The second session of the Twelfth Congress reversed the policy by passing on 2 Jan. 1813 an act which stipulated that in cases where goods owned by U.S. citizens had been shipped from Great Britain, bound for the U.S., between 23 June and 15 Sept. 1812, the secretary of the treasury was directed to remit all fines, penalties, and forfeitures incurred under the terms of the Nonintercourse Act, provided that the usual duties had been paid. The law also required that all legal proceedings concerning those shipments be discontinued (*U.S. Statutes at Large*, 2:789–90). For the debate, see *Annals of Congress*, 12th Cong., 2d sess., 28, 31, 33, 35, 36, 394–402, 403–4, 432–36, 441–43, 450–51, 1250–76.

§ From the Citizens of Greene County, Georgia. *13 August 1812.* "At a meeting . . . held at Greenesborough . . . for the purpose of addressing the President of the United States on the Expediency of taking immediate possession of the Floridas . . . the following address & resolutions were unanimously adopted. . . . The petition . . . Respectfully Sheweth

"That it is an acknowledged Constitutional right, sacred to the people of the United States, peaceably to assemble and to address the Constituted authorities of their Country, upon all subjects of a publick nature, in which they may feel themselves interested. Your pe[ti]tioners are well aware, that upon ordinary occassions, it may not be good policy, too frequently to exercise this privilege; but in times of war, of difficulty, and of danger, a neglect of this privilege would in many cases amount to a deriliction of duty, as good Citizens. If your petitioners were not sensible, at this time, that duty to themselves and their Country, points to the necessity of addressing your excellency, they would not have ventured to impose on you their opinions; but as the subject for their Consideration is one, which materially and vitally affects their dearest interests, they feel constrained to approach you as petitioners.

"Your petitioners however would premise to your Excellency, that they do not come forward with this petition, with any views or wishes, of weakening the arm of Government, of disaffection, or disobedience to the law; on the Contrary they highly approve of the general measures of administration, and they feel themselves impelled by every consideration of duty, interest, and patriotism, to support the measures of Government, whether they relate to the war in which we have lately embarked, or to any other legal and constitutional object. They are the more willing and anxious to support the Government, in the war in which we are engaged, because they have long felt and seen the injuries and insults, which, with an unrelenting hand and heart, have been heaped upon us by Great Brittain. They have seen our excellent Government with the most unexampled degree of patience, exhaust every means of negociation, with that power, whose almost every act, since the establishment of our independence, has evinced the malignity of her heart towards us; And whose injustice and cupidity, again calls us from the bosom of our families, and our homes, to stand forth in the defence of the rights and the Honor of our beloved Country. Under the most solemn appeal to the author of the universe, for the sincerity of their intentions to support our Government in all the measures which they in their wisdom may think proper to adopt, to punish the injustice of our enemy, and bring the present Contest to a speedy, honorable and favorable issue. They will proceed to lay before your Excellency the subject of their immediate consideration. Your petitioners are well aware that it is not unknown to your Excellency, that it is of the utmost importance to the united States, and the more especially to this section of the union, that the Floridas should be attached to, and exclusively belong to the United States. It would be useless for your petitioners, to attempt an enumeration of all the advantages, that would result to the people of this Country, in the event of the Floridas being incorporated with the Union; and it would be equally unnecessary, to point out the many evils that must inevitably accrue to us, should they remain in the possession of Spain, or what is still more to be deprecated, should they become the dependencies of Great Brittain.

"They will only submit to the Consideration of your Excellency, a few of the most prominent reasons, which have influenced them to this Convention; and point out some of the advantages arising to this Country from the possession of those provinces, and some of the disadvantages, necessarily attendant on their falling into the hands of our enemies. The province of East Florida is immediatly contiguous to, and bordering on the State of Georgia.

"It is at this time, claimed by the Regency of Spain in the name of Ferdinand the Seventh; that Regency and Great Brittain are in the most strict alliance: as we are engaged in a war, with Great Brittain and her depen[den]cies, it becomes our indispensible duty, to use every possible means in our power to impair her strength, and diminish her resources, for carrying on the war against us. In what way can the United States most effectually obtain this end? By depredations on her Commerce, and by cutting off her communication with this Continent: In short, by the Conquest of her possessions in the North, and by the Occupation of the Floridas in the South. Admitting for a moment, that we should abandon all intention of taking possession of the Floridas, and they should not be ceded by the Regency of Spain to Great Brittain; yet, as the Regency and Great Brittain are allies, Great Brittain would surely claim of her ally, the privilege of entering her ports, to refit her fleets, to bring in for condemnation, the prizes she might Capture from the U States, and to obtain the necessary munitions of war.

"But your petitioners are Confident, from the relative situation of the United States and the Floridas, that consequences more pernicious than those already enumerated, would result to us, in the event of our forces abandoning those provinces. The patriots of East Florida have openly rebelled against their mother Country, they have formally declared themselves free and Independant, and have proceeded to the adoption of a Constitution of Government.[1] Your petitioners are impressed with a belief, that the patriots of Florida, have been more promt in asserting their claims to the right of self Government, from an expectation that the United States, would extend to them the arm of protection, in the support of so noble a cause: and your petitioners are greatly apprehensive, that the patriots, should they be now abandoned by the U. States, would immediately place themselves under the protection of the Government of Great Brittain, knowing that they would be treated as rebels by the Government from which they revolted. In addition to the reasons already advanced against the policy of abandoning the Floridas at this juncture, and thereby endangering their becoming the depen[den]cies of Great Brittain, may be added the facilities, which will consequently be afforded our enemy, to annoy our Southern Coasting trade, and to pursue with success the odious and abominable practice of smuggling; and in possession of the Floridas, will not our enemy have it greatly in her power, to stir up against us, the merciless and unrelenting Savages, immediately bordering upon us; and from a history of the revolutionary war, have we not much to fear from her seductive overtures to our black population, exciting them to abandon their owners, and perhaps to rise up in rebellion against them. Your petitioners have seen with infinite regret and concern, that a bill which had passed the House of representatives of the United States, by a large majority, and which had for its object, the immediate occupation of the Floridas, was rejected by the Senate.[2] But your petitioners are of opinion, that Under the law of Congress passed in 1811, authorising the president of the United States, to take possession of the Floridas on the happening of either of two events, that your Excellency would be justified and fully authorised in taking such measures, as you might deem Expedient to occupy those provinces, or at least, to prevent our enemy from doing so.[3] That there is every probability that great Brittain, if not anticipated, will possess herself of the Floridas, is too obvious to be questioned. And shall we tamely and qu[i]etly set by, and suffer our open and avowed enemy, to possess herself of those provinces and thus increase her means of annoying us? No, let us not wait till the blow which seals our destiny is given. What will now be the work of a few days, and the loss of little blood, may if delayed, Cost us the lives of thousands, and the labor of years.

"In making the foregoing Representations to your Excellency, your petitioners have been governed, entirely by a sense of the importance of the subject of this petition, to the people of this State, and by a wish to express to your excellency, the confidence they entertain, in the firm, wise and decided measures of your administration. Your petitioners do not presume that they have thrown any new light on the subject of this petition, nor do they believe, that a single reason has been advanced, of which your Excellency was not perfectly apprised. It is foreign from their purpose, in the smallest degree to wish to dictate to their Government; on the Contrary, they wish to inspire Confidence, and to evince their disposition to Co-operate in such measures as may be adopted. They have only a wish, that your Excellency will carry into effect the act of Congress of 1811, so far as that law, in relation to the Floridas will authorise you to go. Whatever expedients may be resorted to by your Excellency to this end, we the people of Greene County of the State of Georgia, do hereby pledge our lives, our fortunes, and our Sacred honors, in Support of the Government, in the pursuit of so laudable and all important an object. And as in duty bound your petitioners will ever pray &C.

"1st   Resolved by this meeting, that a copy of this petition be transmitted to the president of the United States.

"2nd   Resolved that a copy of this petition, be likewise forwarded to the Governor of this State, and to three different printers in this State for publication.

"3rd   Resolved that this meeting, viewing the importance of the subject of its immediate Consideration, do recommend to the other Counties of this State to take the same into Consideration."

RC (DNA: RG 59, ML). 7 pp.; signed by Oliver Porter, chairman, and Ebenezer Torrence, secretary; docketed by Monroe.

1. Following the failure of the efforts of George Mathews earlier in the year to deliver East Florida to the U.S., a group of American settlers in the province organized a convention, presided over by John Houstoun McIntosh, which in July drew up a constitution for East

Florida, to operate until such time as the province could be taken into the Union. Under this constitution McIntosh was elected "Director of the Territory of East Florida," and on 30 July 1812 he wrote to the State Department, urging the administration to provide troops and gunboats for the protection of the province, pending its inclusion in the U.S. (Patrick, *Florida Fiasco*, 154–56, 165–66; John Houstoun McIntosh to Monroe, 30 July 1812 [DNA: RG 59, TP, Florida]).

2. See Memorandum of a Conversation with Augustus J. Foster, 23 June 1812, *PJM-PS*, 4:501–3 and n. 6.

3. The petitioners referred to an act of 15 Jan. 1811 that authorized the president to take possession of East Florida if foreign occupation were threatened (*U.S. Statutes at Large*, 2:666).

§ From Jared Mansfield. *14 August 1812, New Haven.* Recommends Alfred P. Edwards[1] for the consulate at Lisbon.

RC (DNA: RG 59, LAR, 1809–17, filed under "Edwards"). 1 p.

1. Edwards, a native of New Haven, Connecticut, was a successful merchant in New York and the son of Pierpont Edwards, a district judge in his home state (Merchants, Ship Masters, and Insurance Agents of New Haven to Gallatin, 10 Aug. 1812, and Gideon Granger to Monroe, 11 Nov. 1812, with enclosure [ibid.]).

To Albert Gallatin

DEAR SIR   WASHINGTON Aug. 15. 1812

I have just recd. your favor of the 13th. I had proposed to set out for Virga. on friday, and am very glad to learn that you will be with us before that takes place. I expect Mr. Monroe every moment; and Mr. Pinkney being within call, I shall be able to decide with the best advantage the several important questions on hand. Previous to the acct. of the loss of Michillimackin⟨ac⟩ orders had gone for a reinforcement to Hull of 1500 men from Kentucky & Ohio.[1] It is a little strange that no official communication of the revoking order, has yet arrived from G. B. the order being dated on the 23d. of June, and so many motives urging an immediate transmission of it. The solic[i]tude on this point appeared from the hasty communication thro' Halifax before the measure was reduced to its due form. From debates in Parlt. of the 18 & 19 of June, there must have been a sudden transition from the conditional suspension to the shape finally given to the act. Maury writes from Liverpool (June 26), that shipments were taking place, witht. hesitation, of goods to an unexampled amt. for the U. S.[2] It will be an unexam⟨pled⟩ instance of mercantile incaution if passports be not obtaind, to be good in the event of war. The state of things which produced the revocation of the orders, would ensure the granting them, if insisted on.

Enclosed is the new Chancellor of the Exch:'s budget,[3] with an interesting view of the subject by Huskisson.[4] Affece. respects

JAMES MADISON

RC (NHi: Gallatin Papers). Docketed by Gallatin; torn.

1. See JM to Gallatin, 8 Aug. 1812, n. 4.

2. Maury's 26 June letter to Monroe explained that news of the repeal of the orders in council had been received in Liverpool on 25 June, that there was no hesitation about shipping goods directly to the U.S., and that exports "will be unusually ⟨g⟩reat; probably, beyond example" (DNA: RG 59, CD, Liverpool).

3. JM presumably enclosed the 1 Sept. 1812 issue of the *National Intelligencer*, in which Nicholas Vansittart's 15 June budget for Great Britain was published.

4. William Huskisson (1770–1830) was one of the supporters of George Canning in Parliament, an alliance which slowed the progress of his career. He subsequently became a celebrated reformer on the Board of Trade (Alexander Brady, *William Huskisson and Liberal Reform: An Essay on the Changes in Economic Policy in the Twenties of the Nineteenth Century*, 2d ed. [New York, 1967], 1, 5, 7–10, 18–19). The 1 Sept. 1812 edition of the *National Intelligencer* printed Huskisson's criticism of Vansittart's budget, particularly the management of Irish funds. He described a near 10 percent increase in the cost of collecting revenue as "unaccountable" and called for streamlining to prevent such abuses.

From Henry Dearborn

SIR,   GREENBUSH August 15th. 1812

I was this day honored with your letter of the 9th. inst. having been placed in a very unpleasant situation I have endeavored to make the best arrangements for the ultimate success of our Army, that circumstancies permit, the perticular circumstancies which have occasioned the most unfortunate imbarrasments, were my having no orders or directions in relation to uper Canada, (which I had concidered as not attachd to my command,) until my last arrival at this place and my being detained so long at Boston, by directio [sic]. If I had been directed to take measures for acting offencively on Niagara & Kingston, with authority such as I now possess, for calling out the Militia, we might have been prepared to act on those points as early as Genl Hull commenced his opperation at Detroit, but unfortunately no explisit orders have been received by me in relation to uper Canada, until it was too late, even to make an effectual diversion in favour of Genl. Hull all that I could do was done without any delay. If the Troops from the Southward are pushed on soon, I am persuaded that we may yet be prepared to act with effect on uper Canada, and on Montreal, before the season for acting is passed. I have requested Govr. Snyder to send two thousand of the Militia of the Northwestern frontiers of that State, to Niagara, Govr. Tompkins will do everything in his power. Vermont will do well—how many volunteers we shall procure, is uncertain, but there is a prospect of a conciderable number. The months of August & Septr. will give our new troops a seasoning, while they are training for the field, and with such excertions as will be made, for acquiring the necessary knowledge of discipline & camp police, I trust we shall have a body of men capable of effective service—the deficiency in Genl. officers, & in the Commissary of purchases, Department, is felt in every direction, but we must double our excertions and endeavour to overcome all obsticles of whatever kind. The moderate abilities I possess shall be excerted to their utmost stretch—in general, we shall have a respectable corps of Officers, and by the next Spring, we shall have an efficient Army, but measures must be devised for checking the outragious, & Treasonable conduct of our Tories. Their apparent views are open hostily [*sic*] to the Genl. Government and I fear there will be serious & sistematic measures taken for producing a revolution in the Northern States. I most ardently hope that Congress will take early & strong measures for puting down those Treasonable proceedings. I fear you have remained too long at Washington, permit me Sir to entreat you to take care of your health. With sentiments of the highest esteem & respect, I am Sir Your Obedt. Servt.

H. Dearborn

RC (DLC). Docketed by JM.

From Elbridge Gerry

Confidential

My dear Sir,   Cambridge 15th August 1812.

If there is any medical, or other office, which is or may soon be vacant, in or near Boston, it cannot as I conceive be so well applied, as by giving it to Doctor Waterhouse.[1] His history is singular. He has been a Professor thirty years, in our University, & this has long been in the hands of high federalists; such as Ch. Jus. Parsons, the "Boston Rebel,"[2] & similar men. The Doctor was in the first instance, a federalist; but quitted the party with J Q Adams Esq, when our flag was insulted, in the case of the Cheesapeak. Whilst a federalist, his party were disgusted at his moderation; & violent, when he became a Republican. Being lately the only professor of this party, the Government of the College have in every possible way mortified & persecuted him; & have joined such high toned medical men, as envied him, for his reputation in regard to the kine pock, & as successor of D Jarvis[3] at the marine Hospital. Whilst I was in the Chair, & thus officially at the head of the Government of the University, I was a witness of the rancour with which the Doctor was pursued, & of the Exertions made by eminent law characters, to make charges against him, on the ground of his removal from the hospital department. His most inveterate enemies, after long & laborious enquiries, could not bring any charge against him, but have dismissed him by a flimsey pretext, "that it was against the interest of the college, that he should be longer their professor"; a circumstance which confirms the belief here, that misrepresentations to the supreme Executive have been made against him. The vote for his removal by the Corporation, being all of the Essex Junto, has been confirmed by less than one fifth of the board of overseers, whose intriguing conduct is considered by the republicans, & as I am well informed by some high federalists of the University, as being on this occasion, shameful. There was a prospect last year of a vacancy in the medical department of the State Prison, & there was but one mind in the Executive of this State, in regard to Doctr Waterhouse; as the only person to whom it ought to be offered. I have been thus explicit, because we are much indebted to the Doctor for his speculations, over the signature of Salust ⟨sc?⟩.[4] He has a pen which is dreaded by our Enemies, & we wish exceedingly to inlist him as the Editor of the Patriot. But the Government of the University having deprived him of two offices therein, indispensable to the support of his family, has reduced him to the necessity of some pursuit for maintainance. And with aid to accomplish this, he would serve in the other instance, which would afford him but little if any benefit, & be of vast advantage to the cause of our Country. Having a veiw of the whole ground your decision will be conclusive & satisfactory in this quarter.

James Thomas Esq was appointed whilst I was in office, Clerk of the Court in the County of Hancock; & being dismissed from this office by Governor Strong, proposes to join the army of the United States, if a suitable office can be obtained. When he received that appointment, he was a Captain of dragoons, in the service of the U States; & reputed to be a good officer; He is going on to Albany, to confer with General Dearborn on this subject. He appears to me to be a brave man, & I doubt not will do justice to any military office, which may be conferred on him.

William Donnison Junr Esq, son of our Adjutant General, is desirous of joining the army. He is a professed republican, an Attorney at the supreme Court, & I think would with honor fill the office of Captain.

Captain James Miller has produced, from the late Secretary of this State, our Attorney General, Colo Boyd & Major Nye, the recommendation enclosed for sailing master of the Chesapeak, or other similar office.[5] I have no personal knowledge of Captain Miller, except what results from an interveiw, but am inclined to beleive he would make a good sailing Master.

A Young Gentleman by the name of Walter Baker, unknown to me, but recommended by Mr McKean a professor of our University, as appears by his certificate enclosed;[6] & also by a nephew of mine, studying law at Litchfield in Connecticut, at the same law Academy with Baker; wishes for an appointment in the navy, & that any communication on the subject to him may be directed to Hartford in that State.

The frequent applications of individuals on such subjects, whilst troublesome to myself, & I fear more so to our national Executive, indicate the increasing popularity of our military & naval establishments.

In regard to our political concerns, the proceedings of Middlesex, will shew the feelings of republicans in this quarter.[7] The federalists are boisterous, but will not dare to be efficient; at least this is my opinion. If they should be, they will most assuredly be suppressed, or I have mistaken the spirit of my countrymen. Decision cannot fail to promote, as it already has done, our cause. The federalists have formed a coalition with the Clinton party; & the latter has made proposals thro Everett, for purchasing the Patriot,[8] as I am well informed. But I flatter myself the measure will not meet here, as it did in Albany, with success;[9] altho there is danger of it. Ought not an alarm to be sounded, thro'out the states, of such an attempt to carry measures by dint of corruption? What can be more dangerous to the cause of Liberty, than to purchase our best presses? A paragraph in the national Intelligencer, in regard to the disposition of our Government, to meet the british on the ground of accomodation, on the subject of seamen, & also to avoid an alliance with France, has been published in all our papers;[10] & the federalists have triumphed, at this publick concession, as they consider it. Had the same statement been made by reprobating the federal calumnies on these subjects, & by correcting them with the substance of that publication, the effect would probably have been more favorable *here*, to the republican cause; for we find by daily experience, that plain dealing only will answer for the british faction.

Our Governor & his Connecticut Ally, appear to have met with something unpleasant, from the national Government; but the facts have not transpired, being by them carefully concealed.

We are happy to learn that Colo Boyd has the command in this quarter, he is an excellent officer. In what State our fortifications will be placed by the unconstitutional & unprecedented conduct of our Executive, we are yet to learn.

All eyes are on our Government, for an explanation, in due time, of the late measures of G Britain. They are veiwed here as insidious; but whatever may be their true character, an implicit reliance is placed on the wisdom of our national executive, for correspondent measures.

We are unfortunately circumstanced in this section of the Union. Our best writers, in offices, are so occupied by them, as to have no time to write for the Gazettes; & out of office, their families demand their whole time for

supporting them. Whilst G B has pensioned writers amongst us, who overwhelm the publick with misrepresentations & faleshoods [*sic*]; without the
possibility of seasonably confuting them. How this evil is to be corrected,
I know not; but it endangers the overthrow of our republican systems. Accept, my dear Sir, the unfeigned assurances of the highest esteem respect &
regards, of yours, very sincerely

E. Gerry

RC (DLC). Docketed by JM.

1. Benjamin Waterhouse (1754–1846) held the Hersey Professorship of the Theory and
Practice of Physic at Harvard College from 1783 to 1812. He had published his lectures on
the theory and practice of medicine and had lectured and written on such topics as botany,
natural history, the abuses of tobacco, and vaccination against smallpox, which he helped introduce to the U.S. He had been accused of misconduct as a physician while affiliated with the
U.S. marine hospital at Charlestown, Massachusetts, in 1809 (Ford, *Statesman and Friend*,
3 n. 1). For more on Waterhouse's medical career and his relationship with the Federalists, see
Gerry to JM, 20 May 1809, *PJM-PS*, 1:194–95, 196 n. 1.

2. John Lowell Jr. (1769–1840), a Massachusetts lawyer, farmer, and Federalist pamphlet-
eer, earned the nickname "Boston Rebel" after criticizing Gerry in a pamphlet he published
under that name. Disapproving of JM's presidential policies, Lowell was the author of the
1812 pamphlet *Mr. Madison's War*. He suggested that New England should suspend the Constitution and remain neutral during the war (*PJM-SS*, 2:40 n. 3).

3. Dr. Charles Jarvis (b. 1748), a Boston Republican and graduate of Harvard College, had
been a delegate to the Massachusetts ratifying convention in 1788 and served several terms in
the state legislature. He was appointed surgeon at the marine hospital in Charlestown during
Jefferson's administration (Paul Goodman, *The Democratic-Republicans of Massachusetts: Politics
in a Young Republic* [Westport, Conn., 1964], 99; James Spear Loring, *The Hundred Boston Orators Appointed by the Municipal Authorities and Other Public Bodies, from 1770 to 1852* [Boston,
1852], 310).

4. On 22 July 1812 Waterhouse had published a letter in the *Boston Patriot* under the pseudonym "Sallust." He was responding to a 6 July letter "from a Gentleman in a neighboring
State, to his friend in Boston," published in the Boston *Columbian Centinel* on 18 July. Entitled
"The Duty of the Northern States," this letter appeared to be a continuation of a letter with
the same title printed in the 15 July *Columbian Centinel*, which ended, "In my next I will give
you my opinion on the subject of the *Union*." Waterhouse offered sharp criticism of the secessionist message of the *Centinel* publication, arguing that chaos and perpetual war would result from a division of the nation.

5. Enclosure not found. Miller wrote to the secretary of the navy directly on 2 Sept. 1812
to ask whether this enclosure had arrived (DNA: RG 45, Misc. Letters Received).

6. Enclosure not found.

7. On 12 Aug. 1812 the *Boston Patriot* published a memorial from the Republican delegates
of Middlesex County, under the heading "Voice of Middlesex!" The memorial claimed to
counter the conventions, associations, and societies that had recently gathered in the state,
"whose objects and proceedings tend to resistance of government, opposition to the laws, dissolution of the Union, and subjection to a kingdom in actual hostility with the United States."
The delegates saw it as their object to "repel and defeat the seditious attempts of the opposers
of constitutional authorities, to unite in their support, and in the defence of our country
against the invasion of a relentless, perfidious enemy."

8. David Everett had been a publisher and editor of the *Boston Patriot*. His former partner,

Isaac Munroe, continued to own the paper until 1814 (Brigham, *History of American Newspapers*, 1:332).

9. The *Albany Register* was sold by Solomon Allen to Henry C. Southwick on 1 May 1812. Edited by Solomon Southwick, the paper was decidedly Clintonian. Clinton's brother-in-law, Ambrose Spencer, tried unsuccessfully to close the paper by suing the editor for libel and ultimately offering to purchase it outright. Spencer had also founded the short-lived *Albany Republican* in April to counterbalance the influence of the *Register* (ibid., 1:539; Stagg, *Mr. Madison's War*, 104, 238; Donald H. Stewart, *The Opposition Press of the Federalist Period* [Albany, 1969], 617).

10. See, for example, the Boston *Columbian Centinel* of 12 Aug. 1812, which reprinted a 4 Aug. editorial on impressment from the *National Intelligencer*.

§ From the Citizens of Fayette County, Kentucky. *15 August 1812.* "As the people of the United States being citizens of a free goverment, have a natural, unalienable and constitutional right at all times peaceably to assemble and express their oppinions respecting public measures—and as it is Justly deemed highly important in the present interesting crissis, that all *good citizens* should yield their support to the war in which we are now engaged with Great Brittain in defence of our rights and for the redress of the numerous and continued wrongs received at her hands, and also to suggest our oppinion of those measures best calculated to bring it to a speedy and *honorable* termination, not only in retorting the evils of war on the enemy, but that great and permanent adv[an]tages to ourselves may follow—*The people of Fayette County* do therefore, *resolve,*

"1. That we view the present war with Great Brittain, as a war for the protection of the lives and liberties of our citizens, So long and so repeatedly assailed and destroyed by Brittish Tyranny under the name of impressmen⟨t⟩—as a war for the protection of our commerce, destroyed by her arbitrary edicts or orders in council—as a war for our national sovereignty and independence, which she insultingly aims to destroy by her demand that we shall procure her a free trade, with a power over whom we have no controul, and with whom she is at open war herself—and as a war for the protection of our women and children from the tomahawk and Scalping knife of the ruthless and blood thirsty savages, excited to murder them by her agents.

"2. Resolved, That in such a war no sacrafice is too great, no privation too intolerable to ensure our Success.

"3. Resolved, that while we are not insensible to the wrongs of France, and have just claims against her which we hope, never will be relinquished untill fully sattisfied, we view with *abhorrence* those among us who are so lost to the American character as to proclaim that this war has been brought upon us by undue influence or management of France with our Goverment.

"4th. Resolved, That we view the proposition for a repeal of the non-importation law as tending to degrade our nation, by indicating a want of assistance from abroad, even from our enemy, to carry on the war against her—that as its existance has shewn the great distress which it has caused amongst the subjects of that power, even in time of peace, it would be a monstrous folly and inconsistency in any wise to remove it now we are at war, and thus instead of enfeebleing, strengthen her resources.

"5. Resolved, that our country is possessed of abundant raw materials, and the means of producing them, *that our future and permanent prosperity and independence even after the close of the war, will be best secured by the encouragement of our own manufactures*, and that to this end, some permanent system should be adopted by law, which might draw forth the enterprize and capital of our Citizens without the hazzard of loss from *permitting the importation* of similar articles from abroad, *or materials.*

"6. Resolved, that a vigorous war against the savage allies of G. Brittain is the best means of protecting our frontiers, and accelerating and securing the acquisition of the Cannadas, and that the volenteers of this state are competent to this object, if the[y] have such a man as William Henry Harrison for their commander.

"7. Resolved that who ever advocates a dissmemberment of the Union is a traitor—who ever by his speeches, encourages our enemies with hopes of Success, is deserving of punishment—and who ever will not contribute his *exertions, and property* to the support of this contest, is not deserving the protection of our goverment.

"And whereas, we are informed, that some further attemps will be made during the next session of Congress to inco[r]porate a National Bank, and it is firmly believed by us, that no *power* to establish such an institution, or any other description of co[r]poration, is delegated by the federal constitution to that body, which have no other powers than what are derived from that instrument—therefore

"Resolved, that Congress have no power to charter such institutions.

"Resolved, That a coppy of these resolutions be fo[r]warded to the President of the United States, to the President of the Senate & Speaker of the house of Representatives."[1]

RC (DNA: RG 59, ML). 5 pp.; signed by Henry Payne, chairman, and Lewis Sanders, clerk. Cover marked "Via Marietta."

1. On 19 Aug. 1812 the clerk of the meeting added a note to the bottom of the petition pointing out that two regiments of Kentucky infantry and one regiment of riflemen had marched to reinforce Hull. He observed that these men were "badly provid⟨ed⟩ with camp equipage—half of them are without tents, a great number without winter cloathing, & Those that are able to purchase at their own expence are not able to pack it, with their other baggage on their backs."

§ From Robert Cutchins and Others. *15 August 1812, St. Marys, Georgia.* "Sundry Officers of the United States Navy" inform JM that "Batram [*sic*] G. Hipkins,[1] hath for upwards of five Years last past, been a Sailing Master, in the Navy of the United States, and that he hath lately been remov'd therefrom, upon sundry charges, without havaing [*sic*] had an opportunity, of confronting, or refuting the same." Request that the charges against Hipkins be investigated, that he be allowed to defend himself, and that he be "restor'd to the favour of his Country."

RC (DNA: RG 45, Misc. Letters Received, filed at 2 Apr. 1816). 1 p.; signed by Cutchins and three others. Delivered to the Navy Department by William Smoot in February 1813 (Hipkins to William Jones, 12 Feb. 1813 [ibid.]).

1. Batran G. Hipkins was appointed sailing master on 4 Aug. 1807. He was dismissed on 28 July 1812 after several officers complained that he had been making rash statements and cruelly punishing the crew of gunboat no. 63 (Callahan, *List of Officers of the Navy*, 267; Samuel Elbert and others to Commodore Hugh G. Campbell, 6 July 1812 [DNA: RG 45, Misc. Let-

ters Received, filed at 2 Apr. 1816]). Hipkins pressured Hamilton and his successors in the Navy Department for redress (see Hipkins to William Jones, 12 Feb. 1813 [ibid.]), but Secretary of the Navy Benjamin Crowninshield noted on the cover of a 2 Apr. 1816 supporting letter from Monroe that Hipkins had "regularly be⟨en⟩ dismissed from office," that "no new warrant can be grant⟨ed⟩," and that it was not "proper to grant a court martial" (ibid.).

From Thomas Leiper

Dear Sir   PHILADA. August 16th. 1812

The appointment of Captain Callender Irvine to the office of Commissary General gives universal satisfaction. Captain Irvine's friends would have asked you for this favor some time ago but he objected to it and I verily believe his sole reason was he did not like to ask his friends for the security that was necessary. I am informed in a line I have no reason to doubt of the correctness of the information that if Mr William Leonard[1] who now holds the Office of Deputy Quarter master was he to succeed to the Office Captain Irvine held that the business would be conducted much to the Advantage of the service. Mr. Leonard must be well known in the Department of State. I have known Mr. Leonard since 75 true Blue and I do believe has not altered an opinion Religious Moral or Political since that period.

By the bye these are the men and they only who should be appointed into Office for every day's experience shows us there are a set of men amongst us who are to be found not only at Boston but every where else who would sacrifice their country to the interest of Great Britain.

No doubt but it will give you pleasure to be informed that the Republicans in this district are United and I believe it never will be in the power of Duane Binns or Leib to divid[e] us again. Make Mrs. Leiper and my compliments to Mrs Madison. I am with much respect and esteem. Your most Obedient Servant

THOMAS LEIPER

RC (DLC). Docketed by JM.

1. William Linnard (d. 1835), deputy quartermaster in Philadelphia since 3 Apr. 1812, had himself written to Eustis on 11 Aug. 1812 at Irvine's request to solicit an appointment as superintendent of military stores. The appointment went to William Duncan on 26 Aug. 1812. Linnard was promoted to quartermaster general on 12 Apr. 1813 (DNA: RG 107, LRRS, L-162:6; Heitman, *Historical Register*, 1:634).

To Thomas Jefferson

Dear Sir   Washington Aug. 17. 1812

I have recd yours of the 10th. and return as you request, the letter of Mr. Higginbotham. He will probably have understood from Col: Monroe that the consulate of Lisbon is the object of numerous & respectable candidates.

The seditious opposition in Mass. & Cont. with the intrigues elsewhere insidiously co-operating with it, have so clogged the wheels of the war, that I fear the campaign will not accomplish the object of it. With the most united efforts, in stimulating volunteers, they would have probably fallen much short of the number required by the deficiency of regular enlistments. But under the discouragements substituted and the little attraction contained in the volunteer act, the two classes together, leave us dependent, for every primary operation, on militia, either as volunteers or draughts for six months. We are nevertheless doing as well as we can, in securing the maritime frontier, and in providing for an effective penetration into Upper Canada. It would probably have been best if it had been practicable in time, to have concentrated a force which could have seized on Montreal & then at one stroke, have secured the upper Province, and cut off the sap that nourished Indian hostilities. But this could not be attempted, without sacrificing the western & N. W. Frontier, threated with an inundation of savages under the influence of the British establishment near Detroit. Another reason for the expedition of Hull was that the unanimity and ardor of Kentucky & Ohio, provided the requisite force at once for that service, whilst it was too distant from the other points to be assailed. We just learn, but from what cause remains to be known, that the important fort at Machilimackinac has fallen into the hands of the Enemy. If the re-inforcement of about 2000 ordered from the Ohio, and on the way to Hull, should not enable him to take Malden, and awe the Savages emboldened by the British success, his situation will be very ineligible. It is hoped that he will either be strong eno', as he has cannon & mortars, to reduce that Fort, or to have a force that will justify him in passing on towards the other end of Lake Erie, and place the British troops there, between him, and those embodied under arrangements of Dearborn & Tomkins [sic] at Niagara, for the purpose of occupying the central part of Upper Canada. In the mean time the preparations agst. Montreal are going on, and perhaps may furnish a feint towards it, that may conspire with the other plan. I find that Kingston at the East End of L. Ontario is an object with Genl. D.[1] The multiplication of these offensive measures have grown out of the defensive precautions for the Frontier of N. York.

We have no information from England since the war was known there, or even, seriously suspected, by the public. I think it not improbable that the sudden change in relation to the orders in Council, first in yielding to a qualified suspension, & then a repeal, was the effect of apprehensions in the Cabinet that the deliberations of Cong: would have that issue, and that the Ministry could not stand agst. the popular torrent agst. the orders in Council, swelled as it would be by the addition of a war with the U. S. to the pressure of the non-importation act. What course will be taken, when the declaration here shall be known, is uncertain, both in reference to the American shipments instituted under the repeal of the Orders, and to the question between vindictive efforts for pushing the war agst. us, and early advances for terminating it. A very informal, & as it has turned out erronious communication of the intended change in the Orders, was hurried over, evidently with a view to prevent a declaration of war, if it should arrive in time. And the communication was accompanied by a proposal from the *local* authorities at Halifax sanctioned by Foster, to suspend hostilities both at sea & on land. The late message of Prevost to Dearborn, noticed in the newspapers has this for its object.[2] The insuperable objections to a concurrence of the Executive in the project are obvious. Without alluding to others, drawn from a limited authority, & from the effect on patriotic ardor, the advantage over us in captures, wd. be past, before it could take effect. As we do not apprehend invasion by land, and preparations on each side were to be unrestrained, nothing could be gained by us, whilst arrangements & reinforcements adverse to Hull, might be decisive; and on every supposition, the Indians wd continue to be active agst. our frontiers, the more so in consequence of the fall of Machilimackinac. Nothing but triumphant operations on the Theatre which forms their connection with the Enemy, will controul their bloody inroads.

I have been indulging hopes of getting away from this place, in the course of this present week. It is quite possible however that my stay here may be indispensible. As yet I have less of bilious sensations than I could have expected.

Your two letters to Kosciuzco have been duly attended to. Affectionately yours

JAMES MADISON

RC (DLC). Docketed by Jefferson as received 19 Aug.

1. In a 15 Aug. 1812 letter to Eustis, Dearborn had explained that he was "pursuing measures with the view of being able to opperate with effect against Niagara & Kingston," at the same time that he moved "towards Lower Canada" (NHi: Dearborn Letterbooks).

2. The 17 Aug. 1812 edition of the Baltimore *American and Commercial Daily Advertiser* printed a report from the 10 Aug. *Albany Gazette* stating that Col. Edward Baynes, adjutant general of British forces in Lower Canada, had met with Dearborn and Tompkins to report the repeal of the orders in council, announce that Foster had been instructed to open negotiations with the U.S., and convey a message from the governor in chief of British North America, Sir George Prevost, suggesting an armistice until further news could be received from

Great Britain. At a meeting between Baynes and Dearborn in Greenbush, New York, on 9 Aug. 1812, the former attempted to persuade the latter to accept "a cessation of Armes," with Dearborn agreeing that U.S. troops "with perfect safety . . . should Act, merely on the defencive, untill [he] could receive directions from [his] Government." Dearborn added, however, that he "could not . . . include Genl. Hull in such an Agreement, he having received his Orders directly from the Department of War." The War Department repudiated this agreement on 15 Aug. 1812 (Dearborn to Eustis, 9 Aug. 1812 [NHi: Dearborn Letterbooks]).

§ To James Dinsmore. *17 August 1812.* Acknowledges receipt of Dinsmore's letter of 5 Aug. [not found]. Has remitted $407 to Mr. Warnock and has received a receipt. Hopes to be at Montpelier soon.

RC (owned by Robert G. Kaufmann, Wayne Township, N.J., 1985). 1 p.

§ From the Inhabitants of Portland, District of Maine. *18 August 1812.* "We the Inhabitants of the town of Portland in the District of Maine legally assembled in town meeting, and deeply impressed with the Melancholy and alarming situation of our beloved Country, have thought it our duty, in the exercise of our Constitutional rights, to present this Memorial to your Excellency, with a hope that we may soon be enabled to realize the blessings for which we petition, and be relieved from those evils, which we are now suffering.

"We are the Inhabitants of a town which depends on Commerce, not only for its wealth and respectability, but for its very existance. We have once severely suffered under the calamities of War, and have seen and felt its most distressing consequences. We have also enjoyed the blessings of peace, prosperity and harmony. And we cannot but distinctly notice the melancholy constrast [*sic*], while we are peculiarly suffering under the pressure of those evils which distress our Common Country.

"Although we have never been able to discover the necessity or policy of the War, we have hitherto refrained from expressing our sentiments or feelings on the subject. But the recent and important changes which have taken place in the policy and conduct of Great Britain induce us without delay, to assemble and with the independence of Freemen, and the respectful deportment of good and peaceful Citizens, to urge your Excellency to improve the present fortunate opportunity for the restoration of Peace. The revocation of the British Orders in Council, of which Official intelligence has been received, has essentially changed the aspect of British measures, and we believe ought, at once, to produce a correspondent change in American measures. The great question which has so long been agitated between the two Countries is now settled and at rest, the great cause of Complaint is now removed. The obnoxious Edicts are officially declared to be revoked and Annulled.

"We are taught to believe that the Orders in Council were the principal cause which produced a resort to Arms. We are taught to believe this from your Excellency's own conduct and solemn Official acts, in as much as the arrangement made with Mr Erskine, and which restored for a time the commercial intercourse between the two countries, was predicated expressly on the revocation of the Orders in Council, and those only.[1]

"We are sensible that the impressment of our Seamen was also an alledged cause of War. To the wrongs and injuries of that useful and generous Class of Citizens we are feelingly alive, and would resist to the utmost of our power any nation, which should *claim*, and *exercise* the right of siezing and impressing our *native seaman*. But we are assured that Great Britain does not *claim this right*, but only the right of taking *her own seamen* from our merchant vessels. We are also assured that Mr Foster, the late British Minister, requested to be furnished with the names of impressed American Seamen and explicitly offered to cause their restoration. Neither of your predecessors in Office considered impressment as cause of War, but always treated it as a subject of negociation. And we confidently believe that mutual arrangements may be made on this subject, which will effectually secure the rights of Seamen, and preserve the honor of the nation. For this belief we have high authority; for it is well known to your Excellency, that Messrs: Munroe and Pinkney did make an arrangement on this subject, which they pronounced honorable and advantageous to our Country.[2]

"Every important point of difference, except the question of impressment, being thus settled, we can discover no reason for the continuance of a desolating War. And we confidently look to your Excellency for the restoration of peace and Commerce on which our happiness and pro[s]perity depend. Relieved from foreign embarrasments, nothing is wanting but peace and the fostering hand of our own Government to give freedom and prosperity to our Commerce.

"As the revocation of the orders in Council took place but a few days after the declaration of War, as measures of relaxation on *one part*, and hostility on the other, were adopted nearly at the same time, although unknown to the respective powers which adopted them, we presume that, now the facts are all known, as well the motives which actuated the parties, there can be no impediment to the immediate, and honorable termination of the War, in its infancy, before its evils shall be further multiplied before it shall have weakened the sense of moral obligation and the Bonds which unite Society, before its baneful effects shall have poisoned our social intercourse, and a fatal alliance with France, shall have destroyed our Independence.

"For these reasons and under the solemn Considerations, We respectfully and earnestly pray that your Excellency would without delay appoint Commissioners to negociate *Peace* between the United States and Great Britain and restore the freedom of Commerce, or adopt such other mode, as may be deemed proper, speedily to procure for our unhappy Country these inestimable blessings."

RC (DNA: RG 59, ML). 3 pp.; signed by Samuel Freeman, moderator, and Samuel Homer, town clerk. Enclosed in Freeman to JM, 19 Aug. 1812 (ibid.; 1 p.).

1. For David Erskine's agreement with JM, see Presidential Proclamation Restoring Commerce with Great Britain, 15–19 Apr. 1809, *PJM-PS*, 1:117–18.

2. For the Monroe-Pinkney Treaty and the issue of impressment, see Inhabitants of Northampton, Massachusetts, to JM, 1 July 1812, ibid., 4:529–35 and n. 4.

From Albert Gallatin

DEAR SIR   PHILADA. August 19th 1812

I was detained by indisposition & bad weather longer than I expected. I have found here your letter of 15th inst., and wish that you may not leave

Washington as early as you had contemplated. I go there at this time only to meet with you, & will not reach it before Saturday. It is important that I should know your decision on the subject of the large British importations: I have some not unimportant communications to make; and the present crisis, as it relates to our internal concerns or to England, to War arrangements or to armistice (which I disapprove), appears so much more interesting, every decision the Executive may take so much more important in its consequences, than at any former period, that I am earnestly desirous of meeting you before your decisions & departure take place.

I have heard it suggested here that Callendar Irwine [*sic*] was made principal Commissary of purchases. This information has afflicted me with respect to the effect of such extraordinary appointmts. on public mind here. From personal considerations it has hurt me to the quick.[1] If not completed I wish to be heard on the subject. With sincere respect & attachment Your obedt. Servant

ALBERT GALLATIN

RC (DLC: Rives Collection, Madison Papers). Docketed by JM.

1. Irvine was a close friend of William Duane, publisher of the Philadelphia *Aurora General Advertiser*, which had printed many articles highly critical of Gallatin (Brant, *Madison*, 6:27).

§ From the Delegates of Windham County, Vermont. *19 August 1812*. "The delegates from the several towns of Windham County, in the State of Vermont, (being one of the first settled Counties in the state,) convened at the Court House in said County, on the 19th day of August 1812 in conformity to the object of their appointment beg leave respectfully to address the Chief Magistrate of these States, upon the present situation of our Country.

"Conscious and justly proud of our priveleges as *Independent Americans*, as *free citizens of Vermont*, as the favored *owners* & *cultivators* of the soil whereon *we dwell*, it is not with mean and slavish fear & obsequiousness but with bold and undisguised Sincerity and respect, we address you.

"The principles, beauties and practical utility of a Government like ours, cannot exist without this right & liberty in the citizens. The liberty of freely consulting each other on the measures of the Government the liberty of Speech and of the Press, are justly considered as the most efficacious antidotes against the baneful effects of restless, deluded & ambitious partizans.

"Through these organs of public liberty and opinion, our rulers may be enabled to correct the fatal current of destructive party and misrepresentation, and to appreciate more fully the different feelings wishes and interests of the people. Recent occurrences abundantly exemplify the truth of these remarks—a few partial and contemptible meetings of the *War advocates* have made so much parade, and have so misrepresented the feelings and Interests of this state, that some exertion seems necessary on our part to expose this party deception and delusion.[1]

"Far be it from your Memorialists to charge the President or Administration

169

with corruption or wilful mismanagement but they must be allowed to reason and remonstrate against what are deemed unfortunate, unwise or unjust measures.

"It is well known to your Memorialists, as it is to the Government of our Country, that ever since the Revolution in France, that nation has conducted towards this with officiousness, insolence & outrage. She has manifested a disposition to consider us as her devotees & vassals. She has often given us lessons mingled with menace & denunciation—And have we not been too timid, too obedient? And has not such a spirit of compliance been a principal cause of the calamities which threaten to overwhelm our Country? A bold and manly resistance of Gallic interference and outrage would have exhibited to other nations, our national spirit, firmness and love of equal Justice; and must have secured to us their approbation and applause: and the more impositions we patiently bear from a lawless Conqueror like Napoleon the more we invite. We do not ascribe this fatal policy to Corruption but to misfortune and error. Neither do we bring to view the subject as an excuse for British wrongs and aggression; but to shew how much of our losses & national troubles might have been fairly & honourably prevented. It is natural for one nation viewing another as the *Secret ally and abettor* of its most implacable & determined foe, to feel and conduct towards the *suspected secret enemy* with less respect and friendship. And we cannot forbear here to observe, that (as the vital Interests & best welfare of America & Great Britain, so evidently plead for their friendship,) had our Government boldly & resolutely resisted the *French degrees* [sic], issued in violation of a solemn treaty, and without even colour of law or right, we should now have enjoyed all the rights & advantages of an extended & profitable Commerce—*Peace* at home and *Respect* abroad.

"The fate of other acknowledged *friends* & *allies* of *France*, ought to have forewarnd us of the fatal effects of a policy so pregnant with degradation & ruin. Disaffection to their own Government, Corruption of all kinds. An admiration, or slavish fear of Buonaparte—hatred & prejudice towards *his* enemies, the English—war, bloodshed, destruction of Commerce and Industry. And finally *annexation to France*, or perfect submission to her power and princes, all regularly follow such *friendships* & *alliances.* Can we as Americans, as freemen, as Christians, patiently wait the approach of such insidious & fatal scourges, such worse than Egyptian visitations, and not raise our warnings, our remonstrances, our solemn protest against them? And can it be denied that every measure in the present awful and portentous state of the World, which leads to augment the power of Napoleon, and to the downfall of his only rival—as it tends to destroy the balance of Nations, must be highly impolitic, if not vitally dangerous to our Independence. Therefore, the conclusion inevitably follows: That French pretended Alliance and Friendship mingled as it must be with such dangerous consequences and multified [sic] wrongs and outrages unatoned for on her part, is impolitic, hateful & intolerable! It requires no laboured reasoning to shew that *Commerce*, and its efficient Protection, is an object of primary importance to this Country. It is not the merchant alone who gains by it; it is almost every man of industry and business in the Community; compare the present dull and miserable state of the Country with its condition a few Years ago for comments & proofs. All other great and commercial nations have found a degree of naval force as indispensable to protect them as an army or Militia by land. Why should we madly reject the lessons of experience and bewildered in visionary theories, lose more in neglecting what ought to be done, than would twice pay the expence of effecting what our dearest require. If a few ships of war are deemed necessary to our protection, what advantage might not our Country derive from a liberal addition to our maritime force?

"Without attempting to prove which of the belligerents have injured us the most grievously, or have manifested the most unfriendly and wicked disposition towards us, we confess that we cannot find much of favour on the part of France to leave the balance of wrong against Great Britain. The *Blockades* were adopted by the British with an obvious intent to harrass a formidable enemy, but they were limited to a particular coast. The *decrees* were sweeping and unlimited, and destitute of all moral or legal support. The *orders in Council* were retaliatory and not immediately resorted to. The pretended revocation of the decrees was accompanied with acts little less aggravating & requirements little less insulting than the decrees themselves. The repeal of the Orders is as full and specific as that of the decrees.

"The *War* into which we are unhappily plunged, appears to have been declared prematurely, and without that cool reflection and deliberate calculation which a subject so momentous required. We are unprepared: and had our national councils been less precipitate, we might now, as we believe have been in readiness amicably to terminate all controversies between the two nations. Will not the War and the hostile attitude of the two Countries create new obstacles to such an adjustment? And has not the American Government for years past, been abundantly ready to resent and magnify British offences, if not to palliate and secrete those of France? We anticipate with alarm and awful foreboding the disastrous consequences of a long & bloody conflict. In the sad train of national miseries immediately connected with the present system of *offensive War* against the only nation able to injure us materially, and to withstand the deluge of *gallic Conquest* and *domination*, may be classed— *The total destruction of commercial and profitable business, and public morality, industry and prosperity—of all our usual sources and means, of Revenue—the reign of military conscriptions and despotism, and the introduction of grievous exactions.* And your Memorialists apprehend that the renewal or imposition of heavy *land* and other *direct taxes* must prove impolitic and burdensome, more especially while those formerly imposed, remain yet uncollected in some parts of the Union; and your Memorialists cannot foresee any adequate advantages attainable by this War, to counterpoise such afflictive consequences.

"Your Memorialists do most earnestly pray that the Administration may wisely embrace the earliest opportunity for renewing a friendly intercourse with Great Britain, and that the further effusion of human blood, by people of the same religious, moral and commercial habits, allied by kindred blood, and every friendly tie, ought to be terminated as soon as possible—and that the best interests of our hitherto happy & prosperous republic—a due regard to its union, safety and welfare— to the common good of civilized man—all plead for a speedy renewal of fair & frank negotiation and Peace between the two Countries.

"And as it is officially announced that one of the principal Causes of the present War, the *Orders in Council* are removed, and that the British Government have manifested a conciliatory disposition to adjust the other points of controversey, your Memorialists confidently hope and trust that a spirit equally conciliatory will appear on the part of our Government, and that a moment so auspicious as the *pres-*

ent to recommence Negotiation and adjust all political disputes with the British nation, and again to restore our beloved Country to the full enjoyment of all the blessings of free trade prosperity & *Peace*, will not be suffered to pass unimproved.

"Permit your Memorialists also to remark that the liberty of the Press, and the prompt suppression of all insurrections & brutal Mobs, are subjects peculiarly interesting to our feelings as freemen and Americans. We entertain the fond expectation that, if the civil authority of one of our important Cities should continue to connive at, or neglect to suppress the contagious and disgraceful proceedings of the Jacobin Mobs in that City, the President will immediately, (unless he has already in his wisdom done it) order a competent force to that quarter to suppress so daring and dangerous an insurrection, and to protect the citizens in their Rights, liberties, persons & lawful avocations.

"In this address, your Memorialists would abstain from all irritating, and party expressions & reflections, and likewise from that bold & indignant review of French aggressions which our feelings might excite. We wish to merge all minor considerations in the general exertion for the peace & lasting welfare of our beloved Country; confidently believing that the Chief Magistrate of a great and free People, (being actuated by a true spirit of patriotism,) will, at all times, rise superior to party and local considerations, and pursue & maintain an impartial, peaceful and magnanimous policy towards all Governments—A policy which shall again restore these United States to an envied & dignified rank among the nations of the Earth."

RC (DNA: RG 59, ML). 16 pp.; signed by Jonathan Hunt, president, and Jairus Hall, secretary of a meeting at which fifty-four delegates, representing "nearly every town" in Windham County, voted to create a committee to draft a memorial to the president "upon the present alarming condition of our Country" and another committee to report resolutions to be adopted. The draft of the memorial and resolutions was unanimously approved.

1. At this time Vermont was still under Republican control. The state legislature, in a 23 July special session, indicated its support for the war by drafting a memorial to the secretary of war announcing that the order to provide detached militia had been "promptly obeyed." The memorial also requested that more arms be sent to Vermont to protect the frontier from invasion (Walton, *Records of the Governor and Council of the State of Vermont*, 5:341–43).

§ From the Inhabitants of Westport, Connecticut. *20 August 1812*. "The Inhabitants of the Town of Westport, in legal Town meeting assembled August 20th., 1812. ask leave respectfully to state. That they have endured a series of restrictions upon Commerce, which from principle they have disapproved, being according to their understanding, inefficient as respects Foreign nations, and injurious, Chiefly to ourselves. Yet, we presume not to arraign the motives of the Conduct of our Government; in order to obtain redress of injuries which we have sustained from the Belligerent powers of Europe. And after all, that war should be declared against England, (contrary to our expectations and wishes,) we consider premature, Impolitic, inexpedient, and injurious, under the present situation of our Country, being placed by divine providence so remote from the theatre of contention of the European world, the very small naval force we possess, the great length of sea coast that we are bordering on, the defenceless situation of our sea ports in general, the exhausted state of the Treasury, together with the divided Opinion of the public mind, the almost annihilation of Commerce, by which this Country has so rapidly increased in wealth, the Millions of property belonging to our Citizens deposited in England; which will doubtless be sequestered, and the opportunity of her navy, and Cruisers to sweep the Ocean of what navigation is abroad; and almost uselessness of what is at home, the deprivation of employment of hundreds of Seamen, together with the concomitant evils and embarrassments, of all classes of Citizens, with the multiplication of a multitude of Bankrupts and Debtors, the deprivation of the numerous comforts and priviledges which we have been favoured with, both domestic and social, and after all having no possible chance that we can conceive of, to obtain redress, for the wrongs and injuries which we have sustained, any better by remaining in a state of warfare, than by negociation, and further as Britian [*sic*] is so powerful on the Ocean, and the only part of her Dominions which is assailable to us must be Canada, the conquest of which if attained, appears to us would be almost no indemnification, or satisfaction, for the injuries we have suffered and the losses most probable that will ensue in the Conflict, especially to remunerate for the Impressment of our Seamen. And as to the revocation of the Orders in council we understand has taken place, on certain conditions, or modifications; therefore if those were the Ostensible causes of War, is it not now propper and expedient to pause, and again offer for negociation. We are so deeply impressed from every consideration of the subject which presents itself to our Understanding, that we are constrained to express our disapprobation of the present War, and a continuance thereof, and our unwillingness Voluntarily, to be personally engaged therein, believeing that an accommodation and redress of injuries, which we have suffered by Britian, might be more easily, and satisfactorily obtained by negociation, than by War, for we view war as a most awful, and dreadful Calamity which never ought to be resorted unto, but in the defensive, when there has been an actual Invasion, and all hope of negociation at an end. We forbear, to present to the consideration of your Excellency, any further details, of what we anticipate to be the evils, and calamities, incident, and to be the natural consequences of War, both in a Moral and Political view. We do therefore, we trust, from a due regard to ourselves our posterity, and for the Honour, and prosperity of our beloved country, conjure you, to use your utmost endeavours, and influence, for the restoration of peace, on Just and Honourable terms. We therefore pray your Excellency, that Commissioners, may be forthwith appointed on the part of the United States, to negociate with Great Britian. We are at a loss to know, why we as a neutral Nation, should wholly fix our resentment against one of the Belligerent Nations only, when we have received injuries from both. And now by this war we apprehend that the natural consequences will be, to lead to an Alliance with France, which we abhor as the greatest of evils, and the worst of entanglements, the effects of which, we seriously fear instead of defending our own rights, and maintaining our Independence, will be, to help fight the battles of the greatest Tyrant. Whose success, will be our destruction, and loss of Independence, and Power, as has been the fate of all other Powers and Republick's, that have been flattered, allured, and dragged into his deceptive net, whose principal object appears to us, to be Conquest and Dominion.

"From the serious consideration of what your memorialists have herein hinted at, together with many other evils, and distresses which they dread and fear will be the consequences of the present war if continued in and being sincerely attached, both

173

from principle and habit, to a Republican form of Government, and anxiously desireous, that it might be transmitted unimpaired to our Children and successors, and believeing that we express the sentiments and feelings of many thousands of our friends and fellow Citizens we could not forbear expressing them to your Excellency, being impressed with a belief, that under God, the people are the legitimate source of power of Government, and have a constitutional right to make known their grieveances and desires, and ought to be heard. And to conclude, we further believe in the language of the constitution of this Commonwealth, that the end of the institution, maintainance, and Administration of Government, is to secure the existence of the body Politic: to protect it: and to furnish the Individuals who compose it, with the power of enjoying, in safety and tranquility, their natural rights, and the blessing(s) of life; and whenever these great objects are not obtained, the people have a right to alter the Government, and to take measures necessary for their Safety, prosperity, and happiness.

"Pr. Order of the Town in legal Town meeting, by an unanimous Vote."

RC (DNA: RG 59, ML). 4 pp.; signed by Abner Brownell, moderator, and Abner B. Gifford, town clerk.

From Morgan Lewis

DEAR SIR,   ALBANY 21. Augt. 1812

The change of posture given to our national Affairs by the *suspension* of the Orders in Council and the temporary cessation of hostilities, must be my apology for troubling you with a few observations, which I hope may be favorably received. I think it to be regretted that Genl. Hull not being included in the armistice, the movement of Troops was not prohibited. For I cannot but indulge apprehensions, that the enemy will take advantage of the omission, to reinforce the Garrison of Malden, perhaps to an extent which will enable it to act offensively; which he can do without incurring the imputation of a breach of faith; while a counter movement, by way of diversion on our part, would not be equally free from it. I therefore hope that Hull will accede to the Armistice which I understand has been proposed to him also.[1]

Being ignorant of the plan of the Campaign I cannot be presumed to judge correctly of our present positions. I may be permitted to think however, if it was not immutably fixed, that the straits of Niagara would have been a preferable rendevous for our regular Troops, to the position they at present occupy. We should there have held the Enemy in check, have given confidence to our friends in his territory, facilitated the operations of Hull, and avoided many of the discontents which the severity of militia service is producing among our Citizens.

You will pardon me for expressing an Opinion, even though it should not coincide with your own, for it is offered in the utmost Sincerity, that sound policy requires, under existing circumstances, a shew at least of a disposition to negotiate, even though for the sole purpose of gaining time: For I have no hesitation to say, that we cannot take the field during this campaign, but under great disadvantages. We have as yet but the shadow of a regular force—inferior, even in numbers, to half of what the Enemy has already in the field. Ill supplied with Cloathing, Camp Equipage, Ammunition and Ordnance. Not more than a fourth of the Artillery of the Park is mounted—and of that, most of the carriages fail from being constructed of unseasoned Timber. The staff departments are defective in organization, and the war is decreasing in popularity, from the Intrigues of designing and pretended republicans, and the severe duties necessarily imposed on the militia; a body at all times inadequate to offensive operations.

These few remarks are intended for yourself alone. They have but one motive, the public weal with which I consider the support of the present administration intimately connected. With unfeigned Sentiments of Esteem and Respect I have the honor to be Dr. Sir your Obt. Servt.

MORGAN LEWIS

RC (DLC). Docketed by JM.

1. Dearborn wrote to Hull on 9 Aug. 1812, informing Hull of the agreement he had reached that day with Col. Edward Baynes to cease hostilities (see JM to Jefferson, 17 Aug. 1812, and n. 2). Dearborn suggested that Hull concur in the measure "if [his] Orders and Situation would admit of it," but he also warned that the agreement with Baynes did not preclude continuing to prepare for offensive operations or transporting "military & other Stores." "The removal of any Troops from Niagara to Detroit while the present agreement Continues," Dearborn added, "would be improper—And incompatible with the true intent of the Agreement" (NHi: Dearborn Letterbooks).

To the Delegations of Several Indian Nations

MY RED CHILDREN,   WASHINGTON [ca. 22 August] 1812
You have come thro' a long path to see your father but it is a straight and a clean path kept open for my red children who hate crooked walks.[1] I thank the great spirit that he has brought you in health through the long journey; and that he gives us a clear sky & bright sun, for our meeting. I had heard from General Clarke of the good dispositions of several of the nations on & West of the Mississippi; and that they shut their ears to the bad birds hovering about them for some time past. This made me wish to see the principal chiefs of those bands. I love to shake hands with hearts in them.

The red people who live on the same great Island with the white people of the 18 fires, are made by the great spirit out of the same earth, from parts of it differing in colour only. My regard for all my red children, has made me desirous that the bloody tomahawk should be buried between the Osages, the Cherokees, and the Choctaws. I wish also that the hands of the Shawenoe, & the Osage, should be joined in my presence, as a pledge to cherish & observe the peace made at St. Louis.[2] This was a good peace for both. It is a chain that ought to hold them fast in friendship. Neither blood nor rust should ever be upon it.

I am concerned at the war which has long been kept up by the Sacs & Foxes agst. the Osages; and that latterly a bloody war is carried on between the Osages & Ioways. I now tell my red children now present, that this is bad for both parties. They must put under my feet their evil intentions agst. one another; and henceforward live in peace & good will; each hunting on their own lands, and working their own soils.

Your father loves justice. He extends it to all the red tribes. When they keep the chain of friendship with the 18 fires, bright, he will protect them, and do them good. If any make the chain bloody, it must be broken on their heads. The Winibagoes and some other tribes, between the Mississippi & Lake Michigan & the Wabash, have shut their ears to my councils. They have killed men, women and children, and have plundered the white people. They refuse to give up the murderers, and to return the stolen property. Time enough has been allowed them. When they feel the punishment, they must blame their own folly, and the bad councils to which they have listened. I will not suffer my white children to be killed without punishing the murderers.

A father ought to give good advice to his children, and it is the duty of his children to harken to it. The people composing the 18 fires, are a great people. You have travelled thro' their Country; you see they cover the land, as the stars fill the sky, and are thick as the Trees in your forests. Notwithstanding their great power, the British King has attacked them on the great water beyond which he lives. He robbed their ships, and carried away the people belonging to them. Some of them he murdered. He has an old grudge against the 18 fires, because when he tried to make them dig and plant for his people beyond the great water, not for themselves, they sent out warriors who beat his warriors, they drove off the bad chiefs he had sent among them, and set up good chiefs of their own. The 18 fires did this when they had not the strength they now have. Their blows will now be much heavier, and will soon make him do them justice. It happened when the 13 fires, now increased to 18 forced the British King, to treat them as an independent nation, one little fire did not join them. This he has held ever since. It is there that his agents and traders plot quarrels and wars between the 18 fires and their red brethren, and between one red tribe and another. Malden is the place where all the bad birds have their nests. There they are fed with false tales agst. the 18 fires, and sent out with bloody belts in their bills, to drop among the red people, who would otherwise remain at peace. It is for the good of all the red people, as well as the people of the 18 fires, that a stop should be put to this mischief. Their warriors can do it. They are gone & going to Canada for this purpose. They want no help from their red brethren. They are strong enough without it. The British, who are weak, are doing all they can by their bad birds, to decoy the red people into the war on their side. I warn all the red people to avoid the ruin this must bring upon them. And I say to you my children, your father does not ask you to join his warriors. Sit still on your seats; and be witnesses that they are able to beat their enemies and protect their red friends. This is the fatherly advice I give you.

I have a further advice for my red children. You see how the Country of the 18 fires is filled with people. They increase like the corn they put into the ground. They all have good houses to shelter them from all weathers; good clothes suitable to all seasons; and as for food of all sorts, you see they have enough & to spare. No man woman or child of the 18 fires ever perished of hunger. Compare all this with the condition of the red people. They are scattered here & there in handfuls. Their lodges are cold, leaky, and smokey. They have hard fare, and often not eno' of it. Why this mighty difference? The reason, my red children, is plain. The white people breed cattle and sheep. They plow the earth and make it give them every thing they want. They spin and weave. Their heads, and their hands make all the elements & productions of nature useful to them. Above all; the people of the 18 fires live in constant peace & friendship. No Tomahawk has ever been raised by one agst. another. Not a drop of blood has ever touched the Chain that holds them together as one family. All their belts are white belts. It is in your power to be like them. The ground that feeds one Lodge, by hunting, would feed a great band, by the plow & the hoe. The great spirit has given you, like your white brethren, good heads to contrive; strong arms, and active bodies. Use them like your white brethren; not all at once, which is difficult but by little & little, which is easy. Especially live in peace with one another, like your white brethren of the 18 fires: and like them, your little sparks will grow into great fires. You will be well fed; well cloathed; dwell in good houses, and enjoy the happiness, for which you like them, were created. The great spirit is the friend of men of all colours. He made them to be friends of one another. The more they are so the more he will be their friend. These are the words of your father, to his red children. The great spirit, who is the father of us all, approves them. Let them pass through the ear, into the heart. Carry them home to your people. And as long as you remember this visit to your father of the 18 fires; remember these as his last & best words to you.

As we cannot always see one another, the distance being great, My words from time to time will be delivered by General Clarke and others who may be near you. Your words will always come to me through the same hands. I hope they will always be good words.[3]

Draft (DLC). Undated; date assigned here on the basis of evidence presented in n. 1 and JM to Thomas McKenney, 2 May 1825 (DLC), in which JM recalled his "Talk" to "deputations from a number of tribes to the seat of Govt." at the commencement of the War of 1812.

1. JM was expecting two Indian delegations in the summer of 1812. The first, consisting mainly of representatives of the Great and Little Osage, Fox, and Sauk, was escorted to Washington by William Clark, who was at that time the superintendent for Indian affairs in St. Louis. Clark's party arrived in Washington on Saturday, 1 Aug. 1812 (Clark to Eustis, 23 June 1812 [DNA: RG 107, LRRS, C-367:6]; *National Intelligencer*, 6 Aug. 1812). On 8 Aug., Richard Rush reported: "The President . . . gave a grand entertainment yesterday . . . to the Indian chiefs and warriors who are here. They are of three tribes, in the whole 28 in number" (Richard Rush to Benjamin Rush, 8 Aug. 1812, *Letters and Papers of Richard Rush* [microfilm ed.], reel 1). However, this address was probably not given until after the mid-August arrival of a second Indian delegation, consisting of Sioux, Winnebago, and Iowa, under the guidance of Indian agent Nicholas Boilvin. This meeting had been in contemplation since the summer of 1811, but the secretary of war urged Boilvin to delay the trip until the following spring (Boilvin to Eustis, 12 July 1812 [DNA: RG 107, LRRS, B-350:6]; Eustis to Boilvin, 29 Aug. 1811 [DNA: RG 75, LSIA]).

Dolley Madison reported to a young friend on 16 Aug. that "A few days ago We had 29 Indians to dinner wi⟨th⟩ us, attended by 5 Interpretors & the Heads of Depts. makeing 40 persons" (Dolley Madison to Phoebe Morris, 16 Aug. 1812 [DNCD]). A "feast, war dance, and war whoop" were held on 19 Aug. at Greenleaf Point (Richard Rush to Charles Jared Ingersoll, 19 Aug. 1812, *Letters and Papers of Richard Rush* [microfilm ed.], reel 1). The entry for 22 Aug. 1812 in Mrs. William Thornton's diary states: "Mrs Madison sent to invite us to see the Indian Talk—there were 40 of different tribes several of whom made Speeches after the president had done—The presents were afterwards given the whole lasted six hours" (DLC: Papers of Anna Maria Brodeau Thornton, vol. 3).

2. JM referred to a treaty between the U.S. and the Great and Little Osage, concluded at Fort Clark in November 1808 and at St. Louis in August 1809 (*ASP, Indian Affairs*, 1:763–64).

3. Filed with this speech is a three-page document in an unidentified hand headed "Memorandum of the Points which it is proble. the Presedent will take Notice of to the Indians." In addition to outlining JM's address, the memorandum conjectured that JM might mention "The Object of the Factories and their utility in being so arranged as to be Convenient to Such Tribes as are well disposed." JM may well have raised this issue in the final version of his speech, since the location of factories figured prominently in the responses of the Indian delegations on ca. 22 Aug. 1812. The memorandum also dealt with the issue of Indian medals, including JM's suggestion that "As Midals of a Proper description can't be pr[o]cured other midals could be Substituted and a reference made to W[illiam]. C[lark]. to exchange them for Such as could be furnished in a short time from Genl. Mason."

Also filed with JM's address is a one-page document in an unidentified hand headed "The Attawa Chiefs Speech," to which a second unidentified hand has added, "delivered early in the Revolution." The chief claimed that his trip to Washington had allayed his fears and that he would relay what he had heard to his nation. He predicted that "the sunny rays of this days peace shall warm and protect our childrens children from the storms of misfortune." He presented gifts and promised hospitality to Americans visiting his nation.

Speeches of Indian Delegates at Washington

White hair's son[1] spoke first.

My Great father.

I am your little son. I come to see and speak to you this day.

My great father. The first nation who came to speak to you was my nation. My father I therefore speak to you without fear.

My father. When my father came to see you he received good advice. He is now dead.

My great father. All that you promised my father he saw nothing of it— he is dead.

My Great Father.

You ask to see us. I have come to see you. I hope all that has been promised will be performed.

My great father. Those men were present and know.

My great father. Look at me. I am but a young man but your words have penetrated my heart.

My father. All you promised my father should be done at that place. (meaning mill, &ca.)[2]

My great father.

You have put a man to give us good advice. The same advice you have given us this day we hear from him.[3]

My great father.

You have had a factory established on the Missouri; it pleases us much. We sometimes have our men killed going there. The other day we had ten killed. I wish you would have the factory moved to my village.

My great father.

I am now speaking to you. See the nations about you: they wont speak as I do. I speak from the heart and not from the mouth.

My Father. I hope you have heard what I have said to you.

My great Father. When my father returned from visiting you he told me that you had promised him a Mill, a forge and a house.

My great father. My father is dead—but when I look at you and the Secretary of War I do not think him dead.

Clemont chief of the Arkansas band of Osage.[4]

My great Father.

You told me to come and see you—no accident has happened to us, and I am glad.

My great Father. It is a long time that I have been unhappy.

My great Father.

My father has been to see you—the father of the young man who has just spoken has been to see you. My great Father. I know the bad road from the good and know how to take the best.

My great father. My father is dead. I cried. I broke my heart, but he put me in the right road before he died which I followed.

My great father. I once lived with the Osage on the Osage river, but moved to the   5

My great Father. I never saw you before—I have heard from you. I have made peace between the Choctaws, Cherokees &ca. It was in presence of some of your inferior officers.

My great Father. I heard I should see a clear sky when I saw you. I now see a clear sky.

My great Father. In appearing before you I feel as if I was just born. I hope you will build a great fire in my Village.

My Great Father. Of all nations I speak the   .[6] Others may speak from their mouths. I speak from the heart.

My Great Father. We went to the Factory and I was killed—my people were killed.

My Great Father. It is unfortunate for us that we go to the Factory and are killed. I wish you would send goods to my village.

My Great Father. You have heard what I have said to you. I have listened to your words and am pleased with them.

Big Soldier with Wind Son.[7]

My Great Father. I come here with this man—he is an orphan. If any man has ears it is me.

My Father. This is the first time I ever saw you, but I have heard your words and do not sleep without thinking of them. This young man is the son of a man who has seen and spoken to you.

My Great Father.

Here is the son of White hairs—here is Clemont and the Little Chief. White hairs' father gave us good advice and we followed it.

My Great Father. I am pleased with the Factory you have placed near us, but about this Factory we are killed. Why are we killed? All is pleasing to us but being killed.

My Great Father. My ear was bored but never through until now.

My Father. To hear your words my ears are spread as wide as this room.

Sans Oreilles.

My Father. This is the second time I come to see you.[8] The Chief I came with is dead. I am the man to speak for all.

My Great Father. When I returned to my Village my advice kept all quiet. When I rise in the morning I think of your advice and respect it.

My Great Father. We are killed. My young men ask what to do—I tell them to remain quiet. Our Great Father has said so.

My Great Father. Look at what I have on my breast—what you tell me I will follow.

My Great Father. Formerly we had game and peace—since we have   9

My Great Father. See! they look at me—they see I am well made and a man, and can do much mischief yet.

My Father. Since I listened to you we have been killed repeatedly.

Those nations will promise to make peace in your presence, but no sooner out of your presence than they will wage war on us.

My Great Father. My name is No Ears but I have heard your words. I have.

My Great Father. You have placed Mr. Chouteau as our Agent—we wish no other Agent. He gives us good advice and General Clark knows it. All present know it. When he speaks, he speaks to many. I know the manners of the whites and of the red skins.

I have attended at your Council, and my heart is glad. It pleases us that the Factory is near us, but we are killed. This man (Big Soldier) is a man of trust.

My Great Father. This is my Interpreter. What he says I expect is what we said.

I will repeat what I have heard to my people when I return.

Tall Soldier.

My Great Father, this is the second time I have seen you. What White Hairs said to us we followed. He is now dead, but his son follows your advice.

My Great Father. My ears are open to the good advice you have given us this day. From the moment we set out we found no difficulty, and met your doors open to us. The Chiefs have given their hands with pleasure. I give mine with pleasure. All that you had promised old White Hairs I hope you will perform.

My Great Father. The White Hairs is dead, but before he died he left your words.

My Great Father. We are not only a little band, but my village is strong.

My Great Father and Father, my ears are open to your advice.

My Great Father and my Father. I have told you that my ears were open—they will be open with White Hairs. The Factory is pleasing, but it does not please us to be killed.

My Great Father. I beleive we shall always be killed near the Factory—this year ten, last year fifteen and so on. I wish you would send your goods near our Village. I am sorry that we are killed, but I am a man and am ready. We have all ears and will relate what we have heard and seen.

My Father, My Great Father, as you have told us, so we shall return home content.

Young Man brother to White Hairs.

My Great Father. I will follow your words to my Chiefs &c.

Young Man called the Little Chief.

My Great father.

This young man is the son of a Chief, he is not looked on as the son of a Chief. I wish to know for what reason?

My Great Father. I make this man known as the son of a Chief. I hope you will view him as a Chief.

Big Soldier. Little Osage, a common man.

My Great Father. I came with those Chiefs and have heard what you have said to them and what they have said to you. When I return I will make my Nation follow your advice. I am pleased with what has been said and will remember it.

1st. Chief of the Sieux. Ton-ta-gar-wonne. Spoke with a robe pipe & several strings of wampum.

My Great Father.

I am a small man, but I am regarded as a man. Why did not those Nations shake hands as I do?

I shall one day get home. I shall return with pride, and what my Father says I will tell my nation.

My Great Father. I have come a great way.

My Father. When I came along the birds sung about my ears. From what you say I see we shall be happy.

I came along with Mr. Bodwin [10] and the young man whom we know, and hope he will tell you our situation.

When I started from home we set out with the same heart, tho' I hear that those who went to Machinack have been silent; but those are the words they have sent (holding up the several strings of Wampum.) I am glad that you view us all alike. We have come a great way. This young man can tell you all we wish.

The French Crow, a sieux.

My Great Father.

I am happy to hear your good advice, and that we shall be at peace. We shall follow your words.

My Great Father.

I am a red-skin, but what I say is the truth, and notwithstanding I came a long way I am content, but wish to return from here.

My Great Father. We are at war with one nation and we will revenge; but we wish the friendship and attention of the Whites and hope they may come among us.

My Great Father.

You have always given us good advice, and we have followed it, and have prevented the Winnebagoes from doing mischief and killing the whites.

My Great Father. We have seven villages. Last winter the whites abandoned us and one of our villages perished. We hope you will send one of your men with goods to live among us. We wish a Factory in our Country.

(delivered a pipe.)

De-car-rees,[11] Winnebago, and another to intepret.

My Great Father.

We have come like the others to tell our great Father our sentiments, and hear the words of my great Father as my chiefs would not come.

My Father. I was quiet, but all at once there was a shade before my eyes. (alluding to his nation who had gone to Machinack.) When we are disposed to do good we do not go astray. You know that among all nations some will go astray—that is the case with my nation—it has gone astray but my heart is good. I hope my great father will reprove them.

(delivers a pipe.)

1st. Chief of the Sacs. The Blue.

My Great Father.

My great father I have heard your words—what you have said by Agents among us.

They have quarrelled with [12]

My Great Father. I did not know the number of your soldiers. I see that myself.

My Great Father. I came to receive your advice and good counsel. If we do not follow it, it is because there are fools among us as in other villages.

My Great Father. You speak of peace—we know that we ought to be at peace but there are fools among us. When the Great Spirit pleases we shall always assemble.

My Great Father. I am glad to hear your advice, but it is entirely impossible for me to control all my young men.

My Great Father. You have found it wrong that we have communication with the English. We have been in the habit of receiving presents from the English—we cannot leave them all at once—I will do my best.

My Great Father. My heart bleeds. We progress so slowly that I become impatient &c. &c.

My Great Father. I am here in your Village. What would be the situation of your Country if you were in my village? I wish to return and put all well.

My Father. Hear the words of an Indian. Listen to my words though perhaps like that of a white man.

My Great Father. I beleive my great father, I beleive you have not turned your mind to the information we cannot write. It is the people among us that put us right.

My Great Father. The advice we have received from you my father is good, but we cannot bring our young men into the right road in one day.

Quash-quam-ma. (Sac.)

My Great Father. I am happy to see the day that it has pleased the Great Spirit to suffer us to meet—it is a fine day.

My Great Father. You see all these Indians around you. What could they wish more than to be in peace & quietness?

My Great Father. I am happy to hear the good advice you have given us. What we could have done, might have been done much sooner. I am anxious to return.

My Great Father. I have nothing to guide me in my discourse but the dictates of my heart. I cannot write.

My Great Father. When I speak I do not only speak for myself but for all my people.

My Great Father. To speak the mind of all around you would be to speak a great deal. We expect a great many presents.

My Great Father. I see by your discourse that you are well acquainted with our mode of life. When you see it why do you not send us home and prevent our wives and children from starving? I have already seen your towns—it is well for those at home to see them.

My Great Father. You have war—it is very well—defend yourselves. We will do the same with our neighbours.

My Great Father. On my way to see you I heard that you had war with white & red. As to the red I say nothing. I will remain quiet.

My Great Father. From the first time I saw you we have heard the same words. When we saw you first you told us the goods would be at first cost. I do not see it and have come to enquire about it.

My Great Father. I come to enquire what we received for the small portion of land we sold to you?

My Great Father. I come to see you respecting lands. I sold a piece of land, but your people have encroached upon us my great father. I wished to see you and enquire what lands I have sold to you, and whether it was by your directions that those people settled on them.

Ridge. Chief of the Fox.

My Great Father. You have heard what the Chiefs have said—it is all right—we wish to place all right. When I heard your words I did not regret coming to see you.

I was happy to come to see and have all matters adjusted; but I am not the man appointed for that purpose—he will come forward.

My Great Father. I came joyfully to see you, but you have put me in a house on the floor where I have forgot half what I had to say, and begin to think about my wife and children.

My Great Father. You are not ignorant that we are at war with the same Indians that you are, and perhaps at this time some of my people may be laid low. This pipe is a pipe of reconciliation—when I hear your words again I will give it to you.

Big Thunder.

My Village ordered me to come, hear your words, represent them, and carry your words to them.

My Great Father.

The same advice you have given me to day we give to our young men. You compared your people to the stars and to the forest. We did not wish to hear this as we already knew it.

My Great Father. I hope the counsel you gave was not under suspicion of us. We have been true, and have raised some soldiers.

My Great Father. When I heard your advice I heard you were at war— we knew you were at war. We are convinced that you can defend yourself. We are also at war.

My Great Father. I hope you will say that we have done well. We have done so. I hope you will do to us as we do to you, I hope take good words.

My Great Father. You know what length of time we have been absent from our Village. I am tired of rolling about the floor and wish to return home.

My Great Father. I hope for more conversation with you—to hear your words and for you to hear my words. This pipe will be a token of our good understanding.

Waupalathe (Shawanoe chief.)

My Father.

Long ago great troubles took place in our old nation. We divided and went to the other side of the Mississippi where we got lands and were happy. The Osages struck us and I raised a party of Cherokees and Delawares to revenge the injury. We marched with a large party four days when we received General Clark's words which stopped us. We were called to St. Louis and have made peace. We have the hand of our Great Father and will hold it fast. The Americans encroached on our claim but they were removed and we were happy. We wish our land to be marked out. What my Great Father has told you all is true. See that you follow his words. I am at war with no nation—now all is peace.

2d. Ioway Chief.

When I set out from home my nation was to remain quiet and wait my return.

Ioway.

My Great Father.

I am glad to see you—all appear white about you.

Tr, two copies (DLC). Undated; date assigned here on the assumption that these speeches were given in response to JM to the Delegations of Several Indian Nations, ca. 22 Aug. 1812.

1. Sans Oreilles, or No Ears, was a chief of the Little Osage and son of White Hair (d. 1808), the principal chief of the Great Osage (Donald Jackson, ed., *The Journals of Zebulon Montgomery Pike* [2 vols.; Norman, Okla., 1966], 1:288 n. 2, 296 n. 18).

2. In the Treaty of Fort Clark, concluded 10 Nov. 1808, the Osage agreed to give up land and make peace with their Indian neighbors and the U.S. in return for several forms of compensation. The treaty stipulated that the U.S. would build a fort (Fort Osage) "on the right bank of the Missouri, a few miles above the Fire prairie," which would be garrisoned. At this location the U.S. would establish "a well assorted store of goods [a factory], for the purpose of bartering" for Osage pelts and furs. At the fort the U.S. was also to provide for the Osage "a blacksmith and tools, to mend their arms, and utensils of husbandry, and engage to build them a horse mill, or water mill, also to furnish them with ploughs, and to build for the great chief of the Great Osages, and for the great chief of the Little Osages, a strong block house in each of their towns." The U.S. agreed to pay compensation to any inhabitants of the Louisiana Territory claiming to have lost property to the Osage. For the Great Osage the U.S. would deliver yearly to Fire Prairie or St. Louis "merchandise to the amount or value of one thousand dollars" and for the Little Osage "merchandise to the amount or value of five hundred dollars" (*ASP, Indian Affairs*, 1:763–64). For more on this treaty, see ibid., 1:764–67. White Hair was a principal participant in the negotiations that produced the preliminary version of the treaty on 14 Sept. 1808 (ibid., 1:765).

3. This was probably a reference to Pierre Chouteau, who was appointed Indian agent for the district of Upper Louisiana on 17 July 1804 and was assigned as agent to the Great and Little Osage on 7 Mar. 1807. Chouteau helped to negotiate the Treaty of Fort Clark (Dearborn to Chouteau, 17 July 1804 and 7 Mar. 1807 [DNA: RG 75, LSIA]; *ASP, Indian Affairs*, 1:764–67).

4. Clermond, or Gresdanmanses, first chief of the Arkansas Osage, was among the signatories of the Treaty of Fort Clark (Bureau of Indian Affairs, *Treaties between the United States of America, and the Several Indian Tribes, from 1778 to 1837* [1837; reprint, Millwood, N.Y., 1975], 146).

5. Blank left in both Trs.

6. Blank left in first Tr; illegible in second Tr.

7. The Wind had been one of the principal chiefs of the Little Osage and was among the participants in the negotiations that produced the preliminary version of the Treaty of Fort Clark on 14 Sept. 1808 (Jackson, *Journals of Pike*, 1:297 n. 20).

8. Sans Oreilles probably referred to his participation in the negotiations that resulted in the preliminary treaty of 14 Sept. 1808, of which he was a signatory (ibid., 1:296 n. 18).

9. Blank left in both Trs.

10. This was presumably a reference to Nicholas Boilvin.

11. This may have been a reference to either Choukeka Dekaury (ca. 1730–1816) or his son, Konoka Dekaury (1747–1836), both Winnebago chiefs (Hodge, *Handbook of American Indians North of Mexico*, 1:384).

12. Blank left in first Tr; illegible in second Tr.

From William Jones

S<small>IR</small>   P<small>ROVIDENCE</small> Augt 22d 1812

Upon a presumption that my letter of July 22d must have miscarried I now do myself the honor to forward you a Copy thereof, observing to your

Excellency that a supply of Arms &c &c as a part for which an Annual appropriation was made by Act of Congress April 2d 1808[1] is highly necessary, the reception of which would be highly gratifying to the State & very pleasing to me. I have the honor to be with great respect your Excellencys Obedient humble Servant

WM. JONES

RC (DNA: RG 107, LRRS, J-240:6). Docketed as received in the War Department on 31 Aug. 1812.

1. Jones referred to "An Act authorizing the sale of public Arms," which allowed the president to sell public arms to individual states (*U.S. Statutes at Large*, 2:481).

§ From the Citizens of Adams County, Mississippi Territory. *22 August 1812.* At a meeting of "a large and respectable number" of citizens, "a committee of seven . . . reported the following preamble and Resolutions, which were adopted with but two dissenting voices."

"At the present important, and momentous Crisis, of our publick affairs, it becomes the duty of every citizen of the United States to express his faith in the Government of his Country, and in the most explicit manner to evidence to the world his willingness and determination to support it every hazard [*sic*]. Under these impressions; and with a view to promote unanimity and concord with one another, and to inspire the General Government with confidence in our efforts and patriotism;

"Resolved that we approve the Act of the General Government declaring war to exist between the United Kingdoms of Great Britain and Ireland and the dependencies thereof, and the United States of America and their Territories; and that we will unite our best exertions to prosecute the war with energy and vigor until it shall terminate in a happy and glorious peace.

"Resolved that we have the most entire confidence in the President of the United States; and that he will take every measure for the safety, protection, and defence of the Southern frontier: and we pledge our lives and fortunes to enforce to the utmost of our ability, the empire of the laws in this exposed section of the union, and to expel from our shores every hostile foot that shall dare to tread our soil.

"Resolved that the proceedings of this meeting be published in the respective news papers of the City of Natchez; and that one copy of the same be forwarded to the President of the United States, and one to the Governor of this Territory."

RC (DLC). 2 pp.; signed by Joseph Sessions, president, and George Pearre, secretary; postmarked Natchez, 1 Sept.

From Elbridge Gerry

MY DEAR SIR,   CAMBRIDGE 24th August 1812

Our late Secretary, Benjamin Homans Esqr[1] will have the honor of paying his respects, & presenting this to you. His object is to obtain some place, in which he may be employed for the mutual benefit of himself & the Publick. The Consulate to which he was lately appointed would not have enabled him to subsist himself, & his Family. His success in the present pursuit, would afford great pleasure to the republicans generally of this Commonwealth as well as to myself. I have the honor to remain dear Sir, with the highest Consideration & respect Yours very sincerely

E. GERRY

RC (DLC).

1. Benjamin Homans (1765–1823), a Boston native, was nominated by JM to the consulate at Tunis on 1 July 1812. After declining that appointment, he was appointed by William Jones as chief clerk of the Navy Department in 1813 (*PJM-SS*, 2:28 n. 2).

From John Kilbourn

WORTHINGTON, OHIO,

MAY IT PLEASE YOURS [*sic*] EXCELLENCY; SIR,   24th Aug. 1812.

I take the liberty, although, personally, a total stranger, of writing this communication. Dr. E. Tiffin,[1] esqr. can inform you more particularly of me.

The western mail has this moment arrived, and brought the following letter without name. The following is a literal copy from the original now before me.

"August 16th 1812.

Fort Detroit Surrendered[2] to Major Genl. Brock[3] Commanding his Brittanic Majesty's forces in Upper Canada. Gen. Hull the American commandant marched out at 12 o clock with his army unarmed, prisoners of war and in tears at the perfidy of their Genl. The 4th. Article of the capitulation is, (viz) By Genl. Hulls desire a Detachment of the Ohio Troops now under march are considered Prisoners of War.[4] He has politely agreed that those who are at home are at liberty to avail themselves of freedom if they cannot find a leader better disposed to sell them cheaper than he is.

Urbanna August 22nd. m. the express arrived yesterday morning—Capt. Brush[5] this morning & most of his company."

I do not write this letter because I suppose that the substance of the intelligence would not be transmitted previous to the arrival of this; but to give some more particular information of the sentiments of the people generally, which you might not so fully be informed of by the superior commanding officers. The militia in all the interior and western parts of Ohio are risen *en masse*, to march to the north and west. I shall march in 30 minute with the usual habilliments of a privat soldier, but am somewhat fearful, not of the enemy, but that my corporeal abilities will not enable me long to endure the necessary fatigue of a camp, on account of my having been, for a few years, disused to manual labor. But I shall march and assist in my country's defence, so long as my physical powers will permit: until an army of 10 or 12 thousand men can be formed in our rear. Such an army, we country politicians deem necessary.

Col. Cass, now a prisoner, I think would be as popular a commander in chief as we could have, of the new army: if popular opinion was to be observed.

Private letters from the 1st. army, soon after their arrival in Canaday, hinted at what is now talked of openly, and said that "all was not going right."

My haste must be my apology, for the careless manner in which this letter is written; and in the mean time, attribute sir, my presumption in thu⟨s⟩ abruptly addressing you to no improper motive.

There are a number of other particulars, which might be mentioned; but I presume that these now communicated will not be unacceptably received. With great esteem for your character and political sentiments, on many accounts, I am sir your most obedient humble servant

JOHN KILBOURN[6]

RC (DNA: RG 107, LRRS, K-47:6). Docketed as received in the War Department on 14 Sept. 1812.

1. Edward Tiffin (1761–1829), a physician and Methodist minister in Chillicothe, Ohio, was the first governor of the state of Ohio before his election as a U.S. senator in 1806. Tiffin resigned from the Senate in 1808 and was elected to the Ohio House of Representatives the following year, serving as Speaker. JM appointed him commissioner of the General Land Office in 1812, and he became surveyor general of the Northwest Territory in 1814 (Sobel and Raimo, *Biographical Directory of the Governors*, 3:1191).

2. On 8 Aug. 1812 Hull reported to Eustis that he had elected not to attack Fort Malden for the moment because he believed he could not ensure the safety of U.S. posts. He observed that since the fall of Michilimackinac, "the Indian force has been fast increasing in this part of the Country," British troops were advancing on his position from the Niagara peninsula, and communication with his supply network in Ohio had been cut off. Hull moved his troops back to Detroit that same day, leaving 300 men in Upper Canada as a symbol of his intent to return and resume the offensive. A company of Ohio volunteers was bringing supplies for Hull's army but had not moved beyond the river Raisin, and Hull's repeated attempts to send troops to escort them to Detroit did not succeed.

Hull now believed that he was pinned down in Detroit and completely cut off from supplies of equipment and men as the number of British troops and hostile Indians multiplied around him. Preparing for the worst, Hull recalled the troops he had left in Upper Canada on 11 Aug. and sent out a third escort party of 400 men under the command of Cols. Duncan McArthur and Lewis Cass. The detachment departed just as Maj. Gen. Isaac Brock arrived at Fort Malden. On 15 Aug., Brock requested that Hull surrender to avoid an "effusion of blood." Hull's first instinct was to refuse, but after pondering the problem overnight, while British batteries bombarded Detroit, he reconsidered. The next morning Hull received word that British troops were moving by both river and land into position for an attack, and he concluded that it had become "necessary, either to fight the enemy in the field; collect the whole force in the Fort; or propose terms of Capitulation." Weighing his options, Hull chose to surrender on 16 Aug. (Hull to Eustis, 8 Aug. and 26 Aug. 1812, and Brock to Hull, 15 Aug. 1812, *Michigan Historical Collections* 40 [1929]: 437–38, 451, 460–69).

The articles of capitulation, composed that same day and forwarded to Eustis in Hull's 26 Aug. dispatch, stipulated that all troops at Fort Detroit were to be surrendered to the British as prisoners of war, except for Michigan militia that had not yet arrived. All public stores, arms, and documents were to be given up, while private persons and property were to be "respected" (ibid., 40:469–70).

3. Isaac Brock (1769–1812) was born in Guernsey and entered the British army as an ensign in 1785. He had served in the West Indies, the Channel Islands, the Netherlands, and Denmark before being ordered to Canada in 1802. Brock was promoted to major general in June 1811, when he also became president and administrator of the government of Upper Canada during the absence of the lieutenant governor, Francis Gore.

In 1806 Brock had given orders that the marine department on the lakes and rivers of Canada should be placed under the superintendence of the deputy quartermaster general. This action, in large part, made possible his efforts for the defense of Upper Canada in 1812. Brock also advocated a bold policy of limited local offensives and realized the importance of Indian cooperation, developing a working relationship with the Shawnee chief Tecumseh. After Hull's surrender on 16 Aug. 1812 and the capture of Detroit, for which Brock was appointed an extra knight of the Order of the Bath, he returned to the Niagara peninsula, where he was killed in action at Queenston on 13 Oct. 1812 (Halpenny, *Dictionary of Canadian Biography*, 5:109–14, 191, 748).

4. The fourth article of capitulation stipulated that both a detachment from Ohio en route to join the Northwest Army and McArthur's troops that had been sent out from Fort Detroit were included in the surrender, even though they had not been present at the capitulation. The remaining parts of the Ohio militia "as have not joined the Army" were permitted to return to their homes "on condition that they will not serve during the War" (*Michigan Historical Collections* 40 [1929]: 469–70).

5. Capt. Henry Brush, a Chillicothe attorney, was in command of Ohio volunteers en route to Detroit in August 1812 (Alec R. Gilpin, *The War of 1812 in the Old Northwest* [East Lansing, Mich., 1958], 95, 110, 111).

6. John Kilbourn (1787–1833) was the publisher of the short-lived Columbus *Columbian Gazette* in 1815 and the author of the *Ohio Gazetteer*, first published in 1816 (Brigham, *History of American Newspapers*, 2:797; *The Ohio Gazetteer; or Topographical Dictionary* [Columbus, Ohio, 1816; Shaw and Shoemaker 38003]).

§ From the Merchants of Philadelphia. *24 August 1812*. "The memorial of sundry Citizens of the United states and Merchants of Philadelphia respectfully sheweth

"That your memorialists have been for years engaged in the business of importing and vending british manufactures, untill interrupted therein by the unjust orders and decrees of the two great belligerents of Europe, and consequent retaliatory measures of our own government.

"That while friendly negociations were pursuing by the government of the UStates, for the purpose of obtaining a recognition of our neutral rights: We confidently expecting the success they merit'ed were induced to continue our (at that time) lawful pursuits, by the investment of large sums (and otherwise) in England; for the purpose of effecting our customary operations of trade.

"But unfortunately these negociations having failed of producing the desired effect: it was deemed necessary by the UStates, to close the usual channel of our trade, by the passage of a Law prohibiting all importations from GBritain & her dependencies: untill she should relinquish or modify her offensive Edicts, so that they should cease to violate our neutral rights.

"To this measure—although stri⟨k⟩ing at the very vitals of our commercial pursuits, and destroying the means we possessed of obtaining a livelihood for ourselves and families, we chearfully submitted; under the hope that 'ere long it might produce the desired effect on Great Britain, and immediately instructed our agents and correspondents to stop all shipments on our account, untill the usual friendly intercourse between the two countries should be restored.

"In a state of perplexity, we patiently awaited a repeal of the orders in council, which unhappily for us did not occur untill Congress had deemed it necessary to declare that War existed between the United states and Great Britain and her dependencies: a circumstance which being unknown to our Agents in England, could not operate on their minds to prevent the shipment of our property lying there: which they supposed in consequence of the repeal of the orders in council, and the tenor of our non Importation Law, might be legally and safely forwarded to us.

"By this unexpected operation of our Agents in Great Britain, and without the most distant Idea of violating the Laws of our Country, our property to a very large amount is now afloat, and daily expected to arrive, Altho no measure that we know of has been adopted by the Executive to prevent vexatious seizures by the officers of the Customs: and protect us against the rapacity of privateersmen, who have already seized on the high seas, Vessels similarly situated with those conveying our property, and have carried them off for adjudication to ports of the United states at a great distance from that of their destination: thereby rendering it difficult and expensive to obtain redress.

"Neither can we now retrace the steps that have brought us into this dilemma, since unless this property is permitted to enter the ports of the UStates; doubtless a great proportion of it will be lost—a state of War with Great Britain preventing a return of the Vessels to that Country, and likewise the recovery of the value (if captured) on any policy of Insurance effected in Great Britain, such insurance being there deemed illegal.

"Under these distressful circumstances, and conscious of having in no respect intended a violation or evasion of the Laws of our Country, we come forward with full confidence, that you will immediately take into your serious consideration the extreme hardship of our case, and grant us such releif as in your wisdom and consistently with the mild spirit of the government and laws of our country, you may deem us entitled to. . . .

"At the above meeting it was voted that Saml. Harry Merchant and   [1] be a committee to respectfully wait on the president of the United states with the within memorial."

RC (DNA: RG 59, ML). 4 pp.; signed by Charles Pleasants, chairman, and Samuel W. Bradford, secretary.

1. Blank left in RC.

From Thomas Acheson

S<small>IR</small>   W<small>ASHINGTON</small> P<small>ENNA</small>. 25th August 1812

Alarming intiligence which we have Just recd. induces me to call upon the attention of your excellency. Express messengers have arrivd. who bring the dreadful information that *Genl Hull and his Army;* have been Captured by the *British and Indians* after a battle, in which 500 of the brave ohio Volunteers were left on the ground to the Scalping knife of the Savage. The immediate causes which led to this disastrous event we are not yet informd. of but popular disapprobation loudly expressd. has *attached blame* to the department of war, as well as to the unfortunate victim of his own temerity and want of military Science. For my own part I presume not to impeach the Competency or Correctness of the person at the head of that department; but I beg to be indulged in expressing my opinion, that he could not have been truly informd. of the Situation of our enemies Country, when he directed the invasion of it by So inconsiderable a force as that under Genl. Hull. How the British Came to be possessed of the declaration of war at every Military on our frontiers before our own Officers—Why Genl. Hull was permitted actually to enter the enemies territory and plant himself near a Strongly fortified and numerous garrison, and *there to prepare his gun Carriages.* Questions which are agitating the public opinion and public Sensibility in a manner no way advantagious to the reputation of the Secretary at war. As to the military talents of that Gentleman and his Capacity for the Situation he is in—no doubt your excellency is the best Judge. It is obvious however from the late unfortunate occurence that the best and most expedient policy has not been pursued. The only thing that Can now be done to remedy the evil is to prevent the growing Consequences. To that purpose I beg your excellencies attention. The Indians are now in great force (Some Say 5000) advancing with the horrid yell of Savage ferocity upon the back Settlements of ohio and Penna. I have your excellency to paint the dismay and terrors which pervade every heart. For Several years we have felt Safe from the incursions of this most formidable and barberous enemy. Now by one disasterous defeat the best blood of our Sister State ohio, has been immolated on the altar of patriotism; Our frontiers are laid defenceless and open to invasions and the horrid whoop of Indian warfare Sounds in our ears. Express messengers have arrivd. here this morning imploring the aid of our Militia to protect the defenceless Settlements on the frontiers of ohio, whose inhabitants are flying in every direction leaving their property a prey to the enemy. For want of arms ammunition &c. we are unable to render them that efficient assistance which we feel disposd. to do. Our Situation alarmingly Solicits executive interference. Militia always ready to Serve their Country—Calld. upon long ago—we only now demand from your excellency that we may have the immediate means of defending ourselves. Your excellency no doubt is informd. of the Indian character and mode of warfare. If So you will Sympathise with our fears and give the most prompt attention to our alarming Circumstances. I have the honor to assure your excellency that the Penna. militia have not the Same views and ideas of the military duty which the general Government may require from them that the people of Massachusetts appear to have. They are willing to Serve their Country in any place from Main to Georgia and even to march beyond our territorial limits if necessary to Cut off an enemy. Our territory is no [sic] invaded; would it not reconcile the Constitutional objections of Govr. Griswold and Strong to Call the New England militia, to the defence of ohio and at the Same time Order Penna. to march towards the East. Our Country is overrun with disaffected traitors and apostates to liberty who act as a lock chain on the wheels of Government and mar its purposes. Something Should be done to intimidate them. The friends of administration have a vast preponderance. Call upon the friends of liberty, and you will find that the people will rise in majesty and Strength (immediately). Let 5000 men pass into Canada from Detroit. Let 2000 Cut off the Communication between upper and lower Canada—when Canada will immediately fall and our most dreadful enemy be Subdued at once. If Nova Scotia be Subdued by taking Hallifax—the navigation of the St. Lawrence may be embarrassed by our Privateers &c and Qebec will at length fall without bloodshed. The Militia will be Subject to your Call. If a Sufficient number be Calld. out at once it will intimidate the Indians, who always Join the Strongest Side it will assure the Canadians, who are disposed to Join us, that we are able to protect them and it will undoubtedly in the end Save both blood and expence. I beg your excellency to pardon the Suggestions I have intruded upon your notice. They are dictated by a love of Country and a Sincere desire that the armies of our Country and the enemies of administration may be defeated in their malignant views. Rest assured nothing now remains but prompt and vigirous measures to be pursued by the Genl. Government or a total change of political Sentiment not only in the people of ohio but of the population east of the Alegheny Mountain. I Speak not only my own Sentiments but those of 9/10ths of my fellow Citizens. We are now arming ourselves as far as possible and preparing to march to the defence of the frontiers. As the Genl. of this brigade of Penna. Militia I have thought it my duty to make this immediate communication to you of the alarming Situation in which we are placd. by the defeat of Genl. Hull and to Solicit your prompt and efficient attention. Not having the honor of a personal acquaintance I refer your excellency to Mr. Gallatin for my Standing in Society and believe me to be with Sentiments of high respect and esteem Your excellen[c]ys most devoted Hble Servt.

THOS. ACHESON[1]

RC (DLC). Docketed by JM.

1. Thomas Acheson was a merchant in Washington, Pennsylvania, and a member of a Republican party group known after the War of 1812 as the "Washington Club" (James A. Kehl, *Ill Feeling in the Era of Good Feeling: Western Pennsylvania Political Battles, 1815–1825* [Pittsburgh, 1956], 160, 162–63, 196–97).

From the Connecticut General Assembly

[25 August 1812]

At a General Assembly of the State of Connecticut holden at New Haven in said state by special order of his Excellency the Governour on the fourth tuesday of August in the year of our Lord one thousand eight hundred and twelve.

The Legislature of the State of Connecticut, convened to consult the welfare and provide for the defence of the state, at this interesting and eventful period, avail themselves of the opportunity thus afforded to declare and resolve,

That while some of their sister States offer assurances of their unqualified approbation of the measures of the General Government, in respect to our foreign relations, we confidently trust that the motives which influence us to declare what we believe to be the deliberate and solemn sense of the people of this state, on the question of the war, will be justly appreciated.

The people of this State view the war as unnecessary.

Without pretending to an exclusive or superiour love of country to what is common to their fellow-citizens, or arrogating a preeminence in those virtues which adorn our history, they yi[e]ld to none in attachment to the Union or veneration of the Constitution. The union, cemented by the blood of the American people, is endeared to our best affections, and prized as an invaluable legacy bequeathed to us and our posterity by the founders of our empire.

The people of this state were among the first to adopt the constitution. Having shared largely in its blessings, and confidently trusting that under the guardianship of the people and of the States, it will be found competent to the objects of its institution, in all the various vicissitudes of our affairs, they will be the last to abandon the high hopes it affords of the future prosperity and glory of our country.

These sentiments of attachment to the union and to the constitution, are believed to be common to the American people, and those who express and disseminate distrusts of their fidelity to both or either, we cannot regard as the most discreet of their friends.

Unfortunately our country is now involved in that awful conflict which has desolated the fairest portion of Europe. Between the beligerents Great Britain is selected for our enemy. We are not the apologists of the wrongs of foreign nations—we enquire not as to the comparative demerits of their respective decrees or orders. We will never deliberate on the choice of a foreign master. The aggressions of both nations ought to have been met at the outset, by a system of defensive protection commensurate to our means and adapted to the crisis. Other counsels prevailed; and that system of commercial restrictions, which before had distressed the people of Europe, was extended to our country. We became parties to the continental system of the French Emperor. Whatever its pressure may have been elsewhere, on our citizens it has operated with intolerable severity and hardship. In the midst of these sufferings war is declared and that nation of the two is selected as a foe, which is capable of inflicting the greatest injury. In this selection we view with the deepest solicitude, a tendency to entangle us with a nation which has subverted every Republic in Europe, and whose connections wherever formed have been fatal to civil liberty.

Of the operation of her decrees on the American commerce, it is not necessary here to remark. The repeal of them, promulgated in this country since the declaration of war, virtually declares that the American government was not to be trusted. Insult is thus added to injury. Should a continuance of this war exclude our sea-faring and mercantile citizens from the use of the ocean, and our invaluable institutions be sacrificed by an alliance with France, the measure of our degradation and wretchedness would be full.

War, always calamitous, in this case portentous of great evils, enacted against a nation powerful in her armies, and without a rival on the ocean, cannot be viewed by us but with the deepest regret. A nation without fleets, without armies, with an impoverished treasury, with a frontier by sea and land, extending many hundred miles, feebly defended, waging a war, hath not "first counted the cost." [1]

By the constitution of the United States the power of declaring war is vested in congress. They have declared war against Great Britain. However much this measure is regretted, the General Assembly, ever regardful of their duty to the general government, will perform all their obligations resulting from this act. With this view they have at this session provided for the more effectual organization of the military force of the state, and a supply of the munitions of war. These will be employed, should the public exigencies require it, in defence of this state and of our sister states, in compliance with the constitution; and it is not to be doubted but that the citizens of this state will be found, at the constitutional call of their country, among the foremost in its defence.

To the United States is delegated the power to call forth the militia to execute the laws, to suppress insurrection, and repel invasion. To the States respectively is reserved the entire control of the militia, except in the cases specified. In this view of that important provision of the constitution, the Legislature fully accord with the decision of his Excellency the Governour in refusing to comply with the requisition of the general government for a portion of the militia.

While it is to be regretted that any difference of opinion on that subject should have arisen, the conduct of the Chief Magistrate of this State, in maintaining its immunities and privileges, meets our cordial approbation. The Legislature also entertain no doubt that the militia of the State will, under the direction of the Captain General, be ever ready to perform their duty to the state and nation in peace or war. They are aware that in a protracted war, the burden upon the militia may become almost insupportable, as a spirit of acquisition and extension of territory appears to influence the councils of the nation, which may require the employment of the whole regular forces of the United States in foreign conquest, and leave our maritime frontier defenceless, or to be protected solely by the militia of the states.

At this period of anxiety among all classes of citizens, we learn with pleasure, that a prominent cause of the war is removed by a late measure of the British Cabinet. The revocation of the Orders in Council, it is hoped, will be met by a sincere spirit of conciliation on the part of our administration, and speedily restore to our nation the blessings of a solid and honorable peace.

In the event of the continuance of the war, the Legislature rely on the people of Connecticut, looking to Him who holds the destinies of empires in His hands, for aid to maintain those institutions which their venerable ancestors established, and to preserve inviolate those invaluable privileges which their fathers acquired, and which are consecrated by their blood.

The above and foregoing is a true Copy of Record.

Attest. THOMAS DAY, Secretary

At a General Assembly of the State of Connecticut holden at New-Haven in said state by special order of his Excellency the Governour on the fourth tuesday of August in the year of our Lord one thousand eight hundred and twelve

Resolved by this Assembly that His Excellency the Governour be requested to transmit to the President of the United States attested copies of the Resolutions and declarations passed at the present session of the General Assembly relative to the war in which the United States are engaged.

A true Copy of Record Examined by

THOMAS DAY, Secy.

RC (DLC). Enclosed in Roger Griswold to JM, 1 Sept. 1812 (ibid.; 1 p.).

1. Luke 14:28.

From David Jones

I have been about two months in ohio State & am now at this Place on my way to Chester. I think it my Duty to give a Statements of matters here & in the army according to reports, & letters from the army. Reports are so false in ohio State, that I can assert nothing possitively, I will not vouch therefore for the Truth of all I shall write. It is the prevailing opinion here that you have been grosly imposed on to appoint governor Hull as Commander, as it is thought he has not one military Qualification and it is my opinion all his movements have been a full Demonstration of the Fact. Only observe first puting the Baggage on board a vessel without a gard, when it would have been convenient to have sent a Company that way, neither ought they to have gone the East side of the Island opposite to the fort.[1] 2. he crossed over to Sanwich & issued a foolish threat in his Proclamation to put to the Death every man found fighting beside an Indian.[2] 3d. all the Detachments toward malden were weak & could answere no other Purpose than to demonstrate that he was not Qualified to Command, as his Detachments were too small & not supported by proper reinforcements. His Conduct on that side are blunders. It is confidently asserted that he has recrossed to Detroit. Nothing could be worse than this movement, as it will dispirit the Cannadians, and encourage the Indians. 4. he must have known the Number of Indians & brittish at brown's Town. Report says, they were 7 or 800d, while at the same Time he ordered only 400d of Col. Boyds regiment unsupported. The first news said half of them were sacrificed; but the last accounts said only 17 were left Dead. Report says & letters confirm that Colonels Cass, mackarthur & miller asked 500d hundred men, (by the by, his force was not much more than one half enough) to go & burry the Dead. Hulls answere was, let the Dead burry the Dead. This exasperated to [sic] officers so much, that they gave him a Challenge for a Duel. This he did not accept & he ought not. Thus, Sir, you see the army nearly in a State of mutany. Add to all this, it is confidently asserted that he is very often intoxicated; and is very much against him, it is confidently aserted that his Son holds a Commission in the brittish army in malden and that his Daughter is married to a brittish officer there.[3] The Common appelation given him in ohio State is granny Hull. For gods sake Sir, look out an officer fit to command & send him on to suppercede the present Cyfer. Now I have done my Duty to you & my Country, and as I said before, I will not answere for the truth of these facts. If they are not substantiated, it will do[4] harm for you to know that these reports prevail.

Now Sir I shall come home nearer to yourself or Congress, & which to blame I know not. There ought to have been 4 gun boats on this Lake, carrying each two 18 pounders. These would sweep to [sic] Lake of every brittish vessel. For want of this Step, all provisions must be send [*sic*] at an immense Expense & Danger by Land, through the mouth of the Indians, who are fast increasing, & had it not been for the Timely supply from Kentuckey with drafted men from ohio State, with some inlisted Soldiers the Country would have been oblidged to have raised en mass to defend themselves.

By all that I have heard the Conduct of Gen. Dearborn has been little Better; for instead of being at Boston, he ought to have taken the Passes of St. Lawrence & have prevented supplies of Troops from Canada. Also 20 gun boats ought to be built for Lake ontario, which would clear that Lake. Niagara must be taken this fall or the first year will be lost in Blunders. Wishing that god may inspire you with wisdom, I subscribe myself your Sincere friend & humble Servt

DAVID JONES[5]
late Chaplain to gen wayne.

P. S. for want of Time & paper I have sent you this disagreeble Letter without transcribing.

DAVID JONES

RC (DLC: Rives Collection, Madison Papers). Docketed by JM.

1. For the capture of Hull's baggage, see James Taylor to JM, 7 July 1812, *PJM-PS*, 4:572–73 and n. 1. The vessel (the *Cayauga*) was taken as it navigated the Detroit River on the Canadian side of Grosse Île, a route which passed the British fort at Amherstburg (Gilpin, *The War of 1812 in the Old Northwest*, 53–54).

2. Hull's 13 July 1812 proclamation to the inhabitants of Canada announced that the U.S. and Great Britain were at war and explained that to "the peaceable unoffending inhabitant" his invasion brought "neither danger nor difficulty." He promised that the U.S. was "sufficiently powerful" to afford Canadians "every security consistent with their rights." He asked of Canadians: "Remain at your homes, pursue your Customary and peaceful avocations, Raise not your hands against your bretheren." He pledged that they would be "emancipated from Tyranny and oppression and restored to the dignified station of freemen." Hull did not ask for their assistance in the war but stated that if, contrary to their interests, they "should take part in the approaching contest," they would be "considered and treated as enemies." He further warned, "*No White man found fighting by the side of an Indian will be taken prisoner* Instant destruction will be his lot." Hull concluded by saying that if Canadians wished to tender their services to the U.S. voluntarily, "they will be accepted readily" (*Michigan Historical Collections* 40 [1929]: 409–11).

3. Hull's only son, Abraham Fuller Hull (1786–1814), received a captain's commission in the Twenty-third Infantry in April 1812, served on his father's staff, and was on hand at the surrender of Detroit. In April 1813 he joined the Ninth Infantry; he was killed in the Battle of Lundy's Lane in 1814. Hull had three married daughters in 1812. Eliza (1784–1864) was married to New England merchant Isaac McLellan. Ann Binney (1787–1847) was married to Harris Hampden Hickman, a captain in the Nineteenth Infantry in 1812, who served in the U.S. Army throughout the war and was honorably discharged in 1815. Rebecca Parker (1790–1865) was married to Dr. Samuel Clarke of Newton, Massachusetts (Charles H. Weygant, *The Hull Family in America* [n.p., 1913], 493, 509–12).

4. Jones apparently omitted the word "no" here.

5. David Jones (1736–1820), a Baptist minister from Chester County, Pennsylvania, served as chaplain to Brig. Gen. Anthony Wayne's battalion in the Revolutionary War and also during Wayne's expedition against the Northwest Indians in 1794. Jones was appointed chaplain for the Ninth Military District on 2 Apr. 1813 (*PMHB* 36 [1912]: 38 n.; *Senate Exec. Proceedings*, 2:372, 374).

From William Montgomery

SIR   PHILADELPHIA August 25th. 1812

The declaration of war does not I presume affect your power to remove the non-importation Law. The clause in the revocation of the orders in Council reserving the right to renew them can be protested against or denied; and until renewed cannot affect our neutral trade, which I presume after the first of august is free from the operation of the orders. But the war gives a new right. This I hope negotiations will soon remove. If you can make an honourable peace, which perhaps can be now done better than when more money is lost and more lives sacrificed, the applauses of your country will follow your administration and the charge of an attachment to one power and hatred to another will be proved to be groundless. I really believe that the British Government at this moment are disposed to make an honourable peace & such a one as would certainly be more congenial to the interests of our country than a war. The Conduct of France since the declaration that her decrees were repeal'd as to this Country, has not been candid and just but on the contrary insulting, by continuing to burn our ships and to capture them in every sea. In the present war our country is divided—which may lead to civil war or a separation of the Union. The army already raised will enable you to conclude a peace and by placing a force on the Frontiers will secure our influence over the Indians and give the Government a force to invade Canada at any time when we are insulted and before the Enemy will have time to make preparations for resisting such a force. The policy of increasing our territory is much doubted, and without a navy for its protection, it never can be advantageous. This country must have commerce to preserve the union; consider how many people have their all in ships and the greater proportion of the Eastern people supported by them.

Privateers of a few guns it is said are fitting out to capture the goods which are daily expected from England, belonging to our own Citizens of all political opinions. The words in the Law "the President shall issue his proclamation["]¹ and not Knowing of the war, the agents in England have generally shipped the goods owned here. This state of things is novel and deeply interesting. Thousands will be ruined unless our Government interfere, and one Citizen will be seen to possess himself of the property of another, which will increase domestic strife, animosity and discontent. I conjure you, Sir, to give this subject the consideration it solemnly demands and if you can restore a good peace, the blessing of God and the plaudits of your Country will inevitably follow—an honourable armistice would remove hatred and I sincerely hope be the beginning of a lasting peace and cause our country again to flourish and Britain seeing that we will risk a war for our rights, will not invade them. With due consideration I am Your Hble. Servt.

WM MONTGOMERY

P S. I am ¼ owner of some dry goods purchased two years ago—the Agent was forbidden to ship them unless the intercourse was open or other orders given; notwithstanding which they are shipped—this circumstance came to my knowledge since writing the above.

RC (DLC). Docketed by JM.

1. Agents in Great Britain were under the impression that the Nonintercourse Act of 2 Mar. 1811 would lapse even with Congress out of session, since the legislation had stipulated that "in case Great Britain shall so revoke or modify her edicts, as that they shall cease to violate the neutral commerce of the United States, the President of the United States shall declare the fact by proclamation . . . And the restrictions imposed or which may be imposed by virtue of the said act, shall, from the date of such proclamation, cease and be discontinued" (*U.S. Statutes at Large*, 2:651).

From John Ott and Daniel Bussard

SIR   GEORGE TOWN Augt. 25. 1812

Permit us to represent that the appointment of one or more additional Magistrates in George Town would promote the speedy administration of Justice be a convenience to the People and a relief to those in office who have at present for want of assistance more than their share of the Burthen. We beg leave to name Daniel Reintzel[1] as a proper person for the appointment, he at present devotes much of his time in settling disputes among The Citizens and from his having formerly been in Commission has experience to add to his accustomed Industry. Respectfully Your Obedt. Servts.

JOHN OTT[2]
DANL. BUSSARD[3]

RC (DNA: RG 59, LAR, 1809–17, filed under "Reintzal"). A note on the cover indicates that Reintzel was "appointed."

1. JM nominated Reintzel as justice of the peace for the County of Washington, District of Columbia, on 12 Nov. 1812 (*Senate Exec. Proceedings*, 2:303).
2. John Ott, a Georgetown druggist, was justice of the peace for Washington County, Dis-

trict of Columbia, and became president of the Board of Common Council shortly after its formation in 1812 (Oliver W. Holmes, "The City Tavern: A Century of Georgetown History, 1796–1898," *Records of the Columbia Historical Society . . . : The Fiftieth Volume* [1980], 24; *Senate Exec. Proceedings*, 2:305).

3. Daniel Bussard, owner of a blanket factory in Georgetown and a fulling mill in Bladensburg, was named by Congress as one of the incorporators of the Georgetown Lancaster School Society in 1812 (Van Horne, *Papers of Benjamin Henry Latrobe*, 3:384).

From Charles Scott

SIR.   FRANKFORT Augt. 25th. 1812.

Since I had the honor of addressing you under date of the 14th. Inst.[1] feeling the urgent necessity from every information representation and appearance of taking Some decisive and efficient Measure for the relief of the North Western Army under the Command of Brigadr. Genl Hull and well knowing how important an early Step must be to effect this object— Weighing responsibility agt. love of Country; and conceiving that it is of the highest consequence to the Government, and the Successful and Speedy termination of the contest in which we are engage⟨d⟩ which the first impressions Shall make of success or disaster, I have been to [*sic*] induced to call to My aid some of the most respectable and Sincere Friends to the Common Cause, and to Conform to their advice.[2]

Enclosed I beg leave to Submit to you the results of their opinions & advice on this interesting and unexpected State of affairs. The Officer who waits at his post for orders, does well in the General, but cases must & do arise where all is lost to wait for them; and where to anticipate is to obey. The distance of the Seat of Government from the Scene of operation, the thousand unforseen and material occurrences, which call necessarily for some discretion, and the great Stake we have depending—Acting Solely under the Earnest and Ardent desire I have for the prosperity of my Country—all these must be my apology for the course I have ventured to pursue. My own Judgmt. however, much as I distrust it, has been Supported by men in whom the utmost confidence is deservedly placed. Numerous difficulties are not wanting, to carrying the proposed measure into effect. The means of procuring Supplies—who are to furnish them; the want of authority in Settling the command, all Standing in the way. But Something was deemed essential to be done. The force mentioned in the inclosed document, Signed by the Gentlemen,[3] will be immediately (no doubt) completed, if not exceeded including Some Indiana Troops ordered on by Governor Harrison to join the Detachment. The asst. or Depy Commissary, Col. Buford has been requested or rather advised, to furnish the necessary Supplies.[4] It is also evident that a description of force not authorised by any existing regulation, will be highly useful and contribute to the immediate relief proposed: that is mounted infantry or riflemen Say to the number of 500. I have, so far as I could authorised their Employmt. and they with many others must look to the justice of the country for compensation.

The arrangements I have made await the Sanction or disapproval of your orders & pleasure. They were intended merely as provisional, and to meet the pressing exigencies of the case. There is great reason to believe from the enclosed copies of Letters I send you from Officers of Genl Hulls army that it is in extreme danger, and that he has lost their confidence.[5] If the latter be the case; with a more adequate; better Situated; and better appointed force; but little indeed could be expected. You will perceive that many of these Letters contain a freedom of Expression which should be considered confidential, although Copies of them, to be sent to you, Seemed to me necessary, to develope the true temper & situation of the army. A strange and accountable series of failure, or bad management Seem to me also to require a change and point to the necessity of a differen[t] Commander in chief in that Quarter. Their confidence in Govr. Harrison and indeed that of the Western people generally is almost a guarantee for his Success should he be appointed to Command there. Indeed I view it as of so much importance, that the protraction or speedy termination of the war there may depend on it. Enclosed you have a copy of my instructions to him.[6] You will not fail to perceive the necessity of your orders respecting his Command, and of the supply of the Troops with him, being forwarded as speedily as may be, so as if possible to reach him before arriving at Detroit. In all things I have endeavored to act for the best under Existing circumstances. Mr. Clay has written a Letter to my old Friend Col. Monroe on this Subject to which I beg leave to refer you.[7] As I this day close my Administration and shall not from My advanced age, be able again to engage in public life, permit me Sir to express my earnest Wishes for a continuance of your health and useful Services to your Country in the high office you now so ably & satisfactorily fill. I have the honor to be with high respect & consideration, Yr. Mo. Obt. Servt.

CHS. SCOTT

P. S. From the information recd the detachment of Mila. under Genl Payne[8] (1800 or thereabout fine fellows) left cincinnati on their march yesterday they got supplied with arms &c. They will not be delayed by the addition. The Inda. Mila. will join them at Dayton & Poages[9] Regt. before then, the horsemen will soon overtake them, & by the time you receive this they will without an accident be within 100 miles of Detroit.

RC and enclosures (PHi: Daniel Parker Papers). Recorded in the Registers of Letters Received by the Secretary of War (DNA: RG 107) as received in the War Department on 12 Sept. 1812. For surviving enclosures, see nn. 3 and 6.

1. Letter not found.

2. Having received dispatches from Detroit reporting that the situation was grave, Scott called a meeting in Frankfort of Kentucky political leaders on 25 Aug., the last day of the governor's term of office. At the meeting were members of the state's congressional delegation, including Henry Clay, Richard M. Johnson, and Stephen Ormsby. Also present were the incoming governor, Isaac Shelby, and Jesse Bledsoe, John Fowler, former governor Christopher Greenup, Martin Hardin, Samuel Hopkins, Harry Innes, William Logan, and Thomas Todd. Collectively they advised Scott to commission William Henry Harrison as a brevet major general in the state militia, despite the fact that Harrison was not a resident of Kentucky, in order to permit him to command the reinforcements being raised to relieve Hull at Detroit. The meeting also decided to increase the number of those reinforcements from 1,500 to 3,400 (Henry Clay to Monroe, 25 Aug. 1812, in Hopkins, *Papers of Henry Clay*, 1:719–20, 721 nn.).

3. Scott enclosed a copy of a letter to Thomas Buford signed by the thirteen members of the meeting (1 p.; marked "(No. 3)"), advising the deputy commissary that as the requirement for reinforcements to Detroit had been increased from 1,500 to 3,400 men, Buford should increase supplies for the army accordingly.

4. See n. 3, above. Thomas Buford had been appointed a deputy commissary of purchases for Kentucky on 4 June 1812 (Heitman, *Historical Register*, 1:260).

5. Enclosures not found.

6. Scott enclosed a copy of the letter he wrote to William Henry Harrison on 25 Aug. (3 pp.; marked "(No. 2)"), in which he notified Harrison of his appointment as brevet major general of the Kentucky militia. Scott also directed Harrison to take command of the reinforcements being raised for Detroit and authorized him to accept the services of up to 500 mounted volunteers, with the proviso that it would be up to Harrison to guarantee any compensation that might be paid to the latter body of troops. Scott further stated that Harrison was "to receive and confirm [*sic*] to the orders of the President." "In the mean time" he was to conduct himself in ways "so as most effectually to accomplish the views of the Government, and to protect our exposed frontiers."

7. Henry Clay to Monroe, 25 Aug. 1812, in Hopkins, *Papers of Henry Clay*, 1:719–20.

8. John Payne (d. 1854), a general in the Kentucky militia, served under Harrison at the Battle of Mississinewa and the Battle of the Thames (*Collins' Historical Sketches of Kentucky* [1878 ed.], 2:93).

9. Robert Pogue was a Kentucky militia colonel (Esarey, *Messages and Letters of William Henry Harrison*, Indiana Historical Collections, 2:143, 149).

From John Wilson

SIR,   STEUBENVILLE OHIO 25th Augst 1812

With the greatest reluctance I address you on the following subject, why dont your excellency call on the Governors, of Pensylvania & Virginia to send their volunteers to the frontiers as well as the poor Ohio boys and Kentuckians,[1] observe the new states have been very attentive and done as much for there country as any other state, and finding the[y] are oblidged to leave there familys and in fact there small crops, to be exposed to hazard, the remainder of the citizens left, are, quite dissatisfied, there are thousands to my own knowledge, both in Virginia & Pensylvania, who have volunteered, and never received a call, whereas the time is come for there services at Detroit, & my sincere wish is for there success & prosperity, but I cant behold the volunteers from other States waiting in readiness for call and receive none, even in the town of Pittsburgh there are two or three voluntee[r] corps, and in Uniontown all in readiness, and in Frankfort Virginia and great many other places to long for me to relate, I beg you[r] Excellency to not be surprized, at my forwardness, as it would give me satisfaction, to see our American arms, victorious, and the soon⟨er⟩ we bring them savages & british tyrants to there senses the sooner, we should have an honourable peace, Accept the assurance of my due consideration your friend & very Humble Serveant

JOHN WILSON

N. B

There not too, much confidence can be placed in the militiia [sic] of those parts, the dutch will run, nothing like regulars, who are well trained to action, I wish you would send me a Captains commission in the regulars, I should take it as a particular favor,

J.W

RC (DNA: RG 107, LRRS, W-278:6). Docketed as received in the War Department on 1 Sept. 1812.

1. On 1 Sept. 1812 Eustis wrote to the governor of Virginia to request that 1,500 detached militia troops be called and marched to the Northwest. The same day Eustis requested that the governor of Pennsylvania redirect to the Northwest 1,500 troops already preparing to march to Niagara (DNA: RG 107, LSMA).

§ From James McCally. *25 August 1812, Clarksburg.* Encloses a copy of a Harrison County order "relative to a company of Cavalry which I have been ingaged in enlisting."[1] Describes the company as consisting of approximately fifty men and notes that it is prevented from increasing in size by the "oposition made by some disaffected Captains of the Cavalry & Rifle companies." Proposes that if the company was "recognised by the president of the U. S. & the officers commissioned by him," recruitment could proceed "with authority & the citizens Could not be deterred for volunteering."

Relays the wish of the company to join the detachment under General Hull. Expresses concern that unless they are called into service and commissioned by JM, "the purposes for which the[y] have enlisted will have gone past & their assistence in this form lost to the Country."[2]

RC and enclosure (DNA: RG 107, LRRS, M-400:6). RC 2 pp.; docketed as received in the War Department on 5 Sept. 1812. For enclosure, see n. 1.

1. The enclosed court order (1 p.) noted that a company of cavalry had assembled to tender their services to the president. The court recommended James McCally to be captain, "also Jonathan Jackson 1st. Lieutenant, John Wilkinson 2nd. Lieutenant and David E Jackson Cornet" of this troop. At the foot of the page, the company officially tendered the services of these four officers, four sergeants, four corporals, and fifty-three privates.

2. Filed with the letter is a slip of paper with a note in JM's hand: "It wd seem best to send the Commissions in blank to be filled on the spot, so as to combine respect for the law with the choice of the Volunteers." On 8 Sept. 1812 Eustis replied to McCally, forwarding blank commissions for officers and ordering the volunteer company to report at Point Pleasant to Brig. Gen. Joel Leftwich, who would march them to join the Northwest Army (DNA: RG 107, LSMA).

To Richard Cutts

DEAR SIR   [ca. 26 August 1812]

Soon after my last was sent off, I recd. your favor of   .[1] The report of the Capt: relative to what came to his knowledge at Halifax, agrees substantially with accts. thro' other channels. It is pretty certain that the war was little looked for, and that some of its effects are not a little dreaded. Still we ought to be prepared for an angry & malignant prosecution of it, on the B. side, considering the character of the existing Cabinet, and the invitations to it in certain proceedings here. Whether the late advances towards an armistice, which *originated* at Halifax, are to be ascribed to an anxiety to facilitate peace, or an insidious view to gain time, is not known. It is certain however that they were made without adequate authority and clogged with conditions not admissible. We have heard nothing yet from England subsequent to a knowledge there of our declaration of war; and cannot therefore know the impression made by it. The candid having before their eyes the declarations thro' Foster that G. B. would not repeal her orders as to us, in consequence of such a repeal by F. nay that she could not in justice to her allies do so; cannot fail to charge the war, not on our precipitation, but on the tardiness of the B. Govt. in the concessions finally resorted to. You will see in Mr. Gallatins circular, the ground on which importations of British Merchandize will *legally* rest.[2] The importers will be able to appreciate the equitable considerations on which the cases will turn, when before the Authorities which will finally decide on them. From the arrival of some vessels without safe-conducts, and the general delay of the rest, some I find are apprehensive that a knowledge or suspicion of the war may have led to an Embargo. It is probable you will know more of the matter, by the time this reaches you, than is now known here. We are without late accts. from Hull; owing probably to obstructions in the mail & express routes. He has met with difficulties, it wd. seem, not at first anticipated. The Western Country is making zealous exertions to aid him. We are on the point of setting out on a short visit to Montpelier. We should be very happy to have you all with us. Affecte. respects to Mrs. Cutts, & the little family, Yrs. truly

JAMES MADISON

RC (MHi); Tr (NjP: Crane Collection). Undated; date assigned here on the assumption that this letter was written shortly before JM's departure for Montpelier on 27 Aug. 1812.

1. Blank left in RC. Letter not found.
2. For Gallatin's circular, see Gallatin to JM, 13 Aug. 1812, n. 3.

From Richard Cavett

Dear Sir   Chillicothe August 26th: 1812
You have before this heard the melancholy and distressing news of our a[r]my at Detroit, being sold, and surrendered to the British, an army that with a good commander as able to sweep canada to the walls of Quebec. I hope and trust that evry exertion will be made by you in order to organize another a[r]my immediately of sufficient strength to be sure of Vi[c]tory, it will at least now agreeable to my weak opinion take 15,000 men at the lowest calculation with a good General at their head, there will be this week about 4000 men at urbana from Kentucky and this state—if you order out about 5000 from the westren part of Pennsylvania, and about 3000 more from Kentucky and Virginie and the balance from this state this fall is the time, *(not a moment to spair)* the roads will be good ⟨to⟩ Detroit for 3 months yet, & the[y] *are* impracti[c]able in the spring, let the army in the first place cross below Detroit and Take Malden first, then we will be sure of Detroit—it will never do you may rely on it to let the eneny [*sic*] remain there this winter—the war measures would be damped, and the Eastern states in all probability would break off—everything now must be rushed on with the greatest possible energy—the people here are all willing except a nest of Tories in this place, we want arms and amunition the troops from Pennsylvania ought to bring all the cannon possible. I hope you will excuse these lines from a Volu[n]teer who has fought 3 battles, one at the brid[g]e ovr Aux Canards,[1] and two at Browntown,[2] the last we drove the Indians and when Col, McArther was obliged to deliver to the British Officer Elliott[3] I cleared myself those observations although weak I hope will be of advantage to you. I am Respectfully your soldier

RICHARD CAVETT[4]

RC (DNA: RG 107, LRRS, C-447:6). Docketed as received in the War Department on 31 Aug. 1812; torn.

1. Cavett probably referred to a series of mid-July skirmishes between Ohio troops under Lewis Cass and British soldiers and Indians at a bridge across the Canard River about five miles from Fort Malden (Ernest A. Cruikshank, ed., *Documents Relating to the Invasion of Canada and the Surrender of Detroit, 1812* [1912; reprint, New York, 1971], 71–72, 89–90).
2. In the first week of August, Ohio volunteers under the command of Maj. Thomas Van Horne were engaged in a skirmish with Indians in and around Brownstown. The scene was

repeated under the command of Lt. Col. James Miller shortly afterward, but this time the Indians were reinforced with British troops. Van Horne and Miller had been on their way to rendezvous with Colonel Brush's regiment, for which they were to provide an escort to Detroit (*Michigan Historical Collections* 40 [1929]: 438, 463; Cruikshank, *Documents Relating to the Invasion of Canada*, 125–27, 136).

3. Capt. William Elliott received Colonel McArthur's surrender at the river Rouge on 16 Aug. 1812 (ibid., 172).

4. Richard Cavett was a private in Capt. Williams Key's company of Ohio militia (Paul Drake, comp., *Roster of Ohio Soldiers in the War of 1812* [1916; reprint, Bowie, Md., 1995], 25).

From Albert Gallatin

DR. SIR   [ca. 26 August 1812]

Is not the within important?[1] And Might not the Navy dept. give immediate authority to Capt. Chauncey?[2]

A. G.

RC and enclosure (NHi: Gallatin Papers). RC undated; date assigned here on the basis of JM's reply of the same day. For enclosure, see n. 1.

1. The enclosure was a 24 Aug. 1812 letter written from New York by John Armstrong to Gallatin (2 pp.). Armstrong relayed the substance of a conversation with Commodore Isaac Chauncey to the effect that on 1 July 1812, Lt. Melancthon Woolsey had applied to Chauncey for a supply of cannon to arm merchant vessels on the Great Lakes and at Sackets Harbor. Chauncey had responded that he lacked the authority to grant the request, which he had referred "to the proper departt. from which he has since heard nothing." Armstrong endorsed the request "out of a belief that it is not yet too late to effect Woolsey's object." "It's effects will be—to give us the exclusive use of the lake during the Campaign; to give to the Western extremity of your line of operations, (between Lake Ontario & Montreal), an excellent point of support & lastly to cut asunder your enemy's line of communication. Whether Gen. D. operate between the Lakes, Erie & Ontario, or between the latter & Montreal, the advantage will be the same. In both cases the two Canadas will be disjointed and Brock & Prevost will be unable to succor each other."

2. Isaac Chauncey (1772–1840) had served aboard a number of U.S. naval vessels before advancing to the rank of captain in 1807. JM placed Chauncey in command of naval forces on the Great Lakes on 31 Aug. 1812. Based in Sackets Harbor, Chauncey's forces built up a naval presence, cruised Lake Ontario, occasionally engaged the enemy, and lent support to land forces, but were never able to gain full control of those waters. Commodore Stephen Decatur received orders to replace him in 1814, but the change never took place (Hamilton to Chauncey, 31 Aug. 1812 [Dudley, *Naval War of 1812*, 1:297–301]; A. T. Mahan, *Sea Power in Its Relations to the War of 1812* [2 vols.; Boston, 1905], 1:361–63, 365–66, 2:36–41, 51–61, 299–300).

To Albert Gallatin

[ca. 26 August 1812]

The Command of the Lakes is obviously of the greatest importance & has always so appeared. I am glad to find it not too late to have that of Ontario. There must have been some mistake as to the effort to obtain it. It does not appear that any application, such as is intimated has been made to the Navy Dept. Mr. Hamilton has much confidence in Lt. Wolsey,[1] and says that he shall be furnished with what he wants and on orders which will be issued. Affecte respects.

J. M.

We set off tomorrow morning early: the probability of high waters stopped us today

RC (NHi: Gallatin Papers). Written at the foot of Gallatin to JM, ca. 26 Aug. 1812. Undated; date assigned here on the basis of JM's 27 Aug. departure for Virginia.

1. Melancthon Taylor Woolsey (1780–1838) was the ranking officer on the Great Lakes until he was placed second in command to Isaac Chauncey in September 1812. Under Chauncey, Woolsey participated in a number of engagements with the British, including the attack on York in 1813. He was promoted to the rank of master commandant on 24 July 1813 and received a captain's commission on 23 Apr. 1816, at which time he was reassigned to the West Indies (Dudley, *Naval War of 1812*, 1:273, 304–5, 2:495–97, 587; *Senate Exec. Proceedings*, 2:396, 3:44, 47).

From Samuel Spring

HONBL. SIR,   NEWBURY PORT Augst. 26. 1812.

By recurrence to the intimacy which subsisted between us in youth & the pleasant hours I spent at your Seat in connexion with your manner of treating me when I wrote you several years since on a particular subject,[1] induce me to write at this time.

I am oppressed & even overwhelmed with the times. While I respectfully express my sentiments, I hope you will neither consider me as dictating to the President, nor as acting the part of an impertinent Clergy man whose weapons are not carnal, nor political.

I am confident you possess ample means of information relative to the State of the Union. But as far as you have considered the Eastern States, not to mention N. York, ready to enter the Lists in war with G. B. give me leave to say with much deference and submission, you have been deceived. The Mass of men of interest and integrity *here* are wholly averse to the adoption of war measures. The people of these States, on whom you must depend to support necessary war, considering the million of slaves in the Southern

States, who must be carefully watched, will neither relinquish commerce nor in present circumstances fight with England. All the impressions you have received to the contrary by some of the nothern [*sic*] members of Congress are *partial & very erroneous. These States*, with but few exceptions will hazard *all* consequences relative to a civil war & the separation of the Union, rather than to be at war with England & confederated with France. For while *that* government is imperious, *this* is tyrannical & perfidious.

At the present opening, Good Sir, in consequence of the revocation of the French Decrees & the annulment of the orders of Council, is there not opportunity for the adoption of measures which will probably prevent the effusion of much blood & restore harmony between the States? But when with much frankness I make the suggestion, I not only give my own sentiments but the sentiments of thousands of the most valuable inhabitants of this powerful district of the country; that unless the nothern states can be treated with due respect and enjoy reciprocal advantages with the southern states, no matter how soon the contest be decided. We must enjoy our dearly purchased advantages & those which the Creator hath put into our hands. By the rich advantangage [*sic*] of Commerce, which supplied the national Chest with ample revenue previously to the interruption affected by France, both the nothern & southern States were clothed with prosperity and were mutually beneficial: & we hope the wisdom of administration will concert measures which will occasion the recurrence of those happy days.

The loss of harmony between the States must be inestimable: & nothing can prevent it & secure harmony but reciprocal advantage, which depends upon generous & extensive commerce.

Tho' deeply pressed with the weight of national concerns, I hope your excellency will find a moment to let me know the state of your health & that of Lady Madisons. Please to accept my respects & make them to your Lady. From your respectf[ul] friend & hume Servt

SAMUEL SPRING.[2]

RC (DLC: Rives Collection, Madison Papers).

1. Letter not found. Spring had visited JM at Montpelier sometime in the summer or early fall of 1801 (Spring to JM, 20 Oct. 1801, *PJM-SS*, 2:187).

2. Samuel Spring (1749–1819), a Congregational minister and Federalist in Newburyport, Massachusetts, had been JM's classmate at college (Harrison, *Princetonians, 1769–1775*, 166–71).

From Hezekiah Huntington

SIR   NEW HAVEN 27. Augt 1812

Inclosed is Gov. Griswold's message at opening an *extraordinary* session of the legislature, with documents &c, Printed by order of the two Houses.[1]

From their friends, the Administration—doubtless expect *truth* if they speak—but are perhaps more frequently deceived, by their *well meant*, tho' misguided efforts, than from the acts of *open enemies*, against whom they are garded.

A Bill now before the house, reported by a Joint committee, is to receive a third reading tomorrow, I have not seen it, but learn from Members that it Provides for raising an independent Corps, from *exempts*, from Military duty in the Militia, *all*, as many as will volunteer, to be Commissioned: by the Gov. & subject to his immediate Command—& such *Gen.* & Field Officers as he shall Commission—& without the advice of his Council— the Service designated for this Military force by the bill is to Support the laws, of *this State*, & *Surpress insurrections*, but they Cannot be marched out of this State.[2]

It has been said the Silence, of there friends—tended to decieve the Administration respecting the real State of things here in 1809. If things should grow serious—I venture to say—that with Authority to organise independent Companies for the Service of the U. States not to be *marched out* of *this State;* a very respectable force would be immediately organised.

Should we mention reports which conjecture has thrown out in the Course of the day—that the session will be protracted into next week[3] and that expresses are ariving from Boston, Providence &c—of these & many others it would be proper to say, I have not been able to trace them to any respectable Source—but as there *Can be no Ground*, for apprehending Opposition to *Our Laws*, it remains to be assertained, whether, the *real* & *Ostensible*, objects of this *extraordinary* session—& more *extraordinary Bill, are the Same*, inclosed also is a little Newspaper printed here—the editorial remarks may be Considered *half* official. With Great respect have the Honor to be your Excellencys Obedt Servant

Hez Huntington

RC (DLC: Rives Collection, Madison Papers). Docketed by JM.

1. Huntington probably enclosed a pamphlet entitled *Message of His Excellency Governour Griswold, to the General Assembly, at Their Special Session, August 25, 1812* . . . (New Haven, 1812; Shaw and Shoemaker 25147).

2. On 7 Sept. the Hartford *Connecticut Mirror* reported that this bill passed by a vote of 147 to 45. Huntington's account of the bill accords with the final terms of the legislation (see *The Public Statute Laws of the State of Connecticut*, bk. 2 [Hartford, 1817; Shaw and Shoemaker 14767], 93–94).

3. The special session of the state legislature adjourned on 29 Aug. 1812 ("Journal of the House of Representatives at a Special Session of the General Assembly holden at New Haven . . . ," *Records of the States of the United States of America* [DLC microfilm ed., Conn. A.1b, reel 4]).

From Jacob Lewis

SIR   HALIFAX 27th. Augt. 1812

I have been Captured by the Belvidera British Frigate, and Conducted
hither, on my Arival. I was throun into the Common prison; where americans are crouded In a manner, not to be immagined, should malady get
among them, it must be fatal to the whole and in the event of remaining
during the winter Season, they will inevitably perish for want of Cloathing
and other Comforts, it is a general wish of these unfortunate persons that
an Agent for prisoners should be appointed, it is also wished by the ad-
maral, it has been suggested to me to apply for the office, and I have only
to observe if it should be thought expedient to place an Agent here I should
be glad to Serve in that Capacity. With the highest Consideration & respect I am yr. obt. St.

                                                                    J LEWIS

RC (DNA: RG 45, Subject File RP, Prisons, Shore and Ship, box 605, envelope "Correspondence relating to prisons, American and British, 1812–13").

From John Mason

SIR   INDIAN OFFICE 27th. August 1812

I have the honour to state that William M. Stewart appointed by you on
the 10th. Inst. to be assistant Indian agent at Fort Madison, has declined the
acceptance of that office because on account of the Illness of his father he
is not able to leave his family, as promptly as the occasion requires. It being a matter of importance in the present state of the Indian country that
the person intended to fill the vacancy now existing, should go on with the
Indian Deputation now here, some of whom go to the spot. I have lost no
time to look for a person proper to replace Mr. Stewart—and I beg permission to recommend Robert. B. Belt[1] of Prince George County Maryland, he is a nephew of Gov: Bowies & a relation of Osborne Sprigg's[2]—
has been bred to business and I am assured by Doctor Kent[3] member of
congress from that district & others of his correct and regular habits.

As time presses and I know you are so near your departure from the
City—I have used the liberty Sir, in preference to taking up your time, by
asking a personal interview to submit this Gentleman in the first instance
to your consideration in this way and to send the form of an appointment
for him to serve if approved. I return that before made for William M
Stewart cancelled it having never been in his hands. With very great Respect I have the honour to be Sir Your Obt. Servt.

                                                                J MASON S. I. Tr

RC (DLC). In a clerk's hand, signed by Mason.

1. It is not clear when Robert Belt received an appointment, but by 1816 he was assistant factor in the Indian Department at Prairie du Chien (*ASP, Miscellaneous*, 2:338).

2. Osborn Sprigg (ca. 1741–1815) served in the lower house of the Maryland legislature in 1777 and represented Prince Georges County in the 1788 Maryland ratification convention (Papenfuse et al., *Biographical Dictionary of the Maryland Legislature*, 2:764–65).

3. Joseph Kent (1779–1837) had practiced medicine in Maryland before his election as a Federalist representative to the Twelfth and Thirteenth Congresses. Kent was reelected to the Sixteenth and three consecutive Congresses before serving as Maryland's governor from 1826 to 1829. He was elected to the U.S. Senate in 1833, where he served until his death.

§ From the Citizens of Chillicothe. *27 August 1812.* "By a unanimous vote and resolution of a numerous and respectable meeting of the Citizens of this town and the vicinity, the undersigned were appointed a Committee for and on behalf of said meeting to address your excellency on the subject of our national Concerns, as particularly instructed by their resolutions of yesterday which will be published.

"In discharge of the trust Committed to us and yielding to the impulse of our own feelings, we inform your excellency that the individuals Composing the meeting whose names are hereto Subscribed view With great Concern and anxiety for the Welfare of our Common Country and With equal Solicitude for her national honor, the present disa[s]trous situation of our army in the North Western region. They deplore the total defeat of the army under the Command of Bregidier Genl Hull after invading the Enemies Territory With so much Confidence and boldness; and after making such promises of Victory and protection to the poor deluded subjects of that Government as are Contained in that Generals proclaimation to the people of Canada as a great Calamity, the result either of imbicility or Treachery. God forbid, that it should prove to be the latter; tho, we assure your excellency suspicion is awake and strong. The almost unanimous prayer of officer and soldier in that army, and of the Citizens of this State, whose friends and relations are there, for a considerable time before the die was Cast was and yet is—'Oh! for a Commander a General a man of talents and integrity Courage and Conduct, yea *temperance* & *discretion*, destitute of these essential qualities on what foundation rests our faith, our hope of success to our arms, of Victory, of an honorable termination of the war, or an honorable peace.' The valor skill and prudence of Subordinate officers and soldiers, having to Contend With these embarrassments and encounter such difficulties loose their efficacy against the enemy—their spirits are broken—their patriotism sickens—their ardour is Cooled—misdirected in every movement—worn out by useless marches and Counter marches, and in the mean time half starved by design. Can we expect their patience Will last forever?

"In addition your Excellency ought to be informed, that the arms suitable for the Warfare, necessary to be carried on in this Western Country such as Carabines pistols and Sabre's cannot be obtained here. Relief from this Situation of affairs is what your memorialists humbly seek. They love their Country—feel for its honor, and regard its safety. They approve of the War and the measures of the general Government. They promise their aid to the utmost of their ability in carrying on the war, and pledge to your Excellency their fortunes in Support of it, they Can do no more but Want a general in whom they can have Confidence: Such they believe

William Henry Harrison to be, under him they will promptly rally, Confidant of Victory, in whose train follows peace safety and honor—grant it, or one like they beleive him to be and you will have Volunteer soldiers enough. As it is your excellency may be assured they Will march With reluctance because Without hope.

"We further suggest the propriety of directing the secretary at War to furnish the volunteer soldiers of the Western Country With arms suitable to the warfare against such an enemy. Cavalry We Conceive to be essentially necessary—arms and accoutrements for Mounted soldiers, are What is most wanted and Without which your memorialists believe the War Cannot be prosecuted With that Vigor necessary to effect the great Object."

RC (DNA: RG 107, LRRS, F-105:6). 3 pp.; signed by Thomas Scott, chairman, William R. Southward, secretary, and six others; docketed as received in the War Department on 5 Sept. 1812.

From Hezekiah Huntington

Sir,   Friday 28 Augt 11. AM
     The bill for raising a Military force mentioned in my hasty note of yesterday passed the house this morning yeas 147—nays 45, and is Postponed in the other House untill Afternoon.

     The business of a Court now in session leaves me but little opportunity to learn passing events—tis said an elaborate report of a Joint Committee on the subject presented—by the Gov's Message is now under discussion in the House—have not learnd much of it—but it is doubtless such as may be expected from the *Source whence* it eminates.[1] With Perfect respect I have the Honor to be your Excellency's Obdt Servant

                                                    HEZ HUNTINGTON

RC (DLC: Rives Collection, Madison Papers).

1. Huntington undoubtedly referred to the *Report of the Committee of the General Assembly, at Their Special Session, August 25, 1812: On That Part of His Excellency the Governour's Speech, Which Relates to His Correspondence with the Secretary of War* . . . (New Haven, 1812; Shaw and Shoemaker 25149).

From David Jones

Dear Sir,   WHEELING OHIO COUNTY augt 28. 1812.
     The Capitulation of Hull is come to hand. I hope you will condemn every Sentence. It is impossible for me to express the Indignation of the Country here. Not a few reflections are cast on you for appointing such an infamous Rascal to Command. I have vindicated your Conduct, as far as I

could, by asserting that your appointments are made by recommendations, that no Doubt this Plan was laid by Treators in Congress, not Suspected by you. This was the best apology I could make. The Country are not cast down; but much agitated. I now conjure you by all that is Sacred to send immediately gen. Armstrong or some man of Talents to take Command, and appoint some good man for governor; but for god's sake trust no more to yankeys. Good men they have, but office hunters are not in that Class. As I now feel, if you appoint a general to command in the north west, you may appoint me Chaplain in my 77th. year. I wish to die in the Service of my Country. If you wish any further information respecting my Character, I refer you to my old Friend Mr galatin, who has been well acquainted with me many years.

A word now to what must be done to retreive our honour. Give orders immediately to cross the St. Lawrence with 800⟨d?⟩ men, with artilery, & two mortars, and proceed & take the fort opposite to niagara. This can be done, & nothing else can save your honour, & if you do not do it, you need not expect to be reelected President. This I wish to take place, and it depends on your Conduct in this awful Crisis.

I cannot Set out for my home till next week; and you will see under the Signature of the old Soldiers. May the god of heaven direct you, is the sincere Prayer of your humble Servt

DAVID JONES
late Chaplain to gen wayne.

RC (DLC: Rives Collection, Madison Papers). Torn.

From James Wilson and Daniel McMillan

SOUTH CAROLINA

HONOURABLE SIR   CHESTER DISTRICT 28th Augt 1812

Being publickly notified from the department of state in the public prints that all British subjects within the United States are required forthwith to report to the marshals &c. concerning themselves and the various circumstances attaching to them[1] we the undersigned seeing the propriety of such a measure in the present important crisis have accordingly given in our report of this date to the Clerk of this district, at the same time, Honourable Sir we make free to address you with a more particular view of our situation as we have sufficient reason to believe you are possessed of such a disposition as will induce you to hear our reasons with that attention candour moderation and with such feelings as will incline you to make such particular regulations respecting us as will be happily calculated to secure the peace and dignity of the States—and at the same time secure our individ-

ual happiness in this Land of our choise. Honourable sir you will perceive
by our report that we are Emigrants from Ireland—but we hope you will
feell disposed not to rank us amongst the camp of Alien enemies (although
by the Usages of nations) we might be accounted such) we never considered our selves under allegiance to the Tyrant of Britain we expatriated our
selves we hope forever from his Jurisdiction and disclaim every tie to his
Goverment—as friends to civil liberty and the rights of man we do approve of the lovely and leading features of the constitution of the United
States and practising as well as professing such moral Republican principles—and as foes to Tyranny slavery and oppression we have as a Church
emancipated every slave in our possession after the example of the Great
and venerable Washington. Sir we feel our selves farther bound to state to
you that although we are yet standing on back ground as not being formally
incorporated with the national society yet in a physical sence we consider
our selves as constituting a part of the Great National body needing their
energy for the protection of our lives liberty and property likewise on the
other hand we feel our selves firmly bound cheerfully to give every aid and
assistance in our power to repell the unjust aggressions of Great Britain and
the more especially that the mildness moderation and Justice of this Government exercised toward G. Britain had no suitable effect in steming the
torent of their rapacity or allaying their thirst for Tyrany and oppression
Sir if you would wish that we would now seriously and candidly state to you
our principal scrouples which retards us from complying with the full extent of the oath of Naturalization it is not from any hostile views to this
Goverment or from unwillingness to occupy any station or department
which might tend to the peace and happiness of these States but merely because of scrouples wholly religious (Viz) the requiring no acknowledgment
of the universal Ruler of heaven and Earth the Divinity of the Scriptures
nor a future state of rewards and punishments previous to the holding of
office of course the Mahometan the Jew or Infidel are placed on an equal
footing and admitted to the same emoluments with the Christian—yet
Nevertheless we have been always and are at any moment ready to renounce fidelity to Britain and bind our selves by virtue of solemn obligations to aid and assist the United States in the defence of their lawfull rights
and privileges we pray for the peace and welfare of the states and for the administration that they may be enabled to form their civil and political system upon a moral basis which will Grant us the protection of heaven. We
pray for the success of the American arms in the present struggle that they
may become Victorious untill the Eagle of liberty the American Standard
waves throughout the Continent from the frigid to the Torid Zone. We
wish the final and speedy extirpation of all the sowers of sedition and discord in the union and all such as refuse their aid to expell the present enemy. May that noble and illustrous heroe who has entered the confines of

British dominion without interuption where he has the American flag waving on the shores find none untill he subjugates every foe of the union and we hope the virtuous proclamation of that noble General in offering emancipation to the Canadians will cause them to flock in inumerable multitudes to the American Standard were we inhabitants of Canada we would not hesitate one moment to fly to the Eagle. Sir as these are the unequivocal sentiments of our hearts at all times upon this footing we claim your protection and the reason we thus address you as a body is lest we should afterwards be ranked among those who are inimical to the states therefore we hope you will not think us beneath your notice to report what ever measure you think most prudent. Signed by order of our meeting

JAMES WILSON
DANL MCMILLAN

P. S Honourable sir if an article was inserted in the Constitution of the U States to the following import (Viz) the moral law shall be the high and Governing law of the Land and every other article of the Constitution shall be construed to be in subordination thereunto this would remove every Scrouple as an oath is a very solemn act and we wish only to be bound to what is morally Just and we believe a Great Majority of the nation would approve of such an amendment

RC (DNA: RG 59, War of 1812 Papers).

1. For the 7 July 1812 State Department notice concerning alien enemies, see William Farquhar to JM, 17 July 1812, n. 2.

From Samuel Carswell

DEAR SIR   PHILADA. August 29th. 1812

On my return from Bath, my health was so much improved, that I was induced to accept the Office of Comm. Genl. to which I was appointed, thro your favor & friendship. But the sanguine hopes which I then indulged, that it would be reestablished, being dissipated by a return of my complaint, with its former violence, I was constrained to recall the determination I had made & communicated to the Secy. at War.[1] The same reason prevented me from then acknowledging to you, the favor you confered on me, in nominating me to the Senate, & I now tender to you my thanks for it. I was very sorry to decline taking a part, in the service of our Country, at the present time, when it so much requires, all the support & assistance which its friends can give it. Nothing, but the nature of the duties which would have devolved on me, rendered particularly dangerous, both to my person & property, by the delicate state of my health, could have induced me to do so. Death might have made my tenure of the office very short, & in that case, my estate would probably be involved, & I would have left to my family trouble, without having served our Country.

With respect to domestic politics—It is lamentable, that now, when union amongst the friends of the Government, & support of the constituted authorities in the necessary system which they have adopted, is so necessary, to give success to the common cause, & bring about a speedy, & an honorable peace, there should be any division, in the republican ranks. It is unfortunate, both for himself, & the party, that Mr Clinton who held such an honorable & conspicuous place in it, & in whom so much confidence was reposed, should so far loose sight of his own & its Interest, as to suffer himself to be made the instrument of dividing it.[2] Even should he succeed in his views, & attain the object to which he aspires, his reputation would want that lustre, which consistency of character, gives to distinguished talents. However good his chance, of succeeding you in the honorable station which you fill, may have been; by advancing his pretensions at this time, he has done himself an irreparable injury, & I do not think he will ever occupy it. His Commissioners to this City pretend they are willing to continue the policy which you have adopted, pledging themselves, that the war with England shall be prosecuted, till every object shall be attained, for which we fight her. But thinking men take these assurances for what they really are—deceptive—& view with a distrustful eye, the man who is supported by a party, whose principles & policy are totally opposite, to what he professes. If he were a friend to your measures, he would be careful not to divide the party which approves of them. I feel happy in the belief that he will have the support of but a small section of the republicans, & that your election, will be carried by a large majority. Still it is unfortunate, that we should loose any from our ranks. The visit of his Commissioners to this State, has been of little service to him, except in the neighbourhood of Reading, & I am in hopes, that the people there, will return to their old principles, previous to the ensueing election. We are making every exertion here, to promote the common cause. Ten thousand copies of a narrative of the late disturbances in Baltimore, with such remarks as are suitable to the subject, are in preparation, & when ready, will be distributed thro this State & Jersey.[3]

I enclose for your perusal, a letter from my friend Mr. English, dated in London, which will be interesting to you.[4] At the close of it, there are some observations connected with the mention of Mr. Russel which, being of a confidential nature, will of course rest with us. When you have done with the letter, you will please have it returned to me under cover.

Present my compliments to Mrs. Madison, & accept my assurances of respectful consideration. I am very Respectfully Your obliged friend & Hbe. Sert.

SAML CARSWELL

RC (DLC). Docketed by JM.

1. Carswell to Eustis, 5 Aug. 1812 (DNA: RG 107, LRRS, C-415:6).

2. Even after JM was nominated as the Republican presidential candidate by the congressional caucus on 18 May 1812, Republican malcontent DeWitt Clinton retained a great deal of support in his home state of New York. A 29 May caucus of the state legislature nominated Clinton as a presidential candidate with near unanimity, sending a message to Federalists on the lookout for a candidate to defeat JM in November. Hoping to fuse the Federalist party with Republican dissenters in the coming election, Federalists sounded out Clinton as early as July 1812. On 5 Aug., Clinton met with New York Federalists at the home of Gouverneur Morris, where Clinton pledged support for Federalist principles but recommended that an announcement of his plans to accept Federalist backing be delayed in the hope that support for the war would decline. Clinton's agents then began a campaign that capitalized on antiwar sentiment in New York and New Jersey, where the Republican party seemed vulnerable. In pro-war Pennsylvania, however, Clintonians argued that the war had been mishandled and would be pursued more vigorously and successfully under Clinton's leadership (Norman K. Risjord, "Election of 1812," in Arthur M. Schlesinger Jr., ed., *History of American Presidential Elections, 1789–1968* [4 vols.; New York, 1971], 1:252–54, 257–59).

3. Carswell probably referred to *An Exact and Authentic Narrative, of the Events Which Took Place in Baltimore, on the 27th and 28th of July Last: Carefully Collected from Some of the Sufferers and Eye-Witnesses: To Which Is Added a Narrative of Mr. John Thomson, One of the Unfortunate Sufferers* . . . (n.p., 1812; Shaw and Shoemaker 25376). The pamphlet was dated 1 Sept. 1812, and its contents were printed in the Philadelphia *Pennsylvania Gazette* on 19 and 26 Aug. and 2 Sept. 1812.

4. Enclosure not found.

From Hezekiah Huntington

SIR   NEW HAVEN 29. Augt 1812

The bill, organizing a volunteer force underwent some slight Alteration—& passed, in the Senate—it will appear on Monday in the Herald printed in this City.

Since the Mail closed this day a resolution has passed both Houses—taking stronger Ground—it provides for raising two Regts of Infantry—4 Companies of Horse & 4 Do. Artillery.[1]

The necessary appropriations are now made—but further details refered to the October session—this force will be raised from the *Militia*, the Company Field & general Officers to be appointed & Commissiond by the Governor—& the force remain under his immediate Command to be under pay as soon as put in Motion—but Cannot be Marched out of this State—this Sketch is as I have heard it from Members—I sent to the Secretary [to]day for a Copy but Could not obtain it—the Hurry at the Close of the Session it is presumed prevented.

It is obvious, this will operate to extend & increase so far *Exempts* from duty in the Militia of this State, & the Right of the State to extend it to the whole Militia, was asserted in debate by leading Members.

Inclosed is the report of Committee Mentioned yesterday & also a *Declaration* of the Gen. Assembly[2]—so far as I have heard am inclined to believe the *debate* on the declaration was designed for the use & *instruction*, of the Good People of this State—the Printed Declaration to Send abroad—I have before hinted at Permission to Organise Volunteer Companies for the Service of the UStates—to be employed in *this State*, & Presume the Administration will hear further on that Subject Shortly*—& with great Respect Have the Honor to be your Excellencys Obdt Servant

HEZ HUNTINGTON

*A Gent from Hartford has waited on Gen Dearborn at his Head Quarters.[3]

RC (DLC). Docketed by JM.

1. The resolution stipulated that these companies be raised "to hold themselves in readiness for the defence of the state, to enforce the laws of the Union, to suppress insurrections and repel invasions, during the present war, subject only to the order of the Commander in Chief, of this state and to be under pay only when called into the actual service of the State—and that the organization of the same be referred to the General Assembly to be holden in October next" ("Legislative Papers of a Special Session of the General Assembly of the State of Connecticut . . . August 1812," *Records of the States of the United States of America* [DLC microfilm ed., Conn. A.6, reel 14], 30).

2. For the committee's published report, which included the declaration Huntington referred to, see Huntington to JM, 28 Aug. 1812, n. 1.

3. Thomas Tisdale visited Dearborn to urge that a large group of Connecticut volunteers who were sympathetic to the administration be accepted into federal service and supplied with arms by exempts in order to protect the seaboard of Connecticut and neighboring states. Connecticut Republicans desired this measure because they believed that the volunteer act recently passed by the special session of the state's General Assembly was a ploy to put arms and ammunition into the hands of those contemplating a forcible separation of the Union (Dearborn to Eustis, 3 Sept. 1812 [DNA: RG 107, LRRS, D-144:6]).

From David Mead

SIR,   ERIE, PENNYA Augt. 29th. 1812

On the evening of the 16th. Inst. I was apprized at Meadville of the Surrender of Detroit with the whole of the army under Brigr. Genl Hull, and that a number of British vessels were hovering on our coast in Sight of this place, in consequence of the Alarming Situation of the frontier of Pennsylvania bordering upon Lake Erie in circumstances so extraordinary I proceeded immediately with a number of volunteers and arrived here on the 17th.

Having Since my arrival collected from various Sources of undoubted Credit the particulars of the Surrender, and the Surprizing nature of these as well as of the event itself leaving doubts whether a full and Correct communication of all the facts and circumstances may have been duly made to you I have deemed it my duty as well towards the United States as on behalf of this frontier to communicate without delay, the information I have obtained on the Subject.

The bearer Capt. Daniel Dobbins[1] is a man of intelligence and good character who may be fully Credited and having been present and made prisoner At the Capture both of Michilimacinac and Detroit is able to communicate all the material details.

Capt. Dobbins was part owner and Commander of the American Schooner Salina, and has lost his Vessel with his Summers labour and is thrown out of employment, by those Captures. It appears by his Statement and papers that after his release under the capitulation of Michilimacinac his vessel was detained at Detroit by order of Genl. Hull from proceeding on his voyage and consequently recaptured with that place.[2]

The Substance of Capt. Dobbins' Statement[3] Respecting the Siege and Surrender of Detroit is That an inferior force on the part of the enemy was permitted without resistance for two or three days to prepare and complete a battery upon the opposite bank on the Spot from which Genl. Hull had withdrawn. That after a fire from this battery Continued from 4 to 11 PM on the 15th. and from daylight to 6 or 7 oclock on the 16th. upon the town and garrison, although with no other effect than the loss of four men, and Some inconsiderable injury, the enemy effected a landing on our Shore, where resistance ceased, then Marched in close Columns from the place of landing, in the face of our canon and flanked by our troops, Completed the Capitulation, and received possession by 12 oClock the Same day, the Surrender being virtually unconditional Containing as appears not a Single reservation, of which the usages of war Authorised the Surrender in any case.

That the whole force of the captors including indians and Militia was less than one thousand men.

At this place about eight hundred men recently ordered by the Governor are now under arms and expected today. On Yesterday an attack from an Armed brig was hourly expected from about one oclock to Six PM, when She appeared to tow off. About midnight a Communication was received by Bregadier Genl Kelso[4] purporting to be from the Capt. on board, dispatched by his Lieut. Announcing An Armistice between Great Britain and the U. S. The Communications comes however under circumstances questionable and Suspicious the Lieut. as mentioned did not come on Shore nor any belonging to the Vessel, but was handed by the crew of an american boat, which had been taken and released. Nor has any official or Satisfactory information in relation to an armistice been received at this place. Rumours and Conjectures are in Some Currency and the best is hoped for, whatever its general effect may be if true it appears now necessary to the Safety of this place, at which the whole of Genl. Brocks army might assemble with little more difficulty than at Detroit unless, guarded by an efficient force.

For further particulars permit me to refer to the intelligence of the bearer, whom goes to Washington at my request and whose expenses I have to request you will order paid.

The case of Capt. Dobbins appears to be a hard one, he may wish to detail its particulars and to become informed how far he may expect indemnity from Government. I will humbly add that Should there be any vacancy for employing Capt. Dobbins in some active Capacity such as he might accept, I with great confidence recommend him as a man capable trust worthy and highly patriotic—and have the honour to be—Sir, Your Obt. Hume Servt.

DAVID MEAD Majr. Genl.
16 Division Pennsya Militia

RC (DNA: RG 107, LRRS, M-409:6). Docketed as received in the War Department on 14 Sept. 1812. Notes on the cover in Eustis's hand read: "Received Septr 7th & opened by W. Eustis" and "Captn. D.'s accounts confirm those given by Mr Huntington."

1. Daniel Dobbins (1776–1856) of Erie, Pennsylvania, was the captain of the merchant vessel *Salina*, which was captured by the British during the fall of Michilimackinac, released under commercial provisions, and retaken at Detroit. Hamilton appointed Dobbins a sailing master in the U.S. Navy on 16 Sept. 1812 and assigned him to the construction of gunboats at Erie under Isaac Chauncey's command (Gilpin, *The War of 1812 in the Old Northwest*, 90, 208; Dudley, *Naval War of 1812*, 1:311 n. 1, 2:403).

2. In an 11 Sept. 1812 letter to Isaac Chauncey, the secretary of the navy listed the *Salina* among the vessels known to be held by the enemy on Lake Erie (ibid., 1:308).

3. Dobbins's account of Hull's surrender was published in the *National Intelligencer* on 12 Sept. 1812.

4. Revolutionary War veteran John Kelso (1755–1813) was a brigadier general in the Pennsylvania militia in command of a detachment near Lake Erie in the early months of the war (*DAR Patriot Index* [1990 ed.], 2:1654; Esarey, *Messages and Letters of William Henry Harrison*, Indiana Historical Collections, 2:173).

§ From the Inhabitants of Steubenville, Ohio. *29 August 1812*. "The undersigned Committee of Safety & Correspondence, for this Town in the present critical situation of the Country, beg leave to represent to your Excellency—that on the recent alarm occasioned by information of the defection of Gen. Hull, and the surrender of his forces to the British & Indians, all the Troops that could be raised & armed in this & the adjacent counties, proceeded to Lake Erie, there to await orders. Five Companies were marched from this County militia, who, when assembled here were destitute of arms accoutrements, ammunition or provision. A part of them were supplied with the U. States arms that had previously been deposited in this Town, and for the residue arms were procured, either by impressment, with no legal right or justification other than arose out of the *necessity* of the case—or by voluntary surrender of the owners—some of which are very poor, and others absolutely unfit for use & improper to be placed in the hands of a soldier—what provision, ammunition, & camp equipage have been supplied, were procured in the same lawless way, except indeed voluntary donations which have been considerable. By such means aided by the indignation of all classes of people at the traiterous conduct of Hull & their love of country, a small force has been started northward, without half the conveniences due to an army & with provisions for but a few days. The individuals who have readily stepped forth with their donations of money & property, anticipate the approbation of your Excellency and of Administration, and expect that proper steps will be immediately taken, to compensate for the property, and to return the cash, which has been advanced. Should they be disappointed there will be less alacrity in the people on any future emergency, less confidence in the administration of government, & less zeal to avenge the wrongs of their country.

"The undersigned would also call the serious attention of your Excellency, to the precarious situation of those forces which are daily assembling on the shore of Erie. Poorly supplied with arms blankets, tents, ⟨arms &⟩ amunition, they cannot be subsisted unless the attention of the proper officer is immediately directed to the subject by Administration: the undersigned suggest this from a sincere desire that the United States' forces may be at all times efficient & victorious.

"While addressing your Excellency the undersigned cannot refrain from noting, that our infant State and more particularly the northern section of it, in its present imminently dangerous situation, is almost entirely destitute of the means of defence. The Troops which have marched have drained the Country of arms of all kinds; and we have no extensive manufactory from which to furnish a supply—a small invading force might penetrate to the center of our state, with little or no opposition, scattering Desolation and death; and for no other earthly reasons than the total absence of the means of resistance. Should it be within the line of your Excellencies duty, the undersigned humbly solicit your attention to this subject, as one of the first importance to our infant settlements.

"Provisions in this section of our State, at this season of the year are scarce & difficult to be obtained in any considerable quantities, unless the expection of obtaining cash and a good price, gives a new spring to the exertions of the holder: but were a suitably authorized person plac⟨ed⟩ here with cash the time is nigh at hand when vast quantities might be procured with little delay.

"The undersigned feel diffident in making these representations to your Excellency but are prompted to it by an ardent desire for the prosperity of their fellow-citizens abroad in arms, or at home and the success of the national arms; and trust that your Excellency will bestow such attention upon them as in your opinion they are entitled to."

RC (DNA: RG 107, LRRS, H-352:6). 3 pp.; signed by William Hamilton and six others; docketed as received in the War Department on 15 Sept. 1812.

§ From the South Carolina Legislature. *29 August 1812.* "In a Government like ours, which, emanating from the will of all, is strong or weak in proportion to the current of public opinion in its favor, it cannot but be deeply interesting to the servants of the people, to know the light in which their Conduct is considered by those who have invested them with power. Under this impression, and influenced by the consideration that those who have the right to censure where censure is deserved, ought not to pass over with the silence of indifference the merit of their agents, where that merit is conspicuous; the Legislature of South Carolina, called together by the late change in our political relations, cannot separate without expressing the lively approbation they feel at the dignified and decisive appeal to arms, adopted by the President and a Majority of Congress, in vindication of our long outraged rights, and violated Sovreignty as a Nation.

"In other Governments, it has been the constant effort of the real friends of the people, to Curb the angry passions of their rulers, to interrupt the vain dreams of National Glory and foreign conquest, by the melancholy exhibition of ruined Husbandmen and starving Manufacturers; and to shade the deceitful picture of splendid victories and triumphal arches, held up to dazzle and mislead a giddy populace by introducing on the canvass the more faithful and certain representation of individual misery. It was reserved for the United States to present the spectacle, so consolatory to distressed humanity, of a Government uninfatuated by the illusions of National aggrandizement, or the glory of conquest; anxious only to promote the true Happiness of the People, and in deciding on the great question of Peace or War, weighing every drop of blood likely to be shed in the last resort, with the same caution, the same solicitude, as tho' each drop were to be drawn from the veins of those themselves, on whom rested the decision. If the signal for battle can be supposed to have been ever registered in 'Heaven's Chancery,' with any other emotions than those of horror or contempt for human wickedness or folly, it was on the Eighteenth Day of June, 1812. Influenced by no lust of dominion, no unjust spirit of encroachment; but impelled to arms by wanton and continued violations of our best rights, our vital Interests—if ever a war deserved to be denominated Holy, it is this. It is a war of right against lawless aggression, of Justice against perfidy and violence. Thus driven to Hostilities, it is in vain that faction would repress the energy and spirit of the nation, or disaffection depreciate the resources of our Country.

"The Glory of the issue will be commensurate with the righteousness of our cause. If we cannot at this moment, contend with our enemy for the empire of the Ocean, Individual valour and enterprize at length, permitted to be exerted, will ensure to our Citizens no inconsiderable indemnity for the spoliations so long practiced upon thier fair and peaceful commerce. If the acquisition of Canada be of little value in a territorial point of view, in other respects it will not be unimportant. It will remove from us a treacherous and barbarous Neighbor, who at the very moment her envoys were loudest in protestations, of conciliation and friendship, was secretly fomenting by her emissaries, divisions and factions among us; and who has at no time ceased to direct the tomahawks and Scalping knives of her fellow Savages, the indians against the defenceless women and Children of our frontier. From the inconveniences and privations incident to a state of war, we affect not to expect an exemption; but be [*sic*] are willing and able to support them. We shall support them with the more cheerfulness, as they will not fail to be accompanied with more than correspondent advantages. A Commercial, as well as political Independence, predicated upon the improvement and advancement of domestic Manufactures; the extermination of the spirit of faction: a cordial Union of all parties for the common welfare; a happy amalgation [*sic*] of the various, and in some instances, discordant materials, which, to a certain degree, compose our population; in a word, the formation of a National Character—these are some of the benefits confidently anticipated from the present contest. When to these on the one hand, are added, on the other, the accumulated insults and wrongs sustained from Great Britain—wrongs which, if tamely submitted to, must have reduced us to worse than colonial Slavery; we do not hesitate to beleive the war in which we have engaged, wise, necessary and Just.

"Under this conviction, Sir, the Legislature of South Carolina, have deemed it expedient and right not to withhold the full expression of their feelings and opinions . . . Therefore,

"Resolved, that the energy, the patriotism and wisdom of James Madison, President of the United States, manifested in his communication to Congress upon the question of war, give him new claims to the confidence and support of the people of South Carolina.

"Resolved, that in the opinion of this Legislature, the Majority of Congress have consulted the true interests and honor of their country, in declaring war, against Great Britain.

"Resolved, that this Legislature highly approve, of the Conduct of the delegation of this State, in the present Congress."

RC (DLC). 5 pp. Notes at the foot of the document state that the memorial was approved by the South Carolina House on 28 Aug. and by the Senate on 29 Aug. 1812; signed by the clerks of the two houses. Enclosed in Samuel Warren and John Geddes to JM, 1 Sept. 1812 (ibid.; 1 p.), which notes that the address was unanimously adopted by both houses of the state legislature "at an Extra Session" and expresses approval of JM's "public and private virtues." Docketed by JM.

From James Herrington

CRAWFOR COUNTY MEADVILE

MOST HONOURED SIR,   agust the 30th 1812

As a private Citizen I take the Liberty of making the folowing Comunication to your Exelencey.

Dear Sir,

I have no Doubt but that you will have oficialy Received the perticular acount of the serender of the post of MechelleMenack in the Lake Huren—being serendred to our Enemy—and also—the fort of Detroit by His Exelency—Governor Hull Comander in Cheaf at that Station—on his Conduct I wish not to Coment.

I Expect you to have had ⟨a⟩ Comunication from this Country by a Mr. ⟨Dob⟩bins—who was—an Eye witness to the transaction—he is a person that I am not personaly Aquainted with—And will not pretend to sany [*sic*] any thing against his Carecter. I have no Doubt but from what I

have heard of him but that he is a man—that what he says Can be Depended on. However In thes times we have Great nead to wach and Examine farley into Every point as to Intrest and Eviry Subject as a private Citizen. If the war Continues and our westren posts are falen—it would—be
my object—if I had the power to forward Between the out Let of Lake Ontario and the outlet of Erie at Least 25000 men well prepard which would
be suficient to subdue all the forces that Could be posibly—brought by the
Enemy on the north side of the lakes and on taking the full posesion—of
that part of uper Canady would—Cut off all Cuminication to the north
west. I Refer your Honour to the map—of that Country and you may
Clearly see My meaning and the westren posts must fall—if we had the
posesion from the out let of—Lake Erie to the north west Corner of Lake
onterio with the above nombr of men it would be suficint to subdue that
Country—in a few Days which would be—but a small portion above the
Coto of 100000 Melitia—that is now In rediness—by act of Congress. As
the male is about to be Closed I have had not five minits to write, and as a
private person—not wishing to have Any office of Honour trust or profit
only—the Sinciar welfare of my native Country at hart and a free man
born in Pensylvania and my forfathers for three Generations. I have had
the Honour of holding Ofices under this state but at this time I hold none
but that of a Deputy Surveyor of the County of Crawford—for my General Carecter I Refer you to—Mr. Samuel Smith—formerly a Represen-
titive from this Country.[1] I should be hapy to have a Comunication from
your honour—and perhaps it might be of more perticular, service and
benefit for the prosperity of the united—states to lisen to an Indeviduel—
than—to—some men high in power Seeking perferment. &C I Remain
with Esteem—your Most obedient friend and felow Citizen

JAMES HERRINGTON

RC (DNA: RG 107, LRRS, H-353:6). Docketed as received in the War Department on 14
Sept. 1812; damaged by removal of seal.

1. Samuel Smith had been an associate judge in Erie County, Pennsylvania, and a Republican representative to the Ninth, Tenth, and Eleventh Congresses.

From Thomas Jefferson

DEAR SIR   MONTICELLO Aug. 30. 12.
     The mail of yesterday does not tell us whether you have left Washington.
I am this moment setting out for Bedford, & shall be absent 3. or 4. weeks.
Should you be at Monpelier when I return I shall certainly have the plea-

sure of paying my respects to mrs. Madison & yourself. In the mean time accept the assurance of my affectionate esteem & respect

TH: JEFFERSON

RC (MH); FC (DLC: Jefferson Papers).

§ Account with Dinsmore and Neilson. *30 August 1812*. Presents a detailed list of charges totaling just under £1,250 for construction at Montpelier on the west end of the upper story, the dining room, and upper- and lower-story bedrooms. The balance due was £270 15*s.* as of 30 Aug. 1812.

Ms (ViU: Cocke Papers). 2 pp. For a discussion of the construction at Montpelier in the fall of 1812, see Hunt-Jones, *Dolley and the "Great Little Madison,"* 72.

From Tench Coxe

(personal & private)

SIR   Augt. 31. 1812

I am astonished to learn that Mr. B. Mifflin deputy Commy died yesterday suddenly.[1] I entreat your consideration of my name for the office, or for that of Mr. Duncan, under all the circumstances of my family. I say with Sincerity that the times require my appointment to the D. Commys. office. Mr. Irvine is a mere lawyer, unacquainted with the walks of trade. I write at the dawn of day, having been called up by an anxious friend who learned, of a neighbour at a late hour this death so dreadful to the deceased's family. Excuse the imperfections of this letter.

I remain, with every consideration, for your situation and abiding without alteration of heart or conduct, every issue faithfully

T. COXE

RC (DLC). Docketed by JM.

1. Benjamin Mifflin, formerly chief clerk under Coxe in the purveyor's office, had been appointed as a deputy commissary on 27 May 1812 to oversee the transfer of public property from Coxe's office to the new office of the commissary general (Risch, *Quartermaster Support,* 139–40; Eustis to Mifflin, 27 May 1812 [DNA: RG 107, LSMA]).

From Albert Gallatin

DEAR SIR   August 31. 1812

Cleveland being at the mouth of Cayuga,[1] the Huron river at the mouth of which the Ohio militia have been landed, is certainly that which empties into Lake Erie between the rivers Cayuga & Sandusky.[2] The letter being dated 27th instt., Huntingdon cannot be expected within less than a week.[3] In the mean while I am most decidedly of opinion that no information he may bring, can or ought to alter our decision, & that the orders agreed on ought to be transmitted without delay.[4]

The English general treats our militia as Charles the 12th did the Russians after the battle of Narva; and in like manner we will soon be taught by the enemy how to conquer him.[5] With respectful attachment Your's

ALBERT GALLATIN

RC (DLC: Rives Collection, Madison Papers). Docketed by JM. A note in JM's hand at the top of the letter reads: "To be read by Mr. Monroe pro bono publico & returned to J. M."

1. Gallatin probably referred to the Cuyahoga River, which flows into Lake Erie at Cleveland.

2. There are two rivers named Huron in the Lake Erie region, one in southeastern Michigan and one in Ohio. Gallatin referred to the latter.

3. Gallatin probably referred to Elijah Wadsworth's 27 Aug. letter to Eustis, in which he noted that he had sent Samuel Huntington and Lewis Cass to Washington on 24 Aug. to inform Eustis of "many particulars" of the situation in the West (*Michigan Historical Collections* 40 [1929]: 471–74). Huntington arrived in Washington on 3 Sept. to consult with JM's cabinet on the response to Hull's surrender (see Monroe to JM, 4 Sept. 1812, and Eustis to JM, 5 Sept. 1812; Huntington to Elijah Wadsworth, 11 Sept. 1812, *Letters from the Samuel Huntington Correspondence, 1800–1812*, Western Reserve Historical Society, Tract no. 95 [Cleveland, 1915], 149–51).

4. Gallatin probably referred to the plan outlined in Eustis's 1 Sept. 1812 letters to William Henry Harrison and James Winchester. Eustis informed them that JM was determined to "regain the ground which has been lost by the Surrender of Detroit" and to pursue vigorously the objects of the campaign in the Northwest. Harrison was ordered to join Winchester in command of troops intended to reinforce Hull along with additional forces from Kentucky, Pennsylvania, and Virginia. Were Harrison to find himself unable to join Winchester, he was to cooperate as far as possible with him (DNA: RG 107, LSMA).

5. On 30 Nov. 1700 the Swedish army under Charles XII besieged the Russian army in the city of Narva, on the Narova River west of St. Petersburg. This action was the first major battle of the Northern War of 1700–1721. Though the Swedes enjoyed a tactical victory at Narva, they were ultimately unable to win the war. Peter the Great regarded the defeat at Narva as a fortunate turn of events in that "compulsion then drove away sloth, and forced us to labour day and night." Gallatin may have read Voltaire's account of the siege, in which he quoted the czar as saying "the Swedes will beat us for this some time, but in the end they themselves will teach us to beat them" (Andrew Rothstein, *Peter the Great and Marlborough: Politics and Diplomacy in Converging Wars* [London, 1986], 35; Voltaire, *History of Charles XII, King of Sweden*, trans. Winifred Todhunter [London, 1908], 50–54).

From Hezekiah Huntington

SIR NEW HAVEN 31. Augt. 12

The hurry under which circumstances compelled me to write on Saturday[1] will it is hoped apologise for irregularities of expression or Sentiments which may have escaped me—time will shortly decide whether the *alarm felt* here, by the friends, of our *Country*, & the *union* of these *States*, is, or is not, *groundless*.

We may have something to fear from those among us, *openly hostile* to both, but more from *Masked Battories, ostensible friends* but *real enemies*, of the *administration & Continued Union*, of *the States*.

Certain Personal concerns have hitherto Prevented my speaking freely, others differently situated, have long since, *felt*, and now *regret*, they did not *Perform*, the duty.

It is presumed the administration are Correctly informed of the measures taken at the *extraordinary*, Session of our Legislature, by those who had more leisure than I could Command, and also the *impressions*, these measures have left on the *friends* of our Country.

I cannot forbear mentioning again the Subject of Volunteer Companies.

The Act of Congress authorizing the President to accept their Services, is not before me, and its provisions are not familiar, whether such volunteer Companies may be *Organized*, & Commissioned, for the Service of the U. States, & employed *only*, in the States to which they respectively belong, is a question not for me to decide, but the expediency of giving, by Proclamation, or otherwise, a *Construction* to the Act alluded to, allowing, in *all the States*, the Course thought *necessary in this*, is with very great deference suggested, as recommended by Policy—& urged by Considerations Connected with the *Public Safety*.

The militia of the northern States, are the yeomanry—generally industrious mechanics—& small landholders—ever ready to Protect their rights and at their countrys Call, to aveng[e] her wrongs—yet still have, strong inducements & in some measure Peculiar to Men in their Situation—to decline, distant & Protracted Service, for a Compensation less than half the sum Multitudes of them are Constantly paying their Journeymen & Common Laborours. The measure, if Consistent with the Provissions of the Act, while it would apparently, & perhaps essentially, Consult the interest, safety, & *Feelings* of each State, & its *Militia*, would be marked by no invidious distinction, indicating want of Confidence, in the virtue, or Patriotism of any.

But I forbear trespassing further Knowing that where the Nation has Confided its high interests, are all the requisits, of wisdom, power and disposition to devise & execute, whatever the Public Safety demands, and have the Honor to be with great Respect your Excellencys obdt Servant

HEZ HUNTINGTON

RC (DLC: Rives Collection, Madison Papers).

1. Huntington to JM, 29 Aug. 1812.

From John G. Jackson

Dear Sir, CLARKSBURG Augt. 31st 1812

In addition to the information contained in the newspapers several travellers have passed thro' this place confirming the intelligence that the army under Genl. Hull surrendered to the british forces without making any resistance. Those who view things superficially pronounce it to be the result of a perfidious & traiterous plan of the Genl. to sell the army & the distress & consternation that prevails are inexpressible. I have strong fears that the indians will sweep our whole frontiers, if the most prompt & vigorous measures to march a formidable force thither are not immediately adopted. My solicitude is so great that if I possessed any discretionary power as a militia officer I would order out all the efficient men of my Brigade to march immediately. I have examined the laws in vain for some clause that can justify me. We have now at this place about forty officers collected from the Brigade upon public business all anxious to engage even as privates in the public service. This Country was the theatre of indian hostilities even down to the period of Wayne's treaty & affords many men the best qualified for repelling indian warfare.[1] I hope & pray we may be called on, there will be no contests for rank, & I am willing to set the example of descending from the highest grade to the lowest. All we ask is authority to march.[2] My health is so perfectly restored & with it my strength & activity also, that I can endure any service. Previous to hearing this disastrous news we had associated a number of officers as a volunteer company to tender our services under the law concerning the 50,000. The expectation now; that many of us will be called on to command companies battalions &c has defeated that intention for the moment. Offer my affect. regards to Mrs. M. Dr. Sir Your Mo Obt. Servt.

J G JACKSON

RC (DNA: RG 107, LRRS, J-270:6). Docketed as received in the War Department on 12 Sept. 1812.

1. Jackson referred to Gen. Anthony Wayne's victory over the Indians at Fallen Timbers in 1794, which led to the Treaty of Greenville in 1795. The treaty stipulated that Indian nations in Ohio would relinquish their claim to the land south and east of the Greenville line, which comprised almost two-thirds of the state (William C. Sturtevant, ed., *Handbook of North American Indians: Northeast* [Washington, 1978], 401).

2. Under Jackson's supervision, on 2 Sept. 1812 the officers of the Twentieth Brigade and other citizens adopted resolutions requesting that the brigade be called up by the president for immediate service in the Northwest. A copy of these resolutions was sent to Virginia governor James Barbour, but before they could be received, Barbour ordered Jackson's brigade to march to Point Pleasant. At Columbus, Ohio, Jackson and his men joined up with Harrison's forces, which were preparing for an assault on Detroit (Brown, *Voice of the New West*, 113–14).

From Tobias Lear

private.

DEAR SIR, GIBRALTAR, August 31st: 1812.

The long time that has elapsed since the receipt of your respected favor of the 26th of October,[1] with which I was honored on the 18 of december, by the Brig Paul Hamilton, might lead to the suspicion of an unpardonable neglect and inattention on my part, which would be truly distressing to me, did I not think you would be so well assured of the respect and sincere attachment which I have for the writer, as to preclude all suspicion of that kind.

When the Brig Paul Hamilton went on her voyage to Marseilles (of which you have undoubtedly been apprized by my communications to The Honble. The Secretary of State)[2] I expected that, on her return to Algiers, she would proceed to the U. States, and have afforded me the satisfaction of sending by her the Articles mentioned in your letter. Her subsequent fate deprived me of that opportunity. I then waited the arrival of the Ship Allegany, which was long retarded by adverse circumstances; and the unexpected events which took place on her arrival (and which have been fully and repeatedly communicated by me to The Honble. The Secretary of State, to which I beg leave to refer you) again disappointed my hopes;[3] and leaves me in dispair of having fulfilled a commission, the execution of which would have been highly gratifying to me, as well in a public, as in a personal point of view. The expectation of these opportunities of answering your letter effectively, as well as by writing, has prevented my doing the latter until this time. One Ship left Algiers in May, said to be bound to the U. States; but as she was a *licensed* vessel, I could not depend upon her destination sufficiently to put any thing on board her.

I have never known, nor heard of the hessian fly having committed ravages on the wheat in Barbary.

In the Interior of the Regency of Algiers, as well as other parts of Barbary, bordering on the Sahara, is a race of Sheep, from the wool of which is made the fine haikas, and other woollens sometimes brought for sale to the court. These Sheep are said to have been carried into Spain, when that Country was possessed by the Moors, and, mixing with the native Sheep of Spain, produced the true Marino. Whether this account be true or not, I cannot undertake to decide. But for a long time, I had been endeavouring to get some of the Sheep of the Sahara, as they are called in Algiers; and, in May last, succeeded in obtaining, at a considerable expense, compared with the price of Sheep in Barbaru [*sic*], fifteen very fine Rams, (females I could not get at any rate). They appear to have the head, face and horns of the Marino; but the limbs and body are very different. The legs long; and the carcass high and apparently badly formed. They will weigh, when fat, 25#

per quarter, and the meat very fine tasted. I compared the wool with that of the Marino, and found the fleeces of several fully equal to the sample which I possessed; but the fleeces do not weigh in proportion to the carcass, compared with the Marino. Notwithstanding the confusion and embarrassment necessarily attending the manner in which I was obliged to leave Algiers, I got thirteen of these Rams on board the Allegany, and brought nine of them into this Bay, where six still remain on board the Ship. But, besides the unpleasant circumstance of the detention of the Ship, with all other Am. Vessels here, it is next to impossible to procure hay or straw for them, as the Rock of Gibraltar produces none, and the apprehension of the fever prevailing in some parts of Spain, prevents articles of that kind being brought into the Garrison; so that I almost despair of being able to get any of those desireable Animals to the U. States. I shall, however, endeavour if possible, to preserve some of them.

I have further to regret the want of good opportunity to the U. S. from Algiers, as I could have fully answered your wishes with respect to the broad-taild sheep, having a number of very fine ones in my flock, selected with great care, the wool of which was tolerably fine, and the flesh most excellent. And as an aggravation of the circumstance of my being obliged to leave them in Algiers, I could not now find the means of sending them from hence to the U. S. if I should be able to have them forwarded to me here. I can, from my own experience, confirm Judge Peters' account of the longevity of this race of Sheep; for I left several in my flock at Algiers, both Rams & Ewes, the latter bringing lambs this year, which I brought from Tunis in the spring of 1806, and none were then less than 3 years old. At this time they discover no marks of old age in their external appearance.

For several years past I have had the wine which I consumed in my own House, made in Algiers, and have found it far superior to the wine usually imported from France and Spain; besides being much cheaper than those wines have been of late. It was my intention to have sent a pipe of this wine to you, at its cost $35, had there been an opportunity as we wished and expected. I left four pipes in Algiers, and have requested to have one pipe drawn into bottles and sent to me here, if permitted. Should it come, and an opportunity offer of its being sent to the U. S. a part of it at least will be sent to you.

I shall not enter into any particulars relative to the unexpected events which took place at Algiers, as they are so fully detailed in my letter to The Honble. The Secretary of State, of the 29 of July (one of which accompanies this).[4] But I will observe, that good sometimes springs out of evil; for there can be no doubt but the determination of the Dey to break with the U. S. proceeded either from his own opinion, or from the persuasion of others, that his Cruizers could take any number of prizes, and that the U. S. would be ready to redeem the Captives, and renew the Treaty on his own terms. In this he will be sadly disappointed; for, in permitting the Allegany to depart, an opportunity was given of diffusing the information of what had happend at Algiers, which I improved with a promptitude and effect which he hardly expected; and I chose this place as the point from which such information could be best & most readily conveyed to every part of the Mediterranean, as well as to Am. Vessels entering into this Sea. And the war with G. Britain has either kept in port, or detained at sea, almost every vessel of the U. States, which had not received advice from me, so that I should not be surprized to find that the disappointment will produce fatal effects to the Dey, if he was the sole projector of the plan; or to others, if he had advisers to it. And it is not unlikely that propositions may be made, to pass over what has happened, and to renew the Treaty on the former terms. But I presume that that will never be done; and that the Algerines will find true what I have often told them (when they have talked, in their usual stile, of breaking treaties with tributary Nations, to have them renewed on better terms, besides the advantage of prizes and captives) that, while the U. S. would be faithful to such engagements as they had made, however disadvantageous to themselves, so long as the other party preserved their faith; yet, they might be assured, that, should they once break their Treaty with the U. S. it would never be renewed again, but on terms of perfect reciprocity.

The hurried and unexpected manner in which we were obliged to leave Algiers, and the hopes entertained to the last moment, that the differences might be accommodated, prevented our bringing away anything but what could be put in a few Trunks & boxes; so that the bulk of our effects are left to the chance of loss or preservation. I gave them in charge to John Norderling Esq, His Swedish Majestys Consul Genl. at Algiers, to be disposed of for my account, if they were permitted to remain as my property; but at any rate, the loss will be considerable for me.

We have met with hospitality at this place; and as yet have no cause to complain of any personal restraint or inconvenience. But, as is natural to expect from the State of War between the U. S. and G. B. our reception is very different from what it was here nine years ago, when we were on our way from the U. S. to Algiers.

It has given me peculiar satisfaction to find that Mrs. Lear has borne the late unpleasant (and (to an American who has not resided in Barbary) almost incredible Scenes, with a degree of spirit and fortitude which has even astonished me, who knew so well what strength of mind she possessed, accompanied with the truest sensibility.

Two days before the arrival of the Allegany, we were joined by my son, who, having completed his Collegiate education about a year since, had my permission to come to me. Altho' his arrival was in a moment of confusion and anxiety, we considered his presence as a peculiar blessing of Providence; and I have found him very useful to me.

Unless circumstances should make it necessary or proper for me to re-move from this place, I shall remain here until I have the honor of receiv-ing the Orders of Government; as it is the best point for a frequent com-munication with Barbary, and particularly to be informed of what transpires at Algiers.

Mrs. Lear offers her best Respects to your good Lady and yourself, to which I beg leave to join mine. Accept the assurances of sincere Respect and attachment with which I have the honor to be, Dear Sir, Your obliged and Obedt. Servt.

TOBIAS LEAR

RC (DLC). Marked *"(Duplicat)"*; docketed by JM.

1. *PJM-PS*, 3:501–2.

2. Lear had written to Monroe on 30 Apr. 1812 to describe the British capture of the *Paul Hamilton* en route to Marseilles and its subsequent condemnation in Malta (DNA: RG 59, CD, Algiers).

3. As Lear reported to Monroe on 29 July 1812, the *Allegany* arrived in Algiers on 17 July, carrying a cargo of naval and military stores for the dey of Algiers. When the unloading com-menced, the dey declared the stores to be insufficient and ordered the ship, Lear, and all other Americans to leave the regency at once. The dey further demanded payment of $27,000 that he claimed the U.S. also owed him. When Lear refused to pay the money, the dey threatened to put him in chains, confiscate the American vessel and cargo, enslave all Americans in Al-giers, and declare war. Lear then arranged to borrow the money from the business house of Baccri, after which he and his family and several other Americans were allowed to depart. Ob-serving that the dey was "a severe, obstinate and cruel cruel man . . . deprived, at times, of his reason," Lear concluded that Algiers was bent on war with the U.S. As soon as the U.S. settled its differences with Great Britain, Lear urged, the administration should send a naval force to the Mediterranean so that *"Algiers will be humbled to the dust."* The consul ended his account with a discussion of the weaknesses of the Algerine navy (Lear to Monroe, 29 July 1812 [ibid.]).

4. See n. 3, above.

From Robert Taylor

DEAR SIR   ORANGE. August 31st. 1812.

When I saw Genl. Moses Green[1] last he requested me to write you and inform you that if there was a vacancy of a regimental command in the Army it would give him great pleasure to fill it if he could be thought wor-thy of it. He would sooner have made known his wishes had he known that there certainly would have been war, but holding the office of adjutant-general in the State, which yeilds some emolument he did not like to part with it unless for active service. With respect to General Green's qualifications for such a command I expect you are as well acquainted as myself. He is the son of the late Colo. John Green of Culpeper[2] with whose character if not person you were well acquainted and I believe that none of that firmness & martial spirit which characterized the father have been lost upon the son. I find an universal opinion amongst his acquaintance that he would make an excellent officer and that the appointment of him would meet with general approbation. I owe to him an apology for not having made this communication sooner as a fortnight has now elapsed since I saw him, but the delay has arisen from the expectation of your return to this county when this communication might have been personally made. I am yr respectfully

ROBERT TAYLOR

RC (DLC). Docketed by JM.

1. Moses Green represented Culpeper County in the Virginia House of Delegates from 1799 to 1802 and from 1808 to 1811 before serving as adjutant general for Virginia during the War of 1812. Green resigned that post in February 1815, when the state legislature passed a law requiring the adjutant general to reside in Richmond, which he would not do (Butler, *Guide to Virginia Militia Units*, 8–9, 299–300).

2. John Green (1730–1793) had been a soldier in the Seven Years' War before serving with the Continental army throughout the American Revolution. He rose to the rank of colonel in command of the Tenth and Sixth Virginia Regiments before retiring in 1783 (*VMHB* 8 [1900]: 215, 23 [1915]: 103).

From Toppan Webster and Others

SIR,   WASHINGTON Augt. 31. 1812

The undersigned, members of the City Council, residing, in the first ward, Beg leave to recommend Mr. William Waters of said ward as a suitable person for a magistrate, and as we are much in want of one in that section of the City, we pray his appointment to said office.

TOPPAN WEBSTER
WILLIAM WORTHINGTON JUR.
WM. P. GARDNER

RC (DNA: RG 59, LAR, 1809–17, filed under "Waters"). JM also received a 1 Sept. 1812 letter on behalf of Waters from the inhabitants of the first ward of the city of Washington (ibid.; 1 p.; signed by William P. Gardner).

Madison and the Problem
of Mexican Independence:
The Gutiérrez-Magee Raid of August 1812
1 September 1812

EDITORIAL NOTE

The "illegal enterprize" referred to by JM in his 1 September 1812 letter to Monroe was the Gutiérrez-Magee raid, a filibuster into the Spanish province of Texas that had commenced on 8 August 1812. Details of the background and the conduct of this expedition have frequently been recounted by historians with scholarly interests in either the origins of the movement for Texan independence or the troubled diplomatic relations between Spain and the United States in the early nineteenth century. In many instances the narratives thus produced have given rise to significant disagreements over how far JM and his administration might have been implicated in the raid. Specifically, these disagreements center on the question of whether the involvement in the raid of JM's agent to Cuba and Mexico, William Shaler, can be adduced as evidence that JM himself was prepared to sponsor or to condone filibustering as a covert means of making good the claim that the United States had acquired Texas in the Louisiana Purchase of 1803. At the heart of those disagreements is the issue of whether Shaler was acting within or beyond the instructions he had received from the administration when he commenced his mission in the summer of 1810 (Madison and the Collapse of the Spanish-American Empire: The West Florida Crisis of 1810, 20 Apr. 1810, *PJM-PS*, 2:310–11).

As far as JM's instructions to Shaler are concerned, there is little room for controversy. Those instructions expressly precluded Shaler from "interference of any sort" in the "internal system" of either Cuba or Mexico, directing him instead to seek out the likely successor regime to the Spanish government of Mexico for the purpose of commencing conversations on trade prospects and border problems. Because the administration did not want any independent Mexican government to adopt the position that Madrid had taken with respect to the extent of the Louisiana Purchase, in the event of these conversations being "drawn to the South Western boundary of Louisiana," Shaler was authorized to say that "the United States will carry into that discussion, particularly in case it should take place with a neighbouring instead of a foreign authority, a spirit of amity and equity, which, with a like spirit on the other side, forbids any unfavorable anticipations." Vague though that formulation was, these instructions assumed that boundary disputes were to be negotiated and settled by treaties; they did not require or sanction active involvement in filibustering (Robert Smith to Shaler, 18 June 1810 [PHi: William Shaler Papers]).

If Shaler was not authorized to organize or to participate in a filibuster, the question arises how he nevertheless became associated with just such an activity. Here it must be recalled that Shaler's original mission was to travel through Cuba, obtain a passport to enter Mexico at Veracruz, whence he could proceed to the interior, and gather information about the progress of the rebellion against the Spanish authorities and about the regime that might succeed their rule. This aspect of the mission was unsuccessful. Shaler failed to obtain a passport for Veracruz and was expelled from Havana in November 1811, so that he had little choice but to set out for New Orleans, where he arrived in late December 1811 (Madison and the Collapse of the Spanish-American Empire, 20 Apr. 1810, *PJM-PS*, 2:310–11; Shaler to JM, 23 Mar. 1812, ibid., 4:259–60). Moreover, developments in Mexico, as reported in the newspapers of New Orleans in the early weeks of 1812, could have left Shaler with little doubt that it would be impossible for him to reach the interior via Veracruz in the foreseeable future. JM's agent was therefore looking for alternative ways in which he might resume the original purpose of his mission (Shaler to Monroe, 27 Dec. 1811 and 27 Jan. 1812 [NNPM: Shaler Letterbooks]; *Louisiana Gazette and New-Orleans Daily Advertiser*, 14 Feb. 1812).

The arrival of José Bernardo Maximiliano Gutiérrez de Lara in New Orleans, where he and Shaler were introduced by Governor Claiborne in late March 1812, provided Shaler with the opportunity to restart his mission. The agent took the Mexican rebel under his wing, advancing him various sums of money amounting to between $400 and $500 for food, clothing, and accommodation. Shaler then accompanied Gutiérrez to Natchitoches, where they arrived on 28 April 1812. Throughout this journey, and for some weeks thereafter, Shaler not only continued to pay expenses for Gutiérrez but also seized the opportunity to advise him on political matters, assuming that the cultivation of a personal relationship would advance the goals of his mission. Shaler also advised the administration of the course he was taking. Monroe approved these decisions in May 1812, informing Shaler that the president wished him to continue immediately to Mexico to fulfill the purposes of his original instructions (*PJM-PS*, 4:38–39 n. 1, 260–61 n. 2; Shaler to Monroe, 9, 23, and 30 Mar. 1812; Claiborne to Shaler, 7 Apr. 1812 [DNA: RG 59, Communications from Special Agents]; Monroe to Shaler, 2 May 1812 [DLC: William Shaler Papers]).

Gutiérrez was no stranger to Natchitoches. He had passed through the settlement in September 1811 while en route to Washington in the company of another of Miguel Hidalgo's supporters, José Menchaca. In a later account Gutiérrez recalled that he and Menchaca had adopted a plan whereby the latter would recruit troops, including Americans, to march on San Antonio de Béxar and establish a provisional government there. The former would travel on to Washington and purchase arms after Menchaca had informed him of the establishment of the provisional government. While in Washington in December 1811, Gutiérrez learned that Menchaca had betrayed their cause, and it seems likely that when he returned to Natchitoches, he set about trying to renew the schemes and contacts he had established some eight months earlier. How much Shaler knew about these activities of Gutiérrez is difficult to ascertain. That he knew something of them is clear enough from his correspondence with the State Department over the spring and summer of 1812, but the same correspondence shows equally clearly that JM's agent also came to disapprove of many aspects of the conduct of his Mexican traveling companion (Gutiérrez to the Mexican Congress, 1 Aug. 1815, in Gulick et al., *Papers of Mirabeau Buonaparte Lamar*, 1:7–9, 11–12).

Initially, Shaler had taken positively to Gutiérrez, but this did not last. Beginning in May 1812 the agent's letters to Monroe betray growing unease over Gutiérrez's activities, and by July, Shaler concluded that the Mexican was a weak and sorry figure, too easily given to "ridiculous flights of vanity." This discomfort arose in part because Shaler sensed that he had misjudged the character of Gutiérrez, but also, more important, because he suspected the Mexican was acting "a double part" with him with respect to his future plans. So far as Shaler could make out, these plans did encompass a filibuster that would involve Americans in Mexican politics, and Shaler concluded that Gutiérrez had reached "private and confidential" understandings with Americans throughout the southwestern states, including John Adair of Kentucky. Yet the Mexican's plans also seemed to be predicated on his receiving assistance from France, or at least so Shaler believed after learning that an agent of Napoleon had visited Gutiérrez in Natchitoches. None of these arrangements, Shaler supposed, would be favorable to administration interests in the Southwest (Shaler to Monroe, 17 and 22 May, 12 and 23 June, and 12 July 1812 [DNA: RG 59, Communications from Special Agents]).

When Shaler transmitted this news to Washington, he specifically coupled it with clear warnings that a filibuster along the lines that Gutiérrez appeared to be planning could not advance administration policy toward Mexico, and he even pointedly inquired at one stage whether a filibuster was what the president intended. In this context Shaler unequivocally stated that his own preference was not for filibustering but for direct intervention by the United States in Mexico in order to prevent the spread of British influence in the province. That Great Britain would turn its attention to Mexico Shaler took for granted. His reasoning was based on the assumption that the impending outbreak of war between Great Britain and the United States would inevitably lead to war with Spain. Once the latter development had occurred, Shaler believed that Great Britain would remove the Cádiz regency to Mexico—as it had relocated the Portuguese monarchy to Brazil in 1807—and then use the Spanish colony as a base from which to attack the United States (Shaler to Monroe, 17 May, 12 and 23 June, and 12 July 1812 [ibid.]).

Nowhere in the correspondence with Monroe in which Shaler laid out this scenario is there any proof that JM's agent was personally directing the insurgent activities of Gutiérrez as the latter went about organizing the Republican Army of the North that became the vanguard of the filibuster. Shaler did, however, advance Gutiérrez a further $100 on 18 June 1812 as a contribution toward the production of "printed proclamations" that the Mexican planned to send to rebel groups and leaders in Mexico. Whether Shaler realized that this step might be construed as a violation of his instructions is unclear. He merely told Monroe that he thought it "proper" to make the advance, in part, it would seem, in the hope that one of Gutiérrez's couriers would return to Natchitoches within the month "with an exact account of the state of the revolution in the interior of Mexico." At this juncture it was still the mission to Mexico rather than the filibuster that was uppermost in Shaler's mind (Shaler to Monroe, 23 June 1812 [ibid.]).

However, by this stage Shaler had also concluded that it was beyond his power to prevent the raid into Texas anyway. He therefore gave Gutiérrez a warning to the effect that the members of the administration in Washington, no matter how much they might wish for Mexican independence, would not approve of any "unauthorized proceedings, by men unknown, not under their control, and in no manner possessing their confidence," but it was to no avail. The Mexican was almost contemptuous in the manner in which he dismissed such scruples. Yet Shaler had long felt a deep sympathy for, and interest in, the cause of republicanism in Spanish America, and his response to Gutiérrez's conduct was not to withdraw that sympathy and interest but to transfer them elsewhere, namely to Augustus W. Magee, a U.S. Army lieutenant who had resigned his commission in June 1812 and joined the filibuster. Again, the goals of his mission appear to have been Shaler's main concern. The agent hoped that Magee and other Americans in the filibuster would provide a steadying hand and prevent the Mexicans from "running into the extravagance of revolutionary injustice and tyranny." If the raid was "well conducted" and resulted in the establishment of a republican beachhead in northeastern Texas, Shaler predicted that he could then embark on his mission and reach the interior of Mexico. Partly in accordance with the view that he should not enter Mexico prematurely and partly because he was indisposed by illness, Shaler did not accompany the filibuster into Texas. He remained at Natchitoches, biding his time (Shaler to Monroe, 23 June, 18 Aug. [ibid.], and 27 Aug. 1812 [NNPM: Shaler Letterbooks]; Shaler to Claiborne, 25 and 27 Aug. 1812 [ibid.]).

Shaler's conduct at Natchitoches, however, placed him—and by implication the administration—in an ambiguous position. It is quite plausible to maintain that Shaler did not approve of, or contribute very significantly to, the organization of the Gutiérrez-Magee raid. At the same time, though, the agent never concealed the fact that he also intended to take advantage of that raid as a means of realizing JM's instructions. In choosing this tactic, Shaler was probably more guilty of a certain naïveté about the possible consequences of his actions than he was of a deliberate perversion of JM's policy. Shaler had believed he could at least influence, if not control, the conduct of Gutiérrez, but by mid-1812 he had found that he could not. Nevertheless, his decision to follow in the wake of the filibuster in order to gain entry into Mexico inevitably created the impression that the administration had committed itself to supporting the raid. That impression was as unfortunate in its results as it was inaccurate in its representation of JM's intentions, and the reputations of both Shaler and the president have suffered accordingly. To this day it has always been difficult to dispel the notion that a filibuster to seize Texas was the first major policy decision of JM's administration regarding the Mexican nation as it struggled to come into existence.

But even if JM can be acquitted of the charge of intending to organize or to sponsor a filibuster, there remain some other circumstances that have been adduced to support the contention that the Gutiérrez-Magee raid embodied an administration policy to detach Texas from Mexico. Among them are the tardiness of federal and state officials in their efforts to suppress the filibuster under the provisions of the 1794 Neutrality Act and the fact that the ranking U.S. Army officer in the region, Brig. Gen. James Wilkinson in New Orleans, removed a company of troops—which might have been employed to prevent the raid—from Fort Claiborne to Baton Rouge shortly before the filibuster entered Texas. In hindsight, these actions, or failures to act, have been invested with a sinister meaning, and in some cases they have been regarded as clear proof that all American officials along the southwestern frontier tacitly understood that the administration wished to see no obstacles placed in the path of the filibuster. Indeed, even statements from American officials suggesting that they did, in fact, make some effort to suppress the filibuster have been interpreted as evidence that such claims were designed mainly to mislead public opinion and to convince Spain and other nations that the United States could not be accused of violating its obligations as a neutral nation.

Leaving aside the fact that the administration and other American officials probably produced many more statements to the effect that they desired the suppression of the filibuster than any reasonable requirements of plausible deniability might dictate, it is certainly true that these same officials were slow to enforce the 1794 neutrality legislation. Governor Claiborne in New Orleans, for example, knew that a filibuster might be gathering in the Neutral Ground, but he did not direct the appropriate district judges and attorneys to commence legal action until less than a week before the raiding party set out for Texas. Consequently, the governor's official proclamation condemning the filibuster was not issued until 11 August 1812, three days after the expedition had left the Neutral Ground. It cannot be proved, however, that Claiborne delayed his proclamation until he knew the raid had commenced, and the belated timing of his proclamation was regretted by Shaler, who believed, perhaps too optimistically, though not necessarily insincerely, that an earlier expression of official displeasure might have prevented the expedition's departure (Claiborne to Monroe, 10 Aug. 1812, in Rowland, *Claiborne Letter Books*, 6:158–60; Shaler to Claiborne, 25 and 27 Aug. 1812 [NNPM: Shaler Letterbooks]).

Yet it should not be assumed that the enforcement of the law against filibustering was an easy or routine matter. Accurate information about the raid was hard to come by, and the local officials who received Claiborne's directives usually lacked the resources to take on sizable numbers of armed men. Moreover, it was not clear that the Republican Army of the North was in violation of the law anyway. Gutiérrez and his associates had anticipated that contingency by stipulating that volunteers for the raid should "repair to the west of the Sabine river (out of the boundaries of the United States of America) and there arm and equip themselves." John Dick, the U.S. attorney for Louisiana, learned all too well the effectiveness of such precautions when he tried to detain suspected filibusters crossing American territory. The courts, lacking clear evidence that "individuals found with arms" were "engaged in any illegal undertaking," declined to convict, and once on the Neutral Ground, these men were beyond the reach of the law. Shaler too pointed to this difficulty when he wrote to Monroe in August 1813: "The first adventurers in this expedition assembled on the desolate banks of the Sabine, Since that time there ha⟨s⟩ never been within the territory of the United States the least appearance of armament, or military preparation, the Volunteers went out either Singly, or in Small bands, usually armed as hunters, and what few Supplies have been procured here [in Natchitoches] have been furnished in the common way of trade" ("Stipulations to Be Entered into by a Certain Number of Volunteers," enclosed in Claiborne to Monroe, 6 July 1812 [DNA: RG 59, ML]; Shaler to Monroe, 7 Aug. 1813 [DNA: RG 59, Communications from Special Agents]; John Dick to Monroe, 1 Mar. 1816, *ASP, Foreign Relations*, 4:431–32).

As for Wilkinson, it has become difficult for historians to view his conduct as anything other than conspiratorial at best and treacherous at worst. The general did not take up his command in New Orleans until 9 July 1812, and there is no evidence to suggest that the administration had ever alerted him to the assembling of a fili-buster west of the Sabine River. In the period immediately following his arrival on the Gulf Coast, Wilkinson was overwhelmed by the problems of defending a front of over six hundred miles—from Natchitoches to Fort Stoddert—with a force of 1,680 men, no more than half of whom, he estimated, would be disposable troops. His decision to remove men and arms from Fort Claiborne to Baton Rouge was al-most certainly governed by the need to build up the defenses east of the Mississippi River, especially along the border of the recently seized portions of West Florida, which Wilkinson feared would be attacked by Spanish forces reportedly en route from Havana to either Mobile or Pensacola. Wilkinson also claimed that his knowl-edge of developments in the Neutral Ground at this stage was too sketchy to justify any response. He had received reports about raiding parties and believed that they might be under the command of John Adair. That probably gave Wilkinson pause. Adair was still pressing a lawsuit against the general for wrongful arrest during the Burr conspiracy, and he had also testified against Wilkinson at his 1811 court-martial. Wilkinson may well have hesitated to confront the Kentuckian again with-out conclusive proof of his involvement in illegal acts. Instead the general in-sinuated that the goal of Adair's rumored involvement was more likely to be mere plunder than the detachment of Texas or the advancement of Mexican indepen-dence (Wilkinson to Eustis, 11 Apr., 18 May, and 13, 22, and 28 July 1812 [DNA: RG 107, LRRS, W-98:6, W-139:6, W-259:6, W-265:6, W-267:6]).

By the first week in August, however, Wilkinson knew more. He reported to the War Department that Magee headed the filibuster and that its aim was to advance on Nacogdoches and San Antonio, though Wilkinson still suspected that its real purpose was plunder and that its presence west of the Sabine River would, in fact, impede the desire of the Mexican revolutionaries to expand trade and communica-tions with the United States. Wilkinson also informed the secretary of war that he had received a visit from an agent of Gutiérrez, one Pierre Girard of New Orleans, who claimed that the Republican Army of the North would shortly be joined by two thousand men from Louisiana, Kentucky, and Tennessee. The agent therefore wished to know whether the general would furnish official American aid to the cause. Believing these claims to be "not *quite* creditable," Wilkinson gave them short shrift, reminding Girard that the filibuster was illegal and likely to involve the United States in a war with Spain. He threatened to arrest Magee, but in a manner typical of his manipulative style, he also affected great concern for "the poor Native Mexicans" by declaring that he would "die to give freedom to an oppressed people." As he recounted these conversations, Wilkinson also hinted that the administration might take advantage of the disturbances in Mexico "to extend our occupances to our western limits the Rio Grand." He even offered his own services for the task but added that he would not attempt it without instructions (Wilkinson to Eustis, 4 and 10 Aug. 1812 [DNA: RG 107, LRRS, W-286:6, W-303:6]).

Whether the seemingly contradictory impulses embodied in Wilkinson's re-marks prove anything about American policy toward Mexico might be endlessly debated, but in this instance it is unnecessary to decide whether the general hoped to stop the raid or to advance its goals. The administration ignored his hints, ex-pressly instructing him to confine himself to the defense of New Orleans and not to risk hostilities with Spain. As for the filibuster, he was to cooperate with Governor Claiborne to preserve the neutrality of the nation. Moreover, to focus too much attention on the role of Wilkinson at this juncture is to neglect a more important question, namely, can all of these acts of confusion, tardiness, and omission on the part of American officials rightly be viewed as evidence of a tacit agreement on their part to facilitate a filibuster? Might they not, instead, be no more than a chapter of accidents that reflected the limited reach of the early American state? If all of these failures to suppress the filibuster did reflect the administration's policy choices, then the unimpeded departure of the raiding party for Texas on 8 August 1812 was one of the most impressive feats of policy coordination over vast distances that the federal government achieved at this stage in its history. Given the blunders and administrative mishaps that were to characterize the conduct of the War of 1812, this last explanation seems unlikely, and to construe the various activities of JM, Shaler, Claiborne, Magee, Monroe, Wilkinson, and others as evidence of the implementation of a coherent policy is to read more into the documentary record than is there (Eustis to Wilkinson, 26 Aug. and 21 Sept. 1812 [DNA: RG 107, LSMA]).

The final element of JM's policy toward Mexico that has been regarded as proof that he condoned the filibuster is the administration's decision in July 1812 to send Dr. John Hamilton Robinson on a special mission to Nemesio Salcedo, the Spanish commandant-general at Chihuahua in the Internal Provinces of Mexico. The choice of Robinson for this mission certainly seems questionable, inasmuch as he had already made the acquaintance of Salcedo in 1807, during the latter days of the expedition led by Zebulon Montgomery Pike, when the commandant-general had detained the doctor on the suspicion that he was an agent sent to seduce the Comanche Indians from their allegiance to Spain. Yet it was Pike himself—while he was in Washington in June 1812 en route from the Southwest to the Canadian frontier—who suggested that Robinson undertake this mission, and he did so on the assumption that if Mexico broke away from Spain, the Internal Provinces themselves eventually would separate from Mexico. To deal with that development and its likely consequences, the administration might need to open communications with Salcedo in a manner similar to its efforts to make contact with rebels in Mexico. A productive relationship between Chihuahua and Washington was hardly likely to result, however, if bodies of armed men remained free to take advantage of a politically volatile situation by waging "predetory warfare" from the Neutral Ground. It thus became Robinson's assignment to deliver Salcedo an assurance from JM that the president wished to preserve the integrity of the Neutral Ground—as it had been defined by the Wilkinson-Herrara agreement of November 1806—until such time as an "amicable negotiation" on the disputed territory could take place. This assurance was accompanied by an avowal that the pressures of war with Great Britain might drive the United States to seize East Florida and that if such a development did occur, Salcedo should not regard it as evidence that JM was contemplating similar actions beyond the Sabine River (Pike to Monroe, 19 June 1812 [NN: Monroe Papers]; Monroe to Robinson, 1 July 1812 [DNA: RG 59, Correspondence Relating to the Filibustering Expedition against the Spanish Government of Mexico, 1811–1816]).

Such statements, coming when they did, might well be regarded as a classic example of Machiavellian duplicity, intended for no other purpose than to confuse the Spanish about American intentions just as the Gutiérrez-Magee raid got under way. But if it be accepted that the administration had never authorized Shaler to organize a filibuster, if it be accepted that the administration did not regard Shaler's conduct as constituting such an activity, and if the administration further believed that Shaler and others would do whatever they could to prevent the raid, then it is by no means so clear that JM's stated desire to preserve the status quo in the Neutral Ground was insincere. Indeed, when Magee learned about Robinson's mission—in October 1812, as the latter passed through Nacogdoches—he could only assume that its purpose was to thwart the filibuster. His first reaction was to consider preventing Robinson from completing his mission, but he eventually let him continue, after extracting a promise that the doctor would not pass information on to Spanish officials regarding Magee's troops' "position . . . strength or intentions." Yet Robinson did provide the Spanish with a warning about the raid, and it is reasonable to assume that JM intended him to do so (Shaler to Monroe, 6 Oct. [NNPM: Shaler Letterbooks] and 24 Oct. 1812 [DNA: RG 59, Communications from Special Agents]; Robinson to Monroe, 26 July 1813 [DNA: RG 59, Correspondence Relating to the Filibustering Expedition against the Spanish Government of Mexico, 1811–1816]).

As Robinson was traveling to Texas, Monroe also wrote to Shaler, informing him of Robinson's mission, stressing that its goals complemented those of Shaler's mission, and urging the agent to "discountenance" the filibuster, "so far as the expression of [his] opinion [might] avail." No more than Robinson's mission itself is this letter proof that Monroe was being disingenuous. If the secretary of state believed that the filibuster was not under Shaler's control, it would have made no sense for him to instruct the agent to stop it, as opposed to conveying the opinion that JM would not approve of illegal activities. Furthermore, it is difficult to see why the administration should have added Texas as another irritant to the already strained relationship with Spain, especially when any hint of American sponsorship of a raid into the province could have furnished Spain (and its ally Great Britain) with a pretext for commencing hostilities on the southwestern frontier. All of the other information about JM's policy toward Spain at this juncture supports the impression that the president's preoccupations were with security matters and territorial disputes east of the Mississippi and not with the issues of American-Spanish relations to the west of the river. By the time Robinson met up with Shaler to convey that message, however, the latter had concluded that the mission of the former would be too late to affect events already in motion (Monroe to Shaler, 1 Sept. 1812 [PHi: Shaler Family Papers]; Shaler to Monroe, 5 Oct. 1812 [DNA: RG 59, Communications from Special Agents]).

In the longer term, little was to come of the Gutiérrez-Magee raid. The filibuster achieved some early minor successes with the capture of Nacogdoches and La Bahía (Goliad) in the fall of 1812. Its progress was then delayed by the need for further preparations, by bad weather, by skirmishes with royalist forces, and by the prolonged illness of Magee, who eventually died in mysterious circumstances in February 1813. The major accomplishment of the raid occurred on 1 April 1813 with the occupation of San Antonio, after which the Mexicans in the Republican Army of the North drew up a constitution declaring Texas to be both independent of Spain and an integral part of the Mexican nation. Gutiérrez was proclaimed the first governor of the new Texas. Anticipating some of these developments, especially the capture of San Antonio, Shaler had already requested a "general passport" from the State Department in November 1812 to facilitate his movements throughout Mexico once he had commenced the duties prescribed in his 1810 instructions. As he pointed out to Monroe, the papers currently in his possession were hardly "proper . . . to be shewn on unimportant Occasions" (Shaler to Monroe, 10 and 29 Nov. 1812 [ibid.]).

Shaler received his American passport in the first week of April 1813 and, confident of the ultimate success of the raid, made his final preparations for Mexico. He was to be diverted by some unanticipated consequences of the occupation of San Antonio. Always an idealist, Shaler was greatly offended by the Texan constitution drafted by Gutiérrez and his fellow Mexicans. Regarding the document as a betrayal of republican principles, the agent denounced it as "an absurd revolutionary farce" whose provisions would support Gutiérrez in the style of "an Eastern Basha, while everything around him is penury and misery." Even worse was the news that the Mexican rebels, apparently on orders from Gutiérrez, had murdered several Spanish officials following the capture of San Antonio. Appalled, Shaler concluded that the continuation of Gutiérrez at the head of the revolutionary forces would be disastrous for the future of republicanism in Mexico, and he resolved to appeal to the Americans in the ranks of the filibuster to replace Gutiérrez as commander with another Spanish-American rebel, José Álvarez de Toledo, who had arrived in New Orleans from Pittsburgh in the spring of 1813 (Shaler to Monroe, 3 and 18 Apr., 2 and 14 May, and 12 June 1813 [ibid.]).

Shaler's campaign against Gutiérrez was successful, and Toledo took command of the revolutionary forces in the summer of 1813. Those developments, however, brought Shaler a sharp reprimand from Monroe, who reminded the agent in the first week of June that his instructions did not countenance meddling in the affairs of Mexico or "encourage any armaments of any kind against the existing government." The reason for this abrupt decision is often assumed to be that the administration, worried about the faltering course of the war against Great Britain, suddenly became afraid that Shaler's actions would compromise American neutrality with Spain. The more likely immediate reason for Monroe's rebuke of Shaler, though, was the character of Toledo himself. The secretary of state had met Toledo late in 1811, when Gutiérrez was also in Washington, and had entered into understandings with him regarding American policy toward Cuba. Inexplicably, Toledo had failed to honor those understandings, and in October 1812 he had also met with the Spanish minister in Philadelphia, Luis de Onís, to discuss how he might betray revolutionary movements in Spanish America. Both Monroe and Shaler received information about the behavior of Toledo, including the possibility that he might return to the service of the Spanish monarchy, but Shaler, blinded by his disgust with Gutiérrez, chose to disregard the warnings. Monroe did not. In that sense Shaler's openly avowed efforts to turn the leadership of the revolution in Texas over to Toledo did threaten to compromise both American interests in the Southwest and American neutrality with Spain in far more flagrant ways than anything the agent had done during the previous year (Shaler to Monroe, 10 and 14 July 1813 [ibid.]; Monroe to Shaler, 5 June 1813 [PHi: Shaler Family Papers]).

At that point the administration terminated Shaler's mission to Mexico. Shortly thereafter, the Gutiérrez-Magee raid itself came to an end. Shaler received Monroe's reprimand in the first week of August 1813, while on the road to San Antonio. Toledo's forces were defeated in the same month by a reinvigorated royalist counteroffensive at the Battle of Medina. Shaler accepted the reprimand, withdrew to Natchitoches, and informed the State Department that the "fatal disaster" at Medina promised to be "conclusive of the revolution in the neighboring Provinces perhaps forever." He then returned to the United States, reporting on his mission to JM and Monroe in Washington in December 1813. On that occasion Monroe, referring to the filibuster, queried the agent with "friendly politeness": "You know that the U. S. could not take any part in that business?" Shaler admitted that he "knew it well" (Shaler to Monroe, 7 Aug. and 5 and 19 Sept. 1813 [DNA: RG 59, Communications from Special Agents]; Shaler diary entry for 19–21 Dec. 1813 [NNPM: Shaler Letterbooks]).

No matter how the goals of Shaler's mission to Mexico are defined, the mission itself ended in failure. The agent never reached the interior of Mexico to obtain information on the progress of the Mexican Revolution, nor did the filibuster establish an independent Texas as a prelude to the inclusion of that province within the United States. Shaler's presence in the company of Gutiérrez and the Republican Army of the North certainly created the impression that the administration backed the Gutiérrez-Magee raid for expansionist purposes, but a closer examination of the surviving records suggests that this impression was more apparent than real. JM's directive to Monroe on 1 September 1812 that Shaler should do whatever he could to prevent the filibuster is therefore a fairer expression of the president's policy regarding Texas and Mexico at this time than is the assumption that his administration was covertly encouraging policies of a very different nature.

(Secondary sources used for this note: Félix D. Almaráz Jr., *Tragic Cavalier: Governor Manuel Salcedo of Texas, 1808–1813* [Austin, Tex., 1971]; Hubert H. Bancroft, *History of the North Mexican States and Texas* [2 vols.; San Francisco, 1889]; Harold A. Bierck Jr., "Dr. John Hamilton Robinson," *La. Historical Quarterly* 25 [1942]: 644–69; Brooks, *Diplomacy and the Borderlands;* James Morton Callahan, *American Foreign Policy in Mexican Relations* [New York, 1932]; Donald E. Chipman, *Spanish Texas, 1519–1821* [Austin, Tex., 1992]; Isaac Joslin Cox, "Monroe and the Early Mexican Revolutionary Agents," *Annual Report of the American Historical Association for the Year 1911* [2 vols.; Washington, 1913], 1:199–215; Odie B. Faulk, *The Last Years of Spanish Texas, 1778–1821* [The Hague, 1964]; Kathryn Garrett, "The First Newspaper of Texas: Gaceta de Texas," *Southwestern Historical Quarterly* 40 [1937]: 200–215; Garrett, "The First Constitution of Texas, April 17, 1813," ibid., 290–308; Garrett, *Green Flag over Texas;* Griffin, *The United States and the Disruption of the Spanish Empire;* Richard W. Gronet, "United States and the Invasion of Texas, 1810–1814," *Americas* 25 [1968–69]: 281–306; J. Villasana Haggard, "The Neutral Ground between Louisiana and Texas, 1806–1821," *La. Historical Quarterly* 28 [1945]: 1001–28; Mattie Austin Hatcher, *The Opening of Texas to Foreign Settlement, 1801–1821* [1927; reprint, Philadelphia, 1976]; Harry McCorry Henderson, "The Magee-Gutiérrez Expedition," *Southwestern Historical Quarterly* 55 [1951]: 43–61; James E. Lewis Jr., *The American Union and the Problem of Neighborhood: The United States and the Collapse of the Spanish Empire, 1783–1829* [Chapel Hill, N.C., 1998]; Walter Flavius M'Caleb, "The First Period of the Gutiérrez-Magee Expedition," *Quarterly of the Texas State Historical Association* 4 [1900–1901]: 218–29; Thomas Maitland Marshall, *A History of the Western Boundary of the Louisiana Purchase, 1819–1841* [Berkeley, Calif., 1914]; Edward H. Moseley, "The United States and Mexico, 1810–1850," in T. Ray Shurbutt, ed., *United States–Latin American Relations, 1800–1850* [Tuscaloosa, Ala., 1991], 122–96; Abraham P. Nasatir,

Borderland in Retreat: From Spanish Louisiana to the Far Southwest [Albuquerque, N.M., 1976]; Nichols, "William Shaler," *New England Quarterly* 9 [1936]: 71–96; Nichols, *Advance Agents of American Destiny* [Philadelphia, 1956]; Owsley and Smith, *Filibusters and Expansionists;* Julius W. Pratt, *Expansionists of 1812* [New York, 1925]; Richard Stenberg, "The Western Boundary of Louisiana, 1762–1803," *Southwestern Historical Quarterly* 35 [1931]: 95–108; Francisco Valdés-Ugalde, "Janus and the Northern Colossus: Perceptions of the United States in the Building of the Mexican Nation," *Journal of American History* 86 [1999]: 568–600; Henry P. Walker, ed., "William McLane's Narrative of the Magee-Gutiérrez Expedition, 1812–1813," *Southwestern Historical Quarterly* 66 [1962–63]: 234–51, 457–79, 569–88; Harris Gaylord Warren, "Southern Filibusters in the War of 1812," *La. Historical Quarterly* 25 [1942]: 291–300; Warren, *The Sword Was Their Passport: A History of American Filibustering in the Mexican Revolution* [1943; reprint, Port Washington, N.Y., 1972]; A. Curtis Wilgus, "Spanish American Patriot Activity along the Gulf Coast of the United States, 1811–1822," *La. Historical Quarterly* 8 [1925]: 193–215; Wriston, *Executive Agents in American Foreign Relations;* Henderson Yoakum, *History of Texas from Its First Settlement in 1685 to Its Annexation to the United States in 1846* [2 vols.; 1855; reprint, Austin, Tex., 1935].)

To James Monroe

DEAR SIR   OCCOQUON MILLS. Sepr. 1. 1812

The letter from Acheson, should be known in some of its contents. I inclose it to you for reasons on the face of it.[1] I inclose also the letter from Gilbert Taylor,[2] as a memento to the letter you are to write to the Govr. of Tennessee, on the subject of the illegal enterprize on foot in that State.[3] We are so far well on our way. Yrs.

J. MADISON

RC (DLC: Monroe Papers).

1. JM probably enclosed the 25 Aug. 1812 letter he had received from Thomas Acheson on the fall of Detroit.

2. Letter not found. Gilbert Dade Taylor (b. 1791), a grandson of Erasmus Taylor and the son of John and Anne Gilbert Taylor of Orange County, Virginia, was a kinsman of JM. He studied medicine in Philadelphia and moved in 1811 to Giles County, Tennessee. He later served as a surgeon with Andrew Jackson's troops in the Creek War, then in 1819 gave up the practice of medicine to become a Methodist minister (Herbert Weaver et al., eds., *Correspondence of James K. Polk* [9 vols. to date; Nashville, 1969–], 1:584–85; *VMHB* 34 [1926]: 270).

3. On 3 Sept. 1812 Monroe wrote to Gov. Willie Blount to inform him that intelligence had been received suggesting that Tennessee citizens were "collecting in the county of Giles with intention to make an incursion into some of the provinces of Spain to join the revolutionary party in a contest against the existing government" in Mexico. Monroe pointed out that the U.S. was at peace with Spain and that "such a movement is prohibited by law under severe penalties." He conveyed JM's wish that Blount investigate this movement and "give it all discountenance" in his power (DNA: RG 59, DL). On 3 Oct. 1812 Blount informed Monroe that his inquiries had produced no evidence of any such activities in Tennessee (DNA: RG 59, ML).

From Thomas Acheson

S<small>IR</small>   W<small>ASHINGTON</small> 1st Septr 1812

I addressd. your excellency a few days ago on the rumourd. defeat and Surrender of Genl. Hull's Army.[1] Since which we have recd. the detail and it appears that the British have got possession of the important post of *Detroit* in the usual way. Can any faith be held with a Nation So lost to every principle of honor, and So degenerated as to employ no other weapons but *bribery, corruption,* and *intrigue;* Can any Safety be expected while they possess a foot of land on our Continent. Surely not, However dishonorable the Surrender of Hull may be. I am persuaded that good will come out of evil. Be assured the nation were Sleeping or lost in apathy untill now. But having recd. a Shock as of an earthquake. The Spirit of the people is completely rousd. and their indignation against the perfidious *enemy* rolling Eastward like a mighty torrent, which if properly directed must and *will* put down all opposition to carrying on the war with rigour and effect which alone Can Carry Consternation and dismay to the foot of that Blood Staind. Throne which ere long must answer for *"Crimes of a deep dye and a Scarlet hue"* let not the Syren Song of peace, be heard; in our land untill our independence by Sea and land is fully acknowledged and Secured. The inclosd. report of a Committee of Safety appointed by the Citizens of this Borough[2] will Convey to your excellency a faint Sketch of the Spirit of the people in this Western Country. The universal cry was give us *arms* and lead us on to meet the *Savage foe.* I entreat your excellency to ascribe my freedom and Zeal—to my love of Country, and the intire Confidence I have in the upright views and intentions of the Administration. Believe me to be with high Consideration and respect Your excellencys most Obt. Hble Servt.

T<small>HOS</small>. A<small>CHESON</small>

P. S. This moment Major James Dunlap who was Sent express from this place to Cleveland has returnd. and brings the pleasing news that the frontier in that quarter is Safe for the present—report also States that Col. Miller of the Regulars who was Shipped on Board the Queen Charlotte as prisoners of war—destined for fort Erie—had rose on the guard and taken the vessel[3]

RC (DLC). Docketed by JM.

  1. Acheson to JM, 25 Aug. 1812.

  2. Enclosure not found.

  3. The report was incorrect. The *Queen Charlotte* remained in British service until it was captured by the U.S. in the Battle of Lake Erie on 10 Sept. 1813 (Dudley, *Naval War of 1812,* 2:566–67).

From Tench Coxe

Sir   Sept. 1. 1812

I had the honor to write you a hasty line at day light yesterday morning. Suffer me to obtrude upon you a few personal and public considerations. I sincerely believe that a considerable portion of our present difficulties have arisen from the injuries to the operations & system of supply, which have grown out of the measures since the spring of 1809 upon the subject of its organization. I am convinced, that the public in general, without regard to party, would feel that affection of their confidence, which the times require, by my return to the service. I submit to you, Sir, the propriety of a transfer of Genl. Duncan, who has been in the mercantile line, to the office of the late depy Commy, Mr. Mifflin, *in which I will give him every possible aid (so far as in my power)* and of the commitment of the Superintendance of military stores to me. I certainly have seen much of its operations, and with incessant and anxious observation. I even endeavoured to have those anticipations of probable, possible & periodical wants brought into view, which constitute one of the principal aids of the office to the Secy of War. I was in the constant habit of suggesting to the officer & of submitting to the Secretaries those things, which were calculated to improve, quicken & ensure supplies.

As to the object in relation to myself, I understood from the Secy of war & Mr. Mc.Kenney in the end of May that you would have nominated me again; if you had not believed, that I would not be advised & approved.[1] You have seen faithfully stated, what Mr. Gilman asserts.[2] The office at $1500 is below a great number of the Clerkships. To defend our country from the invasion of foreign influence & a monarchy, I, in office, sacrificed my office & family. I have continued with more labor & more sincerity, than any other man the more dutiful course of defence. Suffer as I may, I will still continue that course. The course of my struggles has brought me in contact with persons of *high* standing, who, face to face, have attempted to communicate to me their fears or their infidelities by the most explicit annunciations of assassination, Exile, destruction of my private business, extrusion from office obstructions of my *official business,* Obstructions to the establishment of my family, from 1797 to 1812. and these persons are now in office under the U. S. in a great part, and the rest have been nominated to office since 3d March 1801 or chosen by state Legislatures. I have never made any personal party. I have borne all this fury of the enemies of our institutions, and of our infirm friends, almost broken hearted at times— and alone. The Legislature of my own state, Franklin, Washington, Jefferson, Hamilton, McKean have put a public seal upon my character. I can *prove* the highest encomiums of the Members of the Senate & the Editor, who have for personal reasons, afterwards attempted to misrepresent

247

me[3]—of the latter, I have *written* evidence under his own hand. I understand Mr. McKinney to be twice charged wth. assurances, that my services were appreciated & that you desired to use them. I understood, that the Secy of war had added, that I was considered at Wn. as "the most injured of men." He voluntarily gave me a letter in June, testifying my zeal & fidelity.[4] He added his disposition, his imputation to be able to serve me and his knowledge that his views would be sanctioned. How dreadfully agitated & unorganized have been the business of procuring & superintending supplies since last October.

I conclude, Sir, this letter to Mr. Madison by my reflected affirmation, that I believe that the public service would be most seriously promoted & the public confidence favorably affected, by my restoration to the service in the station lately held by Mr. Mifflin or in that of Genl. Duncan, he going thither. I decidedly prefer the Superintendents office, and I believe it would be best for the public & least susceptible of colorable misrepresentation.

I pray God to fulfil your prayers in preserving the peace liberty and safety of our country being its & your most faithful friend

Tench Coxe

RC (DLC). Docketed by JM.

1. John McKinney had been appointed deputy commissary for the District of Columbia on 25 Apr. 1812. He may have communicated this message when he requested on 29 May 1812 that Coxe turn the official papers of the purveyor's office over to him at the end of May (Hamersly, *Complete Regular Army Register of the U.S.*, 64; Cooke, *Tench Coxe*, 481).

    2. For Coxe's claim regarding Nicholas Gilman, see Coxe to JM, 13 Aug. 1812.

    3. Coxe probably referred to the editor of the Philadelphia *Aurora General Advertiser*, William Duane, who had at an earlier time been one of Coxe's supporters. In 1811 and 1812, however, Duane blamed Coxe for weaknesses in the army supply system, a campaign which coincided with the efforts of Sen. Michael Leib to oust Coxe by abolishing his office (Cooke, *Tench Coxe*, 347, 473–74, 477–79).

    4. Eustis to Coxe, 4 June 1812 (DNA: RG 107, LSMA).

§ From Walker Reid. *1 September 1812, Washington, Kentucky.* Encloses resolutions concerning the Nonimportation Act from Mason County, Kentucky. Apologizes for the poor copy, explaining that he is "in soldiers dress" and will "march in the morning to Join our beloved Harrison—with an elegant company of mounted Riflemen formed in 3 Days."

[Enclosure]

§ From the Citizens of Mason County, Kentucky. *1 September 1812.* "A large and very respectable collection of citizens" met to discuss the "subject of continuing in force or repealing the act prohibiting the importation of British manufactures." The meeting appointed a chairman and secretary. "Judge Beatty[1] then delivered an address on the subject in the course of which he pointed out the abuses of British impressments from the commencement of our Government under Gen. Washington until the present War. The prostration of our rights as citizens and the restrictions of that perfidious nation upon our lawful commerce." He concluded by requesting that the meeting be polled on the question of "'Whether the Act prohibiting the importation of British manufactures ought to be repealed or remain in force during the War' and that a committee be appointed to prepare a resolution in pursuance of the decision of the meeting on said question." A committee was then appointed, and the several resolutions they reported were "amended and finally adopted to read as follows."

"1st. Resolved unanimously that we highly approve of the declaration of War against Great Britain, and that we are clearly of opinion no peace ought to be made, without a relinquishment of the right which she has assumed to impress our Seamen and to regulate and controul our commerce upon the high seas by illegal blockades and orders in council.

"2nd. Resolved unanimously that in the opinion of this meeting it would be highly impolitic to repeal the nonimportation act during the continuance of the War, which now exists between the United States and Great Britain.

"3d. Resolved unanimously as the opinion of the meeting that the prohibition of the importation of British manufactures has produced the repeal of the British orders in council; and that if the U. S. firmly persevere in that measure, it will together with a vigorous prosecution of the War occasion such a degree of pressure and distress on G.B. as will compel her to comply with our equitable demands.

"4th. Resolved Unanimously that we will cheerefully and with pleasure pay our quota of the Taxes necessary to carry on the War and that we spurn with indignation the idea of rep[e]aling the nonimportation Act with a view of raising revenue least the people should be unwilling to pay the necessary internal taxes to carry it on with vigour and Success.

"⟨5⟩th. Resolved unanimously that a vigorous prosecution of the War against the North American possessions of Great Britain is a policy obviously dictated by our interest and our safety and that no honorable means ought to be left untried to accomplish a conquest of them as soon as practicable.

"6th. Resolved Unanimously, that all those who are attempting by covert means to bring about a dissolution of the Union or who countenance or support Great Britain or in any way take part against our Country in the present contest deserve the reprobation and contempt of every honest man in the community.

"7th. Resolved Unanimously that copies of the proceedings of this meeting be forwarded to the President of the United States the President of the senate and to the Speaker of the house of Representatives of the United States."

RC and enclosure (DNA: RG 59, ML). RC 1 p. Enclosure 3 pp.; signed by D. V. Payne, chairman, and Walker Reid, secretary.

1. Adam Beatty (1777–1858) came to Kentucky from Maryland in 1800 and began a law practice in Mason County in 1802. Beatty was elected to the state legislature in 1809, was re-elected for several terms, and was appointed a circuit court judge in 1811, serving for twelve years. He concluded his career in Kentucky politics in the state senate between 1836 and 1839 (*The Biographical Encyclopaedia of Kentucky of the Dead and Living Men of the Nineteenth Century* [Cincinnati, 1878], 139).

From William Eustis

Sir,   Tuesday 2. Septr. [1812]

In forming an answer to Govr. Strong I find some objections which induce me to enclose the papers for a second consideration.[1] It appears that 3 of the 5 companies required for passamaquodda[2] (which implies a greater extent of country than Eastport) have been ordered by the Govr for Eastport. The requisition of G. Dearborn is substantially complied with *at this post*. As it is a frontier post and known to be more exposed than any other, and as it further appears that in the order (published) calling out this detachment *reference* is had to the requisition of the President,[3] (not having the order before me I am not able to state the precise terms of it) it may be worth considering whether under all the circumstances it is prudent to give the proposed answer, untill the volunteers are raised. In great haste & respect—

                                                        W. Eustis

Mr Munroe advises submitting the papers for consideration.

RC (DLC). Docketed by JM. For enclosures, see n. 1.

1. Eustis enclosed a three-page letter he had received from Caleb Strong, dated 5 Aug. 1812, which in turn covered a six-page opinion written by Justices Theophilus Parsons, Samuel Sewall, and Isaac Parker of the Massachusetts Supreme Court (PHi: Daniel Parker Papers; printed in *ASP, Military Affairs*, 1:323, 324). Strong's letter took issue with the assumption that Massachusetts was in danger of invasion and justified the governor's decision to reject the requests made by Eustis and Dearborn that he provide detached militia for the seacoast. Strong and his advisers had also referred the matter to the Massachusetts Supreme Court, and the three responding justices declared that the power to call out the state militia was vested in the governor and not in the president of the U.S. or any subordinate federal officer.

2. On 22 June 1812 Dearborn had requested that Strong provide one company of artillery and four companies of infantry for the defense of Passamaquoddy. Strong ordered out the troops, not because he feared an invasion by "an authorized British force," but because he had been informed by a messenger from the region that the inhabitants there believed "there were many lawless people on the borders from whom they were in danger of predatory incursions" and against whom they needed protection (*ASP, Military Affairs*, 1:322–23).

3. Strong's 5 Aug. 1812 general order, published in the Boston *Columbian Centinel* on 8 Aug., directed Massachusetts militia companies to rendezvous at Eastport to form a battalion for the defense of the frontier under the terms of a 25 Apr. 1812 War Department requisition calling for the detachment of state militia companies in compliance with the act of 10 Apr. 1812 (*PJM-PS*, 4:541 n. 1).

From William Keteltas

NEW YORK 2d Septer 1812

Gnl. Hull and his Army Prisoners at the Onset *Millions* opposed to *thousands* in population In a word the *United States* opposed to two pitiful and Pitiable British provinces seperated from their Guardian by an Ocean of 3000 Miles. *Oh Nature* what a beginning. *Error* some where Methinks ignorance, has assumed the empire of Wisdom *Vice* of *Virtue*, wrong of right, for When opposed to the wrongs of Great Britain, as Colonies, and her Adherents in America, the very reverse of this was the Case.

The Cause of this best presents itself to the real Lover of his Country. I have found it, *Party Self agrandizment*, has almost Sunk first principles and Banished from the Country that Patriotizm which gave us *Independance Honor* and *glory* as a people and a Nation, for the Want of it, we have to bewail this National disgrace.

If their was a want of supplies, this must be owing to the Contractors, Whose Appointments may not be as Censurable as their Continuance in the important trust. Porter at Niagara[1] & Walton at Schen[e]ctady both in this State should be dismis'd if What is Stated is Correct, of one Moments neglect of duty.

They are both inimical to the administration, and wish to bring it into Contempt to Effect a Change at the ensuing Elections.

But why need I Concern myself about its support; when its *Known Enemies* are prefered to its known friends, and where [*sic*] it not for the love of Country it should *Cease* to disturbe My repose.

I have thought it a duty once more to make the follg Communication to the administration in Whose hands all that is dear to America is placed notwithstanding its Neglect of its best friends; then have done with all political concerns; and circumscribe My love of Country to the sole love of My Family and their Concerns Which has been divided with My country, and they the Minor Consideration and Sacrificed at the Shrine of Patriotizm.

I am informd by a Clintonian endeavoring to Cast every odium on the administration for Hull defeat that Walton the Contractor at Schenectady is a half pay British officer and that he Communicated to Gnl. Brock the Situation of *Hull*. You are sufficiently acquainted with the hypocritical Conduct of *Porter* in the Clinton interest on the Question of *War* the touchstone of the American Heart and of American patriotizm. If the *American Army* has been surrendered in the Manner Stated, Hull Must be a *Coward* or a *Traitor*. If he was without powder and Ball & provisions he had his sword in his hand. I Cannot Credit the Scandalous the Monstrous the absurd Tale that 2500 americans on their own ground; Should Yield to an inferior force, with their Bayonetes in their hands. If it Should prove true, we are disgraced and the Stain must without delay be wiped off the Nation.

Having an Eye to the Emperor of france and his extensive V[i]ews to make the most of every thing to gratify his Ambition, it appears to me, the Very time to press our Claims by negotiation for a prompt adjustment of Our rights for if he ever does us Justice it will be While at war with england. Therefore the opportunity should not be let Slip.

England must make a pease with us and that Speedily too, or her Govt. will be Questioned therefore in my humble opinion no time should be Lost in Setling with france, or to bring her Sincerely to the test. Your Obdt Servt.

WILLIAM KETELTAS

RC (DLC). Docketed by JM.

1. Keteltas probably referred to Augustus Porter, brother of Rep. Peter B. Porter, who had a contract to supply troops along the Great Lakes (Risch, *Quartermaster Support*, 157).

From James Monroe

DEAR SIR   WASHINGTON Sepr. 2. 1812

Nothing new is recd. from England; or France. Mr Baker will remain at Fredericktown or some other interior town between this & Phila.[1] Mr Serurier was with me yesterday. He stated many reasons for delay in his govt. to arrange our affairs, but dwelt most on changes in the treaty in discussion between it & Mr. Barlow, proposed by the latter.[2] He mention'd several, all of a commercial nature. He had great confidence that, as soon as it shod be known that we had gone to war, all reasonable accomodation would be afforded.

Nothing is yet recd. from Genl Hull. Many letters are recd. from others, all of a character corresponding with those you have seen.

Mr Duvall express'd a doubt of the fitness of Genl. Winchester to take the command of the troops intended for Detroit. And Captn. Ball,[3] whom I have just seen, and who appears to have much knowledge of that country, & of military affrs, especially those connected with that service, having been in the action & campaign under Genl. Wayne, expresses the same doubt. The latter thinks that Harrison is much better qualified for the trust.

I fear that the failure of Hull will produce much injury to the republican party & cause, till all the explanations belonging to it, are before the publick. Tenderness is due to him, but having lost the army, he is responsible, and it seems to me, that it should appear that the govt. is far from imputing to itself, or allowing it to be imputed by others, any blame.

I have written to Shaler to inform him that the combination of any of our citizens to aid the Mexicans is contrary to law, and ought to be discountenanc'd.[4] I shall write to morrow a letter, to the same effect, to Govr Howard, & to the govr of Tenissee.[5]

Several friends here to the administration, have suggested to me, an idea, corresponding with that on which we conferr'd just as we parted. They think that some marked measure proceeding directly from yourself, will be useful in tranquilizing the people to the westward, & meeting the public expectation generally, in consequence of the late disaster. If on further reflection you should be of opinion that my employment might be useful, I am inclind to undertake it. I know its dangers & difficulties and the an[x]iety to which it would expose me, by separation from my family. If I went my wish would be to serve the active part of the campaign, & then return to my station here. I think I might be back in Novr. In the interim, if my resignation was not deemed indispensable, I would hasten Mr Graham back,[6] & Mr Pleasanton might forward to you till his return, the papers, for your order, or perhaps Mr Rush might act per interim, for me. In case of my resignation which might be most adviseable, Mr Rush might still act per interim till an appointment was made, with a view to keep it open to my renomination on my return, if you approvd. I think I could contribute to the expeditious collection of the troops, could take advantage of the talents of Harrison & winchester, & give the whole some impulse. It would I know lay new & heavy burthens on you, but the motive being seen by the publick, would give satisfaction. If I went, I should wish to take all the idle regular officers of experience whom I could collect. I shod. wish to take Izard, Ball, Bankhead[7] & others, & perhaps old L'Enfant.[8]

Believe me something decisive, that is, of a marked character is necessary. Whether this is the suitable measure I know not. I feel that in being willing to act, I can seriously justify myself to my family, and to others who have great claims on me. I yeild more to zeal in the cause, than to considerations which ought to have weight with me. If I were appointed it would be I presume by Brevitt.

The Garrison of chicago is cut off.[9]

The Secretary at war has deeply interested me in what concerns him in this affair. I have never seen a man more profoundly oppress'd by misfortune than he really is. Mr Hamilton came into my room yesterday & intimated a fear that there was danger of his mind being affected. I saw him immediately afterwards, when there was no evidence of that tendency, & I have been consulted by him on his letters to Winchester & Harrison, which are drawn strictly in the spirit you desired, & forwarded.[10]

I have not yet heard from Onis.[11] I have yours from Occoquan. Very sincerely & respectfully your friend

JAS MONROE

RC (DLC: Rives Collection, Madison Papers). Docketed by JM.

1. Monroe was waiting to hear from Baker regarding a possible exchange of prisoners captured at sea (Baker to Monroe, 29 Aug. 1812 [DNA: RG 45, Misc. Letters Received]).

2. For the commercial treaty that Barlow was negotiating, see Barlow to JM, 22 Apr. 1812, and JM to Jefferson, 24 Apr. 1812, *PJM-PS*, 4:337–38 and n. 1, 345–46, 347 n. 4.

3. James Vincent Ball (d. 1818), a captain in the Light Dragoons, was promoted to major on 16 Sept. 1812 and subsequently served under William Henry Harrison (Gilpin, *The War of 1812 in the Old Northwest*, 143, 153–54; Heitman, *Historical Register*, 1:187).

4. Monroe wrote to William Shaler on 1 Sept. 1812: "As the parties who are said to have combined for the purpose of assisting the patriots, in Mexico, are acting in opposition to a Law of the United States; it will be proper for you to discountenance the measure, so far as the expression of your opinion may avail." The letter also informed Shaler that Dr. John Hamilton Robinson had been "lately appointed" by the president "to reside at the seat of Government" in the Internal Provinces of Mexico. Monroe reassured Shaler that Robinson's appointment would "cooperate" with his "in cultivating a good understanding between the United States and the Governments & people of the Provinces" to which Shaler had been sent (PHi: Shaler Family Papers).

5. For Monroe's letter to Blount, see JM to Monroe, 1 Sept. 1812, n. 3. Monroe wrote to Missouri territorial governor Benjamin Howard on 3 Sept. 1812, acknowledging receipt of Howard's 21 June letter enclosing messages from Louisiana citizens that outlined their plans to visit Spanish provinces (not found). Monroe explained that he concluded from the enclosures that this visit would be "of an unfriendly nature." Monroe communicated the view of the president that since the U.S. was at peace with Spain, a hostile visit to its provinces would be "repugnant" to U.S. policy as well as "positively prohibited by law." Monroe requested that Howard make this sentiment known to the concerned parties (DNA: RG 59, DL).

6. State Department chief clerk John Graham was then traveling in western Pennsylvania and Ohio en route to Kentucky (Graham to Monroe, 28 Aug., 31 Aug., and 7 Sept. 1812 [DLC: Monroe Papers]).

7. Monroe referred to James Bankhead of Virginia (ca. 1780–1856), who had been Monroe's attaché in Europe before receiving a captain's commission in the U.S. Army in 1808. Bankhead was appointed an assistant adjutant general and was promoted to the rank of major in March 1813. In September 1813 he was promoted to the rank of colonel, serving until he was mustered out in June 1815. Bankhead reentered the peacetime army at the rank of captain that same year, serving for the rest of his life. Bankhead received a brevet colonel's promotion in 1838 for meritorious service during the Seminole War and was raised to the rank of brigadier general in 1847 after participating in the siege of Veracruz during the Mexican War (Heitman, *Historical Register*, 1:189; *WMQ*, 1st ser., 14 [1905–6]: 287; *WMQ*, 2d ser., 9 [1929]: 307).

8. L'Enfant was not brought back into active service, but in 1814 he began work on the reconstruction of a fort at Warburton Manor on the Potomac River, later named Fort Washington (H. Paul Caemmerer, *The Life of Pierre Charles L'Enfant* [1950; reprint, New York, 1970], 270–72).

9. Hull had ordered that Fort Dearborn (Chicago) be evacuated at the end of July, but before the commanding officer, Capt. Nathan Heald, could act, Indians in the region began to gather near the post. When Heald eventually attempted the evacuation on 15 Aug., he was able to march only two miles before being engaged in battle and forced to surrender (Gilpin, *The War of 1812 in the Old Northwest*, 126–28).

10. For Eustis's letters to Harrison and Winchester of 1 Sept. 1812, see Gallatin to JM, 31 Aug. 1812, n. 4.

11. In August, Monroe had presented to the unrecognized minister from Spain, Luis de Onís, through the Spanish vice-consul at Alexandria, Pablo Chacón, some propositions and questions relating to East Florida. Monroe offered to relinquish U.S. spoliation claims against Spain in exchange for renunciation of Spanish claims in East and West Florida. He inquired whether Onís was authorized to negotiate a treaty to this effect, when he would come to Washington to do so, and whether officials in Florida would evacuate upon his orders. Monroe also asked whether the formation of the new Spanish government under the Constitution of 1812 would affect Onís's ability to negotiate (Brooks, *Diplomacy and the Borderlands*, 22–23).

From Nelson Nicholas

SIR   LEXINGTON September 2d. [1812]
    I hope you will feel no disposition, as you certainly have no cause, to question my sincerity when I assure you, that the motives which induce me to address you are disinterested, and that my complaints against some of your sub-ministers are dictated by patriotism, and not by enmity to you, or any other individual in power. I wish briefly to disclose the situation of this country, and for a moment to call your attention, to the preperations which have been made in this quarter, to weather the storm of war which has burst on our heads. I am sorry to say, that the country resounds with complaints on these subjects, and I lament extremely, that there is too much ground for these complaints. The public interests have been abused in a manner, which must unavoidably arouse the indignation of every man who feels any solicitude for the welfare of the nation. I feel it to be my duty, as I believe it to be my right, to complain of the negligence or ignorance of public functionaries, whose misconduct has been productive of the most fatal consequences in this country. This misconduct has risen to a most alarming height, and the wrongs of Kentucky call aloud for redress. Listen to her complaints.
    The gallant volunteers who have relinquished the plough to fight the battles of their country, when called to the camp, are marched thro' long and dreary routs, many of them without a cent in their pockets, without baggage waggons, without provisions furnished them, without tents, exposed to all the inclemencies of the weather, and dependent on common charity for support. Those, who when they bid adieu to their homes, laid up what they deemed a sufficient stock of money for the exigencies of the *whole campaign*, find, by the time they arrive at the place of rendezvous, their purses completely exhausted in procuring necessary subsistence for themselves and their more indigent companions; and when they have arrived, there is no money in the military chest to meet their just demands, or satisfy their craving wants. You will readily perceive, sir, that this state of

limited supply and indigent suffering, is very incompatible with the feelings of a people, who have been accustomed to abundant and healthful plenty, who have been taught to rely on their own independent industry for support, and whose stubborn knees reluctantly assume the posture of supplication. When the wearied volunteer, after toiling day after day thro' bad roads, exposed to the burning rays of the mid-day sun, and shivering in unprotected exposure to the chilling dews of night, at length reaches the place of destination, which he vainly expects will be the termination of his sufferings, he is told by his commander, (whose trembling tongue speaks his compassion) that there is no money to remove his distresses. This fatal intelligence sounds like the trump of death to the astonished soldier, who had depended on this supply for his equipment; and who when he contemplates with downcast eye the thread-bare sleeve of his hunting shirt, shakes with chilling anticipation, at the bleak winds of Canada. His spirits droop, and he begins to sigh for the comforts of sheltered home. It is true, he does not think of deserting that post which he has voluntarily assumed; for a Kentuckian will never turn upon his heel when his insulted country points to the enemy and cries aloud for revenge; but he trembles at the chilling blasts of winter, which he is not prepared to repell, and his soul sickens with fears; which the most formidable enemy could never inspire. He is marching to a cold and comfortless climate, with no other covering than a thin linnen dress, which must necessary [*sic*] be reduced to dependent fragments, long ere the term of his service shall have expired. From the unexpected haste with which they have been summonsed to the field, and the great scarcity of that article in this country, our volunteers have been unable to equip themselves with blankets. This is a sad and distressing situation. Without blankets and woolen clothing, it is morally impossible that the army can exist in Canada, and it is equally impossible to procure these necessaries whilst they are on the march without a dollar in their pockets. Unless they are furnished by the government, the army, I fear, will suffer most cruelly during the approaching winter, or be compelled to return to their homes, to avoid inevitable destruction. I, therefore, will presume to suggest the expediency, nay the *absolute necessity*, of forwarding supplies adequate to their wants, and if necessary, deducting the value thereof from their monthly pay. This arrangement, I have every reason to believe, would be very agreeable to our volunteers. They ought likewise to be furnished with tents, for many of the companies neither have, nor are they able to procure them. These men have thrown themselves on the mercy of the government, on whom they are really dependent, and from whose hands they must receive either *death* or *succour*.

Permit me ere I close, to add a few reflection [*sic*] upon some errors, which have been committed in supplying this State with arms; errors, which, I fear, will be attended with serious consequences. Upon the arrival of our troops at New-Port, they were not a little astonished to find, that the public arsenal there contained no arms but muskets. One third of these troops were cavalry or riflemen, who were much surprised to find, that altho' they had been called into service, no arms were provided for them, which they were *compelled* to bear; for having volunteered for different services, they were not *bound* to go as musket-men. But, that they might not disappoint the expectations of the government, or cast any obstacles in the way of success, these gallant patriots, who cannot be too much applauded, resolved to forego their own convenience & wishes and obey the *necessities* of the crisis. Accordingly, the singular spectacle was exhibited, of men awkwardly shouldering the musket, who from their infancy had been taught the use of the rifle, and of horsemen loading themselves with the same cumbrous weapon, which I suspect is unprecedented in the annals of war. The prejudices of the people of this state in favour of the rifle, renders it necessary, that it should be placed in their hands, and their peculiar skill in the use of it, should make the goverment willing to gratify them. Experience has proven it to be the safest and most effectual weapon, with which our Indian enemies can be assailed; and the successes of our revolutionary struggle, teach us, that it may be used with effect even against an English foe. Cavalry are universally acknowledged to be necessary, in all sorts of warfare; but cavalry armed with heavy muskets, will, I suspect, be found to be a dull and useless appendage to an army. Every thing is to [be] expected from the Kentucky volunteers, in their present state, which unarmed men can do; but equip them as soldiers should be equiped, and the myrmidons of despotism will not dare to oppose them.

I beseech you, by that country whose destinies you rule, whose honour and happiness is in your hands, whose prosperity you are sworn to promote, and whose liberty you are bound to guard, that you will weigh well these suggestions, and deliberate cooly on these remarks.

I shall not ask your forgiveness for having trespassed so long on your time and patience, for you are predisposed to pardon the intrusion of one, who infringes the wonted rules of decorum, to speak the language of truth, and advance the happiness of America. With all the respect that is due to your services, and all the freedom that belongs to an *American*, I subscribe myself, Your Fellow-citizen

NELSON NICHOLAS [1]

RC (DNA: RG 107, LRRS, N-58:6). Docketed 2 Sept. 1812 and as received in the War Department on 16 Sept. 1812.

1. Nelson Nicholas (d. 1826), son of lawyer Col. George Nicholas, was a Kentucky political writer (*Collins' Historical Sketches of Kentucky* [1878 ed.], 2:280).

From Thomas Todd

My dear Sir,   Lexington Ky. Septr. 2nd. 1812.

My anxiety & solicitude for the success of the American arms must apologize for obtruding on you any statements or opinions as to military affairs—the disasters which have fallen on the Northwestern army, imperiously require effective measures to be taken—to enable you to do this, correct information is essentially necessary—to possess you of this has induced me to address you.

I presume that you have been fully informed of the proceedings which took place at Frankfort on the 25th Ultimo, in consequence of which the Govr. of this State appointed Govr. Harrison a major General by Brevet.[1] The great confidence which the people of this State & of Ohio repose in Harrison & the still greater confidence of the Officers & soldiers now composing that army will enable him, if continued in Command, to effect every thing which can possibly be done this season.

I also presume that you have received information of the surrender by Genl. Hull of Detroit & his army—of the reduction of Chicago & that Fort Wayne is infested by the enemy—a report reached this place today that it is taken.[2]

The dispatches from the War department recd. here by last mail is said to contain orders to Genl. Winchester to proceed on & take command of the detachment which was destined for the reinforcement of Hull should he do so, it will produce great discontent among the Officers & soldiers & I believe many of the volunteers will leave the army in disgust. Harrison is now with the army making active preparations to retrieve our losses—the Officers & soldiers in high spirits having the fullest confidence in their Genl. that he will lead them on to victory & conquest. Winchester's presence will damp this ardour & mar all their prospects—discontent, nay almost mutiny will certainly ensue.

The public is suffering very much for the want of a Deputy Quartermaster in the Western department—a Deputy Commissary only has been engaged in purchasing provisions & performing also some of the duties of Quartermaster, who, altho a worthy man, is entirely inadequate to discharge those duties[3] I therefore suggest the propriety of appointing a Deputy Quartermaster, whose acquaintance with the duties of the Office will enable him to execute them with promptitude & dispatch. Major James Morrison of this place, having acted for many years as Contractor for supplying the troops & been in the habit of purchasing & tra[n]sporting provisions to the different posts, as well having learnt experience in this kind of business during the revolutionary war, and in point of integrity & respectability standing as high as any man in the State, is in every respect well qualified to fill the Office—some difficulties have arisen from a want of funds & in procuring money for drafts on the Government. Majr. Morrison would experience no difficulties on that score, his personal credit is such, that he could command any sum the exigency might require.

It has been suggested to me that Govr. Howard would accept of the command of a Brigade & carry into Operation the plan submitted to the Government sometime since by Gov. Harrison[4] next to Harrison I believe that he possesses as much of the confidence of the people of this country as any person who could be appointed—in the early part of his life he had some experience in Indian warfare & the promptitude & regularity of the military arrangements for the defence of the frontiers of his Territory, shew his capacity.

I entertain fears that the surrender of Detroit with the ill success of our arms in that Quarter, in addition to other causes, will have considerable effect on the public mind, in attributing these failures to inefficient measures of the Government & that nothing will prevent it, but active, effective & inergetic conduct in the War department, I am Dear Sir with sincere esteem respectfully yrs.

THOMAS TODD

RC (ICHi). Docketed by JM.

1. See Charles Scott to JM, 25 Aug. 1812, and n. 2.

2. This report proved to be erroneous. Fort Wayne, under threat of siege since late August, was not directly attacked until 5 Sept. A series of encounters, mainly with Indians, between 5 and 10 Sept. were repelled by the garrison, which received Harrison's reinforcements without incident on 12 Sept. (Gilpin, *The War of 1812 in the Old Northwest*, 134–37).

3. Todd probably referred to John H. Piatt, a Cincinnati merchant whom Hull had appointed deputy commissary for the Northwest Army. Harrison reappointed Piatt after the surrender at Detroit (Risch, *Quartermaster Support*, 158, 160).

4. On 12 Aug., Harrison had written to Eustis to outline his plan to quell unrest among the Indians by either establishing a chain of posts from the Mississippi River to Chicago or marching troops to Fort Wayne (Esarey, *Messages and Letters of William Henry Harrison*, Indiana Historical Collections, 2:84–88).

From Louis Fromenteau

MONSIEUR   PHILADELPHIE le 3e. Septembe. 1812.

Conçevant par votre Silence, concernant l'humble prière que j'ai eu l'honneur de vous faire par ma lettre du 21e Juillet dernier,[1] que je ne puis espèrer, un emploi Civil, Sous ce Gouvernement, Selon que je m'en étoit flatté, je me Suis d'éterminé à retourner au Canada; a cet effect, après avoir fait m'à déclaration, chez Monsieur le *Marshal* Smith, Conformément à l'acte des Etrangers, je me Suis fait l'honneur d'écrire à Monsieur Monroe Secretaire d'Etat, à l'effect, qu'il me fit passer un permis, pour Sortir de ce païs, n'ayant pas eu de réponse, a quatre lettres, dont la derniere est daté du 27e Août dernier,[2] est ce qui m'à Engagé a vous faire Cette addresse, pour vous représenter, que la Saison Etant d'éja fort avancé, je désire, qu'il vou⟨s⟩ plaise, avoir la gracieuse bonté, d'ordonner, qu'un permis me Soit transmis le plutôt possible, pour effectuer avec Sureté mon retour au Canada, ou j'ai des moyens de Subsister que je ne puis avoir ici: N'étant pas prisonnier de guerre, mais étant venu dans les Etats unis, avec les dispositions que je vous ai marqués, je me flatte, que vous voudrez bien honorer de votre considération, mon humble priere, par l'octroi du permis qui m'est nécessaire, et indispensable pour Sortir de ce païs Sans dangers. Avec un très profond respect j'ai l'honneur d'être Monsieur votre très humble, très obéissant Serviteur

L FROMENTEAU

CONDENSED TRANSLATION

Concludes from JM's silence in response to the humble prayer contained in his letter of 21 July that there is no hope of his receiving a government position. He is therefore determined to return to Canada. After having made that declaration to Marshal Smith, in conformity to the law, he wrote to Monroe asking for a passport. Because he has received no response to his four letters to Monroe, he has addressed JM to request that he order a passport as soon as possible, since the season is already far advanced. He is not a prisoner of war, but having come to the U.S. with the intentions indicated, he hopes JM will grant him the passport he needs in order to leave the country and travel without danger.

RC (DNA: RG 45, Subject File RN, box 574, Correspondence Relating to Aliens, Enemy and Neutral). Docketed by Monroe with the notation "Mr Colvin to write him an answer." Filed at Aug.–Oct. 1813.

1. Letter not found.
2. Fromenteau had written to Monroe, soliciting his aid in finding work in America and requesting a passport to Canada, on 25 June 1812 (DNA: RG 59, LAR, 1809–17, filed under "Fromeantean" [sic]), 3 Aug. 1812 (DNA: RG 45, Subject File RN, box 574), 17 Aug. 1812 (DNA: RG 59, ML), and 27 Aug. 1812 (DNA: RG 59, War of 1812 Papers, Correspondence regarding Passports).

From Robert Johnson

DEAR SR   September 3d. 1812

Some of the people of Kentucky expected when warr was declared that 10,000 men would have been ordered to upper Canada to take that province and enex it to the United States, and at the Same time double the number or more ordered to lower Canada to prevent reinforcements from one place to the other. In this reasonable Expectation they have been (with regret) much disappointed. I have understood Hull was permitted to dictate the force suffitiant to take upper Canada—that he required only the number of men which was sent under his Command, that he has pretended to try, to take Maulden, that his family Connections were in Canada, with the British, that he has by his Conduct Sacraficd a Considerable number of Valluable men, that he has given up Detroet at the loss of all our artilery togather with other Arms and Millitary Stores, when there were 6,000 volenteers ready in Kentucky but were not permitted to go out in defence of their Country because they had no orders, untill near the time we heard that Hull had given up Detroet. The Idea with us is, that Hull is a traitor or nearly an Ediot or part of both. To take a View of the whole of his Conduct, it would seem as if he has played the Grandest Yanke Trick that ever has been played on the U. S. Again, it is understood that Genl. Harrison has been by Brevet Commisioned to take Command of the Kentucky troops and that the Executive of the U S. has Given him a Commission as Bregadier Genl., but if Genl. Winchester shall Go out and Contend for the Command over Harrison; it may make a great deal of uneasiness in the Army. The men have great Confidence in Harrison but with Winchestor they have very little— we are afraid of having a man that is incapable of acting as a good & wise Generall. Something has gone exceedinly rong: and some think Mr Winchester very inadequit to the task. I am not acquainted with that Genteman although I have been introduced to him. I have been informed it was contended on the part of Mr. Winchester to take Command of the army at Newport or Cincinatta Say 1800 or 2000 Volenteers & 350 regulers under Colo. Wells[1] that the off[i]cers discided in favor of Genl. Payne Keeping his Command of the Kentucky volenteers, but when Govr. Harrison over took the army at Sencinatta, there was great rejoicing in the Army: Genl. Payne well pleased. I understand about six or seven thousand men are moving toward Detroit. Being accquainted with you many years past feeling personall frendshep to you, and making no doubt of your Patriotism; I have made free to write these few lines. It has been said a wise man may gather something from a weak man. I hope for the best in future and untill some thing shall appear to make it proper that the Command of the Western Army well not be taken from Genl. Harison and Given to the other, you have the Power & I have no doubt of your doing what you think is Right and best for the good of our Common Country I am with respect

ROBT JOHNSON[2]

RC (DNA: RG 107, LRRS, J-278:6). Docketed as received in the War Department on 16 Sept. 1812.

1. Samuel Wells had participated in a number of skirmishes against the Indians before the war, including the Battle of Tippecanoe. He was promoted to colonel on 12 Mar. 1812 and placed in command of the Seventeenth Infantry. Marching with Harrison to Fort Wayne in September 1812, Wells's detachment destroyed the Potawatomi village of Five Medals on the

Elkhart River. He accompanied Winchester to the river Raisin in January 1813, protesting the exposed situation of his troops and the danger of attack before the battle ensued (Gilpin, *The War of 1812 in the Old Northwest*, 18, 130–31, 139, 165–66; Heitman, *Historical Register*, 1:1018).

2. Robert Johnson (1745–1815) was raised in Orange County, Virginia, relocating to Kentucky in 1779 or 1780. He was a delegate to the first and second Kentucky constitutional conventions, a member of the Virginia-Kentucky boundary commission in 1795, and a member of the U.S. assessment commission for Kentucky in 1798. Two of his sons, Richard M. Johnson and James Johnson, served in the War of 1812 and pursued careers in national politics (*PJM*, 9:130 n. 5).

From John G. Jackson

Sir.   Clarksburg Septr. 4th 1812

I am charged by a numerous meeting of the military & Citizens held at this place on yesterday to forward a copy of their proceedings to you. It is their anxious wish to be employed in repelling the invasion of our Country & chastising the enemy. If 5000 men be a sufficient number to effect this 10,000 will meet with a feeble resistance, & it will be an economy of blood & treasure to strike a decisive blow at once rather than to protract the operations of the army by sending a force incommensurate with the object. I would not thus freely advance these opinions if I did not thereby express the universal desire here—a desire influenced by opinion alone. I ardently hope we shall be called upon by the Government—no Country affords better materials for a warfare with Indians than this does, the men are trained to the use of arms from infancy, & enured to the hardships of the chase: and so great is the anxiety felt here that many will go even if not called on by the constituted authorities. I for one think it criminal to stand by while our Citizens are in such danger. I have the honor to be your Mo. Obt

J G Jackson

[Enclosure]

§ From the Officers of the Twentieth Virginia Brigade. *2 September 1812.* "At a meeting of the . . . officers of the 20th Brigade . . . and many other Citizens," convened at the Clarksburg courthouse "for the Purpose of consulting in what manner the Present alarming crisis of affairs of the Westren [*sic*] Country can be best met," Gen. John G. Jackson gave an account of Hull's surrender and the resultant state of alarm in Ohio and reported "that letters were received from that quarter by the last mail from a Source intitled to respect, urging the necesity of Imediate assistance . . . wherefore on motions made and Seconded, the Meeting adopted the following resolutions unanimously."

"Resolved that it is a Subject of deep regret to us, that we Possess no authority at this moment to Command the requisite means to March forth & Repel any Threatened incursions of the Enimy and to Chastise & drive him out of our Country.

"Resolved, that we conceive it an Indespensible duty to Send a large Military force without delay for that Purpose & that we only wait the Sanction of Government to meet & rally round its Standard.

"Resolved, that many of us have connections and all of us intimate friends in that Country whose welfare is very dear to us, & that we cannot reconcile it to ourselves to remain inactive, while their Safety is Threatened, & when to this feeling is Superadded considerations of regard for the welfare of our Country, we deem it Criminal to Stand by while the Storm of war rages.

"Resolved, that for ourselves & we believe we Speak the Sentiments of our Brother Soldiers of the Militia, we declare our Readiness, and desire to take the field whenever arms are furnished & the Constituted authorities authorise us.

"Resolved that with the Exception of a Few Rifles, we are almost distitute of arms, and that every expedient be tried to Procure a Sufficient number for our use.

"Resolved, that as the crisis admits of no delay, that the sense of this meeting be communicated *directly* to the President of the United States, with a request that he will Imediately Command our services.

"Resolved, that a Copy of these resolutions be Transmited by mail to the President of the United States.

"Resolved that one other Copy be forwarded in like manner to the Governor of virginia, and that the Chairman inform him by Letter, that this departure from the usual course of communications by Military officers would not have occured, had we not deemed any delay to be fraught with danger."

RC and enclosure (DNA: RG 107, LRRS, J-271:6). RC docketed as received in the War Department on 12 Sept. 1812. Enclosure 3 pp.; signed by Jackson as chairman and John Stokely as secretary of the meeting.

From William Kelso

HONERABLE SIR   September the 4—1812

After my asking your pardon I Will inform you that I have Seen this Day a Large Body of men Seting off from this place to assist the Volunteers that Ware Sent to Detroit after We Hard of General Hulls Conduct We Ware affected With it I feel a Very great ⟨etepthey?⟩ against him So great that I feel as although I Would of thanked god that it had of been my lott to haf been With Hull So that I Could of had the pleasure of takeing his life which I Cairtainly Will Do if ever I have the misfortune of being under Such a Comander Honerable Sir there is one favor Which I Shall ask of you that is if you can arange matters So as to get Hull in posetian I Hope you Will Send him to Kantucky Montgumry County Mount Starling and

let me Do With him as I Shall think proper if you Will grant me this I Do
not now that I Shall ever troble you again I ask your Pardon for my takeing this liberty With you if you new my feelings As to Hulls Conduct you
Could not Hesitate one moment as to granting my Request as to my freedom I have a Small family and low in Surcumstances is the Reason of my
Not being in the army at this time I flatter myself that I Shall be With them
Next Sp[r]ing at this time We Will not be able to Do any thing unless there
can be a rainforcement I think if we could have aboute fifteen thousand
men Sent I Should be happy to be one So that We Could Drive them and
Kill all of the indians that Ware unfraindly With us is it posable that We
are to lye under thee misd⟨emeaning?⟩ Which the are allways makeing in
the Westren part of the World Notwiths[t]anding the indians have been
killing our Weomen and Children I feel More fraindship for them than I
Do for Hull all that We Want in this State is to get orders to march I hope
We Will have the Honner of Marching to Detroit With a Sefetiant number of men So that We Can Drive all before us all that I ask is to have the
Honner of being a good and faithfull privet as Soon as your Honner Will
think proper to give orders for a athe [*sic*] Reinforcement to asist those that
are now on there Way to Detroit I hope it Will not be long before the Will
Reach this State it is not in my power to Write or expreess my feelings in
full So Remains your Homble Servent and Well Weashing fraind I hope I
Shall be a true fraind to the united States until Death I am yours

WILLIAM KELSO

RC (DLC). Docketed by JM.

From John Mason

DEAR SIR   GEORGE TOWN 4 Septr 1812
    I entreat you to attribute the Subject of this letter to it's true motive—
the most honest and sincere desire to do public good, in however small a
degree it may be in my power to contribute toward it.
    You will receive Sir, by this same mail a letter from Mr Rush,[1] which has
been written after several earnest and anxious conversations between him
and myself, as to the present Crisis, and contains fully our joint Sentiments—it's Subject has been confined entirely, as it shall ever be to him
myself and Judge Duvall, who agrees altogether with us in opinion, and intends to write to you.[2]
    To what Mr Rush has said Sir, I will only add, my certain and positive
conviction, that at this moment; the appointment of some Man, who has,
in an extraordinary degree, by the weight of his Talents, and personal char-

acter, the means of releiving the public despondency, produced by Hulls infamous Conduct, is necessary; and that no Man in our Community is so well fitted for this, as Mr Munroe, but the objections to his leaving your Cabinet, at this time, can be overcome in no way but by Mr Jefferson in person to supply his Place—and may not the Friends, throughout the Continent, of that great and good Man hope, that he will, on such an occasion, make the Sacrifice?

His Country would hail him with enthusiastic Joy as Secretary of State! and I even will venture to hope that his lofty mind will consider it no Condescension to aid your councils with his Wisdom and his virtue, at such a time. With the highest Consideration & Respect—& great personal Esteem I am Sir Your very obt Sert

J MASON

RC (DLC). Docketed by JM.

1. Richard Rush to JM, 4 Sept. 1812.
2. Gabriel Duvall to JM, 5 Sept. 1812.

From James Monroe

DEAR SIR   WASHINGTON Sepr 4. 1812

I send within a letter from Mr Russell & one from Mr Beasley, which are of no great importance except in relation to the blockade of May 1806.[1]

Every thing we hear of Genl. Hulls conduct increases the high sense at first entertaind of its impropriety. Col: Huntington from Ohio is here, & Col: Cass is expected to day. H. says that even at the moment of surrender our force was sufficient to have driven the British into the river, to have recrossed & in all probability taken Malden.

An account is just recd. of the complete destruction of the Guerrierre by our frigate the constitution, under Captn. Hull.[2] The official document will be forwarded to you.[3]

I have been spoken to by several friends here on the subject of my last. I have no personal sense on the subject; and no motive even to accept but a sincere desire, to support the cause of free govt., & the present admn. on which the cause so essentially depends. To leave my family and incur any hazard, which might possibly affect them, and a possible event, considering the state of my affairs, would deeply affect them, would give me inexpressible concern. But I should hope for the best, & will if the public is likely to be benefited by it, not hesitate, to undertake the trust. Very respectfully & sincerely yours

JAS MONROE

On Mr Dallas's letter be so good as to make a note.[4] It appears to me that the order ought to be left to the court, that the captor shod. make his own case & act as he thinks fit

RC (DLC: Rives Collection, Madison Papers).

1. Monroe probably enclosed dispatches from Jonathan Russell, 26 June 1812 (DNA: RG 59, DD, Great Britain), and Reuben G. Beasley, 25 June 1812 (DNA: RG 59, CD, London). Russell's dispatch described a conversation with Lord Castlereagh concerning the 23 June suspension of the orders in council. Castlereagh had asked whether JM was empowered to restore commerce with Great Britain on the basis of a mere suspension of the orders. Russell replied that "the power in question did not vest in the President until the orders in council w⟨ere⟩ so *revoked* or *modified* as to *cease* to violate the neutr⟨al⟩ rights of the United States," terms which excluded "all idea of a temporary suspension." Russell reported that he had asked whether the blockade of 1806 had been considered as coming under the terms of the order of suspension, to which Castlereagh replied that "he *supposed* it ha⟨d⟩ for it was his opinion that the blockade of 1806 had been merged in the subsequent orders in council and was now extinguished with them." On the question of the entry of armed British vessels into American ports, Russell claimed that Castlereagh had assured him that Britain sought only equal treatment with the armed ships of France. Russell noted that he had told Castlereagh that it was necessary that the question of impressment be addressed in order to establish "a perfect & permanent good understanding between two countries." Russell explained that he had informed Castlereagh that he "wished to know if hostilities should have actually commenced on the other side of the atlantic prior to a knowledge there of the revocation of the orders in council, whether the temper here was such as to seize upon such a circumstance to prolong a misunderstanding between the two countries," to which Castlereagh had replied that "in such case his government would be sincerely disposed to put an immediate end to all hostile proceedings and to cultivate peace & friendship wit⟨h⟩ the United States." The conversation closed with a plea from Castlereagh for U.S. leniency in light of political circumstances that required Great Britain "incidentally to molest neutrals."

Beasley's letter expressed surprise that opponents of the orders in council had "complimented Ministers for the handsome manner, in which, this revocation was made." He argued nevertheless that it would be ill-advised to receive the revocation "with a bad grace," since even the opposition supported it. Beasley believed that with the acceptance of the revocation of the Berlin and Milan Decrees, one difficulty in the way of resolving American spoliation cases with Great Britain had been removed. He noted that Parliament had taken up the question of impressment and had also passed a general enclosure bill. He reported that news of the failure of the effort to obtain a war loan in the U.S. had given Londoners "great pleasure." He closed with a criticism of the high tariffs that would greet loaded ships that had departed for the U.S.

2. Isaac Hull (1773–1843), the son of a mariner, obtained his first command in 1794 and on 9 Mar. 1798, through the influence of his uncle William Hull, was appointed a lieutenant in the U.S. Navy. Isaac Hull participated in Edward Preble's attacks on Tripoli and was eventually promoted to captain in 1806. Hull supervised the building of gunboats on Long Island Sound and in the Chesapeake from 1806 to 1809, at which time he moved to take command of the *Chesapeake*. The following year he assumed command of the frigate *President* for five weeks before taking charge of the *Constitution*. Hull's fame rests largely on his August 1812 victory over the British frigate *Guerrière*, the first American victory of the war and welcome news for JM's administration in the wake of the surrender of Detroit (Linda M. Maloney, *The Captain from Connecticut: The Life and Naval Times of Isaac Hull* [Boston, 1986], 3–138 passim, 185–200, 479).

3. The U.S. frigate *Constitution*, under the command of Isaac Hull, captured the British frigate *Guerrière* on 19 Aug. 1812, burning and sinking it the following day. On 28 Aug., Hull sent the secretary of the navy an official account of the battle (printed in Dudley, *Naval War of 1812*, 1:238–42). On 5 Sept. 1812 the *National Intelligencer* published a detailed account of the capture.

4. Enclosure not found. Pennsylvania district attorney Alexander J. Dallas may have written to Monroe on the subject of the *Superior*, an American-owned vessel transporting a cargo of British goods that was seized by a U.S. gunboat in Delaware Bay. In a 27 Aug. letter to Alexander Murray, printed in the 3 Sept. 1812 issue of the *National Intelligencer*, Dallas expressed his reasons for believing that the vessel had been rightly captured. Monroe acknowledged receipt of Dallas's 1 Sept. 1812 letter in a 17 Sept. response, claiming that he had delayed replying because of JM's absence from Washington. Monroe explained: "The additional instruction to our privateers was issued on the idea that american vessels in the cases therein specified were not subject to capture. It may therefore be considered as an expression of the sense of the executive of the law applicable to the case. The court however before whom any case may be brought, will, of course decide for itself on questions arising out of it" (DNA: RG 59, DL).

From Richard Rush

SIR,   WASHINGTON September the 4th. 1812.

The extraordinary juncture of publick affairs emboldens me to trouble you with this letter, and while I do so with great diffidence I must seek the apology in the motive and proceed to its immediate subject with no other claim to indulgence beyond that which the subject, coupled with the most ardent desires for our countrys welfare, can beget.

The shock given to the publick hopes in the disaster to the army under general Hull requires, in the estimation of many of the best informed of those who look with solicitude to the accomplishment of all the recently formed wise and just plans of the nation, some counter impulse immediate in its application as well as very marked and decisive in its character; something that by its moral impetus shall strongly tend, anterior to the course of any new events, to lift the feelings of the nation from the point of depression to which they are fallen and whence it is much to be feared their course may still, for a time at least—and that time a critical one—be downward; something in short that shall close up, by the power of opinion, and as it were in a moment, the chasm which this wholly unexpected disaster has made.

If Mr Munroe would consent to head an army in the north west!—his name would rally, his talents lead one!—this difficult department of the publick service would be filled up, and so filled up as to collect anew the spirit and draw together, in augmented numbers, the force in that quarter, while it commanded the warmest and most unlimited confidence of the whole country. But—thus far only—and the urgent remedy would go but half way. Who will fill the chasm he would leave? To deprive the nation of the hopes to which it clings in this quarter as to part of the wisdom required in its councils; to deprive you, too, Sir, of such services at such a time would not do! Where, then, is the substitute? Shall I presume to suggest one? not impracticable I trust, effectual—more than heart could wish—I am sure: Where, Sir, is the illustrious Jefferson? I, indeed, can be no stranger, more than all others, to his great age, to his long, useful, arduous, services; to his love of retirement, to his claims to be now exempt from toil. But, Sir, might he not still be prevailed upon to lend the mighty weight of his name—of his venerable years—yet a little longer, to the service of his country when a new crisis addresses itself, as it now would; to his feelings of constant devotion to her cause? May not his venerable and now almost canonized form be seen to step forth to this post; to leave the shades of his secluded and beloved mansion at such a time, at such a call? The sacrifice would, indeed, be great; but, to him, what sacrifice would be too great when his country was in question, her benefit, her highest interests, the stake? Then, Sir, I speak, I am sure, the language of millions when I say, depression would give place to joy, confidence rise to enthusiasm! Then would the great republican family of the union be one—feel with but one heart, rise up in its whole strength! Such an event, Sir, and the best hopes of the patriot are made sure! Such an event, and the glory of the setting days of the then greatest of patriots is more than ever crowned!

I pray you, Sir, to pardon the freedom of these remarks, prompted, as they are, by motives that I feel may be excused. With the highest approbation of the wisdom and virtue of your publick administration, and with sentiments of the utmost personal respect, I have the honor to be your obedient and attached friend and Servant,

RICHARD RUSH.

RC (PHi).

To William Eustis

private

DEAR SIR   MONTPELIER Sepr. 5. 1812

The death of Mr. Mifflin has produced the inclosed applications for the vacancy in the deputy commissiarte [*sic*] held by him.[1] It is probable they will meet others addressed to yourself. If Irvin is to reside or be chiefly in Philada. it does not appear very essential that the office should be filled immediately, if at all. You can judge best. Mr. Coxe has again been brought to my attention; either for that vacancy, if his appointment be reconciliable [*sic*] with his failure in the Senate, or for the place of Duncan or *perhaps* of Lennard[2] in case he should succeed Mifflin. I have known Mr. Cox ever since the Convention of 1806 in Annapolis,[3] of which he was a member, and have had occasion to witness so much of uniformity zeal & useful labor, in maintaining the principles & promoting the success of our republican Institutions, that I think he well merits that species of recommence [*sic*] which the situation of his family requires, as far as public considerations, and comparitive pretensions will authorize. I am aware at the same time of the circumstances which are unpropitious to his wishes, as well as of the precarious value of the superintency [*sic*] of Military Stores. It seems however that even this recourse is desireable to him.

I found on the way that the surrender by Hull had made a deep impression; but as far as I have learnt, the calamity is imputed to his temerity in the first instance, or the opposite extreme, finally. This impression may not prevail elsewhere, nor continue in this quarter; but it exists in this at present; and without any apparent disposition to do injustice to the administration.

I hope you will have been able to put in motion thro' Burbeck or others, the means of dislodging the enemy from the stronghold at Detroit. A knowledge that the effort is making will be useful, even by detaining a part of the force that might otherwise be hastened back to Fort Erie. It has been hinted from friendly quarters, that if Mr. Monroe could in any way be brought into service, his military reputation & Western popularity, might be critically beneficial in giving counsel & impulse to the expedition under Winchester & Harrison, both of whom would feel the requisite respect for his standing. I see the difficulties, and know not that they can be overcome. I wish you however to break the subject to him; and if you concur in any arrangement that will give the expedition, the advantage of his zeal & talents within the requisite time, It shall have whatever concurrence may be wanted on my part. The more I hear of Winchester the more I am persuaded of his worth in general; but I can not say as much of his particular qualifications for commanding the expedition toward Detroit, in comparison with those of Harrison, taking together his intrinsic & adventitious ones. I wish we may not have sacrificed too much to presumed sensibilities, in not transferring W. to another service. Would it be impossible even now to do this, either by a direct order or thro' Dearborn; founding the change, on the change of circumstances produced by Hull's surrender, and the wish of Dearborn for more General officers?

We accomplished our journey in less time than I had calculated, and have not suffered by the fatigue. I am making efforts to render a short stay here, as compatible as possible with some of the objects of the trip; and shall sacrifice the whole of them, to any imperious recall to Washington.

Accept my friendly respects, with my anxious wishes that auspicious events may lighten the burden pressing so particularly on your Department of the public business.

JAMES MADISON

RC (PHi: Daniel Parker Papers).

1. JM may have enclosed Tench Coxe to JM, 31 Aug. and 1 Sept. 1812. The editors were unable to locate any other letters to JM concerning Mifflin's position.

2. JM placed an asterisk by this word and wrote in the margin, "Quere what is Ls. salary?"

3. JM probably referred to the commercial convention held in Annapolis, Maryland, in September 1786, to which both he and Coxe had been delegates (*PJM*, 9:115–16, 118, 122 n. 2).

To James Monroe

private

DEAR SIR   MONTPELIER Sepr. 5. 1812

I recd. yours of the 2d. inst: last night. Your observations on the policy called for by the crisis produced by Hull's surrender are entirely just; and I feel all the value of the aid you offer in meeting it in a proper manner. Both before & since our parting conversation on that subject, the idea has been revolved in the hope that some shape might be given to it worthy both of your standing and of the occasion. This had originally reference to the Eastern operations agst. Canada, rather than to those left by Hull to his successors. Your agency in the latter wd. not be embarrassed with all the delicate considerations incident to the former, tho' possibly not altogether free from them; but on the other hand, the greatness of the distance, the shortness of time, and the uncertainties from these & other causes, make it doubtful whether the public advantage would be commensurate to the sacrifices, public as well as personal, which would be made to the experiment. Without some conspicuous effect, which might be found impossible, the experiment might even have an injurious recoil. Still I feel so much, all that is due to a readiness to make such sacrifices, to the sentiments of some of our friends, & above all to the urgency of the conjuncture, that if on a consultation with the Secretary of War which I shall suggest to him, and an estimate of the prospect of conveying cannon & other appurtenances necessary to success, you should both think your aid can be afforded in season & with effect, I shall gladly embrace it, in whatever form may be thought best. I am much discouraged however by my impression that the form most eligible, a Commission of brevet, is precluded by the terms of the law authorizing such appointments; and by my recollection that no regular commissions remain to be issued of a grade that would be suitable. I am not sure indeed that the appts. of Harrison & Boyd, have not exhausted the Brigadr.

Commissions; if it were practicable to mould one of that grade for the purpose. These are points which will be best ascertained at the War Dept.

Should it be impossible to avail the expedition, of your superintendence, I shall the more fear, that we have sacrificed too much to presumed sensibilities, in not giving it to Harrison instead of Winchester, who it appears is in the opinion of good judges, with all his acknowledged worth, less fitted for it, especially as being less known & confided in than Harrison, by the country volunteering the succours. Harrison wd. certainly attract more troops, and give to the enterprize more impulse. And my anxiety would be sensibly diminished, if a change could yet be brought about, if the question is to lie between those commanders, by a translation of W. to another service, either by a direct order from the War Dept. or thro' Genl. Dearborn.

After all I cannot banish the idea that altho' nothing of a promising nature ought to be untried, yet on the most favorable estimate of the expedition agst. Detroit, less is to be hoped, as to an early antidote to Hull's surrender, from the success of it, than from operations under Dearborn, who will be eager to take advantage of the absence of the B. force, detained perhaps in consiquence of that event.

I think with you that the admn. ought to be protected by just views of the case in point, agst. imputations that belong to Hull, & agst. casualties beyond all human responsibility. Permit me to suggest to you a perusal of Hulls correspondence above.[1] It is short. Affecte. respects.

JAMES MADISON

RC (DLC: Monroe Papers). Docketed by Monroe.

1. JM probably referred to two short letters from William Hull published in the *National Intelligencer* on 3 Sept. 1812. The first, written to Capt. Henry Brush from Detroit on 11 Aug. 1812, informed Brush that "a sufficient detachment" of troops could not be sent from Detroit to the river Raisin "to bring on the provisions with safety." The second, written on 16 Aug. 1812 to Col. Duncan McArthur, informed him that Hull had surrendered Detroit and the Ohio militia under McArthur's command to the British.

From Gabriel Duvall

DEAR SIR,   WASHINGTON, Sept. 5. 1812.

Last evening, Genl. Mason & Mr. Rush made me acquainted with the subject of their letters of yesterday's date to you. Promising that those letters have my entire approbation, I shall make no apology for thus co-operating with them; & my address, of course, will be short.

I am aware that it is expecting a great deal, perhaps too much, of Mr. Jefferson to request at this day, his return to public life, & that he will condescend to act in a station subordinate to that which was the highest in the gift of the people, & which he filled with so much ability & integrity, & in which he gave such universal satisfaction to his constituents. But the present is an important crisis. The unexpected loss of the North Western Army, it is apprehended, will spread, at least, a momentary gloom throughout the United States. To dissipate it, some prompt & signal act of the Government, to inspire general confidence, may be necessary. It is believed that no measure which can be adopted would so completely produce that effect as the appointments suggested, if followed by acceptance. The acceptance of the command of the North Western Army would add to the luster of Col. Monroe's public character. And altho' Mr. Jefferson has already attained the pinnacle of political fame, his condescension to fill the office of Secretary of State would evince such genuine & disinterested patriotism that it could not fail to increase the veneration with which the people of the present age regard his character, & to perpetuate it with posterity.

I congratulate you on the distinguished victory of Capt. Hull in capturing the Guerrier Frigate. I am with every sentiment of Respect & esteem, Your obedt. sert.

G. DUVALL.

RC (DLC). Docketed by JM.

From William Eustis

SIR,   WASHINGTON Septr 5. 1812.

I enclose herewith a Letter from Colo McArthur[1] by Mr Huntington who arrived the day before yesterday & who has this morning taken a carriage to bring in Colo. Cass left about 70 miles from the city in consequence of indisposition, and who may be expected in the course of the day. It appears to be an universal sentiment of the Officers who have come in that the surrender of the post & troops was unnecessary & that they were surrendered to an inferior force. Many circumstances are related by Mr H who is from Cleveland in company with Colo. Cass there were fourteen days provision on hand with an abundant supply within controul of the post, a sufficiency of arms ammunition & willing minds for offensive or defensive measures—it is even stated that the capture of Malden was within the power of our troops from the beginning to the capitulation—such are the reports. The arrival of Colo. Cass will throw more light on the subject.

Genl. Wadsworth whose troops are the nearest to Sandusky & the rapids of the Miami will be supplied with 1500 stands of arms ammunition &

camp Equipage is requested to march 1500 men to the frontiers to protect the settlements, & to join the army which amounting to upwards of 3000 has marched under Genl Winchester who was at Cincinnati on the 27th of August.[2]

I am anxious for fort Wayne. Tecumseh told Genl. Brock "You have done as you pleased at Detroit, let me have my way at F. Wayne":[3] but Mr Huntington says that Brock had ordered 250 regulars to accompany him. Gov. Meigs informs me that fort Wayne will be protected & that he had ordered mounted infantry who would march on the day he wrote. May they be in season & in sufficient numbers![4]

By the enclosed Letter from General Dearborn it appears that at present he contemplates only the conquest of the *South* Side of the St. Lawrence to Montreal for which purpose he is directing his main body of regulars by way of Lake Champlain.[5]

By the mail of this day Letters from General Pinckney are received, enclosing copies of requisitions from the Govr of E. Florida to the Gov's of Havannah &c. for ⟨pr⟩ovissions.[6] These have it is presumed been transmitted from ⟨the⟩ Dept of State, where they were rec'd some says [*sic*] since.

The Letters from Genl. Wilkinson received by the mail of this morning are transmitted[7]—as well as those from Genl. Wadsworth,[8] Colo. McArthur—& Colo. Worthington at Picqua.[9] The return of these Letters with any directions respecting them by as early a mail as may be convenient is requested.

It is mentioned by Mr Huntington that the names of five hundred inhabitants of upper Canada (who had acknowleged allegiance to the U. S. or given some pledge to Gen Hull) had been enrolled in a book, and it was feared that the book had been given up. It is most fervently to be hoped that this may not prove true. The article in the capitulation comprehending "all public records," may have caused the apprehension.

Mr H. presents me the original articles of capitulation which were given to him by Colo. Cass. They do not vary from those which have been published. That they should have been transmitted in this manner accords with ⟨a⟩ll the transactions relative to this catastrophe. Wheatons ⟨le⟩tter will I fear be found to reveal the secret.[10] With perfect respect

W. Eustis

RC (DLC). Docketed by JM; torn. For probable enclosures, see nn. 1, 5, 7, 8, and 9.

1. Eustis probably enclosed Duncan McArthur's two-page letter of 25 Aug. 1812 announcing the surrender of Detroit (DNA: RG 107, LRRS, M-398:6).

2. Eustis sent orders to this effect on 5 Sept. to Maj. Gen. Elijah Wadsworth (1747–1817), in command of the Fourth Division of Ohio militia (DNA: RG 107, LSMA; Drake, *Roster of Ohio Soldiers in the War of 1812* [1995 reprint], 4).

3. On 8 Sept. 1812 the *National Intelligencer* published an anonymous 28 Aug. report from

Pittsburgh that described the fall of Detroit, explaining that Tecumseh had claimed that he "had let the British do as they pleased at Detroit, and he expected the same liberty at Fort Wayne."

4. Gov. Return Jonathan Meigs's 24 Aug. 1812 letter to Eustis enclosed a 19 Aug. letter he had received from James Rhea, commander at Fort Wayne, which expressed concern that the fort was in danger. Meigs informed Eustis that Ohio troops would be mounted the following morning to defend the post (DNA: RG 107, LRRS, M-393:6).

5. Eustis probably enclosed Dearborn's five-page letter of 29 Aug. 1812, which explained that three infantry regiments under Brig. Gen. Joseph Bloomfield and two regiments of artillery had marching orders for Lake Champlain. Dearborn informed Eustis that if he were given command of two or three thousand extra regular troops as well as the militia from New York and Vermont, he "could clear the Southern Shore of the St, Lawrence, to the river opposite Montreal" (DNA: RG 107, LRRS, D-141:6).

6. Thomas Pinckney (1750–1828), brother of Charles Cotesworth Pinckney, was a veteran of the Revolutionary War, governor of South Carolina (1787–89), minister to Great Britain (1792–96), and a member of Congress (1797–1801). In 1812 he received a major general's commission, commanding forces in much of the South throughout the War of 1812 (Edgar et al., *Biographical Directory of the South Carolina House of Representatives*, 3:561–63). Eustis probably referred to 27 and 29 Aug. 1812 letters from Pinckney. The 29 Aug. letter had enclosed translated copies of intercepted letters dated 9 Aug. 1812 from the governor of East Florida, Sebastián Kindelán, to the governor of Cuba, Juan Ruíz de Apodaca (3 pp.), and the commander in chief of the Bahamas, Guillermo Vesey Munnings (3 pp.), requesting provisions. After describing the desperate need for food at St. Augustine, Kindelán explained to the British officer in the Bahamas that the depletion of supplies had rendered his forces unable to thwart the hostile activities of the U.S. He informed Munnings that he had broken "the barrier, with which that band of foragers, who oppose me, obstructed our communication with the Indians; and, having attached the latter to our cause, I induced them to begin their hostilities" (DNA: RG 107, LRRS, P-227:6, P-228:6).

7. Eustis probably enclosed 4 and 10 Aug. 1812 letters from Brig. Gen. James Wilkinson. The first letter (6 pp.) reported on conditions on the southwestern frontier, including the growing strength of forces gathering under Augustus Magee for an invasion of Mexico. Wilkinson suggested that the administration might seize the opportunity "to extend our occupances to . . . the Rio Grande." He also suggested action against Mobile and Pensacola. In the second letter (8 pp.) Wilkinson discussed the defense of New Orleans and requested a ruling on his authority over naval officers (DNA: RG 107, LRRS, W-285:6, W-286:6).

8. Eustis probably enclosed 25 and 31 Aug. 1812 letters from Wadsworth (2 pp. each) reporting on his efforts to protect the inhabitants of the Ohio frontier in the aftermath of Hull's surrender (DNA: RG 107, LRRS, W-283:6, W-284:6).

9. Eustis probably enclosed two 20 Aug. 1812 letters from Worthington. The first, written with Jeremiah Morrow, explained that extra caution would be taken to "keep the Indians quiet" in light of Hull's difficulties. It informed Eustis that British interference and the "unfavourable state of our affairs to the North" would delay the council at Piqua "beyond what might otherwise have been necessary" (printed in *Michigan Historical Collections* 40 [1929]: 457–58). Worthington wrote again later that day (2 pp.) to address problems of supply and to report rumors that the U.S. intended to go to war with the Indians in the Northwest. He expressed his hope that the U.S. would not be "treating and fighting" at the same time (DNA: RG 107, LRRS, W-288:6).

10. No such letter from Joseph Wheaton has been found.

From John Giles

I hope, your Excellency, will not deem me intrusive, in occupying a few minnets of your time. I am not insensible, of the number, nor of the weight, and vast importance of those objects; which must necessarily, claim your attention, and engross your moments. But feeling, and appreciating, as I do, the benefits which flow from your government; I am urgd to offer, this small tribute of my warm gratitude.

Your firm, and undeviating attachment, to the cause of suffering humanity: has stirred the angry passions of corrupt men; whose very *censure*, is praise, and whose wrath, shall praise the Lord, and the remainder of wrath, he will restrain. The good, and virtuous, have, and will, in the existing state of things, be the objects of wicked mens censure, and persecution; but conscious rectitude, will be to us, a sure support.

You will deign, illustrious Sir, to accept the sermons, which accompany this;[1] and tho sensible, that my powers, are too circumscribed, to convey any instruction to your expanded mind: yet they will serve to prove, that even in this place, which is the very sink of Toryism, you have a select few, of warm, and decided friends; who will even dare to speak, the undisguised sentiments of their hearts. Fifteen years experience, has convinced me, of the inestimable value of our privilieges; and that they are worth contending for. My daily aspirations for you, shall ascend to the Eternal Throne: that your life, and health, may be long continued, and that the Almighty, woud inspire you with increasing wisdom, and understanding, that you may continue to fill your exalted station, with dignity, honour, and usefulness. I am, Honoured Sir, with all due consideration, Your humble, and dutiful Servant

J. GILES[2]

RC (DLC). Docketed by JM.

1. Giles undoubtedly enclosed his *Two Discourses, Delivered to the Second Presbyterian Society in Newburyport, August 20, 1812* . . . (Haverhill, Mass., 1812; Shaw and Shoemaker 25519).
2. British-born John Giles (1755?–1824) served as the minister of the Second Presbyterian Church in Newburyport, Massachusetts, from 1803 to 1824, when poor health forced his retirement (John J. Currier, *History of Newburyport, Mass., 1764–1905* [2 vols.; Newburyport, Mass., 1906], 1:285–86).

From James Monroe

DEAR SIR   WASHINGTON 5 Sepr. 1812

I send by the mail a communication from the chr de onis, which was presented to me by mr Chacon.[1] He professes a willingness to make a treaty, but I suspect his powers do not extend to the cession of E. Florida, especially under the new constitution of Spain. Mr Chacon says that the chr. is extremely anxious to prevent hostilities being commenc'd under genl. Wilkn.—that the letter of the Govr. was written to Govr. Claiborne, in consequence of possession having been taken by Genl Wilkinson, of an Island in the possession of the Spn. force, (some ½ dozen soldiers) called dolphin or Dauphin, contiguous to the fort of Mobile.[2] Having just parted with him, & hurrying to take advantage of the post I cannot examine the map, to describe it more accurately. He intimated a sincere desire in Mr onis, to promote on reasonable, but honorable conditions the cession of E. Florida to the UStates, & expressed a hope that no act of hostility on our part, would put an end to the good understanding & commerce of the two countries. He will be here on tuesday or wednesday to confer further on the subject, after I shall have heard from you. He observed that Mr. Onis was desirous of a more formal invitation to come here, than thro Mr Chacon, tho' did not press the idea, on my remarking that the mode adopted ought to have been satisfactory.

I omitted to send you yesterday Mr Duane's letter—it is now enclosed.[3]

My wish is to leave this about the middle of next week. Should you think it adviseable to send me to the Westward, perhaps a volunteers comn. would answer the purpose. It would I am satisfied have equal effect, with Winchester & Harrison, & might look more directly to the object of an early return. A Brevet I believe is only given, where there is an existing rank. I feel, as I have before said, no personal wish about it. I have a letter from Pike which gives a gloomy view of our affairs at Albany;[4] I intended to send it to you, but left it at home. It shall go tomorrow. Affecy yours

                                                                                          JAS MONROE

RC (DLC: Rives Collection, Madison Papers). For probable enclosures, see nn. 1 and 3.

1. Monroe probably forwarded a translation of Onís's 29 Aug. 1812 letter (DNA: RG 59, NFL, Spain; 5 pp.), which gave assurances that the Spanish minister was empowered to "regulate and amicably settle by means of one or more Treaties or Conventions not only the Indemnities which the Executive claimed, for the injuries which the Spanish Govt should have caused to the citizens of the U States but also to terminate & conclude a Treaty of limits mutually advantageous to the two nations as well to the East as the west of the Dominions of the both Powers." Onís stated that as soon as he had informed the new Spanish government of the willingness of the U.S. to enter into such negotiations, he would officially receive the "most ample Powers to terminate amicably all affairs in controversy between the two Countries."

2. On 12 July 1812 the Spanish governor of Pensacola, Mauricio de Zúñiga, wrote to William C. C. Claiborne to complain that armed boats had arrived at Dauphin Island, in the mouth of Mobile Bay, to discharge a landing party. After hoisting an American flag, the invaders told a Spanish detachment that they had four days to leave or they would be taken prisoner. Zúñiga viewed these acts as encroachments upon the rights of the Spanish king. He reported that he was "astonished," as he had "no information" that the U.S. had declared war on Spain and that Claiborne was continuing "the aggressions committed in this part of the pos-

sessions of the King." He claimed that since the U.S. had occupied Louisiana, Spain's rights to free navigation upon the Mississippi River had been compromised, while the U.S. had illegally navigated upon the Tombigbee and Alabama Rivers and Mobile Bay. Zúñiga warned Claiborne that if he did not give orders to withdraw U.S. troops "from the invaded Countries," Spanish officers would "fulfil their duty." Claiborne forwarded a copy of the letter to Monroe on 26 July along with his response (DNA: RG 59, ML). The landing party at Dauphin Island may not have violated Spanish rights, since Dauphin Island was purchased by the Scottish trading house of Forbes and Company in 1806 and given to James Wilkinson for his "use and benefit." The transaction was later legally challenged on the basis of the congressional act of 3 Mar. 1827 regarding land claims adjustments in Alabama (*ASP, Public Lands*, 5:498, 499).

3. No letter from William Duane to Monroe from this period has been found, but there survives a 4 Sept. 1812 draft of a letter from Monroe to Duane, acknowledging the receipt of Duane's "late favor," which evidently expressed great concern about the fall of Detroit and the mismanagement of affairs in the War Department (DLC: Monroe Papers).

4. In a 28 Aug. 1812 letter, Lt. Col. Zebulon Montgomery Pike informed Monroe that preparations in Greenbush did not meet his expectations. He reported that with 5,000 troops on hand, "It is calculated we can take St Johns and possibly Chamble before We make much of a halt," but he questioned whether they should continue to Montreal (NN: Monroe Papers).

To William Eustis

private

Dear Sir   Montpellier Sepr. 6. 1812

I have thought it proper to request the return of the inclosed letters; some of which, though stating facts, & shewing the public sentiment, and on that account worth perusing, contain what ought to consign them to the fire, rather than to the public archives.[1]

The more I hear of the alarm[2] produced in the Western Country by Hull's disaster, and of the incoherent efforts on foot to cure the mischief, the more I am convinced of the critical good to be expected from the presence, the influence, & counsels of Mr Monroe. If he can not be put into command, and would attend as a volunteer, his services would be incalculable. It is impossible to carry on so distant an expedition witht. a latitude of discretion, in a variety of respects, and on the spot, which could in no one be so safely & effectively loosed as in his hands. If Winchester is to retain the command, such an expedient is the more necessary. Any new calamity, or even failure of success, under him, following the oppressive disaster of Hull, would shut every ear agst. arguments for not appointing a Commander, preferred by the public voice. Friendly respects

James Madison

It may be well to let Mr. Monroe peruse some of the letters inclosed. Mr. Hamilton I understand has left Washington

RC (PHi: Daniel Parker Papers).

1. Enclosures not found.
2. JM first wrote "effect" here, then emended it to read "alarm."

To James Monroe

private

DEAR SIR   MONTPELLIER Sepr. 6. 1812

I recd. last evening your favor of the 4th: with a subsequent note covering a letter from Mr. Graham.[1] That from Duane, referred to as inclosed, was omitted.

All the accts., printed & manuscript, coincide with the view given by Mr. Graham, of the Western feeling produced by Hull's disaster. The great point is to seize it and give it proper direction. This requires one mind of the right sort, within the proper sphere, and armed with the just latitude of authority. It is impossible to attain, otherwise, a satisfactory or successful issue to distant expeditions. Hull has shewn himself utterly unqualified for such a trust. Is Winchester equal to it? His want of that enthusiastic confidence on the part of those who are to support & co-operate with him so peculiarly essential to his success, alone answers, this question. Is Harrison, if substituted, every thing that the public would wish? Without disparaging his qualifications, and allowing their great superiority to W.s,[2] his military knowledge must be limited, and a more extensive weight of character, would be of material importance. Should a junction of the two take place what then? No small degree of danger, that jealousies & jars might weaken, more than the union of their talents, would strengthen their measures. I am thus led to the idea, which I find by letters from Rush Mason &c occurs to the best judges among our best friends, of availing the Crisis, if possible of your services. You would carry with you the confidence of all, would be the most unexceptionable depository of the necessary powers, and be most able to give impulse & direction to the only force now applicable to the object. If Winchester cannot be transferred to Dearborn, the interposition of your superint[end]ing. Counsils, acquires peculiar importance. How is it to be brought about? If there be no legal course by which you can be put in command, nothing is left but the expedient of your joining the army as a volunteer, with the known confidence & approbation of the Govt. and with the ready respect that would be paid by the highest in command, to your military judgment and grade of character. If I mistake not, this idea once entered into conversation between us, on the subject of your visiting the other army. In this case it would not be liable to some of the objections occurring in that. I am aware that it is without advantages which would attend an authoritative commission, and I only resort to it, on the supposition that the latter is precluded. Think of it in the same point of view. If it be not admissible in the full extent, think of it as a mere tour to the Western Country, & a visit to the army. In the present temper of both, I am persuaded your presence would be of much use in tranquillizing those under erroneous excitements, and reducing to method and perhaps within necessary limits, the ardent efforts which appear to be on foot. If the alarms which have been excited, should not speedily subside, there appears to be some danger, that scattered bodies of volunteers may be so multiplied as to exceed the means of employing them. Unless the ordnance &c necessary for taking Detroit & invading Canada, can be transported in time, a number competent to defence, till the season will be a defence, ought alone to burden the Treasury, & waste the supplies.

In the event of your embarking in this business, it will be proper for you to take with you a parcel of the Blank Commissions under the volunteer Act. It is possible that under certain circumstances the attachment to the occupancy of Canada, might induce a portion of the Militia volunteers to engage under that act. You will of course arm yourself with all the useful information from the War Dept. as to the resources of arms, & supplies of every sort that can be depended on.

I have dwelt on this subject more than was necessary. But the more I have turned it in my thoughts, & the more I learn of the effect of Hull's catastrophe, the more I am convinced of the public good to be expected from the contemplated measure. I know that less of public spirit than you feel, would shrink from the sacrifices imposed by it. I am sensible also, that your absence from your present duties would be severely felt, but I think the business might be preserved from essential injury, especially if Mr. Graham's absence should be abridged. It will be very happy if affairs should take a turn relieving all of us from the solicitude which projects such taxes on patriotism. Affece. respects

RC (DLC: Monroe Papers). Unsigned; docketed by Monroe.

1. Covering note and enclosure not found, but Monroe probably forwarded a four-page letter he had received from Graham, dated 31 Aug. 1812, from Wheeling, Virginia, which noted that westerners he had encountered expressed "the greatest indignation against Genl Hull" and declared "their readiness to turn out as volunteers to retake Detroit and conquer Upper Canada." Graham noted that Harrison "would be the most popular Commander that could be fixed upon in the Western Count[r]y," though he believed that Monroe's presence in the West, with full authority to command the army, would be "of great advantage" (DLC: Monroe Papers).

2. Someone, probably JM, added "(Winchester)" above the line here.

To Samuel Spring

Revd. Sir   Montpellier Sep. 6th 1812.

I have received your favor of Aug 26. I recollect our Collegiate friendship with the same impressions which it gives me pleasure to find you still retain. Nor have I forgotten the pleasant hours that passed between us at a much later day under my own roof.

We all feel the weight of the times and it is to be regretted that all cannot unite in the measures opposed to them. If it were proper for me, it might not be agreeable to you, to discuss the subjects But I will not conceal the Surprize and the pain I feel at declarations from any portion of the American people that measures resulting from the national will Constitutionally pronounced,[1] and carrying with them the most solemn sanctions, are not to be pursued into effect, without the hazard of Civil War. This is surely not the legitimate course. Neither is it the language, on other occasions, heard from the same quarter; nor a course consistent with the duration or efficacy of any Government.

Permit me to express equal surprise, that this extraordinary opposition to the War declared against Great Britain, is most emphatically rested on an alliance or a connection with France; presumed to exist, or to be intended, in the face of demonstrations to the contrary, with which the slightest degree of candor ought to be satisfied.

Without entering into comparisons between different districts of the Union, with respect to the suffering which led to the war, or the objects at stake in it; it is clear that every district felt more or less the evils which produced it, and is more or less deeply interested in the success of it. It is equally certain that the way to make it both short and successfull would be to convince the Enemy, that he has to contend with the whole and not a part of the Nation. Can it be doubted that if, under the pressure added by the war to that previously felt by G. B. her Government declines an accomodation on terms dictated by justice and compatible with, or rather conducive to her interest it will be owing to calculations drawn from our internal divisions. If she be disposed to such an accomodation, it will be evinced in due time, to the most prejudiced and misinformed, that the earliest and fairest opportunities, are not witheld.

I need scarcely remark that this is a letter altogether *private* and written in confidence that it will be so received.

Mrs. M. acknowledges your kind enquiry after her health; Hers and mine are at present both tolerably good. We hope that yours has been entirely re-established. Accept our friendly respects

James Madison

FC (DLC). Marked "(copy)"; in two hands: the first unidentified, the second the hand of Edward Coles (see n. 1).

   1. From this point, the remainder of the letter is in the hand of Edward Coles.

From James Monroe

DEAR SIR   WASHINGTON Sepr. 6. 1812

I enclose you a letter from Col Humphreys[1] & also one from Col. Pike.[2] I am glad to see by the former that some expln. can be given of the proceedings in Connecticut different from what has been imputed & suspected.

Mr Serurier was with me, to day, & repeated what he had before stated of the cause of delay at Paris, & intimated that if any plan could be devised within the limit of his govt's resources, not to bear too heavily, it would find a favorable disposition in it, at this moment to adopt it. I told him that I should communicate what he had said to you, & take your instruction.[3]

Many of our friends here have expressd to me an earnest desire that you should return as soon as possible, and I own that I am under an impression, that it would produce a very salutary effect. The public confidence in a friend near me, I mean his competency, in this crisis, is undoubtedly gone.[4] Letters to several of our friends have been shewn me, which speak in terms, not only decided but harsh to that effect, and from the most respectable sources. Your absence, when every thing turns on that department, considering the public opinion of its head, may injure you.

If you think proper to send me westward, I should propose to take Wm. Jones of Phila. to lake Erie to build boats, & some agent equally efficient for the quarter masters department. Such men should be sent there let who may have the command. Respectfully your friend

JAS MONROE

RC (DLC: Rives Collection, Madison Papers). Docketed by JM.

   1. David Humphreys's letter has not been found, but it probably related to an act passed by the special session of the Connecticut General Assembly convened on 25 Aug., which called for the formation of volunteer regiments composed of men exempt from regular service. Humphreys later served as the commander of such a company composed of men from his hometown of Derby, Connecticut (Humphreys, *Life and Times of David Humphreys*, 2:392). The act was published in the 7 Sept. issue of the *Connecticut Mirror*.

   2. For Pike's letter, see Monroe to JM, 5 Sept. 1812, n. 4.

   3. In his 2 Sept. 1812 dispatch to the duc de Bassano, Sérurier reported on a lengthy conversation with the secretary of state about Franco-American commercial disputes, particularly spoliation claims and the tariff on American goods entering France. The cause of the "delay

at Paris," however, remained what it had long been—disagreement over whether these matters could be resolved in a new treaty of commerce, which Monroe reminded Sérurier the U.S. had never sought in the first place as a means of settling the outstanding differences between the two nations (AAE: Political Correspondence, U.S., vol. 67).

4. Monroe referred to William Eustis.

From William Crawford

SIR   ADAMS COUNTY PENNA. Septr. 7th. 1812

I hope you will pardon this intrusion in the midst of those momentuous affairs which must now press upon your attention. At the request of Mr. Lloyd[1] I now address you in his behalf. I have witnessed some experiments on his late discovery. I presume not on being competent to decide its merit. But it appears to me worthy of a full & fair trial. As, either in the army or navy, it might be advantageously employed—if success[f]ull. Mr. Lloyd is extremely sollicitous to have the fate of his discovery determined—as, if it shall fail, his family requires his attention to some other pursuits. In the mean time his uncertainty whether he may be soon called on by the government to test his discovery prevents his entering on any business of importance. I understand that he addresses you himself on the subject of his wishes.[2] If consistent with your performance of other public duty—your relieving him from his present anxiety will be highly acceptable to one who is with sincere esteem & High respect your fellow citizen

WM. CRAWFORD

RC (DLC).

1. James Lloyd of Adams County, Pennsylvania, had been working on the construction of a "liquid combustible shell grenade and serpentine rocket," for which he was to receive a patent on 11 May 1813 (*ASP, Miscellaneous*, 2:229).

2. Lloyd to JM, 7 Sept. 1812.

From William Eustis

SIR,   Monday Morng. 7 Septr. 1812

By the mail of this day I have only time to submit for consideration a suggestion which has been made of the expediency of detaining the Indian chiefs as hostages. If their tribes should become hostile it is in my mind doubtful whether they may not be useful with their influence among them; if they are not hostile detaining them will give great cause of offence. On the 24 Aug. Gov Meigs writes from Urbana that fort Wayne "shall be maintained" "Ohio troops mounted go this morning."[1] At Cincinnati it is stated on the 27th. that the post is taken—looking at the map leaves a hope, but the circumstance of 200 citizens of Cin: being lost, shows if true that the force was insufficient & defeated.[2] In great haste

W EUSTIS

Mr Munroe had mentioned the subject and is willing, indeed he proposed to go out.

RC (DLC). Docketed by JM.

1. Meigs stated in this letter that troops would leave the following morning to defend the fort (DNA: RG 107, LRRS, M-393:6).

2. Eustis may have referred to a 23 Aug. account from Cincinnati printed in the Baltimore *American and Commercial Daily Advertiser* on 7 Sept. 1812, which reported: "All is confusion and bustle here. Cincinnati has lost nearly 200, some of them the best citizens we had. This moment 2000 troops from Kentucky have arrived here, on their march to reinforce Gen. Hull, but they are too late."

From Thomas Magrath

SIR,   WASHINGTON CITY Septr 7—1812

About the 25th ult I recd. a draught on me from the Bank of Columbia which I refused accep[t]ing not knowing what it was for & having no orders so to do, in conseq[u]ence of which I recd. the within letter which I thought to send you &c[1] I remain Your Hble. Servt.

THOS MAGRATH[2]

RC and enclosures (DLC). For enclosures, see n. 1.

1. Magrath enclosed a 4 Sept. 1812 letter (1 p.) from the firm of Heth and Randolph stating that the draft for $404 that Magrath had refused to pay was for coal shipped at the request of Isaac Coles "for the use of the President." Accompanying this is a letter from Henry Heth to Isaac Coles, 1 Sept. 1812 (1 p.; docketed by JM), explaining that he had shipped the coal requested and including a bill of lading dated 20 Aug. 1812 (1 p.) to show that the coal had been shipped, and an undated letter to Magrath from Heth and Randolph (1 p.; postmarked 22 Aug.; docketed by JM), also explaining that the coal had been shipped and asking Magrath to honor the draft.

2. Thomas Magrath was a Washington horticulturist who kept a nursery on Uriah Forest's farm near Wisconsin Avenue and Massachusetts Avenue (Bryan, *History of the National Capital*, 1:597–98 n. 5).

From James Monroe

Dear Sir   Washington Sepr 7. 1812

Nothing new has occurrd since mine of yesterday. I have yours of the 5th. Mr Eustis has been with me, & we have communicated on the subject of yours to him. He expresses a strong desire for me to take the command, & thinks that a volunteer comn., would serve the purpose. We will confer fully on this subject to day, and come to a decision, and by to morrow's mail you shall have the result. The principal benefit would be the moral effect the measure might have on the public mind, being one emanating immediately from the govt. itself. Other consequences would be doubtful, the advantages quite precarious, especially in the immediate quarter to which the movement would be directed. On the operations under Genl. Dearborn the effect would be salutary, as it would keep the whole force now in upper Canada still there. This indeed might be done under any one. Your reflections as to the impossibility of any brilliant effect are certainly very forcible. Still an effort, manifesting zeal in the govt. itself, without the aid of any brilliant achievement, might be felt by the nation. We will decide to night. Genl. Mason ought to go at the head of the quarter masters dept. He is best qualified by extent of views, knowledge of all its branches, vigor of mind &ca. and Wm. Jones of Phila., would be a more powerful auxiliary to Captn Chauncey.

I repeat my earnest hope that you would come back as soon as possible. There would be no necessity for bringing Mrs Madison with you, as you might perhaps be able to return again in a short time.

In case I go, as is presumeable, I must get you to write a letter to Mrs. Monroe apprizing her of the obligation I am under, & the difficulty of my declining it. It would contribute to reconcile her to it. Sincerely your friend & servt

                                                    Jas Monroe

A volunteer comn will be the most eligible one

RC (DLC: Rives Collection, Madison Papers).

§ From James Lloyd. *7 September 1812, Gettysburg, Adams County.* "Having wrote you Sometime ago [not found] . . . and Reciving no answer thinking that it never Reached you being Desirous to know the result of an Experiment which has Cost me a great deal of t[i]me trouble & expence not only for my own good but that mankind Should be benefited by it.

"When I was down at the City of washington trying my Combustable having not Suckseeded with it & in want of a Shell Constructed to throw it aney distance with a Cannon or morter But from Varyous Experiments Since and a Great improvement Made on it Both as to its Saffty and Cheapness Simpleness which tend all to its Value having Constructed it in a manner So that I can put up for Land Service in Bottles Containing from one quart to 2 quarts which can be Carried With Saffty into action by men Selected for that purpose When at the Distanc of 70 or 80 feet from the Enemys Ranks to throw them among the Enemy which will when the Bottls Bursts Brake or Explode Set on fire Whare a particle of the Liquid touches Which Burn With fury and must Carry Dismay and Destruction With it. Confident I am with one hundread good men I Could drive one thousand the Bosted Vetrions of England. Provoiding wee ware near a nough to throw it apon them at the Comencment of the action or to Storm a fort or Garison nothing Could Exceed it Let 1000 men outside of the Walls of a fort Run under the Walls having Each two Bottls of the Liquid fire throw them over and on the Ramparts which would drive the men not only from their posts but would imeditly Suficate them Being impregnated With So much Sulpher that no Set of men Could Stand the Stounch as for the Land Service I Can Convince your Excelleny By Experiments that it is practable and Nothing Remains more Sure than I Can perfect it as will for Navel Service. I only Wish I had it in my power that I was plaiced in a Situation to Convince your Excellency and the World in generall that it will Be a means of offence and Deffence Better than Ever heare to fore invented. Being advansed in years and on the Decline of life having a heavy Charge of an helpless family a Small and Contracted Sercumstanc Would Willing leav my family in a living Sercumstanc Venture to make a Sacrifice of Life and all on its Sucksess. I wrote your Excellency Some time Ago proposals to Secure to goverment what Exp⟨ence⟩ that might Occur on its first Experiment Eithr at Land or Sea and my offer to put it practice under your Direction you will Recive a line on the Subject from the Honrable William Crawford Member of Congress his apinion of it and its Effects.[1] I again Request you to Consider on the Subject."

RC (DNA: RG 107, LRRS, L-188:6). 2 pp.; docketed as received in the War Department on 17 Sept. 1812.

1. See Crawford to JM, 7 Sept. 1812.

§ From Christopher Raymond Perry.[1] 7 *September 1812, Newport.* Explains that in 1808 he "procured letters from some of the first Republican characters in this state" recommending him for the office of superintendent of a navy yard[2] but was too late in applying to receive an appointment. JM later appointed him superintendent of the navy yard at Charlestown, Massachusetts, but he was superseded when the previous superintendent returned to the office. Describes his extensive service during the Revolutionary War and his current impecunious situation. Requests that JM appoint him as an agent for the exchange of prisoners in the West Indies.

RC (DNA: RG 59, LAR, 1809–17, filed under "Perry"). 3 pp.; docketed by JM. On the verso of the final page is a copy of a 3 Apr. 1801 letter from Samuel Smith informing Perry that he was to be retired from service.

1. Christopher Raymond Perry had been promoted to the rank of captain in the navy in 1798, was discharged from service under the Peace Establishment Act in 1801, and was appointed collector of the First District of Rhode Island in January 1814 (Callahan, *List of Officers of the Navy*, 431; *Senate Exec. Proceedings*, 2:455, 460).

2. At least ten letters were written on Perry's behalf between 4 Jan. and 5 Mar. 1808 (DNA: RG 59, LAR, 1801–9, filed under "Perry").

To William Eustis

private

DEAR SIR   MONTPELLIER Sep. 8. 1812

I have recd. your favor of the 5th. & return the letters accompanying it. Your last instruction to Wilkinson will I suppose have given him the idea which is for the present to regulate his policy towards the Spaniards.[1] If it be true that a proclamation of neutrality issued at the Havanna, it is a proof that they will not court hostilities with us.[2] In the mean time, the hostile use made of the Indians as disclosed in the intercepted letters from St. Augustine,[3] present a new ground for any decisive course towards the Floridas, which may be expedient. The policy observed by Morrow & Worthington at Pequa, appears to be judicious. I am glad you have been able to supply arms to Wadsworth. Nothing is wanting in the Western Country, to cure the evil proceeding from Hull but supplies of the necessary sorts, and a head to combine & apply the volunteer force every where springing into service. Without such a head, in which all wd. confide, there is danger of much waste of military patriotism & money also; I am the more desirous that Mr. Monroe should patronize & guide the efforts on foot. His appearance in that quarter, as a chargé of military affairs, from the Govt. would of itself do good; and he would be able to regulate & superintend the scattered & crude efforts of the people, in a manner to proportion them both to the object & the resources. It is the more necessary to push the enterprize towards Detroit, as the apparent scantiness of the force under Genl. D. checks our sanguine hopes, of a success in his part of the Campaign, that will redeem it from the reproach elsewhere incurred. Should the Season be found an insuperable obstacle to the recovery of Detroit & the prosecution of the original Object, a great good will be done, by such a display of enterprize & force, as will show that to be the only obstacle, and that the next season will plant our standard wherever we please. The effect on the Savages would be peculiarly salutary; and the Enemy would be rendered less disposed to continue the war, and more flexible in the terms of peace. If Col. Monroe should engage in this service, will it not be best to furnish him with Blank Comissions for volunteer officers, and a blank Majr. Genl: for himself: the whole to be used according to the occasion. A character would then be given to his destination which would place him on better ground than that of a private volunteer.

I shall be with you I expect in a few days, & return the letters from Govr. Strong,[4] to await the result of our personal consultation as to the proper answer. My next will fix the time of my setting out, & probable arrival at Washington. Friendly respects

JAMES MADISON.

RC (PHi: Daniel Parker Papers).

1. In a 26 Aug. 1812 letter Eustis explained to Wilkinson that the "principal object" of his command was "the protection & defence of New Orleans." While acknowledging that offensive measures against the U.S. must be resisted, Eustis noted that there were "reasons of a peculiar & important nature, against exciting hostilities at Pensacola & Mobile" (DNA: RG 107, LSMA).

2. The 7 Sept. 1812 issue of the Baltimore *American and Commercial Daily Advertiser* reported that a 15 Aug. order issued "at the Havana" called "a council of commerce" and summoned "merchants and freeholders, for the purpose of adopting such measures 'as will give immediately that activity to the maritime commerce of the place, which its neutrality requires, during the war between Britain and America.'"

3. See Eustis to JM, 5 Sept. 1812, n. 6.
4. See Eustis to JM, 2 Sept. 1812, n. 1.

To James Monroe

private

DEAR SIR   MONTPELLIER Aug. [September] 8. 1812

I have recd. yours of the 6th. I am sorry to find that Pike confides so little in our prospects. From a letter of Genl. Dearborn to the Secy. of War,[1] it appears that the force at his disposal is more scanty than was hoped. I am not sure whether his immediate plan is to take advantage of the detachments of the B. force from Montreal, by directing his principal operations towards that place, or to draw away the force from above, in order to strike at that at Niagara. Whatever the purpose may be, I perceive no foundation for sanguine hopes, of a success in either quarter that will heal the wound which Hull has given to the Campaign. It becomes the more necessary, to avail ourselves of the western spirit in order to recover if possible what he has lost, and even to accomplish what he might have gained. As men in abundance are already in motion, or awaiting orders, nothing is necessary but to give them a head that will inspire confidence, concentrate their force, and direct the application of it. I am not without hopes that in some way or other this critical service may proceed from you. If neither a regular commission, nor a brevet can arm you with the regular authority, it will only remain to substitute the expedient already suggested, unless it be practicable to cover your services with a Volunteer Commission under the Act of Feby. My impression has been & still is that the enrollment of the Volunteers is to precede the appt. of the officers. But a blank commission of Majr. Genl. might be carried in your Pocket; & it being understood that you were to command such a force, it wd. both promote the enrollment; and in case of failure, give the better gloss to your junction with the army, and guiding its councils if not commanding its operations. Should you go in any capacity, the Secretary of war will doubtless co-operate on your preparatory arrangements. If other than persons in military office be desireable to you, they must of course accompany you as volunteers. I hope the difficulties as to competent ordinance [*sic*] will have been overcome, and that provisions & all other essential supplies may by proper exertions be attainable. Should the lateness of the season be found a bar to success, great good will result from such exhibitions of zeal, of numbers, and of effort, as may demonstrate, that that was the only bar to success. It would have a most salutary effect on the savages; and abroad also; whether there be a desire in the enemy to prosecute the war, which is to be discouraged, or difficulties are to be met in the terms of peace.

Your interview with Onis will, I see, be fruitless. It is clear that he has no powers now, if he ever had, and improbable that he ever had them, to cede Territory. The general terms in his commission, prove nothing. He wd. have sent his instructions along with it, or extracts at least, if his advances had been supported by them. His object is to bring himself into importance, & to gain time. The Spanish anxiety to prevent extremities is seen, in the neutrality avowed at the Havanna.[2] I observe in the intercepted letters of the Govr. at St. Augustine, that he has deliberately employed Indian hostilities agst. us.[3] This will justify his expulsion; if nothing else wd. do it; and the reason seems to be the same as to Mobille & Pensicola. I think it wd. not be amiss, to let Onis know that we have discovered these hostile proceedings on the part of the Spaniards.

If Castlereah was sincere & the ⟨weight⟩ of the Cabinet, in saying to Mr. Russel, that a declaration of war here, without our knowledge of the repeal of the O. in C. would not shut the door to adjustment, we may momently expect interesting communications on the subject.[4] If certain passages in R's letters which are not be [*sic*] used officially, could like one from a former letter, go anonymously to the public, they wd. be seasonable & useful.

Before I recd. your last, I had made up my mind to return to Washington. I expect to be there in very few days. My next will fix the time. Affece. respects

JAMES MADISON

RC (DLC: Monroe Papers). Docketed by Monroe; torn. Misdated 8 Aug. 1812 by JM; date corrected here on the basis of internal evidence.

1. See Eustis to JM, 5 Sept. 1812, and n. 5.
2. See JM to Eustis, 8 Sept. 1812, n. 2.
3. See Eustis to JM, 5 Sept. 1812, n. 6.
4. For Russell's report on the repeal of the orders in council, see Monroe to JM, 4 Sept. 1812, n. 1.

From William Eustis

Dear Sir,   8 Septr 1812 Washington.

By Letters from General Dearborn[1] Genl. Harrison[2] and others from the western country it appears that events of great importance are almost daily occurring: and I cannot refrain from expressing my own with the hopes of all our friends that your return may be found not inconvenient. With great respect

W. Eustis

RC (DLC).

1. Eustis probably referred to a 3 Sept. 1812 letter from Dearborn (DNA: RG 107, LRRS, D-144:6; docketed as received 8 Sept.), which discussed the raising of volunteers in Connecticut, Rhode Island, and New York and enclosed a 31 Aug. letter from Thomas Tisdale on this subject (see Hezekiah Huntington to JM, 29 Aug. 1812, and n. 3).

2. Eustis probably referred to William Henry Harrison's 28 Aug. 1812 letter (DNA: RG 107, LRRS, H-344:6; docketed as received 8 Sept.), which explained the conditions under which he had recently accepted a brevet major general's commission in Kentucky, described his command over most of the troops moving into the Northwest, and announced his intention to reinforce Fort Wayne. He declared that the troops under his command were "the best material for forming an army that the world has produced" but admitted that they lacked training and equipment.

From James Monroe

Dear Sir   Washington Sepr 8. 1812

I have yours of the 6th. I am willing & ready to act in either character alluded to. The effect on public opinion would be greater, if indeed any useful effect might be expected from it, by appointing me to command, than merely making a visit to the country. In the latter case, I would do every thing in my power to promote an organization of the forces, to digest their plan of operations, & facilitate a concert between the generals. In the former I should of course have the direction. The question about the commission is an important one. Mr Eustis thinks that, in consideration of the large bodies of volunteers collecting from the States contiguous to the scene of action, a comn. might be given me to take charge of, to organize & command them, which being that of Major Genl. would carry with it the command in that quarter. He sends you a copy of the act of Congress relating to volunteers, which will enable you to decide. The delay should be as short as possible. I most earnestly hope that you may find it convenient to return, for considerations which have been already suggested. If I take the command, I should write the Govr. of Virga., by whose cooperation a considerable volunteer force of cavalry, may be procurd, as also of infantry.

A Captn. Dobbins from Detroit, since the surrender, who was present at the time, confirms every [*sic*] the most unfavorable representation that has been given of that disgraceful event.[1]

We have nothing new from other quarters. Respectfully & sincerely yours

JAS MONROE

RC (DLC: Rives Collection, Madison Papers). Docketed by JM.

1. See David Mead to JM, 29 Aug. 1812, and n. 3.

§ From the Democratic Citizens of Talbot County, Maryland. *Ca. 8 September 1812*. Report that "a very numerous meeting . . . was held on the court-House green in Easton on Tuesday the 8th. Septr." "The Democratic Citizens of Talbot County feel firmly attached to the constitution of the United States; and ardently adore the liberties we enjoy—actuated themselves by the principles of their revolutionary fathers, and warmly approbating the measures pursued by the General Government, they had confidently expected that when the constituted authorities had summoned the people to the standard of the law in its defence, the voice of opposition would be drowned in the general tone of patriotic emulation, and the struggle of party sunk or forgotten in exertions against the enemy for our liberties and our rights. They considered that in actual War, when union is so essential to success, if not to existence, every act tending in the remotest degree to give encouragement to the enemy would be repugnant to every idea of patriotism, and would be opposed by every citizen feeling an attachment to his country; and they could not suppose that any of their countrymen could be found so wanting to the trust reposed in them by the Patriots of the Revolution, as to forfeit their pretensions to that high character. Differencies [*sic*] of opinion they knew to exist, which, under that blest republican form of Government we have the happiness to live, they never for a moment imagined could cease. Nor did they, in strict conformity with their own character, ever wish to stifle or check them. They relied on that love of country they beleived to be felt by all, that those differences should be managed among ourselves—they never expected to see them promulgated to the enemy, America, and the World in the attitude of Menace and hostility to our own country. But they have been deceived—and when the different addresses which have been issued from several States in the Union are presented to their minds, breathing a spirit of lawless violence and treasonable insubordination engendered in the false conceptions, and loaded with the passions and anti-republican prejudices, we trust of but few, derogatory to the Government and the Nation, and calculated to induce a beleif in the minds of foreign powers of a disaffection and weakness in the American people, the Democratic Citizens of Talbot with heart-felt sorrow confess that they have been deceived. They never calculated on these things; Or, with the same unanimity and patriotism, with which they now act, they long since would have expressed their confidence in the administration of the Government, and have proffered their services, their lives and fortunes to avenge the wrongs and to defend the rights of their injured country.

"Resolved, That we warmly approbate the measures pursued by the General

Government of the United States; and that we are firmly attached to the liberty and independence purchased by the blood of our fathers in the revolution—that we view the present war in which we are engaged equally just, necessary, and indispensable as the war of 1776, and calculated to hand down to posterity the blessings which it procured.

"Resolved, That we have full confidance in the abilities, Integrity, and firmness of James Madison, the President of the United States, called to his office by the voice of a Free People; and that we view with indignation, and hold in contempt, the slanderous intimations that he countenances mobs or is subject to any sinister influence, as the effusions of imbecile minds and malignant hearts.

"Resolved, That we sincerely deplore the recent events in Baltimore; and lament that scenes so little comporting with the dignity of the State should be acted within it. We leave this transaction without comment to the proper Tribunal, which has already taken cognizance of it, to develope its designs, unmask and punish the guilty. Yet we cannot with hold our detestation at the use that is made of it in arraying it against the Government to the service of its enemies.

"Resolved, That we consider the liberty of the Press as sacred, and that it ought to be held inviolate—that we view with sorrow and concern its freedom prostituted, by too many of the papers opposed to Government, to the basest purposes, in waging war against the liberty of the country—in disseminating disaffection—in propagating falsehood, and in traducing some of the best men in the nation with an inveteracy as if their infuriate passions could not be appeased till they had paralized the arm of Government, prostrated our liberty and independence, and offered up the country a hated victim to its enemies.

"Resolved, That we view the manner in which some of the people of this country, from evil council, have been induced to protest against, and oppose, the measures of the General Government, equivalent to giving 'aid and comfort' to the enemy—that this conduct, if persisted in, cannot fail to be highly injurious to the country; to protract the present necessary war, which otherwise would be of short duration, to an interminable length; to cause a great effusion of human blood; and to entail innumerable calamities upon the American people—that all those evils so shocking to the feelings of humanity can only be ascribed to those misguided citizens, who encourage England by their opposition to the General Government.

"Resolved, That the distinguished services and patriotic character of our late Representative in Congress, Robert Wright Esq., merit our confidence; and that we will continue to repose it in him.

"Resolved, that, esteeming merit and patriotism, whereever to be found, whether among Democrats or Federalists, we sincerely lament the death of Lieutenant William Bush,[1] (a native of Talbot County) of the United States Marines, who fell in the defence of his country in the late gallant and successful action of Captain Hull with a British frigate; and that, as a testimonial of our gratitude, and respect to his memory, we will wear crape on the left arm for thirty days.

"Resolved, That these resolutions be . . . forwarded . . . to the President . . . and also that they be published in the 'Republican Star' at Easton, with a request that they be inserted in the 'National Intelligencer' at Washington."

RC (DLC). 10 pp.; signed by Perry Benson, chairman, and Thomas P. Bennett, secretary.

1. Marine lieutenant William S. Bush was fatally shot in the face while attempting to board the *Guerrière* during its engagement with the *Constitution* on 19 Aug. (Dudley, *Naval War of 1812*, 1:246).

§ From the Republican Citizens of Worcester County, Maryland. *8 September 1812.* "Whereas certain Resolutions have recently been entered into by a part of our Fellow Citizens on Tuesday the 25th. Ultimo. at this place,[1] calculated to impress a belief, that the public sentiment in this section of the United States, is Inimical to the present administration of our Government. Holding as we do a deep stake in the interest of this Community and viewing the dangerous Effects that may result from misguided information in this respect more especially at this important crisis, we have thought proper to assemble and express to our Fellow Citizens and to the world our sentiments and Determinations. We had been taught to believe that our Revolutionary War had placed this Nation in an equal Attitude with the other nations of the Earth. That to be Independent we are entitled exclusively to our territorial Possessions. To Choose our own Form of Government, and to administer it in our own way for our own common good. To participate in those Rights that were common to the other Nations of the Earth, and to enjoy unmolested the blessings that Heaven in his wisdom hath bestowed within the reach of the sons of Men. A retrospective view of the Transactions on the Theatre of the world for a few years past will show how far those Rights have been respected by Nations that called themselves civilized. We have seen two Nations engaged in a War of extermination conducted with unrelenting severity. As Belligerents they have assumed rights incompatable with the Peace and dignity of other States that wished to stand on Neutral Ground. By their orders and Decrees the rights of Neutral Trade have been violated and Destroyed. We have seen the productions of our own soil Interdicted from a foreign Mast. Nations at Peace deprived of all Rights and the Commerce of the world usurped and Monopolized by Belligerents alone. And while France in open violation of solemn Treatise has robbed us of our Property and destroyed our Ships and has delayed Indemnification for those wrongs; Great Britain under her Orders in Council has endeavoured to exact Tribute on our Commerce—has Captured and condemned our vessels and Property, Impressed our seamen to fight her Battles, has Insulted our Flag, and within the waters of our own Jurisdiction has murdered our Citizens. We have seen a Foreign Emissary sent among us, avowedly to create dissentions among our Citizens, and dismember our happy Union; We have seen Commercial Posts within our North Western Frontier established to trade with the Indian Nations. And while the Olive Branch of Peace, with the alluring Professions of Friendship are held out, we have seen the savages urged on to Massacre with unrelenting Fury the women and Children of our Peaceful Borders. We have sought redress for our Injuries by Pacific Negotiation—our incessant remonstrances have been answerd by additional wrongs, and new aggressions on our Rights—and while a piratic warfare has been carried on against our Peaceful Commerce, and Insults and Injuries heaped upon us, the Door of Reconciliation has been constantly kept open. To redress our Wrongs the Government of our Country has in it's wisdom sought the last resort of Nations; we have appealed to the god of Battles for the Justice of our cause. We deplore the necessity of a measure that involves us in the destructive horrors of War—a War of Defence in support of our invaluable Rights and Privileges and shall hail the return of Peace as the Harbinger of the future glory of our rising Empire. Under the wise Administration of our Government, we are proud to say that the Growth of our Country in Agriculture, Manufactures and commerce has been unparralleled in the Tide of Times. Abounding in resources our Improvements in every Branch have astonished the Whole World; The Blessings of civil and Religious Liberty in our happy Land are the Pride and Boast of our Citizens, and has become the Envy of Nations. And while the whole Energies of our Country should be exerted to repel the attacks of a Foreign foe—We Cannot but view with Indignation the attempts of Certain Factions within these United States to sow Discord among our Fellow Citizens—To Distract our Public Councils, to array Citizen against Citizen, and to Paralize the Efforts of our Government in an honorable defence of our Just Rights—Against the Hostile Aggressions of a Nation that knows no other measure of Right but her Ambition and her Power.

"Animated by that spirit, that glows in the Bosom of every Freeman that Reverences the Constitution and Laws of his Country; We view with Detestation and horror certain Lawless Assemblies in *Boston* Plymouth[2] and at Baltimore that in the face of the civil Authority have endangered the Peace and harmony of society by substituting violence and Force to gratify their vindictive Passions instead of resorting to the ordinary administration of Public Justice; We consider the actors in those Scenes, Enemies to all order, all Law and all Government. And while those disturbences of the Peace are under Judicial Investigation we see with regret attempts made in different parts to calumniate the fair fame of the chief Magistrate of this state the Mayor of the City of Baltimore, and other Respectable Characters by supposing them capable of Countenancing so gross an Infraction of the Laws. We repel with mingled emotions of Pity and Contempt, the base, wicked, and Mallicious Slanders on the Great Majority of the Good People of the United States, and the Public Councils of our Nation; that they could be influenced by the Tyrant of Europe in Asserting their Rights as Freemen against the aggressions of an haughty foe.

"1st. Therefore, Resolved, that as freemen we hold ourselves individially bound to co-operate with the Constituted Authorities of our Country in the legitimate Exercise of their Duties, as well to suppress internal Insurrections as to repel Foreign Invasions.

"2ndly. Resolved, That we will to the Utmost of our Power and ability, aid in carrying on the present War in which we are engage⟨d⟩ for the Defence of our Just Rights—and will never submit to the Insults and Aggressions of any Foreign Power.

"3dly. Resolved that at the Risque of every thing sacred and Dear to us as Citizens, and as men, we are determined to transmit to our Posterity that Heritage that was purchased by the Blood of our Fathers—Liberty and Independence." In a fourth resolution, recommend four county representatives as delegates to the General Assembly. Resolve further that these resolutions be sent to the president and the governor "and that the same be printed in the Maryland Republican, The Whig, and the Star."

RC (DLC). 4 pp.; signed by James B. Robins, chairman, and Edward Broughton, secretary. Enclosed in Broughton to JM, 21 Sept. 1812 (ibid.; 1 p.).

1. On 11 Sept. 1812 the Georgetown *Federal Republican* printed the proceedings of the 25 Aug. meeting, which expressed reservations about the declaration of war, registered concern that an alliance between the U.S. and France was developing, repudiated mob activity in Baltimore, and praised the antiadministration *Federal Republican*.

2. On 13 July, Federalists had attended a meeting of Boston Republicans in large numbers, their presence promoting "riot and confusion" and causing an adjournment of the gathering (*Boston Patriot*, 15 July 1812). On 3 Aug. 1812 Republican representative Charles Turner Jr. was attacked by a mob in Plymouth, "held by a portion of them, and literally kicked, pushed, and beat, thro' the streets, till he found shelter at the Post-Master's." The potential for violence in Plymouth was sustained into the following day, forcing an adjournment of the court of sessions, of which Turner was chief justice (ibid., 8 Aug. 1812).

¶ To Samuel Carswell. Letter not found. *8 September 1812*. Described as an "Autograph Letter, signed" in Stan. V. Henkels Catalogue No. 698 (1893), item 521.

From James Monroe

DEAR SIR   WASHINGTON Sepr 9. 1812

I have nothing from you to day. Col Cass has arrivd & gives the same acct. heretofore recd. from others of the surrender of Detroit.

Genl Cushing thinks that a power to grant a volunteer comn., to give effect to the law, is a necessary construction of it. I shall, unless some other view be taken in the course of the day, accept such a comn. & set out in discharge of it, in a few days. A short hesitation has taken place in the hope of hearing further from you. But your letter of yesterday is perhaps all that you can say. To morrow we shall probably hear whether you intend to return immediately, & I shall be govd. by your decision. If still at home I shall pass by your house.

The enclosed is interesting to the parties.[1] They say they cannot get to Hallafax in any other mode, & that thier interest depending there is of immense value. The rule must (to accomadate them) either be repealed or modified. Affectionately yr friend

JAS MONROE

RC (DLC: Rives Collection, Madison Papers).

1. The enclosure was probably a 4 Sept. 1812 letter (2 pp.) from the Baltimore firm of Peter Hoffman and Son that had been delivered to Monroe by Walter Smith. The firm and its neighbors, "All native Citizens," sought authority from the State Department to send David Hoffman on a government cartel to Halifax to protect a cargo of British manufactures imported on the *Concordia*, which had been captured by the British. The petitioners also requested of Monroe "whatever, if any, protection you can consistently extend to him in his journey toward, or during his tarry in, the enemy country" (DNA: RG 76, Preliminary Inventory 177, entry 201, Great Britain, Miscellaneous Claims, ca. 1797–1863, folder 15, "Claim of Ship Concordia").

§ From Richard Forrest. *9 September 1812, Washington.* "Agreeably to your request, I wrote to an excellent judge of Wine in Baltimore, to purchase (if he should approve of the quality) a pipe of the prize Wine then about to be sold there."[1] Encloses the letter he received in reply [not found] explaining that the purchase was not made. "The Victory of Capn. Hull, has given great animation to every class of persons appertaining to our navy. The Carpenters at the Yard appear [to] move with a new step, and seem to strike two strokes now, for one formerly."

RC (NN). 1 p.; docketed by JM.

1. JM probably had directed Forrest to inquire about pipes of Madeira from the captured vessel *Henry* that were to be auctioned in Baltimore on 28 Aug. 1812 (Baltimore *American and Commercial Daily Advertiser*, 24 Aug. 1812).

To William Eustis

private

DEAR SIR   Sepr. 10. 1812

I have but a moment to inclose you the letters from Govr: Scott & others.[1] You will communicate to Mr. Monroe what has been done in that quarter. His presence will be useful in getting every thing into system & subordination. A failure in the mail does not allow me time to examine the Volunteer Act, with reference to a Majr. Genl's Comission to Mr. Monroe. But I see no evil from risking the measure, which is not outweighed by the promised good. I shall set out on Saturday Morning, and hope to be in Washington early on Monday. Friendly respects

J. MADISON

RC (PHi: Daniel Parker Papers).

1. JM forwarded Charles Scott to JM, 25 Aug. 1812, with its enclosures, and John G. Jackson to JM, 31 Aug. and 4 Sept. 1812.

To James Monroe

DEAR SIR   Sepr 10. 1812

I have this moment recd. yours of the 8th. & 9th. A failure in the mail, occasioned the recet. of them at the same time. I have not had time to examine the Volunteer Act, which has been forwarded to me, the present mail which brought it, remaining but a short period, & that being occupied in reading papers &c. now sent to the Secy. of War, & others requiring attention. He will shew you those from Kentucky wch. urge your superintendance of things in that quarter. I see no evil in risking your appt. comparable to that which may be obviated by it. The Western Country is all in motion, and confusion. It wd. be grievous, if so much laudable ardor & effort should not be properly concentrated and directed. I shall set out for Washington on Saturday morning, and if I do not say otherwise by the mail of tomorrow evening, shall take the road by Fredg. I shall with great pleasure write a letter to Mrs. Monroe but wait the final result of your mind, before I do it. Affecte. respects

JAMES MADISON

RC (DLC: Monroe Papers).

From Thomas Henderson

STATE OF N CAROLINA MECKLENBURG COUNTY
SIR   Septemr 10th 1812.

It becomes my duty to inform you that pursuant to a publick notice, a large and respectable number of the Citizens of this County convened in the Court house on the 4th. Instant to take into Consideration the State of the Union, After the Assembly was Organised a committee was Appointed to prepare resolutions expressive of the sense of the meeting. The following preamble and resolutions were presented for consideration & unanimously adopted.

Whereas the Government of Great Britain has for a Serious [*sic*] of Years past grossly violated our National rights by proclamations of Blockades, Orders, & other unrighteous edicts, whereby the most ruinous depredations have been committed on the property, and the most daring aggressions on the rights & Liberties of Multitudes of American Citizens.

Whereas every attempt of the Government of the United States by embassies & diplomatic negociations as well as by embargoes & nonimportation laws, to protect the persons & property of our Citizens have been rendered unsuccesful.

And whereas the pacific policy of Our Government has been construed by the Government of Great Britain into pusillanimity, so that she has thereby taken encouragement to persevere in her Offensive measures of impressing our Citizens, Capturing our Vessels, and instigating the Savages on our frontiers to hostilities, Untill our Government has at length appealed to the last resort of injured nations.

Therefore Resolved.

That we consider the declaration of War against England as the only possible means of maintaining our rights, and Supporting our proper Grade in the scale of Independant Nations.

Resolved. That we will cheerfully Cooperate with the Government of our choice in rendering every assistance in our power, to prosecute with Vigour the war we have Justly entered into against the proud Oppressor of humanity.

Resolved. That a copy of the proceedings of this meeting be transmitted by the Secretary to the President of the United States.

THO HENDERSON Chairmn.

ISAAC ALEXANDER Secr'y.

RC (DLC).

From James Monroe

DEAR SIR   WASHINGTON Sepr. 10. 1812

I have yours of the 8th. Having been engaged the whole day in communication with Col. Huntington & Cass, I have only a moment to drop you a line. Cass says that he came here as the representative of all the officers, and indeed as the organ of the army to explain the conduct of Genl. Hull in the sacrifice of the army. He is engaged in making a statment which he wishes to go before the public immediately, to be addressed to the secretary at war.[1] You will arrive in time to decide the mode in which it shall be made public. I am inclined to think that there can be no impropriety in pursuing the one suggested.

The Govr. of Kentuckey has conferr'd on Govr. Harrison the rank of Major Genl. by brevett in the militia of that state. The object either was to give him the command of the Kentuckey Brigrs., or of Winchester; or of both parties. It may create difficulty in respect to the latter, to have the command taken from him in that mode. And as the considerations, or some of them, (in case that should not happen), of a general nature, still urge the measure contemplated from the govt., I have resolved to take the course suggested in your last, of proceeding westwar⟨d⟩ as soon as the necessary arrangments are made, with a volunteer commissn. The Ohio gentlemen seem to wish it; and Mr Clay of Kentuckey, intimates, that the comn. to Harrison would not interfer with any arrangment of the government.[2] I shall set out on saturday or sunday, perhaps by Loudoun[3] (to stay a night there) by your house, to my own, & thence without delay westward. Respectfully & truly yrs.

JAS MONROE

RC (DLC: Rives Collection, Madison Papers).

1. On 10 Sept. 1812 Cass gave Eustis a written report of the surrender of Detroit (DNA: RG 107, LRRS, C-462:6).

2. Clay's 25 Aug. 1812 letter to Monroe noted that Harrison's commission and orders were "altogether provisional, depending upon the President, who will revoke or vary them as he pleases" (Hopkins et al., *Papers of Henry Clay*, 1:720).

3. In 1808 Monroe had become the sole owner of Oak Hill, an estate with a small house in Loudoun County, Virginia (*PJM*, 15:349 n. 1).

From James Taylor

DEAR SIR   CLEVELAND OHIO Sept 10th 1812

Permit me to introduce to your acquaintance Genl. James Findlay a particular friend of mine.

The Genl. Commanded one of the Regiments from this state who were unfortunately Compeled to surrender prisoners of War at Detroit on the 16t. August.

The Genl. has been induced to take Niagara and Genl. Dearborns head Quarter in his way to the City of Washington.

I refer you to Genl. F for any additional Circumstances that may have transpired during our stay at Detroit & Ft Molden which was at least two weeks after Colos. McArthur & Cass le[f]t that quarter.

And I assure you, you may rely implicitly on any information he may give you. I had some Idea of Coming on to Washington my self, but it is thought best that I should go on to the head Quarters of the N. Western Army, you may rest assured that every exertion shall be made in our Power to aid the views of the Government. I refer you to The Genl for the Manner in which Genl Hull endeavored to embarrass me by drawing orders on me for upwards of Four thousand pounds in favor of two Men in Canada[1] and if I had drawn in their favor for that amount there would have been demands for Ten times the amount, but I positively refused to draw for one Cent, and I was threatend with detention both by Military & then Civil detention. Excuse hast[e]. I have the honor to be with great respect & Esteem your Obed. sert.

JAMES TAYLOR

RC (DLC). Docketed by JM.

1. In a 15 Sept. 1812 letter to Eustis, Taylor explained this incident in more detail. Hull had drawn orders on Taylor, the quartermaster general of the Northwest Army, "in favor of two men on account of damage done and property taken while we were in Cannada to the amou[n]t of upwards of Forty five hundred pounds N.Y. currency." Taylor refused, arguing that Hull no longer commanded him, that the enemy would probably not honor his bills, and that the British had wrongfully confiscated military equipment in violation of the terms of the capitulation (*Michigan Historical Collections* 40 [1929]: 485–87).

§ To an Unidentified Correspondent. *10 September 1812, Montpelier.* "The bearer John Neilson[1] has been employed between three and four years by me as a House Carpenter. He has appeared to be unusually skilfull in his profession and very faithfull in the work done by him, I have never heard any thing injurious in the slightest Degree to his integrity, and believe his character in every other respect to be worthy of Confidence."

RC (DNA: RG 42, Records of the District of Columbia Commissioners, Letters Received and Drafts of Letters Sent by the Superintendent of the City of Washington, vol. 21). 1 p.; in a clerk's hand; marked as a "True Copy." Enclosed in Jefferson to Thomas Munroe, 4 Mar. 1815, which recommended Neilson and James Dinsmore for employment in the rebuilding of Washington (ibid.).

1. In an 11 May 1815 letter to Benjamin Henry Latrobe, Jefferson offered high praise for the skills of John Neilson, whom he had hired from Philadelphia in 1804 as a house joiner. Neilson worked for Jefferson for four years at Monticello before going to work for the Madisons (Van Horne, *Papers of Benjamin Henry Latrobe*, 3:673 n. 2). Neilson stayed on at Montpelier until Dec. 1812. His work there focused on the upper southwest end of the mansion, including the installation of ten double-hung windows, four single windows with Venetian blinds, and a "Venetian Door & Side Lights" leading to the roof of the southwest wing. All the remodeling of Montpelier was completed by early 1813, when the Madisons were ready to receive visitors in their home away from Washington (Hunt-Jones, *Dolley and the "Great Little Madison,"* 72).

§ From the Republican Citizens of York County, District of Maine. *10 September 1812.* A convention of "more than six hundred republican citizens," members of the "solid yeomanry," met on 10 Sept. "to consider and resolve on the momentous subjects of public affairs." After attending church services and processing to the courthouse, the convention appointed a committee to prepare a report for consideration. The convention then unanimously approved the following address and resolutions and ordered that they be published and a copy transmitted to the president.

"Fellow Citizens, . . . In times of danger and calamity our fathers were wont to meet and reciprocate their patriotic sentiments, and to improve, inculcate and disseminate those principles which are essential to liberty. In case of threatened or actual war their patriotism was warmed, their zeal animated, their exertions augmented and their strength became equal to the day. Hence have they subdued the wilderness, vanquished the savages, resisted the oppressor and effected their freedom and independence.

"Since our dismemberment from the British empire we have been the envy and admiration of the world. For thirty years had we enjoyed, with little interruption, peace, prosperity and happiness. Spectators of those cruel and vindictive wars which desolated Europe, we could feel for their distresses, deprecate the spirit which dictated them, but could entertain no wish to be involved in their calamities. Pursuing that system of neutrality which Washington adopted and inforced, we had a right to expect from the belligerents, that respect for our rights which was due to us as an independent nation. From the wise, pacific and impartial policy of the American government, the tyrants of Europe could expect no aid to their ambitious views. Each willing to involve us in an unprofitable and destructive contest, each affecting to suspect us of partiality to his foe, and each jealous of our peace and growing prosperity, our course was difficult, critical and dangerous. To avoid contests in which we had no interest, and, at the same time, to secure our commercial privileges, we had taken the precaution to define them by treaty with most of the nations of Europe. But from the close of the American revolution, Great Britain had persisted in violating our neutrality, by forcibly entering our vessels and taking our seamen. We had insisted that *'on the high seas' the flag should protect those who sailed under it;* that for one nation forcibly to take the seamen from the vessels of another is an act of hostility; that altho' Britain has a right to her *own subjects,* who have not become naturalized in the United States, this is not the way to obtain them. Tho' these doctrines had been most conclusively enforced, by men of all parties in the United States, Great Britain had wickedly and wantonly pursued her arbitrary practice of forcibly taking from our vessels, at sea, British subjects, naturalized Americans, foreigners of all descriptions and even native citizens. Thus was the merchant embarrassed in his voyage, the captain deprived of the services of his crew; The poor unfortunate victim dragged from his country, his wife, his children and his liberty to magnify the pride and power of the British nation. Against this outrage upon the rights of the American flag, we had, at all times and under every administration protested. The offence had become insupportable and demanded immediate atonement. Yet, it is said that we ought to endure this intolerable disgrace and submit to the iniquity of the slavery of our citizens rather than enforce a spirit of resentment.

"To such degrading and slavish doctrine this convention cannot subscribe. They are satisfied that this injury alone would justify a prompt and vigorous opposition. But to these insults to our national honor—these attacks upon the liberty of our citizens, are added others of a deeper malignity. Tho' our commerce had suffered by those grosser passions which war excites, it was prosperous and lucrative until the sixteenth of May one thousand eight hundred and six, when England declared all the coast, ports and rivers, from Brest to the Elbe inclusive, in a state of blockade. Thus by a mere declaration, without the possibility of investment, and against every principle of national law, one thousand miles of sea coast, and some of the principal ports and rivers in Europe were subjected to a paper blockade, and the channels of our commerce with near thirty millions of people obstructed. To this was succeeded the French Berlin decree of the twenty first of November one thousand eight hundred and six, blockading the British Islands and their dependencies. However ridiculous might have been the attempt to enforce this monstrous edict, at a time when a French ship durst scarcely venture upon the ocean, it was caught at as a reason for prohibiting our commerce with the enemies of England, and at length of blockading most of the ports of Europe. From this time America has been the sport and prey of the belligerents. Our government has reasoned, remonstrated and protested in vain. Averse to war and disposed to make any sacrifice to peace, short of the honor and independence of the nation and finding that we had nothing to expect but outrage and violence on the ocean, we withdrew from the scene of contention, and attempted the experiment of subsisting on our own resources. The clamors of our own citizens rendered the embargo ineffectual; and a non intercourse was substituted, to cease to operate against that nation which should first cease to violate our rights. At length France officially notified us of the repeal of her edicts, and, with her our commercial relations were restored. From that time our commerce has been subjected to the rapacity of the British cruisers. In vain have we attempted to negotiate. Arguments clear and irresistible have been evaded by empty professions, pitiful pretences and contemptible subterfuges. Finally we were given to understand that the Orders in Council must continue until the French decrees were repealed in cases where they did not affect us. What was to be done? So early as one thousand eight hundred and nine, Congress by a vote nearly unanimous, declared that the United States ought not to submit to these hostile edicts. To add to all this, the merciless savages had been instigated to acts of barbarous, vindictive warfare, and the tomahawk and scalping knife had been raised against the defenceless inhabitants of the frontiers. And to fill up the measure of British iniquity a spy[1] had been detected in attempting to seduce the citizens from their allegiance and to effect a dissolution of the Union.

"In this situation, having for more than twenty years, witnessed the impressment of our citizens, and for nearly six years endured the most wanton and outrageous aggressions on our commerce, having demanded, and in every honorable way sought redress, without the most distant prospect of obtaining it, we have been compelled to resort to arms.

"In a war so just, for the protection of rights so essential, after the endurance of insults so aggravated and encroachments so intolerable, was it to be expected that a murmur would escape on account of the war? Could we entertain a suspicion that there were those who would refuse their aid in prosecuting the war. Is it possible that it has entered into the hearts of the most desperate and wicked to raise the standard of rebellion, and kindle the flames of a civil war, rather than contend for the preservation of those rights and liberties which were purchased by the best blood of our fathers.

"It is with mortification and regret, that this convention perceives that there is a desperate and malignant faction, among us, organized to embarrass the government in prosecuting the war, to aid and encourage the enemy and affect a separation of the Northern from the other states. Within the memory of many of us, the British nation was destroying our property, burning our cities, barbarously butchering our wives and children, and attempting to fix the badge of slavery upon us and our posterity. Now we find among us her advocates from the pulpit, the bar and the bench, applauding her candor and magnanimity, extolling her power, palliating her aggressions and justifying her for the wounds she is inflicting on our country. It is with that indignation which the love of country should always inspire that we perceive that the sacred desk has in many instances been prostituted to base and treasonable purposes. When men so respectable and influential as the clergy pervert their sacred office, and in time of war endeavor to persuade men to acts of opposition and rebellion, it becomes us to watch with unusual solicitude over our rights and withdraw all countenance and support from men who have proved themselves unworthy of their office. At this time it is particularly essential that you be watchful over your liberties. Most of the heroes of the revolution have paid the debt of nature, and after having devoted their lives to the service of their country have gone, we trust, to a happier world. Your Washington is not with you to animate you by his example or instruct you by his precepts. Already are his predictions beginning to be realized. Already you have the testimony of a respectable, honorable and honest federalist that a State convention is summoned for the purpose of taking into consideration the expediency of dissolving the Union. The storm of civil discord is gathering; the thunder roars at a distance; the lightning gleams on the dim mantle of night. Prepare to meet, to resist its fury.

"How do you relish the expressions of joy which you hear at a little British success? What do you think of the man who rejoices at the misfortunes of his country? It is not three years since the federalists were complaining that the government were destitute of energy. The embargo and non intercourse were submissive. We were the tamest people on earth, and *could not be kicked into a war*.[2] How the time is changed. Nothing is, or can be so horrible as war. We are now to be destroyed by the energy of government. When Mr. Madison made an arrangement with Erskine, the federal party said this ought to have been done long before; and that it was what Great Britain had always been willing to do. When England refused to ratify this arrangement, this party blamed Mr. Madison for concluding it at all. The federalists affect to deprecate a treaty with France as the prospect of effecting one increases, and to wish it, as the prospect diminishes.

"The republicans do not fell [*sic*] indifferent to the wrongs and insults which we have received from France. They are satisfied that unless atonement is made, war ought, and must ensue. But the aggressions of one nation are no palliation for those of another. And with what consistency can the professed friends of peace urge a war with both nations at once? Has not the constitutional authority of the United States a right to select one of two enemies, each of which has given us ample cause of war.

"We love peace; we deprecate war. But we apprehend that a peace purchased by the surrender of our essential rights, would render us contemptible in the eyes of the world, and invite aggression rather than prevent it.

"What then is to satisfy the opposers of government? Power! Power! under the auspices and guarantee of Britain! For this they would barter the dearest rights of the country. For this they would wade thro' blood. It is for this they justify the enemy, condemn their own government, and rejoice at the success of England and the misfortunes of America. It is for this the governor has been induced to refuse the militia. It is for this that such high handed measures are intimated to be in contemplation as chill the blood with horror. Despairing of governing the whole, this party would sever the Union that they may govern a part.

"Are you prepared, fellow citizens, to cut the chord which binds us together, and reunite us with Britain? Are your Southern brethren, who fought by your sides and shared with you in the distresses and glory of the revolution, to be abandoned for the vain and dazzling splendors of royalty? Will you raise your hands against your brethren and involve your country in all the horrors of a civil war, merely because certain gentlemen want power? No, fellow citizens, the fire of patriotism must kindle in your bosom. You will indignantly frown at and manfully resist, every attempt to weaken that Union from which you have derived so much prosperity and happiness. What boon are we to obtain by a dismemberment of the Union? After brother has bathed his hand in a brother's blood; after parents shall have sacrificed their children, and children shall have risen up against their parents and caused them to be put to death; after cities are involved in flames, monuments of national grandeur tumbled into ruin and the temples of the most high prostrated in the dust; what new privilege will have been secured, what violated right preserved, what better government established? Weak and unable to protect ourselves, we should be compelled to call to our aid some foreign nation, and surrender our liberties as the price of our protection.

"Let us remember that for thirty years we have enjoyed the rich fruits of our glorious revolution; that our rulers are chosen by, and responsible to, us; that we are not taxed without our consent, that, under the administration of intelligent judges and impartial jurors, our lives, liberties and properties are secured to us by wholesome laws; that our worship is free, and our religion requires no human 'bulwark' to defend it. Let us unite to detect, suppress and resist plots, conspiracies, rebellion and treason, and to defend the honor and glory of the American name, remembering that a vigorous prosecution of the war is the only way to affect a speedy, safe and honorable peace. And looking to the God of armies for his divine protection, we have good reason to hope and believe that he who has so often made bare his arm for our salvation, will lead the United States to victory, glory and happiness. . . .

"The United States are engaged in war for the vindication of their rights upon the ocean. These rights must be maintained or our Independence must be surrendered. Every thing valuable to men in this world is now at stake. Our fate as a nation and as individuals, is to be decided by force of arms. At this awful moment, public spirit should nerve every arm, and love of country swell every bosom. The sublime spectacle of a whole people, regardless of private animosities, rising as one man to save their country, should now be presented to the world. With what disgust and horror, then, must we witness and record, at a moment so portentous, the degrading triumphs of foreign influence; the extended combinations of domestic treason? No sooner is war declared, than proclamation of universal disaffection is made; the country is inundated with seditious, inflammatory publications; high public functionaries side against their country and enlist under the banners of faction; civil war is threatened with all its horrors; our national and state Constitutions are menaced with prostration; a project to dissolve the Union is unblushingly announced; while a disastrous war, a disgraceful peace, are to be among the results of these nefarious machinations; and the elevation of a party into power, hostile to the liberties of the people, who are to rule over the whole or part of the United States, according to circumstances, is to be the glorious consummation of all.

"In such a state of things what remains to be done? Shall an immense majority of the people be silent and suffer the clamors of faction to pass for the unanimous expression of public opinion? While the air is rent with the venal outcries of foreign agents and the frantic ravings of domestic conspirators, against the measures of Government, shall not the voice of reason and patriotism be heard in their favor? That our rulers may be able to place a just and certain reliance on the energy and public spirit of their constituents; that mutual confidence, among the American people, may be universal; the patriotic stand which each section of the Union means now to take, ought to be publicly and solemnly proclaimed.

"Therefore; Resolved, By this Convention, that in this hour of peril, it is the duty of all descriptions of faithful citizens to fly to the standard of their country.

"Resolved, That the war in which we are engaged is, on the part of this country, sacredly just—that it has been absolutely forced upon the nation, that the only way to obtain a safe and honorable peace is to prosecute it with that determined spirit, that patriotic unanimity, that resistless energy which belong to an high minded and powerful people, who, for the maintenance of their rights, have appealed to arms.

"Resolved, That Great Britain, since the American revolution, has never ceased to regard this country with a jaundiced eye; that the achievement of our independence, our commercial prosperity, our republican government, have excited in her rulers, towards us, a deep and deadly hatred; that she has never ceased to cherish the proud hope of our final subjugation to her views of universal maritime domination.

"Resolved, That the English government is at this moment unquestionably making large calculations on our divisions; that she has been led, as appears by official documents, to count assuredly upon a powerful British party among us, who would be able to prevent the sword of this country from being drawn against her, however enormous might be her outrages upon our rights and honor. 'If contrary to all calculation our rulers should be found to possess sufficient energy to resolve on war,'[3] this party was, at once, to compel them to throw away the sword and submit to Great Britain.

"Resolved, That it is now the settled plan of our incensed, relentless, implacable foe, by means of her trade, her emissaries, her agents, her spies and incendiaries; by bribery and corruption; by arraying one half our citizens against the other in a contest for supremacy; by the hopes which the chances of war hold out to faction; at length by open civil discord, to convulse this country to its center, to drench this land in blood, and finally by a dissolution of our union; or by the exaltation of her party into power, by the destruction of our republican institutions, or in either case, by an humiliating, disgraceful peace, effectually to break down the spirit of this people, and ultimately to render this nation the mere instrument of her greatness, the mere appendage of her extended empire.

"Resolved, That it is a fact too plain to be disputed, and which must forever disgrace the page of our history, a fact not to be paralleled except in barbarous ages, or among the most corrupt nations, that these ruthless schemes of conquest and ruin, these diabolical measures to sink the name of our republic, and lay our country low in the dust, are in fatal consent with the conduct of a large portion of our own citizens, who lend themselves to the views of the common enemy, who, having objects of their own which cannot be accomplished without foreign aid, or in a time of national disaster, flatter themselves that the period has now arrived which is to crown their proudest hopes. These political criminals, these traitors to their country, have long formed a combination so powerful; whose devotion to England, whose hostility to their own country, have been so well known in Europe as well as America, that the British Government sent to these men, as we all know, a secret but solemn embassy to form an alliance for the accomplishment of the most horrible purposes. Circumstances put a stop to this negotiation. Late appearances indicate that, in some form or other, it may have since been fully consummated.

"Resolved, That a British party has undeniably existed in this country since the days of the Revolution. This party received a powerful accession by the return of the refugees after the war. No sooner were the tories strangely taken into public favor than this party aspired to power. Strong now by their activity, their wealth and talents, having seduced from the love of liberty many distinguished individuals, having attained to places of high public confidence, an occurrence took place which seemed to establish their fortunes, beyond the reach of accident. The excesses, the fatal termination of the French Revolution had excited universal disgust and horror. It had the effect to produce a surprising influence upon political sentiments in this country. The unpopularity of republican principles soon became apparent. Monarchical and aristocratical opinions, it was evident, daily gained ground. Our own revolution itself became unpopular. To believe that there could be no such thing as a government of the people, and that a limited monarchy, under some name or other, was the best form of civil polity, became the order of the day. The pulpit, the rostrum, the press, resounded the doctrine. Colleges and Academies lent their aid. A large party was soon formed on this ground. Loathing the name of Frenchmen, they soon learnt to adore their enemies, the English. Our former oppressors were suddenly converted into the chosen people of God. England became 'the bulwark of our religion,' the battles which she fought were for the liberties of the world. The leaders of the old British faction had the address to place themselves at the head of this party and to amalgamate it with their own. The clergy had been artfully secured. They were invited to associate piety with all the talents and wealth of the country. And the cloak of religion was borrowed for the whole concern. These parties thus consolidated, thus arrayed, thus directed, became irresistible, bore down all opposition and ere long obtained a decided ascendancy in our public councils.[4] American principles, however, soon had their turn to reign. This great party, which had chosen to term itself federal, and which had entangled in its toils many of our best citizens, now declined Faster than it arose. Driven from the public councils; continually sinking in reputation and in numbers; gradually deserted by all who would not sacrifice their country on the alter of faction; having lost all hope of power but by revolutions, public convulsions, or national disasters; burnt up with ambition, devoured by chagrin; the remains of this party, thus exalted, thus formed, thus fallen, is now dwindled and reduced to a disappointed, remorseless faction, whose bitterness exceeds the bitterness of gall and wormwood; whose venom the poison of the Upas or the Asp. But for the efforts of this faction, the embargo would have saved the country. Great Britain would have receded from her lawless usurpations. And long before this the sunshine of former prosperity would have burst upon us. Unable to prevent a declaration of war, this faction are resolved it shall end disastrously. The good people of America are then to discover that they have no friends but those great politicians who shall have had the magnanimity and patriotism to sell their country to England.

"This faction now plots state confederacies; rebellions backed by state authorities; revolutions and new Governments; and the members of this faction are to lend their aid, if necessary, to guide the destinies of these new empires.

"Resolved, That we can consider the project of a State Convention at Boston;[5] of a convention of States at Hartford;[6] the refusal of the governor of this Commonwealth; as well as of Rhode Island and Connecticut to afford to government the aid of the Militia; the bold proceedings of State Legislatures; The alarming project of state armies, only as so many fearful omens that desperate measures are in serious contemplation; a state of things in which the general government is to be resisted by the sword; when this country is to present a scene of universal desolation, and this land is to be converted into a field of blood.

"Resolved, That it is with profound regret we observe ministers of religion suffering themselves to be dragged into these murderous projects. All men are liable to become fanatical, some are so by constitution. We would regard with tenderness and candor the aberrations of our most useful class of citizens. But when we see pretended heralds of the mild and beneficent gospel of Jesus Christ, throwing off all regard to common decency, outrageously insulting the majesty of the public, sanctioning by their discourses the vilest defamations, proclaiming from the desk the most palpable untruths, exciting among their fellow citizens, bitterness, rancor and hatred; endeavoring to quench every spark of patriotism, and put a stop to the first risings of public spirit, stirring up insurrection, rebellion and civil war, we can view them only in the light of public incendiaries, the decided adversaries of their country, the open auxiliaries of the common enemy, and men who have forfeited all claim to public respect and public support.

"Resolved, That we regard with high approbation the conduct of many distinguished individuals of the opposition, (among whom we notice with great pleasure an eminent citizen of this state,) who on this terrific occasion, have seceded from their former friends, denounced their horrible projects, and joyfully restored themselves to the favor of their country.

"Resolved, That a tribute of national applause is due to the Hon. Joseph B. Varnum, William Widgery,[7] Ebenr. Seaver,[8] Charles Turner and Francis Carr,[9] Esquires, for their independence and patriotism in voting for a declaration of war. We regard the abuse and insults which they have received as outrages upon the whole community; and instead of proceeding from ebullitions of public resentment, as the mere artificial contrivances of a few unprincipled actors behind the scenes, to render the war unpopular and odious.

"Resolved, That should any overt attempt be actually made, as has been repeatedly intimated, to break down the Constitution of this state, and to drive from their seats the patriotic Senate of this Commonwealth because they cannot be bent to the views of faction, we shall feel it our duty immediately to fly to arms! Let those who prepare to execute this project, weigh the matter well. Its perpetration will be resisted by a physical force which they will be unable to meet. They must abide the consequences!

"Resolved, That at this day of danger and alarm, it is rather a time for actions than for professions; that exposed as we are to external, and menaced as we are by internal foes, it is our sacred duty to be prepared for all emergencies; and as the Governor has refused to call out the militia when demanded by the President agreeably to the Constitution; as we have an extensive frontier by sea and land exposed to the enemy; as desperate measures seem to be resolved on by faction; it is therefore hereby recommended to all the friends of our rights and liberties, resident in this county, whether exempted from military duty or not, forthwith to arm and equip themselves for military service, in those cases where it has not been already done, and hold themselves in readiness to act at a moments warning. And it is further recommended that each Town form one or more companies, as aforesaid, appoint their officers and tender their services to Government to support the laws, suppress insurrections and repel invasions!

"Resolved, That the capture of our North Western Army, so far from operating as a disheartening occurrence, will, we trust, produce an universal conviction that the war in which we are engaged must be vigorously prosecuted; that public spirit must be effectually addressed; something like adequate compensation be allowed the brave men who are to fight our battles, and the sleeping energies of our country be called into immediate action.

"Resolved, That we principally rejoice in the brilliant victory lately achieved by the skill and courage of our brave seamen under the conduct of their gallant and able commander, under the sanguine hope that greater dependence will in future be placed on a naval force; and that while no time is lost in pushing on the war by land, the conviction will soon be universal, that the battles for commerce must be fought upon the ocean.

"Resolved, That we have the firmest confidence that the earliest opportunity will be embraced by government to procure a safe and honorable peace. When war could not be avoided with safety or honor, our rulers declared it at the risk of their popularity. They have every inducement to make peace which can influence men. But would the leaders of the British party rejoice at this event? Would they hail an immediate satisfactory settlement of all our difficulties with foreign nations? Would they delight to see the country basking in the sunshine of former prosperity. That an immense majority of the party opposed to the war would, we have not the smallest doubt. Not so with their leaders! Ambitious, unprincipled, they can see no way to greatness, but in their country's ruin. They leave nothing undone which can imbarrass the government and prolong the war. Every patriotic statesman, every advocate of the rights, interests and honor of his country, is mercilessly hunted down. They rend the air with their ceaseless clamors; they load every breeze with the poisonous exhalations of their defaming breath. Is all this to induce Great Britain to sue for peace, upon just and honorable terms? We know the contrary. An immediate return of prosperous times would be regarded by the leaders of the British faction as the greatest misfortune. It would be the destruction of their influence; the ruin of their projects; the death blow of their fondest hopes.

"Resolved, That the deprivations and public burdens, incident to a state of war, will be cheerfully borne by the republican citizens of the county of York. Their patriotism is not to be quenched by the pressure of public calamities. The republican citizens of this county, will stand by their country to the last cent of their property and to the last drop of their blood.

"Resolved, That we need only to be seriously engaged in this conflict, and victory will crown our arms. The nation need only be roused, to carry on the war triumphantly. We have only to employ the means which heaven has put into our hands to obtain a speedy, a solid and a lasting peace."

RC (DLC). 19 pp.; signed by Alexander Rice, president, and Daniel Wood, secretary. Enclosed in Stephen Thasher to JM, 20 Sept. 1812 (ibid.; 2 pp.), in which Thasher declared that "The character which the opposition has assumed, especially in this Commonwealth, seems to render such expressions of public opinion indispensable." Published in the *Boston Patriot* on 19 Sept. 1812. Filed after 31 Dec. 1812.

1. For John Henry, see *PJM-PS*, 4:117 n. 2.
2. See Thomas Shepherd to JM, 24 July 1812, n. 3.
3. The memorialists placed an asterisk here and added at the foot of the page, "See Henry's correspondence." John Henry used words to this effect in his dispatches to James Craig of 7 Mar. and 13 Apr. 1809 (*ASP, Foreign Relations*, 3:549, 551).
4. The memorialists placed an asterisk here and added at the foot of the page: "In vain did President Adams attempt to balance this faction, and restrain it within any bounds. Because he would not sacrifice the country to its views, he himself was to be privately sacrificed. Mr. Adams was not among the last to discover that he was not designed, in reality, for the next Presidency. And he magnanimously gloried in the elevation of Mr. Jefferson to the chair, because, altho' a rival candidate, his election effectually overthrew the tory anti-gallico-anglo faction, and secured the triumph of American principles."

5. The memorialists probably referred to the Boston town meeting of 6 Aug. 1812, which called for a state convention. Though several other town and county meetings also supported such a measure, it never came to fruition (Boston *Columbian Centinel*, 8 Aug. 1812; Morison, *Life and Letters of Harrison Gray Otis*, 2:60–61).

6. Anticipating the Hartford Convention of 1814, some New England Federalists, notably Noah Webster and Thomas Dawes, agitated unsuccessfully for a convention of New England states in the summer of 1812 (Banner, *To the Hartford Convention*, 308–9).

7. William Widgery (ca. 1753–1822) of Portland, District of Maine, served in the Massachusetts House of Representatives from 1787 to 1793 and from 1795 to 1797. He represented Massachusetts in the Twelfth Congress and concluded his career in public life by serving as a judge of the court of common pleas from 1813 to 1821.

8. Ebenezer Seaver (1763–1844) served in the Massachusetts House of Representatives from 1794 to 1802 and was a representative to the Eighth through Twelfth Congresses.

9. Francis Carr (1751–1821) was elected to the Massachusetts state legislature for eleven years between 1791 and 1808, served in the state senate from 1809 to 1811, and was elected to the Twelfth Congress to replace Barzillai Gannett.

To William Eustis

Dear Sir   Montpellier Sep. 11. 1812

Yours of the 8th. has but just come to hand. I return the letters from Genl. D. I shall set out tomorrow morning for Washington & proceed by way of Fredg. expecting to reach Washington on Monday. Meantime will you resolve the arrangement recommended with respect to Connecticut Volunteers? Friendly respects

James Madison

RC (PHi: Daniel Parker Papers).

§ From Matthew Walton. *11 September 1812*, *"Prince Edwd."* Expresses his opinion that William Hull's name should be "wiped off the records Except so far as to shew his Cawardese." Believes that Hull would have surrendered even if given more troops, but "less than 15000 Men aught not to invade upper Cannedy & not less than 25 or 30 aught to invade Lower Kannedy & those men aught be well supplied with every thing necessary." "A line of Forts aught to be established from the Fronteer of Ohio to the Settlemts. in the Michigan Territory Say about 15 or 20 miles a part Made strong & about 2 or 3 Hundred Men left at Each fort, these Forts will be a Safe Deposit for Supplies of every Description, they can be built by the army as they March on. Call the men out there is enough to do all this, prompt measures are the best more especially at the Commencement of a war." Suggests that mounted infantry is the most effective defense in the event of an Indian war, as has been shown by previous experience. "Please to observe the Difference you Send an army of foot in the Indian Country they will Play before you till they find advantage & they will attact always to their advantage if at all but if they find the forse superior & no advantage they will not attack, but on the Contrary send an army of Mounted Riflemen in their Country if they finds there is a party of indians two Strong for them they Can canter off & leave them & go to another plase where they will find a Smaler party & by that means leave the whole Country & Leave them to terms in two or three Campains this Certainly was the case before & I have no doubt woud be the case again to have foot enough to establish forts or a part foot woud not be a miss so that they woud never leave the forts far, the above is my thoughts on this subject you can view them as you think right." Reminds JM that he has recommended Richard Cocke for an Upper Louisiana judgeship left vacant by the death of Judge Shraider[1] and Robert Crouch for a cavalry appointment.[2]

RC (DNA: RG 107, LRRS, W-316:6). 5 pp.; docketed as received in the War Department on 21 Sept. 1812.

1. See Walton to JM, 9 Aug. 1812, and n. 1.
2. Letter not found.

From William Keteltas

SIR   NEW YORK 12 Septm. 1812

I solicited some time past when the State of the Country assumed the aspect of War, a Colo.s Commission of Cavalry;[1] not for Myself, but for My Country. The applicatn was Made from a sense of duty, not from pride and ostentation to Strut about in Regimentals.

That a Man of principle should desire an Office, *Civil*, or *Military* When so Much dishoner and injustice Mark the footsteps of two Characters in particular which I predicted would be the Case, when appointed is not a little extraordinary.

Genl Hulls private Character as informed years past, was as black as stains, could Make it. He has acted himself out, and is a Traitor, or a Coward their is not a doubt, or Shadow of doubt. As a general rule, a man not honest in private life, ought never to be trusted by the goverment. In a word, a Man Morally bad, Cannot be politically Good, so Much for the Conduct of Gnl. Hull.

The next is an appointment in the Civil department, of Judge Talmadge, the name only applying to the *man*, and that only, Never was the Majesty of the people treated with such Indifference, the administration of *Justice*, so trampled upon the Country so degraded; when these Creatures were appointed to those important trusts. The Judge deficient in Capacity. The General a depraved *Traitor* in My opinion; To place him in the most favourable light. A *Coward*.

Many other appointments thro. the Union under the General and State govts. are no better, I will not Venture to Censure the executive for appointments made on the recommendations of others Whose policy it was to deceive him, except he knew they Who recomended the Candidate; were opposed to the Administratn in such Case the president is answerable.

The appointments under the present Administration of this State govt Cannot be excelled in political wickedness. Reverse the Rule, laid down by Mr. Jefferson, in his Inaugural Speech, but never practised and the deformaty appears. It is not the Question is the Candidate *Capable honest* and *faithfull* to the Constitution.[2] But is he weak that we can deceive him, is he unprincipled that we can Corrupt him, will he obeay his Masters will, regardless of the will of the p[e]ople, if so, he shall have an office.

Sir

The unclean hands, and impure hearts Who by intriegue obtained the power in this state and abused it bars Men of principle from accepting any office wether Civil or Military in this State.

If this is the Case as I have Stated; which I aver to be the fact, What but Love of Country, and a Sense of duty can induce a Man of honor to accept a Commission in the Army so well acquainted with the political depravity of the day and be obliged to assosiate with knaves and fools.

Sir

You must percieve by this time, that I speak really like one of the *Sovereign People*. A term politicians Sounded in the Ears of the people as sound only; being one of the Sovereigns and Connected with the Millions, I am for supporting the reality of the Sovereign people, and not that of the Indiv[i]du⟨al⟩ for their is nothing I detest More than the hypocritical sound of the human Voice.

Sir

It is not the *tinsel* of a Commission, which induces me to aske for One. No *Sir* I want to do my duty to my Country in her second Glorious Struggle, and to be *Commissioned* to do it, in such a Manner to be Serviceable to her and honorable to My Self. (I know myself) and set too high a Value on *Virtue* and *patriotizm* to have it sported with or to be neglected for a moment as applicable to myself.

To Enter the army, is against My private interest, having Considered interest and made it the servant of principle thus far in life shall not give up this Just distinction.

The object of this letter is to obtain the presidents refusal to Comply with My request; as an apology for not being in the Army in Support of this Just and holy war waged by the Administration against England, in defence of all that is dear to america in particular, and the world in general. *How Low, How degraded, how Sunk*, are My Countrymen in this city *in degeneracy;* when such a glorious action of Captn Hull's could not obtain a Celebration by any of the political societies in this City. *Societies the ofspring* of which have for their object self agrandizment to obtain which; loose sight of their Country, the *Curse* and cause of all the ⟨injuries?⟩ & disgrace of America, these Very Societies.

To belong to any of them I think is little short of treason against the republic; these Societies are neither More or less, than organized factions in our free and happy Country; Establish'd by some designing knave or knaves to aid his or their ambitious Views.

Was it not from a recollection and participation in the struggle and Sacrifice of our Sages and Heroes to Establish our Independance, as a nation, I might have fallen like others into indifference, what our patriots and heroes May now do, to support that Independance. I have the Honor to Enclose to the president the toasts Drank by a few Gentleman I assembled distinct from party in honor to *Captn Hull*,[3] determined that the *sun* should not set upon the Most Glorious Event, which could grace the Heroes brow; and in its consequences to his Country all important.

WM. KETELTAS

RC and enclosure (DNA: RG 107, LRRS, K-46:6). RC docketed as received in the War Department on 16 Sept. 1812. For enclosure, see n. 3.

1. Letter not found.

2. Keteltas confused the contents of Jefferson's first inaugural with the last line of his 12 July 1801 response to a committee of New Haven merchants who had protested the appointment of Samuel Bishop to the office of collector. On the latter occasion Jefferson declared that in his administration "the only questions concerning a candidate shall be, is he honest? Is he capable? Is he faithful to the Constitution?" (Ford, *Writings of Jefferson*, 8:70).

3. The enclosure is a newspaper clipping describing nine toasts given in honor of Capt. Isaac Hull during a private party at Tammany Hall.

From James Monroe

DEAR SIR   WASHINGTON Sepr 12. 1812

Finding by your letter recd yesterday that you would set out on that or this day, & probably be here to morrow, I resolved to await your arrival, & make a visit in the mean time to Loudoun, rather than take Loudoun in my route to Albemarle. I shall be back to morrow. 6. 24 pounders, 10. 18s. 10. 12s. 6. 6s. & 4. 8 Inch Howitzrs. are orderd to fort Pitt. They are necessary to batter & take Detroit & Malden, and altho, they may not be got there this season, they will be ready for the Spring; Tho' in my opinion, with the suitable effort, they may be carried there with ease, by the latter end of next month. Genl. Mason has undertaken to set them off, with the aid of Col. Burbeck, and they will be in motion immediately.

The gentlemen from Ohio will wait your arrival. Having been conferrd with on the subject by Mr Eustis, they urge my undertaking the business;

and every thing may be put in train, the day after you get here. I leave it however, without any personal feeling, entirely to your desire, for nothing in this world would induce me to undertake it & leave my family, but a confident hope, on my part, & a deep conviction on yours & other friends, that some advantage might result from it.

Mr Eustis recd. a letter yesterday from Winchester,[1] which gave him reason to infer that he would yeild the command to Harrison. This is something, if the fact be so. You will judge whether it comprize all the advantages that might be expected from the contemplated measures.

I proposed to fill the army with all the unemployed regular officers, in the character of adjutants, inspectors &c to train the army; & had thoughts of taking Genl. Carbery with me, as adjutant genl., or Inspector, of appointing Captn. Ball Col. of volunteer horse, & sending him to the Govr. of Virga. to move a regt. Every thing however, remains suspended till you arrive, and reflect further on the subject. Sincerely & respectfully your friend

                                                        JAS MONROE

P S. I have this moment recd. yours of the 10th, & shall send this to meet you at Fredricksbg.

Col: Cass has made a report to the secretary at war of the causes producing the surrender of the army under Hull, which he wishes may be forthwith publishd,[2] & all of us here think that it ought to be, especially, as the other Cols. &, he says, the whole army would concur in it, and the more so as Genl Hull, has not yet renderd any acct whatever. The nation expects an acct of the transaction

RC (DLC: Rives Collection, Madison Papers). Docketed by JM.

1. A 2 Sept. 1812 letter from Winchester (not found), listed in the Registers of Letters Received by the Secretary of War as received on 11 Sept., stated that a letter to the adjutant general (not found) "will explain why he has not joined the Army" (DNA: RG 107).

2. The account of the fall of Detroit written by Lewis Cass on 10 Sept. (see Monroe to JM, 10 Sept. 1812, n. 1) was published in the *National Intelligencer* on 15 Sept. 1812.

From Francis Corbin

THE REEDS. Sepr. 13th. 1812
DEAR SIR   NEAR WH: CH: PO: OFF CAROLINE COUNTY

I did myself the Honor to write to you some time ago,[1] and inclosed my letter to Mr. Monroe, for reasons, which, at that conjuncture, will be obvious to you. As I have never been favored with any Answer, I am inclined to suppose, either that the letter was never received, or, if received, that the weight of business then upon your Shoulders prevented you from replying to it. I embrace this latter Supposition, as the most respectful to Mr. Monroe, and the most grateful to my own feelings.

The Policy of the Fedl. Govt. having been different from what I then imagined it would be, I avail myself of an opportunity by a private hand (Mr. Thos. Grymes of your County) to state to you the *particular* reason that induced me to write that letter to you. My anxiety to preserve, with all Nations, the peace of our Infant Country, in whose welfare I am more deeply interested than most people, by a numerous offspring, my sincere personal Esteem for yourself, and my wish to see your administration popular and Successful, were my *general* Reasons. But my *Particular* Reason was this. I had just then received a Confidential letter from an old English Friend, of no small Consideration in the Politics of that Country, in which, amongst other things, he said—"I think if you would send a Minister here, and be as Studious, in your choice of one, to please the Prince Regent, as you have been in the choice of Mr. Barlow to please Buonoparte, your mission would be successful." Upon this Hint, without waiting to weigh, by grains, the propriety or impropriety of addressing you, I wrote instanter. I wrote then, as I do now, in a profound personal and private Confidence. Both these letters, however, you will be pleased, under existing circumstances, to consider as never having been written, except so far as they go to assure you of my Prayers for a Success and popularity in your Administration equal to my firm conviction of the purity of your Patriotism and motives, and to the Regard with which I am very Sincerely Dear Sir, Your mo: Obt. St.

FRANCIS CORBIN

RC (DLC). Addressed to JM at Montpelier. Docketed by JM.

1. Corbin to JM, 6 Apr. 1812, *PJM-PS*, 4:297–98.

From Samuel Harrison

DEAR AND RESPECTED SIR,   CHITTENDEN September 14th. 1812

The News of the Declaration of War occasioned me to throw by the Letters I had Written to your Excellency on the 11th. to the 24th. of June last, that I did not send them.

The recent Capture of Genl Hull, his Army, Cannon and Military Stores &c. &c. have redetermined me to send them to your Excellency.[1]

I am confident If they had, *then*, been sent, and your Excellency *had paid attention to their Contents, The disgrace of our Country, and the Capture of General Hull would not have occurred.*

I find the same *imbecility in the arrangments under Genl. Dearborne. He will, as certainly, be captured, as Genl. Hull is Captured.*

If a New Leaf is not turned Over.

Excuse, Dear Sir, my Plain dealing. When at Washington in 1806 I had a *Dispensation* granted to me, to use my own *Rules of Etiquette.* The Honour of our Country calls loud for *Peace.* The Interests, the permanent Interests of Both America and Great Britain call for *Peace.* The People The common People of both Countries call for *Peace.* None are hearty in the War, and unless You *hear to the calls of Peace,* The War will terminate dishonorably— it will end in disgrace and will cause Posterity to Curse your Memory—Yes Sir, Your *memory will be Cursed to the latest Generation.* Unless You turn about, before it is too late, *Now is an accepted time now is a Day for our Country's Salvation . . [.] before more blood is Shed . . .*

I still repeat the offer, I made to Your Excellency on the 18th. and 24th. of June, although the Postscript of the 24th. was the Effusions of the Moment. I send it without comment, or Apology.

Read, Sir, those Papers candidly: tho' written in a hurry they *contain Facts. Facts necessary to be known.*

Let my Dear Friend *Genl. Granger read them.* Let Mr Monroe read them. Although I never had any personal acquaintance with the latter the present Secretary of State; I am informed by many, and particularly by the Revd. S. Peters L.L.D who knew him in London, that he is a Candid, honest—humane, real Gentleman. Please to shew them my letter of the 11th of May.[2] I have been informed you have received it, tho' you have not answered it or paid attention to its Contents. I beg of you together with the other Gentlemen to dispense with Etiquette, read my Letters together, not to Criticise on them, but to weigh the reasons, and let your superior Understandings carry you far beyond the Writer. And please to let me hear the result of your deliberations. If you do not comply with my desires pray send me the Papers back; that I may publish them to the World that my Garments may be clean from the *Blood* and *Treasures* and Welfare of my Country sacrificed to the Moloch of inexperience if not of inconsideration. With sentiments of the highest esteem and respect I remain Your most Obedient Servant

SAML HARRISON

P. S. I have just seen a Gentleman directly from Montreal who on Monday last Saw Genl Hull and his Son on the Parade amongst some British Officers in that City.[3]

S H

RC (DNA: RG 59, ML).

1. Harrison's letters to JM of 11, 18, and 24 June have not been found.
2. *PJM-PS*, 4:374–77.
3. Sir George Prevost released Hull from Montreal on 9 Sept. 1812 on the condition that he would avoid military service in "any capacity whatever, untill regularly exchanged." Hull returned to the U.S., passing through Dearborn's Albany camp en route to Newton, Massachusetts, where he awaited further instructions from the government (Hull to Eustis, 19 Oct. 1812, *Michigan Historical Collections* 40 [1929]: 494; Dearborn to Eustis, 14 Sept. 1812 [DNA: RG 107, LRRS, D-168:6]).

To William C. C. Claiborne

DEAR SIR   [ca. 15 September 1812]

I have reecived [*sic*] your favor of the 2 Ulto. and very sincerely congratulate you on the high proof given you of the Confidence & affection of your fellow Citizens of Louisiana. The event is important in several political views, as well as gratifying to your personal friends. To myself it is a source of unfeigned pleasure.

I say nothing on public affairs: because I could say nothing which will not reach you with more certainty, & probably in less time than this letter, through printed vihitcles [*sic*]. Accept my sincere esteem & friendly regards.

                               Signed   JAMES MADISON

Printed copy (Rowland, *Claiborne Letter Books*, 6:191–92). Undated; date assigned here on the assumption that Claiborne's 2 Aug. 1812 letter arrived in Washington approximately a month after it was sent. At that time JM was at Montpelier and probably did not answer the letter until after his return on 14 Sept. JM's letter was entered into Claiborne's letterbook between 13 and 16 Oct., suggesting that it was sent from Washington approximately a month before.

From Pierce Butler

SIR   PHILADA. September 15: 1812

It is with reluctance I again intrude on You. By a letter I this day recd from the Island of Great St Simons in the State of Georgia, I learn that Your kind intention of affording protection to that Island has not been carried into execution[1]—allow me to give you an extract from the letter, by which You may form an opinion—"I will first inform You respecting the Gun-boats and Barges—The kind and feeling attention of the President, which You inform'd Us of, reliev'd the feelings of all the Settlers on the Island; but they are again depressd, as no protection has come to the Island. About three weeks past, information came from Savannah, that there were four Barges on their way from the Northward to St Simons; for the protection of this Island; one of them came as far as Doboy, and return'd. It has since been reported, that the Barges are at Sunsbury in Liberty County. About one week past, two Gun-boats came to this County; one is station'd at St Simons sound; the other is gone up Turtle River; one of the Gun Boats ought to be Station'd at the North end, say Long Island inlet, for the protection of Great St Simons; and for the protection of the Altamaha River, and the Settlers thereon—One Gun boat at the South end of Great St. Simons; the Barges used in rowing between, woud afford ample security—In Our Judgement there has been some foul-play, as regards the Barges, or they would not have been station'd at Sunbury. Even if these Six Barges were intended to move from place, to place, as a look out for the whole Sea-Coast of Georgia, St Simons is assuredly the proper place for head quarters—If Sunsbury is a place of so much consequence, why erect the Light House on St Simons!"

The Interest I have myself in common with many respectable Residents on the Island of St. Simons, will plead my apology for this intrusion. I am respectfully Sir Your most obedient

P. BUTLER[2]

RC (DLC). Docketed by JM.

1. On 4 July 1812 the inhabitants of St. Simons Island addressed JM to express their concern that the island was vulnerable to attack and to request protection (*PJM-PS*, 4:557–58). No response from JM or Eustis to either Butler or the inhabitants of St. Simons has been found.

2. Pierce Butler (1744–1822) of South Carolina had been a member of the Continental Congress in 1787 and 1788, the Federal Convention of 1787, and the U.S. Senate from 1789 to 1796 and from 1802 to 1804.

From Eli Simpson Davis

SIR,   ABBEVILLE, SO. CAROLINA, Sepr. 15th. 1812

In obedience to a resolution to that effect, I have herewith forwarded the proceedings of the people of this district, and village.[1]

Their transmission has been procrastinated in consequence of your departure from Washington having been announced. Your Excellency will excuse the crude, but sincere effusions of our minds developed in those proceedings; they are the legitimate expression of our souls. The people here, view with becoming feeling and anxiety the procellosity[2] of the North, and should they not have the pleasure of participating personally in the pending conflict, their first prayers accompany the brave patriots to whom providence has assigned the glorious task of redressing the wrongs of an injured country. The defeat of Gen. Hull I am apprehensive may encourage our red neighbours to become troublesome; as yet however, they are held in perfect contempt as to their formidableness. Accept individually, the respect and regard, with which, I am &c.

ELI SIMPSON DAVIS.

RC (DLC).

1. Enclosure not found.
2. *Procellous:* stormy (*OED,* 2d ed.).

§ From the Delegates of Hillsborough County, New Hampshire. *15 September 1812.* "One hundred and eighty nine Delegates from all the Towns in the County of Hillsborough and State of New Hampshire have convened at Weare. They are attended by more than fifteen hundred of their constituents. Among us are many, as their signatures will show, who are proud to have participated in our Revolution; and also to behold as their associates in this Convention the flower of our Yeomanry our Mechanics and Manufacturers. Such numbers and character will perhaps justify us in addressing the Chief Magistrate of our Union, and without presumption expecting from him a regard to the sentiments we may express as emanating, at least from an honest and respectable source. The citizens of this County, Sir have in common with their countrymen suffered long from aggressions of the European Belligerents. And though their pressure has fallen more directly and more heavily on some others; yet the circuitous evils of them have visited us with no small privations. But complaint has hitherto been foreborn from a reliance on the wisdom and integrity of our own Government. This confidence, we are happy to perceive, was not misplaced. After a series of injury and negotiation, and indignities, which would long before have exhausted the patience of any people and rulers, less wedded to peace than the American ones—they have at length rose in the violated majesty of a nations rights and hurled the gauntlet at our oppressors. Even France they are pledged to attack, unless atonement shall be proffered by her, ere satisfaction has been wrested from England. This bold magnanimous deed of the twelfth Congress was beheld by many with sentiments of approbation. In fancy the Heroes of our Revolution re-appeared, proclaiming the charter of American Independence; and we fondly anticipated that all *its friends* would once more press forward in support of it, and, as our ancestry devote 'their lives, their fortunes and their sacred honor.'[1] Has this hope been disappointed or are its *foes—the enemies of Republics—* those alone who raise the cry of distrust and sedition? The latter, patriotism as well as facts would induce us to believe, is more probably the truth; for while ancient differences of party have vanished, and men of integrity—of genius the most brilliant and reputation the most extensive—rally round our constituted authorities; the voice of complaint vibrates now as ever from a few relicts of our Revolutionary opposition—a few sys[t]ematic revilers of the people and a clan of their respective sycophants. That voice elevated against an administration which vast majorities have selected, stigmatizing its measures, of whatever character, with imbecility, corruption or wickedness—that voice, hoarse with threatening resistance to law and summoning all the myrmidons of monarchy and faction to demolish our confederacy—that voice has blown the tocsin of alarm over our retired vilages and awakened the Republicans of Hillsborough County to refute in a collective manner its misrepresenation of their sentiments. What shall such panders of sedition and their newspaper hirelings, and the merchants of British capital with their deluded disciples and abject dependents—shall these men dare to guide or speak the oppinions of our great mechanic, manufacturing and agricultural phalanx⟨?⟩ Shall they describe us ali[e]nated from the Administration; because agonizing under that injustice of the Belligerents against which its Administration amicably negotiated till the olive withered? Shall they describe us hostile to War; because it remains the sole weapon to wield against their indignities and aggressions—their rooted animosity and ferocious jealousies? Shall they describe us, ripe for rupture of the Union and all the horrors of civil butchery; because that Union was created by the founders of our Independence, ⟨m[e]ntored?⟩ by their example, and enforced by their precepts? Because its benefits are innumerable—extending ov[e]r our empire and augmenting our opulence—a rainbow in Peace and meteor in War? These things, Sir, have constituted *a crisis*, acknowledgedly momentous and alarming; yet being forced on us, according to our belief by the joint iniquity of foes domestic and foreign we will never, though deprecating its ⟨inviable?⟩ evils, *never* flee from it as cowards or traitors; but rather face undaunted the enemies of our Republic with our full portion of the energies that God has lavished on seven millions of Freemen. In such emergencies, an *enlarged* exposition of the feelings and opinions of Electors are seldom unacceptable to those Elected. It is therefore

"*Resolved*, That we consider the great compact, which binds in confederation these United States, a national act—an act which should be supported, and reverenced, and perpetuated as the Ark of our political salvation; for, among other reasons, having legally emanated from a vast majority of the People, it has become *a Law*—one too of the highest obligation—one as to all others what God's are to man's; and which as Washington, that Father and Hero of our Country enjoined we should not ever *speak* of but 'as the Palladium of our Liberties'; not countinence so much as 'a *suspicion*, that it can in any event be abandoned.'[2]

"*Resolved*, That all Laws, enacted under this Confederation and according to its provisions ought to be fulfilld, encouraged and respected; because they are formed with our consent, constitutionally expressed through a majority of our Representatives; and have thus not only received the engagements of all, but the allegiant *oaths* of many to their support; and consequently a breach of them will entail upon its authors deliberate faleshood [*sic*] or flagrant perjury, as well as jeopardize the whole fabric of our civil polity.

"*Resolved*, That it is not with acquiescence but with astonishment—not with emotions of sympathy, but with abhorrence and detestation—we have witnessed men, who *call themselves* Americans, threatening to prostrate all these barriers of moral and political duty—scattering disaffection and revolt into the very bosom of our families, and assailing that Union and those Laws with the firebrands of calumny, rebelion and death: and our reasons for indulging this sentiment are that though the leaders of an 'artful and enterprising minority'[3] have often avowed contempt for our Republic and hostility to our Confederation; though suspected of intrigues for even the ove[r]throw of the one and dismemberment of the other; though they have once disconserted of our Government by an approximation to that catastrophe [*sic*]; and for diverting the people from a scrutiny of their machinations have brought every unholy engine to bear upon the passion, prejudice and sordid interests of community; though as Arnold accused the Congress of '76 with subjection to French influence,[4] so have *Arnold* geniuses accused that of 1812; though as the *Rivingtons*[5] of our Revolution strove to excite sectional interests between the North and South and to taint our fraternal blood with jealousies the most reprobate, so have hirelings at the present day; though as Washington himself, being a Virginian, was branded with southern partialities and, according to *Marshall* menaced in the very midst of our struggle for Independence with removal from office,[6] so has been the fate of many of his surviving copatriots and disciples; though in alliance with these, whole hosts of perturbed spirits have been conjured up from that pride and ambition, which had 'rather rule in Hell than serve in Heaven';[7] and this at the very crisis, where each link in their chain of Union should be brightened to a sunbeam—*yet, we continue still undismayed.* The friends to our Constitution—whether Republican or Federal, will form a pillar of adamant, which shall break this tempest, that beats around it. And though surprised at such depravity, its very hidiousness will arm them to its discomfiture with an indestructible energy—an energy, sanctified by the justness of our cause and a reliance on that same arm, which was made bare for the salvation of our Fathers.

"*Resolved;* That after the passing of laws, deliberation should form a space yielding to action. Time for opposing their policy has been enjoyed; and a competent tribunal have rendered judgment. By that we will abide till all legislative acts, presumptively good, because approved by a majority, are after full experiment ascertained to be bad. The people and their representatives will then personally realize this; and their repeal inevitably ensue. But as the disorganizing and turbulent have attempted by *Assemblages* to misrepresent popular opinion, particularly on the late measures of our Government, we feel constrained to come forward and express in their favor our detailed and almost unqualified approbation; and this among a myriad of other reasons, because the conduct of both the great belligerents has towards this country been long and systematically hostile. For evidence of that we rely not on declamation, but appeal to facts. It is perhaps enough for us to forget the attack on our liberties, the conflagration of our seaports, and murder of our ancestors during the war for Independence; and that these outrages were inflicted only because we had previously fled thither to a wilderness and barbarians, as less ferocious than our British persecutors; because we had here laid in tears and blood the base of a new empire, which presented wealth for their plunder and power for their jealousy. But that perfidy originating from the *same principle* which appeared in a noncompliance with some articles of the subsequent reluctant Peace—particularly in a retention of the Western Posts, that produced the desolation of our frontier in the burning and butcheries of Indian warfare, and humiliated us by tribute to the Savages, and planted in their breasts thorns of revenge, which have grown, rankled and devasted to the present moment—these we confess cannot so easily be forgotten. And though *Jay's* Treaty however disapproved by many of the wise and good, and even by Washington considered but as a *choice of evils;* though that might have imposed on us silence, while strictly adheared to and its temporary provisions existing; yet the subject of Impressment was *collusively* excluded from it; and all its articles but the permanent ones have long since expired amidst our wishes and endeavors for its renewal on an honorable basis. This last assertion let the arrangement with Erskine corroborate—let the labors of Pinkney and Monroe confirm. For the very persons, who rail so loudly at the rejection of their contemplated Treaty, ought to be conscious that it contained what clearly demonstrates England's exorbitant pretentions and America's conciliatory spirit. One glance at the instrument must convince them, that its clauses on the East Indian trade[8] and enforcement of our commercial restrictions, if no others, were totally inadmissible. Distinguished Statesmen of both parties have also pronounced this. The question of Impressment too was agin, as in Jay's Treaty, postponed to a supplement. Indeed this last topic, so incalculable in its interest had early as 1792, rendered it in Washinton's opinion 'necessary that their Goverment should explain themselves on the subject and be led to *disavow and punish* such conduct.' This he directed to Jefferson, his illustrious Secretary[9] as also to inform our minister at the Cabinet of St. James, that 'the vessel being American should be evidence that the seamen on board her are such'; and if 'a settlement of this point' was not soon completed there would be 'difficulty in avoiding our making *immediate reprisals* on their seamen here.['][10]

"Mr Jay ought on this basis to have effected 'that settlement' our political Father considered thus indispensable and momentous; but in the hurry of concluding his Treaty says Pickering, 'among the articles left unadjusted, one of the *most interesting* nature regards the impressing of American seamen';[11] and that, with others, as before observed, was expressly stipulated to be afterwards supplied. The credulous Ambassador left England, under this belief and also indulging as he observes, 'a pleasing expectation that orders will be given, that Americans impressed' be immediately liberated; and that persons honored with his majesty's commissions do in future abstain from *such violence*.[12] But Mr. King was sent out—Mr. Liston[13] arrived—negotiations were recommended; and all these 'pleasing expectations' terminated, not in an additional article to the Treaty—not in a release of our countrymen—not in subsequent forbearance from *such violence;* but in a mere proposal which even President Adams reprobated; and our minister himself, since Federal candidate for Vice President, (Mr. King) indignantly spurned, as sanctioning 'a principle, which might be productive of greater evils than those it was our aim to prevent.'[14] And can they be friends to our country, who even now reiterate, that Great Britain has *always* been willing to honorably adjust this barbarous custom? In 1806, to be sure, Mr. Monroe⟨,⟩ after much toil, obtained from her a mere con[ce]ssion on Impressment 'both honorable and advantageous to the United States'; yet even that consesion was refused by her to be incorporated with his Treaty and has since been disclaimed by proclamation and practice. And could Mr. Foster in his boasted letter intend any thing else but adding insult to injury by proposing to release all who should be proved Natives of America?[15] For have not we the same privilege as England to naturalize foreigners, and then protect them, with other citizens *by our flag?* This denial to others, what she claims to herself, says Chief Justice Marshall, converts 'the practice into a question of power and not of right.' But even '*Natives of America,*' says he, '*they* are impressed; *they* are dragged on board British ships of War with evidence of their citizenship *in their hands,* and forced by *violence* there to serve, until conclusive testimonials of their birth can be obtained.' [']These,' says he, 'must generally be saught for on this side of the Atlantic. In the mean time acknowledged *violence* is practiced on a *free* citizen of the United States, by compelling him to engage and continue in foreign service.' 'The mere release of the injured, after a long course of *service* and *suffering*, is no *compensation* for the past and *no security* for the future.'[16] If then such be the facts—such the principles and such their authority we ask, what measures should have been adopted? To liberate one citizen from confinement, Greece welcomed a ten years war. Will the opponents of Government then inform us how much longer time ought to have been employed to use the Judge's language, in 'unsuccessful remonstrance and unavailing memorials,'[17] with above Six Thousand of our citizens in bondage!

"But the rapacity of England could not so violate the rights of person without assailing also those of property. A commerce bleaching every sea was too tempting a pray. Jealousy of our naval greatness—a dearth of resources to support her own vast expenditures, and that wantonness, that abandonment of principle, which power frequently engenders in a conflict with mere right—all combined to produce those gradual aggressions on our neutrality; which have augmented to their present heinousness and ruin. In 1805 they burst forth in a manner the most flagrant and unwarrantable. The rule of '56 was revived. A measure, which by one fell sweep, conveyed almost our whole carrying trade into the grasp of British cruizers. No provocation—no state necessity—no settled principle of national law, could or was pretended to extenuate this deed of piracy. And hence a long year before Blockades or Decrees or the Orders in Council all our Seaports covered the tables of Congress with supplications for War—War against *England.* Even the Senate, that body so grave and deliberate, with not one dissenting vote, pronounced it an 'unprovoked aggression upon the property of the citizens of these United States—a violation of their neutral rights and an encroachmen⟨t⟩ upon their national Independence.'[18] And can some of these very men now protest that Great Britain has done us 'no essential injury'? That the War is [']impolitic, unnecessary, unjust'? That 'France was the first aggressor'! We have not time, had we the disposition, to wade through that morass of Blockades, Decrees and Orders, which succeeded this wanton attack on our commercial rights. All of them, however, and particu[lar]ly the last, even Mr. Bayard denominates, 'destructive to neutrals' and 'covering injustice with the cloak of retaliation.' 'They violate (says he) the plainest rights of the nation.' 'It is a doctrine, which we must resist.'[19] And we have resisted it. Honor, interest, justice, all summoned us to resist it. The insulting repetition, too of Mr. Foster, but a few weeks prior to the 18th. of June, 'that Great Britain cannot relinquish her retaliatory system on France,' or, in other words, her determination and right in contending with Bonaparte to sacrifice the commerce of America, unless we compelled him to 'recind absolutely and unconditionally' his Decrees[20]—that is, in relation to *all the world,* as well as the United States—this we believe was not wanting to *fill* the cup of insolence and iniquity. And though by us it is regretted, that six years since 'the Republican banner' had not been 'unfurled' against the then only aggressor, before Nine Hundred And Seventeen of our ships had fallen victims to her injustice; yet we consider the postponement of hostilities a proof, incontestable as solemn of our invincible attachment to peace. It is known, and even demonstrable, that neither the present or past Administrations are lovers of War. In avoiding it, their forbearance became the very theme of *ridicule*. But it was a failing, that 'leaned on virtue's side';[21] and from which to redeem themselves, their preparatory measures have already produced a *suspension* of the English Orders; an honorable repeal of which with the adjustment of all points in dispute, we confidently believe energy and fortitude in the Cabinet will eventually effect. This war is regarded as one of resources, and not simply of men or ships: while therefore occasional disasters darken the lustre of frequent victory, we still look to no distant termination of it. But may the greatest caution be exercised in renewing negotiations with that Court, which disavowed the arrangement of Erskine, and whose present prime minister pledged himself to reward *Henry* for encouraging the dismemberment of our Union. This last act of perfidy and crime, whatever may have been its success or reward, is among all governments regarded in its patrons, advocates, or abettors, as equally abhorrent. 'It is' says Vattel, 'a violation of the law of nations to persuade those subjects to revolt, who actually obey their sovereign, though they complain of his government'—'an *atrocious* injury' 'if any one attempts' it 'by his emissaries.'[22] And aught a free people—an independent sovereignty, tamely to submit to be thus trifled? Is it to be endured, that amid the rotation of all their miserable expedients to benumb our public feeling avert merited reprisals, and palsy if not annihilate our national spirit—is it to be endured, we say, that not only Spies shall be missioned into the heart of our country; but the Savages also, their merciless and now open allies, be let loose on our frontiers 'to wake the sleep of the cradle'—butcher our wives, and apply the midnight torch to our dwellings?

"Because these and a host of other offences cried for vengeance, we therefore approve of War—War against the *first* aggressor and *greatest* aggressor—against *one* at a time instead of *both:* and if before an adjustment with *this*, the other Belligerent shall not atone for his plunder, we pledge our-selves with equal sincerity to assail her wherever vulnerable.

"*Resolved,* That this contest, however, ought not to be prolonged unecessarily— but still we revolt from its cessation till there has been procured restitution for injuries and security for our rights. Because, although the trade, navy, and seaports of America should be *exterminated;* yet a peace without that restitution and security could be neither permanent or honorable. Some of these calamities we have now partially endured and the others if happening shall rather than depress only inspire us with redoubled ardor in their redress; for as freemen we dread submission worse than misfortune—deprecate insult alike with aggressions, and welcome poverty before disgrace. Indeed without these sentiments, so indispensable to respect, Independence and national honor, we should richly merit, what England seems long to have meditated, the conversion of our affluence, our liberty, yea life itself into an infamy and a curse. In our desire for speedy, if honorable 'peace with all nations,' let it however be understood, that we entreat for 'entangling *alliance* with none.'[23] British Fraternity and French Fraternity are equally our abhorrence; and while others with much parade disclaim a fondness for the last and aversion to the first, we, in our Republican simplicity, detest *both*. For perhaps almost as little exists, deserving admiration, in 'that bulwark of our religion' which even now tears from all our theological sects but one of the privileges of freemen, which ha⟨s⟩ burnt hundreds of us at the stake and exiled as many thousands more to the mercy of barbarians—in 'that champion for the liberties of the world,' who on[c]e jeopardized ours—who recently robbed Denmark of the power to defend hers, and who at this moment makes the commerce of most its plunder, the seamen of some its slaves, and whole regions of the East with unhappy Ireland her *vanquished and guiltless* tributaries—in 'that last hope of nation⟨s'⟩ who has really favored few, that she has not gangrened with corruption, and leagued with as few, that have not perished in her embrace: it is seriously repeated, that in *this* we can perceive but little more to admire, than in the fickle, perfidious and sanguinary Corsican. But finally if an internal foe, as many appearances indicate, has conspired with the external one and shall actually co-op[e]rate to cut the Gordian knot of our Union, as well as surrender those rights already so violated—

"Resolved, That we will embody around the Const[it]utions of our Fathers and their elected Guardians; and never assent to peace or alliance till victory or death; for if our republic is to be overturned; if this fair fabric of freedom is destined *thus* to fall, rather than survive the catastrophe, we deem it more eligible, as well as magnanimous to *bury* ourselves under its splendid ruins."

RC (DNA: RG 59, ML). 12 pp.; signed by Robert Alcock, president, and Henry B. Chase and John Bromam, secretaries.

1. The memorialists quoted from the final sentence of the Declaration of Independence (Boyd, *Papers of Jefferson*, 1:432).

2. In his farewell address Washington referred to the Union as "the Palladium of your political safety and prosperity," cautioning the public to guard against "even a suspicion that it can in any event be abandoned" (Fitzpatrick, *Writings of Washington*, 35:219).

3. Washington used this phrase in his farewell address to refer to minority faction leaders (ibid., 35:225).

4. In the fall of 1780 Benedict Arnold published a tract that explained his decision to abandon the Revolutionary cause as a reaction to the alliance between the new government and France (*To the Inhabitants of America* [New York, 1780; Evans 16701]).

5. The memorialists referred to James Rivington (1724–1802), a bookseller, printer, and newspaper publisher in New York during the American Revolution. *Rivington's New-York Gazetteer* became an object of criticism from patriots during the war because it featured loyalist as well as patriot opinions. After his printing press was destroyed by a party of Connecticut Sons of Liberty in 1775, Rivington rebuilt the press and resumed publication of his paper in 1777 with a decidedly loyalist slant (Brigham, *History of American Newspapers*, 1:686).

6. The memorialists may have referred to the Conway Cabal of 1777 as described in Marshall, *Life of George Washington*, 3:336–38.

7. The memorialists quoted Milton's Satan in *Paradise Lost*, book 1, line 263: "Better to reign in hell than serve in heaven" (John Milton, *The Complete English Poems*, ed. Gordon Campbell [New York, 1992], 156).

8. Article 23 of the unratified Monroe-Pinkney treaty of 1806 effectively restricted the free access to the British East Indies that had been granted in Article 13 of the 1794 Jay treaty (see *ASP, Foreign Relations*, 3:145, 151).

9. On 12 Oct. 1792 Jefferson sent to Thomas Pinckney, the U.S. minister to Great Britain, a letter from two Virginia merchants complaining that sailors on their vessels had been impressed. Jefferson noted in his covering letter that "So many instances of this kind have happened that it is quite necessary that their government should explain themselves on the subject, and be led to disavow and punish such conduct" (Boyd, *Papers of Jefferson*, 24:472–73).

10. See Jefferson to Pinckney, 11 June 1792, ibid., 24:62.

11. Pickering to Rufus King, 8 June 1796, *ASP, Foreign Relations*, 3:574.

12. Jay to Lord Grenville, 30 July 1794, ibid., 1:481.

13. Robert Liston, British minister to the U.S. from 1796 to 1800, had been authorized to negotiate a supplement to the Jay treaty regarding impressment but was unable to do so (see ibid., 3:576–81).

14. King to JM, July 1803, ibid., 2:504.

15. Foster had promised Monroe in a 15 Apr. 1812 letter that should it be claimed that native-born American citizens were aboard British vessels, "no exertion shall be wanting on my part to procure their discharge" (ibid., 3:454).

16. Marshall to King, 20 Sept. 1800, ibid., 2:489.

17. Ibid., 2:490.

18. The Senate unanimously passed a resolution to this effect on 12 Feb. 1806 (*Annals of Congress*, 9th Cong., 1st sess., 91).

19. On 16 June 1812 Sen. James A. Bayard of Delaware used words to this effect during a speech urging that a declaration of war be delayed until the following fall (ibid., 12th Cong., 1st sess., 295).

20. Foster to Monroe, 30 May 1812, *ASP, Foreign Relations*, 3:455, 456–57.

21. Oliver Goldsmith, *The Deserted Village*, line 164.

22. Emmerich de Vattel, *The Law of Nations; or, Principles of the Law of Nature* (1st U.S. ed.; 3 vols.; New York, 1796), 3:131.

23. The memorialists paraphrased Jefferson's first inaugural address of 4 Mar. 1801 (Ford, *Writings of Jefferson*, 8:4).

§ From Jonathan R. Spann. *15 September 1812, Charleston.* Observes that his court-martial proceedings will be forwarded to JM for a final decision.[1] Requests JM's "particular attention, to the testimony, on the different Charges & Specifications." Refers JM to his defense in the court-martial record, an affidavit from one of the men in his company, and a statement he had published in the newspaper.[2] Requests that JM "Suspend a desison in the Cace" until all Spann's papers can be laid before him.[3] Intends to proceed to Washington as soon as possible.

RC (DNA: RG 153, Court-Martial Orders, 1810–24). 3 pp.

1. The court-martial of Spann, a captain in the Light Artillery Regiment, commenced on 15 July and concluded on 3 Sept. 1812. He was found guilty of conduct unbecoming an officer, specifically cheating at cards, failing to purchase gaiters after appropriating money from his troops for that purpose, failing to distribute bounty money to his troops, and stealing the pay of one of his men, Thomas Bryant. He was also charged with violating Article 12 of the rules and articles of war by "Taking a private of his Company a few miles from Charleston & giving him a furlough for several months" and Article 36 by embezzling public clothing for the use of his slave (DNA: RG 153, Proceedings of Courts-Martial, vol. 4, entry 14).

2. On 12 Sept. 1812 the Charleston *Times* published a statement from Spann denying the charge that he had misappropriated government property when he ordered that his slave be clothed from public stores.

3. Several other letters from Spann requesting a review of his case and a new trial are listed in the Registers of Letters Received by the Secretary of War but have not been found (DNA: RG 107). Eustis replied to Spann on 30 Oct. 1812 to explain that there were no grounds for a new trial (DNA: RG 107, LSMA).

From Jonathan Dayton

[ca. 17 September 1812]

Your political enemies are taking every possible advantage of our unaccountable disasters at Detroit, to render your Presidency unpopular, &
your cabinet Council odious & contemptible. This is not doing by *Federalists* alone, but with equal zeal, tho' greater caution by "the *Democratic Republicans.*" The great object of the former is to remove the Chief magis-
tracy, not from you only, but from the State of Virginia, whom they
pronounce hostile to commerce, & to the growth of the Eastern section of
the Union, & to give it to a New Yorker, known to be favorable to both
these objects, without regarding the minor features of his political character. The views of the Democrats more limited & personal, but equally decided, are directed to the elevation of a single individual, who is the idol of
their party. These are sparing neither of pains nor expense. They have addressed circulars to almost every Democrat of influence in the Eastern &
middle States, recommending their man—& they have a Committee for
secret correspondance, who communicate very confidentially with certain
characters in Pennsylvania & Maryland, who pretend openly to be perfectly friendly to you. There are also men very near you, in office at the seat
of Government, who are in secret conspiracy to supplant you. These in-
triguers here profess to be very certain of all the Eastern States, N. York &
N. Jersey, & calculate confidently on three or more of the five States of
Pennsyla Delaware, Maryland, No. Carolina & Ohio. Preparations have
been making for the forming of a system of operations,[1] & two prominent
characters H. G. Otis[2] & Colo. Thorndike[3] of Boston are just arrived in
N. York, for the sole purpose of maturing & organizing it. One of their
friends came over to see the writer yesterday, with the view of ascertaining
what the Federalists in this quarter were, or might be disposed to do, in the
event of a formidable competitor in York State arising against you. There
are other emissaries instructed & qualified to confer with the Democrats,
as to their bias & disposition, who have funds at their command. My wishes
are sincerely for your success, & therefore I warn you of these machinations, that the proper measures may be taken to counteract them, but I assure you sir, that your friends, must not sleep on their posts, nor feel themselves too confident.

If the prospects of peace should brighten, or if our Arms should be attended with such success in the interior, as to give us speedy possession of
Montreal, & of the British posts between Ontario & Erie & the latter & St.
Clair, the causes of discontent, & the clamours agt. your Administration
would be diminished at a critical season. If these are to be effected this year,
they must be before the end of October, & may be done, if proper measures have been taken, & shall be promptly pursued.

The blunders committed by Genl. Hull were of the grossest & most unpardonable kind. If he required more men & provisions for his expedition, twenty days delay would have given them to him, & he should have availed himself of this time to send expresses to Genl. Dearborn, urging him to have a diversion made in his favor at the other extremity of the lake. He ought never to have crossed to the British side of the river, until prepared to carry fort Malden by assault, if not surrendered on the first summons. By going over & remaining at Sandwich for reinforcements & supplies, he removed from a straight & nearer line of communication with our posts & settlements, to a circular & more distant one—he enabled the enemy the more easily to intercept them, by their water excursions from Fort Malden—he put it more in their power to ascertain the number & quality of his troops, to learn the extent of his reinforcements as they were coming up to join him, which would not have been practicable if he had remained within our lines, with better accommodations & less severe duty, until he was prepared to carry all before him. The surrender which followed this series of blunders, was the most unpardonable of all. If thro' want of numbers or discipline he could not venture to meet the British forces in the field, or thro' want of provisions or ammunition, he could not shut himself up in the fort, & receive & beat them there, he ought to have proceeded with all the effectives of his army by rapid march to join Colo. Miller's detachment, & with them, to meet Majr. Brush & his provisions at the river Raisin, instead of ordering up Colo. Miller & his Regt. to swell the number of prisoners, & the enemy's triumph. For such conduct there can be no good excuse. He knew that his provisions were stopped at the river Raisin, & that the communication could not be kept open by mere detachments from his army, & therefore if fighting was out of question, he had but one course as a military man to pursue, which was to have marched, with all that could march, & with such as were able to ride, tho not walk, on all the horses that could be collected (two on a horse) in order to meet his provisions, to gather up his detachments, & to approach & protect the other posts & settlements in Ohio, which he would have been perfectly adequate to do, with little or no loss, leaving in the garrison, a subaltern's command of effectives, & all the non-effectives of the Army to enter into the usual capitulation.

The uncertainty whether the Legislature would eventually declare the war, prevented without doubt the taking of one of the most important preparatory steps for acquiring a superiority on the lakes, which should have been commenced in Jany. or February by sending up a corps of artificers to cut & prepare the timber by hewing & sawing, for building the vessels in the spring. Green timber would have answered every purpose, for the superiority, once acquired, would never have been lost, & the movements, operations & supplies of our Army would have been rendered easy, cheap & successful by our command of the water—the Indians could have been kept in check, fewer troops could have done the business, as detachments would be less necessary, & the garrison could not be strengthened from the Lower posts. This might all have been done with proper exertion, even after the appointment of the Commander in chief, who himself committed another great error in not approaching & threatening fort Erie, at the very time when Hull was advancing upon Malden. Had that been done, Genl. Brock could never have spared a soldier to the upper post, & still less would he have gone there to act in person. The projected armistice was, on our part a weak, indiscreet measure, for it left them free to act with all their force above, without endangering their lower posts, & the noise of it served greatly to check the military spirit & ardour of our militia. If it even prevented the enemy during it's temporary continuance, from bringing the war across the line into our territory, it did us thereby no service, for such an advance would inspirit & unite our people far more than a purely defensive system on their part. Be assured sir, by one who has himself made such a campaign, that *a winter* campaign in Canada cannot be carried on by such troops as are now collecting for the expedition. All they have to do this year, must be done before the end of October, & ought to be, by the middle of it, after which, if your soldiers are kept in tents, you will lose more than the half of them, by sickness. The capture of Montreal will have the double advantage of giving eclat to our military operations, & good quarters for our soldiers, as well with a view to their comfort, as our early operations in the spring. If after crossing our line against Malden, Erie, & on the rout to Montreal, the troops proceed with rapidity to their objects, they must succeed, if well commanded, but if, after crossing, they linger or delay, from whatever cause, their failure & defeat must be inevitable.

This communication is made from motives of friendship towards you, & of purest attachment to our country's cause & welfare. The writer has no views to office, for nothing would ever induce him to take one. Should the information he gives, be acceptable, & any thing further from him be desired on any subject, an anonymous line to this effect, addressed to "Mr. Levi Canning in Elizabeth town N. Jersey" will be properly attended to.

The writer has this moment received a verbal message that Mr. H. of Baltimore,[4] who has been & is now in N. York, attending a large private meeting, will call & see him on his way back to Maryland.

RC (NjP). Undated; date assigned here on the basis of the postmark, which reads "Elizh Town, Sep. 17." Unsigned; correspondent identified on the basis of JM's docket, which reads "Anon: from J. D," and by comparison with the handwriting of Dayton's "Cyrus" letters (see *PJM-PS*, 1:210–11 and nn., 4:249–50 and n. 5, 257–58 and n.). A note on the verso of the cover in Dayton's hand reads: "The enclosed to be opened by Mr. Madison only, & therefore to be sent to him, if absent from Washington, in case this should be opened by one of his Secretaries. It relates to private concerns."

1. A convention of more than sixty Federalists from eleven states met in New York on 15–17 Sept. 1812 to select a candidate for the upcoming presidential election. The delegates failed to agree on the nomination of DeWitt Clinton as a Federalist candidate and passed instead a series of resolutions that left party members at the state level free to endorse a candidate who seemed the most likely to oppose the policies of JM (Morison, *Life and Letters of Harrison Gray Otis*, 1:308–11; John S. Murdock, "The First National Nominating Convention," *American Historical Review* 1 [1895–96]: 680–83).

2. Harrison Gray Otis (1765–1848), a Boston lawyer and Federalist representative to the Fifth and Sixth Congresses, enjoyed a long career in Massachusetts politics, serving in the state House of Representatives from 1802 to 1805 and from 1813 to 1814 and in the state senate from 1805 to 1813 and from 1814 to 1817. Otis was among the organizers of the Hartford Convention of 1814 (Fischer, *The Revolution of American Conservatism*, 38–40; Morison, *Life and Letters of Harrison Gray Otis*, 1:308–10).

3. Israel Thorndike (1755–1832) was a successful merchant from Beverly, Massachusetts, active in Federalist party politics, who served in the state House of Representatives and senate between 1802 and 1815 (Fischer, *The Revolution of American Conservatism*, 262; Forbes, *Israel Thorndike*, [7], 99, 101, 121–22).

4. Dayton probably referred to Robert Goodloe Harper, formerly a Federalist representative from South Carolina, who had retired to Baltimore and who had attended the convention in New York (Murdock, "The First National Nominating Convention," *American Historical Review* 1 [1895–96]: 683).

From William Eustis

[ca. 17 September 1812]

Colo. Cass is of opinion that the Penva. troops at Pittsbg will not be required by Genl. Harrison. It remains to be considered 1st that having been advised of them G. H. may have made his arrangements accordingly[1]—by dismissing a part of his other troops—by ordering a part to the Iillinois [*sic*] or otherwise. 2. A part of the Penva. troops particularly those in the vicinity of Pittsburg prefer the western to the Eastern Route having friends in the former.

Again it is to be considered that the march to Detroit by the way of Cleveland is near 300 miles—that to Niagara not much more than 200, the former thro' a wilderness, the latter principally thro' a settled country. A man of good judgment and of proper authority could determine at Pittsburg what under all circumstances would be best.

Provisions to and at Niagara more plentiful and less expensive by 50 prcent.

RC (DLC). Unsigned. Undated; dated 1812 in the *Index to the James Madison Papers*; date assigned here on the basis of evidence presented in n. 1.

1. Eustis wrote on 17 Sept. 1812 to give Harrison command of the Northwest Army, promising him "the Volunteers & militia of Kentucky Ohio" and "Three Thousand detached Militia from Virginia & Pennsylvania" (Esarey, *Messages and Letters of William Henry Harrison*, Indiana Historical Collections, 136–37).

From David Jones

MY DEAR SIR,   EASTOWN CHESTER COUNTY PENNA Sept. 17. 1812.

The Tenth Day of June last, I left home, to make a Tour through this & ohio State. I had some Business of my own, & an ardent Disire to know the minds of the people, in this important Crisis. I mixed in all Companys, of all Ranks, conversed freely & preached very often. I have reason to beleive that my Labour was not unsuccessful. On my return, I wrote to you two letters from wheeling in ohio County virginia. One before I heard of Hull's Treachery, & the other after.[1] I can assure you that never was a people more unanimous than the State of ohio, with a few Exceptions. Some at marrietta are devoted to the Interest of England, and may be for any thing I know, in brittish *Pay;* but more of them are deceived by the men of the East, receiving *Secret Service money,* and I gess these are not a few. When I was at marriotta, a good looking man steped into my room, and introducing Politics asked me, if I thought the war would continue? My answere was, that it was my opinion that it would continue till england would *fall.* At which he shewed violent Passion; & said then the union would be dissolved, by the with drawing of the N. England States, adding as a reason, that they were a Commercial People, & the Middle States were agricultural. I would not admit that they were more commercial than we were, except in a few articles such as fish, Cabbage, potatoes, onions with Lumber & live Stock. They were oblidged to come to our ports flour [*sic*], &c. and if they withdrew, he might be sure, we would never suffer one of their vessels to enter our ports while the world stood. From our Conversation, I am fully perssuaded that some in N. England have entered into a secret Combination with England; but we have this Comfort, viz. there is more there for us than against us. The vile Hypocritical Preisthood are against us, and all, who are Preist ridden, and no more. It will be your Duty Sir to call for volentiers, and their Tory governors will not be able to prevent them to the Confusion of all Treators.

I would now call your attention to ohio State. They are new Settlers & very scarse of blankets. They are willing to pay for them, but they are not be had [*sic*]. It will be incumbent on you Sir, to send two or three Thousand before winter to marrietta or Cincinati before winter. Col. Duane told me they can be had in the manifactories near Philadelphia. It is universally the opinion of the People that Dr ustis is not properly Qualified for his Station, it is expected that you will displace him, as he has not the Confidence of the People, and appoint another. Through some neglect, there is neither arms, nor amonition Sufficient in ohio State. I have know Companeis to march from Zanevill with only 4 rounds a peice. There is now 30.000d Stand of arms ready at Harper's ferry. This I had from one of the manifactorers. And I have not seen one bayonette fit for action. I told you this last march in Conversation, but nothing has been done on the Subject. From wheeling I recommended gen. Armstrong to command the Northwestern Army. From my acquintance with him last war, I beleive him to be a man of firmness & Judgement. I have recommended him warmly to the State of ohio, I shall wait with Solicitude to hear of his appointment. Governor Harrison is my friend & a good man; but there is some thing wanting in him for that Station; he might answere for second in Command his Conduct in his last Campaign was so imprudent, that he cannot be acceptable, excepting with a few of his Friends.

I will now give you my opinion of Pennsylvania. They are generally warm whiggs; but there are too many Tories among them, especially in Philadelphia. These do all in their power to impede your operations, & bring your administration into disgrace. They are not very formidable, but they are guilty every Day of Treason; and if no Notice is taken of them by men in Power, you may depend on it, some serious Consequences will follow. We unite now under the Name of whiggs, and by this Term we mean all who approve of the present measures. By Tories we mean all whining, canting fellows, who affect to be friends of Peace, but in fact are wolves in Sheeps Cloathing, and openly declare the war unnessesary & ruinous. These are all for Dewit Clinton for president, asserting that you want Energy. I sorry [sic] that for months past, you given [sic] them so much room for their assertion. Never was there a greater blu[n]der than the omission of building gun boats on the Lakes, and not securing the St Lawrence. However it is better to mend *late* than never do well. The present operations minister a pleasing prospect. Your ordering ship Carpinters to the Lake is what ought to have been done long ago, and before winter all upper Canada will be in our Possession. This will retreive our honour and damp the Spirit of the Savages. Before long, you will See my Ideas on this Subject. You deceived yourself in appointing worthington to act in the ill Judged & untimely Treaty, for his very Name is abhorred by many in the State. Nothing could injure your Election in this State more than taking any Notice of worthington. You must learn to know your real Friends better, or you will soon have very few. The News Papers will inform you that great Exertions are making in this State for Dewitt Clinton as president. I shall oppose this with all the Energy & influence I can command, & so will Duane, for he told me so this Day. Some of my Reasons are, that governeur Morris is at the head of the Business. I have watched him for more than 30 years, & in all that Time I never knew him to do one good act. With me this is reason enough to oppose Dewitt Clinton. Morris is in my opinion one of the most unprincipled men on Earth, & a vile Intriguer.

Another reason determines me against Clinton, which is that all the Tories are for him; and where they are concerned there can be no good in view. The reason assigned for Chosing Clinton is, they want at present a man of Energy, & they say you possess it not. I am Sorry that this year's administration has left too much room to say so; but I am not discouraged, I hope this Campaign will Terminate *gloriously*, and convince your Enemies, that you possess more Energy than Suits them. My Dear Sir, if you must die politically, die *gloriously*, the present prospect, to me is very pleasing. I am willing to trust the Event to god.

Before I cloase, I think it my Duty to observe that general Dearborn has done nothing till lately that discovers any Talents for his Station. If the news Papers are correct, he has Sauntered away his Time Shamefully instead of Concentrating his army near the Lakes. I know not who originated the Project of buying land opposite to albany.[2] A more ridiculous plan was never devised. A mere waste of publick money, and the ruin of the army. The very firewood would there cost an immence Sum of money. Barracks should never be near any Town, or in the Spring of the year your army will be ruined with the *lues venerea*.[3] Remember Sir in 1777. we built our Cabins at the valley Forge, and in other winters, we pursued the Same Plan. You ought to have your military cantoonment in a woody Country between albany & the Lakes, and let the Soldiers may[4] their own Cabins as we did at greenville, and if this is not done, there can be no greater Demonstration that Something is wanting somewhere. Now my Dear Sir I have discharged, what I deemed a Duty to you & my own Conscience. Perhaps my reward, will be your Displea[su]re, be it so, yet beleive me there is not a man in the union wishes your administration better than myself. And may the god of heaven give you wisdom & prudence to conduct our publick affairs to his glory & the good of the Country is the honest & sincere desired of your humble Servt.

DAVID JONES

P. S. Joseph Biggs[5] of Bellmont County, State of ohio wished me to let you know that he would Serve you in the army as a Major or even a Captain. In the last war he fought 16 battles with the Indians. Which is as high recommendation as can be given.

RC (DLC: Rives Collection, Madison Papers); draft (NRAB). Draft dated 15 Sept. 1812; a note at the foot reads: "This is the Copy in Substance of a letter sent to James Madison."

1. Jones to JM, 25 and 28 Aug. 1812.

2. Jones referred to the army camp at Greenbush, outside Albany, New York (Heitman, *Historical Register*, 2:504).

3. Syphilis.

4. Draft has "make."

5. Joseph Biggs (1755–1833) had been an ensign from Virginia during the Revolutionary War. He appears to have performed two tours of duty as a private in Capt. Robert McElwain's company of Ohio militia in 1812 and 1813; he later became eligible for a pension for this service (*DAR Patriot Index* [1990 ed.], 1:252; Drake, *Roster of Ohio Soldiers in the War of 1812*

[1995 reprint], 111; Virgil D. White, comp., *Index to War of 1812 Pension Files* [2 vols.; Waynesboro, Tenn., 1992], 1:164).

From Richard M. Johnson

SIR,   IN CAMP, AT FORT WAYNE. Sept. 18th. 1812

I have the honour of commanding the only Battalion of Mounted Riflemen now attached to the army at this place. I have been present with the army & have been a Strict observer of men & things and let me inform you that no event is now so important to the cause of our Country in this quarter as the giving Gov. Harrison the command of the forces from Kentucky destined for Canada. He has capacity without an equal. He has the confidence of the forces without a parrellel in our History except in the case of Genl. Washington in the revolution. Genl. Winchester has this evening arrived & the united exertions of us all cannot reconcile them to the transfer of the Command.[1] I speak what I know & you cannot do wrong in acting accordingly. I have just returned from the Expedition to the Elkhart village upon the River of that name, which village we destroyed. To morrow we commence an expedition composed of mounted men, the object of which is to drive the Savages from our limits & distroy all we can find. We have considered the Miamies as enemies. The evidence of their hostility is complete. I shall not be in the City untill a week or two after the Commencement of the Session. I am sure I can be of more service here for twenty days than any where else, as I am at the head of the most choice men I have ever seen—who are now serving without pay & who volunteered Knowing that pay was not authorised. Your friend

RH: M: JOHNSON.

RC (DLC). Docketed by JM.

1. On 19 Sept. 1812 Harrison issued general orders announcing that "The President of the United States having designated Brigadier General James Winchester to the Command of the army originally destined to relieve General Hull and that officer having arrived at this place, the command is accordingly relinquished to him." Harrison enclosed the order in his letter to Eustis of 21 Sept. 1812, in which he explained that he had proposed to Winchester that they "divide the force and act in support of each other." After Winchester refused to agree, Harrison began making plans for a separate military expedition against the Indian villages below Lake Michigan (Esarey, *Messages and Letters of William Henry Harrison*, Indiana Historical Collections, 2:141, 143–47).

From Philip S. Physick

DEAR SIR,   PHILADA. 18th. Septr. 1812

Having been made acquainted with many circumstances of the medical department of our army which lead me to believe that much advantage would accrue from having it under the immediate control of some accomplished medical character I have been induced to trouble you with a request that you would be so obliging as to inform me whether it is the intention of the executive to institute the office of Surgeon General to the army at the next session of Congress.[1]

My Nephew Doctr. John Syng Dorsey[2] having received a complete medical education in this and in foreign countries—having been for ten years engaged in very extensive business and being perfectly conversant with the various modern improvements of surgery wishes to be considered as a candidate for this distinguished post. It is proper also to inform you that Dr Dorsey has for several years been Adjunct Professor of surgery in the University of Pennsyla.

I have no hesitation in assuring you that every confidence may be placed in him for the faithful and zealous performance of his duties and I make no question that the appointment would prove highly beneficial to the interests of the army and of course highly honourable to him who receives it. Requesting you to present my best compliments to Mrs. Madison I have the honour to be with the highest respect your most Obedient and very faithful servant

PHILIP S. PHYSICK

RC (DLC). Docketed by JM.

1. Congress created the office of physician and surgeon-general by an act of 3 Mar. 1813 (Heitman, *Historical Register*, 1:41). The office was first filled by James Tilson in June 1813 (*Senate Exec. Proceedings*, 2:352, 353).

2. John Syng Dorsey (1783–1818) received his medical degree from the University of Pennsylvania in 1802. He joined the faculty of that school in 1807 and from 1810 to 1818 was also a surgeon at Pennsylvania Hospital. Dorsey published a well-received volume on surgical techniques in 1813 and was elected to the chair of materia medica and later to that of anatomy (Howard A. Kelly and Walter L. Burrage, eds., *American Medical Biographies* [Baltimore, 1920], 321–23).

§ Petition Recommending Irenée Amelot de Lacroix. *Ca. 18 September 1812.* "The Petition of the Subscribers, Citizens of the United States, on behalf of themselves and many others, *Most respectfully sheweth,*

"That your petitioners and a great number of their friends, feeling the necessity of pursuing with vigor the just and necessary war now subsisting between the United States and Great Britain, and by that means to obtain an honorable peace, are anxious to see every reasonable means adopted, that we may be able, by well directed exertions, to reach that desirable end.

"Past experience has convinced your petitioners and the world, that our gallant troops want nothing but discipline, well directed and well enforced, to render them equal to the best armies of Europe; and it is an indisputable truth that this can only be obtained by placing skilled and experienced officers at their head. A long peace, during which most of our revolutionary heroes have disappeared from the scene, has made us forget, in a great degree, the knowledge which we had once acquired in the art of war. The men who, under Washington, led us to victory, are no more. The small number of those who remain are, with very few exceptions, enfeebled by honorable age, and pains have unfortunately not been taken to raise successors to them worthy of their names and glory. Under similar circumstances, under circumstances much more auspicious, other nations have had recourse to skillful and experienced foreigners, and employed them even in the highest grades to great advantage. France has had her Berwick, her Saxe, and her Lowendahl. Spain her Conetable [Constable] of Bourbon. Prussia her Keith. Austria her Eugene. Great Britain her Solms, her Ruvigny, her Ligonier, and many others. At this moment Sweden glories in her Bernadotte; Russia regrets her Moreau, and in the ranks opposed to *us*, we see the De Rottenburgs and the Wattevilles honorably employed. In fine, America will always recollect with pride the names of Fayette, De Kalb, Steuben, Pulaski, and a host of other revolutionary worthies, who had not the happiness to be born among us, but who did not serve our cause with the less zeal and fidelity, to the great advantage of our country, and to their own immortal honor.

"For these and many other obvious reasons, your petitioners are of opinion that the same advantage and honor would redound to our country if she were to avail herself, in the present contest, of the knowledge and talents of some European disciplinarian, skilled and experienced in the military profession, and as such they beg leave to recommend to the particular notice of government, Ireneé Amelot De La Croix, formerly a Colonel in the armies of France and afterwards in that of the United States; the brave defender of the French colony of Guadeloupe, who, in consequence of his gallant defence of that island, was surnamed the Intrepid, and did in fact deserve that name. Your petitioners are all acquainted with that brave and excellent officer, honor his person, and esteem his merits, and are convinced that if he were employed in our army, with a suitable grade and command, he would prove of the most essential service to our cause. His name and talents are well known among us, and your petitioners are well satisfied that if he shall be so appointed, thousands will flock to his standard, and be eager to serve under his command.

"Your petitioners therefore respectfully again beg leave to recommend to your excellency the appointment of Colonel De La Croix as a General in the army of the United States, and with such a command as may enable him to display his military talents to their full extent, to the honor of our country and terror of our enemies."

Printed copy (*Portrait of Colonel I. A. de La Croix, Baron de Vanden Boègard: Written by His Former Secretary, and Afterwards His Adjutant Major*, trans. Mme de Lacroix [Baltimore, 1814; Shaw and Shoemaker 32553], 172–75). The petition was signed by "near three thousand subscribers, among whom are three Major-Generals, six Brigadier-Generals, eleven Colonels, fifteen Lieutenant Colonels, fourteen Majors, and more than one hundred and fifty subaltern officers; the others were respectable native Americans" (ibid., 175). Undated; date assigned here on the assumption that the petition was forwarded with Lacroix's note to JM of 18 Sept. 1812 seeking a commission to raise volunteers (see William Keteltas to JM, 11 Oct. 1812, n. 2).

To Mathew Carey

private

Sir   Washington Sepr. 19. 1812.

The sermon inclosed with your last of the 3d. instant is now returned.[1] It is a strong proof of the baneful spirit for which your proposed plan is meant as an antidote. I wish not to diminish your laudable solicitude on the occasion, nor to question the powerful tendency of the resource which it has suggested to you. But I can not suppress my hope that the wicked project of destroying the Union of the States is defeating itself. The great body of the people in the Quarter to which it has been addressed, have too palpable an interest in their connection with the other States, to be easily seduced into an exchange of it, for a foreign connection which presents rivalship instead of reciprocity in all the great branches of national prosperity. I observe also that in Connecticut, if no where else, the friends of the Union & the Genl. Govt. are already pursuing a very strong & decided mode of supporting both agst. their disorganizing adversaries. If local efforts can be employed with success they are preferable, to a national one, more especially under the patronage of the National Govt. The latter can only be recommended in an extreme case. In making these remarks, I repeat my unwillingness to derogate from the meritorious vigilance & active zeal, of which you have made me a witness, and which I doubt not will be continued & proportioned to the manifestations of dangerous hostility to the Unity & Institutions of our Country. Accept my respects & friendly wishes.

James Madison

RC (NjP). Docketed by Carey as received 21 Sept. and answered 24 Sept. 1812.

1. Letter and enclosure not found.

From George Joy

Dear sir,   London Septr: 19th. 1812.

Mr. Maury has transmitted to Monroe M.S. copy of a peice that I had the good fortune to get into the Times of the 24th. Ult.[1] I am not advised of his having had an opportunity of sending the enclosed rejoinder to a note of the Editor thereon which however he has refused to insert from, among other things, "the absolute want of room for new correspondents when the Journal cannot afford space even to its old ones, whose opinions are congenial to its spirit."[2] Such is his reply to a mercantile house in the city (Messrs. Mullett & Co.) through whom it was conveyed to him without announcing the Author.

Sir Wm. Scotts judgment on the Snipe[3] is rich in evidence of the necessity for a tribunal differently constructed to decide ultimately on these subjects. I have noted largely upon it with a view to publication in case of need. But while the door is open to a proposition for a mode of adjustment which may not incur his powerful opposition; the severity of censure is best repressed. If, as I observed many years ago, the redress of injury is to be preferred to the revenge of insult; and the former only to be applied as subsidiary to the latter; the irritation of individuals is not to be excited at the expence of the property of our fellow citizens; & least of all is the gratification of the individual instead of his punishment to be thus blindly promoted. If the great end is to be obtained by the retreat of the enemy without annoyance let him back out in God's name. It is with a view to this conciliatory mode of adjustment that I have referred, in the enclosed note to Lord Sidmouth, to Mr Forster's late correspondence with Mr Monroe on the subject of impressments.[4] And though I have since been informed that Lord Castlereagh has said it was unauthorized, yet as he himself has certainly made use of it in parliament as an evidence of the desire of this Government to come to a reasonable adjustment with us on that head, I would willingly leave it as a pretext if they are desposed to make it such.

The object of my meeting Lord S. referred to in the within and on which among other things I spent an hour with him about three weeks ago was to deprecate the admission of Mr Canning into the Cabinet (which I had heard from pretty good authority was in serious contemplation) while the hope of conciliation with America remained. I referred him to an extract from the National Intelligencer in the Morning Chronicle of the 8th. Novr: 1808 "We pronounce this charge a gross and palpable falsehood" &c[5] and to an unsatisfactory apology in a note from Canning that Mr Pinkney read to me at the time.[6] I also mentioned a conversation I had had with Count Bernstorff, in which he charged C. with that gross misrepresentation which destroyed all confidence. And though I had little faith in the report of Mr Thornton going to Denmark,[7] and still less in his effecting any thing, I stated my apprehension that as well there, as with us, his (Mr C.'s) coming into office would be considered as a signal of hostility.[8] It is now pretty certain that he will not be employed before the meeting of parliament; and whether he will then or not is doubtful.

I have considered the insertion of the above mentioned peice in the

Times as fortunate; because the effects of it in promoting a change of opinion in many quarters were immediately announced to me. I was not aware in time to justify the anticipation of any good effects, of the influence of my former publications. Indeed, I have now reason to believe that efforts were made to suppress the conviction produced by them in places of some consideration. Could I have anticipated this, I should not from a false delicacy have been backward to announce it. Without better evidence of it than any that fell in my way it would have been wrong, as well as indecent, to have promised any thing from them. Indeed, I have very little to boast either as a prophet or a priest; for both the court of Admiralty, and Parliament have passed over the subject of the date of the French decree of April 1811 without noticeing the obvious inconsistency of its want of promulgation with the requisites of the Duke de Cadore's letter of the 5th. of Aug: 1810 although the former has quoted that very letter; and in contempt of my salutary intimation (Letter to a Noble Lord page 4.) has in that quotation omitted the words that I had marked in Italics.[9] The Duke of Sussex too, who is a reading man, and with whom I spent an hour last week, mortified me by observing that we claimed the privilege of free ships free goods, although I had sent him, at the time it was published, under a blank cover, a copy of said letter which I now acknowledged was my own. I am however not easily mortified, nor discouraged in the pursuit of what I think right and I shall continue my endeavours to get rid of this abominable impressment of seamen, though a source of that emolument which would fall to me in the situation I have proposed for myself. I rest always most truly, Dear sir, Your friend and servt.

GEO: JOY.

RC and enclosures (DLC: Rives Collection, Madison Papers). RC in a clerk's hand, signed by Joy; postmarked Baltimore, 3 Dec. Note on cover reads: "Custom House Baltime Decr 3 1812 / Recd & forwd by J H McC." Docketed by JM, "Joy Geo. 19 & 21. Sep. 1812." For enclosures, see nn. 2 and 4.

1. In his 20 Aug. 1812 dispatch, James Maury had enclosed six manuscript pages of an article that appeared above the signature of "A Cosmopolite" in the London *Times* on 24 Aug. 1812 (DNA: RG 59, CD, Liverpool). Joy's article, couched as a response to a critique of JM's 1 June message to Congress that had been printed in the same paper on 12 Aug., took issue with the notion that impressment was insufficient grounds for war. Joy denied the charge that the U.S. had long been willing to tolerate impressment, arguing that neither JM nor his predecessors had been "content to be passive on the subject for one moment," in spite of their desire to maintain favorable relations with Great Britain. Instead, Joy faulted Great Britain for failing to redress the grievance in light of its disavowal of any right to impress native-born Americans. Nor, he argued, could it be proved that the U.S. had given cause for impressment by encouraging the desertion of British seamen. Joy explained that, on the contrary, the U.S. had declared a willingness to aid in the discovery and return of British sailors as part of an agreement to protect the rights of its own. Joy observed that while British naturalization laws were designed to recruit foreign seamen, British sailors could find no inducement in Ameri-

can naturalization practices to defect. He concluded that since few British seamen were actually recovered during searches on the high seas, their recovery could not be the true object of such acts, which "so often deprived the American ship of her own proper seamen, and left her not unfrequently with an insufficient crew to keep her off a lee-shore."

Joy also took exception to the implication in the earlier article that U.S. policy was guided by French influence. He argued that JM had taken pains to point out French transgressions on American maritime rights and had stated publicly that the U.S. should avoid entangling alliances with foreign powers. Joy expressed the hope that British policy makers would "perceive, which is the true fact, that Americans are not Frenchmen; neither are American principles French principles."

2. Joy enclosed an unpublished response (3 pp.) to the charge of French influence on American policy, which appears to have been inspired by an extract from a meeting of the citizens of Columbia County, New York, published in the 24 Aug. London *Times*. The meeting had objected to the war because it connected the destinies of Americans "with those of the French Empire." Though France stood to gain from a war between Great Britain and the U.S., it was Joy's opinion that such an outcome was not an object of the war. He observed that JM had urged Congress to avoid entanglements "in the interests or views of other powers." He pointed to the willingness of the Senate to support a war against France as further evidence of his point, referring to his published pamphlets on the subject of British-American relations for further treatment of this matter.

3. In his 30 July 1812 opinion in the case of the *Snipe*, Sir William Scott declared that the French decree revoking the Berlin and Milan Decrees was "altogether obscure, involved, and contradictory." He pointed out that repeated requests by Great Britain for a copy of the decree had been denied, leading him to the conclusion that the document was "a false and fraudulent instrument, without good faith, without authenticity, and without promulgation." Scott argued that its fraudulence hardly mattered in any case, because the real question was whether it was appropriate for France to select a single neutral power as the beneficiary of the supposed revocation while leaving restrictions in effect with respect to other neutral nations (*The Times* [London], 28 Aug. 1812).

4. Joy enclosed a copy of his 12 Sept. 1812 letter to Lord Sidmouth (2 pp.), which had enclosed a reprint of a 4 Aug. 1812 editorial on impressment from the *National Intelligencer*. Joy alluded to measures taken by the British government to open negotiations on the subject before the declaration of war, probably referring to Foster's 15 Apr. and 1 June 1812 letters to Monroe. In the former, Foster promised that when American-born citizens were found upon British vessels, "no exertion shall be wanting on my part to procure their discharge." In the latter, Foster claimed to be under orders to inform Monroe that "the Government of His Royal Highness the Prince Regent will continue to give the most positive orders against the detention of American citizens on board His Majesty's ships" any longer than necessary to determine their citizenship (*ASP, Foreign Relations*, 3:454, 459–60).

5. This edition of the London *Morning Chronicle* reprinted an extract from a 2 Sept. 1808 editorial from the *National Intelligencer* criticizing George Canning's 24 June 1808 speech in Parliament. The extract claimed that Canning's misrepresentation of the relationship between the U.S. and Great Britain, the orders in council, and the *Chesapeake* affair had the effect in the U.S. of promoting opposition to the administration on the eve of several important elections. The editorial took exception to Canning's charge that the U.S., indifferent to restoring harmony with Great Britain, had failed to submit remonstrances against the orders in council while keeping the lines of communication open with the French. Declaring such a charge to be a "gross and palpable falsehood," the editorial claimed that redress had been demanded of both nations whenever an infraction of the neutral rights of the U.S. had been committed. The editorial further argued that Canning had himself received and ignored remonstrances against the orders in council, thus closing all avenues of recourse.

6. Canning's 22 Nov. 1808 letter to William Pinkney explained his delay in responding to

the American minister's comments on the implementation of the orders in council as the result of the pressure of business and his own misunderstanding of Pinkney's authority and intentions (ibid., 3:237–39).

7. On 10 Sept. 1812 the London *Times* reported that Sir Edward Thornton, British minister to Sweden, had been in Denmark, where he had failed to negotiate a peace treaty.

8. Canning had been a member of the ministry that had ordered the bombardment of Copenhagen in 1807, a measure taken to prevent the neutral Danes from forming an alliance with France (see Rory Muir, *Britain and the Defeat of Napoleon, 1807–1815* [New Haven, 1996], 23–25).

9. In his pamphlet *A Letter, from a Calm Observer, to a Noble Lord* (see Joy to JM, 16 May 1812, *PJM-PS*, 4:389 n. 1), Joy had italicized the phrase "conformément à l'acte que vous venez de communiquer," referring to Macon's Bill No. 2.

From William Duane

Sir,   Phila Sepr 20. 1812

If I did not believe that the motive which actuates me would justify me even under the possibility of my conceptions being erroneous, and that you would receive the suggestions of an individual who has no other views than the general and common interest I should not venture to address you. The efforts of the humblest individual may at least contribute to the direction of the ex[e]cutive mind towards objects of great public importance; and I address you without reserve under these impressions.

The letter of General Hull[1] goes to vindicate the Administration in every thing that relates to the unhappy events at Detroit, except in the single point of the neglect of Machilimacknac; and altho' this cannot justify the misconduct of the Officer, it is a point upon which he may escape every imputation but that of incapacity or cowardice.

I offer this opinion with no other view than to indicate the absolute necessity of being provident, on other vulnerable points, and in doing this I must attempt to anticipate by first considering what is possible, the necessity of guarding against what is probable.

The U. States may be assailed at its two extremities, that is at some point of Florida or Louisiana, on the South; and at some point between the Long island Sound and the Bay of Casco, or betw⟨ee⟩n N. York and Portsmouth in N. Hampshire. The necessary means for the defence of the South I have no doubt have been properly pointed out by the able Officer who has charge of N. Orleans; if the Government have provided the means requisite there, and in such hands there is no doubt of their being well managed, it will be unnecessary to touch a point so much better occupied. But the most vulnerable point at this moment is the section on the East which I have referred to.

What renders it particularly indispensible at this time and not an hour should be lost, is the peculiar circumstance of the Eastern states and the facilities which their superior naval force afford to the enemy to select any point of that section of the Union upon which they may think fit to make an impression.

I do not believe that disaffection is either so extensive as the seditious in that quarter represent; nor do I think that left to themselves without external influence, their clamors or the most treasonable efforts they could make would end in any other than their own destruction and the greater security of the government.

But as in all political affairs, as well as in military affairs, the effects of human passions acted upon by sudden and alarming events, must be always taken into view, it may be safely assumed, that the landing of a force of from three to five thousand troops of the enemy on any point of that Section, would encourage disaffection, and what is most to be apprehended, appal the virtuous. The effect need not be minutely examined it is within the measure of every man's conceptions.

But it may be presumed that as the disaffection is more in clamor than in reality, there is not so much danger. This would be just reasoning if we had any reason to think the British government to be wiser now or less credulous when their wishes were their counsellors, than at former periods. If we wanted any evidence to satisfy us, the speeches in the Parliament of England in the last Session, the mission of Henry, and the audacious insolence and temerity of the adherents of England in our seaports and at the seat of the government itself, would declare that the British Government calculates largely on the disaffection in all parts of the Union, but particularly in the three maritime states next adjoin[in]g to N. York. That they will act in some shape upon these calculations, I believe there can be no doubt. Whether they will resort to private emissaries and largesses, or to public offers of alliance and association with those states; or whether they will employ their naval force to land an army on the Eastern coasts is uncertain; I think they will attempt all these means. It may be very truly urged, that they could derive no permanent advantages from such attempts; that they would be driven off in disgrace or their troops compelled to surrender; or that the[y] could not send a force sufficient for any durable conquest. But admitting all these results as certane, the event is not the whole of the consideration, they could accomplish great and heavy afflictions—they would paralyse the efforts and obstruct the resources of prosperity over a large surface of country: the alarm would be even greater than the danger or the evil perpetrated, but the evil would not be wholly local its effects would be felt to the extreme of the union as the disastrous but comparatively trivial event at Detroit now is.

It may be well to consider what they can and may do. The importance which they necessarily and truly attach to the Station of Halifax, super-

added to the importance of Quebec will induce them to send out a considerable force to Halifax, arriving early they might enter the St. Lawrence at
any time in the ensuing month of October, vessels to my knowlege have
entered in November, and a vessel has been known to sail early in December; however, they can enter Halifax at any Season. They may upon ten
ships of war and 20 transports send 10000 men to Halifax. They can provision them by the temptations which they have held forth to the avarice of
our people to carry provisions to Bermuda, or direct to Halifax; but even if
provisions should not be abundant, the[y] would then have a fresh stimu-
lant to keep their troops in action and discipline, to transport a body of
5000, to some part of our coasts where by the previous advices of their
emissaries, they would find means to subsist their troops or satiate their
rapacity.

Perhaps by an *understanding with their friends* they may not at first touch
Boston; but the greater probability is that their first attempts would be in
that quarter; but secure within Cape Cod, with a superior fleet, they could
select any place in that Bay particularly Plymouth; the waters of Rhode Island and all along the Sound to New Rochelle, they might depredate without danger, and land troops under cover of their ships; 5000 men landed on
Long Island could carry off every thing upon it, and bombard and lay N.
York in Ashes, and retire before any force competent to resist them could
be brought to act.

I draw this sketch rapidly tho' its scope is extensive, because altho' they
could not operate on all that line of coast at once, yet they having the choice
of the point of attack it is indispensible to consider how far and how much
they may be able to go and do.

That such is the course a powerful and skilful enemy would pursue, I believe will admit of no question; and without supposing them to possess all
the Skill in the world, it can hardly be presumed that they are so little acquainted with the management of military operations as to overlook such
advantages as our circumstances present to them.

These views press upon the consideration of the government, the importance of an early and adequate preparation against such contingencies;
and there [are] other motives no less cogent which call imperiously for effective and prompt preparations.

Measures of prevention are of all others the most wise; th[e]y do not
carry the eclat of victory but they secure the consolations of virtue; they do
good by preventing evil. The means by which I would guard against them,
is by acting upon the *offensive* I would not wait for his assault, I would compell him to remain within his strong hold, if I could do no better; and if I
could take it from him, I would prefer it; but at any event I would keep him
so effectually in check, that he should not be capable of moving without
danger, and I should thereby protect myself.

In a paper which I published a few days ago, I threw out a loose sketch of these conceptions,[2] but I confess that *there was an object upon which I would not publicly touch*, which is of no less moment; perhaps of the greatest moment. I shall state it, when I have suggested the means to which I would have recourse.

I would embody and encamp a force of 10000 men in two divisions; 5000 regulars, 5000 Volunteers, or such militia as would perform a tour of duty for six months, in which case, they should go at the end of every month, after the first three, one thousand men, and be preceeded by 1000, who should be as exactly disciplined as the regulars; with these corps, I should threaten to march to Quebec in the first instance by the Kennebeck & Chaudiere; but I should by marches of discipline, change their direction and menace Halifax; if Halifax should be found accessible (and I know it is) it might be taken after two or three feints; if not taken the troops would at least be disciplined to war by the movements, and the enemy, apprized of the state of preparation, would be cautious of Exposing his post by sending his troops upon marauding expeditions or to be taken by a force so much more capable from its local advantages of repelling them.

I need not point out the advantages to discipline, and to the acquisition of an Efficient force for any service, the embodying a compact army of 10000 men would prove. But what I before referred to is the importance of having it embodied in the *very neighborhood of disaffection*—its presence, without a single act of rigor, its discipline without being employed on any other duty, would not only destroy every disposition to treason, but it would disconcert the enemy, by occupying the very ground, upon which *he had been invited to raise his standard.*

A force of this kind would attract attention, the faithful citizen would feel a confidence which he is now a stranger to—the army itself would circulate its pay and give activity to local industry; the voice of patriotism would be heard where treason now mutters curses upon the government which is too mild to punish it; and the operations in other quarters would instead of being interrupted or weakened, they would derive confidence and strength from the very knowlege that such a force existed.

I have expressed what I conceive to be in itself more important than I can describe it—but I sincerely believe it would be a measure of the greatest importance in all the views in which I have presented it. I am Sir with great respect your obed sert

WM DUANE

RC (DLC). Enclosed in a note from Duane to JM, 20 Sept. 1812 (DLC; 1 p.; docketed by JM), which requested that the letter be considered a "private communication" to be shared only with Monroe (printed in the *Proceedings of the Massachusetts Historical Society*, 2d ser., 20 [1906–7]: 355). A note in an unidentified hand attached to the verso of the final page reads: "The two parties opposed to the present administration, who had delegates at Lancaster—

have quarreled and separated in ill blood—without agreeing on any object relative to the Governmental or Presidential Election—a good omen." This was probably a reference to the meeting of Democrats and Clintonian Republicans in Lancaster, Pennsylvania, on 26 Aug. 1812 (see Higginbotham, *Keystone in the Democratic Arch*, 259).

1. Duane referred to Hull's 26 Aug. 1812 letter to Eustis, enclosing the articles of capitulation at Detroit and offering his explanation for the surrender (*Michigan Historical Collections* 40 [1929]: 460–69). Duane published the letter in the *Aurora General Advertiser* on 21 Sept. 1812.

2. In the 8 Sept. 1812 issue of the *Aurora General Advertiser*, Duane had suggested that Halifax was an attractive target for an American offensive.

§ From Samuel Turner. *20 September 1812, Hormuz, "His Majesty's Ship Salvador del Mundo."* "Presumeing that you are already acquainted with the particulars of my capture, I feel it a duty incumberent on me most respectfully, to acquaint you that I have been kept a close prisoner on board His Majestys Britannic Ship Salvador del Mundo laying as a guard Ship at this Port, since the 29 of June last, never been once suffered on shore, however urgent my private affairs were.

"I deem it a duty due to my Count[r]y to make you acquainted with such *particular* circumstances as immediately fell under my own observation. Fifteen American Subjects were *forced* by Captain James Nash of the Salvador to go on board H. M. ship Clarence Seventy four Guns where they now are, one of whom, Lewis Bancel a native of New-York wrote me on the Subject. I accordingly stated, what I knew as to their being american Subjects—and offered Captn Nash to make my affidavit—but it had no effect.

"I do therefore Sir most humbly implore that you will take the peculiar hard case of myself & my unfortunate countrymen into your very benign consideration, and adopt such measures for our releif, as in your superior Judgment may deem the most expedient. I think it necessary to add that I am clas'd with the Petty officers with seamans allowance.

"I have made repeated official applications, to know how I am to be considered, but cannot obtain my answer.

"For your better information I have enclosed the Copy of a letter I sent to the admiralty, also one I received from Lewis Bancell."

RC (DNA: RG 59, Letters Received regarding Impressed Seamen, box 10). 3 pp.; docketed as received 15 Nov. and as "Sufficient." Enclosures not found.

To James Monroe

Dear Sir   Washington Sepr. 21 1812

Not a word from abroad, or the West, since you left us. Dearborn has still one eye on Montreal, and the other on Niagara: forcing the attention of the Enemy to both, with a purpose, doubtless of striking, himself, at either or both according to circumstances.[1] The story of an armament agst.

Plattsburg is groundless. Niagara was very weak at the last date, and more in danger of attack, than Plattsburg. But Dearborne counted on about 3,000 regulars & 4000 militia, as soon to be there. Proofs multiply daily, of the difficulty of obtaining regulars, and of the fluctuating resource in the Militia. High bounties & short enlistments, however objectionable, will alone fill the ranks; and these too in a moderate number. This plan wd. have give [*sic*] us a greater force in July, when the Enemy were unprepared, than we shall have in Novr. when it is possible reinforcements may have reached Canada from England. D. has allotted a Brigade at Niagara, to Smith. This has given rise to the pretensions in his letter to you;[2] which I am persuaded go beyond the intentions of Genl. D, as well as beyond military rules. How Van R. is to rank, without commanding him in a conjoint operation, is not understood; or why he shd. not do so without the limits of the U. S. if under their Govt., any more than without the limits of N. Y: as in the case of such an operation in Vermont, is also to be explained. Besides, an older Brigadr. as Winchester, may take the Command of the regulars at that place. If you answer his letter, I think it wd. be best to refer him to Dearborne for explanatory directions on those points; with an intimation not to act on his own ideas in the mean time. Affecte. respects

JAMES MADISON

RC (DLC: Monroe Papers).

1. In his 14 Sept. 1812 letter to Eustis, Dearborn declared that he could "calculate on no movement, with any prospect of success, unless we can ultimately succeed at Niagara." The general also discussed troop movements, his decision to give the command of a brigade at Niagara to Brig. Gen. Alexander Smyth, and his belief that command of the upper lakes should constitute an urgent strategic goal. He informed Eustis of his plan to send nearly 5,000 regular troops and militia to Plattsburgh under Brig. Gen. Joseph Bloomfield, with orders to draw British forces away from Upper Canada (DNA: RG 107, LRRS, D-168:6).

2. Letter not found.

From George Joy

DEAR SIR,   LONDON 21st septr: 1812

Mr: Russell has sometimes said he wished I would give a lesson to some of my federal friends; and it has occurred to me, at the moment of despatching the within to take the liberty of passing it under your eye.[1] No objection will be made to the publication of any part of it, as extract of a letter from an American in London to his friend in Boston.

I have already written you by this Conveyance; and remain very respectfully, Dear sir, Your friend & Servt:

GEO: JOY

I should have observed in the above that the 2nd and 3rd sheet were all I would trouble you to look over. The general Letters of the George Washington were delivered here yesterday Morning; but there were none rec'd for Mr Russell as late as 3 o'Clock yesterday. I presume as the wind is [*sic*] that he sailed from Plymo: this morning in the Lark.

RC (DLC: Rives Collection, Madison Papers). Marked "(Copy) 1st. ℔ Lark via N. York." This letter covered Joy's dispatch of 19 Sept. 1812.

1. Enclosure not identified.

From Edward Coles

DEAR SIR   GREEN MOUNTAIN Sep. 22d '12
When I had the pleasure to see you at Montpellier I expected long before this to have been with you in Washington. It is with much concern I inform you that I have been, and shall, Dr. Everette[1] thinks, necessarily be detained between three and four weeks longer by a serious indisposition. If my absence should be attended with any very serious inconvenience to you, and you should know of any one to take my place, who will be equally satisfactory to you and Mr. M., I beg that you will permit no feelings of delicacy to me for a moment to prevent you from doing that which will be most agreeable. When I say this I feel persuaded you will justly appreciate the motive, and that you are too well acquainted with the high regard and filial affection I entertain for you and Mrs. M. to believe that I am influenced by any other consideration than that which relates to your convenience and pleasure.

As Dr. Everette is waiting to convey this to the post-office I must conclude, but not without tendering my most affectionate regards to Mrs. M., and assuring you of the imperishable gratitude & affection of your friend
                                                    EDWARD COLES

RC (ICHi). Docketed by JM.

1. Dr. Charles Everett (d. 1848) received his medical degree from the University of Pennsylvania in 1795 and settled in Albemarle County, Virginia. He served as a representative to the Virginia House of Delegates and was personal physician to James Monroe (Wyndham B. Blanton, *Medicine in Virginia in the Eighteenth Century* [Richmond, 1931], 82; *Tyler's Quarterly* 4 [1922–23]: 96).

From Thomas Lawton

SIR, Sept 22, 1812

I address you upon a subject, which I claim no right to, except that of humanity and of the public benefice.

As our Country is now involved in War and the mite of every one is highly requisite to extirpate that foe who has thought proper to excite our indignation, I think that every means within our limits, to strengthen our Armies; ought to be resorted to.

In the US. Army, there are many Prisoners who have rendered themselves so, by different foiables, the principal part of them by Desertion and this crime, generally is, without doubt occasioned by the ill as well as inhumane conduct of Officers towards Soldiers, that induces them to do that, which necesity in manner obliges them to.

There are Prisoners of the description already mentioned, in the US. Service, whose hearts palpitate with desire to take an active part in the present contest, and many of whom, are within the knowledge of my researches.

Tis seldom that you see an idiot or a person destitute of common sense in confinement for the above mentioned Crime; and in fact these Prisoners, whom I allude to, would in reality, compose the flower of the Army, were they allowed to occupy their Arms.

It is a common expectation among people in general, that when War, takes place—that Prisoners would be released & return to duty; but this suggestion it seems has not as yet been verified, which causes this address.

As a Citizen I only intreat that the President would think proper to proclaim their pardons, and allow them to return to their duty; as this measure would much strengthen the active force of the Army with no expence, more than they now incur to the Public.

All of which is respectfully submitted to your Excellency's, consideration. I am your Obedient Humble Servant.

THOMAS LAWTON

RC (DNA: RG 107, LRRS, L-209:6). Docketed as received in the War Department on 1 Oct. 1812.

§ From William Eustis. *Ca. 22 September 1812*. Informs JM that Henry Glen was appointed assistant deputy quartermaster on 1 July 1812 on the recommendation of Morgan Lewis. Lewis, however, subsequently withheld the appointment, "finding some objection." Glen has failed to return his letter of appointment; Lewis will be written to on the subject.

RC (DLC). 1 p. Undated; dated 1812 in the *Index to the James Madison Papers;* date assigned here on the basis of Eustis's 22 Sept. 1812 letter to Lewis requesting the return of Glen's letter of appointment (DNA: RG 107, LSMA).

To James Monroe

Dear Sir   Washington Sepr. 23. 1812.

Still without authentic information from Abroad. The Halifax papers expect Adml. Warren with a naval force, and an offer of peace. It appears that Wellington has gained a victory over Marmont;[1] The extent of it not ascertained. From the West the accounts are that a B & Indn. force amounting to about 600 left Malden after the surrender of Detroit, to attack F. Wayne, & in case of success, to proceed to F. Harrison & Vincennes.[2] As it is pretty certain F. Harrison was invested, it is apprehended that F. Wayne may have fallen. According to the latest dates however, that is to say the 13th. inst: from Urbanna, no such information had come to hand.[3] Harrison has finally determined to push on himself towards Fort Wayne; having left Piqua on the 6th. inst: with the rear of the Army, & an intention to overtake it by forced marches. The force then immediately with him will be about 3000. Affce. respects

JAMES MADISON

Good supplies of tents, Blankets & other articles have been sent from Pittsburg, as well as from Philada. for the N. Western Expedition.

RC (DLC: Monroe Papers).

1. On 22 July 1812 the duke of Wellington won a decisive victory over French forces commanded by Auguste-Frédéric-Louis Viesse de Marmont at the Battle of Salamanca in northern Spain (Tulard, *Dictionnaire Napoléon*, 1144, 1745).

2. Harrison's 5 Sept. 1812 letter to Eustis provided this news. The general explained that the perilous situation of Fort Wayne had prompted his decision to leave Piqua in order to reinforce the fort (DNA: RG 107, LRRS, H-366:6).

3. Meigs's 13 Sept. 1812 letter to Eustis reported that Harrison had marched from Piqua on 6 Sept. with 3,000 troops "for the relief of Fort Wayne," but Meigs provided no news of the condition of the fort (ibid., M-424:6).

From Jonathan Dayton

Septr. 23. 12

The writer of this did not intend to follow up the late communication[1] with any other, until he learned thro' the channell he had pointed out, whether they were acceptable, but considerations, not only personal to yourself, but important to the welfare of our country have impelled him so far to change his intention. The Assembly of the *Notables* (as they are ludicrously called) convened lately in the city of New York, have broken up. The first object of their discussion was to ascertain whether there was any hope of carrying a Federal President—this being unanimously decided in the negative—the next enquiry was, whether, under present circumstances it would be adviseable to put up a Federal candidate, on whom to expend all the Federal votes. The discussion on this point was a long & animated one. Mr. Rufus King & a few others coming out strongly in support, & Mr. H. G. Otis leading in opposition, & carrying with him a large majority. The plan of course now is, for all those States who can carry Federal electors, to reserve themselves as make-weights in the scale of competition between the two great rival, Republican competitors. There was neither proposition nor any argument nor hint in relation to a severance of the Union. It would have been unsafe & most impolitic to broach it before the men who were from the States south of the Hudson, especially those from Penns. & Maryland.

Upon the subject of future operations agt. Canada, the writer will venture to suggest a plan which appears to him by far the most adviseable, & which you sir, & your cabinet can estimate at what it is worth. Instead of directing your forces towards Montreal this season, where their success from various causes will be very doubtful, let their destination be agt. the British posts on lakes Ontario & Erie & the waters of communication between them. Instead of sending or stationing troops along lake Champlain, remove every soldier from thence beyond one company—leave no stores of any kind at Plattsburgh or it's vicinity to invite invasion, but barely provide for keeping complete command of that lake. Let a corps of observation *not of operation* (it's number depending upon circumstances) be stationed upon the St. Laurence between Ogdensburgh & the outlet of Ontario, & let Genl Dearborn's army file off to the left & approach Niagara, dismissing previously however such part of his force as may be considered supernumarary for the object, especially those of the militia drafts which may be the worst clothed or armed, or apparently the most reluctant. The forts Erie & George, opposite Niagara & black rock must inevitably fall to him, & a part of his troops may occupy for the winter, the settlements of the Canadians on the west side.

In like manner & at same time, the operations of Genl. Harrison must be carried with sufficient force & decisive effect agt. Malden, & desultorily agt. the settlemts. & towns of all those Indians whose warriors have taken any part agt. us. The proper artificers must be employed at proper & secure stations to build & equip vessels for taking & keeping command of both lakes, & in addition thereto, such boats & water craft as will be useful for the descent of the St. Laurence in the spring. To this extent, success, under even tolerable management on the part of the Commanders, must be certain—the Indians will be checked & destroyed or under controul—the lakes under subjection to us—our soldiers will have time & means for discipline & for the fit preparations for the more arduous task in the ensuing campaign of invading lower Canada, and encountering the whole British force. From what we learn of this force, and from what we know of our own, which latter must be made up in great measure of raw recruits or irregular militia, there is reason to fear that in their attempt *even upon Montreal,* this season, they will be defeated. If the writer could seriously think otherwise, or could believe the danger less than he has represented it, he should have been very far from making this suggestion, but he is so strongly impressed with the evil consequences of a second disaster in our military affairs this season, that he could not, in justice to his feelings, his best wishes for the prosperity of the country, & (he takes the liberty of adding sir) for your success also, forbear to make this communication. It is however sir, intended for your perusal only, but with full permission & expectation that you make such use, as you think proper, of the information & opinions it contains, for your own benefit, or that of the country.

This is hastily written, within one hour before the departure of the mail—there are many arguments & inducements in favor of the plan of operations above proposed, & against those now carrying on, upon the side of Montreal & next to Champlain, which there is not time to detail.

RC (NjP). Unsigned; correspondent identified on the basis of JM's docket, which reads "J. D. apparently," and by comparison with the handwriting of Dayton's "Cyrus" letters (see *PJM-PS*, 1:210–11 and nn., 4:249–50 and n. 5, 257–58 and n.).

1. Dayton to JM, ca. 17 Sept. 1812.

From Abraham G. Lansing

Sir   Albany Septr. 23d. 1812

I take the Liberty of soliciting your patronage for my Son John Y. Lansing[1] who is a Surgeon in one of the Regiments of detached Militia of this State and who I wish to have transfered in the same Grade to the regular Army or Hospital—he has been liberally educated, has creditably compleated his Course of Medical Studies and received Diplomas both in Philadelphia and New York.

That I have the Honor to address you unsupported by others, is owing to my Indisposition to apply to the two prominent Characters here thro' whom it is generally believed Applications of this kind can only be successful and who tho' they probably profess to be your Friends, if their Sentiments are to be inferred from their Actions are only aiming to subserve their own views regardless of those professions—with them I could not consistant with the opinion I entertain of them have any Connection until their Conduct is less equivocal, altho I have no Doubt from their late Behaviour towards me that I could procure any Recommendation I wished on my Application.

With my worthy Friend General Smith I have had an unreserved Conversation a few Days since—on the Subject of our political Affairs in which we perfectly accorded and he has been so good as to undertake the Transmission of my Letter under his Cover. I have the Honor to be with the greatest Respect Sir Your obedient & very humble Servant

ABM. G LANSING.

RC (DLC). Docketed by JM.

1. JM appointed John Y. Lansing (b. 1788) to the rank of regular army surgeon on 15 Oct. 1812 (*Senate Exec. Proceedings*, 2:300). John's father, Abraham Gerrit Lansing (1756–1844), was state treasurer for New York in 1803 and 1810 (Lee C. Lansing Jr., comp., *Genealogy of the Lansing Family in America, 1640–1985* [n.p., 1985], T, 11, 19).

From James Monroe

DEAR SIR   ALBEMARLE Sepr 23. [1812]

I have just received yours of the 21st. Smiths pretention is entirely unfounded. A major genl. in the militia takes rank of a Brigr. in the regular service, whether within or without the UStates, indeed the circumstance of being within or without our limits, can make no difference. The relation between the troops, and the officers commanding them is the same, in each case. I will write him on the subject, and after giving my own opinion, refer him to genl Dearborn. The claim to a brevet is equally unreasonable. The other Brigs, especially of the old army, would have just cause of complaint if he was preferr'd above them.

I found Mrs Monroe much indisposed on my arrival, with a bilious complaint. She is better, and I hope will be able to set out, on our return, to Washington early next week.

Altho a state of inactivity at Niagara, and below it, is to be regretted, if imposed by necessity, it is much better than a repulse. I think a repulse at either place at this time would produce a very bad effect. A false step would be much worse than none. The cause of the latter might be explaind, and the nation not feel itself dishonor'd by it; but it would be otherwise in the other case.

The affair of Hull has not injurd the govt. in this quarter. It tends rather to make the opposition more odious, by the simpathy which it excites for the sufferers to the westward, and the mortification which most feel at the stain it has fixed on our national character. I am told that the sentiment is of general impression that untill we efface this stain, no terms ought to be accepted from G Britain. Respectfully & sincerely yours

JAS MONROE

RC (DLC: Rives Collection, Madison Papers). The year "1812" is appended to the date-line in JM's hand. Misdocketed by JM "Sepr. 23. 1813."

From William Plumer

NEW HAMPSHIRE—EXECUTIVE DEPARTMENT
SIR,   EPPING September 23, 1812.

Having in common with every good citizen of the United States an anxiety, that the present necessary & just war against Great Britain & her savage allies, should be prosecuted not only with vigor but with success, I know your candor will excuse the freedom I indulge, in suggesting the propriety of allowing higher wages to the soldiers. In New England, the demand for laborers is so great, & the price of labour so high, that the terms offered by Congress are considered inadequate.[1] The laborer, whose toil is not severe, whose diet & lodging is good, & who is not exposed to danger, receives much more than the soldier. The bounty in land that the soldiers are to receive at the termination of their service, is by them generally greatly underated. Present pay, has to that class of men, stronger inducements than a larger, but distant reward. In these parts, I impute the want of success in the recruiting business, much more to the lowness of wages, than to an indisposition to support the war. In a new country, like the United States, where land is cheap & labour of course high, & the objects inviting industry numerous, it cannot be expected we should obtain soldiers for the same wages as they do in the old cultivated countries of Europe. If the wages of new recruits should hereafter be raised, I am sensible that of those already enlisted should, from the same period, be also encreased, otherwise they would complain. And I cannot think the raising of the wages would eventually enhance the cost of the war; but would bring such a force into the field as would bring it to a more speedy termination.

I most cordially congratulate you on the success of the Republican election in Vermont.[2] It has given a great shock to that fatal measure, which too many of the leaders of Eastern federalism have adopted, the *dismemberment of the Union*. If we succeed in New Hampshire in our November elections, & I trust we shall, it will, at least for the present, put that dangerous question at rest.

351

The war appears to grow more popular; & I think much of the clamour against it will subside with the December elections.

Have you any overtures from Great Britain that will warrant the hope of accomodation on *just principles?*

Should you have a leisure moment any communication you will please to make will be duely appretiated. I have the honor to be with sentiments of much personal respect & esteem Sir your most obedient humble servant

WILLIAM PLUMER

RC (DLC); letterbook copy (DLC: William Plumer Papers). RC docketed by JM.

1. The rate of pay for privates in the U.S. Army had been set at $5 per month in 1802. In 1812 the money bounty for a five-year term of enlistment was $16; the land bounty upon discharge was 160 acres (*U.S. Statutes at Large*, 2:133, 672).

2. On 19 Sept. 1812 the *National Intelligencer* printed a letter from Vermont reporting that preliminary election results for state offices, including the governorship, showed a "nett republican gain" of 1,220 votes.

From James Taylor

SIR   NEW PORT KENTUCKY Sept 23d 1812

I have the honor to inclose you a Copy of a statement made at Cleveland in order to send on to our Army which I supposed was proceeding on toward Detroit.[1]

I did myself the honor to give one to Genl Wodsworth & to forward to Genl Harrison & Gov Meigs each one. When I arrived at Urbana I was very unwell & indeed became ill before I left that place.

I fully intended to have seen Genl Harrison, but for my indisposition and the difficulty of finding him short of Ft Wayn⟨e⟩ & indeed no Certanty even at that place. Colo McArthur went on & I got him to add some other impressions and that inteligent officer would be able to add a great Many useful hints.

I sincerely lament & deeply deplore the loss we have met with at Detroit. I am not concious of having omited to do any thing which it was my duty to have done as far as my Capacity would enable me to do.

I was one of those who took upon my self the responsibility of writing & sending to Gor. Scott by express beging him to send us on all the Troops he could possibly raise for we had lost all confidence in Genl Hull or nearly so & thought it our duty to make some exertions to save the Country. The raising the flag was like a panic to the great body of the officers & Men. I happened to be out of the fort at time or should have certainly aided Colo Findlay in prevailing upon Colo Miller to assume the Command or aid Colo F. but I was attending to some business in the Town at the time & did not get in to the Fort 'till the aid decamp rode up, and then it was too late. On the refusal of Colo Findlay to join in drawing up the articles of Capitulation he sent for me & requested me to join Colo Miller but I refused to do so telling him perhaps he could get some one whose mind was more congenial with his & one who could perhaps do more justice to the Case. The Genl Called no council as to the delivery as far as I have understood but have no doubt You have receivd from Colos. Cass & Findlay a Correct statement. I had left the Ft. about one & a half hours I presume before the Flag was raised & never was more supprised when I saw it up. I can assure you with Truth that every one of the Colonels & myself who was generally one were anxious to go on to Malden & protested against leaving the Canada side, but all was to no effect. I declare to you I think the whole course of proceeding the most weak cowardly & imbecile that ever came within my notice.

I have not time at this time to say more, I refer you to my letters to the Honbl the Secy of War.[2] I gave you a little hint that Genl Hull had drawn orders on me to considerable amount. This was near detaining me, but I persisted & came off clear. I have the honor to be with great respect & esteem in hast sir Your obed serv

JAMES TAYLOR

RC (DLC). Docketed by JM.

1. Enclosure not found, but it may have been a list of arms and supplies in the possession of the American forces at the surrender of Detroit. Such a list was published in the *National Intelligencer* on 29 Sept. 1812.

2. Taylor probably referred to his letters to Eustis of 15 and 16 Sept. 1812, which discussed the pressure he was under to relinquish his funds to the British (DNA: RG 107, LRRS, T-161:6; Registers of Letters Received by the Secretary of War [DNA: RG 107]).

From Mathew Carey

(Private)

SIR,   PHILADA. Sept. 24. 1812

Your favour of the 19th. which I duly recd is before me.

I am rejoiced that you, who have so much better opportunities than I have, feel so confident of a favourable issue of the present state of affairs. Altho' your opinion has allayed my apprehensions in some degree, yet I cannot feel quite so sanguine as you are.

I owe it to myself to explain one part of my letters, which you have misconceived. It was not my wish or expectation that the government should openly interfere in the establishment of the societies that I regarded, & still regard as the only sovereign remedy for the treasonable attempts made to

353

the eastward. No such thing. I merely wished that their friends in New England should be encouraged in the undertaking by the knowledge that it was regarded with a favourable eye by the administration.

That the views of the leaders of the party are to the last degree hostile to the existing form of government—that if any favourable opportunity offers for putting their treasonable projects into execution, they will gladly avail themselves of it—that the vicissitudes of war, especially under the alarming disparity of naval forces, might in a week afford them such an opportunity—are truths most undeniable—& as awful as they are undeniable. Under those circumstances, to neglect taking every fair means to secure the country from the menaced ruin, would, in my opinion, be most lamentable infatuation. I am, sir, respectfully, your obt. hble. servt.

MATHEW CAREY

RC (DLC).

From Joel Barlow

private[1]

DEAR SIR,   PARIS 26 Sep. 1812.

Your letter of Aug. 11. has *excited serious reflections* in several eminent men to whom I have communicated in confidence its principal points. I had many times lately explained to them the same ideas. It is very useful to have it in my power to inforce them by your authority.

I have never yet despaired of obtaining such an arrangement as would be *acceptable to you* both as to the past & the future. But *the Emperor* for the last six months, has been so *totally absorbed in his Russian war* that he has thought of very little else. And this I believe has been the principal cause of *the delay* of which I have not ceased *to complain.* The *Treaty* might have been agreed upon and signed long ago, if it were not for the *indemnities for past spoliations* some arrangement for which I insisted on to accompany *the treaty.*[2]

The prospect in regard to these has never been *brilliant.* I believe you had no decided *expectation of obtaining* any part of them, and since I did not feel authorised to listen to any thing like *indemnity arising* out of a convention of *limits for Louisiana* and a *cession of East Florida* (for which objects however *five millions of dollars* had been repeatedly offered, and *offered to France*) *this unpromising work* became still more *difficult* to manage. It is now however, *in discussion* and seems to *promise more than I ever expected.* In consequence of my note of the *11th. June*[3] on that subject, & of many informal communications to the *Duke D'Alberg*[4] and other persons of the *Emperor's confidence here*, they are *assailing him with my arguments* and their own.

Propos[i]tions have frequently been made to me to *separate the cases* that occured *previous to Novr 1810* from these that have happened since. And *D'Alberg* has assured me that the *latter would be compensated.* I have always *opposed* the distinction, referring, for argument to *my note of the fifth June.*[5]

Prince Cambaceres[6] gives it as his opinion that the whole included in *both periods will be* allowed, & he desired me yesterday in confidence *to express this opinion to you. Prince Talleyrand* is of the same opinion.

The Ministers of *commerce & of police have ventured* out of the line of *their official duty* to urge this *subject with the Emperor.*

I have indeed *great hopes to recover* the whole by *perseverence* in the use of *arguments* especially if the *Emperor returns to Paris in November* which is expected.

I am sensible that the state of *the public mind* both in and out *of Congress* is such as not to be *satisfied* with *opinions and hopes* instead of *facts* and for this reason I do not dwell upon *them in my official dispatches* to the *Secretary of State.* But it is with great *solicitude* that I impart them in *confidence* to you, fully impressed with the belief that the best interests of our country demand a *little more patience* on this subject before *recurring to measures of hostility.*

Cambaceres who understands the interests of the two countries as well as any man & who seems almost equally *desirous of promoting* the *prosperity of each* assures me that he has not the *least doubt but* that the present *attitude* taken by *the United States* will induce the *Emperor* the moment he can *get half an hour to read* and reflect on the subject, to *agree* to all we can *reasonably desire* and he thinks the principle of *indemnity as we* have stated it, is undeniably *just.*

Your letter has showed them the necessity of a *speedy decision.* Your observations are already *transmitted* to the *Emperor* thro *more channels* than one. And so has been the piece under *the Washington* head in the *National Intelligencer* of the *fourth of August*[7] which I assure them contains your sentiments & those on which *Congress will probably act.*

Articles written in that spirit, combining *moderation and energy* and holding clearly up to view the honest tenor of our policy, may be generally turned to *good account.*

Indeed it is true, & we may as well say it among ourselves as not, that *the wisdom of our Government & the dignity* of our national character are the *admiration of all Europe.*

There is not a foreign minister here who does not *bow down to us* in this respect; and they all *assure me* that such is the *sentiment of their Courts.*

Permit me in confidence to make one observation on the *double war* to which you allude.

It appears to me, of great importance, founded partly on a fact, which from local circumstances has struck my mind with more force than it probably has yours, if indeed it has been known to you at all.

Burr's project for dividing the U. States between France & England was not disliked by either government. *Fouche's disgrace* had nothing to do with it.[8] On the contrary the part he took in *listening* to it and putting it into *shape* was rather applauded by *his Master.*

The plan was laid aside for *that time* because the *parties* could not then *agree on a peace between* themselves. But it is believed to be only *adjourned* to be *resumed and attempted* with all the force of these *two nations* whenever stronger *passions* which now *oppose it* shall subside. And this aspect is rendered more *threatning* by the situation of *Spanish America* which greatly augments the interests naturally calculated to draw their attention to that *side of the world.* Now it is reasonable to suppose, indeed it is certain, that a *war declared* against them *both at once* would have a powerful tendency to *calm the violence* of their present *animosity against* each other & smooth the way to a *speedy peace between* themselves. When they would have *armies and navies* on hand *competent* (when *acting in concert*) to the *greatest enterprizes* ever undertaken in *distant regions.*[9]

It is with *great inquietude* that I contemplate these *possibilities.* And why should we *give them a pretext* by uniting *them against us* when they would have *real vengeance* as well as a *supposed interest to prompt them in pursuing our destruction.* And be assured they both *hate the principles* of our *Government* with an *equal hatred* and would *sacrifice* a great deal to *accomplish its overthrow.*

I am not supposing that they would *succeed* in their *project* tho that is *not impossible* for surely with all their *ships and men* nothing but the want of *motive* would *hinder them landing on our shores two hundred thousand* of the most *effective troops* that ever went *to war.*

Should we not rather *look on* at a *distance* and see their *present rage* with its unexampled *means of mischief* turning to the *East* as it possibly may do, & spending itself *in Turkey Persia and India?*

The violent *bodily exertions* and the *unbridled passions of Napoleon* added to the *hazards of battle* and of *assassination* forbid the expectation of a *long career.*

If in the next year *he drives* for *Constantinople* (which *he* probably will if we do not *call him off*) there is more than an even chance that *he will not live* to revisit his *own Capitol.*

His death would produce *tranquility* at least *for us.* For tho the *agitations* (might survive)[10] they never would *shake* the *Western shores* of the *Atlantic* nor greatly disturb our commerce; as I take it for granted that *England* will soon be brought to acknowledge *the principles for which we now contend.*

Excuse my speculations. They have led me far, but I think not beyond my subject. *Have but patience* a little longer with *my endeavors* to accomplish the *object* of *my mission.*

I promise you *nothing but zeal* but I have strong *hopes of success.*

I beg you not to suffer any of the *names of persons mentioned in this letter* to be made *public* in any way. It would greatly *injure them* as well as me, and prevent any *informal services* from them or others *in future*. Be assured of my perfect attachment and respect

J. BARLOW

RC (DLC); Tr (DLC: Rives Collection, Madison Papers). RC docketed by JM. Unless otherwise noted, italicized words are those encoded by Barlow and decoded interlinearly by JM; key not found.

1. Underlined in RC.
2. For Barlow's attempts to negotiate a commercial treaty with France, see Barlow to JM, 1 Jan. 1812, *PJM-PS*, 4:110 and n. 1.
3. Barlow's note has not been found.
4. Emmerich Joseph, duc de Dalberg (1773–1833), descended from a German aristocratic family, grew up in Mannheim, and studied law in Göttingen. In 1803 he was appointed Baden's ambassador at the French imperial court. Napoleon named him duke in 1810 and appointed him to serve on the council of state. Dalberg later conspired against Napoleon and participated as second French ambassador at the Congress of Vienna (Gisela Bergsträsser, "Joseph von Dalberg as a Collector of Drawings," *Master Drawings* 22 [1984]: 28–30).
5. Barlow's 5 June 1812 letter to Dalberg was enclosed in his dispatch to Monroe of 13 July 1812 (DNA: RG 59, DD, France).
6. Jean-Jacques-Régis de Cambacérès (1753–1824) was second consul of the French republic and the unofficial head of the administration of justice under Napoleon (*PJM-SS*, 2:140 n. 1).
7. See Gerry to JM, 15 Aug. 1812, n. 10.
8. For JM's earlier knowledge of the circumstances relating to Aaron Burr and Joseph Fouché, duc d'Otrante, see John Armstrong to JM, 5 Aug. 1810, *PJM-PS*, 2:461, 463 nn. 5 and 8.
9. At the foot of the page at this point, a penciled note in JM's hand reads: "If such a plan was really favored by the two powers was it not with a view in each to dupe the other into a war with the U S. A successful & satisfactory division of the Spoil could not be seriously counted on by either. J. M."
10. JM inserted "(might survive)" in pencil above the line.

From John Geddes

(Private)

SIR.   CHARLESTON September 26th. 1812.

By this days Mail you will receive the Unanimous Address of both branches of the Legislature of this state approbatory of your political Conduct as Chief Magistrate of the United states.[1] I, at the same time, take the Liberty of stating to you, that the result of the late proceedings of our Legislature, at our Extra Session evidence a determination on the part of this state, to aid the General government, in the prosecution of the war which has commenced, with vigour and spirit. And to the utmost of their power, to meet the views of government, and to assist in placing the state in a respectable posture of defence—liberal appropriations were made, and every munition of war, was ordered to be procured, with zeal and alacrity.

It may not be deemed improper, to remark, that the federal party have recently held federal Caucus's in this City, and that they have already agreed on opposing the re-Election of our distinguished member Mr. Cheves,[2] by bringing forward Col. Rutledge[3] in opposition to him. The friends of Mr. Clinton have not been inactive in their endeavours to promote a change in the friendly opinion of the Citizens of this state towards you—and the present administration of the United States. They have lately forwarded and distributed the Address of the New york corresponding Committee—to which a reply is preparing for the Members of the Legislature of this state previous to the choice of Electors of President & Vice President. Major Noah[4] of this City with much Zeal and talents, has manifested his attachment to the Republican cause, and has written several members in support of your re-Election, in opposition to Mr. Clinton. I have been induced, to take the Liberty of mentioning the name of this gentleman to you, from a conviction that you are at all times desirous of knowing those political friends who have laboured in effecting the permanent Security of Republican Interest.

The failure of General Hull, and the subsequent disasters which have occur'ed to his Army, it is believed, will stimulate the Citizens of the United States under the direction of the government, to carry on the War with additional vigour, in order to regain by strong, decisive, and successful operations the ground we have unfortunately lost. The failure, notwithstanding the efforts of your enemies to the Contrary, will be attributed to its proper cause, and there is a firm persuasion that no blame can attach itself to the Administration. I think myself warranted in Stating to you, and I state it with great pleasure, that you will unquestionably receive the Unanimous Vote of South Carolina. In this procedure you will at once observe, that we never desert those Citizens who have served us faithfully, and whose sole object is to secure the rights, maintain the honor, and promote the prosperity of the Union. I have the honor, to be with great respect & Esteem your obedient Servant.

JOHN GEDDES.

RC (DLC). Docketed by JM.

1. See South Carolina Legislature to JM, 29 Aug. 1812, and n.

2. Langdon Cheves (1776–1857) was a Republican representative from South Carolina to the Eleventh, Twelfth, and Thirteenth Congresses. A successful planter who had already enjoyed a distinguished career in South Carolina politics before his arrival in Washington, Cheves served as chairman of the committee on naval affairs during the first session of the Twelfth Congress and as chairman of the Ways and Means Committee and as Speaker of the House during the Thirteenth Congress. He turned down JM's offer of the office of secretary

of the treasury in 1815. Returning to South Carolina, Cheves took up a career on the bench. He then became the director of the United States Bank in 1819, relocating to Philadelphia. He served on the commission to settle War of 1812 claims from 1823 to 1827 and retired from public life in 1852 (Edgar et al., *Biographical Directory of the South Carolina House of Representatives*, 4:111–14).

3. Col. John Rutledge Jr. (1766–1819), son of John and Elizabeth Grimké Rutledge, was a Federalist representative from South Carolina to the Fifth through Seventh Congresses. At the urging of Harrison Gray Otis, Rutledge organized a campaign to oust JM from office in the fall of 1812 and made an unsuccessful bid for Cheves's seat in Congress (ibid., 4:500–502; Archie Vernon Huff Jr., *Langdon Cheves of South Carolina* [Columbia, S.C., 1977], 66–68).

4. Geddes referred to Mordecai M. Noah, whose anti-Clintonian views were published under the pseudonym "Diodorus Siculus" as *A Letter Addressed to the Members of the Legislature of South-Carolina, Examining the Claims and Qualifications of Dewitt Clinton, to the Presidency of the United States* (Charleston, 1812; Shaw and Shoemaker 25274) (Sarna, *Jacksonian Jew*, 11–12, 165–66).

¶ From Pierce Butler. Letter not found. *26 September 1812, Philadelphia.* Offered for sale in the American Art Association Catalogue, Frederick B. McGuire Collection (1917), item 22, where it is described as a one-page letter giving "information regarding John Ryan, a British Spy under sentence of death."

To Jonathan Dayton

[post 26 September 1812]

The letters to be answered under address to Mr Levi Canning &c. has [*sic*] been recd. The friendly motives & public objects which they manifest, as well as the interesting observations contained in them, entitle the writer to acknowledgments. Any further communications having in view the public good will of course be acceptable.

Draft (NjP). Unsigned. Addressee not indicated; identified on the basis of Dayton's letters of ca. 17 and 23 Sept. 1812. Undated; date assigned on the assumption that JM wrote this note sometime after the receipt of Dayton's 23 Sept. letter but before Dayton wrote his ca. 28 Dec. letter, which acknowledged JM's note.

§ From Zabuel June. *27 September 1812, North Salem, Westchester County, New York.* Expresses his opinion that "political parties aught to Unite together for Common Defence." Believes that it is the duty of all citizens to support the war, to "cease to Slander the Administration," and to abandon attempts "to Sacrifice the Liberty and honor of their Country to Gratify their unholy th[i]rst for power." Points out that the Federalists blame the administration for "Every unforeseen incident," including Hull's defeat, naval weaknesses, and difficulties in conquering Canada. Describes the Federalists as "accusing the Government with french Influence partiality and injustice" while claiming that there is no cause for war. Some state governors refuse militia quotas, and "Governor Griswold is attempting to Raise an

Army to Defend Connecticut which whispers Revolt from the federal Compact." Claims that "there are men Enough in Connecticut to Drive the Gove[r]nor from his thron[e] if Necessity Shoud. Require it." Suggests that the only remedy is to "prosecute the war with vigor" and to make no peace "till the Canadas are ours," because as long as the British possess Canada, "the tomahawk and Scalping Knife in the hands of the Savages will be the awfull Scourge of our frontiers."

RC (DLC). 2 pp.; docketed by JM.

To Edward Coles

DEAR SIR   WASHINGTON Sepr. 28. 1812
Yours of the 22d. came to hand yesterday. We regret extremely the indisposition which disappointed our expectation of seeing you on the arrival of the last stage. In such good hands as Dr. Everard's you will soon be restored. Don't risk a relapse by entering on the journey prematurely. We sha⟨ll⟩ look for your return with confidence as soon as your health will justify, but with the patience due to that consideration. Accept our affecte. respects and tender them to all around you.

JAMES MADISON

RC (NjP: Edward Coles Papers).

From William Jones

SIR   PROVIDENCE Septr 28th 1812
As it is possible my letters of July 22d & of August 22d may not have reached your Excellency, I am advised by the Council of War of this State to forward a triplicate[1] & to inform your Excellency that in consequence of an Alarm by the appearance of three British Frigates near point Judith on the 13th Inst the Citezens of the Island of Rhode Island with a promptness that does them very great credit appeared at their Alarm posts ready to render any service in their power to protect & defend the Island &c when to our mortification they were found without ammunition & with but a very few Arms on which any dependance could be placed in case of attack.

Suffer me to notice to your Excellency that at the declaration of War by the Congress of the United States against Great Britain this State was found materially in debt & with no other means of raising monies than by a dry Tax, which in common times is attended with difficulties that under our present privations are insurmountable. Such being our situation we are

under the necessity of applying to your Excellency for this States proportion of the Arms &c for which an Annual appropriation was made on
April 23d 1808[2] of $200,000 for the purchase of Arms directing them to be
transmitted to the several States & Territories to be distributed by the legislatures thereof, of which this State as yet have received no part.

It will be useless to offer to your Excellency any information relative to
our exposed situation as your Excellency must be possessed of a compitant
knowledge thereof, I shall therefore only add the urgency of the case and
rely with confidence on your Excellencys readiness to attend to the request
of this State in furnishing the Arms Ammunition &c for which I was directed to apply. I have the honor to be Your Excellencys Obedient & Very
humble Servant

WM. JONES

RC and enclosures (DNA: RG 107, LRRS, J-306:6). Docketed as received in the War Department on 5 Oct. 1812. For enclosures, see n. 1.

1. Jones enclosed a copy of his 22 July 1812 dispatch and its enclosure.
2. See *U.S. Statutes at Large*, 2:490–91.

From James Monroe

DEAR SIR   ALBEMARLE—Tuesday [29 September 1812]
I set out today, but being forc'd thro Caroline by some private concerns
with the family of my late sister,[1] shall not be able to reach Washington till
the last of the week. I shall hurry on as fast as possible.

The enclosed from Mr Crawford, it is proper that you should see.[2] In its
relation to two gentlemen, of real virtue (in my judgment) however they
may stand with the public, or fit they may be in all respects for their stations, it is necessary to know, what is thought & said of them however
painful. I think in relation to a circumstance alluded to as to one, there is
an error. But as you only will see it, no injury can result to him or either,
of them. I bring Mrs Monroe, who has sufficiently recoverd to undertake
the journey. Your friend

JAS MONROE

RC (DLC: Rives Collection, Madison Papers). Postmarked Milton, 30 Sept. Undated; date
assigned on the basis of JM's later docket, "(probably 1812)," and the fact that 30 Sept. 1812
was a Wednesday.

1. Monroe's sister was Elizabeth Monroe Buckner (1754–1802), wife of William Buckner
of Mill Hill estate in Caroline County, Virginia (Hugh Montgomery-Massingberd, ed.,
Burke's Presidential Families of the United States of America, 2d ed. [London, 1981], 142).

2. Monroe enclosed a 9 Sept. 1812 letter he had received from William H. Crawford (DLC: Monroe Papers; 4 pp.), which expressed astonishment at the surrender of Detroit and offered sharp criticism of cabinet secretaries Eustis and Hamilton. Crawford also discussed the possibility of receiving East Florida from Luis de Onís. He understood that a cession would require the recognition of Onís as Spanish minister, which would be inconsistent with previous U.S. policy. Yet it was his view that the loss of slaves to Florida and the "depredations of the Indians" were sufficient reasons to desire the cession under any terms. In his view, if Onís was indeed empowered to cede the territory and could cause the Spanish governors to carry out the cession, the transfer would be legal, would silence senatorial malcontents, and would be inoffensive to Napoleon as well. Crawford went so far as to claim that he would be glad to see East Florida received even if these terms were not entirely met.

From an Unidentified Correspondent

FRIEND,   [29 September 1812]

Thou may'st deem it wonderful that I, professionally a quaker, should write to thee on the subject of war, a thing so obstinately opposed by the mass of my brethren. Quakers are but men, and subject as other men to frailties; and holy writ is so translated that it admits of numberless constructions. Therefore he who interprets scripture most to the glory of the Omnipotent and the General Instruction of man, deserves highest applause as a commentator. I believe the bible authorises me to resist when my life and rights are in danger or my property is assailed. Under such conviction I differ very materially from the more bigotted and passive quakers, as touching war waged in behalf of these great immunities. The illustrious St Paul assures us, that magistrates are not to bear the sword in vain, and that we must respect and obey men of authority. Also this holy sage represents the law as being made not for the righteous but disobedient and gainsaying, which convinces me that God never desired good men to surrender life and freedom at the nod of despots and presumptuous impostors. In short, nothing but groveling enthusiasm, treachery or cowardice could dissuade American freemen at this time, whatever might be their religious creed, from arming against the Prince Regent and his "horrible bloodhounds of savage war,"[1] who are now exterminating, in the usual manner of Britain, "all ages, sexes, and conditions" of our frontier inhabitants. God forbid I should believe he has ordained tyrants to riot in the massacre of upright people. It is mu[c]h more compatible with the merciful and just attributes of an Almighty Deity, to suppose virtuous men naturally inspired with detestation of oppressors, and created for the purpose of humbling them in the dust by force & vengeance instead of being chained like brutes to their "Adamantine throne." Whilst such is the state of things and tyranny is put down, the whole catalogue of human privileges, civil, political and religious, becomes perfectly secure, and virtue gains a glorious ascendant over vice. Now, friend James, as thou has received my candid opinion in regard to resisting England, unfriendly as she is towards America, I rely upon equal candor from thee, when I impute error to thee, in sending so feeble an army into Upper Canada.[2]

Thou art the supreme constitutional agent for equipping the soldiery & for proportioning its force to existing difficulties, and the way to shorten this war, save lives & money, would [be] to detach a complete and efficient army at once for Canada. Say ten thousand men might be located at the north end of Lake Ontario, ten thousand men at fort Malden, and an equal number in the vicinity of the south & west Indian Towns—ten thousand at St John's, the north end of Lake Champlain. Such a dispersion of this army would occasion a division between the British and Indians, to oppose it at different points, and such an augmentation of the late detachment which commenced the war would speedily end it. By this management thou mightest acquire laurels as a soldier equal in splendor to thy political renown. But if thou sufferest our men to be murdered in small parties for want of means to baffle the enemy, thy public fame must inevitably suffer, which would penetrate me with keen distress, since I am greatly attached to thy virtues, talents and worth, and hope never to see them tarnished by neglect or clouded through misfortune. Send not thy generals to fight the foe at sections of the country where interest or connections might pollute their fidelity. . . . The disaster at Detroit, although the result of one man's weakness alone, should and must, friend James, arouse thee to caution hereafter in dispensing command to trusty characters. Another thing—I am alarmed that some of our agents should be so remiss in duty, failing in many important cases to apprise government of the hostile movements of the savages, in time enough either to prevent or punish their murders and depredations. Friend James, if thou respectest these my plain and friendly intimations, as I do thy amiable and illustrious traits of character, may they not humbly conspire, with the reason and justice of things, to stimulate thee to retrieve the honor and advantages we lost by Hull's surrender. Moreover we must, if possible, have Canada, Nova Scotia and New Brunswick, as a fresh addition of territory to our beloved Union. Notwithstanding the howlings of federal bull-dogs and the secret tricks of traitors, thy election next March is as certain as fate. For myself, I indulge an assured hope that thou wilt wind up thy career in an honorable manner and retire like JEFFERSON to private life, shaded by garlands of endless repute. I remain thy very humble servant and real friend,

I. C.

Printed copy (*National Intelligencer*, 29 Sept. 1812). Headed "From an Aged Quaker."

1. In his 18 Nov. 1777 speech in the House of Lords, William Pitt, first earl of Chatham, denounced the British government for employing Indians, "these horrible hell-hounds of savage war," to defeat the American colonists.

2. The editor of the *National Intelligencer* placed an asterisk here and a note at the bottom of the column, explaining that he had given space to this piece "in compliance with the earnest request of a hoary-headed whig" but wished to point out that the author "seems not to be aware that no peremptory orders were given to This army to enter Canada." The editor observed that the orders were provisional and that "it was not, the intention of administration that Canada should be invaded by any force that was not completely adequate to the object in view."

§ From Marinus Willett.[1] *29 September 1812, New York.* Informs JM that Armstrong has appointed Evert A. Bancker[2] to the office of judge advocate. Praises Bancker and requests confirmation of his appointment.

RC (DNA: RG 107, LRRS, W-331:6). 1 p.; docketed as received in the War Department on 5 Oct. 1812.

1. Marinus Willett (1740–1830), Revolutionary War veteran and former sheriff of New York City and County, served as mayor of New York from 1807 to 1811 and was defeated in his bid for the lieutenant governorship of the state in 1811.

2. On 14 Oct. 1812 Willett wrote to Gallatin to request that he pass on to JM Willett's support for Bancker, whom he described as "a Counciler of law, of respectable connection of good moral charector Amiable disposition and well qualified to perform the duties of the office" (DLC; docketed by JM). JM later nominated Bancker to be judge advocate for the Third U.S. Military District effective 18 Mar. 1813 (*Senate Exec. Proceedings,* 2:371).

From Henry Dearborn

SIR,   HEAD QUARTERS GREENBUSH, Sept. 30th, 1812

Unless the Troops destined for Detroit & Niagara, with those on the Eastern shore of Lake Ontario & Upper St Lawrence, aided by the Naval Preparations, now commencing in that quarter, shall be fortunate enough to penetrate Upper Canada, before winter sets in, we shall have the credit of an unfortunate Campaign.

After it become [*sic*] necessary to detach a large proportion of the regular troops, to Niagara, & Lake Ontario, that had been originally destined for (what I considered my immediate command) Lower Canada—I was compelled to relinquish all ideas of offensive operations against Montreal or its dependencies this year, & to confine my movements in that quarter, to a *feint*—which would operate as a diversion in favor of our operations on the great Lakes. That object has been so far effected, as greatly to alarm Montreal & its vicinity, & to detain a considerable number of the regular forces there, which otherwise would have gone to Upper Canada.

I shall continue such movements towards Montreal, as will threaten their outposts. If the Enemy fortunately delays his attack at Niagara, a few days longer, we shall be prepared not only to meet him on our side, but to attempt carrying his posts. But I have been in hourly expectation of hearing that our Troops had been obliged to fall back, if nothing worse, for the disaster at Detroit enabled Gen. Brock, to immediately concentrate a force at Niagara, that would have empowered him to drive Gen. Van. Rensalaer from his position, before the reinforcements could reach him. I have detached upwards of sixteen hundred regular troops from this camp, for Niagara & Lake Ontario; some have arrived there & the remainder will reach there in eight or ten days, about which time, the four small Regiments from Virginia, Maryland, & Pennsylvania, with the two thousand Pennsylvania Militia & a considerable number from this State will probably arrive at the same place. I calculate strongly on the exertions of Capt, Chauncey especially on Lake Ontario; he has gone on with about seven hundred fine seamen, exclusive of Marines & Carpenters. We have made an unfortunate beginning, but we shall ultimately I hope do well. Gen. Hull has been at Head Quarters, & several of the Officers captured with him. His story will not satisfy the most intelligent & candid part of community. The tedious delays in the appointment & organization of the Quarter Master, Commissary of Purchase & Ordnance & Pay Masters Department, as *well as the deficiency of Major Generals*, have had an unfortunate effect on all our measures. I am averse to complaining, but I have been so incessantly engaged in the minute details of those Departments, as well as the usual employments in organizing the Troops & preparing them for service, as to have rendered my duties perplexing & painful. I hope & trust that measures will be early taken by Congress, & by the Executive that will place the Army on such a footing in point of organization & strength as will render it competent to the services expected from it by our country.

I am far from being convinced that One Man can manage the War Department. Something must be done: it is impossible to get on, as we are at present. I doubt whether an army of sufficient strength can be brought into the field, without additional encouragements. We should have a regular force next campaign of not less than fifty thousand men. The expences of the Militia are enormous, & they are of little comparative use, except at the commencement of war, & for special emergencies. The sooner we can dispense with their services, the better, on every consideration.

If I should be continued in my command, I hope & trust that it will not, as at present, extend to such distant points, as will render it impossible, to perform the duties, in a manner, the good of the service requires. *There should be at least five Major Generals North & West of* Washington & four additional Brigadier Generals. The Quarter Master General should be allowed to appoint an additional number of Deputies, & Assistants.

There now appears to be a prospect of forming considerable bodies of Volunteer Corps, but the encouragement is not sufficient to ensure success. The Officers of these Corps should have one or two months advance pay, when called into service, & the men should either be supplied with cloth-ing, or receive at least twenty five dollars each in lieu of clothing, to enable them to purchase it, before they march. By giving additional encour-agement—say eight dollars pr month instead of five, I presume an Army may be raised, competent to all purposes. It should be recollected that at the commencement of our Revolutionary war, the best of hands could be hired to labor for five dollars pr—month—& we gave our Soldiers forty shillings—& now such laborers can have ten or eleven dollars pr month & the pay of a soldier is thirty shillings.

I presume the greatest part of *that description of men*, that can be enlisted for five dollars pr month, is already engaged. I find that the Regiments, in Pennsylvania, Maryland & Virginia, are less than one half of their com-plement of men. The Northern Regiments are not much better, except in the State of New York. I engage Sir, not to trouble you soon, with another such a long & tedious letter. I have the honor, Sir, to be with the highest Consideration & respect, your Obedient & humble servant

H. Dearborn

RC (DLC); letterbook copy (NHi: Dearborn Letterbooks); Tr (MeHi). RC docketed by JM.

¶ From Ephraim Webster. Letter not found. *30 September 1812.* Acknowledged in Eustis to Webster, 12 Oct. 1812, as having been received and transmitted to Eras-tus Granger, agent for the Six Nations in New York, "with the inclosed Talk" and with instructions "to enquire into the facts therein stated" and "to keep the Indians quiet if possible" (DNA: RG 75, LSIA).

§ From Louis B. de Niroth. *1 October 1812, Washington.* "Some years Past I had the honnor to be entrodused to you in the time of your Predecesor. I am a Percicuted Stranger and have with me a Morther Les Daugther ho is Now with stranger with home I am not aquanted the in Closed Letter will Prove I Come here with a com-munication to the Secratarie of war this Communication is of Sireius Counci-quance to the governement of the united St: I was not three ours in the City I was thrown in the Debtors gaill for Debts Contracted by an unfortunet under Teaken. But verry fortunetly have Compromised with My Creditors.

"And Now only de-taned for the Gaill fees which amounts a bove 20 Dollars destance from all my aquantance I must Teact the Libertey to implore and apiall to your Excellences humanetey and beg for that assistance to gain My Libertey for the Preserevation of my unhappe Daugther and allso that I Can Proceed with my Com-munication which I Cannot do duren my Confindment."

RC (DLC). 2 pp.; docketed by JM. Enclosure not found.

From Thomas Jefferson

DEAR SIR   MONTICELLO Oct. 2. 12.

I take the liberty of inclosing to you a letter from mr Meigs,[1] heretofore President of the University of Georgia. This has been delayed by the same absence from home which prevented my having the pleasure of delivering it to you personally at Mon[t]pelier. I do not know mr Meigs personally, but have always heard him highly spoken of as a man of science. He was selected for the university of Georgia by our late friend Baldwin,[2] and I remember he was considered as a great acquisition there. Of the state of the place he asks for I am ignorant: but if in that or any other place you can benefit the public by employing him, I am sure you will do it as well on their behalf as from your own disposition to patronise science. I avail myself of this as of every other occasion to renew to you the assurance of my constant friendship & wishes for your health and success in the awful charge you have on you.

                                           TH: JEFFERSON

FC (DLC: Jefferson Papers).

1. JM nominated Josiah Meigs surveyor general of the U.S. on 12 Nov. 1812 (*Senate Exec. Proceedings*, 2:303, 304).

2. Abraham Baldwin (1754–1807), a graduate of Yale and first president of the Board of Trustees of the University of Georgia, had been a representative from Georgia to the First through Fifth Congresses and a U.S. senator from 1799 to 1807 (Dexter, *Biographical Sketches of the Graduates of Yale College*, 3:432–34).

From William Eustis

                                           [ca. 3 October 1812]

In making out the order, as the Militia were to rendezvous at Pittsburg, at which place they would of course wait for further orders, it was thought sufficient by this mail to direct detachments on the requisition of Captn. Piatt[1] for the Cannon & Stores, without adding "you will wait further orders"—taking the chance (which is very small) of any part of them proceeding without orders.

I observe that in one of Harrison's proclamations[2] (not now before me) that he calls for men for *one month:* it appears safe to wait another mail.

                                           WEUSTIS

Nothing from Genl. D. or from any quarter by the mail of this day.

RC (DLC). Undated; dated 1812 in the *Index to the James Madison Papers;* date assigned here on the basis of evidence presented in n. 1, below.

1. Eustis wrote to William Piatt at Pittsburgh on 30 Sept. 1812 to inform him of his appointment to the office of deputy quartermaster general and to request that he forward mounted ordnance to the frontier immediately, while the roads remained passable. Piatt was also instructed to direct as much ordnance as possible to the rapids of the Maumee River while awaiting Harrison's orders. On 3 Oct. 1812 Eustis wrote to the commanders of militia troops at Pittsburgh, requesting that they detach troops upon the requisition of Piatt for purposes of escorting ordnance and military stores to the Northwest Army (DNA: RG 107, LSMA).

2. In Cincinnati, Harrison issued a circular on 21 Sept. 1812 calling for mounted volunteers to serve from thirty to forty days (Esarey, *Messages and Letters of William Henry Harrison,* Indiana Historical Collections, 2:147).

§ Edward Coles to Dolley Payne Madison. *5 October 1812.* Sends this letter by his cousin Edward Carrington, son of Judge Paul Carrington. "You will find Mr. Carrington an amiable and intelligent young gentleman; full of indignation at the wrongs and insults under which his Country suffers, and animated with an ardent zeal to avenge them by his personal efforts in the field; he attempted to raise a Volunteer Company, but having failed in this he goes to Washington to endeavour to procure a commission in the Army.[1]

"May I ask the favor of you just to say to Mr. Madison that Walter Coles, who is now a second Lieut. in the Cavalry, has written to me that a first Lieut. of his Battalion has resigned, and that he wishes to be considered an applicant to fill the vacancy.[2]

"I have this moment received Mr. Madisons kind letter with its enclosures.[3] Dr. Everette cheers me with the assurance of my being well and capable of travelling in two or at most three weeks more."

RC (NN). 2 pp.

1. JM nominated Edward Carrington as second lieutenant of the Virginia Light Dragoons on 9 Nov. 1812. He was promoted to the rank of captain in 1814 (*Senate Exec. Proceedings,* 2:296, 301, 506, 511).

2. On 10 Mar. 1814 JM recommended Walter Coles (1790–1857) for promotion from second lieutenant to captain of riflemen. The son of Isaac Coles, Walter was a member of the Virginia House of Delegates in 1817, 1818, 1833, and 1834, as well as a representative to the Twenty-fourth through Twenty-eighth Congresses (*Senate Exec. Proceedings,* 2:505–6).

3. JM to Coles, 28 Sept. 1812.

To William Plumer

Sɪʀ   Wᴀsʜɪɴɢᴛᴏɴ October 6. 1812

I have duly received your favor of the 23. Sepr. Your observations on the deficiency of the inlistments & the remedy for it are entirely just. The recommence [*sic*] provided by law for those who are to serve in the ranks, whether of the regular army, or the volunteer corps, has every where failed to fill them. Justice as well as policy should make amends to the soldier for what is given up by the Citizen. It is to be hoped that Congress, will be sufficiently taught by experience, what was not sufficiently understood without it. Many other defects in the military system will be brought to their attention by the same monitor. We have had no authentic information from G. B. by which we can decide on her views with respect to the war, or the conditions on which she is disposed to put an end to it. We are equally uninformed of the final measures of France as to the questions depending with her. The tardiness of her decisions, does not encourage favorable expectations. We have this day recd. communications from Genl. Harrison,[1] charged with the North Western Expedition. He had relieved Fort Wayne, destroyed the towns of several hostile tribes of Indians, and was making vigorous arrangements for regaining the ground lost by his predecessor, and if possible giving to his operations, an effectual bearing in favor of those at Niagara. His force will amount to 8, 10, or 1200 as he may chuse to make it: and the advanced part of it was on the 27th. of Sepr. the date of his dispatches, on its way from Fort Wayne to F. Defiance. His prospects are not discouraging. The promptitude with which such a force has taken the field will at least have the salutary effects of proving to the Enemy that the public Spirit has been roused, not depressed by the event at Detroit, and of making the Indians feel that they can never have security in the protection held out to them from Canada. Accept Sir assurances of my high esteem, and my friendly respects.

JAMES MADISON

RC (NjP: Crane Collection).

1. JM probably referred to Harrison's 24 and 27 Sept. 1812 letters to Eustis. The former was docketed as received in the War Department on 6 Oct. (printed in Esarey, *Messages and Letters of William Henry Harrison*, Indiana Historical Collections, 2:149–51, 156–58).

From Lafayette

MY DEAR SIR   LAGRANGE October 6th. 1812.

Our friend M. Barlow has communicated to me the article of your Letter relative to my affairs.[1] So far I am from Wondering at a delay of the decision of Congress on the report of their Commissioners, That I feel much obliged to you to have mentionned it, under the actual pressure of affairs, in your Last dispatch. It is however of Great importance to me that the Business of those two patents be concluded as soon as possible.

My former Letters have informed you that the two remaining Titles to Locations of thousand acres each had been purchased at the Rate of sixty francs, about twelve dollars, by Mr. Seymour an English Gentleman.[2] One half of the monney has been paid. The other half shall be delivered on the Receipt of those two patents. But if they are not come before the End of the Year, instead of being Creditor for this half bearing interest, I become a debtor for the interest of the received monney, and in case M. Seymour is not in possession of the patents in the Course of the other Year, the Whole must be refunded and the Bargain is Void.

That arrangement has been on my part consented to because I had your Kind Letters stating that the patents were already in your hands and wanted only to be signed by you, a confirmation by Congress of the settlement of Claims made by their Commissioners.[3] It appeared to me next to Certainty that their decision given upon the spot should be confirmed in Congress. But, in the Contrary Case, you have been pleased to promise a new Location as soon as possible which would make no odds in my Bargain with M. Seymour, The particular Spot having not been designated. M. Seymour has Liberally depended on your expressed intention, if the two patents in your hands were not approved by Congress, to have the next best Lands immediately Located for me.

I Know, my dear friend, it suffices, to insure your Kind Exertions, that my Situation in that respe[c]t be Laid before you. And as the War with England makes a Correspondance very unsafe, I beg Leave to forward as many Copies of this Letter as there are American Vessels going this month—permit me also to request that, when you have been able to obtain the Confirmation by Congress of those two patents, I may be on my part enabled as soon as possible to fulfill the Conditions of my Bargain with Mr. Seymour.

Of the 520. acres which it, more than ever, becomes so important for me to obtain within two miles of the City I shall here say nothing, having by several opportunities fully writen to you on that subject. Enough of your Time has been intruded upon, and with hearty apologies for the foregoing long mention of private Concerns, I shall only add the expression of my affectionate gratitude, friendship, and respect.

LAFAYETTE

RC (PHi). In a clerk's hand, signed by Lafayette; marked *"Duplicate"*; cover marked *"private"*; docketed by JM.

1. See JM to Barlow, 11 Aug. 1812.

2. See Lafayette to JM, 21 Nov. 1811 and 22 Apr. and 6 July 1812, *PJM-PS*, 4:29–30, 340–41, 563–65.

3. No letter from JM to Lafayette to this effect has been found, but the two surveys were enclosed in John K. Smith to JM, 25 Aug. 1811, *PJM-PS*, 3:432 and n.

§ From William Tatham. *6 October 1812, Washington.* Expresses his concern that "the Administration is exposed to considerable danger of being suddenly siezed by the enemy, without any efficient, and reasonably practical, means having been hitherto thought of as a precaution for their information and safety." Believes that "this danger is threatened from the following considerations: 1st. there are many disaffected persons among our Citizens; 2dly. the similarity of manners, habits, and language of the parties admits of so little discrimination that spies may be in the midst of our Councils without discovery. 3dly. British gold has long been known to be an Engine employed on base minds; and they do not spare it when it is likely to turn to good account; 4thly. the Wood-land & thinly settled condition of our country is favorable to partisan enterprize; and, 5thly, the navigable waters of the Chesapeak permit an Enemy's fleet to approach undiscovered, within the 'striking distance' of our Nights expedition." Has invented "a nocturnal tellegraph, or beacon," to prevent "any such disaster," a sketch of which is enclosed; the invention is explained "by a reference which is hereunto annexed."[1] Believes that each station would cost five dollars. Estimates that the sixty-six miles from the president's house to the mouth of the Potomac could be covered with thirty stations at a cost of $150, and "a line of twelve miles would apprise Norfolk when a fleet entered the Capes, if that addition was deemed advisable." Offers to survey and make arrangements "to carry this design into immediate effect; or to superintend a similar duty at any other post or posts along our maritime frontier."

RC and enclosures (DNA: RG 107, LRRS, T-27:8). RC 2 pp. For enclosures, see n. 1.

1. The enclosures are a sketch of the signaling device (1 p.) with the caption "Tellegraph proposed by Wm Tatham in 1810; for short sights" and a two-page description of the workings of the invention, titled "Reference to the Model, &c." The description makes reference to letter markings that do not appear on the sketch.

To Henry Dearborn

Dear Sir   Washington October 7. 1812.

I have recd. your favor of Sepr. 30. I am glad to find that you have succeeded in producing such apprehensions at Montreal as to prevent reinforcements from that quarter to the posts above. It would have been fortunate if you could have derived such Militia & Volunteer aids from Vermont & Eastward of it, as might have substantially have [sic] a like controul on Prevost, and thereby have augmented the regular force ordered to Niagara. Appearances denote a better spirit or rather perhaps a better use of it, in the Eastern Quarter; but it may be too late & too distant to answer immediate purposes; unless indeed the volunteers of Maine, and the Militia or Volunteers of N. H. should be, in sufficient numbers and forwardness, to prevent descents on our maritime frontier, by a show towards Nova Scotia which would excite defensive attention at Halifax. The advance of the season, would I presume render a measure of that sort unavailing at Quebec. Yet *there* is undubitably the Sensorium, to which projects of alarm may be most succes[s]fully addressed, when not too palpably chimerical. You will receive from the War Office, the last information from Harrison. He has a prospect of doing something towards retrieving the campaign. The promptitude and numbers of the force under his command, will at least save the military character of that part of the nation; will satisfy G. B. that the tendency of defeat is to rouse not depress the American Spirit, & will stamp deep on the Indian mind, the little security they have in British protection. As Harrison seems to be making sure of food for his army, & the measures taken promise seasonable supplies of other necessaries, I see nothing to prevent his reaching Detroit early in this month. And if the great exertions on foot to give him cannon should not fail, it may be hoped, he will not only be in possession of that place, but of Malden also; and proceed towards a still more effectual co-operation with the forces at Niagara. Nor do we despair of his success, should the cannon not reach him in time, if the B. Garrisons be such as are represented & he can carry with him the force he has in view; since he will be able to proceed with a very impressive portion, & leave sufficient investments & precautions behind. The artillery sent from this place had travelled nearly to Pittsburg at a rate which promised a good chance for its reaching Detroit before November, if not by the 20th of this month. As Hull's army was lost, it is to be regretted that the misfortune did not take place a little earlier; and allow more time, of course, for repairing it, within the present season. This regret is particularly applicable to the great Lakes. What is now doing for the command of them proves what may be done. And the same means would have been used in the 1st instance if the easy conquest of them by land held out to us, had not misled one calculation. The command of the lakes, by a superior force on the water, ought to have been a fundamental point in the national policy, from the moment the peace took place. Whatever may be the future situation of Canada, it ought to be maintained, without regard to expence. We have more means for the purpose & can better afford the expence than G. B. Without the ascendency over those waters, we can never have it over the savages, nor be able to secure such posts as Makinaw. With this ascendency we command the Indians, can controul the companies trading with them; and hold Canada, whilst in Foreign hands, as a hostage for peace & justice.

I dont wonder you are oppressed with labor, as well from the extent of your command rendered necessary by the mutual relations between its objects, As from the deficiency of General Officers; and particularly the difficulty and delay in bringing the Staff Department even into its present state. The effect of these circumstances in burdening you with details, has been severely felt here, in throwing them where they as little belonged. To carry on the War with due advantage; more effectual inducements at least must be put into the hands of recruiting Officers.

The Volunteer system must be essentially improved; the use of the militia secured to the constitutional authority; and an addition made to the

Genl officers both of Divisions & Brigades. It will be equally essential, to discriminate better the functions of the several Staff Departments, and to have heads of them in immediate contact with the war department. Experience enforces these truths; and nothing but that will ever sufficiently inculcate them.

We have nothing important from abroad but what is in the Newspapers. Health & success with friendly respects.

J. M.

FC (DLC). In a clerk's hand, signed by JM; marked by JM "private / copy / To Majr. Genl. Dearborn." A note on the cover in JM's hand reads: "in relation to the state of the war at that period."

§ To Albert Gallatin. *7 October 1812.* In accordance with a 3 Mar. 1809 act of Congress,[1] directs "that the sum of seventy thousand dollars be applied out of the appropriation of Pay & subsistence of the Navy to Contingent expenses."

RC (DLC, series 7); letterbook copy (DNA: RG 45, entry 4, Letters to Secretary of Treasury). RC 1 p.; in a clerk's hand, signed by JM. At the foot the letter is redirected in Gallatin's hand to "Mr Anthony" with the instruction "Please to attend / A. G."

1. "An Act further to amend the several acts for the establishment and regulation of the Treasury, War and Navy departments" (*U.S. Statutes at Large,* 2:535–37).

§ From the Delegates of Strafford County, New Hampshire. *7 October 1812.* "Possessing equal rights with our fellow Citizens, and constitutionally assembled, to consider the great evils which we feel, and to avert the greater consequent Evils, which we fear, while we address you with the frankness of independent Freemen, we approach you, with that high deference and respect, due to the chief Magistrate of a great Nation, over whom you have the honor and felicity to preside.

"The Assembly who now address you, are composed, in part, of those who have been habituated from their infancy, to commercial pursuits; but principally of freeholders & Cultivators of the earth, men who gain their subsistence, *by the sweat of their brow*, and who all consider Agriculture & Commerce as inseperably connected; *that they are twin sisters*, growing with each other's growth, and strengthening, and strengthened by each other's strength, that they sympathize, flourish or languish together; *and being entwined* & united by the God of nature, none but a sacriligious hand can put them asunder.

"We consider, Sir, all legitimate Government as originating with the people, and founded in their consent; that it's end, is the public good, and the preservation of the rights of the governed. That in a republican Government, constituted like ours, the administration of it rests, in a high degree on *public opinion:* that the Citizens have a right, and that it is at all times, their paramount duty, with candor and decorum, to canvass the conduct of their rulers, and that their deliberate voice, on subjects to them important, and of which they have the means of judging, should not only be presented with respect; but listened to with attention.

373

"We were permitted, by that Providence, with whom are the destinies of Nations, to see the time, when, under the administration of a *Washington*, the prosperity and happiness of this Nation, was great beyond the most sanguine expectations: when like another chosen people, we were conducted to a land of plenty—concord and peace reigning over a happy Land: joy sitting in every face, content in every heart; a Treasury, apparently exhaustless; a people unoppressed, undisturbed, unalarmed; every man 'managing his own concerns in his own way'; our Ships covering the ocean, and their canvass whitening every Port, & asserting with *pride* and *triumph* the honor of the American Name as far as waters roll or winds could waft them.

"'But *yesterday*, America could have stood against the world; *now*, none so poor, to do her reverence.'[1]

"It might be deemed invidious, to contrast in detail, those halcyon days, with the present disasterous situation of our common Country. But Sir, the Americans are not a stupid people, neither are they blindfold. Endowed with as large a portion of understanding, as is ordinarily alloted to the sons of men, is it not their duty in sober seriousness, to enquire whence this sad Reverse, and to endeavour to trace the Evil to it's origin?

"We do not hesitate to declare our opinion, that the principal, if not the sole cause, of the Evils which we now suffer, is, what is commonly called, 'the restrictive System' a fixed, permanent, and determined resolution in the general Government to enforce the *Fiat* of your last predecessor in office, 'to retire from the Seas, and to provide for ourselves those Comforts and Conveniences of life, for which it would be unwise ever more to recur to distant Countries.'[2]

"This opinion *was enforced* by a deleterious and dessolating course of *Restriction Non-Importation, Non-Intercourse,* & *Embargo.* By these, Poverty entered our doors, and brought accumulated distress even to our fire-side. We were deprived of the customary means, which we, and our fore-Fathers used, and which had been sanctioned by the Usage of nearly two Centuries, of supporting our wives and children; and many, very many, were reduced to a state of insolvency and Ruin.

"But it seems this is but a portion, of the suffering, to which this people has been devoted.

"Crushed under the ponderous weight of these evils, and vainly believing, that the Cup of our Calamities was now full, another Vial of wrath has been poured fourth, and caused the waters of bitterness to overflow.

"We are plunged into a War, without preparation, of dubious success—incalculable in extent, and perhaps interminable in duration!

"Unmindful of the parting advice of our Father, the political Saviour of his Country, 'We are quitting our own to stand on foreign ground, and by interweaving our destiny with that of Europe we are about to entangle our Peace and Prosperity in the toils of European Ambition, Rivalship, Humor or Caprice.'[3]

"We have, with anxious solicitude and attention, perused your Manifesto, in conjunction with the Report of the Committee of Foreign Relations,[4] in the hope of extracting evidence on which the weary mind could safely repose, that this war, was, under the existing circumstances of our Country, either *just, honorable or necessary;* and give us leave to observe, Sir, with the frankness for which we pledged ourselves in the outset, that we are constrained to say, that in our opinion, it will bear neither of those characteristics.

"You will not find among our number, an apologist, for the unjust or wanton demands of any Court, whether of St James or St Cloud; neither will we on this occasion undertake the task of deciding (which however we do not think herculean) which of the great Belligerents has done us 'the most harm.'

"That we have received from both, Injuries very greivous to interests & humiliating to our pride, is a fact, on which there can be no divided opinion. Still, however, we are by no means satisfied, that it was either wise or expedient, in the present defenceless situation of our Country, to appeal to the dernier resort of Nations, even against England, who has been selected as the greatest enemy.

"For the outrageous attack on the Chesapeake which excited, and excited so justly the sensibilities of the Nation (protesting it was an act unauthorized by her Government) she had offered terms of reconciliation and atonement, which our own Government received as satisfactory. We mention this, merely as indicative of a disposition, on her part, to negotiate on all the other great points of difference between the two Nations.

"Our Complaints of Impressment although vastly exaggerated in the manner in which they have been usually treated, we view to be a subject of great difficulty and importance. That the Right of search has in many instances been abused, we have no doubt; and we must observe with regret, that no small number of them are attributable to the *facility* and *falsity* with which American Protections are obtained.

"Can it be expected, or ought it in justice to be said that 'the American Flag shall give the American Character to all who sail under it.' This subject (no one knows better than yourself) has been cause of complaint most of the time since the United States became a Nation, and yet, neither the Administration of Washington, Adams or Jefferson, ever deemed it *cause of War*. They considered it, as in truth it is, a subject of negotiation, of modification and amicable arrangement. England has ever professed a disposition so to consider it. She pretends to no right of impressing *our Seamen*, but claims a right, recognized by the Law of Nations, *the Right of Service in her own Subjects*.

"And can you think, Sir, by waging War against that country, and involving our own, in the greatest of all calamities, you will compel England, a Nation great in strength, ample in resources, Empress of the Ocean, and at this moment contending for her very existence, *altogether* to abandon this principle?

"Give us leave to suggest that in our opinion such expectations are vain.

"You may take Nova Scotia, conquer both her Canadas, and make inroads on her other dependencies; she will view them as *dust in the Balance*, compared with this Right. Dereliction of the Principle would be, in her, at this time, political suicide.

"On the subject of Blockade, we can have no doubt, both the great Belligerents 'feeling power and forgetting right'[5] have taken ground which cannot be justified by the Law of Nations, or sanctioned by former usage.

"We meddle not with the question how far these measures, were measures of Retaliation. Yet, when we find that Mr. Monroe then Minister at the Court of Great Britain, & now Secretary of State, in his Correspondence with yourself on this Subject in May 1806 at the moment this offensive step was taken, unhesitatingly & unequivocally gave his opinion that the Orders were made *to favour American views & Interests*, when he tells you on the 20th. of the same month that the Orders (of the 16th) appeared to be 'highly satisfactory to our commercial interests.'[6] When we find the British Government expressly and formally disavowing the principle, that

375

any Blockade, can be justifiable or valid, unless supported by an adequate naval force destined to maintain it. When they acknowledge the very doctrine of the Law of Nations, for which the American Government contend. When we so clearly perceive these things, we cannot consent that the subject of Blockade *is sufficient cause of War.*

"The orders in Council, constitute the most prominent feature in the alledged causes of War. However greivous may have been this cause of complaint, and greivous it most assuredly was, we are happy, that we can, at this time, congratulate you Sir, each other, and our countrymen at large, that this cause *now ceases to exist.* England, before she could have known of your Declaration of War (would to Heaven that Declaration might have been postponed for one short month) retraced her steps. These Orders are revoked, and of this revocation we trust your Excellency has in possession evidence equal, if not greater, than you have *now, or ever had* of the revocation of the Berlin & Milan Decrees.

"We are not aware, nor can we anticipate any material obstacle that can now exist, to the restoration of the two countries to their former habits of harmony and commercial intercourse.

"We shall *dispatch* the case of Henry as he has *dispatched* himself—*in great haste.* He has appeared in one short scene, strutted his short hour on the Stage, principally in dumb show—and made his *exit.*

"The *Unity of Time* would not permit him to tarry longer. We view with surprise, mingled with other emotions, the importance attached to him in a paper of State as seemingly with intent to injure the Reputation of a fair portion of our fellow-citizens pre-eminent in worth, talents, integrity and patriotism. Verily the Traitor has his *reward.* He has been suffered to escape the justice of an offended nation, in a national vessel ready to receive him, flying on the golden Wings of *five thousand American Eagles!*

"The continuance of the War under the present aspect of things, we shall consider as tremendously portentous. That it portends the greatest of all earthly evils, an alliance with France. We have in too lively view, the fate of Spain, Holland, Switzerland, and a large portion of continental Europe, now agonizing under the Iron Sceptre of the Colossian Tyrant of the House of Corsica, ever to consent to this; and we now enter our *Solemn Protest* against any such Alliance, of any description or character. Every conscript of France landed on our shores, we shall view as an enemy in disguise.

"'The smile on his cheek, will warn us of the Canker in his heart.'

"Your Memorialists, cannot in justice to themselves, and the Public, leave you on this occasion without expressing their sentiments on other subjects, intimately connected in their minds with the common Weal.

"We deem, to use the words of our Constitution 'the Liberty of the Press essential to the security of Freedom' and that it ought to be inviolably preserved—and the Freedom of Deliberation, Speech, and Debate, essential to the Rights of the People; and we view with alarm and Terror the prostration of the former by a *murderous mob,* finds an apology in a paper of our Government[7] and that the latter has received a *death wound,* in being denied to a distinguished member of the House of Representatives, when addressing them on a subject of vital importance to the interest honor and welfare of his Country.[8]

"We shall cling to the Federal Union, as the political Ark of our Nation's *Salva-*

tion and the main Pillar of Freedom's sacred Dome. Anathematized be the voice, and the hand, of that man who shall attempt to sever it. Far distant be the day of such a Calamity. But if the period should ever arrive, when a majority of Congress, shall be composed of men, who suffer their prejudices and passions to usurp the seat of Reason, shall indulge in national partialities, and pursue a course of measures, tending to excite jealousies, dissention, and dissatisfaction in the different sections of our country—shall persevere in a system, tending to the total destruction of Commerce, and the annihilation of Trade, impose on us Burthens 'greater than we can bear,' and take from us our life, 'in taking whereon we live'—who shall intend nothing by serving the public, but to feed their own vanity, and aggrandizement, without the sense of any duty they owe to God, or man. Should these events ever happen we shall consider them as the knell of our Country's departed Freedom, and as placing the *'Hic jacet'* on the Tombstone of the last Republic on Earth.

"Think not Sir, that our remarks on the subject of the present War are dictated by our personal fears.

"We have among us men who are inured to 'watchings, abstinence and toil'[9]— who have once and again bared their bosoms to the thunderbolts of War.

"They are not unmindful of the honorable distinction attached to our Troops *on those occasions*—we have among us younger men, who are not to be appalled at the prospect of a like conflict.

"Shew them a war, which they can clearly and distinctly perceive to be *just, necessary & honorable* and the hardy yeomanry of New Hampshire, will be found among the foremost to vindicate their Country's Rights, and to avenge her wrongs. But Sir, the object of this assembly, is neither to palliate or varnish the wrongs of conflicting Belligerents, to foster the animosities of party pride, or to distract the Counsels of the Cabinet.

"We sue only for Peace, and Peace only, on honorable terms.

"It would be indecorous in us, to prescribe to you; the mode in which this most desirable of all human Blessings may be attained, and we are slow of heart to believe that the *Flos de Luce* of France can have greater charms than the *Olive Branch* of Peace."

RC (DLC). 17 pp.; signed by Jonathan Steele, chairman, and John Mooney, secretary; enclosed in Steele and Mooney to JM, 7 Oct. 1812 (ibid.; 1 p.).

1. "But yesterday the word of Caesar might / Have stood against the world; now lies he there, / And none so poor to do him reverence" (Shakespeare, *Julius Caesar*, 3.2.118–20 [*Riverside*]).

2. The memorialists paraphrased Jefferson's 2 Aug. 1808 address to the New Hampshire legislature (Lipscomb and Bergh, *Writings of Jefferson*, 16:307–8).

3. The memorialists paraphrased Washington's farewell address (Fitzpatrick, *Writings of George Washington*, 35:234).

4. The memorialists referred to JM's message to Congress of 1 June 1812 (*PJM-PS*, 4:432–38) and the report of the House committee on foreign relations of 3 June 1812 (printed in *ASP, Foreign Relations*, 3:567–70).

5. The memorialists alluded to Jefferson's first inaugural address, 4 Mar. 1801, in which the U.S. is described as "A rising nation spread over a wide & fruitful land, traversing all the seas with the rich productions of their industry, engaged in commerce with nations who feel power and forget right" (Ford, *Writings of Jefferson*, 8:2).

6. The memorialists referred to Monroe's letters to JM of 17 and 20 May 1806 (printed in *ASP, Foreign Relations*, 3:124–25, 125–26).

7. The memorialists referred to the publication in the *National Intelligencer* on 13 Aug. 1812 of a "Report Of the Committee appointed to enquire into the causes and extent of the late commotions in Baltimore," which somewhat minimized the role of the crowd in the riots.

8. The memorialists referred to John Randolph, who was ruled out of order on 29 May 1812 for arguing that the Berlin and Milan Decrees were still in force and that there existed in the administration "a fatal French bias" driving the U.S. toward war with Great Britain. The Speaker of the House stopped Randolph in midspeech by ruling that no issue might be debated before the House until a motion had been made, seconded, and committed to writing and the House had agreed to consider it. Randolph eventually offered a motion that "under existing circumstances, it is inexpedient to resort to war against Great Britain," but the House voted not to debate the motion. Randolph protested being silenced and ultimately defended his position in the pages of the *National Intelligencer* on 18 June 1812 (*Annals of Congress*, 12th Cong., 1st sess., 1451–79).

9. "Dost thou love Watchings, Abstinence, and Toil, / Laborious Virtues all? Learn them from Cato: / Success and Fortune must thou learn from Caesar" (Joseph Addison, *Cato*, 2.1.290–92).

§ From Louis B. de Niroth. *7 October 1812, Washington.* "On the first of this Month I took the Libertey to adresed a Letter to you which was of Counciquance to me, and allso too the Governement as soon I obtaine my Libertey, it is usles to repite any ting more on that Subjecte I am not alloane Concerned in the Communication wat I alludet to and in Particcullar I have Teaken an oath not to comunicate any thing to paper.

"And as I have received Now answer from your Excellency I must Perrich in this Bastele Which is Keped by one of the greatest Barberigen I will Teact it as a Particcullar favor if you send me the in Closed Letter Bak which is from my daugther."

RC (DLC). 1 p.; docketed by JM. Enclosure not found.

§ From William Rice. *7 October 1812, Brunswick, "Richardsons P. O."* Informs JM that a volunteer company in Brunswick County [Virginia] is gathering and that a battalion will no doubt be formed from the brigade to which he is attached. Holds the rank of major in the Ninety-sixth Virginia Regiment. Offers his services as major of a battalion and claims to be ready to march at a moment's notice "whereever my countrys Interest may require my services."

RC (DNA: RG 94, Letters Received, filed under "Rice"). 2 pp.; docketed as received in the War Department on 21 Oct. 1812.

From William Duncan

SUPERINTENDANTS OFFICE

U.S. ARSENAL Octr. 8th. 1812

SIR,

I am induced from a sense of duty to our much injured Country, to communicate to your excellency the following information received as

matter of fact, from Mr. Tolado[1] a Spanish Gentleman resident in Philadelphia, of whose Character I understand you possess some knowledge.

"In pursuance of a communication of an official nature, by Dn. Lewis De
Onis, to the Council of Regency in Spain, respecting the occupation of
East Florida by the troops of the United States, and of their conduct towards Spain;[2] The Council of Regency sent a copy of the communication
of Onis to the Cortes, accompanied by their opinion that it was necessary
to declare War immediately against the United States, but that the circumstances in which Spain now existed would prevent so speedy a declaration
as would be requisite. The Cortes after mature deliberation, resolved to remit the documents to the Regency, to be communicated to the English
Government, requesting at the same time the sentiments of that Government on that particular. The Court of London replied by stating their concurrence in the opinion expressed by the Regency; adding that it was necessary to attend a more favorable opportunity."[3]

How the foregoing information was obtained by Mr. Tolado I have not
been informed, but whether it is authentic or not, I rest satisfied that it will
be received in the spirit in which I take the liberty of communicating it.
With sentiments of the highest esteem & regard I have the honor to be
Your excellency's Obedt. Very huml. Servt.

WM. DUNCAN

S M S

RC (DNA: RG 59, ML).

1. José Álvarez de Toledo y Dubois (1779–1858), a Cuban who had been an elected representative from Santo Domingo to the *cortes* in 1810–11, arrived in September 1811 in Philadelphia, where he began circulating schemes favoring the independence of Spain's colonies
in the Antilles and their subsequent union with Mexico and possibly with the U.S. as well. In
December 1811 he traveled to Washington, where he met not only with Monroe but also with
José Bernardo Maximiliano Gutiérrez de Lara. Just as Monroe had encouraged Gutiérrez to
return to Mexico to continue working for Mexican independence, so too did he urge Toledo
to return to Cuba, presumably for a similar purpose, and he gave Toledo a letter of introduction to JM's agent to Cuba and Mexico, William Shaler. Fearing entrapment, however, Toledo decided against returning to Cuba, and he remained in Philadelphia for most of 1812.
Eventually Toledo opted to go to Texas, apparently determined to wrest control of the Republican Army of the North from Gutiérrez and Augustus W. Magee. He arrived in Natchitoches in the first week of April 1813, where he found that both Shaler and the Americans in
the Texan republican army, horrified by the execution of royalist officials after the capture of
San Antonio, were willing to support his bid to displace Gutiérrez. Toledo took command of
the Texan republican army in early August 1813, but the royalists rallied from their earlier set-
backs and defeated Toledo's forces at the Battle of Medina on 18 Aug. 1813.

Following this failure, Toledo returned to the U.S. Thereafter, he was to remain intermit-
tently involved in schemes promoting the independence of Spain's American colonies until
1816, but at the same time he never wholly severed his connections with representatives of the
Bourbon cause in Spanish America, most notably Luis de Onís, whom he kept informed from
time to time of developments in the various rebel causes with which he was associated. In December 1816 Toledo petitioned Ferdinand VII for a pardon. Returning to his former allegiance to the Spanish monarchy, he ended his career as Spanish ambassador in Naples (Cox,

"Monroe and the Early Mexican Revolutionary Agents," *Annual Report of the AHA for 1911*, 1:202–5; Joseph B. Lockey, "The Florida Intrigues of José Alvarez de Toledo," *Fla. Historical Quarterly* 12 [1934]: 145–78; Harris Gaylord Warren, "José Alvarez de Toledo's Initiation as a Filibuster, 1811–1813," *Hispanic American Historical Review* 20 [1940]: 56–82; Harris Gaylord Warren, trans. and ed., "José Álvarez de Toledo's Reconciliation with Spain and Projects for Suppressing Rebellion in the Spanish Colonies," *La. Historical Quarterly* 23 [1940]: 827–33).

2. This could have been either Onís's 23 June 1812 dispatch to Spanish secretary of state José Pizarro or his 19 July 1812 dispatch to Pizarro's successor, Ignacio de Pezuela. Both letters dealt with American efforts to seize East Florida earlier in the year (see Pilar León Tello, *Documentos relativos a la independencia de Norteamérica existentes en archivos españoles* [11 vols. in 14; Madrid, 1976–85], 3:458, 465).

3. Ignacio de Pezuela's 10 Sept. 1812 letter to Onís explained some of these transactions. After learning of the American declaration of war against Great Britain, the regency government in Cádiz informed the British minister there of its desire to continue the friendship and the alliance of the two nations. As far as relations with the U.S. were concerned, the regency informed Onís that although Spain had long had cause for war with the U.S., the dependence of the Iberian peninsula on American supplies of flour and wheat required the adoption of "a policy of temporizing with the American government." This policy was to be conducted in ways that did not harm the interests of Great Britain, while care was also taken "not to give pretext to the American government to carry the excess of its complacency toward France to the point of making a war which could suit neither Spain nor England" (Brooks, *Diplomacy and the Borderlands*, 21).

Presidential Proclamation

[8 October 1812]

Whereas information has been received that a number of individuals, who have deserted from the Army of the United States have become sensible of their Offences, and are desirous of returning to their duty:

A full pardon is hereby granted and proclaimed to each and all such individuals as shall, within four months from the date hereof, surrender themselves to the commanding officer of any Military post within the United States or the territories thereof.

In Testimony whereof, I have caused the seal of the United States to be affixed to these presents and signed the same with my hand.

Done at the City of Washington the Eighth day of October A.D. 1812; & of the Independence of the United States the Thirty Seventh.

By the President   JAMES MADISON

                                             JAS. MONROE Secretary of State.

Ms (DNA: RG 107, LRUS, P-1812); letterbook copy (DNA: RG 59, PPR). Ms in a clerk's hand, signed by JM and Monroe. Printed in the *National Intelligencer* on 10 Oct. 1812.

§ From Benjamin Stone.[1] *9 October 1812, Warren, New Hampshire.* Informs JM that he is a Revolutionary War veteran who views the current war as a just cause. Writes to offer advice from the belief that it is "an incumbant duty injoined on all the friends to this nation at this momentious Crisis—more Peticular on account of the desaster of our Northwestern army."

Has examined the statements of Cass and Hull. "It appears that Hull is not to be acquited with haveing done his duty. Let him Pretend what he in his immagination might Conceive I knew him in the army in the revolution. He did not appear to me when at tieconderoga to be a man that was not affeard of gun Powder. He was in favour of a retreat from that post previous to the Same. We had Conversation on that Subject a day or two before it was put in Execution he avoided being in the Battles we had with Burgoin. He was a fanncy Parade officer. This was my estimate on him in that day he has turned out as I Expected a man of not much foresight and less varasity.

"Sir, those disasters usuly take plase in the begining of a war and Espceially a nation under the Circumstance we are under—filled with internal Enemys Who Spare no pains nor Property to distroy our goverment—and as money is tempting to Men without princaple; and those who are less deserveing are the most anctious after Promotion and at this time after plases of trust and in that they Can do us the greatest injury. No doubt all this has Consenterated in Genll. Hull." Recommends changes in the system for raising an army. Suggests that the terms are too long, the regiments too large, the pay to noncommissioned officers and privates inadequate, the number of troops too small to guard the vast extent of frontier territory, and recruiting officers too restricted in their duties.

"For Suposition was an army Enlisted for one year at a time many Men who will not Enlist for five years would for one a Man who has a family cannot leave them so long.

"A Regmet. to Contain five hundred rank and file Commanded by a Colonal Commidant and two Majors—would give twelve field officers to two thousand men—field officers are as liable to Cassultyes as others and on the field of action may be killed or wounded and good bold interprizing officers make their Soldiers the Same. I have been in a great number of Battles and I always found the Soldier to Performe well if the officer did likewise the Salvation of an army under god is in the ⟨Cursedy?⟩ and good Conduct of the officers—and on this depend, the victory and Salvation of the Cuntry. Your luke warme Slow men never Carry any great interprize officers Should be filled with that military grit that move Quick and with Resolution—and not lay on their oars till the enemy has Reinforsed and then must Capitulate or flee.

"As to the Pay not being adiquate to the Servises to be Performed—is obvious to Every man. When a Common labourer Can have from his neighbour ten dolla[r]s pr. month to labour on his farme and have a good bed to lodgon and his Regulor food and no risk of being tomihawked—will he Enlist as a Soldier. The answer is plain he will not—this has been Proved to a demonstration in drafting the melitia we have been Constrained to give them an adition to make their pay ten dollars pr month. This is done by the republicans—but they Cannot Continue and have the Rich toryes go free and not only that but doing all in their Power to prevent men from going at all. If the goverment was to give this in that Case they would be obliged to pay their Proportion. My oppinion is to pay and find well and Persue with Resolution and vigure—and the interprize will be ours.

381

"As to the number our armys are Composed of now are not addequate to the Servises to be Performed—not less than one hundred thousand Men are Sufficient for the Reduction of Canada. That Cuntry is Extenesive and we have the Savages to incounter they are lurking in Slygh plases—and must be watched with the greatest Caution. And we must not ⟨luk?⟩ to the frunt but to the rear and flank also. And Ellowing for garrisons and Casultyes—not more than forty thousand will arrive before Quebeck. They must be divided into two devisions one on the plains of abram and the other at Point levy—and Each being able to incounter with their main body in case of an attack on Either point and be able to Repulse them without the assistance of the other.

"And that fortris must be reduced by a regular Seage by haveing heavy ordinance and morters well found—and the Same Commence Early in the Season. For to attempt the reduction as was pland in the revolution will no doubt terminate as that did. We must go to work Sistimaticuly if we Expect to Suceed.

"The Restrictions on the Recruteing—has a tendancy to reteard its Progress—viz.

"A mans body Should be free from arrest for debt and he Should not be kept under the Controle of a Tory Creditor and the Restraint as to miners should be removed. But few men will give their Consent to have their Sons go into the army—neither will a man Consent to have his apprentis go—and the tory Party are unannimus in this. I have lived and been an acter in two wars and I never knew those restraints put in the way of Recruteing till know."

Urges Congress to pass laws against opponents of the war and advises JM to choose his officers with care. Has known Dearborn since he was sixteen years old and served with him in the Revolutionary War. "He is a man in whome I think I Can plase Confidence—but he never has been acquainted with Beseageing Strong Castles—and hear he must be indebted to Some other Person of more knowledg⟨e.⟩ . . .

"I am of an Opinion that let the plan be as it may for this Campain—it has not been Prosicuted with that Pollicy and military Skill that I Could have wished. It Seems from genll. Hulls own Statement he had but a Small number of men when he tuck Possesion of Sandwich, and there he found ⟨fir⟩st his gun Carridges was rotten. He it Seems was ⟨no⟩t attentive to his duty in Seeing that they were always ready for Service. His conduct after he had taken Possesion of Sandwich in laying on his oars and playing bo peap at the bridg in Sending Small partyes to give the Enemy a Challange and waiting for them to Reinforse—all Caryes a Simton at least of his inability and not-understanding much about the arts of war. I also Should have Suposed that Genll. Dearborn would have moved on to Plats burg at the time Genll. Hull moved into upper Can[a]da So that the attention of the Enemy would have been at least attracted this way—and that would have prevented their Sending reinforsements to Malden. The Pollicy of the Request of the enemy for an armistick might have been Seen into without much Millitary knowledge. . . . Genll. Dearborns Conduct in this movement Coroberates with what I have already Stated as to his Military Experiance. Great Ellowances must be made we are all young in the arts of war. . . . But it appears to me we Shall not have a more favourable time by which we might have wone Possesion of all Canada Expt Quebeck this Campain—and have Silenced the Savages—but now we must double our deligence or we Shall have heard work another year. No doubt but Brittan will Reinforse to the best of her Power—and withstand us in all directions—and Sir, I am of an oppinion that we Cannot adopt a better Scheam than what I have Proposed that will be likely to be Caryed into affect—as the Toryes are numerous and are planing in all directions to miss lead and Procrasterate all the opperations of goverment—and unless Some thing decisive is done we Shall be under most disagreeable Circumstances. . . .

"Our internal Enemyes are not only numerous but Impudent and they do not hissitate in Saying and Publishing the most inflamitory Sedetious Scanditious Publications and are magnifying Every thing against us—and Palliateing the Conduct of our enemyes—and the Common People are missled by them—and they are imbarissing them in all directions—and laying the Same to the goverment—and unless goverment give the Pople Some assuerance of their being put into a Differant Situation by a better Prospect of haveing adiquate Compensation for their Servises I am affeard that instead of our army augmenting it will Decrease—and those Republicans who have as yet Stood fast will loose their influence over the Commonourity and they Shift Sides and Joine the toryes and Brittan."

RC (DLC). 7 pp.

1. This was probably Benjamin Stone (d. 1820), who was a captain of the Third New Hampshire Regiment during the Revolutionary War (Heitman, *Historical Register Continental*, 523).

To the South Carolina Legislature

Ocr. 10. 1812

I have recd. fellow Citizens, your joint address transmitted by the President and Speaker.[1]

In the unanimous determination to support the war in which our Country is engaged, you have given a conspicuous proof of your fidelity to the national rights, and sensibility to the national character. It is a war worthy of such a determination; having its origin neither in ambition, nor in vain glory; and for its object, neither an interest of the Govt. distinct from that of the people; nor an interest of a part of the people, in opposition to the welfare of the whole. It is a war which was forced by persevering injustice, on exhausted forbearance. And having been called for by the public voice, every motive ought to be felt, to bear its necessary pressure with cheerfulness, and to prosecute it with zeal to a successful issue.

The approbation you have been pleased to express, of the agency which fell to my lot, in resorting to the only mode left of maintaining for our Country the rights and the rank of our Independent Nation, claims my acknowledgments. I tender them, with my fervent wishes that a general emulation & exertion of the patriotism exhibited by the Legislature of South

Carolina, may speedily secure to the U. States, the blessings of a just and honorable peace.

Draft and partial draft (DLC). Partial draft consists of an earlier version of the first two paragraphs.

1. South Carolina Legislature to JM, 29 Aug. 1812.

From an Unidentified Correspondent

Sir   Octr. 10th. 1812 Virginia

It is one of the greatest blessings of our republican Goverment and administration; the Ease, and facility with which, any man can approach the chief magistrate of the nation; and however weak he may be in his political opinions, if he has the love of his Country at heart, it will be a free pasport to his president, under these considerations I have taken the liberty to suggest some few Opinions with gr[e]at defference and respect to your excellencys better opinions and judgment; indeed, I have never thought you have erred in any single instance in the Various departments you have filled, I have had the presumption, to think that your predecessors did err altho great and Good men, in a point or two, but without a compliment I have never thought so of you; their is a firmness, and decission in your Charactor, that has never been possessed by even Genl Washington or Mr Jefferson in so emminent a degree, this is not only my opinion, but the Stern republican opinion of the nation. I know full well that all matters, and things coming immediately under yr cognizance will go on well, and I think it is very hard that any president of the U States should be responsible for the agents of the government in all its ramifications and I think also that the nation ought not complain on every little disaster; it is the chance of war, and we must, and ought to calculate, on ⟨Sceares?⟩, and changes, no president ought to be blamed for the treachery, or cowardice of a General. Gen Washington had his Arnold; but you are not sensured by any Patriot, or man of Honour in the U States but the cry is raised by Traitors, tories, Randolphits, and Burrites and the friends of D, W, Clinton, to promote his Election have joined in the cry, but I hope in God they will all be made to cry in earnest the first monday in November next or as soon there after as they can hear of the election in the different States. I am astonished that the martials in the different states do not take the Alian Enemies for their are a great many, and send them, ought of the country, if congress does not make some wholesome provisions relative to the tories, and traitors, at the next session, I am convinced the people will tare & feather, them, cane, & kick them, out of the country. We are astonished that Aaron Burr should be permitted to come, and remain in peace in this country, after his treason, he comes into the very face of justice, but I veryly believe if he was to come before the Chief justice of the united States; before he would have him taken on his recognizance and sent for trial, he would dine with him as he once did at Wickham's when he was brought before him to be tried for high treason;[1] You may rely upon it Sir that if Aaron Burr is not taken up soon, that the Tories and traitors, will complain and say, that the government wants Energy and can not stand, as it wants Energy to bring a traitor to punishment, for what will not Tories and traitors do & say I expect that Ad. Warren & Sir Sydney Smith will soon be here, to make offers of peace,[2] I have just been reading, that in the year, 1778 the Earl of Carlisle, William Eden, Eqr. and George Johnstone, arrived at philadelphia the begining of June as commissioners for restoreing peace, between G Britain & America; but the Government of America refused to treat with the british commissione[r]s unless the independance of the united states was acknowledged, or the Kings fleets and armies were withdraw[n] from America So in the same spirit we hope that the Goverment of the united States will demand of England the acknowledged right of the liberty of the seas, the giving up of our unfortunate seemen impressed on board of british ships of war, and a Stipulation that they will not impress any m⟨ore?⟩ then and not til then, [*illegible*] I hope the president will attend to any propositions that the commissioners may make until thos⟨e⟩ points are first conceaded in the mean time I hope the war will be carried on both by sea, and land with the greatest forse and vigoar, Harrison, Dearborn, & Bloomfield will soon be in sufficent forse to carry every thing before them the invasion of Canada will not be delayed I hope a moment, Harrison say's he will take Malden before chrismass and Dearborn and Bloomfield will do as much so that when all the forse of the different divisions of the army is united they will give the finishing blow to Quebeck. I am your excellency's most Obedient humble Servant

A TRUE MADISONIAN

RC (NN). Damaged by removal of seal.

1. One week after his acquittal on treason charges in April 1807, Aaron Burr, along with his counsel, John Wickham, had dined with Chief Justice John Marshall in Richmond, Virginia (see Abernethy, *The Burr Conspiracy*, 232).

2. On 24 Sept. 1812 the *National Intelligencer* published a 9 Sept. report from Halifax that Admiral Sir John Borlase Warren, in command of a British squadron en route to the U.S., was expected any moment and that it was understood that he was invested with the power to negotiate for peace or, failing that, to "unkennel the dogs of war." On 13 Oct. the paper reported that Warren had arrived in Halifax on 27 Sept. but was "not possessed of those diplomatic powers with which busy rumor had clothed him." In a 30 Sept. 1812 letter, Warren informed Monroe of the repeal of the orders in council and requested that the U.S. "instantly recall their letters of marque and reprisal against British ships, together with all orders and instructions for any acts of hostility whatever against the territories of His Majesty or the persons or property of his subjects," on the understanding that Warren would likewise immediately issue

a command that British measures of war be terminated. He explained that should the U.S. accede to his proposal, he was authorized "to arrange with you as to the revocation of the laws which interdict the commerce and ships of war of Great Britain from the harbors and waters of the United States; in default of which revocation . . . the orders in council of January, 1807, and April, 1809, are to be revived." Monroe responded on 27 Oct. 1812 that it would be "very satisfactory" to JM to "meet the British Government in such arrangements as may terminate, without delay, the hostilities" but that "A suspension of the practice of impressment" would also be necessary (*ASP, Foreign Relations*, 3:595–96).

§ From Henry Foxall.[1] *10 October 1812, "Spring Hill, near Geo. Town."* "Sence I had the Honour of Speaking to you on the Subject of the Situation of the poor unfortunate John Ryan,[2] now in Buffaloe Jail I have endevoured to Obtain some evidence of what I then communicated to you respecting the time he came to this country, the place where he landed, and as fare as could be obtained, of his Carrecter and conduct, sence he landed in America." Encloses letters to prove that Ryan "was not settled in canada, nor has no wife, nor family there."[3] Expresses his belief that Ryan "came to this country with the most pure Intentions, of filling up any Sittuation Providence might place him in, as a *good* and *faithful* Citizen."

RC and enclosures (NN). RC 1 p.; docketed by JM. For surviving enclosures, see n. 3.

1. Henry Foxall (1758–1823) was a British-born Methodist lay preacher who emigrated from Ireland to Philadelphia in 1797. Foxall relocated to Georgetown in 1800, where he established the Columbia Foundry, an important source of government munitions during the War of 1812 (Madison Davis, "The Old Cannon Foundry above Georgetown, D.C., and Its First Owner, Henry Foxall," *Records of the Columbia Historical Society* 11 [1908]: 38–41).

2. On 13 Aug. 1812 British subject John Ryan was convicted of being a spy and sentenced to death by a general court-martial in Lewiston, New York. JM granted him a pardon on 14 Nov. 1812 (DNA: RG 59, PPR).

3. Enclosed are a 1 Oct. 1812 letter (1 p.) from the Reverend Thomas Sargent to Foxall, marked "No. 3," promising that Sargent was making every effort to gather information concerning Ryan's case, and a 6 Oct. 1812 letter (2 pp.) from Sargent to Foxall, marked "No. 4," transmitting three certificates (not found) testifying to Ryan's good character. Foxall claimed to have also enclosed letters from himself to Ryan and Sargent.

§ From the Inhabitants of Stonington, Connecticut. *10 October 1812.* The petitioners request that JM turn his attention to their port, which they consider endangered by the existing state of affairs and their incapacity to defend themselves against enemy attack. "That we are exposed to such an attack a reference to a survey of this coast will shew and experience has testified to its probability. Having before stated these circumstances in a communication to the Government it may be unnecessary to repeat them,[1] although it may be proper to observe that since that time our citizens have been much alarmed by the appearance of a hostile fleet off the mouth of our Harbor, whose tenders or boats might have taken out our Vessels and pillaged our Village before a sufficent force could have been collected to have repelled them, particularly had it been undertaken in the night season.

"In the year 1808 when it appeared probable that our Government would be constrained to resort to hostile measures to procure redress for wrongs offered the

Country, a petition was preferred from this Borough to the Executive, praying their attention, which was followed by precautionary measures; That is an Arsenal was built and two pieces of Ordnance with proper ammunition have been placed in it. An Officer of Engineers visited here and selected a suitable site for the erection of a sufficient Battery, and an Agent for the War Department settled the terms of purchase for the Premises; but all operations have since been suspended and our unacquaintance with any circumstances which could lead to it. When the danger then only apprehended is actually approaching, induces us again to petition your Excellency to take it into consideration. The two Gun Boats which are stationed in this neighborhood have yet been too seldom in or off our Harbour to be able to render us any certain assistance. If such a force was permanently stationed off this place and suitable works erected on shore with a small force to support them, under whom the Citizens would be authorised to act should emergency require, we should feel all the security which a state of War will admit. The Guns which are placed here can afford us but small prospects of security, while laying in an arsenal a considerable distance from the shore, and with none whose duty it is to use them who are acquainted with their proper exercise, nor any prudent station in which to place them where they could be efficiently improved.

"Two associations have formed and been on duty for their exercise & use, but knowing of no existing law whereby they could be vested with authority to act & their services be located, we have no reliance on their aid.

"Abandoning a reliance upon any force which our State Government may organise separate from the Militia and they having been withheld from service we must now look to the Government of our Nation and our own exertions for protection & support in defending our Port & sustaining our part in the prosecution of the present War, which we consider undertaken solely for the purpose of asserting and supporting the honor & Interests of the United States."

RC (DNA: RG 107, LRRS, P-274:6). 3 pp.; attested by Peleg Brown, clerk; enclosed in Amos Palmer, Amos Denisin, and Gurdon Trumbull to JM, 12 Oct. 1812 (ibid.; 1 p.); docketed as received in the War Department on 19 Oct. 1812.

1. The memorialists probably referred to a petition from the inhabitants of Stonington that was laid before the House on 26 Feb. 1808 and then forwarded to Jefferson. The petition described the unprotected nature of the port and requested that provision be made for its defense (*Annals of Congress*, 10th Cong., 1st sess., 1689).

§ From Michael Sweetman. *10 October 1812, "Scotland Neck Halifax County N Carolina."* Reports himself to the president, stating that he is a native of Ireland, has resided in the U.S. for two years, is twenty-four years old, has no family, and is employed as a clerk. Adds that he has not yet made his intention to become a U.S. citizen known in court but intends to do so at the November session.

RC (DNA: RG 59, War of 1812 Papers, Letters Received regarding Enemy Aliens). 1 p.

From Albert Gallatin

Dear Sir   Sunday evening Ocr. 11. 1812

The exchange of places which you suggested[1] would, in my opinion, have a most salutary effect on the conduct of the war: but, on mature reflection, I apprehend that it would not satisfy public opinion and would be more liable to criticism than almost any other course that could be adopted. Respectfully Your's

ALBERT GALLATIN

RC (DLC). Docketed by JM.

1. The details of this proposed change have not been found, but it may have involved Monroe's replacing Eustis in the War Department (Brant, *Madison*, 6:120).

From William Keteltas

Sir   N. York 11 Oct 1812

It is with pleasure I assure You of the great gratification the release of the Schooner Industry[1] belonging to the poor English Widow and Children prize to the franklin Privateer afforded the friend and foe to the administration in this City. It has ever been My pride and ambition to prevent the honor of My Country, and its Govt., from receiving any & every Stain, and that no Spot or wrinkle should in the least degree tarnish its Character and reputation.

I have not received any answer to My application for a Colo. Commission of horse, which I offered to raise for the Service of the United States, but found on My return to the City, the Appointment of *A Colo. Dela Croix a frenchman.*[2] This May be well enough and proper, provided Colo. dela Croix Can raise a regiment of french emigrants as a tribute of gratitude for the hospitality and protection the Americans Afforded Frenchmen against the desolating Guilitoine of *Robert Spere* in the bloody revolution of France, and an Assylum under the usurpation and tyranny of their Master Bonaparte Since, Which Acts of those two *Tyrants* blasted the efforts in the Onset of The best Men of France to Emancipate the french people from the Shackles of an Absolute Monarchy.

Americans will never nor ought they to be Commanded by foreigners; it is impolitic and Unnatural Their proud Souls Abhor the humiliation. This seems to be the difficulty with Colo. dela Croix at present as I am informed in raising his regt., and no wonder. If he ever raises a regiment they Must be as they ought to be frenchman; for Americans Cannot will not Yield their Honbe Pride to be Commanded by Foreigners.

I hope the president does not look for a pledge of *devotion* to support his reelection to Obtain the Commission asked for. No this Cannot be; it would be d[i]shonbe. to the president, degrading to myself, and destructive of that independance of A freeman ruinous in the end to the Liberties of the people.

Not to Obtain the approbation of the world would I Make this Ignoble Sacrifice, as A Man and as an *American.*

My Military pretention is My love Of Country; and a wish to defend it, Which I did as a Volunteer in infancy in our glorious revolution. I had the honor to be engaged in the first attack of the British upon the people of Connecticut in the Year 1776. A people Who now Sin politically Speaking if I May be allowed the expression against the Holy *ghosts, of Patriots Slain.* They Sin against light and the Conviction of their own Consciences. If their Crime is not unpardonable upon repentance, May their Country forgive but never forget them.

The War Entered into with Great Britain, I believe *Holy Just* and *right,* and will if prosecuted with Vigour and Maintained with fi[r]mness redeem us from our fallen State as a people: to oppose which Ambition has raised its Cursed Crest, but when opposition like Lucifers against his God will end in its own ruin.

Great Britain Must Yield sooner or later to our Just Claims or her Govt., will fall, if Conducted as it has been by a wicked and profligate administration, perhaps she has already passed the Rubicon. Your Obd. Servt

WM. KETELTAS

RC (DLC). Cover marked "private"; docketed by JM.

1. On 13 Oct. 1812 the *National Intelligencer* reported that the schooner *Industry* had been captured by the *Benjamin Franklin*, brought into New York, and "delivered up to the owner Mrs. Wheelan, who, with her daughter were passengers."

2. Irenée Amelot de Lacroix had written to JM on 18 Sept. 1812 (not found; acknowledged in Eustis to Lacroix, 22 Sept. 1812 [DNA: RG 107, LSMA]), probably seeking a commission in return for raising a corps of French-speaking volunteers in New York City. Eustis forwarded Lacroix's letter to Brig. Gen. John Armstrong, leaving the matter to his discretion, subject to the proviso that "Commissioned Officers are to be Citizens of the UStates" (Eustis to Armstrong, 22 Sept. 1812 [ibid.]). Armstrong evidently granted Lacroix the authority to raise volunteers, a decision that caused some controversy in the newspapers (see, for example, the N.Y. *Columbian*, 6 Oct. 1812).

From Elkanah Watson

Sir   PITTSFIELD MASSTS. 12h Octr 1812

The Inclosed Sample of Cloth was made of my wool—under my direction 12/4 wide from loom, finished a little Short off 7/4—with elegant hair lists. At the Cattle Show & Fair in this place—this ps. obtained the prize of 50$ a struggle of 4 Counties—which I surrendered to the workmen.

The result fairly devolopes a very important item in the resources of Our Country, the ps. was 23 yds. long. One half will be exhibited t'morrow befor the Ligeslatur in Boston—the other half—has gone to different public char[a]cters in the State of New York—except a Patern of 2¼ yds—Inclosed in a Packet & directed to you Sir. & will be delivered by the Honl. ⟨Mr?⟩ Bacon Member from this County or rather district.[1]

It was my intention to have transmitted it by an eairlier oppertunity—as that is imposible I Judg'd it proper to apprize you off the intention. I am Sir with profound respect & esteem Your Obt. St.

ELKANAH WATSON[2]

RC (DLC).

1. The Republican representative from Pittsfield was Ezekiel Bacon, who wrote to Gallatin from Pittsfield on 13 Oct. 1812 to complain about deficiencies in army pay and clothing. Gallatin apparently forwarded the letter to JM (DLC; 3 pp.; docketed by JM).

2. After several failed business ventures in Europe and the U.S., Elkanah Watson (1758–1842) settled in Albany in 1789, where he organized the Bank of Albany and promoted several canal projects and other internal improvements. Relocating to Pittsfield, Massachusetts, in 1807, Watson turned his attention to scientific farming and husbandry. He is most widely known for his promotion of agricultural fairs, beginning with his hosting of a "Cattle Show" in 1810, which led to the formation of the Berkshire Agricultural Society later that year (William R. Deane, *A Biographical Sketch of Elkanah Watson, Founder of Agricultural Societies in America, and the Projector of Canal Communication in New York State* [Albany, 1864], 3–11, 14).

§ From Samuel Fulton. *12 October 1812, Baton Rouge.* Wrote to JM in 1802[1] reporting his arrival in the U.S. and expressing his desire to become "usefull to my own Country by entering into its amediate Service, after having Spent Eight years of my Life in that of France." Acknowledges JM's response [not found], which informed him that his name would be placed on the list of appointments. States that he is ready to accept any post he may be thought capable of filling, but would prefer to serve in the cavalry or rangers. Notes that in West Florida under the Spanish government, he was "Charged with organising and Training the Militia as Commandant, and now under the Teritorial Government of Louisiana as Colo. of the Militia."

RC and enclosure (NN). RC 2 pp.; docketed by JM. The enclosure (2 pp.), entitled "A Statement of S Fultons Military Services—whilst in France," is dated 15 Oct. 1812 and signed by Fulton.

1. Fulton to JM, 10 Aug. 1802, *PJM-SS*, 3:470.

§ From Hugh Chisholm. *13 October 1812, Charlottesville.* "I have this day drawn on you at eight to pay moses Sammuel and James Leitch for the Some of two hundred dollars I hope it will be convenient for you to honor I was sorry that I Could not see you when you was in Orrang on the account of sickness."

RC (DLC). 1 p.; docketed by JM. A note at the foot of the page in JM's hand reads, "$200 pd. as drawn."

§ From James Dinsmore. *13 October 1812, Park Mills.* "I received your favour of Septr 25 [not found] & have agreeable to Request given an order on you, in favour of James Leitch for 600 Dollars which he will want paid in Baltimore from whence he will probably send the order. I wish to get a few more Sheets of the Iron if you Can Spare it & will thank you to mention it to your Manager at Montpelier."

RC (DLC). 1 p.; docketed by JM. A note at the foot of the page in JM's hand reads, "$600 pd. as drawn."

§ From William Eustis. *13 October 1812, War Department.* By an act of 3 Mar. 1809,[1] "it is provided that all warrants drawn by the Secretary of war, or the Secretary of the Navy, on the Treasurer shall specify the particular appropriation to which the same should be charged; and that on application of the Secretary of the proper department the President is authorized to direct that a portion of the monies appropriated for one branch of expenditure be applied to another, in the same department." Informs JM that appropriations to the Quartermaster's Department are nearly exhausted and requests that JM direct that $500,000 appropriated for the pay of the army be applied to defray expenses in the Quartermaster's Department.[2]

RC (DLC); FC (PHi: Daniel Parker Papers); letterbook copy (DNA: RG 107, LSP). RC 2 pp.; docketed by JM. FC is a letterpress copy. A note at the foot of the first page of the RC in Daniel Parker's hand reads, "This letter was prepared to submit to the President when the order was given by him to transfer from one approp[r]iation to another & is now sent that there may be record of the transaction in the War Office."

1. See *U.S. Statutes at Large*, 2:535–37.
2. In the margin of the letterbook copy is written a letter of the same date from JM to the secretary of the treasury: "In pursuance of an Act of the 3d March 1809—entitled 'an Act further to amend the several Acts for the establishment of the Treasury War & Navy Depts'—I do hereby direct that the sum $500,000 of the fund appropriated for the pay of the Army, be applied to that of the Qr. M. Dept: signed J M."

§ From the Vermont General Assembly. *13 October 1812.* "Resolved, That the constituted authorities of our country having declared war between the United States and Great Britain, and her dependencies, it is our duty as citizens to support the measure; otherwise we should identify ourselves with the enemy, with no other distinction than that of locality. We therefore pledge ourselves to each other, and to our Government, that, with our individual exertions, our examples and influence, we will support our Government and country in the present contest, and rely on the Great Arbiter of events for a favorable result.

"Resolved, That his Excellency the Governor be requested to forward a copy of this resolution to the President of the United States."

RC (DLC). 2 pp.; attested by William D. Smith, clerk, Rollin C. Mallary, secretary, and Thomas Leverett, secretary of state, "In Council Octr 17th 1812"; docketed by JM, "Resolution of Vermont from Govr. Galusha Ocr. 13. 1812." Enclosed in Jonas Galusha to JM, 7 Nov. 1812 (ibid.; 1 p.; docketed by JM as received 29 Nov. 1812).

To Thomas Jefferson

DEAR SIR   WASHINGTON Ocr. 14. 1812

I recd. your favor of the 2d. inclosing the letter from Mr. Meigs. The place he wishes, has been long allotted to Mr. Mansfield, who preferred it to that of the Surveyorship held by him; and who has just obtained the exchange; and a Commission for the place vacated, has just been sent to Mr. Meigs, who was long ago recommended for it; and who it was understood wished it. It is the more probable that it will be acceptable to him, as he has connections in the W. Country, particularly the present Govr. of Ohio.

I see so little chance of being able to peruse the lucubrations of Faronda you were so good as to send me, that I replace them, for the present at least in your hands.[1]

The last intelligence from the Westward left a military crisis near Fort Defiance.[2] Winchester with about half the army, was encamped within 3 miles of the encampment of about 300 British troops with some field pieces & a body of Indians stated at 2000, or 2500. It is probable they were destined agst. Fort Wayne; with the general view of finding employment for our forces on their way to Detroit untill the Season should be spent, or Brock could send troops from below. Of our affairs at Niagara & the neighborhood of Montreal, it is difficult to judge, the force of the Enemy being imperfectly known, & that under General Dearborn, depending so much on circumstances. Our best hopes for the campaign rest on Harrison; and if no disaster, always to be feared from Indian combats, befall him, there is a probability that he will regain Detroit, and perhaps do more. He has a force of 8 or 10,000 men at least, enthusiastically confiding in him, and a prospect of adequate supplies of every sort, unless it be Cannon, which tho' on the way, may possibly encounter fatal delays. This article however he appears not to make a sine qua non; nor will it be wanted for Detroit, if it be true as is reported that every piece has been withdrawn by the British.

The latest accts. from Europe are in the Newspapers.[3] The ideas of which Foster & Russel are put in possession, will soon draw from the B. Govt. some evidence of their views as to peace. From France we hear nothing; and shall probably meet Congs. under the perplexity of that situation.

The current Elections bring the popularity of the War or of the administration, or both, to the Experimentum Crucis.[4] In this State the issue is not favorable, tho' less otherwise than would appear. In the Congressional Districts the Republicans I believe, have not lost ground at all, notwithstanding the auxiliaries to federalism. In the State Legislature, they will be in a minority on a joint vote.[5] Penna. altho' admitted to be shaken, is represented to be safe.[6] New Jersey is doubtful at least. The same is the case with New Hampshire.[7] North Carolina also is reported to be in considerable vibration.[8] The other States, remain pretty decided on one hand or on the other.

You will be amused with the little work of the Author of several humurous [sic] publications, Irvine[9] of N. York. It sinks occasionally into low & local phrases, and sometimes forgets the allegorical character. But is in general good painting on substantial Canvas. Affece. respects.

JAMES MADISON

RC (DLC). Docketed by Jefferson as received 17 Oct.

1. See Jefferson to JM, 5 Aug. 1812.

2. On 15 Oct. 1812 the *National Intelligencer* printed extracts of several letters from the Northwest describing Winchester's impending encounter with British troops and Indians near Fort Defiance. JM probably also derived his opinions from Elijah Wadsworth's 27 Sept. 1812 letter to Eustis, which specified the number of British troops and Indians involved (DNA: RG 107, LRRS, W-330:6). Harrison's 13 Oct. 1812 letter to Eustis gives a full account of these events (Esarey, *Messages and Letters of William Henry Harrison*, Indiana Historical Collections, 2:173–78).

3. On 29 Sept. 1812 and for four subsequent issues, the *National Intelligencer* printed summaries of the arguments heard in Parliament in favor of repeal of the orders in council. On 15 Oct. the *National Intelligencer* reprinted William Cobbett's address to the prince regent, originally published in the 4 Aug. 1812 edition of *Cobbett's Weekly Political Register*. Defending the U.S. decision to prosecute the war, Cobbett argued that the repeal of the orders in council was not sufficient to ensure peace and that impressment and possession of the Floridas still remained to be addressed.

4. *Experimentum crucis:* crucial experiment.

5. JM probably referred to the Maryland election results, which were printed in the *National Intelligencer* on 8, 10, and 15 Oct. 1812. The paper reported that fifty-two Federalists and twenty-eight Republicans had been elected to the House of Delegates, "So that there will be a sufficiently large majority in the House of Representatives to outweigh the Republican Senate, and ensure the election of a Federal Governor and Senator in Congress, at the next meeting of the Legislature." Maryland sent six Republicans and three Federalists to both the Twelfth and Thirteenth Congresses (Parsons et al., *U.S. Congressional Districts, 1788–1841*, 92–95, 158–60).

6. In spite of intense Clintonian activity before the election, Pennsylvania's 25 electoral votes for JM proved decisive in his victory over Clinton by a margin of 128 to 89. The state sent twenty-two Republicans and one Federalist to Congress and maintained a Republican majority in the state legislature as well (*Niles' Weekly Register* 4 [1813]: 268; Higginbotham, *Keystone in the Democratic Arch*, 265–68).

7. JM was rightly concerned about New Jersey. The state sent two Republicans and four Federalists to the Thirteenth Congress, gave its electoral votes to Clinton, and elected a Federalist majority in the state legislature. Similarly, New Hampshire elected six Federalists to the Thirteenth Congress and gave its electoral votes to Clinton (*Niles' Weekly Register* 4 [1813]: 268).

8. Sometime in the fall of 1812, JM received the following note from William Blackledge relating to politics in North Carolina: "Nothing which art and intrigue can effect, is or will

be left undone in this State by the Clintns. & F. d's. A proposition I am informed has been made by Govr. Tomkins to Govr. Hawkins, that the Cltons. will support the late Govr. Stone for Vice, if the vote of this State can be secured to Clinton for President. The knowledge which we have however of Stones character I think will justify the Conclusion that he will treat the overture with the disdain it merits. I shall write him by the first mail on the subject what is said & request an answer addressed to me at Washington.

"Under cover of another package I will send a copy of a letter to Cap Taylor and his answer if he has kept one—on the subject of the Presidency recd. from one of the Cltns. at New York" (DLC: Rives Collection, Madison Papers; 1 p.; unsigned; undated; filed at 30 Sept. 1812). North Carolina, however, remained Republican, supporting JM's reelection, sending a predominantly Republican delegation to the Thirteenth Congress, and electing a Republican state legislature (*Niles' Weekly Register* 4 [1813]: 268).

9. JM later placed an asterisk before this name and wrote at the foot of the page, "'John Bull & brother Jonathan' rather by Paulding." He probably enclosed a copy of James Kirke Paulding's *The Diverting History of John Bull and Brother Jonathan, by Hector Bull-us* (New York, 1812; Shaw and Shoemaker 26392).

From an Unidentified Correspondent

Sir   New York Octr. 14th. 1812

Although I have not the honor to be personally acquainted with you, yet I shall take the liberty to write you a few lines. I am acquainted with the different political parties in this City, and throughout the State; and am in the freequent habit of discussing different Political subjects, with Federalists, Clintonians &c; and in general, with such as have not made up their minds, at all events, to decry every measure of their opponents, I have found no difficulty in defending the measures of the late and present Administrations. But, Sir, the recent proceedings of Mr. Sanford,[1] (which I am credibly informed, have been fully represented to the secretary of the Treasury) in libeling the Goods, which have lately arrived here from England, in a manner calculated to put the Importers to as much expence as he possibly can, with the view of encreasing his own Costs, *probably cannot be defended!* As Sanford libels, in each vessel, the Goods of each Importer separately, some have to pay him considerable sums; and others, whose Invoices are small, have to pay nearly as much as the Goods are worth! And most assuredly a plan might be devised, to save Importers such vexations and expence: the natural tendency of which, is to encrease the impression, already too prevalent, that the present Admn. are enemies to Trade, and desirous of hampering the merchants all they possibly can! For my part, I know perfectly well, that the opposition given to the Orders in Council, by the late and present Administrations, from first to last, was correct, and what our Interest, as well as our honor, demanded; and that we should have been robbed of millions of property, *for years and years to come*, under those very Orders, had our Govt. submitted to them; but I know that many worthy men, consider your Admn. as enemies to Trade; and, as a person ardently desirous of your re-election to the Presidential Chair, I now take the liberty to suggest, that in my opinion it would be an act of justice, as well as of advantage to the Republican cause, to relieve Importers from future oppressions of the kind I have mentioned. The Bonds might be taken, I should think, before the Goods were libelled; or the whole Cargo might be included in one libel. I shall only add, that I am neither directly, nor indirectly, concerned in Importations of any kind, and that my motives in writing this letter are fully express'd in the declaration, 'that I feel anxious for your re-election.'

A FRIEND TO THE JEFFERSON AND
MADISON ADMINISTRATIONS

RC (DLC). Docketed by JM "Gallatin A. / Ocr 14. 1812." A note on the cover in Gallatin's hand reads: "I believe the fact to be as here stated: at least I was so informed before I left N. York. Thus if there be sixty consignees having prohibited goods on board one vessel; instead of embracing the whole cargo in one libel, there are sixty distinct ones, giving to the dist. atty., clerk, & marshals sixty fees instead of one. As this abuse, if it be one, should in fact be most properly corrected by law, or by the Court, I asked Mr Dallas respecting the propriety of the course & his own practice. He does not dislike fees, but at once told me that he would not consider such proceeding as strictly honorable, & that he never had made but one libel for the whole cargo in all such cases. He knew that Sanford & several other district attornies acted otherwise. The office is so little profitable that, if it had not been for the immense number of prosecutions thus arising from the late British importations, the practice might have passed un-noticed. The question now is whether an executive remedy will be attempted. I see no other than to refer the subject to the Comptroller who may write a circular to the dist. attornies disapproving the practice. A. G."

1. Nathan Sanford (1777–1838) was U.S. attorney for the district of New York from 1803 to 1816. He served as a state assemblyman in 1810 and 1811, as a state senator from 1812 to 1815, and as a member of the U.S. Senate from 1815 to 1821 and from 1826 to 1831.

From George Dayton

[ca. 15 October 1812]

The Present Governor of St. A:[1] I believe to be a benevolent good man a Soldier & States man & that he will never surrender the Place at least the fort untill compelld. by force—or want of *Provisions*—of wch. there were when I left on 11h. Augt: 2 or 3 months *allowance* for the Garrison & militia. Since wch. time I have learnt of supplies having arrivd. safe from H: & Nassau for St. A: & it was *confidently* believd. when I left there that they shd. not want for a reasonable supply of money troops & Provisions from H——na wch. were daily expected—and it was also expected that B——sh cruisers wd. be off an[d] on to keep the *Patriots* in Awe—but were the Amer:n. Govt. to Come *generously* forward there is little doubt that an arrangement wd. immediatly take place to the *advantage* of *all* Parties. This Arrangement or Capitulation—or what you may chuse to call it wd. most probably be *Conditional*—leaving it for the Cortes, or at any rate the Capt. General of the island of Cuba to ratify, wch. I believe wd. certainly be done knowing that sooner or later the 2 Floridas *must* be Am——n & a treaty securing the friendship of the two Powers & guaranteeing to the loyal Inhabitants—possession, restitution of their property or Compensation for their losses wd. be an object of such Importance as to ensure an easy acquiescence on the Part of Spain. And You may rest assurd. unless the Amer: Govt. send a greater force agt. it *than it is* probable they can conveniently spare at present; the Place will not be given up to men *who have threatend. a general and indiscriminate Massacre & Plunder.* Nevertheless there are *some* People in St. A: who secretly favor the opposite side & who have been endeavouring to create disaffection among the *Black* troops. The Indians to the No. of 9.000 were down before I left St. A: & 14.000 were appointed in all—to make war agt. the Americans & Patriots. It is supposed by many that the Spanish Govt. have instigated them to this[2]—*how ridiculous*, their wives & relatives out in the country who cd not get into town *have* been equel sufferers with the Insurgents. Frank Fatio[3] is bereaft of *all* his Property by the Indians & with difficulty savd. his & his wife's Lives. The Indians being so hostile to the Americans is owing to a dread of being deprivd. of their territory & Property—shd. the Amer. get a footing in the Country. I apprehend the contest will be *long* & bloody—& have given up all Intentions of ever settling in E: F: but The Probable fate of the Province can only *as yet* be guessed at—the above is my *true & unbiassed* Sentiment, & deliverd. according to the best of my knowlege & Judgement. There is no communication between Augustin & the united States at present.

G.D.

RC (DLC). Undated in the *Index to the James Madison Papers*. Conjectural date assigned here on the basis of internal evidence and the information presented in n. 2.

    1. Sebastián Kindelán (1763–1826), formerly governor of Santiago de Cuba, had become governor of Spanish East Florida in 1812. Throughout the latter half of 1812, after the Madison administration had disavowed the actions of George Mathews (see *PJM-PS*, 4:294–95 n. 2), Kindelán was engaged in negotiations with Georgia governor David B. Mitchell over the security of the property and persons of Americans who had supported Mathews's efforts to overthrow the Spanish regime and transfer the province to the U.S. (*Enciclopedia universal ilustrada*, 28:3446; Owsley and Smith, *Filibusters and Expansionists*, 76–80).

    2. In the final weeks of the summer of 1812, reports from East Florida had circulated to the effect that the Spanish were supporting Indian and black uprisings, culminating in the news, printed in the Augusta *Mirror of the Times* on 12 Oct., that a ship had sailed from Augusta to St. Augustine in late September "to supply the more savage Spaniards who have encouraged and rewarded the blood-thirsty savages to spread desolation and horror through all East-Florida." Dayton's letter may have been a response to such reports. For a description of the conflicts between Americans, blacks, and Indians in East Florida at this time, see Patrick, *Florida Fiasco*, 195–210.

3. Francis Philip Fatio owned a plantation on the St. Johns River. His farm was attacked by Indians on 13 Aug. 1812 (ibid., 48, 187).

From George Hubbard

SIR   STONINGTON. CT. Octr. 15. 1812.

Inclosed herewith You have a List of the Crew of the private Armed Schooner "Lewis" of Stonington:[1] which Privateer was captured about the 14th. August last and sent into Halifax.

It so happens that very few if any prizes are bro't into Connecticut; it, of course, becomes very difficult to procure English Prisioners [sic] to be exchanged for the *brave Crew* of the "Lewis." I am requested by a person concerned in the "Lewis" to state to your Excellency that the Crew, are really in a straitned condition, especially as it respects their living, being kept on a very scanty allowance. In addition I can say, as it respects the greater part of the Crew, they would doubtless be of much service to our Common Country. I beg your Excellency to give such instructions to Mr Mitchel at Halifax as will insure the speedy return of the Crew of the "Lewis." Your Obt Humb Servant

GEO HUBBARD

RC (DNA: RG 45, Subject File RE, box 589); enclosure (DNA: RG 45, Subject File RA, box 570). Redirected in JM's hand to "The Secy. of State"; docketed by Monroe. A note at the top of the page reads, "exchd in Halifax." For enclosure, see n. 1.

1. The enclosed list (1 p.) of thirty-seven crew members is marked "excha. in Halifax."

§ From L. Marchand. *15 October 1812, Augusta, Georgia.* "My motives in writing you these lines are no others than the warm interest I feel for this my adopted land, happy if what experience I have acquired in european wars can forewarn the false steps so common in the beginning of a war, to a nation who have been blessed with thirty years peace & prosperity. . . .

"The northern frontier presents a military position which will ensure the final Success of the war to those who will know how to take advantage of it; The late disasters at Detroit may in the Sequel prove favourable to the country, first by rousing the Spirit & energies of the nation, & by drawing the english forces in the Wilderness where their efforts will be harmless; But the point of attack must be by lake Champlain, & its communications by Water with the St Lawrence. The first step is therefore an attack on St John & Chambli both on Sorrel river. These two fortresses being in our power will become the point from which all the operations will be directed; they will Secure the Communications with the State of New-York, from whence by means of Steamboats, which should navigate the Hudson to its head, and others which should depart from the southern extremity of lake George, the warlike stores would be transported with a great promptitude as far as the rapids of St John, & then forwarded to the different divisions of the army. The army while encamped between St John & chambli, would be in a position almost inexpugnable; one of its wing protected by a fortress, its back by Sorrel river, & some redoubts in its front would present a fortified Camp, which would be during the whole war the place of reserve, where the recruits should be sent & instructed, & from whence the reinforcements should be forwarded where wanted. As soon as the army should have Succeeded in taking St John & Chambli, the General commanding must divide it in three columns, the left of about six thousand men, will march against Montreal; the right column of eight thousand men must descend Sorrel river & attack Trois rivieres & the center column of four thousand men must direct its march so as to cross the St Lawrence in the most convenient place between Montreal & Trois rivieres, so as to be able to bring assistance to the right or left division as necessity may require; But the march of the three division must be calculated in reason of the distance & the difficulties of the road, so as to attack on the Same day & the same moment; it would be advantageous that the army now opposite Detroit should make Some attacks on that town a few days previous to the real attack. The english have Succeeded in one of their Scheems which was of attracting the attention of the americans towards the northwest, where the country being almost unsettled they hope to render war without object & Victory without fruit, having nothing at Stake but a pathless Wilderness, while they preserve their rich & populous provinces from the evils of war; But their cunning may be retorted upon them & while an army of militia will keep them in awe in that quarter & oblige them to reinforce their army with regulars, the theatre of war being carried below, they will find themselves inadequate to the contest, & if they extend their line out of proportion with their strength they will fall an easy prey & meet with disasters everywhere. The passage of the St Lawrence being effected, the center division must unite with the right & take a position on the right shore of the easternmost river which empties itself in the St Lawrence at Trois rivieres. The advantages of placing the american lines on its shores, are that by keeping possession of that town the communications with lake Champlain are secured, without having any troops Stationned on the left bank of the St Lawrence, & the keeping of the peninsula la prairie between Sorrel river & Montreal can be trusted to the militia which will not meet there with a harder service that [*sic*] can be expected from them. The brave mountaineers of Vermont bordering on the eastern Shore of lake champlain will present a barriere sufficient to resist the detached parties of the ennemy if they were willing to interrupt the communications on the rear; and the powerfull & fruitfull state of New-York would supply provisions, & a numerous militia who without going out of the state could render the most imminent Services, in taking on the frontiers the place of the regulars who should be sent to the army. But connected with this plan is the safety of New-York, for if the ennemy were coming & storm that place they would oblige the northern army to withdraw to its assistance & war should be carried on american land which should be a great evil to the country. However if the english General is a man of skill & spirit, he will not fail instead of opposing the invasion of Canada, to attack New-York, & with eight thousand men he will oblige it to capitulate in three days; He will land unexpected in York bay, in the same place where the english landed last war & Marching to Brooklyn he will establish his batteries opposite New-York & summon it to Surrender. Such a rich

& populous city instead of exposing itself to destruction will capitulate, & the forts raised with so much expense for its defence, will be given up without firing. From hence the necessity of throwing up some works at Brooklyn; a fort there would be of the greatest importance, but if time is too short to have one constructed, a palissaded entrenchement protected by redoubts, would add to the security of the city, & ensure the operations of the northern army. This in the lines of Trois rivieres, will wait till frost will have blocked up the river & obliged the ships of war to withdraw to halifax, and will advance to Quebec which is distant about five days march. The Strength of the place will make a blocus[1] necessary, therefore the troops will be Stationned on the plains of Abraham, at point Levy on the Island of Orleans & on the eastern shore of Charles river; a Strong line of circonvallation raised & palissaded, & batteries of bombs & red hot Iron ball erected, in order to burn if possible the stores & magazines of the ennemy & to hasten its reduction. The rigors of a canadian winter may be partly avoided by constructing for the soldiers huts twelve feet square terminating in a Conical form at the top at the heigth of nine feet; this shape is the best calculated to support the weight of snow & when covered with it they are warmer than Brick houses; eight men can be quartered in each. It is probable that if Quebec was blocked up in the beginning of Winter it could not hold out, till it should be relieved by troops from Europe, who could not reach it before the beginning of May; therefore the english of Halifax could perhaps attempt to succour it, & by way of preventing it, a sham expedition against nova scotia, should be prepared somewhere in the district of Maine, with a great ostentation either by land or by sea. As long as the season would permit it, it would be necessary that the army destined for detroit should make excursions & continue a petty warfare, in order to keep the ennemy busy & prevent them from detaching any reinforcements to the troops in lower Canada.

"This hasty Sketch of a campaign is susceptible of extension & I have omitted many important circumstances to not extend the limits of this letter. Permit me to conclude it with this observation that a board of war composed of experienced officers who should devise the plans of campaigns would perhaps be one of the best methods to ensure their success."

RC (DNA: RG 107, LRRS, M-502:6). 4 pp.; docketed as received in the War Department on 17 Nov. 1812.

1. *Blocus:* blockade (Fr.).

§ Jonathan Coffin to Albert Gallatin. *15 October 1812, Nantucket.* Requests that his salary be raised to place him "on A footing with other keepers of light housses" and that a dwelling be built for him near the lighthouse.

RC (DNA: RG 217, Manning File). 1 p. On the verso is a note of the same date from four selectmen of Nantucket attesting to the correctness of Coffin's letter. On the cover sheet Gallatin redirected Coffin's letter to JM and wrote a note requesting that the salary be raised to $166.67. Below this note JM added "Approved" and his signature.

From the Tennessee General Assembly

[ca. 17 October 1812]

At the second session of the ninth General Assembly of the state of Tennessee, holden at Nashville in said state, the following Preamble and resolutions were passed—viz:

Whereas from the genius of the government and people of the United States it has always been an object of the highest importance to cultivate peace and harmony with all nations, and more especially with those, with whom they have had commercial regulations. And Whereas there is in the opinion of this General Assembly no one instance in which the American Government has failed to observe the strictest rules of justice and impartiality towards the government of G. Britain, in return for which they have under their orders in Council (containing principles wholly repugnant to every rule of national love as well as to every notion of natural Justice) captured and burnt our ships and destroyed all american commerce which has fallen into their piratical hands—they have impressed thousands of American Citizens who are detained against their will in ships of war, and groaning beneath severities inflicted on them far from their families and Country, and then compelled to fight the battles of their own and Country's enemy, and that too against their beloved Country; they have murdered many more, wantonly, whose blood is still unatoned for. They have basely and contrary to the rules or policy of any other civilized nation on earth, attempted by an unauthorized agent, to seperate these United States and to sow sedition among the Citizens thereof, at a time too when they were professing the most fri[e]ndly disposition towards the American Government; not contented with this black catalouge of crimes against an innocent and unoffending nation. The[y] have induced the wretched savage tribes within our limits and on our borders, to raise their tomahawks against our peaceable and innocent citizens, thereby exciting and Contributing to the support of a war for the indiscriminate murder of our aged fathers, Mothers, wives and helpless Children; a war commenced and prosecuted for the purpose of extermination, by which disgraceful and insideous policy they have already spilled the blood of some of the best Citizens of our western Country, in a midnight attack in which they assisted the Indians on the wabash, after lulling them into security by professions of friendship and a wish for peace. And Whereas in consequence of these enormities, and others not here enumerated, the Congress of the united states did on the 18th. day of June last, declare that war existed between the U: States and Great Britain and Ireland and their dependencies—and Whereas since the declaration of war (altho' a measure in itself so just and necessary) many of the Citizens of the united States have most basely vilified and traduced the present administration for the measure; thereby in effect surrendering the rights of the people of this Country, in favour of the domineering policy of our Common enemy.

Therefore, Resolved unanimously by the General assembly of the state of Tennessee, that we view the late declaration of war against G. Britain and Ireland and their dependencies as an act of indispensable necessity for the sovereignty, welfare, happiness and safety of the government and people of the United States, and in our opinion further submission to the unjust measures of the British Government, would have been too degrading for a free people, and would have amounted to a sacrifice of the Independence, which our fathers nobly acquired at a vast expence, and with the loss of much of the best blood of America in a contest with the same enemy.

Resolved that we veiw any and every attempt to divide the people of the U: States, whether by a foreign government, by the state governments respectively, or by any of those stiling themselves citizens of either or any of the states, as an act in the first place too mean, degrading and barbarous, ever to have been countenanced by any other civilized government than that of our present enemy, whose policy has for a series of years been marked by no single act of magnanimity or justice; but on the Contrary by a constant and unvarying determination to sacrefice every principle of justice, humanity or honor.

Resolved that while we ourselves feel the highest confidence in the constituted authorities, to support these measures in the prosecution of this just and necessary war, we pledge our lives, property and sacred honor. We see with sorrow, the attempt of many persons within our bosoms to defeat the measures adopted for our safety and happiness, and thereby in effect serving the Cause of our enemy.

Resolved that it is the opinion of this General Assembly that the Government of the U: States ought to prosecute the war with energy and vigor, in order that it may be effectual, and that they ought neither to spare men or money in the prosecution thereof, beleiving as we do that we have patriots enough in our Country to carry into effect any just or necessary measure that the government may find it necessary to resort to; and we feel confident that our citizens will be as ready to pay their money as to jeopardize their persons in support of the war.

Resolved—That the Senators in Congress from this state, be instructed, and the Representatives be requested to use their best endeavours to induce the general government to adopt the measures recommended in the foregoing resolution, as the course to be pursued in this war.

Resolved that a copy of the foregoing resolutions be forwarded by the executive of this state, to the President of the United States, and to each of the Senators and representatives in Congress from this state, signed by the speakers of the respective houses of this general assembly.

RC (DLC). Undated; dated 1812 in the *Index to the James Madison Papers*; date assigned here on the basis of the memorial's having been adopted by the Tennessee General Assembly on 17 Oct. (*Journal of the House of Representatives, at the Second Session of the Ninth General Assem-*

bly of the State of Tennessee [Nashville, 1813; Shaw and Shoemaker 29931], 131–34). Unsigned; docketed by JM.

From Thomas Wilson

(Essay)

SIR,   ERIE, PENNSYLVANIA, October 17th. 1812

The Indians must be either enslaved, exterminated, deprived of forign aid and, for a time at least, of arms; or they will during our wars continue more and more to scourge our extended frontiers.

To cut off British intercourse by the St. Lawrence and prohibit all supplies of guns from any source to any Indian whatever seem to be at once the most practicable and effectual measures; But to hold as hostages a number of the most leading amongst even those tribes who profess friendship but are suspicious ought not in the mean time to be neglected.[1]

The fullness of time is now come when an effective Naval force of some description must be erected and maintained. This truth is demonstrated by 1st. the arguments in congress last winter 2d. by the facts and experience of last summer, and 3d by the geographical structure of the American continent. The Mississippi waters a country like a world in itself, and will soon conduct to the "high way of nations" more tonnage than all the other rivers &c. of America. Its mouth is but 1560 miles from Porto Bello and that but 54 from Panama; Possession if obtained while favourable opportunities occur, of these ports and the intervening Isthmus can be forever maintained with the command of trade to china by the united States. This is evident. The cheapness and inexhaustable abundance of provisions and Naval materials which this river will afford, together with the shortness of passage to the Isthmus; defies alike in war or Peace the power and competition of Great Britain. That power must build & victual a Navy for this trade by purchases at five times our prices and then transport four times our distance, through Stormy Seas. The odds is more than 20 to one. This subject is connected with futurity indeed; but it is wise to look forward.[2]

In the mean time our safety most immediately depends upon the preparation of a vigorous land force—not that it is escentially necessary to make extraordinary sacrifices solely with a view to the *Speedy* conquest of all the Canada's.[3] We can easily take and maintain possession of the St. Lawrence above Quebec by a well concerted arrangement for the speedy augmentation and reduction from time to time of an army which must be stationed for this purpose at or near three river point. When this is effected the country is conquered. The fortress below remains; and unless a favourable opportunity occurs for the purpose it may not be best to attempt its hasty reduction. It would cost more than it will for a long time be worth. Without peace or a navy we cannot use its advantages; and would have it, with others, to maintain at much hazard and expense.[4] The British will probably be most distressed by holding it occupied and defended as it must be by strong land and Naval forces, and these maintained at enormous expense without advantage in return.

But at all events we must have a Strong and Stationary force on the St. Lawrence with the best possible arrangement for the Speedy transportation of troops and Stores between that and the Hudson. The Fleet of Britain gives her the great advantage of coming by Surprize; not to the St. Lawrence only—but desperate attemps may be made on the Shores of the a[t]lantic. To *embody* troops with *speed* and *move* them with *rapidity* must become a principle object.[5] In these respects our greatest defects exist at present. An Army can be embod[i]ed in England and landed at Norfolk in less time than we can raise 2000 militia men in one state and station them in another *in many instances.*[6]

Contracts must be liberal in proportion to the despatch required and importance of the object in view. This will prove real economy: a contract for provisions ought not to be suffered at Starving prices but such as will *command* the exertions and the capital of able men.[7]

In providing Arms and ships something should be done to give fame to America and to the age. It is practicable. By a single contract for 200,000 muskets at $10 each a perfection in their quality and facility in construction may be acquired that would ensure all additional supplies at $4 and of the best—in a few years time a gun for every man and not a workman robbed from other trades. This alone would humble Europe—and prove us able to suceed in every necessarey branch.[8]

The writer of this is ready to engage by Contract all he asserts so far as relates to subjects of contract—would he make a fortune by that proposed for guns? He would; he ought; and thus devote that fortune to his country in its applications, so as to realize whatever effect he promises from what he states. As in the instance of Muskits he will contract to furnish 200000 at $10 in four years and 600,000 more at $4.00 each (100,000 Yearly). In this proposition the writer states a more naturel and common effect of a given cause—one however to which due attention is rare. In general the effect is not closely enough observed and ascertained—and all Governments more or less neglect to avail themselves of it to due advantage. They neglect the latter Stipulation; and thus suffer the advantage to be engrossed by the Spirit of monopoly and patent right. It is however a principle, properly applied and managed, that will not fail to accomplish whatever is practicable.[9] I am Sir with high respect Your Obt. Servt.

THOS. WILSON

The rolling or whirling of cannon-balls in firing might be prevented by a thin socket of sheet-iron, in the cylinder form, but terminating at one end in a semiglobe, the axis equal to that of the balls *and cut in two equal* segments lengthwise, quite assunder (except a very small space at the bottom) so as to part from the ball immediately at the muzzle.[10]

RC (DNA: RG 107, LRRS, W-349:6). Docketed as received in the War Department on 26 Oct. 1812.

1. To the left of the first two paragraphs Wilson added a brace and the word "Indians."
2. In the left margin Wilson wrote, "Navy / present & future effects of."
3. In the left margin Wilson wrote, "Immediate necessity for a strong land force."
4. In the left margin Wilson wrote, "Quebec."
5. In the left margin Wilson wrote, "Speedy movements all important."
6. In the left margin Wilson wrote, "now tardy."
7. In the left margin Wilson wrote, "Liberal contracts."
8. In the left margin Wilson wrote, "Muskets."
9. In the left margin Wilson wrote, "wherein want of attention is common to all governments in different degrees."
10. In the left margin Wilson wrote, "Firing Cannon."

From Paul Hamilton

[ca. 20 October 1812]

All the public vessels, worthy of repair, have been put in requisition—& the following are now in actual service,

frigate	President
	Constitution
	United States
	Congress
	Essex
Ship—	John Adams
"	Wasp
"	Hornet
Brig	Siren
"	Argus
"	Vixen
"	Enterprize
"	Viper
"	Oneida
	Scorpion

& all the gun boats

The frigates Constellation & Chesapeake have been repaired & are expected to sail in a few days.

The frigate Adams is now repairing; but will probably not be ready for sea before spring.

*At new orleans, in consequence of the late Hurricane, heavy expenditures became necessary & were authorized[1]—& in addition to the naval force stationed in those waters, two block ships, & as many small vessels as might in the opinion of the commg military & naval officers be deemed essentially necessary for the defence of n'orleans; were authorized.

At new York, Telegraphs have been established to convey information from the Hook—fire ships have been authorized to be built; & all the public vessels have been put in requisition for the defence of that harbour.

On the Lakes Ontario & Erie, extensive naval operations have been authorized—with the view to our obtaining the Mastery on those Lakes.[2]

On Lake Champlain—the same.[3]

At Charleston—12 barges have been authorized—six of which are stationed at Sunbury.[4]

Note. None of these expenditures,[5] were contemplated in the Estimate for the year 1812—of course they are all extraordinary—their amount will probably not fall short of $750,000.

In our operations against the Enemy, we have lost

The brig Nautilus[6] of 12 guns—commd. by Lieutt Crane.[7] The result of a court of Enquiry leaves us no cause to blush on that occasion! All acted well. She was captured by a squadron of large ships.

We have captured

The Alert—a national brig of 18 guns—captd by the Essex.[8]

The Guerriere a national frigate of 49 guns—" Constitution[9]

& 22 merchant Vessels.

Lieutt. Elliott,[10] on the 8th Octr., proceeded with 2 boats to Fort Erie, & cut out two British vessels of war, viz. brig Detroit (late U S brig Adams) & brig Caledonia. This enterprize was effected under circumstances very perilous & highly honorable to the Party performing it.

RC (DLC). Undated; dated 1812 in the *Index to the James Madison Papers*; date assigned here on the assumption that news of the 9 Oct. 1812 capture of the *Detroit* and the *Caledonia* on Lake Erie could not have reached Washington before mid-October and that Hamilton submitted this report to aid JM in the writing of his annual message to Congress of 4 Nov. 1812. Unsigned.

1. On 19 Aug. 1812 a hurricane struck the Mississippi Delta, seriously damaging U.S. gunboats and other vessels at anchor. On 25 Sept., after the news had reached Washington, Hamilton authorized the commanding officer in New Orleans, John Shaw, to "make every necessary provision to supply the place of any boats, that may have been lost, & to defend the Water passes to new orleans" (Dudley, *Naval War of 1812*, 1:407).

2. See Gallatin to JM, ca. 26 Aug. 1812, n. 1.

3. On 28 Sept. 1812 Hamilton ordered Lt. Thomas Macdonough to assume command on

Lake Champlain, where he was to oversee the preparation of two gunboats and six vessels then under construction. Hamilton also directed thirty seamen under Commodore Chauncey's command to be sent for Macdonough's immediate service and promised Dearborn's assistance as well (Dudley, *Naval War of 1812*, 1:319–20).

4. On 9 July 1812 Hamilton ordered John H. Dent to send six completed barges to Sunbury, Georgia, and to build an additional six for Charleston (DNA: RG 45, Letters to Officers).

5. Above the line here Hamilton wrote, "from *."

6. On 16 July 1812 Capt. Philip Broke's squadron captured the *Nautilus* less than a day out of New York, marking the first U.S. naval loss in the War of 1812. On 26 Sept. a court of inquiry was held aboard the *United States* in Boston (Dudley, *Naval War of 1812*, 1:209, 476 n.).

7. William M. Crane (d. 1846) received his lieutenant's commission in 1803. During the War of 1812 he rose through the ranks quickly, becoming a commander in 1813 and a captain in 1814 (Callahan, *List of Officers of the Navy*, 137).

8. On 14 Aug. 1812 the U.S. frigate *Essex*, commanded by Capt. David Porter, captured the first British vessel in the war, forcing the *Alert* to surrender after less than ten minutes of battle (Dudley, *Naval War of 1812*, 1:218–19 and n. 1).

9. For the capture of the *Guerrière*, see Monroe to JM, 4 Sept. 1812, nn. 2 and 3.

10. Lt. Jesse D. Elliott (d. 1845) participated in the Battle of Lake Erie in 1813 and was promoted to the rank of master commandant in July of that year. He became a captain in 1818, despite alienating many of his peers by his quarrels with popular naval leaders, particularly Commodores Perry and Decatur (Callahan, *List of Officers of the Navy*, 181; Dudley, *Naval War of 1812*, 1:327).

From John G. Jackson

DEAR SIR,   FRANKLINTON October 21st 1812

I arrived at this place a few days since with a small party of my friends from Clarksburg to join the North Western army destined to Detroit; & cooperate with them as a corps of mounted Riflemen. On our Arrival we found Govr. Meigs here. Genl. Harrison returned from Chelicothe on Monday. I communicated to them our wishes & expectations; namely that we were anxious to be actively employed in the service of our Country, & we expected to be furnished with forage & rations on public account as it was impossible for us to supply ourselves. On finding that Genl. Harrison was vested exclusively with authority in relation to the ulterior operations of the army my application was made conformable to that state of things, & I had the pleasure to learn from the General that he would employ us, altho the laws made no provision for any such case. In reply to his intimation that he had no authority to engage any compensation to the party, I stated that altho some of them might expect & wish it I would obviate any difficulty on that score by assuming upon myself the responsibility of paying them. I am anxious therefore to learn from you how far I may expect an indemnity for this expence I shall thereby incur as it may be necessary for me to discharge some of them if my pecuniary resources are incommensurate to it. For myself I neither wish, or will accept any compensation whatever. Having long been convinced of the justice & necessity of the war, & determined to participate in it if my strength enabled me, I shall find in the consciousness of having aided its success with my best exertions, an adequate reward. General Harrison intends setting out for Mansfield on the Waters of Muskingom, tomorrow. I shall follow him in a few days, & would accompany him were I not prevented by an arrangement made with some of my friends to meet with them at Urbanna which I expected would be in the road to Genl. Harrison's head quarters. I have sent on today for them to join me here & on their arrival will pursue the route of the Genl. Your letters under cover to him will reach me with most expedition & safety.

The interest I take in the success of his Campaign has led me to make the most minute enquiries in relation to his force, supplies &c &c. I find that there are at Fort Defiance under Genl. Winchester about 1800 effective men. On their way from Urbanna to Fort McArthur under Genl. Tupper[1] about 1000 men marching by Chelicothe on to this place 1500 Virginians under Genl. Leftwich[2] and about 1300 Pennsylvanians on their march from Pittsburg to Mansfield; & exclusive of these about   [3] men principally Cavalry. For these the supplies of all kinds coming on are unquestionably ample, including a fine train of Artillery. But on enquiry I find that the Genl. has no Artillerists & but one Officer qualified for the command or capable of teaching them. This is an obvious defect which should be remedied: otherwise the Artillery are worse than useless, for it is a fact that among the militia Officers not one in an hundred knows how to load a Cannon, much less the art of annoying the enemy or protecting our Army with them. Among my associates is a Capt. Davisson[4] who commands an artillery company of Militia, & altho he is a fine intelligent Officer he knows nothing of the practical use of cannon; and I hazard little when I express my belief that few if any of them know more. It seems to me of the utmost importance that proper Officers be sent on without delay, & as many of them are doubtless at your disposal they can join the army before it reaches Detroit. I know my dear Sir you will excuse the freedom of my remarks because you know the sincerity with which they are communicated. Previous to my departure from home I resigned the Office of Commissioner to ascertain the boundary line of the Virginia Military reservation with which I had been entrusted by the Executive of Virginia. As it is, I regret that I ever accepted the appointment or solicited the delay of commencing that business which you were pleased to grant.

Offer my affectionate regards to Mrs. Madison—tell her that I left Mrs. Jackson & little Mary in good health at Marietta, & that when the War is over I will bring them to see her. Dr. Sir yours truly

JG JACKSON

RC (DLC). Docketed by JM.

1. Edward W. Tupper held the rank of brigadier general in the Ohio militia (Drake, *Roster of Ohio Soldiers in the War of 1812*, 4).

2. Joel Leftwich (1759–1846) had held the rank of brigadier general of the Twelfth Militia Brigade since 1809. He served under Harrison in the Northwest in 1812 (Butler, *Guide to Virginia Militia Units*, 302; *CVSP*, 10:167, 168–69).

3. Blank left in RC.

4. Jackson may have referred to George J. Davisson, of Harrison County, Virginia, who was an artillery captain with a separate command during the War of 1812 (Butler, *Guide to Virginia Militia Units*, 270).

From David Howell

SIR,   PROVIDENCE 22d October 1812.

To assure you of the steady & persevering adherence of Governor Fenner & all *his* Friends, who are more than ninetenths of the Republicans in this State, to your person & administration, I have enclosed *The Providence Patriot* of October 17th Instant containing Resolutions passed at a Republican Convention of Delegates from all the Towns in this County.[1]

These Resolutions were written by Governor Fenner & presented to the meeting in his own hand writing as the Chairman has informed me—for I was not present: but at Boston on publick business.

The depression of our party here could not have been effected by Embargoes, nor by restrictive regulations of Commerce, however grieviously felt in this little commercial State, without the aid of a Faction, or Schism among ourselves, which, openly, & in a printed circular Letter dispersed throughout the State, denounced Governor Fenner; by which means and by their own corrupt practices, the adverse Party succeeded, by a very lean majority in May 1811.[2]

We consider these Schismaticks, tho' few in number, more bitter enemies to our Cause than Federalists. The Clintonian Schism of N. York, fatal as the Trojan Horse, threatens a like Catastrophe to the United States. Our faction stands on tiptoe, eager to join Clinton, hoping thus to gain the ascendancy over us at Washington, of which they despair during the continuance of pure Republicanism in the U.S. Cabinet. For several years past they have openly & contumaciously refused to accord with the proceedings of our General Republican Convention—and, it is said, they have some organ, through which they labour to thwart our nominations at Washington. One of their number hath lately been to New York—spent some time there & returned here [a] Clintonian Agent.[3]

To describe the malignity & virulence, with which party rages in this Town, & State, would require the pen of *Thucydides*, which painted the plague, at Athens, in the time of the Peloponnesian War.[4]

My very dear & only Son will have the Honor to deliver you this Letter: and to present you with my highest respects. I have the Honor to remain, Sir, your assured Friend and obedient Servant

DAVID HOWELL

RC (DLC).

1. On 10 Oct. 1812 "a Convention of Delegates representing the Republican Citizens of all the Towns in the County of Providence" unanimously approved eleven resolutions. The resolutions upheld the powers of Congress and the primacy of the federal union, called for an end to impressment, supported the war effort, reprobated the conduct of France, and endorsed the nominations of JM and Elbridge Gerry in the upcoming election (*Columbian Phenix: or, Providence Patriot*, 17 Oct. 1812).

2. On 17 Apr. 1811 Federalist William Jones defeated James Fenner to become the governor of Rhode Island by a margin of just over two hundred votes (*Providence Gazette*, 20 Apr. 1811).

3. Howell placed an asterisk here and wrote at the bottom of the page, "This was discovered by his tampering with one of the Printers of the Patriot." The printers of the *Columbian Phenix: or, Providence Patriot* were Bennett Wheeler and Josiah Jones.

4. Thucydides, *History of the Peloponnesian War*, bk. 2, chap. 7.

§ From Winney Love. *22 October 1812*. Requests that her son be released "from the Regelar troups as he is under adge & has inlisted a gance My will and he is the onely Son of the Surport of a Pore widde womman hou has a Large famely of Small Childeran." "My Sons Name is Charls Love[1] under the Command of Cpt Thomes P More[2] at Clarksburg Harrason County Vargina."

RC and enclosure (DNA: RG 94, Letters Received, filed under "Love"). 1 p.; cover addressed "to the Secretary of Ware or the Presentden of the United States"; docketed as received in the War Department on 12 Nov. 1812. The enclosure, addressed to the secretary of war, is a 31 Oct. 1812 petition (1 p.) by Winney Love for her son's discharge, signed by thirteen supporters.

1. Charles Love, an eighteen-year-old farmer from Clarksburg, Virginia, enlisted for eighteen months' service on 19 Aug. 1812 and was discharged in 1814. His mother's petition was unsuccessful (DNA: RG 94, Registers of Enlistments, 1798–1914, 14:236).

2. Thomas P. Moore was a captain in the Twelfth Infantry Regiment; he received a major's commission in the Eighteenth Infantry Regiment on 20 Sept. 1813 (Heitman, *Historical Register*, 1:723).

§ From Abijah Peck. *23 October 1812, Warwick, Orange County, New York*. Informs JM that he manufactures bridle bits "to considerable extent with but a very small Capital and succeeded finely with it till the great influx of English bits arived this faul." Has returned from New York and Philadelphia, where he "sold to great disadvantage a pretty large quantity." Hopes the government "will conduct so as to make the English Merchant regret that he has shipped so many goods and . . . make the Amer[i]can Merchant wear a longer face than at present." Claims that he will be forced to abandon his business if importation of British bridles does not cease. Believes that farmers prefer to purchase his bits but that merchants prefer to sell British products. Hopes that JM "will not be terified by the clamour let loose upon you by Newspapers." "They certainly do not convey the sentiments of the People there is not one to Hundred of Mr. Clintons friends that will argue in favor of his Election they dislike the company that they are oblidge to keep so much if they do it. I know they extreemly regret of ever putting him in nomination and I beleive will almost to [a] Man dersert him if he persists in his claim to the Presidency. I Sir have never been able to discover that wavering in your conduct that has been attributed to you by your enemies."

RC (DLC). 3 pp.

From Henry Dearborn

SIR,   GREENBUSH Octobr 24th. 1812

The Secretary of war has undoubtedly informed you of the unfortunate event at Niagara.[1] It undoubtedly originated with two or three indiscreet ardent spirits, whose political and personal feelings could not brook the Idea of having any share of the honour of an effective movement attached to those officers and men that were more immediately under the direction of the U. S. But Genl. Van Renssellaer did not, I presume, partake of those feelings, he was pressed into the premature measure by being deceived into a belief that the Militia Generally were so eager for the measure, that unless he consented, they would all leave him—several officers of the regular Troops that happened to be near, were induced to volunteer their services, probably from an apprehention that they might suffer in reputation by declining, but that he should have countenanced such a premature and extraordinery measure, is not easey to account for, especially after having been fully informed by me, of the strength of the force destined for his command, and of the object contemplated, and having been reminded of the expediency of consulting the principle officers, on the time & points of attack, and that it would be necessary to be prepared if possable for crossing with 5000, men at once, with Artillery &c. instead of being so prepared, only 13 boats out of from 80 to 90, were collected at the point of cross[i]ng, and instead of being prepared to act in concert with Genl. Smith & the main body of the Troops which were at Buffalo, the attempt was made with from 800 to 1000 men, with boats sufficient for transporting not more than 500 men, at once. Genl. Van Renssellaer having intimated a desire to be relieved from his command, I have directed him to give the command over to Brigadr. Genl. Smyth, and I have authorised Genl. Smyth to take upon himself the command, and I have been explisit in my directions to him, I have proposed his giving Col Parker[2] the command of a Brigade—every effort in my power has been made for sending on reinforcements, and Military stores, and I do not yet dispair of some effective movements, both at Niagara, and towards Montreal, but from some strange fatality, I have not been able to obtain the necessary supply of musket cartridges and have been compelled to the necessaty of sending powder & lead to be made up by the respective Regts. I have not deemed it practicable to leave this place, without exposing the service to such imbarrasments as would probably much more than ballance any services I could contemplate at any one point—and until the respective commands are defined, and within such limits, as to enable each commander to actually superintend and direct in person, whatever relates to his command, we must expect misfortunes and disappointments. I have not been insensable of the difficulties & imbarrasments that we must unavoidably encounter at the commencement of a war, especially an offencive war, but we shall ultimately overcome all difficulties and shew the world that alth'o we make a clumsey begining, we are nevertheless capable of prosicuting a war with vigour & effect. Perhaps it is best, all things concidered, that we should find it difficult to commence war. We might otherwise be too ready to ingage in wars. With the highest respect I am Sir your Humbl. Servt.

H. Dearborn

RC (DLC). Docketed by JM.

1. Dearborn referred to Stephen Van Rensselaer's decision to lead his mixed force of regular army and militia across the Niagara River into Upper Canada on 12 Oct. 1812. His troops, reduced in number due to the refusal of many militiamen to leave U.S. territory, occupied Queenston Heights briefly but were forced to surrender within days. Van Rensselaer then resigned his commission on 16 Oct., leaving Alexander Smyth in command of the Niagara forces (Louis L. Babcock, *The War of 1812 on the Niagara Frontier* [Buffalo, N.Y., 1927], 42–51, 54–55).

2. Thomas Parker (d. 1820) of Virginia, a Revolutionary War veteran, was colonel of the Twelfth Infantry Regiment. He was promoted to the rank of brigadier general on 12 Mar. 1813 (Heitman, *Historical Register*, 1:770).

§ From Benjamin Forsyth. *24 October 1812*, *"Ogdensburg River St. Lawrence."* Informs JM that he has served as a captain in a rifle regiment for four years without promotion and made every effort to keep his regiment full with five-year enlistments. Desires a brevet appointment for long and meritorious service.[1]

RC (DNA: RG 107, LRRS, F-129:6). 2 pp.; docketed as received in the War Department on 4 Nov. 1812.

1. JM nominated Forsyth for promotion to major on 20 Jan. 1813 (*Senate Exec. Proceedings*, 2:323–24).

From John Armstrong

Sir Maysville Oct. 26th 1812

I feel myself in duty bound to return you my Sincere and ardent thanks, for that Wisdom and Magnanimity, that have marked all your proceedings, as the Chief Magistrate of this flourishing and Extensive Continent Since yr. Inauguration to yr. Station—and trust in that God who rules the destinees of nations that this Happy Land will be So greatly Blessed as to have the Same Chief Magistrate to conduct us thro. the toils & Calamities of War, and through whose benign administrations of the Laws we hope to have an Honourable Isue of the present Contest before the Lapse of four more revolving years, and Sir, permit me as a Warm friend to your administration to Express a hope that your Excellency will not Suffer a peace to be made with that haughty and Domineering nation (the Brittish) and their Murderous allies the Savages, unless we first obtain full and ample compensation for the multiplied Wrongs, that this highly favoured but much Injured country have Suffered, for a number of years past, not wishing to dictate to yr. Excellency my own Sentiment but I believe the Sentiment of the Greatest number of the Citizens, of the West we could be content to Lend our Support to the present administration Untill Such times as the Brittish Government, Compleatly revoke her orders in Council, Relinquish the Right She pretends She has, to Search the Vessels of Neutral Nations thereby Impressing our Brave Seamen. Make Such compensation as our Gove[r]nment may deem Sufficient for the Insults and Injuries already received and for a further Security for the Peace and Happiness of our frontier Citizens the Intire Abandonment of at Least upper Canady. I am Happy to Inform your Excellency that the State of Kentucky have furnished her Quota of Men & also have provided & forwarded a Sufficient Quantity of Cloathing for her Brave Sons & have no doubt in their patriotism of furnishing More Men & Cloathing when they are Called on.

Shall Esteem it as a particular favour If yr. Excellency will allow yr. Secty. to Drop me a line for our Encouragement. With Sentiments of profound Respect I Am Sir yrs.

Jno. Armstrong [1]

RC (DLC). Docketed by JM, "Armstrong Jno. (Kentucky)."

1. John Armstrong (1779–1851) was born in Ireland, settling in Maysville, Kentucky, between 1790 and 1800. He was instrumental in building up the town and promoting internal improvements in the area (*Biographical Encyclopaedia of Kentucky*, 381–82).

§ From James Timmonds. *26 October 1812, Cumberland, Allegany County.* Expresses his wish that JM be reelected to office. Is surprised that enemies of the government are not "Made Examples of to the publick." Hopes "Such proseedings will in A

Short Time be checked." Is thankful that war was declared. Compares Commodore Rodgers to David "when he Slew Golia[th] very Uneaquil in Size and Strenth Untill God strenthend David and soon Slew his Antagonist." "So we are Not to Boast of our selves as of our Selves But our Sufitiency is from God, and I hope his all Seeing Eyes will aid Direct and Instruct us to fight those Tyrants and the Enemy of our country as the Depradations comitted was not by us. . . . May God of his Mercies guide and direct the citizens of These U. S. in Prudence wisdom and Knowledge in Shewing and Proveing Their zeal and paying Their homage as dutifull Children To their parents Espetially at the Time of Need which is at hand." Also prays that "Good and faithfull Brave Men" may be recommended to JM as officers. In a postscript explains that "with the aid of washington county we will Gain in this District as this County alone is chiefly A damd Tory one."

RC (DLC). 3 pp.; docketed by JM.

From William Garrard

Sir   Opelousas Octr 27th 1812

The very extraordinary movements of the People from this State and the adjoining Territory, in the invasion of the Spanish Province of Texas was my only inducement in making any direct communication to you heretofore,[1] on the State of our affairs in Louisiana being personally unknown to you, and my situation humble in life. Perhaps I may have been thought busy and Officious in doing so but I trust however a proper construction on my views will do away any impression of that kind; and of its being attributable only in the zeal I have for the honour, the interest, and happiness of my Country. The open declaration those People make of the approbation of the Government, is what I do not credit, but consider as a scheme to draw the ignorant, and innocent People to the West, to subserve the ambitious and interested motives of a few individuals. Information very recently recvd from the West, state that Colo Magee[2] is in quiet possession of St Antonio,[3] with a force of at least One thousand Men, where he intends making his stand untill reinforc'd by such numbers as will justify and insure success in penetrating into the interior Provinces. I still am of the opinion, that the project of cooperating with the Spanish Patriots must eventually fail; a Gentleman of information lately arriv'd from that Country, informs me of the little disposition great numbers of the party have to submit to military dicipline, I am not surpris'd at it, for the greater part I have seen are such characters as can't possibly be restraind by any regulation whatever altho their safety so much depends on it. Genl Adair[4] has been two or three times expressly sent for to take the command but refuses I am told unless the expedition was sanction'd by Government, it is suppos'd this Army would have more confidence in him than their present commanders; they are frequently passing by this place in considerable numbers. I am informd

413

lately that frequent desertions take place. They find their dreams of plun-
derd wealth all vanish, the Country they have invaded is said to be miserably poor, and the inhabitants very little more civiliz'd than the neighbouring Savages. The absence of such numbers to the Spanish Country,
leaves their men greatly expos'd, nothing as yet has transpir'd to create
alarm. Great indignation is express'd by the real Americans at the cowardly
conduct (to give it no harsher term) of Genl Hull in the surrender of Detroit. But, it gives me infinite pleasure to state to you sir that no censure has
been thrown on the Executive; not even by those stiled Federalists and who
are suppos'd innimical to the Administration. The whole Nation have been
deceiv'd in the character of Genl Hull, the first annunciation of his appointment to the command of the North Western army; gave us in this
quarter great pleasure, his military talents, his good name, and his suppos'd
Geographical knowledge of the Canadys, induc'd a belief that his appointment was a very judicious one, and I do most sincerely wish that yr enemies
Sir, may derive no more advantage in the ensuing Presidential election
from the misfortune attending that Army; than they will in this State. Sorry
I am to see malignant opposition arising at this momentous crisis of our affairs, but I trust the good sense of the People will prevail and that you will
soon have high evidence of their confidence in yr worth, talents, and services. I have the honour to be Sir with great respect yr Ob Servt

WM GARRARD

RC (DLC). Docketed by JM.

1. No earlier correspondence from Garrard on this subject has been found.

2. Augustus W. Magee (d. 1813) was a second lieutenant in the U.S. Army stationed at
Natchitoches with orders to suppress unlawful activities in that area. He resigned his commission on 22 June 1812 to aid José Bernardo Gutiérrez Maximiliano de Lara with his filibuster into Mexico (Heitman, *Historical Register*, 1:683; Madison and the Problem of Mexican Independence: The Gutiérrez-Magee Raid of August 1812, 1 Sept. 1812).

3. This report was erroneous. Although Magee's forces had easily captured the Mexican
town of Nacogdoches in August 1812 and were pushing on toward Goliad, they did not capture San Antonio until the following spring, after Magee had died (Nichols, "William
Shaler," *New England Quarterly* 9 [1936]: 90–91, 92, 94; Madison and the Problem of Mexican Independence, 1 Sept. 1812).

4. Garrard referred to John Adair (1757–1840) of Kentucky, who served in the state house
of representatives for many of the years between 1793 and 1803 and was elected to the U.S.
Senate to complete the term of John Breckenridge in 1805. Adair's reputation suffered from
his involvement in the Burr conspiracy, but his service at the Battle of the Thames and the
Battle of New Orleans did much to restore his good name. Adair became the governor of Kentucky in 1820, a U.S. senator in 1825, and a U.S. representative in 1831 (*Biographical Encyclopaedia of Kentucky*, 647).

§ From Levett Harris. *27 October 1812, St. Petersburg*. "The present will be handed
You by my nephew, Mr John L. Harris, who returns home the bearer of dispatches
from Mr Adams from Count Romanzoff & from me.[1] He will have the honor of

paying his respects in person to your Excellency. I take the liberty of thus introducing him to you & of recommending him to your protection & notice."

RC (NN). 1 p.; dated "15/27 October 1812" in the Julian and Gregorian calendars; docketed by JM.

1. John Levett Harris probably carried Adams's 17 and 24 Oct. 1812 dispatches to Monroe, Count Nikolai P. Rumiantsev's instructions to Andrei Dashkov of 12 Oct. 1812, and Levett Harris's 27 Oct. 1812 dispatch to Monroe.

Adams's 17 Oct. letter explained that he had received a 9 Sept. 1812 letter from Jonathan Russell announcing the closure of his mission in London and the British government's rejection of his proposal to suspend hostilities. Adams described a meeting with Count Rumiantsev during which he informed the count of the contents of Russell's letter and mentioned that Rumiantsev had reacted to the news by repeating his earlier offer to mediate between the U.S. and Great Britain, both "from the sentiment of friendship to see the parties reconciled to each other" and from "a strong interest of his own in their reconciliation." Adams explained that Rumiantsev had prepared a letter to Dashkov instructing him to offer mediation, requesting that Adams find a safe means of transmitting it (Ford, *Writings of J. Q. Adams*, 4:401–2). Adams's 24 Oct. dispatch discussed the means by which his and Rumiantsev's letters were to be transported to the U.S. (DNA: RG 59, DD, Russia).

Rumiantsev's 12 Oct. letter to Dashkov explained the Russian emperor's view that war between Great Britain and the U.S. would "create great obstacles to the commercial prosperity of nations," so that he was compelled to do "all in his power to thrust aside the harm that this war augurs for even those nations which do not take part in it." The emperor, Rumiantsev declared, entrusted Dashkov to propose mediation and, should it be accepted, to request that Adams be furnished with the necessary power to begin the negotiation (Bashkina et al., *The United States and Russia*, 880–82).

Harris's communication reported that trade to St. Petersburg had been "totally suspended" by the American war with Great Britain. He noted that most of the ships that had sailed before news of the declaration of war arrived had been captured and carried to Great Britain. He reported that he was seeking reimbursement for $2,000 spent to support several destitute American seamen who had arrived in ships with false American registers. He calculated that "there is now here in store American and colonial produce, brought the present year in our ships and belonging to American citizens, to the value of three and a half million dollars, which, from the stagnant state of commerce occasioned by the present war, cannot be sold, and which, in the event of the French arms reaching this city, will be exposed to great danger" (ibid., 894–95). Harris may also have enclosed copies of his 16 May and 22 Aug. letters to Monroe (DNA: RG 59, CD, St. Petersburg, vol. 2).

From an Unidentified Correspondent

VIRGINIA Octr. 28th. 1812

We have heard today, the capture of another part of our Army, under Gen. Van Ranselear the death of 400 brave men in the field is nothing; but the surrender of one army after another, is Extreamly distressing to the people of this country; they remember with exultation to this day, the surrender of Genl Burgoine and Lord Cornwallis with two considerable british Armeés; and they can not reconsile it to themselves when they are now twise as strong to see their countrymen surrending to a few English Canadians & indians, we have not heard the perticulars, we trust that the circumstances are more favourable than it has been represented; the only circumstance that seems to afford relief to our minds is that the 13th. American regiment, drove the british 42nd regiment several miles; their is a universal cry among us, of mismanagement some where; but no body beside Giles, Randolph, and the tories pretend to lay any censure at the door of the president; The commanders on the lakes ought certainly to have concentrated thier forse it is very painful to the friends of the country, & Government to hear the disaffected, and tories predicting the overth[r]ow, and surrender ⟨of our?⟩ Army's, because the forse is not sufficent, they say to make any ⟨serious?⟩ impression on Canada. Giles was publicly stateing the other day, that the forse was intirely insufficent to make any serious impression on Canada, *he stated it as a fact that their was nearly 3,00000 people in upper and lower Canada, that every Canadian was as well disiplined as any british soldiar, that they were conplely Armed &c. he stated these things as facts* and that he *had warned the government, that their would be defeated &c with the forse at present applyed, Mr. Jno Randolph has turned prophet and told the people in his district after the event had hapned that Hull would fail.* God forbid that these men should profisy truely again. It is the wish of the people of the UStates, that they be called in sufficent numbers to overrun Canada at once; Their is at last in the State of Virginia, between, 10 or 15 thousand men, Volunteers & drafts armed an[d] in complete uniform, these men are willing, and desirous that the president should call on them they would be ready in a day or two, to march to Canada, the same number of men might be called from Pensylvania, &c &c, which would insure success. We see it stated in the paper that Genl. Harrison ta[l]ks of sending back all the Volunteers from Kentucky, and Ohio, except 4,000 which he will take on to Canada, this forse will not do; and for God sake let us have no more defeats and surrender's call out a sufficent forse at once, and let Canada be over run at any rate this winter. The State of Virginia can furnish the Government with 10 thousand men above the falls of the Rivers, and would march chearfully to Canada if called on, money is raising in every county for their accomodation and they are not only willing, but solicitous, that the Government should call on them, immediately; I will venture to say they will act better than the New York Malicia, they want no change in a president, North Carolina, Tennesee, Kentuckey, & Ohio would conqueer Canada if permitted to turn out in sufficent number's, certainly this winter; the representation from Virginia we expect will be instructed to vote to raise 50,000 regular troops immediately, and increase the navy as much as possible, a recommendation of this kind would come well from the president to congress the laying any kind of an Embargo would have a very bad effect, it would alianate the Eastern States more, the trade to Spain & Portugal, in furnishing the british troops with provision is certainly a very dishonourable trade, but it is not worth while to attempt to stop what is already gone to those ports. We trust, and hope that the president of the United States, will not think of a peace on any terms with the enimy until we have an opportunity of retreaving the disgrace, on our Arms, by such surrenders such an inglorious peace which would now be on any terms; would breake down, the national sperit, and render the republican administration infamous forever we trust Sir, if one of your General ever agrees to an armistice again, that you will strike him off from the list of your Officrs forever; after the disavowal of the arrangement which you made with the british minister (with so much promptness as little Jack Randolph said) no attemps even at arrangements will be made on any turms until we wash out with the very best blood of the nation the disgrace on our Arms by two successive defeats and surrenders, let us now implore the president of the U States to call into the service of the ⟨U⟩ States the very best Offi[c]ers Armst[r]ong, Monroe & & &c &c the choise of the president would be the choise of the nation, a new Secretary of War would be at any rate a very popular appointment. The Secretary at War, has not the confidence of the people, and that is sufficent of itself in a goverment like ours without specifiing any objection. The business of inlistment has certainly been conducted in the most miserable manner indeed, 25 thousand regulars might have been inlisted in the state of Virginia alone if the Officers had come a mong the people. The Secretary at War, was informed of this from time to time, but nothing has been ever done it has been the universal complaint all th[r]o' Virginia, and we suppose that is the case all th[r]o' the United States, that off[i]cers would not come a mong them with music &c &c. We submit it to your Excellency's better judgment if it would not be good policy to advise the Govournors of Kentuckey & Ohio &c to invade the indian settlements this fall, & winter, in the spring they will ⟨swarm⟩ but in the winter they may be distroyed like Bees in a hive. The people of Virginia will support you handsomely on the first monday in November next. We are

"WE THE PEOPLE"

RC (NN). Docketed by JM, "Anonymous / Ocr. 18. 1812"; damaged by removal of seal.

From William Eustis

Sir,   War. Dept: October 29. 1812

I have the honor to inform you that the existing appropriations applicable to the Clothing Department are nearly expended & to request that you will be pleased to direct that the sum of Five hundred Thousand Dollars appropriated for the pay of the Army be applied to defray further expenses in the Clothing Department.

W. Eustis.

RC (DLC); letterbook copy (DNA: RG 107, LSP). RC in a clerk's hand, signed by Eustis; docketed by JM.

§ To Albert Gallatin. *29 October 1812.* In accordance with an act of 3 Mar. 1809,[1] directs "the sum of Five hundred thousand Dollars, of the fund appropriated for the pay of the Army, be applied to that of the Clothing Department."

RC (owned by Albert C. Wilkerson, Richmond, Va., 1961). 1 p.; in a clerk's hand, signed by JM.

1. See *U.S. Statutes at Large*, 2:535–37.

§ From Adolph Ehringhaus.[1] *29 October 1812, Philadelphia.* Informs JM that he wrote to the secretary of war on 16 Sept., enclosing "a Memorandum shewing the Costs of raising a Corps of Husars." Having received no answer, expresses suspicion that his plan either was not explicit enough or was contrary to the department's views.[2] Explains his desire to be useful to his adopted country of fourteen years in his area of expertise, "having been an officer in a German Husar Corps in the french army in 1793." Invites JM to inquire about him and offers to provide a recommendation. "I know that I can raise 400 men from amongst my Countrymen, most of whom have seen Service, who—altho considered in its fullest extent as regular enlisted U. S. Soldiers, yet under the alluring name of Volunteer free Corps, would flock to the Standard—and having a German Commander enlist freely— serve for such a time as your Excellency would designate." Pledges that in four months he would be ready to march. Expresses his belief that a hussar corps "at the late Battle of Lewistown would have turned the Scales, by swimming through the St Lawrence—understanding that the Voice of the Commander could be distinctly heard on the American side." Informs JM that he currently commands the first hussar corps formed in the U.S., which has offered its services to the state governor.

RC (DNA: RG 107, LRRS, E-108:6). 3 pp.; docketed as received in the War Department on 4 Nov. 1812.

1. Adolph Ehringhaus was a broker in Philadelphia (John A. Paxton, *Philadelphia Directory and Register, for 1813* [Philadelphia, 1813; Shaw and Shoemaker 29456]).
2. On 6 Nov. 1812 Eustis responded to Ehringhaus: "I have the honor to inform you that the two Regiments of Dragoons belonging to the army, with such volunteer mounted Troops

as had been accepted before the receipt of your Letter to this Department are deemed a sufficient force of that description" (DNA: RG 107, LSMA).

From Samuel Harrison

DEAR SIR   CHITTENDEN VT. Octr. 30th. 1812

While the direful calamity of War is scourging our once happy Country, I shall not apologise for troubling your Excellency with my Lamentations upon the Horrific subject. I was in hopes that the hints I communicated in May last,[1] would have led you into a Train of Reflections, by which the woful miseries, to which, we are now subjected, might have been procrastinated; if not prevented.

The Reasons I penned in June, and sent to you in September[2] why it was *improper to go to War;* with many other, still continue permanent; and are yet powerful Arguments against its continuance; What were Reasons, *then,* against its *Commencement,* are Reasons, *now,* against its *prolongation.*

I could wish for the Tongue of an Angel, or the Pen of a Seraph; that I might be enabled to communicate to your Excellency my views of the misseries to which we are subjected by the *Ferocity of Man.*

Dear Sir *Must the Sword, forever, be the only Arbiter of Right and Wrong? Must Evils be, forever, multiplied? Because Evil exists.*

But you are at a distance, and do not feel them, and thus remain callous to the Misseries of your fellow Creatures.

Place yourself, Dear Sir, for a Moment, in a Frontier situation; either in Georgia, Indiana, Ohio, N York, or Vermont, listening for the dreadful War hoop, and Savage Yell of the ferocious Indian! as the only Warning of the Awful, and ensuing Massacre, of your Wife, and helpless Children! And the Conflagration of your only dwelling! *Behold the dreadful Tomahawk! lifted up over your darlings! ready to cleave their innocent heads! Or the Arm of the Barbarian stretched out! with the bloody scalping knife! reeking with the Gore of your next Neighbor! ready to plunge into the bosom of your best beloved Wife!!! Or the suspended War-Club! bespattered with the Blood, and Brains of your nearest Relation! ready to break your own Scull! and dash out your own Brains!!!* And then say, *I am unconcerned at the Consequences.* And then say, if you can; That the Calamities of War are Exaggerated by those that oppose it, and its direful effects will not enhance the Calamities of the Nation!!! This is not Painting.

This, Sir, is not Idle Preaching—*it is what must,* and *will take place;* in *many, too many, instances, should your present Measures continue.*

But Why Should I be only answered with a Sneer, and my Letters be thrown by with a Bundle of uninteresting Papers, without Notice, like the

Petitions of the Americans, by the Court of Great Britain, before the Commencement of the Revolutionary Contest? I know not.

My Introduction to your Excellency merits better treatment.

Why have you not, either, answered my Papers? Or sent them back as requested?

You cannot say that I have exaggerated any of the Subjects; Or the tendency of your Measures—Or deny one point of Fact that I have represented.

Are Despots, alone, to be reproached with feeling uninterested at the flowing of the Blood, and the squandering the Treasures; and sporting with the feelings; and lives of their Subjects?

I thought Republicans were amenable to their Constituents; for their Conduct, in order to ensure the tranquility of their Country; and the Confidence, of those who Placed them in their Stations.

If I have Erred in any respect I am Sorry. It must be imputed to an excess of Zeal—to an *Independence of Sentiment I contracted when Fighting, and Bleeding, and Suffering for FREEDOM which has not been eradicated, by being placed in the vicinity of the Green mountain; I Glory in the Appellation of Green Mountain Boy;* of being a *VERMONTEER who has never crouched at the Frowns; or been seduced by the Flatteries, of either Sycophant, or Tyrant. I yet feel a spirit of Independence; That I will write my Sentiments, and will warn you to Flee from the Wrath to come. Whether you will hear, or whether you will forbear. My Writings will arise against you, in Futurity and Historians will point at this Beacon, which has warned you of Destruction.*

Had your Excellency been advised by me and paid attention to my Letter of May 11th. 1812, there would not have been such a cry of Treachery in our Land. Had you listened to Me, General Hull would not have disgraced the Annals of your Presidency by the *inglorious Surrender of Detroit, his Army, Cannon, scanty stores, and the whole territory of Michigan.*

Had you considered the Reasons, I penned in June, why it was improper to declare War—*The Unfortunate Vn. Ransalear might, now, have had whole limbs*[3]—*Scott, Christie, and Fenwick might have, now, had their Liberty,*[4] *and Wadsworth, and Stranahan, been employed in Ameliorating the Miseries of Man:*[5] *and the Blood of fifteen hundred brave Heroes would not have Deluged, and fattened the Corn fields, and Orchards, on the heights of Queenstown.*

Would you yet, Sir, hear to my Advice. *The Defeat and Disgrace of Generals Dearborne, and Bloomfield, and their companions in Arms, in our Northern Army may still be prevented.*

What I wrote to your Excellency on the 14th of Sepr. and to Genl. Gideon Granger on the 15th., and 16th., days of the same month, which I desired him to shew you, are facts.

"Soldiers are not made in one Day."

And Soldiers must be taught; before they can perform wonders; They must be taught; before they can get to Montreal; They must be taught; before they can arrive at Quebec; They must be taught; and *a great number, must be taught; before they can conquer Canada; They must be taught before they can b(eco)me Veterans.*

And were I General, I should not feel *so much disgrace to take seven Trumpets of Rams horns, and March, in Procession, seven times, Seven times* around, that well provided Fortress, and attempt to prostrate the Walls of Quebec,[6] *As I should, to command our Present Army, with their present numbers, their present Discipline, and their present supplies, and their present support, from our present Lacual Force, to attempt the Conquest of the Canadas in their Present situation.* The Arrangements of the Campaign—The method of supplying the wants of the Troops—The transporting Cannon Ball from Philadelphia 400 Miles when they might be purchased at a cheaper Rate in Plattsburg, Highgate, Sheldon, Newhaven, Vergennes, Pittsford, Clarendon, Tinmouth, Bennington and Albany, &C. &C. Must, to a Person acquainted with Military Operations, appear like a *revival of the Days of Chivalry;* And the appeal of my Namesake Genl Harrison—to the *Patriotism of the Ladies of Ohio to furnish his Southern Brethren,* with *Lindsey Doublets* to enable them to brave the Borean Blasts of Canada, must appear Quixotic, and look more like *Knight Errantry*—Than a well digested Economical System calculated to subjugate those Frozen Regions of Canada to the Government of the United States—and drive the British Government to our own terms—*Soldiers must have Blankets and plenty of thick woolen cloathing* or they will *Freeze* in Canada *instead of Conquer them.* You must excuse me I can *Negociate*—but I hate to Fight it is so with ⅗ of the Country and although I speak plainly I am really your Friend; a true friend to the U.S. and your Obt Servant

SAML. HARRISON

RC (DLC). Docketed by JM.

1. Harrison to JM, 11 May 1812, *PJM-PS*, 4:374–77.

2. Harrison to JM, 14 Sept. 1812.

3. Solomon Van Rensselaer (1774–1852) fought in the campaign against the Northwest Indians in 1794 under Gen. Anthony Wayne and was wounded in the Battle of Fallen Timbers. He served as the adjutant general for New York in 1801–9, 1810–11, and 1813–21. In 1812 he returned to active military service as Stephen Van Rensselaer's aide-de-camp. He led an advance party in the Battle of Queenston, sustaining several severe wounds, which incapacitated him early in the conflict (*National Intelligencer*, 24 and 27 Oct. 1812).

4. Lieutenant Colonels John Chrystie of New York, John R. Fenwick of South Carolina, and Winfield Scott of Virginia were reported to have been captured by the British during the Battle of Queenston (ibid., 27 Oct. 1812). Colonel Fenwick "distinguished himself at the unfortunate battle of Queenstown, and received a number of dangerous wounds" (Philadelphia *Aurora General Advertiser*, 1 Jan. 1813).

5. On 27 Oct. 1812 the *National Intelligencer* reprinted a 20 Oct. report from the *Albany Gazette* that claimed that Brig. Gen. William Wadsworth and Lt. Col. Farrand Stranahan of the New York militia had been captured in the Battle of Queenston.

6. Harrison paraphrased the biblical instructions Joshua received for besieging Jericho (Josh. 6:3–5).

§ From James M. Harris. *30 October 1812, "Pine Hill Post office."* "I . . . Request . . . that you will give me by letter the prominent articles of your Religious Creed, the reason of such A singular request being solicited, is in Consequ[e]nce of the wonderful controversies that are kept up here concerning your Religious Sentiments."

RC (DLC). 1 p.; docketed by JM.

From Samuel Carswell

DEAR SIR   PHILADA. October 31st. 1812

The pleasure of acknowledging the receipt of your letter ⟨of t⟩he 8th. of Septr.[1] is much augmented, by having it in my power to congratulate you on the success of republican principles, in the election that was held in this place, yesterday. We carried it by a majority, in the City & Liberties, of twenty two hundred,[2] & I am of opinion, that the collected votes of State, will give to the republicans, a majority of at least twenty one thousand. This triumph may be attributed, chiefly to the energetic character of the measures which were adopted last winter, & I have no doubt, that a perseverance in them, will be attended with the happiest consequences to the country.

I am happy to inform you that I have, in a great measure, recovered my health. With Respectful & friendly considerations Your Most. Obdt. Sert.

SAML CARSWELL

RC (DLC). Torn.

1. Letter not found.
2. Carswell's figures were somewhat optimistic. On 2 Nov. 1812 the Philadelphia *Aurora General Advertiser* reported that in the city of Philadelphia, the district of Southwark, the townships of Moyamensing and Passyunk, and Penn Township, JM had received 4,276 votes to Clinton's 3,135 votes. For statewide election results, see JM to Jefferson, 14 Oct. 1812, n. 6.

From Thomas Jefferson

DEAR SIR   MONTICELLO Oct. 31. 12.

This will be handed you by Monsr. de Neufville[1] a person of distinction from France who came over to this country with his family some years ago,

& is established as an Agricultural citizen near New Brunswick in Jersey. He brought recommendations from some friends of mine which established his merit, as well as his right to any service I could render him. Since his settlement in Jersey I have heard him spoken of as one of the most amiable & unoffending men on earth. He has asked a letter of introduction to you, as he goes on to Washington to sollicit the reception of his nephew in the military school at West point. The nephew is 15. years old, & so far has recieved an education très soignée. I have apprised M. de Neufville of the possibility that the number of competitors for places in that school may produce difficulties & delays, that the principles of our government admit little exercise of partialities in it's public functionaries, and have prepared him of course for a possible disappointment proceeding from circumstances unconnected with the dispositions of the Executive. So that should he succeed he will be made the more happy & thankful. In any event he will be very sensible to any kindnesses & attentions which shall manifest a recognition of the personal merit of which he cannot but feel a consciousness. The favor will at the same time be acknoleged by myself on behalf of friends beyond the water who have claims of gratitude on me towards a person recommended by them. Accept always the assurance of my constant friendship and respect.

TH: JEFFERSON

FC (DLC: Jefferson Papers).

1. Jean-Guillaume Hyde de Neuville had written to Jefferson on 19 Oct. 1812 to request this letter of introduction (ibid.).

§ To Albert Gallatin. *31 October 1812.* In accordance with a 3 Mar. 1809 act of Congress,[1] directs "that the sum of fifty thousand dollars be applied out of the appropriation of Sulphur & Salt Petre to Provisions & twenty five thousand dollars out of the same appropriation to Contingent expenses."

Letterbook copy (DNA: RG 45, Letters to Federal Executive Agents, 1798–1824). 1 p.

1. See *U.S. Statutes at Large,* 2:535–37.

§ From Cary F. Dunn Jr. *31 October 1812, "State of New York Queens County Jamaica."* Was introduced to JM by Mr. Vining[1] when JM was a member of the U.S. House of Representatives meeting in New York. Holds a commission as a judge of the New York Court of Common Pleas for the county of Queens and was a magistrate for the city and county of New York for seven years. Seeking to support his family, requests from JM "a Nomination with his interest to the Senate." Infers that *"Old Servants of the Revolution"* will not be forgotten by "the Virtuous President and his friends, particular at this momentuous day." Informs JM that "it is the Opinion of our political friends that the Removals of the present incumbents call'd the Col-

423

lector, Naval Officer, Surveyor, and Marshel of the District Court in the City of New York Should be carried in effect in due time." "Their long continuance and lucrative places is inconsistent with the principels of a free goverment to the exclusion of those whose Merits are more deserving and competency more evident." Encloses this letter to Ebenezer Sage, who will present it but is unacquainted with its contents.

RC (DLC). 3 pp.; marked "copy" and *"confidential"*; docketed by JM, "Dunn, C. F. Jr / 1812 / 1813." Cover marked "To the particular care of Doctor Sage."

1. John Vining (1758–1802) of Delaware had been a member of the Continental Congress, 1784–85, of the First and Second Federal Congresses, 1789–93, and of the U.S. Senate, 1793–98.

§ From John Wayles Eppes. *31 October 1812, Petersburg.* Reports that "Many respectable citizens of this place are anxious for the appointment of Mr. Peter Purryear as the successor of our unfortunate friend George Jefferson."[1] Informs JM that Puryear comes from Mecklenburg County, Virginia, and has "acquired reputation and wealth unaided by Foreign connection or capital." "For his character and standing as a merchant," refers JM to a testimonial from some inhabitants of Petersburg.[2] Reports that he has known Puryear for many years and knows him to be an "undeviating Republican" and to have "supported those principles which so distinctly mark in general the line between native & adopted citizens."

RC (DNA: RG 59, LAR, 1809–17, filed under "Puryear"). 1 p. A postscript dated "3rd. Novr. 1812" and signed by Peterson Goodwyn and Thomas Gholson Jr. reads: "Having been long acquainted with Mr. Puryear, we fully concur in the above statment."

1. For the vacancy in the Lisbon consulate, see James Leander Cathcart to JM, 22 June 1812, *PJM-PS,* 4:497 and n. 2.
2. A 31 Oct. 1812 testimonial from Joseph Jones and others, "merchants and citizens of the town of Petersburg," recommending Puryear for the Lisbon consulate, is filed with this letter. JM also received a 31 Oct. 1812 letter on Puryear's behalf from Jerman Baker (DNA: RG 59, LAR, 1809–17, filed under "Puryear").

From William Eustis

[ca. 1 November 1812]
After war had been declared, it was deemed necessary, for the security of the maratime frontier, to order the recruits to the posts on the seaboard, which had a tendency to check the recruiting service, and has retarded our military operations on the no[r]thern frontier.

The surrender of the army & post of Detroit opened the N. Western frontier to the incursions of the Savages and rendered it necessary to resort to volunteers and detachments of militia to protect the frontier settlements, to recover the territory which had been lost, and to pursue with energy the operations against the enemy in that quarter. The Officer who entered into the capitulation having returned to the U. States on his parole, an investigation of his conduct will be had, as soon as the public service will permit, by a court martial[1] whose proceedings will explain this unexpected and disastrous event—(or will be bro't before a court martial as soon &c. to account for this &c. event).

On the 13th of October an attack on the enemy's post at Queenstown near Niagara was made by a detachment of the American troops under the command of Major Genl. Van. Ranselear of the militia of the State of New York, in which it appears that our troops displayed great gallantry and were for a time victorious, but for want of proper support were defeated in their object.

A revision of all the Laws relating to the Militia and to the army of the U. S. with a view to supply defects disclosed by experience, and to render the system uniform & efficient.

RC (DLC). Unsigned; undated; dated 1812 in the *Index to the James Madison Papers;* date assigned here on the basis of internal evidence and the assumption that Eustis composed these remarks to assist JM in preparing his message to Congress of 4 Nov. 1812.

1. Hull's court-martial was originally scheduled to commence on 25 Feb. 1813 but was postponed until 3 Jan. 1814 (Gilpin, *The War of 1812 in the Old Northwest,* 232).

From Albert Gallatin

DEAR SIR   1 Nov. 1812

I send the two paragraphs.[1] I believe the whole to be sufficiently distinct, with the exception perhaps of the last sentence of the first paragraph. If the forfeitures are not remitted at all, there will be considerable injustice, great discontent, & 8 to 10 millions of dollars put in the pocket of the collectors. If they are altogether remitted, the importers will make unreasonable profits, & there will be equal & as well founded dissatisfaction. To attempt to discriminate between cases will be an invidious & endless task. I think that the best & most equitable mode will be to authorise a remission of all the forfeitures of american property, on condition that the importers will lend to Govt. the sum equal to the prime cost. With respect to British property, a sequestration seems the most eligible mode.

The object of the sentence alluded to is to indicate this course or any other modification answering the same purpose, which may appear more eligible, or prove more palatable. Respectfully Your obedt. Servt.

ALBERT GALLATIN

RC (DLC). Docketed by JM.

1. Enclosure not found.

From an Unidentified Correspondent

Sir.   Philada. Novemr. 2nd. 1812

I do not mean to dictate but only as a friend to your Administration and as one of the family of the Union to communicate my sentiments in a few particulars as briefly as I can conveniently.

I have suggested to you a mode of raising an hundred thousand troops or militia by classing the Citizens of the United States in such a manner as that the amount of the State tax each class annually pays in their respective States shall be alike, equal, and of the same amount.[1] And that each class shall find one man by giving him a bounty and also find him a military Coat & hat to make him look a little like a soldier and each man of the class to pay his proportion of the expence in proportion to the said tax he pays.

Let the class stand during the war and then it will be their interest to inlist the men during the war. However let them inlist them for three or five years or during the war as they may choose or can contract with them and furnish another when the time is expired if that shall happen while the war continues and so repeatedly Until the close of the war.

Black men perhaps might be taken to the Amount of one fourth of the number. In the eastern and middle States they are most of them free and receive the same protection that white people do and why not let them fight for it as well as the others.

In cases of death or removal out of a district let the class be filled up with those that move into it or arrive to a taxable age and if there be a supernumerary number of the latter let them be required to pay their proportion as above proposed towards filling up the ranks in cases of death or inlistments [*sic*] in the regular Army and if that be insufficient lay the residue in the same proportion on all the classes in the state. Thus will an efficient militia force be established during the war to be called on if wanted or otherwise to remain at their homes in readiness.

These men being so engaged would, many of them, for the sake of a new bounty and the land given to the regular troops be likely to enlist among them and thus probably the regular regiments would be Easily kept full.

It may easily be effected thro' the medium of the Marshals they may be authorized to appoint and quallify deputies in the Counties who may be authorized to appoint and quallify township deputies to class the Citizens and attend to the whole business so far as respects their particular townships. Any assessor of a Township will probably do it for a trifle perhaps a cent a name with being exempt from military duty and exactions as being favorable to his fellow Citizens and preventing the horrors of a draught. Nevertheless the services of Volunteers may be accepted and when necessary be called upon to act. It would be ungenerous if their patriotism should be slighted. I kept no Copy nor had I any idea of this when I wrote my former communication and if there be in this, a few repetitions of that, I hope they may be excused also that a zeal for my Country's good and the success of your Administration which has been my inducement may be considered as an excuse for them. *I am &c. yours.*

RC (DNA: RG 107, LRRS, A-223:6). Unsigned; postmarked Philadelphia, 7 Nov.; docketed as received in the War Department on 11 Nov. 1812.

1. No previous correspondence with JM on this subject has been found.

Annual Message to Congress

WASHINGTON November 4th 1812

Fellow Citizens of the Senate and of the House of Representatives

On our present meeting, it is my first duty to invite your attention, to the providential favors which our Country has experienced, in the unusual degree of health dispensed to its inhabitants, and in the rich abundance with which the Earth has rewarded the labours bestowed on it. In the successful cultivation of other branches of industry, and in the progress of general improvement favorable to the national prosperity, there is just occasion also, for our mutual congratulations and thankfulness.

With these blessings are necessarily mingled, the pressures and vicisitudes incident to the state of war, into which the United States have been forced, by the perseverence of a foreign power in its system of injustice and aggression.

Previous to its declaration, it was deemed proper, as a measure of precaution and forecast, that a considerable force should be placed in the Michigan Territory; with a general view to its security and, in the event of war, to such operations in the uppermost Canada, as would intercept the hostile influence of Great Britain over the Savages, obtain the command of the Lake on which that part of Canada borders, and maintain co-operating relations with such forces, as might be most conveniently employed against other parts. Brigadier General Hull was charged with this provisional service; having under his command, a body of Troops composed of regulars, and of volunteers from the State of Ohio. Having reached his destination after his knowledge of the war, and possessing discretionary authority to act offensively, he passed into the neighbouring territory of the Enemy, with a prospect of easy and victorious progress. The Expedition, nevertheless, terminated unfortunately, not only in a retreat to the town and Fort of Detroit, but in the surrender of both, and of the gallant corps commanded by that Officer. The causes of this painful reverse, will be investigated by a Military Tribunal.

A distinguishing feature in the operations which preceded and followed this adverse event, is the use made by the Enemy, of the merciless savages under their influence. Whilst the benevolent policy of the United States invariably recommended peace and promoted civilization, among that wretched portion of the human race; and was making exertions to dissuade them from taking either side in the war; the Enemy has not scrupled to call to his aid, their ruthless ferocity, armed with the horrors of those instruments of carnage and torture, which are known to spare neither age nor sex. In this outrage against the laws of honorable war, and against the feelings sacred to humanity, the British commanders cannot resort to a plea of retaliation: For it is committed in the face of our example. They cannot mitigate it, by calling it a self defence against men in arms for it embraces the most shocking butcheries of defenceless families. Nor can it be pretended that they are not answerable for the atrocities perpetrated; since the Savages are employed with a knowledge, and even with menaces, that their fury could not be controuled. Such is the spectacle which the deputed authorities of a nation, boasting its religion and morality, have not been restrained, from presenting to an enlightened age.

The misfortune at Detroit was not, however, without a consoling effect. It was followed by signal proofs, that the national spirit rises, according to the pressure on it. The loss of an important post, and of the brave men surrendered with it, inspired every where, new ardor and determination. In the States and Districts least remote, it was no sooner known, than every Citizen was ready to fly with his arms, at once to protect his brethren against the bloodthirsty Savages let loose by the Enemy on an extensive frontier, and to convert a partial calamity, into a source of invigorated efforts. This patriotic zeal, which it was necessary rather to limit than excite, has embodied an ample force from the States of Kentucky and Ohio, and from parts of Pennsylvania and Virginia. It is placed, with the addition of a few regulars, under the command of Brigadier General Harrison; who possesses the entire confidence of his fellow Soldiers, among whom are Citizens, some of them volunteers in the ranks, not less distinguished by their political stations, than by their personal merits. The greater portion of this force is proceeding on its destination, towards the Michigan Territory; having succeeded in relieving an important Frontier post; and in several incidental operations against hostile tribes of Savages, rendered indispensible by the subserviency into which they had been seduced by the Enemy; a seduction the more cruel, as it could not fail to impose a necessity of precautionary severities, against those who yielded to it.

At a recent date, an attack was made on a post of the Enemy near Niagara, by a detachment of the regular and other forces, under the command of Major General Van Renssalear of the militia of the State of New York. The attack, it appears, was ordered in compliance with the ardor of the troops; who executed it with distinguished gallantry, and were for a time victorious; but not receiving the expected support, they were compelled to yield to reinforcements of British regulars and savages. Our loss has been considerable, and is deeply to be lamented. That of the Enemy, less ascertained, will be the more felt, as it includes among the killed, the commanding General who was also the Governor of the Province; and was sustained by veteran troops, from inexperienced soldiers, who must daily improve in the duties of the field.

Our expectation of gaining the command of the Lakes, by the invasion of Canada from Detroit, having been disappointed; measures were instantly taken to provide on them, a naval force superior to that of the Enemy. From the talents and activity of the Officer charged with this object, every thing that can be done, may be expected. Should the present season not admit of compleat success, the progress made will ensure for the next, a naval ascendancy, where it is essential to our permanent peace with, and controul over the Savages.

Among the incidents to the measures of the war, I am constrained to advert to the refusal of the Governors of Massachusetts and Connecticut, to furnish the required detachments of Militia, towards the defence of the maritime frontier. The refusal was founded on a novel and unfortunate exposition, of the provisions of the Constitution relating to the Militia. The correspondences which will be before you, contain the requisite information on the subject.[1] It is obvious, that if the authority of the United States, to call into service and command the Militia, for the public defence, can be thus frustrated, even in a state of declared war, and of course under apprehensions of invasion preceding war; they are not one nation for the purpose most of all requiring it; and that the[2] public safety may have no other resource, than in those large and permanent military establishments; which are forbidden by the principles of our free Government, and against the necessity of which, the militia were meant to be a constitutional bulwark.

On the coasts and on the ocean, the war has been as successful, as circumstances inseparable from its early stages, could promise. Our public ships and private cruisers, by their activity, and where there was occasion by their intrepedity, have made the enemy sensible of the difference between a reciprocity of captures, and the long confinement of them to their side. Our trade, with little exception, has safely reached our ports; having been much favored in it, by the course pursued by a Squadron of our Frigates under the Command of Commodore Rodgers. And in the instance, in which skill and bravery were more particularly tried with those of the Enemy, the American flag had an auspicious triumph. The Frigate Constitution commanded by Captain Hull, after a close and short engagement, compleatly disabled and captured a British Frigate; gaining for that officer and all on board, a praise which cannot be too liberally bestowed; not merely for the victory actually atchieved; but for that prompt and cool exertion of commanding talents; which giving to courage its highest character, and to the force applied its full effect, proved that more could have been done, in a contest requiring more.

Anxious to abridge the evils from which a state of war cannot be exempt, I lost no time, after it was declared, in conveying to the British Government, the terms on which its progress might be arrested, without awaiting the delays of a formal and final pacification.[3] And our chargé d'affaires at London was, at the same time, authorized to agree to an armistice founded upon them. These terms required, that the Orders in Council should be repealed as they affected the United States, without a revival of blockades violating acknowledged rules; and that there should be an immediate discharge of American Seamen from British ships, and a stop to impressments from American ships; with an understanding that an exclusion of the seamen of each nation, from the ships of the other, should be stipulated; and that the armistice should be improved into a definitive, and comprehensive adjustment of depending controversies. Although a repeal of the Orders, susceptible of explanations meeting the views of this Government, had taken place before this pacific advance was communicated to that of Great Britain, the advance was declined; from an avowed repugnance to a suspension of the practice of impressment, during the armistice, and without any intimation that the arrangement proposed with respect to Seamen, would be accepted. Whether the subsequent communications from this Government, affording an occasion for reconsidering the subject, on the part of Great Britain, will be viewed in a more favorable light, or received in a more accomodating spirit, remains to be known. It would be unwise to relax our measures, in any respect, on a presumption of such a result.

The documents from the Department of State which relate to this subject, will give a view also, of the propositions for an armistice which have been received here, one of them from the authorities at Halifax and in Canada, the other from the British Government itself, through Admiral Warren; and of the grounds on which neither of them could be accepted.[4]

Our affairs with France retain the posture which they held, at my last communications to you.[5] Notwithstanding the authorized expectation of an early, as well as favorable issue, to the discussions on foot, these have been procrastinated to the latest date. The only intervening occurrence meriting attention, is the promulgation of a French Decree, purporting to be a definitive repeal of the Berlin and Milan Decrees. This proceeding, although made the ground of the repeal of the British Orders in Council, is rendered by the time and manner of it, liable to many objections.

The final communications from our Special Minister to Denmark, afford further proofs of the good effects of his mission, and of the amicable disposition of the Danish Government.[6] From Russia, we have the satisfaction to receive assurances of continued friendship, and that it will not be affected by the rupture between the United States and Great Britain. Sweeden also professes sentiments, favorable to the subsisting harmony.[7]

With the Barbary powers, excepting that of Algiers, our affairs remain on the ordinary footing. The Consul General residing with that Regency, has suddenly and without cause, been banished, together with all the American Citizens found there.[8] Whether this was the transitory effect of capricious despotism, or the first act of predetermined hostility, is not ascertained. Precautions were taken by the Consul, on the latter supposition.

The Indian Tribes, not under foreign instigations, remain at peace, and receive the civilizing attentions which have proved so beneficial to them.

With a view to that vigorous prosecution of the war to which our national faculties are adequate, the attention of Congress will be particularly drawn to the insufficiency of the existing provisions for filling up the military establishment. Such is the happy condition of our country, arising from the facility of subsistance, and the high wages for every species of occupation, that notwithstanding the augmented inducements provided at the last session, a partial success only has attended the recruiting service. The deficiency has been necessarily supplied, during the campaign, by other than regular troops, with all the inconveniencies and expence incident to them. The remedy lies in establishing, more favorably for the private soldier, the proportion between his recompence and the term of his enlistment. And it is a subject which cannot too soon or too seriously, be taken into consideration.[9]

The same insufficiency has been experienced in the provisions for volunteers, made by an act of the last session. The recompence for the service required in this case, is still less attractive than in the other. And although patriotism alone, has sent into the field some valuable corps of that description, those alone who can afford the sacrifice can be re[a]sonably expected to yield to that impulse.

It will merit consideration also whether, as auxiliary to the security of our Frontiers, corps may not be advantageously organized, with a restriction of their services to particular districts convenient to them.[10] And whether the local and occasional services of Mariners and others in the seaport-Towns, under a similar organization, would not be a provident addition to the means of their defence.

I recommend a provision for an increase of the General officers of the Army, the deficiency of which has been illustrated by the number and distance of seperate commands, which the course of the war, and the advantage of the service, have required.[11]

And I cannot press too strongly on the earliest attention of the Legislature, the importance of a re-organization of the Staff Establishment; with a view to render more distinct and definite, the relations and responsibilities of its several departments.[12] That there is room for improvements which will materially promote both economy and success, in what appertains to the army and the war, is equally inculcated by the examples of other countries, and by the experience of our own.

A revision of the Militia laws, for the purpose of rendering them more systematic, and better adapting them to emergences of the war, is at this time particularly desirable.[13]

Of the additional ships authorized to be fitted for service, two will be shortly ready to sail; a third is under repair; and delay will be avoided in the repair of the residue. Of the appropriations for the purchase of materials for ship building, the greater part has been applied to that object, and the purchases will be continued with the ballance.

The enterprizing spirit which has characterized our naval force, and its success, both in restraining insults and depredations on our Coasts, and in reprisals on the Enemy, will not fail to recommend an enlargement of it.

There being reason to believe that the act prohibiting the acceptance of British licences, is not a sufficient guard against the use of them, for purposes favorable to the interests and views of the Enemy; further provisions on that subject are highly important.[14] Nor is it less so, that penal enactments should be provided, for cases of corrupt and perfidious intercourse with the Enemy, not amounting to Treason, nor yet embraced by any statutory provisions.

A considerable number of American vessels which were in England, when the revocation of the orders in council took place, were laden with British manufactures, under an erroneous impression that the non-importation act would immediately cease to operate, and have arrived in the United States. It did not appear proper to exercise on unforeseen cases of such magnitude, the ordinary powers vested in the Treasury Department to mitigate forfeitures, without previously affording to Congress an opportunity of making on the subject such provision as they may think proper. In their decision they will doubtless equally consult what is due to equitable considerations and to the public interest.[15]

The receipts into the Treasury, during the year ending on the thirtieth of September last, have exceeded sixteen millions and a half of dollars, which have been sufficient to defray all the demands on the Treasury to that day, including a necessary reimbursment of near three Millions of the principal of the public debt. In these receipts is included, a sum of near five millions eight hundred and fifty thousand dollars, received on account of the loans authorised by the acts of the last session: the whole sum actually obtained on loan, amounts to eleven Millions of dollars; the residue of which, being receivable subsequent to the thirtieth of September last, will, together with the current revenue, enable us to defray all the expences of this year. The duties on the late unexpected importations of British manufactures, will render the revenue of the ensuing year, more productive than could have been anticipated.

The situation of our country, fellow Citizens, is not without its difficulties, though it abounds in animating considerations, of which the view here presented, of our pecuniary resources, is an example. With more than one nation we have serious and unsettled controversies; and with one, powerful in the means and habits of war, we are at war. The spirit and strength of this nation are, nevertheless, equal to the support of all its rights; and to carry it through all its trials. They can be met in that confidence. Above all we have the inestimable consolation of knowing, that the war in which we are actually engaged, is a war, neither of ambition nor of vain glory; that it is waged, not in violation of the rights of others, but in the maintenance of our own; that it was preceeded by a patience without example, under wrongs accumulating without end; and that it was finally not declared, until every hope of averting it was extinguished, by the transfer of the British Sceptre into new hands, clinging to former Councils; and until declarations were re-iterated to the last hour, through the British Envoy here, that the hostile Edicts against our commercial rights and our maritime Independence, would not be revoked; nay, that they could not be revoked without violating the obligations of Great Britain to other powers, as well as to her own interests. To have shrunk under such circumstances from manly resistance, would have been a degradation, blasting our best and proudest hopes: It would have struck us from the high rank, where the virtuous struggles of our fathers had placed us, and have betrayed the magnificent legacy which we hold in trust for future generations. It would have acknowledged that on the Element, which forms three fo[u]rths of the globe we inhabit, and where all independent nations have equal and common rights, the American people were not an independent people, but colonists and vassals. It was at this moment, and with such an alternative, that war was chosen. The nation felt the necessity of it, and called for it. The appeal was accordingly made, in a just cause, to the just and all powerful Being, who holds in his hands the chain of events, and the destiny of nations. It remains only, that faithful to ourselves; entangled in no connections with the views of other powers, and ever ready to accept peace from the hand of justice, we prosecute the war with united councils and with the ample faculties of the nation; until peace be so obtained, and as the only means, under the divine blessing of speedily obtaining it.

JAMES MADISON

RC and enclosures (DNA: RG 233, President's Messages, 12A-D1); printed copy and enclosures (DNA: RG 46, President's Messages, 12A-E1); partial draft (owned by Ralph Earle, Philadelphia, Pa., 1958). RC in the hand of Edward Coles, signed by JM. Printed copy (1 p.) is an "extra" of JM's annual message from the *National Intelligencer*. Minor variations between the draft and RC have not been noted. House copy referred to the Committee of the Whole on 4 Nov. (*Annals of Congress*, 12th Cong., 2d sess., 16, 139). Enclosures filed with House copy consist of twenty-two extracts (119 pp.) from letters and other documents concerning U.S. relations with Great Britain and Denmark (for enclosures, see nn. 4 and 6). Senate copy received and ordered printed on 4 Nov. Enclosures filed with Senate copy consist of six extracts (54 pp.) from letters and other documents concerning U.S. relations with Denmark. Annual message printed with twenty-two numbered enclosures in the *National Intelligencer*, 5, 10, 12, and 14 Nov. 1812. Enclosures relating to U.S. relations with Great Britain also printed in *ASP, Foreign Relations*, 3:432–34, 585–87, 589–90.

    1. On 6 Nov. 1812 JM transmitted to Congress correspondence with the governors of New England states relating to their refusal to call out the militia, including Eustis's 15 Apr. 1812 circular to New England governors, Eustis to Caleb Strong, 12 June and 21 July, Dearborn to Strong, 22 and 26 June, Strong to Dearborn, 26 June, Strong to Eustis, 5 Aug. (with enclosure), 21 Aug., and 10 Sept., Roger Griswold to Eustis, 20 Apr., 17 June, and 13 Aug., Eustis to Griswold, 12 June, John Cotton Smith to Eustis, 2 July, and Eustis to Smith, 14 July (printed in *ASP, Military Affairs*, 1:3[21]-26).

    2. Partial draft ends here.

    3. For JM's and Monroe's statements to Foster concerning conditions for peace, see Memorandum of a Conversation with Augustus J. Foster, 23 June 1812, *PJM-PS*, 4:501–3 and n. 8.

    4. JM enclosed Monroe to Russell, 27 July 1812, extracts from Monroe to Russell, 26 June and 21 Aug. 1812, Graham to Russell, 9 and 10 Aug. 1812, Russell to Monroe, 26 June, 2 July, and 1 and 3 Sept. 1812, John Borlase Warren to Monroe, 30 Sept. 1812, and Monroe to Warren, 27 Oct. 1812 (printed in *ASP, Foreign Relations*, 3:432, 434, 585–88, 590, 595–97).

    5. JM referred to his message to Congress of 1 June 1812, which closed with a brief account of the unresolved state of negotiations in Paris over French violations of U.S. maritime rights (*PJM-PS*, 4:437–38).

    6. JM enclosed George W. Erving to Monroe, 12 Apr. (two letters), 17 Apr., 18 Apr., 20 Apr., and 9 May 1812 (printed in the *National Intelligencer*, 10, 12, and 14 Nov. 1812, where the 20 Apr. letter is dated 12 Apr.). Erving's dispatches and his enclosed correspondence with the Danish minister of foreign affairs, Niels Rosenkrantz, documented the resolution of a number of difficult prize cases against American vessels in Danish courts.

    7. JM probably referred to information conveyed in a series of letters written by commercial agent John Speyer to Monroe on 31 Mar., 14 Apr., and 18 May 1812, to the effect that Sweden, even as it opened its ports to British goods and vessels, would also offer port facilities to American merchants, that American vessels would be permitted to enjoy the protection of Swedish convoys in the Baltic, and that the Prince Royal intended to send a minister to the U.S. (DNA: RG 59, CD, Stockholm).

    8. See Tobias Lear to JM, 31 Aug. 1812, and n. 3.

    9. After some debate Congress passed a bill, which JM signed into law on 12 Dec. 1812, to raise the pay of noncommissioned officers, musicians, privates, and others in the U.S. Army. The pay of army privates was increased from $5 to $8 a month (*Annals of Congress*, 12th Cong., 2d sess., 22, 23–24, 25, 153, 155–66, 167–93, 211, 217; *U.S. Statutes at Large*, 2:788).

    10. Congress passed an act on 25 Feb. 1813 to raise "ten additional companies of Rangers" (*U.S. Statutes at Large*, 2:804).

    11. A 24 Feb. 1813 act authorized JM to appoint "six major generals, in addition to those already authorized by law . . . and six brigadier generals" (ibid., 2:801).

    12. A 3 Mar. 1813 act reorganized the U.S. Army staff. The act outlined the organization of the adjutant and inspector general's branch of the army and required the secretary of war "to prepare general regulations, better defining and prescribing the respective duties and powers of the several officers in the adjutant general, inspector general, quartermaster general, and commissary of ordnance departments, of the topographical engineers, of the aids of generals, and generally of the general and regimental staff." The act also created the office of physician and surgeon general and allowed the president to appoint assistant deputy quartermasters on his own and all other officers named in the act with the consent of the Senate (ibid., 2:819–20).

13. The only legislation passed by the second session of the Twelfth Congress respecting the militia was a 2 Feb. 1813 act requiring the reporting of all fines levied against militiamen to the Treasury Department and increasing the pay and benefits of active noncommissioned volunteer and militia corps during the war to parity with that of similarly ranked U.S. Army personnel (ibid., 2:797).

14. The second session of the Twelfth Congress passed no legislation on this subject.

15. For congressional action on forfeiture cases, see Gallatin to JM, 13 Aug. 1812, n. 3.

To John G. Jackson

DEAR SIR   WASHINGTON NOVr. 4. 1812

I have recd. your favor of the 21st. I cannot too much applaud Your zeal & that of your associates, in efforts to retrieve what has been lost by the want of that or something else in others. The present sacrifices you are yourself making call for peculiar acknowledgments. I am constrained at the same time to remark that according to the view taken here, of the prospects before Genl. Harrison, it must be doubtful whether an additional *mounted* force will be required, or if otherwise, whether *forage* can be relied on at the approaching season & thro' the winter; and moreover, as you seem to be aware, that the law has made no provision for a force of the description in question. So much confidence however is placed in Genl. H. that if his judgment decides that the corps you have provided will be wanted & can be supported, the Executive will do all in their power towards defraying the expence of it as proposed by you; that is to say, the case will be stated and recommended to the justice of Congres⟨s⟩ [*illegible*] [1] footing is the only one on which it can be put. You can appreciate all the circumstances attending it, and particularly the expediency, of dim[in]ishing the expence to be defrayed, as far as consists with the plan, should under the explanations here given be pursued [*sic*]. We have not been unaware of the want of Artillery Office⟨rs⟩ for the Expedition to Detroit &c. But the truth, that there so few [*sic*] of them who have had experience or even the preparatory education, that they are already appropriated under the other commanders where their services cannot be spared. The officers appointed to the new Corps, are as yet as raw as those of the Militia. I learn indeed that there are some under Genl. Wadswirth, who have more acquaintance with Artillery, than any not of the old Corps. We shall however not lose sight of this object, and will do all that can be done. In much haste yrs.

J. MADISON

RC (InU: Jackson Collection). Torn; damaged by hole punch. Written at the foot of the second page is Return Jonathan Meigs to Jackson, 23 Dec. 1812.

1. Several words are obscured by tape here.

From an Unidentified Correspondent

S<small>IR</small>. P<small>HILADA</small>. Novemr. 4th. 1812

In order to prosecute a war effectually in a republic it seems necessary the people should be willing to support it or otherwise when that is not the case, of consequence, or of course I would have said, Compulsion is inevitable. As there is a Scism among the people I shall propose an efficient mode easily effected on the indubitable principles of Justice partaking of both.

To observe our national and State Governments in opperation is an excellent school to learn the principles of representative establishments. The mode of representation in the national senate of two members from a State the time they serve &c. is perhaps as well as may be, but the representation is unjust as respects the states individually. New-York and Pennsylvania have but four members whereas the five New-England States, New-Jersey, and Delaware have fourteen altho' taken altogether have not so many people as the other two.

Some of the States have refused to obey an evidently constitutional Law of the Union and ought therefore in Justice to be deprived of their State sovereignty, considered as mere territory of the United States and incorporated with some of the other States who pursue correct principles. This would be a good example for refractory states in future. It is not an unprecedented thing to alter the boundaries of territory and why should not the United States for the sake of a more just representation in Senate be fashioned to a more equal size say fifty thousand square miles, about an eligible size for them, or as near it as may be convenient and the nature of the case may admit of, considering also the probable future population.

In the State of Connecticut the people have it is said, some of them associated for the purpose of supporting the present just and unavoidable contest with Britain. Such associations ought to be set on foot in all the Tory States in the Union, the officers proposed to class the militia could take the signatures correctly, and in such States as have forfeited their sovereignty the Associators authorized to choose delegates to meet some patriotic State in Convention, if that State agrees to it, to modify its Constitution if thought necessary or form such a new one as they may agree upon to incorporate them into one and to disfranchise the nonassociators at least Until the close of the war but it would be more advisable if forever. If they will not support a war that could not be avoided on our part but with the loss of our independance as a Nation, A war which the Brittish had waged previous to our Government's having declared it, they ought never to be entitled to elect nor be elected. During the revolutionary war when the Constitution of New-Jersey was formed none but Associators were allowed to vote for the delegates who composed the Convention who formed it how it was with respect to that in the other States I am not informed.[1] The refugees being permitted to return after our revolutionary war and they and the Tories being admitted to the free full right of franchise, has ever since, been a principal cause of our political misfortunes.

If the old part of Massachusetts, Connecticut and Rhode Island could be given to the State of Vermont, The District of Maine to New-Hamshire⟨,⟩ New-Jersey to Pennsylvania, And if Virginnia would spare twenty thousand square miles of her territory to receive Maryland and little Delaware to be formed with it into one the representation in senate would be more just the power of the tories almost annihilated and other important advantages produced which to be brief I shall not notice considering it unnesesary. If the whole of it cannot be effected it may in part may-be and while Congress is taking a slice off the Missisippi territory why not give it to South Carrolina rather than Georgia which is large enough already. The territory not adjoining is but an unimportant consideration. When a State is pretty large, the people living somewhat remote from each other and possessing a diversity of political interests it is said they are in less danger from ambitious intrieguers colleagueing together and concerting measures dangerous and injurious to the well-being of the republic. *I am &c. Yours.*

RC (DNA: RG 107, LRRS, A-223:6). Enclosed with and written in the same hand as Unidentified Correspondent to JM, 2 Nov. 1812. Unsigned.

1. New Jersey's 1776 constitution was written by a group selected by the colony's provisional congress and was adopted by that congress without a general vote (Julian P. Boyd, ed., *Fundamental Laws and Constitutions of New Jersey* [Princeton, N.J., 1964], 26, 28–29).

§ From Henry Smith and Others. *4 November 1812, Providence.* "The District Judge of this district having deceased, we beg leave to recommend Asher Robbins Esqr. as a suitable successor.[1] . . .

"His pre-eminent qualifications for a seat in the Supreme Court having, as is presumed, been completely unfolded to your view on a late occasion,[2] it is only necessary for us to offer our names in his favor for the present vacancy, forbearing to dwell on his rare merits."

RC (DNA: RG 59, LAR, 1809–17, filed under "Robbins"). 2 pp.; signed by Henry Smith, Seth Wheaton, Thomas Coles, Christopher Ellery, and Samuel Thurber.

1. For this vacancy, see James Fenner to JM, 3 Aug. 1812, and n. 1.
2. For Robbins's unsuccessful bid to replace William Cushing on the U.S. Supreme Court in 1810, see Christopher Ellery to JM, 21 Dec. 1809 and 30 Sept. 1810, Constant Taber and Others to JM, 24 Sept. 1810, David Howell to JM, 26 Nov. 1810, Charles Collins and David A. Leonard to JM, 27 Nov. 1810, and John Pitman Jr. to JM, 24 Oct. 1811, *PJM-PS,* 2:140–41 and nn., 566–67 and n. 2, 553–54, 3:10 n., 27–28, 31, 497–98.

To Congress

November 5th 1812

The Bill entitled, "An Act supplementary to the Acts heretofore passed on the subject of an uniform rule of naturalization" which passed the two Houses at the last Session of Congress,[1] having appeared to me liable to abuse by Aliens having no real purpose of effectuating a naturalization, and therefore not been signed; and having been presented at an hour too near the close of the Session to be returned with objections for reconsideration; the Bill failed to become a law. I recommend that provision be now made in favor of Aliens entitled to the contemplated benefit, under such regulations as will prevent advantage being taken of it, for improper purposes.[2]

JAMES MADISON

RC (DNA: RG 46, President's Messages, 12A-E2). In the hand of Edward Coles, signed by JM. Transmitted to both houses of Congress on 6 Nov. 1812 (*Annals of Congress*, 12th Cong., 2d sess., 17, 141).

1. On 27 June 1812 Rep. Abner Lacock of Pennsylvania pointed out to the House of Representatives that because of the declaration of war, current law required courts to deny naturalization to all foreigners, regardless of whether they had met conditions for citizenship. A naturalization bill to allow resident foreigners to become U.S. citizens was then passed by the House on 2 July and by the Senate on 4 July. The bill permitted alien enemies to receive U.S. citizenship if they declared their intention to be naturalized within six months of the passage of the law (ibid., 12th Cong., 1st sess., 318, 1561, 1571, 1574).

2. JM's message was referred on 6 Nov. 1812 to a House select committee, which reported "An act supplementary to the acts heretofore passed on the subject of an uniform rule of naturalization" on 18 Nov. The bill stipulated that all naturalization laws already in force would continue to operate regardless of the state of war between the U.S. and Great Britain, provided that "no alien enemy shall be admitted to the rights of citizenship, who shall not within nine months after the passing of this act make his application, and such declaration of his intention, as is required by law," and provided that this law should not be construed "to interfere or prevent the apprehension and removal, agreeably to law, of any alien enemy at any time previous to the actual naturalization of such alien." This version of the naturalization bill passed the House on 23 Feb. 1813 and the Senate on 3 Mar. but was not signed into law (ibid., 12th Cong., 2d sess., 120–21, 141, 152–53, 1110).

§ From John Armstrong. *5 November 1812, "Head Qurs. New York."* "Mr. Benjamin Romaine of this City proposes to visit Washington[1] and seeks the honor of an introduction to you.[2] He is a gentleman of intellegence and integrity."

RC (DLC). 1 p.; docketed by JM.

1. Romaine traveled to Washington to lobby for a scheme that John Armstrong had proposed to the War Department, namely that Congress amend the volunteer laws to allow the president to accept the services of up to three thousand volunteer artillerists who would serve for the duration of the war defending New York and the surrounding area. Armstrong regarded this measure as preferable to making constant calls on the state militia (see Armstrong to Eustis, 5 Nov. 1812 [DNA: RG 107, LRRS, A-215:6]). Later, on 28 Feb. 1814, JM ap-

pointed Benjamin Romaine deputy quartermaster general for the Third Military District (Hamersly, *Complete Regular Army Register of the U.S.*, 132).

2. In a letter to Dr. Nicholas Romayne, postmarked 15 Nov. 1812, Romaine described his 14 Nov. meeting with JM: "Was ushered, without any ceremony, to his presence, when three gentlemen immediately left the room (which rule I observed in about twenty minutes after when a gentleman entered in a like manner). First topic—if I had an agreeable passage (after reading my introduction from Genl. Armstrong). Second respecting the Genls: health. Thirdly on the improving facilities of tra[n]sport by Steem; and Fifthly [*sic*], I took occasion to state the probabel advantages of a defencible local force, if some regulation was provided for by law to embody those men above the age of forty five and such as had, in N. York, served in the artillery four years which had freed them from further millitary duties other than that of volunteering—that such provision would, in all probability, speedily produce an organization of a respecticable force for local defence. Of this he approved, and hoped, if the U. S. did not make such arrangement, that the several states would. His mild and agreeable manner brought me instantly at home. I mentioned the movements in the Tammany Society on the above plan, of which he had heard" (ViU).

§ From Nehemiah Rice Knight.[1] *5 November 1812, Providence.* Transmits a copy of the constitution of the Whig Society of Rhode Island,[2] the author of which was David Howell, "whose exertions in the cause & principles delineated therein induced the Branch meeting of the Town of Providence to elect him their President."

Howell and his "coadjutors" have not achieved so complete a success as they and their supporters anticipated, in spite of their "industry & zeal" in the Republican cause. Their failure is attributed to dissenting Republicans, who united themselves "with the Systematic opposers of the General Government" and "by their joint efforts & management succeeded . . . in '*prostrating his Excellency Govr. Fenner*' and with him the whole Republican interest in this State." "Yet a considerable band of faithful citizens true to their Country's rights & interest remain undismayed & look to you as the polar Star in their political Horizon."

Encloses "a copy of the catalogue of the Officers & Students of Brown University by which you will learn the office Mr. Howell holds therein."[3]

RC (DNA: RG 59, ML). 2 pp.; signed by Knight as "Sec'y to the Genl. meeting of said Society." A note on the cover reads: "Containing the Constitution of the Washington or Wig Society at Providence Rhode Island."

1. Nehemiah Rice Knight (1780–1854) was a member of the state House of Representatives in 1802, clerk of the circuit court for the District of Rhode Island, 1812–17, governor of Rhode Island, 1817–21, and member of the U.S. Senate, 1821–41 (Sobel and Raimo, *Biographical Directory of the Governors*, 4:1337).

2. Knight probably enclosed a copy of the *Constitution of the Society Called the Rhode-Island Disciples of Washington, or Whig Society, for Promoting Constitutional Information* (n.p., 1812; DLC: Madison Collection, Rare Book Division).

3. Knight probably enclosed a copy of the *Catalogue of the Officers and Students of Brown University* (Providence, 1810; listed, but not reproduced, in Shaw and Shoemaker 19656).

§ From Constant Taber and Others. *5 November 1812, Newport.* Recommend Asher Robbins to fill the place of the late David Leonard Barnes in the office of district judge. Refer JM to the previous recommendations of Robbins to fill the vacancy occasioned by the death of Judge Cushing on the U.S. Supreme Court.[1] Declare Rob-

439

bins to be a Republican "in this State, of the first grade, both as to principle, and as to talents." Describe Robbins as a lawyer "equal to any in the State . . . peculiarly qualified for the Judicial seat, by the coolness and prudence, and moderation which accompany his legal knowledge." Express the belief that Robbins's appointment would be "far more agreeable to the people of this State, generally, to the opposite parties, Republican and Federal, than the appointment of any other person." Mention that as Rhode Island "has always been divided into North and South, these districts have always insisted and agreed on an equality in Offices." "At the commencement of our present National Government, the Officers of the United States, were too, almost equally distributed, but for some time past, Sir, and at the present moment, it is too true, that the County, or rather the bitterly Federal Town of Providence has had, and now has all the general Offices of the United States, in the State of Rhode Island. The County of Newport, where Mr. Robbins is an Inhabitant— The County of Newport, which first revolutionized the State from Federal to Republican principles, the County of Newport, which has been always zealous, and always energetick has not one—The Counties of Washington, of Bristol and of Kent have not one—Providence has all." Ask, were a man in Newport equal or superior in all respects to a man in Providence, whether "the man in Newport ought not to be considered, and especially considered on the ground of an equal distribution of the Offices of the United States." Point out that it would be advantageous to have the officers of the district court residing in Newport, since most foreign vessels and prize vessels arrive there, even in severe winters.

RC (DNA: RG 59, LAR, 1809–17, filed under "Robbins"). 2 pp.; signed by Constant Taber, John Slocum, W. Nichols, Benjamin Fry, Nathaniel Hazard, Daniel Denham, Thomas G. Pitman, and Samuel Vinson.

1. See Henry Smith and Others to JM, 4 Nov. 1812, n. 2.

From Thomas Jefferson

DEAR SIR   MONTICELLO Nov. 6. 12.

I inclose you a letter from Colo. Gibson Secretary under Governor Harrison.[1] I suppose he has addressed it to me on the footing of a very old acquaintance. He is a very honest man, very old in public service & much esteemed by all who know him. All this I believe however is known to yourself, & possibly he may be personally known to you.

The seeing whether our untried Generals will stand proof is a very dear operation. Two of them have cost us a great many men. We can tell by his plumage whether a cock is dunghill or game. But with us cowardice & courage wear the same plume. Hull will of course be shot for cowardice & treachery. And will not Van Renslaer be broke for cowardice & incapacity? To advance such a body of men across a river without securing boats to bring them off in case of disaster, has cost us 700. men: and to have taken no part himself in such an action & against such a general could be nothing but cowardice. These are the reflections of a solitary reader of his own letter.[2] Dearborne & Harrison have both courage & understanding, & having no longer a Brock to encounter, I hope we shall ere long hear something good from them. If we could but get Canada to Trois rivieres in our hands we should have a set-off against spoliations to be treated of, & in the mean time separate the Indians from them and set the friendly to attack the hostile part with our aid. Ever affectionately your's

Th: Jefferson

RC (DLC: Rives Collection, Madison Papers); FC (DLC: Jefferson Papers).

1. Enclosure not found. In his epistolary record of 4 Nov. 1812, Jefferson noted the receipt of a 14 Oct. 1812 letter from John Gibson (DLC: Jefferson Papers) in which Gibson apparently solicited reappointment as Indiana territorial secretary or governor. Gibson also requested this appointment in his 14 Oct. letter to Eustis (Carter, *Territorial Papers, Indiana*, 8:209–10), in which he mentioned having written to the president on the same subject. Gibson (1740–1822), a Revolutionary War veteran, was Indiana territorial secretary, 1800–1816, and served as acting governor during the War of 1812.

2. Van Rensselaer's 14 Oct. 1812 letter to Dearborn, giving an official report on the Battle of Queenston, was printed in the *National Intelligencer* on 29 Oct. 1812.

From Levi Wheaton

Sir, Providence Novr. 6. 1812.

The office of District Judge for the District of Rhode Island having been lately vacated by the death of David L. Barnes Esqr., you have ere this perhaps been solicited in behalf of a Successor. Who or what the number of Candidates for the vacant office may be I cannot pretend to say. I have perceived however that Mr *David Howell* has long been waiting with impatience for the Mantle of the departed Judge—ordinary men would have had the delicacy to have concealed their views in such a case, but the Self love which in others is found compatible with some regard to social feeling, some pride of character and consistency, is with this Man a beastly instinct which driving at its object outruns his wit and tramples upon decency. It may seem officious, & perhaps ill-natured, in an obscure Individual like myself to attempt the portrait of a Man who has so long filled an important office, and who has at several periods of his life acted a conspicuous part in public affairs—but persuaded as I am that his character is not sufficiently well known, that he is undeserving the station which he now fills, and has still less pretensions to that to which he aspires—I cannot resist the impulse which I feel respectfully to address you on the subject. I do this with the greater freedom from a consciousness that I am actuated by no impure or interested motive—that the suggestions I am about to make are dictated by a zeal for the honour of your Administration as connected with the public good, and that I shall speak the language of the great body of my fellow Citizens who know the man—traits of him indeed have often appeared in Newspaper publications, but so evidently intended to subserve party purposes as to leave but a vague & transient impression—whilst he has been able to shelter himself under the *licentiousness* of the press, and dextrously to make common cause with men who having some pretensions to character have confessedly suffered in this way much unmerited abuse.

It were sufficient perhaps to annihilate his claims upon the present Administration to expose the duplicity of his conduct in regard to the decisive measure lately adopted by the government—at one time declaiming upon the rights & wrongs of the Country & gasconading his readiness to vindicate them by the sword as the only alternative—at another boastting his exertions in influencing the vote of his son,[1] and whining like a Quaker against the War as a ruinous & impolitic measure—always aiming to adapt his discourse to his Auditors, with a meanness & inconsistency of which he alone is capable—but a sketch of his history may better elucidate his character. He first made himself known as a political man in those times when the good people of this State set their faces against the *five percent* impost, recommended by the old Congress[2]—he was found a fit instrument to pamper their prejudices, and keep up the delusion, and in the discussions which took place on that subject, it can not be denied that he contributed much to defeat the measure, and acquired some reputation for talents— whilst his political integrity could not fairly be questioned, because it had not fairly been tried—but his antifederal creed, and the reputation he had acquired in its defence, were equally shortlived—the prediction of Thomas Paine was soon verified—"He rose like the rocket & fell like the Stick"[3]—a little experience taught the necessity of a more energetic federal Government, with powers as far transcending *that* which he had represented so formidable, as his emoluments under this Government have exceeded his deserts—and his subsequent history has proved to the satisfaction of every body, that he was on this, as on later occasions, the same time serving, mercenary Wretch—always ready to sell himself to the highest bidder, that is to say to the dominant party.

At the close of Mr Adams' Administration (under which he had received about Eleven thousand dollars for a few Weeks devoted to the adjustment of our Eastern boundary) when the reelection of this Gentleman was confidently looked for, he wrote what he called his best political piece—advocating the federal policy & repelling the claims of Mr Jefferson—but upon the revolution which unexpectedly took place, he with the versatility of a true Vicar of Bray[4] fell to eulogising the great talents and virtues of Mr Jefferson, and so well did he manage that many of our most respectable Republicans were induced to recommend him to fill the vacant office of District Attorney—there being at the time no practitioner at the bar in this State who was not a decided Federalist—with what ability he has discharged the duties of this office I do not pretend to judge. I speak only of his moral & political character—of which it would not be too much to say there is none more universally despised.

Yet other Men have been time servers, Adulterers, Hypocrites—"and practised falsehood under Saintly shew"[5]—without becoming wholly detestable—some lingering virtue, some semblance of Manhood has preserved them from utter contempt—not so with this Man of acknowledged learning and abilities, Men shun his society as a pestilence, and his Old Mare is perhaps the only Female of his acquaintance who would admit him into hers—he is not known to a decent family into which he would introduce himself without the risque of being insulted—his Children repel him from their board—and why is this? It is because he has not the feelings—the spirit of a Man—in a word it is because he is known to be destitute of *honour!*

How he has found favour in the eyes of the Fenner family is easily explained—he has long been their *obsequious Tool*—and this family like the Clinton of New York (and the parallel might be extended) has been remarkable for their gratitude to their *humble Servants,* especially when they could remunerate them at the public expence—through this channel I suspect he has been recommended to the notice of Govr. Gerry—for surely Govr. Gerry could not have known the estimation in which he is held by the Community in which he lives—or he may have been mislead by the figure he has sometimes made in the Republican prints of this town and of Boston—always written or procured by himself.

His removal from his present office would I doubt not give *almost* universal pleasure—but of this it may be said that his liability to be removed may operate as a Check upon his aberrations from duty—whereas let him once be made a Judge, leave him nothing farther to hope or fear from a *Republican* Administration—and his leanings & prejudices (I say nothing of his *principles*) will be on the side of Federalism—immediately surrounded by the wealthy & influential to whom he has been accustomed to bow with servility—his convenience & sordid views of Interest will prompt him on all occasions to subserve their purposes—and the same reasoning will apply to the *vote* of the Senator.

My primary object, Sir, as I have stated, was to present you a faithful picture of a Man whom I considered undeserving your patronage—but as the office of District Judge must soon be supplied by some One—I will take the liberty to recommend to your attention Samuel Eddy Esqr.[6] our present Secretary of State as a Gentleman well qualified for the Station. Mr Eddy was educated at the University in this town, studied law under the late Judge Bourne,[7] and was for several years a Copartner with him in professional business—but for the last ten or twelve years has held the office of Secretary of State—the duties of which he has discharged with much ability. He has ever been considered an able Lawyer by the Gentlemen of our Bar—and altho' not a Practitioner at present, is still often consulted in that capacity, and his opinions always highly respected—of a strong retentive deliberating mind, of which a sound Judgement is the characteristic feature—he is very popular in this State, and universally esteemed not only as an able, but as an honest & a religious Man. Mr E. altho mingling little with political circles has been an undeviating Republican, and an uniform Supporter of your Administration and that of your illustrious predecessor. *Just' et tenacem propos'ti Virum*[8]—he is a Man of honour, of inflexible Integrity & a feeling heart—he is about Forty years of age—not rich but unembarrassed & free in his Circumstances—in short I feel a confidence that there is no Man in this State who on every account is so well entitled to the Office of District Judge.

His delicacey would not allow him to be a *competitor* for this office—nor would he knowingly suffer a recommendation with any number of signatures to go forward in his favour—yet from sounding him on the subject I feel assured he would accept it if conferred upon him. Mr E. is the particular friend of Mr Russell our Chargé d'affaire at London, who were he present would be warmly interested in his favour. He is well known to the Gentlemen of our Delegation—especially to Messrs. Potter[9] & Jackson,[10] who altho' his Antipodes in politics will do justice to his Character.

Besides the intrinsic merits of Mr Eddy, I have been induced to recommend him to your attention as a likely mean of silencing the conflicting claims of rival Candidates—his appointment cannot be disapproved by the friends of either party, and I well know that the Gentlemen of this Vicinity who have signed a recommendation in favour of one of them, would most chearfully have done the same for Mr E. could they have supposed him willing to become a Candidate.

Excuse Sir, the freedom of this communication, and be pleased to accept assurances of my high consideration & respect, with my best Wishes for the honour success & continuance of your Administration.

LEVI WHEATON[11]

RC (DLC). Docketed by JM. Cover marked "to be returned."

1. For Jeremiah Howell's vote against the declaration of war, see *PJM-PS*, 4:510 n. 1.

2. Howell led the Rhode Island congressional delegation in opposition to the impost of 1781, which had been designed to free Congress from dependence upon the states by providing a means for raising revenue directly. Though the measure had the support of every other state, Rhode Island's noncompliance eventually resulted in its defeat (E. James Ferguson, *The Power of the Purse* [Chapel Hill, N.C., 1961], 146, 152–53).

3. "And the final event to himself has been, that as he rose like a rocket, he fell like the stick" (Thomas Paine, *Letter Addressed to the Addressers* [New York, 1793; Evans 25957], 3).

4. "The Vicar of Bray" was a popular eighteenth-century song of uncertain origin. The vicar was a timeserving parson who boasted that he had accommodated himself to the changing religious views of British monarchs and that "whatsoever king may reign," he would remain the vicar of Bray (Margaret Drabble, ed., *The Oxford Companion to English Literature* [6th ed.; Oxford, 2000], 1058).

5. Milton, *Paradise Lost*, 4.122–23: "That practisd falshood under saintly shew, / Deep malice to conceale, couch't with revenge."

6. Samuel Eddy (1769–1839) was a delegate to the Rhode Island ratifying convention, secretary of state for Rhode Island, 1797–1819, a trustee of Brown University, 1797–1805, a member of the U.S. House of Representatives, 1819–25, and a Rhode Island Supreme Court justice, 1826–35 (*Historical Catalogue of Brown University* [1905 ed.], 73).

7. Benjamin Bourne (1755–1808) was a trustee of Brown University, 1792–1808, a member of the U.S. House of Representatives, 1790–96, and a U.S. district court justice for Rhode Island, 1801–8 (ibid., 524).

8. *Iustum et tenacem propositi virum:* "The man tenacious of his purpose" (Horace, *Odes*, 3.3.1, in *Horace: The Odes and Epodes*, Loeb Classical Library [1914; reprint, Cambridge, Mass., 1978], 179).

9. Elisha R. Potter (1764–1835) was a member of the Rhode Island House of Representatives, 1793–96, 1798–1808, and 1816–35, a member of the U.S. House of Representatives, 1796–97 and 1809–15, a trustee of Brown University, 1802–35, and an unsuccessful candidate for governor in 1818 (*Historical Catalogue of Brown University* [1905 ed.], 31).

10. Richard Jackson Jr. (1764–1838) was a member of the U.S. House of Representatives, 1808–15, and a trustee of Brown University, 1809–38 (ibid., 31).

11. Levi Wheaton (1761–1851) was a trustee of Brown University, 1798–1851, a professor of medicine there, 1815–28, and a physician in New York State and Providence (ibid., 72).

§ To Congress. *6 November 1812*. Transmits "copies of the correspondencies [*sic*] between the Department of War and the Governors of Massachusetts and Connecticut, refered to in my Message of the fourth instant."

RC and enclosures, two copies (DNA: RG 233, President's Messages, 12A-D1; DNA: RG 46, President's Messages, 12A-E2). First RC 1 p.; in the hand of Edward Coles, signed by JM. For enclosures (34 pp.), see Annual Message to Congress, 4 Nov. 1812, n. 1.

§ From William Eustis. *6 November 1812*. Lists proposed promotions and appointments in the U.S. Army for JM's approval.

Letterbook copy and partial letterbook copy of enclosure (DNA: RG 107, LSP); printed copy and printed copy of enclosures (*Senate Exec. Proceedings*, 2:296–302). Letterbook copy 1 p. On 9 Nov., JM forwarded to the Senate Eustis's list of recess promotions and appointments in the Corps of Engineers, the Regiment of Artillerists, the Regiment of Light Artillery, the First through Seventh Regiments of Infantry, and the Rifle Regiment, along with a list of recess appointments from Massachusetts, New York, Pennsylvania, South Carolina, Vermont, Tennessee, the Indiana Territory, Delaware, Ohio, Georgia, Connecticut, Virginia, New Jersey, Kentucky, Rhode Island, North Carolina, the Mississippi Territory, Maryland, the District of Maine, and New Orleans (ibid., 2:296–302).

From Elbridge Gerry

CAMBRIDGE 8th Novr 1812.

I have read, my dear Sir, with inexpressible pleasure, your message to Congress; embracing, in my veiw of it, every important point, & every requisite observation thereon, compatible with elegant precision. Had Congress adjourned to an earlier period, this important document would have probably had a salutary influence on the elections.

I observe with pleasure, that there is soon, to be a legal investigation of the causes of the incomprehensible conduct of Brigadier General Hull. In no instance have I been so unprepared as for that event. It did not, in my mind, exist within the compass of possibilities. My recommendation of him has been a source of mortification.[1] I am informed, for I have not seen him, that he professes to be easy on the subject, from a conviction of good grounds for his Justification. On the possibility of this, I can give no opinion. If the trial, which must attract public attention should be in Boston, or the Vicinity, And you have not selected a Judge advocate, I know of no Lawyer in this State, who would do stricter Justice to the subject, than my son in law James T Austin Esqr.

The conduct of our citizens in their Congressional Elections is mysterious. It does not present a favorable prospect of those for our national Executive.[2]

I addressed Sir a letter to you on the 15th of August, on various subjects, & have the honor to remain with the highest esteem & respect, very sincerely your obedt. Sert

E. GERRY

RC (DLC). Docketed by JM.

1. See Gerry to JM, 12 and 27 Dec. 1811, *PJM-PS*, 4:64, 93.

2. Gerry referred to the rise in the number of Federalists elected to the Thirteenth Congress (see JM to Thomas Jefferson, 14 Oct. 1812, nn. 5 and 7). As Gerry feared, the results presaged a steep decline in the number of Massachusetts Republicans voting in the presidential election. In the April 1812 election for governor, Massachusetts Republicans polled 51,326 votes, accounting for 49.3 percent of the votes cast; in the presidential election, the Republicans cast only 27,272 votes, representing 34.9 percent of the turnout (Banner, *To the Hartford Convention*, 361).

§ From the Inhabitants of Bristol County, Massachusetts. *9 November 1812, Easton.* "At a cricis like the present, while our Country calls for the zeal of her Patriots; we feel it our duty to rally around its standard and prepare ourselves for action, to defend the rights and liberties achieved us by our forefathers.

"We, inhabitants of the United States, citizens and residents within the County of Bristol and commonwealth of Massachusetts the land which through the blessing of Kind Providence has reared us from childhood and commands our inviolable attachment; as additional Military forces appear competent to the security of our rights, particularly in this State, we have deemed it expedient to form ourselves into a company signalized by the term 'Madison Volunteers,' Under the provisions of an act of Congress of the 6th February and the supplementary thereto of the 6th July last, do hereby place ourselves in conjunction with other volunteer military corps, with the privilege of being stationed within this, or any of its adjacent States. Not that we would cowardly turn from the utmost extremity of our country, were it necessary to proceed thither; but as several of the young volunteers desire to be stationed near their dwellings as possible, we are induced to make this exception.

"The small number of men within the fortress' at Boston; the nesessary erection of other batteries; and the late indisposition of Govr. Strong in refusing to call forth the detached militia on the requesition of General Dearbo[r]n; you doubtless are not unacquainted with.

"In our opinion Sirs, to place volunteer troops within the forts at Boston is highly requisite, it will relieve the heavy burthen that now presses on that scanty number, there: but should it prove that the addition of our little band, were more than sufficient to man them, (provided you admit us,) they can be taken to the frontiers or any other place whither your excellency may please to call them.

"Should it please you to accept us, you shall ever receive the thanks of Americans whose hearts are united to their country, and ever ready to defend it, to spend their last drop of blood in the establishment of its injured rights.

"The young men who have join'd this company are of good families and can individually obtain a maintainance independant of resorting to the Army, but their love of Country; the ardour that animates the trueborn Patriot has stimulated them thus to present their services as privates: they have signed an enrollment, binding themselves to conform to the provisions of the act of congress which gave rise to this company.

"Enclosed you will find a certificate[1] of the presiding Gentlemen, attested by the clerk pro-tempore at a Meeting of the 'Madison Volunteers' legally notified and convened according to the constitution of the Company, which neither infringes on the laws of the United-States regulating the militia or the act. And should you think it expedient to grant commissions to us who are chosen to command the company, we will transmit to you a complete list of Musicians, Privates and such non-commissioned officers as shall hereafter be appointed, together with the whole transactions coppied from our Register.

"To conclude, we solicit your immediate attention to the foregoing address, and should it meet the approbation of your excellency, the earliest information by mail is requested. In the mene time every step will be taken to discipline and render respectful this little corps, who will give a good account of themselves should they chance to meet our enemy with Powder and Ball or Bayonet.

"After the first day of January next, should you view it expedient, we will arrain ourselves and be at your command and will march to any place (not far distant,) that you should think proper to order us; and, if the errection of other Batteries are nesessary, will repair to, and assist in fortifying against the shot of our enemy.

"Though utter strangers to your excellency, it is hoped that the subject alone will sufficiently apologise for our presumption.

"Recommendations from the most respectable Republicans of this county will be forwarded as soon as information is received that commissions can be granted us, with whom we are personally acquainted."

Add in a postscript: "NB. we omit to send you the names of those who signed the enrollment, for should you accept our offer and deem it expedient to call us without the neighbourhood of this State, about one half of them would desire an arasement, to which we would feel ourselves bound to assent, from our verbal agreement with them. If the above receives your attention, or at least excites so much as to communicate any intelligence, please direct to Saml. Hodges, jun. Easton (Mass.)."

RC and enclosure (DNA: RG 107, LRRS, K-60:6). RC 3 pp.; signed by Edward Kingman, Daniel Rogers, Samuel Hodges Jr., and Martin Torrey. Cover addressed to William Eustis; letter addressed to "His Excellency the President of the U. S. and the Honourable Secretary at War." Docketed as received in the War Department on 24 Nov. 1812. For enclosure, see n. 1.

1. The enclosure (1 p.) is an 8 Oct. 1812 certificate stating that the majority of "Madison Volunteers" had elected Edward Kingman as captain, Daniel Rogers as first lieutenant, Samuel Hodges Jr. as second lieutenant, and Martin Torrey as ensign.

From Wade Hampton

Sir,   Mississippi State of Louisiana, Nov. 10th. 1812.

I received from Major Genl. Pinckney, soon after my return to Carolina last summer, a letter, authorizing my attention to my private concerns, until the state of the service should require a call to the discharge of my military duties; which, on account of the slow progress made in the recruiting service, I was given to understand, was not very soon to be expected.

About the middle of September I was induced to enquire, whether I was at liberty to consider this indulgence as extending so far, as to authorize a short visit to my plantation on this river, and was answered, in the affirmative.

The enquiry was dictated by the circumstance of my sudden and unexpected recall from this country,[1] and by the change in our foreign relations which immediately followed, and which rendered a correspondent disposition of my affairs in this quarter, indispensable—in a word, my object was to place my concerns every where upon the *war establishment*, that I might be prepared to devote myself entirely to my public duties.

My return to Carolina will not be prolonged beyond the month of december. I shall then be prepared to meet from my government any orders with which it may be pleased to honor me. And as this is a subject of more Public interest to my feelings than any which has at any time occurred, I have availed myself of the opportunity which offers by my friend Mr. Hamilton, to renew to you the expression of my wishes as relating to it. You will not have forgotten what passed in a conversation, I had the honor to have with you, a few days before I left the seat of government, relating to the proposed military operations. Should events prove my opinions to have been *in part* erroneous, my only regret is, that they had not turned out *wholy so.* All things considered, I did not think it possible that any beneficial operations, of a decisive character, could be attempted against Canada, before the Spring; and I had a strong anticipation of *disaster,* if they should be attempted.

Notwithstanding these impressions, which were expressed (perhaps with more zeal than discretion) in the conversation alluded to, it was then added, that a *real command* in the north, would be greatly preferred to the indulgence which was accepted purely to avoid a mere *nominal* one. But so far, as respects myself, I shall not murmur. It only remains for me to ask of you Sir, in terms as earnest as respectful, to cause me to be placed, before the opening of the ensuing campaign, in command over that portion of the Army to which I am distinctly Attached, and which has not been confided to my Senior in rank of that Establishment.[2] My earnestness in this request, is dictated by the most sacred considerations. If it should not be granted, or an active command assigned me of equal importance with the one solicited, it will be impossible for me to consider myself within the pale of that honorable competition in the service of my country, which must have constituted one of the motives for entering the Army. I neither presume to solicit any seperate command, nor to affect any extraordinary military pretensions. My desire, is to be imployed. And above all, to avoid the imputation of being thought unworthy of commanding the troops of my own Corps, and of sharing their danger, & honors.

I regret extremely the necessity of troubling you upon a subject, which would more properly have been addressed to [the] head of the War department. Some circumstances of delicacy forbid the latter course, and compel the former. All I can do, is to throw myself upon your own sense of justice. Mr. Hamilton is perfectly in my confidence, and his movements will be governed by your determination. I have the honor to be Sir, very respectfully, Yr. Most Obt. Servt.

W. HAMPTON

RC (DNA: RG 107, LRUS, H-1812); Tr (NHi). RC docketed as received in the War Department on 1 Jan. 1812 [1813].

1. Hampton had been reassigned on 6 Mar. 1812 from his post at New Orleans to a command in South Carolina, where he was ordered to relocate "with as little delay as may be" (DNA: RG 107, LSMA). He informed Eustis on 19 May that he intended to depart the following day for Baltimore and would travel to Washington immediately, en route to South Carolina (DNA: RG 107, LRRS, H-254:6).

2. Here Hampton was indicating that he did not wish to be placed in a command with or under James Wilkinson. On 2 Mar. 1813 Hampton was promoted to the rank of major general, and on 7 Apr. 1813 he was given command of the Fifth Military District, headquartered in Norfolk (DNA: RG 107, LSMA).

From Thomas Lehré

S<small>IR</small>   C<small>HARLESTON</small> (S. C.) Nov: 10th. 1812

I have just this Moment received from a friend, a Copy of your Message to both Houses of Congress. It has produced a wonderf⟨ul⟩ effect here. It has raised the spirits of ⟨your⟩ friends, and depressed that of your enemies. The manly attitude you have taken in your Message, has given, most completely, the lie, to the base, and unprincipled insinations [*sic*] which a certain set of men & British agents here, have circulated with the greatest industry against you. Several thousand Copies of your Message, have been printed Extra, and circulated throughout this State, to undeceive many of our fellow Citizens, who have been grossly imposed upon, by a certain set of men, who like Esau of old, would sell their Country for a Mess. of porridge.[1] On the 20th. Inst. I shall leave this City, for Columbia, to meet our Legislature there, where I expect your enemies will bring into operation, every thing they can, to defeat your Election, however, I think they will not be able to obtain their ends.[2] The accounts I daily rece[i]ve from some of the Members elected, assure me, that I am not wrong in my Conjectures on this head. Nevertheless, permit me Sir, to ⟨su⟩ggest to you the propriety of Keeping your frien⟨ds w⟩ell and early informed upon every matter you wish made public, that they may be able to meet the Feds, & British agents at every point, and rebut the falsehoods & Calumny their [*sic*] may utter against you, any time before the Election of Electors. As soon as I arrive at Columbia, I shall inform you by the first Mail after, of the prospect of affairs there. I remain with every sentiment of esteem Sir Your Obedt. Humble Servt.

T<small>HOMAS</small> L<small>EHRÉ</small>

RC (DLC). Docketed by JM; damaged.

1. Gen. 25:29–34.
2. South Carolina's electors voted unanimously for JM and Gerry on 2 Dec. 1812 (Schlesinger, *History of American Presidential Elections*, 1:272).

From Christopher Ripley

S<small>IR</small>,   W<small>ASHINGTON</small> Novr. 10th. 1812.

The condescending attention with which you have heared what I have said respecting the affairs of our Country at London, has inspired me with the liveliest sentiments of gratitude, and, I know that I ask much, when I ask for more of your valuable time: but, believing as I do, that it is your wish to do perfect justice to all the public servants, and, knowing that this cannot be done without a complete knowledge of their cases, I beg leave to call your attention to the three Documents herewith transmitted: two of them are short,[1] and the other (the Copy of Mr. Dickins's letter to the Secretary of State dated Septr. 27th. 1811)[2] perhaps you read last year, if not, I hope that you will now do it. I am, Sir, With the greatest respect, Your very humble Servant,

CHRISTR. RIPLEY[3]

RC and enclosures (DNA: RG 59, LAR, 1809–17, filed under "Dickins"). For enclosures, see nn. 1 and 2.

1. Ripley probably enclosed two letters in support of Asbury Dickins's candidacy for the London consulate: a copy of a 27 Sept. 1811 testimonial (1 p.) signed by William Vaughan and thirteen other American merchants in London and a 7 Apr. 1812 letter (2 pp.; in French) written by Capt. Joseph Louis de Beaulieu.

2. For Dickins's letter to Monroe and additional correspondence recommending Dickins for the London consulate, see William Cobbett to JM, 12 June 1812, *PJM-PS*, 4:471–72 and n. 1.

3. Ripley was employed in the American consular office in London from April 1810 to August 1812. JM later nominated him to be a captain in the Thirty-seventh Infantry Regiment effective 30 Apr. 1813 (Ripley to Monroe, 17 Nov. 1812 [DNA: RG 59, LAR, 1809–17, filed under "Dickins"]; *Senate Exec. Proceedings*, 2:431).

§ From James T. Austin. *10 November 1812, Boston.* Encloses an offer of his services "as Judge Advocate in the trial of General Hull." "I am induced to do this not with a view to any pecuniary recompence which may be attached to a discharge of such duty, but by a professional ambition which I hope is not exceptionable."

RC (DLC). 1 p.; docketed by JM. Enclosure not found.

§ From David Meade Randolph. *10 November 1812, London.* "The public papers announce that the 'Americans are building Schooners of one hundred and twenty feet in length for privateers' against England; a circumstance that excites much apprehension here, in the minds of Naval men—and, particularly those from whose information I was able to make you certain communications last winter, on the subject of an 'Improved system of Naval Architecture.'[1] The party interested in this subject, feel disquieted, lest they incur some unfavorable imputation, and, consequent reprehension by their Superiors." Expresses confidence in JM's "correct direction of the project submitted to your consideration," which has enabled him to assure the inventors that they will be remunerated "for all the benefits that shall result from the adoption of their principles." "Shoud therefore, either the public, or private individuals have essaied these principles, I pray you will have the goodness to order a reply hereto, directly or indirectly through the medium of my Son,[2] by whom I learnt that you had received the Documents[3]—to-gether with whatever circumstance can serve as a basis for the ultimate hopes of the *party*, whose *political dispositions* had so readily accorded to me discoveries deemed of much vast importance to our Common country." Transmitted copies of the same documents to "Mr. Quincey . . . with a view to the advancement of my speculati[o]ns."

RC (DLC). 3 pp.; docketed by JM.

1. Randolph to JM, 16 Dec. 1811, *PJM-PS*, 4:69–70.
2. It is unclear whether Randolph referred to his son William Beverley Randolph (1789–1868), a lieutenant of cavalry during the War of 1812, or to another son, Richard Randolph (1782–1859), a fourth corporal of Richmond horse troops during the War of 1812 who became an adjutant of a squadron of Gen. Robert Porterfield's brigade (*WMQ*, 1st ser., 9 [1900–1901]: 183, 250).
3. Randolph probably referred to communications he had sent to Eustis in the fall of 1811, which have not been found but are mentioned in Randolph to JM, 16 Dec. 1811, *PJM-PS*, 4:69.

§ From Dutee J. Pearce. *11 November 1812, Newport.* Although unknown to JM personally, requests the president's attention to the subject matter of this letter. Suggests that David Barnes's office as district judge should be filled by "one who is a Republican in principle & in action, & friendly to the present Administration; & one who will not Lean in his Decision one way nor the other, whether the United States, or an individual is a party to the Action that may come before him." Points out that David Howell of Providence and Asher Robbins of Newport are the two competitors for this office. "The former is now District Attorney & his son in Law, Marshall & his son Senator in Congress. If the talents of these two men were equal I see no reason why one family should monopolize all the offices of trust or emolument. Mr Howell is a Man to be sure *who is well read in the Law*. But his practice for the last fifteen Years has been confined to the Duties of the office of District Attorney & to the Discharge of these important Duties, he would have been totally inadequate, had he not received the aid of Mr. Robbins in every Case of weight & of Consequence. Mr Howell is very often erroneous in his opinions, capricious in his Nature & is scarcely ever confirmed in his own Judgement unless he is convinced that it coincides with the Judgement of another man."

Expresses his belief that Robbins is second to no writer in Rhode Island, the productions of his pen having filled the columns of most of the Republican newspapers of New England. Refers JM particularly to "his remarks under the signature of Franklin."[1] Explains that as a lawyer Robbins "holds the first Rank & has been highly complimented for his argumentative powers by the Supreme Court at Washington." "His talents are not yet on their wane nor have they reached their zenith. Should the Life of Mr Robbins be protracted to any Considerable Length of Time, He will undoubtedly become one of the first jurists in the United States. I have no hesitation in saying that there is No comparison between the two men on the score of abilities & the appointment of Mr Robbins would be more conducive to the interest of the Republican party in this State & perhaps in the United States. And whether the District Judge resides in this Town or in the Town of Providence is a matter which I conceive to be of little.[2] The admiralty Business of this Town is Greater than that of all the other parts of the state in the aggregate & always will be in a time of War, owing to causes too obvious to be mentioned. I would only ob-

serve that the Town of Providence has now nearly all the offices of the General &
State Government."

RC (DNA: RG 59, LAR, 1809–17, filed under "Robbins"). 2 pp.

1. Pearce probably referred to a piece in the 3 Jan. 1810 issue of the Newport *Rhode-Island
Republican* entitled "Reflections on the Proceedings of Our Government with Jackson, the
British Minister," which was continued in four subsequent issues and signed "Franklin."

2. Pearce apparently omitted a word here.

§ To Congress. *12 November 1812.* "For the further information of Congress relative to the pacific advances made on the part of this Government, to that of Great
Britain, and the manner in which they have been met by the latter, I transmit the
sequel of the communications on that subject received from the late chargé d'affaires at London." [1]

RC and enclosures, two copies (DNA: RG 233, President's Messages, 12A-D1; DNA: RG
46, President's Messages, 12A-E2). First RC 1 p.; in the hand of Edward Coles, signed by JM;
printed in *ASP, Foreign Relations,* 3:585. For enclosures, see n. 1.

1. JM transmitted a copy of Russell's 19 Sept. 1812 letter to Monroe (1 p.; printed ibid.,
3:590–91), announcing that Lord Castlereagh had rejected the offer of an armistice, subject
to Great Britain's agreeing to the conditions for ending the orders in council, illegal blockades, and impressment, that Monroe had proposed in his 27 July 1812 instructions to Russell
(printed ibid., 3:586).

Russell's two 12 Sept. 1812 letters to Castlereagh (2 pp. and 4 pp.; printed ibid., 3:591) informed the British foreign secretary that he had received additional instructions to propose a
convention to end hostilities pending the appointment of commissioners by the U.S. and
Great Britain to negotiate a treaty providing for the security of both nations' seamen, the regulation of their commerce, and "all other interesting questions now depending between
them" and that he regretted to learn that Lord Castlereagh was "out of town."

Two communications from Lord Castlereagh and his secretary, William Hamilton, to
Russell on 16 Sept. 1812 (1 p. each; printed ibid., 3:591) announced that Castlereagh would
reply to Russell in a few days and would agree to meet Russell that same evening. Russell's 16
Sept. reply to William Hamilton (1 p.; printed ibid., 3:592) stated that he regretted the delay
and that he would leave London on 20 Sept. to embark for the U.S. Castlereagh's 18 Sept. response (3 pp.; printed ibid., 3:592) rejected Russell's proposals for a convention and treaty negotiations on the grounds that they differed little in substance from proposals that Great Britain had already rejected.

Russell's 19 Sept. 1812 letter to Monroe (1 p.; printed ibid., 3:592) covered a copy of his
19 Sept. letter to Castlereagh (2 pp.; printed ibid., 3:592) expressing disappointment at the
British rejection of his offer and denying Castlereagh's contention that there were no substantial differences between the American proposals. Russell's 7 Nov. 1812 letter to Monroe
(1 p.; printed ibid., 3:593) informed the secretary of state that he expected to land in New
York that day, that he would set out for Washington as soon as possible, and that as a consequence of the British rejection of his armistice proposals, "a vigorous prosecution of the war
appears to be the only honorable alternative left to us."

§ David Bailie Warden to Dolley Payne Madison. *12 November 1812.* Sends "nine
other copies of the Engraving of the portrait of the President,[1] to whom and to the

family I pray you to present my respects." "I took the liberty of writing to him by the *mary amore*, and of sending him some *brochures*.[2] I hope soon to hear of his re-election, and of complete success to his patriotic administration." Sends "this by Dr morell,[3] who is a Very promising young man, and attached to the government." "I hope that the circumstance of his detention in France, from ill health, will not operate against his views of employment in the navy or army of the United States."

Letterbook copy (MdHi: Warden Papers). 1 p.

1. These engravings have not been identified.

2. No letter to JM matching this description has been found, but see Warden to JM, 24 Nov. 1812.

3. Dr. Robert Morrell had been appointed a surgeon in the navy in 1810 and was last known to have been in service in New Orleans in 1815 (Callahan, *List of Officers of the Navy*, 391).

From Lafayette

My dear Sir   La Grange 13h November 1812

While You are Honorably Engaged in patriotic Concerns for which my feelings Have not Ceased, during Six and thirty Years, to be truly American, I don't Like to intrude on Your time With observations Relative to My private affairs. Yet the Correspondance is Now So Uncertain that I will not miss a Good opportunity to trouble you with a few Selfish Lines. I am much pleased to preface them with the Hopes Which the invitation Given to Mr. Barlow Cannot fail to Excite.[1]

You Have Received, my dear friend, Multiplied information of the Several Bargains Which make it more than Ever important for me that the tract Within two miles of the City may with propriety Be Located for me. I shall to day Mention only the two patents, Each of thousand Acres, Which were waiting for the Approbation By Congress of the decision given By their Commissioners. The Sale of those, or other Such patents, Has Been made in terms Which turn the interest Against me if they are not delivered Before the End of this Year—it does not Behove me to Hurry the public transaction of that Business, But as Soon as it is Settled, I Beg Leave to Suggest the idea to Send the patents duplicate or triplicate if it may Conveniently Be done.[2]

How far My Heart feels proudly and Affectionately interested in Every Military Account from the United States you Will Judge, My dear Sir, from the Sentiments which Have made me one of their Earliest Soldiers and now to my Last Breath one of their More devoted Veterans. Receive the affectionate Expression of My old, Grateful, and Everlasting friendship

Lafayette

RC (PHi). Docketed by JM.

1. In his 20 Oct. 1812 dispatch to Monroe, Barlow reported that a commercial treaty and a plan for payment of indemnities had just been sent from Paris to Napoleon at Moscow, and Barlow was hopeful that the provisions they contained would be acceptable to all parties. However, five days later he reported that the duc de Bassano had invited him to Vilna on the emperor's orders to conclude the treaty without further intervention of intermediaries (DNA: RG 59, DD, France). Barlow hastily left for Vilna, arriving on 18 Nov. (Barlow to Monroe, 23 Nov. 1812 [ibid.]).

Barlow would not see his hopes realized. On 15 Jan. 1813 Barlow's secretary informed Monroe that he had heard that the commercial treaty "is finished & ready to be signed; Indemnities are included in it." But that letter also bore the news that Barlow had fallen ill and died on his return trip to Paris in December, leaving no one to conduct the business of the minister's office (ibid.).

2. For Lafayette's efforts to secure these patents, see Lafayette to JM, 6 Oct. 1812, and n. 2.

§ From William Keteltas. *14 November 1812, New York.* "I had the Honor of mentioning the subject before to Your Excellency[1] I repeat it again. If You will give Me the Command of a Regt. of horse or foot I will endeavour to do My duty to My Country." Believes that to achieve peace in the spring, the U.S. must take Canada this winter and that to reach this goal the administration need only "will it to be done." If his tender of military service is not accepted, asks "for the appointment of marshal of this district should the present Enemy of the administration be removed," in order to provide his family with "those Comforts they have been deprived of by My Efforts in support of the Constitutional rights of Man."

RC (DLC). 2 pp.; docketed by JM.

1. Keteltas to JM, 12 Sept. and 11 Oct. 1812.

From John Adams

DEAR SIR,   QUINCY November 17th. 1812.

My Election to the Presidents office, was but by a majority of one or at most two votes. Mr Jeffersons was by no majority of the people and by a majority of one only in the house after thirty or 40 votes had been equally divided between him and Mr Burr. Mr Jeffersons second election was by a great majority and his third would have been by a greater still if he had not declined. Your Election was I believe by as great a majority as his second.[1] I have entertained hopes that no such meager Elections as mine and Mr Jeffersons first, would ever have been seen again, Indeed I wished, hoped, and expected that your second Election would have been more unanimous than any since Washingtons. I still am confident that your re-Election is certain but by all appearances it will be by a smaller majority than your first. There is a strange appearance at present I know not how to describe it. The light souls of all parties seem to have mutually transmigrated out of and into one another. I really should not be surprized if our Hyperfederalists in Boston should four years hence set up Ben Austin, whom they hate more than they do the Devil, for President.[2]

But to be more serious the Elections in New England hitherto demonstrate a discontent from the Potomac to Nova Scotia which is alarming and it is to be feared will embarress and weaken the administration at a time when it ought to be the most energetic and the most unanimously and cordially supported: the causes of such a change are too numerous, besides the inherent and inalienable fickleness of the people to be detailed at present.

There is one of many years standing which has been constantly increasing in its operation and has had a more malignant effect in our late Elections than a stranger could well imagine. I mean the claim to the Georgia Lands.[3] It has ever been my opinion and that of every other Lawyer in New England whose judgment was worth one farthing to his Client in any case and the opinion of every other man of honour and candor that the title of the claimants is good and valid in Law.

Nor is there any doubt here among reasonable men that their title is good and valid in Equity. The transaction on the part of the purchasers was bonâ fide. They had no suspicion of buying a controverted title. They had no intimation of any design to attempt a repeal: and indeed if such notice had been given them it was impossible they could have beleived it serious or feasible. They are now great sufferers. Many are of respectable situations in society. Many are reduced to poverty, by the interference of Georgians and the consequent interference of the United States to injure a title which stood on the legal constitutional and authentic records of the highest authority of a sovereign state. They paid an adequate and at that time an ample consideration. These facts are notorious and universally beleived here; and the Characters of many persons concerned render it extremely improbable in the public opinion, that the general opinion in this respect is erronious.

Such a case as this has a tendency to weaken the confidence of the people in the justice and impartiality of the nation and to propogate and countenance an apprehension that the government of the United States is an Enemy to the northern part of them. And it really has in too great a degree that Effect.

Far from me be the thought of proscribing for the government—but as every citizen has a right to his own opinion and to give it I may venture mine in unison with the universal opinion in this quarter: that government ought either to remove all obstacles to the claimants possessing the lands, or to take them for the nation by the consent of the purchasers paying them an adequate and liberal indemnity for all their advances and damages. Neither myself nor any of my Connections have any lot or portion in this business. As [*sic*] sense of public and private justice a love of the union and an ardent desire of its continuance in harmony are my only motives for giving you this trouble.

I am too sensible of the impropriety of your committing yourself to any individual without necessity upon a subject like this that I neither expect nor wish for any acknowledgment of this letter, which is intended only to communicate the sense of the public with which in this case that of the individual coincides.

Wishing you health, honour, and long life in and out of office. I remain Sir with great respect and esteem your most obedient Servant.

JOHN ADAMS

Letterbook copy (MHi: Adams Papers). The RC has not been found.

1. In the 1808 presidential election JM received 122 electoral votes. His competitors, Charles Cotesworth Pinckney and George Clinton, received 47 and 6 electoral votes, respectively (Brant, *Madison*, 4:467).

2. Benjamin Austin Jr. (1752–1820), a Boston artisan and Revolutionary War patriot, was best known for his writings in opposition to Massachusetts legal procedure in the 1780s. He was a member of the state senate in 1787, 1789–94, and 1796 but fast fell out of favor in Massachusetts because of his increasing passion for Republican views. Jefferson appointed him commissioner of loans in 1804 (*Senate Exec. Proceedings*, 1:476, 477).

3. Adams referred to the continuing controversy over the Yazoo claims of the shareholders in the New England Mississippi Land Company. The U.S. Supreme Court in its 1810 ruling in *Fletcher* v. *Peck* had upheld the claim of the New Englanders that the repeal of the Yazoo land sales by the Georgia legislature in 1796 had violated their contractual rights, but the ruling did not provide for financial indemnification. The New England land speculators were thus required to seek a federal compensation law, and their campaign was ultimately successful in March 1814 when Congress passed a law making up to $5 million available for compensation (see Magrath, *Yazoo*, 85–100).

§ To Congress. *17 November 1812.* Transmits "copies of a letter from the Consul General of the United States to Algeirs, stating the circumstances preceding and attending his departure from that Regency."[1]

RC and enclosure, two copies (DNA: RG 233, President's Messages, 12A-D1; DNA: RG 46, President's Messages, 12A-E2). First RC 1 p.; in the hand of Edward Coles, signed by JM. For enclosure, see n. 1.

1. JM transmitted an extract from Tobias Lear's 29 July 1812 dispatch to Monroe (34 pp.; printed in *Annals of Congress*, 12th Cong., 2d sess., 1222–35). For the contents of the dispatch, see Lear to JM, 31 Aug. 1812, and n. 3.

§ To Congress. *18 November 1812.* "I transmit . . . copies of a communication from Mr. Russell to the Secretary of State.[1] It is connected with the correspondence accompanying my Message of the 12th instant, but had not at that date been received."

RC and enclosure, two copies (DNA: RG 233, President's Messages, 12A-D1; DNA: RG 46, President's Messages, 12A-E2). First RC 1 p.; in the hand of Edward Coles, signed by JM. For enclosure, see n. 1.

1. Russell had arrived in Washington on 15 Nov.; the next day he handed Monroe a letter dated 16 Nov. (1 p.; printed in *ASP, Foreign Relations*, 3:593), covering his dispatch of 17 Sept. 1812 (16 pp.; printed ibid., 3:593–95). Russell's 17 Sept. letter was an account of his 16 Sept. meeting with Lord Castlereagh to discuss the American proposals for an armistice and negotiations (see JM to Congress, 12 Nov. 1812, and n. 1). The British foreign secretary began by doubting that Russell had the authority to negotiate at all, since his diplomatic functions had ceased, a circumstance that would place Great Britain on "unequal ground," as it would require Castlereagh to pledge the faith of his nation while leaving the U.S. "free to disregard its engagements." Russell's instructions from Monroe, moreover, had been written without taking into account the 23 June 1812 repeal of the orders in council, and the issue of impressment, Castlereagh continued, "was attended with difficulties" of which neither Russell nor the U.S. was aware. Here Castlereagh alluded to the "great sensibility and jealousy of the people of England on this subject," adding that "no administration could expect to remain in power that should consent to renounce the right of impressment."

Russell urged Castlereagh to overcome these difficulties, warning that "in the mean time, the war would be prosecuted, and might produce new obstacles to a pacific arrangement." He assured Castlereagh that the cessation of impressment could be handled "in the most *general terms*" and in conjunction with the passage of laws that would prohibit the employment of native-born and naturalized citizens of one nation on the vessels of the other. Russell also proposed a similar course with respect to the definition and implementation of blockades. These "moderate and liberal" propositions, he reported, were treated in a manner which forbade him "to expect their acceptance," with Lord Castlereagh's secretary even going so far as to request that the U.S. should "*deliver up* the native British seamen who might be naturalized in America."

Russell concluded that the "predetermination" of the British government was to reject any proposal relating to impressment, and he feared that he might have appeared too eager to bring about a suspension of hostilities when Castlereagh observed, "somewhat loftily, that if the American Government was so anxious *to get rid of the war*, it would have an opportunity of doing so on learning of the revocation of the orders in council." Russell countered with the remark that the wish of the U.S. "*to get rid of the war* was only a proof of the sincerity with which it had constantly sought to avoid it."

§ From Charles Collins and David A. Leonard. *18 November 1812, Bristol.* Recollect that when Cushing's seat on the U.S. Supreme Court was vacant, Asher Robbins of Newport was "held up as a suitable Candidate by the lawyers & several others, whose motives, in our view, were not worthy an object so important." Thought at that time that it was their duty to "express to the Executive our thoughts upon the subject."[1] Distrusted Robbins because he was "so warmly recommended by the people whom we knew to be opposed to the government of their country," though they did not object to his character or suitability for the office. "Whatever we may have suggested at the time that may now be prejudicial to the character of Mr R. we are ready & willing to retract. We now believe he is to be found among the firmest friends of his Country & government, & those of his profession who advocated his appointment, at the time above mentioned, did it merely to remove out of their way a powerful rival. We think him the best character the state affords to supply the vacancy recently made in the District court by the decease of Judge Barnes. We considered it our duty to take this early opportunity to forward you a letter to this effect which will but a few days precede another touching the subject of a new appointment in our District Court, signed by an additional number of our citizens."

RC (DNA: RG 59, LAR, 1809–17, filed under "Robbins"). 2 pp.

1. See Collins and Leonard to JM, 27 Nov. 1810, *PJM-PS*, 3:31.

From Albert Gallatin

[ca. 19 November 1812]

Memoranda

Mr Armstrong's letter[1]

1. Preference to be given to contracts for supplying the army with provisions. This is so indubitable that how any hesitation on the subject could take place is not easily understood. That branch of military expenditure is the only one (pay excepted) which is well administered & under a good accountability. If it was practicable to extend the same system (of contracts) to other branches, the advantages would be immediately felt. But where the practice exists & has answered it should not certainly be changed. The contracts are not yet made for any important quarter & ought without hesitation to be promptly entered into.

2. Recruiting service. Its immediate organization is absolutely necessary & there is no time to be lost. We will otherwise be without the requisite number of men in April next. To organize & to act without delay is indispensible. The encrease of pay may be relied on. An encrease of officers for that service & their distribution are the points to be attended to & decided. The encrease either by encreasing the number of regiments (diminishing the number of men in proportion in each regiment) or the addition of a recruiting company, or of some supernumerary officers to each regiment, might, whichever principle be adopted, be arranged in all its details in half a day. The selection of persons to fill the new appointments is more difficult & on that account to be attended to at once. If this subject be not immediately attended to, it will be February before the recruiting parties are properly & actively employed.

3. Local force. Unless the measure be general it may be objectionable to raise it for New York alone. The only objection which I can perceive to the general plan is that it may at this moment impede the recruiting service. Perhaps to have a law only at the end of the session & not to act on it till the other recruiting service is nearly over would be most eligible.

Next year revenue & expences.

The expences are. 1 for civil list, miscellan. diplomatic		1.600.000[2]
2. for public debt including all necessary demands of which 3 million for Treasy. Notes		8.000.000
3. army alone, as pr. prest. est. & indian Departmt.		13.396.000
4. navy as it now stands		4.926.000
		27.822.000
add deficiency in militia appn. for this year		1.000.000
		28.822.000

The resources are

1. Revenue estd. for the whole	12.000.000	
2. Treasury notes to replace those which will be reimbursed	3.000.000	
3. Loan	14.000.000	
		29.000.000

But we must add to war estimate

1. encrease of pay & officers	1.500.000	
2. volunteers & militia, at least	2.500.000	
		4.000.000

and to the naval estimate

building 4 74s & 6 frigates		3.000.000
		7.000.000
which added to the above		14.000.000
would make 1813 loan		21.000.000

I think a loan to that amount to be altogether unattainable. From Banks we can expect little or nothing, as they have already lent nearly to the full extent of their faculties. All that I could obtain this year from individual subscriptions does not exceed 3.200.000 dollars. There are but two practicable ways of diminishing the expenditure. 1. by confining it to necessary objects. 2. by introducing perfect system & suppressing abuses in the necessary branches.

1. In the War department, to reduce the calls for militia and above all to keep the controul over those calls & other contingent expences: in the navy to diminish greatly the number of gun boats, and to strike off all supernumerary midshipmen, pursers, sailing masters & other unnecessary officers.

2. System requires skill in forming & decision in executing. Both the preparing & executing such plans must rest almost exclusively with the heads of the departments. I have no doubt that knowledge & talents would save several millions & the necessary business be better done.

RC (DLC). Undated; dated 1812 in the *Index to the James Madison Papers;* date assigned here on the basis of evidence presented in n. 1. Unsigned; docketed by JM, "Gallatin A. / 1813 / Autumn previous to meeting of Congress."

1. Gallatin referred to a 16 Nov. 1812 letter he had received from John Armstrong in New York, in which Armstrong mentioned that "it is proposed to supply the army with food, otherwise than by contract, & that the old plan of buying and issuing, is seriously spoken of." Armstrong warned Gallatin against abandoning the contract system for fear of waste. He reminded Gallatin that the "pause between the labors of the fall & those of the winter" made for conditions "highly favorable to recruiting," so the recruiting stations should be opened. In his closing paragraph he informed Gallatin that he would be able "to raise thirty companies here of 100 men each, to serve during the war, on condition, that their service be confined to this Post and its dependencies" (*Papers of Gallatin* [microfilm ed.], reel 25).

2. Printed copy in Henry Adams, ed., *The Writings of Albert Gallatin* (3 vols.; 1879; reprint, New York, 1960), has "$1,500,000" here (1:528).

From Albert Gallatin

[ca. 19 November 1812]

Is it proper to enlist volunteers, under the existing act, for local & special services? Is not this a distinct organisation such as was contemplated when thinking of a local force? And would it not be better to have a general law for that object, reserving the volunteers for more active service?

If Gen. A. is not controlled, he will draw for the defence of New York a much larger permanent force than, taking the whole ground into consideration, we can spare & support.[1]

RC (DLC). Undated; dated 1812 in the *Index to the James Madison Papers;* date assigned here on the basis of the documents cited in n. 1. Unsigned; docketed by JM, "Gallatin A. / 1813" and "Albert Gallatin / 1812–3."

1. For John Armstrong's proposal to change the volunteer laws, see Armstrong to JM, 5 Nov. 1812, n. 1, and Gallatin to JM, ca. 19 Nov. 1812 (first letter), and n. 1.

From an Unidentified Correspondent

Sir   [19 November 1812]

Since the perusal of your late Message, I have been led to reflect upon the actual situation of our country, of which your communication to Congress professes to be a faithful exposition; and as I cannot bring my mind to the same results with your Excellency, I trust you will allow me the liberty of expressing some doubts, with my reasons for them, in regard to the prosperous state of our affairs, so highly vaunted in the message. I would premise, in the first place, that a sagacious statesman never calculates upon, or takes comfort from, the casual or unlooked for circumstances which, for a time only, may afford some relief to his country, or shed an evanescent lustre upon its affairs.

In one of your concluding paragraphs you say—"The situation of our country is not without its difficulties; though it *abounds* in animating considerations, of which the view here presented of our pecuniary resources is an example." What other example you could quote as holding forth "animating considerations," I am at a loss to conjecture; and of this particular, when examined, there may not be much cause for exultation. You state the receipts for the past year in a gross sum of 16,500,000, of which sum 5,850,000 dollars arises from a loan, leaving an actual revenue of 10,650,000. As I am now ignorant of the particular sources from whence this revenue is derived, I can only say that it must, in a great measure, arise from importations made previous to the declaration of war, and assisted latterly by a double duty. You further state that the "late unexpected importations of British manufactures will render the revenue of the ensuing year more productive than could have been anticipated"—And now from these facts and circumstances what cause is there for animating reflections? Mr. Gallatin has doubtless informed your Excellency how difficult he found it, after repeated trials, to obtain the amount of the loan; and in what manner the residue of it, not yet received into the Treasury, has been disposed of, I know not—but certain it is, that at this moment the books are open for subscriptions, "in sums to suit purchasers," upon the original terms. So that if any Banks, or others, have engaged to take the amount deficient, they are willing to share the advantage with any applicant. And what is there animating in this prospect? Why truly that with six months labour, the government has borrowed as much money as, under other circumstances, might have been obtained in as many hours. And with regard to the revenue—because an "unexpected importation of British manufactures" has been made, which, with a *double duty*, will for a moment replenish the coffers of the treasury, we are called upon to regard this casual, unexpected circumstance as an "animating consideration." Verily, this is short sighted calculation. I will allow, however, that upon the eve of an *important election*, it would not be good policy to say any thing concerning *direct taxes* and increased burdens. The foregoing observations apply only to the government; and now one word for the people. Is it an "animating ⟨consi⟩deration" with them, bowed down as they are under the accumulated pressure of this disastrous war, with their commerce, their navigation, and their accustomed means of support entirely cut off, and with the price of all taxable commodities and the necessaries of life enhanced by double duties, that their government, with the aid of these fortuitous and burdensome expedients, and the further hope of borrowing, will be enabled to exist one short year, without the necessity of resorting by direct taxes to an already impoverished community? Is it an "animating consideration" with either the government or people, that after expending their blood and treasure in this unnecessary and hopeless war, they and their posterity are to be loaded with an enormous *publick debt*, which will require many years of uninterrupted peace to lessen or discharge? So much for the prosperous state of our finances. Let us now look at the army. Your Excellency confesses that a "partial success" only has attended the recruiting service; and that owing to the *plentiful lack* of patriotism, volunteers cannot be relied upon as an effective force. Is this an "animating consideration" with the government? I will allow that with the people it is; and I can further inform your Excellency, that additional pay will gain you but few soldiers, and that nothing but absolute starvation staring the people in the face, will induce any portion of them to enter the ranks in this war of *conquest*, which has been so wickedly waged. And your Excellency will learn also that the people rejoice in that "novel and unfortunate exposition of the constitution," as it is termed, which denies to the President the use of the militia for any and all purposes to which he may choose to compel them; and although your Excellency speaks with some complacency of "large and permanent military establishments," as a last resource, the people are consoled with the reflection that the militia are not now to be converted into a *standing army*, and that there is yet some prospect of maintaining their liberties.

Without adverting to the adroit manner in which your Excellency dismisses the capture of two armies, and passing over other parts of your message, I will only ask your Excellency, in what sense you intended the people should understand that part of it which relates to the proposition for an armistice and the impressment of seamen. With regard to the latter, the grievance has been generally understood as affecting *American seamen*, and when you say that the British government declined the overture "from an avowed repugnance to a suspension of the practice of impressment during the armistice," did you intend that the people should be led to believe that England still insists upon a right to impress American seamen? If you did thus intend, I am apprehensive the facts will not justify you in this disingenuous statement. On the contrary, the British claim no such right, notwithstanding mistakes may have been made in the exercise of their *undoubted right* of taking *their own seamen*. I can hardly believe that a war can ever be necessary or just which is waged for the purpose of protecting under our flag any other than *native Americans*. Nor do I deem it necessary to mislead and inflame the public mind upon the only remaining point of dispute between Great-Britain and this country.

ONE OF THE PEOPLE.

Printed copy (*Boston Gazette*, 19 Nov. 1812).

§ From William Eustis. *19 November 1812, War Department.* Lists proposed appointments in the U.S. Army for JM's approval.

Letterbook copy (DNA: RG 107, LSP). 2 pp. On 20 Nov. 1812 JM forwarded to the Senate Eustis's list of nominations in various army regiments from North Carolina, Pennsylvania, South Carolina, Massachusetts, New York, Kentucky, Rhode Island, and Maryland (*Senate Exec. Proceedings*, 2:305–6).

§ From the Mississippi Territorial Legislature. *19 November 1812.* "Resolved . . . That the Conduct of the General Government in declaring war against the Kingdoms of Great Britain and Ireland and their dependencies has met with their warmest approbation.

"Resolved that We will support the Administration of the General Government in a vigorous prosecution of the war to the utmost of our abilities so as to produce the most efficient result, a glorious and honorable peace."

RC, two copies (DLC). First RC 1 p.; signed by Cowles Meade, Speaker of the house of representatives; Thomas Barnes, president of the legislative council; Thomas B. Reed, house clerk; and Felix Hughes, council secretary; docketed by JM, "Mississippi Territory / Novr. 1812 / Resn. approving Declr. of War."

§ From an Unidentified Correspondent. *19 November 1812, Newport, Rhode Island.* "It is generally believed among the Republican Citizens of this Town, that Mr. William S. Rogers has gone to the City of Washington, an applicant for some appointment under the authority of the Government,[1] it wou'd be equally repugnant to ev'ry Republican that this Gentleman shou'd be favor'd in his views, Particularly so, as his aversion to the Present Administration has been very Publickly declared, the Writer assures you Sir that he is influenced by no Private or Personal animosity toward Mr. Rogers, but is induced by the General Principle of human Nature. Them that Love me, will I love. It is a cause of deep concern & regret that we have already amongst us, those who ought to be the Servants of the Government, Men holding Commissions, who are the first and most clamorous in denouncing it, and it is much to be wished that this Gentleman may not be added to the Number."

RC (DNA: RG 59, LAR, 1809–17, filed under "Rogers"). 1 p.; signed "A Citizen of Newport."

1. On 21 Dec. 1812 JM nominated Rogers to be a purser in the U.S. Navy (*Senate Exec. Proceedings*, 2:312).

From Alexander Wolcott

Sir   Middletown 21 Novr 1812

I have never entered on a subje[c]t with so much reluctance and hesitation as on that t⟨o⟩ which this letter will be devoted. This reluctance is owing to many causes, all applying to feeling, and which nothing could forc[e] me to resist, but a settled opinion that a public evil exists and that the public service impereously demands the application of the proper remedy.

When Mr. Huntington was appointed Attorney for this District, application was made to me to recommend him to the President. He then considered me, and with justice, as one of his most fast friends. He was considered as [sic] man of respectable mental endowments, of a steady and decisive charecter, and the tide of opinion among the leading republicans in this state was in his favour. An intimate acquaintance with him, at the bar, had shown me that, in legal information he was deficient, and to that degree that, with the strongest wishes to promote his interests, I felt myself obliged to withold any active agency in his behalf. It is true I could not object to an experiment, in which every body except myself (I mean of his political friends) seemed to have confidence. He was recommended[1] and appointed, and unfortunately the worst of my forbodings has been more than realised. It was natural to expect that practise would improve him in his profession; but whether it is that the harsh treatment he has received, not only from his political enemies, but from a quarter whence it was not to have been expected, has cowed and broken his spirit, or from whatever cause it proceeds, his powers seem to have withered and decayed, to that degree, that the imbecility of the Attorney is notoriously and professedly calculated on as diminishing the danger of violating the laws, and it is but too true that an opinion so pernicious is greatly strengthened by the multitude of causes that are decided against the United States on the ground of some insufficiency of the prosess, or on account of inattention, or neglect of the prosecutor. This portrait, Sir, will appear to you to be drawn in strong colours. It is however a true one, and the task of drawing it is to me most painful, and, what gives vast increase to this pain is that Mr. Huntington considers me, and has for several years considered me inimical to him, and he believes, or affects to believe that I have exerted myself with you Sir, to procure his removal. He knows little of me not to understand that if I have personal and private grounds of controversy with him it must be a powerful motive with me for witholding all exertion against him.

I know that, long since, exertions were mad[e] to procure his removal, and I was applied to, to aid them, but, as I disliked the motive and the manner of proceeding I refused. I advised Mr Huntington, on his applying to me for advice, to resign an office productive, to him, of mortification only. This he assured me he would in a few months do. A report got abroad, a year or two ago, that his removal was determined on, and I have been informed, by a Mr. Whitman,[2] that, at the request of Mr. Huntington, he wrote a letter, addressed to you, requesting a suspension of the removal, for a short time, which letter was signed by several Gentlemen, friends of Mr. Huntington[3]—that their motive was not to conduce to the continu-

465

ance of Mr Huntington in the office, but to afford him an opportunity of quietly withdrawing himself, which he pledged himself to do, at a given period, which has, long since, passed—that Mr. Huntington does not now recognize any such agreement, and that the gentlemen feel themselves to be in an awkward situation, as they consider themselves as having given a pledge which they cannot redeem. This I state on the authority and at the request of Mr. Whitman. My troubling you, Sir, with an account of what I have done and what I have refused to do will I fear have the appearance of extraordinary egotism. As the strong statements I now make would seem to be inconsistent with my former silence I have wished, as far as truth will bear me out, to excuse this seeming inconsistency. Perhaps, however, Sir, I ought principally to make my excuses for troubling you at all. I certainly should not have taken the liberty but from a perfect persuasion of your wish to be informed of whatever the public good requires to be made known to you, and a pretty strong persuasion also that you are not aware of our precise situation relative to this subject. I hope my being perfectly unreserved and explicit will not be displeasing to you. If it be deemed of importance to know what is the general impression respecting this subject I can with perfect saf[e]ty state that the incapacity of the Attorney is too frequently and too publicly the subject of animadversion to admit of any mistake, as to public opinion and I do assure you Sir, with great sincerity that with the exception of Mr. Huntington alone I do not believe there are two opinions entertained on the subject.

In case Mr. Huntington resign his Office, or a change shall be deemed expedient may I be permitted to express an opinion respecting a successor? I believe there are but two men who have been spoken of, in reference to such an event. Mr. Bristol of New Haven whose christian name has at this moment escaped my memory, is one. He is a respectable man and a respectable lawyer, amiable and of Gentlemanly manners. He is son in law to Mr Edwards the District Judge. It is, I believe, a prevailing opinion that this circumstance will be thought an objection to him, especially as the Clerk of the court is son to the judge. If it shall not be thought advisable to have the Judge, the Clerk, and the public prosecutor, so nearly connected, indeed from one family, Mr. John Thompson Peters,[4] of Hebron in this State is in every respect equally respe[c]table, and liable to no objection that I know of. Either of these gentlemen would, I am confident, perform the duties of the office in a perfectly honourable and satisfactory manner, but my opinion is in favour of the latter, (Mr Peters), partly on account of the circumstance above stated, and partly because he is a few years the oldest lawyer and many years the oldest republican. He is besides, I think, of a firmer and more decisive and steadier temper than the other. I am, Sir, with perfect respect, your Obedt. Servt.

ALEX. WOLCOTT

RC (DNA: RG 59, LAR, 1809–17, filed under "Bristol").

1. Robert Fairchild and others to Gideon Granger, 25 Jan. 1805 (DNA: RG 107, LAR, 1801–9, filed under "Huntington").

2. Lemuel Whitman (1780–1841) was a judge of the Hartford County Court, 1819–23, a member of the state senate in 1822, and a member of Congress, 1823–25. He was probably the last signatory of the 9 Apr. 1811 letter on Huntington's behalf (see n. 3, below), the bottom of which is torn and the final signature partially obscured.

3. Jonathan Bull and Others to JM, 9 Apr. 1811, *PJM-PS*, 3:253 and n. 1.

4. On 17 Jan. 1814 JM nominated John Thompson Peters as collector for the Fourth Connecticut District (*Senate Exec. Proceedings*, 2:455).

§ From Larkin Smith. *22 November 1812, Norfolk*. Addressed "a short letter" to JM "the day before yesterday, stating the wishes of Mr. Miles King jr. to fill the Navy Agency at this place, made vacant by the recent death of Mr. Theodorick Armistead" [not found]. Without detracting from King's merits, states his opinion "that the claim of Mr. John Fawn is better founded."[1] Fawn is Armistead's half-brother "and has had the exclusive management of the Navy Agency, as well as extensive establishments of the manufacture of leather and rope for several months past." "Mr. Armistead before his death associated Mr. John Fawn with him as a partner in these works, and made arrangments for continuing them in operation, under the exclusive direction of Mr. Fawn, these establishments would be greatly b⟨e⟩nefitted, by having the Navy Agency attached to them; a⟨nd⟩ I think the family of no person, can have a stronger claim upon the Govern⟨ment⟩ than that of this most valuable departed citizen." Was unacquainted with these facts when he addressed JM about King.

RC (DNA: RG 45, Misc. Letters Received). 2 pp.

1. On 8 Dec. 1812 JM recommended John Fawn as navy agent for Norfolk, Virginia, in the place of Armistead (*Senate Exec. Proceedings*, 2:310).

From Samuel Harrison

DEAR SIR   CHITTENDEN VT. Nov 23th. [*sic*] 1812.

On the 30th. of last Month I addressed your Excellency, again, on the Subject of War.

And I must exclaim, "My Bowels, my bowels! I am pained at my very heart, my heart maketh a noise in me. *I cannot hold my Peace*, because thou hast heard O my Soul, the sound of the Trumpet, the Alarm of War."[1]

When I view the desolation and destruction of War, when I behold the Multitudes of Blessings sacrificed to the *Moloch* of Inconsideration, and inexperience, I must lament, I cannot help but proclaim to your Excellency, "Destruction upon Destruction is cried, for the whole land is spoiled, suddenly are my Tents spoiled, and My Curtains as in a Moment."[2]

I told your Excellency that my name Sake's, Genl Harrison's appeal, to the Patriotism, of the Ladies of Ohio, to supply his southern Brethren, with Lindsey Roundabouts, looked more like Knight Errantry, than an ["]Economical, well digested System"; &c. The Event has proved it— Genl. Tupper has confirmed it and he verifies an important consideration, I communicated to your Excellency, on the 11th. of May.[3] He writes thus to General Harrison. "Thus Sir has terminated an Expidition at one time capable," &c. "The man whose courage and Patriotism expires when his Rations are reduced, ought never to place himself between his Country, and its enemies."[4]

The Arrangements of the Whole Campaign, indicate inexperience, or Blindfold Ignorance. But I will not exclaim! I will relate an Anecdote directly to the Point.

A Gentleman in a Sea Port took a Great fancy to a Particular breed of Dogs, whose docility was remarkable, he procured a Puppy, and brought it home; and called his Servant. John, take particular care of this Puppy, feed him well, and as soon as he is capable, teach him all that is Possible for a Dog to learn. A few days elapsed, the Servant was called, and interrogated. Well, John, how does your charge come on? Very well, Sir, he grows finely; he is very fat. After seven, or eight days more he was, again, Interrogated. And John made the same reply, that he grew finely, but was yet Blind, and feared he would remain so, as the time for the Canine species, to Open their Eyes, was nine Days; and more than double, that time had expired; Well, keep him Nine days longer, and if he does not open his Eyes, in that time, You may kill him. The Nine days expire, the Puppy does not open his Eyes; John takes a Cord fastens a large Stone to one End, the other he fastens round the neck of the puppy; and launches him into the Water. His Master again calls John, to enquire about the Puppy: John relates the circumstances, that he had Obeyed his Orders, the Puppy remained blind, until his last Agonies; *And just when drowning, and when alas! too late! he opened his Eyes.*

I will not apply this Anecdote, the Application is obvious. I hope your Excellency and all the Advocates of War may be enabled to discover the true Interests of the United States; before the Cord is fastned, and the Nation precipitated, into remediless Ruins for then, it will be too late to open your Eyes. I remain with Respect and Esteem Your most Obedient Servant.

SAML. HARRISON

RC (DLC). Cover addressed to Sen. Stephen R. Bradley; marked "Pittsford Decr. 1t"; docketed by JM, "Harrison Saml. / Novr. 28. 1812."

1. Jer. 4:19.
2. Jer. 4:20.

3. *PJM-PS*, 4:374–77.

4. Harrison quoted from Tupper's 12 Oct. 1812 letter to William Henry Harrison (printed in Esarey, *Messages and Letters of William Henry Harrison*, Indiana Historical Collections, 2:167–72).

§ Approval of a Resolution by the City of Washington. *23 November 1812*. "I approve the object . . . for which it is proposed to raise, by lottery, the sum of ten thousand dollars by the corporation of the City of Washington."[1]

Printed copy (*Records of the Columbia Historical Society* 2 [1899]: 254).

1. JM was responding to two resolutions passed by the Board of Aldermen and the Board of Common Council of the City of Washington on 19 Nov. 1812 to raise funds to build and endow two public schools "on the Lancastrian system." A third resolution required the mayor of Washington to forward these resolutions to JM for his approval (ibid., 2:253–54).

§ From Aaron Haight Palmer and Henry B. Hagerman.[1] *23 November 1812, New York*. Signed a paper addressed to JM, "purporting to be a Representation of the superior Officers of the Regiment of New York Volunteers,"[2] and now deem it their duty to explain that they were induced to sign it by their faith in "Colonel De la Croix declaration of the facts as therein set forth," which, they regret to state, "have subsequently proved to be groundless misrepresentations."

Inform JM reluctantly that "the Colonel has not equalled the expectations we had sanguinely entertained of his talents and reputation as a gentleman and a soldier, which has determined us on receding from the engagement into which we had entered to serve under his command; at the same time assuring Your Excellency that we hold ourselves in readiness, at the call of our Country to Volunteer our services in the defence of her rights and liberties."

"We respectfully refer Your Excellency to General Armstrong for more particular information on the subject of this letter; to whom we have imparted our objections to serve under Colonel De la Croix, and who suggested to us the propriety of the present communication."

RC (DNA: RG 107, LRRS, P-19:7). 2 pp.; redirected by JM to the "Secy of War"; docketed as received in the War Department on 15 Jan. 1813.

1. Henry B. Hagerman was a captain in the Fifth Militia Regiment from New York County in 1812 (Hastings, *Military Minutes of the N.Y. Council of Appointment*, 2:1300).

2. It is uncertain to which paper JM's correspondents referred. Possibly they were signatories to the petition urging JM to appoint Lacroix as a general in the U.S. Army (Petition Recommending Irenée Amelot de Lacroix, ca. 18 Sept. 1812), or they may have signed a later petition (not found but dated 31 Oct. 1812) requesting that the volunteer companies raised in New York City "be inspected, mustered and received" (John Armstrong to Lacroix, 8 Nov. 1812 [printed in *Portrait of Colonel I. A. de La Croix* (Shaw and Shoemaker 32553), 171]).

From Return Jonathan Meigs

Sir,   Chilicothe Novr 24 1812

A report is here in Circulation that General Harrison is suspended—or superceded in the Command of the N W Army—& creates a general Anxiety. I truly hope that arrangements may be made to reconcile or obviate any diffeculties which may oppose his retaining the Command of the Army.

It is in my Opinion all important that he should command that Army, if he should not I fear that the Objects of the Campaign may be lost.

Nothing but the sincerest Desire of the ultimate Success of that Army would permit me to obtrude my Opinion. I have the Honor to be respectfully yr Obt St

R J Meigs

RC (DLC). Docketed by JM.

From David Bailie Warden

Sir,   Paris, 24 november 1812.

I have the honor of sending you two *brochures* of the national Institute, the contents of which are very interesting. I also inclose some french gazettes which contain some details concerning the situation of the french armies. Letters, which I have now received from the united States, announce the pleasing intelligence, that you will be reelected by a great majority. I have taken the liberty of writing a note to Mrs Madison by Dr Morell.[1] I am, Sir, with profound respect your most obedt & humble Servt.

D B. Warden

RC (PPAmP); letterbook copy (MdHi: Warden Papers).

1. Warden to Dolley Payne Madison, 12 Nov. 1812.

§ From Benjamin B. Mumford and Others. *24 November 1812, Newport.* Recommend Asher Robbins for the office of district attorney.[1] "No Gentleman can be better qualified than he, for the discharge of the duties of that office, not only possessing moral, but political and legal talents. Our former recommendations of this Gentleman bespeaks [*sic*] his worth, & to discribe anew his talents, natural & acquired, & his moral virtues, would only be a repetition of his merits. We beg Sir your attention to the splendid Abilities of this Gentleman, convinced as we are, that he will honor the appointment; & give universal satisfaction to the public in that capacity." Refer JM to their former recommendations of Robbins.

RC (DNA: RG 59, LAR, 1809–17, filed under "Robbins"). 2 pp.; signed by Mumford, Constant Taber, William Wilbour, Thomas G. Pitman, W. Nichols, James Peny, and Joseph Briggs.

1. On 8 Dec. 1812 JM nominated Robbins to replace David Howell as U.S. attorney for Rhode Island, and his nomination was approved by the Senate the following day (*Senate Exec. Proceedings*, 2:310). Robbins wrote to JM accepting the post on 16 Dec. 1812 (DNA: RG 59, Acceptances, 1813–20).

From Henry Middleton

(private)

Sir,   Columbia (S. Ca.) Novr. 25th. 1812.

I take the liberty of enclosing you my last communication to our State Legislature.[1] I am aware that its *local* topics can claim but a small share of your attention, and that its *general* are only a repetition of what has been often better expressed. I conceive however that it must be gratifying to you to learn that we are willing to go all lengths in the prosecution of the just objects of the war. I may add with confidence that you will obtain the undivided vote of our State for a re-election. I have the honor to be, Sir, with the highest esteem & regard yr. obt. Sert.

HENRY MIDDLETON

RC (DLC). Docketed by JM.

1. Enclosure not found, but it was probably Middleton's message to the South Carolina legislature of 24 Nov. 1812, which expressed support for a "vigorous prosecution of the war" (*National Intelligencer*, 10 Dec. 1812).

§ From William Eustis. *25 November 1812, War Department.* Lists proposed appointments in the U.S. Army for JM's approval.

Letterbook copy (DNA: RG 107, LSP). 2 pp. On 27 Nov. 1812 JM forwarded to the Senate Eustis's list of nominations in various army regiments from Virginia, New Jersey, South Carolina, Tennessee, New Hampshire, Rhode Island, Georgia, and Massachusetts (*Senate Exec. Proceedings*, 2:307).

§ Ruth Baldwin Barlow to Dolley Payne Madison. *25 November 1812, Paris.* "I wrote you in my last that my husband was on his way to Wilna, sent for by the Emperor, & this you doub[t]less, knew before, by Mr. B's letters to the President & Dept. of State, of which he sent in different directions six copies before his departur⟨e⟩.[1] He left Paris with the most flattering hopes of being able to communicate directly with the Emperor & of being able to convince him that in doing us Justice he would advance his own interest & Glory. This hope, gave Mr. B courage to undertake this long cold journey 650 leagues at this inclement season. The roads from Berlin to Wilna are generally bad, & not very safe. I had a letter dated about 50 leagues this ⟨si⟩de Köningsborg, all well he enjoyed perfect health, th'o he had only slept part of two nights. That is, he had been in bed but twice in bed [*sic*]. The Emperor was expected in Smolensk the 8th. of this month & it was supposed was going on to Wilna, this however, I have not from authority. Yet, from the best authority I have it, that he is not coming to Paris. . . . I recd. a letter from the daughter of the Marquis St. Simon (who is in Prison with her Father) to desire me, to beg you, to recall to the remembrance of the President, the affairs of her Father, which Mr. Barlow wrote to him upon, last winter.[2] I do not explain any thing, as the President will doubtless recollect the subject. They are in great distress."

RC (ViU); FC (MH). RC 3 pp.; torn.

1. See Lafayette to JM, 13 Nov. 1812, n. 1.
2. No such letter to JM has been found, but on 30 Mar. 1812 Barlow wrote to Monroe suggesting that the U.S. government "interpose its good offices" on behalf of Claude-Anne Rouvroy, marquis de Saint-Simon-Montbléru, who had fought in the American Revolution and subsequently become a naturalized Spanish citizen. Following the French invasion of Spain in 1808, Saint-Simon was made a general in the Spanish army and fought against the French. He was captured, brought to France, and found guilty of treason, and he was said to have escaped the firing squad only because of the exertions of his daughter on his behalf. Barlow explained that the marquis was languishing in prison and that his situation might be improved should the French government be urged by the U.S. to consider him a Spanish prisoner rather than a French traitor (DNA: RG 59, DD, France).

§ From Nathan Williams.[1] *26 November 1812, Utica, New York.* Introduces Alexander Johnson,[2] "a respectable young merchant of this place, who will spend a few days in Washington City, for the sake of amusement & information."

RC (DLC). 1 p.; docketed by JM.

1. Nathan Williams (1773–1835), a prominent Utica attorney and civic leader, was president of the village corporation and president of the Manhattan Bank. He also served as a Republican representative in the Ninth Congress between 1805 and 1807 (*The Utica Directory for the Year 1817* [Utica, N.Y., 1817; Shaw and Shoemaker 39653], 18, 23).
2. Alexander B. Johnson was a director, secretary, and treasurer of the Utica Insurance Company (ibid., 10).

To Jonas Galusha

SIR   WASHINGTON NOVr. 30. 1812

I have just recd. your letter of the 7th. instant[1] communicating a Resolution of the General Assembly of Vermont pledging their co-operation with the General Govt. & with the Nation, in the present Contest with a Foreign power. Had this Contest originated in causes appealing with a less indiscriminate force to the common interests & honorable feelings of every portion of our fellow Citizens, that respect for the will of the majority, regularly proclaimed, which is the vital principle of our free Constitution, would have imposed on all, the sacred duty which is thus laudably recognized by the State of Vermont; and the discharge of which is enforced by the powerful consideration, that nothing can more contribute to prolong the Contest and embarrass the attainment of its just objects, than the encouragement afforded to the hopes of the Enemy, by appearances of discord & discontent among ourselves.

In doing justice to the patriotism which dictated the Resolution transmitted, I take a pleasure in remarking that it is heightened by the particular exposure of Vermont to the pressure which the war necessarily brings with it, and in assuring myself that proportionate exertions of her Citizens, will add new lustre to their character. In the war which made us an Independent Nation, their valor had a conspicuous share. In a war which maintains the rights and attributes of Independence on the ocean, where they are not less the gift of Nature and of Nature's God, than on the land, the same zeal & perseverence may be confidently expected from the same pride of liberty & love of Country. Accept Sir assurances of my high respect & best wishes

J. M

Draft (DLC).

1. See Vermont General Assembly to JM, 13 Oct. 1812, n. Republican Jonas Galusha (1753–1834) served as governor of Vermont, 1809–13 and 1815–20 (Sobel and Raimo, *Biographical Directory of the Governors*, 4:1564–65).

From David Jones

Dear Sir,   EASTOWN CHESTER COUNTY Nov. 30. 1812.

God has given you the hig[h]est Station in the united States. It is in your power to do much good or much evil. It is your Duty, to obey the will of the People expressed by the Majority. It must be your wish to know what the People think, if they are in the habit of thinking on our publick affairs. Suppose my Communications are disagreeable to you, it can do no harm to know my Mind, for other Persons may think as I think. The Newspapers inform us of some kind of Proposals for an armistice. It is my opinion this is desinged [*sic*] to gain Time, & I know some of the best Pollititians are of the Same opinion. Their view is to amuse you & throw you off your gard, and relax your Exertions for war. Never was England in a worse Situation than at present, and knows not what to do. She Justly fears insurrections. Trade is ruined, & never will be regained. The Inhabitants are enraged.

What is to be done? They must pretend to be willing to redress our Rongs. But all is Deception, they are not yet reduced low enough. Will they give up the Lake Trade totally? I beleive they will not till they are compelled. Besides the Indian war has been very expensive, and we cannot, on Just Principles, make Peace without a Compensation; and must at least give up upper Canada. I told you last march that I feared taking Quebec would cost too much blood. Let us take all the rest of Canada, & Quebec will fall of Course. You must not depend on Militia only on Immergencies. They are extreamly useful, but they soon wish to return home to attend to their domestic affairs. You will see several Numbers in Duanes paper under the Signature of *the old Soldier*,[1] I am the author. My object was to demonstrate, that our old Custom of Treaties is rong. That we must never solicit a Treaty. That we must humble the Savages. That they must, as a Conquered People ask for peace. That we must grant it only on Condition that they shall apply themselves to a farming Life, and abandon their former mode of Life.

With respect to the north west army, I beleive Harrison will be Equal to the Task, if he can be properly supported. It is my opinion, he will meet with little opposition on his way to Detroit. But what can he do there? He cannot attempt F. Maulden without two mortars and heavy artiliry, for no Doubt, the british have made it Strong. I have heard of no artiliry sent to Harrison. The Israelites could not make brick without Straw. I received a letter from New Connecticut, which gave information that one of Gen. Hull's Captains Named Rose said that after his Capture, a briti[s]h officer told him, that the briti[s]h did not intend to fight, if the americans had approached the fort. The Terms of Capitilation were drawn up & ready to be signed, but Hull retreated as a Drunkard, & Coward & a Treator. If he is fooll enough to appear on trial, he must be condemned as a Treator or a Coward, either of these Charges is sufficient to condemn any man in a Court martial.

I hope a large army will be raised to make short work 20000d may not be too Large for Canada. We should run no risque. I am pointedly against a large Navy. It is impossible for us to equal England. I should think it much more eligible to apply to France for 5 or 6 frigats to come to our Coasts, where they can Serve France more effectually than at home, where they are roting. I meet with no man of any military knowledge pleased with the Commander in Cheif of the army. I hope some man better Qualified can be found. In the Circle of my acquaintance, there is no man Superior to general Armstrong, but your knowledge may be more extensive.

When I had the honour of conversing with you last march, I told you I had no thoughts of Serving in the army as a Chaplain; but I have changed my mind on the Subject, & from Patriotism, I cannot stay at home, it rest with you to say whether I shall visit the army on my own Expenses or the

Publicks. I think I know well the Duty of that Station, and if there should be a vacancy I will accept of it at least for one year.

Should Clinton succeed in the Tory Ticket, I shall stand no Chance, for he will soon be informed, that I have used all my Influence against him.

Should you see proper to w[r]ite to me, you must direct. The Revd. David Jones Eastown Chester County Pennsylvania. To be left at the spread Eagle post office LanCaster Turn pike.

Should you wish for any information about me, I would refer you to Mr Smiley, mr Roberts, mr Finley who all are well acquainted with me.

Praying you may be directed by him who is the fountain of grace & wisdom, & that you be enabled to direct the helm through the present Storm I am with much respect, your most obedient & humble Servt.

DAVID JONES

RC (DLC: Rives Collection, Madison Papers); FC (NRAB). RC docketed by JM. FC dated 26 Nov. 1812; marked, "A Copy of this was Sent to the President Nov. 30. 1812."

1. Letters signed with the pseudonym "The Old Soldier" appeared in the Philadelphia *Aurora General Advertiser* on 21 Oct., 14 Nov., and 24 Nov. 1812. Their contents discussed such subjects as British corruption, Toryism, and policy toward the Indians.

§ From Charles Collins. *30 November 1812, "Collector's Office District of Bristol."* Has been informed by David Howell that he has "ceased to be the district attorney for the Rhode Island district." Recommends Asher Robbins for that office.

RC (DNA: RG 59, LAR, 1809–17, filed under "Robbins"). 1 p.; torn.

§ From William Eustis. *30 November 1812, War Department.* Lists proposed promotions and appointments in the U.S. Army for JM's approval.

Letterbook copy (DNA: RG 107, LSP). 1 p. On 1 Dec. 1812 JM forwarded to the Senate Eustis's list of nominations for Corps of Engineers promotions and army appointments from Pennsylvania, New York, and Maryland (*Senate Exec. Proceedings*, 2:309).

§ From Benjamin King.[1] *30 November 1812.* Begs forgiveness for addressing JM, "but when I look round me, and see my six children and an aged mother depending on my exertions and industry for their support, the motive must plead strongly in a parent's breast." Was "dismissed the Public service on the 14th. instant without any other cause than that of absence for three or four days, through personal illness, after a faithful service of Eleven years to my country, during which I have by my invention and labour brought this Navy Yard, in my department, to a pitch of perfection, not Known in any other part of the Union." Mentions a patent for preserving iron scrap, which he has shown JM, that he has employed "without emolument." This, together with some newly constructed pumps, which have met the approval of Captains Rodgers, Hull, Decatur, Stewart, Smith, and Porter and "indeed every other nautical man, ought to have had some weight." Is gratified by the patronage he has received from Captain Gordon[2] and hopes that his services in Baltimore "may soon turn to the same utility with these, which are so evident here, for the benefit of my country." Wishes to provide for his family but has "laid out about 7000 dollars in property which has put it totally out of my power to procure the necessary tools, unless great sacrafice of the property, truly belonging to my children, is made." Believes that with JM's patronage he will "have the work of those vessels which may be repaired in Baltimore, and perhaps those that may be hereafter built." "A trifling advance from the Government would save me from many unpleasant embarrassments which advance I can give the government necessary security for."

RC (DNA: RG 45, Misc. Letters Received). 2 pp.; docketed in an unknown hand, "to be reinstated Master Blacksmith / Washington."

1. Benjamin King was a Scottish-born ironworker who had worked for several years for Benjamin Henry Latrobe on the Capitol and in the Washington Navy Yard (Van Horne, *Papers of Benjamin Henry Latrobe*, 1:532 n. 4).
2. King referred to Master Commandant Charles Gordon of Maryland (d. 1817), who was currently stationed in Baltimore and planning to rebuild the frigate *New York*, which had been laid up since 1805. Gordon had served as captain of the *Chesapeake* when it was attacked by the *Leopard* in 1807. He was promoted to captain in the navy on 2 Mar. 1813 (Callahan, *List of Officers of the Navy*, 224; Dudley, *Naval War of 1812*, 1:26, 27, 592–93).

§ From Stanley Griswold. *1 December 1812, Kaskaskia.* "Edward Hempsted, Esqr.[1] the Delegate from Missouri territory, now on his way to the city of Washington, knows my wishes—which remain the same as heretofore made known to you, particularly by Col. Mansfield, late Surveyor General, the last summer. If however the vacancy occasioned by the resignation of the latter gentleman might be obtained, it would please me better than going to Detroit.[2]

"The longer I experience this climate, the more I am convinced of its incongruity with a northern constitution, and of the impossibility of enjoying our health here."

RC (DLC). 1 p.; docketed by JM.

1. Edward Hempstead (1780–1817) of New London, Connecticut, relocated to St. Louis, District of Louisiana, in 1805. He served as attorney general of the Upper Louisiana Territory, 1809–11, and as a territorial assemblyman in 1812. After the Missouri Territory was formed in June 1812, Hempstead was its first delegate to Congress. He was also elected to the Thirteenth Congress.
2. Griswold wrote to James Monroe on 2 Nov. 1812 requesting the nomination as judge of the Michigan Territory, the position having been left vacant by the appointment of Judge Augustus B. Woodward as secretary under the British occupation (Carter, *Territorial Papers, Michigan*, 10:416–17).

§ From Isaac Wilbour.[1] *1 December 1812, Little Compton, Rhode Island.* Is told that Asher Robbins is willing to accept the office of district attorney for the District of Rhode Island. Believes that if the office goes to Robbins, "the duties there of will be discharged with Honor to him selfe & the Goverment."

RC (DNA: RG 59, LAR, 1809–17, filed under "Robbins"). 2 pp.

1. Isaac Wilbour (1763–1837) served in the Rhode Island House of Representatives, 1805–6, and was lieutenant governor of the state, 1806–7 and 1810–11. Wilbour was a Republican representative in the Tenth Congress, and he served as associate justice on the supreme court of Rhode Island in 1818 and as chief justice, 1819–27 (Patrick T. Conley, *Democracy in Decline: Rhode Island's Constitutional Development, 1776–1841* [Providence, 1977], 175).

From William Eustis

SIR, WAR OFFICE December 3rd. 1812

The constitution of the War Department as well as that of the military force rendered the duties of the Secretary of that department necessarily arduous during a time of peace. When war was declared the augmentation of duty, the great responsibility attached to the department, together with a belief that some other citizen might be selected, possessing greater military knowlege and commanding in a higher degree the public confidence, induced me to propose to retire from office. These considerations operating on my mind with increased force at this time have determined me again to tender my resignation in the hope that advantages may be derived to the public service, and that the interests of our common country may be advanced.[1]

With best wishes for the prosperity of your administration and with the highest personal respect, I have the honor to remain, your most obedient and humble servan⟨t⟩

⟨WILLIA⟩M ⟨EUSTIS⟩

RC (DLC: Rives Collection, Madison Papers); FC (MBSpnea). RC docketed by JM; torn.

1. Eustis remained in office until mid-December, when Monroe temporarily took over his duties (Brant, *Madison*, 6:123, 126; *National Intelligencer*, 8 and 15 Dec. 1812).

From John Williams

IN CAMP ONE MILE FROM KNOXVILLE

SIR December 3rd. 1812

Late intelegence shews a want of troops in East Florida to check the hostile savages. A considerable part of the Georgia Militia it is said have refused to afford relief to the troops of the United States Stationed at St. Johns from a fatal exposition of the constitution relative to the militia.[1] And believing from the course of political events that the Government of the United States will shortly wish to occupy the Floridas, I determined to collect some military force and march directly to that Quarter.[2] Upon short notice one hundred & sixty five mounted men convened at this place on Tuesday the first of this month and will march on tomorrow under my command for St. Johns—where it will afford us pleasure to execute the orders of the President. In executing your orders not a man in this corps will entertain constitutional scruples on the subject of *boundaries.* Accept Sir assurances of my high respect

JOHN WILLIAMS[3]

RC (DNA: RG 107, LRRS, W-14:7); Tr (DNA: RG 46, TP, Florida). RC docketed as received in the War Department on 12 Jan. 1813.

1. The role of the Georgia militia in East Florida was a subject of discussion at the fall 1812 session of the Georgia state legislature. Responding to rumors that the Spanish were encouraging Indian and black insurgency against Americans in East Florida, Gov. David B. Mitchell opened the session on 3 Nov. 1812 with an address describing "The present force in Augustine" to be "of a description which we can not tolerate" and the mode of warfare that the governor of East Florida had commenced to be "so savage and barbarous, that it is impossible for an American to hear of it without feeling the utmost indignation and resentment against the power that commands or even permits it." Mitchell expressed his belief that JM would "proceed in the business" of occupying East Florida, should Congress allow it, an event which he viewed as crucial to the "peace and happiness" of the state, and he recommended that the legislature take the situation under consideration. The state senate referred the matter to a committee, which reported on 9 Nov. 1812 that "immediate and decisive measures ought and must be adopted by the General or State Government, for the possession and occupancy of said Province." The committee reasoned that a state could engage in warfare without the consent of Congress only in the event of an invasion or when in such danger "as will not admit of delay." In their view "the facts are before the public, that a warfare has been commenced on the frontiers—that murders have been perpetrated under the sanction, or with the connivance of the governor of East Florida—and that a savage warfare is still in operation under the sanction of the said authority—which surely places our fellow citizens immediately exposed to its effects in imminent danger, and a danger too, not admitting of delay." The committee argued that if the General Assembly admitted to "a danger of this complexion," the state was vested with the power to organize a force to march into and occupy East Florida, "the occupation to be relinquished by the State troops, so soon as the National Legislature shall have adopted efficient measures to relieve the people, from the imminent danger with which they are now menaced." The committee then submitted a bill authorizing the occupation of East Florida, but it was read once and dropped.

On 17 Nov. the committee issued a report, which was sent to the U.S. Congress, describing the dangers posed to Georgia's citizens by the current situation in East Florida and explaining that only their reverence for the Federal Constitution kept the legislature from "avenging the manifold injuries they have received." The memorial promised that if "the constituted authorities of the United States shall deny them that aid which the safety, the honor and interests of the southern frontier of the Union, the state they represent, so imperiously require; they will deeply regret the necessity, which shall compel them to resort to those means which God and nature has placed within their reach" (*Journal of the Senate of the State of Georgia* [Milledgeville, Ga., 1813; Shaw and Shoemaker 28622], 5, 6–7, 9, 12, 23–25, 41–43).

2. For several weeks Williams had been preparing a force of Tennesseans to fight in East Florida. On 23 Nov. 1812 he placed a call to arms in the Nashville *Democratic Clarion and Tennessee Gazette*, explaining that there was a "want of troops in East Florida to check the hostile Indians" and requesting that Tennesseans come forward "well mounted, and prepare to march to Saint Johns." On 12 Dec., Gov. Willie Blount wrote to the secretary of war to express his support of the Tennessee mission to East Florida (Patrick, *Florida Fiasco*, 226–27).

3. John Williams (1778–1837) of North Carolina, cousin of Marmaduke Williams, relocated to Tennessee and took up the practice of law in Knoxville in 1803. In 1812 he became colonel of a corps of Tennessee mounted volunteers, which he led on an expedition against the Seminole Indians in 1813. At the same time he held a captain's commission in the regular army and was promoted to the rank of colonel in 1813. In that capacity he fought against the Creek Indians in Alabama and participated in the Battle of Horseshoe Bend in March 1814. He was elected to complete George W. Campbell's term in the U.S. Senate and was then reelected, serving from October 1815 to March 1823 (Powell, *Dictionary of North Carolina Biography*, 6:209–10).

To William Eustis

Dear Sir   December 4. 1812

I have received your letter of yesterday, with the impressions which could not but result from your purpose of retiring from an office so nearly related to that which has been entrusted to me, in which your services have been co-eval with mine, and in which I have witnessed the zeal and constancy of your exertions for the public good, under difficulties peculiarly arduous & trying. In bearing this testimony, I indulge my own feelings, as well as pay a tribute which is so justly due.

I take the liberty of adding a hope, that it will not be inconsistent with your arrangements, to continue your official attentions untill they can be replaced by a successor.

I thank you for the kind wishes you have expressed, and I offer the best of mine for your welfare and happiness.

JAMES MADISON

RC (MHi: Eustis Papers); draft (DLC).

§ From Thomas Lehré. *4 December 1812, Columbia*, "In the Ho. of Representatives 4 oClock P.M." Informs JM that both branches of the South Carolina legislature have reelected John Gaillard to the U.S. Senate. Gaillard received 118 votes to Governor Middleton's 37, and there was "one lost Vote." Gaillard's reelection proves South Carolina's attachment to JM, because he firmly supported JM's administration. "There were certain persons here from New York, but we kept such a watchful eye over them, as to render abortive every thing they could say, or do against you."

RC (DLC). 1 p.; docketed by JM.

§ Petition from Sailors on the *San Antonio.*[1] *4 December 1812, "Portsmouth harbour."* A number of U.S. seamen who have been captured or given themselves up as prisoners of war from British vessels, "now in close confinement on board of the St Antonio, beg leave to address your Excellency."

Declare "That the greatest part of your petitioners have been in this situation for the space of 3 or 4 Months, very few less than 2, during which time Suffered Considerably in our health not only through the want of sufficient nourishment in regard of provisions which has been kept from us but also from our being entirely destitute of warm clothing, an article so necessary and essential to our comfort during the Severities of an approching winter, which also is not allowed us."

"Seeing this to be the case and being likewise fully convinced that we can obtain no redress for our just complaints except from the Government of our own Country your petitioners judged it most fit to address your Excellency on this subject (at the same time flattering ourselves that this conduct would not be deemed reprehensible) to beseech your Excellency to cause this our humble petition to be laid before the Congress of the united States.

"That if it would not be attended with any inconvenience Speedy measures may be taken to procure our exchange in any manner which may appear most fitting to the interests of our Country as we are as anxious to obtain our liberty through a desire of again serving it as we are through the wish of escaping from a situation so irksome to us as this. But if on the contrary our wishes on this head cannot be acceded to, we humbly pray that our situation may be a little mollified through the interposition of our Government, and as there are a number of us who have Considerable Sums of prize money due to us for captures made prior to our being taken, we humbly pray those sums may be remitted to us (if not attended with too much difficulty) a little assistance in pecuniary matters would be of the greatest benefit to us in procuring such necessaries as we are most in need of."

List in a postscript "those vessels to whose crew prise money is due part of whose men is at present in this prison," including forty-six men from the *James Madison*, twenty men from the *Decatur* of Newburyport, and twenty-five from the *Baltimore* of Baltimore.

RC (DNA: RG 76, Preliminary Inventory 177, entry 123, France, Convention of 1803 [Spoliation], Misc. Claims, folder 63). 2 pp.; signed "The prisoners to the number of 185 at present confined in the St Antonio."

1. The *San Antonio* was a 74-gun Spanish ship of the line before it passed into French service and was renamed the *Saint Antoine*. It was then captured by a Royal Navy force under the command of Admiral Sir James Saumarez off Gibraltar in July 1801 and taken into British service. After being sent to Portsmouth, however, it never went to sea again and presumably served as a prison hulk (William Laird Clowes, *The Royal Navy: A History from the Earliest Times to the Present* [7 vols.; London, 1897–1903], 4:309 n., 466–67 and nn.).

§ Account with Dinsmore and Neilson. *4 December 1812.* Lists charges for work done since September 1812, including the purchase of venetian blinds, "side lights," a door, shutters, bolts, and nails. Also lists charges for four days' labor by Neilson and a "Boy" and another day's labor by Neilson for putting in a window frame. The total cost was £21 13s., which Dinsmore added to a bill rendered in September for

£1,247 5s., making a total of £1,268 18s. Against this sum Dinsmore set credit for other bills paid by JM for cash charges, a walnut plank, sheet iron, and various orders on James Leitch for a total of $3,874.50 or £1,162 7s., leaving a balance due of $355.16 or £106 11s.

Ms (ViU). 1 p. For additional accounts (ibid.) covering work done at Montpelier by Dinsmore and Neilson, see *PJM-PS*, 2:45 n. 1.

§ From the Illinois General Assembly. *Ca. 5 December 1812.* "The General Assembly impressed with the importance and danger of the approaching crisis and believing that the energies of our General Government will be necessary to save our fellow Citizens their wives and Children from the indiscriminate Slaughter of an extensive Confederacy of hostile irreated Savages, or even to maintain any part of this Territory against their attacks—Beg leave most respectfully to Solicit, that a Garrison of at least two Companies may be immediately erected at Pioria, in which event we take the liberty of recommending Capt. William O Allen of the 24th. Regiment United States Infantry as Commandant thereof, if consistant with your arrangements. We are far from a wish to seem to dictate and we are sure a decent and respectful expression of our wishes, will not be Offensive to you, although you may find it improper to gratify us.

"Our predeliction for Capt. Allen arises from our acquaintence with him. He is known to be a Gentleman of Science, bold and enterprizing, has resided so long among us as to have contracted those intimacies and friendships which to us would be a pledge for the Zeal with which he would discharge his duty on account of our fellow Citizens as well as for his own honor. At the same time his intimate knowledge of the Geography of the Country of the number, residence, Customs, and habits of our Savage neighbours, would we think render him infinitely better able to anticipate and disappoint their views, than any one who either had not had an opportunity of acquiring those advantages or who had not fully availed himself of them.

"Resolved that the above address be signed by the Speaker of the House of Representatives and by the president of the Council and that his Excellency the Governor be requested to transmit the same to the President of the United States."

RC (DLC). 1 p.; signed by George Fisher, Speaker of the house, and Pierre Menard, president of the legislative council; enclosed in Ninian Edwards to JM, 9 Dec. 1812 (ibid.; printed in Carter, *Territorial Papers, Illinois*, 16:275). Undated; date assigned here on the basis of the fact that the memorial was signed by the president of the council on 5 Dec. and forwarded to the territorial governor on that day ("Journal of the House of Representatives of the Illinois Territory, 1812," *Records of the States of the United States of America* [DLC microfilm ed., Ill. A.1b, reel 1], 29). A note in the margin reads: "Origionated [*sic*] in the House of Representatives and was passed the 4th. day of December 1812 / *Wm. C Greenup* Clk."

§ From John Whitehead. *5 December 1812, Burke County, Georgia.* Explains that in August 1789 the Creek Indians took from his Liberty County plantation "Four Negroes women and One man, the property of your Petitioner." Calculates that these slaves and their increase "amounting in December las[t] to twenty one (who can be indisputably identified) are now in the Nation." States that he has used "all due diligence" to recover his property under the provisions of the "Treaties of New York and Colerain."[1] Claims to have traveled to the Creek Nation several times and had several interviews with the agent for Indian affairs, "who has informed him that the Indians had made arangements to give up property in this situation when directed to do so by the Government of the United States." Explains that the agent has further consented to lay his case before the president but fears that the agent has been prevented from doing so[2] and that further delay will entirely deprive him of the opportunity of asserting his claim. Requests that JM take his case into consideration, have his claim investigated, and "give such directions to this Agent for Indian Affairs as shall be just and reasonable."

RC (DNA: RG 59, ML). 2 pp.; docketed by Monroe, "For the President."

1. In the Treaty of New York, signed in 1790, Upper, Middle, and Lower Creeks and Seminoles ceded much of their hunting land to the federal government and agreed to hand over runaway slaves to federal officials (Frederick E. Hoxie, ed., *Encyclopedia of North American Indians* [New York, 1996], 650). Article 7 of the Treaty of Coleraine between the Creek Indians and the U.S. government, signed in 1796, required that "all citizens of the United States, white inhabitants and negroes," being held as prisoners be handed over to the superintendent of Indian affairs under the provisions of the Treaty of New York and that all such persons and property taken since the treaty also be returned (*ASP, Indian Affairs*, 1:609).
2. No correspondence from Creek Indian agent Benjamin Hawkins addressed to JM or to the secretary of war concerning Whitehead's case has been found.

From Hubbard Taylor

DEAR SIR   CLARKE COUNTY Decr 6th. 1812
Notwithstanding the length of time since I addressed a letter to you, be assured it has not been in the least degree owing to the want of respect for your person, or a steady adherance and full confidence, in the wise political system you have invariably recommended, and so far as depended on yourself decisively adopted, to promote the peace, happiness & preservation of our much beloved Country; but it has been entirely occationed by a full conviction of the great pressure of important & w[e]ighty pub[l]ic official duties, necessarily devol[v]ing on you, and having no Matter of private concerns absolute[l]y requiring any special communicati[o]n. The little I have to transact for you, is duly attended to.

My avocation being at present exclusively agricultural I have no great oppertunity to collect as much of public opinion as at some other periods of my life, but I am still on the enquiry. Your Message to Congress is highly approved, if they will act up to its contents with considerable uninimity, and decision, we shall have noth[i]ng to fear in the reseult. The measures that has been persued towards Great Britain ought to give satisfaction to all true Americans, and cement us together as a band of brothers, but unfortunately this is not the case, for notwiths[t]anding the little deviation from the prenciple in this State, and some others it is very different in Many other states, and shame to the American charector thet such should be the case. But, I do yet believe, we have a sufficient proportion of Virtue & patriotism, to bear us out successfully in the Contest.

I am extreamly sorry that Genl. Hopkins failed in his first expedition against the Indian villages,[1] the cause of this is variously represented, by those of the party. I hope the Animosities and hart burnings thet seems to be at present Kindleng up, on thet subject will soon subside and be extinguished. Many of the offic[e]rs I have seen attatches no blame to the Genl. thet he was in extream ill health is admited by all—and the charge of intemperence I am assured by those on whom I can implicitly rely is not well founded. The Difficulty of restraining Volunteers within the due bounds of dicipline is almost at the first command impossible, I have no doubt, the incapacity & Electioneering policy of many of the subordinate officers as well as, many of the privates of the like temper, with some other causes I am not acquainted with, all combind to defeat the object particularly the ignorence or design of the Pilots & guides. I flatter myself thet the Expedition on which the Genl. is now gone[2] will terminate more advantagiousley. The former one probably saved Russell & Edwards, by drawing out the Indians in persuit of the Genls. troops. The Increase of the pay of the troops that has been recommended in your Message and likely to be adopted is particularly pleasing to the Citizens in this Country.

The only fear as to our No W. Army is the difficulty of supplies of pro[v]isions & Cloathing for the Six months Volunteers in Service, they went out thinly Clad not Knowing thet their Winter Cloathing would have been taken on at the public expence, & believing too, thet they would be in Canada before the Winter sit [sic] in, & further they had been led to believe Cloath[i]ng could be there obtained, this I know from my own Knowledge, Much has, & much more will be said on this subject & the Mismanagement of regulateions for C[l]oathing & provisions, in the public prints from different motives, first the Fideral party both in & out of the Army from this quarter spares no pains to abuse ev[e]ry thing thets done secondly the Malcontents of the Republican's partially gives into it—& indeed some others without reflecting on the extream difficulties attending the transportati[o]n by land, thro such a Country at such a distance rather acquiescess in the Complaint instead of searching in to the real causes and seting th[e]m in clear light before the public—thet the hu[r]t may not have been done in every instance is highly proba[b]le, but the means thet have be[e]n adopted were at thet time the best advised I have no doubt: and I am fretted to see men who cannot have lenity enough to believe in the honest integrity of the department thet directs those matters specially, without imputing it to ignorenc[e] and neglect, when it is so evident, thet it has been in a great degree owing to the peculiar situation of things and circumstances so mixed & so far distant from the department of War. I have mentiond these things thet you might see as far as my weak judgemnt can direct me, what course I am persuing—for I always want to unite, instead of widin the bond of all parties in this the time of danger.

I have had the satisfacti[o]n again to be an Elector we met on the 2d. Int: and gave a Unanimous Vote for yourself and Mr. Gerry. I do assure you Sir, thet I can with pleasure say the Vote was not the only gratification I had, but the warm expressions of high respect & personal attatchment, for you, and the gr[e]at Zeal for the political System you have persued in your department, & recommended to Congress, was I might say, unlimited & believed to pervade the districts thet they represented almo[s]t as Universally.

The advices you get from the Army will be so much more correct then we get from private hands thet I shall not trouble you with any thing on thet head. My Son Hubbard is out with the Army. He equiped himself as a Horse man, & set out before he heard of the serrender of Detroit, he then joind Colo Re. M. Johnstens troops of Mounted Riffle men, & since there return, was about doing business in the quarter Master's depart. for my Brother James, & since the appointment of Colo. Morrison he is Acting A. Q M. to him for Genl. Tuppers Brigadge,[3] his last letters says he intends to see Canada this winter if the troops to which he is attached are permited to advanc[e] which he sincerely wishes may be the case. He also speaks of the very great difficulty of the transportation of provisions & Military Stores th[r]ough thet Country his last was dated at McAuthers Block House about Forty Miles from Urbanna, and about 60 from the Rapids.

I spent an evening a few days ago with our friend Judge Todd, who and Mrs Todd were in good health, it was some time after there arrival before I had an opportunity of an acquaintance, I am much pleased indeed.

You will be pl[e]ased to present my best respects to gether with Mrs Taylors to Mrs Madison and accept our best wishes for her & your health and happin[e]ss. Mr. George Shannon[4] takes in the Votes of the Electors, he is the Young Man thet lost his leg in the Battle with the Indians in taking home the Osaage Indian Chife and was also in the Expedition with Lewis & Clark to the Pecific Ocean, he intends to petition for some Compensation, in consequence of his being disabled. I must beg you will excuse any improper remarks I may have made in this hasty letter & be assured I am with great esteem Dear Sir Yr: affe. Friend & ob srt

HUBBARD TAYLOR

RC (DLC). Docketed by JM.

1. On 15 Oct. 1812, in an effort to pacify hostile Indian groups in Illinois, Kentucky militia brigadier general Samuel Hopkins began marching mounted volunteers from Fort Harri-

son toward Peoria, where they were to rendezvous with Col. William Russell's rangers and the militia coming from Vincennes under the nominal leadership of Ninian Edwards. Several days later Hopkins's troops believed themselves to be in imminent danger of attack after being driven across the prairie by Indians. Hopkins could not prevent his men from retreating to Fort Harrison, even by pointing out the danger of attack from the rear (Hopkins to Isaac Shelby, 6 Oct. 1812 [*National Intelligencer*, 5 Dec. 1812]; Gilpin, *The War of 1812 in the Old Northwest*, 147–49).

2. After failing to reach Peoria, Hopkins organized an expedition against Prophetstown. Arriving on 19 Nov., he found the village deserted and ordered that it and two other settlements be burned. On 22 Nov., Hopkins and his men rode into an ambush, in which they suffered heavy casualties, and were unable to give chase due to heavy snows (Hopkins to Shelby, 27 Nov. 1812 [*National Intelligencer*, 24 Dec. 1812]; Gilpin, *The War of 1812 in the Old Northwest*, 149–50).

3. Harrison appointed Hubbard Taylor Jr. deputy quartermaster on 27 Nov. 1812 (Esarey, *Messages and Letters of William Henry Harrison*, Indiana Historical Collections, 2:246).

4. George Shannon (1785–1836) was the youngest member of the Lewis and Clark expedition, having been one of the "nine young men" who enlisted with Meriwether Lewis in Kentucky in October 1803. He lost his leg in 1807 after being wounded in an encounter with the Arikara Indians while returning the Mandan chief Sheheke to his people. He returned to Kentucky, where he studied law, and later he settled in Missouri (Gary E. Moulton, ed., *The Journals of the Lewis and Clark Expedition* [13 vols.; Lincoln, Neb., 1983–2001], 2:521–22).

§ From the Citizens of the Big Creek Settlement. *6 December 1812, Illinois Territory.* "The Memorial, of the undersigned Citizens of the united States Humbly Sheweth ... That whereas Many thousands poor Industrious Inhabitants, faithful Citizens of the United States, are now Struggling under heavy Burthens for the want of a necessary portion of the soil of the united States; and whereas many Millions of acres of land, lying West of the river Ohio and Mississippi, ar⟨e⟩ unoccupied, and are likely to lie so for many Years, unless some provisions are made for the more speedy Settlement thereof—you[r] Memorialists solicit that Some More favorable measures May be taken, that the poor Industriou⟨s⟩ people may obtain a Suffic[i]ent Quantity of land for the support of them and their families to Enable them to enjoy the sweets of liberty and indipendenc⟨e⟩ and so become useful and loyal Citizens. Many have hitherto been Cruelly Oppressed, for want of their equal natural rinights [*sic*]: many of us, Who fough⟨t⟩ for Indipendence, and Sufered every thing but death, are now in a State of Indigence, and can not enjoy the Common Comforts of life; and the lands for which we have fought, are at this time So dear, and money so Scarce that it is Impossible for us to purchase (at that rate) a Sufficient Quantity to produce the Comforts of life, and enable us to enjoy the realities of Independence.

"It is Impossible for us (without Stooping to the mean paths of Intrigue which We Scorn) to remedy ourselves In the present Crisis. We humbly Conceive, that the Most grievous Complaints among the white people of America have been Occasioned by being Cruelly deprived of our or[i]ginal right of Inheritance. We Conceive, that every free Male Citizen of the united States at 18 years of age and upwards; and every female head of a family, ought to be allowed to hold a Sufficient

Quantity of what is Called Congress Land for their Support that no one ought to be allowed to hold more than 200 acres by Improvement, We humbly Conceive, that if Each Citizen aforesaid, was allowed to hold 200 acres of land by Improvement at 12½ Cents pr. acre payable In 7 years (without Interest) after Settlement, that the taxes arising from them, would Soon produce a greater revenue, than disposing of the lands In the present way. We also Conceive that being put in possession of freeholds Estates, would produce loyalty in each Citizen prevent Rebellions, remove animosities, Cement an union, and promote happiness throughout each department of the family of the united States. We your memorialists humbly pray, that this subject May be taken m⟨or⟩e fully Into Consideration, be laid before the Senate and Representatives of the union, and such Measures taken as shall be Conducive of the general good."

RC (DNA: RG 59, TP, Illinois). 2 pp.; signed by Thomas Morrow Sr. and 137 others; addressed to the president and Congress. Printed in Carter, *Territorial Papers, Illinois,* 16:272–75.

§ From William Tatham. *7 December 1812.* "Last evening I recieved information, accidentally, that the Committee had acted on my Memorial concerning the subject of topographical documents, without investigating the vouchers or surveys prepared in support of my statement.[1] This being a matter of surprize to myself, . . . I have this day applied to the Chairman for information.

"I learn . . . that the Committee (being persuaded they would be interfereing with the executive duties, and believing that the annual appropriations afforded that branch of Government were an ample contingent fund) had directed their Chairman to move that I should have leave to withdraw my Memorial. This I have done Sir, under an assurance from the Chairman, that, should the executive desire the possession of such powers as I have offered them; and think the ordinary appropriations insufficient, there is no doubt that any aid they require will be chearfully granted by the house.

"It becomes my duty, Sir, to submit this state of the matter to your consideration without delay; and I accordingly transmit the memorial and vouchers.[2] The British and other military surveys remain arranged and labeled in one of my appartments fitted purposely for the committee: they will continue subject to such examination as you may direct, or be removed to the Presidents house for your conveniency, if such a disposition is agreable.

"If, in the interim, the public service requires any portion of the copies of them which I have offered, they shall be executed by faithful and competent assistants, so soon as funds are appropriated to enable me to employ them."

RC (DLC). 2 pp.; docketed by JM. Printed in McPherson, "Letters of William Tatham," *WMQ,* 2d ser., 16 (1936): 394–95.

1. On 23 Nov. 1812 Nathaniel Macon of North Carolina presented a memorial from William Tatham stating that "for the last twenty years" Tatham had been "collecting, at great trouble, risk, and expense, a quantity of topographical materials," for which he now sought compensation. Some of these materials appear to have been very similar to those that Tatham

submitted to Congress in 1806 (see Tatham to JM, 26 July 1812, and n. 1). The petition was referred to the House committee on military affairs, but on 4 Dec. 1812 the chairman, David R. Williams, moved that the committee be discharged from consideration of the petition and that Tatham be given leave to withdraw it (*Journal of the House of Representatives of the United States, at the Second Session of the Twelfth Congress* [Washington, 1813; Shaw and Shoemaker 30189], 562–63, 574).

2. On 24 Dec. 1812 JM transmitted to the Senate a letter from Tatham "on the subject of maritime defence, referring to sundry documents enclosed." It seems likely that these documents included eighteen pages describing various proposals for fire rafts, pontoons, and portable bridges, among other things, that Tatham assembled in December 1812 under the heading "Schedule of sundry important military, and economical acquisitions and improvements communicated, in aid of the public safety and prosperity" (DNA: RG 107, LRUS, T-1812). JM was to forward another letter to the Senate from Tatham on the same subject on 18 Feb. 1813, and the Senate referred all these materials to the secretary of war for a report (*Annals of Congress*, 12th Cong., 2d sess., 36, 90).

Draft of a Message to Congress

[ca. 8 December 1812]

Considering that the U. S have a just claim on Spain for indemnities to a large amt. the justice of which has been admitted & for the satisfaction of which the Spanish possessions on the S Borders of the U. S. were brought into negociation; that these possessions, under the existing Circumstances of the Spanish Monarchy are every day liable to be occupied by the Enemy of the U. S. whence that security for the payment of the debt due to them must be endangered & may be eventually lost; that in the mean time they are rendered by the peculiarity of their geographical relations auxiliaries to the British schemes for a clandestine & corrupting intercourse with the inhabitants of the U. S. whilst an extensive territory appertaining as a part of Louisiana, continues to be witheld from the U. S. and finally, it being ascertained that the Spanish authorities in those possessions not only violate their neutral obligations by unlawful privileges in their ports to G. B. but have armed & excited different Tribes of Savages to a merciless war agst. the U. S. thus making themselves parties thereto introducing at the same time into their garrisons troops of a character & colour well calculated to [*illegible*] revolt among tha⟨t⟩ [*illegible*] of the Cont[i]guous [*illegible*] of the U. S I recommend to the consideration of Congress the justice & expediency of authorizing an immediate occupancy of the Spanish Territory Eastward of the river Perdido not as act [*sic*] of hostility but subject to future amicable negociations for adjusting all differences between Spain & the U. S.[1]

Draft (DLC). Undated; date assigned here on the basis of evidence presented in n. 1.

1. JM appears to have drafted this message in response to developments in Spanish East Florida sometime between 21 Nov. and 10 Dec. 1812. On the former date the *National Intelligencer* published Gov. David B. Mitchell's 3 Nov. 1812 address to the Georgia legislature, complaining of Spain's employment of Seminole Indian auxiliaries against the U.S. forces in the province and predicting that the president, if authorized by Congress, would respond by occupying East Florida (see John Williams to JM, 3 Dec. 1812, and n. 1). On 8 Dec. 1812 Monroe informed Maj. Gen. Thomas Pinckney that because of the "connection between Great Britain and the Spanish regency . . . East Florida has become essentially a British province," and he insinuated that the U.S. would not tolerate this state of affairs indefinitely. In the interim Pinckney was to concentrate his troops for the purposes of "chastising the savages who have committed hostilities" and "watching the movements of England, and of the Spanish forces acting under English influence" (*State Papers and Publick Documents of the United States from the Accession of George Washington to the Presidency*, 2d ed. [10 vols.; Boston, 1815–17; Shaw and Shoemaker 36007], 9:188–91). JM may well have composed this draft at this time but did not send it to Congress, probably because Sen. Joseph Anderson of Tennessee, on 10 Dec. 1812, introduced a resolution calling for a committee to consider legislation "to authorize the President of the United States to occupy and hold the whole or any part of East Florida, including Amelia Island, and also those parts of West Florida which are not now in the possession and under the jurisdiction of the United States" (*Annals of Congress*, 12th Cong., 2d sess., 124).

From George Luckey

DEAR PRESIDENT   HARFORD Decr. 8. 1812

Many strange & unexpected things have happened since I received Your last favour.[1] The present period is eventful. The United States have enjoyed peace liberty & safety longer than is common for nations. Luxury & its concomitant evils have followed, & the most high would deal With us otherwise than he has dealt With nations, if he does not bring us low; to humiliation & repentence; or destruction, if the people will not hear & obey.

A Theologist would say of our times; as happened at the redeemers first coming; there should be wars & rumours of wars; so we look for the same before he comes to reign on the earth a thousand Years—the last effort of the crooked serpent in Wars & cruelty will be his worst: We do not know how long it may be permitted; but soon republicanism the form of government sent from heaven shall take place every where & glory fill our land. In the mean time let us do our duty. Israel was not delivered without fighting many hard battles & were often defeated thro the want of reliance on the God of battles. Go on in so good a cause & prosper, You have all the men of real Virtue & religion on Your side. I congratulate our country on your re-election. As far as man can see, an happy event! Republicans lovers of their country & liberty are three fourths of the people—Are determined to remain free or perish in the ruins of their country. Our intestine enemies have ever proved themselves pusillanimous; may we go forth With the sword of the Lord, & of the United States—the Lord reigns—he being our shield We are in safety. With esteem & regard; ever Yours

GEORGE LUCKEY

RC and enclosure (DLC). RC docketed by JM. The enclosure is a three-page tract in Luckey's hand, entitled "Maxims in politicks," in which he described the dangers inherent in "Kingly government" and explained the advantages of a republican system. He described the threat to republicanism posed by a "predominant spirit in the people of dictating to their rulers, & discontentment from a presumption that every man knows better than the ruling power" and posited that the current troubles of the U.S. "arise from impatience of moral restraint & giving loose reins to the Vitious desires of degenerate man." Luckey concluded: "No nation will long be in peace & enjoy liberty, where the bulk of the people do not suitably regard christianity."

1. Letter not found, but it may have been a response to Luckey's 1 Apr. 1812 letter to JM (*PJM-PS*, 4:284).

§ From the Illinois General Assembly. *Ca. 8 December 1812.* "The general Assembly of Illinois Territory, as the representatives of the good people thereof, beg leave to address you upon a subject highly interesting to them, both as it respects their property, & their very existence, not doubting that this appeal to your Justice, and that of the nation, will have all that consideration to which it is entituled. Recent events which we have no doubt have been communicated to you by the Governor of this Territory[1] must convince you, that this part of the community, is doom'd to bear a very considerable proportion of the calamities and dangers resulting from the war which the injustice of an unprinciple'd, ambitious, foreign power, has forced the American Government to declare.

"For years past we believe the british Government (adopting a policy equally inconsistent with humanity, and disgraceful to any civilised nation,) have been constantly machinating & intriguing with the savages to render them hostile to us, and to engage them in the war which their unfriendly conduct in ploting to divide our happy union, and their dispotic usurpation, and disregard of our rights, induced them to anticipate. M[u]ltiplied instances of depredations upon our property, and frequent repetitions of the indiscriminate, slaughter of men, women, and children afford too many melancholy evidences of the success of those intriaguers. Manaced as we are by an extensive hostile confederacy thus formed on our very borders, admonished by the past, and warned of the future, by information lately received[2] we should be unfaithful to our trusts and regardless of the claims that our constituents have upon us, were we not to ask of the General Government assistance adequate to those emergencies which the horrid aspect of our affairs too clearly indicates. An inspection of the map of this country with a knowledge of the residence of the hostile Indians will prove that no part of the American fronteer, is in more danger than this Territory, all of which from its thin and dispersed population seems to be equally exposed to savage inroads, already has this fact been clearly demonstrated, by the hostile invasion that we have lately witnessed, and we have now received information, on which we can rely that a considerable number of British traders and emissaries have arrived on the Mississippi, with supplies of Merchandize unusually large, and having felt the effects of the influence of those men during the last season when they were badly supplied with goods, and even before a declaration of war had taken place, we cannot doubt that their success will now be much greater and our danger proportionably increased, the more especially as they will not venture to return to Canada, in the spring without collecting a great number of the savages to accompany, and protect them—how soon we may witness a return of the scenes that have passed we know not, the winter in general is not the time that our enemies, select for war, but it ought to be remembred that they are subtil & enterprizing, and that they commenced their hostilities early last winter—prudence requires that we should be prepar'd for them at all times, when they are known to be hostile.

"WE therefore earnestly solicit on behalf of our fellow citizens that the Governor of this Territory may be furnished with assistance as soon as possible, and authorized to take proper measures for our defence, without which we do most seriously apprehend that this country will *be abandoned.* With the management of a campaign of a General nature we know it is not our business to interfere, but we trust that the defence of our Territory will be under the control and direction of the Governor thereof, whoes measures under divine providence we verily believe have saved this Country from *devastation, ruin,* and *desertion.* Well informed as to the residence, number, and dispositions of the enemy, and vigilent to discover their designs—we have never found him disappointed, or surprized, and notwithstanding many difficulties and unasisted by any force except that which his exertions his influence, and the patriotism of our fellow Citizens enabled him to collect. He has always been ready at the critical moment to repel hostile invasion. With a firmness that commanded strict subornation [*sic*] amongst the officers and men under his command, he has conciliated their esteem and won their affections of which they universally bear him the most honourable testimony. His unparallelled success in the defence of our fronteer upon a plan peculiar to himself, and his well timed and distinguished Expedition against the savages at the head of Peoria lake[3] prove his capacity to plan with *Judgement,* and to execute *with energy,* they have entituled him to the gratitude, and have secured him the good wishes of the people of this Territory, we therefore hope for a continuation of his services. We beg leave also most respectfully to invite your attention to the claims of the militia of this Territory, nearly one half of them have been till lately engaged in its defence, and to whoes exertions its salvation may be justly attributed. We are persuaded that no militia has ever performed services more arduous and honourable to themselves, or more beneficial to their country—some of them were in service last year—others since last spring, but as yet none of them have receeved any compensation whatever. Situated as this Territory, is with relation to the savages, the citizens thereof are risquing their lives by their residence in it, which we think contributes more to support our Government, and upon Cheaper terms than the service of regular soldiers, wherefore we beg leave to offer our petition to congress[4] praying that the inhabitants of this Territory, may be made interested in the soil by donations of land equivalent to the protection they afford, the risque they run & the inconvenience they are subjected to, by being forced into stations and prevented from pursuing their usual & regular avocations. Please to receive the humble testimony of our approbation, of your administration and our sincere wishes, that you may long continue to enjoy that share of public confidence, which the history of your life, proves you emminently intituled to.

"Resolved. That the foregoing address be Signed by the Speaker of the House of Representatives and by the President of the Legislative Council, and that the Said address be Sent to the Governor of this Territory with a request that he transmit the Same to the President of the United States."

RC (DLC). 4 pp.; signed by George Fisher, Speaker of the house, and William Biggs, "Prest. of the Legislative Council Pro tem." Undated; dated 1812 in the *Index to the James Madison Papers;* date assigned here on the basis of an 8 Dec. 1812 resolution of the Illinois Legislative Council that the address be signed and sent to the territorial governor with a request that it be forwarded to JM ("Journals of the Legislative Council of the Illinois Territory, at the First Session of the First General Assembly," *Records of the States of the United States of America* [DLC microfilm ed., Ill. A.1a, reel 1], 9–10).

1. JM's correspondents may have referred to a 18 Nov. 1812 letter sent to the War Department by Gov. Ninian Edwards, describing his efforts to defend the Illinois Territory over the summer and fall of 1812 (printed in Ninian W. Edwards, *History of Illinois, from 1778 to 1833; and Life and Times of Ninian Edwards* [Springfield, Ill., 1870], 69–72).

2. The legislators probably referred to Edwards's 28 Nov. 1812 message to the territorial legislature, which provided a history of the conflicts with the Indians throughout Illinois (ibid., 78–84).

3. Illinois militia and Indiana rangers led by Edwards and Col. William Russell had destroyed a Kickapoo village north of Peoria in late October (Gilpin, *The War of 1812 in the Old Northwest,* 149).

4. The legislators may have referred to their 30 Nov. petition to Congress, which pointed out the danger of attack on the Illinois frontier and requested "some positive assurance of a corresponding remuniration for the Sacrifice and peril incident to a Soldiers life" for those who defended it. This petition was sent to the territorial governor with instructions to send it to Washington so that the territorial delegate might lay it before both Congress and JM (Carter, *Territorial Papers, Illinois,* 16:271–72).

From Richard M. Johnson

[ca. 10 December 1812]

Plan of a Winter Campaign of mounted force against the Savages, hostile to the U. States

The Objects

1st to secure the North Western frontier from Fort Wayne to the Mississippi 300 miles a direct course.

2d To prevent the North Western Army from having convoys of provisions destroyed, when the Army shall be lessened in the Spring

3d to furnish some inducement for the neutrality of the Savages in future.

The Indians of the Ilianois have left Piorias, & will winter about Fox River which runs into Ilianois *at least 600 Warriors,* The Indians of the

Wabash have been routed from Tippicanoe by Genl Hopkins, & have determined to concentrate their forces upon the head of Wabash at least 300 Warriors. At Chicagu the Inds have collected & will spend the winter there say 300. On the St Joseph, & on L Michigan from its mouth to Chicagu Pottawattamies & others stragling 300 warriors, on the West of L Michigan up towards Green Bay a number of villages of the winebagoes & others, where 100. 150. & 200. warriors may respectively reside, in the winter these Tribes could not collect, want of provisions, & the care of the Squaws & children would prevent. Indians have been so harrassed & their wants made so imperious—by Russell Hopkins & Harrison, that the Spring will be more anxiously looked for, to take satisfaction on the Frontiers.

2ndly The Force & its organization

Two regiments each amounting to 640. men amply sufficient to traverse the whole country mentioned and disperse and destroy the various tribes within that circle—good officers & brave men alone will accomplish it. A company to consist of 80 men 4 companies 1 Battalion—2 Battalions 1 Regiment—the men to choose their officers—the Governor to commission them. A general order will answer the purpose of commissions if necessary—the force can be raised in Kentucky in 30 days. Take Fort Wayne as the point to commence operations—on account of its being a more secret rout & the enemy's retreat would be cut off—or take the grand pass on Illinois 80 miles below from Piorias, which would be best on account of the contiguity of a rich settlement near the mouth of the Illinois which would afford forage & provisions, & the Illinois is navigable in Edward's large bullet-proof boat up to Piorias. We take Fort Wayne as the place in supposition, and all things considered it is the best. The army may be considerd as at Fort Wayne, as all agree in the practicability of reaching to that post, there being only 85 miles frontier.

3rd. Preparations for the march from Fort Wayne. None can doubt the practicability of the campaign as to the men, if the horses can be provided for. In 30 lbs of the most nutritious food, such as Bacon, biscuits, sugar, coffee &c &c. each man would have 50 days provision, this without depending on resources in the enemy's country. The horses present the only objection & this is more in imagination than reality. Mr Bond from Illinois[1] & Mr. Greely of Michigan[2] both say, a horse in that country with a quart of Salt would live the winter & not be in low order if not hardly used. The tops of trees in all seasons furnish nourishing food for horses—these would be cut down daily for night fortifications—the grass in some places is green—in no place (if dry) is it deprived of its nourishing quality. Horses, therefore, that would be selected would perform a journey of 30 days, 25 miles a day without grain—from Fort Wayne, Mr. Greely says in the dead of Winter traders go to the Mississippi from Detroit & no provision is ever made for horses, but depend on the natural growth—this is without any calculation of a supply in the enemy's country—there is a quantity of corn in every village not already destroyed, particularly at Chicago & its vicinity—a number of Canadian French are here settled & with large farms—near lake Michigan on the St. Joseph at a Potawattamie village there is a quantity of corn, so at Masisinniway on the Wabash if not destroyed by a detachment from Genl. Harrison's army—so there is on the Illinois near a river called Fox river running into Illinois. In addition to this a horse will live 20 days upon 3 pints of corn per day the 4 first days & afterwards on one quart per Day—make a deposit of grain at St. Mary's or Fort Wayne, which could be done with ease, for 20 days. Each man could start from Fort Wayne with ten days forage for his horse & 30 for himself & no burthen, as the men would prefer to walk much to keep warm, unless in case of pursuing the enemy & forced marches. Another idea, 50 or 100 pack horses of grain to march with the army to lake Michigan 6 days, at which time dismiss the packs and take all the grain & food except what would carry the men to Fort Wayne—there would be no danger in the return to Fort Wayne—at the same time send back the *sicks*, the *broken dow(n)* the Sick & all incumbrances—our numbers would be lessened some little, but we should be in better condition as to force and provision, than at Fort Wayne. The rout through the enemy's country to be governed according to circumstances. From Fort Wayne 20 Beeves might be carried along to lessen the burthen of the horses without inconvenience 26 miles a day. The difficulties are now surmounted or if not the plan might be extended to very valuable purposes, in which case the whole force under Col. Russell and the Governors of the territories (the force in actual pay) might cooperate. By making deposits of forage and rations for 20 days at Fort Harrison & as high up the Illinois as would be safe with a company or two of rangers—the purchases to be made and the transportation to begin, the time fixed for the main army leaving fort Wayne. This would always be a sure fund to the army of mounted men—they would be in 6 or 8 days of forage & provisions, & if any part of the country should be left unexplored, the deposits at those places would enable the Campaign to go on again after dismissing the disabled, sick, worn down &c. as a less force would now be sufficient, the strong holds of the enemy being broken up. This is the outline, there are details not necessary to be entered into. Ten or 12 guides can be had whose fidelity will not be doubted, well acquainted with every foot of the Indian country. The campaign must be over by the 20t of March or first of April, or the waters of the Spring will make the country impassable for months. If the force should assemble too late it will furnish a valuable reinforcement to the North western army about that time lessened as it will be by the loss of the 4000 Kentucky volunteers.

The force here contemplated will be valuable if raised, not a minute ought to be lost. The proposition for this campaign has made the West rejoice. They expect something to be done. If the deposits should not be used by the mounted men, other troops will use them. The plan here presented in so many forms may be too complex and too expensive. It may be simplified in several particulars & perhaps it would be as well. 1t. all pack horses might be dispensed with, & also all deposits, giving the men one dollar a day to find themselves—here the expense will be lessened. 2d the deposits on the Illinois & Fort Harrison dispensed with, & if Colo Russell cooperated, he could pursue his rout in the same way, the men finding themselves at one dollar per day which is much the cheapest force.

The expence may be under 80,000$—it would not exceed 100,000—upon the plan in its extent. If successful how much more usefull than to keep troops inactive upon the frontiers.

Any verbal explanations will be given[3]

RH: M: JOHNSON

RC (DNA: RG 107, LRRS, J-386:6); FC (OCHP: Robert Clarke Papers). RC marked "a Copy"; addressed to "James Munroe / Sec: of State &c &c."; docketed by Monroe; docketed as received in the War Department on 26 Dec. 1812; a note on the cover reads: "Copy sent to Genl Harrison Decr. 26." FC in a clerk's hand, signed by Johnson; undated; a note in Johnson's hand at the foot of the final page reads: "A detailed outline of a Campaign submitted to the President of U. States By R M Johnson—submitted 10th or 15th of December." FC varies in wording from the RC. FC enclosed in Johnson to Robert B. McAfee, 4 June 1814 (OCHP: Robert Clarke Papers), in which Johnson noted that "the outlines of the proposition for a winter campaign" had been submitted to the president and the War Department, "out of which the authority to me to raise a mounted Regt arose."

1. Shadrach Bond (1773–1832) was born in Maryland and relocated to Kaskaskia, then in the Indiana Territory, in 1794. He was a member of the Indiana Territorial Legislative Council from 1805 to 1808 and was a delegate from the Illinois Territory to the Twelfth and Thirteenth Congresses, taking his seat on 3 Dec. 1812. He later became the first governor of Illinois, serving 1818–22 (Sobel and Raimo, *Biographical Directory of the Governors*, 1:365).

2. Aaron Greeley (d. 1820) was a surveyor of private land claims at Detroit from 1806 until his death (Carter, *Territorial Papers, Michigan*, 10:157 n. 49).

3. On 26 Feb. 1813 Johnson was authorized by the secretary of war to "organize and hold in readiness a Regiment of Mounted Volunteers" (DNA: RG 107, LSMA). His regiment of Kentucky militia commenced service under Harrison on 22 May, too late to implement this winter plan (Gilpin, *The War of 1812 in the Old Northwest*, 200).

From Charles Pinckney

DEAR SIR   IN COLUMBIA [ca. 10] December 1812

I wrote you the other day recommending to you a gentleman who will forward the letter[1]—since this as I stated to you we have on the 2d given to you an unanimous vote by our Electors[2] & North Caroline having done the same[3] fixes you in the Chair for 4 Years more on which Event I congratulate yourself & our Country—it is one I never had any doubt of but as there was a stir in some of the northern states, & attempts seriously made in North Carolina & ⟨e⟩xpected in this I thought it my duty (having been elected for Charleston) to attend the present session at Columbia—a Clintonian Emissary of some official consequence was here, but soon finding how vain any attempt would be, he departed. I lament extremely Mr. Clintons conduct, & view it as inexpressibly aggravated by the time & by its holding out to our Enemy the appearance of Division & disaffection as well to your administration, as to our Union & a belief that they are ready at any time to sacrifice their rights to the benefits of commerce.

I fear from what I have heard You are not in good health nor should I be surprised at it—the cares you have had & which must still surround you are sufficient to wear out the strongest constitution, & as neither you or myself are as young as when we formed the Constitution You must feel it more & the unexpected disasters at the commencement of our Land War must have increased your uneasiness. We look with anxiety to Canada & to the Ocean & to the difference of Opinion which will probably prevail in England when the intelligence of our Elections reaches them—to the first for the repair of our disasters & to the last for the return of peace under the conviction that our Enemy seeing all hope of succeeding by obtaining majorities in our councils at an end will yield to your reasonable propositions. I wrote to you some months agoe on the subject of General Joseph Alston[4]—that gentleman is this moment elected Governour of this state[5] & will of course have the honour to address you on the particular situation of this State: & its maritime frontier. With great regard & Esteem, & best wishes for your happiness & honour I am dear sir always Yours Truly

CHARLES PINCKNEY

Since writing the within we have heard of the capture of the Frigate Macedonia[6] on which I congratulate you & trust this & the guerriere will be the means of inducing Congress to increase our Vessels of War

RC (DLC). Docketed by JM. Dated December 1812 in the *Index to the James Madison Papers;* date assigned here on the basis of evidence presented in n. 5.

1. Letter not found.
2. For the presidential election in South Carolina, see Thomas Lehré to JM, 10 Nov. 1812, and n. 2.
3. For the elections in North Carolina, see JM to Jefferson, 14 Oct. 1812, and n. 8.
4. Letter not found.
5. Joseph Alston was elected governor of South Carolina on 10 Dec. 1812 and served until December 1814 (Sobel and Raimo, *Biographical Directory of the Governors*, 4:1393).
6. The British frigate *Macedonian* was captured by the *United States*, under the command of Stephen Decatur, on 25 Oct. 1812 between the Azores and the Cape Verde Islands (Dudley, *Naval War of 1812*, 1:548–49).

§ From Joseph Wheaton. *10 December 1812, Canton, Ohio.* Explains that he received an assistant deputy quartermaster's appointment on 10 Aug. 1812 [1] and was directed by the secretary of war on 14 Aug. to proceed to Pennsylvania to deliver commissions to three captains and the officers of three infantry companies who had tendered their services to JM "and to furnish those companies with funds instead of rations & transportation to enable them to reach the rendevous, their place of distination." [2]

Before he had completed this task, news of Hull's surrender reached him. Having had a full opportunity to learn the feelings of the people on the matter, he decided to await the secretary of war's further commands [3] and in the meantime to make himself useful. He stopped in Pittsburgh for some time, sending the secretary of war several letters from that place, [4] and he viewed troops of cavalry, infantry, and riflemen, which he also supplied, in addition to the first three companies he had been directed to supply and march. He also viewed for four weeks those who had tendered their services to the governor of Pennsylvania, as well as the drafted militia of that state that had assembled at Meadville and on the Allegheny River opposite Pittsburgh. Believed that the volunteer companies that had tendered their services to JM "would behave Some thing like Soldiers" because of the regard they expressed for JM and their zeal, and he "was led to Say much to the Secretary at war respecting them." However, several of those companies have exhibited conduct "indescribable base, by desertion, robbery—and every Species of disorder—those from the neighbourhood of Union Town Pa. particularly." But he has learned that Butler's [5] troops from Pittsburgh and Alexander's [6] from Greensburg are with General Harrison and have acquitted themselves well.

"The Brigaid which rendesvous'd at Meadville under Command of Genl. Tannehill [7] were little Short of an organised band of robbers—and those near Pittsburg commanded by Genl. Crooks were of the Same charecter and discription—and of the 2000 men which were to constitute each Brigade, I am persuaded—they cannot now muster twelve hundred each—that from all the concuring circumstances—of desertion robbery's disorderly & Mutinous conduct with waist of public property—together with the disgust given to the inhabitants, and the hard expressions levelled at yourself and the Secretary at war—it is Self evident that nothing substantial can be expected, or looked for, in this Species of troops—to say nothing of how much the Honor of the country is Shattered where ever they march."

Believes it would not become him to ask JM to recommend an additional 30,000 infantry regulars, but it is his opinion "that Such an encrease properly officered would Save Millions of expence to the nation—insure Success to every interprise, and create an additional Glory around your Head."

"The attention which the legislature has been called to give to the Soldiers compensation—If it could have been an increase of bounty to have induced the Soldier to inlist would have a most beneficial effect—but Sir Such are the habits of Soldiers—that experience has Shewn, that the less money he gets the better his health is preserved when he is well fed and cloathed—and consequently the more Service he renders to His country—because when he has money he will lay it out for ardent Spirrits and with it he will be intoxicated, confined, & punishd."

The ordnance and military stores in the care of Captain Gratiot [8] of the Corps of

Engineers and himself are on their way to General Harrison, from whom they had an express "this day" from Franklinton. "We were Obliged to halt at this place three days, to Shoe our horses, and to repair gun carriages and wagons which have received considerable injury from the very uncommon bad roads." These repairs will be completed in two days, and he expects "to reach Wooster on Wednesday." Hopes to reach Mansfield by Sunday. "The frost for three days past gives us hope of firmer roads."

RC (DLC). 3 pp.; marked *"Confidential"*; docketed by JM.

1. Eustis to Wheaton, 10 Aug. 1812 (DNA: RG 107, LSMA).
2. Eustis's 14 Aug. letter to Wheaton instructed him to proceed to Fayette and Huntington Counties, Pennsylvania, to supply transportation for the volunteer companies of Captains Thomas Collins, John Philips, and Robert Allison, who were to join the army at Niagara, New York (ibid.).
3. Wheaton wrote to Eustis on 27 Aug. to explain that news of Hull's surrender had reached him and that he had decided to delay directing the volunteer troops to Niagara on the assumption that new orders would be forthcoming to change their destination to Ohio (DNA: RG 107, LRRS, W-280:6).
4. Wheaton wrote to Eustis from Pittsburgh on 30 Aug., 10 Sept., and 15 Sept. 1812 to express his opinions on Hull's surrender, describe the formation of volunteer forces in the area, and urge acceptance of their offers of service (DNA: RG 107, LRRS, W-287:6, W-302:6, W-312:6).
5. James R. Butler was a captain in the Pittsburgh Blues (John H. Niebaum, "The Pittsburgh Blues," *Western Pennsylvania Historical Magazine* 4 [1921]: 112).
6. John Byers Alexander was captain of the Greensburg Rifle Company (ibid., 4:113, 122).
7. Adamson Tannehill (1750–1820) relocated from his native Frederick County, Maryland, to western Pennsylvania after serving in the Revolutionary War. He left his post as a brigadier general of the Pennsylvania militia in December 1812 to serve as a Republican in the Thirteenth Congress.
8. Charles Gratiot (d. 1855) received a captain's commission in 1808 and was promoted to the rank of major in 1815. A career army officer, he received a brevet brigadier general's commission in 1828 for meritorious service and general good conduct (Heitman, *Historical Register*, 1:470).

To Congress

WASHINGTON December 11th 1812

I transmit to Congress copies of a letter to the Secretary of the Navy,[1] from Captain Decatur[2] of the Frigate "United States," reporting his combat and capture of the British Frigate, Macedonian. Too much praise cannot be bestowed on that officer and his companions on board, for the consummate skill and conspicuous valour, by which this Trophy has been added to the naval arms of the United States.

I transmit also a letter from Captain Jones[3] who commanded the sloop of war, Wasp, reporting his capture of the British sloop of war the Frolic, after a close action, in which other brilliant titles will be seen, to the public admiration and praise.

A nation feeling what it owes to itself and to its Citizens, could never abandon to arbitrary violence on the ocean, a class of them, which give such examples of capacity and courage, in defending their rights on that Element: examples which ought to impress on the Enemy, however brave and powerful, a preference of Justice and Peace, to hostility against a country, whose prosperous career may be accelerated, but cannot be prevented by the assaults made on it.

JAMES MADISON

RC and enclosures (DNA: RG 46, President's Messages, 12A-E2). RC in the hand of Edward Coles, signed by JM. For enclosures, see nn. 1 and 3.

1. JM transmitted Decatur's 30 Oct. 1812 letter to Paul Hamilton, reporting his 25 Oct. capture of the British frigate *Macedonian* (3 pp.; printed in *ASP, Naval Affairs*, 1:280–81).

2. Stephen Decatur Jr. (1779–1820) entered the navy in 1798 as a midshipman. He rose quickly through the ranks and for his efforts in the Tripolitan War was rewarded with a captain's commission in 1804. Decatur's major achievement during the War of 1812 was the capture of the *Macedonian*, after which his ship, the *United States*, was blockaded in New London until the war's end. In March 1814 Decatur took command of the *President* in New York harbor, where he was in charge of naval defenses. On 15 Jan. 1815, after evading a pursuing squadron of British vessels off the Long Island coast and surviving a pitched battle with the *Endymion*, Decatur's ship was captured by the British squadron. A court of inquiry declined to censure him for the loss of the *President*. After brief service off the coast of Algiers, Decatur closed out his naval career on the Board of Navy Commissioners (Leonard F. Guttridge and Jay D. Smith, *The Commodores* [New York, 1969], 83, 202–4, 246, 264–66, 273, 281).

3. Jacob Jones's 24 Nov. 1812 letter to Paul Hamilton reported the capture of the British sloop *Frolic* on 18 Oct., a feat which was followed by the capture of the *Wasp* on the same day by the British ship *Poictiers* (3 pp.; printed in *ASP, Naval Affairs*, 1:281). Jones and his crew were then imprisoned in Bermuda. After being exchanged, Jones (1768–1850) was given command of the *Macedonian* and received a captain's commission in March 1813. In 1814 he commanded the *Mohawk* on Lake Ontario. Between 1815 and 1827 he held several positions overseas; he then served in a series of shore posts until his death (Callahan, *List of Officers of the Navy*, 301; J. Worth Estes, "Commodore Jacob Jones: A Doctor Goes to Sea," *Delaware History* 24 [1990]: 109–22).

From Albert Gallatin

DEAR SIR   Decer. 11. 1812

The enclosed letter[1] asserts positively that Hutchinson is warmly attached to the present administration. That from his connections & residence at Lisbon, he will be the most respectable & best appointment, I really believe. On those grounds, permit me once more to renew my application in his behalf. Cathcart is already placed, & will certainly give much less satisfaction to the commercial part of the community. He has no important political or mercantile connections. Respectfully Your obedt: Servt.

ALBERT GALLATIN

RC (DLC). Docketed by JM.

1. The enclosure was probably an unaddressed 9 Dec. 1812 letter from Joseph S. Lewis on behalf of Israel P. Hutchinson (DNA: RG 59, LAR, 1809–17, filed under "Hutchinson, Israel P."). JM nominated Hutchinson to be consul at Lisbon on 31 Dec. 1812 (*Senate Exec. Proceedings*, 2:313).

John G. Jackson to Dolley Payne Madison

MY DEAR SISTER   CLARKSBURG Decr. 11th 1812

I am again at Clarksburg after an absence of two months, worse than mispent in the western Country. I have not even the consolation to believe that any benefit has resulted to the community from my expedition, & therefore there is no offset for ⟨m⟩y in⟨di⟩vidual sacrifices of time & money. I left General Harrison at Franklinton about the 1st. instant & the Virginia troops at Delaware four or five days afterwards. After the maturest reflection I have formed the opinion that H will not be able to march his Army to Detroit this winter; the transportation is very tardy & the state of the roads so impassible that it is difficult to supply the respectiv⟨e⟩ detachments of the Army with provision at their various encampments. A few days before I left Genl. H he sent about 700 men principally mounted; to attack the Indians on the Wabash.[1] I determined with the *expressed* approbation of Genl. H and of Colo. Campbell[2] who commanded the expedition as well as Major Ball & Colo. Simmerell,[3] who went under him to accompany them, those officers invited me to partake of their tents &C & I had no doubt that they honestly felt the friendly dispositions they expressed towards me. Judge then of my surprise when I learned on the next day that Campbell & Ball signified to the Genl. that altho they felt well disposed towards me, and had no doubt that nothing would occur to interrupt that feeling, yet as theirs was a subordinate command & neither of them held the rank which I did, & altho I had no command, my *standing* was such as to induce a belief that whatever credit was acquired would be so divided as to assign a large share to me, & in so far diminish theirs. I never dreamt until this discovery that I would have to encounter a temper so illiberal—for I had supposed that in proportion as the characters commanded [. . .] conspicuous so would the credit of their commanders be enhanced, and as I had no command & would not assume any my case could not furnish an ex-

499

ception. They it seems reasoned differently, & by doing so presented an obstacle to my going further or remaining longer to my mind insurmountable and I resolved to return home. Genl. H *expressed a willingness* that I should be with him as a volunteer aid & said he would write me when he took up his line of march & I *could* then join him. On these terms we parted. I cannot say on retrospecting the conduct of the Genl. that I have any cause to be dissatisfied with it, & it may be that the letter which he shall write me will induce me to return to the army, having looked forward so long & determinately I dislike very much to abandon the enterprise. Altho I did not kill any of our enemies I was daily spilling the blood of the deer &c on my route. I carried my Rifle all the way threw away my cane & never enjoyed better health. I am now almost as strong as ever. I heard that Mr M had written me in answer to mine from Franklinton[4] but I never recd. his letter it was h⟨an⟩ded about so as never to reach me. I re⟨joice⟩ exceedingly that he has triumphed over Federalists, apostates, tories & all the combined crew of ⟨o⟩ppose⟨rs⟩. I have been much pressed to offer for Congress & if my services were of any value or my vote could influence the measures which I espouse I would consent to it but I have no faith in either; &, as at present inclined if I do not fight for my Country I shall stand aloof entirely. I saw John Payne at Franklinton acting as an assistant to the Q Master Colo Morrison. I hope & believe he will do well.

I enclose a letter to Mr. Forrest cant you get him to answer it, I have not been able to extract one line from him since I was at Washington.

We are all well & send you much love. Yours truly

J G JACKSON

RC (ViHi). Torn.

1. On 25 Nov. 1812 Harrison ordered Lt. Col. John B. Campbell to take action against Miami Indian villages along the Mississinewa River, part of the Wabash River system. Harrison believed that the inhabitants of those villages posed a danger to Winchester's supply routes. On 17 Dec., Campbell's forces arrived at a minor Miami village, attacked, and took prisoners. The following day Campbell's forces were themselves attacked. After an hour-long battle, they drove back the Indian forces with moderate casualties, successfully neutralizing the threat from that area (Harrison to Campbell, 25 Nov. 1812, and Campbell to Harrison, 18 Dec. 1812, in Esarey, *Messages and Letters of William Henry Harrison*, Indiana Historical Collections, 2:228–31, 248–49).

2. John B. Campbell of Virginia was serving as a lieutenant colonel in the Nineteenth Infantry Regiment in the fall of 1812. He was promoted by brevet to the rank of colonel on 18 Dec. 1812 for his efforts in the Mississinewa expedition and was killed at the Battle of Chippewa on 5 July 1814 (ibid., 2:179 n. 1; Heitman, *Historical Register*, 1:278).

3. Jackson referred to James Simrall (1781–1823), colonel of a regiment of Kentucky Light Dragoons (Esarey, *Messages and Letters of William Henry Harrison*, Indiana Historical Collections, 2:145 and n. 3).

4. Jackson probably referred to JM's 4 Nov. 1812 letter in reply to Jackson's of 21 Oct.

From Albert Gallatin

DEAR SIR   12 Decer. 1812

In support of the suggestions heretofore made against permitting Gen. Armstrong to raise a volunteer force on different principles from those recognized by law and adopted elsewhere, I enclose 3 advertisements from the late New York papers.[1]

Whilst such improper encouragement is given for a local force, it will be impossible to recruit for the army or for general purposes; and the general object of providing an efficient offensive force will be sacrificed to a local object. This mode also destroys the general plan of a local force, which is founded on the practicability of raising men to be paid only when employed or in proportion to their time of service. But here full pay &c. are promised for local services not to exceed 5 or 8 days in each month. This does indubitably secure at an enormous expence for Gen. A. all the force he wishes. But every other consideration of economy, uniformity, & even of the recruiting service, is sacrificed to that sole object. Respectfully Your obt. Servt.

ALBERT GALLATIN

RC (DLC). Docketed by JM.

1. For Gallatin's objections to Armstrong's plans, see his two letters to JM, ca. 19 Nov. 1812. Gallatin probably enclosed advertisements similar to one printed in the *New-York Evening Post* on 8 Dec. 1812, which called for six volunteers to perform local duty approximately five days per month for a $36 muster payment and $12 per month of regular pay.

From Elbridge Gerry

DEAR SIR,   CAMBRIDGE 12th Decr 1812

I am happy, extremely so, in the prospect of your re-election; for the reverse of this would, in my mind, have given to G Britain, a complete triumph over our most meritorious administration, & Legislature, & Would have been considered by her, & probably by all Europe, as a sure pledge of the Revocation of our Independence. If the issue of the Election should be such, as is here anticipated by all parties, I wish to be confidentially informed, whether the Senate (or new Congress) will be immediately convened, & how long it will probably be in Session.[1]

Accept my hearty gratulations on the repeated & brilliant success of our Navy; & my best wishes for your health & welfare. With the highest esteem & respect yours very sincerely

E. GERRY.

RC (DLC); FC (NjP). RC docketed by JM.

   1. The first session of the Thirteenth Congress convened on 24 May 1813 and adjourned on 2 Aug.

§ From Phineas Stevens.[1] *12 December 1812, Andover.* Informs JM that for five years he successfully commanded an infantry company that included Revolutionary War veterans before requesting and obtaining an honorable discharge two years ago because his command was incompatible with his business. Since the declaration of war, his acquaintances have urged him to join the army. Has complied with their request and in one week has enlisted forty volunteers for one-year terms. Expects to fill the company in the next twelve days. Encloses "the invitation to the Soldiers to enlist"[2] and, as he has set forth his feelings in that document, adds only that he offers his services "with diffidence . . . lest I should not be able to put in execution my good intentions." Recommends "Liet. Natht. Stevens for the second Liet. & Charles Cummings Ensighn." "The first Liet. is absent for . . . this reason I would defer the appointment untill his return." Asks for these commissions at this time because the company wishes "to randezvouze one or two months before we march for Canady in order that we may not appear inferior to any company & we would wish that we may Randezvouze in Adover [*sic*] untill after the first Monday in April in that we may have an opportun[i]ty to endeavour to prevent the same obstical being thrown in the way of the General Government by having the same executive we hav had this year by our Constitutional Right's." His company wishes "to know the sum each man is to recieve for his uniform & when & where we are to recieve our armes? & whether we may draw our pay & rations from the time we Randezvouze? And whether detatched hav not the liberty of enlistment?"

   RC and enclosure (DNA: RG 107, LRRS, S-491:6). RC 2 pp.; docketed as received in the War Department on 30 Dec. 1812. For enclosure, see n. 2.

   1. Phineas Stevens (1776–1844) was a millwright in Andover, Massachusetts (*Vital Records of Andover, Massachusetts, to the End of the Year 1849* [2 vols.; Topsfield, Mass., 1912], 1:350, 2:551).
   2. The enclosure is a one-page printed broadside entitled "To Men of Patriotism and Courage."

§ From Elkanah Watson. *12 December 1812, Pittsfield.* Is gratified to hear from Ezekiel Bacon that JM has received the "elegant Cloth" Watson manufactured for a coat. Believes that if double duties continue on fine cloth, New England will soon rival Great Britain "in that essential prop to that Sinking power." Though the recent state of things has generated in New England "a temporary and a lamentable predilection t'wards our enemies," he believes that [Jonathan] Russell's recent communications will "produce a re'action in the public mind, tending to Union, and a vigorous Support of national measures."[1]

   "The bearer Jos. Watson Esqr[2] my nephew has resided in the territory of Michigan about Six years; many of the principal Officers who resided at Detroit, have testified to me his exemplary deportment—his inteligence and great usefullness as a public officer. His singular & commanding influence among the Canadians of that

Country fully evinced by his Successfull exertions in withdrawing about 360 from the british Garrison at Malden as I have been credibly informed. He has shared largely in the misfortunes of the N. western Army, & altho' aid-du-Camp to Genl. Hull,[3] he was shamefully rob'd off [sic] all his property after the Surrender off Detroit. Confident of his integrity, abilities, and patriotism; I take the liberty to Solicit for him, the appointment of Sec[r]etary of the territory of Michigan.

"It is not his wish to prejudice the Claim of the late Sec[r]etary. He married the daughter of Judge Wetherel late off Detroit, & is anxiously waiting the issue of events to enable him to return to his former residence under some respectable appointment in the U. States Service.

"Permit me Sir to add—his intimate Knowledge of Michigan—his strict & faithfull attention to business—his perfect Knowledge of the French language by being educated in France; and in consideration off the Offices he has heretofore Sustained in that District—I trust will not fail haveing their merited weight in Supporting his Views and wishes."

RC (DNA: RG 59, LAR, 1809–17, filed under "Watson, Joseph"). 3 pp.

1. See JM to Congress, 18 Nov. 1812, and n. 1.
2. Joseph Watson served as secretary to the governor and judges of the Michigan Territory in 1808. JM nominated him to be a second lieutenant of infantry on 6 Mar. 1812. Watson declined the appointment but served as an aide to William Hull during his unsuccessful invasion of Upper Canada (Carter, *Territorial Papers, Michigan*, 10:256, 382, 424; *Senate Exec. Proceedings*, 2:226).
3. Above the line here in another hand is written, "as Commander in Chief of Michigan."

From Henry Dearborn

SIR, ALBANY Decemr. 13th. 1812

I confidently hope that the Campaign that has now closed, has afforded sufficient evidence of the necessaty of having a regular Army fully competent for all offensive opperations,[1] from fifteen to twenty additional Regiments, ought in my opinnion, to be raised North of the Potomack, what additional force will be necessary to the South, & west, I have found no opinnion. If an adaquate force could be raised in season, the latter part of February, or first of March, would be a favourable time to take possession of Montreal, It would not require a very large force to take possession of that place at that season, but we ought not to enter Canada with an Army that would not at all events be able to hold Montreal and the adjacent Country, against not only what force the Enemy could muster under present circumstancies, but such additional force as may arrive in May or June. I think we ought not to attempt more than we can with certainty accomplish, delay would be a serious evil, but defeat would be a much greater misfortune. I should think it more advisable to act on the defencive the next campaign, than to attempt more than the strength of our regular force would be fully competant to, my having volunteered the foregoing opinnions & remarks may be concidered as officious, but I must rely on the purity of my intentions as my only apology. I fear that the close of our Campaign will occasion some uneasiness, and probably much censure, I must expect my full share of it. I am not intirely satisfied with what has taken place at Niagara,[2] but I trust that on more particular information, It will appear that the measures were dictated by sound discretion, but unfortunately, the commanding officer has not been as popular as could have been wished—in relation to myself, I have expressed my sentiments in my last letter to the Secretary of War with frankness and candour.[3] It will be eaqually agreably [sic] to me, to imploy such moderate talents as I possess, in the service of my Country, or to be permited to retire to the shade of private life, and remain a mere, but interested, spectator of passing events. With sentiments of the highest respect I am Sir your Humbl. Servt.

H. DEARBORN

RC (DLC). Docketed by JM.

1. Dearborn's plans to launch a winter campaign against Montreal faltered due to poor road conditions, the unwillingness of some militia companies to cross the Canadian border, and sickness in the camp. Dearborn's final effort of 1812 was to give the appearance of an excursion into Lower Canada, as a diversion to aid western U.S. troops, and then to retreat into winter quarters. However, even this modest goal could not be reached without incident. While attacking an outpost at Lacolle Mill as part of this operation on 19 Nov. 1812, Col. Zebulon Montgomery Pike reported that his men were so overzealous and undisciplined that "the fire of the volenteers and ours was in a direction to endanger the lives of our own men" (Dearborn to Eustis, 24 Nov. 1812, enclosing Pike to Dearborn, 20 Nov. 1812 [DNA: RG 107, LRRS, D-254:6]).

2. On the Niagara Peninsula troops under Brig. Gen. Alexander Smyth had prepared to cross the Niagara River in force from his camp near Buffalo, New York. Smyth believed that 3,000 regulars, volunteers, and militia were ready to make the crossing, the number mentioned in his orders from Dearborn. On 27 Nov. he sent two parties across in advance, one to "capture a guard & destroy a bridge about five miles below Fort Erie" and the other "to take and render useless the Cannon of the enemies Batteries, and pieces of light Artillery." The first group took prisoners but did not destroy the bridge. The second group destroyed some enemy artillery but then in confusion brought all of the boats back, stranding Capt. William King and his men in Canada. King made the most of the situation, taking captives, destroying batteries, and finding boats to send the prisoners and some of his men across the river before he and his remaining troops were captured. However, this turned out to be the full extent of Smyth's invasion. On two occasions he called for a general embarkation but could not raise more than 1,500 troops for the crossing. He particularly noted that the number of regular troops was declining rapidly. He and his officers deemed it inexpedient to attempt the crossing under these conditions, and after the second failed embarkation on 1 Dec., Smyth called off the operation altogether, ordering that huts be constructed to house the regulars over the winter (Smyth to Dearborn, 4 Dec. 1812 [DNA: RG 107, LRRS, D-262:6]).

3. Dearborn's 11 Dec. 1812 letter to Eustis, enclosing Smyth's 4 Dec. report (see n. 2, above), expressed his view that "something like fatality has pervaded our military operations, through the course of this campaign." Expecting censure for the failure of military operations

in the East, he claimed to be happy to yield his command to someone more talented and popular (ibid.).

From John Graham

[ca. 14 December 1812]

In corroboration of what is stated in this Letter, it may not be improper to remark to the President that a Gentleman who was recently in this City from Caracas (Mr Picornell)[1] stated to Mr Thos Brent that Mr Scott[2] was held in some measure as a Prisoner and not permitted to carry on any corresp[ond]ence. This if true, accounts for the circumstance of no Letter having been received from him.

[Enclosure]

[Jacob Clement to James Monroe]

SIR,   PHILADA December 12th 1812

    I beg leave to acquaint you that I have received information from several sources of the condemnation at Laguira by the royal party of the american vessels employd by government to carry out their donation to the sufferers in that province by the earthquakes last spring.[3] Two vessels belonging to me were of the number, one of which was commanded by my son for whom I am extremely uneasy not having heard from him since June last. Notwiths[t]anding two vessels have arrived direct from these ungrateful people not a single letter has been received by them, by any American. And on inquiry I find they dare not bring an american as a passenger. I fear the crews of these vessels (and there must have been a number of them there[)] are suffering for the means of subsistance or immured in a Spanish prison. As the intercourse is in a measure stop'd and deprives those that would transmit succour to their freinds it would give them infinite pleasure if Government would despatch a small vessel for them. I am not much mistaken, when I say there is upwards of one hundred at Laguira & Porto Cavello. Be pleased sir to take the situation of these men under consideration and make it known to the President. If the President should Conclude to send for them I will cheerfully give my aid under the direction of Mr. Steel the collector as I feel more than common interest. I am sir with great respect your Most Obt Hbl Servt

JACOB CLEMENT[4]

RC and enclosure (DNA: RG 59, ML). RC unsigned; undated; date assigned here on the basis of the enclosure. A note in Monroe's hand on the cover of the enclosure reads: "For the President / Mr Clement / relative to vessels & men at Laguira."

1. Juan Bautista Mariano Picornell y Gomila (ca. 1759–1825) was born in Majorca and later moved to Madrid, where he became a teacher and writer. Influenced by Freemasonry, he participated in revolutionary activities against the Spanish monarchy, for which he was sentenced to death in 1796. His sentence was commuted to life imprisonment at La Guaira, but he escaped in 1797 and spent several years wandering around the Caribbean, continuing to conspire against Spanish authority in the New World. He returned to Venezuela after its declaration of independence in July 1811 only to flee to Philadelphia in July 1812. There he was to associate himself with José Álvarez de Toledo and his filibustering activities against Texas in 1813. After the failure of Toledo's plans at the Battle of Medina in August 1813, Picornell established himself briefly as the president of a provisional government in Mexico in 1814. He then renounced this position and sought reconciliation with the Spanish crown, which finally pardoned him in 1816. His last years were devoted to uncovering or suppressing revolutionary activities against the Spanish state (Harris Gaylord Warren, "The Early Revolutionary Career of Juan Mariano Picornell," *Hispanic American Historical Review* 22 [1942]: 57–81; Warren, *The Sword Was Their Passport* [1972 reprint], 56, 58, 84–89, 113–14, 131).

2. Alexander Scott was sent by the U.S. to Caracas, Venezuela, in the spring of 1812 to administer foreign aid. He arrived in La Guaira on 27 June 1812 and reported to Monroe in a 16 Nov. 1812 letter that the country was in a "deplorable state," its cities and agriculture destroyed by severe earthquakes while Francisco de Miranda's "republicans" fought unsuccessfully against royalist forces. Scott also reported widespread anti-American sentiment in Venezuela. Domingo Monteverde, the royalist general, seized some of the five U.S. vessels that transported the flour and corn for Venezuelan relief and then sold the donated goods at inflated prices. Scott and Robert K. Lowry, the U.S. consul at La Guaira, eventually secured the release of the vessels. By December 1812 all American citizens residing in Venezuela were ordered to leave the country. At the request of Venezuelan officials, in January 1813 Scott and Lowry were ordered to leave the country within forty-eight hours. Denied permission to land at Curaçao, they stayed at Puerto Cabello, Venezuela, until they were able to return to Washington in May 1813 (DNA: RG 59, CD, La Guaira; James Johnston Auchmuty, *The United States Government and Latin American Independence, 1810–1830* [London, 1937], 32–33, 34–35; Bierck, "The First Instance of U.S. Foreign Aid: Venezuelan Relief in 1812," *Inter-American Economic Affairs* 9 [1955]: 47, 52, 54–58).

3. For the humanitarian aid that Congress authorized for Venezuela, see *PJM-PS*, 4:349 nn. 1 and 2.

4. In 1813 Jacob Clement was listed in the Philadelphia city directory as a merchant on Water Street (Paxton, *Philadelphia Directory and Register for 1813* [Shaw and Shoemaker 29456]).

§ From the Tammany Society of Cincinnati. *14 December 1812*. "The Tammany society belonging to Wigwam No. 3 in the State of Ohio, at this time deem it their duty (as freemen and Republicans) to express to you their Chief Magistrate, their opinions and feelings as they relate to the present crisis in our National affairs. They are Sir induced to this course most particularly, from the hostile spirit and want of unanimity; which we learn through the medium of Newspapers exists and prevails among our Eastern Brethren, on the subgect [*sic*] of the just and necessary War in which we are engaged. War we conceive to be a calamity; but nevertheless we do think that there are cases and situations, which will justify that measure and require the energies and valour of the nation to be brought into action in its support. We do humbly conceive that if ever such a period did arrive in the affairs of a nation, it had arrived with us, from the aggressions & unprincipled conduct of Great Britain, in her relations with these United States—a Conduct without precedent in the history and laws of civilized Nations—a conduct founded on no principle of Justice and supported only by arrogance of superior power and prowess in war—a conduct which if pusillanimously submitted to by us would shortly annihilate us from the list of Nations, by destroying our commerce, imprisoning and making vassals of our brave Tars and the destruction of our frontier brethren by the savage tomahawk and scalping knife. We then Sir, although but a small part, of the great community of the Union, do claim our right to make it fully known to you that we approve of the War in which we are engaged and of an energetic prosecution of it. That we do think abundant cause had existed for years past for the commencement of such a state of things and that our forbearance has been construed by our enemies to arise from fear & want of spirit. We Sir cordially approving of the acts of our Representatives in placing the Nation in an attitude to resent & resist the injuries which she has long suffered under, do solemnly pledge our lives and property in the defence and support of so necessary a measure. Signed on behalf and by order of the Society."

RC (DLC). 3 pp.; signed by Daniel Symmes, grand sachem, and Thomas Henderson, secretary.

¶ To James Dinsmore. Letter not found. *Ca. 14 December 1812.* Offered for sale in the American Art Association Catalogue, 2–3 Dec. 1926, item 331, where it is described as an "Autograph Letter Signed . . . franked, December 14, 1812, . . . regarding an account."

From Tench Coxe

SIR   PURVEYOR'S OFFICE ROOM Decemr. 16th. 1812.

It is only from a desire to reserve from the public files of the war department an application, which might wear the appearance of complaint, where none is intended, that I have ventured to do my self the honor to address the requests in this letter to you.

In the week preceding the cessation of my operations as Purveyor, I made applications to the war department for the name of an officer authorized to receive all public property and all things, which I ought to deliver, from me within the time fixed by law: and for the means of settling my accounts, for which clerkship and funds were necessary.[1] From the state of the service, the refusal of the Commissary general's office by several, the non appointment of a deputy here, the nature of the times, the urgent request of the Secretary of war, and from my own sense of duty, I continued to act with the utmost energy in my power in the business of the supplies till 11 O'Clock at Night on the 31st. of May.

The manner in which the late depy. Commissary Mr. Mifflin construed or attended to the letter written to him by the Secretary of War[2] in regard to the books and papers necessary to settle my accounts, and in regard to giving me access to the books, accots. and other papers prevented me from obtaining any of the means to settle my accounts during his life, which unhappily terminated in the latter part of August. Three months were thus lost, tho' I attended every day in this room with one clerk, and had another ready at my call, for some time. I ought to have mentioned, Sir, that the delivery of all the public property in my hands, including my books, letters, receipts, contracts and other papers, were all made by order of the Secretary of War, in the end of may, to John McKinney Esqre., who, I believe, delivered the whole on the 1st. or 2d. of June to Mr. Mifflin. I offered personally or by letter to all the officers of the new department every aid and facility in my power and gave the same in numerous cases to a great amount with the utmost promptitude, as my letters and theirs will shew.

When Mr. Irvine the Commissary General was appointed, I applied to him for the necessary papers and got so many as quickly to settle the ordinary and principal accounts down to the 31st. of may.

But a difference of opinion, as to the settlement of the accounts of certain agents, whom I was instructed to employ in other places, existed in the mind of the Secretary of war (whose instructions I thought it my duty to respect, as if I were still in office) and the accountant of the war department, who is clothed with certain powers under the laws. The latter explicitly and urgently required me to settle with the Agents, and then to settle (so as to include those settlements) with him, to which I had no objection. But I could not obtain the use of the Agents accot's. nor even the sight of them. The Secretary of war had considered it not inconvenient that those Agents, should settle with Mr. Mifflin Dy. Cy. or Mr. Irvine Commy. Genl. after his death. *This constitutes one of the points,* upon which I do myself the honor to request that you would be pleased to cause proper order to be taken, as there is a vacancy in form, in the department of war. I beg leave to observe that it will be particularly comfortable to me, if Mr. Monroe and Mr. Eustis will be so good as to bestow their personal or official consideration upon this subject, as I perceive they are both said to have a present relation to the war department.

From the omission to grant one extra clerk to the Purveyor's office for 1811 tho' recommended by the two Secretaries of War and until late in the first quarter of 1812, the gentlemen employed assured me they were unable to keep the books up with the course of my operations. I believe they were unable. This fact, the extreme and increasing urgency of supplies, the difficulties of purchase before the Amelia Island goods and the late goods arrived and other circumstances render it particularly a duty from me to the United States, the sellers and contractors, my sureties and myself that I should have the books carefully revised, completed & settled. To omit it would be imprudent, dangerous and perhaps very injurious to some of those persons or parties. The Secretary of war, in July I think, authorized my freest admission to the books & papers in a letter to the deputy Commissary Mr. Mifflin. As that letter is now among the papers handed over by Mr. Mifflin's family to Mr. Irvine Commy. genl. I applied in writing to the latter. But to my first application, Mr. Irvine returned an answer declining the permission, as, in his opinion, unnecessary.

I wrote a second letter to him some weeks ago and added to the general and official reasons, that I had a cause pending in court in preparing for which examination of my official books and papers was necessary. To this second letter Mr Irvine has not replied.

The cause was marked for trial at a Nisi Prius[3] sitting of one of the Judges of our Supreme Court from the 30th. of Novemr. to the 12th of Decr. It fortunately happened, that the cause was not quite reached. It was very painful to me, that, by advice of eminent counsel, I was obliged to prepare a deposition stating the facts and declaring, that I could not go safely to trial without an opportunity to inspect my late office papers. My feelings were however saved, for I kept the deposition in reserve between my counsel and myself, and the cause went off for the time. It will soon come up again and is about the 3d or 4th. on the list. Such a deposition concerning an officer, who, in truth, succeeds me, would be very uncomfortable and of ill effect.

These circumstances present the second point of my request, which is that the officer (Mr. Irvine) who at present holds the Books and papers of the late Purveyor's office, which relate to my time from August 1803 to June 1. 1812, may be instructed to let me have free access to them from time to time, as I may find such access necessary.

I never refused such access to any person, having apparent reason; and the case has several times occurred.

The correct settlement of public accounts and the promotion of justice being matters, which cannot fail to engage your general good wishes, I trust Sir, that my requests will be granted: and I beg permission to add, that I feel a sincere and respectful confidence, that any thing which may do me a right without occasioning any other person a wrong will not be unsatisfactory to you. I have the honor to be with perfect respect, Sir, Your most obedient Servant.

TENCH COXE

RC (DNA: RG 107, LRRS, C-558:6); draft (PHi: Tench Coxe Papers). RC in a clerk's hand, signed by Coxe; docketed as received in the War Department on 30 Dec. 1812.

1. Coxe probably referred to his letters to Eustis of 24 and 27 May 1812, which touched upon these subjects (DNA: RG 107, LRRS, C-308:6, C-312:6).

2. Eustis's 30 June 1812 letter to Mifflin stated that Coxe should be allowed "every facility of reference to the Books and papers in your possession, appertaining to the late Office of Purveyor of public Supplies, for the purpose of enabling Mr. Coxe to Settle his accounts" (DNA: RG 107, LSMA).

3. "The *nisi prius* courts are such as are held for the trial of issues of fact before a jury and one presiding judge" (*Black's Law Dictionary* [6th ed.], 1047).

From Henry Dearborn

SIR,   ALBANY Decemr. 16th. 1812.

Permit me to observe that I concider it of the utmost importance that improvements should be effected as soon as may be in the Staff Departments of the Army, and especially in that of the Quartr. Mastr. Genl. and it is indispen[s]able that the Q, M, G, should be a real man of business, in addition to good talents, general information & integrity, he should be habitually industrious, energetic & prompt, in the descharge of the important duties of the office, and should possess a capacity for inspiring all his under officers with zeal & activity, in short a Q, M. G should see every thing, anticipate every thing, so as to be prepared at all times, as far as humane foresight will admit, for every emergency. Many Gentlemen may be very well qualified for a Genl. officer in the line, who would not be well qualified for the office of Q. M. G. I most sincerely wish that Genl. Lewis, who I have a great respect for, might be satisfactorily provided for in the line, he would like the change, and if several additional Majr. Genl. should be appointed he would be a prominent candidate for one of them. I am not personally acquainted with any Gentlemen who I think as well qualified for the place of Q, M. G as Genl. Wim. King[1] of Massachusetts, and I most ardently hope that he, or some other Gentleman eaqually well qualified will be appointed to that important office. It will be impracticable to carry on another Campaign, without great improvements in the Q M——s Department, and such a change as I have alluded to, might undoubtedly be made to very great advantage to the public service.

On mature reflection I have concidered it my duty to observe, as my deliberate opinnion, that measures ought to be taken without delay, for raising such an additional regular force North of the Potomack and on the Ohio as would, with those already authorised by law, amount to 30,000. men to be apportioned on the several States nearly as follows,

Ohio	1300	Connecticut	1 300
Kentuckey	2000	Rhode Island	400
Maryland	2000	Massachusetts	5 500
Deleware	200	New Hampshire	1 600
Pennsylvania	6000	Vermont	1 500
Jersey	1200		10 300
New York	7000		19 700
	19700		30,000

What additional force may be necessary to raise South of the Potomack, I have not concidered. To raise the force I have proposed, will require only one thirteenth part of the enrolled Militia of the respective States, or five men from each Company of Militia consisting of 75 men, and if so very small a proportion of our Countrymen cannot be induced to enter the Army, we ought not to think of prosicuting a war with a view to any Offencive opperations, nor indeed, any war whatever. I have concidered it my duty to express to you Sir, the foregoing opinnions, and I cannot but hope that you may concider it expedient to urge on Congress the absolute necessaty of being prepared for prosicuting the war with such effect, as will command a speedy & honourable peace. I am fully persuaded that a *strong* message to Congress, urging the propriety of raising a large additional regular force, would have a desirable effect in several respects, and that it is generally expected, and by your best friends concidered necessary. I must beg you Sir, to excuse the freedom with which I have expressed my sentiments & opinnions, I am persuaded you will not impute to me other than honest motives. With sentiments of the highest respect I am Sir your Obedient Servant

H. DEARBORN

RC (NN: Monroe Papers).

1. William King (1768–1852), half-brother of Rufus King, was a successful merchant and shipbuilder in Bath, Maine. He was a representative to the Massachusetts General Court in 1795 and 1803–6 and to the state senate in 1807–8. A militia major general, he received a colonel's commission in the U.S. Army on 18 July 1813, serving in the adjutant general's office. King took an active role in the movement to separate Maine from Massachusetts and served as Maine's first governor, 1820–21 (Sobel and Raimo, *Biographical Directory of the Governors*, 2:595; Hamersly, *Complete Regular Army Register of the U.S.*, 87).

§ From Jacob Kimball and Others. *16 December 1812, "Bridgeton (Maine)."* Explain that under the direction of J. D. Learned[1] they have been recruiting volunteers to be organized into a regiment. As soon as five companies had been filled, "several others being then in forwardness," the captain and subalterns thought it proper to recommend field officers and accordingly did so. "Soon after this had been done certain individuals . . . men who had no connection with, or right to interfere in this business; men who had never offered the least assistance to their country in raising this regiment; men who during the Presidential contest, while the Clintonian faction raged, never dared open their lips in behalf of their bleeding country, (for reasons well understood) stepped forth & have recommended one Robert Ilsley to command this corps, a man who has never turned on his heel to assist volunteering; a man who is not known in this transaction & one in whom we cannot have confidence; and this too in a way, & by a series of measures which we deem neither honorable or Just. We would not be understood to dictate to the Executive, but we trust that your Excellency will not deem it presumptive for us to recommend the officers to be placed immediately over us, men in whom we have the highest confidence, and to pray your Excellency so far to consult the feelings of a patriotic corps of volunteers as to allow them to remonstrate with effect against the appointment of others, either unknown to them or in whom they have no confidence."

RC (DNA: RG 107, LRRS, C-16:7). 2 pp.; signed by Capt. Jacob Kimball and eight others; docketed as received in the War Department on 18 Jan. 1813.

1. On 18 Feb. 1813 JM nominated Joseph D. Learned to be colonel of the Thirty-fourth Infantry Regiment (*Senate Exec. Proceedings*, 2:325, 326; Heitman, *Historical Register*, 1:621).

§ From the Pennsylvania General Assembly. *16 December 1812.* "Viewing the present state of our foreign relations We with astonishment and regret behold the Emperor of the French withholding from our Country those indemnifications which ought to have been rendered with liberality and promptness. After the Aggressions of Great Britain had by long continued practice been regarded by her Government as right—After the forebearance of the American Government had assumed the appearance of Cowardice; War, is reluctan[t]ly—unavoidably, but decisively declared. Animated by the most sincere love of peace, the President of the United States in the same dispatch announces to the British Government the existence of War; and the equitable easy and honorable means by which its progress might be arrested, and its calamities permanently prevented; but this extraordinary proof of a humane and pacific disposition is treated with contempt, familiarized with the slaughter of Man around the Globe the British Government prefers the effusion of human blood to a suspension of the inhuman practice of impressment, even during the short space of an armanstice agreed on for the purpose of negociating a just and honorable peace—Nay, notwithstan[din]g the offer made by the Government of the United States to exclude British subjects from our Merchantmen and navy. But what atrociti⟨es⟩ are too enormous to be found in that Government, whose Characteristical features are cruelty & perfidy, which stimulates the savage to drench his tama hawk and scalping knife in the blood of our frontier men, Women and infants, which making the most solemn professions of friendship and peace strives by the Malignant breath of its secret em⟨is⟩saries to kindle in our nation dissatisfaction, discord, rebellion and Civil War with all their Sanguinary and horrible consequences. Thus is extinguished in the American Government, and every American bosom, the last hope of finding in the conduct of Great Britain toward the United States a single voluntary Act of Justice or humanity. . . .

"Resolved that the declaration of War against . . . Great Britain . . . was the result of solemn deliberation, sound Wisdom and imperious necessity.

"Resolved, that the sword being drawn should never be sheathed till our wrongs are redressed— our Commerce unfettered, and our Citizens freed from the danger of British impressment— of imprisonment in the floating dungeons of the British Navy, and the painful necessity of fighting the battles of an inveterate enemy, against their fathers—their brethren—their native Country and their friends."

Resolved that it is the duty of every citizen "to exert all the energies of his body and of his mind, and to devote his property to bring the existing War to a speedy, just and honorable issue, and to teach our insolent foe, that the Americans are as free from timidity and weakness in battle as from covert and disguise in negociating."

Resolved that they contemplate with regret the refusal of some state executives to furnish, at the president's request, "their quota of Militia for the defence of the sea coast" and that they confidently expect Congress to give this matter its prompt attention.

"Resolved that the promptness and the Zeal with which the Governor of this Commonwealth executed the military orders of the President since the commencement of hostilities entitle him to the gratitude of this General Assembly of Pennsylvania and of the nation.

"Resolved that the Governor of this Commonwea⟨lth⟩ be instructed to transmit a Copy of these resolutions to the President . . . with a request that he communicate them to Congress."

RC, two copies (DNA: RG 233, President's Messages, 12A-D1; DNA: RG 46, President's Messages, 12A-E2). First RC 4 pp.; in a clerk's hand, including the signatures of John Tod, Speaker of the Pennsylvania House of Representatives, and P. C. Lane, Speaker of the state senate. Notes at the foot of the last page add that the memorial was read and adopted in the state senate on 10 Dec. and in the state house of representatives on 16 Dec., as attested by Joseph A. McJimsey, clerk of the senate, and George Heckert, clerk of the house. Certified as a true copy by N. B. Boileau, secretary, on a separate sheet. The memorial was transmitted to Congress by JM on 30 Jan. 1813 (ibid.; 1 p.). Printed in *ASP, Miscellaneous,* 2:203.

§ From Marinus Willett. *16 December 1812, New York.* Requests JM's "Indulgence to the talk of an Old Soldier." "It is not however a little humiliating while I use this appelation as a claim to Indulgence when I reflect on the conduct of some of my old Cotemporaries who have been invested with Command in the late Campaign. Imbecility a want of decition and unsolderly Conduct has marked their proceedings and made our first Campaign an Inglorious one." Does not censure the measures pursued by the government but notes that there is "a great contrast . . . between them and the measures of the first Campaign in our revolutionary war." "The want of all the munitions for war at that time require no Illustration, they are known to every body, yet, with the very small means we had, much was effected, System, Spirit and energy pervaded our movements; Permit me to Illustrate this assertion by events in which I was engaged. On the 28th of June 1775 I received a Captains Commission in the first New York regiment, on the 8th of August I embarked with three other Companies of the same regiment Compleatly equipt Clothed and furnished with tents. The Musquets and Bayonets with which we were armed were taken from the 18th British regiment who were quartered in this city at the time the battle of Lexington was fought. On the sixth of September we landed at St Johns in Canada, accompanied with a regiment from Connecticut and a few other troops making in the whole about 1000, under the Command of generals Schuyler and Montgomery. And Shortly after having received some small reinforcments the Garrison at that place was regularly Invested. The scarcness of ammunition obliged us to be very sparing of our powder and shot, Untill by a well executed enterprise a small Fort at Chambly Commanded by Major Stopford[1] with part of the Seventh British regiment was taken, which put us in possession of amunition sufficient to enable us to advance our approach and increas our fire so as to obtain the Surrender of the Garrison at St Johns on the third of November, The effect of this Surrender was the possession of Montreal and all the Country from thence down to Quebeck. What a Contrast is here to the first Campaign we have made which appears a series of blunders mistakes and want of decition. The question now is how to improve these missdoings. The want of experience has no doubt been one cause of our missfortunes. That the few old officers who have been employed Justify the Conclution that they are not equal to the trust they have had or their experience Joined to requisite tallents would have opperated more to the advantage of their Country. A new Commander in Chief is most Indubitably essential, And if we look at the atchievments of our little Navy all of which have been performed by Young men, they become powerfull lessons to Instruct us in the propriety of having the young blood of our Country sought after to lead our Soldiers as well as our Saylors to Glory. In the selection of these materials, all distingtions but those of Patriotism, spirit Courage and skill are to be disregarded." Believes there are plenty of men of this description "who if properly selected and encouraged will vie for the palm of Glory with the Young Gentlemen of our Navy." Because the war "has become serious and will probably last long, a perminent regular well deciplined army is Essential." The selection of officers for this army is important. "One good officer can do a great deal, But poor dull Cowardly officers are a Curs to the army." Mentions Samuel Swartwout,[2] the son of a captain in his Revolutionary War regiment, whom he believes "will be equal to General Wain in spirit and enterprise and superiour to him in understanding." Ordered Swartwout to the attention of the secretary of war "last winter,"[3] but objections were made to him because of his previous connection with [Aaron] Burr. Believes it "is not to be thought strange" that a young man should have been led astray by Burr, nor should this circumstance "by any means . . . prevent his Country from receiving the benefit of his services." "I am satisfied his heart is pure, With a mind that thirsts for fame and a spirit suited to stand forth in his Countrys defence." Mentions that Swartwout has a brother,[4] who was in command on Staten Island while the militia were stationed there. "He is now employed in raising a Volunteer regiment at this place and Contemplates having his Brother Samuel for his Lieutenant Colonel. Samuel is at present in the Volunteer service at Niagary. My hearty wish is to see both these Brothers in the perminent Army. Neither of them know any thing of this address in their favour."

RC (DLC). 4 pp.; docketed by JM.

1. Maj. Joseph Stopford was in command of the Seventh British Regiment at Chambly in 1775 (*A List of the General and Field-Officers, As They Rank in the Army* [Dublin, 1775], 15, 61).

2. Samuel Swartwout (1783–1856), son of Abraham Swartwout, was arrested, tried, and acquitted as an accomplice to Aaron Burr in 1807. During the War of 1812 he served as a militia captain. From 1829 to 1838 he was collector for the port of New York, but upon his leaving office his accounts were reported to be in arrears by more than a million dollars. Swartwout traveled to England in hopes of raising funds to settle the accounts, but he ultimately avoided prosecution only by surrendering his personal property in the U.S. (B. R. Brunson, *The Adventures of Samuel Swartwout in the Age of Jefferson and Jackson* [Lewiston, N.Y., 1989], iii, 1–5, 28, 44, 59, 159–80).

3. A 21 Dec. 1811 letter from Willett, recommending Samuel Swartwout for a military appointment, was received by the secretary of war on 26 Dec. 1811 (DNA: RG 107, Registers of Letters Received by the Secretary of War).

4. Robert Swartwout (d. 1848) was a New York merchant and militia colonel who received a brigadier general's commission and replaced Morgan Lewis as quartermaster general on 21 Mar. 1813 (Risch, *Quartermaster Support*, 153; Heitman, *Historical Register*, 1:939).

§ From James Monroe. *Ca. 17 December 1812*. Lists proposed appointments in the U.S. Army from North Carolina, Pennsylvania, New Hampshire, Virginia, Vermont, Ohio, New York, South Carolina, Connecticut, Delaware, and Tennessee.

Letterbook copy (DNA: RG 107, LSP). 1 p.; undated; date assigned here on the basis of JM's letter dated 18 Dec. 1812 submitting these appointments to the Senate (*Senate Exec. Proceedings*, 2:312).

§ From Marinus Willett. *17 December 1812, New York*. After sending his letter to JM to the post office "Yesterday," was informed that Samuel Swartwout had arrived from Niagara. "I called to see him but had little opportunity of talking with him, from what little I heard it appeared, that the health of the troops at that place is not properly attended to." Swartwout informed him that he was going to Washington with dispatches for the secretary of the navy. Wishes JM "would take some opportunity of Conversing with Mr Swartwout while he remains at Washington." Also learned that Col. Robert Swartwout has gone to Washington. Reminds JM that he is acquainted with Willett's opinion of these men. "I therefore need not repeat to you how much I wish that they may be placed in the perminent army." Believes they will "do honor to their Country."

RC (DLC). 1 p.; docketed by JM.

§ From the Kentucky Legislature. *Ca. 18 December 1812*. "The Legislature of Kentucky fully impressed with the importance of Unanimity amongst the several States Composing the Union, On the Subject of the War we are engaged in with Great Brittain, believing that at no time, since the revolution, which established our Glorious independence, has there been a Crisis so eventful as the Present, deem it Proper to declare to their Sister States to the General Government, to our Enemies, and to the World, their Own sentiments, and those of the State they represent. Wherefore; Resolved, that we are firmly convinced that the Government of the United States has been forced into the Present War with Great Brittain by a long Series of unprovoked injuries and injustice, by a pertinacious adherence to Claims which no independent Nation ought to Submit to, And in our Opinion the Government of these States would have manifested a Culpable neglect of the dearest rights of the People, and have abandoned the high trust committed to its charge, if the Power of the nation had not have been called into resistance by War. 2. Resolved, that the State of Kentucky is prepare⟨d⟩ to contribute whatever of her strength, shall be required for the vigorous and effectual Prosecution of this war, to the Attainment of an honorable peace, founded upon the recognition of our rights and indemnity for past injuries.

"3. Resolved, that our confidence in the General Government is unshaken, And we view with abhorrence the attempts of some who call themselves Americans to weaken the confidence of the People in the Constitutional Authorities, and inspire our enemies with the hopes of disunion."

Resolve to send copies of these resolutions to the president and the Kentucky delegation in Congress.

RC (DLC). 1 p.; in a clerk's hand, including the signatures of Joseph H. Hawkins, Speaker of the Kentucky House of Representatives, and Richard Hickman, Speaker of the state senate. Undated; date assigned here on the basis that the resolutions were adopted by the house of representatives on 11 Dec. and approved by the senate on 18 Dec. (*Journal of the Senate, of the Commonwealth of Kentucky* [Frankfort, Ky., 1812; Shaw and Shoemaker 28871], 32–33, 57–58). A note at the foot of the page reads: "Approved Decr. 22d 1812 / Isaac Shelby."

From Elbridge Gerry

Dear Sir,   Cambridge 19th Decr 1812

I had the honor on the 12th, to address a line to you, requesting information whether there probably will be a Session of Congress or of the Senate on the 4th of march next, & if so, of what duration? The principal object of this enquiry was to ascertain, in case of the success of the republican ticket for President & Vice President, & of no Session of Congress, or of the Senate on the day mentioned whether it will be requisite for the latter officer to take a journey of five hundred miles, in february, merely for the purpose of being inaugurated to office?[1] The Constitution & laws of the UStates, I believe, are silent on the subject, & if an administration of the Oath by a federal Judge in a public manner is admissible, it will save a journey out & home of a thousand miles; a species of amusement, which few are fond of, at an inclement season. Any indulgence incompatible with rule, or the public interest, is not expected; & such as is consistent with reason, will undoubtedly be readily adopted. Accept dear Sir the highest esteem & respect of your very sincerely

E. Gerry

RC (DLC); FC (MHi: Elbridge Gerry Papers). RC docketed by JM.

1. On 4 Mar. 1813 Gerry became vice president, taking the oath of office at Elmwood, his Massachusetts estate (George Athan Billias, *Elbridge Gerry: Founding Father and Republican Statesman* [New York, 1976], 135, 324).

From James Monroe

DEPT. OF STATE Decr. 19th. 1812.

The Secretary of State to whom was referred the Resolution of the House of Representatives of the 9th. Instant,[1] requesting information touching the conduct of British Officers towards persons taken in american armed Ships, has the honor to lay before the President the accompanying papers marked A. B. C.[2] from which it appears that certain persons, some of whom are said to be native, and others naturalized Citizens of the United States, being parts of the Crews of the United States armed Vessels the "Nautilus" and the "Wasp" and of the private armed Vessel the "Sarah Ann," have been seized under the pretext of their being british Subjects, by british Officers for the avowed purpose, as is understood, of having them brought to trial for their lives, and that others being part of the Crew of the Nautilus, have been taken into the British service.

The Secretary of State begs leave also to lay before the President the papers marked D & E.[3] From these it will be seen, that whilst the british Naval Officers arrest as criminals such persons taken on board american armed Vessels as they may consider british Subjects, they claim a right to retain on board british Ships of War american Citizens who may have married in England or been impressed from on board british Merchant Vessels—and that they consider an impressed American when he is discharged from one of their Ships, as a Prisoner of War. All which is respectfully submitted.

JAS MONROE

RC and enclosures (DNA: RG 233, President's Messages, 12A-D1). RC in a clerk's hand, signed by Monroe. Transmitted to the House of Representatives by JM in a letter dated 21 Dec. (ibid.; 1 p.; in the hand of Edward Coles, signed by JM) and referred to the committee on foreign relations on 28 Dec. (*Annals of Congress*, 12th Cong., 2d sess., 438–40). For enclosures, see nn. 2 and 3.

1. On 9 Dec. 1812 the House of Representatives had approved a resolution offered by Nathaniel Macon of North Carolina that "the President of the United States be requested to cause to be laid before this House any information which may be in his possession touching the conduct of British officers towards persons taken in American armed ships" (ibid., 351).

2. The enclosures marked "A" include an extract (1 p.) from F. H. Babbitt to William M. Crane, 13 Sept. 1812, enclosing a list (1 p.) of U.S. seamen who voluntarily went into British naval service and promising a list of those involuntarily taken to Great Britain under suspicion of being British subjects; John Borlase Warren to Monroe, 30 Sept. 1812 (2 pp.), complaining that twelve British seamen who had been taken prisoner off the *Guerrière* were being held contrary to an exchange agreement; and Monroe to Warren, 28 Oct. 1812 (1 p.), promising an investigation of Warren's charges. The enclosure marked "B." is George S. Wise to Paul Hamilton, 17 Dec. 1812 (1 p.), forwarding a list (1 p.) of twelve U.S. seamen taken from the *Wasp* by John Beresford, captain of the British ship *Poictiers*, under suspicion of being British subjects. The enclosure marked "C." is Thomas Pinckney to William Eustis, 4 Nov. 1812

517

(1 p.), explaining that Charles Grandison, commander of naval forces at Charleston, had informed him that six U.S. seamen who were taken off a U.S. privateer by the British had been transported to Jamaica and tried for treason as British subjects. Pinckney informed Eustis that in response Grandison had requested that the marshal retain twelve British seamen. The marshal had sought Pinckney's advice on this point, and it was Pinckney's opinion that the prisoners should be detained until JM's views were known. Pinckney enclosed a 14 Oct. 1812 letter from Richard Moon, commander of the U.S. privateer *Sarah Ann*, describing the six prisoners taken from the vessel (3 pp.; printed in *ASP, Foreign Relations*, 3:597–99).

3. The enclosure marked "D" is John Borlase Warren's letter to John Mitchell, agent for U.S. prisoners at Halifax, of 21 Oct. 1812 (2 pp.), explaining that Mitchell's letter and enclosures relative to captured seaman Thomas Dunn had been received and that their records showed that Dunn was married in England, had been in British service for eight years, and received a government pension. Also, as Dunn had not applied for discharge, he would continue aboard the prison vessel *Statira*. The enclosure marked "E" is a letter received by Monroe from William H. Savage, agent for American seamen and commerce at Jamaica, of 1 Dec. 1812 (1 p.), enclosing four letters exchanged between himself, British Vice-Admiral Charles Stirling, commander of the Jamaica station, and Charles Stirling Jr., secretary to the vice-admiral. The letter marked "No. 1" is Savage to Stirling, 6 Aug. 1812 (4 pp.), requesting an order of discharge for four U.S. seamen held aboard H.M.S. *Sappho*, describing enclosed documents proving the citizenship of twenty-one other impressed seamen, and describing an enclosed list of forty-six others for whom relief was requested. The letter marked "No. 2" is Stirling Jr. to Savage, 7 Aug. 1812 (1 p.), explaining that all captured seamen who could prove U.S. citizenship were to be transferred to a prison ship to await exchange. The letter marked "No. 3" is Savage to Stirling Jr., 16 Sept. 1812 (5 pp.), requesting that three more captured seamen be removed from duty aboard the British schooner *Découverte* on the basis of their U.S. citizenship. The letter marked "No. 4" is Stirling Jr. to Savage, 19 Sept. 1812 (2 pp.), explaining that the vice-admiral did not believe that the three seamen mentioned in Savage's previous letter had sufficiently proved their U.S. citizenship (printed in *ASP, Foreign Relations*, 3:599–601).

§ From Thomas B. Eyre.[1] *19 December 1812, Philadelphia.* Requests "with much diffidence" that JM consider him "When deciding on the Builders of National Vessels." "For Character, for Capability, for Execution, for dispatch I would refer you, if necessary to the Collector of the port of delaware, Allen Mclane Esqr. Thomas Newbold Member of Congress, or Merchants of Philadelphia."

RC (DNA: RG 45, Misc. Letters Received, filed at 7 Feb. 1813). 1 p.

1. Thomas B. Eyre (d. 1845) was presumably a member of the Philadelphia Eyre family, all of whom were merchants and shipbuilders and prominent in local Republican party politics (see Scharf and Westcott, *History of Philadelphia*, 3:2217; *PMHB* 26 [1902]: 344).

From Paul Hamilton

SIR, NAVY DEPARTMENT 21 Decr 1812

On the subject of the Resolution of the honorable the House of Representatives, of the 16th: instant,[1] I have the honor to state:

That in pursuance of the Resolution of congress of the 3rd March 1805, a gold medal, emblematical of the attacks on the town batteries & naval force of Tripoli, by the squadron under commre. Preble's command, was presented to commre. Preble—in the manner stated in the enclosed letter dated May 17. 1806:[2]

That one month's pay was allowed, "exclusively of the common allowance, to all the petty officers, seamen & Marines of the squadron, who so gloriously supported the honor of the American flag, under the orders of their gallant commander in the several attacks":[3]

That no sword has been presented to either of the commission officers or midshipmen, who distinguished themselves in the several attacks:

And that it is not known to this Department, that there ever was made by Congress, a specific appropriation of 20.000$ for the purpose of carrying into effect the Resolution referred to.

With respect to that part of the Resolution which "requests the President to cause a sword to be presented to each of the Commission officers & midshipmen who distinguished themselves,["] it is presumed that the President saw what to his mind appeared, difficulties of great delicacy, from the peculiar language of the Resolution. By the Resolution he was requested to present swords to such only as had distinguished themselves; and all having been represented to him, as having acted gloriously, he could not, in justice, draw with precision, a line of discrimination. He felt it is presumed a repugnance to the making of a selection which, by implication, would necessarily have cast an unmerited reproach upon all not therein included. A degradation of that kind, might have greatly injured the Service; & could not possibly have been grateful to the honorable feelings of the favored officers. I have the honor to be with the greatest respect Sir Y. most O S

PAUL HAMILTON

RC and enclosure (DNA: RG 233, President's Messages, 12A-D1); letterbook copy (DNA: RG 45, LSP). RC in a clerk's hand, signed by Hamilton. Transmitted to the House of Representatives by JM on 23 Dec. (DNA: RG 233, President's Messages, 12A-D1; 1 p.; in the hand of Edward Coles, signed by JM) and referred to a select committee (*Annals of Congress*, 12th Cong., 2d sess., 451–52). For enclosure, see n. 2.

1. On 16 Dec. 1812 the House of Representatives had approved a resolution offered by Josiah Quincy of Massachusetts that JM provide "a statement of the proceedings which have been had under the resolution of Congress of the 3d of March, 1805, whereby the President of the United States was requested to cause a gold medal to be presented to Commodore Ed-

ward Preble, and a sword to each of the officers and midshipmen who distinguished themselves in the attack on the town, batteries, and naval force, of Tripoli"; that JM provide the
names of those officers; and that he account for the expenditure of the $20,000 appropriation
made for these purposes (ibid., 402–3).

2. Hamilton enclosed a letter from Robert Smith to Edward Preble, dated 17 May 1806,
presenting Preble with a medal "emblematical of the attacks on the town, batteries, and naval
force, of Tripoli, by the squadron under your command . . . as a testimony of your country's
estimation of the important and honorable services rendered by you" (1 p.; printed in *ASP,
Naval Affairs*, 1:282).

3. Hamilton quoted from the congressional resolution of 3 Mar. 1805 (*U.S. Statutes at
Large*, 2:346–47).

§ To the Senate. *21 December 1812*. Nominates seven men, "Midshipmen since
1806, and now acting Lieutenants," to be lieutenants in the U.S. Navy and nine, including Samuel P. Todd, to be pursers.

Printed copy (*Senate Exec. Proceedings*, 2:312).

§ From M. Pontoire. *22 December 1812, Nantes*. Offers his services as a military or
naval engineer.

RC (DLC). 1 p.; in French.

§ From Daniel D. Tompkins. *22 December 1812, Albany*. "The peculiarity of the
case of Mr David S. Wendell of Troy, for whom I am desirous of obtaining a Commission of Lieutenant in the Army, is my apology for troubling you with this recommendation." "He was orderly Sergeant of the 'Invincibles,' an Independent uniform Company of Militia in the Village of Troy," which Tompkins sent "to the
Northern Frontier" in September. "At that time Mr. Wendell was clerk and agent
for the original proprieter of the Land upon which the Village is Situated, and for
his services as Such clerk and agent received, I am informed, about 500 dollars per
year. His employer being an inveterate opponent of the administration used every
persuasion to prevent Mr Wendell from going with his Company and even offered
extra compensation to induce him to refuse the performance of his duty in the
Corps. He, however, went and performed his tour of duty faithfully; was with the
Company under Major Young[1] at the Surprise and Capture of the Voyageurs[2] at St.
Regis and Volunteered his Services with the rest of the Company and went up on
the expidition into Canada with *Col. Pikes* Regiment of Regulars."[3] After serving for
three months, Wendell was discharged, "& although His former employer needs
his Services he will not continue Mr. Wendell in the clerkship and agency, by way,
I presume, of punishing him for his patriotism."

RC (DNA: RG 94, Letters Received, filed under "Wendell"). 2 pp.; docketed as received
in the War Department on 1 Jan. 1812 [1813]. Printed in Hastings, *Public Papers of Daniel D.
Tompkins*, 3:213–14.

1. Guilford Dudley Young (d. 1818) was a major in the New York volunteers in 1812. He
received a major's commission in the U.S. Army in February 1813 and was promoted to the
rank of lieutenant colonel in April of that year (Heitman, *Historical Register*, 1:1067).

2. Tompkins probably referred to the Voltigeurs, a volunteer regiment primarily composed of French Canadians and Indians under the command of Maj. Charles de Salaberry. Sir George Prevost created the regiment in the spring of 1812 to protect the Canadian border. On 23 Oct., Americans attacked and overpowered the Voltigeurs at the Indian village of St. Regis, New York (Everest, *The War of 1812 in the Champlain Valley*, 36–37, 67, 73; C. P. Lucas, *The Canadian War of 1812* [Oxford, 1906], 62).

3. For Pike's expedition into Canada, see Dearborn to JM, 13 Dec. 1812, n. 1.

From Joseph Wheaton

EXCELLENT SIR   WOOSTER Decr. 23d. 1812

Since I wrote: has fallen into my hands the Pittsburg paper, the commonwelth,[1] in which I with great pain read the disasterous affair at Black rock or opposite Queenstown—but indeed Sir My daily discoveries of desertion and insubordination evinces to Moral certainty that nothing effectual can be done by Such troops—and that no alternative is left but to resort to an efficient regular Army—a bounty of fifty dollars pr. Man—with necessary Strictness in discipline—commanded by Selected Officers will effect every purpose—you will pardon me for expression, the result of observation, with truth—it is the interest of the country & your glory I Seek—pray Sir give to the officers of the Quartermaster Generals department—(not of the line of the Army) Military rank—in proportion to their worth & experiance—with the homage of my heart I am Excellent Sir faithfully your devoted Servant

JOSEPH WHEATON

RC (DLC). Docketed by JM.

1. Several issues of the Pittsburgh *Commonwealth* contained news of the events at Queenston. As Wheaton's last letter to JM is dated 10 Dec. 1812, it is uncertain which issue he referred to here. Articles on the "Battles of Queenston" and "War Events at Black Rock" appeared in the 4 Nov. 1812 issue, an "Official Account of the Battle of Queenston" appeared in the 11 Nov. 1812 issue, and "Another View of the Battle of Queenstown" appeared in the 2 Dec. 1812 issue. The 16 Dec. 1812 issue contained an update on the "Progress of the War on the Niagara Frontiers" as well as George McFeeley's official report to Alexander Smyth describing an attack on Fort Niagara from Fort George.

§ From James Monroe. *24 December 1812, War Department.* Proposes for JM's approval various "Promotions in the Army of the United States."

Letterbook copy (DNA: RG 107, LSP). 1 p. Monroe's suggestions for promotions in the Fifth and Seventh Infantry Regiments were recommended to the Senate by JM on 31 Dec. (*Senate Exec. Proceedings*, 2:313).

§ From Daniel D. Tompkins. *24 December 1812, Albany.* Brings to JM's attention Capt. John E. Wool[1] of the Thirteenth Infantry Regiment, who was "Commandant on Queenstown heights for a part of the 13th of October & lead the party which attacked and carried the British works on the high ground in which he received a wound." Is informed by Van Rensselaer and others of Wool's good conduct and gallantry during that engagement; recommends him "to the notice & patronage of Government."

RC (PHi: Daniel Parker Papers). 1 p.; docketed as received in the War Department on 13 Jan. 1813.

1. John Ellis Wool (1784–1869) of Troy, New York, enjoyed a long and successful military career. He entered the U.S. Army as a captain of the Thirteenth Regiment in April 1812. After being wounded in the Battle of Queenston, he was promoted to the rank of major in April 1813 and to the rank of lieutenant colonel by brevet in September 1814 for gallant conduct at the Battle of Plattsburgh. After the war he became a full colonel and in April 1816 inspector general of the army, a post he held for twenty-five years. Wool was involved in the resettlement of the Cherokee Nation in 1836 and was a key participant in the Mexican-American War, with the rank of brigadier general. After successive commands of the Eastern Military District, the Department of the Pacific, and the Department of the East, Wool was given command of the Department of Virginia during the Civil War, receiving a major general's commission in 1862. He retired from active service the following year (*A Sketch of the Life and Public Services of Maj. Gen. John E. Wool* [New York, 1851], 4–7, 10; Samuel Rezneck, "The Civil War Role 1861–1863 of a Veteran New York Officer Major-General John E. Wool [1784–1869]," *New York History* 44 [1963]: 237, 238, 245).

§ From Robert Wickliffe. *24 December 1812, Lexington, Kentucky.* Recommends James Blair[1] for "judge of The Superior Court In the Missouri Territory."

RC (DNA: RG 59, LAR, 1809–17, filed under "Blair, James"). 1 p. Addressee not indicated but assumed to be JM on the basis of the fact that Wickliffe's letter is filed with a similar letter he wrote to Monroe on the same day.

1. James Blair was a lawyer in Lexington who had previously served as attorney general for Kentucky (Hopkins et al., *Papers of Henry Clay*, 1:78, 91, 124, 125 n. 7).

§ From Edward Cutbush.[1] *25 December 1812, Philadelphia.* Has been a U.S. Navy surgeon since May 1799, serving in the West Indies, in the Mediterranean, and at a hospital in Syracuse. Upon returning to the U.S. from Sicily, found that Dr. [Thomas] Ewell had been appointed a navy surgeon and stationed at Washington without having been on a single cruise at sea. "Conceiving that an ⟨o⟩lder surgeon, whose life had been exposed to the vicissitudes of climates, and the perils of the Ocean, and who had graduated at the most respectable Medical School in the Union, had a greater claim to be stationed at HeadQuarters than Dr. Ewell, I waited on Mr. Smith, then Secretary of the Navy, to urge my claims to the situation, who informed me, that it was the will of th⟨e⟩ President (Mr. Jefferson) in consequence of the friendship which had subsisted between Dr. Ewell's father and himself, he disapproved of the arrangement, and made frequent assurances, both verbal and by letter, that should the place be vacated *justice* would be done me." Having received news that Ewell is about to relinquish his post, requests JM's intervention in his favor. Has addressed the secretary of the navy on the subject.

RC (DNA: RG 45, Letters Received from Commissioned Officers below the Rank of Commander). 2 pp. Cover docketed in an unidentified hand, "Dr. Cutbush Complaining of Dr. Ewell's being appointed over him with a letter from Adam Seybert of Ph(i) respecting his being appointed hospital surgeon at Washn. in room of Dr Ewell" (see Seybert to JM, 29 Dec. 1812).

1. Edward Cutbush (1772–1843) graduated from Philadelphia College in 1794, after a medical internship at Pennsylvania Hospital. He was appointed a surgeon in the U.S. Navy in 1799 and on 5 May 1813 was ordered to Washington by the secretary of the navy, William Jones, to take up Thomas Ewell's post as surgeon at the Washington Navy Yard. Jones subsequently ordered Cutbush to oversee the establishment of a navy hospital in Washington (Dudley, *Naval War of 1812*, 1:143 n. 2, 2:124; Jones to Cutbush, 5 May 1813 [DNA: RG 45, Letters to Officers]).

From David Meade Randolph

DEAR SIR,   LONDON 26th December 1812

The subject of my communication to you last winter,[1] appearing of still greater importance, I am induced to a repetition of the liberty under which I then wrote to you. The accompanying packet[2] to my Son, contains the duplicate of a letter I wrote to the Honl. Mr. Quincey by a private hand last fall on the same subject, as also a transcript of a correspondence I was *permitted to make* between the professional character alluded to in my letter, and a certain Naval Lord under the *vain* expectation of removing from the minds of the Admiralty, that old prejudice which alone prevents the adoption of the new system of Naval Architecture set forth in the "prospectus" furnished you. The duplicate of that letter and the transcript, I shall be happy if you wou'd condescend to read—they will be delivered to you, shoud you do me the honor to ask them of my Son, to whom they are transmitted for preservation—and, that nothing can be found in my possession, which it woud be indiscrete to have subject to the Eye of *Authority here.*

Se[e]ing that 20 frigates are to be built,[3] I am doubly anxious to have my speculations put to the test of practice. And, shoud you authorise me to *improve my opportunity*, or, encourage the *Adventurers* by patents as heretofore suggested, I am persuaded that my zeal, and sources of information may tend greatly to the advancement of my Country's success in its present contest, and permanent honor.

The packet also contains private letters to my family; and, in thus addressing them to your care, I persuade myself that your own congual [*sic*] feelings will justify my temerity, since I am, otherwise unprovided with any safe medium for their transmission. And, you will also perceive the more clearly my justification when you are assured, that I am ignorant of any one particular as to the condition of my family sinc[e] July last! Your goodness will moreover, excuse me for asking your attention to the forwarding any communicati[o]ns from them by the first conveyance at command. As you will doubtless have little leisure to think of this part of my request, I wou'd most respectfully hope that Mrs. Madison will be so good as to give her kind attention to the subject; and, if she can suggest any possible thing for me to do here in return, I pray that she will equally believe in my sincerity and faithfulness—assuring of those feelings of respect and esteem with which I am continually your friend and Huml. Svt.

D M RANDOLPH

RC (DLC). Docketed by JM.

1. Randolph to JM, 16 Dec. 1811, *PJM-PS*, 4:69–70.
2. Randolph wrote in the margin of the first page, "Withdrawn for fear of implicating certain persons here, if this shou[ld] be opened here," presumably referring to the enclosures, which have not been found.
3. Randolph probably alluded to the 3 Dec. 1811 recommendation made by Paul Hamilton to Langdon Cheves, chair of the House naval affairs committee, in response to his 19 Nov. 1811 letter requesting Hamilton's input on the increase of the navy (see *ASP, Naval Affairs*, 1:248–49).

§ From Thomas L. Dillehay. *26 December 1812, "Near Hagerstown Md. Washington County."* Requests that JM take no "umbridge at the following lines, as they come from one you never saw, and perhaps, never heard of." "On the 14th. inst. it pleased God to make me Father of two Sons! which was yesterday noon Christened and call [*sic*] James Madison and Thomas Jefferson." Adds in a postscript, "The Hon. S. Ringgold knows me well, Tho' should not wish him to Know I dared to address you."

RC (DLC). 1 p.; postmarked Hagerstown, 10 Jan.; docketed by JM.

§ From Henry King. *26 December 1812, Buffalo, New York.* "It is with extreme regret that I am Thus compeled To address you for my Liberty. It is not Sir that I dispise the Servis nor is it the Least Spark of fear in me for I have shared in all the Toils and dangers of this Frontier. But Sir it is on account of a Letter that I have recently received informing me of the distresed Situation of my pore wife and five infant children which I Left in Virginia. Through the perswations of men that appeared To Be noing and Told me that the thing would be done with in the course of Six months and that wee should be at home with our famlys again believeing The cause of a war To be a just one I the more willingly entered in To it.

"It now appears that it will not end very soon and the thoughts of my Little children Being fully 600 miles from me and that of More sufference comeing so recently To my ears is things so combineed To gether that it has allmost run me mad noing that it is by and through you only that I can Leave the army in an Honerable way and To Leave it by any other means I hope will never enter my head and my not haveing the Honor of being acquainted with you makes me affraid that you will not Take my distresed situation in To Serious consideration for if you ware Sir I will no that you would have me discharged immediately."[1] Suggests that Col. John Tayloe "of Washing city," whom he served for eight years, could inform JM about his character and situation. Notes that many men "of Low principal" are deserting on the frontier, but he "would Sooner never See wife or Children again" than desert, "as it might be an induce⟨ment⟩ for many To follow me, by my influence I have prevented many from forsakeing there Collours." Is the first corporal in Capt. Thomas Sangster's company of the Twelfth Infantry Regiment. "I will add that I am 43 years old and wish To Spend the ballance of my days with my Children."

RC (DNA: RG 94, Letters Received, filed under "King"). 2 pp.; docketed as received in the War Department on 8 Jan. 1813. A note on the cover in JM's hand reads: "Does not such a case merit a favorable attenti⟨on⟩." Following this, a note in Daniel Parker's hand reads: "This note is by the President & I suppose the Adjt Genl. will think proper to discharge the man D. P."

1. On 9 Jan. 1813 the adjutant general, on the authority of the secretary of war, wrote to Moses Porter "or Officer Comg. near Buffalo N.Y.," ordering a discharge for Henry King (DNA: RG 94, Letters Sent).

§ From John Vawter.[1] *26 December 1812*, *"Town of Madison Jefferson County I Ty."* Upon "Reflecting on the important principals of our Goverment a Republic in which every man are eaqually entitled to the benifit of the Law Speech & press," claims it to be a right that "every part of the union or Republic" be maintained "undesterbed" and that every citizen be "made Secure in his person property & family," and on that basis believes "a communication of this kind might in Some way contreebute to the much desired end."

Was born in Virginia and relocated to the Indiana frontier. Represents "our pecular cituation in case of hostillities with our neighbouring Indians next Spring—as being a case—lamentable & miserable beyond Expression in asmuch as the larger portion of our citizens have become purchasers of land of the united States believing they would be Supported & maintained in the peacable enjoyment & possession of the Same in which case they would be enabled to comply with the Requisitions of the land office department otherwise must loose all moneys payed on former instalments, lands & improvements without any recourse which would be extremely hard on any individual & much more So when applyed to a respectable portion of good Citizens of this Territory that will give up all in the coming Spring unless Goverment Should take Some immediate & prompt measures for the better Security & Safety of those Rights Guarranteed to them by the first principals of our Goverment." "It would be Indecorous in me to dictate nor do I design going So fare in this letter although I give it as my opinion that Should our armies effect little or nothing this winter we may look for warme times on the braking up of winter, & for our Safety would Submit the following plan (Viz) let the General Goverment appoint & Commition a Captain Lieutenant & Ensign in each & Every county in the Territory who Shall Enlist in or out of there county a company of men to Serve for one year unless Sooner discharged on the fronteers of there Said county & not else where (unless in persuit of the enemy when doing mischief on an adjoining county) & them to be provided for by law as other ranging companyes are & this mode of procedure will quiet the minds of many as well as give Security to there persons & property—you may ask why not call out the militia for that purpose my answer is if you call them there families must be removed & the moving of one will cause ten perhaps to do the Same & in this way I have witnessed the entire disertion of many Settlements in our country & why Such Sufferings for want of a little Energy in a parental Goverment. I infur (that it must be what is Every bodyes business is no-bodyes & the old proverb becomes verrifyed) that it is the neglect of the citizens to represent their case fairly & State facts for I have full confidence & do believe Goverment will extend there Support to us as Soon as any other part of the union upon a fair Statement of facts. I was one who witnessed the affecting Scene at the pegeonruist Settlement[2] about 30 miles from my place of residence where 20 persons was intered having been Shamefully put to death by Savages Saw the bones of 2 who was burnt in one of 5 dwelling houses that were burnt with every article therein with many out houses & a number of Cattle killed on the ground—these are facts Sufficient to make every mans Bosom warm with resentment & Seize the first opportunity of avenging the rongs of his injuryed Country as well as those innocent persons who are nomore—my object in having the officers appointed within the county they are to Guard is that they will be acquainted with its cituation & have an interest in the welfare of the Same which will ensure the more vigilance on my own part I have but little property, but have determined it & myself will die together (Viz) I will not run away & leave it as many do, neither do I write with a view of receiving any benifit from a change in the land law myself as my Small tract is paid for, but for others—my portion in life appears but Small although the confidence of the good people of my county have been Such that they have recommended me to His Excellency William Henry Harrison Governor of our Territory to fill the office of Sheriff and Major in the county aforesaid both which appointments were accordingly confured on me by His Excellency & now although it would be fareign to my interest would take charge of a company to be raised as aforesaid & Serve one year on the fronteer of our county for the prosperity of my countryes cause but believe there are men much better quallifyed would they accept thereof I cannot omit before I close this letter Stating that we have the utmost confidence in the Exertions of the Honourable Jonathan Jennings Delegate in congress in behalf of us."

Adds in a postscript that "on Saturday night last the Indians Stole Seven head of horses in this county & about 17 miles from my residence & it is believed they were Delawares as the[y] made a Severe push for the Delaware Towns but was not overtaken."

RC (DNA: RG 107, LRRS, V-4:7). 3 pp.; docketed as received in the War Department on 1 Feb. 1813.

1. John Vawter was appointed marshal for the Indiana Territory on 27 July 1813 and ran unsuccessfully for lieutenant governor of the territory in 1816 (*Senate Exec. Proceedings*, 2:400; William Wesley Woollen, *Biographical and Historical Sketches of Early Indiana* [New York, 1975], 163).

2. On 3 Sept. 1812, after an attempted siege on Fort Harrison, a group of Indians attacked the Indiana settlement of Pigeon Roost, killing more than twenty people (Edmunds, *Shawnee Prophet*, 129–30).

From Thomas Leiper

DEAR SIR   PHILADA. Decr 27th 1812

I know what is well meant will be well received by you. From that circumstance I will proceed and I trust I shall put nothing on record but what shall have a tendence to the public good. I am pleased to a very high degree that the Secretary of State has sent for the bearer Captain Callender Irvine[1] this no doubt is with a view of obtaining information and in my opinion their are few men more capable and moreover what he retails to you you may rely on for he is a man of the strictest honor.

I hope you will desire of him to speak freely of men and things which I am certain he can give much information on this subject from his own personal knowledge.

The first thing you did on the formation of the Army which I thought materially wrong was appointing General Dearborn at the Head. When I first heard of the appointment I said we shall have no war for I reasoned with myself thus if we are to have a War the President would certainly not [have] commissioned him to the first command.

General Dearborn is a good man but their is some thing more required. If General Dearborn was Thirty Five years of Age he might do to command a Regiment but at the present period of his life I very much doubt if he is qualified for that station. Courage and Heels are absolutely necessary in a soldier the former he may have but the later from his age he cannot, complete victories are never obtained but by the Army who posseses both.

If I had the formation of an Army the Rank and file should be from 18 to 30 the Officers from 20 to 40 and the Commander in Chief should not exeed the last number if he can be procured.

We have been extremely unfortunate in our Generals. We are of the opinion here you cannot do better than put Wilkinson at the Head of the War Department from his long services he must be better Qualified for the Appointment than [any] man in the Army. Apothecarys will not do you may rely on it unless you mean to Ruin yourself and I may add your Country. Do what is right and good effects will follow.

Our Opinion here [is] that General Armstrong is better qualified to command than General Dearborn. On the Judicious appointments eve[r]y thing depends. I intended to have added much more but I am affraid I have said too much. I am with much respect & esteem Your most Obedient St

THOMAS LEIPER

RC (DLC). Docketed by JM.

1. On 19 Dec. 1812 Monroe, as acting secretary of war, wrote to Irvine to request that he come to Washington immediately to arrange the affairs of his department "in relation to the next Campaign." In particular, Monroe expected to discuss "the distribution of Cloaths

throughout the United States for the accommodation of the Recruits & to promote the Recruiting Service." Irvine was directed to bring a statement of all his disbursements and to describe the condition of his department (DNA: RG 107, LSMA).

From Jonathan Dayton

[ca. 28 December 1812]

Letters of congratulation are not the object of the writer, altho' no one more sincerely rejoices at the defeat of your enemies. No one more deeply laments that the military arrangements, movements & disasters of the late summer campaigns, improperly imputed to the Head of the Governmt. had, for a moment shaken the confidence, or alienated the affections of some portions of the community. The means & powers were sufficient, if they had been judiciously employed & directed, & the mass of the people will ere long be convinced of this, & return to their former attachment. I must speak plainly & frankly, since your last addressed to L. C.[1] invite it, *where the public good requires it.* You have very near you sir, a most insidious, artful & decided enemy in the Post master General,[2] who was deeply engaged in the plans for changing the Administration. To no man is the caution of the Roman more applicable. *"Hic niger est, hunc tu Romane caveto."*[3] Your Commander in Chief, tho not unfaithful as the former, is miserably incompetent, & if not changed, disaster will be added to disaster—disgrace to disgrace, & discontent of course to discontent. The defects of all his plans & systems, if indeed he ever had any, are now plainly perceptible. Only one Regt. of regular troops was wanted for the whole frontier from St. Laurence to Champlain—the further force required there by way of feint, should have been made up of militia, for here could not be the brunt of battle, because our unprepared state, & the advanced stage of the season rendered our advance to Montreal unadviseable & impracticable, which the Comr. in chief & Secy. of War, above all other men could & should have foreseen, & acted accordingly. Under such an arrangemt., the enemy would never have crossed the line, for there would be no military stores to take or destroy, & if they had crossed for purposes of devastation, they would have roused & brought agt them the New England hives, with sharpened stings, who otherwise would be disposed to remain quietly in their cells.

Two additional regular Regts. should have been sent to the vicinity of Niagara, where it was most important that our operations should have been carried on vigorously & successfully, & every British post subdued. This force, under proper direction would have ensured it, & your troops might then have wintered on that side in safety, & to great advantage. Harrison required at least one full Regiment of Regulars more than he had. This would have taken 4 out of 5 of the regular Regts. at Plattsburgh, & a part of the 5th. Regt. should have been stationed at Oswego & it's vicinity, & the other at or near Sackett's harbour. It is a perfectly well ascertained fact sir, that in order to ensure the services of 2000 militia in the field, you must have at least 4000 under pay & subsistence, & to ensure the services of 2000 regulars in the field, would require from 24 to 2500 under pay & subsistence. In favor too of the 4 or 500 non-effectives of the latter description, they may mostly be useful for garrison duty, but militia *non-effectives* are of no use. This will be found nearly just on ordinary calculations, but there may be a variance arising from extraordinary causes. In comparing the value of Regular & Militia effective soldiers, we need not recur to the experience of our Revolutionary war, for the present one (short as it has already been) will guide us. In every case except invasions into the heart of our country, 2000 Regulars are more to be relied upon for success, than 4000 militia, altho' these may be individually equally brave. To attack or to defend, either by or agt. regular approaches or assault, a fortified post—to invade an enemy's country—to fight in battle array in open plain—to sustain sudden onsets of Cavalry, or the charge of the bayonet, there is scarcely a comparison in point of value—it is in skirmishing or irregular fighting only, that the Militia can succeed when they have a Regular Army, as now, opposed to them, for these remarks do not apply in so great force, altho' even then in no small degree, to a contest with Indians only. The result of all this is, that with *2500* Regulars engaged for the War & under pay & subsistence, more can be effected than with *8000* enrolled, paid & subsisted militia. This is not said to disparage the latter, but merely to lead to a right course & proper system for carrying on the War, which I pray to God, may be successful, & terminate in a speedy & honorable peace. Forgive & excuse me, respected sir, for speaking plainly, as it arises from a most earnest desire to remove from your Administration the unpopularity attendant upon ill-planned measures or systems, & thereby to promote the great interests of my country, in which I hold too great a stake, to be an indifferent or unconcerned spectator. My communications, being anonymous, will consequently be entitled to no more weight, than they appear to your own enlightened mind, intrinsically to merit. So long as they are acceptable, I shall continue to make them, when any thing of sufficient importance occurs. If any subject or plan arises, upon which the opinion of the writer is desired, an intimation of it, in a line addressed as the last to "Levi Canning" will draw a ready answer.

Indulge me sir, in some other remarks on an important subject, & ascribe them not to presumption, but to the purest intention. *Unity*, in all the branches of the Executive Department has certainly many advantages, but in times of war & a heavy pressure of duties, they may be overbalanced by the advantages arising from a *Board of three* well selected, to each one of whom should be assigned his distinct province, or portion of the duties of the Department, for individual management, but brought into Joint Council, whenever the President should require, or any two of the three should request, their opinions, as a Board. The war (if it continues for one or more years longer (as is now very probable) will be a very extensive & complicated one, requiring new & greatly enlarged systems, arrangements & establishments. There is no beaten path to follow—no sure directory or guide—much, very much is to be done, far more indeed than one head can conceive, or one man execute, unless there should be found one preeminently superior, a task not very easy since the deaths of Hamilton & Carrington, who, it is believed, have not left behind them, any one equally competent, singly to discharge so great a trust, at such a crisis as the present. Both were well known to the President himself.

The opposers of the Government & of your reelection are (to use a familiar sea phrase) shaking in the wind, perplexed, embarrassed, hesitating & undecided as to their future measures. Uniting only in one great object, that of the change of Presidency, but differing as to almost every other, they begin to discover that they can go together no longer. The steady loyalty of Pennsa. defeats entirely one projected plan of endeavouring by means of a Convention of deputies from the States North of Maryland, to throw off a connection with the Southern part of the Union, & to form a *compact & strong one* of their own. New York would then have been the centre, and the make-weight or arbiter of this new confederacy, but she will not venture to connect herself alone with New England, where her influence would be lost, altho' the Yankies would rather have that State & New Jersey without Pennsa. than with it. They have made the most they could of the indescreet movements & disasters of our Armies in the interior, with a view to the Presidential contest—this failing, they now again return to the former hope of a separation, but they w⟨ish⟩ (what Archimedes wished for in vain) the *Pou stein*,[4] & they begin to flatter themselves with delusive expectations, that either the new & necessarily heavy taxes, or a French alliance or both together, will give them that ground on which to stand, in order to shake & sever the Union. They speak with great confidence, tho' I cannot learn certainly on *what authority*, or *upon whose assurance*, that the next year's hostile operations will be so managed and directed as to dishearten, weaken, harrass & distress the whole of the Southern States, to render the war most burthensome & unpopular in that quarter. Such an event they regard as likely to aid & promote their views in two very important respects. These suggestions of the writer are certainly not sufficient grounds of conduct, so far as to found upon them preparations for warding off, or properly meeting the threatened dangers, but they may produce further enquiry & greater vigilance in relation to those more vulnerable parts of our Union, which the enemy would delight to invade & lay waste, from special motives of hatred & revenge, more than the general policy of an honorable warfare.

RC (NjP). Undated; date assigned here on the basis of the postmark, which reads, "Elizth. Town, Decr. 28"; "1812" has been added to the postmark date in JM's hand. Unsigned; a note on the cover in an unidentified hand reads: "avowed by Jonathan Dayton tho' not signed by him." Docketed by JM, "Recd. December 30. 1812." A penciled note on the cover in JM's hand reads: "proviso—New ⟨Act⟩ not to ⟨suspend?⟩ enlistmts under former Volr Act option between 5yr & war—⟨depending?⟩." Damaged by removal of seal.

1. Levi Canning (see JM to Dayton, post 26 Sept. 1812).
2. In the presidential election of 1812, as in 1808, Gideon Granger showed decidedly Clintonian leanings. The New York congressional delegation returned home in July 1812 bearing letters from Granger supporting northern opposition to JM (Alexander, *Political History of New York*, 1:202).
3. "That man is black of heart; of him beware, good Roman" (Horace, *Satires*, 1.4.85, in *Horace: Satires, Epistles and Ars Poetica*, Loeb Classical Library [1970 reprint], 54, 55).
4. Dayton probably meant "pou sto," from the Greek meaning "where I may stand." The term comes from a saying of the Greek mathematician Archimedes (ca. 287–212 B.C.), who is credited with inventing the compound pulley as a means of moving unwieldy objects and boasting of it, "give me (a place) where I may stand, and I will move the earth" (*OED*, 2d ed.; Charles Coulston Gillispie et al., eds., *Dictionary of Scientific Biography* [16 vols.; New York, 1970–80], 1:213).

§ From the Inhabitants of Harrison County, Indiana Territory. *28 December 1812.* "Your Memorialists have settled on the extreme Frontiers of this Territory bounded as follows on the N & N E by Driftwood, on the S Mishkakitac and S E by the Pigeon Roost Settlement where we have been and are still constantly assailed by the Horrid and relentless fury of the Inhuman and remorseless Savages. Three of our most Respectable Citizens have already fell a Sacrifice to the Tommy Hawk & Scalping Knife and we know not how soon it may be our Fate. It is true that the Executive of this Territory have provided us with a guard but we beg leave to assure your Excellency that it is by no means effecient for the protection of our Persons or Property for since it has been stationed here we have lost property (horses) stolen by the savages to the amount of Two thousand Dollars and two of our Citizens murdered we therefore most humbly solicit that some speedy relief may be granted us without which, we shall be compelled to abandon our Crops & property and the little wh we have been for years accumulating. We beg leave to recall your Excellency's attention to the Evils which will result both to us and the U. S. Government by an abandonment of this settlement in the first place the payment which we have already made to the General Government for our Land will together with the Land be lost to us and forfeited to the U S for in our present situation it will be impossible for us to dispose of our Property or Produce every avinue to the market being frequently ambuscaded by the Indians—in the second place the U. S. must and will be considerably injured. For in that event it will be the means of detering others from purchasing and of puting a Stop to the Sale of the U. S. Land on this Frontier a most Beautiful Fertile & Luxuriant Tract of Country. The serious consequence of such a measure will no doubt be instantly recognised by yr. Excillency. We beg leave further to assure your Excellency that we entertain too just an opinion of you than to suppose that you would knowingly permit any part of that Country or its Citizens over which you Preside by the voice of your Countrymen to remain under any serious Calamity that you could redress on being apprised thereof but that you would with promptitude & Chearfulness so far as in your power remedy the Evil. We therefore most humbly solicit from your Excellency a Competent force for our protection and if we may presume to advise with you on the subject we would recommend that there might be a Company of Mounted Rangers consisting of 100 or 120 men permanently Stationed here untill the Storms of War be blown over or the Savage Power completely checked or entirely subverted. At this Present moment we have been compelled to fly from our Farms & habitations for the Safety of our Lives as well as that of our Wives & Children and take refuge in Forts & Block Houses, our Property Crops and Houses exposed to the lawless depredation of the Savages and further it will perhaps [be] necissary to inform your Excellency that our settlement is only distant from the Delaware Nation of Indians one hundred Miles and from the Prophets Town one hundred & twenty."

RC (DNA: RG 107, LRUS, P-1812). 3 pp.; signed by forty-two citizens. Cover marked "Corydon I. Ty Jany 17"; docketed as received in the War Department on 14 Feb. 1813.

From Joseph Wheaton

Confidential

SIR   OHIO—MANSFIELD—Decr. 29. 1812

We arrived at this post 27. at noon after a march of 36 days—the most difficult of any I ever experienced in any period of Service I have Seen— the Season of the year most of all unfavorable, and it was So rainy and damp that the Sun has not appeared to us five days of the time—that we have been plunging through mud mire and frost cotinually [*sic*]. The whole country through which we have passed is intirely new, and forage become Scarce on account of the numbers of teams and troops which had gone before us. The Ohio Militia many of them—the Brigade of Genl. Crooks and Several troops of horse—and yet I believe altho two thousand men have used this rout, there has not been any detachment of pioneers to make the least repairs consequently we have cut 2 Crooss [*illegible*] about 60 Miles or near one half of our intire distance—160 Miles from Pittsburg to this post—these distressing circumstances has made havock of our wagons and often our gun carriages in every part—wheels, axletrees, tonges, hound— wagon body. Broke the limbs of horses and many have died—tho that I expected owing to Lt. Johnson A D Q Master at Pittsburg furnishing me with the very worst Kind. Mares with fold. horses Sick of the Glanders, and many So lame as compelled me to leave three of my number on the ground—the axes too which he has Supplied, made by his Brother in Law, are after the enormous expence of transporting to this place not worth their weight in Iron. General Crooks's Brigade tho 1400 men at Pittsburg has not in their three month Service, it is believed done one days work on the road, or any other thing but insult, and distress the inhabitants where ever they have appeared—at this place where they have been encamp'd Six weeks, the inhabi[tants] Sorounded me, and with united complaints that made the heart Sick, and the countenance turn pale. It is believed that this Brigade, tho it was to have been two thousand men at Pittsburg—will not march into camp at Sandusky (for which place they marched last wednesday) more than Eight hundred men. The virginia Militia, I am informed have deserted in about the Same proportion, what General Harrisons Object will be after our arrival I cannot Say—but Such troops are enough to break down the Spirits of any man and defeat any measure. I State these plain truths from observation and evidence, and being So, to induce an enlargement of the regular System, to enable the government to carry their views into effect and Secure the object of the war, at an infinite less expence—and honorable to the Nation. The present System only creates enemies to the government, and expence to the Country. Captn. Grat[i]ot of the Engeniers with this Convoy has recd. orders from Genl. Harrison—by his Adjt. Genl. to leave four Six pds at this place with the carriages, and complains that no more than five Eighteen pds were forwarded. It was well to leave the four four pds. for all the Carriages recd. at Pittsburg Made by Majr. Craig[1] are actually So rotten, as to be unfit for Service—we leave this as Soon as I can get Six days forage to carry us to Sandusky forty Eight Miles—without house or any possible resource for Supply—every possible Exertion has been and will continue to be made by me and, the party with this convoy for the interest of the country. I hope to leave this tomorrow—& will if the two hundred horses now out for forage return this day as I expect. I write Sir for the information of the Secretary at war—but Seeing in the papers that Mr. Eustis tendered his resignation and not Knowing a Successor, take the liberty of addressing to you—the post is waiting or I Should enlarge. With perfect Respect I am Excellent Sir faithfully your Obedient Servant

JOSEPH WHEATON Capn
A. D. Q. Mastr. N. W. Army

RC (DLC). Docketed by JM.

1. Isaac Craig (1741–1825) was born in Ireland, came to America in 1765, and served in the artillery, infantry, and marines during the Revolutionary War. After the Revolution he settled near Pittsburgh, acquired land, and constructed a glassworks (Daniel Agnew, "Address to the Allegheny County Bar Association, December 1, 1888," *PMHB* 13 [1889]: 43–45).

§ From Adam Seybert. *29 December 1812, Washington.* "It is reported, that Doctor Thomas Ewell, a surgeon in the Navy of the United States, has tendered his resignation, and that a successor, to the vacancy of Hospital Surgeon at the marine barracks of this City, is to be appointed. Allow me to lay before you the pretensions of Doctor Edward Cutbush, a native of Philadelphia and now a surgeon in the Navy of the U. S.—he ranks second on the list." Informs JM that he has been acquainted with Cutbush for more than twenty years. Describes Cutbush's educational background and naval service and explains that Cutbush must support his family on a navy surgeon's pay.

"The Rules & regulations intended for the Navy Hospitals of the U. S. which were, at the last session of Congress, referred to a select committee, all of whom were Medical men, were reporte⟨d⟩ with the following resolution 'Resolved, Tha⟨t⟩ no person shall be appointed a surgeon t⟨o⟩ any of the navy hospitals of the Unite⟨d⟩ States unless he shall have been previously *in actual service in the Navy of the United States during a period of seven years.*'[1] This resolu⟨tion⟩ received the unanimous vote of the Committees. The protracted state of the session precluded any further order on the subject."

RC (DNA: RG 45, Letters Received from Commissioned Officers below the Rank of Commander). 4 pp.

1. On 26 May 1812 the secretary of the navy had submitted to the House of Representatives a paper "containing rules and regulations for the government of the navy hospitals," which was referred to a committee of which Seybert was the chairman (*ASP, Naval Affairs,* 1:270–73; *Annals of Congress,* 12th Cong., 1st sess., 1437, 1487).

From Paul Hamilton

S<small>IR</small>   C<small>ITY OF</small> W<small>ASHINGTON</small> December 30th. 1812

Having devoted unremittedly more than thirty years of my life to public service, in various situations, in all of which, I feel a consciousness of having done my duty according to my best judgment and understanding; and being now about to withdraw from the Office of the Secretary of the Navy with which you honored me, permit me to ask you whether, in your opinion, there has been any thing in the course of my conduct, in that station, reprehensible.[1]

Your goodness of heart, Sir, will induce you, as I trust, readily to excuse this intrusion, when you reflect that if this enquiry is answered as my conscience leads me to expect it will be, you will put me in possession of what may be a valuable Legacy to my Children. Wishing you Sir every earthly blessing I have the honor to be with great respect yrs.

P<small>AUL</small> H<small>AMILTON</small>

RC (DLC). Docketed by JM with the added notation "his resignation."

1. According to rumors circulating in the capital, this letter was written after two meetings between JM and Hamilton. At the first, held on 28 Dec. 1812, JM mentioned that there had been complaints about Hamilton's management of the Navy Department; during the second, held at JM's request the next day, the president informed Hamilton that Congress would not vote for naval appropriations until there had been a change in the department. Hamilton attempted to vindicate his conduct, then submitted his resignation. On 31 Dec. 1812 the *National Intelligencer* announced that "in pursuance of what he has for some time past contemplated, the hon. PAUL HAMILTON has resigned the office of Secretary of the Navy." Hamilton took offense, declaring that the wording of the announcement was "erroneous," and complained of "the harsh conduct of the President towards him." On 8 Jan. 1813, after a discussion with the editors of the *National Intelligencer*, Hamilton wrote a letter of clarification in which he conceded that the newspaper had not misrepresented the situation with respect to its announcement of his resignation, adding that he had hoped to retire "with the return of peace" but that "things have taken a different course" (John A. Harper to William Plumer, 5 Jan. 1813 [DLC: William Plumer Papers]; James A. Bayard to Caesar A. Rodney, 31 Jan. 1813, "James Asheton Bayard Letters, 1802–1814," *Bulletin of the New York Public Library* 4 [1900]: 239–40; *Daily National Intelligencer*, 11 Jan. 1813).

To Paul Hamilton

DEAR SIR   Decr. 31. 1812
   I have recd. your letter of yesterday, signifying your purpose to retire from the Dept. which has been under your care.
   On an occasion which is to terminate the relation in wch. it placed us, I can not satisfy my own feelings, or the tribute due to your patriotic merits & private virtues, without bearing testimony to the faithful zeal, the uniform exertions, and unimpeachable integrity, with which you have discharged that important trust: and without expressing the value I have always placed on that personal intercourse, the pleasure of which I am now to lose.
   With these recollections & impressions I tender you assurances of my affectt. esteem, and of my sincerest wishes for your welfare & happiness.
                                                              J. M.

Draft (DLC).

From Tench Coxe

SIR   PURVEYORS OFFICE ROOM Decemr. 31. 1812
   I respectfully trust you will excuse this second letter, when you know the circumstances, under which it is written. Since I had the honor to address you on the 17th. Instant,[1] I have received very urgent tho' polite applica-

tions from Jacob Eustis, Esquire, of Boston,[2] Messrs. Gansevort & La-grange of Albany & Aaron R. Levering, Esquire, of Baltimore all late agents for this office to Settle or to procure a Settlement of their accounts. Mr. Levering had the trouble to Come to Philada. on the subject. There are balances due to most or all of the above Gentlemen as they alledge & I think probable. Some monies are due from them to contractors. Mr. Levering assured me that he believed he could not at this time, purchase upon good terms, in the name of the United States in Maryland because he had been thus delayed in payment of several accounts beyond the Stipulated and customary times. I anticipated this state of things and confess my belief in its present existence. The Gentlemen are all perfectly moderate and polite, but considerably anxious & pained.

Suffer me to add that my counsel has also spoken to me upon the subject of the information necessary for me. But I refrained from any further application however respectful.

This day I have received an unexceptionable letter from the accountant of the War Department[3] to whom I sent all my accounts so far as I could get the means within a month or two of the time of my being allowed my vouchers. I am detained from prompt & dutiful completion *only* by the open agents accounts & the open accounts of Contractors, to whom advances were made, necessarily equal to the sum the accountant mentions: *for no monies ever came into my hands.* I always endorsed the Treasurers orders for cash, with a direction to pass them into the Bank, indicated by the Secretary of the Treasury, to the *official* credit of T. C. Purveyor of public supplies. Thus I avoided even to touch the public funds. The monies are drawn out in regular discharge of public dues from the office & I have, by a little, actually over paid. So that I can have no money. Yet you will perceive, Sir, that I am not allowed, by circumstances uncontroulable by me, to see my books and papers & settle my accounts. Wh⟨at⟩ I do is too much in the dark for custom or reason. I have been kept from the last of May to this day in the most hard and painful form of public duty, without being permitted to proceed in my settlements. My receipts & vouchers for cash, my orders or checks on the bank, and every thing to which agents of decent character usually have access are kept from me. It was thus that while I was in office I was occasionally prevented from doing my duty & serving the United States. Suffer me most respectfully to add that had all such things been and if they shall be avoided the public service would not have exhibited and will not in future exhibit various uncomfortable appearances & evils, of a nature to render wise and good men uneasy, and others of less estimable qualities, censurers and opposers.

From the gross miscolourings & misrepresentations, which have occurred, orally and in print, I doubt not that serious untruths may have circulated even to your presence. I have ever been ready to submit all such explanations as the service or my personal situation may appear to require. There are some very great and intrinsic difficulties, in the business of our supplies, but there are many which I conceive might have been and might yet be prevented avoided or dimi[ni]shed.

With the most sincere and earnest personal and public solicitudes for the success of your administration. I have the honor to be with perfect respect, Sir, Your most Obedient & hum Sevt.

TENCH COXE

There are goods in the hands of Mr. Levering undelivered, tho purchased under my orders of last spring, and there is a small balance due from the office to the Bank of Pennsylvania, and there is a want of a small fund to defray clerkship & other contingencies occurring in the settlement of my accounts, on which I would respectfully request that ord⟨ers⟩ might be directed to be taken by the gentleman administering the department of war, as I receive applications on these subjects.

RC and enclosure (DNA: RG 107, LRRS, C-3:7); draft, two copies (PHi: Tench Coxe Papers). RC in a clerk's hand, except for Coxe's signature and postscript; docketed as received in the War Department on 4 Jan. 1812 [1813]; also docketed "Philadelphia / Decr 28 1812." First draft dated 23 Dec. 1812; text crossed through. Differences between the 23 and 31 Dec. versions have not been noted. For enclosure, see n. 3.

1. Coxe referred to his letter to JM of 16 Dec. 1812.
2. Jacob Eustis had served as military agent in Boston until he was appointed to the office of deputy quartermaster on 8 Apr. 1812, during the reorganization of the military supply departments (*Senate Exec. Proceedings*, 2:242, 244; Risch, *Quartermaster Support*, 138).
3. Coxe enclosed a copy of a 28 Dec. 1812 letter sent to him by the accountant of the War Department, William Simmons, reminding Coxe of the balance "of upwards of 250.000 Dollars in favor of the United States." Coxe was directed to render the residue of his balance "without delay" so that a complete settlement of his public transactions for the duration of his agency could be made.

From Joseph Wheaton

EXCELLENT SIR   MANSFIELD Decr. 31. 1812

As I Stated in my last I Sent of[f] two hundred horses to the Mohecan Settlement where I had made arrangemts for forage—on the 27—they returned yesterday and this day—though Eighteen Miles from this—and packed and brought me 600 Bushels of corn—in the mean time all my hands left that could handle a tool was imployed in Shoeing horses, and repairing wagons—Making axletrees—&ca—this afternoon they have all moved of[f] for Sandusky. I am only waiting this might [*sic*] to pay of[f] all my bills and follow them to Morrow Morning by day light. I have been 36.

days coming to this place—others have taken 62 days on the average—the distance to Sandusky is 50 Miles. I allow Myself to Tuesday next to reach it—others, take 10. & 11 days—you may expect to hear from me when I reach that post (Head Quarters). I beg leave to Mention Capt. Johnson of the Pensylvania Militia who Marched with me from Pittsburg. I cannot Say enough of this gentleman he has Supported that order & regularity which Might be expected from men better acquainted with Service, and he has regularly kept 25. Men on Severe duty as pioneers and greatly aided in faci[li]tating the March by cutting new & repairing the old road and cross ways—and Indeed Sir the only Man or Company from whom I have heard of their doing any good—permit me to ask your recollection of him. I am Sir faithfully your Obdt. Servant

JOSEPH WHEATON

A D Q M. N. W. Army

If Mr. Eustis is with you please pass this to him

RC (DNA: RG 107, LRRS, W-36:7). Cover marked *"Private"*; docketed as received in the War Department on 1 Feb. 1813.

From Tobias Lear

[January 1813]

On the 31st. *Decr the Regency of this Kingdom presented to the Cortes General and Extraordinary what they termed an exposition* of the *conduct* of the *United States toward Spain before* the *revolution in Spain* to the *present time.*[1] *This paper enters generally*[2] into the *conduct adopted* by the *agent* of the *United States resident here,*[3] *The possession* of *East Florida,* the *numerous incendiaries employed* by the *Executive* of the *United States* in *different parts* of *their American possessions, naming several, particularly a Doctor Robinson,*[4] *The forces collecting near baton rouge, as intended* to *join* the *insurgents in mexico: but more particularly* the *correspondence of the Chavalier Onis, which exhibits many unfounded speculations,* and *false conclusions upon subjects that he* is *totally unacquainted with, or which he has viewed thro a false medium. The Regency concludes with saying that they should recommend a declaration of war instantly, if* the *actual circumstances* of this *kingdom did not forbid it,* and the *hope* that *clinton,* the *friend* of *onis* and of *Spain* and *her ally, would succeed* to the *President before, in which case* the *alternative would be unnecessary. This Paper was, in secret session, committed* to a *commission* to *report thereon. It is supposed no report*[5] *will be made for some considerable time say two months. I am led* to *think* that neither the *british minister nor Lord Wellington* had *any thing to do* in this *affair, which I deem* of *too much importance not* to make *an attempt to communicate it.*

538

RC (DLC: Monroe Papers); FC (owned by Stephen Decatur, Garden City, N.Y., 1961). RC undated; date assigned here on the basis of internal evidence and information presented in n. 3. RC unsigned; addressee not indicated, identified as JM by Stephen Decatur; docketed by Monroe, "To be decypherd"; a note on the cover in John Graham's hand reads: "This Paper came under a Blank Cover. Mr Lears Cypher was used to read it." FC undated; inserted between pages in Lear's letterbook at January 1809. Italicized words are those encoded by Lear's clerk and decoded interlinearly by Graham (key is in the Lear family papers [ibid.]).

1. This report was sent to the *cortes* by Pedro Labrador, minister of state for the regency of Spain. Much of its contents complained of the presence and activities of U.S. agents in various parts of the Spanish-American Empire that had recently experienced revolutionary disturbances, most notably Buenos Aires, Caracas, East and West Florida, and Mexico. Spain accused the U.S. of failing to prevent the activities of seditious and filibustering parties as well as of seizing Spanish territory, including Amelia Island, West Florida to the Perdido, Dauphin Island, and Nacogdoches. It was alleged that the administration had dispatched agents to the other Spanish-American provinces for the purpose of encouraging declarations of independence from Spain. A twenty-five-page copy of this report (dated 31 Dec. 1812; in Spanish) may be found in the Library of Congress (DLC: Spanish Affairs, 1810–16), where it is accompanied by an eleven-page summary and translation in the hand of John Graham (docketed by Graham, "Report of the Regency to the Cortes of Spain—relative to the measures taken by the UStates"). A second copy of this report is filed at 31 Dec. 1812 in the State Department records at the National Archives (DNA: RG 59, ML; 22 pp.). A short summary of the report may be found in León Tello, *Documentos relativos a la independencia de Norteamérica*, 4:485.

2. Encoded "fully."

3. Lear almost certainly referred to the U.S. consul in Cádiz, Richard Hackley. In his 27 Feb. 1813 letter to Monroe, Hackley mentioned that Lear had been with him for some "considerable time." Hackley continued: "I have deemed it better in the state of things to converse fully with that Gentleman and to give him every information in my power relative to our Affairs here, which by Information *you will have received and will Obtain by this opportunity* will be found not to stand upon a good footing, on the contrary I have my fears that (and *well grounded*) that we shall not be long exempt from the most serious difficultys with this power" (DNA: RG 59, CD, Cádiz).

4. John Hamilton Robinson (1782–1819), a native of Augusta County, Virginia, received a medical education in Philadelphia, after which he settled in the Louisiana Territory. He accompanied Zebulon Montgomery Pike on his exploration of the Colorado region in 1806–7, during the latter stages of which he was detained by Commandant-General Nemesio Salcedo before being allowed to return to the U.S. Robinson was then employed as an army surgeon's mate and later as aide-de-camp to the brigadier general of militia in the Illinois Territory. In June 1812 Pike recommended him to Monroe to undertake a special mission to Salcedo to explain administration policy regarding the Neutral Ground. While on this mission Robinson encountered the filibustering party led by Gutiérrez and Magee near Nacogdoches, and he was interrogated by Magee and others before being allowed to proceed. His mission to Salcedo was unsuccessful. Salcedo decided that Robinson lacked the proper credentials to undertake negotiations, and the agent returned home, reporting back to the administration in July 1813. By late 1813 Robinson was developing filibustering schemes against Mexico. None of these schemes came to fruition before the end of the War of 1812, and he received no support from the administration for them. He continued to plot against the Spanish authorities in Mexico after 1815, but ill health forced him to abandon many of his plans, and he retired to Natchez, where he died (Harold A. Bierck Jr., "Dr. John Hamilton Robinson," *La. Histor-*

ical Quarterly 25 [1942]: 644–69; see also Madison and the Problem of Mexican Independence: The Gutiérrez-Magee Raid of August 1812, 1 Sept. 1812).

5. Encoded "reply."

From Richard Rush

SIR.   January 1. 1813.

Mr Ingersoll has sent me on the enclosed letter[1] from Philadelphia, which, for the sake of the sentence it contains about impressment, I venture to enclose for your eye.

Mr Ingersoll is not, as Mr King supposes, engaged in any publication upon this subject. He is investigating it, with others, preparatory to his congressional career, which I please myself with the hope will be prominent and useful.[2] With the most respectful attachment, I have the honor to be your obt. Servt.

R. RUSH.

RC (MiU-C). Docketed by JM.

1. Enclosure not found, but it was probably a letter from Rufus King to Charles Jared Ingersoll. Rush added in a postscript to his letter to Ingersoll of 7 Jan. 1813: "I wrote you the enclosed last night, and forgot to mention that I received Mr King's letter. I sent it to the President. When he returns it you shall have it again" (*Letters and Papers of Richard Rush* [microfilm ed.], reel 2).

2. In his letter to Charles Jared Ingersoll of 28 Dec. 1812 (ibid.), Rush wrote: "I am glad to hear you say you have been investigating more thoroughly the question of impressment. *I* went farther last July than any body had ever gone publickly up *to that period*, I mean placing the matter on a more footing [*sic*] of natural, abstract, eternal, moral, damnable, enormity, without introducing papers, documents, or the long list of principles from international law. But you may doubtless go much farther than I did on all the points."

From William Wingate

DEAR SIR,   NEW SHARON January 1st 1813.

I feel it my duty at So alarming a Crisis of our National Goverment as this moment exhibits, for to address you on So important occasion, not doubting you all will give it its due weight. Firstly, Shall observe that a *regular* Army has become the *only* Safety and bullwork of our Country, and that the *drafted* Malitia and Volunteer Corps are more fatal and dangerous than our open Enemies, this has already been verified in *Several* important instances, principally asscribed to *Their treaterous Commanders*, and in Case they are further made use off either on the Sea board or frontteir, they will

most assuredly prove the overthrow of our Republican Goverment, for in-
stance it is evident that the Nothern States are determined for to Stand
Nuter, and it is also evident that the Southern States are Seriously divided,
the Malitia in the Nothern States are *now* nearly all commanded by Federal
Governors, Major Generals &c down to corporals and They may all Justly
be considered our Sworn Enemies and more dangerous than an equal
Army of Brittish, for they have it in their power for to Surrender up all our
Fortresses, Men, Public and Private property under their Command at
pleasure, as *Hull, Ransaleer* and Smith has done, no doubt all the rest of
them will do the Same whenever they have a Similar oppertunity, this is not
all, let us view other dangers and difficulties our Army has mett with, They
have Suffered for the want of Provision, Cloathing, Tents, Barracks, Doc-
tors, and even for *Ammunition* in the time of *Battle* no doubt owing to our
Contractors and officers being Enemies to their Country Cause, I here ask,
how easily Such Men by Such Conduct may effect a Change of our present
Goverment and by the help of the Brittish plant their Standard in the
Nothern States, and by Uniting their forces on the North River, and at the
Same time imploy the Savages and Negroes on the Frontier and all over the
Southern States, with Admiral Warren[1] on the Sea board with a body of
Troops Joined by the Federalists to Assassinate and kill all the leading Republicans in the Southern States and plant the Brittish Standard there,
these are Serious Questions and worth my Friend Your *Serious and immediate* attention. Here I will State to You the *only* remedy that will be able for
to prevent this awfull Scene taking place the next campaign this present
year. Congress will act wisely for to raise immediately *Fifty thousand regular* Troops during the War, to be stationed at *Greenbush* untill the Wars
end, as an Army of *observation* and to Act as Circumstances may require.

And as it has become an object of the greatest importance to our Brethren who live on the Frontier, that we Should So far Conquer our Enemies
as will induce or Compell the *Indeons* for to Stand *Nuter*, also for to regain
the Confidence of the Canadians which we have forfeited, it makes it absolutely necessary that we Command Fort *Malden*, Fort *George* and *all* the
Lakes, (otherwise I Should Strongly recommend not to advance one Inch
into Canada), in order for to obtain the above objects. Congress will act
wisely for to raise immediately Twenty five thousand *regular* Troop during
the w⟨ar⟩ to be Stationed at Detroit untill the *war ends*—order one third
part of this army for to attack Fort Malden—one third as an army of reserve for to reinforce the Invadors instantly if necessary—the other third
to be kept at a proper place to cover their retreat in case of a defeat, and
guard the wounded, Provisions, and Public Stores, if in Case they take Fort
Malden, for to *demolish* it immediately and return to Detroit. Congress will
act wisely for to raise Twenty five thousand *regular* Troops during the War
to be Stationed at Niagara untill the *war ends*—order this army to proceed

as above Stated, and in Case they take Fort George for to *demolish* it immediately and return to Niagara—it will require Several thousand of these armies for to guard our Supplies &c on the road from Ohio &c, besides Several thousand of each army will either be killed, wounded and otherwise unfit for duty. Congress will act wisely for to raise *double* the number of *Seamen* and *marines* that is required at any one time for to man our Vessels and Boats on *each Lake* allowing one half to be killed and unfit for duty in the Course of one Campaign. These also to be enlisted during the war. Congress will act wisely for to raise one hundred thousand *regular* Troops during the war to be Stationed on the Sea Board from Louisiana to Eastport, in this Case the drafted Malitia may be disbanded. Volunteer Corps may Still be accepted upon the Condition that the President appoint all the Commissioned officers. In Case Congress Should Se[e] fit for to take Montreal it will require Fifty thousand more *regular* Troops not a man too many. In Case Congress should further Se[e] fit for to take Quebec it will require one Hundred thousand more *regular* Troops during the war, not a man too many. As I have no Idea that the two last Cases will be attempted or provided for this Season Shall add no more on either head. The Soldiers wages ought to have been *Ten* dollars per month and *must* be before you will be able for to raise a Sufficient Army even for to Act on the defencive, every Soldier ought for to receive all his Cloathing at the Instant he passes muster, and afterwards punctually and of a good quallity, and each Soldier ought to have a good *Great Coat* and a good pair of cowhide *Boots* and as *many* pair of Shoes as are found wanting, or they must often Suffer and die for Such neglect, their provision ought always to be good, and there ought always to be Six months provision in *advance* at *every Station*, also Tents, Barracks and Straw, and every Contractor that is found delinquent in furnishing *any* article in his Contract to forfeit a large penalty and immediately discharged as it tends for to distroy the lives of the Soldiers and prosecution of the War, this has already been verified, and our Internal Enemies have made great use of it to discourage our raising an Army, I refer you to all the Federal and even our Republican Newspapers.

Congress will act wisely for to authorise the President for to borrow at least one hundred Millions of Dollars if wanted and when wanted for to carry on the war, this will be a wise and necessary Step, as I am Confident that Congress will Soon have a Federal or Clintonian majority,[2] in either Case They will not vote to raise a Cent for to Carry on the War, now is the only favorable oppertunity for the Republicans in Congress for to Cloath the President with ample power, So as no future Congress can revoke it, You must be Sensiable Sir, that they have So far and no doubt will persevere for to defeat all your measures untill they actually effect a Change of our present Goverment. I am feelingly Sensiable that the Judgments of God are loudly threatened against the whole Humane Family, God has hardened the Hearts of our internal Enemies, we are a divided people and if the Scripture is true we Shall finally be left for to devour one another, Still it is our duty for to Contend for our Liberties and Country and leave the event to God. I have enclosed a Letter[3] to Sattisfy you how much I was Concerned in peacable times to have an Enemy removed out of office, how much greater my Concern must now be to Se[e] So many traitors appointed in the first onset of the present War, and God only knows how many more are now in office and will be unless the President and Senate will act more cautiously in future. The President will do well for to recommend to Congress for to appoint immediately a Sutable *Committee* for to inspect our armies, with regard to their provisions, Cloathing, and in every other respect, and make a monthly return to the Secretary at War. Such a Step would not only defeat the false rumors of our internal Ene-⟨mies⟩ but encourage the raising of an Army.

The President and Head Department ought not to hold Their Offices longer than *Eight* Years, it is not only unpopular but extremly dangerous in a Republican Goverment, Therefore Congress will act wisely for to establish this as an invariable rule in future, Mr. Eustis did well in resigning at this moment. Mr. Galliten in particular will do well for to resign his office *immediately*, and in Case He neglects to do it, the President will do well for to *remove* Him *immediately*, *all* the Federalists and *most* of the Republicans now Say that They ought to be removed, and I am often told by the Federalists that Mr Gallitin will prove to be a defaulter for thirty Millions of Dollars, Therefore Congress will do well for to chuse a Committee immediately for to Settle his Public accounts, let one third be Federalists and two thirds Republican, otherwise the Federalists will accuse the Committee of acting partial.

The Federalists all Say that they never will advance or pay a Cent towards Carrying on the War, unless they are Compelled to do it, Congress are all knowing to this fact. Therefore They ought not to have remitted the Merchants Bonds &c, besides Congress ought to be extremly Cautious not to Spend their time in making that or any other Laws, that will take as much time for to repeal it, in fact in the present Case it opened a door for bribery, how can the people Judge otherwise when those Bonds were all given by the Federalists; therefore now was the time for the Republicans to make the Federalists help Support the war, but alas it is now too late. I hope They will act more wisely in future, If Sir there is no more prospect of peace than our Newspapers inform us, I Shall be Surprised that Congress has not raised an army equal to the one I have proposed, Shall only add, that unless my proposals are immediately adopted and the whole army raised by the first day of June next and arrive at each Station, I now pledge my life that our Goverment will [. . .] this Season be obliged for to abandon the War, may God order it otherwise is my Sincere prayer.

Sir, please to excuse my incorrectness and expressions, and believe me to be with Sentiments of the highest Essteem and Respect yours and the Republicans well wisher.

WILLIAM WINGATE[4]

NB. you may return the enclosed Letter or not as you Se[e] fit.

RC (NN). Headed, "Circula⟨r⟩ to be laid before the Head department, General Dearborn and General Varnum"; docketed by JM; torn.

1. Sir John Borlase Warren (1753–1822) had been the British commander in chief of the Halifax station from November 1807 to July 1810. Educated at Emmanuel College, Cambridge, and serving in North America during the American Revolution, he held a seat in Parliament from 1774 to 1807 and commanded a frigate squadron that captured most of a similar French force on 23 Apr. 1794, for which victory he was made a Knight of the Bath. On 3 Aug. 1812 he was appointed to the Halifax, Leeward Islands, and Jamaica stations, whose commands had been united, so that he directed the overall naval strategy of the war. Warren advised Sir George Prevost, the military commander in North America, to build more ships on the Great Lakes and to reinforce the region. He also devised a defensive strategy off the North American coast for the protection of trade while maintaining a limited blockade of American waters through the spring of 1814. When Warren was relieved of his duties in March 1814, the blockade had extended beyond the Delaware and Chesapeake Bays to include New York, Charleston, Port Royal, Savannah, and the Mississippi River. It included not only named ports but all inlets southward as far as the Florida boundary, with New England still exempted (Halpenny, *Dictionary of Canadian Biography*, 6:802–3; Mahan, *Sea Power in the War of 1812*, 2:10–11).

2. The political composition of the Thirteenth Congress was 27 Republicans and 9 Federalists in the Senate and 114 Republicans and 68 Federalists in the House of Representatives (*Niles' Weekly Register* 4 [1813]: 268).

3. Enclosure not found.

4. William Wingate (1745–1821) of Haverhill, Massachusetts, and Hallowell, Maine, was married to Mehetable Bradley and was the younger brother of Paine Wingate, a jurist and U.S. senator from New Hampshire in the First and Second Congresses and a representative in the Third Congress (Charles E. L. Wingate, *Life and Letters of Paine Wingate* [2 vols.; Medford, Mass., 1930], 1:38; 2:438–39, 518, 540).

§ To Thomas Lloyd.[1] *1 January 1813.* "J. Madison will see Mr. Lloyd as he requests tomorrow morning at 10. OC."

RC (PPACHi: Thomas Lloyd Papers). 1 p. Dated "Jany. 1."; year assigned on the basis of evidence presented in n. 1.

1. Thomas Lloyd (1756–1827), a Federalist sympathizer and skilled stenographer, had edited the Pennsylvania ratification debates on the Constitution published in 1788 and had reported the debates of the First Federal Congress (*PJM*, 10:375 n. 1). After this meeting with JM, Lloyd evidently moved to Alexandria, where he began teaching shorthand and writing a book on the subject (Lloyd to JM, 29 Apr. 1813 [DLC]).

§ From Robert Patterson. *1 January 1813, "Mint of the U. States."* Forwards an annual report on the operation of the Mint.[1] Enumerates gold, silver, and copper coins struck, amounting to $1,115,219.50 in value. "The supply of gold & silver bullion still continues to be abundant; the deposits for coinage, at this time in our vaults, amounting to upwards of half a million of dollars."

RC and enclosures, two copies (DNA: RG 233, President's Messages, 12A-D1; DNA: RG 46, President's Messages, 12A-E5); FC (DNA: RG 104, Letters Sent by the Director). First RC 1 p. Forwarded by JM to Congress on 4 Jan. 1813; printed in *ASP, Finance*, 2:599–600. For enclosures, see n. 1.

1. Patterson enclosed a one-page statement of the coins struck at the U.S. Mint in 1812 and a one-page abstract of the ordinary expenses of the Mint for 1812.

§ Presidential Proclamation. *1 January 1813*. Revises building terms and conditions for the city of Washington. Suspends the first and third articles of the 17 Oct. 1791 building regulations until 1 Jan. 1814.[1] Adds an exception that "no wooden covering more than three hundred twenty square feet, or higher than twelve feet from the sill to the eve [*sic*] shall be erected, nor shall any such house be placed within twenty four feet of a brick or stone house."

Ms (DLC: Commissioners of the District of Columbia Collection, 1791–1869); photocopies of Ms (DLC: U.S. Executive File; DNA: RG 42, Records of the Office of Public Buildings and Grounds, entry 4). Ms 1 p.; in a clerk's hand, signed by JM. Printed in the *Daily National Intelligencer*, 8 Jan. 1813.

1. See Presidential Proclamation, 1 Jan. 1810, *PJM-PS*, 2:157 and n. 1.

§ From John Binns and Others. *2 January 1813*. "At a very numerous and respectable meeting of citizens of the United States, natives of the United Kingdom of Great Britain and Ireland, held in the city of Philadelphia January 2, 1813, to consider the proclamation of the Prince Regent of the 26th October, 1812[1] (a copy of which is enclosed), it was resolved to communicate to you, sir, the sentiments of the meeting on this proclamation, and respectfully, yet very earnestly, solicit such information as you may think proper to communicate on this very important subject. We are instructed to give the most unequivocal assurances of the sincere confidence they repose in the justice of the present administration of the General Government, of a devoted attachment to the Constitution of the United States, and a determination, with heart and hand, life and property, to defend the rights, the honor, and interests of the nation. The meeting, sir, were duly sensible of the peculiar delicacy and embarrassment of their situation.

"As citizens of the United States, they know that they are entitled to the protection of the Government, and they are not unmindful that you, sir, as Secretary of State, have informed the British minister that 'it is *impossible* for the United States to discriminate between their native and naturalized citizens.'[2] These facts are impressive, and would, even under the proclamation of the Prince Regent, have been altogether conclusive, were it not that facts, apparently in contradiction, are busily circulated and too often misrepresented not to induce fears and opinions calculated to injure the public service. Many thousands are the hearts which beat with anxiety to know the result of this application; yet their feelings, their fears, or forebodings are, in our judgment, but of small account compared with the public interests which are involved in the inquiry. Our opportunities enable us to see, and hear, and know the extent to which this proclamation has carried apprehension and excited distrust—an extent scarcely credible to persons whose situations and stations concur to preclude such opportunities, and shut every avenue to such knowledge, except from formal representation.

"May we not hope, sir, that these circumstances will by you be accepted as an apology for occupying so much of your time. Our motives, we trust, will excuse our errors, if our zeal should lead us into error. We affirm, not merely for ourselves, but for thousands, whose hearts are known to us, that we are desirous to be satisfied; we wish to be convinced; we are anxious that no loop be left on which skepticism or disaffection should hang a doubt to overshadow the minds of the timid or the wavering. Our feelings, our principles, our attachments are all embarked in the just and sacred cause of this our chosen, our adopted country.

"Here are our families, here our fortunes, here all that is most dear and precious to us, and it would wound us sorely if any device of the enemy should scatter such suspicion as to thin our ranks, when they were to be mustered to fight the battles of the United States.

"We arraign not the motives of those who go about and take pains to state that the hanging of a naturalized citizen at Halifax, taken from on board a national ship, in time of peace;[3] the not seizing hostages for those of the crew of the Wasp, put in irons and threatened with execution, and this with a knowledge of the regent's proclamation, are regarded as symptoms of an indifference to the fate of naturalized citizens; certain, however, we are that such statements have excited, and continue to excite, fears which we believe to be groundless, but which we certainly know to be injurious to the public service.

"Independent of all considerations connected with public or private armed ships, it is within the knowledge of this meeting that many persons who have enlisted in the army from the purest and most patriotic motives, men who enlisted determined to conquer or die, are now pausing and considering consequences, and some are actively employed in devising ways and means to procure their discharge, or otherwise to be permitted to leave the service.

"Similar feelings and fears prevent many at this time from enlisting. It is also a fact that a volunteer company, in this city, one hundred strong, principally naturalized citizens, whose zeal had prompted a tender of their service to the United States, have become so alarmed, under the proclamation, that the company will rather disband than hazard being hung as traitors. No inconsiderable portion of the militia of this State and of the States of New York and Maryland are naturalized citizens, principally natives of the United Kingdom of Great Britain and Ireland, and we regret to state, but we know the fact, that this proclamation has caused much conversation, which has awakened apprehensions which cannot fail to strengthen and to be productive of evil, if some means be not taken to eradicate them, and restore that perfect confidence which existed previous to the proclamation.

"We trust, sir, that the circumstances which have given rise to this letter, our apprehensions as to the probable magnitude of the evil, and the facts we have stated, will justify us to you for the length of this communication, and induce you to give such an answer as will dispel all fear, reanimate confidence, and make gratitude and patriotism burn with a still brighter and more vivid flame."[4]

Printed copy (John Binns, *Recollections of the Life of John Binns* . . . [Philadelphia, 1854], 214–17). Signed by Binns as chairman and by a committee consisting of William Smiley, John W. Thompson, Francis Mitchell, John Maitland, and George Palmer. Undated; date assigned here on the basis of internal evidence. "The above letter was forwarded addressed to 'The Hon. Richard Rush, acting Secretary of State,' to be by him laid before the President of the United States" (ibid., 217).

1. On 26 Oct. 1812 the prince regent issued a proclamation that was published in the 31 Dec. 1812 issue of the *National Intelligencer*. The proclamation declared that every native of Great Britain and Ireland taken in the service of the U.S. should be subject to "pain of death, and all other pains and penalties of high treason and piracy." Twenty-three English and Irish prisoners taken from the U.S. Army were sent to Quebec under this proclamation, then transported to England for trial. The episode provoked a lengthy debate in Congress over how the U.S. might respond. A bill authorizing the president to retaliate by inflicting similar punishments on British prisoners of war emerged from a Senate select committee formed on 9 Nov. 1812. The retaliation bill was debated and amended in both houses until 1 Mar. 1813, when it finally passed in the Senate, becoming law on 3 Mar. 1813. The bill authorized the president to resort to "full and ample retaliation" for any violation of the "law and usages of war." It also stipulated that the president could retaliate upon the British for injuries done by the Indians. The main objections to the bill arose not from opposition to the principle of retaliation but from the belief that such a power already existed (*Annals of Congress*, 12th Cong., 2d sess., 70–71, 89, 90, 112, 154–55, 1080, 1143–44, 1145–46; *U.S. Statutes at Large*, 2:829–30). After the bill became law, Secretary of War John Armstrong ordered the confinement, on 15 May 1813, of twenty-three British prisoners as hostages (*ASP, Foreign Relations*, 3:634–35).

2. Although the editors have been unable to locate the quotation Binns attributed to JM, the latter, while secretary of state, did remind British special envoy George Rose during their negotiations on the *Chesapeake* affair in February 1808 that "it would be impossible for the U. States to view natural-born subjects of G. Britain, who had been naturalized here, in any other light than as American Citizens whilst within American jurisdiction" ("Negotiations with Mr. Rose," 8 Feb. 1808, in Madison, *Writings* [Hunt ed.], 8:4–5).

3. Binns referred to the execution at Halifax of one of the sailors captured during the *Chesapeake-Leopard* affair in June 1807. Alleged to be a British deserter, the accused sailor, Jenkin Ratford, claimed to be an American named John Wilson. A native of London, Ratford was charged with deserting the British ship *Halifax* in March 1807 and thereafter serving on board the *Chesapeake*. He was court-martialed and sentenced to death on 26 Aug. 1807, having been found guilty of "mutiny, desertion, and contempt (insolence to a British naval officer)." On 31 Aug. 1807 he was hanged from the fore yardarm of the sloop *Halifax* (*The Trial of John Wilson, Alias Jenkin Ratford, for Mutiny, Desertion and Contempt: To Which Are Subjoined, a Few Cursory Remarks* [Boston, 1807; Shaw and Shoemaker 13737]; Tucker and Reuter, *Injured Honor*, 113).

4. Rush replied to Binns on 27 Jan. 1813: "I should have written to you before this upon the subject of the address you transmitted to me from our naturalized fellow-citizens to be laid before Mr Munroe, but that I was under the impression Mr Munroe himself would specially reply to it in a manner due to its importance. The reason I presume why he has not is, that he has not, as yet, felt himself enabled to say any thing in an official shape. . . . Besides the general conversations I have had with him upon the subject of the address it gives me great pleasure to say, though I do it unofficially, that I had an interview with him the day before yesterday and another this morning; that he says the President has had this interesting subject under his very special consideration; that he is determined this portion of our citizens shall stand upon a footing of the most undoubted security and receive, in all respects, the most sacred protection" (*Letters and Papers of Richard Rush* [microfilm ed.], reel 2).

§ From J. A. P. Poutingon. *2 January 1813, "Criminal residence," Washington.* Reports having been sent by JM five times to the office of the secretary of war: "and when I go for Justice in that office, I am ordered out by a Clerk." Repeats his appeals to "Generous James Madison," seeking a five-minute audience with JM to prove himself.[1] "When I loosed all what I had, I lost the Key, who open the mouth of the Attorneys." "If I was rich, I should not be in goal. . . . If I was to appears at this Court, I should wait for Justice, but I have nothing to wait, when I am confined only, but because I am a poor." Requests that JM "order my liberty."[2]

RC and enclosure (DLC). RC 4 pp.; undated; date taken from enclosure. Notes on cover in Poutingon's hand read: "To be forwarded immediately it comes from a man yet alive and in the grave" and "Your Excelency, will be bail for me I am confident, because I do not know nobody." For enclosure, see n. 2.

1. James Monroe, acting as secretary of war, wrote to Poutingon on 1 Jan. 1813, informing him that JM had appointed him riding master in the Second Regiment of Light Dragoons. Monroe noted that if Poutingon received and accepted the nomination, which was contingent on the consent of the Senate, "you will immediately repair to Albany, report yourself to Colonel Burn, & receive his orders" (DNA: RG 107, LSMA). That there is no record of the Senate's ever considering this nomination might suggest that Monroe and JM changed their minds after reading the contents of Poutingon's letter.

2. In the two-page enclosure Poutingon offered thoughts under the heading "Discovery or Service" on militia service and also on the constitutional extension of the territory of the Union. He included a brief piece for the Boston *Columbian Centinel*, addressed to the American government, on harbor fortifications. For a similar piece for the same newspaper, see the note Poutingon enclosed with his letter to JM of 30 Jan. 1811 (*PJM-PS*, 3:142 n. 3).

§ From Levin Winder.[1] *2 January 1813, Annapolis.* Transmits to JM "a Copy of a law passed by the General Assembly of Maryland" and requests that he "lay it before the Congress of the United States at their present Session."[2]

RC and enclosure (DNA: RG 233, President's Messages, 12A-D1); letterbook copy (MdAA: Executive Letter Book, fol. 225). RC 1 p.; in a clerk's hand, signed by Winder. For enclosure, see n. 2.

1. Levin Winder (1757–1819) had been inaugurated as the Federalist governor of Maryland in November 1812, replacing Republican Robert Bowie. Reelected in 1813 and 1814, Winder left the governor's chair in January 1816 and was elected the same year to the state senate, where he served until his death (Sobel and Raimo, *Biographical Directory of the Governors*, 2:653–54).

2. Winder enclosed a three-page summary of the proceedings of the Maryland General Assembly at its 1812–13 session, during which, on 2 Jan. 1813, the Maryland legislature passed an "act to incorporate a company for the purpose of cutting and making a canal between the river Delaware and the Chesapeake Bay." The Maryland legislature offered to take 250 shares in the Chesapeake and Delaware Canal Company if the commonwealth of Pennsylvania would subscribe for 375 shares, the state of Delaware for 100 shares, and the U.S. government for 750 shares in the same company. In its winter session of 1812–13, the Pennsylvania legislature also passed an act authorizing a subscription to the canal company if the U.S. government and the state of Delaware would subscribe in proportional amounts. On 13 Jan. 1813, at the request of the Maryland General Assembly, JM transmitted to Congress "copies of their Act passed on the 2d instant" (DNA: RG 233, President's Messages, 12A-D1; 1 p.), which was read before the House of Representatives on 14 Jan. and the Senate on 15 Jan.

On 26 Jan. 1813 Maryland representative Stevenson Archer "presented a bill authorizing the Secretary of the Treasury to subscribe for shares in the Chesapeake and Delaware Canal Company, in behalf of the United States" (*Annals of Congress*, 12th Cong., 2d sess., 46, 51–52, 804, 893). As with past subscription proposals to Congress from the canal company, Congress delayed consideration of the bill by referring it to committee. In 1816 the suspended canal project was linked with the chartering of the Second Bank of the United States, but hopes for federal aid for internal improvements were shattered by JM's subsequent veto of the 1817 Bonus Bill (see Joshua Gilpin to JM, 28 Aug. 1809, *PJM-PS*, 1:342 and n. 1, and Gray, *The National Waterway*, 24).

From Joseph Wheaton

Confidential   CAMP 10, MILES FROM MANSFIELD.
EXCELLENT SIR,   ON MY ROUT TO UPER SANDUSKY Jany 3d 1813
    I wrote you from Mansfield Decr. 31. and detailed to you the measures taken to insure a Speady March to Head Quarters. The ordinance & Stores moved about two Miles on that day in hopes of making considerable distance the next. Unfortunately the thawy weather had much more broken up the road than was immagined, and the next day 1st. Jany it raind incessantly very hard & wa[r]m all day. Capt Gratiot who had been with me the whole rout and was Commanding officer of the whole received orders from Genl. Harrisons Asst. D. Adjt. Genl. to leave the command of the troops & convoy with me, and tooke his leave at ½ past Six A.M. yesterday Morning in a very Severe Snow Storm which has continued ever Since—and the Snow is now Sixteen inches deep. I commenced our March immediately after his departure, but the warm rain had So effectually Softened the ground, taken the frost wholly out that the gun carriages only Made four Miles and the wagons very few came up—one of the tongues of a Six pdr. Broke, and an axletree of a twelve pd. But not a wagon moved without being Stalled. Several tongues, axletrees, & coupleing poles broke. The Snow has now been falling thirty three hours, and is continuing. I in this Situation have thought it prudent, and advisable to detach the light Six pd carriages in front and the twelve pdrs in rear to Sandusky in order to keep open the road that the wagons may go, on as Soon as I can have them repaired—but Sir I assure you all my resourses are now in requisition. Captain Matthew Johnson[1] of Greenburg, Pa. his Compy of fifty men With Liut Walker of thirty men were all the force that Majr. Stodard allowed me as guards and pioneers. Capt. Johnson his officers and Men have therefore been on the most Laborous and Severe duty ever Since I left Pittsburg, and yesterday with unequalled patience, perseverance and zeal, without a Murmor or complaint, redoubled their exertions, with Screws, pries, & ropes to haul out the wagons, and assist the horses in every instan[c]e of difficulty up to their hips in water mud & Snow, but all our exertions and force failed

about twenty wagons are fast in the mud and tho we have Strength enough to hew them all to pieces we cannot move them. The Mud with the Snow Make the wheels a Sollid body and holding them in the Soft Ground they become fast. To Captain Matthew Johnson of Greersburg his officers and men, I owe to them to State to you Sir that all that could be done by men has been done, their Labour has been constant and every exertion made to aid this convey [sic]. To Mr. James Anderson, and Mr. Paul Anderson my wagon Master & Forage Master I have receved every possible aid, their fidility, zeal, and exertions with Superior abilities fitter for more ellevated Situations has been imployed on every occasion. I apprehend with much concern that I Shall have to return Some horses to the Mohacan Settlement near thirty miles for forage and provision before I Shall be able to Make Sleads Sufficient to overcome this difficulty. Of Brigadier General Crooks Also I feel Myself bound to State that he Marched from Pittsburg about the 15th. Octr. with 1400 or 1500 men, that he arrived at Mansfield the last day of November. On all of his rout I cannot find that he had out a Single party as pioneers, or on fatigue duty, nor a Single instance when he mended or improved the road. At Canton Captain Gratiot wrote him in the most urgent Maner to Send four or five Companies of enfantry to aid the convoy in getting forward—he returnd him for answer that Captain Johnsons command was Sufficient, refusing any additional aid—at Mansfield where he lay four weeks—nothing was done for the imp[r]ovement of any road, no kind of discipline was observed in his camp, and if the united testimony of public officers and inhabitants is to be regarded, a genel. depridation was committed upon their Cattle, their Hogs, their Cornfield, their poultry—household furniture, Blankets cloathing, untill the general appearance of the inhabitants are as tho they possessed nothing. I never have Seen apparently so destitute a Set of people, these people expressed as much joy and Gladness at their departure as if So many Savages had left them. They Say they are deprived of every thing but their land and their lives. On this rout to Sandusky plains 25 Miles it was expected Something would have been done to have facilitated the movements of this convoy So invaluable to Genl. Harrisons Army, but Sir if anything has been done it is greatly to its injury by le⟨ad⟩ing me in to a Swamp where Some of my wagons must winter. Unfortunately I fear we must loose Several of Capt Johnsons men their exposure has been such, their health is gone and I apprehend Several will sink under it I have neither medicine, nor medical aid to relieve them. The impositions too put on the public in the article of axes by a Lt. Johnson A D Q M at Pittsburg I have before mentioned to the Secretary at war, there are about 2000 Made by his brother in law now lying at Mansfield, and deemed worth less than comon Iron. They are only ground up to disappoint all who take them, and tho I have to Commence Making Sleads to Morrow to Move all the Stores with me I have only Six axes fit for use, having all the rest returned or left because useless. My Heart is Sick with the ignorance the folly or wickedness of those in public Service. I write you Excellent Sir not knowing who May now be the Secretary at war—hoping however it May be Mr. Monroe—if that good man Eustis has retired—and with a frankness arising from your knowledge of me—and I am Excellent Sir with the Homage of my Heart faithfully your Obedient Servant

JOSEPH WHEATON Capt. M. D. C
& Asst Depty Qutr. Mastr. N. W. Army

Excuse any encorrectness. I write with very cold fingers under my tent in the Snow
   The Snow is Still falling and is now 18 inches deep

RC (DLC). Docketed by JM, "Jany 3. 8. 1813."

1. Mathew Johnson (d. 1853) of Greensburg, Pennsylvania, served as captain of a company of Pennsylvania militia from October 1812 to April 1813 (White, *Index to War of 1812 Pension Files*, 2:1088).

§ From Philip Sisson. *3 January 1813, Tiverton.* Has read in the newspapers that JM is "to cause to Be Bult an addition to our Navy four Ships fit for Battle Ships and Six forty gun frigits."[1] Offers to "have one of them Bult within the State of Rhode-island or the town of troy State of masachusetts."

RC (DNA: RG 45, Misc. Letters Received). 1 p.

1. Sisson had read the act to increase the navy, which was approved on 2 Jan. 1813. The naval buildup grew out of a recommendation in JM's annual message of 4 Nov. and a Senate resolution on 9 Nov. 1812 to create a select committee under the leadership of Samuel Smith "to report thereon by bill or otherwise." On 30 Nov., Smith introduced the bill in the Senate, where it was debated from 12 Dec. until it passed on 15 Dec. Burwell Bassett, who had chaired the naval committee in the House of Representatives and introduced the bill there on 27 Nov., had consulted with Paul Hamilton to obtain estimates of the expenses of building and equipping ships of war as well as of the force needed to protect U.S. commerce. The bill to increase the navy authorized the president "to cause to be built, equipped and employed, four ships to rate not less than seventy-four guns, and six ships to rate forty-four guns each" and appropriated $2.5 million for this purpose. It was further debated in the House from 16 Dec. to 23 Dec. On 24 Dec. the Senate concurred in an amendment to the bill adopted by the House (*Annals of Congress*, 12th Cong., 2d sess., 18, 25, 31, 32, 33, 34, 35, 142, 201, 404–28, 429–30, 436–37, 440–41, 443–50; *ASP, Naval Affairs*, 1:275–80; *U.S. Statutes at Large*, 2:789).

To Creed Taylor

SIR   WASHINGTON Jany. 4. 1813
   Understanding that a Clerk will be wanted for a Chancery Court at Fredg. I have yielded to the request of the friends of Mr. R. M. Chapman, who is my neighbor & acquaintance, so far as to join them in bearing tes-

551

timony to his personal worth & reputed qualifications for the duties of such an appointment. Being ignorant of the other names which may be before the Judges, it would not be in my power, if it were less improper, to enter into the comparative estimates, by which their selection will be guided. I could not do less however than express my belief, that if this should fall on Mr. Chapman the object of the Court would not be disappointment. Be pleased to accept assurances of my esteem & respect.[1]

JAMES MADISON

RC (ViU: Creed Taylor Papers). Addressee not indicated.

1. Creed Taylor (1766–1836) was a lawyer and judge in Cumberland County, Virginia. He served under Capt. Charles Allen during the Revolution and later worked in the law office of Col. George Carrington Jr. Taylor was a member of the Virginia House of Delegates in 1788 and of the state senate from 1798 to 1805. In November 1805 he was elected judge of the General Court and in June 1806 chancellor of the superior court for the Richmond District. Taylor was the founder and director of the Needham Law School (Robert K. Brock, *Needham Law School, 1821–1842* [Farmville, Va., 1935], 10–11).

From Albert Gallatin

DEAR SIR   Monday [4 January 1813]

I do not believe that the appointmt. of Govr. Tompkins[1] would be either eligible or calculated to inspire confidence. No person thinks him equal to the place at such time as this. The office requires first abilities & frightens those who know best its difficulties. Dearborn & Mr Monroe have shrunk from it, & so will, I suspect, Crawford.[2] Respectfy. Yours

ALBERT GALLATIN

RC (DLC: Rives Collection, Madison Papers). Undated; date assigned here on the basis of the fact that 4 Jan. 1813 was the last Monday before JM nominated John Armstrong as secretary of war on 8 Jan. (*Senate Exec. Proceedings*, 2:315).

1. Above the line here in JM's hand is written "(Secy of war)."
2. JM hoped that James Monroe would take over the duties of the War Department on a permanent basis. Monroe, however, was concerned about how such an appointment would affect his prospects in the 1816 presidential race and declined the position. Reinstating Henry Dearborn in the post he had occupied during the Jefferson administrations seemed ill-advised after the military defeats in the fall of 1812. JM also considered William Harris Crawford as a possible replacement for Eustis, but Crawford also refused (see Brant, *Madison*, 6:126–28).

From Benjamin Morgan

Sir   New Orleans Jany 4th 1813

On the 21st of June last I received a letter from the Secretary of War informing me that I was appointed Deputy Commissary for this District and desiring If I accepted of the appointment to forward on my bond with two surities for the sum of ten thousand dollars for the faithful performance of my trust. Being assured by my Northern friends that our Country would be involved in War with Great Britain & willing to contribute my Services in the way they would be most useful to wit the Staff department I wrote to Mr Eustis on the 23d of June that I accepted and again on the 29th of the same month enclosing the Bond required and desiring he would send me instructions since which I have never receivd a line from him.

Early in the Month of August I was called upon by General Wilkinson to enter upon the duties of my office I began my purchases without hesitation seeing the Publick service required it altho without a Commission or Instructions. Early in November I receivd Instructions from Callender Irvine Esqr Commissary General with whom I have since Corresponded.

I trouble you with this detail to shew that the Secretary of War has by his inattention hazarded the Publick Interest in this quarter and placed me in a very unpleasant situation by Obliging me to Act without proper Authority or information or see the Service suffer And to solicit that you will cause a Commission to be sent me with directions from the War department to Act under the orders of & Account with the Commissary General in future If that is as I presume it must be the intention of the Government. I am with great respect Your Most Obt Servant

                                       Benjn Morgan [1]

RC (DNA: RG 107, LRRS, M-21:7). Docketed as received in the War Department on 1 Feb. 1813.

1. Benjamin Morgan (d. 1826) was appointed to the legislative council of the Orleans Territory in 1804 and in 1806 was a representative of Orleans County in the territorial legislature. He was one of the principal merchants of New Orleans, an alderman for the city from 1806 to 1811, and a director of the New Orleans Navigation Company and the New Orleans Insurance Company. He was appointed president of the New Orleans branch of the Bank of the United States in 1811 and president of the New Orleans branch of the Second Bank of the United States when it was established in 1816 (Van Horne, *Papers of Benjamin Henry Latrobe*, 3:120 n. 8).

§ From the Ohio General Assembly. *4 January 1813*. "It has pleased Divine Providence, that this general assembly should convene under circumstances, new, replete with interest, and of great national concern. While the moral and political convulsions of Europe have shaken empires from their centre, this nation has, alone pursued a peaceful policy. It has grown in wealth, it has increased in importance, until its power has become a cause of jealousy among the nations of the old world, and its wealth has but too effectually invited their rapacity.

"Endeavoring to surmount injustice with its view fixed on peace and with exertions never suspended, the American administration has been determined if practicable, to elude the evils of war, mildness has characterised its manner, and justice has been its whole demand: But forbearance has been in vain. Forgetting the principles of justice and regardless of our unquestioned rights, the great contending powers of Europe have reduced plunder to system, and in that system, unremittingly persevere, nor is this all; the British nation has superadded personal oppression and the cruel enslavement of our citizens; and even when professedly at peace with the United States she has been perfidiously accessary to the murder of our frontier inhabitants, by instigating and aiding her savage allies whose cruel mode of warfare is disgraceful to humanity. Still, was she invited to be just, while the sword was yet starting from its scabbord, the olive branch was cordially offered to the enemy; but this offer is refused, and the only republic which has survived the general wreck of nations is in open war.

"Impressed with a full conviction that the war in which this nation is involved is on our part just and necessary, that the cause pursued by the administration in recommending the measure, and in its mild, conciliatory and continued efforts to secure to this nation an honorable peace, merits the entire approbation of this general assembly and that, not only the honor and dignity of this people, but its continuance, as a free and independent nation, depends upon a vigorous prosecution of the war: Therefore,

"*Resolved by the general assembly of the state of Ohio,* That in the name and in behalf of our constituents we pledge ourselves, to aid the national government in the present emergency to the extent of our resources: And we do this in the hope that the goodly heritage of our freedom may descend from us, to posterity, as we received it—excellent and unimpaired.

"*Be it further resolved,* That we have seen, with emotions of much concern, the protracted delay of the French government, to render justice to this nation, for its outrageous depredations upon us, and that we will afford, to the constituted authorities in whose wisdom and firmness we place confident reliance, our utmost support in their efforts to sustain the honor of the nation, and to obtain suitable amends for its injuries.

"*Be it further resolved,* That in the opinion of this general assembly, every republic is now peculiarly called upon by all honorable and honest motives, to sacrifice, at the shrine of his country, political dissentions and personal animosities, and with united efforts to rescue from danger, that civil and political liberty, for which our fathers so arduously struggled and so freely bled.

"*Be it further resolved,* That the governor be requested to transmit to the president of the United States, to the president of the senate, the speaker of the house of representatives, and to our senators and representative in congress, one copy each of the foregoing declaration and resolutions."

Printed copy (DLC). 1 p.; signed by John Pollock, Speaker of the Ohio House of Representatives, and Thomas Kirker, Speaker of the Ohio Senate. Enclosed in Return Jonathan Meigs to JM, 10 Jan. 1813 (DLC; 1 p.).

To Elbridge Gerry

private

DEAR SIR   [5 January 1813]

Your two favors of   ¹ have been some time on hand. I believe it may
be assumed, that no meeting of Congress will take place immediately after
the 4th. of March. The Senate has usually been detained a few days, for the
sake of appointments growing out of the laws of session. It is always possible, and must be so considered at present, that other business requiring
their decision, may prolong their stay, or an early return, after their adjournment. Nothing is known here, more than you know, on which a calculation as to the latter must be founded. Should the call on you be limited
to the case of the ordinary business of deciding on nominations, you have
the sanction of precedent as well as the length of the Journey & season of
the year, in yielding to your personal accomodation. The oath of office may
I believe be taken *any where*, before the Judge & within the time prescribed.
After stating this side of the subject, allow me to remind you, that one half
of the difficulty arising from the distance & the season, may be avoided by
proceeding Southwardly instead of returning Northward. Your friends in
Virga will then be the gainers, & among them none more than Yrs. very
sincerely

J. MADISON

RC (owned by Mr. and Mrs. Philip D. Sang, Chicago, Ill., 1958). Postmarked Washington,
5 Jan.; docketed by Gerry: "President Madison without date—recd Jany & copy of my answer
26 Jany 1813." Undated; date assigned here on the basis of the postmark and Gerry's docket.

1. Blank left in RC. Gerry's previous two letters to JM were dated 12 and 19 Dec. 1812.

§ From Alexander Stuart, Shadrach Bond, and Edward Hempstead. *5 January 1813,
Washington.* "The Undersigned beg leave . . . to State to the President . . . that they
Consider Nathaniel Pope Esqr Secretary of the Illinois Territory as a Gentleman
of the first intelligence, talents, work, and integrity. That the office he now holds
cannot in our opinion be filled by any One with more ability than by him, and that
his reappointment to that office will give general satisfaction to the inhabitants of
that Territory."¹

RC (DNA: RG 59, LAR, 1809–17, filed under "Pope, Nathaniel"). 1 p.; enclosed in
Shadrach Bond to James Monroe, 5 Jan. 1812 [1813] (ibid.). Printed in Carter, *Territorial Papers, Illinois,* 16:284.

1. JM nominated Pope for reappointment as secretary of the Illinois Territory on
29 May 1813 (*Senate Exec. Proceedings,* 2:347).

§ From an Unidentified Correspondent. *5 January 1813, Walpole, New Hampshire.*
Writes to communicate to JM "the principle of a long desired discovery . . . , that

of perpetual motion." Uses the example of waterwheels to demonstrate the usefulness of force. Because he does "not think it right to sell the efforts of reason in discoveries," he will "make a present of it" to his country.[1] Does not "even think proper at present to reveal" his name but may do so "in time": "it will be known by the producing the piece of paper cut from this and the original."

RC (DLC). 2 pp.; marked "Duplicate"; signature clipped; docketed by JM, "perpetual motion / 1813."

1. Many "inventors" of perpetual motion machines sought to make a fortune by charging admission to demonstrations of their contraptions. In 1812 Charles Redheffer set up a machine in Philadelphia that many people flocked to observe. The Philadelphia *Aurora General Advertiser* became a clearinghouse for the ongoing battle between the advocates and detractors of perpetual motion. William Duane, editor of the *Aurora*, reported on 9 Jan. 1813 that "some unknown person" brought an advertisement to be inserted into his paper about the perpetual motion machine and "when asked by whose order, or to whose account," answered only, "on account of the proprietors of the machine." (For a more detailed account, see Arthur W. J. G. Ord-Hume, *Perpetual Motion: The History of an Obsession* [New York, 1977], 125–33.)

From William Harris Crawford

Sir.   Senate Chamber 6th Jany. 1813

The very Kind and flattering manner in which you offered me a seat in the Cabinet,[1] yesterday, has made a very deep impression upon my mind. Under the influence of this impression, and with a sincere desire to act in conformity with your wishes, I have reviewed the reasons which then induced me to decline that honorable distinction. This review has terminated in the conviction, that I am not qualified to discharge the duties which would devolve upon me, by obeying your call, with reputation to myself, and with advantage to the Country.

In communicating this determination, I beg leave to assure you Sir, that in the present Situation of the nation, nothing but a deep Sense of my incapacity to discharge the duties of the office, which your Kind partiality had intended for me, would induce me to decline the honor. I am Sir respectfully your most obt. & humbe Servt

Wm H Crawford

RC (DLC: Rives Collection, Madison Papers); Tr, two copies (ViHi; DLC: Samuel Smith Papers). RC docketed by JM.

1. See Gallatin to JM, 4 Jan. 1813, and n. 2.

From Albert Gallatin

Dear Sir   7th Jany. 1813

Since, from this morning's conversation, it appears that the choice of a Secy. of War must fall on Govr. Tompkins or on Gen. Armstrong, permit me to state the reasons which, after fixing my thoughts on those two gentlemen alone, incline me in favour of the last.

Personally acquaintted with both, I feel no hesitation in saying that as respects talents & military knowledge, Gen. Armstrong is much superior to the Governor, who I fear would prove inadequate to the task of organizing the department & the army. Public opinion has also assigned a standing to Gen. Armstrong both as a military man & as a man of talents, which will shield him & the administration from the attacks to which the other gentleman would be as much exposed as Dr. Eustis.

In point of temper, Govr. Tompkins would perhaps have the advantage;[1] but this consideration, at this time, should, in my opinion, yield to those I have mentioned, unless there should be some stronger objection than I understand to exist on your part or on that of Mr Munroe. The fate of your administration, of the Republican cause, perhaps of the Nation depends so essentially on the proper management of the War department, that from the beginning I never could be reconciled to the selection of an inferior character for that station. Gen. Dearborn I did not consider as such.

The objection of indolence does not strike me very forcibly: from self experience I infer that a sense of duty & fear of disgrace may, even in a man much less ambitious than Gen. Armstrong, prevent any sensible inconvenience from that cause. And it is much more important for the head of a department that he should think & act well than that he should work much.

Neither of them has much personal influence either in Congress or amongst the people; but Armstrong will certainly inspire more general confidence, although he probably has more enemies. In the present political situation of New York, it seems also more eligible to leave Govr. Tompkins there, than to throw the immediate Government in the hands of De-Witt Clinton & to lose the only chance of a Republican Governor at the April election.

The only difficulty in my mind is that Gen. Armstrong may not bring in the administration that entire unity of feeling, that disinterested zeal, that personal attachment, which are so useful in producing hearty co-operation & unity of action. And this is felt by me with particular force, because the Treasury department stands most in need of that co-operation and is most seriously affected when perfect cordiality & disposition to accommodate do not exist. I can only say that, although Mr Munroe, Mr Crawford & Gen. Dearborn would in other respects have appeared preferable, & in that view been every thing that could be desired, and although it is not improbable that Govr. Tompkins would at least be more accommodating, I am willing so far as relates to myself to run the risk of being associated with Gen. Armstrong. I believe that without having the strong feelings to which I have alluded, he is upon the whole personally well disposed; and that he has too much sense not to perceive that his only chance of success will depend on a cordial union with all of us, & that once embarked he can not save himself if we are shipwrecked. Respectfully & truly Your's

ALBERT GALLATIN

I forgot to say that it is the circumstance of my being the only person in the adminn. personally acquaintted with Govr. Tompkins which has prompted me to write. I have already mentioned that I am on the most cordial footing with him.

8th. Let me add that I think that you do not appreciate the several departments at their real actual rate of importance. If the choice is to fall on a man not professional, I will be ready (Mr Monroe still refusing) to accept the War dept. with all its horrors & perils. And let Tompkins take the Treasury. That at least would be better than to give the War dept. to him.

RC (DLC: Rives Collection, Madison Papers). Docketed by JM.

1. John Armstrong had a reputation among his acquaintances for being indolent, irascible, and quick to make enemies. Charles Biddle wrote that Armstrong "has very superior talents, but they are almost useless, he is so extremely indolent" (see Skeen, *John Armstrong*, 20, 115–16, 205).

From Charles W. Goldsborough

SIR,   NAV DEPT. 7th Jan. 1813.

Agreeably to directions received from you yesterday, I have the honor of transmitting a paper which exhibits a view of the vessels purchased & built, since the last session of congress, without being previously authorized by Law—with their cost as far as it can be ascertained.[1]

It is a subject of great regret to me, that owing to the very loose manner in which the Books of money warrants & drafts have been kept, for some time past, the State of the appropriations cannot, in any reasonable time, be prepared. With great respect I have the honor to be sir yr o st

CH: W: GOLDSBOROUGH

RC (DLC). Docketed by JM.

1. Enclosure not found.

From John Winthrop

SIR,   BOSTON Jany. 7. 1813

It may appear presumptuous in a private individual like myself to address the chief majistrate of a nation, but when the interest of a beloved country is at heart, when those all important ties which ought to unite, as an integral, ev'ry member of the Union are daily diminishing from causes which are, in a great measure, kept hid from your knowledge & prompted by my own sufferings produced by my adherence to the republican cause, I deem it my sacred duty to address you upon the subject.

When Docr. Eustis was first called to the War Departmnt. I was in habits of frequent intercourse with him; & the subject of Executive appointments, among others, being introduced, I stated to him the necessity of your being correctly informed as to the characters of candidates for Offices, & above all, as to the characters and influence of those who recommended them, & further that the republican cause had been greatly injured in this section of the Union, by injudicious appointments. I attached no blame to Mr Jefferson; I loved, honored & respected him; but censured those who from the basest sinister motives had wilfully misled him. The Docr. fully coincided with me in opinion, & said that he would take the Liberty as he thought it a duty, to suggest these facts to you. Yet, Sir, pardon me the remark, the same system has been unfortunately persevered in ever since, & although I have orally & by letters both to Docr. Eustis & Mr Hamilton protested against it, my monitions have been slighted or but partially regarded, untill the most deleterious consequences have followed, even in a more rapid and fatal succession than I predicted. You have had men recommended to you, as competent to fill responsible and lucrative offices, who five or six years ago kept wine cellars, were Shoemakers & were some of a lower grade, who possessed no one requisite for the Offices to which they were appointed, except being violent partizans: Many of them destitute of education or influential family connections & have little or no weight of character among the well inform⟨ed⟩ part of the community where they reside. Several me⟨m⟩bers of Congress from this State, have, as I am informed been very active in recommending their subordinate agent⟨s⟩ to your favor, without discovering to you their own dir⟨ect⟩ or remote interests; but Sir, I hope you will pardon my presumption, if I recommend the adoption of the latin mott⟨o⟩ "Audi alteram partem."[1] Then you will receive the whole truth. The public voice has been loud in its disapprobat⟨ion⟩ of many of our delegates, & their influence in the counties th⟨ey⟩ represent is merely nominal. Had I not the most exalt⟨ed⟩ opinion of the purity of your motives & your earnest wish to consult the best interests of your country I should not venture to be thus explicit; I have ineffectually tried to convey the truth thro' the heads of Departments, & I now a⟨d⟩dress the source of their power. You may rely on the fact, that nearly one half the opposition to your Govern⟨ment⟩ in this State has grown out of these causes. Men who had suffered great mortifications, had been excluded from the benefit of monied institutions, and even from visit[i]ng good society, solely from their attachment to an elective government; have been left, to buffet the storms of party, in neglect, whilst others of the description be-force [*sic*] mentioned have basked in the sunshine of Executive patronage. It is impossible any government whose basis is the principal of universal suffrage, however modified in this country, can long sustain itself, unless by the most vigilant attention to the appointment, of its subordinate officers. Men of talents and strong family interest have become disgusted, some of them in orde⟨r⟩ to screen themselves have united with the Federalists, but a far greater portion have kept aloof and would tak⟨e⟩ no part in the late elections. They could not in their con⟨s⟩ciences justify placing power and emolument in such improper hands, & they were determined to suffer in silence, but not under the additional reproach of vindicating such appoint-ments. Those and similar causes combined with the severe pressure of just, tho' unfortunate War, have amalgamated many of the most violent party antipathies, & produced in New England, a solid & prodigious mass of op-position to your administration. There is scarcely a single man of tolerable respectability who now advocates the cause.

The person who now has the honor of addressing you, has suffered se-verely under the mortifications & disappointments he discribes. For a year past he has been boyed up by the most delusive promises from Docr Eustis & Mr Hamilton, and while espousing a sinking cause has been crushed in its fall. Immediately on my return from Europe, & in conjunction with Mr Erving I warmly embraced the republican cause, & in several public meet-ings in this Town, openly advocated the election of Mr Jefferson, as I con-sidered the measures he would pursue, essentially opposed to ev'ry thing resembling an heredetary establishment. I entered life with flattering pros-pects, a good estate and extensive family connections. 'Tis now nearly twelve years since I have been labouring under the morbid effects of my first political attempt I have never, 'till within the past year, solicited an office, nor have I, in any manner, received countenance or patronage from the government in whose cause I suffered. My early friend⟨s⟩ and acquain-tance have refused extending their assistance, because I had professed the opinions of a party, they chose to consider, as unpopular as they were de-grading. Owing to these circumstances, for some years past, I have been compelled to quit my accustomed occupation & have done business under other names. But the calamities of War have checked that source, & the loss of a considerable property coming from New Orleans & taken by the Brit-ish, together with the increasing expenses of a young family, render me in-competent to provide for my annual expenditures. Col Hichborn[2] my father in law, & well known to Col. Munroe, is also very infirm, & needs my assistance.

Under these circumstances Sir, I presume to address you. To state facts with which Mr Lloyd and Docr. Eustis are conversant & to request you would interest yourself in my favor, by placing me in some Office where my exerti[o]ns may prove useful to myself and country. My relations are all strongly republican, & my uncle James Winthrop has been an elector of Mr Jeffersons.

Should you deem it proper to acknowledge the receipt of this letter, & wish any further evidence of the facts contained in it; you will confer a lasting obligation on one, who has the honor to be Sir, Yr Most Obt. respectful servant

JOHN WINTHROP [3]

RC (NN). Docketed by JM.

1. *Audi alteram partem:* "hear the other side."
2. Benjamin Hichborn (1746–1817), a noted Boston orator and barrister, graduated from Harvard in 1768 and was an ardent patriot, serving as a lieutenant colonel and as a member of the Boston Committee of Correspondence during the Revolutionary War. With Perez Morton he organized the Boston Independent Corps in 1776. In January 1779 he was involved in a widely publicized incident in which he reputedly shot Benjamin Andrews in the head by accident while seated at Andrews's dinner table. In February 1780 he married Hannah Gardner Andrews, the widow of Benjamin Andrews, and cared for her children. He served as a justice of the peace and in the 1780s and 1790s as an elected member of the General Court, where he represented Boston and, later, Dorchester. After becoming a widower, Hichborn traveled in France. Upon his return, he married Hannah Pendexter in 1801 and was elected a state senator from Norfolk (Loring, *The Hundred Boston Orators*, 130–32; Clifford K. Shipton, *Biographical Sketches of Those Who Attended Harvard College in the Classes 1768–1771*, vol. 17 of *Sibley's Harvard Graduates* [Boston, 1975], 37–44).
3. John Winthrop (1778–1819) of Boston graduated from Harvard in 1796, whereupon he traveled to Europe. He inherited land in the District of Maine upon his father's death in 1800. On 9 Nov. 1801 he married Ann Halsey Hichborn. After her death in 1813 he traveled to Europe again, and upon returning to the U.S. he relocated to Baton Rouge, where his brother Adam was prospering and where his unmarried sister Harriet had moved with his children (Lawrence Shaw Mayo, *The Winthrop Family in America* [Boston, 1948], 352–55).

§ From Albert Gallatin. *7 January 1813.* "I enclose the usual account of the contingent expences of Govt.—which is sent by yourself to each house of Congress. The triplicate remains with you." [1]

RC and enclosure (DLC); enclosure, two copies (DNA: RG 233, President's Messages, 12A-D1; DNA: RG 46, President's Messages, 12A-E2). RC 1 p.; docketed by JM. For enclosure, see n. 1. JM transmitted the message in a letter to Congress dated 11 Jan. 1813 (DNA: RG 233, President's Messages, 12A-D1; 1 p.; in the hand of Edward Coles, signed by JM).

1. According to the enclosed one-page account, prepared by Joseph Nourse and dated 6 Jan. 1813, the contingent expenses of government from 1 Jan. to 31 Dec. 1812 were

$16,844.72. The account included $120 in favor of Gideon Granger for the "expenses of taking possession of a part of West Florida under the Presidents Proclamation of October 1810; and for which . . . Claiborne is charged."

§ From Charles W. Goldsborough. *7 January 1813.* "With great deference—but for *very special reasons*—C W Goldsborough would propose to the President the immediate revocation of the order, to which the enclosed letter is an answer; [1] & which was unknown to C. W. G. till this moment."

RC (DLC). 1 p.; docketed by JM. Enclosure not found, but see n. 1.

1. On 31 Dec. 1812 Paul Hamilton had directed George Harrison, naval agent at Philadelphia, to deliver to Thomas Ewell, hospital surgeon at the Washington Navy Yard recently turned government contractor, "Sixty thousand lbs of Saltpetre either crude or refined—and ten thousand lbs of sulphur taking his receipt for the same" (DNA: RG 45, Misc. Letters Sent). In a pamphlet he was to publish on 22 Jan. 1813, Goldsborough revealed that he had long been on bad terms with Ewell and that they had quarreled over the terms of Ewell's gunpowder contracts with the Navy Department. On this occasion Goldsborough objected to a contract made on 31 Dec. 1812, the fulfillment of which was contingent on the above order and which would pay Ewell "*twenty-two and a half* cents per pound, for every pound of Powder made by him for the Navy Department." Goldsborough claimed that the contract was "*so twisted and turned*, and *cunningly contrived*, that the contractor will receive *more than twenty-two and a half cents!*" He also objected that "In this contract, *no security* was taken—the quantity of Powder to be made was undefined—no stipulation as to the period of delivery—besides other informalities and defects" (Charles W. Goldsborough, *To the Public* [n.p., 1813; Shaw and Shoemaker 51307], 24–25). This contract, Goldsborough believed, had been written by Ewell himself, and Goldsborough declared that he "knew nothing of it till the 7th January, 1813" (ibid., 24), when he was alerted to its existence, apparently by a 5 Jan. 1813 letter from George Harrison (not found, but acknowledged in Goldsborough to Harrison, 7 Jan. 1813 [DNA: RG 45, Misc. Letters Sent]). After meeting with JM, Goldsborough directed Harrison to suspend the order "till further directions shall be sent to you upon the subject," and he signed his letter "by order of the President" (ibid.). In one of his many responses to Goldsborough's intervention, Ewell stated that it was his understanding that JM suspended the order for the saltpeter and sulfur until the time of William Jones's arrival in Washington to take up the duties of secretary of the navy (Thomas Ewell, *Conclusion of the Evidence of the Corruption of the Chief Clerk of the Navy Department* [n.p., n.d.; DLC: Rare Book and Special Collections Division], 12).

§ From John Hall and Others. *7 January 1813, "Marine Barracks Washington."* Members of the court-martial for Lt. John Brooks [1] "gave their deliberate ⟨d⟩ecision, on the charges produced against that ⟨o⟩fficer, on Thursday the 24th. Decr., and . . . a ⟨r⟩econsideration of the Sentence was ordered by ⟨th⟩e Hono. Secretary of the Navy and the Court re⟨a⟩ssembled and came again to a decision on ⟨T⟩hursday the 31st. Ultimo; since which time, ⟨t⟩he Accuser, the Accused and the Court have been ⟨k⟩ept in a most unpleasant state of suspense, ⟨to⟩ which it is our prayer you will put an end." Ask that JM either act on the matter himself "or authorise the Commandant of the Corps to do so," as the office of the secretary of the navy lies vacant. [2]

RC (DNA: RG 45, Misc. Letters Received). 2 pp.; signed by John Hall and five others; redirected in JM's hand to Charles W. Goldsborough.

1. John Brooks Jr. (1783–1813), the son of general and later Massachusetts governor John Brooks, was born in Medford, Massachusetts, and studied medicine with his father after graduating from Harvard in 1805. He was commissioned a second lieutenant in the U.S. Marine Corps in 1807 and promoted to first lieutenant in 1809. He served on board the *Congress* and the *Wasp*, as well as at the navy yards in Boston, New York, and Washington. In April 1813 Brooks was ordered to Lake Erie after being accused of cheating at cards in Washington. During the Battle of Lake Erie he commanded a marine detachment on board the *Lawrence* and was reputedly speaking to Oliver Hazard Perry when he suffered a fatal cannonball blow to the hip (Gerard T. Altoff, *Deep Water Sailors, Shallow Water Soldiers: Manning the United States Fleet on Lake Erie, 1813* [Put-in-Bay, Ohio, 1993], 130).

2. On 29 Dec. 1812, one day before his resignation as secretary of the navy, Paul Hamilton had written to Col. Franklin Wharton of the Marine Corps that the proceedings of Brooks's court-martial presented "an aspect so very extraordinary, that I can't but feel unwilling to act upon them, before the Court shall have had an opportunity of reconsidering them." William Jones, Hamilton's successor, wrote to Wharton on 22 Feb. 1813: "The proceedings of the Court Martial convened at the Marine Barracks for the trial of Lieut. J Brooks of the Marine Corps, and the Sentence pronounced by that Court on the 24th. Decr. 1812 have received the attention due to a decision involving consequences of the most serious nature.

"To approve would be to sanction an act subversive of all correct military principles and to substitute the rude ebbullition of passion for the rules of law, order and decency.

"The language used by Lieutenant Miller was highly irritating and certainly unbecoming an officer and a gentleman; but how the Court could 'honorably acquit' an officer who had violated every principle of military discipline and decorum by publickly inflicting a disgraceful blow upon a junior officer who dared not return it without committing a capital offense, it is extremely difficult to conceive.

"I cannot allow myself to question the correct intentions of the Court, they no doubt were fair, impartial and honorable; but it is impossible to sanction their judgement in the Case.

"The Sentence of the Court is therefore disapproved; but as Lieutenant Brooks has hitherto sustained the character of a correct and honorable officer, I do hereby, in the hope that he will be more circumspect in future, direct, that his Sword be returned to him, and that he be ordered on duty" (DNA: RG 80, Records of the Office of the Secretary of the Navy, entry 1, Letters to the Commandant and Other Officers of the Marine Corps, 1804–86, vol. 1).

§ From Aaron Lyle.[1] *7 January 1813, "Washington City."* "I take the liberty of Recommending James M. Riddle of Sommerset County Pa. as I believe a suitable caracture" to fill one of the two vacant territorial judgeships.

RC (DNA: RG 59, LAR, 1809–17, filed under "Riddle"). 1 p.; docketed in an unidentified hand, "recommends Mr. Riddle as Judge in Louisiana or Indiana Territories."

1. Aaron Lyle (1759–1825) of Washington County, Pennsylvania, was a member of the state house of representatives and the state senate prior to serving as a Republican representative from Pennsylvania to the Eleventh and three succeeding Congresses, 1809–17.

From Joseph Wheaton

Excellent Sir   Janry 8. 1813.

On the 6th. after Six days the most Severe labor and fatigue I Succeeded in getting together all our wagons without the loss of a flints worth of the public Stores, and yesterday I ordered the principle wagon Master Mr. James Anderson, whose zeal activity and exposure had been very great with the men, to have all the 18 pd. Gun Carriages to be made ready, with the remaining 12vs. & Six's—with Six horses to the 18ns. five to the 12vs. and four to the Six'es—with Seven wagons loaded with powder, & fixed amunition, and attempt reaching Sandusky (Head Quarters—) the remaining horses fit for duty—with two Asst. Wagon Masters, and Mr. Paul Anderson the Forage Master to return back to the Mohecan Settlement for forage thirty miles—and for provision—the Snow is 20 inches deep on the level in these woods, and I was informed by My express from Sandusky that the Snow on the plains was belly deep to a horse—yet I had the satisfaction to learn by him that my first detachment had Succeeded in Making their way with the light Sixes and would arrive yesterday—thus opening the rout by breaking through the Snow and mud which has Sufficiently frozen by last mights [sic] excessive cold. So Sir; I trust; by the time the Wagon Master can return to me I Shall be able to provide Sufficent forage and provisions, repair the damaged wagons, and be ready to move with the remainder of My Charge.

I Should have gone on with Making Sleads but upon examining My axes after Supplying what was necessary for these detachments for the purposes of roads, and to cut their firewood by night—I had not enough to cut firewood for the troops.

I cannot fully discribe to you Sir the waste & distruction of Genl. Crooks Brigade. It is as true, as astonishing that to complete the climax of their disolation: on leaving Mansfield they with their ax poles Broke all the Grindstones in the town. I have ordered one to be packed from Mohecan found there on a farm the family being killed lately by the Indians, and I have not had the use of one Since leaving Canton.

May I take the liberty to Say to you Sir, the System of Militia is destructive of the best interist of the Nation, and disgusting, and distressing to the inhabitants where ever they March.

I write you Sir for the information of yourself and the Secretary of war, (whoever he may be only) and please to rest assured, in every Situation of my Zeal & my fidility and best exertions for the public Service. With Great respect I am Sir your Devoted Servant

Joseph Wheaton Capt. M. D. C
Asst. D. Q. M. N. W. Army
Comdg. Convoy & detachment

Excuse this—I write in My Cold tent My ink on the Coals. My pen freezing.

RC (DLC).

§ From James Monroe. *8 January 1813, War Department.* Forwards "copies of the several letters[1] which have passed between the Secretary of War and his Excellency the Governor of Tennessee and Colonel Benjamin Hawkins, Agent near the Creek Nation, relative to murders committed by the Indians in the State of Tennessee and its vicinity."[2]

RC and enclosures (DNA: RG 46, President's Messages, 12A-E6); letterbook copy (DNA: RG 107, LSP). RC 1 p. RC and enclosures forwarded by JM to the Senate on 11 Jan. 1813; printed in *ASP, Indian Affairs,* 1:811–14. For enclosures, see n. 2.

1. On 24 Dec. 1812 the Senate had approved a resolution requesting that the president provide "any correspondence that may have taken place between the Secretary of War and the Governor of Tennessee, and Mr. Hawkins, agent near the Creek nation, relative to the murders committed by Indians within the State of Tennessee" (*Annals of Congress,* 12th Cong., 2d sess., 36).

2. Monroe enclosed extracts and copies (31 pp.) of twenty-one letters exchanged by William Eustis, Benjamin Hawkins, and Willie Blount between 6 Apr. and 24 Nov. 1812. The correspondence concerned a series of murders committed by the Creek Indians of white settlers living along the Duck and Tennessee Rivers. For the murders of Thomas Meredith Sr., William Lott, and members of the Crawley family, as well as the capture and torture of Mrs. Crawley, Hawkins suggested that "a show of force will be necessary within the [Creek] agency." In his 25 June 1812 letter to Eustis, Governor Blount also recommended that the government order a campaign against the Creeks to punish them for their crimes. The Creek Council promised to avenge these crimes themselves, and Eustis hoped that the swift administration of justice on the offenders would obviate the need to campaign against the Creeks. Hawkins informed the secretary of war and the Tennessee governor that the Creeks intended "to punish the guilty, and look for nothing but friendship." By the end of August 1812 they had "executed eight for murder, and seven are cropped and whipped for theft." Subsequently Hawkins obtained "reiterated assurances from the Creeks and Cherokees, of their unanimous determination to be in peace and friendship with the United States, and of their unbounded confidence in the justice of their President."

From Thomas Ewell

Sir,   Saty. night 10th Jany. 1813.

It is with the utmost consternation I have this moment learnt that you have on the false representations of the clerk of the navy Departt. countermanded an order of the late Secy. of the navy to deliver to me materials for making Gun Powder in my manufactory.[1] So unusual a step—without any reference to me on the spot—must necessarily excite impressions that fraud has been practised: And it is a wretched affliction for an individual to have arrayed against him—*a condemning act* of the Chief of the

Country. A misfortune I have not deserved and which I trust you will speedily avert.

The sufferings I endure at your having for a moment yielded to the representation that it was possible for me to have defrauded the public, is somewhat allayed by the reflection that it was made by one of the most corrupt men of the City—Charles W. Goldsborough. His villany has been such, that a few days since I sent to the press for publication, his true Character, which is not yet quite completed.[2] But of his Guilt—as an officer— I have evidence, which if you prefer I will call and submit to your inspection in private.

I should also seize the opportunity to explain the conduct of the pure and the good Mr. Hamilton—as it respects his transactions with me—which will satisfy you of the baseness of the supposition that he acted basely.

Your order—is anxiously waited—& will be respectfully attended to by yr. most obedt Servant

THOMAS EWELL

RC (DLC).

1. See Goldsborough to JM, 7 Jan. 1813 (second letter), and n. 1.

2. Ewell referred to a broadside that would appear on 11 Jan. 1813 under the heading "TO THE PUBLIC," in which he accused Goldsborough of cowardice—for failing to respond to Ewell's challenge to a duel—and of abusing his position as chief clerk in the Navy Department in order to enrich himself at public expense. Ewell prefaced his attack by invoking "THAT sense of duty which impels every man to cry out *Mad-Dog* on the approach of a rabid animal." Describing Goldsborough as "one of the most cunning scoundrels with whom I have ever come in contact," Ewell listed three instances of the clerk's manipulation of government business for his own advantage. One of these had required that Ewell purchase medical supplies from a shop in which Goldsborough was a "secret partner," and Ewell claimed that he had never been forgiven for interrupting Goldsborough's "monopoly" by declining to do so and "by opening a shop of my own." Goldsborough reproduced Ewell's broadside in a counterbroadside addressed to "DR. THOMAS EWELL," which he published in Washington on 12 Jan. 1813. On that occasion the chief clerk refuted some of Ewell's allegations and dismissed the others as "Chaff" (Shaw and Shoemaker 51306).

§ From John Coburn.[1] *10 January 1813, Maysville, Kentucky.* Resigns his commission as judge in the Missouri Territory following passage of a congressional act making it "indispensible" for judges to reside in the territories over which they preside.[2] Has performed the duties of his office "under circumstances extremely unpleasant—Traversing a wild and savage country in ten different journies."

RC (DNA: RG 59, LRD). 2 pp. Printed in Carter, *Territorial Papers, Louisiana-Missouri,* 14:622–23.

1. After resigning his judgeship, Coburn participated in the 1813 campaign in the Northwest. On 17 Jan. 1814 JM nominated him as a collector of the revenue for Kentucky (*Senate Exec. Proceedings,* 2:457, 461).

2. Coburn referred to "An Act concerning the District and Territorial Judges of the United States," which Congress approved on 18 Dec. 1812 (*U.S. Statutes at Large*, 2:788).

From Bernard Smith

SIR.   NEW BRUNSWICK NJ. Jany. 11. 1813.

The writer of the enclosed letter requested me to forward it to you with some information respecting him. Mr. Eastburn, is a very respectable old Gentleman, and belongs to the Society of friends, and altho' his religious principles make him the advocate for peace, he is not of the description of persons, who for deceptive purposes have assumed the appellation of "friends of peace"[1]—on the contrary he is a decided Republican, & has been a supporter of Govt., since the commencement of Mr Jefferson's administration, and possesses considerable influence in this State, particularly among the people called Quakers.

I avail myself of this occasion to tender to you my congratulations on your re-election, and assurances of my high respect & consideration.

B: SMITH[2]

[Enclosure]

I CONGRATULATE THEE   NEW BRUNSWICK N JERSEY 1 mo 11th 1813 on thy Continuance in thy office nott Because I vew thee as Some are pleased to Represent thee: as one that Delights in warr: that most Aufull Calamity: butt I hope that is not True—butt that peace would be thy Desire. I vew it as A Truth that the Nation with whomb we are Now unhappily ingaged in warr has Done us Essential Injuryes haveing unjustly Taken our Vessyles & Impressing Thousands of our Seamen Depriveing them of there Liberty & oblidging them to fight there Battles Even Against there Near freinds & it is Believed they have Influenced & Aided the Indian Nations to murder our Defenceless Inhabitants these are Great Evils & must be Allowed to be Great provocations & probably no Nation on our Globe Situateed as we are would have Born So patiantly & So Long as we have Done this I think has been well Done on our part butt the Inquirey may Arise is there no other meanes or manner for us to persue than that of the Destructions of mens Lives it may be Answerd other meanes have been Tryed butt by various Causes they have been Inefectual this Appears Truly A matter of Great Lamentation that more virtue & Stability Should nott have been Evidenced in nott Adhearing to the Imbargo & Non Intercoarse Lawes but our presant unhappy Condition is warrs & Rumers of warrs witch has Already Caused Great Calamities in Battles Deseases Sufferings

& Deaths of Numbers in that Extreem Seveer Nothern Climate Seveer to our poor Sothern Soldiers & would Appear perhaps to make it an object of Desire to Remove from that Land: & though it may be vewed in one Sence on our part as Self defence yett as it Resepts [*sic*] the Country we Attempt to Invade may it nott be Inquired is it nott in this Case the opposit & Should ours Appear to be of an offencive Nature as it may Relate to many of the unoffending Inhabitants of that Country it may Cause Great Sorrow pleas to Excuse me in my attempts of Inquirey Losses have no Doubt Attended us & all men Are Lyable to Err both in Judgment & practice nor is there any Surety of Being in the Right butt being under the Divine Direction & protection & this we all Stand in Need of both for time & Eternaty but we Say we Desire A Just & an honerable peace: butt with Rispect to Justice it appears Brittons Governers has nott A disposition to do Justice & there pride Leads them to Acts of Extreem violence Regardless of the Direfull Sufferings of there own fellow men & Less of thos of A distinct Body from them butt I possess A hope that we are Governed by Better motives— our Supreem Rightfull Soveraign hath Expressly Declared that it is our Duty Rather to Suffer Rong than to do that witch is So the Being Instrumental of Depriving our poor Destressed fellow men of there Existance is allowed to be an Aufull Consideration butt Espetially when there is Just Doubts of A preperation for Sutch A Chainge as Death makes butt with Respect to honer as an Eminent Carrector Expresses it to be A puff of Noisey Breath yett men Expose there Blood & venture Everlasting Death to Gain that Airey Good[3] Easily Tarnished & quickly Departed Except it be that honer that Comes from Above & will Indure when all worldly Greatness Shall Seease to be I Do no[t] pretend to Degtate what mode to persue butt if Imbargo or non Intercoars Laws may nott be Thought best to be Renewed: would it nott be thought well to prohibit the Exportation of all kinds of provetions & may I Nott Express a Desire of peace oh that Great that Rich Blessing that precious object of Inestimable vallew oh Dear freind while I plead with my Exalted Soveraign may I Nott allso plead with thee that thou would be pleased to use thy utmost Rational Indevours that peace may Again be Restored to this our fertile Land we have A Large Extent of Country to Govern & as to the poor unhappy Government of Brittan they appear Standing on A Slipary precipice Ready to Slide Beyond all possable Recovery there haughtiness there kingly Government: I Believe to be of Short duration they Surely are nott objects of Envy by us butt there Inhabitants are Greatly to be pitied & many of them Desire our Good with there own: butt the poor haughty vain men that Govern—they Appear Ignorent of there own best Good & they Rule as with A Rod of Iron over the Suffering multitude butt while this appears there unhappy Condetion may ⟨y⟩ou be favoured of heaven to be Truly wise both for time & Eternity is the Desire & prayer of thy freind

ROBERT EASTBURN

I Just farder Remark that where there is two Contending partie Each one Commonly Aimes at the mastory butt if there Appears A Disposition to prevail towards A Giving way on the one part it Sometimes is thought to have A Softening tendency on the opposit part

perticularly when it tend to mercy.

I Send A peice that I have Handed forward for publication of Late time desireing thy kind Acceptance of them to use & distribute According to thy wisdom & pleasure[4]

I though[t] to Send more Butt have no Desire to Burden thee

I have thought of the petition of an Atiant poit Saying Teach me to feele an other's wo[5]

RC and enclosure (DLC). Docketed by JM.

1. Smith referred to the Clintonians.
2. Bernard Smith was surveyor and inspector of the revenue in New Brunswick (see *PJM-PS*, 2:164 n.).
3. Eastburn quoted from the hymn "The World's Three Chief Temptations," by Isaac Watts: "Honour's a puff of noisy breath; / Yet men expose their blood, / And venture everlasting death / To gain that airy good" (Isaac Watts et al., *The Works of the Reverend and Learned Isaac Watts . . .* [6 vols.; London, 1810–11], 4:327).
4. Enclosure not found.
5. "Teach me to feel another's Woe; / To hide the Fault I see; / That Mercy I to others show, / That Mercy show to me" (Alexander Pope, "The Universal Prayer," in *Minor Poems*, ed. Norman Ault and John Butt [New Haven, 1954], lines 37–40).

From William Wirt

Jany. 11. 8113 [1813]

I understand that we have lost Judge Tyler[1] and that his place is to be immediately filled, will you give me leave to bring to your recollection for the appointment St Geo Tucker, late judge of our court of appeals. I do this without the privity of Judge Tucker much less without his authority; but I am under the impression that he will probably accept & I know of no one who would do more justice or honor to the appointment. I need not speak to you who know him so well, of Mr. Tuckers intellectual vigor, of his extensive legal science, or his most extraordinary habits of application to business.[2] It may be proper tho' to observe to you that Mr Ts resignation of his office in the court of appeals arose from causes very different & remote from either aversion or incapacity for business—his faculties are still in their zenith & he may long be highly useful to his country. It may be proper also to state to you that Mr. T is & has ever been a warm & undeviating friend & supporter of the administration: & is one of the few remaining soldiers of the Revolution. I am dear Sir yo. ob Sert.

WM. WIRT

Letterbook copy (MdHi: Wirt Letterbook).

1. In January 1811 JM had nominated John Tyler as federal district judge for Virginia, a position made vacant by the death of Judge Cyrus Griffin (*PJM-PS*, 3:86 n. 1). After Tyler died on 9 Jan. 1813, JM nominated St. George Tucker for the position on 18 Jan. 1813 (*Daily National Intelligencer*, 21 Jan. 1813; *Senate Exec. Proceedings*, 2:316, 317).

2. St. George Tucker (1752–1827), a native of Bermuda, had replaced Edmund Pendleton on the Supreme Court of Appeals of Virginia, serving from 1803 until 1811. He rendered important and dissenting opinions in this capacity. In *Turpin* v. *Lockett*, his opinion sustained the constitutionality of the act of 1802 by which the glebes of the Episcopal Church were to be applied to the relief of the poor in each parish. Tucker had published poetry and was known for his juridical writings, which included essays on slavery, trade, and the Louisiana Purchase. In 1803 he also annotated a five-volume edition of *Blackstone's Commentaries* ("The Judges Tucker of the Court of Appeals of Virginia," *Virginia Law Register* 1 [1896]: 792–94).

§ From Joseph Watson. *11 January 1813, Washington.* "Candour and the respect that I entertain for R. Attwater Esquire compel me to state unequivocally that were I not impressed with the idea that his merits are destined for a higher circle of action, the recommendation which I now present would have been withheld;[1] Should my expectations in this respect not prove fallacious I would beg leave to mention that I shall feel disposed to exert my slight abilities in the service of my country, and I dare presume to say that Messieurs Varnum and Robinson of the Honourable Senate and MM: Shaw, Bacon, Fisk, Mitchell and Pond of the House of Representatives will vouch thus far *if not farther.*"

RC (DNA: RG 59, LAR, 1809–17, filed under "Attwater"). 2 pp. Printed in Carter, *Territorial Papers, Michigan*, 10:424.

1. On 5 Jan. 1813 Reuben Attwater's petition requesting "compensation for extra services rendered as Secretary of the Michigan Territory, and remuneration for losses sustained from depredations of the enemy on his private property, after the surrender of Detroit, in consequence of his having acted as Governor," was presented to the Senate (*Annals of Congress*, 12th Cong., 2d sess., 39). Watson's affidavit in support of Attwater's petition, sworn on 11 Jan. 1813, included accounts of the latter's exercise of the functions of governor and commander in chief during Hull's absences from the territory and his reorganization of the territorial militia after the Battle of Tippecanoe. On 28 Jan. 1813 the Senate committee reviewing the petition recommended an award of $500 "as full compensation for all ex officio services, rendered by the petitioner" (Carter, *Territorial Papers, Michigan*, 10:425, 427–28).

To William Jones

SIR   WASHINGTON Jany. 12. 1813

The inclosed commission will inform you of your appointment to be Secretary of the Navy.[1] I hope it will not be incompatible with your views, to aid the public, especially at the present conjuncture, with your valuable talents; and that you will be able, without delay, to enter on the important duties of the Department committed to you; no temporary provision having been made for the vacancy produced by the resignation of Mr. Hamilton. Accept assurances of my great esteem & friendly respects.

JAMES MADISON

RC (PHi: William Jones Papers).

1. Enclosure not found, but a photocopy of Jones's commission, dated 12 Jan. 1813 and signed by JM and Monroe, may be found in the Historical Society of Pennsylvania (ibid.). JM had already nominated Jones on 8 Jan. 1813 (*Senate Exec. Proceedings*, 2:315).

From Tench Coxe

SIR   PHILADELPHIA Jan. 12. 1813

Mr. Eustis, the late Secretary of War, on his way to Boston, remained two or three days here. During the time I conversed unreservedly with him. He informed me that it had been understood at Washington that I was in a very good way in business. I had no opportunity to learn from what source such a representation could have arisen. I understood that it had reached you & was probably credited by you. I determined therefore to venture on the liberty of noticing the subject in a letter, as might injure me.

When the various and long operations in respect to the purveyors office terminated in its discontinuance, I was prompted by many duties to endeavour to get into business. I had little or no expectation, and but little hope. I however made two distinct and successive attempts at plans of business, and I have used every endeavour, which occasion has presented or ingenuity could devise. But it is a truth that the moderate expences attending those endeavours have *greatly* ex[ceeded?] the trifling benefits. I remain with my large[1] without income, without a prospect. I ventured to submit a suggestion to you with respect to the office of Superintendent of Military Stores, which I hope may yet receive your consideration & approbation.

I will not trespass on your time or feelings. I apologize for the only subject, which compelled me to write, as a matter of duty. I could not resist. I have the honor to be with entire respect Sir yr. mo. obedt. & mo. hum. Servant

TENCH COXE

RC (DNA: RG 94, Letters Received, filed under "Coxe"). Docketed as received in the War Department on 1 Feb. 1813.

1. Coxe evidently omitted a word here.

From James Taylor Sr.

Dear Sir   Mt. Sion 12th. Jany. 1813

As I intend this as a private letter shall address you as a friend & not as a Public character, & therefore in the first place must acknowledge myself great[l]y indebted to you for your kindness, in informing me of the safety of my son, which was truly gratifying, I have since recd. a Lre from James dated at his Brothers in Kentucky, at which time our friends in that quarter were well, Taylor Berry a Grandson of mine & assistant to James, has likewise returned, but I have still three Grandsons with Genl. Harison & altho I greatly lament the loss of our army, do not regret that James was with them as he has returned in safety. I hope this may find you & Mrs. Madison well & after presenting Mrs. Taylors & my best Respects takes the liberty of reminding her promise of sending us both your likeness, it being what we should much prise. I beg leave to say a word in favr. Capt. Reuben Tankersley,[1] the berer of this Lre, but having wrote Colo. Monroe of this date wherein have given my Opinion of Capt. Ts. qualifications to commd. a Company, shall beg leave to refer you to that Lre. I have now turned four Score & find my self declining fast, so that can hardly expect to see the end of our conflict with G. B. & her Savage Allies, that you may out live those troubles & enjoy every felicity this world can afford is the cincere prayer of your Affe. Friend and Mo. Obt. &c &c

                                                        J. Taylor

RC (DLC).

1. Reuben Tankersley of Caroline County, Virginia, was a captain in the Thirtieth Virginia Regiment (Butler, *Guide to Virginia Militia Units*, 64, 65, 288).

From William Montgomery

Sir   Philadelphia Jany. 13th. 1813

As an American born citizen I view, with lively interest every passing event. I cannot conceive that much benefit will result from the acquisition of the Canadas—but while in the possession of the British, we may consider them some security for their proper treatment of the rights of our country. As to the Indians, in time of peace they must see that they are at the mercy of the U. States, which will secure us their friendship.

Our country is much divided now with respect to carrying on the war, and it cannot be done without incurring an immense expense—money to a very considerable amount, cannot be obtained on Loan, & taxes, in some parts of the U. States cannot be collected. I observed the extent of the offers of Mr Russell and the reply[1]—Sailors under our Flag and on the Ocean ought to be exempt from impressment, to render our Commerce secure; but not to cover the subjects of any country, when called for. If our Govt. were to pass a Law, with suitable penalties, prohibiting the employment in our service of British Seamen, including those naturalized hereafter, and provide a mode of furnishing our Sailors with a proof of their having been born in such a place, and when naturalized, I say, if this were done, in good sincerity—no more British seamen would come to the U. States to follow the sea, and really we do not want them, but could do better without them.[2] If all our merchant vessels were compelled to take a certain number of apprentices—in a few years we might have a sufficient number of seamen, on whom we could rely. As our language is the same with theirs: the more our commerce is extended, the more our interests will clash. A liberal adjustment of this critical business, may secure the future peace of both countries with each other. If our Govt. were fairly to pursue such a course, and a peace could not be made, then, I presume the war would be supported by a majority in all parts of the Union. A cessation of hostilities, to come at such a settlement, cannot injure us, as it will require five months to collect such an army, on the borders of Canada⟨,⟩ as we ought and must have, to insure succe⟨ss⟩ to our arms—and very little can be done by cruizer⟨s⟩ at this season of the year—indeed I fear that we shall lose more than we shall gain during the winter months. If, sir, you can make a peace on some such terms, I am confident that you will be applauded by 9/10ths. of all the reflecting people of this country. These are my views, dictated in a plain manner, but with feelings warm for the good of my country. If the war must be continued God only knows, what will be the result. My motive in troubling you with my sentiments on this occasion, is love of country, which only actuates—Your Hble. Servt.

WM. MONTGOMERY[3]

RC (DNA: RG 59, ML). Damaged by removal of seal.

1. See Annual Message to Congress, 4 Nov. 1812, n. 4.

2. The Seamen's Bill was first introduced into the House on 29 Jan. 1813 and passed on 12 Feb. before being sent to the Senate, where it passed on 27 Feb. "An Act for the regulation of seamen on board the public and private vessels of the United States" was approved on 3 Mar. 1813. It stipulated that only U.S. citizens and "persons of colour, natives of the United States," were to be employed on board public or private U.S. vessels and that naturalized citizens could be employed only if they exhibited certified copies of their naturalization papers to a customs collector. The law also gave the president the authority to issue supplemental regulations and directions respecting seamen employed on public vessels. The law additionally imposed penalties or fines on commanders and shipowners for employing persons not qualified according to its terms and punished persons guilty of forging citizenship certificates (*Annals of*

Congress, 12th Cong., 2d sess., 83, 84, 85, 92, 108, 111, 937, 1022–55; *U.S. Statutes at Large,* 2:809–11).

3. William Montgomery (1736–1816) was a representative from Pennsylvania in the Third Congress, 1793–95. He was commissioned a major general of the Pennsylvania militia in 1793 and served for fourteen years. In 1808 he was a presidential elector for the Madison-Clinton ticket.

From Larkin Smith

Sir   Norfolk 13th. January 1813

The Death of Judge Tyler, which has occurred within a few days past, renders it necessary that a successor should be appointed; and it will be attended with much inconvenience, if it is delayed. There is now in this Port, one or two valuable Prizes, and a Ship from Liverpool with a Cargo, all of them waiting the decision of a Court; and other cases may be daily expected to occur. It is therefore hoped that no time will be lost in supplying the vacancy alluded to. I know not who will be presented to the Government, except the present District Attorney, who I am informed wishes the appointment, and I have no doubt, that he is well qualified to fill that office. In this event, from my long experience in the disadvantage sustained by the Government in it's prosecutions, and other Judicial proceedings, from not having an Attorney to reside in this place; that I would most strongly recommend, as a thing of real public importance, to select a character residing in Norfolk. Had this been the case, throughout the operation of the restrictive Systems; I veryly believe that it would have been some hundred thousand dollars in the way of the Government. A great proportion of the public[1] of the State, is transacted here; and will rather increase than diminish. Under these circumstances, I will take the liberty to mention Mr. Littleton W Tazewell[2] as the most able, and advantageous appointment that the Government could make in the State. And I am convinced that the advantages of this appointment are scarcely to be estimated. It will be necessary however to observe, that altho' I believe there is no doubt but that this Gentleman will accept the office; he nevertheless as relates to himself, from motives of a private nature, would not wish to interfere with any pretentions set up by Mr. Wirt; and he is delicately situated in another respect, he is at present engaged for the defendants in all the important prosecutions now pending, and some of them already argued. These objections are however in my Judgment, of no importance when compared with the permanent advantages, that will most certainly result to the Government in making the appointment of this Gentleman. I have the honor to be Sir with sentiments of high Esteem & respect your Excellencies most Obt. Servant

Larkin Smith

RC (DLC). Docketed by JM.

1. Smith evidently omitted a word here.

2. Littleton Waller Tazewell (1774–1860) was elected to several terms in the Virginia House of Delegates, serving from 1798 to 1800 as the representative for James City County. He filled the vacancy left by John Marshall in the U.S. House of Representatives from 26 Nov. 1800 to 3 Mar. 1801. He again served in the House of Delegates, 1804–6 and 1816–17. In 1807 he became the spokesman for the city of Norfolk in its defiance of the British fleet after the attack on the *Chesapeake* by the *Leopard.* Tazewell was later elected to the U.S. Senate to fill the vacancy caused by the sudden death of John Taylor of Caroline and served in this capacity from 1824 to 1832. From 1834 to 1836 he was governor of Virginia (Sobel and Raimo, *Biographical Directory of the Governors,* 4:1636–37).

§ To the Senate. *13 January 1813.* Transmits to the Senate "copies of the correspondence called for by their Resolution of the 7th instant."[1]

RC and enclosures (DNA: RG 46, President's Messages, 12A-E2). RC 1 p.; in a clerk's hand, signed by JM. For enclosures, see n. 1. Printed in *ASP, Naval Affairs,* 1:282–84.

1. The clerk inserted an asterisk here and added at the foot of the page: "Resolved That the secretary of the navy be directed to lay before the Senate, any correspondence that may have taken place between him and Captain Chauncey and Lieut. Elliott relative to the capture & subsequent disposition of the British armed brigs Detroit and Caledonia on the 8th. of october 1812." In response JM forwarded copies (numbered 1 through 7) of Jesse D. Elliott to Paul Hamilton, 9 Oct. 1812 (4 pp.), detailing the capture of the British brigs *Detroit* (formerly the U.S. brig *Adams*) and *Caledonia;* Elliott to Hamilton, 10 Oct. 1812 (2 pp.), postponing sending a list of the officers and men engaged in the capture of the brigs; Elliott to Isaac Chauncey, 10 Oct. 1812 (2 pp.), announcing his capture on 7 Oct. of the *Detroit* and the *Caledonia* with two men killed and five wounded; Chauncey to Hamilton, 16 Oct. 1812 (2 pp.), reporting that Elliott, accompanied by sixty sailors and several volunteer militia, left Fort Erie and, while running the *Detroit* and *Caledonia* for Black Rock, grounded the vessels, which he still hoped to save; Chauncey to Hamilton, 27 Oct. 1812 (1 p.), praising the actions of Elliott; Harris H. Hickman to Elliott, 8 Jan. 1813 (1 p.), giving an account of the armaments and stores that were on board when the British captured the *Adams;* and Hamilton to Elliott, 27 Oct. 1812 (1 p.), acknowledging receipt of Elliott's letter of 9 Oct. and conveying JM's "particular thanks" to the officers and men involved in the expedition to Fort Erie.

§ From Gideon Granger. *13 January 1813, "Genl. post Office."* Encloses the answers of Charles Burrall, postmaster at Baltimore, to "a part of the queries put to him by the House of Representatives of maryland."[1]

RC and enclosure (DLC). RC 1 p.; docketed by JM. For enclosure, see n. 1.

1. The seven-page enclosure, dated 18 Dec. 1812, contained Burrall's deposition, including answers to "all the questions which have been propounded" about the incidents surrounding the riots at the Baltimore office of the *Federal Republican* on 22 June 1812.

§ From an Unidentified Correspondent. *13 January 1813, New York.* Writes JM "in behalf of Aliens." Recounts an episode in which [Barent] Gardenier "was sued by a female alien servent for wages [*sic*] amounting to 35$," which he refused to pay.

Relates another example of Federalist mistreatment of aliens, in which "A respectable Englishman"[1] became intoxicated and consequently unguarded in his speech and accused Washington of being a British Tory. An altercation ensued, and a Major Horn cut the Englishman's ear "in two then gave him three contusions." "I need not point out to you the benefit foreigners have been to the United States they deserve to be protected. From the above correct statement I beg to appeal to your humanity in getting a bill passed for the relief of British subjects residing within the United States or order them to quit the country." Reminds JM in a postscript that "as the Law stands now in the minds of the multitude a british alien is liable to be robbd maime⟨d⟩ and murdered publicly with impunity."

RC (DNA: RG 45, Subject File RN, box 573). 3 pp.; signed "a friend to Humanity." A note on the cover reads: "Anonymous letter respecting the treatment of alien enemies in NYork— Stating that in actions for debt the defendants had pleaded the alien character of the Plaintiff by which the proceeding was quashed. Among others mentioned as having so acted is Mr Gardinier. M. C." Redirected in Monroe's hand to "Mr Colvin / Relative to a British officer."

1. In a second postscript the author added: "Since writing the above I have learned the man is a Yorkshire-man of good habits & is a Woolen cloth Manufacturer has resided in America four years & is at present manufacturing blankets. The brave Major has reported the man to the marshal whos name is Stephen Marsland he is in hourly expectation of receiving his warrant."

To John Armstrong

DEAR SIR   WASHINGTON Jany. 14. 1813
   The inclosed Commission will inform you of your appointment to the direction of the Department of War.[1] I hope it will not be incompatible with your views, to avail the public of your services in that important trust; and that you will be able, without delay, to relieve the Secretary of State, who has been charged ad interim, with that addition to his other duties. Accept assurances of my great esteem and friendly respects.

                                                    JAMES MADISON

RC (owned by Mrs. Richard M. C. Aldrich, Barrytown, N.Y., 1961); FC (DLC).

1. Enclosure not found. JM's nomination of Armstrong was sent to the Senate on 8 Jan., and an 18-to-15 confirmation vote was taken on 13 Jan. Nine Republicans, one-third of the Republican membership, voted against confirmation (*Senate Exec. Proceedings*, 2:315, 316).

To the Senate

January 14th 1813

I transmit to the Senate a Report of the Secretary of State complying with their Resolution of the 22d December.[1]

JAMES MADISON

[First Enclosure]

DEPARTMENT OF STATE January 14. 1813

The Secretary of State to whom was referred the Resolution of the Senate of the 22d ult. has the honor to report to the President, that no precise information has been communicated to this Department, of any movement of British troops, for the purpose of taking possession of East Florida. The Secretary presumes that if that measure should be adopted, the intention and the act will become known at the same time. As Great Britain is at War with the United States and under the necessity of sending troops to Halifax, the West Indies and other parts of America, it will be easy for her to disguise the destination of any particular embarkation, until it reaches our coast. It will therefore be easy for her to land such force in East Florida, and to take possession of St Augustine, or of any other post which she may wish to hold, without opposition from the United States.

Of the disposition of the inhabitants of East Florida to be received under the protection of the United States, satisfactory evidence was afforded, by the revolutionary movements in that province, and by the cession made of it by the inhabitants, to Genl. Matthews. Other evidence of that disposition is contained in the paper marked A.[2]

The paper marked B contains a return of the force at Point Petre and other stations on the southern frontier of Georgia, and also of such other force as has been ordered there under the command of Major Genl Pinckney.[3]

The paper mark'd C contains a return of the force under the command of Major Genl Wilkinson.[4]

The papers D give the best information in possession of this Department, of the Spanish force in St Augustine, Pensecola and Mobille.[5]

E is a copy of the instructions to the Governor of Georgia to whom the powers before given to Genl Matthews were transferred and of the correspondence of the Govr of Georgia with this Department. It contains also a copy of Govr Mitchells correspondence with the Govr. of East Florida, of the instructions since given to Major Genl Pinckney, and of the correspondence of this Department with him.[6]

The Secretary of State presumes that it was not the intention of the Senate, in requiring information of any negotiation which may have taken place, for the settlement of differences and claims between the United States and Spain not heretofore communicated, to bring into view any negotiations with the Spanish Government prior to the act of Congress of the 15th January 1811 which authorized the Executive to take possession, on certain contingencies, of East Florida. He understands it to be the object of the Senate, to obtain information of such communications only as may have passed between the Executive and the Agents of the persons exercising the Government of Spain for the adjustment of those differences, and cession of East Florida to the United States, since the last Session of Congress.

On this subject the Secretary of State has the honor to report, that on the suggest[i]on of Mr. Chacon the former Consul of Spain, residing at Alexandria, who has continued to exercise the functions of that office since the deposition of Charles IV., that the Chevr Onis had power to accommodate the differences between the United States and Spain, and to cede E. Florida to the United States, in satisfaction of their claims on Spain, an attempt was made to ascertain the powers of the chevr Onis, with a view to take the same into consideration.[7]

The President was willing to obtain peaceable possession of East Florida, at a fair equivalent from those who held that possession, without making the United States in any degree, a party to the controversy relative to the Spanish Monarchy. It appeared however, that the Chevr Onis had no power to make the proposed Cession, or to enter into the desired arrangement, and from a provision in the new Constitution of Spain, it is to be inferred that none could be contemplated by the Spanish Regency.[8]

It was the policy of the former irresolute and tottering Govt of Spain, to protract a decision on the just claims of the United States for spoliations and other wrongs. The same policy animates the Regency. There does not appear to be the slightest cause to hope that any fair adjustment will be made by the United States with the Regency, to indemnify them for losses, either by the payment of money or by the cession of territory, at its just value. The paper marked F is a statement of losses sustained by Citizens of the United States by spoliations and otherwise, which was presented to the Govt. of Spain in 1805, no part of which has since been paid.[9]

Whether the British Govt. has it in contemplation to take possession of E. Florida, and in that case, at what time it may carry the intention into effect, it is impossible by any evidence in the possession of this Department to ascertain. It is to be presumed that the policy of the British Govt. will be regulated by its interest. That Great Britain has long entertained a desire of acquiring possessions in Spanish America, has been distinctly seen. Without detailing other enterprizes that were in contemplation, it is known that an expedition was actually set on foot in 1807 against Buenos Ayres,[10] for that purpose. If it is not considered the interest of Great Britain that Spain should take part with her in the war against the United States, it cannot be doubted that she will decline any measure tending by inevitable necessity to produce that result. And while her operations in the peninsula are essentially dependent on supplies from the United States, it is equally probable that she will not be disposed to involve Spain in the controversy. But should a change of circumstances occur either by her gaining the complete dominion of the peninsula or by her expulsion from it, it is believed that her views with respect to this Country will become more decisive and hostile. Commanding the peninsula her means of aggrandizing herself in this hemisphere would be considerably augmented. Expelled from it, the same result would follow, as she might apply on this side of the Atlantic, the force now employed there, aided as she then would be by all the forces of the Regency; for there is cause to believe, that it is contemplated, in that event, to transfer the Regency to Mexico.[11]

The Spanish Regency may now be considered as essentially under the controul of the British Govt. It is not probable that future events will make it less so. It is more probable that they will produce the opposite effect. At this time it is evident that the possession of East Florida, by Spanish troops is, in effect, a possession by those of Great Britain. If Great Britain held the province with the same influence over the neighbouring indians, as is enjoyed by the means thereof by the Spanish authorities there, the force remaining the same, a more unfriendly direction towards the United States could not be given to it.

It seems to be the inevitable destiny of Spain to become a temporary appendage at least, either of Great Britain or France. It can hardly be doubted by any impartial person who has observed with attention the course of events, that Spain must receive her ruler from the will of one or other of those powers. France has openly grasped at the Sovereignty of that Country, and now holds its monarch in captivity. England approaches the same object in a different way. Professing to acknowledge the Sovereignty of Ferdinand a captive in France, a nominal character only, she profits of the national prejudice in his favor, and thus by a refined policy, gradually, extends her own authority, over every portion of the state, in opposition to France. The British force in the peninsula has the ascendency there; British Generals command their combined armies; Spanish officers are advanced to power or expelled from it, by British influence. In fact, Spain cannot be said to exist as an independent nation. England and France are the only efficient parties to the controversy, and the triumph of either over the other, fixes the destiny of that Country. Whether it be England or France which succeeds the United States can have no reliance on either as to indemnity for past spoliations. If the United States suffer East Florida to pass into the hands of either of those powers that resource for justice perhaps the only one, may be lost. All which is respectfully submitted

JAS MONROE

RC and enclosures (DNA: RG 46, TP, Florida). RC in the hand of Edward Coles, signed by JM. First enclosure in a clerk's hand, signed by Monroe. The record of JM's transmission of this message has been deleted in the manuscript copy of the Senate journal (DNA: RG 46, Journals, 12A-A3), and it did not subsequently appear in the printed version (see *Journal of the Senate . . . , Being the Second Session of the Twelfth Congress . . .* [Washington, 1812; Shaw and Shoemaker 30191], 115). Enclosures printed in *State Papers and Publick Documents* (Shaw and Shoemaker 36007), 9:155–98. For remaining enclosures, see nn. 2–6 and 9.

1. This confidential resolution of the Senate, dated 22 Dec. 1812 and first submitted by Michael Leib of Pennsylvania on 16 Dec., requested that the president lay before the Senate "any information which he may have of the intention of the enemy to take possession of East Florida, and of the disposition of the people of that Territory to be received under the protection of the Government of the United States; the amount of the American force in that neighborhood, and under the command of General Wilkinson; and the quantum of the Spanish or other force in St. Augustine, Pensacola, and Mobile; and respecting any negotiation that may have been had for the settlement of differences and claims existing between the United States and Spain, not heretofore laid before the Senate; respecting any proposal or negotiation that may have been made, or had, by or with any person or persons exercising the powers of the Government of Spain, or claiming to exercise the powers of said Government, or with their respective agents, for the cession of East Florida to the United States; respecting any proposal to or from the local authorities of East Florida, (not heretofore communicated,) for the cession, surrender, or occupancy thereof, to or by the United States; and also, any information respecting the relations of the United States with Spain or said Territory of East Florida, which the President may deem proper to communicate" (*Annals of Congress,* 12th Cong., 2d sess., 124–25). A confidential 14 Jan. 1813 letter from the clerk of the House of Representatives to JM also resolved that "the Committee on Foreign Relations be instructed to enquire into the expediency of authorizing the President to occupy East and West Florida, without delay, and that they have leave to report by bill or otherwise" (DNA: RG 59, ML).

2. Enclosure "A" is a copy of an undated letter from John Houstoun McIntosh to Monroe (6 pp.), summarizing McIntosh's activities as "Director of the Territory of East Florida" following JM's disavowal of George Mathews's efforts to deliver the province to the U.S. in April 1812 (see Mathews to JM, 16 Apr. 1812, and JM to Jefferson, 24 Apr. 1812, *PJM-PS,* 4:326–29 and n. 5, 345–46). McIntosh lamented the president's failure to accept the offer of the American settlers to cede East Florida to the U.S., and he described their fear of the dangers of slave unrest and attacks by the Creek Indians. He implored JM to maintain a sufficient number of troops and gunboats in the region "until a cession of the country shall be accepted by the United States."

3. Enclosure "B" is a copy (1 p.) of John Williams to JM, 3 Dec. 1812, accompanied by a copy (4 pp.) of Willie Blount to Eustis, 12 Dec. 1812, describing the hostile disposition of the Creek Indians and the measures taken in response by volunteer militia from East Tennessee. Filed with these documents is an extract from a letter from Thomas Flournoy to Thomas Pinckney (1 p.; forwarded to Eustis on 12 Dec. 1812), stating that there were "between eight hundred and a thousand troops in Augustine, consisting of about four hundred blacks, the rest men & boys—They have lately been well provided with provisions & ammunition to last them several months, and upwards of 20000 Dollars in money to pay the troops."

4. No enclosure "C" has been found, but there is an enclosure marked "D" (1 p.) consisting of two extracts from letters from Brig. Gen. James Wilkinson to Eustis, dated 22 July and 22 Sept. 1812, to the effect that a new governor and 130 men ("blacks") had been sent from Havana to Pensacola and that two armed Spanish schooners had been sent from Havana to Mobile with 160 troops.

5. A second enclosure marked "D" is a 13 Jan. 1813 letter from Thomas H. Cushing to the secretary of war, estimating that the Spanish force at St. Augustine was 900 men, at Pensacola 500 men, and at Mobile 250 men (1 p.).

6. Enclosure "E" includes (1) a copy of Monroe to David B. Mitchell, 6 July 1812 (4 pp.), stating that he had transmitted "some time since" documents relating to the declaration of war against Great Britain and informing Mitchell that the Senate had rejected the bill authorizing the president to take possession of East Florida. In light of the Senate's action, Monroe advised Mitchell to withdraw American troops from East Florida, partly for health reasons, provided British troops had not recently landed in the province in numbers superior to those of the American forces. Monroe also directed Mitchell to negotiate with the Spanish authorities "the best Conditions in your power in favor of the Revolutionary Party." He further stated that the U.S. claim to the Floridas was "not to be considered as abandoned" and anticipated circumstances that would "induce Congress, at the next session, to authorise the President to take possession of the Country." In a postscript Monroe added that if British troops had landed in East Florida, Mitchell should maintain his ground, provided that could be "done consistently with a due Regard to the safety of our Troops." Also included are (2) extracts (2 pp.) from Mitchell's 17 July 1812 letter to Monroe, expressing disappointment at the Senate rejection of the bill to take possession of East Florida, forwarding copies of his correspondence with the new Spanish governor, and adding his opinion that circumstances did not permit the withdrawal of American troops from St. Augustine; (3) a translation (2 pp.) of Sebastián Kindelán's 11 June 1812 letter to Mitchell, advising Mitchell of his arrival at St. Augustine and demanding the withdrawal of American troops from the town within eleven days of the date of this letter; (4) a copy of Mitchell's 16 June 1812 reply to Kindelán (2 pp.), refusing to withdraw the troops until the governor provided an explanation for a Spanish attack on these forces made after the president had disavowed their unauthorized use in the effort to seize East Florida; (5) extracts (6 pp.) from Mitchell to Monroe, 19 Sept. 1812, describing the dangers to the southern frontier in the event of American troops being withdrawn from East Florida, including threats from the Indians, the British, and "restless" blacks, to which Mitchell added, "I trust the President will not send any peremptory Order to recall the Troops, but that he will let us gain a little time, and probably some Circumstances may arise out of our present situation that will bring us Relief"; and (6) a copy of Monroe's 12 Oct. 1812 reply to Mitchell (3 pp.), noting the president's "regret" and surprise at the conduct of the governor of East Florida, reiterating American claims that wrongs committed by Spain fully justified the U.S. in taking possession of the province, and expressing JM's approbation of Mitchell's conduct to date. Monroe also notified Mitchell of JM's intention to transfer his duties on the East Florida frontier to Maj. Gen. Thomas Pinckney in order to allow the governor to resume his executive tasks in Georgia. Further included are (7) a copy of Mitchell's 13 Oct. 1812 letter to Monroe (3 pp.), reporting renewed Indian attacks on American settlers, as described in an enclosed 22 Sept. 1812 letter he had received from Lt. Col. Thomas A. Smith (5 pp.), and including Smith's recommendation that he be given reinforcements to permit him to reduce St. Augustine and destroy Indian settlements in East Florida; (8) a copy of Mitchell's 19 Oct. 1812 letter to Monroe (4 pp.), conveying news of the hostile disposition of the Seminole Indians and the likely movements of British forces toward St. Augustine and Pensacola, as described in an enclosed 20 Sept. 1812 letter and reports Mitchell had received from Benjamin Hawkins (10 pp.), and concluding with Mitchell's statement of his intention to raise a force to assist Smith; (9) a copy of Monroe to Thomas Pinckney, 3 Nov. 1812 (2 pp.), transmitting instructions, "The President having committed to you . . . the management of our concerns in East Florida, confided in the first instance to the late General Matthews, and afterwards to Governor Mitchell, of Georgia"; (10) a copy of Pinckney to Monroe, 14 Nov. 1812 (4 pp.), acknowledging receipt of Monroe's 3 Nov. letter and seeking further clarification of his assignment, especially with respect to the reinforcement of Smith and his troops at St. Augustine; and (11) a copy of Monroe to Pinckney, 8 Dec. 1812 (4 pp.), forwarding copies of Mitchell's correspondence with the State Department and defining Pinckney's duties as "partly of the Civil and partly of the military Character," to the extent that they permitted him either to accept a surrender of East Florida from the local authorities or to take posses-

sion of it in the event of its occupation "by a foreign power." Force could be used only in the latter contingency, but on the assumption that Great Britain had "a complete ascendancy over the Spanish Councils" and that "East Florida has become essentially a British province, for British purposes," Monroe directed Pinckney "to maintain the ground on which you now stand" and to take "such ulterior measures, as may be found to be proper and necessary." Filed with these enclosures is a copy of Pinckney to Monroe, 29 Dec. 1812 (5 pp.), forwarding copies of communications he had received from Mitchell in a 17 Dec. 1812 letter relating to his negotiations with the governor of East Florida (16 pp.) and including Pinckney's statement of his reasons for deciding against further negotiations with the Spanish authorities for the present. To these reasons Pinckney added a description of forces at his disposal and observed that the U.S. would not be ready to attempt military operations against the Spanish before the middle of March 1813.

7. See Monroe to JM, 5 Sept. 1812, and n. 1.

8. Article 172 of chapter 1 in caption 4 of the Spanish Constitution of 19 Mar. 1812 prohibited the king from alienating, ceding, renouncing, or transferring any place in, or any parts of, the Spanish territories, no matter how small. The said territories, including "las dos Floridas," were defined in the Constitution as consisting of all Spanish possessions in both the Eastern and Western Hemispheres (see Juan E. Hernández y Dávalos, *Coléccion de documentos para la historia de la guerra de independencia de Mexico de 1808 a 1821* [6 vols.; 1877–82; reprint, Liechtenstein, 1968], 4:87–88, 100).

9. Enclosure "F" includes two statements (2 pp. each) of French seizures of 168 American vessels in Spanish ports since 1 Oct. 1796 and the judicial proceedings against them. The statements had been presented to the Spanish government on 12 May 1805.

10. Following the spectacular but short-lived occupation of Buenos Aires in 1806 by forces led by Brig. Gen. William Carr Beresford and Royal Navy captain Sir Home Riggs Popham, the British ministry in 1807 committed forces totaling about 11,000 troops under the command of Lt. Gen. John Whitelocke to the task of taking possession of Spain's province on the Río de la Plata. Due to supply problems and bad weather, the expedition failed to accomplish its goals, and it surrendered to the defending local forces on 7 July 1807 (Peter Pyne, *The Invasions of Buenos Aires, 1806–1807: The Irish Dimension*, University of Liverpool, Institute of Latin American Studies, Research Paper 20 [Liverpool, 1996], 5–56).

11. In his letters to the State Department in the spring and summer of 1812, executive agent William Shaler had referred to the possibility that Great Britain would transfer the Spanish regency to Mexico (see Madison and the Problem of Mexican Independence: The Gutiérrez-Magee Raid of August 1812, 1 Sept. 1812).

From William Jones

Sɪʀ   Philada. Jany 14. 1813

I am honored with your letter of the 12th Inst enclosing my Commission as Secretary of the Navy for which mark of your confidence I pray you to accept my sencere acknowledgements.

Having seen my nomination in the public prints[1] I had given to the subject the consideration due to so weighty and important a trust, and although I feel the full force of the responsibility proposed to be vested in me, and that your own and the public confidence far transcends my merits,

I have determined to accept the appointment and devote my humble talents to the discharge of the duties you have assigned to me.

My own private interest, domestic convenience and a just estimate of my own qualifications would have forbidden my acceptance, but the sacred cause in which we are engaged and my confidence in and attachment to the administration of our Government demands the sacrifice of every personal consideration. Therefore after four or five days of partial arrangement of my private affairs (or sooner if possible) I will set out for the seat of Government, trusting to the probable chance of a short relaxation after the adjournment of Congress to arrange finally my private concerns. With the most perfect respect and regard I am Sir Your Obdt

W JONES [2]

RC (DLC). Docketed by JM.

1. The announcement of Jones's nomination as secretary of the navy appeared in the 11 Jan. 1813 issue of the Philadelphia *Aurora General Advertiser.*

2. William Jones (1760–1831), a native of Philadelphia, had served in the Continental navy under Thomas Truxtun. From 1801 to 1803 he sat as Philadelphia's Republican representative in the Seventh Congress. Prior to his appointment by JM as secretary of the navy, he had refused an assignment in 1810 to be a special minister to Denmark. Jones reorganized many of the routine duties of the Navy Department before resigning in September 1814 and vacating the office by 1 Dec. From May 1813 until February 1814, he also served as acting secretary of the treasury. In July 1816 Jones was elected the first president of the Second Bank of the United States; he resigned from this post amidst rumors of financial indiscretion in January 1819. In his later years he operated a shipbuilding company with Joshua and Samuel Humphreys and served as collector of customs for Philadelphia from 1827 to 1829 (Edward K. Eckert, *The Navy Department in the War of 1812* [Gainesville, Fla., 1973], 16; Edward K. Eckert, "William Jones: Mr. Madison's Secretary of the Navy," *PMHB* 96 [1972]: 169–82).

§ From Thomas Gholson. *14 January 1813.* Transmits a letter from Mr. Johnson of the Virginia legislature, recommending James Semple to fill the "vacancy occasioned by the death of Judge Tyler."[1] "Mr. Semple[2] who is at this time a Judge of the general court of Va. is a man of talents, and would, I have no doubt, discharge with ability, the duties of the office solicited for him."

RC and enclosure (DNA: RG 59, LAR, 1809–17, filed under "Semple"). RC 1 p. For enclosure, see n. 1.

1. The enclosure is James Johnson to Gholson, 12 Jan. 1813 (1 p.).
2. James Semple (1768–1834) was a professor of law at the College of William and Mary. In December 1795 he married Anne Contesse Tyler, the eldest daughter of Judge John Tyler (*Tyler's Quarterly* 8 [1926–27]: 142).

§ From William Tatham. *14 January 1813.* Suggests the "propriety of an immediate application to the State Sovereignties of Delaware Maryland Virginia and North Carolina (perhaps Circular to all the States might be well) for Acts authorizing the President of the United States to provide for the public safety, by causing surveys to be made of the inland hydrography of the Maritime frontier, by the construction of such Military and Maritime Works, and by the extension of such Canals Military and Commercial roads, as he may deem useful in the general defence of the United States; by means of any public or private appropriations which he may have power over in this particular, whether established by act of special incorporation, or otherwise, in such manner & form as he may deem advisable." Reminds JM of the possibility that the Virginia legislature might adjourn without having made adequate provisions for "the defence of Norfolk as the *Maritime Citadel of the United States.*" [1]

RC (DNA: RG 107, LRUS, T-1813). 1 p.

1. Tatham had repeatedly argued for fortifications and military defenses in Norfolk. A motion presented by Charles Yancey to the House of Delegates on 20 Jan. 1813 resolved "That the Governor of this Commonwealth be requested to renew his correspondence with the Executive of the U. States, in relation to the defence of the maritime frontier of this State; and, for that purpose, to recommend to the Executive of the United States to call forth and embody so many of the militia of the State as may suffice to furnish, at least, one company thereof, for the security of each of those places of deposit (excepting the city of Richmond) of the munitions of war which may be provided by law" (Norma Lois Peterson, ed., *The Defence of Norfolk in 1807, As Told by William Tatham to Thomas Jefferson* [Chesapeake, Va., 1970], 97, 98, 104; Richmond *Va. Argus,* 21 Jan. 1813).

Governor Barbour communicated the resolution on 28 Jan. to Monroe, who passed it on to JM. Monroe responded to Barbour on 3 Feb. that for the protection of coastal towns and ports, "much reliance ought to be placed on the local force in aid of the measures which may be adopted by the General Government for that purpose" (DNA: RG 107, LSMA). John Armstrong, the new secretary of war, replied to Barbour on 10 Feb.: "Colonel Freeman commanding at Norfolk has been instructed to concentrate the Recruits raised in that Vicinity, and is authorized to require of Your Excellency such Detachment of Militia as may be found necessary for the effectual defence of the Harbour. . . . The President is assured of your zealous cooperation in such measures as may be adopted for the protection of the Country & the support of the Government" (ibid.). By early February, however, Norfolk had been "effectually blockaded by the enemy's squadron under Admiral *Warren*" (Richmond *Va. Argus,* 11 Feb. 1813).

§ From William Tatham. *14 January 1813.* "I presume the late measures concerning the increase of the Navy will require wet and dry Docks for Seventy fours: Believing my experience in this branch to be at least at par with any other person, and my economical methods superior, I beg it may be understood that I offer my services as chief Engineer ⟨or?⟩ Supervisor." Describes the process by which the engineers or architects for such projects are selected in Europe.

RC (DNA: RG 45, Misc. Letters Received). 2 pp.

From Henry Lee

DEAR SIR   ALEXA. Jany 15th. 1813

I cannot refrain from expressing to you my apprehensions on a subject which mater[i]ally affects the public interest, & which from yr. course of life may escape your attention until too late for yr interposition.

I would have waited on you for this purpose, but my painful face & the coldness of the season alike forbid me.[1]

The corps lately under the command of Brigadier Smythe have been placed in winter quarters twelve miles only from the water which washes the enemys post at Queenstown. This water is narrow, less than one quarter of a mile as I am informed & the country from thence to our camp, open & easy of penetration. General Brock is dead & his successor is considered as very inferior to him in activity & enterprize. But it does not require a leader of Brocks sagacity & fire to seize the inviting opportunity of breaking up our winter quarters & the most cogent considerations urge the enemy to the attempt.

I humbly conceive that the subject is worthy of yr immediate consideration & I cannot help declaring as my unalterable opinion, that the corps ought to be removed at least twenty five miles from the enemys post. This change in our position removes the danger of a sudden nocturnal attack & is equally convenient for the resumption of offence in the spring, as that now occupied, which is only half the distance from the enemy.

I am sure you will impute my address to the motives which alone dictate it, & will only add my sincere & respectful wishes for yr. health & prosperity.

HENRY LEE

RC (DLC). Docketed by JM.

1. In the course of defending Federalist newspaper editor Alexander Hanson in Baltimore in July 1812, Lee was beaten and placed in jail, where he was again attacked and crippled. He never fully returned to health. Federalists urged him to write an account of the Baltimore riot, and *A Correct Account of the Conduct of the Baltimore Mob, by Gen. Henry Lee, One of the Sufferers* (Shaw and Shoemaker 31243) was published in Winchester, Virginia, in 1814, although it may have been written by another member of Hanson's party rather than by Lee himself. In an attempt to find respite from his wounds, political enemies, and debts, Lee settled in the West Indies for five years before dying in 1818 on Cumberland Island, Georgia (Royster, *Light-Horse Harry Lee*, 3, 7, 232–33).

§ From James Monroe. *15 January 1813*. Proposes for JM's "approbation the enclosed appointments in the Army of the United States."[1]

Letterbook copy and letterbook copy of enclosure (DNA: RG 107, LSP). Letterbook copy 1 p. For enclosure, see n. 1.

1. The enclosure (1 p.) lists twenty-three regimental appointments from North Carolina, Georgia, South Carolina, Tennessee, Ohio, Maryland, New York, Connecticut, Pennsylvania, Massachusetts, and the Missouri Territory. From this list, which JM forwarded to the Senate on 18 Jan., nine appointments were approved the following day and the rest by 18 Feb. (*Senate Exec. Proceedings*, 2:316–17, 319, 325, 326).

§ From Louis B. de Niroth. *15 January 1813, Washington.* "I repaired to the seat of government about four months ago and laid before the proper departments [a] project, which my long experience had suggested, and which could not, I am convinced, fail of producing the most important advantages, even to the saving of millions of dollars, and, what is of still greater importance, the preservation of thousands of lives."[1] Delays have protracted his stay, causing him to incur debts and to suffer the seizure of his "cloths desk and papers." Requests "a grant or . . . a loan" so that he can regain possession of his papers, proceed to Philadelphia, and make arrangements to repay his debts.

RC (DLC). 2 pp.; docketed by JM.

1. See Niroth to JM, 1 Oct. 1812.

§ From P. Woods. *Ca. 15 January 1813, Frederick County, Maryland.* Proposes a plan to increase the efficiency of troops in battle. "The plan is that an instrument, which may be called a rest, be placed in front of each platoon of infantry formed in line of battle." Gives seven arguments for adopting the plan: "1st, Two or three volleys well directed against the enemy in the open field would operate so general, so similar and so instantaneous that a total discomfiture of all in front of the rests would most certainly be the consequence indeed it is quite probable that one volley might decide a battle.

"2nd, The muskets of the front and rear ranks bearing on the rests would be so close and all operating alike in consequence of all having the same level that scarcely a man in the front line of the enemy could escape the first fire.

"3d Firing on the rests might commence as soon as the enemy would be within killing distance—this might cause the whole loss to be on the enemy's side as armies seldom begin firing at that distance.

"4th The men who have charge of the rests, having nothing to do but solely to attend to levelling, and understanding how to level on declining or ascending ground, or in case of smoke may still take proper aim, must act with greater certainty than soldiers firing in the heat of action can possibly do in such cases.

"5th. In consequence of fewer motions in charging and being under no concern about taking aim further than bearing on the rests, men can fire oftener in the same space of time than in the present mode.

"6th, This improvement, so simple in its construction, so easily understood and acted on, and so certain in its effects, can be possessed by an army with hardly any ditriment to the present mode of warfare—for the instrument maybe so formed that it can be fixed or unfixed in about the same time a soldier is employed in fixing and unfixing his bayonet and the men who have charge of it by placing the stand on their backs, which can be done by means of a strap would be completely armed with their halberds to make or repel a charge if necessary.

"7th. This plan is most admirably adapted to street firing or where it would be convenient for men to fire and then file off."[1]

RC and enclosure (DNA: RG 107, LRRS, W-20:7). RC 3 pp.; undated; date assigned here on the basis of the docket. Docketed as received in the War Department on 18 Jan. 1813. For enclosure, see n. 1.

1. Enclosed is a two-paragraph commentary (1 p.) signed by Col. Decius Wadsworth of the Ordnance Department on the effectiveness of the proposed plan. The second paragraph reads: "Some Advantage might be gained by the proposed Mode of firing, could the Ideas of the Inventor be realized in Practice, which can only be ascertained by an Experiment. On the whole it does not appear to me to promise sufficiently to warrant a Change in the Mode of exercising the Troops. If it be thought deserving of an Experiment, it should be referred to the officers of the Infantry to decide upon its Merits."

From Jonathan Dayton

[16 January 1813]

I took the liberty of writing to you lately on the subject of our affairs,[1] & will now trouble you once more, for my anxiety is extreme. The contemplated plan of raising 20,000 men for one year is a most erroneous one. By the time they are made good soldiers they must be disbanded, another army enlisted. Your troops would always be raw, the expenses enormous— the delays incalculable. Besides the double expense & delay, the desertions will be more than double where you raise 20,000 men for one year, & a like number to supply their place for the next year, what they would be if raised at once for two years.

If the term of enlistment be predicated on the belief that the Canadas, upper and lower, can be taken in the next Summer's campaign, let me assure you, Sir, that there will be the most fatal disappointment. No force you can collect & send there, however great, can so far succeed as to reach & take Quebec by the first year's operations. All you can do (& this is certainly very practicable) will be to take the whole of upper Canada, & all the British fortresses as low down as Montreal. *Here*, your army should pass their winter, having their communications open & free with the lakes Champlain & Ontario & Erie, where there would no longer be an enemy post or vessel, & here, they would be in excellent quarters, preparing for their descent ag't Quebec as early in the spring as the roads would admit, which would be more than a month before any vessels bringing reinforcements or supplies could venture to enter the St Lawrence. As soon as the proper measures should be taken with a competent force for completely investing the town, the most favorable positions between it & the gulph should be taken & fortified for beating back, taking or destroying every ship that should appear in the river. This latter respecting the river force is now mentioned in order to impress the conviction that a larger army will be absolutely necessary, than what might be deemed sufficient on a strict calculation to carry the fortress & town of Quebec, with its garrison alone. If I were to speak in reference to the present state of things, I should say not less than 25,000 nor more than 30,000 men; but you will be able to spare, in order to make up this force, nearly or quite two thirds of the troops which had been employed in taking forts Malden, George, Erie, Amherstburgh, &c, & for the descent of which men with cannon, stores, &c, batteaus may be built at proper points on the lake, as was done for Sir Jeffrey Amherst's army in the old French war, when they descended ag't Montreal. * * *[2] I cannot conclude without expressing the hope (& praying your pardon for doing so) that the vapouring of Mr Quincey about cabinet influences, electioneering projects & such stuff, will not prevent the appointment (if it were contemplated) of Mr Sec'y M. to the command of the army.[3] His talents of every description are so greatly superior, his promptitude & decision so much greater, & his views so far more enlarged as to admit of no comparison between him & the present commander, & besides all this, the confidence of the Army would be infinitely greater in him, than the other, & most deservedly so. This matter of confidence too is of no small importance at any time, but more than ever essential now, after so many of our Generals have so greatly disappointed the public expectation.

Printed copy (Stan. V. Henkels Catalogue No. 694 [1892], item 169). Undated; dated 16 Jan. 1813 in the lists probably made by Peter Force (DLC, series 7, container 2), where it is described as a two-page letter from Elizabethtown.

1. Dayton to JM, ca. 28 Dec. 1812.
2. Asterisks in printed copy.
3. In a long and vitriolic speech to the House of Representatives on 5 Jan. 1813, Federalist Josiah Quincy of Massachusetts asserted that the plan for the next invasion of Canada would serve as "a means for the advancement of the objects of the personal or local ambition of the members of the American Cabinet." He railed against the "despotic" nature of a cabinet "composed, to all efficient purposes, of two Virginians and a foreigner," declaring that its policies for the past three years had been intended to ensure that "James the First should be made to continue four years longer" and that its project for the next three years was that "James the Second shall be made to succeed, according to the fundamental rescripts of the Monticellian dynasty." Quincy also denounced the plan to create the rank of lieutenant general for the commander of the army. Assuming that Monroe would seek the position, he predicted that the appointment would be "ominous to the liberties of this country" (*Annals of Congress*, 12th Cong., 2d sess., 560–67).

From Charles Pinckney

DEAR SIR   January 16 [1813] IN CHARLESTON

I had the honour to write to you from Columbia immediately on the close of the last Election[1] & to congratulate you & our Country on its succesful & honourable termination, & afterwards on the subject of Colonel John Taylor.[2] I now take the liberty of addressing you for the purpose of introducing to you Major Noah[3] of this City who having as I understand some public business at Washington wishes the honour of an introduction to Yourself & Colonel Monroe & as he is a gentleman of character & talents & a strong republican, I do it with pleasure & will Thank you to mention my wish to such Gentlemen of your Executive Departments as he may have business with.

I am very hopeful soon to send my son,[4] who has just graduated, to pay his respects to Yourself Mr Jefferson—Colonel Monroe & Mr Gallatin, as I well know you would all give him a friendly welcome such as I trust he will deserve—he is destined to grow up in the pursuit of those principles which have so distinguished yourself & them, & so much honoured & benefited our Country. When you see those gentlemen please present me affectionately to them & believe me always dear sir with the greatest & most affectionate respect & regard & best Wishes for Your honour & happiness Yours Truly

                                                    CHARLES PINCKNEY

RC (DLC). Docketed by JM. Year assigned here on the basis of evidence presented in n. 4.

1. Pinckney to JM, ca. 10 Dec. 1812.
2. Letter not found.
3. Mordecai Manuel Noah.
4. Henry Laurens Pinckney (1794–1863) was the only son of Charles Pinckney Jr. and was named for his maternal grandfather. He graduated from South Carolina College in 1812 and read law in the office of his brother-in-law, Robert Young Hayne. He served as a state legislator, 1816–32, editor of the *Charleston Mercury*, 1823–32, and congressman, 1833–37 (Edgar et al., *Biographical Directory of the South Carolina House of Representatives*, 3:555, 558).

§ From Ninian Edwards. *16 January 1813, Kaskaskia, Illinois Territory.* Is apprehensive about "the predatory incursions of the Indians and their allies." Received information "Some time ago . . . that Dickson[1] was preparing for a descent upon this country at the head of a number of Canadians & Indians." "I have again conversed with Colo Menard who assures me that he has no doubt that such an attempt will be made—he gets his information from a quarter that I think is much to be relied on—indeed I am convinced that there is nearly as regular communications between Mackinac & this country as between Washington City & it.

"Great quantities of goods have been deposited at Makinac St Joseph' & I believe at Praire de Chien—which will enable the british to keep up the war between the indians & us. So long as the British war continues, the enemy will not cease to employ the savages against the U. S. and if Upper Canada should be taken by our troops, the weight of the hostile confederacy must fall upon the Missisippi country—the confederacy will last as long as the British can supply goods and untill our supplies can substitute those they have been accustomed to make—for I lay it down as as [*sic*] undeniable position that British influence is much greater with the savages than ours, & if neither of us shall be able to furnish competent supplies their influence must of course preponderate and subject us to the continuance of a predatory warfare at least.

"If Genl Harrison succeeds as I hope he will, no doubt it will eventually lead to very beneficial consequences, but prudence requires that we should not prematurely anticipate them."

Conjectures on Indian movements if Malden is taken. "Last year Tecumseh with about 12 Warriors passed on by Fort Wayne to Malden on his arrival at that place he declared himself in favor of the British. Sometime afterwards the Prophet with about one hundred followers went to Fort Wayne, making great professions of friendship &c. . . . The Kickapoos & Miamies that I defeated at the head of Peoria lake run off to Rock river and are now with the Sacs a majority of whom I believe to be as hostile as any other tribe whatever. Their proximity to us and their numbers render them formidable. Too long have we confided in Indian professions, the most melancholy consequences have resulted from it—& I hope we shall hereafter profit of our experience—for my own part I have been deceived as little as any one. You may rest assured that nothing but fear re[s]trains any of them—and with what they wd consider a sufficient support to promise success they would all declare against us—the number of those who could attack us conveniently is stated in my letter to the Govr of Kentucky a copy of which was transmitted to the War Department & published in the National Intelligencer as well as I remember on the 20th of Sepr last.[2] . . .

"We must soon expect desultory attacks at least upon our settlements. I would advise the employing of a regiment of mounted men who should be ready to persue all invaders—and who should be kept out constantly in the country between us & the enemy. Any other species of force they regard not. Witness the number of lives lost in Inda Ty last year while an immense force was in service at Vincennes. For defence of the territory I wd not give one regt of mounted men for ten of infantry—the Indians generally come in detachments to their rallying points none of their detachments will ever be too strong for a regt & by Keeping it out it wd have an opportunity of cutting off some and detering others. Upon this plan I have hitherto succeeded for two years—and I cannot relinquish my predilection for it. The mounted regt could afford this protection till a campaign cd move and would then be an excellent appendage to it—and in this way it would cost the U. S. less to defend the country than any other."

Recommends employing armed boats at river entrances to prevent water attacks and building forts "as precautionary measures." "And we should also have excellent positions to command a permanent influence over the indians—that wd be usefull to us at all times hereafter. We should have hard fighting to accomplish these objects but peace is not to be obtained without it. The advantage of this line of march cannot be fully understood without a correct Knowledge of the geography of this country. . . .

"A sufficient portion of mounted men should at all times be used on any campaigne because otherwise the indians know[i]ng that they cannot be persued will be constantly making attacks on the army when it reaches their own country."

RC (DLC). 8 pp.; docketed by JM. Printed in Carter, *Territorial Papers, Illinois*, 16:285–89.

1. Robert Dickson (1765–1823) was a Scottish-born fur trader operating in the Great Lakes region in competition with American fur-trading interests run by John Jacob Astor. After the commencement of the war, he raised Indian allies for the British crown and participated in the first British success of the war, the capture of Michilimackinac on 17 July 1812. In January 1813, so that he could continue his recruitment of Indians for the British, he was appointed agent and superintendent for the western Indian nations (Halpenny, *Dictionary of Canadian Biography*, 6:209–11).

2. The 22 Sept. 1812 issue of the *National Intelligencer* included an extract of a letter "from a very intelligent gentleman in Illinois territory, dated August 20, 1812," which gave detailed information about the theater of operations in the Northwest Territory, outlined specific Indian tribe strengths and alliances, and expressed concern about a united Indian front.

§ From Thomas Tenant.[1] *16 January 1813, Baltimore*. Writes as "a resident merchant in the city of Baltimore" and as "the owner of the Brig or vessel called the Herald that was captured on the twenty fifth of December last, on the American Coast by a British Squadron, being then in the prosecution of a voyage from Bordeaux in France to the port of Baltimore."[2] Requests JM's permission to "dispatch a vessel in the character of a Cartel" to Bermuda "for the purpose of bringing home the officers and crew of the said vessel" and returning "several Prisoners of War now in the port of Baltimore, belonging to the Island of Bermuda who might also be sent back to their Homes in the same vessel."[3]

RC (DNA: RG 59, War of 1812 Papers, Requests for Permission to Sail from the U.S.). 2 pp.

1. Thomas Tenant (1769–1836), a Federalist, was a Baltimore merchant, shipowner, wharf owner, and prize agent. He served as a major in the Sixth Regiment of the Maryland militia. Tenant was director of the Bank of Baltimore and the Baltimore Insurance Company and vice president of the Charitable Marine Society of Baltimore (Garitee, *The Republic's Private Navy*, 269).

2. The *Niles' Weekly Register* for 16 Jan. 1813 reported: "The British squadron off the Chesapeake have captured the very valuable brig Herald, from Bordeaux for Baltimore. The brig had encountered a gale of wind off the Western islands, in which she carried away her fore-top-mast, part of her foremast, and was otherwise crippled. She was becalmed to the leeward of the squadron, which came down upon her with a stiff breeze, and she did not take it until they were within 30 yards of her. She still attempted an escape, and had 150 shot fired at her before she struck!"

3. Tenant wrote in a 29 Jan. 1813 letter to Alexander McKim, "I am inform'd that the permission to send a Cartel to Bermuda is granted me." He expressed his belief that there were 300 to 500 prisoners at Bermuda and his desire to return to Bermuda two boys captured on the British brig *Porgia* by the schooner *High Fleet* (DNA: RG 59, ML).

From John Adams

Sir QUINCY Jan. 17. 1812 [1813]

A young Gentleman, and his Father, have requested me to mention his Name to The Secretary of The Navy. I choose rather to mention it to you.

The youth has a fine Person, an elegant Figure, a fine Countenance, healthy vigorous and robust. His Education has been Accademical and mercantile in a very respectable House. His Father Served five years in our Revolutionary War, and his Grandfather was one of our Conquerors of Louisburg in 1745. I have uniformly observed that when once a military Tang, gets into a Family many Generations pass before the Taste is wholly lost. This young Man has accordingly been Seized with an ardent Ambition for the Naval Glory of his Country, and an Enthusiasm to participate in it. He wishes to be appointed a Midshipman: and as it was always my delight to promote young Persons of respectable Connections and promising Genius in the Navy, I have great Pleasure in recommending this one to your Consideration. His Name is John Marston Junior.[1] His native Town and place of Residence Boston.

I am also requested to mention another Name, that of William G. Smith a native of Newbury Port, whose Family and connections are very respectable, his Education mercantile. He has travelled in Russia Denmark &c been captured and plundered Under the Orders in Counsel. He wishes to be appointed a Purser. I believe him to be qualified for the Trust.

I have no other Connection with either of these Families than a transient acquaintance.

I am also requested to mention another Name, that of Josiah Quincy Guild, a Native of Boston now resident with Widow Mother in Newton. He had a liberal Education, went into the Mercantile Line, went abroad was captured travelled in France and returned pillaged. He wishes to be a Purser.

This is of a Family that has been in a Sort familiar to me from my Cradle. That Circumstance however ought to have no weight with me and certainly will have none with you. I believe him to be qualified and worthy of the Trust. With great and Sincere Esteem I have the Honour to be Sir, your most obedient Servant

JOHN ADAMS

RC (NjP); FC (MHi: Adams Papers). FC dated 17 Jan. 1813.

1. On 13 Apr. 1813 William Jones wrote to John Adams that because more midshipmen had been appointed than were legally sanctioned, he had "been precluded from gratifying the ardour of many a gallant youth." Jones assured Adams that with the naval increase, Marston would be "among the first appointed." In the meantime he encouraged Marston to volunteer with Commodore Rodgers. John Marston (d. 1885) received an appointment as a midshipman on 15 Apr. 1813 (MHi: Adams Papers; Callahan, *List of Officers of the Navy*, 353).

From John Armstrong

Sir,   New York 17th. Jan. 1813.
I have this moment had the honor of receiving your letter of the 14th. instant and the commission it enclosed.

Accept Sir, my thanks for this new mark of your confidence & my assurances that no personal consideration shall delay my journey southward a single moment. I do believe however that an interview with Gen. Dearborn, preliminary to my entering on the duties of the War Department, would be so useful, if not indispensable to a prompt & regular discharge of these, that I shall set out this evening or to-morrow morning for Albany, Whence, I shall proceed directly to Washington. I have the honor to be, Sir, with the highest respect, your most [. . .]

RC (DLC). Docketed by JM. Signature and remainder of complimentary close clipped; author identified on the basis of JM's docket.

From Lemuel Sawyer

Sir   17th Jany. [1813]
I hope you will excuse me for taking the liberty to call your attention to our fellow citizen Richard W Meade, merchant in Cadiz. The regency has thought proper, for some pretense or other, to throw him into prison where he is confined without any hope of deliverance but from the interposition of this government.[1]

His father in law, Anthony Butler is my freind & neighbour, & looks for our good offices in Mr. Meades favour. I do not presume to interfere farther than to presume you might not have been apprised of these facts, & of the impossibility of his release without a demand on our side. I am very Respy. Sir. your Obt Sert.

L Sawyer

RC (DNA: RG 59, ML). Dated 17 Jan.; year assigned on the basis of John Graham's docket.

1. For Meade's imprisonment in 1812, see *ASP, Foreign Relations*, 4:150–51.

From George Logan

DEAR SIR   STENTON Jany: 18th: 1813

An editorial notice in the national intelligencer, "that it was intended to introduce into the Legislature, a proposition for excluding by law, foreign seamen from the public and private vessels of the UStates," gives general satisfaction to your fellow-citizens.[1] A few individuals among us, influenced by the basest motives, may censure every act of the Government, calculated to restore peace and prosperity to our distracted country. The clamours of such profligate characters, should not for a moment influence our public councils.

I consider the contemplated law,[2] consistent with justice, sound policy and national honor; and therefore wish you to have the merit of recommending it to the attention of Congress. From my conversation with members of different political opinions, during my late visit at Washington, I am satisfied, it will be supported by a great majority of both Houses, particularly if proposed by yourself; as a measure of peace; on which you may negociate a treaty of friendship & commerce with Great Britain. Notwithstanding some unfavorable appearances; a *peace may yet be obtained* between the United States and Great Britain, *equally honorable* and *beneficial* to *both countries.* I speak on this subject with confidence, founded on intimate conversations with men of all parties, and in every situation of life; when last in England. Their best informed men acknowledge, that it is not the interest of their country to be at war with the United States. Should the war be protracted and the american nation, after years of bloodshed and devastation, become conquerors, qui bono?[3] I appeal to your own accurate knowledge of history. What miseries were inflicted on Sweden by the mad ambition of Charles XII, and on France by the conquests of Lewis XIV? In the fatal war of 1756, France lost great part of the flower of its youth, more than half its current money of the kingdom—its navy commerce and credit. It was believed it was very easy to have prevented all these misfortunes by friendly negotiation, but some ambitious persons to make themselves necessary and important, plunged France into this fatal war.

A great statesman will banish war, generally terminating in the mutual destruction of nations—miserable notions of policy, which substitute vengeance, hatred jealousy & cupidity, to those divine precepts which constitute the true glory and happiness of nations. Accept assurances of my friendship

GEO LOGAN

RC (DLC); FC (PHi). RC docketed by JM.

1. An editorial on "Free Trade and Sailor's Rights" in the 13 Jan. 1813 issue of the *Daily National Intelligencer* reported: "A disposition is indicated in Congress to pass a law which shall

remove the only pretence heretofore set up by the British government as a justification of the practice and principle of impressment."

2. For the Seamen's Bill, see William Montgomery to JM, 13 Jan. 1813, and n. 2.

3. *Cui bono*: to whose advantage?

From Spencer Roane

SIR.   RICHMOND, Jany. 18th. 1813.

The venerable Judge Tyler having departed this life, a vacancy exists in the office of Judge of the federal Court, for the district of Virginia.

I am authorized to say, that George Hay Esquire, of this City, would be glad to succeed to the Vacancy; and I presume upon the liberty of naming him to you, as a Candidate for that office. Of a man so well known, as Mr. Hay is, to the public, and doubtless to yourself, it would be impertinent in me to say much. As, however, I have had considerable opportunities of being acquainted with him & his qualifications, I take the liberty to say, that I consider him as a very sensible man, & an Eminent lawyer, and that, from his attendance on the federal courts, in his character of Attorney for the United States, he must be well acquainted with many legal topics, usually occurring in those Courts, with which Lawyers in general, may be in a great measure unacquainted. Mr. Hay is, also, in the prime of life, & capable of rendering many years service, in a Department which has suffered, in this respect, in relation to the two last worthy & respectable Characters Who filled it. I will only add, that, as far as I can collect the opinions of the public, & the members of the bar, at this place, the appointment of Mr. Hay would be Entirely satisfactory. I have the honour to be, with great consideration & respect, Sir, yr: mo: obt: St:

SPENCER ROANE

RC (DLC). Docketed by JM.

§ From Samuel Warren and John Geddes. *18 January 1813, Charleston.* Support "Mr [Mordecai] Noah of this City, appointed Consul for the port of Riga in Russia," who "contemplates making application to the administration of the United States, for the purpose of procuring a change in his place of destination in Consequence of the War, now existing in the North of Europe, as well as a desire of being more actively employed."

RC (DLC). 1 p.; docketed by JM.

From James Barbour

Sir   Richmond Jany. 19th. 1813

The office of District Judge for this State having been vacated by the death of Judge Tyler, I presume, a successor will, shortly, be appointed. Knowing that a difficulty some times occurs in making a Judicious selection, from a want of knowledge of fit Characters, I take the liberty (unsolicited) to present to your view Mr George Hay. His standing both as to talents, and integrity is so high, and so universally known, as to supersede the necessity of Comment. But I beg leave, particularly, to impress upon You that the professional pursuits of Mr Hay, (being in a great degree confined to the Federal Court and Courts of Admiralty) do in an emenent degree, point him out, as one of the most eligible Characters which can be selected in Virginia. I should not have troubled you with this communication, had I not heard, some Characters mentioned for that office, who I do not think will be very agreeable to a large portion of the Commonwealth. I write to you very frankly from no other motive than a disposition to see a Gentleman introduced into the Federal Court whose appointment would be acceptable; and I have no other solicitude in favor of Mr Hay, than that inspired by his merit. This communication is intended entirely for yourself and if Mr Hay should not be placed in nomination it is wished that his willingness to accept this appointment may not be mentioned. With very great respect I am yours &c.

Js Barbour

RC (DLC). Docketed by JM.

§ From David Holmes. *19 January 1813,* "*Town of Washington.*" "By the inclosed transcript from the journals of the House of Representatives of this Territory [not found], you will see that Nathaniel A Ware,[1] and Abner Green, are nominated to supply a vacancy in the Council, occasioned by the death of Alexander Montgomery Esq. Both the Gentlemen in Nomination are respectable. From the Number of votes that Mr. Ware obtained, I presume he would be the most acceptable to the Legislature. He is a Gentleman of good information and of unquestionable integrity."

RC (DNA: RG 59, LAR, 1809–17, filed under "Ware"). 1 p. Printed in Carter, *Territorial Papers, Mississippi,* 6:354.

1. On 16 Feb. 1813 JM nominated Ware "to be a member of the Legislative Council" of the Mississippi Territory, "being one of two persons nominated to me by the House of Representatives, of the said Territory, to fill the vacancy occasioned by the death of Alexander Montgomery." The Senate confirmed Ware's appointment on 26 Feb. 1813 (*Senate Exec. Proceedings,* 2:324–25, 328).

§ From Christopher Meyer.[1] *19 January 1813, Bordeaux.* Requests an appointment as U.S. consul for "the port of Bayonne or any other port in the French Empire."

RC (DLC); RC (DNA: RG 59, LAR, 1809–17, filed under "Meyer"). First RC 1 p.; docketed by JM.

1. Meyer served as chancellor and subsequently as vice-consul in the port of Bordeaux from October 1803 to January 1813 (see Meyer to Monroe, 19 Jan. 1813 [ibid.]).

From Andrew Ellicott

Sir,   Lancaster Jany. 20th. 1813.

In several of our publick prints, I have observed the conduct and character of Col. Hawkins, one of our agents of indian affairs, ungenerously attacked.[1] Having been acquainted with Col. Hawkins for more than 20 years, I can say with truth, that during the whole of that period, I have not known a more humane, and benevolent character, nor a firmer friend to the interest, and liberty of his country.

While I was in the Carolinas, and Georgia about a year ago, it was not uncommon to hear the Col. censured with great severity; but this opposition to him originated in the worst of motives. The Col. in his agency has been careful to protect the indians in their rights, which has given great offence to a numerous band of speculators, who have for years past had their attention directed to the best lands in the Creek country, and had it not been for the firmness, and integrity of the Col. the Creeks, over whom he presides, would either have been exterminated, or driven over the Mississippi before this time.

Believing as I do, that improper attempts have been made, and are still making to injure the Col. in the estimation of his fellow citizens, I should be wanting in a duty which I owe to my own conscience, did I not come forward and bear my testimony in his favour, and which I request may be considered a sufficient apology for addressing this note to you.

My compliments to Mrs. Madison, and believe me to be with due respect, your fri[e]nd and hbl. servt:

                                         Andw. Ellicott.

RC (DLC). Docketed by JM.

1. Several Tennessee newspapers reported on the "manufactured . . . falsehood" of Benjamin Hawkins's report with regard to the Creeks' execution of the Indians who assisted in the massacre at the mouth of the Duck River (*Democratic Clarion and Tennessee Gazette*, 11 Sept. 1812). In September 1812 Gen. John Cocke offered the Tennessee legislature a resolution "in consequence of the false representations, or Indian statements, of Ben. Hawkins, agent for the

U. States in the creek nation." The governor was to call forth ten thousand Tennessee militia-men to the frontier to prevent a repetition of the murders. If the murderers were not deliv-ered up within twenty days of receiving notice, the governor would "order out a sufficient force to exterminate the Creek nation." These resolutions were to be forwarded to the presi-dent. A further resolution demanded that "the senators and representatives from this state to the Congress in the United States, be instructed and requested to use their best endeavors with the proper authority, to have Ben. Hawkins removed from the Creek agency" (*Nashville Whig*, 30 Sept. 1812).

From Thomas Ewell

SIR,   20th Jany. 1813

The unnoticed note I addressed to you a few days since[1]—was intended in the highest feelings of respect; altho its fate suggests the fear that it was otherwise considered. It is in the same feeling & with the same motive, of securing reparation to the good Mr. Hamilton & to myself, that again I en-treat a moment of your consideration. Assuredly the greatest man in the country would not be offended—if it were the meanest who entreated for Justice. I am correctly told, that a representation has been made to you, that I attempted to convert the nitre received in Phila. from the Navy Dept. into money.[2] This is indeed untrue: as you will credit—from the certifi-cate of Dr. Ott & Geo. Harrison of Phila. which yesterday I shewed to Mr. Coles. Since then Mr. Todd has written on the same subject—& in a day or two I shall have another letter from Phila. all shewing the truth of the statement of Dr. Ott & Mr. Harrison. The first certifies that he had pressed me to take 15,000 lbs. nitre in this place—& Mr. Harrison declares that at the time I stated to him that I wished to dispose of the same quan-tity which Dr. Ott offered me in Washington—so as to save the enormous insurance from british capture which is 15 pr. cent. The originals of these I will deposit in the navy. Dept. on the arrival of the new Secretary: or leave with yourself.

Indeed so cautious was I—that when offered a sum for a part of the ni-tre by Mr. Lehman—as will be proved—I refused it—un⟨til I c⟩ould as-certain at what Ott's could be obtaine⟨d.⟩[3] This exchange is of immense im-portance to me; and if I am prevented from making it with the 15,000 lbs. proposed—the loss will be to the public.

My powder mills were built upon solemn assurances of the Heads of the navy & war Depts. to give extensive employment.[4] They would have cru-elly ruined me—if they had not have complied. The Secy. of the navy fulfilling a prior engagement—on a formal contract—orders the navy agent of Phila. to deliver me 60,000 lbs nitre. This agent orders the storekeeper—who delivers officially the article—takes my receipts—& then gives me his receipt—declaring that he holds the article in his *private capacity* subject to my order. Now when a most judicious exchange is in my power—*it is ordered to be suspended!*—which besides an injury to me equal to ten cts pr. pound—clearly reflects on the conduct of Mr. Hamilton— whom I would not for a limb—have to suffer so unjustly.

To me it is no object—to have in hand more raw materials than will keep the mills in regular work. As more than this is rather an incumbrance—I cannot hesitate agreeing to have the article deposited in this navy yard— subject to my control for manufacture, or if required—I would give double security! One of these modes is assuredly the proper mode of *securing safety* to the public propert⟨y⟩, and as it is consistent wi⟨th⟩ th⟨e⟩ Law—I hope you will be pleased not to delay suspending the violent method resorted to in the first instance, of *undoing* what had been *done*. Respectfully I have the honor to be yr. ob. St.

THOMAS EWELL

RC (DLC).

1. Ewell to JM, 10 Jan. 1813.

2. Goldsborough had evidently made this charge in his meeting with JM on 7 Jan. 1813, and he was to repeat it, along with several other charges that accused Ewell of trying to fix prices in his contracts, in his pamphlet *To the Public* (Shaw and Shoemaker 51307; see pp. 24– 26). The explanation Ewell gave to JM in this letter is a condensed version of a more detailed response that he was to provide on two later occasions. The first was in a four-page, undated letter to incoming navy secretary William Jones, a copy of which Ewell forwarded to Edward Coles on 27 Jan. 1813 with a one-page note requesting that Coles "lay the enclosed before the President" (DLC). The other was in his pamphlet *Conclusion of the Evidence of the Corruption of the Chief Clerk of the Navy Department* (DLC: Rare Book and Special Collections Division). On each occasion Ewell explained that after receiving the 31 Dec. 1812 order that permitted him to obtain saltpeter and sulfur in Philadelphia, he went to that city to complete the transaction. He took delivery of the barrels from navy agent Harrison, of whom he inquired about the costs of their insurance and transportation. Upon hearing Harrison's estimate that he should add 15 percent to his costs for insurance, Ewell consulted him on "the propriety of disposing of so much in Philadelphia as I could at once secure in this place [Washington] of Dr. Ott, namely 15,000 pounds." David Ott and Company, druggists in Georgetown, furnished a certificate stating that they had pressed Ewell "to take the nitre," which Ewell said he had "promised to do, if practicable." Ewell also claimed that both Harrison and navy purser Samuel P. Todd (nephew of Dolley Payne Madison) had been informed of the transaction and that there had been no intent "to speculate in public property" (Ewell, *Conclusion of the Evidence*, 12).

3. William Lehman was a Philadelphia druggist in the firm of William Lehman and W. Smith and Son. In his *Conclusion of the Evidence*, Ewell reproduced an extract from a letter he received from Lehman, dated 28 Jan. 1813, confirming that Ewell had been prepared to sell saltpeter, "substituting some which you bought or could buy in Washington or Baltimore— 15,000 lbs we offered to buy—at 45 cts. which price you declined accepting" (ibid., 12, 14).

4. For Ewell's earlier dealings with the Navy and War Departments, see *PJM-PS*, 4:440

n. 2. Throughout his *Conclusion of the Evidence*, Ewell sought to justify his understanding of the bases on which his contracts rested. Driven into contracting because neither his surgeon's salary nor an income from private practice could support his growing family, Ewell had explained his circumstances to Paul Hamilton, adding that his gunpowder mill could not succeed unless the Navy Department made "advances towards the completion" of the business. Ewell also argued that he had to undertake the capitalization of his business alone and that it was essential that he receive the same price for his gunpowder from both the Navy and War Departments, and he evidently thought that this arrangement should be on a permanent footing, regardless of the prices that prevailed for gunpowder on the open market. While Hamilton seemed reluctant to sign contracts that did not allow for prices to be varied *"according to the price of the best manufactories,"* he gave Ewell assurances of "extensive employment" and agreed to the "customary and liberal allowances," notwithstanding the prospect of "other manufactures combining to underwork and ruin [his] enterprize." It was on that basis that Ewell approached Hamilton again in late December 1812, seeking to obtain from Philadelphia the order for saltpeter and sulfur that provoked the ire of Goldsborough (Ewell, *Conclusion of the Evidence*, 4, 5, 11, 12).

§ From the Inhabitants of Franklin County, Indiana Territory. *20 January 1813.* "At a meeting of the Inhabitants of Franklin County Indiana Territory at the House of William H. Eady in Brookville," the citizens resolved unanimously "that when we examine the Frontier of an extensive Territory and its exposed situation to savage ferocity and also the many insults and depredations committed and offered to us by the British, and add to that their influence with the savages, and their aid in inducing them to attack our Citizens, we believe the wound too great for America as an independant nation to yield." "And as we believe that the experience of General Harrison in Indian warfare is all important and competent to cut off all communications with the Indians & British in upper Canada, which would relieve our frontier from savage cruelty and retard British insults, by remaining at the head of the powerful army now under him, and finding that he is shortly to retire from the same," the inhabitants of Franklin County announce their adoption of four resolutions: urging JM and the Senate to appoint Harrison as a major general of the Northwest Army, urging Harrison to accept such an appointment if nominated, directing the chairman and secretary of the meeting to transmit the proceedings to JM and the Senate with petitions from the Indiana Territory to follow, and asking the printers in the western country "to publish the above resolutions a fiew times."[1]

RC (DNA: RG 94, Letters Received, filed under "Harrison"). 2 pp.; signed by John R. Beaty, chairman, and John Test, secretary; docketed as received in the War Department on 14 Feb. 1813.

1. JM nominated William Henry Harrison to the rank of major general on 26 Feb. 1813; the Senate consented on 1 Mar. 1813 (*Senate Exec. Proceedings*, 2:329, 330).

From Mathew Carey

SIR,   PHILADA. January 21. 1813.

I hope & trust, you will believe that I sit down to trespass on you once more, with no small degree of diffidence & reluctance. There is so strong an appearance, at least, of presumption in an obscure individual obtruding his opinions, liable from his situation to great error, on a chief magistrate whose means of information are so much superior, that nothing short of the alarming explosion with which the nation is menaced, could have impelled me to the measure. But with the strong & irremoveable impressions that exist in my mind, silence would be guilt. If my anticipations be erroneous, my error will be sufficient apology. If otherwise, the step I take is an obvious duty, & requires none.

I hold that the following positions are in whole or in part obvious to, & must command the assent of, almost every observing individual in the Community.[1]

1. A most daring, powerful, unprincipled and formidable conspiracy exists in New England, particularly in Massachusetts.

2. It embraces probably two thirds of the gentlemen of the bench, the bar, the pulpit, & the mercantile interest.

3. They are daily preparing the public mind for a separation of the states, & for a northern Confederacy, connected with Great Britain.

4. They avail themselves of forgery, perjury, hypocrisy, & the most atrocious calumny, to delude the public.

5. Although the mass of their followers at present may reprobate the idea of a separation, yet a continuation of the frauds & artifices that have been so successfully employed for years back wd. probably reconcile them to it finally. Or they may be, as they have been, gradually led to the verge of the precipice before they are aware, & committed by some desperate act, so as to leave no door open for a return.

6. The experience of all ages & all nations, proves that 1000 men employed to overturn a government, have more energy & efficacy than 20,000 who wish it to be supported.

7. There has hardly ever been a conspiracy so openly & daringly avowed. In all former cases, the conspirators have convened in dens, & caverns, & garrets, & cellars, under solemn adjurations of secrecy. But the existing conspiracy avows itself in the gazettes, in the pulpit, on the bench, in the Coffee house, & in the Senate chambers.

8. A separation of the states wd. produce in all probability a bloody civil war—lay us prostrate at the feet of the European nations—wholly de-

stroy our form of government—crush republicanism for centuries—& probably subject a portion of the Country at least to the tyranny of a military despot.

9. During the whole of this frightful state of things, growing worse daily, it does not appear that any efficient step has been taken by the government, either legislative, executive, or judiciary, to repress the evil, or ward off the catastrophe. Whatever laws are in existence for the punishment of treason or conspiracy, if any such there be, have been as completely a dead letter, as if they formed a part of the code of China or Japan. No new law has been made to designate the penalty due to the insurrectional proceedings that threaten, & but too speedily, the dissolution of civil order & government— Acts & publications, of the most pernicious tendency, which in any other country, would have drawn down the vengeance of the violated laws, here pass off with the most perfect impunity, & without the slightest animadversion, as totally harmless. In many parts of the union, the conspirators against the peace, happiness, & sovereignty of the nation, have a complete ascendency over, & browbeat the friends of law, order, and the constitution.

Never has the sun shone upon a nobler cause, on one better calculated to excite all the energies of the human mind—&, shame upon the nation, under so high a responsibility to posterity, it may be fairly asserted never was a cause more wretchedly managed. While the enemies of human liberty are a solid, compact, well-organized body, who act in concert & implicitly follow their leaders—we have no harmony—no union—no organization. They are the solid impenetrable Macedonian Phalanx—we the disorderly Persian rabble.

Such a state of things cannot continue. We are on the eve of a most tremendous explosion. Whether after the apathy that has prevailed, it be possible to prevent that most horrible of all human calamities, civil war, I know not. But certain I am, that nothing can avert that calamity, but a total change of system. We have hitherto been like the miserable wretch, the wagoner in the fable, calling upon Hercules to aid us. But God helps those that help themselves. And we must put our shoulders to the wheel, or we may fast & pray forever in vain.[2]

I am fearful the evil has gone too far to admit of a remedy. But perhaps I am wrong. If that be the case—if I overrate the danger, I feel convinced at all events, that but two measures afford even a gleam of hope. One I have repeatedly urged for four years—but alas! in vain. I mean the formation of Union Societies throughout New England, & perhaps elsewhere. The more I reflect on the probable, indeed I might say the certain consequences of this measure, the more seriously am I distressed that it has not been resorted to early. It would combine & concentrate the energies of the friends of the existing form of government. It wd. inspire them with zeal, activity, &, what is of infinite importance, with confidence. And in proportion as it excited their courage, it wd depress & dismay the conspirators. It wd. effect more without bloodshed before an explosion, than an army of 20,000 men would by the sacrifice of a thousand lives after such a hideous event. It wd. convert a party who are now a mere undisciplined rabble, into a solid, effective phalanx, capable of paralyzing & prostrating their enemies.

Viewing the measure in this point of light, I most ardently implore you to use your exertions to give it a fair trial. It is not necessary that you should appear prominently in it. But if you should do so, & it should be universally known, what sentence will the wise & good of the present & future times pronounce upon the fact. Merely, that you, the executive magistrate of a great & growing nation, entrusted with the care of the welfare & happiness of a cotemporaneous eight millions of people, & of posterity for ages to come, had, to preserve the sacred ark of our liberties, employed a portion of that activity, which a most traiterous & perfidious confederacy have displayed to destroy it. Surely, sir, in a review of a long & pure life, devoted to the performance of public duties, this would form one of its brightest ornaments.

The other measure I must defer till next mail. Mean while, I remain, with sincere esteem, Your obt. hble servt

MATHEW CAREY

RC (DLC: Rives Collection, Madison Papers).

1. Carey further disseminated these ideas in his 1814 publication *The Olive Branch* (see Carey to JM, 1 Aug. 1812, and n. 2).
2. Carey paraphrased Aesop's fable "Hercules and the Wagoner."

From Charles W. Goldsborough

SIR,   6 oClock 21 Jany 1813
I have this moment received information, which I deem it my duty to lay before you without a moments delay.[1]

A gentleman of great integrity & patriotism—has stated to me that Mr. Salvador Catalano[2] Sailing master in the navy & generally employed to prove the powder &c. residing near the navy Yard here, is ready to make oath.[3]

1st that Capt Tingey *gave him orders* to pass all the powder, made at Docr Ewells mills, that would carry a 24pd ball *80* yards—when in Mr Catalano's judgment he ought not to have received any that would not have carried the ball *100* yards.

2d. that when Lt. Neill (who has no experience in proving powder) was going to Docr. Ewell's powder mills to prove the powder for the Constellation, Capt Tingey ordered Mr Catalano to attend but *not to say a word!*

3rd. that Mr Catalano did see Docr Ewell privately put in the Prouvette, a paper (which he verily believes contained powder) which was partly *concealed in the Sleeve of his coat, after the regular charge, viz 1 oz., had been put in!!*

4h. That Mr Catalano, who is a very honest man & a very competent judge, does from these & other facts known to him, verily & sincerely believe that the Powder which has been sent on board of the Constellation is entirely unfit for use.[4]

If these facts be as stated, the Constellation would not be able to contend with an Enemy's Sloop of war; & if Capt Stewart should under these circumstances proceed to sea: seeking as I know he will the Enemy, his capture is inevitable.

In order to satisfy yourself as to the correctness of these facts, I respectfully would suggest your sending immediately for Mr. Catalano: as, if they be true, an express ought, I should think, to be sent to Capt Stewart to stop him.

Excuse this hasty scrawl. This intelligence has excited feelings which I can not well suppress even in addressing you. With the highest respect & esteem, I have the honor to be sir yr mo o st.

CH: W: GOLDSBOROUGH

The bearer Jos Sutherland will if commanded by you proceed immediately for Mr Catalano[5]

RC and enclosure (DLC). For enclosure, see n. 3.

1. Goldsborough's information related to a test that had been made at Bladensburg, probably on 15 Jan. 1813, of gunpowder manufactured in Ewell's mill and reported in the *Daily National Intelligencer* three days later. Lt. Benedict Neal of the USS *Constellation*, John T. Frost, and Fielder Parker all swore certificates to the effect that Ewell's gunpowder, with the exception of only one barrel, could throw a twenty-four-pound cannonball a distance of at least 200 yards, the standard of proof required by the navy. Accompanying these certificates was one sworn by Thomas Tingey, superintendent of the Washington Navy Yard, on 28 Oct. 1812 that he had tested 250 barrels of Ewell's gunpowder and found, "with the exception of very few barrels," that it was "of good and sufficient proof and quality." These certificates accompanied the announcement that Ewell's mill was "now in complete operation" and "in hope of securing a continuance of public patronage" (*Daily National Intelligencer*, 18 Jan. 1813).

2. Salvadore Catalano (d. 1846) was appointed sailing master on 9 Aug. 1809 (Callahan, *List of Officers of the Navy*, 106).

3. Goldsborough enclosed a 19 Jan. 1813, one-page note he had received from Thomas Carbery, stating that Catalano was reluctant to respond to Goldsborough's summons to the Navy Department without having received "an *official order*" from either Goldsborough or JM: "he is a timid man & is fearfull of Comod Tingeys turning him out of the yard." Once Catalano received written instructions, Carbery added, he would "go & relate all the facts relative to the Powder before the President."

4. In his pamphlet *Conclusion of the Evidence of the Corruption of the Chief Clerk of the Navy Department* (DLC: Rare Book and Special Collections Division), Ewell responded to the four charges made by Goldsborough as follows: (1) He stated that Catalano was "an ignorant fellow; deluded by Mr. Goldsborough, and until within a few days stated to commodore Tingey,

that the powder was excellent." Ewell added that he would seek a court-martial of Catalano on the grounds that he could not have witnessed all the tests made of Ewell's gunpowder. (2) He stated that Lieutenant Neal, who had loaded the eprouvette, had showed "great resentment" at Goldsborough's allegation that he had practiced deception in the test of the gunpowder. Ewell also published a certificate from John T. Frost to the effect that Frost had carried a letter from Ewell to Capt. Charles Stewart of the USS *Constellation* offering to retest the powder and that Stewart had replied that he had been satisfied by the first test. (3) Ewell stated that the eprouvette used in the test had been found to be faulty and that "it was only as an experiment, when the Eprouvette was dirty, that the ball was forced in." Ewell conceded that on the day of the test, some of his powder had been damp and thought to be faulty, but it had been tested again "and at this moment the powder which is not damp is as good as any in the country." (4) Ewell declared that Catalano was "a most ignorant Italian" and that he had "expressed the strongest approbation of the powder." Ewell concluded this rebuttal by reaffirming that his gunpowder was "superior to most the public have heretofore had" and that representations made to JM to the contrary were not to be believed (6, 13).

5. Aside from agreeing to hear Catalano's testimony (see Goldsborough to JM, 22 Jan. 1813), JM appears to have made no further intervention in the Ewell-Goldsborough quarrel. After reviewing the matter, the new secretary of the navy, William Jones, decided to offer the chief clerk the option of resigning or being discharged. Goldsborough chose the former, but Jones, who did not wish to offend Goldsborough or his friends throughout the naval officer corps, took pains to emphasize that nothing more should be inferred from Goldsborough's resignation than the fact that he had intended to retire from his position (Jones to Goldsborough, 27 Feb. 1813, Goldsborough to Jones, 8 Mar. 1813, Jones to James Ewell, 10 Mar. 1813, and Jones to Eleanor Jones, 22 Mar. 1813 [PHi: William Jones Papers]).

From Richard M. Johnson

Sir,   Capitol. Jan. 21st. 1813

I have just been informed by the chairman of a select committee of the Senate to whom was refered the nomination of Docr. Hanson Catlett that his name is improperly Spelt. vz. "Catett" this I was requested to communicate for correction.

Ten days since I handed to Mr Munroe the resignation of Governor Harrison. The letter was enclosed to me. He is under a hope that he will be appointed Maj Genl. if an opportunity occurs untill which time he acts under his Brevet Commission of Maj. Genl. from the Gove[r]nor of Kentucky when that shall expire he will act under the Commission of Grigadier [*sic*] untill he has accomplished the objects of his appointment. vz. the regaining the Country which we have lost.

Genl. Harrison has expressed a willingness to accept the appointment of Brigadier with a view to hold it permanently untill regularly promoted provided he should be made third or fourth in rank, which it is probable will be done, according to the rule about to be established viz. having a reference to former services & grade in the service of the U States.

But this acceptance will result from the want of an opportunity to appoint him Majr. General as I believe none doubt his capacity & his merit for Such appointment. With considerations of Sincere respect you[r] ob. Sert

RH: M: JOHNSON

N B His resignation is of his civil appointment.

RC (DLC).

§ Isaac Clason and Others to James Monroe. *21 January 1813, New York*. "Several persons, neutral foreigners, as well as Americans, whose private affairs require their presence in England have applied to us to procure them passages, and having now in this Port a very fine ship lying idle, we ask permission to send her to England as a cartel to be commanded by our Cap. Joseph Skinner and Cap N. Willis or one of them." Remark that the cartel business in New York "has been almost exclusively in the hands of the avowed and implacable enemies of the administration" and that "The correspondence which is maintained, by the means of such agents is of the most pernicious Cast; grossly misrepresenting the feelings of the people of the United States, and the views and conduct of our rulers." "To prevent the necessity of a recurrence to such perfidious agents we have associated, and offer to furnish hereafter at very short notice and at any and all times, a Ship or vessel of any description, or any number of them as may be required by the Government for a cartel or for an express to any part in the world or for such other purposes as may be required."

RC (DNA: RG 59, ML). 2 pp.; docketed by Monroe, "For the President / Captn Skinner." A note on the cover in another hand reads: "Application of I. Clason, Joseph Skinner, and N. Willis, for permission to send a cartel to England. They offer to contract to supply the Govt. with cartels whenever wanted."

From Charles W. Goldsborough

SIR,   Jany 22. 1813.

I have just received some samples of powder—which appear to confirm the correctness of Mr. Catalano's opinion.[1] Mr. Catalano says the powder of which these are Samples is now in the Magazine in this city—that that which was manufactured by Mr. Lorman[2] (at ⅔rds the price given to Docr Ewell) was proved by him—that Docr. Ewell's was proved & certified by capt. Tingey himself—that these are perfectly fair Samples; & that by a re-examination of the powder now in the Magazine this fact, with the correctness of the opinion he had the honor of expressing to you last night, will be established.

The Express left this for St Marys this morning—I will arrive there about 12 oClock tomorrow.[3] As it is possible the Constellation may have left there & proceeded to Hampton, I sent this day, by mail, a duplicate directed to the Navy agent at Norfolk—with a request that he would cause it to be delivered without delay to capt Stewart. I have the honor to be with great respect sir yr mo ob st.

Ch: W: Goldsborough

RC (DLC). Docketed by JM.

1. See Goldsborough to JM, 21 Jan. 1813. In his pamphlet *To the Public* (Shaw and Shoemaker 51307), Goldsborough repeated the charges he had made against Ewell in that letter (see pp. 26–28).

2. Goldsborough probably referred to William Lehman of Philadelphia.

3. In a 25 Jan. 1813 letter to Capt. Charles Stewart, Navy Secretary Jones informed him of the doubts about the powder on his vessel and ordered him not to proceed until he was "sattisfied that the quality . . . is good—which You are to ascertain, by reproving, & reexamining it—this You will do, without delay, & report to me immediately the result" (DNA: RG 45, Letters Sent to Officers).

From Jonas Humbert Jr.

Sir   New York Jany 22d. 1813.

Impelled by a sence of Duty I owe to myself, and wishing to be informed from yourself of the rectitude of my conduct, while doing Duty on the Fortress on Ellis's Island relative to my takeing away therefrom a quantity of Wood, that has caused the then General Armstrong to Issue an Order causeing the stopage of My pay for One Month and an Half, Amounting to about $73. inclusive of Rations Servants wages etc. whatever Wood other Officers of the same Regiment took I do not hold myself accountable for, consequently the Issueing a General Order to stop the Pay of all the Officers without discrimination, and from report only I think to be both arbitrary and unjust the A. D. Q. M. General reported to the General 70 Chords on Bedlous Island left by the Detachment when according to his own Measurement he made it 88 Chords, luckily Capt Crane happened to be with him and gave his Certificate to the fact othe[r]wise the Regiment would have been Saddled with 18 Chords more than what I conceive to be the unjust pretentions of the General, However by your decision I am willing to abide; the Regulations says that Each 2d Lieutenant (the capacity that I had the Honor of serving in) shall have 1⅓ Chords per Month for the Winter Establishment, Therefore I was entitled to 4 Chords provided the 3 Months I served was all in the Winter Establishment but 15 Days is to be deducted therefrom that is included in the Summe⟨r⟩ establishment Makeing it something less. The Officers on Ellis's Island not being all in affluent circumstances, (of which unfortunately I have to include Myself in that Number) agreed instead of Burning Wood in Eight Fire Places (the Quantity they were intitled to) to Burn it only in two and put up with a little inconvenience hopeing to enjoy the Benefit from saveing their Fuel, as they were almost all precluded the Benefit of carrying on their Business, and a hard winter likely to sett in they considered this mode of conduct the wiseest [sic] they could adopt, and in the Winter Season people generally think themselves well off if they can make both ends meet in the Spring, I Sir, had a peculiar task to perform, being a Baker, and my custom entirely depended on a Daily supply, must either Resign my Commission, or Sacrafice my three Month Business in a great Measure, as it is but illy Done by another, this being the first call of my Country on me for my services, what was to be done? I must ignomeniously Resign or make the sacrafice. I sir, unhessitatingly choosed the latter altho' having a Wife and four Small Children to Maintain, you sir, will easily percieve that I could not support Myself as an Officer and render the necessary comfort to My Family, and be enabled to save any of my Wages, Therefore Sir, I thoug[h]t Myself at least entitled to all that the Regulations allowed. And not knowing that they were subject to alterations as it related [to] the Malitia, I have presumed to take away from Ellis's Island 10½ loads of Wood being my share as equalized by the arrangement, (the Captns, & Majors being equalized With the Lieu[t]enants) for this my pay has been stopped! The General allowed one Months Wood to be taken away, from what authority I know not, but if I was entitled on any principle to take away one months Wood I thought I was entitled to the Ballance after deducting what I Burnt, to you Sir, I have made this appeal not as the Slave of a Foreign Despott appealing for Favor but as an American Citizen appealing to an enlightened Head for Justice and no More, Permit, me Sir here to observe that the Eleventh Regiment did more Duty than both of the others put together nay, the Garrisson on Ellis's Island performed more Duty than the 2d. Regiment altogether as their Garrisson was contigious to their Homes and ours at a Distance, we sir had to pay upwards of $20 Dollars for Water that was found there in abundance, and Sir the expence of Bargemen Amounted to for Ellis's Island alone to $180. together with hireing Pettiauguas[1] to transport the Men in Boisterous Weather amounted almost to a total of $300, and after undergoing all these difficulties to Carp at officers for takeing what the regulations says they are entitled to is I think a stigma on the Government. The above expences the 2d. & 9th Regiments were totally exempt from, and not one Private that was on Guard more than ten Days During the whole 3 Month, when the Privates of the Eleventh Regiments were on guard generally speaking more than four times ten Days, Permit me Sir, to inform you that at a general Meeting of the Officers a Motion was made that a Dinner should be given to Genl. Armstrong by the Brigade, and that the other two Regiments suggested the Propriety of makeing it a Brigade expence the Officers of 11th Regt conside[r]ing that those Regiments had been stationed in town and at no expence could very easily afford to pay for a Dinner provided the Eleventh Regiment Paid one third, they having also almost two Officers to their one the assessments on them would be very light, and theirs very heavy, and that the General had reviewed those Regiments but had not paid us that compliment to say the least of it, if it was not his Duty, they further considered that they could not offer Public testamonials to a Man that they conceived had not done his Duty not having once reviewed them, he having twice mad[e] the appointment and after making every preparation they were as many times deceved and Therefore they unanimously rejected the proposition and I believe this has caused the Generals Ire! and that being the case I have no cause of regret in having voted in the negative. To you Sir without any other acquaintance than your Public acts give me leave to tender My hearty congratulations for your complete success in triumphing over Clintonian Duplicity and inordinate ambition, I have nothing further to communicate but that I require your early attention to this subject as I think the Commander in Chief will be willing to do that Justice that I think is withheld from me. I do not ask for your interference for reward but for my pay as I have sacraficed $500, for that I have not yet obtained, I sir would just inform you that, I have a Father that sacrafised his all in promoting your elevation it was his Pen under the signature of Diodoros Siculus[2] that laid Cheetham Prostrate those Numbers you well know and for the writing them his reward from Clintonians, was dismissal from Office, an Office that neated him about 1400 Dollars per year, and supported him and a numerous Family, at a time when he was Sick and the last shilling expended, and no means of obtaining any support for his Family those Myrmydons of Clinton turned him out of Office after trying to seduce him by offering to retain him if he would leave off Writing, he refused and I have informed you of the result, for him if you could appoint or procure him an appointment I only ask and save him from ultimate distress. If I found an Enemy in as much difficulties I think I would at least alleviate them and how much more ought to be done for one that has sacrafised his all, he would have come to Washington but the state of his Finances are such that he is totally disenabled. Altho' it is a circumstance truly to be deplored in this Country but Nevertheless it is the case if he was rich and only had the cupidity to ask an office he would inevitably by some means or other obtain it, how these things get the upper hand of a Republic I cannot Divine Witness Peter A. Schenck worth a Million of Dollars at least, but I suppose is as poor as any body in pretence when wanting an office & D Gelston Genl. Bailey & Sam. Osgood all Clintonians but never mind they are Rich one would suppose that when men gets rich by an Office they would be satisfied but the more they get the more they want and the poor Patriot must live on what he has done and if that will not suffice why he must turn Cammelion. Thes[e] observations I have made to you as Freely as I would to one of my acquaintances leaving you to decide on their thruth [*sic*] or Falsity. Yours with Due Defference but not Flattery

JONAS HUMBERT JUNR[3]

N.B An European Despott would Answer this Epistle by silence of the Halter

To James Madison President of the United States of America Free Sovereign & Independant may she remain so as long as she shall continue to Deserve it and no longer for what is it to the t[r]ue lover of Liberty what Name is given to the soil. The enjoyment of Civil Liberty constitutes the Glory of Man and without its genial influen[ce] sways our Rulers its is only a Name like wearing Baubles to sett of[f] Prostitution the sight of wich only serves to put him in Mind of his Degredation[4]

J. H.

RC (DLC). Docketed by JM, "Humbert Jonath. Jr / Jany. 28 1818."

1. Piraguas.
2. See *PJM-PS*, 3:375–76 n. 2.
3. Jonas Humbert Jr., son of the Tammany official of the same name, was a second lieutenant in the Third Artillery Regiment of the New York County militia in 1811. By 1814 he had been promoted to first lieutenant in the Eleventh Regiment from New York County (Hastings, *Military Minutes of the N.Y. Council of Appointment*, 2:1218, 1495).
4. Filed with this letter is a second, undated letter from Humbert (1 p.): "Please to inform me of the fate of this Letter as it relates to my pay and if you can Do any thing for my Father. He knows nothing of this letter nor has he any Idea of it whatever, but if you really could procure him a situation may Heaven continue to prosper you in all your laudable undertakeings and be assured of my most liberal and cordial Support in the prosecution of the same. The circumstance of stopping the Officers pay has been very predjudicial to the Volunteering service as I know that it has detered some valueable officers from entering, and it behoves us to make as many friends as possible in these times, The Officers only took as much wood as the Regulations allowed them and I suppose did not leave enough behind for Mr A D Q M G. but I think it illy became the Genl. to interfere as nobody would suppose that he could reap any benefit but the warmth in which he took it up has excited som[e] suspicion but I believe without foundation."

From William Plumer

SIR,   EPPING (NH) January 22d 1813.

As a law has recently passed for building ships of the line, with an additional number of frigates, permit me to suggest for your consideration, the propriety & expediency of building one of the seventy fours at Portsmouth in this State. The harbor is not only good, but the situation & means for building is convenient. In that place the *America* was built, the only ship of the line, I beleive ever built in the United States.[1] I think the harbor safe against the attacks of our enemies, & with little additional expence may be rendered absolutely so. There is a very considerable quantity of well seasoned timber on an island near the town, the property of the United States, & I presume the remainder can be easily obtained from our forests.[2] There are many excellent carpenters, & other mechannics ready to perform the necessary labor of building the ship. The employment, & the money that would be expended in such an undertaking, would have a favorable effect upon the great mass of the people in the eastern & northern part of the State, who would derive real benefits from it: a circumstance, in times like these, worthy of notice, to a government that in a great measure is founded in public opinion.

Being an entire stranger to the present secretary of the navy, & having no other motive but to promote the public good, you will, I trust, excuse the freedom I have taken in addressing you on this subject. I am with sentiments of respect & esteem, Sir, your obedient servant.

WILLIAM PLUMER

Letterbook copy (DLC: William Plumer Papers).

1. Construction on the *America*, a seventy-four built by Col. James K. Hackett in Portsmouth, began in May 1777. Lack of materials, skilled labor, and funds delayed the work. In early June 1779 Congress ordered Robert Morris to complete the ship as quickly as possible and later appointed Capt. John Paul Jones her commander and supervising inspector. Construction still lagged, however, and the *America* was not launched until 5 Nov. 1782 (Howard I. Chapelle, *The History of the American Sailing Navy: The Ships and Their Development* [New York, 1960], 80–83).

2. Construction at Portsmouth on the seventy-four *Washington* began in the spring of 1813 and was completed in October 1814. The commandant of the navy yard at Portsmouth, Isaac Hull, spent the spring of 1813 trying to collect the necessary timber and frequently advertised for live oak in the local newspapers. By July 1813 he was compelled to lay off most of his carpenters and use white oak as a substitute in some of the ship's construction. Competition for the wood was especially keen because William Bainbridge at Charlestown, Massachusetts, was overseeing the construction of another seventy-four, the *Independence*, which was launched in June 1814 (*New-Hampshire Patriot*, 6 Mar. 1813; Dudley, *Naval War of 1812*, 2:43, 91, 195). For construction at the Portsmouth navy yard, see Maloney, *The Captain from Connecticut*, 211–57.

§ To Congress. *22 January 1813*. Transmits "copies of a correspondence between John Mitchell, agent for American Prisoners of War at Halifax, and the British Admiral commanding at that station."[1] Also transmits "copies of a letter from commodore Rodgers to the Secretary of the Navy."[2]

RC and enclosures, two copies (DNA: RG 233, President's Messages, 12A-D1; DNA: RG 46, President's Messages, 12A-E2). First RC 1 p.; in the hand of Edward Coles, signed by JM. RC and enclosures printed in the *Daily National Intelligencer*, 25 Jan. 1813. For enclosures, see nn.

1. A provisional agreement for the exchange of naval prisoners of war was concluded at Halifax on 28 Nov. 1812 by Richard John Uniacke, the advocate general for Nova Scotia; William Miller, British agent for prisoners of war at Halifax; John Mitchell, late consul of the U.S. at Cuba and American agent for prisoners of war at Halifax; John Mason, commissary general for prisoners of the U.S.; and Thomas Barclay, royal agent for prisoners of war. Monroe ratified the cartel on behalf of the U.S. on 14 May 1813 (DNA: RG 59, War of 1812 Papers, Agreements for Exchange of Prisoners of War).

The enclosures that JM transmitted included an extract (4 pp.) from John Mitchell to James Monroe, 5 Dec. 1812, covering Mitchell's correspondence with John Borlase Warren and expressing concern over proof of nativity and application protocols; a copy of Mitchell to Warren, 1 Dec. 1812 (2 pp.), directing the release of American citizens impressed on board the *Centurion* and *Statira*; a copy of Warren to Mitchell, 1 Dec. 1812 (3 pp.), claiming to allow the discharge of impressed Americans with proof of their nativity and permitting men on board British ships to make application only through their commanding officers; a copy of Mitchell to Warren, 3 Dec. 1812 (2 pp.), requesting clarification of the policy of not receiving applications from impressed seamen claiming U.S. citizenship; and a copy of Warren to Mitchell, 4 Dec. 1812 (2 pp.), responding to the policy that any address by men on board British ships must be made directly through the commanders of the vessels.

2. The enclosure is a copy of John Rodgers to Paul Hamilton, 14 Jan. 1813 (2 pp.), which covered a package containing two muster books of the British vessels *Moselle* and *Sappho*, found on board the British packet *Swallow*. Rodgers sent these to Hamilton to prove that the British had been detaining American citizens on board their ships of war, despite their assertions to the contrary.

§ From Albert Gallatin. *22 January 1813, Treasury Department.* Submits statements in conformity with the resolution of the Senate dated 20 Jan.[1] "For all the Treasury notes which have been disposed of, credit has been given, by the respective Banks, to the Treasurer of the United States, on the days from which such notes, respectively, were dated & commenced to bear interest."[2]

RC and enclosures (DNA: RG 46, President's Messages, 12A-E4). RC 1 p. For enclosures, see n. 2. JM transmitted Gallatin's report in a letter to the Senate dated 23 Jan. 1813 (ibid.; 1 p.; in the hand of Edward Coles, signed by JM). Printed in *ASP, Finance*, 2:600–601.

1. On 19 Jan. 1813 James Lloyd of Massachusetts introduced the following motion, which was approved on 20 Jan.: "That the President of the United States be requested to cause to be laid before the Senate an account of the sale or disposition of three millions one hundred and eighty thousand dollars of Treasury notes, subscribed for by various banks, as stated in the annual report of the Secretary of the Treasury, with the time and terms of sale to such banks respectively; and the state of their several accounts with the Treasury Department, from the time of such sale or subscription, to the first day of the present month of January" (*Annals of Congress*, 12th Cong., 2d sess., 54, 57).

2. Gallatin enclosed a one-page statement "exhibiting the weekly state of the Treasurer's account with sundry Banks purchasers of Treasury Notes, from the dates respectively when such purchase was made, to the 4th. Jany. 1813, taken from the weekly returns of the Treasurer of the U. States to the Secretary of the Treasury," and a statement of "3,180,000 Dollars in Treasury Notes, sold to, or contracted for by sundry Banks, previous to the 4th. Decr. 1812; shewing the time when the same were sold or contracted for, the days on which they were dated, and on which their amount was credited, or engaged to be credited to the Treasurer of the United States." The participating banks are listed as "State Bank Boston / Man-

hattan Company / Mechanic's Bank New York / Trenton Bank / Bank of Pennsylvania / Farmer's & Mechanic's Bank / Union Bank Georgetown / Farmer's Bank of Alexandria."

From Samuel Latham Mitchill

SIR   CAPITOL HILL: Jany 23rd 1813

At the request of the Governor of Newyork, I have the honour of submitting to the eye of the President Judge Tiffany's Description of the peninsula of Upper Canada.[1] Though I have personally visited the region which lies between the great Lakes, I must confess, the present writer has given me much additional information. My persuasion that it may be relied upon for its genuineness and authenticity, determines me to forward it, without a day's delay; knowing that in the arrangements necessary for the ensuing campaign, every article of sound information is valuable. I have the honour to renew the assurance of my high respect

SAML L MITCHILL

RC and enclosures (DLC). RC docketed by JM. For enclosures (docketed by JM, "Tompkins D. D. (Govr) / Jany. 12. 1813 / inclosing I. H. Tiffany's information as to Canada."), see n. 1.

1. Mitchill enclosed a letter from Gov. Daniel D. Tompkins to Mitchill of 12 Jan. 1813 (2 pp.), covering a letter from Judge Isaac Hall Tiffany to Tompkins of 3 Jan. 1813 (3 pp.), which enclosed a copy of a letter from Tiffany to Tompkins of 30 June 1812 (3 pp.) as well as Tiffany's description of Upper Canada (21 pp.). Also enclosed was a "Millarium" (2 pp.) or list of distances between points, including the distances from Niagara and Albany to several destinations in the Michigan Territory and Upper Canada. Tiffany's detailed description, portions of which were printed in the *Daily National Intelligencer* on 26 Jan. 1813, contained observations on the boundaries, soil, produce, climate, geography, population, manners, policy, government, and Indian allegiances of the peninsula of Upper Canada. He stressed the economic importance of the region: "Upper Canada is peculiarly valuable to the British as it can afford great supplies of provision for the garrisons at Quebeck, Halifax & in the West Indies for the navy ⟨at⟩ the American Stations as also Staves & lumber for the Indias when not furnished by the U. States."

In his 3 Jan. 1813 letter, Tiffany remarked to Tompkins that this description was based "upon actual & intimate observation" and that all of his character was "pledged to the fidelity of the remarks & my confidence in the schemes or projets of invasion submitted." He noted that in his June correspondence with Tompkins, he had suggested a plan which "in its season, would have been deemed adviseable, nay self evident, to most of them who have travelled that country with a forecast to war." "But under the present disposition of the forces of the U. S. that plan may not be preferable. The reduction of U. Canada will familiarize, your legions, in some degree to danger before they approach Quebec or Halifax. Exercise & manouvre may be taught; but veterans are only made by the fatiagues [*sic*] & perils of the field. But in Whatever manner & time an invasion of that province may fall, the observations are, in many instances, calculated to interest those from among whom the ranks of the army are to be filled."

From Mathew Carey

Philada January 25. 1813

   Had the associations which I recommended in my last letter, been
adopted fo[u]r or five years since, when they were first urged, they could
not, I am persuaded, have failed of success.[1] At that period, the spirit of
treason, insurrection, & rebellion, was in its cradle, & might easily have
been strangled. It was confined to a few persons, part of them probably in
the pay of England, and the rest panting for the honours & dignities &
affluence, which they hoped to acquire under an independent sovereignty
in New England, in the establishment & perpetuation of which they wd.
play a distinguished part. That spirit has unfortunately since arrived at a
most formidable maturity. Never in the whole history of mankind had a
conspiracy such encouragement, such impunity as has been experienced by
the traitors who are indefatigably plotting the subversion of our government: and, as I stated in my former letter, never was a conspiracy so openly,
so daring, so fearlessly avowed. What a few years back was a puny infant,
whose efforts might have been despised, is now a Hercules, who, in a
struggle with our government, will most inevitably be triumphant, unless
a more energetic system be pursued—unless that government does more
than it has hitherto done for its own defence. And indeed I am strongly inclined to doubt whether any measure that can be devised will at present
avail. The old wise rule—obstare principiis[2]—has been totally & fatally
neglected. But while there is life there is hope. And however alarming the
crisis, we ought not to give way to despair. We ought to try every fair &
honourable means that can be devised, which affords any reasonable prospect of salvation.

   As an auxiliary to the measure I lately suggested, some man of powerful
talents ought to reside in Boston, whose particular province it should be, to
illuminate the public mind—to detect & expose to public infamy the horrible falsehood to which the enemies of the liberties of this country, have
daily recourse—to trace the progress of treason—to strip it of its mask—
& above all to dilate upon the tremendous consequences of a separation, &
the horrors of a civil war, its certain offspring. In a word, to put into requisition all the means which a sound head, a good heart, & the liberty of the
press, afford, to defend the ark of our liberty. The press, the noblest instrument of human happiness ever devised, has in New England for years
been perverted to the most hideous purposes. It has been unceasingly arming man against man—poisoning the sources of happiness in the social intercourse—& sowing the seeds of the most tremendous scourges that ever
afflicted human nature. It owes the nation a heavy expiation. And such a
man as I contemplate, wd. be able to perform miracles by judicious man-

agement. He might readily enlist a phalanx of powerful coadjutors, who would chearfully & effectually cooperate with him.

He ought to publish in the federal papers, particularly the detections of falsehood & calumny. To secure admission into them, or, in the event of a refusal, to cover their editors with infamy, his lucubrations ought to be dispassionate, candid, argumentative, & resting wholly on the basis of truth & fact. He ought to shun, as he wd. the bite of a rattlesnake, making a single assertion which could be disproved, or stating a single fact that he could not establish as clearly as the noonday sun.

Where, it will be asked, is a suitable person for such an arduous office to be found? I believe there are numbers. That one may be had, I feel no doubt. I have a suitable person in my eye. Jonathan Russel is a man of transcendent talents. He is perhaps the only person who has represented this country abroad with uniform ability. I had made a comparison between his communications & those of our other diplomatic characters, in order to shew his superiority. But I wave it. Suffice it to say, that those of Mr Russel, were marked with dignity, dec[e]ncy, strong talents, & irrefragable conviction. They reflect honour on the cause—on the officer—& on the Country that produced him.

Where he is now, or what he is doing, I cannot tell. But I have been informed that he became a bankrupt previous to his departure for Europe. And it is therefore probable that his circumstances are not such as to preclude him from engaging in this undertaking, for a suitable recompense. For it cannot be expected, that he should devote himself wholly to the public, & Sacrifice his other pursuits without a recompense.[3]

I presume 2000 or 2500 Dollars per annum, wd. be quite enough for such services. And so much do I dread a convulsion—so sincerely desirous am I of steering clear of the rocks & quicksands that at present threaten us—so perfectly am I convinced, that if we escape the dangers now impending over us, our form of government may last for centuries—& so much faith have I in the efficacy of the plan, if it be not now too late for any thing to save us, that rather than not give it a fair trial, I should not hesitate, though I cannot afford it, to pay even one half of the salary for one year. But this is a sacrifice unnecessarily great for any individual. Most chearfully, however, will I be one of twenty or even of ten persons, to make up the sum requisite.

In aid of the exertions of Mr Russel, or any other person chosen in Boston, something ought to be done in New York & here. And this leads me to a case of very great hardship, which reflects dishonour on the Country. I mean the case of Mr Coxe, which it is impossible to reflect upon without a mixed sensation of distress & disgust. Except Editors of papers, many of whom are mere Hessians, whose party has been not unfrequently decided by chance, & whom circumstances might have arrayed on the opposite side of the question, no man in this country has written half so much to promote the public good. No man has more ably advocated the rights of the nation in opposition to the wild & indefensible claims of the belligerents. No man has more openly defended the tenets & proceedings of the republican party. And no man has for his political labours made himself so many rancorous, cut-throat, & irreconcileable enemies. And what is his reward? It is enough to sicken the Heart of every man of feeling acquainted with the case. He has been immolated to the vengeance of some of the worst men in the country—men pretending to profess the same principles with himself. His office has been insidiously taken from him—& after the meridian of his life has been past in labouring for the public, he is now, with a large & interesting family, cast upon the world, to seek some new business to Support that family. He is placed in this situation under almost every possible disadvantage—his mercantile connexions entirely dissolved—his habits of business forgotten—those friends & connexions, on whom he might rely for support, alienated & rendered hostile by his elaborate defences of a party which has shamefully & ungratefully abandoned him.

This is, to be sure, a hideous picture—& not more hideous than true. A remedy ought to be applied. And it is fortunate, that the public good may be highly promoted, & private justice done to Mr Coxe, by the extension of this plan. If an office could be given him which wd. support his family, & the duties of which wd. not be very onerous, he might very materially & powerfully aid the gentleman in Boston, in the exposure of the scandalous frauds that are unblushingly employed to overturn the government.

Never was a cause so miserably managed as ours. Hardly a day passes but circumstances occur and disclosures are made of the views of the anti unionists, which if properly used, wd afford immense advantages, by opening the eyes of their deluded followers, among whom are to be found a very large portion of the very best citizens in the nation, who are under a degree of infatuation & insanity, of which I know no example in history, except in the days of Oates & Bedlow in England. These favourable circumstances are almost unnoticed—or when they are the subject of animadversion, it is in so feeble & desultory a mode, that more than half the advantages they might afford are wholly lost. I have seen single paragraphs in the Federal Republican, the Repertory & the Centinel, which in proper hands wd furnish ample texts for a month, & make converts of all those readers whose minds were open to conviction. One of these paragraphs lately expressed a strong wish that the British might not be inveigled into a suspension of hostilities, & that the treasury might become bankrupt. And some time in April last, the Editor of the Federal Republican deprecated as the most Serious of evils, the repeal of the orders in Council. The first of those paragraphs, if duly employed by a man of powerful talents wd. probably have given Massachusetts a democratic Governor & assembly, & produced the same effect in New Hampshire. What an incalculable difference would not this make in the existing state of things! How different wd. be our present prospects of peace & union! At a million of dollars it wd. have been a cheap purchase.

These things pass almost wholly unnoticed. And this villainy is encouraged fearlessly to run its career. Every undetected lie is a sort of premium for future mendacity. When it is considered that the choice of a governor, a senator, or a board of electors, may depend upon twenty—ten—or even five votes, it is inexpressibly lamentable that fraud, falsehood, forgery, perjury, hypocrisy, & treason, which are so unceasing & industrious in their efforts to delude & deceive the unwary & well meaning, & so fatally successful in these efforts, are allowed to perpetrate their deeds of darkness & villainy, without any systematic or regular opposition, & have little or nothing to dread but the desultory & disorderly efforts of newspaper editors, few of whom have the talents, & probably none the leisure requisite for such a grand & sublime undertaking, an undertaking in which more might be done by a powerful individual than perhaps in any other mode in which his time & talents could be employed.

This reminds me of a "sore evil under the sun."[4] Some men of transcendent talents enjoy lucrative situations under the government, & take no more pains to defend it, than if it were as tyrannical & abominable as that of Nero or the emperor of Morocco. Mr Dallas & Mr Bishop may be instanced. The former is among the most powerful political writers in this country. The latter for strong, sarcastic, overwhelming humour is probably little inferior to Dean Swift. I have strong doubts whether either of them ever wrote a column in defence of the government from the day of his appointment to the present hour.

In your reply to one of my former letters, you expressed a strong doubt of the propriety of an executive magistrate, as you are, interfering in this business.[5] But how is it possible a question can be made upon the point? Is it not a most imperious duty of a citizen to whom is confided the destiny not merely of eight millions of his cotemporaries, but that of a hundred millions of their posterity, which depends upon the result of the present crisis—is it not, I ask, his duty to take every just & honourable precaution ne quid detrimente respublica capiat?[6] To object to such proceedings, on the ground of informality, wd be as absurd, as to condemn a pilot, who when a vessel under his care was on the point of sinking, thrust open a door to get at the means of saving her.

Public functionaries, sworn to defend the constitution, men of high standing, powerful connexions, & commanding influence, are openly arrayed, under the hypocritical mask of Washington Benevolent Societies, for the destruction of that constitution.[7] And shall the first public functionary of the Country, equally sworn to defend it, hesitate about the employment of means, perfectly honourable & just, & upright, to defend that Country & that Constitution, & defeat nefarious projects pregnant with incalculable, perhaps interminable miseries. Forbid it, honour; forbid it, justice; forbid it, good sense; forbid it, patriotism.

To such conscientious scruples have the happiness & liberty of mankind, been a thousand times sacrificed. While the honest & upright part of the community are pausing, and doubting, & deliberating about the correctness & justice of the means necessary to avert impending perdition, the nefarious conspirators against the republic, totally regardless of the means, and determined to carry their point *per fas nefasque*,[8] have hunted them to the earth, & demolished the fabric of human happiness. Scruples of this kind immolated Brissot, Claviere, Vergniaud, Gensonne, & Roland, with their illustrious associates on the altars of rapine & slaughter, erected by Danton, Legendre, Marat, Le Bon, Couthon, St Just & Robespierre. And pray heaven these scruples may not immolate James Madison, Thomas Jefferson, & James Munroe, to the vengeance of Jacob Wagner, A. C. Hanson, Gen Lee, Kilgour, & Timothy Pickering.

I now close this trespass on your time & patience—perhaps I shall never again obtrude upon you. Should my importunity fail of its effect—should that deleterious, destructive, & never-enough-to-be-deplored reliance upon the good sense of the public continue, to which I think the future historian will ascribe the awful crisis we are in—should the horrid trump of civil war sound through the land—should state be arrayed against state, father against son—& brother against brother—should we renew the horrible scenes of the Peloponnesian war in Greece, the Social war of Rome, the white & red Rose in England, the Guelphs & Ghibelens in Italy & Germany, & the holy league of France—*as I much fear will be the case*—I shall have the melancholy consolation, which I shall carry with me to the Grave, that I foresaw the issue, & urged a preventative above four years ago—that I have exhausted all the energies of my mind to accomplish a plain, simple, salutary object, which required but a slight effort to insure its success, & which I am unalterably convinced wd. have averted the perdition which, like the sword of Damocles, is suspended over our heads by a slender thread! I am, respectfully, your obt. hble servt

MATHEW CAREY

RC (DLC).

1. See Carey to JM, 21 Jan. 1813.
2. *Obsta principiis:* "Withstand beginnings; resist the first approaches or encroachments" (*Black's Law Dictionary* [6th ed.], 1077).
3. Jonathan Russell returned to the U.S. in November 1812 (see JM to Congress, 12 Nov. 1812, n. 1).

4. "There is a sore evil which I have seen under the sun, namely, riches kept for the owners thereof to their hurt" (Eccles. 5:13).

5. Carey probably referred to JM's letter to him of 19 Sept. 1812.

6. *Ne quid detrimenti respublica capiat:* that the republic is not harmed. An allusion to the Roman Senate: "When the Republic was in danger, the senate might confer unlimited power upon the magistrates by the formula *'videant consules, ne quid respublica detrimenti capiat,'* which was equivalent to a declaration of martial law within the city" (William Smith, ed., *A Dictionary of Greek and Roman Antiquities* [3d ed.; New York, 1843], 868).

7. The Washington Benevolent Society was a Federalist political organization that operated as a charity. Carey was to claim in *The Olive Branch* that the society originated in Boston; however, the first society was founded in Alexandria, Virginia, in 1800, and by 1816 there were at least 208 such societies in eleven states. Drawing on the broadest possible membership base, the societies attracted anyone with a vote and generally posited three requirements for membership: U.S. citizenship, "good moral character," and "a firm attachment to the constitution." Ostensibly serving as humanitarian associations, the societies provided clothing and firewood, medical care, financial aid, and legal advice to alleviate the burdens of the "unfortunate individuals within the sphere of our personal acquaintance." Members also nominated candidates for office and supervised electioneering campaigns (Carey, *The Olive Branch* [10th ed.; 1969 reprint], 481; William Alexander Robinson, "The Washington Benevolent Society in New England: A Phase of Politics during the War of 1812," *Proceedings of the Massachusetts Historical Society* 49 [1916]: 275; Fischer, *The Revolution of American Conservatism*, 114–28).

8. *Per fas nefasque:* by right or wrong.

From Albert Gallatin

DEAR SIR   [ca. 25 January 1813]

I enclose the recommendations &a. for sundry offices either vacant or where removals should take place. The pressure of more important business had prevented an earlier attention to those minor subjects, all of which have been delayed too long & most of which are earnestly urged by the respective members of the vicinities. The designations of offices and names of candidates are as followeth.

1. Collector of the district of Vermont and Inspector of the revenue for the port of Allburgh.
   Cornelius P. Van Ness of Vermont

2. Collector of the district of Mumphreymagog and Inspector of the revenue for the port of Mumphreymagog.
   Roger Enos of Vermont

3. Collector of the district of Erie and Inspector of the port of Cayahoga
   Ashbel W. Walworth of Ohio

4. Collector of the district of York *Maine* & inspector of the revenue for the port of York
   Jeremiah Bradbury of Massachussets

5. Collector of the district of Têche & inspector of the revenue for the port of Nova Iberia
    Jesse M'Call of Louisiana

6. Collector of the district of Great Egg harbour and Inspector of the revenue for the port of Great Egg harbour
    Ezra Baker of New Jersey

7. Register of the Land office for the eastern district of the State of Louisiana, being the New Orleans district
    Columbus Lawson of Louisiana

8. Receiver of public monies for the land office of the eastern district of the State of Louisiana, being the New Orleans district.
    Lloyd Posey of Louisiana

9. Receiver of public monies for the land office of the western or Opelousas district of the State of Louisiana
    William Garrard of Louisiana

10. Register of the land office of Madison County in the Mississippi Territory.
    John Reed of Mississippi.[1]

Observations

1. vice Buel to be removed—general & it is believed well founded complaints for connections with illegal importers from Canada. After some hesitation on the part of Judge Robinson & of Mr Shaw for whom the office was wished by his friends, Mr Van Ness now district attorney is generally recommended.
    Note In that case, but to be subsequently nominated John Hutchinson is recommended by Fisk & Strong as district attorney

2. vice   [2] who has never resided or attended personally to the duties which have been accordingly much neglected, & illegal trade carried on. This collection district is in Mr Fisk's district; and he recommends Mr Enos.
    Note Both Buel &   [3] had been appointed on Bradley's recommendation.

3. vice his father Walworth deceased. The son is recommended by ____[4] Edwards Member of Congress elect for that district, by Colo. Worthington &a.

4. vice M'Entire to be removed for not accounting & laxity in executing the non-importation. Mr Bradbury recommended by Mr Cutts.

5. vice Wren resigned. Mr M'Call recommended by Mr Magruder & known to Georgia Senators

6. vice Somers resigned. This district has always been distracted. Mr

Hufty now federalist evidently leans to Risley & next to Leeds. Before the late schism, the delegation was generally in favr. of Baker who besides respectability had taken no share in local quarrels. I still prefer him. The objection to his present residence has no weight, as by law he must reside within 2 miles from Somers point. Next to him Leeds though young & deputy of Somers who will probably appear delinquent is preferable to Risley.

7. vice Grimes who has deserted the State & his post. Lawson was clerk of the board, is honest, understands thoroughly the business & is recommended by the Member Mr Robertson

8. new office necessary to be filled in order to decide on the claims. Lloyd Posey is son of the General who will not accept this office. He & Clay recommend the son, and Magruder acquiesces.

9. new office as the other. Wm. Garrard as Commissioner has some claim on the public & is recommended by Magruder

10. vice Dixon resigned. Reed was the clerk, is recomd. by Govr. Blount, Campbell of Tenessee &a. Poindexter acknowledges that he is preferable to Moore a member of the territorial legislature recd by his colleagues. They have generally recomd. one another for land offices. Respectfy. Submitted.

ALBERT GALLATIN

RC (DLC). Undated; date assigned on the basis of evidence presented in n. 1. Docketed by JM.

1. On 27 Jan. 1813 JM forwarded to the Senate his nominations of Van Ness, Enos, Walworth, Bradbury, McCall, Baker, Lawson, Posey, Garrard, and Reed for these positions (*Senate Exec. Proceedings*, 2:318).

2. Blank left in RC. The previous collector for Memphremagog, Vermont, was Josiah Demming (ibid., 2:187).

3. Blank left in RC. Gallatin presumably referred to Demming (see n. 2, above).

4. Blank left in RC. Gallatin referred to John S. Edwards.

§ From James Ewell.[1] *25 January 1813, Washington.* Submits for JM's perusal letters to be presented to the head of the Navy Department. "If the recommendations submitted to you should be deemed sufficient to entitle me to the office I solicit, I shall ever be grateful for your acquiescence which I flatter myself will be the only thing wanting to ensure me success."

RC (DLC). 1 p. Addressee not indicated. Enclosures not found.

1. James Ewell (1773–1823), a physician, author, and brother of Thomas Ewell, was appointed by Paul Hamilton to a clerkship in the Navy Department when his predecessor, Samuel P. Todd, Dolley Madison's nephew, became a navy purser in July 1812. On assuming control of the Navy Department in January 1813, William Jones was eager to dismiss James Ewell, who was notorious for his lack of accounting and handwriting abilities (McKee, *A Gentlemanly and Honorable Profession*, 21).

§ From James Monroe. *25 January 1813*. "The Secretary of State to whom was re-ferred the Resolution of the Senate of the 18th. Instant,[1] has the honor to submit to the President the enclosed Papers marked A & B."[2]

RC and enclosures (DNA: RG 46, President's Messages, 12A-E3). RC 1 p.; in a clerk's hand, signed by Monroe. Enclosures (20 pp.) forwarded by JM in a letter to the Senate dated 26 Jan. 1813 (ibid.; 1 p.; in the hand of Edward Coles, signed by JM); printed in *ASP, Foreign Relations*, 3:602–4. For enclosures, see n. 2.

1. The resolution of 18 Jan. 1813, introduced by Outerbridge Horsey of Delaware on 15 Jan., called for the president to lay before the Senate "the French decree, purporting to be a definitive repeal of the Berlin and Milan decrees, referred to in his Message of the 4th No-vember last, together with such information as he may possess, concerning the time and man-ner of promulgating the same; and, also, any correspondence or information touching the re-lations of the United States with France, in the office of the Department of State, not heretofore communicated, which, in the opinion of the President of the United States, is not incompatible with the public interest to communicate" (*Annals of Congress*, 12th Cong., 2d sess., 53, 54).

2. The enclosures marked "A" consist of extracts from correspondence concerning the proof that the Berlin and Milan Decrees had ceased in November 1810, including Joel Bar-low to Monroe, 2 May 1812, Barlow to the duc de Bassano, 1 May 1812, Barlow to Monroe, 12 May 1812, and the duc de Bassano to Barlow, 10 May 1812. The enclosures marked "B," mentioning Barlow's plans to travel to Vilna to participate in negotiations between France and the U.S., consist of copies of Barlow to Monroe, 25 Oct. 1812, and the duc de Bassano to Barlow, 11 Oct. 1812, and an extract from Barlow to the duc de Bassano, 25 Oct. 1812.

§ From Simon Snyder. *25 January 1813, Harrisburg, Pennsylvania.* "Having my at-tention accidentally drawn to an act of the Legislature of this Commonwealth, passed 20th of March 1811, a certified Copy of which I have the honor herewith to transmit,[1] I perceive by the 4th section thereof that its preceeding sections cannot go into operation without the consent of the Congress of the U. States. I have deemed it my duty to transmit a Copy of the said Act with a request that you would please to lay the same before Congress for their approbation."

Letterbook copy (PHarH). 2 pp.

1. Snyder referred to "A supplement to the act, entitled 'An act to establish a board of war-dens for the port of Philadelphia, and for the regulation of pilots and pilotages, and for other purposes therein mentioned'" (*Laws of the Commonwealth of Pennsylvania* . . . [5 vols.; Phila-delphia, 1812; Shaw and Shoemaker 26414], 5:213–15; Samuel Hazard et al., eds., *Pennsylva-nia Archives* [138 vols.; Philadelphia and Harrisburg, 1852–1949], 9th ser., 5:3306).

From Elbridge Gerry

confidential

DEAR SIR,   CAMBRIDGE 26 Jany 1813

Accept my sincere thanks for your friendly favor, without date;[1] & for the cheerful manner of your meeting my request. At the time prescribed,

& before the District Judge & a circle of my friends, I propose to take the oath, agreably to your information; unless it should be requisite, for public purposes, to be then at Washington, in which event I shall claim no indulgence.

Nothing delights me more, than the prospect of paying my respects to my Virginian Friends, & to yourself & your Lady, in a particular manner. Long absence sublimates friendship, & produces a due estimation of it's worth. Accept my best wishes & respects, & altho unknown, present them to Mrs Madison. Yours very sincerely dear Sir

E. GERRY

RC (DLC); FC (owned by Mr. and Mrs. Philip D. Sang, Chicago, Ill., 1958). RC docketed by JM. FC marked "answer"; written on the verso of the cover of JM to Gerry, 5 Jan. 1813.

1. JM to Gerry, 5 Jan. 1813.

From David Bailie Warden

SIR,   PARIS, 26 Jan. 1813.

The mournful event of mr. Barlows, death, has placed in my hands, the affairs of the Legation.[1] In supplying this vacancy, it shall be my utmost endeavor to merit your approbation.[2] It is unfortunate, that the negotiation is averted, at a moment, when the mind of this Government seems earnest for arrangement. Dr. Stephens, whom I send as a confidential messenger, will communicate to you the current news, and a summary of facts which I think prudent not to commit to paper.

I take the liberty of sending, for your inspection, the outline of a treatise on Consular establishments, which, with your approbation, I propose to publish.[3] I should be much gratified, by your permission, to dedicate it to you. The sudden departure of Doctor Stephens, to whom I have confided it, does not allow time to prepare a corrected copy; and I send this rough sketch merely to give you an idea of the manner in which the subject is treated. I am, Sir, with great respect; your most obedt and very humbe Servt

DAVID BAILIE WARDEN

RC (DLC); letterbook copy (MdHi: Warden Papers).

1. Ruth Barlow wrote to Monroe on 10 Feb. 1813, stating that she had intended to send her nephew, Thomas Barlow, to the U.S. to convey "some communications" but that "Mr. Wardens indelicate, & I think incorrect conduct has obliged me to detain him to protect the private papers which regard the negociations" (DNA: RG 59, ML).

2. In a circular letter addressed to consuls and dated 19 Jan. 1813, Warden claimed that on the basis of an official letter from the duc de Bassano of 16 Jan. 1813, he was "the only Com-

missioned agent and organ of our Government, at Paris," and he invited all consuls to correspond with him "on subjects relating to the interests of our Citizens and government" (DNA: RG 59, CD, Paris). For Warden's alleged misdemeanors and breach of protocol, see Isaac Cox Barnet to Monroe, 23 Feb. 1813, enclosing extracts from George Erving to Barnet of 3 and 17 Feb. (ibid.). Monroe forwarded Barnet's letter with a note on the cover: "For the President." Warden continued to act as the official representative of the U.S. to France until William H. Crawford dismissed him in May 1814. JM, writing to Jefferson on 23 Oct. 1814, admitted that Warden, after the death of Joel Barlow, "behaved badly to Mrs. Barlow, and having made himself acceptable to the French Govt thro' his intimacy with subalterns, he seized, with its concurrence, the station for which he had as little of qualifications as of pretensions" (DLC).

3. Enclosure not found. Warden's treatise was later published as *On the Origin, Nature, Progress and Influence of Consular Establishments* (Paris, 1813). Warden dedicated it "To the President and Senate of the United-States . . . as a public memorial of the respect and gratitude of the author" (3).

From Marinus Willett

DEAR SIR,   NEW YORK January 26th. 1812 [1813]
    The advantages resulting from having Command of the Lakes are so many and so great that effectual measures ought to be taken to destroy the Naval force of the Enemy as soon as the weather will permit. This object is so very important that to ensure its success all the Ship builders from the Atlantic ports and all the Sailors from our Vessels of war if requisite should be ordered to those parts that the defeat of the Enemy may be prompt and certain. After having procured the Command of the Lakes, but a small force will be required to retain it, and the subsequ[e]nt opperations against Canada will be much facilitated. I do most earnestly pray that the Command of the troops destined for that object may be confered on an officer of activity and Spirit, With sentiments of the highest esteem I am Sir your very Obedient Servant

                                                    MARINUS WILLETT

RC (DLC). Docketed by JM, "Willett Marinus / Jany. 26. 1812."

William Henry Harrison to James Monroe

No. 38.   HEAD QUARTERS N. W. ARMY PORTAGE RIVER
SIR,   15. MILES FROM THE MIAMI RAPIDS. 26 Jany. 1813.
    I have the honor to enclose herewith a duplicate of my letter of the 25th. Inst: together with the official report of Col: Lewis, to Genl. Winchester of the Action of the 18th. Inst: (No 1.)[1]

That you may be enabled to judge of the propriety of the Steps which were taken by me previously to the unfortunate event at the River Raisin, I proceed to give you an account of the Situation of the troops and the arrangements I had made for their advance. The left wing of the army under the immediate orders of Genl. Winchester, consisting of the 6th. Regts. Kentucky troops a Battalion of Ohio Infantry and a Detachment of Regulars under Colo Wells. The importance of keeping a considerable force on this line After the advance of the Army, from its vicinity to the Indian tribes of the Wabash and Lake Michigan induced me to direct Genl. Winchester to take with h⟨im⟩ 3 Ky. Regts. and the Regular Troops only—with these amounting to about Thirteen hundred men he marched from his Camp 5 Miles below the mouth of the Auglaise River, on the 31st. Ulto. on the evening before he dispatched an express informing me of his intention to March the Next Morning. This express was sent thro' the woods to Genl. Tuppers Camp 44 Miles advanced of Urbanna upon Hulls Road. A violent Snow Storm prevented it from reaching Genl. Tupper untill 9th. Inst. and it was not untill the 11th. that it came to me at Upper Sandusky. I immediately gave orders for Several droves of Hogs which had been Stopped on their Route to proceed to wards the Rapids & I directed the Artillery to be prepared to progress as soon as the Generals arrival at the Rapids should be announced, which I directed him to do by an express to be sent immediately to U. Sandusky. Not hearing from the Genl. for some days I began to conclude that his progress had been Stoped by a considerable thaw— which took place about the 1st. of the Month. On the evening of the 16th Inst. I receeived a Letter from Genl Perkins enclosing one from Genl. Winchester to him of the 15th. informing of his arrival at the Rapids on the 10th. That it was his intention to advance against the enemy and directing him (Genl Perkins) to send a reinforcement to the Rapids of One Battalion, alarmed at this information, I dispatched an Express with the enclosed Letter (No 2)[2] by the direct route to the Rapids and set out myself to lower Sandusky & reached it on the evening of the 17th. On the morning of the 18th. The Battalion which Genl. Winchester applied for marched from Lower Sandusky. About 2 oclock on the morning of the 19th a Letter from Genl. Winchester was received of which the enclosed is an extract (No 3)[3] I gave immediate orders for the 2nd Regt. of Perkins Brigade (which consists of two Regts only) to march immediately for the Rapids and proceeded thither myself. On my way I received the Genls. Letter of the 19th. informing me of the success of Colo. Lewis—a copy of which I had the honor to enclose you from the Rapids. Upon my arrival at the Latter place on the morning of the 20th. I found that Genl. Winchester had marched the preceding day having left Genl Payne with about Three hundred of the Kentucky Troops. It was not untill late on the 21 Inst. that Majr Cotgrave was enabled to extricate his Baggage, & the peeice of Artillery, he had in charge from the Horrid Swamp which Seperates the Miami and Sandusky Rivers. He encamped t⟨hat⟩ evening near the Miami Bay and by Marching early on the following morning he had arrived with in fifteen miles of the River Raisen when he was informed of the total defeat of our Troops there.[4]

The 2nd Regt. of Perkins Brigade arrived on the 21st. and I immedeately ordered the remaining part of the Kentucky troops under Genl. Payne to proceed with all possible expidition to the River Raisen. I was still uneasy for the Troops there, but supposing that Genl Winchester had obtained the best information of the Strength of the disposable force of the Enemy—And as I had Sent him Three hundred Men more than he deemed Sufficient for maintaining his Ground (See his Letter of the 21st. No 4.)[5] and as there were a Thousand reasons which made it necessary to Maintain it if practicable—I did not think it proper to Order him to retreat, altho' the advance in the first instance was Contrary to my wishes and opposed to a princeple by which I have been ever governed in Indian warfare ie never to make a detachment but under the most urgent circumstances. Amongst the many reasons why the Post at the River Raisen Should be maintaind, The protection of the French Inhabitants was not the least. The greater part of these people had received our Troops with Open Arms Many of them had Sallied out of thier houses upon the arrival of Colo. Lewis with thier Arms in thier hands and had even in the Opinion of Some of our Officers Won the palm of valor from our Troops they attacked and Killed the Strugling Indians whereever they met them, their Houses were all open to our men, they offered to give up the whole of the provisions which yet remained to them, upon Condition that they Should not again be abandoned to the fury of the Savages, or subjected for what they had done, to be immured in the Prisons of Malden. I had also been informed, that the Supplies to be procured there were considerable, (See Days letter enclosed in No 3.)[6] and the assistance to be derived, from the Carioles of the inhabitants was an object of the greatest importance. The former of these Motives had made so strong an impression upon the Minds of the Genl. And his Troops, that I am persuaded, that nothing but a reiterated order to retreat, would have produced Obedience upon the part of the Latter. These Reasons, together with the respect which it was necessary to Shew, to the Opinion of an officer of high rank and experience, whose oppertu⟨ni⟩ty of procuring the most Correct information, was much better than mine, produced the determination, to support rather than with draw, the detachment from the River Raisen, indeed it appears that there was not time for either, after my arrival at the Rapids. When I left upper Sandusky—The Artillery was ordered to be sent on immediately to the Rapids, escorted by Three Hundred Men. Detachm[e]nts were also ordered for the Pack Horses, Waggons and Sleds, which were Constantly progressing thither. An other

Battalion could also have been drawn from Lower Sandusky so that the troops at the Rapids would have been almost daily increased. On this day they would have Amounted to Twenty five hundred with two pieces of Artillery—and in four or five days more the Virginia Brigade and Pensylvania Regt would have increased them to Thirty Eight hundred, with a furthur supply of Artillery. By the 5th. of Febry. the whole force Four thousand five hundred, which I contemplated assembling at the Rapids, would have been there; and provisions and Munitions of war in abundence.

I should have been enabled to advance to the Rapids again this day or tomorrow, but for a most unfortunate rain, which has broken up the roads, so as to render them impassable for the artillery altho it is fixed on Sleds. The whole train is stopped Twenty five miles from this. I have reason to believe that the Miami River has broken up.

I have the honor to enclose You a Report made to me by Major McClanehan, the Senior, of the two officers, who escaped from the action at the River Raisen,[7] It requires no comment from me. I have the honor to be With great Respect Sir. Yr. Obt. Sert

WILLM. HENRY HARRISON

RC and enclosures (DNA: RG 107, LRRS, H-38:7). RC docketed by Armstrong with the added notation, "to be covered & sent to the Presidt." For enclosures, see nn. 1–3 and 5–7.

1. The enclosure marked "No 1." is a copy of James Winchester to Harrison, 21 Jan. 1813 (1 p.), enclosing William Lewis to Winchester, 20 Jan. 1813 (5 pp.), which recounted the events of 18 Jan. 1813, describing the Americans as "steady and composed" during an assault in which 13 Americans were killed and 54 wounded.

2. The enclosure is a copy of Harrison to Winchester, 16 Jan. 1813 (1 p.; marked "No 2"), stating that Harrison would wait to hear from Winchester before forwarding supplies to the rapids.

3. The extract from Winchester to Harrison, 17 Jan. 1813 (2 pp.; marked "No 3."), enclosed a copy of Isaac Day to Harrison, 12 Jan. 1813 (1 p.) (see n. 6, below).

4. In the second week of December 1812, Harrison, hoping to capture Fort Malden before the winter set in, had ordered Winchester to proceed with his troops to the rapids of the Maumee River. Upon his arrival Winchester disregarded these orders, deciding instead to protect settlers at Frenchtown, where he dispersed a small British detachment on 18 Jan. 1813. Col. Henry Procter, with his combined force of 1,300 British troops and Indians led by the Wyandot chief Roundhead, organized a counterattack against Winchester's smaller force of about 1,000 men. On 22 Jan., during the surprise attack by the British and Indians, Winchester was captured and surrendered all his troops. While precise casualty figures are unavailable, there were over 197 Americans killed or missing and hundreds taken prisoner; only 33 escaped. The following day 60 prisoners were murdered by a band of intoxicated Wyandot Indians who sought revenge for atrocities committed earlier by the Kentuckians. The pro-war American press used the events at the river Raisin as propaganda against the British. Harrison remained at the rapids of the Maumee River and began building a stockade, which was later named Fort Meigs (Gilpin, *The War of 1812 in the Old Northwest*, 158, 163–71; George F. G. Stanley, *The War of 1812: Land Operations* [Toronto, 1983], 143–48).

5. In Winchester to Harrison, 21 Jan. 1813 (2 pp.; marked "No 4."), Winchester stated, "I would rather that my force, was encreased to 1000 or 1200 effective men, Sufficient to repel

any force that could be brought against me." He reported that he was not yet able to inform Harrison of the amount of provisions required, and he added that "No pains or reasonable expence" would be spared in obtaining "the necessary information concerning the enemy."

6. In Day to Harrison, 12 Jan. 1813 (see n. 3, above), Day claimed that he could secure flour and wheat if a detachment of cavalry and riflemen was sent. He also reported that the British were gathering Indians to rally at the river Raisin "for the purpose of giving battle."

7. The enclosure is marked, "Report of Maj. McClanehan & Capn. Graves [sic] To Genl. Harrison." In his letter to Harrison of 26 Jan. 1813 (5 pp.), Maj. Elijah McClanahan described himself as "the senior officer who escaped" and recounted the events of the Battle of the River Raisin on 22 Jan. Also enclosed is Capt. Michael Glaves to Harrison, 26 Jan. 1813 (1 p.), concurring with McClanahan's report (printed in Esarey, *Messages and Letters of William Henry Harrison*, Indiana Historical Collections, 2:338–41).

§ From Shadrach Bond, Edward Hempstead, and John B. C. Lucas. *26 January 1813, Washington.* Recommend Silas Bent of St. Louis to fill the "Vacancy in the office of Judge of the Superior Court of the Territory of Missouri, occasioned by the resignation of Mr: Coburn."[1]

RC (DNA: RG 59, LAR, 1809–17, filed under "Bent"). 2 pp. A note at the foot of the RC is signed by A. Lacock, A. Lyle, Robert Brown, and David Bard as concurring in the recommendation. Printed in Carter, *Territorial Papers, Louisiana-Missouri*, 14:626.

1. A few days later Lucas sent JM an undated letter outlining Bent's qualifications for a judicial appointment (DNA: RG 59, LAR, 1809–17, filed under "Bent"; 1 p.; printed in Carter, *Territorial Papers, Louisiana-Missouri*, 14:626–27). JM nominated Bent for the judgeship on 16 Feb. 1813, and the Senate confirmed the appointment two days later (*Senate Exec. Proceedings*, 2:324, 326).

To Thomas Jefferson

DEAR SIR   WASHINGTON Jany. 27. 1813

I snatch a moment to intimate that Dr. T. Ewell is under circumstances which induce him to surround himself with respectable names as far as he can.[1] Yours has been already brought into print, and he is availing himself to the utmost of your alledged patronage of him. I think it probable that he will endeavor to draw from you by letter whatever may be yielded by your politeness or benevolence; and I cannot do less than put you on your guard.

Congs. proceed with their usual slowness even on the most essential subjects; and the under-current agst. us is as strong as ever. I have not time to explain the late changes in the Ex: Dept, if I were disposed to trouble you with them. Bonaparte, according to his own shewing is in serious danger; and if half the official accounts of the Russians be true, his own escape is barely possible, and that of his army impossible. The effect of such a catastrophe on his compulsory allies may once more turn the tables quite round in the case between France & Engld. You will have seen the Speech of the Regt.[2] The debates on it have not reached us. Wellesley's party attack the

Ministry for not prosecuting the war more vigorously agst. us. Nothing but the difficulty of their affairs will open their ears, & that without opening their hearts to peace. In the Peninsula, the French are dr[a]wing Wellington back to Lisbon, and there now is no doubt that the late harvest is a very short one, and the quality for the most part bad. Their expenditures also are enormous, beyond former years; and their bank paper 35 per Ct. below specie. I have for you a Copy of Cooper's Justinian,[3] which I will forward by next mail. Yrs. always & affecy.

J M

RC (DLC). Docketed by Jefferson as received 29 Jan.

1. JM referred to an undated broadside published by Ewell offering "a few more remarks on the guilt of the Chief Clerk of the Navy Department." Ewell provided further examples of Goldsborough's practice of arranging contracts in ways that benefited him as a private citizen and expressed surprise at the chief clerk's efforts to damage the reputation of his powder mills, "even after reading the distinguished evidence of their excellence in the public prints!" Ewell further claimed that he was moved to publish by "a sense of what he owes to the great and good Mr. Jefferson who gave him his office—and to the generous and the patriotic Mr. Hamilton, who befriended him in it." Ewell remarked that he had "constantly remembered that the late President saved him from [the] machinations" of his enemies and that he had been warned that those same enemies, "in spite of President Jefferson," would "yell [him] from the face of the city." JM's copy of this broadside is located in the Library of Congress (DLC: Madison Collection, Rare Book Division).

2. Extracts relating to American affairs from the prince regent's address to Parliament on 30 Nov. 1812 had been published in the *Daily National Intelligencer* on 25 Jan. 1813. They reported that the regent regretted that efforts to restore peace between Great Britain and the U.S. had not been successful; that the U.S. had attempted, without success, to invade Great Britain's Canadian provinces and "to seduce the inhabitants of them from their allegiance" to the king; and that until peace could be restored *"without sacrificing the maritime rights of Great Britain,"* the regent would expect parliamentary support for "a vigorous prosecution of the war."

3. JM referred to the *Institutiones*, or *The Institutes of Justinian, with Notes by Thomas Cooper* (Philadelphia, 1812; Shaw and Shoemaker 25764).

From David H. Robinson

SIR,   BOWLING GREEN K. 27th. Jan. 1813.
That I am an American Citizen must be my appology for the liberty I take in addressing you: but through the medium of my address you will not view a Sycophant standing cap-in hand soliciting an appointment; nor a petulant Censor faulting measures for which his imbecile brain cannot suggest a reason. No Sir, I am none of those, I profess that my motive is publick good: You will readily agree with me when I say that the practical blessings of a Republic would be Jeopardised if men, untried, and apperently destitute of merit, through the specious recommendation of their friends should be appointed to fill the most important offices in the nation.

I am informed through a source to which I attach Credit, that the friends of Capt. Anthony Butler, of Russellville, Kentucky, have designated him as a proper Successor for the illustrious Wm H. Harrison in his gubernatorial seat! Had you possessed a personal knowledge of Capt Butler, the necessity of this Epistle would have been superceded, for I, as well as the rest of the Citizens of Kentucky rely with the proudest confidence on your superior discernment and ability: but expecting the information [you] would receive on this subject would be altogether on *one side* I have taken the liberty to state a few unvarnished facts.

About five years ago Capt Butler emigrated to this Country, from S. Carolina & in that short time has successively solicited an Appointment in the U S Army, the place of the Judge of the Court of Appeals in this State, an Appointment by the people as Representative in Congress in which he was left out by an overwhelming majority—An Appointment by the legislature of this State of Senator of the U. S. in Congress but in every effort for advancement he has been superceeded by men in whom the people could repose confidence. The people of Kentucky, I believe, have been uniform in their attatchment to Republicanism & the[y] prefer having political servants "not only chaste but *unsuspected.*"

When Capt Butler first arrived at Russellville he figured as a Gentleman of easy fortune who had retired from the profession of the law to sip the pleasures of life this he certainly done [*sic*] in what some call a *Gentleman like manner*; but in a manner not altogether approbated by the People: But in his congressional Canvass with the people he repeatedly disclaimed having ever practiced as an Attorney: I believe the fact to be that he has practiced as a Lawyer in S. Carolina but soon found it was not his path to eminence. His *fashionable course* has attached some men to his interest but I know of nothing else to recommend him; at least you will discover that from his repeated solicitation for offices there is no danger of damping the genious of unassuming merit. Sir, with the highest consideration your Mo't Ob't

DAVID H. ROBINSON.

RC (DLC). Docketed by JM.

From St. George Tucker

DEAR SIR,   WILLIAMSBURG January 27. 1813.

I have this moment concluded an official Letter to the Secretary of State, notifying my Acceptance of the Commission which by your direction was sent to me from his office the last week.[1] In that Letter I took the Liberty of offering you my respectful acknowledgements for what I deemed a testimonial of your approbation and Confidence; but the sense I entertain of your Conduct on this Occasion will not permit me to rest satisfied with such an acknowledgement: Permit me to look upon this occurrence as an unequivocal mark of your friendship, also. In that light, believe me, Sir, I have more pleasure in recieving it, than I could derive either from the Honors or Emoluments of the office. Of the former I was not ambitious; of the latter I was not in the least desirous. I had retired, as I thought, forever, from a public station, & from public notice. Among the Inducements which I have to emerge from my obscurity, the Idea that in so doing I should manifest a respect for your opinion, & good Wishes, holds a distinguish'd place.[2]

I beg you Sir to accept this friendly expression of my feelings towards you in good part; and with it my most sincere Wishes for the health of yourself & Mrs. Madison (to whom be pleased to offer my respectful Compliments) and for your mutual happiness; added to my fervent prayers for the honourable Issue of your patriotic Endeavours to advance & preserve the honor and Interests of our common Country. I am with sincere respect & friendship, Dear Sir, your most obedt. Servt.

St: G: Tucker

RC (DLC); FC (ViW: Tucker-Coleman Papers). RC docketed by JM.

1. In his letter to Monroe, Tucker acknowledged receipt of his commission as a district judge for Virginia and expressed his gratitude to the president (Tucker to Monroe, 27 Jan. 1813 [ibid.]).

2. Tucker initially considered declining the position and drafted a long letter to JM on 23 Jan. 1813 stating his reasons for this decision (ibid.). Appended to the 23 Jan. draft is a paragraph dated 27 Jan.: "The persuasions of several of my friends induced me to take further time to deliberate on the step I was about to take. Unwilling as I was, & still continue, to enter again into public Life, the Consideration *that all my means of support* being now invested in Banks, which might be ruin'd by the War, it might be well to accept an office the Salary annext to which, might in Case of such an Event, defend me from Beggars. This consideration has prevaild, & I have this day acceptd the office—May Heaven support me under it!!!" The Senate had confirmed Tucker's nomination on 19 Jan. (*Senate Exec. Proceedings,* 2:317).

§ To the Senate. *27 January 1813.* "I transmit to the Senate a Report of the Secretary of War, complying with their Resolution of the 7th instant."[1]

RC and enclosures (DNA: RG 46, Executive Proceedings, 12B-D2). RC 1 p.; in the hand of Edward Coles, signed by JM. For enclosures, see n. 1.

1. On 7 Jan. 1813 the Senate passed a resolution that had been presented by Samuel Smith of Maryland on the previous day, directing the secretary of war to lay before the Senate "a return of the commissioned, non-commissioned officers, musicians, and privates, who have enrolled themselves" in accordance with JM's charge "to accept and organize certain volunteer military corps" (*Annals of Congress,* 12th Cong., 2d sess., 40). In response JM forwarded a 26 Jan. 1813 letter from James Monroe, as acting head of the War Department, to the president

of the Senate (3 pp.), explaining that in the interests of efficiency, blank commissions had been sent to army generals authorizing them "to organize and embody" volunteers with the regular troops and that the returns had not yet been transmitted to the department. He added that the War Department had organized companies of volunteers from Petersburg, Baltimore, Pennsylvania, and Alexandria and that several other troops from the District of Maine "are in service, with the several Armies, called Volunteers, who have not complied with the provisions of the Acts, and can only be considered as Militia from the several states, where they have been raised." Monroe also enclosed a return from the adjutant general, dated 11 Jan. 1813 (1 p.), listing a total of 747 privates in nine regiments as the number of "non commissioned officers, musicians and privates enlisted into the Army of the United States for eighteen months, under the act entitled 'An Act in addition to the act entitled "An Act to raise an Additional military force" passed January 11th 1812.'"

§ From Thomas Gholson. *27 January 1813.* Encloses a recommendation [not found] of Judge Waller Taylor for the office of governor of the Indiana Territory. "Mr. Taylor is certainly a meritorious man. I have been long acquainted with him. He is honorable intelligent & brave; and if it be reconcileable with the views & policy of the Government to appoint a person residing within the Territory, I imagine Judge Taylor would be the best selection that could be made."[1]

RC (DNA: RG 59, LAR, 1809–17, filed under "Taylor, Judge"). 1 p. Printed in Carter, *Territorial Papers, Indiana,* 8:232.

1. On 26 Feb. 1813 JM nominated Thomas Posey to replace John Gibson as acting governor of the Indiana Territory. The Senate confirmed the appointment on 3 Mar. (*Senate Exec. Proceedings,* 2:329, 333).

From Armand Duplantier

MONSIEUR   Ce 28 janvier 1813
    Jai L'honneur de vous joindre ici copie de La Collocation que jai faite pour Le gl. Lafayette des terres appartenant à L'état, derierre Les Communes de La ville, Le Long du canal Carondelet,[1] Comme je Crois vous en avoir prevenus dans Le tems. Jais quelques raison pour croire que Les representant de L'état de La Louisianne pourroit en faire La demande au Congres. C'est pour Cette raison que jai L'honneur de vous adresser Cette Copie. Le Congres a eû tant de bonté pour cet état, que je craindrois pour Les interets du general, qu'il Lui fit encore ce don, S'il ignoroit Cette Collocation, Ce qui Lui feroit Le plus grand tort.
    Je viens de recevoir des Lettres du gl. par Lesquelles il m'inform⟨e⟩ qu'ayant fait une vente tres avantageuse de Ces terres audessus de La pte. Coupée,[2] et son plus fort acquereur, par Les informations qu'il a reçu, croyant avoir payé Ces terres beaucoup trop cher, pour L'indemniser il Lui

a donné un interets dans celles que jais Colloqué Le Long du canal, et aussi en assurant Son marché, cela Lui donne un moyen d'amélliorer, et mettre en valeur Cette portion de terre. Si par Ces amis, et La constante bontée du gt. il peut L'obtenir, Son acquereur Lui offre de fournir Les moyens necessaires pour La mettre en valeur, d'apres Ce qu'il me marque, C'est tout Ce qui lui resteroit du don magnifique que Lui a fait Le gt. Le produit des ventes qu'il a faites Suffisant à peine pour payer ces dêtes. Il vous aurat Surement écris pour reclamer de nouveau, vos bons Service, et votre amitie à ce Sujet, il me marque n'avoir reçu aucune nouvelles de vous depuis Longtems, ni L'avis de Lenvois des plans des dernieres Collocations que je vous ais adressé, L année derniere, par L'entremise de Mr. Smith.[3] Je n'ais pas crus devoir faire arpenter Les terres Sur Le Canal, je n'y trouverois pas La quantité que je désire, il Seroit bien à Souhaiter que Cela pourroit être finé de Suite en faveur du gl. vus que La Compagnie de navigation a enfin commencé à fouiller Le Canal, et cela doit donner de La valeur à ces terres, qui, quoique tres basse, en y faisant des travaux, quelques dépenses, deviendroit un objet de valeur, ayes La bontée de me dire, ce que je dois faire à ce Sujet, pour Le mieux des interets du gl. jais tant de preuves des bonnes intentions de ces amis au nort, et de votre bonté et amitie pour Lui, que jai tout espoir qu'il obtiendrat cette portion de terre Je me féliciteres du Succes que jai eu, grâce à vos soins. Jais L'honneur d'être avec respect Monsieur votre tres humble et obéissant Serviteur

DUPLANTIER

CONDENSED TRANSLATION

Forwards a copy of the list he made for General Lafayette of the state lands behind the city commons along the Carondelet Canal, believing that the Louisiana representative in Congress might ask for it. Congress has been so generous to the state that were it to make the gift again to the general in ignorance of this list, it might do him an injustice. Has just received letters from the general informing him that, having sold his lands above Pointe Coupee and believing that the largest buyer paid too much for them, Lafayette has given the buyer a stake in those alongside the canal. In addition to securing the deal, this gives him a way to improve this portion of the land. If he can obtain the land, his buyer will provide the means to develop it. This is all that remains of the government's generous gift to him, the sale of which scarcely suffices to pay his debts. The general will surely have written to JM, calling again on his assistance and kindness. Lafayette reports that he has not heard from JM for some time, nor has he been notified of the forwarding of the previous lists, which Duplantier sent to JM last year by Mr. Smith. Has not deemed it necessary to survey the canal lands, not believing that he would find the necessary quantity there. Wishes this matter could be settled soon in the general's favor, as the dredging of the canal has begun, which should add value to the land. Asks JM to instruct him what to do to serve the general's interests. Is confident that with the goodwill of his friends and JM's kindness, the general will obtain this portion of land.

RC, two copies (DLC). First RC docketed by JM, "Duplantier / Jany. 23. 1813." Second RC dated 15 May 1813; marked *"duplicata"*; docketed by JM, "May 15 1813."

1. Enclosure not found.
2. Between 1810 and 1812 Lafayette sold all of his Pointe Coupee lands. His main buyers were Alexander Baring, Sir John Coghill, and Henry Seymour. For JM's role as agent for Lafayette, see Madison and Lafayette's Louisiana Lands, 26 Oct. 1809, *PJM-PS*, 2:35–38.
3. See John K. Smith to JM, 25 Aug. 1811, ibid., 3:432.

From William Eustis

confidential

DEAR SIR,   BOSTON Jan: 29. 1813.

I cannot bear to see the recruiting season which expires in the month of March, passing away without the success which I am confident would result from proper measures & exertions. By a late arrangement Colo. Ripley stationed in Portland has charge of a district in Maine Lt Colo. Darrington in N. Hampshire, Colo. Tuttle in Boston, Colo. Larned in Pittsfield Masstts., with a view it is presumed to their personal convenience & supposed influence. The two latter are indolent & will get nothing which does not *come to them*. The two former may do a little better. I have conversed with Boyd, Major Eustis & others. It is very evident that altho' they do in fact get men, ten might be had for one by suitable exertions. Officers commanding districts should be ordered to visit every recruiting post once at least in every week or ten days—to remove every officer & every post which is not successful—to transport (for I find they doubt whether they are authorised to incur the expence, and to all I see I give notice that every necessary expence will be allowed) cloathing, camp equipage & arms in waggons or sleighs to each rendezvous—to march (& to hire transport for provision & baggage) from one post to another, to display some pride & circumstance of war from village to village—they the commanders of districts instead of their fire sides should have positive orders to be on horse back—to put the recruits to the drill the moment they are raised. Two thousand men who may with great certainty be raised in this section in two months will bring 1500 or 2000 more and have a greater effect in silencing the opposition than any measure within my contemplation. But there must be a revolution in the practice, and as I apprehend in the men, in some of them at least. It grieves me to observe the time lost, in which alone the objects of the next campaign can be provided for. The vis inertia of a part of these district officers might be removed by an order forbidding them to *rest*. Having recovered from a heavy cold I was about making an arrangement with G. Boyd to effect a change and a more vigorous execution, but he will not I fear have time to visit the different posts, being ordered on the Court Martial.

It was reported to me yesterday that the District Officers had not received money. Twenty thousand dollars & a General Officer with twenty aids might be employed with equal use & œconomy on this all important branch at this precious time. Being uninformed of the arrival of Genl Armstrong & the characters of the officers being of a delicate nature I have trusted to the importance of the subject an apology [*sic*] for addressing you and am as ever with the greatest respect

W. Eustis

RC (DLC). Docketed by JM.

§ Andrew C. Mitchell to James Monroe. *30 January 1813, Washington.* Seeks an appointment as agent for the exchange of prisoners of war at Quebec, "the only vacant Post, where an agent for that purpose is admitted under the late arrangement between Sir John Borlasse Warren & my father."[1] Urges the establishment of an agency at Quebec on the grounds that "at the commencement of the ensuing campaign . . . a first Engagement may place Prisoners of Rank & Importance in the hands of either party, the immediate Exchange of which might be highly advantageous to the United States," that "The Information which might be obtained from an Agent before the Commencement of hostilities without subjecting himself to the character of a Spy, might be advantageous to the Regulations and distributions of our armies," and that "In case of Peace even before our arms were carried into Canada," an agent in Quebec could help the U.S. "endeavour to obtain a free navigation of the River St Laurence."

RC (DNA: RG 59, LAR, 1809–17, filed under "Mitchell, Andrew C."). 4 pp. A penciled note on the cover in JM's hand reads: "If there be *now* occasion for such an Agent at Quebec, a person belonging to Detroit was recomended by Genl Dearborn as proper & in distress."

1. Andrew C. Mitchell was the son of John Mitchell, American agent for prisoners of war at Halifax. For the agreement governing the exchange of naval prisoners of war, see JM to Congress, 22 Jan. 1813, n. 1.

From John Adams

Dear Sir   Quincy January 31st. 1813
I have subscribed with Mr Gray[1] and others a recommendation of Hendrick W Gordon Esquire[2] a copy of which is enclosed. As he requests a seperate Certificate, I enclose his letter and can sincerely say that from an acquaintance with him, of several years, I believe that what is said of him,

in the Certificate, and in his letter, to be no more than he deserves; He is a civil, well bred man, capable industrious, and faithful in business, I have the honour to be very respectfully Sir your most obedient Servant

JOHN ADAMS

Letterbook copy (MHi: Adams Papers).

1. William Gray (1750–1825), a prominent shipowner and merchant in Salem, Massachusetts, had been a member of the Salem militia during the Revolutionary War. In 1792 he became the first president of the Essex Bank. Serving in numerous civic capacities throughout his life, Gray was a state senator in 1807, 1808, and 1821, a lieutenant governor of Massachusetts in 1810–11, a nominee for governor in 1816, and president of the Massachusetts electoral college in 1824. Unlike many of his fellow New England merchants, Gray supported the Embargo Act of 1807, subsequently realigning himself with the Republicans, moving to Boston, and thereafter upholding government measures during the War of 1812 (Edward Gray, *William Gray of Salem, Merchant: A Biographical Sketch* [Boston, 1914], 12, 39, 41, 82–83).

2. Gordon had been appointed a prize agent by Capt. Samuel Evans, commander of the *Chesapeake*, and he wrote to JM on 23 Feb. 1813, "a Valuable prize to that Ship, having arrived safe at Portsmouth NHampshire," to request "the agency of the part which accrues to the Goverment by law." On 17 Jan. 1814 JM nominated Gordon for the office of collector of direct taxes and internal duties for the Tenth District of Massachusetts, but the nomination was rejected by the Senate. On 8 Mar. 1815 Gordon requested from JM a consular appointment in a European port, which he did not receive. He wrote to JM on 4 July 1815 that if he was not appointed consul to a European port, he would accept "the same office" at any port or place JM would send him. When he did not receive a consulate, Gordon wrote to Monroe on 9 Dec. 1815 requesting any other situation for which he was qualified. On 17 Sept. 1816 he wrote to JM seeking to fill the vacancy in the consulate at Palermo (DNA: RG 59, LAR, 1809–17, filed under "Gordon"; *Senate Exec. Proceedings*, 2:455, 468).

From James Monroe

Jany 31. [1813]

By the enclosed communication from General Dearborn, it appears, that Genl Prevost declines the proposed exchange of Genl Hull, & the officers designated here, for a reason, which is not warranted by any fact known to us.[1] I suspect, it is a sequel, of the ⟨arbritary?⟩ exchanges made at Halifax without our consent. The letter to Genl Dearborn, written in haste, wh. I leave open for your inspection, notices the subject.[2]

I send him a copy of the exply observations relative to late acts on military affrs.,[3] which appeard to be necessary, as he declines coming here.

If you see no objection to the letters going on be so good as seal, & deliver to bearer.

RC (DLC: Rives Collection, Madison Papers). Unsigned; dated "Jany 31."; docketed by JM "Jany. 31. 1813." For enclosures, see nn.

1. The enclosure was an extract from Dearborn to Monroe, 25 Jan. 1813 (DNA: RG 45, Area File 7; 1 p.), which forwarded a four-page extract from Sir George Prevost to Dearborn, 11 Jan. 1813, in response to Dearborn's 2 Jan. 1813 letter, which had transmitted to Prevost "a List of American prisoners of war" considered by Monroe and Dearborn "as exchanged in conformity to the principles agreed on and put in practice by the British admiral at Halifax, and requesting [Prevost's] approbation to that schedule, which was annexed, being an account for the exchange of Brigr. Genl. Hull, and certain officers named, belonging to the army of the U. States, for the officers, non-commissioned officers, and private soldiers of his majesty's first regiment of foot, captured on board the Samuel and Sarah Transport, by the United States frigate the Essex, capt. Porter" (ibid.).

Prevost expressed "some surprize at receiving this communication" and regretted "that circumstances will not allow me to afford my concurrence." By way of explanation, Prevost alluded to a dispatch he had received in September 1812 from Sir John Coape Sherbrooke in Halifax, from which "it must be inferred that the receipts from the American Agent for the crew of the United States Sloop Nautilus, and a sufficient number of other seamen belonging to the United States, have expressed [sic] as being in exchange for the British soldiers taken on board the Samuel and Sarah Transport, by the United States frigate Essex." For details of the capture of the Nautilus by a British squadron on 16 July 1812 and Porter's seizure of the Samuel and Sarah, see Dudley, Naval War of 1812, 1:209–11, 217, 255–56, 446, 487 n., 558–59.

2. In his 31 Jan. 1813 letter to Dearborn, Monroe acknowledged receipt of Dearborn's letter of 25 Jan. (see n. 1, above) and expressed astonishment at Prevost's conduct, adding that "we had no knowledge of any such exchange of the men taken at sea by the Essex, as he suggests" (Hamilton, Writings of Monroe, 5:241–42).

3. Monroe referred to his "Explanatory Observations," sent to George Washington Campbell, chairman of the Senate select committee on military affairs, on 23 Dec. 1812. Upon Monroe's assumption of the duties of the War Department in December 1812, he was given a congressional directive to report on the manpower requirements for the war. Monroe outlined the forces needed for coastal defense, especially to prevent a British seizure of Florida, and for offensive operations in Canada in 1813. He called for the expansion of the army beyond the authorized strength of 35,000 and proposed a bill to recruit an additional 20,000 men for twelve months' service with the intention that such a bill would replace the volunteer laws of 1812. Monroe also recommended that the president be given authority to appoint all officers below the rank of field grade in the latter force rather than let the men choose them, as had been the policy under the 1812 legislation. Congress approved Monroe's recommendations, altering only the amount of the bounty for enlistments from the suggested $40 to $16. The bill became law on 29 Jan. 1813, although the Senate insisted on its right to confirm all officer appointments and several congressmen doubted whether the term of one year of service was adequate (Ammon, James Monroe, 315–16; Hamilton, Writings of Monroe, 5:227–35; U.S. Statutes at Large, 2:794–96).

From James Taylor

DEAR SIR,   BELLE VUE NEAR NEWPORT Jany 31st 1813

I most sincerely congratulate you on the Certainty of your being again called on to Preside over the destinies of my beloved Country, but I more particularly congratulate my country, as I conci[e]ve it a most fortunate occurrence that could have happened, both as it relates to the Man & principle.

I hope Genl Harrison will be more fortunate with the Present N. W. Army than the a[r]mies lower down the lake. Indeed I find Gen Winchester has got on as far as the river raisen & in a skirmish there our arms proved victorious.[1]

The Circumstance of Genl. Hulls surrender[2] prevented many of us from Participating in the honors which awaits our arms in that quarter, and I sinc[e]rely regret that I cannot be actively engaged there, but I hope the time is not far distant when I may be. No exertion shall be wanting on my part to aid the glorious cause, every energy of my mind & body have been directed to that end. I had three Nephews and my self actively engaged in the first N. W Army, and I have in Genls Harrisons four Nephews beside a number of relations and connections and I have not failed both by precept and example to stimulat[e] them & all others to join in the contest.

Two of these Nephews have been brought up by my self. James Taylor Eubank I have had with me from a child Genl Harrison & Colo Morrison were so pleased with his capacity & disposition to do business that he has been appointed a Deputy Q. Master and is the first in the appointments index Genl H only appd. one of the same rank in that army my brothers son Hubbard is appd an asst. Deputy he is a fine young man. They were both doing business for me at the time of Colo Morrisons & Mr Hunts appointments & were with the army. My Nephew Taylor Berry (son to Washington Berry Esqr one of our assistant Judges) was one of my assistants & the principal one, & was taken prisoner with me at Detroit. He is a fine young man & I will venture to say did as much business as it was possible for one Man to do during the whole Campaign, for I was robed of my other two assistants. Mr Beall was taken prisoner in the vessell & Mr Carniot[3] I permitted to come on to bring on dispatches & transport the detachment sent for to our relief.

Mr Berry is anxious to serve his Count[r]y in the line of the army prov[id]ed he can get a first Lieutenancy and I do assure you I do not think he ought to accept any thing under that grade. He is about of age about six feet high & stout in proportion dark hair & eyes and as good a looking young man as you will see in a thousand, drinks no ardent spirits and is completely the man of business and a soldier. During the affair at Detroit he was with Lt. Dallaby[4] at his Battery during the whole time & when Gen Hull ordered it silenced, He shouldered his firelock & marched on to join Genl Findlay Regt when he found them marching in to the Fort.

I Know Colos Findlay McArthur & Cass think highly of Mr Berry for I have heard them frequently express it and I expect some if not all of them may drop you or the Secy of War a line on the subject. I am sure Leut. Thomas S. Jesup now at Washington will corroborate what I have stated and thro Mr. Coles he could be called on to state the facts to the Secy of War or any one else.

I Know your situation as[5] those appointmnts but it appears to me that if you were to suggest to the member from our district or the State that you wished one or two appointments made that they would chearfully aquecse [*sic*].

I have written to Mr Clay & Mr Johnson on the subject but our friend Richard with all his good qualities is so fond of popularity that he regards that more than merit & has made some of the worst appointments in the state.

Alfred Sandford son of the Genl.[6] would make a first rate Military Man brave to a fault, he is now out as adjutant to the late Colo Scotts Regt. He applied for a Captaincy last winter.

I wrote to Mr Johnson on the subject but he informed me no such rank could be had for him. The fact is Johnson & Gen S were competitors & a coolness took place & it is still Kept up in some measure between these Gent. Sandford is a man of fine education & is reading Law. He married the daughter of Major Thos. Martin & as the Major is an old Revolution-ary officer & has no son Capt. Sandfords claims to an appointment might be the stronger.

If both him & Mr Berry could be gratified & they could be arranged to one Company it would be the more pleasing but not of great importance, but I will pledge my reputation that there would not be two better officers of their grades in the service than they would be.

Will you be so good as to mention me to my worthy friend Mrs Madi-son in termes of great respect & freindship and to your whole household, and believe me to be with the highest respect & friendship, You[r]s truly

JAMES TAYLOR

P S.

You no doubt recollect the circumstance of Doct. Hosea Blood being wounded by the cannon ball at Detroit that Killed Lt Hanks &c. The Doct was imployed by Genl Harrison on the Tippacoe expedition & attended the Hospital with Doct Foster & after he left it. He came on with the 4h Regt Went on to Detroit with a Doct. Edwards being appd to do the duty of Sergt to that Regt Doct Foster took Dot Blood in to the Hospital dept when he came on to Detroit. I attended the Hospital frequently & had an opportunity of seeing the amputations & it was given up on all hands that Doct Blood was the most skilful man among them all, and also that he did more real duty than all the rest of the Medical department for all the sick & wounded mostly was under his charge & Doct Foster was able to give him little or no assistance. This man ought to be attended to as a Treasure. Steady & laborious as possible & of a fine constitution & solid mind, but not briliant, he moves on & discharges his duty faith fully. He is a Yanky but latterly from Mr Ormsbys district, but I am told he is not acquainted with him. I wrote to Mr. Ormsby on the subject. I hope you will pardon me for thus troubling it is my wish to serve my Country

J. T.

RC (DLC).

1. Winchester's initial skirmish of 18 Jan. at Frenchtown was a short-lived American victory. Taylor evidently had not yet heard of the events at the river Raisin on 22 Jan., in which approximately 300 Americans were killed (see William Henry Harrison to James Monroe, 26 Jan. 1813, n. 4).

2. For Hull's surrender of Detroit, see John Kilbourn to JM, 24 Aug. 1812, and n. 2.

3. Taylor probably referred to Thomas Davis Carneal.

4. James A. Dalliba (d. 1832) of Connecticut was a graduate of the U.S. Military Academy who received a commission as a second lieutenant in artillery in March 1811 and was promoted to first lieutenant in March 1813. He served as master of ordnance for the Northwest Army in 1812 and later testified in the court-martial of Hull (James Dalliba, *A Narrative of the Battle of Brownstown* [New York, 1816; Shaw and Shoemaker 37382], 11; Forbes, *Report of the Trial of Brig. General William Hull* [Shaw and Shoemaker 32628], 79–84, 126; Heitman, *Historical Register*, 1:351).

5. Taylor evidently omitted a word here.

6. Thomas Sandford (1762–1808) was a Kentucky congressman from 1803 to 1807 (*Biographical Encyclopaedia of Kentucky* [1980 reprint], 128).

From Edmund Edrington

SIR   STAUNTON VA. Feby. 1st. 1813

You will no doubt be surprised at being addressed by an obscure individual and an utter stranger to you; and perhaps still more so when the cause which has induced him to address you is know[n]: it is to ask a favour, and a pecuniary one too, that I have presumed to trespass upon your important engagements: I am a young man of a respectable but not wealthy family, and of a somewhat better education than poor boys usually recieve in our state; I have a small farm and a few slaves; with this I was satisfied; but to save a large and respectable family from ruin and absolute want I some time since assumed for them a responsibility which I am unable to meet; and unless I can obtain a loan of 2000$, all the little I have will be taken from me; I shall be cut short in the prosecution of a study (that of Medicine) in which I have been some time engaged, and an aged mother, who is dependent on me, will be brought to taste the bitterness of poverty and want. I feel great diffidence in making this application; but when I reflect that it is a loan only that I ask, that such a loan would enable me to save my property from sacrifice, and cheerfully to pursue my studies; that I can give the most unquestionable security on property for the repayment of the money at the end of two years: I have some hope of success: It is not known to any person, nor shall it be known, that I have made this application to you: If you can save me from ruin, it could be done through the instrumentality of a friend, and you not known in the transaction, or I would go to Washington if necessary: I can produce the most satisfactory and creditable testimonials as to my character and conduct: I am known to Mr. Taliaferro who represents the District of which King George is a component part, but I would rather not be known unless you can render me the great kindness I ask. I shall be very thankful to hear from you, that if my application is successful I may go on my way rejoicing, if otherwise I may be delivered from a state of suspense.[1]

In publica commoda peccem, si longiore sermone Morer tua tempora.[2] Most respectfully Your Excellency's Obdt. Servt.

EDMUND EDRINGTON

RC (DLC).

1. In a letter to JM of 14 Feb. 1813, Edrington thanked the president for his prompt reply of "the 8th. Inst." (not found). Presumably JM did not provide the requested loan, because Edrington remarked that the reply "has saved me from expectations which I might have hoped would be fulfilled" (DLC).

2. "In publica commoda peccem, si longo sermone morer tua tempora, Caesar": "I should sin against the public weal if with long talk, O Caesar, I were to delay your busy hours" (Horace, *Epistles*, 2.1.3–4, in *Horace: Satires, Epistles and Ars Poetica*, Loeb Classical Library [1970 reprint], 396, 397).

From James Taylor

SIR,   [ca. 1 February 1813]

I had the pleasure of seeing Govr. Howard lately and was much pleased in hearing from his own lips an account of his efforts in protecting the frontier of his Territory.

Would it not be well to confer the rank of Brigadier Genl on Gov Howard. He is a Military Man & it appears to me that all the Troops in his Territory ought to be under his command. He would accept of it & receive either the emoluments of that or the Governorship alone.[1]

You recollect I named this Gent with Genl. Harrison Gen WClarc as persons meriting appointments. I am still of the same opinion. With either of these Men at our head what would We not now be master of in Canada? Indeed if we had had no one except the four Colonels, we should have done well I am convinced.[2]

Men raised in the Wilds of the Western Country have a boldness of thought & action on military subjects different from those rocked in the cradle of ease & luxury. Pardon my intruding my opinions on you, my object is good.

J T.

P S.

What is to be the consequence if Genl. Harrison leaves the N. W. Army. That army is now our best & only hope for this campaign.

He decid[ed]ly is the 2d. best Genl in the U:States Genl Wilkinson I consider the first. If it was practicable to give him a Majr Genl berth or brevette rank so as for him to Command the N W Army I should be pleased otherwise I fear we have no one competent to the task Genl Winchester is too old & inactive.

I am told the senate of our state have refused to approve the Br[e]vette appointment of Genl Harrison, indeed I do not Know that they could do otherwise, this is not from any want of merit in Genl H. in their opinion but as unwarranted by the constitution or Laws of our state.[3] This information is only from report

J. T.

RC (DLC). Undated; postmarked Cincinnati, 1 Feb. 1813; dated February 1812 in the *Index to the James Madison Papers*. Docketed by JM, "Taylor Js / Feb. 1813."

1. On 12 Mar. 1813 Benjamin Howard was given command of the Eighth Military Department. He was nominated to the rank of brigadier general by JM on 15 June 1813 with the approval of the Senate on 21 June (*Senate Exec. Proceedings*, 2:356, 373).

2. The four colonels Taylor referred to were Lewis Cass, James Findlay, Duncan McArthur, and James Miller.

3. Harrison's appointment in 1812 violated Article 6, Section 11 of the Kentucky Constitution of 1799: "all militia officers shall reside in the bounds of the division, brigade, regiment, battalion, or company to which they may severally belong" (Francis Newton Thorpe, *The Federal and State Constitutions, Colonial Charters, and Other Organic Laws of the States, Territories, and Colonies* . . . [7 vols.; Washington, 1909], 3:1287).

From John Adams

Dear Sir   Quincy Feb. 2 1813

I am very apprehensive that the liberties I So frequently take of writing to you, will appear importunate, if not impertinent. But I beg it may be fully understood that none of my letters are to be answered; and that I shall perfectly acquiesce, in your decisions well knowing the multiplicity of

Candidates, the difficulty of making the Selections and that The President is the only Ultimate and rightful Judge.

There is one Gentleman whose Character and Situation lies with much weight on my mind.

I am constrained to acknowledge, Tho' with great reluctance, that a great majority of all the litterary Corporations in this State have been in Systematic opposition, for the last twelve years, to the national Administration. And I must add that they have countenanced measures in Some of our Seaport Towns and in the Legislature, that have appeared to me intemperate and unwise. Dr Benjamin Waterhouse[1] has never united with them, and this Conduct has brought upon him resentments and opposition which have ended in his Deprivation of his Employment which he has held for thirty years, with reputation. Of his litterary Character, which has been long known and established in Europe and America, it would be idle in me to Speak. I have known him more than thirty years and have never Seen a Stain upon his moral Chara[c]ter. I Scarcely know a more benevolent or exemplary Person. Though I am not minutely acquainted with the Circumstances which occasioned his removal from an Office under the U. S; I have reason to believe that his Error proceeded from his ardent zeal to place the Hospital in the best possible Order; without any Intention of deviating from the Strict line of Integrity. It is perhaps improper to mention any Thing in particular. If it is, I beg your pardon for Suggesting, that if Congress Should establish an Office of Surgeon general and another of Physician General; and I know it to be the opinion of the best Judges, that both ought to be established; perhaps Waterhouse might fill that of Physician General to Advantage. I mean not however to recommend him for any particular Employment: but if there Should be any opening, adequate to his Age, Experience, and Character, in my opinion, his professional moral, litterary and political character is Such as to give a fair claim for his being a Candidate. With great respect, I have the honour to be, Sir your most obedient Servant

JOHN ADAMS

RC (DNA: RG 107, LRUS, R-1813); letterbook copy (MHi: Adams Papers); Tr (NN: Monroe Papers).

1. See Elbridge Gerry to JM, 15 Aug. 1812, n. 1. In June 1813 JM nominated Waterhouse as hospital surgeon, and the Senate confirmed the appointment (*Senate Exec. Proceedings*, 2:379–80).

§ From James Monroe. 2 *February 1813*, *War Department*. Lists proposed promotions in the U.S. Army for JM's approval.

Letterbook copy (DNA: RG 107, LSP). JM forwarded the list of promotions in the Light Artillery Regiment, the First Light Dragoon Regiment, the Rifle Regiment, and the First through Seventh Infantry Regiments to the Senate in a message of 3 Feb. 1813 (*Senate Exec. Proceedings*, 2:320–23).

From John Melish

S<small>IR</small>   P<small>HILADELPHIA</small> 5 Janry [February] *1813*

I duly received your esteemed favour of the 30th. ulto.,[1] in compliance with which I have sent by this mail a Copy of the Travels in plain binding, price $6.—which may be remitted to myself.[2]

The work, I trust, will meet your approbation on perusal [*sic*]. I had a letter sometime ago from Mr Jefferson in which he bestows on it almost unqualified approbation; and concludes by stating that he considers it so lively a picture of the real state of the Country that if he can obtain opportunities of conveyance he will send a Copy to a friend in France, and another to one in Italy, who he Knows will translate and Circulate it as an antidote to the misrepresentations of former travellers.[3] I am with much respect Sir your ob. Servt.

J<small>OHN</small> M<small>ELISH</small>

RC (DLC). Misdated 5 Jan. 1813 by Melish; date assigned here on the basis of evidence presented in n. 3. Docketed by JM.

1. Letter not found.
2. Melish sent JM a copy of his *Travels in the United States of America, in the Years 1806 and 1807, and 1809, 1810, and 1811* (2 vols.; Philadelphia, 1812; Shaw and Shoemaker 26062). During his travels Melish met JM in Washington on 1 June 1811, and he provided the following account of the occasion: "He [JM] received me very politely in a drawing-room, and we had a long conversation, principally regarding the relations between Britain and America. Mr. Madison observed, that he would have gone to the country before this time, but was waiting for Mr. Foster, now daily expected, and he sincerely hoped that on his arrival something would be done to accommodate the differences between the two countries. He remarked that he was happy to observe the favourable disposition of the prince of Wales towards neutral trade, and it was a considerable ground of hope, that he was so popular in his own country. He had done nothing as yet, but it appeared that he had hitherto sacrificed his own opinion to his filial regard for his father, and this circumstance, though it militated against a free trade between England and America now, yet it was in favour of the prince's personal character; and he thought there could hardly be a doubt but he would change the ministry and restore a free trade, when he succeeded to full power.

"On the stopping of the trade itself, he remarked that, the immorality and injustice of the measure out of the question, it had always astonished him that the British ministry should persevere in a system so evidently impolitic, and which militated more against the interest of England than any other nation; and it could not be from ignorance, for the operation and tendency of the orders in council had been very amply exposed in England, particularly in Mr. Baring's pamphlet, and Mr. Brougham's speech; both masterly productions, and which placed the question between the two countries in as clear a point of view as words could convey it. He observed that the effect of the orders in council were very injurious in this country, as they tended to distress the sea-ports, and to divide the people; and there was now no alternative but to sacrifice the national honour, or to resist. Resistance had been determined on by congress, and would in all probability be persevered in till justice was obtained; nor did he believe that any supposed opposition in the eastern states would now have any effect on altering that determination, it being well known that the mass of the people in these states were determined republicans; and, notwithstanding the difference of opinion on commercial subjects, he was well assured that in the day of trial they would stand as firmly by their own government as any section of the union.

"He regretted that a number of the merchants did not take ⟨a⟩ more extended view of the subject, and prefer their permanent interests to a precarious and temporary interest, ⟨li⟩able to be cut off every day. It was evident that, independent of the principle which the orders in council involved, that during their operation, the trade must necessarily be very limited, and subject to great contingencies; and without a free trade *to* the continent, there could be no free trade *from* England: so that, although the government were even to sacrifice the national honour, and allow the merchants to regulate the commerce of the country, the trade would soon cease of itself. *Goods could only be imported to the extent of the exports,* and these being confined to England, and her dependencies and allies, it must necessarily be so limited, that many of the merchants would be in a losing concern, and domestic manufactures would ultimately supercede foreign commerce.

"On the subject of manufactures he observed, that they had progressed in a wonderful degree, and went far to supply the internal demand, which was one great and permanent good that had arisen out of a system fraught with many evils. And so firmly were these manufactures now rooted, that they would unquestionably flourish and increase. On the other hand, such had been the increase of population and wealth in the United States, that there would still be a very great demand for British manufactures, were the trade opened. Mr. Baring had pointed out in his pamphlet, that the exports from Britain to America, amounted to 12,000,000 sterling, and he had no doubt but they would continue to be equal to that amount if the trade were free; and this consideration alone might have induced the British ministry to cultivate a friendly intercourse with a nation, who were disposed to be friends, in place of seeking a precarious commerce by means of special licences with their enemies.

"The conversation lasted nearly an hour, and embraced several other topics, but these are the most material; and I left Mr. Madison with sentiments of friendly regard, and high esteem" (ibid., 2:13–15).

3. Jefferson conveyed these sentiments, in almost identical words, in a letter to Melish dated 13 Jan. 1813 (DLC: Jefferson Papers).

To Henry Dearborn

private

DEAR SIR   WASHINGTON Feby. 6. 1813

Your two favors of Decr   [1] have lain long without acknowledgment. For some [2] after they came to hand I delayed it in expectation of such further information as to Gen. Smith, as would enable me to judge better of his case; and latterly I considered it as probable that I might have an opportunity, not now expected, of making that as well as other matters, subjects of conversation with you here. I know not how Gl. S. will reconcile his appeal to your orders, with his previous language in a letter to you;[3] or how he will explain the several unfavorable appearances in his military management. The call is growing strong for some public step towards him; & it is the louder since his omission to seek a regular investigation has been followed by his inclosed appeal to the public thro' the press.[4] I have not yet had any conversation with the new Secy. of War, on the subject.

We have been a little uneasy, lest the Enemy at Niagara, should beat up the Quarters of Col. Porter, which appear to be within reach of it; whilst they are too distant to support the troops at Black Rock &c. and save the vessels in preparation, in case these should be objects of enterprize. Another apprehension has been, that a part of the Enemy's force in that quarter, might, be detached to oppose Harrison's operations if they should reach Malden or Detroit. How far there may be occasion for any of these anxieties, can be so much better decided, by those possessing better information & nearer the scene that I take refuge in that consideration agst. disagreeable anticipations. The two last mails have brought nothing from Harrison. The cold weather had so far favored transportation, that he began to hope from a continua[n]ce of it, that he should still prevent an entire abortion of his undertaking.

We have been under some anxiety also for the safety of the stake at Sackets Harbour. The latest information strengthens our hope, that it is made proof agst. an enterprize from Kingston. We are even encouraged by the possibility of some handsome dash by Chauncy agst. the latter. We learn however as you will doub[t]less have done, that the Enemy are making transcendent exertions to equip a naval force that will command the Lakes. Whatever theirs may be, ours ought to go beyond them. Nothing ought to be left to hazard on this subject. If they build two ships, we should build four. If they build thirty or 40 gun ships, we should build them of 50 or 60 Guns. The command of those waters is the hinge on which the war will essentially turn, according to the probable course of it.

You have seen the arrangement for the recruiting service. The prospect of enlistments is said to be flattering; but much will depend on the attention & activity of the *superintending* officers to whom every spur should be applied, that can make them spur those under them.

It appears that Bonaparte has secured his retreat or escape, but not without unexampled sacrifices. On the other hand Wellington appears to be falling back to Lisbon, and probably under a pretty severe pressure from the United armies commanded by Soult.

We have no accounts from England subsequent to the arrival there of the communications thro' Warren, or even of those made to Congs. Accept my best wishes

JAMES MADISON

RC (owned by Joseph Rubinfine, West Palm Beach, Fla., 2002).

1. Blank left in RC. Dearborn's last two letters to JM were dated 13 and 16 Dec. 1812.

2. JM evidently omitted a word here.

3. In giving the command of the American forces on the Niagara peninsula to Brig. Gen. Alexander Smyth on 21 Oct. 1812, Dearborn had directed the general to prepare a force of "3000 men, with artillery," before attempting an invasion of Canada (NHi: Dearborn Letterbooks). In a report he sent to Dearborn on 4 Dec. 1812, after his invasion had been called off, Smyth reported that he had assembled a force in the region of 3,000 men and that he therefore deemed himself "ready to 'cross with 3000 men at *once*,' according to your orders." However, in the same letter Smyth also reported that when he assembled this force in boats on 1 Dec. before crossing the Niagara River, he found that, without the officers, it amounted to little more than 1,500 men. He asked his officers, *"Shall we proceed?"* and found that his officers were unanimously opposed to making the attempt (*National Intelligencer*, 24 Dec. 1812).

4. In a 28 Jan. 1813 letter to the editors of the *Daily National Intelligencer* (published on 8 Feb. 1813), Smyth provided a defense of his conduct during his unsuccessful attempt to invade Canada from Black Rock, New York, between 28 Nov. and 1 Dec. 1812. Smyth drafted this defense in response to claims made by Peter B. Porter that Smyth had "4500 *effective* men" under his command on 27 Nov. 1812. Smyth countered by arguing that he had only 3,500 such men, of whom not more than 1,500 could be ordered across the Niagara River. On 1 Dec. 1812, Smyth added, the number of men "armed with muskets, who were at the navy-yard, embarked or not embarked, did not exceed 2000."

From John Love

Sir   Alexana. Feby 6th 1813

A company which has been incorporated by an act of the virga. assembly, are now engaged in making a road from a point in the little-river turnpike road, towards Thorntons gap, passing near Fauquier court house and affording the most direct rout from Washington to the Kanhawa country, a few miles in the commencement of the road are finished and as many more contracted to be made as will afford a passage across the marshy country, well recollected I am sure by You called the *blackjack*. We need however much aid to carry this measure of utility into effect, and agreeably to an order of the board of Directors, making it incumbent on me to address letters of solicitation to such gentlemen as may be most likely to encourage the work, I now take the liberty to ask for your aid and the Patronage of your name, as a stockholder. The amount of each share as fixed by the law is 100$—payable at such times as the President & Directors may require, We have fixed the periods in equal payments of nine eighte[e]n and twenty seven months. Should You find it consistent with your pecuniary arrangements We shall hope for your aid, and that you will be pleased to address a letter to me at *Buckland* directing to what amount of shares You will become a Stockholder which shall accordingly be entered on the books still remaining open for Subscription. I am Sir with very great regard and the highest respect Your most obedient Servant

Jno Love

RC (DLC). Docketed by JM.

From an Unidentified Correspondent

Sir.   Philada. 6th. Feby. 1813

On reading in one of our Public prints a definition of Treason given as by one of the Circuit Judges of the United States I was led to reflect whether or not it be timely and Advisable to amend or modify the Constitution of the United States so as to make it Treasonable to attempt to dissolve the Union or to aid or encourage it by writing publishing or pronouncing anything that might be considered to have that tendency or the excitement of local prejudices tending to that purpose. Internal Enemies are sometimes the worst of Enemies and the perpetuation of the Union of so much importance to the well-being and proba[b]le future happiness of the people that any attempt to dissolve it must be wicked in the extreme: but I only suggest the idea. I am &.

RC (NN). Unsigned; docketed by JM.

§ From John Binns and Others. *6 February 1813.* "The Naturalized Citizens of the United States residing in the City and vicinity of Philadelphia, natives of the United Kingdom of Great Britain and Ireland have at various meetings had under their serious consideration the Proclamation of the Prince Regent under date of the 26th. October 1812, upon which subject, with all the respect due to the enlightened Chief Magistrate of a Free people and with all the solicitudes and anxieties which so important a subject demands we, a committee appointed for the purpose, address your Excellency. The inhuman threat, the barbarous policy which is manifested in the Proclamation are presumed to have issued from counsellors, determined & desperate enough to dare to do that which they have dared to threaten. With the Sheild of the Constitution and the Laws between them and the vengeance of the Prince Regent, the Naturalized Citizens would have stilled the tumultuous throbbings of indignation and apprehension which this Proclamation had caused were not their bosoms from time to time agitated and distracted by statements of Naturalized Citizens having been taken from among the prisoners in the United States Army and Navy, put in Irons and sent to the United Kingdom to be tried for High Treason in having taken up Arms against their Natural and lawful sovereign George III.

"These statements do, indeed they cannot fail, to damp the warmth of Patriotism and check the ardor of devotion to the public service which otherwise would and which previously did glow in the hearts of Naturalized Citizens toward the country of their adoption which is made dear to them by the most sacred principles of truth, by the most interesting associations and the tenderest ties of gratitude and affection. On the justice of the Constituted Authorities of the United States we repose with the most entire confidence and their assurance that the rights and persons of the naturalized Citizens proscribed in the Prince Regent's proclamation should be protected would be entirely satisfactory and would invigorate their arms in every contest against the Enemy of the United States, that cruel enemy whose persecution and Tyranny drove us from the land of our fathers and would vindictively pursue us even to death in the only country whose hospitable arms are open to receive the persecuted and oppressed.

"The committee feel assured that you sir, have given this momentious subject a consideration commensurate with its extent of bearing and importance of effects & we pray you to be assured Sir, that considerations connected with the public weal, as intimately as they involve the rights & feelings of those whom we represent, could alone have induced us to tresspass upon your time and very respectfully yet not less earnestly solicit from you some information as to the course which the Executive of the United States are determined to pursue in the event of the Prince Regent carrying into effect the measures threatened in his proclamation."

RC (DLC). 2 pp.; signed by John Binns, William Smiley, John W. Thompson, Francis Mitchell, John Maitland, and George Palmer. Undated; date supplied from printed copy in Binns, *Recollections of the Life of John Binns*, 217–18. Docketed by JM with the added notation "answd. Feby. 11. 1813."

From William Blackledge

WASHINGTON CITY Feby. 7th. 1813

Captain James Taylor late Collector of the Port of Ocracock is at this time in the City of Washington with his two daughter [*sic*] & one Son, I have known him for more than twenty years, and much the greater part of the time intimately. Captain Taylor is reduced in circumstances by Causes which few men could have withstood. Had he been corruptable he might have been as wealthy as he pleased. To his inflexible integrity in enforcing the Embargo & other restrictive measures of the government, is only attributable a scene of hostility against him by the principal Merchants, & directors of the Bank of Newbern, which have eventuated in his ruin. Captain Taylor tho' has his faults; they may be concenterd in the single one of wanting strength of mind to bear with fortitude the change of Circumstances which he saw approaching. He for a time yielded to a course which frail human nature is too apt to give way to, for the purpose of drowning painful reflections. The duty he owed to his family and friends, and the triumph he was affording his relentless enemies I am happy to see have triumphed at length over the weaknesses of his nature, and he has come on to endeavor to establish his daughter in this place as an instructress of the

French & Italian As well as the English languages, and at the same time to settle his accounts as late Collector of the Port of Ocracock.[1] And Sir if any appointment could be given him in the City or District which would enable him to reside near his daughter, I should not only feel under obligation, but am convinced & would guarantee if necessary a faithful discharge of the duties of the appointment, as well as a correct & satisfactory deportment on his part. I should in fact tell him myself, what I have already assured him I would advise, that he was to be removed without hesitation, if his Conduct did not Comport with my assurances. But Sir I should not wish him to be appointed, but from a conviction that this admonition from me will not be necessary. He was one of the agents of the State of North Carolina, for setling the accounts of that State with the United States, was raised a merchant, and is well qualified to fill any of the accountantships, or clerkships in any of the offices of the War or Navy Departments. He is well acquainted with the topography, productions, & principal characters of the State of North Carolina, & in the recess might I should imagine be useful to you in giving information which from the want of some person to be relied on at this place could not perhaps be otherwise so well obtained. I will only add that there is not within my Knowledge a man from that State in any of the offices here, and with sentiments of the highest respect remain Your Obdt Servt

WM. BLACKLEDGE[2]

RC (DLC). Docketed by JM.

1. James Taylor was removed from office and replaced by Thomas S. Singleton in 1812 as collector at Ocracoke, North Carolina. Taylor's enforcement of the Embargo and Nonintercourse Acts had earned him the dislike of the New Bern merchant community, who were opposed to war with Great Britain (Blackledge to Paul Hamilton, 25 Nov. 1812 [DNA: RG 45, Misc. Letters Received]; *Senate Exec. Proceedings*, 2:278, 279; *ASP, Miscellaneous*, 2:317).

2. In 1812 William Blackledge (d. 1828) was defeated in his bid for reelection to the Thirteenth Congress by the Federalist attorney William Gaston of New Bern (Powell, *Dictionary of North Carolina Biography*, 1:166).

From S. Potter

SIR,   W. CITY Feb. 7th. 1813.

It has once more gain'd belief with me, that you will again be call'd by the American people to fill the chief Chair of state, & as I told you Sir, four yea[r]s past,[1] so I now tell you, that in my humble opinion, its a great indignity to the Chair to fill it with a man who is in any degree concern'd in enslaveing any part of the human family. To say the least of such a man, he is dishonest, and facts within the daily observation of every man who breaths in these southern climes would justify me in saying, that such a man is not only dishonest, but is inhuman, irriligious, tyranical & barbarous, & depriv'd of moral virtue & Religion, & unworthy to fill that dignified station.

Such language may sound rather harsh Sir, in the ears of a man, who has all his days been nurs'd, educated & daily exercis'd in tyranny & oppression, but to a man possess'd of real piety, virtue & Religion, & one too, who has all his days been taught by his father & the divines of his time to believe, that freedom is a gift of almighty God, and not to be violated, but with his wrath: to such a man Sir, the language seems mild, & is the least he can say of all such men.

If you wish, Sir, to secure the love & friendship of all good men, & to escape the Divine wrath, you must, before you again enter upon the duties of that office, not only immancipate all your slaves, but you must use your utmost influence to cause others so to do, who are in the habit of keeping open that execrable market where man is bought & sold.

Now, Sir, whether we consider the practice of enslaveing the people of Colour who are brought in, or born in these states as incourag'd by individuals, corporate bodies, or by the ministers of the Gospel, it presents to our immagination a dreadful preeminance in wickedness—An equal degree of enormity and sin—A crime which not only involves the best interest of all who are concern'd in it, but a crime, which will ere long draw down the divine displeasure upon this beautiful flourishing country. Witness South America.

If you have no concern, Sir, for your own soul, nor for the good of the present race of men, do have some little regard for the riseing age, & the honour & good of your country, & use your best means to wipe away from it, this dreadful sin & shame.

For what end Sir, do you profess a Religion, the dictates of which you so flagrantly violate? How long will you continue a practice, which a wise policy rejects, justice condems & piety revolts at?

You do Sir, to the utmost of your power, by this inhuman practice, weaken the union, & desolve the universal tie, which binds & unites societies & individuals together, & thereby destroy all the sweets of social life. You practice what you execrate in others, & ought to exclaim against as the utmost excess of barbarity & wickedness: and thereby, instil into the minds of all whom you enslave, the most despisable opinion of you, your piety virtue & Religion.

In consequence of this unmerited, bruitish servitude, you sacrifize you[r] conscience, your reason, your humanity your virtue, your charity, your love, & your Religion, for an unnatural sorded gain.

You have, Sir, you & your coagitors, by this inhuman, barbarious practice of slavery, reduced millions of the human family to circumstances far more miserable than the brute creation.

You have torn thousands of these unfortunate people from their homes,

& from every object of their affections, & drag'd them together into these southern states to the horrors of a mutual servitude, that ends only with their lives! You are daily driving them in droves like cattle & horse; linked together in chains from one state in the union to another, where they & their children are brought up in ignorance & hardships, & expos'd to every vice & folly, which is disgraceful to man & abhorant to God!

Galling them in chains with an unrelenting spirit of barbarity, inconceaveabl[e] to all, but the unhapy victims of their rage, or the spectators of these horred scenes.

By this means, you seperate men from their wives, & little children from their parents, which causes them to cry and mourn, & gray hairs to go down in sorrow to the grave.

This is but a faint picture, Sir, of the sufferings of these unfortunate people, nor of the barbarity & wickedness of those who have inflicted the smart. But the attempt to enumerate the crimes of such monsters would be like the attempt to number the sands of the sea-shore, which has been so often stain'd with the blood of those innocent & innofencive people.

To be short, Sir, your, Dogs, Cattle & Horses are use[d] in a much more civil & becoming manner—Sick or well—Hungry or naked—Wet or dry—Hot or cold—Blow high or blow low, the poor weather-beaten slave must go—Guilty or innocent he must bear the whole shower of your wrath.

Such is the practice of thousands who call themselves pacifick, inlighten'd Americans—Reform'd Christians. Thus have you profited by example, by your education, & by an express Revelation of your duty from Almighty God! Will not the blessing which you have so shamefully & wickedly abused, testify against you at the bar of Almighty God? Will not the innocent blood which has been so wantonly spilt, cry from the ground for vengance upon your guilty heads? You call the Moors a knot of inhuman barbarous ruffins, for enslaving your sons & daughters, and are daily complain[ing] of G. Britain for pressing and enslaving a few thousands of your seamen, & yet you southern Nabobs, to glut your avrise for sorded gain, make no scruple of enslaving some millions of the sons and daughters of Africa, & their desendants, and take away all their honest labour, for the vile purpos of aggrandizeing yourselve and families, at their expence.

Notwithstanding, Sir, you preach up humanity, love & liberty to all mankind—Bend the sainted knee, & call on God to bless and prosper you[r] labours, while you hold in one hand the Gospel, & in the other the bloody whip, wet with the blood of some innocent person of colour, who has unfortunatly offended you in some trifle or other, or for refuseing to labour for you without some reward.

What a dreadful prospect! How profound a subject for contemplation! How little are you both in your morrals and Religion. By such base conduct Sir, you take the most effectual measures to prevent the spread of the Gospel, by rendering it a scheme of power and barbarous oppression. You even make yourselves enemies to the natural priviliges of human kind, and by such despotism & fraud, tread under foot all your bills of human right, & one of the best instruments of human composition—Your Declaration of Independence.

That this heavy charge may not rest on my sholders alone—In support of which, I give the following extracts.

1st. "With what execration should that statesman be loaded, who per-miting one half the citizens thus to trample on the rights of the other; transforms those into despots & these into enemies; destroys the morrels of the one part, & the amor patria of the other. And can the liberties of a nation be tho't secure, when we have remov'd their only firm basis, a con-viction in the minds of the people, that these liberties are the gift of God? That they are not to be violated, but with his wrath. Indeed I tremble for my country, when I reflect that God is just, & that his justice cannot sleep forever: that considering numbers, nature & natural means only, a revolu-tion of the wheel of fortune; and exchange of situations is among possable events; That it may become provable by super-natural interferance." See Notes on Virg. By Tho. Jefferson Esq.[2]

2d. "With regard to the Slave-Trade, Root & Branch, First & Last, in all its motives, measures, concomitints and consequences, if ever any human undertaking merited the deepest abhorance of man, & the heavi[e]st curse of Almighty God, it is surely that." See a Compend. of history, By Saml. Whelply.[3]

3d.   "O! execrable son, so to aspire,
        Above his brother, to himself assigning,
        Authority userpt, from God not given;
        He gave us only over beast, fish, fowl
        Dominion absolute, but man over man
        He made not Lord, such title to himself
        Reserving, human left from human free."
                    See the great Milton.[4]

4th. "They, who go out as Piraters, & take away poor Africans, or people of any other land, who never forfeted life or liberty, & carry them into slav-ery, are the wo[r]st of Robbers, and ought to be consider'd the common en-emies of mankind, & that all they who buy them of those inhuman Robbers & use them as mere beasts of burthen for their own convenience; regard-less of their spiritual welfair, are fitter to be called Demons than Chris-tians." See Richd. Baxters Christian Directiory.[5]

It will be seen by these quotations, Sir, that the practice of slavery is not only odious to me, but is execrated by men whose names are immortaliz'd in history, & stand on record as patterns of piety, virtue & religion; who have denounced the judgments of God against all who are in the habit of keeping open this execrable market where man is bought & sold.

When I seriously reflect on the despotism, inhumanity, wickedness & barbarism of the legislators of these southern states, and the misery & distress to which they have reduced so many thousands of their citizens, I cannot avoid crying out, O sacred Tree of Liberty, where are thy fruits! Was this sacred & rare plant set in the earth—water'd & nourished with the blood of heroes—Tears of widows & orphans, for the vile purpose only, to shade & nurish a few of Burr's best blood of America—Dr. Johnson's great men—family, birth, blood and extraction, &c. I say, if this was the intention of the fathers & polititions of that day—If their sons bleed & died to drive out the tyrants of Europe, in order that they might step into their shoes, & enjoy the fruits of the Tree of Liberty only—Then—O! then, did the blood of heroes, & tears of widows & orphens flow in vein.

It would seem to a reflecting mind, as If virtue, humanity, love & religion were fled from off the face of the earth. For let us survey what quarter of the Globe we pleas; we find in all, nearly the same spirity [*sic*] of oppression, luxury, vice & folly.

If, instead of this inhuman conduct, the nations which bear the Christian name, were generally engaged in the great world of refformation—Were desirous to meliorate the condition of the human race; they might, by a proper line of good conduct, ere long remove from their minds, all those deep-rooted prejudices, which have so long destroyed the peace & harmony of the human family, & transform'd thousands of them into wolves & tygers; who seem now to bid defience to all rational law, virtue, humanity & religion.

> . . . My ear is pain'd, (says Mr. Cowper)
> My soul is sick with every day's report
> Of rong & outrage with which this earth is fill'd,
> There is no flesh in man's obderate heart,
> That does not feel for man. The natural bond
> Of brother-hood is sever'd as the flax,
> That falls assunder at the t[o]uch of fire.
> He finds his fellow guilty of a skin
> Not colour'd like his own, & having power
> To force the rong for such a wicked cause,
> Dooms & devotes him as his lawful prey.
> Land interspread by a narrow frith
> Abhor each other. Mountains intersposed,
> Make enemies of nations, who had else
> Like kindred drops, been mingl'd into one.
>   This man devotes his brother, and destroys;
> And more than all, & most to be deplor'd

As human natures broadest, foulest blot,
Chains him, tasks him, & exacts his sweat,
With stripes, that mercy with a bleeding heart
Weeps, when she sees inflicted on a beast.
Then, what is man? & what man seeing this
And having human feelings, does not blush
And hang his head to think himself a man."[6]

Its verry surpriseing Sir, that the agents of the people in these southern states, who talk in a very high strain of freedom & political liberty, should make no scruple of reducing one half or more of their whole population into circumstances, by which they are not only depriv'd of property, but almost of every species of human right, and degraded below the bruits that perish.

Do you think, Sir, that the people of colour can suffer all this w[it]hout a decline of love for this country, or indeed, without feeling that love turned into hatred, & seeking the bitterest revenge?

I might here make a catalogue of all the consequences of slavery, if my heart did not recoil at the horred tale. I shall therefore, content myself by saying, this barbarous, inhuman practice, has destroyed the morrals, manners, industry & religion; & spread corruption, disease, wickedness & folly, to the greatest body of the inhabitance of six or eight of the finest states in the union, and involved in misery, poverty and distress, & bound down to worse than Egyptian slavery, one half or more of their whole population: Yea this horred practice is pregnat with every evil that is disgraceful to human nature, injurious to man, abhorant to God; & offends against all the laws of morality, and rights of human kind. And its much to be feared, that this malignant disease will not only distroy the morrals, manners, industry & religion of the inhabitance, but will ere long subvert your very Constitution, & throw the U. S. into anarchy, & give a death blow to the Tree of Liberty.

Pause, Sir, for justice & mercy sake pause, before you find yourself & children swallow'd up in this dreadful tempest!

"It is the immutable d[e]cree of God himself, (says Esq. Poydras) that no man, or set of men, shall be unjust with impunity. The consequences of injustice are dreadful & unavoidable. A people oppressed by tyranny are like the body when afflicted by sickness—a stranger to ease, & anxious to obtain it; every position is try'd untill one less painful than the othere is found; that may suffer the sick person to take a little rest. So the victim of tyranny is ever resles [sic] in search of relief from his oppressor.

I know of no other basis for a government to rest upon, but justice; place it upon any other, & it will be like a house erected on the sand—when the winds blow & the rains desend it will be sweept from its foundation."[7]

Since I've again got in to quotations, I'll give one more & then close the subject, for I fear that writeing to you Sir, on the practice of slavery will be time lost, but I shall have this for consolation in my last hours, that I've done what I conceived to be my duty in striving to list you on the side of virtue & humanity, in order, if possable to ward off the impending danger which awaits you, & hangs over this devoted country. Before you spurn such language as this, or treat with contempt the author of it, you'll do well to consider his motives, & the wait of evidence which he has produced in support of what he has wrote. I've not[8] a syllable against your character or person, other than what is herein expres'd. Clear your skirts of this inhuman practice, & then you'll have my warmest support. But as long as you continue this inhuman barbarous practice, I shall laugh at your calamities, & mock when your fear comes.

"Laws to be just & equitable should protect the weak & innocent, & defuse blessings upon all with a liberal hand. Just laws give vigor & proportion to every part of the body; but slavery aggrandizes one part of the community at the expence of the other, & is cruel and unmerciful. To accuse a people of cruelty, who pride themselves of being the most human upon earth, is a bold unde[r]taking. How can that be rong (says the slave-holder) which has been the sanction of the fathers & polititions so many years, & which is the source of our wealth, ease & happines?

In cases like the present, multitudes, antiquity, wealth, eas[e] & happiness, prove nothing. The fact is, here are millions of men, women & children, deprived of the rights of their nature, and suffering all the consequences of that deprivation. They have in despite of all the rights of humanity, been forced across the ocean; & they & their posterity bound to the severest labour. The consequences, alass are obvious & too painful to relate.

Immortal soles in slavery! Subjects of the grace of God, & the purchase of the precious blood of Jesus Christ in slavery! Beings capable of all the blessings of civil society, deprived of them all, to administer to the vices & pleasures of others!

Hail ye sons of benevolence! will ye sing with the Poet,

> "That mercy I to others show,
> That mercy show to me!" Pope.[9]

Will you make this the criterion of the favours of God & Man? Do you expect to be judged by this rule?

It is not imposable that you & your children may have the same measure meated back to you again. It is no uncommon thing with God to reward men according to their works, even in this world.

Slavery omits the waiter [*sic*] matters of the law, therefore its unlawful & unscriptural. A Christian must do unto others, what he would that others should do unto him; but no slave-holder would have others to enslave himse[l]f: therefore, slavery is contrary to christ[i]anity. Love worketh no ill to his neighbour, but slavery worketh the greatest ill, therefore, slavery is contrary to love." From yours most respectfully.

S. POTTER

RC (DLC). Docketed by JM.

1. No previous correspondence between Potter and JM has been found.

2. Thomas Jefferson, *Notes on the State of Virginia*, ed. William Peden (1954; reprint, Chapel Hill, N.C., 1995), 162–63.

3. Samuel Whelpley, *An Historical Compend: Containing a Brief Survey of the Great Line of History . . .* (Morristown, N.J., 1806–7; Shaw and Shoemaker 11862), 134.

4. John Milton, *Paradise Lost*, 12.64–71.

5. Richard Baxter, *A Christian Directory; or, A Summ of Practical Theologie, and Cases of Conscience*, bk. 2, *Christian Oeconomicks; or, The Family Directory* (London, 1673), 559.

6. William Cowper, *The Task*, 2.5–28.

7. Julien Poydras de Lalande, *Speech of Julien Poydras, Esq., the Delegate from the Territory of Orleans, in Support of the Right of the Public to the Batture in Front of the Suburb St. Mary* (Washington, 1810; Shaw and Shoemaker 21129), 15.

8. Potter may have omitted a word here.

9. Alexander Pope, "The Universal Prayer," lines 39–40.

§ From Charles P. Harrison. *7 February 1813, Philadelphia.* "Desirous of engaging the patronage of the enlightened and most distinguished men of our country, I submit to you the accompanying annunciation for a subscription list,[1] which I am anxious to render as honourable to the patriotism of the present period in our annals, as contributory to the advancement of the Fine Arts in the United States: arts which have ever flourished, and always attained the acmé of glory and perfection in a republic."

RC and enclosure (DLC: Madison Collection, Rare Book Division). RC 1 p.; printed, with date, address, and signature in Harrison's hand. For enclosure, see n. 1.

1. Harrison, a Philadelphia copperplate printer, enclosed a one-page printed prospectus, headed "ADDRESS," for a "subscriptive Print" of *The American Tar.* Emphasizing the influence of the fine arts on the "elevation of national greatness," Harrison hoped that a nation that supported the arts would not fail to support the relief of seamen's widows and orphans, the beneficiaries of his print sales (Paxton, *Philadelphia Directory and Register, for 1813* [Shaw and Shoemaker 29456]).

Index

NOTE: Persons are identified on pages cited below in boldface type. Identifications in earlier volumes of this series are noted within parentheses. Page numbers followed only by n. (e.g., 272 n.) refer to the provenance portion of the annotation.

Abbeville, S.C.: letter to JM from inhabitants of, 316
Acheson, Thomas, 194 n. 1, 245 and n. 1; letters to JM, 192–93, 246
Adair, John, 237, 240, 413, **414 n. 4**
Adams, John: administration of, xxv, 95, 168, 320, 375, 442; corresponds with W. Jones, 592 n. 1; and election of *1796*, 455; and Federalist party, 307 n. 4; makes recommendations, 635–36, 643; letters to JM, 455–57, 592, 635–36, 642–43
Adams, John Quincy, 158, 414; corresponds with Monroe, 415 n. 1
Adams (U.S. brig), 405, 575 n. 1
Adams (U.S. frigate), 405
Adams County, Miss. Territory: letter to JM from citizens of, 187
Adams County, Pa., 282 n. 1
Addison, Joseph, 378 n. 9
Adeline (ship), 96
Aesop, 603 n. 2
Africa: slaves from, 18–19 and n. 1, 652
Alabama: Creek Indians in, 479 n. 3; and land claims, 276–77 n. 2
Alabama River, 276–77 n. 2
Albany, N.Y., 10, 113, 390 n. 2, 421, 536, 548 n. 1, 613 n. 1; Dearborn at, 133, 134 n. 3, 151, 159, 315 n. 3, 593; Dearborn ordered to, 13 n. 1; encampment at, 12, 331 and n. 2
Albany Gazette, 166 n. 2, 421 n. 5
Albany Register, 162 n. 9
Albany Republican, 162 n. 9
Albemarle County, Va., 311, 345 n. 1
Alburg, Vt., 619
Alcock, Robert, 323 n.
Alert (British brig), 405, 406 n. 8
Alexander I (of Russia), 415 n. 1

Alexander, Isaac, 297
Alexander, John, 51 n.
Alexander, John Byers, 496, 497 n. 6
Alexandria, Va., 96, 255 n. 11, 544 n. 1, 578, 619 n. 7, 631–32 n. 1
Algiers, 498 n. 2; T. Lear's departure from, 231, 232, 233 n. 3, 431, 457; navy of, 233 n. 3; sheep in, 230–31; wine in, 231
Ali Dey (of Algiers), 231–32, 233 n. 3
Alien enemies, 214–15, 384
Alien Enemy Act (*1798*), 42 n. 2
Aliens: and naturalization laws, 438 and nn.
Allegany (U.S. ship), 230, 231, 232, 233 n. 3
Allegany County, Md., 413
Allegheny Mountains, 65, 193
Allegheny River, 496
Allen, Charles, 552 n. 1
Allen, John, 68, **68 n. 1**, 98; letter to JM, 83–84
Allen, Solomon, 162 n. 9
Allen, William O. (*see* 3:247 n. 7), 481
Allison, Robert, 497 n. 2
Alston, Joseph (*see* 4:393 n. 1), 495 and n. 5
Altamaha River, 316
Amelia Island, E.Fla., 488 n. 1, 508
America (U.S. ship), 611 and n. 1
American and Commercial Daily Advertiser (Baltimore), 41 and n. 1, 135 and n. 1, 166 n. 2, 283 n. 2, 287 n. 2, 295 n. 1
American Question: A Letter, from a Calm Observer, to a Noble Lord, on the Subject of the Late Declaration Relative to the Orders in Council; see Joy, George, "Calm Observer" letters
The American Tar, 657 n. 1
Amherst, Jeffrey, 10, 588

cornell as president of, 506 n. 1;
relations with Spain, 241, 242, 245
n. 3, 379 n. 1; relations with U.S.,
254 n. 4; revolutionary activity in,
538, 539 n. 1; and Spanish regency, 579, 582 n. 11

Meyer, Christopher: letter to JM, 597

Miami Indians, 332, 499, 500 n. 1, 590

Miami River (Miami of the Lake
River); *see* Maumee River

Michigan Territory, xxiii, 308, 420,
427, 428, 476 n. 2, 502, 503 n. 2,
613 n. 1; governor of, 214; militia,
189–90 n. 2

Michilimackinac, Mich. Territory, 182,
183, 339, 372, 589; surrender of,
151–52 and n. 2, 156, 165–66,
189 n. 2, 220, 221 n. 1, 224, 591
n. 1

Middlesex County, Mass., 149 and n. 3,
160, 161 n. 7

Middleton, Henry (*see* 3:88 n. 2): governor of S.C., 471 n. 1, 479; letter
to JM, 471

Mifflin, Benjamin, 226 and n. 1, 247,
248, 268–69, 270 n. 1, 507–9 and
n. 2

Mifflin, Samuel, 58, 59 and n. 2

Military supplies, 78–79, 122, 202,
251, 279, 286, 528, 575 n. 1; for
Algiers, 233 n. 3; camp equipment, 175, 273, 634; at Detroit,
189–90 n. 2, 261, 298 n. 1, 313,
353 n. 1, 420; mismanagement of,
483–84; for Northwest Army,
201, 367, 368 n. 1, 372, 392, 407,
483, 491, 549–51; provisions, 222,
255, 271 n. 1, 272, 288, 459, 461
n. 1, 483–84, 491, 541, 543, 626,
627, 628 n. 6; at St. Augustine,
395; tents, 163 n. 1, 222, 255,
256, 347, 513, 541, 542; transport
of, 175 n. 1, 397, 403, 410–11,
483–84, 496, 634; *see also* Arms
and ammunition; Clothing;
Commodities

Militia, 127, 170, 174, 342, 348, 350,
390, 398, 575 n. 1, 631–32 n. 1;
contrasted with regular troops,
204, 529; expenses of, 365, 460;
governors refuse to detach, xxiv,
17 nn. 4–5, 127, 129, 134, 250

n. 1, 305, 306, 359, 387, 429, 434
n. 1, 447, 513; laws, xxvi, 126 n. 2,
225, 425, 432, 435 n. 13, 447;
power to call out, 195–96, 250 nn.
1 and 3, 463; at Queenston, 410,
411 n. 1; recruiting efforts, 344,
426; state quotas, 83–84, 88; unre-
liability of, 175, 365, 474; and use
of artillery, 407, 435; U.S. reliance
on, 133, 165, 424; *see also under individual states*

Miller, James, 159, 161 n. 5, 197,
206–7 n. 2, 246, 326, 352–53,
641, 642 n. 2

Miller, John, 57 n. 1

Miller, William, 612 n. 1

Mill Hill estate (Caroline County, Va.),
361 n. 1

Milton, John, 323 n. 7, 445 n. 5, 653,
657 n. 4

Milton, Va., 47 n. 2, 136, 137 n. 1, 361
n.

Mint, U.S., 545 n. 1; annual report of,
544–45

Miranda, Francisco de, 130 n. 6, 506
n. 2

Mirror of the Times (Augusta, Ga.), 396
n. 2

Mishkakitac; *see* Muscatatuck River

Mississinewa, Battle of (*1812*), 99 n. 1,
203 n. 8, 500 nn. 1–2

Mississinewa (Indian village), 493

Mississinewa River, 500 n. 1

Mississippi Delta: hurricane in, 405
n. 1

Mississippi Republican (Natchez), 98

Mississippi River, 3 n. 2, 176, 240,
242, 276–77 n. 2, 402, 485, 490,
491, 492; blockade of, 544 n. 1;
and Indians, 175, 185, 259 n. 4,
597

Mississippi Territory, 437, 596 and
n. 1; governor of (*see* Holmes,
David); letter to JM from legislature of, 464

Missouri River, 179, 186 n. 2

Missouri Territory, 254 n. 5, 259, 476
and n. 1, 586 n. 1, 641; J. Coburn
resigns as judge of, 566 and n. 1,
628; governor of (*see* Howard,
Benjamin); recommendations for
office in, 522, 628 and nn.

Semple, Anne Contesse Tyler
(Mrs. James), 583 n. 2
Semple, James, 583, **583 n. 2**
Senate, U.S., 87 n. 6, 216, 338 n. 2,
423, 433 n., 501, 570 n. 1, 605,
624 n. 3, 631 n. 1, 636 n. 2; and
appointments, 471 n. 1, 555, 576
n. 1, 596 n. 1, 621 n. 1, 628 n. 1,
632 n. 1, 643 n. 1; JM transmits
letters to, 487 n. 2, 565 n., 622 n.;
JM transmits reports to, 612 n.,
631 and n. 1; members of, 126
n. 2, 189 n. 1, 212 n. 3, 247, 316
n. 2, 367 n. 2, 395 n. 1, 414 n. 4,
424 n. 1, 439 n. 1, 479, 479 n. 3,
570, 575 n. 2; messages from JM,
520, 575, 577, 631; and military
appointments, 464 n., 471 n., 475
n., 515 n., 521 n., 548 n. 1, 586
n. 1, 600 and n. 1, 637 n. 3, 642
n. 1, 644 n.; passes naturalization
bill, 438 nn. 1–2; passes retaliation bill, 547 n. 1; passes Seamen's
Bill, 573 n. 2; political composition of, 544 n. 2; rejects bill to occupy E.Fla., 155, 581 n. 6; rejects
T. Coxe's nomination, 150–51,
268–69; resolutions of, 321, 324
n. 18, 551 n. 1, 565 n. 1, 575 and
n. 1, 577, 580 n. 1, 612 and n. 1,
622 and n. 1, 631 and n. 1; state
representation in, 436
Sérurier, Louis-Barbé-Charles (see
3:164 n. 2), 252, 281 and n. 3;
corresponds with Bassano, 281
n. 3
Sessions, Joseph, 187 n.
Seven Years' War; see French and Indian War
Sevier, John: governor of Tenn., 51
Sewall, Henry, 17 n. 3
Sewall, Samuel, 250 n. 1
Seybert, Adam, 523 n., 534 n. 1; letter
to JM, 534
Seymour, Mr.: Lafayette sells land patents to, 369–70
Seymour, Henry, 634 n. 2
Shakespeare, William: references to
works of, 148, 149 n. 1, 374, 377
n. 1
Shaler, William: agent to Mexico and
Cuba, xxvi, 235–39, 241–44, 379

n. 1, 582 n. 11; corresponds with
Monroe, 236, 237, 239, 242, 243,
244, 253, 254 n. 4
Shannon, George, 484, **485 n. 4**
Shaw, John, 405 n. 1
Shaw, Samuel, 570, 620
Shawnee Indians, 176, 185, 190 n. 3
Sheaffe, Roger: as I. Brock's successor,
585
Sheep, merino, 230–31
Sheffield, John Baker Holroyd, first
earl of, 47, 49 n. 1
Sheheke (Mandan chief), 485 n. 4
Shelby, Isaac, 203 n. 2; as governor of
Ky., 417, 516 n.
Sheldon, Vt., 421
Shepherd, Thomas, 71, 77 and n.; let-
ter to JM, 70
Sherbrooke, John Coape, **88 n. 2,** 637
n. 1; letter to JM, 87–88
Shipbuilding, 91, 326, 330, 348, 432,
451, 460, 476 and n. 2, 523, 551
n. 1, 583 n. 2, 610–11 and nn.
1–2, 624, 646
Shoemakers, 559
Shrader, Otho, 135, 309
Sidmouth, Henry Addington, Vis-
count (see 2:542 n. 3), 36, 38 nn.
1–2, 84–86, 87 n. 7, 336; corre-
sponds with G. Joy, 338 n. 4
Silver: in U.S. Mint, 544–45
Simmons, William: War Department
accountant, 508, 537 n. 3
Simrall, James, **99 n. 1,** 499, 500 n. 3;
letter to JM, 98–99
Singleton, Thomas S., 650 n. 1
Sioux Indians, 178 n. 1, 182
Siren (U.S. brig), 404
Sisson, Philip: letter to JM, 551
Skinner, Joseph, 606 and n.
Slavery, 66 nn. 3–4, 570 n. 2; opposi-
tion to, 149 n. 2, 215, 650–57
Slaves, 35 n. 1, 155, 208–9, 324 n. 2,
362 n. 2, 481, 482 n. 1, 580 n. 2,
640
Slave trade, 18–19
Slocum, John, 440 n.
Smallpox: vaccination, 161 n. 1
Smiley, William, 547 n., 649 n.
Smilie, John, 475
Smith, Bernard, 569 n. 2; letter to JM,
567